South African Constitutional Law *in Context*

PUBLIC LAW

South African Constitutional Law *in Context*

PUBLIC LAW

PIERRE DE VOS (EDITOR)
WARREN FREEDMAN (EDITOR)
DANIE BRAND | CHRISTOPHER GEVERS
KARTHIGASEN GOVENDER | PATRICIA LENAGHAN
DOUGLAS MAILULA | NOMTHANDAZO NTLAMA
SANELE SIBANDA | LEE STONE

OXFORD
UNIVERSITY PRESS
SOUTHERN AFRICA

OXFORD
UNIVERSITY PRESS

Oxford University Press is a department of the University of Oxford.
It furthers the University's objective of excellence in research, scholarship,
and education by publishing worldwide. Oxford is a registered trade mark of
Oxford University Press in the UK and in certain other countries.

Published in South Africa by
Oxford University Press Southern Africa (Pty) Limited

Vasco Boulevard, Goodwood, N1 City, Cape Town, South Africa, 7460
P O Box 12119, N1 City, Cape Town, South Africa, 7463

First published 2014

South African Constitutional Law in Context

ISBN 978 019 599137 6

Fourth impression 2015

Typeset in Utopia Std 9.5 pt on 12 pt
Printed on 70 gsm woodfree paper

Acknowledgements
Publisher: Penny Lane
Development editor: Jessica Huntley
Project manager: Marguerite Lithgow
Copy editor: Jeannie van den Heever
Proofreader: Annette de Villiers
Indexer: Michel Cozien
Typesetter: Barbara Hirsch
Cover: Catherine Watts
Printed and bound by ABC Press, Cape Town
123503

The authors and publisher gratefully acknowledge permission to reproduce copyright material in this book. Every effort has been made to trace copyright holders, but if any copyright infringements have been made, the publisher would be grateful for information that would enable any omissions or errors to be corrected in subsequent impressions.

To Lwando Scott

Pierre de Vos

To my wife, Margot, and my daughters, Jessica and Emily

Warren Freedman

Contents in brief

Contents

Preface

The 1997 Australian comedy, *The Castle*, tells the story of the Kerrigan family's fight against the compulsory acquisition by the government of their home to make way for an expanded runway at the airport. The father, Darryl Kerrigan, hires an incompetent lawyer acquaintance, Dennis Denuto, to assist the family, but when asked by the judge what section of the Constitution he is invoking to challenge the expropriation, Dennis is unable to assist the court. 'There is no one section,' he hesitantly tells the court. 'It's just the ... the *vibe* of the thing, your Honour.'

After the Kerrigans lost the case, Lawrence Hammill, a retired Queen's Counsel, decides to argue it *pro bono* on appeal before the High Court of Australia. Lawrence makes a persuasive case that the Kerrigans have the right to just compensation under section 51(xxxi) of the Australian Constitution and closes by paraphrasing Darryl's own comments that his house is more than just a structure of bricks and mortar: it is a home built with love and shared memories. The Court rules in favour of the Kerrigans and their case becomes a landmark precedent.

To some extent this textbook takes its inspiration from *The Castle*. It recognises that a proper appreciation of South Africa's Constitution requires a keen understanding of *both* the 'vibe' of the Constitution, specifically its broad aims of preventing a recurrence of the horrors of apartheid and of promoting the social and economic transformation of our society, *and* a detailed and precise understanding of the individual provisions of the Constitution. It also requires an understanding of the jurisprudence of the Constitutional Court that fleshes out these provisions.

This textbook therefore aims to provide students (and others interested in the manner in which the Constitution must be interpreted and applied) with a relatively succinct, yet comprehensive, overview of the constitutional law of South Africa. The text is premised on the fact that South Africa's colonial and apartheid past continues to exert an influence on the attitudes and social and economic circumstances of those who live in the country as well as on the prevailing political culture. It embraces the notion that ours is a transformative Constitution aimed at facilitating the creation of a fair, equitable and just society in which the human dignity of every person is respected and protected.

Given South Africa's colonial and apartheid past, the individual provisions of the Constitution can be understood as having the collective purpose of ensuring (in the words of the late Nelson Mandela, the first democratically elected President of South Africa) that 'never, never and never again shall it be that this beautiful land will again experience the oppression of one by another.' As such, this book aims to situate the study of South African constitutional law within the political, social and economic context of present-day South Africa to enable readers better to understand the provisions of the Constitution and their interpretation, especially by the Constitutional Court.

The book aims to achieve this purpose by including tables, diagrams and 'learning boxes' containing relevant factual information about the socio-economic and political realities in the country and its history, opinions from a wide array of sources as well as excerpts from academic writing (which are also aimed at encouraging critical thinking about the Constitution and its interpretation). We hope that it provides a crisp yet detailed overview of most of the pressing constitutional law issues in South Africa today, issues which are not normally addressed in other courses in the standard LLB curriculum. We further hope that the book signals that many constitutional law issues can be approached from different angles, thus encouraging further reading and critical analysis and engagement with many of the most pressing constitutional law issues that are often hotly debated in the South African media.

The editors deliberately recruited a team of dedicated authors with different levels of experience from many different academic institutions in order to utilise and showcase the diverse talents of constitutional law academics in South Africa. It is not surprising that working with a large team of authors presented some challenges. The editors worked hard to ensure that the contextual focus is retained throughout the book and that the book retains a coherent tone and an even level of complexity. We hope that the end result reflects at least some of this hard work. However, the book would not have been possible without the assistance of the authors whose dedication, we hope, is reflected in the final product. We would therefore like to thank Danie Brand, Chris Gevers, Karthy Govender, Patricia Lenaghan, Nomthandazo Ntlama, Douglas Mailula, Sanele Sibanda and Lee Stone for their hard work in making this book a reality.

Apart from the authors, we would also like to thank the staff of Oxford University Press, and especially Penny Lane and Tarryn Talberg, for their hard work and patience. But we wish to single out Jessica Huntley from Oxford University Press, whose diplomatic skills, tireless attention to detail and unstinting support and encouragement sustained us throughout the process of editing the book. Without Penny, Tarryn and Jessica's commitment to this book, it might not have seen the light of day.

Pierre de Vos and Warren Freedman
December 2013

About the authors

PIERRE DE VOS (Editor)
BComm (Law), LLB, LLM (Stellenbosch), LLM (Columbia, NY), LLD (Western Cape)
Pierre de Vos holds the Claude Leon Foundation Chair in Constitutional Governance in the Department of Public Law at the University of Cape Town, where he lectures on constitutional law. Prior to joining the University of Cape Town, he lectured and held a Professorship at the University of the Western Cape. He is Chairperson of the Board of the Aids Legal Network, and is a Board member of the Triangle Project. Author and co-author of numerous articles for academic publications, Pierre also writes regularly, from a constitutional law perspective, for his widely read and quoted blog which addresses social and political issues.

WARREN FREEDMAN (Editor)
BComm, LLB (Witwatersrand), LLM (KwaZulu-Natal), Advanced PG Certificate in Higher Education (KwaZulu-Natal)
Warren Freedman is Associate Professor in the School of Law at the University of KwaZulu-Natal, Pietermaritzburg where he lectures on constitutional law, environmental law, and property law. His particular research interests include sub-national constitutional law, local government law, land use and planning law, and coastal zone management law. Warren has published a wide range of articles on constitutional law and was a member of the panel of experts appointed to advise the KwaZulu-Natal Provincial Legislature on the drafting and adoption of a provincial constitution in 2004/2005.

DANIE BRAND
BLC (Pretoria), LLB (Pretoria), LLM (Emory), LLD (Stellenbosch)
Danie Brand is Associate Professor in the Department of Public Law at the University of Pretoria, where he lectures on aspects of constitutional law, administrative law and land reform law, and publishes in the fields of constitutional law and theory. Danie is a member of the University of Pretoria Centre for Human Rights, the International Association of Constitutional Law, and the editorial board of the Pretoria University Law Press (PULP). He is an Advocate of the High Court of South Africa, and an Associate Member of the Pretoria Society of Advocates.

CHRISTOPHER GEVERS
LLB (KwaZulu-Natal), LLM (London School of Economics)
Christopher Gevers is a Lecturer in the Faculty of Law at the University of KwaZulu-Natal in Durban, where he lectures on human rights and international law. His research focuses broadly on international law, with a specific interest in international criminal law and international humanitarian law, as well as international legal theory. He has acted as adviser to litigants in cases concerning international law both in South Africa and abroad. Christopher also acts as a consultant on issues relating to human rights and international law for various non-governmental organisations.

KARTHIGASEN GOVENDER

LLB (London), LLB (KwaZulu-Natal), LLM (Michigan)

Karthigasen Govender is Professor in the School of Law at the University of KwaZulu-Natal, Howard College campus, and is a Colenso Fellow to St Johns College, Cambridge. In 1996 he was appointed to the South African Human Rights Commission by President Mandela, and in 2002 was reappointed for a second term by President Mbeki. He is a Senior Arbitrator for the South African Local Government Bargaining Council. Karthigasen is a Barrister (Middle Temple, Inns of Court, United Kingdom), an Associate Member of the KwaZulu-Natal Society of Advocates, and an Advocate of the High Court of South Africa. He has also acted as a Judge of the High Court of South Africa. He has published work in the fields of constitutional and administrative law.

PATRICIA LENAGHAN

BLC LLB (Pretoria), LLM, LLD (Western Cape)

Patricia Lenaghan is Associate Professor in the Department of Mercantile and Labour Law at the University of the Western Cape where she specialises in international trade law, regional integration and development, and European Union law. Patricia practised in Gauteng as an Attorney, Notary and Conveyancer of the High Court of South Africa before joining the University of the Western Cape to pursue her academic interests.

DOUGLAS MAILULA

B Proc, LLB, LLM, LLD (South Africa)

Douglas Mailula is Chair of Department for the Department of Public, Constitutional and International Law at the University of South Africa, where he previously lectured in constitutional law and advanced constitutional law and fundamental rights. He is an assistant editor of the Comparative and International Law Journal of Southern Africa. Douglas was formerly a Deputy Director of Mineral Policy Development in the erstwhile Department of Minerals and Energy. He has published academic research in his areas of special interest, including constitutional law, customary law, family law and child law, and has presented papers on mining and mineral law at various national conferences.

NOMTHANDAZO NTLAMA

B Juris LLB (Fort Hare), Certificate in Comparative Human Rights, LLM (Stellenbosch), LLD (South Africa)

Nomthandazo Ntlama was Professor of Law in the Department of Public, Constitutional and International Law at the University of South Africa before joining the University of KwaZulu-Natal, where she is currently the Dean of Research in the College of Law and Management Studies. Previously, she was a Researcher on Equality at the South African Human Rights Commission, and a Lecturer and Coordinator of the Human Rights Projects attached to the UNESCO 'Oliver Tambo' Chair of Human Rights, at the Nelson Mandela School of Law, University of Fort Hare. Nomthandazo was a board member of the Women on Farm's Project in Stellenbosch, and also a member of the Verloren van Themaat Centre, and the Centre for Indigenous Law at the University of South Africa.

SANELE SIBANDA

BA LLB (Cape Town), LLM (Witwatersrand)

Sanele Sibanda is a Senior Lecturer at the School of Law at the University of the Witwatersrand where he teaches constitutional law and the law of persons. His research interests lie within the areas of constitutional law, customary law reform, decolonial theory and liberation theory. He has taught, researched and published work on questions related to separation of powers, administrative law, customary marriage, customary law reform and South African constitutionalism from a critical perspective.

LEE STONE

LLB (Free State), LLM (Pretoria), Diploma in the Justiciability of Economic, Social and Cultural Rights (Abo, Finland)

Lee Stone is a Senior Lecturer in the Department of Public, Constitutional and International Law at the University of South Africa, where she lectures in constitutional law at both undergraduate and postgraduate level, and refugee law. She is also an extraordinary lecturer at St Augustine University, Mwanza (Tanzania). Lee is an Attorney of the High Court of South Africa, and a member of the Board of Directors of Agenda, a feminist non-governmental organization based in South Africa. Previously, Lee held a research position for the Refugee Rights Project at Lawyers for Human Rights, South Africa, worked for the African Commission on Human and Peoples' Rights in The Gambia, was a Legal Officer at the Institute for Human Rights and Development in Africa (a Pan-African NGO based in The Gambia), and worked at the Legal Resources Centre in Durban. Prior to joining the University of South Africa she was a Senior Lecturer in the School of Law at the University of KwaZulu-Natal's Howard College campus, Durban. Lee has published research in the areas of international criminal law, the African regional human rights system, refugee law, gender and the law, and constitutional and human rights law.

About the book

South African Constitutional Law in Context is a pedagogically rich learning resource. This book is designed to form a strong foundation of understanding, to develop the skills to engage independently and judiciously with legal principles, and to create skilled and proficient professionals.

Brief description of the features:

Pause for Reflection: This feature instils a broader and deeper understanding of the subject matter. It invites readers to interrogate or reflect upon specific questions and issues, thereby stimulating discussion, supporting independent intellectual thought, and developing the ability to analyse and engage meaningfully with relevant issues.

Critical Thinking: This feature supports and encourages readers' ability to engage critically and flexibly with concepts and perspectives discussed in the text. The content of this feature may highlight areas of controversy, specific criticisms of the law, or possible options for law reform. It builds an awareness of various opinions about a particular principle, assists readers to engage with issues and debates from various perspectives, and develops readers' skills in formulating and analysing legal argument.

This Chapter in Essence: Primarily directed at supporting readers' orientation, this section maps the key areas and core topics which are covered within each chapter in a succinct list of essential points.

Glossary: The text is supported by a comprehensive glossary that succinctly explains and contextualises the key terms and concepts which appear in the text. All terms which are included in the glossary words are styled as bold-grey text within the book.

Diagrams: These Figures provide visual overviews for some concepts in the book. This feature reinforces understanding, helps to clarify key concepts, and illustrates the interrelationship between distinct legal concepts.

PART ONE

Principles and structures of government

Chapter 1

South African constitutional law in context

1.1 Introduction

A constitution is often said to be the founding document of a nation as the authority of the state is derived from it. It sets up the structures of government and authorises as well as regulates the exercise of power by the elected branches of government and the judiciary (and, in some instances, private institutions and individuals). It also places limits on the exercise of that power and sets out the ground rules according to which a country must be governed. However, democratic constitutions are not mere technical legal documents that contain detailed provisions prescribing the manner in which the legislature, the executive, the judiciary and other organs of state exercise public power and setting limits on the exercise of those powers to protect citizens. Hence, we cannot profitably study the constitutional law of a democratic state in the abstract, as if the historical context out of which the constitution emerged and the current social, economic and political realities of this state have no bearing on an interpretation and evaluation of the various provisions of a written constitution.[1] Nor can we ignore the broader global context within which the constitution operates. Constitutional law can therefore arguably be described as the most 'political' branch of the law.

1 Not all constitutions can be found in one or more formal written documents. For example, the British or Westminster Constitution has evolved over a long period of time but has never been fully codified in any written official form. See De Smith, S and Brazier, R (1994) *Constitutional and Administrative Law* 7th ed 6.

In critically evaluating the manner in which constitutions actually operate in practice and in judging the successes and failures of various aspects of a constitutional design, we should start with, but cannot exclusively rely on, the text of the constitution to gain a comprehensive picture of how this constitution operates. We also need to consider the wider context in which that constitutional text finds application. Constitutions are often said to represent a snapshot of the hopes and dreams of a nation at the time of its writing or – more cynically – to represent a snapshot of the relative political power and influence of various political formations involved in the drafting of that constitution.

However, constitutions are also living documents that judges have to interpret and apply in an ever-changing political, economic and social environment. A constitutional text often contains open-ended and relatively general language. In constitutional democracies, therefore, judges have to interpret, apply and flesh out the meaning of the constitutional text. The interpretation and application of the various provisions of a constitution will not necessarily remain static. Judges will often reinterpret and reapply the text. These judges are, after all, human beings who do not float above the world like disembodied ghosts completely untouched by the society in which they live. Judges are the products of the society in which they live. They will, despite their best efforts, interpret the often open-ended and general provisions of a constitution in ways that are not entirely 'objective' and may change over time as social, economic and political circumstances change. Many of the justices of South Africa's Constitutional Court have tentatively acknowledged the open-ended nature of the language of the South African Constitution. They have admitted that there may be a need to refer to extra-legal values and texts, including the South African political context and history, to justify their decisions.

PAUSE FOR REFLECTION

Approaches to interpreting a constitution

In the first decision handed down by the Constitutional Court of South Africa in *S v Zuma and Others*, Kentridge J signalled an awareness of (but skirted) the issue of what judges should do when confronted with a constitutional text that contains sometimes vague and open-ended phrases when he remarked:

> **I am well aware of the fallacy of supposing that general language must have a single 'objective' meaning. Nor is it easy to avoid the influence of one's personal intellectual and moral preconceptions. But it cannot be too strongly stressed that the Constitution does not mean whatever we might wish it to mean.[2]**

One of the most perplexing questions in law relates to the manner in which judges should interpret the often open-ended or even vague provisions of a constitution. If judges merely make the constitution mean whatever they wish it to mean, they will be accused of being politicians and not judges. If they are not constrained by the text of the constitution or by other extra-legal but objective criteria, their decisions may lack legitimacy as judges are not elected and cannot be seen to make up the meaning of the constitution as they go along. This is why judges often state that they are constrained by the text of the constitution and, if the text is vague, why judges resort to factors such as context or the history of a country to give meaning to the provisions in a constitution.

2 (CCT5/94) [1995] ZACC 1; 1995 (2) SA 642; 1995 (4) BCLR 401 (SA); 1995 (1) SACR 568; [1996] 2 CHRLD 244 (5 April 1995) para 17.

In this chapter we therefore discuss the constitutional history of South Africa, a history that has been dominated by **colonialism** and **apartheid** and the resulting struggle for freedom and democracy which finally led to the adoption of South Africa's 1996 Constitution. We explore the manner in which the South African Constitution came into being and the nature of South Africa's transition from an **authoritarian** race-based autocracy to a constitutional democracy. We also explore the current social, political and economic context within which the South African Constitution must operate, We focus, in particular, on the legacy of apartheid and the role of political parties in South Africa's current one-party dominant democracy.[3] We then briefly introduce the main features of the South African Constitution and pose questions about how this Constitution may be classified and how it should be interpreted.

1.2 The historical-legal context: from colonial conquest to democracy

South Africa's political history is often wrongly said to have begun in 1652 when Jan van Riebeeck arrived in South Africa and the process of colonisation formally commenced. Similarly, South Africa's constitutional history is often said to have begun in 1910 when the South African state in its present form was created and the Union of South Africa came into existence with the passing of the Union of South Africa Act, 1909 (the South Africa Act or the Union Constitution) by the British Parliament.[4] This decidedly colonial approach to history, which views history through the eyes of those settlers who arrived in South Africa from Europe, is no longer viewed as either tenable or credible. It ignores the fact that Khoisan-speaking hunters and herders already occupied western parts of the country while agro-pastoralists occupied large parts of the eastern part of the country at the time when settlers from Western Europe arrived at the southern tip of Africa.[5]

However, it is difficult not to revert to colonial imposed markers when discussing the historical context out of which the modern democratic state in South Africa emerged. There are a number of reasons for this. First, pre-colonial history was never written down. Second, there is insufficient clarity about the multitude of governing structures through which pre-colonial **indigenous populations** of South Africa governed themselves. Third, South Africa with its current borders legally came into existence only in 1910. In the section that follows we nevertheless attempt to draw attention to the fact that South Africa's political and legal history can be viewed through various lenses and that we cannot ignore the legal pluralistic nature of South African society and legal culture when discussing the historical context out of which South Africa's 1996 Constitution emerged.

1.2.1 Pre-Union developments

It is important to understand the complex nature of pre-democratic governance structures in South Africa as these structures continue to have an effect on South Africa's democratic constitutional order. A number of centrally governed societies emerged in the geographical

3 See Choudhry, S (2009) 'He had a mandate': The South African Constitutional Court and the African National Congress in a dominant party democracy *Constitutional Court Review* 2:1–86.

4 See Currie, I and De Waal, J (eds) (2001) *The New Constitutional and Administrative Law, Vol 1 Constitutional Law* 40–3.

5 See Kuper, A (1997) Review: *The Mfecane Aftermath: Reconstructive Debates in Southern African History* by Carol Hamilton *Current Anthropology* 38(3):471–3; Woolman, S and Swanepoel, J 'Constitutional history' in Woolman, S and Bishop, M (eds) (2013) *Constitutional Law of South Africa* 2nd ed rev service 5 2.6.

territory now known as South Africa from the seventeenth century onwards. In colonial enclaves in the Cape in the western parts of the region and in parts of Natal in the east, the development of constitutional forms mirrored those of other British colonies with large European settler populations.

In the Cape, executive government emerged with a British-appointed Governor and an advisory council of white settlers. In 1853, this developed into a representative form of government with an appointed Governor but an elected legislature. Finally, in 1872, a system of responsible government emerged with a Governor-General representing the British Crown and an elected legislature whose support was needed for the formation of an executive council.[6] This meant that locally representative executives governed these territories, but the British-appointed Governor-General had to approve legislation. The Governor-General, in effect, had a veto power over bills which could be exercised on the advice of the British government. Moreover, the British government also had the power to 'disallow' bills passed by the colonial legislatures within a period of one year from the date the bill was passed. This in effect nullified these bills.[7] The governance structures therefore mirrored the **Westminster system** in place in Britain although the arrangement retained final control over the colonies for the British government.

Nevertheless, these governing structures firmly established the principle of the supremacy of the legislature on South African soil.[8] This meant that the legislature by and large had a free hand to pass any legislation it wished as long as it followed the requisite procedures. Courts were not empowered to test the laws passed by the legislature against a bill of rights and could not declare legislation invalid even where that legislation infringed on the rights of citizens.

To the north of the Cape, two Boer Republics (the Orange Free State and the South African Republic, also known as the Transvaal Republic) emerged in the mid-nineteenth century. Both these Republics rejected the Westminster system described above. Under the influence of the constitutions of the United States, France and the Netherlands, the Boer Republics embraced a form of governance based on the principle of the separation of powers with directly elected presidents. The Orange Free State also had a justiciable Bill of Rights that guaranteed rights of peaceful assembly, petition, property and equality before the law. In addition, rigid rules were prescribed for the amendment of the Orange Free State Constitution of 1854.[9]

However, despite the fact that the Orange Free State Constitution formally recognised the right of courts to review legislation, this power was used only once. Moreover, the protections in the Constitution were of limited application as they were interpreted to be reserved for white males only.[10] This early tentative experiment in constitutionalism was thus tainted by a notion of racial citizenship which later came to dominate constitutional law and practice in a unified South Africa.[11]

6 Currie and De Waal (2001) 42; Dugard, J (1978) *Human Rights and the South African Legal Order* 17. See generally Klug, H (2010) *The Constitution of South Africa: A Contextual Analysis* 8–11.

7 Currie and De Waal (2001) 42.

8 Dugard (1978) 14–18.

9 Hahlo, HR and Khan, E (1960) *The Union of South Africa: The Development of its Laws and Constitution* 72–83. See generally Carpenter, G (1987) *Introduction to South African Constitutional Law* 64–72.

10 In *Cassim and Solomon v The State* (1892) *Cape Law Journal* 9:58, the High Court of the Orange Free State reviewed a law which prohibited 'Asians' from settling in the state without permission of the President on the ground that it violated the guarantee of equality before the law. However, the Court upheld the law, arguing that the constitutional guarantee had to be 'read in accordance with the *mores* of the Voortrekkers'. See Dugard (1978) 19.

11 Klug (2010) 11.

In the South African Republic (Transvaal), the Constitution of 1858 was blatantly racist. It provided that 'the People desire to permit no equality between coloured people and white inhabitants, either in Church or State'.[12] In the Transvaal, an attempt in 1892 by Chief Justice JG Kotze to review and strike down legislation of the legislature (*Volksraad*) on the basis that it conflicted with the Constitution created a constitutional crisis.[13] President Paul Kruger rejected the right of the court to review and strike down legislation and eventually fired the Chief Justice. When swearing in a new Chief Justice, President Kruger warned the judges that 'the testing right is a principle of the devil', which the devil had introduced into paradise to test God's word.[14]

Those parts of South Africa not directly subjected to colonial domination exhibited various forms of indigenous governance structures loosely centred on the concept of chiefdoms. These chiefdoms usually had a similar governance hierarchy consisting of a chief, a paramount chief or a king. Below them were headmen who were representatives of leading families. Headmen were responsible for affairs within a defined geographical area and reported to the chief. The chief, together with his headmen, constituted a council. Below the chief and headmen were family or kraal heads. The chief's role was to adjudicate disputes fairly and to provide for the well-being of his people by applying a living **customary law** which developed through its application by chiefs. To empower the chief to meet his obligations, he was vested with secular powers and was granted certain privileges that he was entitled to exercise.[15]

The selection of a chief was rooted in ancestry and traditional leaders were born into the role rather than selected and trained. We must be careful not to evaluate the traditional leadership structures through the lens of Western-imposed governance structures. It is therefore not profitable to evaluate these structures with reference to concepts such as the separation of powers or parliamentary sovereignty. Nevertheless, although chiefs had wide powers, these were not unlimited. Chiefs were generally required to consult with their councillors in certain matters and were always required to act for the benefit of their people.[16] Potential challenges to the office of the chief also acted as an incentive to ensure that chiefs acted appropriately.[17]

The emergence of the Zulu Kingdom, which eventually spanned large parts of what is now known as KwaZulu-Natal, represents a modification to this governance model. The Zulu Kingdom began with the reign of Dingiswayo, Chief of the Mthethwa, who ruled from 1808 to 1818. King Dingiswayo conquered several chiefdoms with the assistance of a reorganised military. This had important sociopolitical implications since it weakened the influence of territorially based kinship relations. Dingiswayo also changed the political order by centralising power over the conquered area.[18]

After the death of King Dingiswayo, King Shaka seized power. Shaka gathered a large number of chiefdoms into one entity and incorporated the defeated troops into the Zulu military. Although some chiefdoms were able to disperse into other territories, Shaka's wars resulted in the merging of some 300 formerly independent chiefdoms into the Zulu Kingdom. Shaka ordered his warriors to remain unmarried and controlled the organisation of his

12 Dugard (1978) 20.
13 *Brown v Leyds NO* (1897) 4 Off Rep 17.
14 Dugard (1978) 24.
15 Bennett, TW (2004) *Customary Law in South Africa* 103.
16 Bennett (2004) 104.
17 Bennett (2004) 104–5.
18 Deflem, M (1999) Warfare, political leadership, and state formation: The case of the Zulu Kingdom, 1808–1879 *Ethnology* 38(4):371–91 at 376–7.

military regiments. This further weakened traditional kinship ties and the powers of the elders in favour of his central authority. However, the purported authoritarian rule of Shaka still relied on a delicate system of delegated chiefly powers. Shaka was assisted by a staff of chiefs who surrounded him in the royal kraal (a territorial dwelling unit with the house of the King located at the centre). While Shaka needed the chiefs to execute his will, he was careful to limit their effective powers and it is argued that he stirred rivalry among them so that they would check one another but never dispute his will.[19]

COUNTER POINT

Different viewpoints on the evaluation of indigenous governance structures

There is a fundamental difference between the governance structures of the indigenous societies of South Africa and the governance structures imposed by the British colonial regime. Some commentators argue that the indigenous structures valued community and the relationships between individuals and groups. This mitigated what may appear from the vantage point of the modern state to be an autocratic and undemocratic arrangement. Chiefs relied on the goodwill of their subjects, so it is argued, and hence were required to rule wisely and humanely. Where this did not happen, chiefs could be removed and this acted as a check on the power of the chiefs. Others point to the essentially patriarchal nature of the arrangement and contend that the arrangement was, at the very least, deeply sexist as it negated the role of women in society.

When evaluating these various governance structures of the era, it would be difficult to do so except through the distorted twenty-first century lens. However, it can be argued that the governance structures of traditional indigenous societies in South Africa have something to offer a South African constitutional law scholar as they are often said to have been based on a kind of communalism. This indirectly finds resonance in the co-operative government provisions in the modern South African Constitution. Nevertheless, if we judge these structures from the modern-day vantage point, they may seem problematic as they are not based on the same democratic principles that we take for granted in a modern constitutional state.

The various forms of governance and the customary powers of traditional leaders described above remained largely intact as the British extended their colonial domination across southern Africa. Nevertheless, over time – as the territorial expansion of colonial governments proceeded apace – indigenous South Africans were increasingly subjected to the authority of the colonial powers. This led to a situation in which colonial governments became the primary source of the traditional leader's authority.

In 1894, the Glen Grey Act[20] was passed in the Cape Colony. This Act effectively excluded the vast majority of Africans from the Cape Parliament. It also weakened the authority of the system of chiefs by replacing them with a system of government-appointed district councillors. In addition, the Act introduced separate 'reserve' areas where Africans were supposed to stay if they were not selling their labour to white-owned institutions in cities and towns. The Act was thus designed to set a pattern of African land-holding – individual plots in separate 'reserves' – throughout the 'Cape African reserves'.[21] It assigned certain

19 Deflem (1999) 377–8.

20 Act 25 of 1894.

21 Davenport, TRH (1987) *South Africa: A Modern History* 3rd ed 181.

geographical areas for use by blacks and others for whites under a distorted version of the communal system of land tenure. The Glen Grey Act can therefore be said to be a forerunner of the more all-encompassing segregationist and apartheid measures, especially the creation of territorially separate areas for African occupation after 1910.[22]

By 1903, the Native Affairs Commission (the 'Langden Commission') had developed a vision for a future South African union based on the territorial segregation of black and white as a permanent mandatory feature of public life.[23] The Commission endorsed the practice of creating 'native reserves' and accepted the notion that this involved special obligations on their part to the colonial state. 'Natives' were seen as having special rights to these pieces of reserved land as the 'ancestral land held by their forefathers'. 'Native reserves' were held communally and administered by tribal chiefs who were said to have transferred their sovereign rights over land and their absolute political authority to the Crown through a process of 'peaceful annexation'.[24] The assumption of the 'peaceful annexation' of land was a fiction which served the interests of the colonial rulers. These developments set the scene for the formation of a **bifurcated** state when the various territories now known as South Africa were unified into the Union of South Africa in 1910 and can clearly be seen as the precursor for the elaborate system of apartheid.[25]

PAUSE FOR REFLECTION

Recognition of traditional governance structures in the Constitution

Constitutional law textbooks have often ignored the governance structures of indigenous South Africans as well as the customary law applied by chiefs during the pre-Union period. They have tended to focus exclusively on the imposition of the Westminster model by the British and on the importation of Roman-Dutch and English **common law**. This is not surprising as such textbooks have been written from a Western perspective.

Today, the Constitution partly recognises traditional governance structures. However, as we shall see, these traditional governance structures were transformed in their encounter with the colonial rulers and this affected their development. These developments help to explain the present arrangement in South Africa in which traditional leaders and the application of customary law are made subject to the provisions of the 1996 Constitution.

1.2.2 The Union of South Africa and the bifurcated state

After the British defeated the armies of the Boer Republics during the Anglo-Boer War of 1899–1902, the territory now known as South Africa largely came under the influence of the British government. However, as part of a policy of granting self-rule to white colonists in its various colonies, Britain facilitated negotiations that led to the formation of the Union of South Africa in 1910. Black South Africans were not invited to take part in these negotiations. This process of negotiation resulted in the drafting of the South Africa Act (the Union Constitution). This Act brought together the four settler colonies – Cape, Natal, Orange Free

22 Hendricks, F and Ntsebeza, L (1999) Chiefs and rural local government in post-apartheid South Africa *African Journal of Political Science* 4(1):99–126 at 102.

23 Davenport (1987) 152.

24 Woolman and Swanepoel (2013) 2.14.

25 Klug (2010) 8; Davenport (1987) 112–15; Mamdani, M (1996) *Citizen and Subject: Contemporary Africa and the Legacy of Late Colonialism* 67–9.

State and Transvaal – as well as the various indigenous groupings in South Africa in a single unitary state known as the Union of South Africa. The Constitution establishing the Union in essence granted parliamentary democracy to the white minority within the borders of present-day South Africa. However, this settlement largely ignored the political aspirations of indigenous South Africans and subjugated the black majority to autocratic administrative rule.

It is true that the drafters of the Union Constitution reached a compromise that allowed the Cape to retain its provision for limited voting rights for black citizens.[26] However, the northern provinces were allowed to exclude all participation by black South Africans in the electoral process. The retention of this very limited franchise for black South Africans in the Cape did not change the essentially racist and paternalistic nature of the founding Constitution of South Africa. African society was presented as essentially 'traditional' and was to be governed by chiefs under the paternalistic 'protection' of the white government. The South African polity was therefore divided into two distinct spheres – one white and one black. This reflected the colonial character of South Africa's legal culture in which 'professed legalism with its accompanying rhetoric of justice' coexisted with the racist abuse of power by the state.[27] Thus section 147 of the Union Constitution stated that the 'control and administration of native affairs ... throughout the Union shall vest in the Governor-General in Council'. The Governor-General in Council was given 'all special powers in regard to native administration'.

This 'colonialism of a special' type thus established a Westminster-style parliamentary system. Under this system, a pseudo-democratic white state co-existed with an authoritarian order in which the majority of the country's people lived under a classic system of colonial indirect rule.[28] Traditional versions of South Africa's constitutional history produced before 1994 ignore this bifurcated nature of the South African state between 1910 and 1994.[29]

As noted above, the Constitution establishing the Union of South Africa was largely applicable to white citizens only. This Constitution followed the British model and opted for a Westminster-style system of parliamentary government and a form of **parliamentary supremacy**. The Union Parliament consisted of two Houses, the House of Assembly and the Senate. The House of Assembly was directly elected by the limited number of male citizens who had the right to vote. The members of the Senate were partly indirectly elected by the House of Assembly and partly nominated. South Africa was also established as a unitary state rather than a federal state. However, the four former colonies were retained in the form of four provinces and each province had equal representation in the Senate.

The most striking aspect of the Union Constitution was, however, the fact that it retained a system of parliamentary supremacy. Despite this, the South African legislature was restrained, initially at least, in two important ways which imposed limits on the sovereignty of the newly created Parliament.

First, until the British Parliament adopted the Statute of Westminster in 1931, Parliament was, in theory, still bound by the provisions of the Colonial Laws Validity Act, 1865. This meant that the Union Parliament could not legislate extraterritorially or in a manner

26 In the Cape Colony, every man over the age of 21 who was a British subject and who owned property worth at least 25 pounds or who received a salary of at least 50 pounds per year was granted the vote. Although few black men qualified, there was no formal racial restriction in the Cape franchise and this was retained after unification. Similar provisions applied to the Natal Colony. However, black men and women in the other two provinces were not allowed to vote.

27 Chanock, M (2001) *The Making of South African Legal Culture 1902–1936: Fear, Favour and Prejudice* 22.

28 Klug (2010) 9.

29 See, for example, Basson, DA and Viljoen, HP (1988) *Suid-Afrikaanse Staatsreg* 2de uitg 36–7.

repugnant to any Act of the British Parliament which had been made applicable in South Africa. All bills passed by the South African Parliament had to be sent to the Governor-General (as representative of the British Crown) for assent before they could become law. The Governor-General could assent to the bill, refuse his assent or reserve it for the King's decision. The King made his decision based on the advice of the British cabinet. The British monarch also had the power to disallow a bill within one year after the bill had received the assent of the Governor-General, a power once again exercised on the advice of the British cabinet. In practice, little or no control was ever exercised and the powers referred to above were never used before they were scrapped by the Statute of Westminster.[30]

Second, a small number of clauses in the Union Constitution required Parliament to use a special procedure before they could be amended. These entrenched sections protected the limited franchise for blacks in the Cape[31] and the guarantee of the equality of the two official languages (English and Dutch).[32] Thus, Parliament could amend any section of the Constitution with a simple majority in each of the Houses of Parliament sitting separately. However, section 152 of the Union Constitution required that any alteration of the above sections (as well as section 152 itself) would only be valid if the bill was passed by both Houses of Parliament sitting together and agreed to at the third reading of the bill by not less than two-thirds of the total number of members of both Houses.[33] Despite the procedural protection of the limited franchise, all African voters (those who lived in the Cape Province and had retained their right to vote in the deal struck in 1909) were nevertheless removed from the common voters roll and given separate representation in 1936.[34]

The Union's first full-blown constitutional crisis arose after the National Party (NP) narrowly won the parliamentary election in 1948 on the basis, among others, that it would impose absolute racial segregation on South Africa. In 1951, the NP attempted to remove 'coloured' voters from the common voters roll by adopting the Separate Representation of Voters Act.[35] A group of voters challenged the Act on the basis that the procedure required by section 152 of the Union Constitution was not used. In *Harris and Others v Minister of the Interior and Another*,[36] a unanimous Appellate Division (AD) found that the Separate Representation of Voters Act was of no force because the correct procedure had not been used to pass the amendments. After further legislative and judicial manoeuvres, in which the NP was again thwarted, it increased the size of the AD from five to 11 judges and also increased the size of the Senate.

When this legislative move was again challenged in *Collins v Minister of the Interior*,[37] 10 of the 11 judges upheld the challenged amendments to the Union Constitution.[38] This brought an end to the limited voting rights enjoyed by black South Africans and until partial reforms were introduced in 1983, only white South Africans could vote in parliamentary elections. In 1958, the whites-only Parliament adopted the South Africa Amendment Act.[39]

30 Currie and De Waal (2001) 44–5.

31 S 35 of the Union Constitution.

32 S 137 of the Union Constitution.

33 See Currie and De Waal (2001) 44–5.

34 Native Representative Act 12 of 1936. The Act was challenged in *Ndlwana v Hofmeyer NO and Others* 1937 AD 229, but the courts refused to intervene.

35 Act 46 of 1951.

36 1952 (2) SA 428 (A).

37 1957 (1) SA 552 (A).

38 The only judge to dissent, Oliver Schreiner, was later twice overlooked when a new Chief Justice had to be appointed. See Dugard (1978) 286; Haynie, SL (2003) *Judging in Black and White: Decision Making in the South African Appellate Division, 1950–1990*.

39 Act 1 of 1958.

This Act prohibited any court of law in South Africa from enquiring 'into or ... pronounc[ing] upon the validity of any law passed by Parliament' other than those affecting the clause dealing with the two official languages.[40] When South Africa became a Republic in 1961, a new constitution was adopted which confirmed the supremacy of Parliament. Section 59 of the 1961 Constitution thus stated that: 'Parliament shall be the sovereign legislative authority in and over the Republic, and shall have full power to make laws for the peace, order and good government of the Republic'. This extreme form of parliamentary supremacy, which became dominant in South Africa after 1948 and the rise of Afrikaner nationalism, is said to have 'brought about the debasement of the South African legal system' and brought it to its 'logical and brutal conclusion' to the detriment of a respect for human rights.[41] However, it may well be argued that it was the **combination** of this extreme form of parliamentary sovereignty and the inherently racist nature of the bifurcated constitutional system which gave the South African state its particularly brutal character before the advent of democracy in 1994.

COUNTER POINT

An extreme version of parliamentary sovereignty

In *Sachs v Minister of Justice; Diamond v Minister of Justice*,[42] the AD had to consider the validity of a banning order issued by the Minister in terms of the relevant provisions of an applicable Act. Banning orders prohibited a person from being present in specific areas because the Minister was satisfied that the person 'is in any area promoting feelings of hostility between the European inhabitants of the Union on the one hand and any other section of the inhabitants of the Union on the other hand'.[43] Banning orders were a powerful tool used by the authorities to restrict the political activities of those opposed to the policies of the government. In rejecting the challenge to the banning order, Stratford ACJ made the following statement about the nature of parliamentary sovereignty in South Africa:

> [O]nce we are satisfied on a construction of the Act, that it gives to the Minister an unfettered discretion, it is no function of a Court of law to curtail its scope in the least degree, indeed it would be quite improper to do so. The above observation is, perhaps, so trite that it needs no statement, yet in cases before the Courts when the exercise of a statutory discretion is challenged, arguments are sometimes advanced which do seem to me to ignore the plain principle that Parliament may make any encroachment it chooses upon the life, liberty or property of any individual subject to its sway, and that it is the function of courts of law to enforce its will. In the present case we were referred to many decisions dealing with the exercise of discretionary powers. In this division, at all events, no decision affirms the right of a Court to interfere with the honest exercise of a duly conferred discretion. For the sake of greater caution I should perhaps add, that in exercising a conferred discretion, the procedure laid down in terms of its

40 Klug (2010) 12.

41 Dugard (1978) 36. Dugard contrasts this extreme notion of parliamentary supremacy to that which holds sway in the United Kingdom where political traditions, conventions and respect for the rule of law act as a control on the system of parliamentary supremacy.

42 1934 AD 11.

43 S 1(12) of the Riotous Assemblies and Criminal Law Amendment Act 27 of 1914 as amended by the Riotous Assemblies Amendment Act 19 of 1930.

> **grant must, of course, be observed as essential conditions of its exercise. Interferences when they have occurred are justified on one of two broad grounds, either that (a) the exercise has not been honest or (b) that the discretionary power has been exceeded.[44]**

The view expressed by Stratford ACJ represents an extreme version of the nature of parliamentary sovereignty. It is also far less compatible with the notion of democracy than a view which limits the power of the legislature to adopt legislation that encroaches on the rights of citizens and allows judges to review and set aside legislation and the actions of members of the executive if this is needed to protect and safeguard the rights of individuals. This is because democracy itself can be subverted if the rights of citizens to exercise their democratic rights are not protected.

After the Union of South Africa was established in 1910, the bifurcated nature of the South African state led to the adoption of several laws by the Union Parliament aimed at developing legal mechanisms to entrench further a classic form of indirect colonial rule. The Black Administration Act of 1927 (BAA)[45] was a lynchpin in this system which reaffirmed the rule of chiefs within so-called 'reserves' and that subordinated their rule to the power of the 'white' government and its officials.[46] The BAA made the Governor-General the supreme chief with the authority to create and divide tribes and appoint any person he chose as chief or headman - even in the face of popular opposition from a community.[47] The BAA to some extent built on the Glen Grey Act and further subverted the traditional governance structures based on chiefs selected via kinship. It allowed for the appointment of traditional leaders from outside the ruling families, creating scope for a body of government lackeys, who were compliant with entrenched party political interests, to assume the role of traditional leader. It has been remarked that the BAA:

> **was intended to shore up the remains of chieftaincy in a country-wide policy of indirect rule, which would allow for segregation in the administration of justice. The policy was aptly named 'retribalisation', giving chiefs the semblance of power and hoping that this would safeguard the allegiance and acquiescence of the Reserve residents.[48]**

The BAA conferred civil jurisdiction on chiefs who could apply the customary law to their subjects in most private law civil disputes. However, in practice, Africans had a choice of courts to which they could take their civil case - the magistrates' courts or the chiefly authority. The magistrates obviously wielded much more power than the chiefs in relation to the central government, but the chiefs were given a niche in the local arm of administration which 'they seized with alacrity'.[49]

44 *Sachs v Minister of Justice; Diamond v Minister of Justice* 1934 AD 11 paras 36–7.

45 Act 38 of 1927.

46 S 12.

47 S 1. See Mqeke, RB (1997) *Basic Approaches to Problem Solving in Customary Law: A Study of Conciliation and Consensus amongst the Cape Nguni* 83–4.

48 Hendricks and Ntsebeza (1999) 104. See also Lacey, M (1981) *Working for Boroko: The Origins of a Coercive Labour System in South Africa* 94–119.

49 Hendricks and Ntsebeza (1999) 104.

As the confidence of the ruling NP government grew in the years after 1948, it stepped up political repression while simultaneously trying to create a system based on ethnic nationalism within a tribal context. Thus, the implementation of a system of indirect rule accelerated with the adoption of the Bantu Authorities Act[50] in 1951 and, by 1959, legislation which created a system of homelands.[51] The system divided South Africa into several 'self-governing' territories where each ethnic group was accommodated in a separate homeland (the former 'native reserves'). These homelands were envisaged as the sole mechanisms through which Africans would be able to exercise their political aspirations. People classified as 'coloured' or 'Indian' were not accommodated in this system at all. Eventually, certain of the homelands were granted 'independent' status[52] but other homelands never achieved or refused to take up an offer of 'independence'. Chiefs held half the seats in the legislative assembly of the homelands *ex officio* and thus assured the leading parties of support.[53]

It is important to note that this social engineering had devastating consequences for the traditional governing structures of indigenous South Africans. It transformed chiefs by bringing them directly into the service of the state. It became more and more difficult for chiefs to claim legitimacy, to win respect from their followers and to implement the provisions of the Bantu Authorities Act at the same time.[54] With the advent of democracy, the role of traditional leaders, and especially chiefs, has become controversial given the manner in which the system was manipulated during the colonial and apartheid eras. This role is perceived to be inherently undemocratic and patriarchal as it is both hereditary and reserved for men.[55] However, despite concerns surrounding the undemocratic essence of tribal leadership, it remains an important part of South Africa's cultural heritage which, despite allegations of corruption, receives some popular support.[56]

By the late 1970s, the apartheid state had come under increasing pressure both internally and externally as opposition and resistance to apartheid and white minority rule increased and the struggle for freedom by the black majority gathered momentum.[57] In response, the apartheid government of Prime Minister PW Botha (who became Prime Minister in 1979) opted for a process of so-called 'reform' to try to reincorporate people classified as 'Indian' and 'coloured' under the apartheid system into the political system. This led to the 1983 Constitution[58] which extended the franchise to coloureds and Indians in a tricameral legislature.

This new constitutional system (whose introduction was fiercely resisted by the majority of South Africans) created three separate Houses of Parliament: one chamber for whites, one for Indians and one for coloureds. The jurisdiction for each House was distributed according to whether an issue dealt with an 'own' affair or 'general' affair. Own affairs were vaguely defined and were deemed to be matters 'which specially or differentially affect a population group in relation to the maintenance of its identity, traditions and customs'.[59]

---

50 Act 68 of 1951.

51 The Promotion of Bantu Self-government Act 46 of 1959.

52 Transkei in 1976, Bophuthatswana in 1976, Venda in 1979 and Ciskei in 1981.

53 Bennett (2004) 111.

54 Hendricks and Ntsebeza (1999) 106.

55 There is one exception, the Balobedu tribe. See further Pieterse, M (1999) Traditional leaders win battle in undecided war *SAJHR* 15:179–187; Motshabi, KB and Volks, SG (1991) Towards democratic chieftaincy: Principles and procedures *Acta Juridica* 104–15 at 104–5.

56 For a discussion of the controversial nature of chieftaincy, see Bennett (2004) 111–13 and 120–3; Pillay, N and Prinsloo, C (1995) The changing face of 'traditional courts' *De Jure* 1:383 at 383–4.

57 See Woolman and Swanepoel (2013) 2.21–2.22.

58 Republic of South Africa Constitution Act 110 of 1983.

59 S 14 of the 1983 Constitution. See Basson and Viljoen (1988) 152.

Each House was given powers to deal exclusively with these 'own affairs'. 'General affairs' were defined as matters which were not own affairs.[60] The white minority government retained control of this system through a provision in the Constitution that stated that the State President took the final decision on whether an issue dealt with an own affair or a general affair.[61]

Each House enacted legislation dealing with 'own affairs' related to its race group while all three Houses of Parliament dealt with general affairs. However, in effect, the tricameral Constitution ensured that the exercise of power would remain firmly entrenched in the hands of the dominant white majority party - the National Party. This was done, first, by centralising the running of the government under the State President who was given extraordinary powers in both the legislature and executive arena.[62] Moreover, all significant decisions within the tricameral legislature - such as the election of the President - would be automatically resolved by a 4:2:1 ratio of white, coloured and Indian representatives.[63] This ensured that even if the Indian and coloured Houses voted in unison, the will of the white House would prevail.[64]

Despite these 'reforms', the African majority continued to be excluded from the constitutional scheme. The apartheid government maintained that South Africa would eventually be divided into one section over which the tricameral Parliament would hold sway and the several homelands which would obtain 'independence' and would govern all Africans living within the original borders of the Union of South Africa. Africans living outside the homelands were all deemed to 'belong' to one of the homelands and had no political rights in the areas in which they actually lived. These 'reforms' backfired spectacularly and resistance to the apartheid government became ever more fierce. Finally, in 1990, State President FW de Klerk lifted the restrictions placed on liberation movements such as the African National Congress (ANC), the South African Communist Party (SACP) and the Pan Africanist Congress (PAC), and ordered the release of Nelson Mandela and other liberation leaders from prison. The period of negotiations then commenced.

1.3 The transition to democracy

1.3.1 The run-up to the first democratic election

The Constitutional Court has described South Africa's past as that of a 'deeply divided society characterised by strife, conflict, untold suffering and injustice' which 'generated gross violations of human rights, the transgression of humanitarian principles in violent conflicts and a legacy of hatred, fear, guilt and revenge'.[65] As the struggle against this system intensified, the minority government, backed by a powerful security apparatus, became more oppressive and authoritarian.[66]

60 S 15 of the 1983 Constitution.

61 S 16 of the 1983 Constitution.

62 Klug (2010) 13. See generally Pottinger, B (1988) *The Imperial Presidency: P.W. Botha, the First 10 Years.*

63 For example, the State President was elected by an 88-member electoral college, 50 of whom were from the white House, 25 from the coloured House and 13 from the Indian House. These delegates were elected by each House with a simple majority, thus ensuring that the majority party in the white House would retain overall control over the election of the President.

64 Klug (2010) 13. See also Currie and De Waal (2001) 56–7 and Basson and Viljoen (1988) 50–1.

65 *Certification of the Constitution of the Republic of South Africa, 1996* (CCT 23/96) [1996] ZACC 26; 1996 (4) SA 744 (CC); 1996 (10) BCLR 1253 (CC) (6 September 1996) para 5, quoting from the postamble to the 1993 Constitution.

66 *First Certification* para 9.

Distinct but sometimes overlapping movements led the resistance to this system of white minority rule: the ANC and the SACP with their internal allies, the United Democratic Front (UDF) and large sections of the trade union movement, as well as the PAC and the Black Consciousness Movement, including the Azanian People's Organisation (AZAPO). The ANC was officially formed on 8 January 1912 and has a long and complicated history of resistance to white political rule. Its stature grew as it took a more defiant stance against the apartheid policies of the newly elected NP after 1948 – especially after its Youth League under the auspices of Oliver Tambo and Nelson Mandela successfully pressed the organisation to adopt more militant methods in resisting the apartheid regime.

In June 1952, the ANC initiated the Defiance Campaign which employed passive resistance strategies to resist the newly imposed legal restrictions on black South Africans in general and Africans in particular. The ANC then helped to engineer the drafting and adoption of the Freedom Charter with the assistance of other opponents of apartheid, including the SACP, the Natal Indian Congress and others.[67] This Charter contained claims and expressed the aspirations of large sections of the South African citizenry oppressed by the apartheid regime, formulated in the format of a charter of rights with a strong emphasis on non-racialism. As such, the Freedom Charter is often seen as one of the founding documents of the human rights culture which later found expression in the Bill of Rights contained in South Africa's 1996 Constitution.[68]

PAUSE FOR REFLECTION

Extracts from the Freedom Charter

The People Shall Govern!

Every man and woman shall have the right to vote for and to stand as a candidate for all bodies which make laws;
All people shall be entitled to take part in the administration of the country;
The rights of the people shall be the same, regardless of race, colour or sex ...

The People Shall Share in the Country's Wealth!

The national wealth of our country, the heritage of South Africans, shall be restored to the people;
The mineral wealth beneath the soil, the Banks and monopoly industry shall be transferred to the ownership of the people as a whole ...

The Land Shall be Shared Among Those Who Work It!

Restrictions of land ownership on a racial basis shall be ended, and all the land re-divided amongst those who work it to banish famine and land hunger;
The state shall help the peasants with implements, seed, tractors and dams to save the soil and assist the tillers;
Freedom of movement shall be guaranteed to all who work on the land;
All shall have the right to occupy land wherever they choose;
People shall not be robbed of their cattle, and forced labour and farm prisons shall be abolished.

67 The notion of a Charter was first mooted at the annual Congress of the ANC in August 1953. Prof ZK Mathews formally suggested convening a Congress of the People (COP) to draw up the Freedom Charter. The idea was adopted by the allies of the ANC, the South African Indian Congress, the South African Coloured People's Organisation and the South African Congress of Democrats.

68 Woolman and Swanepoel (2013) 2.28.

All Shall be Equal Before the Law!
No-one shall be imprisoned, deported or restricted without a fair trial;
No-one shall be condemned by the order of any Government official;
The courts shall be representative of all the people ...

All Shall Enjoy Equal Human Rights!
The law shall guarantee to all their right to speak, to organise, to meet together, to publish, to preach, to worship and to educate their children;
The privacy of the house from police raids shall be protected by law ...

There Shall be Houses, Security and Comfort!
All people shall have the right to live where they choose, be decently housed, and to bring up their families in comfort and security;
Unused housing space shall be made available to the people;
Rent and prices shall be lowered, food plentiful and no-one shall go hungry;
A preventive health scheme shall be run by the state;
Free medical care and hospitalisation shall be provided for all, with special care for mothers and young children ...

It is often said that the Freedom Charter is the intellectual source for many of the provisions contained in South Africa's Bill of Rights. Like the Bill of Rights, the Freedom Charter addresses both traditional civil liberties such as the right to vote and the right to a trial as well as social and economic rights concerns relating to housing and land, among others. Although the historical and political context in which the document was formulated influenced the content of the provisions of the Charter and the way in which the demands were formulated, it is remarkable that it addresses many of the same concerns addressed in the Bill of Rights.

The Sharpeville Massacre took place on 21 March 1960, a date now commemorated as Human Rights Day in South Africa, when the South African police opened fire on a protesting crowd, killing 69 people (including eight women and 10 children), and wounding over 180. As a result of the massacre, the ANC decided to change tactics and formed Umkhonto weSizwe (MK) which was charged with using various forms of violence to sabotage the apartheid state.[69] The ANC as well as the PAC were subsequently outlawed and their leaders went into exile or were captured.

During the Rivonia Trial of 1963 and 1964, 10 members of the ANC – including Nelson Mandela, Walter Sisulu, Govan Mbeki and Rusty Bernstein – were tried for sabotage. Eight were found guilty and sentenced to life imprisonment. Many other ANC leaders – including long-time ANC President Oliver Tambo – fled into exile from where they orchestrated the ANC's resistance campaign against the apartheid state by mobilising international opinion against the apartheid regime and orchestrating internal resistance.

As the apartheid state increased its repression of political dissent, resistance grew. From 1976 to 1990, ANC-aligned internal resistance (under the flag of non-racialism and non-sexism) focused on the efforts of the labour movement led by the Congress of South

69 Woolman and Swanepoel (2013) 2.26.

African Trade Unions (COSATU) and the UDF. These internal allies of the ANC played a significant role in putting pressure on the apartheid state, gradually bringing the leaders of the governing NP to the realisation that it would eventually have no option but to cede power and allow the formation of a democratic state.

Meanwhile, the PAC had broken away from the ANC in 1959 because they felt the ANC was too accommodating. They also believed that liberation in South Africa had to be led by Africans without assistance from white, coloured and Indian allies. Under the leadership of the charismatic Robert Sobukwe, the PAC organised mass-based resistance campaigns leading a nationwide protest against the hated Pass Laws which required African people in so-called 'white areas' to carry a pass book at all times. Sobukwe led a march to the local police station at Orlando, Soweto, to defy openly the laws, which led to the Sharpeville Massacre. Following Sobukwe's arrest, he was charged and convicted of incitement, and sentenced to three years in prison. After serving his sentence, he was interned on Robben Island. The new General Law Amendment Act[70] was passed, allowing his imprisonment to be renewed annually at the discretion of the Minister of Justice. This procedure became known as the 'Sobukwe clause' and went on for a further three years. Sobukwe was the only person imprisoned under this clause and he remained imprisoned on Robben Island until his release in 1969.[71]

The founding of the Black Consciousness movement is usually credited to Steve Biko. However, the movement was probably also influenced by the philosophy espoused by Robert Sobukwe and the PAC as it held that liberation could not be achieved by multiracial institutions, parties or movements. Biko challenged the notion – often said to be the root cause of racism and racial domination inherent in South African society of the time – that 'whiteness' was 'normal' and that 'blackness' was an aberration. He aimed to infuse into the black community a sense of pride and self-respect.[72]

The Black Consciousness movement influenced the Soweto uprising which commenced on 16 June 1976, but Biko was later arrested, detained and tortured. He died at the hands of the police in 1977. In the absence of a strong leader and a viable organisation in exile, many young South Africans, who fled the country after the Black Consciousness-inspired uprising, joined the non-racial ANC whose influence and political dominance grew. The political struggle in South Africa appeared to reach an impasse in the 1980s as the UDF increasingly managed to make the country ungovernable and as state repression increased through the application of various States of Emergency.

But then, according to the Constitutional Court, our history suddenly took a turn for the better. In the 1980s, it became manifest to most people that our country was heading for disaster unless the conflict was reversed.[73] Thus, 'remarkably', the country's political leaders 'managed to avoid a cataclysm by negotiating a largely peaceful transition from the rigidly controlled minority regime to a wholly democratic constitutional dispensation'.[74] Tentative and highly secretive talks between members of the ANC and the NP commenced in mid-1980. When FW de Klerk became President in 1989, he was able to build on the previous secret negotiations with the imprisoned Nelson Mandela. The first significant steps towards

70 Act 37 of 1963.

71 Woolman and Swanepoel (2013) 2.26.

72 Biko, S (1978) *I Write What I like* 45–53.

73 *Azanian Peoples Organization (AZAPO) and Others v President of the Republic of South Africa and Others* (CCT17/96) [1996] ZACC 16; 1996 (8) BCLR 1015; 1996 (4) SA 672 (25 July 1996) para 2.

74 *First Certification* para 10.

formal negotiations took place in February 1990 with the unbanning of the ANC and other banned organisations such as the PAC by State President FW de Klerk, and the release of political leaders such as Nelson Mandela from prison.[75] Exiled leaders of the ANC and the PAC returned to South Africa and eventually negotiations about the transition to democracy commenced.

1.3.2 CODESA, the MPNF and the two-stage transition

The Congress for a Democratic South Africa (CODESA) was convened in late 1991 and it was this body – comprising all the major political formations in South Africa[76] – which was tasked with the drafting of the **interim Constitution**. CODESA was preceded by intense negotiations, particularly between the NP and the ANC, to try to reach agreement on the basic premises that would guide the negotiating process.

The Declaration of Intent signed when CODESA was set in motion on 21 December 1991 already recorded a common view that the new constitution would ensure:[77]

> **a. that South Africa will be a united, democratic, non-racial and non-sexist state in which sovereign authority is exercised over the whole of its territory;**
> **b. that the Constitution will be the supreme law and that it will be guarded over by an independent, non-racial and impartial judiciary;**
> **c. that there will be a multi-party democracy with the right to form and join political parties and with regular elections on the basis of universal adult suffrage on a common voters roll; in general the basic electoral system shall be that of proportional representation;**
> **d. that there shall be a separation of powers between the legislature, executive and judiciary with appropriate checks and balances;**
> **e. that the diversity of languages, cultures and religions of the people of South Africa shall be acknowledged; and**
> **f. all shall enjoy universally accepted human rights, freedoms and civil liberties including freedom of religion, speech and assembly protected by an entrenched and justiciable Bill of Rights and a legal system that guarantees equality of all before the law.**[78]

However, negotiations stalled in June 1992 when the ANC walked out in protest at the slow pace of progress and CODESA was eventually replaced by the Multi-Party Negotiating Forum (MPNF).[79] This body finally adopted the interim Constitution in 1993 before it was ratified by the apartheid Parliament.

The negotiating process was not without its difficulties as the major political parties had very different visions about the transition to democracy. On the one hand, the ANC was

---

75 Sparks, AH (1994) *Tomorrow is Another Country: The Inside Story of South Africa's Revolution.*

76 By the time the interim Constitution was finalised, the Inkatha Freedom Party (IFP) and its allies in the Freedom Alliance (consisting of various Bantustan governments and pro-apartheid white parties) had walked out of the negotiations.

77 See Venter, F (2010) Liberal democracy: The unintended consequence – South African constitution-writing propelled by the winds of globalisation *SAJHR* 26(1):45–65 at 53. Venter notes that this wording was developed by a working group of the Steering Committee established by the 19 participating parties that committed themselves to CODESA in the course of November and December 1991. It was partly foreshadowed in chapter 1 of the National Peace Accord signed on 14 September 1991 by some 40 parties and organisations.

78 Available at http://www.anc.org.za/show.php?id=3968&t=Transition.

79 The MPNF emerged after intense negotiation which led to the Record of Understanding signed on 26 September 1992 and which is available at http://www.anc.org.za/show.php?id=4206.

committed to the drafting of a constitution by a democratically elected body and the formation of a majority government. On the other hand, the NP favoured the drafting of a final constitution by the unelected MPNF, followed by a long transitional government with power shared among the most popular parties in a manner that would effectively provide a veto for coalition parties. After many twists and turns, the ANC and the NP managed to reach a compromise model for the transition to democracy. While the ANC and the NP agreed that it would be necessary to draft a constitution containing certain basic provisions, those who negotiated this commitment were confronted, however, with two problems. As the Constitutional Court explained:

> **The first arose from the fact that they were not elected to their positions in consequence of any free and verifiable elections and that it was therefore necessary to have this commitment articulated in a final constitution adopted by a credible body properly mandated to do so in consequence of free and fair elections based on universal adult suffrage. The second problem was the fear in some quarters that the constitution eventually favoured by such a body of elected representatives might not sufficiently address the anxieties and the insecurities of such constituencies and might therefore subvert the objectives of a negotiated settlement. The government and other minority groups were prepared to relinquish power to the majority but were determined to have a hand in drawing the framework for the future governance of the country. The liberation movements on the opposition side were equally adamant that only democratically elected representatives of the people could legitimately engage in forging a constitution: neither they, and certainly not the government of the day, had any claim to the requisite mandate from the electorate.**[80]

The impasse was resolved by a compromise – typical of the constitution-making process – which required a programmed two-stage transition from the apartheid state to a democratic state instead of an outright transferral of power from the old order to the new. In the first stage of the transition, the unelected negotiating parties at the MPNF negotiated the interim Constitution which was adopted by the apartheid Parliament in terms of the 1983 Constitution and which became binding immediately after the first democratic election of April 1994.[81]

The interim Constitution provided for the establishment of an interim government of national unity and the country was governed on a coalition basis with both the ANC and the NP represented in the executive. This coalition government was provided for in clauses in the interim Constitution that allowed for a form of power sharing among the major political parties for a minimum period of five years. In the second stage, a Constitutional Assembly was then to draft a final constitution after the first democratic election.[82]

80 *First Certification* para 12.

81 Murray, C (2001) A constitutional beginning: Making South Africa's final Constitution *University of Arkansas at Little Rock Law Review* 23:809–38 at 813.

82 The procedure for the adoption of the final Constitution was laid down in ss 68–73 of the Constitution of the Republic of South Africa Act 200 of 1993.

Table 1.1 The two-stage constitution-making process

Interim Constitution	Final Constitution
Negotiated before the first democratic election by unelected MPNF.	Negotiated after the first democratic election by the elected Constitutional Assembly.
Contains power-sharing agreement allowing the ANC and the NP to share power for five years and provides for two Deputy Presidents - one from the ANC and one from the NP.	Does not provide for any formal power-sharing agreement - after the 1999 election the winner of the election governs the country on its own.
Contains 34 Constitutional Principles and provisions to regulate the adoption of a final constitution, including provisions for the **certification** of the constitution by a newly created Constitutional Court.	Certified by the Constitutional Court as complying with 34 Constitutional Principles after it was first rejected by that Court and sent back to the Constitutional Assembly.
Contains a Bill of Rights protecting all basic human rights.	Contains an extensive Bill of Rights protecting both civil and political as well as social and economic rights.

Chapter 5 of the interim Constitution prescribed the basic framework and rules for the drafting of the **final Constitution**. Section 68(1) provided that: 'The National Assembly and the Senate, sitting jointly for the purposes of this Chapter, shall be the Constitutional Assembly.' In terms of section 68(2), read with sections 68(3) and 73(1), the Constitutional Assembly had to adopt a new constitutional text within two years of the first sitting of the National Assembly. For such adoption, section 73(2) required a majority of at least two-thirds of all the members of the Constitutional Assembly. Section 71(2) then required that: 'The new constitutional text passed by the Constitutional Assembly, or any provision thereof, shall not be of any force and effect unless the Constitutional Court has certified that all the provisions of such text comply with the Constitutional Principles referred to in subsection (1)(*a*) [Constitutional Principles].'[83]

The Constitutional Principles, negotiated before the first democratic election and thus included in the interim Constitution, contained wide-ranging provisions. In addition, the relatively open-ended language afforded considerable power to the Constitutional Court to interpret and apply these provisions when it was called on to certify the final Constitution. The basic structures and premises of a new constitutional text contemplated by the Constitutional Principles were described as follows by the Constitutional Court:

(*a*) **a constitutional democracy based on the supremacy of the Constitution protected by an independent judiciary;**

(*b*) **a democratic system of government founded on openness, accountability and equality, with universal adult suffrage and regular elections;**

(*c*) **a separation of powers between the legislature, executive and judiciary with appropriate checks and balances to ensure accountability, responsiveness and openness;**

(*d*) **the need for other appropriate checks on governmental power;**

83 See also *First Certification* paras 16–19.

> **(*e*) enjoyment of all universally accepted fundamental rights, freedoms and civil liberties protected by justiciable provisions in the NT [final Constitution];**
> **(*f*) one sovereign state structured at national, provincial and local levels, each of such levels being allocated appropriate and adequate powers to function effectively;**
> **(*g*) the recognition and protection of the status, institution and role of traditional leadership;**
> **(*h*) a legal system which ensures equality of all persons before the law, which includes laws, programmes or activities that have as their objective the amelioration of the conditions of the disadvantaged, including those disadvantaged on grounds of race, colour or creed;**
> **(*i*) representative government embracing multi-party democracy, a common voters' roll and, in general, proportional representation;**
> **(*j*) the protection of the NT against amendment save through special processes;**
> **(*k*) adequate provision for fiscal and financial allocations to the provincial and local levels of government from revenue collected nationally;**
> **(*l*) the right of employers and employees to engage in collective bargaining and the right of every person to fair labour practices;**
> **(*m*) a non-partisan public service broadly representative of the South African community, serving all the members of the public in a fair, unbiased and impartial manner; and**
> **(*n*) security forces required to perform their functions in the national interest and prohibited from furthering or prejudicing party political interests.**[84]

The interim Constitution determined that the decision of the Constitutional Court certifying that the provisions of the new constitutional text complied with the Constitutional Principles would be final and binding. It also prohibited any other court of law from enquiring into or pronouncing on the validity of the text.[85] It is important to note that once the Constitutional Court had certified the text of the final Constitution, compliance or non-compliance of any aspect of the text with the Constitutional Principles could never be raised in any court of law again. This means that the Constitutional Principles, while of utmost importance in guiding the work of the Constitutional Assembly and the process of certification by the Constitutional Court, have played their role and cannot now be relied on by any party who wishes to challenge an amendment to the Constitution.

COUNTER POINT

Was the constitution-making process undemocratic?

The process which brought into being the 1996 Constitution has been criticised as being essentially undemocratic. Botha summarises – without necessarily endorsing – this argument as follows:[86]

> ... the sovereignty of the people, in whose name the Constitution was adopted, was systematically weakened by a two-stage process that bound the people's elected representatives to prior agreements between political elites. As a result, it might be argued, the voice of 'the people' was drowned out by the buzz of elite

84 *First Certification* para 45.

85 S 71(3) of the interim Constitution.

86 Botha, H (2010) Instituting public freedom or extinguishing constituent power? Reflections on South Africa's constitution-making experiment *SAJHR* 26(1):66–84 at 69–70.

bargaining, the noisy arguments of lawyers and the pronouncements of judges. Sovereignty was splintered by a political deal which fragmented the constitution-making process and turned it into the preserve of lawyers, judges and technocrats. Constituent power was effectively reduced to constituted power, which had to comply not only with the procedural requirements entrenched in the interim Constitution, but also had to heed the 'solemn pact' represented by the Constitutional Principles. The requirement of judicial certification of the constitutional text, which is unprecedented in the history of constitutionalism, contributed further to the weakening of popular sovereignty.

As we shall see, despite the constraints placed on the Constitutional Assembly, it could be argued that the provisions of the 1996 Constitution more or less reflected the relative influence and power of the negotiating parties in the Constitutional Assembly. As the ANC was by far the strongest party in the Constitutional Assembly, the large majority of provisions of the Constitution most closely reflect its vision for a democratic society.

1.3.3 Drafting and adoption of the final 1996 Constitution

The 1994 election - in which the Inkatha Freedom Party (IFP) along with all other major parties decided to take part after a last-minute deal - delivered an overwhelming majority for the ANC. However, the ANC did not gain the two-thirds majority required to write the Constitution without the support of other political parties. Table 1.2 indicates the final election results and the number of seats gained by each party in the National Assembly.

Table 1.2 The final 1994 election results[87]

Party	Votes	%	Seats
African National Congress (ANC)	12 237 655	62,65	252
National Party (NP)	3 983 690	20,39	82
Inkatha Freedom Party (IP)	2 058 294	10,54	43
Freedom Front (FF)	424 555	2,17	9
Democratic Party (DP)[88]	338 426	1,73	7
Pan Africanist Congress (PAC)	243 478	1,25	5
African Christian Democratic Party (ACDP)	88 104	0,45	2

Because the ANC did not obtain a two-thirds majority and because its negotiators were inclined to seek consensus, it tried hard to gain the necessary support for the various provisions from its long-standing opposition in the negotiating process, the NP. An enormous public participation programme and a programme of political discussions were also launched to ensure popular participation in the negotiating process which, it was believed,

87 See Elections in post-apartheid South Africa *SA History Online* available at http://www.sahistory.org.za/elections-post-apartheid-south-africa.

88 The Democratic Party is the forerunner of the Democratic Alliance, that was formed when the DP merged with the NP.

would lead to popular acceptance of the outcome reached.[89] Despite the Assembly's commitment to transparency, meeting away from the watchful eye of the press was probably essential to resolve some of the most fundamental disagreements between the parties. Technical legal advisers also played an important role in formulating alternative options relating to some of the most controversial clauses.[90] However, it is widely accepted that the consensus, which ultimately emerged, favoured the dominant party – the ANC.[91]

The interim Constitution contained several mechanisms to break any deadlocks in the negotiations. A panel of constitutional experts, consisting of lawyers, was empowered to advise the Assembly to try to resolve deadlocks. The interim Constitution also provided that if a draft constitution did not command two-thirds of the vote but did gain the support of the majority of the members, it could nevertheless become the country's constitution if it was supported by 60% of the voters in a referendum.[92] However, neither of the major parties was keen to resort to the referendum option and eventually the Constitutional Assembly voted to pass the new Constitution with only two no votes and 10 abstentions.[93]

COUNTER POINT

Was the public participation programme influential in the constitution-making process?

In a submission to the Constitutional Assembly, Sampson Moholoane – one of the more than two million South Africans who made submissions to the Constitutional Assembly – wrote:

> I want to stress one area which I believe as a citizen of South Africa one should have access to at all times. That is a welfare programme that will leave no South African from being able to afford three square meals a day. It must be a citizen's right to be able to have shelter and food even when he is not working, even if he is a destitute. The new Constitution must make this compulsory ...[94]

Some commentators argue that the public participation programme run by the Constitutional Assembly was not decisive in influencing the form and content of the provisions of the final Constitution as these submissions often contained vague wish lists concerned with problems of poverty and a low standard of living. Others point to the set of social and economic rights (discussed in chapter 16) as proof that the process did play an important role in giving voice to the aspirations of ordinary people in the drafting of the Constitution.

After the Constitutional Assembly had adopted the final Constitution, the document was submitted to the Constitutional Court for certification. All political parties involved in the negotiations, except for the ANC and the PAC, lodged objections to the text with the

89 Murray (2001) 816. The Constitutional Assembly's slogan, 'You've made your mark now have your say', invited the many millions of South Africans who had voted for the first time in 1994 to contribute to the country's first democratic Constitution – and over two million did so. See generally Ebrahim, H (1998) *The Soul of a Nation: Constitution-making in South Africa*.

90 See ss 72–3 of the interim Constitution. A panel of constitutional experts comprising two practising lawyers and five academic lawyers was to review the final Constitution. The panel had a month to come up with 'deadlock-breaking' ideas.

91 Woolman and Swanepoel (2013) 2.41.

92 See s 73(8) of the interim Constitution.

93 Murray (2001) 832.

94 As quoted in Murray (2001) 821. This particular submission was dated 16 May 1995.

Constitutional Court. Because the document had emerged through negotiations, many of these parties were not happy with certain clauses in the draft text and challenged these provisions in the hope that the Constitutional Court would refuse to certify the text for failing to comply with the 34 Constitutional Principles.

The Constitutional Court saw its task as measuring the text of the final Constitution against the Constitutional Principles to determine whether the text complied with those principles. The Court held that the Constitutional Principles had to be 'applied purposively and **teleologically** to give expression to the commitment "to create a new order" based on "a sovereign and democratic constitutional state" in which "all citizens" are "able to enjoy and exercise their fundamental rights and freedoms"'.[95] The Principles therefore had to be interpreted holistically and in a manner that was not too technically rigid.[96] The Constitutional Court evaluated the text of the final Constitution in two distinct ways. First, it asked whether the basic structures and premises of the final constitutional text were in accordance with those contemplated by the Constitutional Principles.

> **If such basic structures and premises do not comply with what the [Constitutional Principles] contemplate in respect of a new constitution, certification by this Court would have to be withheld. If the basic structures and premises of the [final Constitution] do indeed comply with the [Constitutional Principles] then, and then only, does the second question arise. Do the details of the [final Constitution] comply with all the [Constitutional Principles]? If the answer to the second question is in the negative, certification by the Constitutional Court must fail because the [final Constitution] cannot properly be said to comply with the [Constitutional Principles].[97]**

In *Certification of the Constitution of the Republic of South Africa, 1996*,[98] the *First Certification* judgment, the Constitutional Court found that the text did comply with the structural requirements. The Court then proceeded to consider the details of the text and found that it was not compatible with the Constitutional Principles on nine discrete grounds. It also set out in fairly unambiguous terms the changes that were necessary if the constitution was to meet the test of the Principles.[99] This meant that the Constitutional Assembly was found to have adopted an unconstitutional constitution and that the Assembly had to amend the text to comply with the Constitutional Court judgment. Although the constitution was therefore adopted by a democratically elected body, the Constitutional Court had the final say on whether the provisions agreed on by this body were compliant with the Constitutional Principles negotiated by the unelected MPNF.

As soon as the Constitutional Court decision was handed down, the Constitutional Assembly reassembled and amended the constitution as required by the Constitutional Court judgment. The Constitutional Court finally certified the amended draft of the constitution in *Certification of the Amended Text of the Constitution of the Republic of South Africa, 1996*, the *Second Certification* judgment, as being compliant with the 34 Constitutional Principles in December 1996.[100] President Nelson Mandela signed the final version of the 1996 Constitution on 10 December 1996 and it came into effect on 4 February 1997. It is this text – and its subsequent amendments – which forms the subject of this book.

95 *First Certification* para 34.
96 *First Certification* paras 36–7.
97 *First Certification* para 44.
98 (CCT 23/96) [1996] ZACC 26; 1996 (4) SA 744 (CC); 1996 (10) BCLR 1253 (CC) (6 September 1996).
99 See *First Certification* para 482.
100 (CCT37/96) [1996] ZACC 24; 1997 (1) BCLR 1; 1997 (2) SA 97 (4 December 1996).

COUNTER POINT

The unique birth of the 1996 Constitution

Some commentators and politicians have argued that the way in which South Africa's final Constitution came into existence was unique in the world. A newly created Constitutional Court actually declared unconstitutional a constitution drafted by a democratically elected constitution-making body. However, so they argue, this approach represented a wise compromise that helped to allay the fears of the minority NP but that ultimately allowed the dominant ANC to have a determinative influence on the text finally agreed to and adopted. Perhaps, they say, the text would not have looked so very different even if the Constitutional Assembly had not been required to comply with the 34 Constitutional Principles. This is because neither the NP nor the ANC could muster the support of two-thirds of the members of the National Assembly to push through their own agendas and were therefore forced to make compromises.

1.4 The South African Constitution of 1996

1.4.1 The transformative nature of the Constitution

Formally, the South African Constitution, adopted by the Constitutional Assembly in 1996, creates a sovereign democratic state founded on the values of human dignity and the advancement of equality, non-racialism and non-sexism, the supremacy of the Constitution, the rule of law, universal adult suffrage and a multiparty system of democracy in which free and fair elections are held regularly.[101] Unlike the Westminster-style Constitutions of the colonial and apartheid eras, parliamentary sovereignty has been replaced by constitutional sovereignty. This means the Constitution is the supreme law of the Republic, law or conduct inconsistent with it is invalid and the obligations imposed by it must be fulfilled.[102] It contains a detailed Bill of Rights that sets out a list of civil, political, social and economic rights. The Bill of Rights also places both a negative and a positive obligation on the state and – in some cases – a further obligation on private individuals and institutions, to respect, protect, promote and fulfil the rights in this Bill of Rights.[103]

The courts – with the Constitutional Court at the **apex** – are the guardians of the Constitution in general and the Bill of Rights in particular. They have the power to declare invalid any act or any legislation inconsistent with it. To this end, the Constitution sets up three branches of government (the legislature, the executive and the judiciary) and a system of separation of powers between the three branches. It also guarantees the independence of the judicial branch in relation to the other two branches to allow the judiciary to interpret and enforce the law and the provisions of the Constitution without fear, favour or prejudice.

The Constitution is avowedly a **democratic** one, guaranteeing the right to make political choices. This includes the specific rights to form a political party, to participate in the activities of that party and to campaign for a party or cause. Moreover, citizens have the right to free, fair and regular elections for any legislative body, as well as the right to stand for and hold public office and vote in those elections.

---

101 S 1.
102 S 2.
103 S 7(2).

The Constitution also recognises the institution, status and role of traditional leadership according to customary law. It makes provision for the functioning of a traditional authority that observes a system of customary law, subject to any applicable legislation and customs. The Constitution also enjoins courts to apply customary law when that law is applicable, but always subject to the Constitution and any legislation that specifically deals with customary law.[104] In addition, the Constitution provides authority for various legislatures to adopt legislation that provides for a role for traditional leadership as an institution at local level on matters affecting local communities. To deal with matters relating to traditional leadership, the role of traditional leaders, customary law and the customs of communities observing a system of customary law, national or provincial legislation may provide for the establishment of houses of traditional leaders and national legislation may establish a council of traditional leaders.[105]

We will discuss these technical aspects of the Constitution in detail in subsequent chapters of this book. However, it is important to note that we must also view the Constitution of 1996 through a less formalistic lens to capture the unique nature of the document and to come to grips with the manner in which the Constitutional Court has interpreted its provisions. In particular, we must be alert to the fact that the Constitution was written in response to the social, economic and political history of South Africa and is often described as a transformative Constitution,[106] a document committed to social, political, legal and economic **transformation**.

In fact, the transformative nature of the South African Constitution has been confirmed in several judgments of the Constitutional Court.[107] But what does this mean in practice? The Constitution is said to have set itself the mission of assisting with the transformation of society in the public and private spheres. It rejects 'that part of the past which is disgracefully racist, authoritarian, insular, and repressive' and facilitates a move towards a more democratic, universalistic, caring and aspirationally egalitarian society.[108] South African constitutionalism thus attempts to transform our society **from** one deeply divided by the legacy of a racist and unequal past **into** one based on democracy, social justice, equality, dignity and freedom.[109]

Exactly how the end product of this metamorphosis should look and when, if ever, it will be achieved must necessarily remain uncertain and dependent on the outcomes of this continuous interaction. However, the outcome should simultaneously not be conceived as so vague as to preclude meaningful and deliberate participation in the process. Traditional liberal constitutions are said to authorise, regulate and check the exercise of public power,

---

104 S 211.

105 S 212 of the Constitution.

106 See Klare, K (1998) Legal culture and transformative constitutionalism *SAJHR* 14(1):146–88; Chaskalson, A (2000) The third Bram Fischer lecture: Human dignity as a foundational value of our constitutional order *SAJHR* 16(2):193–205 at 199; Pieterse, M (2005) What do we mean when we talk about transformative constitutionalism? *SA Public Law* 20:155–66; Langa, P (2006) Transformative constitutionalism *SLR* 17(3):351–60; Moseneke, D (2009) Transformative constitutionalism: Its implications for the law of contract *SLR* 20(1):3–13 at 4; Davis, DM and Klare, K (2010) Transformative constitutionalism and the common and customary law *SAJHR* 26(3):403–509.

107 *Mkontwana v Nelson Mandela Metropolitan Municipality* (CCT 57/03) [2004] ZACC 9; 2005 (1) SA 530 (CC); 2005 (2) BCLR 150 (CC) (6 October 2004) para 81; *Soobramoney v Minister of Health (Kwazulu-Natal)* (CCT32/97) [1997] ZACC 17; 1998 (1) SA 765 (CC); 1997 (12) BCLR 1696 (27 November 1997) para 8; *Investigating Directorate: Serious Economic Offences and Others v Hyundai Motor Distributors (Pty) Ltd and Others In re: Hyundai Motor Distributors (Pty) Ltd and Others v Smit NO and Others* (CCT1/00) [2000] ZACC 12; 2000 (10) BCLR 1079; 2001 (1) SA 545 (CC) (25 August 2000) para 21.

108 *S v Makwanyane and Another* (CCT3/94) [1995] ZACC 3; 1995 (6) BCLR 665; 1995 (3) SA 391; [1996] 2 CHRLD 164; 1995 (2) SACR 1 (6 June 1995) para 262.

109 See Davis, D (1999) *Democracy and Deliberation: Transformation and the South African Legal Order* 44.

but supposedly allow voters and politicians to decide in which direction a society will move and at what pace that movement will occur. By contrast, the South African Constitution is said to contain a commitment to creating a society that will look fundamentally different from the one that existed at the time when the Constitution was being drafted. When interpreting the text of the Constitution, it is therefore necessary to look both backward and forward. We need to look backward at the history of South Africa and to ask what negative aspects of our past this document aimed to address and to transform, to what extent the transformation was required and at what pace. At the same time, the Constitution also signals a tentativeness, suggesting that it is a permanent work-in-progress, always looking forward, always subject to revision and improvement to try to achieve the society it envisages.[110]

This vision of the transformative nature of the Constitution is at least partly derived from the text of the Constitution itself. The text acknowledges that the new dispensation arose in a particular historical context and requires an acknowledgement of the effects of past and ongoing injustice. The notion that the Constitution is a transformative document is also captured by referring to it as a post-liberal document. This is so because while the Constitution contains many provisions that mirror provisions in other constitutions in liberal democracies (such as the US Constitution), it also departs from liberalism as it envisages a move towards an 'empowered' model of democracy.[111] The transformative or post-liberal nature of the South African Constitution manifests with reference to several unique characteristics of the document which were first highlighted by Klare: it is social, redistributive, caring, positive, at least partly horizontal, participatory, multicultural and self-conscious about its historical setting and transformative role and mission:[112]

- **Social rights and a substantive concept of equality:** The Constitution endorses the view that political freedom and socio-economic justice are inextricably linked. There is therefore a close connection between political rights, such as freedom of expression and the right to vote, and socio-economic rights such as the right to housing and health care. Democracy and the democratic rights that make democracy possible only have meaning if they lead to the creation of a new kind of society in which people actually have the social resources they need to exercise their rights meaningfully. The chief purpose of classical liberal bills of rights is to ensure that the government of the day does not interfere with the liberty of individuals and the property rights of the middle classes. By contrast, the South African Constitution embodies the idea that the power of the community can (and must) be deployed to achieve goals consistent with freedom. This is why the Constitution contains a pervasive and overriding commitment to the achievement of substantive (redistributive) equality.
- **Affirmative state duties:** A traditional liberal bill of rights places only negative restraints on a government to stop it from interfering with the liberty of individuals. By contrast, the South African Bill of Rights, in addition to negative restraints, also imposes positive or affirmative duties on the state to combat poverty and promote social welfare, to assist people in authentically exercising and enjoying their constitutional rights, and to

110 See ss 1 and 7 of the Constitution. The Constitution's historically situated character has been recognised in several Constitutional Court judgments. See, for example, *AZAPO* para 50: 'constitutional journey from the shame of the past to the promise of the future'; para 42: '[w]hat the Constitution seeks to do is to facilitate the transition to a new democratic order'. See also De Vos, P (2001) A bridge too far? History as context in the interpretation of the South African Constitution *SAJHR* 17(1):1–33.

111 Klare (1998) 152.

112 See generally Klare (1998) 153–6.

facilitate and support individual self-realisation.[113] For example, the Bill of Rights places a positive duty on the state to take reasonable steps progressively to ensure access to socio-economic welfare in areas such as housing, health care, food, water, social security and the protection of children.[114]

- **Horizontality:** Traditional bills of rights in liberal constitutions are said to be concerned with the vertical relationship between citizens and the state, limiting the power of the state to interfere in the lives of individuals or private institutions. However, the South African Bill of Rights has an explicit **horizontal application**. This means that in certain cases the Bill of Rights does not only limit the power of the state to interfere in the lives of individuals or citizens, but also binds individuals and institutions and, in some cases, requires them to respect the rights of others. Thus section 8(2) states that the Bill of Rights binds private parties in certain cases. Private parties are expressly barred from engaging in invidious discrimination and government is obliged to enact legislation enforcing that command.[115] Moreover, section 39(2) requires courts to take into account the spirit, purport and objects of the Bill of Rights when they interpret and develop the common law and customary law which, to a large degree, regulate private relationships.
- **Participatory governance:** As we shall see, the nature of the democracy established by the Constitution focuses on the participation of citizens at all levels and at all stages of decision making. The Constitution envisages inclusive, accountable, participatory, decentralised and transparent institutions of governance and contemplates that government will actively promote and deepen a culture of democracy.[116]
- **Multiculturalism:** South Africa is a multicultural society and it is said that the Constitution celebrates multiculturalism and diversity within a framework of national reconciliation and *ubuntu*.[117] It expressly promotes gender justice and rights for vulnerable and victimised groups and identities, explicitly including protections for gay men, lesbians and the disabled. It also protects language diversity and respect for cultural tradition and diversity and the 'right to be different'.[118]
- **Historical self-consciousness:** The Constitution is said to reject the notion of a constitution as a social contract entered into by citizens, presenting a snapshot of that society at the time of its conclusion and requiring the protection of the *status quo* at the time of its adoption. Unlike traditional liberal constitutions, it is said to reject the notion that its aim is to protect the pre-existing hierarchy and distribution of social and economic power. It accepts that legal and political institutions are chosen, not given, that democracy must be periodically reinvented, and that the Constitution itself must constantly be interpreted and reinterpreted to reflect the evolving understanding of the needs and problems a society faces. The 1996 text also contains numerous passages acknowledging that constitutional provisions are not self-executing, but are evolving texts that must be interpreted and applied.[119]

---

113 See s 7(2) of the Constitution which states that the state has a duty to respect, protect, promote and fulfil the rights in the Bill of Rights and *Minister of Finance and Other v Van Heerden* (CCT 63/03) [2004] ZACC 3; 2004 (6) SA 121 (CC); 2004 (11) BCLR 1125 (CC); [2004] 12 BLLR 1181 (CC) (29 July 2004) para 24.

114 See ss 26–8 of the Constitution.

115 See s 9(4) of the Constitution.

116 See generally ss 40(2) and 41(1). See also s 32 (access to information); s 33 (right to fair and just administrative action); and ss 34 and 38 (access to courts) and s 234 (charters of rights).

117 *Makwanyane* paras 224 and 263.

118 See *National Coalition for Gay and Lesbian Equality and Another v Minister of Justice and Others* (CCT11/98) [1998] ZACC 15; 1999 (1) SA 6; 1998 (12) BCLR 1517 (9 October 1998) para 135: 'The Constitution acknowledges the variability of human beings (genetic and socio-cultural), affirms the right to be different, and celebrates the diversity of the nation.'

119 S 1(*a*); s 7(1); s 39(1).

PAUSE FOR REFLECTION

The need for a transformative Constitution

Generations of children born and yet to be born will suffer the consequences of poverty, of malnutrition, of homelessness, of illiteracy and disempowerment generated and sustained by the institutions of apartheid and its manifest effects on life and living for so many. ... It will take many years of strong commitment, sensitivity and labour to 'reconstruct our society' so as to fulfil the legitimate dreams of new generations exposed to real opportunities for advancement denied to preceding generations initially by the execution of apartheid itself and for a long time after its formal demise, by its relentless consequences.[120]

1.4.2 Interpretation of the South African Constitution

When interpreting the Constitution, the starting point will always be the text of the relevant provisions in the Constitution. However, we should not read these provisions in isolation; instead we should assume that the various provisions of the text are in harmony with one another and we should read it holistically. The specific textual provisions alone will not always provide a clear and definitive answer as to their meaning. Courts are required to interpret and apply these provisions and, through this interpretation, the meaning of the Constitution will evolve over time.

A fundamental question arises regarding the power of judges to interpret the text and to what extent contextual factors as well as the normative commitment of judges may and should play a role in the interpretative exercise. On the one hand, many of the justices of the Constitutional Court have tentatively acknowledged the open-ended nature of the language of the Constitution and the inherent need to refer to extra-legal values and texts, including the South African political context and history, to justify their decisions.[121] On the other hand, some judges have warned that it is not permissible to revert to general philosophical or moral values to try to flesh out their understanding of the constitutional text.[122]

The Constitutional Court has since often declared its commitment to the centrality of the constitutional text in constitutional interpretation. However, the Court has also acknowledged that any such interpretation can only be conducted with the assistance of objective or objectively determinable criteria, or, at the very least, with reference to criteria that are somehow distanced from the personal views, opinions and political philosophy of the presiding judge.[123] The criteria the Constitutional Court employs to do the work in the

---

120 *AZAPO* para 43.

121 *Makwanyane* para 321 per O'Regan J: the language of fundamental rights is 'broad and capable of different interpretations'; para 207 per Kriegler J: '... it would be foolish to deny that the judicial process, especially in the field of constitutional adjudication, calls for value judgments in which extra-legal considerations may loom large'; para 266 per Mahomed DP: 'The Constitution must be examined with reference, *inter alia*, to the text, context and the factual and historical considerations'; para 382 per Sachs J: 'in seeking the kind of values which should inform the court's approach to interpretation the "rational and humane adjudicatory approach" must be preferred'.

122 See also *Makwanyane* para 207 per Kriegler J: '... methods to be used are essentially legal, not moral or philosophical ... it would be foolish to deny that the judicial process, especially in the field of constitutional adjudication, calls for value judgments in which extra-legal considerations may loom large. Nevertheless the starting point, the framework and the outcome of the exercise must be legal'; para 349 per Sachs J: 'Our function is to interpret the text of the Constitution as it stands. Accordingly whatever our personal views on this fraught subject might be, our response must be a purely legal one'; para 266 per Mahomed DP: '... difference between a political election made by a legislative organ and decisions reached by a judicial organ, like the Constitutional Court, is crucial'.

123 See Klare (1998) 172–87 for examples of this kind of reasoning by the judges of the Constitutional Court.

interpretation of the constitutional text have varied. The Court has resorted to an array of traditional devices such as references to common law, its own precedent established in previous judgments, the history of the drafting of the Constitution, international law or foreign case law, and canons of constitutional interpretation. At times, the Court has also resorted to less traditional factors such as the surrounding circumstances of a case, the social context of a case, the economic, political and social environment in South Africa (including the continued existence of vast inequalities between the rich and the poor) or the general history out of which the Constitution was born.

PAUSE FOR REFLECTION

The interpretative approach of the Constitutional Court

In *S v Makwanyane and Another*, Mahomed DP summarised the approach of the Constitutional Court to the interpretation of the Constitution as follows:

> What the Constitutional Court is required to do in order to resolve an issue, is to examine the relevant provisions of the Constitution, their text and their context; the interplay between the different provisions; legal precedent relevant to the resolution of the problem both in South Africa and abroad; the domestic common law and public international law impacting on its possible solution; factual and historical considerations bearing on the problem; the significance and meaning of the language used in the relevant provisions; the content and the sweep of the ethos expressed in the structure of the Constitution; the balance to be struck between different and sometimes potentially conflicting considerations reflected in its text; and by a judicious interpretation and assessment of all these factors to determine what the Constitution permits and what it prohibits.[124]

It will be difficult to claim that the Constitutional Court has systematically developed a clear and unambiguous approach to the interpretation of the Constitution in general or even of the provisions of the Bill of Rights more specifically. Nevertheless, it is safe to say that apart from its use of traditional methods of interpretation to signal the 'legal' (as opposed to 'political') nature of its task, the Court has also developed what can loosely be termed a 'contextual' or 'teleological' approach to constitutional interpretation. In applying its contextual approach, the Court has often found guidance in the more recent decisions of the Canadian Supreme Court.[125] In line with Canadian Supreme Court jurisprudence, the Court has often referred to the historical context in which the Constitution was adopted. Of

124 (CCT3/94) [1995] ZACC 3; 1995 (6) BCLR 665; 1995 (3) SA 391; [1996] 2 CHRLD 164; 1995 (2) SACR 1 (6 June 1995) para 266.

125 See *Zuma* para 15: the reference to *R v Big M Drug Mart Ltd* (1985) 18 DLR (4th) at 321; *President of the Republic of South Africa and Another v Hugo* (CCT11/96) [1997] ZACC 4; 1997 (6) BCLR 708; 1997 (4) SA 1 (18 April 1997) para 41; *Prinsloo v Van der Linde and Another* (CCT4/96) [1997] ZACC 5; 1997 (6) BCLR 759; 1997 (3) SA 1012 (18 April 1997) para 32 quoting from *Egan v Canada* (1995) 29 CRR (2d) 79 at 104–05. On the use of history, see, for example, *Zuma* para 15 per Kentridge J: '... regard must be paid to the legal history, traditions and usages of the country concerned ...'; *Makwanyane* para 39 per Chaskalson P: 'we are required to construe the South African Constitution ... with due regard to our legal system, our history and circumstances ...'; para 264 per Mahomed DP: 'It is against this historical background and ethos that the constitutionality of capital punishment must be determined.'; paras 322–23 per O'Regan J: '... the values urged upon the Court are not those that have informed our past...' and in '...interpreting the rights enshrined in Chapter 3, therefore, the Court is directed to the future'; *Executive Council of the Western Cape Legislature and Others v President of the Republic of South Africa and Others* (CCT27/95) [1995] ZACC 8; 1995 (10) BCLR 1289; 1995 (4) SA 877 (22 September 1995) para 61 per Chaskalson: the nature and extent of the power of Parliament to delegate its legislative powers ultimately depends 'on the language of the Constitution, construed in the light of the country's own history'.

course, it cannot be said that the Court always uses a contextual approach, or that it always uses it in the same manner, or even that the different judges understand and apply this approach in the same way. Yet, in case after case, the various judges of the Court have carefully sketched the political and social context within which the Constitution operates before proceeding to give an interpretation of the relevant provision of the Constitution.

The contextual approach to constitutional interpretation purportedly employed by the Court is a complex and multifaceted endeavour.[126] Essentially, the Court has embraced the idea that textual provisions can only be understood with reference to the historical and political context in which the interpretation takes place. When interpreting the Constitution it is important to keep in mind what the Constitution aimed to achieve. To do so, we need to recall South Africa's unique history and understand that the Constitution was drafted at least in part to ensure that the horrors of the apartheid past are never repeated.

PAUSE FOR REFLECTION

A grand narrative acts as an interpretative tool

It has been argued that the Constitutional Court attempts to use South Africa's history as a 'grand narrative' - a meaning-giving story - to justify its interpretations and to avoid allegations that it interprets the Constitution based on 'political' rather than on 'legal' considerations:

> While many of the provisions in the constitutional text do not have one objective meaning, and while the meaning of a text (often) depends on the context in which it is being interpreted, the grand narrative provides exactly such a context (or at least the major tenets of such a context). This context seemingly enables lawyers, legal academics and judges to interpret the Constitution without recourse to their own social, moral and political opinions. This strategy holds the promise of allowing the court to move away from the traditional liberal or modernist view of legal texts as holding one distinct and fixed meaning - a view that has become unsustainable in the age of constitutional interpretation - without doing away with the distinction between law on the one hand and politics on the other. The text of the Constitution may not always have one objective meaning, so it is said, but if we read it in the context of our history it will pretty much tell us what we want to know without us having to have recourse to our own personal, political or philosophical views. I therefore contend that the grand narrative acts as an interpretive tool, a tool deployed with the aim of safeguarding the legitimacy of the process of constitutional review and interpretation itself.[127]

Of course, South Africa's history may well be a useful reference point for understanding the various provisions in the Constitution. If we assume that the Constitution was drafted to ensure that no government would ever again act in a way that fundamentally breached the rights of citizens and to prevent a recurrence of the injustices of the past, we may well argue that our history can teach us much about the purpose of the various constitutional provisions included in the Constitution.

126 For a short review of contextual interpretation by the Constitutional Court, see Currie, I and De Waal, J (2013) *The Bill of Rights Handbook* 140–5.

127 See De Vos (2001).

However, the context in which the Constitution needs to be interpreted also includes the political, economic and social context. The nature of the South African democracy, as well as the lingering effects of the system of racial discrimination and minority rule, may well inform the way in which courts interpret the constitutional text.

1.4.3 Context: an inegalitarian society and a one-party dominant democracy

The South African Constitution does not operate in a political or economic vacuum. South Africa is an inegalitarian society with vast discrepancies in wealth between rich and poor citizens. These factors must play a role when interpreting the provisions of the South African Constitution. As the Constitutional Court pointed out:

> **We live in a society in which there are great disparities in wealth. Millions of people are living in deplorable conditions and in great poverty. There is a high level of unemployment, inadequate social security, and many do not have access to clean water or to adequate health services. These conditions already existed when the Constitution was adopted and a commitment to address them, and to transform our society into one in which there will be human dignity, freedom and equality, lies at the heart of our new constitutional order. For as long as these conditions continue to exist that aspiration will have a hollow ring. The constitutional commitment to address these conditions is expressed in the preamble which, after giving recognition to the injustices of the past, states: 'We therefore, through our freely elected representatives, adopt this Constitution as the supreme law of the Republic so as to – Heal the divisions of the past and establish a society based on democratic values, social justice and fundamental human rights; Improve the quality of life of all citizens and free the potential of each person.'**[128]

This passage underlines the transformative nature of the Constitution. The Constitution aims to address the unequal nature of South African society and imposes an obligation on the state and other relevant actors to address the needs of the most vulnerable and marginalised members of society. When interpreting the provisions of the Constitution – especially the provisions of the Bill of Rights – the Constitutional Court has signalled an acute awareness of the unequal and unjust nature of South African society and the vulnerability of many groups who lack economic or political power and who require protection or advancement from the legislature and the executive as well as the judiciary.

However, the political culture and the nature of the South African democracy must also play a role in interpreting the provisions of the Constitution. It finds application and must be interpreted by the courts with reference to the specific nature of South Africa's political culture and the role that political parties play in the political system. Political parties play a decisive role in the South African system of government, first, because of the nature of the electoral system currently in operation in South Africa and, second, because of the dominant position of former liberation movements in current politics. It would be impossible to come to grips with the manner in which the various provisions of the Constitution operate without understanding – in broad terms – the South African political landscape. As we have seen, the ANC overwhelmingly won the first national democratic election in 1994. The ANC has won every national election ever since. In 1999 it increased its support to 66,3% of the total vote and in 2004 this further increased to 69,7% of the vote. Its closest competitor has been

128 *Soobramoney* paras 8–9.

the DA which won only 9,56% of the vote in 1999 and 12,37 in 2004. Table 1.3 illustrates the standing of parties in 2009.

Table 1.3 The 2009 election results[129]

Party	Votes	%	+/-	Seats[130]
African National Congress (ANC)	11 650 748	65,90	-3,80	264
Democratic Alliance (DA)	2 945 829	16,66	+4,29	67
Congress of the People (CoP)	1 311 027	7,42	+7,42	30
Inkatha Freedom Party (IFP)	804 260	4,55	-2,42	18
Independent Democrats (ID)	162 915	0,92	-0,81	4
United Democratic Movement (UDM)	149 680	0,85	-1,43	4
Freedom Front Plus (FFP)	146 796	0,83	-0,06	4
African Christian Democratic Party (ACDP)	142 658	0,81	-0,80	3
United Christian Democratic Party (UCDP)	66 086	0,37	-0,38	2
Pan Africanist Congress (PAC)	48,530	0,27	-0,45	1
Minority Front (MF)	43 474	0,25	-0,11	1
Azanian People's Organisation (AZAPO)	38 245	0,22	-0,03	1
African People's Convention (APC)	35 867	0,20	+0,20	1

It is therefore clear that since 1994, one party, the ANC, has enjoyed electoral dominance and continues to win free and fair elections with all other parties lagging far behind. Such a system in which one political party continuously wins overwhelming electoral victories in free and fair elections is often referred to as a **dominant party democracy**.[131] Although this description is disputed as far as South Africa is concerned, it is important to note that the

129 See South Africa: 2009 National Assembly Election Results, Electoral Institute for Sustainable Democracy in Africa, available at http://www.eisa.org.za/WEP/sou2009results1.htm.

130 The number of seats refers to the number of representatives of each party in the National Assembly.

131 See Choudhry (2009) 1–85. Whether South Africa can indeed be characterised in this manner has been the subject of intense debate. See Southall, R (1994) The South African elections of 1994: The remaking of a dominant-party state *Journal of Modern African Studies* 32(4):629–55; Giliomee, H (1998) South Africa's emerging dominant-party regime *Journal of Democracy* 94:128; Southall, R (1998) The centralization and fragmentation of South Africa's dominant party system *African Affairs* 97(389):443–69; Friedman, S 'No easy stroll to dominance: Party dominance, opposition and civil society in South Africa' in Giliomee, H and Simkins, C (eds) (1999) *The Awkward Embrace: One Party Domination and Democracy* 97; Giliomee, H, Myburgh, J and Schlemmer, L (2001) Dominant party rule, opposition parties and minorities in South Africa *Democratization* 8(1):161–82; Southall, R (2001a) Opposition in South Africa: Issues and problems *Democratization* 8(1):1–24; Southall, R (2001b) Conclusion: Emergent perspectives on opposition in South Africa *Democratization* 8(1):275–84; Alence, R (2004) South Africa after apartheid: The first decade *Journal of Democracy* 15(3):78–92 at 78; Hamill, J (2004) The elephant and the mice: Election 2004 and the future of opposition politics in South Africa *The Round Table: The Commonwealth Journal of International Affairs* 93(377):691–708; Lodge, T (2004) The ANC and the development of party politics in modern South Africa *Journal of Modern African Studies* 42(2):189–219; Southall, R (2005) The 'dominant party debate' in South Africa *Afrika Spectrum* 40(1):61–82; Suttner, R (2006) Party dominance theory: Of what value? *Politikon: SA Journal of Political Studies* 33(3):277–97; Handley, A, Murray, C and Simeon, R 'Learning to lose, learning to win: Government and opposition in South Africa's transition to democracy' in Friedman, E and Wong, J (eds) (2008) *Political Transitions in Dominant Party Systems: Learning to Lose* 191.

electoral dominance of one political party has the potential to influence the manner in which various constitutional structures in a democracy operate.

Advocates of the dominant party thesis have described a number of consequences flowing from the continued electoral dominance of one political party. They argue that the dominant status of one political party in a democracy has the tendency to erode the checks on the power of the executive created by a democratic but supreme Constitution. Legislative oversight over the executive in Parliament may be stymied and opposition parties may be marginalised where one political party dominates the legislature. There is also a danger that a dominant party may 'capture' various independent institutions – including the judiciary and other bodies such as the prosecuting authority, the police service and other corruption-busting bodies – by deploying its members to these institutions to remove effective checks on the exercise of power by the government. In a one-party dominant democracy, so they argue, the formal mechanisms through which power is exercised become hollowed out while the separation between the political party and the state breaks down. This essentially shifts the centre where real decisions are made from the formal constitutional structures – the Presidency and the Cabinet on the one hand and the legislature on the other – to the decision-making body of the governing party.

In such a system, they argue, the leadership of the dominant party makes all important decisions which are then merely formally endorsed by the constitutional structures. This process is characterised by a blurring of the boundary between party and state. This has the effect of reducing the likely formation of independent groups from within civil society that are autonomous from the ruling party. It is also characterised by a growing preponderance of political power, leading to abuse of office and arbitrary decision making. This undermines the integrity of democratic institutions, particularly that of the legislature and its ability to check the executive. If this is true, it will influence the manner in which the legislature, the executive, the judiciary and other constitutional institutions operate as the dominant party will have a disproportionate influence on these institutions, thus posing difficulties for their effective operation.

Whether the electoral dominance of the ANC has turned South Africa into a one-party dominant democracy is a hotly contested issue. Critics of this thesis argue that there are external checks that operate outside the constitutional system on the ANC which serve as functional substitutes for the internal check provided by the formal institutions of parliamentary democracy that the ANC's dominance has eroded. Because of the fact that the ANC is a 'broad church', so the argument goes, and because there is a high degree of internal democracy in the ANC, this provides not merely opportunities for debate, but for the reversal of official policy.[132] The ANC is also in an alliance with the SACP and the trade union federation COSATU, both with their own membership and views. These alliance partners play an important role in keeping the leadership of the ANC in check and ensuring that the government of the day addresses the needs of the majority of its citizens.

In the chapters that follow, we will discuss the formal provisions of the Constitution that set up various institutions and structures and that regulate the governance of the country. When evaluating these institutions and structures and when determining how well these structures operate in practice, it is important to keep in mind arguments about the one-party dominant nature of the constitutional democracy in South Africa. The view we take about this issue will influence the judgment we make about how effective and successful the structures set up by the Constitution function in reality and interact with one another as

132 Lodge (2004) 205–7.

required by the Constitution. Those who believe that South Africa is indeed a one-party dominant democracy will have a more negative assessment of the way in which the Constitution succeeds in establishing a fully functioning multiparty democracy in which the will of the people guides the governance of the country. They will argue that the legislature does not always hold the executive accountable, will worry about the 'capture' of the judiciary and whether it remains independent, and will warn against the abuse of power by the executive. Those who reject the one-party dominant thesis will argue that the constitutional structures, on the whole, work well, that the executive remains accountable to the legislature and that the independent judiciary acts as a bulwark against abuse of power by state officials and elected representatives of the people.

SUMMARY

South Africa's constitutional history before 1994 was characterised by extreme forms of racial segregation and discrimination, creating a bifurcated state with one system with its own structures and sets of rules applying largely to white settlers and other structures with their own sets of rules applying to indigenous peoples. This essentially racial division is also to be found in the law that is applicable in South Africa even today. The common law, introduced by the colonial rulers, at first largely applied to the white population while customary law developed by indigenous peoples applied to black South Africans. Today, the common law and customary law both apply to different people in different contexts.

In 1910, the Union of South Africa formalised the bifurcated nature of the state by establishing a Westminster system of government that largely applied to the white population while allowing traditional governance structures centred around chiefs to continue to operate for indigenous South Africans but under the control of the white government. The Westminster system established an extreme form of parliamentary sovereignty in which Parliament was supreme and could make any law it wished as long as it followed the correct procedure. This changed in 1994 with the transition to democracy.

The transition to democracy occurred in two stages: the first transitional stage was guided by an interim Constitution which allowed for power sharing between the major political parties for a period of five years and also contained 34 Constitutional Principles which would bind the drafters of the final Constitution. The interim Constitution also prescribed the manner in which the final Constitution had to be adopted. The final Constitution was drafted by the Constitutional Assembly, comprising the democratically elected National Assembly and the indirectly elected Senate, but this body was bound by the 34 Principles. The Constitutional Court had to certify that the final Constitution complied with these principles, which it eventually did after first referring the Constitution back to the Constitutional Assembly because it had not complied in all aspects with these Principles.

The final Constitution is said to be a transformative Constitution. This means it responds to the social and economic history of our country. It aims to facilitate the transformation of our society away from an unequal and uncaring society in which racial discrimination and the marginalisation of women and other vulnerable groups was the order of the day and vast inequalities remained towards a fairer and more equal society in which the human dignity of all is respected and protected. This Constitution often contains vague provisions that judges must interpret. Judges use a purposive method of interpretation and often refer to South Africa's history to guide them in their interpretative task.

Chapter 2

Basic concepts of constitutional law

2.1 Introduction

To obtain a sound command of South Africa's constitutional law, it is important that we consider certain fundamental concepts at the outset. This is necessary to establish some level of common understanding of the principles, doctrines and concepts that lie at the heart of how our Constitution operates, the context that gave rise to it as well as the context in which it operates. These concepts lie at the heart of the South African Constitution and find expression in many of the provisions of the Constitution. When studying specific aspects of the Constitution, this needs to be done against the background of the concepts discussed below.

The principle aim of this chapter is therefore to introduce some of the more important overarching ideas that are pivotal in both explaining and contextualising the development of South African constitutional law. Although we focus on constitutional developments that have taken place in the period after South Africa's transition to **democracy**, we also briefly consider some important constitutional moments from bygone colonial and apartheid periods for purposes of context. We will also attempt to locate these constitutional developments within a broader historical and political context that recognises the influence of the constitutional law and practices of other countries.

2.2 Constitutionalism

2.2.1 Understanding the nature of constitutionalism

Constitutionalism as an idea or a term is not easy to define. The term 'constitutionalism' is sometimes used to convey the idea of a **government** that is limited by a written constitution: it describes a society in which elected politicians, judicial officers and government officials must all act in accordance with the law which derives its legitimacy and power from the constitution itself.[1] Constitutionalism, in this sense, is thus concerned with the problem of how to establish a government with sufficient power to realise a community's shared purposes and to implement the programmes for which a specific government has been elected by voters. At the same time, at issue is how to structure that government and control the exercise of power by the various branches of that government (and other powerful role players in society) in such a way that oppression and abuse of power is prevented.[2] As such, constitutionalism is closely related to the notions of democracy and theories of governance.

As a starting point, we can identify some characteristics of constitutionalism that will assist us to understand its nature:

- First, constitutionalism is concerned with the formal and legal distribution of power within a given political community in which a government is ordinarily established in terms of a written constitution.[3]
- Second, constitutionalism provides for the establishment of the institutions of governance, such as the legislature, the executive and the judiciary.
- Third, constitutionalism brings about the creation of binding rules or laws for the regulation of the political community, its institutions of governance and the governed.

---

1 See Hogg, P (2007) *Constitutional Law of Canada* 5th ed 2.

2 See generally Currie, I and De Waal, J (2001) *The New Constitutional and Administrative Law, Vol 1 Constitutional Law* 10.

3 The British constitutional system, to be discussed in detail below, is one notable exception in that the Constitution is not contained in one written document.

- Fourth, constitutionalism plays an important role in determining the nature and basis of relations that exist between institutions of governance and those they govern.
- Last, and implicit in the previous points, constitutionalism prescribes limits on the exercise of **state** power and provides mechanisms to ensure that the exercise of power does not exceed the limits set by the constitution.

While this is by no means an attempt at a definition, in identifying these characteristics, we attempt to expose the types of matters with which constitutionalism would ordinarily be concerned. In the section that follows immediately below we elaborate further on what constitutionalism is.

Accepting the characteristics of constitutionalism described above, we can conclude that, in essence, constitutionalism is about the notion that a constitution must **both** structure and constrain state power. On the one hand, a constitution must allocate power to various branches of government to allow for the effective governing of a state. On the other hand, it must limit and/or disperse that power to ensure that it will not be abused.

While constitutionalism seeks to achieve what are clearly important, if not sometimes conflicting, goals, we must acknowledge that constitutions are not self-executing documents nor do they contain identical provisions. The development of a particular system of constitutionalism and its relationship with other important constitutional law concepts, such as the **rule of law**, the protection of **human rights** and democracy, therefore, will depend on which constitution is under consideration, the relevant political and social history of the society in which it is being established and the particular rules, principles and institutions it establishes. Consequently, over the centuries during which the concept has evolved, different understandings as well as different models of constitutionalism have developed. The development of these models depended on how a particular constitution structured and allocated power and which **norms** were emphasised as foundational to the system by the text of the constitution and/or by the interpretation and application of that text by judges. We consider some of these understandings and models below.

PAUSE FOR REFLECTION

The unique nature of South African constitutionalism

In *S v Makwanyane and Another*, Mahommed J made the following statement which, arguably, captures the unique nature of South African constitutionalism:

> All Constitutions seek to articulate, with differing degrees of intensity and detail, the shared aspirations of a nation; the values which bind its people, and which discipline its government and its national institutions; the basic premises upon which judicial, legislative and executive power is to be wielded; the constitutional limits and the conditions upon which that power is to be exercised; the national ethos which defines and regulates that exercise; and the moral and ethical direction which that nation has identified for its future. In some countries, the Constitution only formalizes, in a legal instrument, a historical consensus of values and aspirations evolved incrementally from a stable and unbroken past to accommodate the needs of the future. The South African Constitution is different: it retains from the past only what is defensible and represents a decisive break from, and a ringing rejection of, that part of the past which is disgracefully racist, authoritarian, insular, and repressive and a vigorous identification of and commitment to a democratic, universalistic, caring and aspirationally egalitarian ethos,

> **expressly articulated in the Constitution. The contrast between the past which it repudiates and the future to which it seeks to commit the nation is stark and dramatic.**[4]

This passage highlights the fact that South African constitutionalism must be understood as relating to more than the mere technical legal regulation of the exercise of state power (and the limits placed on the exercise of that power) by the various branches of government. South African constitutionalism is thus not only a **descriptive** doctrine, factually describing what institutions should exercise power in what particular manner. It is also a **prescriptive** doctrine as it prescribes how state power should be exercised in a legitimate manner, which is related to the democratic legitimacy of the exercise of that power, and it prohibits the exercise of state power in certain ways. It is also **normative** as it sets out the **values** that must be adhered to in the governing process. This limits the kinds of actions that any state institutions, and sometimes also private institutions, are permitted to perform. We explore these aspects further below.

2.2.2 Constitutionalism as a descriptive doctrine

We can view constitutionalism as a descriptive doctrine or, put slightly differently, we can understand it in a descriptive sense. Understood in this way, constitutionalism seeks to provide a factual description of the institutions, procedures and structures that make up the constitutional system of a particular state.[5] This understanding of constitutionalism is formalistic in nature: it focuses on explaining the distribution of power, the relations between the branches of government and the limitations on power as provided for in a given constitution. It does not concern itself with whether state power is being used in contravention of democratic or human rights norms. In other words, it does not seek to make value judgments as to whether the state in question adheres to or upholds its own constitutional limits or rules or whether it provides for an essentially democratic system of government.

Constitutionalism as a descriptive doctrine tends to represent a practice that has largely fallen out of favour as it reduces constitutionalism to a mere explanation of a constitution's structure and operational design. It was in this descriptive sense only that we could, prior to the advent of democracy in South Africa, speak of South African constitutionalism. This was similar to other colonial territories where there was a constitution but the constitution failed to establish a truly democratic system of government, and concepts of equal rights or even equal **citizenship** for both black and white inhabitants were absent. This form of constitutionalism could at best be described as an empty form of constitutionalism as it focused on form rather than on substance.

PAUSE FOR REFLECTION

Constitutionalism as a descriptive doctrine in practice

The purely descriptive form of constitutionalism discussed above can be illustrated with reference to the facts and reasoning of the Appellate Division's decision in *Harris and Others v Minister of the Interior and Another*,[6] in which amendments to the Union

4 (CCT3/94) [1995] ZACC 3; 1995 (6) BCLR 665; 1995 (3) SA 391; [1996] 2 CHRLD 164; 1995 (2) SACR 1 (6 June 1995) para 262.
5 Currie and De Waal (2001) 10.
6 1952 (2) SA 428 (A).

Constitution then in place were challenged on procedural grounds.[7] The Union Constitution required that constitutional amendments be passed by the two Houses of Parliament sitting together (unicamerally) with a two-thirds majority. However, a constitutional amendment, removing coloured people from the common voters roll, was passed bicamerally (both Houses of Parliament sitting separately) with a simple majority.

The Court held that the failure on the part of Parliament to pass the constitutional amendment in accordance with the procedure set out in the Union Constitution resulted in such legislation not being recognised as an Act of Parliament and was therefore invalid. The Court could not enquire into whether the removal of coloured people from the common voters role would diminish the democratic aspects of the Union Constitution or whether the right to vote would be infringed. It was empowered merely to determine, on procedural grounds, whether the amendment was valid or not.

2.2.3 Constitutionalism as a prescriptive doctrine

More recently, the understanding of constitutionalism has evolved. This evolution has seen constitutionalism become a prescriptive doctrine that seeks to define in general terms the manner in which state power is allocated and exercised. In terms of this understanding, constitutionalism assumes some prescriptive force that establishes the norms and principles that define what may be termed to be a constitutional government.[8] Constitutionalism, thus understood, demands that a particular constitutional system adhere to the following norms and principles: **separation of powers**; the rule of law; democratic self-government; the protection of human rights; and the existence of an independent judiciary.[9]

We discuss certain of these norms and principles in more detail below. However, before doing so, we briefly discuss three different models of constitutionalism that have influenced South Africa's constitutional development.

2.2.4 Models of constitutionalism

Constitutions, while broadly serving the same purpose, can vary widely in terms of their structure and content. One factor that influences the form and substance of a constitution is the peculiar history of the country in which it was drafted. The issues addressed by a constitution usually reflect the specific period and place of the drafting, as well as the prevailing power relations between political and economic actors in that society. Also influencing the content of the constitution are the social, political, legal and cultural traditions of that society[10] and the shared norms of that society (or at least the norms embraced by the elite who drafted the constitution).

However, as the nation-state has become the most dominant form of government in the world, so too has there been some level of coalescence around the general framework and content of constitutions[11] as well as around models of constitutionalism. This has led to two

7 Discussed in ch 1.

8 Akiba, O 'Constitutional government and the future of constitutionalism in Africa' in Akiba, O (ed) (2004) *Constitutionalism and Society in Africa* 5.

9 Akiba (2004) 5–6.

10 For example, a society that has a monarchy or other form of traditional leadership which enjoys popular legitimacy may make provision for the recognition of such persons within the constitutional framework.

11 Currie and De Waal (2001) 26–31 list the main features that constitutions contain as follows: (1) a preamble; (2) a chart of the state system; (3) an amending provision; (4) a bill of rights; and (5) financial provisions.

major constitutional models that have greatly influenced the development of constitutionalism over the past 50 years. We refer here to the Westminster constitutional model and the United States (US) constitutional model which we consider in turn below. Both these models have had a great influence on South African constitutional history. We also consider a third model, namely the German model, which has also been influential in the South African context, more especially in the post-apartheid era.

2.2.4.1 The Westminster constitutional model

The Westminster constitutional model has its origins in Britain.[12] The Westminster model evolved over an extensive period during which it came to be characterised by certain distinctive features.[13] One particularly interesting fact about the Westminster constitutional model is that, as a model, it is premised on Britain's Constitution which to date remains unwritten. In fact, what is commonly known as the British Constitution is actually a series of conventions and ordinary laws in the form of **statutes**, **common law** and **case law** that broadly regulate state power as well as the relations between the state and its citizens.[14] These laws taken collectively comprise the British Constitution. However, where the Westminster model has been adopted, particularly in former British colonies such as pre-democratic South Africa, Botswana and Zimbabwe, the practice has been to reduce the constitution to writing.

At the heart of the Westminster model is the legislative branch, namely Parliament. In Britain, Parliament comprises the House of Commons (the directly elected lower House) and the House of Lords (the unelected upper House). Parliament is of central importance as it exercises sovereign or supreme law-making powers. This means that any law made by Parliament cannot be undone by anybody or any organ except by Parliament itself.[15] This characteristic feature of a Westminster-style constitution is also known as parliamentary supremacy or parliamentary sovereignty. This means that in Britain there is, in principle, no fundamental law which cannot be altered by ordinary parliamentary action and there is no bill of rights which denies Parliament the power to destroy or curtail liberties. Parliament is said to have the power to make any law on any subject.

The contemporary position is, however, not so clear cut. First, the United Kingdom's accession to the European Union has subjected Parliament, to some degree, to the laws of the European Community.[16] Second, it has long been recognised that there are certain measures that it would be politically impossible to adopt and whose enactment would never be attempted.[17] Parliamentary sovereignty in Britain, properly understood, thus 'denotes only the absence of legal limitations, not the absence of *all* limitations or ... inhibitions, on Parliament's actions'.[18] Such exceptions notwithstanding, the fact that Parliament is the ultimate law-making authority does not excuse or exempt it from being bound to respect the rule of law. We discuss the rule of law later in this chapter.

Another notable feature of this constitutional model is the formal separation between the head of state and the head of government. In practice, the head of state in Britain is the

12 See generally Bogdanor, V (2009) *The New British Constitution* and King, A (2007) *The British Constitution.*

13 Modern British constitutional conventions and arrangements are said to have their origin in the English Charter called the Magna Carta that was enacted in 1225 AD.

14 There have at various times been calls for the adoption of a written constitution. In this respect see Institute for Public Policy Research (1991) *A Written Constitution for the United Kingdom.*

15 Dicey, AV (1885) *Introduction to the Study of the Law of the Constitution* 10th ed (1959).

16 See De Smith, SA and Brazier, R (1998) *Constitutional and Administrative Law* 8th ed ch 4.

17 See Mann, FA (1990) *Further Studies in International Law* 104.

18 Munro, CR (1999) *Studies in Constitutional Law* 2nd ed 135.

monarch (currently Queen Elizabeth II) while the head of government is the Prime Minister. After an election, the monarch calls on the leader of the majority political party in Parliament (or the person chosen by a coalition of parties where no party has achieved an overall majority and a coalition has been formed) to form a new government. The Prime Minister is the head of this new government and is usually the leader of the majority party in Parliament. The government is formed and governs in the monarch's name as long as it retains the support of a majority of Members of Parliament.[19] Therefore, with this model, political parties play an important role in forming a government and retaining it in power.

A closely related feature of the Westminster constitutional model is that of parliamentary government. Parliamentary government means that the executive **branch of government**, namely the Prime Minister and the Cabinet, are all drawn from and continue to be Members of Parliament. The Prime Minister and his or her Cabinet thus serve both as members of the legislature and as members of the executive at the same time.[20] There is therefore no strict separation of powers between the legislature and the executive as is the case in the US system discussed below. The Prime Minister engages in regular question-and-answer sessions in Parliament during the Prime Minister's questions time where he or she verbally spars with the leader of the opposition and other members of opposition parties. The effect of this practice is that Parliament continues to exercise an oversight role over the executive. Members of the executive are required to account to Parliament as to how they exercise their powers in conducting government business, including the development of policy and the implementation of the law, on a continuous basis.

We now turn our attention to the courts. The courts' function in this model must be viewed in light of the doctrine of parliamentary supremacy discussed above. As an incidence of parliamentary supremacy, the courts under this model enjoy no powers to decide on the constitutionality of legislation although they may review administrative decisions of the administration.[21] The effect of this limitation on the courts' powers is that it makes them institutionally less powerful than the legislature. However, this does not mean that the courts do not enjoy significant powers nor that they are any less important than the legislature within the entire scheme of governance under this constitutional model. While the courts may not have constitutional review powers, they do, when adjudicating matters, have a significant opportunity to influence how the law is applied as well as its impact in a given situation.

In 1998, the British Parliament adopted the Human Rights Act[22] which gives effect in British law to many of the provisions of the European Convention for the Protection of Human Rights and Fundamental Freedoms (1950). However, in theory, Parliament retains its sovereignty although the courts must now interpret legislation consistently with the provisions of the European Convention whenever possible. Some of the national courts are empowered to issue declarations of incompatibility if they find legislation to be in conflict with the norms embodied in the European Convention. This triggers the possibility of fast-track amendments by means of administrative legislation. If this is not sufficient, the provisions of the Act can be challenged before the European Court of Human Rights. Although Parliament can, in theory, depart from orders of this court, it seems politically ever less feasible that it will do so.[23]

19 Motala, Z (1994) *Constitutional Options for a Democratic South Africa: A Comparative Perspective* 48.
20 Currie and De Waal (2001) 14.
21 But see the discussion of the Human Rights Act below.
22 Available at http://www.hmso.gov.uk/acts1998/42/data.pdf.
23 See Elliot, M (2004) United Kingdom: Parliamentary sovereignty under pressure *International Journal of Constitutional Law* 2(3):545–627 at 553.

Because of the important role played by the courts, the Westminster constitutional model demands as one of its defining features that the judiciary be independent. It thus requires that the judiciary function independently of Parliament and the executive. Remaining judicially independent means that judges must not be subjected to any undue influence either by Parliament or by the executive while they discharge their duties. This has necessitated the inclusion of mechanisms that seek to guarantee judicial independence, including the following:

- First, judicial independence is guaranteed by way of security of **tenure** that requires that judges are appointed for life.
- Second, judges cannot be removed from their judicial office except where they are found to have contravened the law or otherwise engaged in serious misconduct.
- Third, judges' salaries are guaranteed and cannot be reduced while their tenure continues.[24]

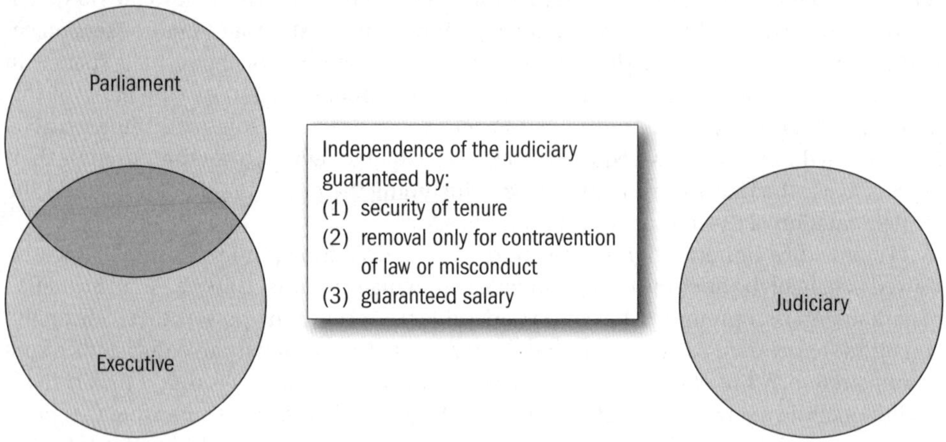

Figure 2.1 The overlap between the legislature and the executive indicates that the members of the executive are drawn from Parliament

2.2.4.2 The United States constitutional model

The United States (US) constitutional model[25] originates, as its name indicates, in the United States of America. The US constitutional model can immediately be distinguished from the Westminster model by way of the history of its making. While the Westminster model evolved organically over centuries, the US model was the product of 'a deliberate process of constitution-making' in the late 1780s involving 13 former British colonies that had been established in the territory.[26] In coming together to form a federation under the banner of the United States of America, these former colonies established a Constitution and a constitutional system that today endures as the longest-surviving system based on essentially the same written Constitution.[27] In the following section we discuss some of the characteristic features of US constitutionalism.

24 Currie and De Waal (2001) 15.

25 See generally Chemerinsky, E (2009) *Constitutional Law* 3rd ed; Hall, DE, Bailey, SJD and Barron, C (2006) *Constitutional Law*; Curtis, MK, Parker, C, Douglas, D and Finkelman, P (2010) *Constitutional Law in Context: Volume 1* 2nd ed.

26 Currie and De Waal (2001) 17.

27 Motala (1994) 50.

As a constitutional model that arose out of 'a deliberate process', a process which aimed to unify 13 independent colonies, one of the main issues of concern was that of the exercise of political power; more precisely, how to limit the exercise of political power by the federal government. To achieve an effective balance between regulating the former colonies' collective interests on coming together and ensuring that power was not overconcentrated in one source, the drafters of the US Constitution divided power along two lines. In the first instance, the drafters created a two-tier federal state with a central federal government on one level and state governments on another level. This federal division of power resulted in certain specified powers and functions being allocated to the national federal government. The remainder or residue of powers and functions was left to the states which came together to form a 'more perfect union'.[28] The result of this division of power is that it ascribes exclusive functions and competencies to each level of government. Ultimately, as a constitutional principle, federalism serves as an important limitation on an overly powerful central government. At the same time, it promotes diversity and local autonomy by allowing each state to deal with many of the day-to-day issues affecting its citizens.[29]

The second line along which the US Constitution limits power is in terms of the concept of separation of powers adopted by the drafters of the Constitution. The doctrine of separation of powers dictates that governmental power be divided according to function (and, in the most rigid cases, of personnel too) between three primary branches of government, namely the legislature, the executive and the judiciary. The US constitutional model provides for the most stringent separation in respect of the branches, their functions and personnel. While a similar separation of branches exists under the Westminster model, the US's model is radically different in that the separation between the three branches is far more absolute. For example, the US model of separation of powers provides for a complete separation of personnel between the three branches of government - no one may be a member of more than one branch at any given time.[30] Contrast this with the Westminster system of parliamentary government where members of the executive (the Prime Minister and his or her Cabinet) are also necessarily Members of Parliament.

The US model does not, however, demand a complete separation of powers in all respects. Instead, the US model introduced an important innovation from a constitutional law point of view, namely a system of **checks and balances**. This system of checks and balances allows the three branches to enjoy a limited amount of power to check the exercise of power by the other branches in prescribed circumstances in order to maintain a balance of power among them. The US model ensures that no one branch can function completely independently of the other while ensuring that no one branch accumulates excessive powers.[31] It is based on the assumption that the concentration of power in one body would lead to a possible abuse of power. For example, while the legislative branch enjoys the power to legislate, this power is subject to the presidential veto in terms of which the President can block legislation from coming into force despite the legislature having passed it. Equally, another example of a check is where a court declares a statute to be unconstitutional in spite of the fact that such legislation was properly passed by a legislative majority.

---

28 Tenth Amendment of the US Constitution.
29 Currie and De Waal (2001) 19–20.
30 Motala (1994) 51.
31 Currie and De Waal (2001) 18.

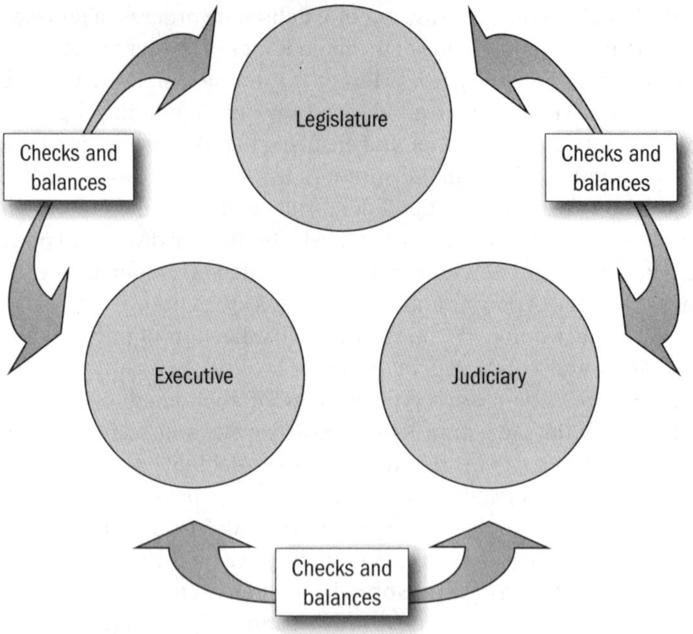

Figure 2.2 Checks and balances in the US model of constitutionalism

Another defining feature of the US constitutional model is that of constitutional supremacy. Contrasted with parliamentary supremacy under the Westminster model, constitutional supremacy is premised on the notion that the constitution is the highest law and requires all other law and conduct to comply with its provisions. Put differently, constitutional supremacy means that the constitution is the ultimate source of all law and lawful exercise of authority. Subject to the constitution being amended, the appropriate court must declare invalid any law passed by the legislature or conduct by a governmental body or organ that is in conflict with or is otherwise inconsistent with the constitution.

The inclusion of a Bill of Rights by the drafters[32] is another important contribution made by the US constitutional model. The importance of a bill of rights is that it also serves as a limit on the power of government by setting out those individual freedoms and liberties on which the government may not encroach. Constitutionally protected rights, in other words, serve as a protective mechanism for safeguarding rights-holders' interests against governmental trespass. Of course, remember that although the language of the US Bill of Rights was couched in universal terms and would later serve to inspire many other countries in their quest for independence, the US Bill of Rights was a product of its times. So while the Bill of Rights proclaimed that 'all men [*sic*] are created equal' and that their rights are 'inviolable' in 1789, it did not protect native Americans and Africans (many of whom were brought to the US and held in slavery). Women also did not originally enjoy equal rights with men.

32 The Bill of Rights was not contained in the US Constitution originally adopted but was introduced by the first 10 amendments to the Constitution, which were ratified on 15 December 1791. Several further amendments adding to the Bill of Rights were subsequently adopted.

The final feature of the US model that we consider here is the institution of judicial review. The US Supreme Court asserted its power of judicial review for the first time in *Marbury v Madison*.[33] This power is an important check on the legislature and the executive as it empowers the courts to declare unconstitutional any law or conduct found to contravene the constitution. However, the US Constitution does not expressly provide for this checking power exercised by the courts on the other branches of government. This fact, alongside the fact that the power of judicial review essentially permits courts to overrule a majority decision taken by the legislature on behalf of millions of citizens, also known as the counter-majoritarian dilemma,[34] has ensured that to this day the power remains controversial in the US.

We deal with **counter-majoritarianism** in more detail below. For present purposes, it is imperative that we point out that the overriding importance of judicial review is that for a constitutional system premised on the doctrine of constitutional supremacy and providing for a bill of rights to have excluded powers of judicial review would have weakened the system immensely.[35] The reason for this is that there would otherwise be no politically non-partisan **organ of state** charged with upholding and enforcing the constitution.[36]

PAUSE FOR REFLECTION

Justification for the courts' power of review

In *Marbury v Madison*, then US Chief Justice Marshal established the principle that the courts have the right to review and set aside legislation that contravened the Constitution. He made the following argument to justify his decision:

> This theory is essentially attached to a written constitution, and is consequently to be considered by this court as one of the fundamental principles of our society. It is not therefore to be lost sight of in the further consideration of this subject. If an act of the legislature, repugnant to the constitution, is void, does it, notwithstanding its invalidity, bind the courts and oblige them to give it effect? Or, in other words, though it be not law, does it constitute a rule as operative as if it was a law? This would be to overthrow in fact what was established in theory; and would seem, at first view, an absurdity too gross to be insisted on. It shall, however, receive a more attentive consideration. It is emphatically the province and duty of the judicial department to say what the law is. Those who apply the rule to particular cases, must of necessity expound and interpret that rule. If two laws conflict with each other, the courts must decide on the operation of each. So if a law be in opposition to the constitution: if both the law and the constitution

33 5 US (1 Cranch) 137 (1803).

34 The classic discussion of this dilemma can be found in Bickel, AM (1962) *The Least Dangerous Branch: The Supreme Court at the Bar of Politics*. See also Ackermann, BA (1984) The Storrs lectures: Discovering the Constitution *Yale Law Journal* 93:1013–72 and Chemerinsky, E (1989) Foreword: The vanishing Constitution *Harvard Law Review* 103:43–102.

35 The US Supreme Court said in *Marbury v Madison* para 176: 'The powers of the legislature are defined and limited; and that those limits may not be mistaken, or forgotten, the constitution is written. To what purpose are powers limited, and to what purpose is that limitation committed to writing, if these limits may, at any time, be passed by those intended to be restrained.' See also para 177: 'The constitution is either superior, paramount law, unchangeable by ordinary means or it is on a level with ordinary legislative acts, and like other acts, is alterable when the legislature shall please to alter it. If the former part of the alternative be true, then a legislative act contrary to the constitution is not law: if the latter part be true, then written constitution are absurd attempts, on the part of people, to limit a power, in its own nature illimitable.'

36 Currie and De Waal (2001) 20.

> apply to a particular case, so that the court must either decide that case conformably to the law, disregarding the constitution; or conformably to the constitution, disregarding the law: the court must determine which of these conflicting rules governs the case. This is of the very essence of judicial duty. If then the courts are to regard the constitution; and the constitution is superior to any ordinary act of the legislature; the constitution, and not such ordinary act, must govern the case to which they both apply. Those then who controvert the principle that the constitution is to be considered, in court, as a paramount law, are reduced to the necessity of maintaining that courts must close their eyes on the constitution, and see only the law. This doctrine would subvert the very foundation of all written constitutions. It would declare that an act, which, according to the principles and theory of our government, is entirely void, is yet, in practice, completely obligatory. It would declare, that if the legislature shall do what is expressly forbidden, such act, notwithstanding the express prohibition, is in reality effectual. It would be giving to the legislature a practical and real omnipotence with the same breath which professes to restrict their powers within narrow limits. It is prescribing limits, and declaring that those limits may be passed at pleasure. That it thus reduces to nothing what we have deemed the greatest improvement on political institutions - a written constitution, would of itself be sufficient, in America where written constitutions have been viewed with so much reverence, for rejecting the construction. But the peculiar expressions of the constitution of the United States furnish additional arguments in favour of its rejection. The judicial power of the United States is extended to all cases arising under the constitution. Could it be the intention of those who gave this power, to say that, in using it, the constitution should not be looked into? That a case arising under the constitution should be decided without examining the instrument under which it arises? This is too extravagant to be maintained.[37]

This passage contains the classic justification for judicial review in a system where the constitution is supreme and the rule of law is adhered to. It is premised on the idea that a supreme written constitution would be of little use if the courts could not declare invalid those laws that contravene sections of the constitution. Where promises are made in a constitution, but no impartial body is empowered to enforce those promises, they may very well remain illusory. However, it does not deal with the question of whether unelected judges - or individuals belonging to another institution or body - should be awarded the power to declare invalid laws duly passed by the democratically elected legislature.

One major contribution to constitutional law that can arguably be attributed to judicial review has been the development of a body of law that deals with how governmental power under a supreme constitution is to be properly exercised. This body of law also deals with how the relations between the different branches or levels of government should be balanced and resolved on the basis of constitutional principles rather than politics. The US form of judicial review, based on its Bill of Rights, has also greatly influenced the development of human rights norms and standards.

37 *Marbury v Madison* 5 US (1 Cranch) 137 (1803) paras 177–9.

Table 2.1 A comparison of constitutional supremacy and parliamentary supremacy

	Constitutional supremacy	Parliamentary supremacy
Country of origin	US	UK
Supreme source of law	Constitution	Parliament
Effect of supremacy of such law	The Constitution is supreme and any law or conduct established to be inconsistent with the Constitution stands to be struck down by the courts	Parliament is the supreme law-making authority. Laws made by Parliament cannot be struck down except where they have been enacted without following the correct procedures

2.2.4.3 The German constitutional model

Thus far we have considered the two constitutional models that, first, have endured substantially unchanged for several centuries and, second, that are recognised as being significant contributors to the development of our understanding of constitutionalism, especially in South Africa. There is, however, one other model that we shall consider that has been of some influence before turning to the South African constitutional model. This is the German model.[38]

Germany has a long constitutional history that dates back at least to the 1800s. Despite this long history, Germany has gone through several significant constitutional changes and configurations caused by shifts in state power, state form and, more importantly, the intervention of two world wars. As such, our interest in the German constitutional model commences from 1948 after the Second World War and the fall of the Nazi regime.[39] The constitutional model established in this period was in many ways a reaction to Nazi atrocities in much the same way that parts of the South African Constitution were drafted in reaction to South Africa's apartheid past. The German model sought to ensure that the inhumane excesses of the period could never be re-enacted under a new constitutional dispensation. The Constitution that was produced in response to this history is one from which South African constitutional law has drawn as it has also sought to deal with South Africa's own past of racial violence, exploitation and exclusion. In this section, we highlight some of the most significant features of this model, especially those that we believe resonate with the current South African constitutional dispensation.

Like the US constitutional model, the German model is premised on the notion of constitutional supremacy. However, in developing its unique constitutional model, Germany has, by the inclusion of constitutional values, added another important layer to the notion of the constitution being supreme. In this respect, the drafters of the German Constitution sought to establish a value-based democratic order that attempts to 'secure democratic rule in Germany by binding the democratic process to the values and principles expressed in the constitution'.[40] The Constitution is thus not viewed as a neutral document that merely regulates state power, but as a document that aims to impose a normative value system on

38 See generally Heun, W (2010) *The Constitution of Germany: A Contextual Analysis* and Crosby, MB (2008) *The Making of a German Constitution: A Slow Revolution.*

39 Davis, D, Chaskalson, M and De Waal, J 'Democracy and constitutionalism: The role of constitutional interpretation' in Van Wyk, DH, Dugard, J, De Villiers, B and Davis, D (eds) (1994) *Rights and Constitutionalism: The New South African Legal Order* 69–70.

40 Davis et al (1994).

that country.[41] This means that where the German Constitution is applied or interpreted, it should entail an application or interpretation that accords with and promotes the values embodied in the Constitution. Central to this value-based order is the value of human dignity which, under the German Constitution, is declared to be 'inviolable' and cannot be amended.[42] The dimension that this value-based democratic order adds is that it recognises the importance of establishing a constitutional culture of broadly shared values and that such values may actually be just as important as the rules, processes and institutions established under the constitution.

The concept of ***Rechtsstaat*** is yet another defining feature of the German constitutional model.[43] In terms of *Rechtsstaat*, the Constitution is established as the higher law with which all other laws and state conduct must comply.[44] However, the importance of the concept of *Rechtsstaat* in the German constitutional system is that it demands more than mere formal constitutional compliance or procedural safeguards that prohibit the arbitrary exercise of power. It also demands that the law and state actors must 'strive to protect freedom, justice and legal certainty'.[45] With regard to legal certainty, the concept of *Rechtsstaat* is closely linked to the notion of the rule of law as it also encompasses the idea that legal rules must be clear and enforced equally.[46] However, it is often said to encompass a more substantive aspect: in a *Rechtsstaat*, the Constitution, as interpreted by the Constitutional Court, ensures the normative preconditions on which the realisation of the rule of law and especially the formulation of individual human rights claims are based.[47] In this sense, a German understanding of the *Rechtsstaat* will always be bound to the context of the democratic and social constitutional state. If the democratic or the social welfare aspects of the state are fundamentally eroded, the *Rechtsstaat* will no longer be respected.

Another major feature of the German constitutional model is that it established Germany as a social state.[48] By establishing Germany as a social state, the Constitution places the state under an obligation to provide for the basic needs of members of German society, including housing, water, electricity and education.[49] The social state is premised on the value of

41 The German Constitutional Court affirmed this, using the German phrase, 'eine objektive Wertordnung' in BVerfGE 39, 1 para 41: 'The jurisprudence of the Federal Constitutional Court is consistently to the effect that the basic right norms contain not only defensive subjective rights for the individual but embody at the same time an objective value system which, as a fundamental constitutional value for all areas of the law, acts as a guiding principle and stimulus for the legislature, executive and judiciary.'

42 See Arts 1 and 79(3) of the German Basic Law for the Federal Republic of Germany. This is the German Constitution. The position with respect to the basic rights contained in Art 1 (dignity) and Art 20 (constitutional principles) is that they also cannot be amended.

43 Since 1949, the term '*Rechtsstaat*' has appeared in Art 28 para 1 which states that 'the constitutional order in the *Länder* shall conform to the principles of the republican, democratic and social state governed by the *Rechtsstaat* within the meaning of this Basic Law'. Since the revision of 21 December 1992, the expression has also appeared in para 1 of the new Art 23 dealing with the European Union which states that 'with a view to establishing a united Europe the FRG shall participate in the development of the European Union, which is committed to democratic, *Rechtsstaat*, social and federal principles as well as to the principle of subsidiarity, and ensures protection of basic rights comparable in substance to that afforded by this Basic Law'.

44 See Blaauw-Wolf, L and Wolf, J (1996) A comparison between German and South African limitation provisions *SALJ* 113:267–96 at 268 who, while conceding that '[a] coherent concept of *Rechtsstaat* has not yet been developed', tell us that the concept is one that has a formal and a material conception. The authors say of *Rechtsstaat* that '[t]he formal concept consists of a number of elements for which no uniformly accepted definition exists. The material concept ... is based on the idea of justice in law and in administrative decisions'.

45 Stern, K (1977) *Das Staatsrecht der Bundesrepublik Deutschland Volume One* 615 quoted in Blaauw-Wolf and Wolf (1996) 268.

46 Stern (1977) 615 quoted in Blaauw-Wolf and Wolf (1996) 268.

47 Kunig, P '*Der Rechtsstaat*' in Badura, P and Dreier, H (eds) (2001) *Festschrift 50 Jahre Bundesverfassungsgericht* 421–44 at 434.

48 See Art 20(1) of the German Basic Law.

49 Motala (1994) 54.

human dignity. It holds that every person has an inherent value as a human being which was denied by the Nazi government. As such, the state has an obligation to create an environment in which people can reach their full potential as human beings. The social state is, therefore, about more than just state welfare. It is a philosophical principle which assumes that the value of human dignity can only be respected where the state plays a role in protecting individuals and by providing the basics which make living one's life meaningful. Although the German Constitution clearly establishes a social state, it interestingly does not expressly include any socio-economic rights in its Bill of Rights in the sense of individually enumerated rights.[50] Instead, under the notion of a social state and underpinned by a strong culture of entrenched human rights, the German model establishes an effective balance between limiting the power of the state and upholding the rights of citizens, including providing for the basic material needs of a life worth living.

COUNTER POINT

The notion of a social state versus a free-market system

A social state can arguably be said to reflect the same concerns expressed by adherents to the values of *ubuntu* as it focuses on the idea of human solidarity. It represents a rejection of an overly individualistic worldview and affirms the importance of community and the fact that all people in society are demeaned when some people do not have their basic social and economic needs met. Bauman describes the social state in the following manner:

> A state is 'social' when it promotes the principle of communally endorsed, collective insurance against individual misfortune and its consequences. It is primarily that principle – declared, set in operation and trusted to be in working order – that recast the otherwise abstract idea of 'society' into the experience of felt and lived community through replacing the 'order of egoism' (to deploy John Dunn's terms), bound to generate an atmosphere of mutual mistrust and suspicion, with the 'order of equality,' inspiring confidence and solidarity. It is the same principle which lifts members of society to the status of citizens, that is, makes them stakeholders in addition to being stockholders: beneficiaries, but also actors – the wardens as much as the wards of the 'social benefits' system, individuals with an acute interest in the common good understood as a network of shared institutions that can be trusted and realistically expected, to guarantee the solidity and reliability of the state-issued 'collective insurance policy'.[51]

Some critics of the social-state principle argue that, in essence, it establishes an unfree or even undemocratic state that does not protect the free market as it does not sufficiently restrict the ability of a government to intervene in the economy. The freedom of individuals to act as they see fit, and to make a profit and exploit their own talents to the best of their abilities, would be better protected in a less welfarist state. This, they argue, is required to enable freedom to flourish, something that is fundamental to the proper functioning of a constitutional democracy. They reject the notion that unbridled capitalism would be fundamentally unjust to a large majority of citizens in a state and that while some would reap huge financial gains, it would visit misery on others. They

50 Davis et al (1994) 71.

51 Bauman, Z (2007) *Consuming Life* 140.

argue that a more radical free-market system would unleash economic growth that would eventually benefit all members of society. This, in turn, would better safeguard democracy.

Those who express these views are often, perhaps unkindly, called market fundamentalists. The views of market fundamentalists who oppose - to different degrees - the introduction of social welfare elements in a constitution are difficult to square with the provisions in the South African Constitution and with the idea that the South African Constitution is transformative in nature.[52] As we will see later, the South African Constitution includes a set of justiciable social and economic rights. This gives credence to the proposition that, like the German Constitution, it creates some form of a social state.

The German constitutional model also incorporates a system of separation of powers. The system divides power along the usual lines into the three branches, namely the legislature, the executive and the judiciary. In terms of this system, a bicameral Parliament is established that comprises a *Bundestag*[53] (the lower House) and the *Bundesrat*[54] (the upper House). Apart from law making, the lower House is responsible for the election of the Federal Chancellor, the equivalent of a prime minister, who is usually the leader of the dominant party in the Parliament.[55] The Chancellor selects his or her Cabinet and is responsible, with the Cabinet, for developing public policy and executing laws.[56] The German Constitution also makes provision for a President whose main function is to serve as a ceremonial head of state akin to the role played by the British monarch.[57] The system also has a system of administration of justice that includes a Constitutional Court.[58] The primary function of the Constitutional Court is to adjudicate constitutional matters arising from disputes between state organs, as well as between the state and private citizens, especially in instances of alleged rights violations.[59]

The final feature that bears mentioning for our purposes is that of the federal system. The German Constitution establishes Germany as a federal republic. Under the federal government are the provincial or *Länder* governments.[60] Although the *Länder* governments have their own constitutions, such constitutions must generally be in conformity with the German Constitution.[61] The German Constitution also provides the *Länder* governments with the authority to regulate their own affairs subject, of course, to limits placed by it. The Constitution stipulates areas or subject matter over which the *Länder* have exclusive competence to legislate and others over which they have concurrent competence with the *Bundestag*.

2.2.5 Constitutionalism in South Africa: a brief overview

We discussed South Africa's constitutional history in chapter 1 and will therefore not repeat it here. Instead, the aim of this section is to demonstrate the influence that the different constitutional models discussed above have had on the development of the various

52 See ch 1.
53 Arts 38–49 of the German Basic Law deal with the *Bundestag*.
54 Arts 50–3 of the German Basic Law deal with the *Bundesrat*. The *Bundesrat*'s involvement in law making is limited to matters concerning the *Länder* (provinces) only.
55 Art 63 of the German Basic Law.
56 Arts 64–5 of the German Basic Law.
57 Arts 54–61 of the German Basic Law. See also Motala (1994) 55.
58 Arts 92–104 of the German Basic Law.
59 Art 93 of the German Basic Law. See also Davis et al (1994) 75–7.
60 Arts 20–37 of the German Basic Law.
61 Art 28 of the German Basic Law. See also Davis et al (1994) 75.

constitutional models in South Africa since the formation of the modern South African state in 1910. As noted in chapter 1, we do not agree with the view that South Africa's constitutional history can be explained solely with reference to the formal structures imposed by the colonial rulers and that South Africa's constitutional history started in 1910. Nor do we wish readers to lose sight of the bifurcated nature of the constitutional arrangements in place from 1910 to 1994. However, as the governance traditions of indigenous South Africans have had a limited impact on the provisions of the South African Constitution, we focus here on the colonial history of constitutionalism in South Africa. We therefore do not claim that the models considered here are the only ones that have influenced South African constitutional developments, but it is most certainly arguable that they have had the most significant and identifiable influence on the constitutional structure and content of present-day South Africa.

2.2.5.1 The era of the dominance of the Westminster constitutional model

As discussed in chapter 1, the 1910 Union Constitution[62] established a colonial government that was tied to the British monarchy in several significant aspects. Apart from such formal colonial ties, another significant way in which such ties were manifested was in the constitutional model adopted at the National Convention of South Africa in 1908–9 which led to the Union Constitution of 1910. The Union Constitution adopted a manifestly Westminster form of government which made no provision for a bill of rights and provided little by way of constitutional guarantees limiting the power wielded by Parliament.

In 1961, South Africa cut ties with the British Commonwealth and adopted a republican Constitution.[63] Institutionally, very little changed from the previous Westminster-style Union Constitution, save that the head of state was no longer the British monarch and the position of a state president was created to serve a similar ceremonial role previously served by the monarch.[64] In terms of the 1961 Constitution, the prominence of parliamentary sovereignty as a defining constitutional feature was left in no doubt as the doctrine was provided for in explicit terms. Section 59 of the 1961 Constitution reads as follows:

> **Parliament shall be the sovereign legislative authority in and over the Republic, and shall have full power to make laws for the peace, order and good government of the Republic.**
>
> **No court of law shall be competent to enquire into or to pronounce upon the validity of any Act passed by Parliament other than any Act which repeals or amends or purports to repeal or amend the provisions of section one hundred and eight or one hundred and eighteen.**[65]

62 The Union of South Africa Act, 1909. This Act was passed through both Houses of the Imperial Parliament in the United Kingdom exactly as it was forwarded after the South African Convention was held. King Edward VII assented to the Act on 20 September 1909. A Royal Proclamation of 2 December 1909 declared the date of the establishment of the Union to be 31 May 1910.

63 Republic of South Africa Constitution Act 32 of 1961.

64 Ss 7–15. See also Dugard, J (1978) *Human Rights and the South African Legal Order* 35.

65 Ss 108 and 118 entrenched English and Afrikaans as the two official languages of South Africa with equal status and prohibited amendment of the entrenched sections except with the support of two-thirds of the members of the House of Assembly and the Senate. However, a later amendment allowed homelands to recognise one or more of the other indigenous languages for that particular self-governing territory.

Given the bifurcated nature of the state and the apartheid policies of the National Party (NP) which governed South Africa from 1948–1994, it is not surprising that during this period the NP government used parliamentary supremacy as a powerful instrument to secure political power for the white minority. In addition, the NP government used parliamentary supremacy to insulate the many legal provisions which discriminated against black South Africans and which restricted the basic rights of citizens from effective judicial scrutiny.

Having said this, however, we must be careful not to confuse the substance of the Westminster constitutional model with the abuses to which it was put and can potentially be put. The British experience with parliamentary supremacy is markedly different from that of South Africa and bears testimony to the fact that as a model of constitutionalism, there is nothing inherently flawed or problematic with the Westminster model. Like all other constitutional models it has its strengths and weaknesses, but any weaknesses it may have are not directly responsible for the system of racial exclusion and apartheid. Often, such weaknesses can be traced back to problems with the political culture and political parties and not necessarily with constitutional structures.

However, the tainted history of the Westminster system in South Africa most likely contributed to its not being wholly adopted as the preferred model during constitutional negotiations in the early 1990s.[66] While the end of apartheid brought with it an end to the era of parliamentary supremacy in South Africa, aspects of the Westminster system nevertheless found their way into the South African Constitution in amended form.

2.2.5.2 The era of constitutional supremacy

We discussed the history of the constitutional negotiations in chapter 1 and detailed the context that informed the choices made by the drafters of the Constitution. In this section, we therefore describe and discuss the prominent features of South Africa's democratic Constitution that arose from constitutional negotiations.

2.2.5.2.1 Constitutional supremacy

By far the most definitive feature of South Africa's post-apartheid constitutional system is that of constitutional supremacy. This notion of a supreme constitution is an important one on which South Africa's democratic constitutional dispensation is based. The Constitution in its founding provisions[67] expresses supremacy first as a foundational value, and second, declares the supremacy of the Constitution as a binding and enforceable rule in no uncertain terms. Section 1(*c*) of the Constitution provides:

> **The Republic of South Africa is one sovereign, democratic state founded on the following values ... [s]upremacy of the Constitution and the rule of law.**

Section 2 of the Constitution provides:

> **This Constitution is the supreme law of the Republic; law or conduct inconsistent with it is invalid, and the obligations imposed by it must be fulfilled.**[68]

---

66 The post-1994 Constitutions did adopt a form of parliamentary government usually associated with the Westminster constitutional model as – unlike in the US system – most members of the executive remain members of the legislature.

67 Ch 1.

68 These provisions are augmented by s 165(5) of the Constitution which states that '[a]n order or decision issued by a court binds all persons to whom and organs of state to which it applies' while s 172(1) states that '[w]hen deciding a constitutional matter within its power, a court must declare that any law or conduct that is inconsistent with the Constitution is invalid to the extent of its inconsistency'.

The decision by the drafters to make the Constitution supreme has had far-reaching implications for how the current democratic state operates, how the various structures and institutions relate to one another and how governmental power is exercised. The meaning of constitutional supremacy has already been dealt with above and that understanding applies with equal force to South Africa. What is, however, of interest to us here (and this is a question that is peculiar to the South African Constitution) is whether there is a difference between constitutional supremacy as a **value** captured by section 1 of the Constitution and the declaration of constitutional supremacy as a binding and enforceable **rule** set out in section 2. Notionally, we would assume that there should be some difference or significance to the drafters having included the idea of constitutional supremacy in two different provisions with two differing connotations in the Founding Chapter of the Constitution.

However, judging from the case law, it appears that the courts have made nothing of the difference between the two concepts. In fact, we find that there are few references in the case law to these provisions, save for passing, unsubstantiated references to the fact that the Constitution is supreme.[69] With respect to the declaration of supremacy in section 2, a possible reason put forward for the lack of judicial consideration of it is 'due to the clarity of the rule it states'.[70] In other words, there is little room for alternative interpretations of the provision. This position finds support in the General Provisions Chapter[71] of the Constitution in which section 237 demands that 'all constitutional obligations must be performed diligently and without delay'.

There is a difference in the procedure for the amendment of section 1 and section 2. On the one hand, the Constitution imposes a higher threshold for the amendment of section 1 where it requires the supporting vote of at least 75% of the members of the National Assembly (NA) and the support of six provincial delegations in the National Council of Provinces (NCOP).[72] For section 2, it requires the supporting vote of two-thirds of the members of the NA.[73] However, it is doubtful that Parliament would be able to amend section 2 without infringing on the values set out in section 1. If this happens, the constitutional question will arise whether the amendment of section 2 in effect amends section 1 and thus requires the more onerous amendment procedure to be followed to be validly passed.

While little seems to turn on whether constitutional supremacy is appealed to as a value or a binding and enforceable rule, constitutional supremacy is certainly a defining feature of South African constitutionalism as it renders the entire Constitution justiciable. Any law or conduct can thus potentially be tested against the provisions of the Constitution and must be declared invalid if it fails to comply with these provisions. Given the **justiciability** of the Constitution, an important incidence of constitutional supremacy is therefore the institutionalisation of judicial review which enjoins the courts to declare any law or conduct inconsistent with the Constitution invalid.[74] This power vested in the judiciary is an important one that secures the rights of all rights-holders under the Constitution as well as

69 See, for example, *Pharmaceutical Manufacturers Association of South Africa and Another: In re Ex parte President of the Republic of South Africa and Others* (CCT31/99) [2000] ZACC 1; 2000 (2) SA 674; 2000 (3) BCLR 241 (25 February 2000) para 44. See also Roederer, C 'Founding provisions' in Woolman, S and Bishop, M (eds) (2013) *Constitutional Law of South Africa* 2nd ed rev service 5 13.18. Roederer is of the view that the role of the proclamation of supremacy in s 2 is to specify further the value in s 1(*c*).

70 Roederer (2013) 13.25.

71 Ch 14.

72 S 74(1).

73 S 74(3).

74 See *S v Mamabolo* (CCT 44/00) [2001] ZACC 17; 2001 (3) SA 409 (CC); 2001 (5) BCLR 449 (CC) (11 April 2001) para 38.

securing the Constitution itself against violation as no authority or law is higher than the Constitution. We discuss the institution of judicial review further in this and subsequent chapters of this book.

PAUSE FOR REFLECTION

Exploring the effects of the supremacy of the Constitution on the legal system

Chaskalson CJ conveyed the primacy (or supremacy) of the Constitution lucidly and strongly in *Pharmaceutical Manufacturers Association of South Africa and Another: In re Ex parte President of the Republic of South Africa and Others* where he stated: 'There is only one system of law. It is shaped by the Constitution which is the supreme law, and all law, including the common law, derives its force from the Constitution and is subject to constitutional control.'[75] This declaration by the Constitutional Court is pivotal for South African law in general as it affirms the Constitution as the founding law of the Republic. It also affirms the unity of the South African legal system which derives its legitimacy and its binding force from the Constitution alone. Michelman explained the further significance of this passage as follows:[76]

> In those two sentences, the CC [Constitutional Court] claims for the Final Constitution [FC] not just one special virtue as compared with the rest of South Africa's laws but three of them, two of which go well beyond the claim (which also is there) for the Constitution's supremacy in the unadorned, norm-trumping sense declared by FC s 2. The first of these additional claims is for the pervasiveness of the Final Constitution's norms - 'all law ... is subject to constitutional control.' The second is the claim for the Final Constitution's status as the basic law of South Africa - 'all law ... derives its force from the Constitution.' Certainly there is no other law in South Africa of which it may be said either that all (other) law is subject to its control or that the force of all (other) law flows or stems from it. Now, a law to which these unique virtues are ascribed, along with trumping-sense supremacy, would be about as superlatively - or 'radically' - supreme as a law can get. Suppose, then, that the CC's attribution to the Final Constitution of the three special virtues combined could be seen to posit or reflect a value to which South Africa's embrace of the Final Constitution could defensibly be said to have committed the country; a value, that is, that stands distinct from and additive to the other human and societal goods posited as founding values by FC s 1. If we could see the threefold attribution in such a light, then we might understand 'supremacy of the Constitution' as it occurs in FC s 1's list of founding values to be the textual pointer toward the CC's claims in *Pharmaceutical Manufacturers* for the pervasiveness and the basic-law status, as well as the normative-trumping force, of the Final Constitution.... 'Supremacy of the Constitution' names the value of legal-systemic harmony in the service of the vision of the good society staked out by the entire list of founding values set forth in FC s 1 and instinct in the rest of the Final Constitution. We deal here with the value of the unity of the legal system — meaning the system's normative unity or, as one might say more poetically, its visionary unity. The value in question is the value of having all the

75 (CCT31/99) [2000] ZACC 1; 2000 (2) SA 674; 2000 (3) BCLR 241 (25 February 2000) para 44.

76 Michelman, F 'The rule of law, legality and the supremacy of the Constitution' in Woolman and Bishop (2013) 11.37–11.38.

institutional sites in which the legal order resides – and especially all of its courts of law – pulling in the same and not contrary directions, working in ultimate harmony (which is not to say without difference and debate) toward the vision (the elements of which must always be open to interpretation) of a well-ordered South African society depicted in very broad-brush fashion by the other founding values listed in FC s 1: human dignity, equality, human rights and freedoms, non-racialism, non-sexism, and the basic accoutrements of an open, accountable, representative-democratic system of government.

If Michelman is correct, it means that the Constitution, and the norms or values enshrined in it, must now animate all aspects of South African law (as interpreted, developed and applied by all South African courts) in the pursuit of justice. The supremacy of the Constitution then signifies not only the absolute unity of the legal system, but such a unity that stands in the 'service of transformation by, under, and according to law'.[77] No aspect of South African law, including the common law and customary law, would then be immune from the influence of the basic values of human dignity, equality, human rights and freedoms, non-racialism and non-sexism, as well as the basic accessories of an open, accountable, representative-democratic system of government which are embodied in the Constitution. Any development of the common law and customary law will have to occur with reference to these basic constitutional values. The principle of constitutional supremacy, in this understanding, will thus have a far more profound effect on the legal system than merely indicating that all law inconsistent with the specific provisions of the Constitution will now be unconstitutional. The trajectory of the development of all forms of law in South Africa will be fundamentally altered by the supremacy of the Constitution, thus understood. This radical aspect of South Africa's constitutional model is not always appreciated by lawyers and judges who continue to work with the common law, customary law and legislation as if these are entirely insulated from the norms enshrined in the Constitution.

2.2.5.2.2 A value-based constitutional system

Section 1 of the Constitution affirms that the South African constitutional model is not only descriptive but prescriptive. This section sets out some of the most important values on which the South African constitution model is founded. Section 1 reads as follows:

> **The Republic of South Africa is one, sovereign, democratic state founded on the following values:**
> **(*a*) Human dignity, the achievement of equality and the advancement of human rights and freedoms.**
> **(*b*) Non-racialism and non-sexism.**
> **(*c*) Supremacy of the constitution and the rule of law.**
> **(*d*) Universal adult suffrage, a national common voters roll, regular elections and a multi-party system of democratic government, to ensure accountability, responsiveness and openness.**

77 Michelman (2013) 11.38.

Section 1 of the Constitution is of profound importance as it sets out the foundational values on which the current constitutional dispensation is based. In so doing, it is self-evident that these values espoused in the provision reflect a break from the past and establish the foundations of a new society in the making. This society is governed by law, but the law derives its force from the Constitution and its development is animated by the values contained in section 1 of the Constitution. The importance of these values within the overall constitutional scheme is reflected in the fact that section 1 is an entrenched provision that can only be amended subject to special procedures and majorities being attained in Parliament.[78]

COUNTER POINT

Amending the founding provisions of the Constitution

The founding provisions are often lauded as being central to South African democracy and, as Michelman points out, to the legal system as a whole. However, we will see below that the values they protect are not inviolable. Amendment may be made to the founding provisions provided 75% of the members of the NA and six provinces in the NCOP vote for such an amendment. Therefore, Parliament could alter the provision that states that the Constitution (and not Parliament) is supreme if a required majority of members of the NA and delegations in the NCOP support this. So too could the provisions that state the values of human dignity, the achievement of equality and the advancement of human rights and freedoms. If Parliament were to make an amendment of this kind to the Constitution (an unlikely scenario as no political party has ever acquired the 75% majority in the NA), it would be possible to restore Parliament to the position of supremacy it enjoyed during the apartheid era. Such a Parliament would also be able to abolish the rule of law.

Some critics argue that it would have been more prudent of the drafters of the Constitution to have made section 1 unchangeable (something the German constitution-makers did)[79] to safeguard the democratic and non-racial character of the South African constitutional system. Others argue that circumstances and the political, economic and social context in a country may change over time and that future generations should not be absolutely and finally held to ransom by the drafters of the 1996 Constitution. Such a system, they say, would in extreme cases invite the government of the day that enjoys legitimacy and overwhelming electoral support to suspend the Constitution in its entirety.

How a person views this issue will depend on his or her commitment to the values enshrined in section 1 as well as on his or her view of the political landscape and whether an elected Parliament would ever be able to muster the requisite heightened majority to abolish the basic values on which the 1996 Constitution is based.

It is therefore clear that in addition to the clearly articulated values found in section 1, there are also some unarticulated values embodied in the Constitution which, together with those in section 1, form the normative basis of how the South African Constitution is to be

78 See s 74(1)(*a*) and (*b*).

79 Art 79(3) of the German Basic Law states: 'Amendments to this Basic Law affecting the division of the Federation into *Länder*, their participation on principle in the legislative process, or the principles laid down in Articles 1 and 20 shall be inadmissible.'

interpreted.[80] In other words, our Constitution does not simply set out the rules, processes and structures that place limits on governmental power. The Constitution also expresses itself on the ideals and characteristics to which we, as a society, deem worthy to aspire. This idea should be familiar to us as it is derived from the notion of a value-based democratic order as found in the German model discussed above.[81] In the South African context, the courts have recognised the significance of the value-based constitutional system where they have asserted that the democratic constitutional order has established an 'objective normative value system'.[82] However, this notion, while appearing to be incredibly important, has not been the subject of much attention from the courts[83] or academic commentators in South Africa.[84]

2.2.5.2.3 Co-operative federalism

The final characteristic of South African constitutionalism that we shall discuss in this section is that of the federal division of power. The Constitution provides for what can be deemed a quasi-federal division of power across three levels or spheres of government, namely national, provincial and local spheres. This system differs from the traditional federal system where the powers and functions of different levels of government are clearly delineated and where each sphere is empowered to deal exclusively with certain distinct subject matters.

According to Chapter 3 of the Constitution, the model adopted is that of co-operative federalism or co-operative government. Chapter 3 makes it clear that while the three spheres of government are distinct, all three spheres are expected to work together to deliver the vision of the Constitution.[85] Rather than competing with each other, the Constitution envisages a co-operative relationship between the three levels of government that entails their sharing responsibilities in a mutually supportive fashion.[86]

Co-operation between the three levels of government is not always easy, especially if different political parties govern different entities in different spheres. For example, if the African National Contress (ANC) governs nationally, the Democratic Alliance (DA) governs the Western Cape Province and a coalition of political parties governs one of the municipalities in the Western Cape, this will present specific challenges. In terms of Chapter 3, the ANC national government, the DA Western Cape government and the coalition municipal government are required to co-operate with each other. This task is made even more difficult as the national government, the provincial governments and municipalities sometimes are all empowered to deal with a specific subject matter, for example the provision of housing. If political parties are unable to work together, the governments in the various spheres will not

80 See Roederer (2013) 13.3–13.8 where he makes the point that section 1 does not explicitly contain all the foundational values, for example separation of powers, *ubuntu*, transformation, social justice and constitutionalism. The courts have recognised these values and several others and we will discuss them in the chapters to follow.

81 See Woolman, S 'Application' in Woolman and Bishop (2013) 31.93–31.94.

82 See *Carmichele v Minister of Safety and Security* (CCT 48/00) [2001] ZACC 22; 2001 (4) SA 938 (CC); 2001 (10) BCLR 995 (CC) (16 August 2001) para 56 where the Constitutional Court confirmed that the Constitution contained an 'objective value system', but declined to discuss what this value system might be. See also Roederer (2013) 13.9–13.15.

83 See *Carmichele* and *Geldenhuys v Minister of Safety and Security and Another* 2002 (4) SA 719 (C) 728G–I where the Court affirmed that the 'objective normative value system' seeks to establish a society based on human dignity, equality and freedom 'and institutions of government which are open, transparent and accountable to the people whom they serve. The content of this normative system does not only depend on an abstract philosophical inquiry but rather upon an understanding that the constitution mandates the development of a society which breaks clearly and decisively from the past and where institutions which operated prior to our constitutional dispensation had to be instilled with a new operational vision based on the foundational values of our constitutional system.'

84 However, see Woolman (2013) 31.90 as well as Michelman (2013) 11.40.

85 S 40(1) describes the three levels of government as being 'distinctive, interdependent and interrelated'.

86 See s 41(1)(*h*)(i) to (vi). See also Currie and De Waal (2001) 119–20.

be able to deliver on their housing mandate in an effective manner. This is why the provisions of Chapter 3 are of utmost importance for the smooth running of the country. We will discuss the details of co-operative federalism in chapter 8 of this book.

2.3 Separation of powers

2.3.1 The purpose and principles of the doctrine of separation of powers

Constitutional restrictions on the exercise of public power can be both procedural and substantive in nature. Substantive restrictions are achieved through a justiciable bill of rights and the constitutional commitment to other values such as the rule of law. The exercise of public power can also be restricted in a procedural way. One of the most important mechanisms through which this is achieved in a constitutional democracy is through the separation of powers.[87] The separation of powers doctrine seeks to limit the powers of each individual branch of government: the legislature, the executive and the judiciary. The doctrine is therefore the basis for an institutional, procedural and structural division of public power to create a society in which the abuse of power by government is curtailed and public power is exercised wisely, or at least prudently, and not in an abusive manner.

The South African Constitution makes no express mention of separation of powers. However, the Constitutional Principles that formed part of the interim Constitution required that the final Constitution contain a separation of powers between the three branches of government as well as the appropriate checks and balances on the exercise of power of each of these branches to 'ensure accountability, responsiveness and openness'.[88] It is thus against this background that the doctrine of separation of powers must be seen as forming an integral component of South African constitutionalism.

Historically, as a means of limiting governmental power, separation of powers is primarily concerned with establishing procedural limits on the exercise of power. As a mechanism to achieve this broad aim, separation of powers seeks to ensure that power is not concentrated in one institution or branch, or in one person or office. This is to prevent abuses of power by an all-powerful government which has concentrated all power in one body or in one individual such as a president. Separation of powers can be said to be premised on the understanding that rather than trusting in the benevolence of rulers, a more predictable and transparent way to prevent tyranny is by distributing power between different branches of government which can, individually, be better held to account. Such distribution seeks to limit the possibility of an overconcentration of power in any one branch and also to create some level of exclusiveness or specialisation of functions in each of the branches.

Beyond limiting governmental power by distributing it, the modern conception of separation of powers is also closely associated with the protection of human rights more generally in addition to safeguarding political liberty. This is so because separation of powers aims to protect society against the abuse of political power, something that is required to protect human rights. The procedural nature of the separation of powers can therefore be seen as having a substantive aim – the protection of the human rights of all and the prevention of the abuse of power.

87 Seedorf, S and Sibanda, S 'Separation of powers' in Woolman and Bishop (2013) 12.1.

88 Constitutional Principle VI of Schedule 4 of the interim Constitution provided: 'There shall be a separation of powers between the legislature, executive and judiciary, with appropriate checks and balances to ensure accountability, responsiveness and openness.'

Before discussing separation of powers in some depth, it is worthwhile to lay out the four principles that make up the modern conceptualisation of the doctrine.[89] The four principles are as follows:

- First, there is the **division of governmental power** across the three branches, namely the legislative branch (parliament), the executive branch (president/prime minister and cabinet) and the judicial branch (the courts). This division is often referred to as the *trias politica*.
- Second, the principle of **separation of functions** entails conferring distinct areas of responsibility and authority on each of the three branches of government and preventing one branch from taking responsibility for the tasks allocated to another branch.
- Third, the principle of **separation of personnel** entails that each branch of government must have assigned to it specific persons who are responsible, often exclusively, for the performance or execution of that branch's function.
- Last, the provision of **checks and balances** entails that one branch can be held accountable by other branches to check the exercise of power by that branch. In certain circumstances, this allows one branch to veto the actions taken by another branch. This ensures, first, that the branches remain connected in the discharge of their functions, and second, that the branches hold each other to account where provided for by the constitution.

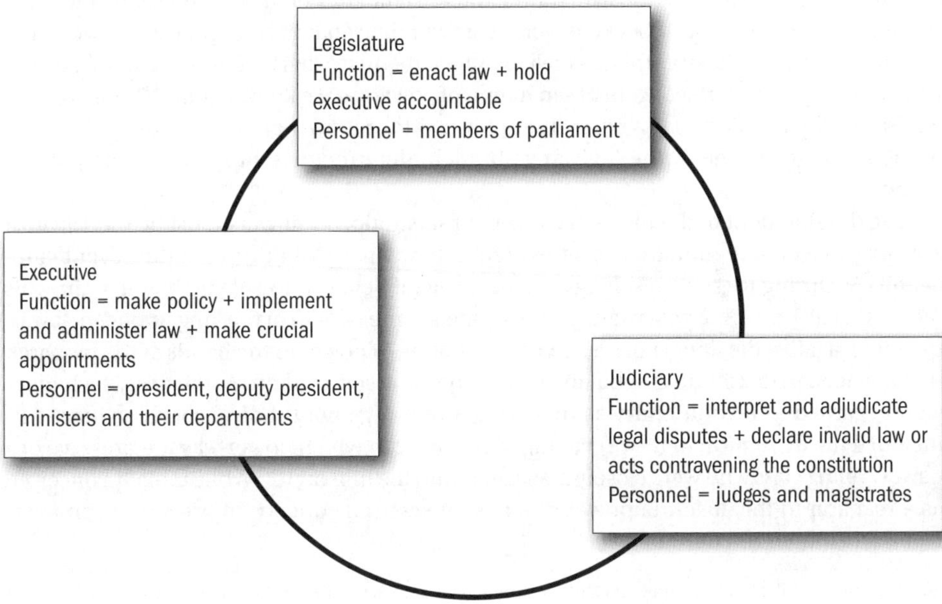

Figure 2.3 *Separation of powers doctrine*

The principles set out above are generally accepted as the pillars on which the doctrine of separation of powers is based. However, it is acknowledged that no constitutional system encompasses a full separation of governmental authority where power is exercised by each

89 The two classical texts on this subject are Vile, MJC (1967) *Constitutionalism and the Separation of Powers* and Gwyn, WB (1965) *The Meaning of the Separation of Powers: An Analysis of the Doctrine from its Origin to the Adoption of the United States Constitution.*

individual branch of government in isolation from the others.[90] Instead, the division of power, functions and personnel, and the provision for checks and balances, differ extensively among constitutions that subscribe to the doctrine.

2.3.2 A brief history of the doctrine of separation of powers

The doctrine of separation of powers as a distinct theory of government is often said to have its origins in the political philosophy of the Enlightenment in seventeenth-century Europe.[91] However, this may be an oversimplification. Although no separation of powers as currently understood existed in pre-colonial southern African societies because traditional leaders performed all functions of government,[92] traditional leaders were nevertheless expected to consult with an advisory body or to seek approval from the population at large. They could not take any important decision without discussing it first in the council. This allowed for a check on the exercise of power by the relevant chief.[93] Nevertheless, the modern concept of separation of powers is said to have emerged as a model to explain the English constitutional model developed by John Locke.[94] Locke's writing on this topic emerged in the wake of the constitutional developments in England which ended the absolute power of the monarch. Locke was concerned that absolute monarchic power should not be replaced by absolute parliamentary power. His writing therefore wrestled with ways of countering the power-accumulating tendencies of those in power and the tendency of those in power to abuse the power they accumulated.[95] Locke never envisaged the separation of powers between the executive and the judiciary. This task fell to French theorist, Charles Baron de Montesquieu, who devised the modern concept of separation of powers as we know it today.[96] This concept envisaged the division of governmental power into the *trias politica*, namely the three branches of government, the legislative branch, the executive branch and the judicial branch.

The development of the modern concept of separation of powers must be seen against a history of absolute monarchy that existed in many parts of Europe in the seventeenth century.[97] During these times, kings or queens were believed to rule by divine right. This meant that all powers of governance were located in the person of the king or queen. It was, therefore, against the danger of an overconcentration of power in the hands of the monarch that the need to distribute and balance power became self-evident. At the time, such ideas were regarded as revolutionary as they sought to bring about radical social change. This included the disruption of the prevailing social order in which power was the preserve of a narrow ruling class who were closely associated with the monarch.[98] While initially conceived as a reaction to the absolute power of kings, the central concern of preventing an over-

90 See Rautenbach, IM and Malherbe, EFJ (2012) *Constitutional Law* 6th ed. See also Pieterse, M (2004) Coming to terms with judicial enforcement of socio-economic rights *SAJHR* 20:383–417 at 386.

91 See Calabresi, SG, Berghausen, ME and Albertson, S (2012) The rise and fall of the separation of powers *Northwestern University Law Review* 106(2):527–50 at 529–36.

92 See ch 1.

93 See Bennett, T and Murray, C 'Traditional leaders' in Woolman and Bishop (2013) 26.4 and 26.53. See also Seedorf and Sibanda (2013) 12.3 for a discussion on the roots of this doctrine.

94 Locke, J (1690) *Second Treatise on Government* (1986) 143–4, 150 and 159. See also Van der Vyver, JD (1993) The separation of powers *SAPL* 8:177–91 who points out that Locke's initial conception of separation of powers classified the threefold governmental powers as legislative power, executive power (including adjudication) and federative power (foreign relations).

95 Seedorf and Sibanda (2013) 12.5.

96 De Montesquieu, C (1748) *De l'Esprit des Loix* (Nugent, T (tr), Neumann, F (ed) (1949) *The Spirit of the Laws*).

97 For an overview on the history of separation of powers preceding this era, see Seedorf and Sibanda (2013) 12.3–12.10.

98 Seedorf and Sibanda (2013) 12.1.

accumulation of power remained at the core of the development of the doctrine as constitutional theorists, such as Locke, warned against the dangers of any one institution, even parliament, having too much power.[99] This modern concept was to find its earliest, clearest expression in the adoption of the US Constitution wherein the idea of separation of powers provided a basis for the distribution of power and the very structure of government.

2.3.3 Separation of powers: the South African experience

As mentioned above, Constitutional Principle VI in the interim Constitution required that the final Constitution incorporate a system of separation of powers. However, this Principle was silent as to the exact nature of the distribution of power between the three branches and the institutional limits to be put in place on the exercise of power by each of the branches. Instead, what Constitutional Principle VI did specify was the purpose for which the separation of powers had to be incorporated into the 1996 Constitution. This purpose was to uphold and safeguard important democratic values and norms, namely 'accountability, responsiveness, and openness'.[100] It was, therefore, left to the drafters of the 1996 Constitution to determine how the South African model of separation of powers was to be conceptualised and incorporated.

Note that there is no universal model of separation of powers. Moreover, in democratic systems of government in which checks and balances result in the imposition of restraints by one branch of government on another, there is no separation that is absolute.[101] The concept can be incorporated in a constitution in different ways: it can require a more or less strict separation of functions and personnel as well as more or less powerful mechanisms that would allow one branch of government to enforce checks and balances on another. In interpreting separation of powers in the South African context, what is clear is that the Constitutional Court is reluctant to measure the South African model against the standards of other countries or other models of separation of powers. It is, therefore, important to recognise that we must interpret and judge South Africa's model of separation of powers with our own historical experiences and political context in mind.[102] In this respect, the Constitutional Court has captured this idea crisply in *De Lange v Smuts NO and Others* when Ackermann J wrote as follows:

> **I have no doubt that over time our courts will develop a distinctively South African model of separation of powers, one that fits the particular system of government provided for in the Constitution and that reflects a delicate balancing, informed both by South Africa's history and its new dispensation, between the need, on the one hand, to control government by separating powers and enforcing checks and balances, and, on the other, to avoid diffusing power so completely that the government is unable to take timely measures in the public interest.**[103]

The Constitutional Court has previously held that although there is no explicit reference or mention of separation of powers in the Constitution, it is implicit in the Constitution and is of equal force as an express constitutional provision.[104] However, this apparent omission

99 Seedorf and Sibanda (2013) 12.5.

100 These values are enshrined in s 1(*d*) of the Constitution.

101 *Certification of the Constitution of the Republic of South Africa, 1996* (CCT 23/96) [1996] ZACC 26; 1996 (4) SA 744 (CC); 1996 (10) BCLR 1253 (CC) (6 September 1996) para 108.

102 See *S v Dodo* (CCT 1/01) [2001] ZACC 16; 2001 (3) SA 382 (CC); 2001 (5) BCLR 423 (CC) (5 April 2001) para 17.

103 (CCT26/97) [1998] ZACC 6; 1998 (3) SA 785 (CC); 1998 (7) BCLR 779 (28 May 1998) (CC) para 60.

104 *South African Association of Personal Injury Lawyers v Heath and Others* (CCT27/00) [2000] ZACC 22; 2001 (1) SA 883; 2001 (1) BCLR 77 (28 November 2000) paras 18–22.

must be read against the structure of the Constitution which clearly makes provision for the separation of powers in terms of its institutional and substantive arrangements.[105] We can infer the implicitness of the doctrine in the Constitution from the manner in which governmental power is actually distributed primarily between the legislative, the executive and the judicial branches of government. Other provisions in the Constitution also support this implicit inclusion of the separation of powers doctrine. These provisions include the regulation of the distribution of functions; the identification of the appropriate personnel to perform the functions; and, more generally, the framework of control and interaction between the branches of government and the personnel therein. To demonstrate the substance of this implicit doctrine, we discuss the methods by which separation of powers manifests in the Constitution below.

COUNTER POINT

Does the legislature in South Africa in fact hold the executive accountable?

In *Certification of the Constitution of the Republic of South Africa, 1996*,[106] the Constitutional Court had to deal with arguments that the South African Constitution, which provides for members of the executive also to be members of legislatures, contravened the principle of the separation of powers. The reason for this was that it did not allow for a complete separation of personnel between the legislature and the executive as members of the Cabinet remain members of the legislature. By virtue of their positions, Cabinet members are thus able to exercise a powerful influence over the decisions of the legislature. In rejecting this criticism the Constitutional Court noted that there is more than one model of separation of powers and stated that:

> While in the USA, France and the Netherlands members of the executive may not continue to be members of the legislature, this is not a requirement of the German system of separation of powers. Moreover, because of the different systems of checks and balances that exist in these countries, the relationship between the different branches of government and the power or influence that one branch of government has over the other, differs from one country to another. The principle of separation of powers, on the one hand, recognises the functional independence of branches of government. On the other hand, the principle of checks and balances focuses on the desirability of ensuring that the constitutional order, as a totality, prevents the branches of government from usurping power from one another. In this sense it anticipates the necessary or unavoidable intrusion of one branch on the terrain of another. No constitutional scheme can reflect a complete separation of powers: the scheme is always one of partial separation. In Justice Frankfurter's words, '[t]he areas are partly interacting, not wholly disjointed'. ... As the separation of powers doctrine is not a fixed or rigid constitutional doctrine, it is given expression in many different forms and made subject to checks and balances of many kinds. It can thus not be said that a failure in the [final Constitution] to separate completely the functionaries of the executive and legislature is destructive of the doctrine. Indeed, the overlap provides a singularly important check and balance on the exercise of executive power. It makes the executive more directly answerable to the elected legislature.[107]

105 The Constitutional Court made this point in *First Certification* paras 106–113.
106 (CCT 23/96) [1996] ZACC 26; 1996 (4) SA 744 (CC); 1996 (10) BCLR 1253 (CC) (6 September 1996).
107 *First Certification* paras 108–12.

It is unclear whether this view of the Constitutional Court has proven to be correct. Although – as we will see – the executive is in theory accountable to the legislature, in practice this accountability can seem illusory. This is because the members of the majority party in the legislature are required to hold accountable the members of the executive who are also, more often than not, members of the leadership of the political party to which the majority of members of the legislature belong. It is not always easy for the members of the legislature to hold the executive to account when this would require them to challenge the authority of the leaders of the political party to which they belong. This difficulty is further exacerbated by the fact that members of the legislature are not individually elected. Because of the electoral system in operation in South Africa, they depend for their election to the legislature on the leadership of the party to which they belong.

2.3.3.1 The legislature

A strict version of the separation of powers doctrine requires the creation of a separate legislature with its own personnel empowered to exercise its powers independently from the other branches of government.[108] Chapter 4 of the Constitution creates a slightly less strict separation between the legislature and other branches of government. As far as a separation of functions is concerned, the Constitution vests the national legislative authority in Parliament[109] which consists of the National Assembly (NA) and the National Council of Provinces (NCOP). Chapter 4 also determines that the exercise of legislative authority, broadly speaking, entails the power to make laws. This includes amending the Constitution, making general laws as well as the power to assign or delegate Parliament's legislative powers.[110] When Parliament exercises its legislative authority, it is only constrained by the fact that it must act in accordance with and within the limits of the Constitution.[111] Chapter 4 also specifies in whom the powers to legislate vest. These powers are conferred on members of the legislature who comprise members of the NA[112] and members of the NCOP.[113] In their capacity as Members of Parliament, the Constitution empowers both members of the NA as well as members of the NCOP respectively to regulate their own processes.[114] Closely related to this power, the Constitution confers on the members of both Houses **parliamentary privilege** for all speeches made in Parliament and its committees.[115] We will discuss the content and limits of these powers and privileges in chapter 4 of this book.

However, the Constitution does not provide for a strict separation of powers between the legislature and the executive. First, while it establishes Parliament as the distinct legislative branch with its particularised function of law making and its own personnel, the Constitution also makes provision for the involvement of the executive in the performance of the

108 See ch 4.
109 See ss 43(*a*) and 42(1).
110 S 44(1)(*a*) read with s 44(2)(*b*).
111 S 44(4) provides that when Parliament exercises its legislative authority, it is only bound by the Constitution and must act in accordance with and within the limits of the Constitution.
112 See ss 46 and 47 for provisions relating to the composition, election and membership of the NA.
113 See ss 60 and 61 for provisions relating to the composition and allocation of delegates to the NCOP.
114 See s 57 in respect of the NA and s 70 in respect of the NCOP.
115 See s 58 in respect of the NA and s 71 in respect of the NCOP.

legislative functions.[116] Apart from being allowed to introduce legislation in the NA, members of the executive are given the power to develop and implement policy, as well as to prepare and initiate legislation.[117] In addition to this, the executive enjoys limited law-making powers in that it is empowered to make subordinate legislation, a power usually conferred on the executive in the empowering legislation.[118]

Second, there is an overlap in personnel between the legislature and the executive: apart from the President and a maximum of two other members of Cabinet, all members of the executive are also required to serve as members of the NA.[119] This connection between the legislature and the executive can be seen simply as being rooted in and a continuation of the Westminster tradition of parliamentary government as discussed above. It can be argued that this overlap of the personnel in the legislature and the executive should be judged in light of the injunction in Constitutional Principle VI that there be checks and balances between the branches. Viewed thus, the close involvement of the executive in the legislative process could be argued to serve the purpose of promoting efficiency and accountability between these two branches, especially considering that governing has and continues to become more and more complicated with an ever-increasing need for regulation. Members of Parliament do not always have the expertise to make complex decisions on specialised topics. They therefore rely on the executive to formulate policy and to translate policies into draft legislation that is then scrutinised by the legislature. Where the members of the executive and members of the legislature overlap, this process (so it is argued) will run more smoothly, improving the efficiency of both the legislature and the executive.

COUNTER POINT

Does South Africa's electoral system weaken the power of the legislature?

The electoral system in force in South Africa requires that political parties compile electoral lists from which members of the NA and provincial legislatures are then drawn after an election. Some argue that this system weakens the legislature in relation to the executive. This is because the leaders of the majority party, who will often also be members of the executive, may have a decisive say in who appears on the party's election lists. According to this argument, members of the majority party in the legislature may be reluctant to hold the executive to account – they have to safeguard their position in the legislature and they have to respect party discipline which requires strict adherence to the dictates of the party. Such members of the legislature may even bend over backwards to implement the legislative programme of the executive. This weakens the system of checks and balances that goes hand in hand with any effective

116 S 73(2) permits members of the Cabinet or Deputy Ministers to introduce Bills in the National Assembly. S 79(1) enjoins the President to assent to and sign a Bill which has been passed by Parliament.

117 See s 85(1)(*b*) and (*d*).

118 See *Executive Council of the Western Cape Legislature and Others v President of the Republic of South Africa and Others* (CCT27/95) [1995] ZACC 8; 1995 (10) BCLR 1289; 1995 (4) SA 877 (22 September 1995) para 51. See also *AAA Investments (Proprietary) Limited v Micro Finance Regulatory Council and Another* (CCT51/05) [2006] ZACC 9; 2006 (11) BCLR 1255 (CC); 2007 (1) SA 343 (CC) (28 July 2006) paras 49, 93 and 122–3; *Constitutionality of the Mpumalanga Petitions Bill, 2000* (CCT 11/01) [2001] ZACC 10; 2002 (1) SA 447 (CC); 2001 (11) BCLR 1126 (5 October 2001) para 19; *Executive Council of the Province of the Western Cape v Minister for Provincial Affairs and Constitutional Development and Another, Executive Council of KwaZulu-Natal v President of the Republic of South Africa and Others* (CCT15/99,CCT18/99) [1999] ZACC 13; 2000 (1) SA 661; 1999 (12) BCLR 1360 (15 October 1999) paras 123–4; *Justice Alliance of South Africa v President of Republic of South Africa and Others, Freedom Under Law v President of Republic of South Africa and Others, Centre for Applied Legal Studies and Another v President of Republic of South Africa and Others* (CCT 53/11, CCT 54/11, CCT 62/11) [2011] ZACC 23; 2011 (5) SA 388 (CC); 2011 (10) BCLR 1017 (CC) (29 July 2011) para 53.

119 See s 91(3).

system of separation of powers. Moreover, it is often argued that in a modern state in recent times, the legislature has declined in political influence in comparison to the executive which 'has burgeoned in size, influence over the legislature and power over the citizenry'.[120] This has turned the legislature into an ineffective body in relation to the executive whose members also dominate the legislature and help to emasculate it.

However, it is unclear whether a change in the electoral system would automatically strengthen the separation of powers and improve the ability of the legislature to hold the executive accountable. It has been pointed out that at the local government level half the municipal councillors are **not** elected via the electoral list system, but rather in constituencies. This has not necessarily improved accountable and responsive government. According to this view, merely changing the electoral system will not change much. Unless the power of the leaders of political parties to decide who is nominated to represent them in constituencies is weakened, the power of political leaders who serve in the executive over the Members of Parliament who are their juniors in the political party will not be broken. How can even independently elected members of the legislature hold the executive accountable if they know that they will only be renominated as a candidate in a specific seat to contest the election on behalf of the majority party if they do not upset the leadership of the party?[121]

The Constitutional Court has had occasion to consider questions about the power of the executive to interfere with the law-making functions of the legislature in the important early Constitutional Court judgment of *Executive Council of the Western Cape Legislature and Others v President of the Republic of South Africa and Others*.[122] This case involved a challenge to provisions in an Act of Parliament which delegated powers to the President, allowing him to amend the Local Government Transition Act[123] by proclamation. The Constitutional Court readily accepted that in a modern society, the act of governing would require some level of delegation of law-making power to the executive. Chaskalson P, writing the majority judgment, wrote as follows:

> **In a modern state detailed provisions are often required for the purpose of implementing and regulating laws, and Parliament cannot be expected to deal with all such matters itself. There is nothing in the Constitution which prohibits Parliament from delegating subordinate regulatory authority to other bodies. The power to do so is necessary for effective law-making. It is implicit in the power to make laws for the country and I have no doubt that under our Constitution parliament can pass legislation delegating such legislative functions to other bodies.**[124]

However, in this case, the delegation in question was found to be unconstitutional. In coming to this decision, the judges of the Court delivered several judgments, all concurring that the delegation was invalid but for different reasons. A common thread, though, among the judgments was the fact that while delegation of legislative power is indeed permissible, the

120 See Pieterse (2004) 388.

121 See De Vos, P (2012, 14 August) Towards a parliament for the people *Constitutionally Speaking* available at http://constitutionallyspeaking.co.za/towards-a-parliament-for-the-people/.

122 (CCT27/95) [1995] ZACC 8; 1995 (10) BCLR 1289; 1995 (4) SA 877 (22 September 1995). See also *Justice Alliance*.

123 Act 209 of 1993.

124 *Executive Council of the Western Cape Legislature* para 51.

doctrine of separation of powers demands that there be limits to the **nature** or the **extent** of the power to be delegated by Parliament to the executive. It was with respect to the determination of the extent or even the factors to be taken into account that the judges failed to reach agreement.[125] However, in spite of such disagreement, all the judges concurred on the point that Parliament could not delegate its plenary powers to make or amend a statute to the executive branch. By attempting to do so, Parliament had contravened the separation of powers principle inherent in the structure of the Constitution.

2.3.3.2 The executive

Chapter 5 of the Constitution vests executive authority in the President[126] who is both Head of State and head of the national executive.[127] The Constitution provides a broad definition of the scope of the executive function. In terms of the Constitution, the executive is responsible for the development, preparation and implementation of national policy and legislation as well as for co-ordinating the functions of state departments and administration.[128] More generally, the executive is responsible for the execution and implementation of law, policy and administration.

In the President's capacity as Head of State and head of the national executive, he or she is duty-bound to uphold and defend the Constitution as the supreme law of the Republic.[129] In terms of the Constitution, the President exercises executive authority together with the Cabinet which comprises the Deputy President and Ministers.[130] The President as head of the executive has the power to appoint and dismiss the other members of the Cabinet who serve at the President's pleasure.[131] Although enjoying the power to select the Cabinet of his or her own choice, the President is constrained by provisions of the Constitution that require him or her to select all but two members of the Cabinet from the NA.[132]

While the executive function is undoubtedly an expansive one and has significant powers, these powers must be viewed in light of other constitutional provisions that place the executive under the scrutiny of Parliament. In particular, the Constitution provides that members of the Cabinet are accountable individually and collectively to Parliament.[133] Although the accountability is to 'Parliament' as a whole, section 55(2) affirms that, in effect, this power resides with one of the two Houses, the NA.[134] Cabinet members must also provide full and regular reports concerning matters under their control.[135] Beyond this, the Constitution confers on the NA the ultimate checking power, namely the powers to remove or recall the executive. These powers, on the one hand, permit the NA to remove the entire Cabinet or only the Deputy President and Ministers by way of a vote of no confidence by a majority of the members. This is essentially a political power where the majority of members of the NA have lost confidence in the Cabinet or in the President.[136] On the other hand, these

125 See also Currie and De Waal (2001) 98–102.
126 S 83(*a*).
127 Ss 84(1) and 85(1). For a discussion as to the import of the distinction between these two capacities in which the President exercises power, see ch 5.
128 S 85(2)(*a*)-(*e*).
129 S 83(*b*).
130 S 91(1).
131 S 91(2).
132 S 91(3).
133 S 92(2).
134 The dominant role of the NA becomes apparent if we compare s 55 with the comparable s 68 dealing with the powers of the NCOP. The latter section makes no mention of an accountability or oversight role for the NCOP.
135 S 92(3)(*b*).
136 S 102 establishes two different motions, one that provides for the removal of the Cabinet excluding the President and another motion that provides for the removal of the entire Cabinet, including the President.

powers also permit the NA to remove the President by way of a two-thirds vote by the members where the President is found to have violated the Constitution or the law, engaged in serious misconduct or when she or he is found to be no longer able to perform his or her functions of office. This is essentially the power of impeachment.[137]

2.3.3.3 The judiciary

Unlike the relationship between the executive and the legislature, there is an absolute separation in personnel and (arguably)[138] also in powers between the legislature and executive on the one hand and the judiciary on the other.[139] This is the bedrock principle of the separation of powers doctrine in a constitutional state. Thus, Chapter 8 of the Constitution vests judicial authority in the courts,[140] establishes a hierarchy of courts comprising the Constitutional Court, the Supreme Court of Appeal (SCA), the High Court of South Africa and the magistrates' courts,[141] and establishes the Constitutional Court as the apex court in all matters.[142]

The primary function of the courts is the adjudication of legal disputes, including those that require the interpretation and application of the Constitution.[143] For present purposes, our primary focus is on courts' constitutional jurisdiction, in particular the courts' powers of judicial review.[144] As discussed above, the essence of judicial review is that it empowers the courts to declare as constitutionally invalid any law or conduct found to contravene the Constitution. The legislation or actions declared invalid in this way will have no legal force or effect. This means that the courts – with the Constitutional Court at the apex – have enormous power to check the exercise as well as the abuse of power by the other two branches of government. Unlike the US Constitution where it took the Supreme Court's own doing to assert its powers of judicial review, the South African Constitution clearly makes provision for judicial review in several ways. This includes specifically conferring on the courts, including the High Court of South Africa and the SCA, the power to declare law or conduct to be invalid to the extent that such law or conduct is inconsistent with the Constitution.[145]

The Constitution also provides for the appointment of judges. Owing to the important role played by the courts in enforcing the Constitution, the process of the appointment of judges is carefully detailed and regulated by the Constitution.[146] In particular, the Constitution makes provision for structures and procedures for the appointment of judges that involve all three branches of government and other relevant bodies and organisations through the involvement of the Judicial Service Commission (JSC).[147] A major part of the

137 S 89(1).

138 Because of the proliferation of quasi-judicial administrative bodies within the executive, this absolute separation of functions is becoming less clear.

139 See also ch 6.

140 S 165(1).

141 S 166(*a*)–(*e*).

142 S 167(3)(*a*).

143 See s 34 which confers on everyone the right to access the courts.

144 Owing to the fact that s 170 precludes the magistrates' courts or other courts of a status lower than the High Court from reviewing the constitutionality of legislation or conduct of the President, this discussion necessarily excludes magistrates' courts.

145 S 172 details the various types of orders that the courts can make in relation to constitutional matters. It is important to note that in so far as Acts of Parliament, Acts of the provincial legislatures and conduct of the President are concerned, only the Constitutional Court may issue an order of final invalidity, after which point such an order has full force and effect (s 167(5)).

146 S 174.

147 See s 174 wherein the procedure for the appointment of judicial officers is set out. See also s 177 which deals with the provisions in respect of the removal of judges.

reasoning underlying the need to include such detailed provisions and procedures for the appointment of judges is the need to secure the independence of the judiciary.

Judicial independence is a fundamental concept of constitutionalism in as far as the functioning of courts is concerned and is a pivotal requirement for the effective functioning of the separation of powers doctrine. This is evident in the manner in which the Constitution provides for it. The Constitution demands that the courts, in the exercise of their judicial authority, shall be independent and subject only to the Constitution and the law which they must apply impartially and without fear, favour or prejudice.[148] As a safeguard for the independence of the courts, the Constitution creates a prohibition against interfering with the functioning of the courts that applies to everyone, including other branches and organs of state.[149] In addition to this, the Constitution places a positive duty on organs of state to take measures to assist and protect the courts in ensuring their independence, impartiality, dignity, accessibility and effectiveness.[150] These constitutional provisions seek to protect an important element of independence, namely the institutional independence of the courts. In this respect the Constitutional Court in *South African Association of Personal Injury Lawyers v Heath and Others* made the point as follows:

> **The separation of the judiciary from the other branches of government is an important aspect of the separation of powers required by the Constitution, and is essential to the role of the courts under the Constitution ... Under our Constitution it is the duty of the courts to ensure that the limits to the exercise of public power are not transgressed. Crucial to the discharge of this duty is that the courts be and be seen to be independent.**[151]

The other important element of judicial independence relates to the personal independence of judges. This is of crucial importance if they are to perform their functions with impartiality and without fear, favour or prejudice. The Constitution provides for such independence by way of guaranteeing the judges' security of tenure,[152] as well as their salaries and benefits which may not be reduced as long as they remain in office.[153]

The judiciary, like the other branches, is subject to important checks on its power. Judges may be removed from office before the end of their designated tenure where they are proven to be suffering from incapacity, or they have been found guilty of gross incompetence or gross misconduct.[154] The process for the removal of a judge entails the JSC conducting an investigation and then making a finding on one of the grounds previously mentioned.[155] Thereafter, the matter would come up for the consideration of the NA which must adopt a resolution supported by two-thirds of all its members ordering the removal of the judge in question. Where such a resolution is successfully passed, the President is then obliged to effect the removal of the judge in question.[156]

---

148 S 165(2).
149 S 165(3).
150 S 165(4).
151 (CCT27/00) [2000] ZACC 22; 2001 (1) SA 883; 2001 (1) BCLR 77 (28 November 2000) para 25.
152 See s 176(1) and (2) which stipulates how long judges remain in office. In terms of this section, Constitutional Court judges serve for a maximum term of 12 years or until such time as they attain the age of 70, whichever occurs first. Other judges remain in office until they are discharged from active service which is normally at the age of 75.
153 See s 176(3).
154 See s 177 which deals in detail with the procedure in respect of the removal of judges.
155 The process that must be followed by the JSC when a complaint is laid against a judge is set out in the Judicial Service Commission Act 9 of 1994.
156 S 177(2).

Table 2.2 *The manner in which checks and balances are effected by each branch of government on the others*

Checks	Legislature	Executive	Judiciary
Legislature		The executive checks the legislature by: • developing and implementing policy • preparing and initiating legislation • making subordinate legislation • assenting to Bills passed by the legislature.	The judiciary checks the legislature by: • invalidating laws enacted by the legislature that do not comply with the Constitution • ensuring the legislature complies with the procedural requirements prescribed in the Constitution.
Executive	The legislature checks the executive by: • requiring members of the executive to provide full and regular reports concerning matters within their control • appointing the President • removing or recalling national executive members • approving the extension of states of emergency.		The judiciary checks the executive by: • invalidating acts by members of the executive that do not comply with the Constitution • ensuring that the executive fulfils its constitutional obligations diligently and without delay.
Judiciary	The legislature checks the judiciary by: • indirectly taking part in the appointment of judges through selected representatives on the JSC • taking part in the removal of judges who, before the end of their designated tenure, are proven to be suffering from incapacity or have been found guilty of gross incompetence or gross misconduct • passing legislation (in conformity with the Constitution) to respond to judicial decisions (structured dialogue).	The executive checks the judiciary by: • taking part in the appointment of judges as some of its members sit on the JSC which appoints judges • formulating legislation (in conformity with the Constitution) to respond to judicial decisions (structured dialogue).	

2.3.4 The counter-majoritarian dilemma

In a constitutional democracy, like that established by the South African Constitution, the constitution and not parliament is supreme. The judiciary is independent and empowered to review and set aside the actions of the other two branches of government. The judiciary thus necessarily wields enormous power even though its members are not democratically elected. Although this is a necessary result of the particular system of separation of powers and judicial review adopted by the drafters of the South African Constitution, this system raises many conceptual and practical difficulties. A system which affords the power of judicial review to courts and thus permits an unelected judiciary (which is arguably the least accountable branch of government) to declare unconstitutional and invalid laws made and actions taken by democratically elected and accountable members of the legislature and executive can appear to be anti-democratic.

It is true that judicial review is an institution that is generally accepted as being of central importance to the South African constitutional project. However, judicial review, rather than serving to answer or resolve important constitutional questions, raises many of its own that go to the heart of our understanding of democracy and separation of powers. For example, if we accept judicial review as being a legitimate practice in a constitutional democracy, how do we account for the fact that judicial review allows for the invalidation of laws supported by a majority?[157] How is it possible that the judiciary can substitute its own decision for that of the executive when declaring a particular government policy to be unreasonable, even in instances where the executive has consulted widely?[158] What makes the decision of a few unelected judges carry more weight than the choices of the majority?

These questions are commonly referred to as the counter-majoritarian dilemma or difficulty. The essence of the dilemma is that judicial review, while recognised as having a legitimate purpose in the main, involves the courts taking undemocratic decisions that often go against the popular will.[159] The obvious underlying apprehension is that while the constitutional system may be founded on democratic principles and practices, judicial review allows for the democratic will to be displaced by unelected and seemingly unaccountable judges.

With the US constitutional system being rooted in constitutional supremacy while making no explicit provision for judicial review, it is not surprising that the institution of judicial review has, for a long time, been the subject of much controversy among US constitutional law scholars.[160] At its core, the enduring controversy around judicial review relates to concerns regarding the nature and extent of the power that it places in the hands of an unelected judiciary and that allows judges to make decisions with overtly political consequences and to encroach on the domain of the other branches. These controversies have led to much debate on the precise nature of the democratic curtailment and the separation of powers issues raised by judicial review and how to resolve them or otherwise

---

157 See *Makwanyane* paras 87–9.

158 See generally *Minister of Health and Others v Treatment Action Campaign and Others (No 2)* (CCT8/02) [2002] ZACC 15; 2002 (5) SA 721; 2002 (10) BCLR 1033 (5 July 2002).

159 See Bickel (1962) 16.

160 See Friedman, B (2002) The birth of an academic obsession: The history of the counter-majoritarian difficulty, Part five *Yale Law Journal* 112(2):153–260.

account for them as being somehow aligned with democracy.[161] In the main, attempts to account suitably for counter-majoritarianism have elicited three main types of responses:

- Some view judicial review as being a severe constraint on the participation of citizens in political decisions affecting them and, as such, see judicial review as being irreconcilable with the ideals of majoritarian democracy.[162]
- Others downplay the significance of the difficulties judicial review poses. They instead regard encroachments occasioned by judicial review as contributing to the democratic process.[163]
- Yet others attempt to establish a workable interpretative theory in terms of which judicial review can be justified as legitimising judicial interventions in a manner that contributes to the attainment of substantive democratic ends.[164]

While we must concede that most of the debates have been conducted in a US context, we must ask whether similar counter-majoritarianism concerns arise in the South African context, particularly in light of the fact that our Constitution clearly makes provision for judicial review. The short answer to this question must be an unqualified yes. We will explore why this is the case below.

The fact that the Constitution makes explicit provision for judicial review is important as it confirms that the democratically elected Constitutional Assembly freely chose a system of judicial review, thus bestowing some democratic legitimacy on the process of judicial review. However, apart from directly answering the question of the constitutional basis for judicial review, such fact alone does not account for why we should accept judicial review as a legitimate feature of South Africa's democracy. Because judicial review operates in essentially the same way irrespective of the jurisdiction and tends to result in the curtailment of democracy in a generalised sense, it will also be an issue in South Africa. Of particular interest, however, in the South African context, is the question of how we ensure that the courts perform judicial review in a manner that balances the need to promote and respect the majoritarian nature of our democracy while at the same time ensuring that the Constitution's transformative vision is enforced. In other words, while the Constitution may provide for judicial review, it is unable to determine in advance how judges will use the power of judicial review. Because enforcement of the Constitution via judicial review necessarily entails judicial interpretation, it becomes important how judges make their decisions and whether they are possibly influenced by their own political, religious, moral or cultural viewpoints.[165] Bearing this in mind, an important question then becomes how

161 See Lenta, P (2004) Democracy, rights disagreements and judicial review *SAJHR* 20(1):1–31 for a detailed account and critique of some of the various arguments in support of and against judicial review contributing to the ideals of democracy.

162 One of the views discussed by Lenta (2004) 4 is that of Waldron, J (1999) *Law and Disagreement* who argues that judicial review is undemocratic. According to Lenta, Waldron premises his argument on the fact that judicial review negates the democratic right of citizens to participate equally in decisions concerning them and their interests. The arguments put forward by Waldron seek to dispel the notion that there is something about the courts that makes them especially equipped to make better decisions on constitutional rights or questions of political morality. Instead, according to Waldron, the right to participate being a foundational element of democracy is unjustifiably diminished when judicial review denies citizens an opportunity to participate in decisions that are made the preserve of the courts.

163 See Lenta (2004) 5 for a discussion of Ely's view that judicial review is legitimate or justifiable on the basis that there are times when the courts may be called on to guarantee or safeguard the democratic process (Ely, JH (1980) *Democracy and Distrust: A Theory of Judicial Review*).

164 See Lenta (2004) 6 for a discussion on Dworkin's conception of a constitutional democracy where Dworkin argues that judicial review is an integral part of a democracy in that it sees democracy as being more than simple majoritarianism (Dworkin, R (1986) *Law's Empire*). See also generally Davis et al (1994) 6–7.

165 Lenta (2004) 5–6.

society safeguards against judges using their powerful positions to advance their own political, religious or moral interests. Put differently, how do we as society guarantee that judges, while performing the function of judicial review, are, in fact, enforcing the Constitution rather than simply imposing their own will or morality on the majority?

COUNTER POINT

Does public acceptance of a court's decision as legitimate suffice to address counter-majoritarianism concerns?

Let us take a moment to consider the case of *Makwanyane*, the Constitutional Court decision that struck down the death penalty. This matter resulted in the judges of the Constitutional Court handing down 11 different concurring decisions, all of whom determined that the continued use of the death penalty was not in keeping with the letter and spirit of the Constitution. This decision was in stark contrast to the prevailing majority or popular sentiment that the death penalty was in keeping with public morality and the demands of a crime-riddled, divided society.[166] In capturing the prevailing public attitudes of the majority and their influence on the judicial review, Chaskalson P opined as follows:

> The Attorney General argued that what is cruel, inhuman or degrading depends to a large extent upon contemporary attitudes within society, and that South African society does not regard the death sentence for extreme cases of murder as a cruel, inhuman or degrading form of punishment. It was disputed whether public opinion, properly informed of the different considerations, would in fact favour the death penalty. I am, however, prepared to assume that it does and that the majority of South Africans agree that the death sentence should be imposed in extreme cases of murder. The question before us, however, is not what the majority of South Africans believe a proper sentence for murder should be. It is whether the Constitution allows the sentence.
>
> Public opinion may have some relevance to the enquiry, but in itself, it is no substitute for the duty vested in the Courts to interpret the Constitution and to uphold its provisions without fear or favour. If public opinion were to be decisive there would be no need for constitutional adjudication. The protection of rights could then be left to Parliament, which has a mandate from the public, and is answerable to the public for the way its mandate is exercised, but this would be a return to parliamentary sovereignty, and a retreat from the new legal order established by the 1993 Constitution. By the same token the issue of the constitutionality of capital punishment cannot be referred to a referendum, in which a majority view would prevail over the wishes of any minority. The very reason for establishing the new legal order, and for vesting the power of judicial review of all legislation in the courts, was to protect the rights of minorities and others who cannot protect their rights adequately through the democratic process. Those who are entitled to claim this protection include the social outcasts and marginalised people of our society. It is only if there is a willingness to protect the worst and the weakest amongst us, that all of us can be secure that our own rights will be protected.

166 See *Makwanyane* para 88 for the views of Chaskalson P on the place of public opinion in constitutional adjudication.

> **This Court cannot allow itself to be diverted from its duty to act as an independent arbiter of the Constitution by making choices on the basis that they will find favour with the public.[167]**

Interestingly, despite public opinion opposing the abolition of the death penalty, South Africans nevertheless accepted the Constitutional Court decision as legitimate. The question still remains, however, whether public acceptance of a decision as legitimate alone suffices to address the counter-majoritarianism concerns raised above. We would argue that it does not for at least three reasons:

- First, public acceptance of a court decision need not necessarily mean that judges have acted in a manner that actually promotes constitutionalism or democracy.
- Second, what the public is willing to accept at any given time does not necessarily reflect what is acceptable in a democratic constitutional state.
- Third, and most importantly for us presently, public acceptance takes us no closer to providing us with a sound theoretical basis that justifies why or even how judges should exercise powers of judicial review. In other words, for judicial review to be palatable and address the concerns raised by the counter-majoritarian dilemma, we need to have some acceptable theoretical basis that assures us that when judges decide a matter, they are applying criteria of sufficient determinacy to enable judges of different political, religious or moral predispositions to arrive at generally consistent results when faced with similar facts or circumstances.

In light of the above, an obvious question that then bears asking is why include judicial review in South Africa's constitutional system if it poses so many difficult conceptual and practical questions. A better question, though, may be what the justification is for the inclusion of judicial review in South African constitutionalism taking into account the curtailment of democracy it necessarily entails. Before putting forward some arguments in support of the inclusion of judicial review, it is necessary to concede that due to the nature of judicial review, it can never be fully reconciled with a purely majoritarian concept of democracy.[168] The nature of the adjudicative function and the powers exercised therein simply do not lend themselves to being exercised by a plurality of the population in a democratic society. Therefore, if we accept that the judiciary is to play a legitimate part in upholding the Constitution, then we must be able to justify, in a reasoned manner, why important decisions affecting millions should be left in the hands of a relatively few unelected judges whose decisions may not necessarily be wiser, more principled or moral that those of the majority in a democracy. Despite inherent counter-majoritarian concerns, there are several good arguments or justifications that have been put forward in support of judicial review. We will discuss a few of these below:

- While judicial review does tend to diminish democracy from a majoritarian point of view, democracy, when viewed substantively and especially in a plural political society, is never simply majority rule. While the elected representatives of the political majority must exercise political power in a democratic society, this does not necessarily give the

167 *Makwanyane* paras 87–9.

168 See Lenta (2004) 1 for a detailed account and critique of some of the various arguments in support of and against judicial review contributing to the ideals of democracy. See also Van der Walt, J and Botha, H (2000) Democracy and rights in South Africa: Beyond a constitutional culture of justification *Constellations* 7(3):341–62 at 350.

majority a blank cheque to govern in whatever way it desires. There are in place mechanisms that regulate and **limit** the exercise of power in a way that seeks to secure the welfare of all members of a particular political community. Those subscribing to this view would argue that where all people enjoy the same rights in a democracy, all people are entitled to be treated as equals irrespective of whether they are part of the majority or not.[169] So understood, democracy entails much more than conferring power on a particular majority on any given day. It also necessarily entails finding a balance between enabling those in the majority to govern and limiting the things that they can do while in power, especially where such power can be used to violate the rights of others or undermine the very nature of the democracy.

- Another argument in support of judicial review holds that the judiciary is ideally positioned to decide on disputes and matters of principle. The reasons for this are the specialised nature of judges' adjudicative expertise, the judiciary's detached institutional positioning relative to the other democratically elected branches and its entrenched independence. According to those who hold this view, the courts are institutionally stronger and better positioned than the other two branches for purposes of protecting rights and upholding democratic principles as they do not have to pander to the demands that may be placed on the other branches by an electorate.[170]
- Another argument in support of judicial review, related to the preceding one, is that the courts can be seen as a forum that can actually enhance democracy, particularly deliberative democracy. Those subscribing to this view argue that the courts provide an important platform where citizens may challenge the decisions or actions of their elected representatives. In effect, citizens can enter into a structured dialogue with elected representatives through the courts.[171]

COUNTER POINT

Counter-majoritarianism opening up the possibility of a non-technical ethics

Van der Walt and Botha have a distinct view on the counter-majoritarian difficulty and approach the matter from a theoretically more critical perspective:[172]

> We wish to make clear from the outset that we have no solution to the counter-majoritarian problem. We believe it is irresolvable ... [However,] the problem must be addressed. Irresolvable problems are, after all, the only ones we can address. Resolvable problems are not real problems. Resolvable problems are fake problems, temporary technical hiccups, often spectacularly disguised as crises. The counter-majoritarian problem and the problem of significant social dissent are not technical hiccups. They constitute aporias. They allow no way through. They confront us with the impossible. Paradoxically, however, this impossibility opens up the possibility of social deliberation that would exceed technical procedure. It opens up the possibility of a non-technical ethics. It gives politics a chance.

In this view, although the counter-majoritarian problem cannot be resolved, it can tentatively be addressed by admitting that there will always be a tension between the

169 See Lenta (2004) 10–11 where he discusses Dworkin's substantive conception of democracy that demands that a balance be struck between collective decisions and individual rights by placing limitations on the majoritarian legislatures by means of mechanisms such as judicial review (Dworkin (1986)).
170 See Lenta (2004) 17–18.
171 See Pieterse (2004) 391–2.
172 Van der Walt and Botha (2000) 353–5.

demand for democratic accountability on the one hand and the demand for judicial review on the other. How these demands are balanced against each other in a given case will depend on many factors and may well change over time. This approach is often associated with a view of the Constitution as flexible and open-ended.

These arguments briefly set out above merely represent some of the views that have been put forward in an attempt to justify or account for the inclusion of the institution of judicial review in a democratic system of government. In and of themselves, they can be challenged and can be found wanting in as far as completely dispelling accusations that judicial review does tend to curtail or subtract from majoritarian democracy. However, judging by the acceptance of judicial review in some democratic societies, including South Africa, we can conclude that there is some level of acceptance of the idea that there should be a branch of government that must be tasked with the role of interpreting and upholding the constitution and the rights of all citizens. Put differently, there appears to be some acceptance that for constitutional democracy to flourish, it is sometimes necessary to employ some outwardly undemocratic means to achieve long-term democratic ideals such as inclusiveness, broad representativity, accountability and transparency. It has been suggested that instead of glossing over judicial review's democratic deficit, there is a need to think of constitutions such as South Africa's as being mixed constitutions. The mixture in this sense is that such constitutions, although grounded in democratic principles and practice by necessity, also include an anti-democratic practice such as the inclusion of judicial review.[173]

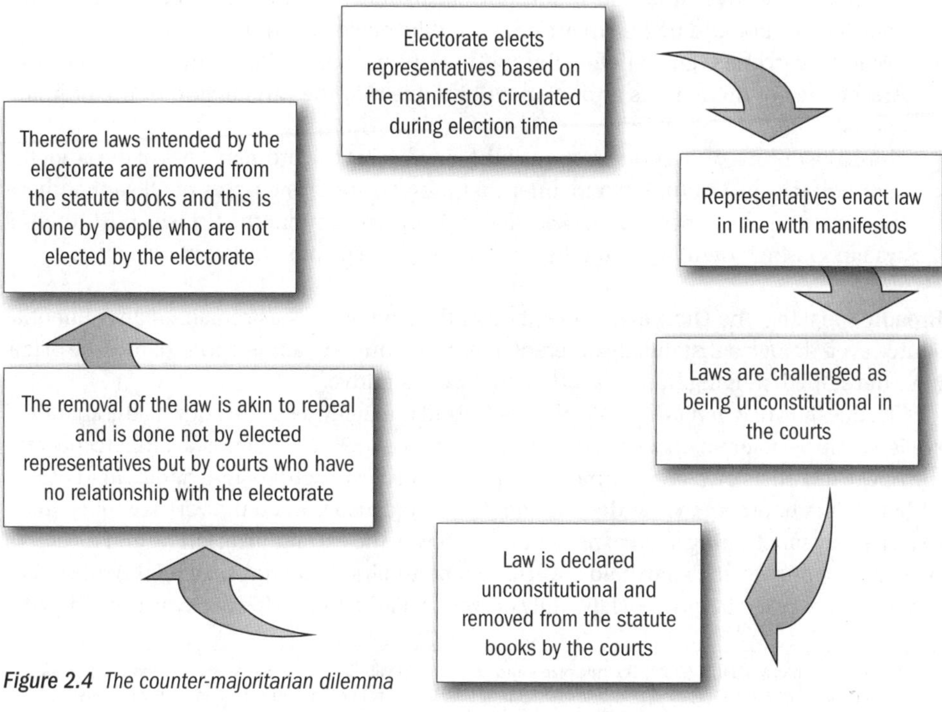

Figure 2.4 The counter-majoritarian dilemma

173 Lenta (2004) 31 makes this point as follows: 'They are mixed because, even if the people are deemed to have agreed to the inclusion of rights in their constitution, their consent cannot be taken to extend to controversial judicial interpretations.'

2.4 The rule of law

An elemental feature of South African constitutionalism is the principle of respect for the rule of law. The rule of law is often equated with the German principle of the *Rechtsstaat* discussed above, but although there are many similarities between the two concepts, the rule of law is arguably a more limited concept than the *Rechtsstaat*. The two terms are nevertheless often used interchangeably and below we consider whether the inclusion of the rule of law as a founding value in the South African Constitution should require us to view it as being akin to the *Rechtsstaat* principle known from German constitutional law. The importance of the rule of law in South African constitutional law is clearly demonstrated by the fact that the rule of law is a founding value entrenched in section 1 of the Constitution. However, there is some difference of opinion about the scope and content of the rule of law and this is the subject of much debate among constitutional law scholars.[174] Apart from being a value, the rule of law is also recognised as an enforceable principle on which the exercise of public power and legislative acts can be challenged. In this section we briefly consider the rule of law in order to detail its historical understanding under apartheid and then its development and how it has been received by the courts in the constitutional era.

2.4.1 A brief history of the rule of law

To understand the evolution of the rule of law it is is helpful to consider an early formulation of the concept put forward by Dicey who is considered to be the earliest proponent of the principle of the rule of law.[175] According to Dicey, the rule of law comprises three main principles:

- First, since the law is supreme, public power can only be exercised in terms of authority conferred by law and no one may exercise public power arbitrarily.
- Second, everyone is equal before the law, the law must be applied equally to all persons irrespective of their status and all must be subject to the jurisdiction of the ordinary courts.
- Third, the ordinary courts are responsible for enforcing the ordinary laws of the land, the common law and statute in a manner that protects the basic rights of all so that these laws function as a constitution. (Recall that Dicey wrote about the British constitutional system in which there was, and there still is, no written constitution in place.[176])

Broadly speaking, the Diceyean conception of the rule of law has remained an influential source even though substantially different interpretations and applications of the rule of law have developed, ranging from the formal to the substantive.

The question of whether the rule of law was fundamentally respected during the apartheid era is a controversial one. The discussions about this issue highlight the fact that respect for the rule of law on its own is not sufficient to protect the basic rights of individuals in a society. Although it later emerged that the apartheid state had also flouted the very laws it claimed to respect by sanctioning in an explicit or implicit way the extrajudicial killing and torture of political opponents, the apartheid government maintained that it respected the rule of law because it governed in terms of laws duly passed by Parliament. However, in as much as the

174 See, for example, Magen, A (2008) The rule of law and its promotion abroad: Three problems of scope *Stanford Journal of International Law* 45(1):51–116 and Rosenfeld, M (2001) The rule of law and the legitimacy of constitutional democracy *Southern California Law Review* 74(5):1307–52.

175 Dicey(1959) xcvi–cli (also referred to in Currie and De Waal (2001) 75–7).

176 Dicey (1959) 45–54. See also Dugard (1978) 37.

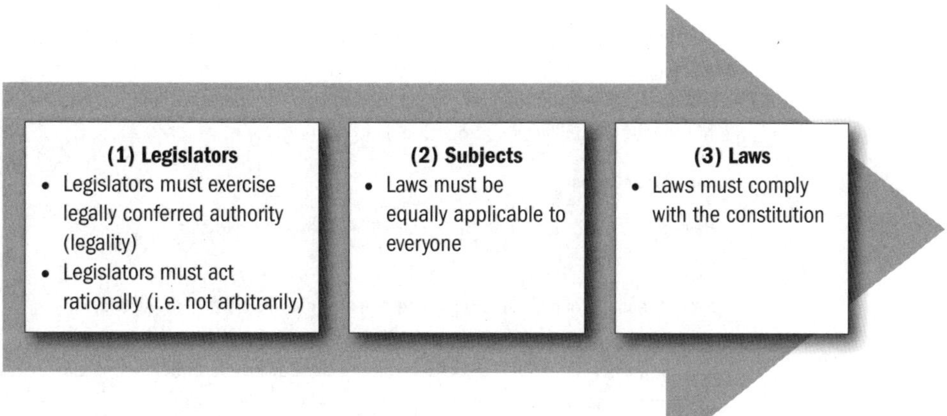

Figure 2.5 *The Diceyean conception of the rule of law*

apartheid government did so, it was only in the formal sense that it could ever have been said to respect the rule of law. The apartheid government relied to a large extent on the law to enforce unjust and oppressive policies fashioned under the legislative freedom conferred by parliamentary supremacy. It is well documented how racist and violent laws were crafted, enacted, executed and enforced through the combined force of state organs, including the courts, acting in unison to bring about the NP's mission of an exclusive white state.[177] The inherent unjustness and inequality of the system at the time, however, did not prevent some from still speaking of the system as being premised on the basis of the rule of law.[178] This equation of 'rule of law with rule by law'[179] represents a formalistic understanding of the importance of law as an instrument of governance rather than a substantive understanding that also concerns itself with the content of the laws.[180] Therefore, the understanding of the rule of law under apartheid was mostly formalistic. This means that as long as there was a legislative provision enabling governmental conduct, then the enforcement of such law was generally considered to be lawfully warranted.[181] Such an approach clearly emasculated the concept of the rule of law and subjected it to much justifiable criticism.

COUNTER POINT

The Law of Lagos

In 1960, the NP was consolidating its rule in South Africa via the formation of an exclusive white republic rooted in parliamentary sovereignty and a narrow, formal conception of the rule of law. In numerous other parts of the African continent the period of decolonisation and independence was just commencing. In an apparent response to these changes from the authoritarianism that accompanied colonial rule, a movement developed that was driven by the International Commission of Jurists (ICJ). The ICJ sought to promote the rule of law in countries undergoing the process of decolonisation. In 1961, the ICJ met in Lagos, Nigeria at a conference on the rule of

177 See Klug, H (2010) *The South African Constitution: A Contextual Analysis* 225–9 where the author describes how the courts (especially the magistrates' courts) were 'part of the state's disciplinary machinery'.

178 Dugard (1978) 43.

179 Dyzenhaus, D (2007) The pasts and future of the rule of law in South Africa *SALJ* 124(4):734–61 at 738.

180 See Dyzenhaus (2007) 738–9.

181 See Klug (2010) 32 where he describes how a substantive conception of the rule of law developed as part of human rights law. See also Dugard (1978) 39ff.

law to deliberate on the role of the rule of law in Africa. At the end of that conference the delegates produced what was to become known as the Law of Lagos. We reproduce the Law of Lagos below so as to contrast the evolving conception or approach to the rule of law internationally to that developing in South Africa at the time.

The Law of Lagos

Having discussed freely and frankly the rule of law with particular reference to Africa, and

Having reached conclusions regarding human rights in relation to government security, human rights in relation to aspects of criminal and administrative law, and the responsibility of the judiciary and of the Bar for the protection of the rights of the individual in society,

NOW SOLEMNLY

Recognises that the rule of law is a dynamic concept which should be employed to safeguard and advance the will of the people and the political rights of the individual and to establish social, economic, educational and cultural conditions under which the individual may achieve his dignity and realise his legitimate aspirations in all countries, whether dependent or independent,

Reaffirms the Act of Athens and the Declaration of Delhi with special reference to Africa, and

Declares:

1. That the principles embodied in the Conclusions of the Conference which are annexed hereto should apply to any society, whether free or otherwise, but that the rule of law cannot be fully realised unless legislative bodies have been established in accordance with the will of the people who have adopted their constitution freely;
2. That in order to maintain adequately the rule of law all governments should adhere to the principle of democratic representation in their legislatures;
3. That fundamental human rights, especially the right to personal liberty, should be written and entrenched in the constitutions of all countries and that such personal liberty should not in peacetime be restricted without trial in a court of law;
4. That in order to give full effect to the Universal Declaration of Human Rights of 1948, this Conference invites the African governments to study the possibility of adopting an African Convention of Human Rights in such a manner that the Conclusions of this Conference will be safeguarded by the creation of a court of appropriate jurisdiction and that recourse thereto be made available for all persons under the jurisdiction of the signatory states;
5. That in order to promote the principles and the practical application of the rule of law, the judges, practising lawyers and teachers of law in African countries should take steps to establish branches of the International Commission of Jurists.

This Resolution shall be known as the Law of Lagos.[182]

182 See Centre for Human Rights University of Pretoria available at http://www1chr.up.ac.za/images/files/documents/ahrdd/theme36/rule_of_law_lagos_1961.pdf.

Although much could be said about the Law of Lagos, we will limit ourselves to two comments that highlight important substantive advances in the way the rule of law is conceived here. First, the rule of law is conceived as a 'dynamic concept'. But what was meant by this? Why was it important to isolate the rule of law, draw attention to it and seek to entrench it as an overarching principle applicable to any society, free or otherwise? From the proceedings of the conference, it seems that against the background of colonialism and the demands of decolonisation, there was a recognition of the dangers presented by a narrow and formalistic conception of the rule of law. As such, the Law of Lagos sought to transcend this by presenting the rule of law as a positive rights-reinforcing principle that promoted not only political rights, but one that also self-consciously recognised its role as a significant contributor to the attainment of the socio-economic well-being of people. Second and most significantly, the rule of law was here closely associated with the ideas of the protection and promotion of human rights and democracy rather than simply being seen as a guarantee of the supremacy of the law and the equal application of the law. This latter view was being demonstrated in South Africa and other colonies where it was deemed to be compatible with laws that were patently unjust and unequal.

2.4.2 The rule of law under the 1996 Constitution

In spite of its chequered history in pre-democratic South Africa, the rule of law has assumed a pre-eminent role in the current constitutional dispensation. As already mentioned above, the rule of law, alongside the supremacy of the Constitution, is enshrined as a founding value in section 1(*c*) of the Constitution. This inclusion of the rule of law as a founding value in the Constitution may at first glance seem peculiar and unnecessary. This is so because the Constitution also establishes the supremacy of the Constitution and contains an enforceable Bill of Rights. The provisions of the Bill of Rights provide more extensive and far-reaching protection against the abuse of power and the infringement of human rights than could ever be afforded by the principle of the rule of law. We may therefore ask whether we should read or interpret this coupling to have more meaning than mere drafting convenience. In other words, should the declaration of the rule of law as a value alongside that of constitutional supremacy influence our understanding of the rule of law in South Africa? Alternatively, is the manner in which the rule of law is captured in our Constitution more in keeping with the *Rechtsstaat* idea derived from German constitutionalism or is it closer to Dicey's conception? To gain a better understanding of the place of the rule of law in South African constitutionalism, it is necessary to consider how it has been applied in cases before the courts.

Interestingly, the rule of law continues to be an important foundational concept in South African constitutional law. Its prominence is evidenced by the manner in which the courts have invoked the rule of law as a mechanism primed to limit, regulate as well as give more precise meaning to how governmental power is exercised. As such, the rule of law has emerged as a powerful practical principle that can be invoked before our courts to ensure that the exercise of state power conforms to basic minimum criteria. The rule of law, as a constitutional principle, has been invoked in many cases where it has been raised as the basis of a constitutional challenge against Acts of Parliament or the executive. This has occurred in cases where the actions of the legislature or the executive were not challenged on the basis that these actions somehow infringed on any of the rights contained in the Bill of Rights.

An early example of such a matter was that of *Fedsure Life Assurance Ltd and Others v Greater Johannesburg Transitional Metropolitan Council and Others*.[183] This matter was decided under the interim Constitution and entailed a challenge by Fedsure to the Johannesburg local government's powers to levy substantially higher property rates. Fedsure initially instituted the challenge on the basis of an alleged breach of its constitutional right to administrative justice.

The Constitutional Court held that the powers under which the local government acted were not administrative in nature and, therefore, could not be tested against the constitutional right in question. Nevertheless, the Court went on to hold that the powers exercised by local government remained subject to the Constitution and, in particular, the exercise of such powers was constrained by the rule of law. The Court held that the local government was permitted only to exercise powers that it had had lawfully conferred on it. In particular, the Court stipulated that the principle of legality – as an incidence of the rule of law – is what determines whether public bodies act lawfully or not. The Court made its point as follows:

> **The rule of law – to the extent at least that it expresses this principle of legality – is generally understood to be a fundamental principle of constitutional law. It seems central to the conception of our constitutional order that the legislature and the executive in every sphere are constrained by the principle that they may exercise no power and perform no function beyond that conferred upon them by law.**[184] **(our emphasis)**

From the *Fedsure* case and subsequent cases it would appear that the principle of legality has become possibly the most important and oft-invoked principle of the rule of law.[185] An obvious question at this stage must be what the principle of legality is and why it has risen to such prominence in our understanding of the rule of law. It is to this question that we shall turn briefly before discussing its application in more detail below.

The principle of legality, as an incidence of the rule of law, can be described as the notion that the exercise of public or governmental power is legitimate and valid only where it is lawful. In other words, the principle of legality demands that where individuals or institutions exercise public power, those acts are binding only in as far as they are authorised by law, notwithstanding the fact that such law may itself be challenged for its constitutionality. The principle of legality has developed into an important constitutional law principle in that it has general and residual application.[186] Thus understood as underlying all exercise of public power, the principle of legality can be applied seemingly to any and all instances of the exercise of public power which can be tested to determine whether they conform to this principle. This idea of the generality of the principle in constitutional law is cogently captured

183 (CCT7/98) [1998] ZACC 17; 1999 (1) SA 374; 1998 (12) BCLR 1458 (14 October 1998).

184 *Fedsure* para 56.

185 See also *President of the Republic of South Africa and Others v South African Rugby Football Union and Others* (*SARFU III*) (CCT16/98) [1999] ZACC 11; 2000 (1) SA 1; 1999 (10) BCLR 1059 (10 September 1999) paras 38 and 148; *Pharmaceutical Manufacturers* paras 20–21; *Affordable Medicines Trust and Others v Minister of Health and Another* (CCT27/04) [2005] ZACC 3; 2006 (3) SA 247 (CC); 2005 (6) BCLR 529 (CC) (11 March 2005) para 49; *Albutt v Centre for the Study of Violence and Reconciliation and Others* (CCT 54/09) [2010] ZACC 4; 2010 (3) SA 293 (CC); 2010 (2) SACR 101 (CC); 2010 (5) BCLR 391 (CC) (23 February 2010) para 49; *Democratic Alliance v President of South Africa and Others* (CCT 122/11) [2012] ZACC 24; 2012 (12) BCLR 1297 (CC); 2013 (1) SA 248 (CC) (5 October 2012) para 12.

186 See Hoexter, C (2007) *Administrative Law in South Africa* 321.

in the following *dictum* by Ngcobo J in *Affordable Medicines Trust and Others v Minister of Health and Another*:

> **The exercise of public power must therefore comply with the Constitution, which is the supreme law, and the doctrine of legality, which is part of that law. The doctrine of legality, which is an incident of the rule of law, is one of the constitutional controls through which the exercise of public power is regulated by the Constitution ... In this sense the Constitution entrenches the principle of legality and provides the foundation for the control of public power.**[187]

As a constitutional principle deriving from the rule of law, the principle of legality is extremely useful in that where there is no right or specific constitutional provision, rule or principle that crisply and directly addresses a question before a court, as was the case in *Fedsure*, then the principle of legality may be readily invoked. In such an instance, the principle of legality demands that, even where there is an enabling law in place, for an exercise of public power in terms of such law to be legitimate, then the body or official in question must have acted only within the limits of the powers conferred on the body or official by the law. In other words, the act or conduct must not be arbitrary or a demonstrable abuse of power or discretion.

A case that clearly demonstrates this point is that of *Pharmaceutical Manufacturers*. In this matter, the President had mistakenly brought into force legislation that required the prior or simultaneous promulgation of regulations and schedules so that it could be implemented properly.[188] There being no specific rule or law permitting the President to undo an erroneous action that he had taken lawfully in terms of powers conferred on him by the Constitution, the Constitutional Court had to decide whether his actions were reviewable and the basis on which this could be done. The Court found that:

> **The President's decision to bring the Act into operation in such circumstances cannot be found to be objectively rational on any basis whatsoever. The fact that the President mistakenly believed that it was appropriate to bring the Act into force, and acted in good faith in doing so, does not put the matter beyond the reach of the Court's powers of review. What the Constitution requires is that public power vested in the executive and other functionaries be exercised in an objectively rational manner. This the President manifestly, though through no fault of his own, failed to do.**[189]

The courts' employment of the rule of law has not been limited to its appeal to the principle of legality. The courts have also had occasion to use the rule of law to demand that public officials not act in an arbitrary way and that they must exercise their powers in a rational manner related to the purpose for which the power was given.[190] In *Lesapo v North West Agricultural Bank and Another*, the legislative provision in question allowed for the respondent bank to seize and sell the property of defaulting debtors without any recourse to the courts.[191] In the matter, Mokgoro J denounced the use of public power to perform such

187 (CCT27/04) [2005] ZACC 3; 2006 (3) SA 247 (CC); 2005 (6) BCLR 529 (CC) (11 March 2005) para 49.

188 *Pharmaceutical Manufacturers* para 66.

189 *Pharmaceutical Manufacturers* para 89.

190 *Lesapo v North West Agricultural Bank and Another* (CCT23/99) [1999] ZACC 16; 2000 (1) SA 409; 1999 (12) BCLR 1420 (16 November 1999).

191 (CCT23/99) [1999] ZACC 16; 2000 (1) SA 409; 1999 (12) BCLR 1420 (16 November 1999) para 1.

acts and described them as self-help which is inimical to the rule of law. In capturing the rule of law principle forbidding self-help, Mokgoro J said the following:

> **Self help, in this sense, is inimical to a society in which the rule of law prevails ... Taking the law into one's own hands is thus inconsistent with the fundamental principles of our law.[192]**

Mokgoro J added further:

> **The Bank, as an organ of State, should be exemplary in its compliance with the fundamental constitutional principle that proscribes self help. Respect for the rule of law is crucial for a defensible and sustainable democracy. In a modern constitutional state like ours, there is no room for legislation which, as in this case, is inimical to a fundamental principle such as that against self help. This is particularly so when the tendency for aggrieved persons to take the law into their own hands is a constant threat.[193]**

There are numerous other instances where a court has invoked the rule of law as a principle in deciding cases or in its reasoning of the cases. A few examples of such instances are as follows. The rule of law has been invoked to demand that rules must be conveyed in a clear and accessible manner for them to comply with the standards required by the Constitution.[194] The rule of law has, further, been invoked to challenge legislation for vagueness and uncertainty where the provisions of the legislation in question conferred broad discretionary powers on a Minister.[195] The Constitutional Court has also held that judicial independence and impartiality are implicit in our understanding of the rule of law as a constitutional principle.[196]

Overall, the rule of law seems to occupy pride of place as a constitutional value alongside that of constitutional supremacy. The rule of law simultaneously operates as an independent and enforceable principle with an important and equally useful derivative in the form of the principle of legality. We can thus argue that the current conception of the rule of law is one that extends beyond the formal Diceyean understanding. Judging from the manner in which the rule of law has been invoked in our case law, it is evident that under the rubric of the rule of law, we are now also concerned with the impact of laws on those affected, the substantive content of laws as well as how public officials and bodies exercise their powers even in the face of enabling laws. In short, our conception of the rule of law under the Constitution has evolved.

COUNTER POINT

Formal versus substantive conceptions of the rule of law

Some commentators[197] have argued that the inclusion of the rule of law as a founding value in the South African Constitution may be of little effect if the rule of law is conceptualised in a narrow way as requiring little more than legality and rationality

192 *Lesapo* para 11.

193 *Lesapo* para 17.

194 *Dawood and Another v Minister of Home Affairs and Others; Shalabi and Another v Minister of Home Affairs and Others; Thomas and Another v Minister of Home Affairs and Others* (CCT35/99) [2000] ZACC 8; 2000 (3) SA 936; 2000 (8) BCLR 837 (7 June 2000) para 47.

195 *Janse van Rensburg and Another v Minister of Trade and Industry and Another* (CCT13/99) [2000] ZACC 18; 2001 (1) SA 29; 2000 (11) BCLR 1235 (CC) (29 September 2000) para 25.

196 *S and Others v Van Rooyen and Others (General Council of the Bar of South Africa Intervening)* (CCT21/01) [2002] ZACC 8; 2002 (5) SA 246; 2002 (8) BCLR 810 (11 June 2002) para 18.

197 See Dyzenhaus (2007) 734–61.

from law makers and state officials acting in terms of the law. They point out that if the rule of law exists when the principle of legality is observed, then the apartheid government also largely observed this principle. The fact that law was used as an instrument of apartheid ideology would then simply show that the principle of legality or the rule of law is by itself morally insignificant. What matters is the content of the law – the nature of the ideology of which the law is the instrument. It follows, then, that the explicit commitment in the final Constitution to the supremacy of the Constitution and the rule of law is in itself empty. What matters is not that commitment but that the final Constitution guarantees a list of rights and liberties. In addition, it gives to the judiciary the authority both to ensure that the exercise of public power has a legal warrant and that any legal warrant is consistent with constitutional guarantees.

However, this limited conception of the rule of law is controversial in legal theory and was contested in legal practice during apartheid. Lawyers who mounted challenges to government oppression through law often argued in court that the judiciary should read statutes in the light of common law presumptions protecting the individual interest in liberty and the equality of those subject to the law. According to this view, only to the extent that a statute explicitly requires that these interests are not to be protected by the statute should judges countenance that the legislature intended to subvert rather than serve the interest of all those subject to the law in liberty and equality. The idea is that the commitment of the legal order to the supremacy of the Constitution and to the principle of legality includes constitutional, albeit unwritten, commitments to protecting these interests. Should officials implement statutes in ways that go beyond these unwritten constitutional constraints, so judges should find that they acted outside the scope of their legal authority. This latter, more expansive, conception of the rule of law is often referred to as a substantive conception of the principle. The question arises whether such a substantive conception of the rule of law is required in South Africa, given the existence of a supreme Constitution and a justiciable Bill of Rights which includes the right to fair administrative action.

2.5 Democracy

One of the major rallying calls informing the struggle for liberation in South Africa was the demand of 'democracy for all'.[198] As unambiguous an aspiration as that sounded, what it concealed was the fact that the concept of democracy is one that can and has been described as 'controversial'[199] or is at the very least contested.[200] The supposed 'controversy' underlying democracy is related to the fact that as a concept, democracy has proven immensely difficult to define in a singular and uncontested manner, with many writers preferring to provide their own definitions or understandings of the word. Contributing to the supposed 'controversy' is the fact that the term 'democracy' is commonly used in conjunction with

198 In a press statement issued in 1992 by former President Nelson Mandela, he described 'democracy for all South Africans' as the final goal of negotiations. Available at http://www.sahistory.org.za/archive/press-statement-nelson-r-mandela-president-anc-ancnp-summit-meeting-world-trade-centre-johan.

199 Motala (1994) 19.

200 See, for example, Kurki, M (2012) Democracy and conceptual contestability: Reconsidering conceptions of democracy in democracy promotion *International Studies Review* 12(3):362–86; Benhabib, S (1996) *Democracy and Difference: Contesting the Boundaries of the Political.*

other concepts such as 'liberal', 'constitutional' or 'majoritarian'. Despite this supposed 'controversy', democracy's pre-eminence as one of the dominant political ideas of modern times is unassailable. Certainly in the South African Constitution, the idea of democracy is a prominent one that permeates virtually all aspects of the Constitution. Beyond the Preamble, section 1 of the Constitution ushers in democracy by declaring South Africa to be 'a sovereign, democratic state'. Section 1(*d*) builds further on this by setting out the democratic values and principles on which South Africa is founded, namely '[u]universal adult suffrage, a national common voters roll, regular elections and a multi-party system of democratic government, to ensure accountability, responsiveness and openness'. While not defining what democracy means in South Africa, the section goes a long way towards making explicit those elements of democracy that are paramount in the South African constitutional context.[201] In this section we consider the idea of democracy and its place in the South African constitutional system.

2.5.1 Conceptions of democracy

Although having already conceded that democracy as a concept defies singular definition, it is nonetheless imperative that we put forward an understanding of what democracy entails. One conception that we have found useful, particularly in a constitutional law setting, is that put forward by Roux who attempts to encapsulate the foundational social idea of democracy as well as the contemporary political understanding of democracy in practice. Roux tells us that:

> **[t]he core idea – that decisions affecting the members of a political community should be taken by the members themselves, or at least by elected representatives whose power to make those decisions ultimately derives from the members – is more or less settled.**[202]

This description, while it does not seek to be comprehensive, serves as an adequate starting point as it can be adapted to speak to various conceptions of democracy from the perspective of the persons affected or from a perspective that recognises that modern democracy is exercised mainly through institutionalised politics that entails citizens electing individuals or organisations to represent their interests. This idea of democracy is therefore linked to the notion that the will of the people should prevail and that people should have a say in how they are governed. It does not seek to convey any idealised form of democracy. Instead, it seeks to convey the foundational reason for democracy, namely that of enabling members of a political community to act together in matters that affect them and to take decisions collectively with respect to such matters. The fact that it also lends itself to a variable understanding of democracy is of particular use in studying the Constitution as the Constitution clearly embodies several different conceptions of democracy. A study of the constitutional text will reveal that there are several different conceptions or understandings of democracy that can be identified, namely direct democracy, **representative democracy** (such as a multiparty democracy), **participatory democracy** and **constitutional**

---

201 While not a definition of democracy, the principles and values in section 1(*d*) do, to a significant degree, tend to tally with certain elements or practices which have been identified and are said to be indicative of a democratic society. For example, (1) government based on consent of the governed through free and fair elections; (2) the active participation of the people, as citizens, in politics and civic life; (3) protection of the human rights of all citizens; (4) respect for the rule of law; (5) majority rule and respect for minority rights; and (6) constitutional limits of government. In general, see Beetham, D (2004) Towards a universal framework for democracy assessment *Democratization* 11(2):1–17.

202 Roux, T 'Democracy' in Woolman and Bishop (2013) 10.1.

democracy.[203] The presence of the varied conceptions of democracy in the Constitution serves to demonstrate not only the varied understandings of democracy, but also the centrality of democracy in defining the type of society post-apartheid South Africa seeks to become. We turn to discuss the different conceptions below.

2.5.2 Direct democracy

Direct democracy means a system of governance that entails direct participation on the part of the citizenry, rather than elected representatives, in the rule and decision making of their political community.[204] Historically, direct democracy is generally regarded as the 'purest' form of democracy that comes closest to achieving the rule of the people.

In the context of the modern **nation-state**, examples of direct democracy are not always self-evident since most decisions are taken not by the citizenry but by their elected representatives in legislatures. Owing to numerous factors, not least its complex structure and internal workings, the modern nation-state has left little room for direct democracy. Direct democracy would, in practice, demand a vote on every piece of legislation by every eligible member of society. Instead, prevailing democratic systems of governance usually comprise elected legislatures whose rule is premised on a mandate from the citizenry who periodically confer the power to decide on their behalf to selected political organisations, such as political parties, or individuals.

As a result of this, it seems widely accepted that direct democracy, where it does exist, exists in a limited sense in modern democracies. That is to say, there is virtually no modern example of a political system that operates primarily in accordance with the basic tenets of direct democracy as outlined above. The same is true for South Africa, save to say that there are elements of South Africa's conception of democracy that can be said to be premised on ideas of direct democracy. We turn to consider these manifestations of direct democracy in the South African constitutional scheme below.

The Constitution makes no mention of or reference to the concept of direct democracy in its text. However, the constitutional expression of direct democracy is to be found in several provisions that guarantee and recognise mechanisms for citizens to act directly in influencing decisions. An important instance where the Constitution makes provision for direct citizen action is by guaranteeing everyone's right to assemble, demonstrate, picket and present petitions peacefully and unarmed.[205] In terms of this guarantee, all citizens are free to engage to make their views known and to seek to influence decisions affecting them unhindered subject to the limitation that they do so unarmed and maintain the peace. As an expression of direct democracy, this right is pivotal as it recognises that despite the predominance of representative governance, citizens must always enjoy the space to advance their own agendas or paths with respect to any issues that they believe affect them as individuals or groups.[206]

Other expressions of direct democracy identified in the Constitution are to be found in the provisions that allow for the executive to seek citizens' views on a particular issue or set

---

203 See *Doctors for Life International v Speaker of the National Assembly and Others* (CCT12/05) [2006] ZACC 11; 2006 (12) BCLR 1399 (CC); 2006 (6) SA 416 (CC) (17 August 2006) paras 96–117.

204 See generally Scarrow, SE (2001) Direct democracy and institutional change: A comparative investigation *Comparative Political Studies* 34(6):651–65 at 654–65.

205 S 17.

206 Woolman captures the importance of s 17 as follows: 'By creating political space for crowd action, s 17 vouchsafes a commitment to a form of democracy in which the "will of the people" is not always mediated by political parties and the elites that run them.' Woolman, S 'Assembly, demonstration, picket and petition' in Currie, I and De Waal, J (2013) *Bill of Rights Handbook* 6th ed 397–8.

of issues directly through the ballot by way of referenda.[207] Although to date no referendum has been called in the post-democratic era, this is a potentially important mechanism in as far as it allows citizens to have an unmediated voice on a particular issue. One criticism that can be levelled against these provisions as representing an instance of direct democracy is that it is actually at the discretion of the President or Premier to call the referendum. There are no mechanisms by which the citizenry can initiate or even demand that a referendum be held, nor are there directives or guidelines as to which matters should require a referendum be held.

PAUSE FOR REFLECTION

To what extent does the Constitution provide for direct democracy?

Merafong Demarcation Forum and Others v President of the Republic of South Africa and Others[208] was a matter brought before the Constitutional Court concerning the manner in which the legislature had opted to deal with the location of Merafong City. Prior to an amendment to the Constitution Merafong City had straddled North West and Gauteng Provinces. The issues in this case focused on public participation and the duty of the legislature to facilitate public involvement. Interestingly, in this matter there had been a consultative process that allowed the community to air their views on relocation. The majority were opposed to the local municipality being located in the North West Province (74% of the residents were prior to the relocation Gauteng residents).[209] However, in spite of this opposition by a majority of the residents, the constitutional amendment was effected and upheld by a majority of the Constitutional Court who held that the legislature had fulfilled its duty to facilitate public involvement and had acted rationally in the face of opposition.

The decision of the majority in the Constitutional Court, while legally defensible, must be viewed against the background of events on the ground, so to speak, within the municipality. Building up to the decision to relocate the municipality and subsequent to it, the community had vociferously made their disaffection with regard to relocation known. They had done this through public meetings, written submissions, mass public protests, marches and ultimately widespread civic disobedience characterised by public violence and the destruction of private and public property.[210] Ultimately, when the matter came before the Constitutional Court, parts of Merafong, particularly the township of Khutsong, had become 'ungovernable' and resembled a war zone as residents refused to accept the decision to relocate the municipality.[211]

This judgment raises some searching questions about the content and limits of direct democracy in South Africa. For example, does South Africa's Constitution actually entail a substantive form of direct democracy that allows citizens to take decisions about things that affect them directly and where those decisions are binding? Or do the expressions of direct democracy we identify above more accurately represent a

207 Ss 84(2)(*g*) and 127(2)(*f*) of the Constitution confer this power on the President and provincial Premiers respectively.

208 (CCT 41/07) [2008] ZACC 10; 2008 (5) SA 171 (CC); 2008 (10) BCLR 968 (CC) (13 June 2008).

209 *Merafong* para 29.

210 See the dissenting judgment of Moseneke J in *Merafong* paras 133–40. For a more detailed description of how the civic protest unfolded, became violent and its impact on the residents of Merafong, particularly in Khutsong township, see Kirshner, J and Phokela, C (2010) *Khutsong and xenophobic violence: Exploring the case of the dog that didn't bark* particularly 8–14. Available at http://www.gcro.ac.za/sites/default/files/News_items/Xeno_reports_July2010/case_studies/5_Khutsong_reprint_lowres.pdf.

211 See Kirshner and Phokela (2010).

right to be heard as seems to be the essential holding of Merafong? Would there be any purpose served by making provision for citizens to demand that certain matters be subject to referenda? Does the fact that we now live in a more technologically connected age not present opportunities to make some advances in making direct democracy more possible to implement?

2.5.3 Representative democracy

Representative democracy as a conception of democracy entails a system of governance in which the members of a political community participate indirectly through elected representatives in the governance of their community.[212] In other words, at its heart, this form of democracy presupposes that citizens elect representatives who govern on their behalf for a limited period of time until the next election. Political parties are often central to this form of democracy because electoral systems require voters to vote for political parties as opposed to individual representatives. Also, political parties influence the choices of voters and often lead people to elect representatives partly because of their party political affiliations.

Representative democracy, as mentioned above, has become the predominant form of democracy in the nation-state system.[213] Since the emergence of the nation-state as a political entity that occupies a particular geographical space and houses a sizeable population, representative democracy has become widely accepted as the only 'workable' system of democracy.[214] A major reason for this is said to be that as a matter of practicality, governance is far too complex to expect government to operate in a fashion that takes account of each individual citizen's viewpoint on decisions that affect them or even simply to afford them such an opportunity. There are multiple hurdles such as a lack of information, geographical spread, unequal access to resources and citizen apathy among others. Also, the sheer enormity of the task of gathering and collating all these views has made the development of political parties or similar civic organisations as the vehicles of representative democracy appear to be inevitable. The result has therefore been that structurally and procedurally a constitution is tailored towards political parties playing a pre-eminent role in the governance of the country. It is, after all, a political party or a coalition of political parties that forms a government.

As noted above, the presence of political parties in a system of representative democracy has become integral to the functioning of modern democracies. Political parties, by organising, campaigning and electioneering, act to represent the interests of their members who will usually share a common agenda or vision. The role of political parties is further enhanced in South Africa by the electoral system and by strict party discipline. Therefore, while the Constitution does not overtly regulate the establishment, financing or activities of political parties, it does nonetheless recognise that political parties are very much a part of the modern democratic political system and have an important role to play in constituting South Africa's democracy.[215]

Evidence of this recognition of political parties by the Constitution is found in certain constitutional clauses, both substantive and procedural. These clauses make it explicit that

212 See generally Kateb, G (1981) The moral distinctiveness of representative democracy *Ethics* 91(3):357–74.

213 Sachs J in a concurring judgment in *Doctors for Life* stated that 'representative democracy undoubtedly lies at the heart of our system of government ...' para 229.

214 Roux (2013) 10.13.

215 See Currie and De Waal (2001) 86.

the type of democracy contemplated by the drafters was a representative one in which political parties have a major role to play. For instance, according to section 1 of the Constitution, South Africa is founded on, among other values, the democratic values of '[u]niversal adult suffrage, a national common voters roll, regular elections and a multi-party system of democratic government ...'[216] The primary organ of citizen representation is the NA that is elected to represent the people and to ensure government by the people.[217] Furthermore, provisions relating to the composition of the NA demand that its members must be elected in terms of an electoral system that, in general, results in proportional representation.[218] In prescribing a system of proportional representation, the Constitution goes further by demanding that representation of citizens through their political parties must be provided for in the internal arrangements, proceedings and procedures of the NA.[219]

The High Court decision of *De Lille and Another v Speaker of the National Assembly*[220] highlighted the importance of ensuring that the citizenry is properly represented in the working of the NA. In this matter, the Court was required to decide on the constitutionality of a decision by an *ad hoc* committee of the NA to suspend a member of the NA as a form of punishment for statements she had made before it.

In answering the question in the negative, the Court recognised the NA's constitutional powers to regulate its own affairs. However, the Court held that such powers did not include the power to suspend a member for contempt as a form of punishment.[221] According to the Court, such action, if permitted, would be inconsistent with the requirements of representative democracy. The reason for this is that it would punish not only the member who was found to have acted contemptuously, but also the party and the citizens who had voted for her party. This would deprive them of their proportionate representation in the NA.[222] Although this finding was not the main basis for the final outcome, the Court's reasoning that connects the the most important reason for the member being in the NA with the electorate is important. Its importance lies in the Court's recognising that the NA should take into account the interests of the electorate as a whole in the decisions it makes; it cannot simply focus on the individual concerned.

Even the rights concerning voting are clearly crafted towards a system of representative democracy. The Constitution makes it clear that this is one of the primary conceptions envisioned by the drafters by capturing the effect of representative democracy in the political rights provision of the Bill of Rights. Section 19 is an important democratic right in the sense that it grants citizens the right to participate in various ways in the political life of the country. Again, while not directly mentioning that this right to participate is within a political system of representative democracy, this idea is implicit in the way the right is framed. Section 19(1) confers on citizens the right to make political choices. It also seems to envisage that citizens exercise these choices within or via a party political system. Hence, the section explicitly states that the right includes that of forming, joining or campaigning for a political party. Section 19(2) further cements the implicitness of the political system being that of representative democracy by stipulating that the citizens have the right to free and fair

216 S 1(*d*).
217 S 42(3).
218 S 46(1)(*d*); 105(1)(*d*); 157(2)(*a*).
219 See s 57, in particular subsecs (1)(*b*) and (2)(*b*).
220 1998 (3) SA 430 (C).
221 *De Lille* para 27.
222 *De Lille* para 27.

elections. Finally, section 19(3) adds to this by conferring on every adult citizen the right to vote in elections, to stand for public office and to hold such office if elected.

The courts have on several occasions pronounced on the right to vote and its significance for democracy.[223] The courts have also had occasion to consider the relationship between the citizenry and their elected representatives. In the main, the courts have considered this relationship within the context of constitutional democracy. Some of the pronouncements also serve to shed much light on how the courts view representative democracy in South Africa. O'Regan J's comments in *Richter v The Minister for Home Affairs and Others* shed much light on the democratic nature of and the responsibilities that characterise the relationship between voters and their elected representatives:

> **The right to vote, and the exercise of it, is a crucial working part of our democracy. Without voters who want to vote, who will take the trouble to register, and to stand in queues, as millions patiently and unforgettably did in April 1994, democracy itself will be imperilled. Each vote strengthens and invigorates our democracy. In marking their ballots, citizens remind those elected that their position is based on the will of the people and will remain subject to that will. The moment of voting reminds us that both electors and the elected bear civic responsibilities arising out of our democratic Constitution and its values.**[224]

Section 19 of the Constitution, read in conjunction with section 1(*d*) of the Constitution, underscores the idea that an integral aspect of our conception of representative democracy is that it is a multiparty democracy rather than a one-party state or some other formulation that places limits on political participation at a party-political level. In *United Democratic Movement (UDM) v President of the Republic of South Africa and Others (No 2)* the Court made the point as follows:

> **A multiparty democracy contemplates a political order in which it is permissible for different political groups to organise, promote their views through public debate and participate in free and fair elections. These activities may be subjected to reasonable regulation compatible with an open and democratic society. Laws which go beyond that, and which undermine multiparty democracy, will be invalid.**[225]

PAUSE FOR REFLECTION

The controversial constitutional amendment that allowed floor crossing

The *dictum* in the *UDM* case quoted above was made with respect to a controversial constitutional amendment that allowed for floor crossing in spite of the fact that South Africa's electoral system is based on proportional representation and a list system. The amendment, in effect, permitted members of the NA representing one political party to change political parties between elections and still maintain their seat in the NA. The effect of this was that member 1, whose membership in the NA came about as a result of being on party X's list, could defect during a specified period and join party Y

223 For example *New National Party v Government of the Republic of South Africa and Others* (CCT9/99) [1999] ZACC 5; 1999 (3) SA 191; 1999 (5) BCLR 489 (13 April 1999); *August and Another v Electoral Commission and Others* (CCT8/99) [1999] ZACC 3; 1999 (3) SA 1; 1999 (4) BCLR 363 (1 April 1999); *Minister of Home Affairs v National Institute for Crime Prevention and the Re-Integration of Offenders (NICRO) and Others* (CCT 03/04) [2004] ZACC 10; 2005 (3) SA 280 (CC); 2004 (5) BCLR 445 (CC) (3 March 2004).

224 (CCT03/09, CCT 09/09) [2009] ZACC 3; 2009 (3) SA 615 (CC); 2009 (5) BCLR 448 (CC) (12 March 2009) para 52.

225 (CCT23/02) [2002] ZACC 21; 2003 (1) SA 495; 2002 (11) BCLR 1179 (4 October 2002) para 26.

while retaining the seat he or she occupied owing to being a member on the electoral list of party X. In a highly criticised decision, the Constitutional Court held that the constitutional amendment was constitutional. This was despite the fact that the provision clearly robbed the voters of party X of their representation by allowing an individual for whom they may not necessarily have voted to cross the floor with their party's seat. In justifying its decision to uphold the amendment as constitutional the Court had this say:[226]

> **This case is not about the merits or demerits of the provisions of the disputed legislation. That is a political question and is of no concern to this Court. What has to be decided is not whether the disputed provisions are appropriate or inappropriate, but whether they are constitutional or unconstitutional. It ought not to have been necessary to say this for that is true of all cases that come before this Court. We do so only because of some of the submissions made to us in argument, and the tenor of the public debate concerning the case which has taken place both before and since the hearing of the matter.[227]**

The Court went on to add the following passage in the judgment:

> **None of the rights specified in section 19, seen on its own or collectively with others, is infringed by a repeal or amendment of the anti-defection provisions. The rights entrenched under section 19 are directed to elections, to voting and to participation in political activities. Between elections, however, voters have no control over the conduct of their representatives. They cannot dictate to them how they must vote in Parliament, nor do they have any legal right to insist that they conduct themselves or refrain from conducting themselves in a particular manner.[228]**

In light of the above here are some questions to consider:
- What are we to make of these statements made by the Court in this case?
- Can law and politics be separated in the manner suggested by the Court here?
- Is the practice of democracy simply to be left to the determination of Parliament even where the effect of the constitutional amendment in question seems to violate the right to vote?
- How do we reconcile floor crossing with representative democracy and at the same time take voting rights seriously?

In the final analysis, the controversy fuelled by floor crossing was such that the law permitting it was reversed early in 2009.

In conclusion, it is important to acknowledge that against the background of South Africa's struggle against apartheid where the right to vote was acquired or denied on the arbitrary basis of race, this right came to assume an overriding significance. The establishment of a system of representative democracy has succeeded in affirming and recognising the equal

226 For a critical appraisal of the disconcerting implications of this passage, see Roux, T (2009) Principle and pragmatism on the Constitutional Court of South Africa *International Journal of Constitutional Law* 7(1):106–38 at 128–30.

227 *UDM* para 11.

228 *UDM* para 49.

citizenship and political agency of all, especially for those who previously suffered the indignity of being denied the franchise. However, it is equally important to realise that there are limitations of the system that may have long-term consequences. We briefly outline a few of these below:

- The failure to regulate political parties in the Constitution may give rise to an elite-driven democracy. The fact that there is no requirement that the parties practise some form of internal democracy ultimately has the effect of conferring a huge amount of power on the party leadership who may dominate party affairs and impose their preferred representatives.
- The lack of opportunity for the electorate to influence directly their representatives outside the five-year election intervals is also less than ideal. In similar fashion to the point raised above, it leaves the electorate in the position of onlookers as elected representatives take decisions in the name of the electorate without an opportunity to oppose independently unpopular decisions.
- Another major limitation of the system is that it makes it difficult for people who are not actively involved in political parties to make an impact on legislative and policy issues affecting them. In other words, for those without party affiliations and therefore no representative, the opportunities to contribute their views effectively are severely limited.
- Finally, and possibly most controversially, the fact that the South African political landscape is dominated by one party, namely the ANC, presents its own challenges. This situation is referred to as a dominant party democracy.[229] It is of particular concern as it affects democratic accountability and limits democratic participation by making the governing party the primary site for all debate and decision making. The fact of one-party dominance does not in and of itself present an immediate crisis of democracy. However, in the long run, it has been shown to lead to an entrenchment of a system of patronage, erosion of the separation between party and state, and, ultimately, the domination of all aspects of national life by the party.[230]

2.5.4 Participatory democracy

In the section above the picture we sought to convey was that of representative democracy being at the heart of the South Africa's democracy both in terms of the structures that the Constitution establishes as well in terms of how democracy works in practice. With this in mind, it is also equally important that we point out that representative democracy is subject to its own limitations. In particular, representative democracy in the way it operates carries with it the potential to be disempowering as far as the citizenry is concerned. Elections take place periodically, usually every five years in South Africa. This inevitably entails citizens' conferring their mandate on a political party to represent their interests over a period of time. It is quite conceivable that in a system of representative democracy, decision making on matters of national concern can be made without taking citizens' views into account. There is, therefore, a need to somehow counteract this potentially disempowering aspect of

229 See Choudhry, S (2009) 'He had a mandate': The South African Constitutional Court and the African National Congress in a dominant party democracy *Constitutional Court Review* 2:1–86 at 23; Southall, R (1994) The South African elections of 1994: The remaking of a dominant-party state *The Journal of Modern African Studies* 32(4):629–55; Giliomee, HB (1998) South Africa's emerging dominant-party regime *Journal of Democracy* 9(4):128–42; Friedman, S 'No easy stroll to dominance: Party dominance, opposition and civil society in South Africa' in Giliomee, HB and Simkins, CEW (eds) (1999) *The Awkward Embrace: One Party Domination and Democracy* 97; Alence, R (2004) South Africa after apartheid: The first decade *Journal of Democracy* 15(3):78–92 at 78.

230 See Choudhry (2009) 24–5.

representative democracy. The Constitution does this by including in its conception of democracy the element of participatory democracy.

Participatory democracy is primarily concerned with ensuring that citizens are afforded an opportunity to participate or otherwise be involved in decision making on matters that affect their lives. Put differently, it adds a participatory element to representative democracy, augments and enhances it, but does not replace it. As a conception of democracy, it is in a sense a derivative of representative democracy as it seeks to ensure that while citizens may confer a mandate on elected representatives, they are not totally excluded from the decision-making process in matters that concern them. In essence, participatory democracy seeks to ensure that citizens are afforded real opportunities to participate meaningfully in decision making that affects them.[231] The Constitution recognises participatory democracy as a vital element of South Africa's democracy. In *Doctors for Life International v Speaker of the National Assembly and Others,* Ngcobo J, writing for the majority, captured this idea as well as elucidating on what participatory democracy entails when he wrote as follows:

> **In the overall scheme of our Constitution, the representative and participatory elements of our democracy should not be seen as being in tension with each other. They must be seen as mutually supportive. General elections, the foundation of representative democracy, would be meaningless without massive participation by the voters. The participation by the public on a continuous basis provides vitality to the functioning of representative democracy. It encourages citizens of the country to be actively involved in public affairs, identify themselves with the institutions of government and become familiar with the laws as they are made. It enhances the civic dignity of those who participate by enabling their voices to be heard and taken account of. It promotes a spirit of democratic and pluralistic accommodation calculated to produce laws that are likely to be widely accepted and effective in practice. It strengthens the legitimacy of legislation in the eyes of the people. Finally, because of its open and public character it acts as a counterweight to secret lobbying and influence peddling. Participatory democracy is of special importance to those who are relatively disempowered in a country like ours where great disparities of wealth and influence exist.**[232]

In recognising the importance of these participatory elements of democracy, the Constitution contains various provisions that seek to underscore the fact that this form of democracy is an indispensable feature of our system of governance. At the national and provincial levels of government, the Constitution places the legislatures under a duty to facilitate public involvement in their legislative and other processes, including their committee work.[233] The exact nature of this duty or whether, in fact, it constitutes a justiciable constitutional duty was determined in *Doctors for Life.* In this case, the issue before the Court related to a complaint from the applicants that in passing certain pieces of legislation, namely four Bills affecting health professionals, the NCOP had failed to involve the public as demanded by the Constitution. The applicants contended that the NCOP and the affected provincial legislatures had failed to provide for public involvement by failing to call for written submissions and hold public hearings. At issue in the case was the question as to the nature and scope of the duty to facilitate public involvement and the extent to which

231 Currie and De Waal (2001) 87.

232 (CCT12/05) [2006] ZACC 11; 2006 (12) BCLR 1399 (CC); 2006 (6) SA 416 (CC) (17 August 2006) para 115.

233 See ss 59, 72 and 118.

such duty was justiciable.[234] In making its determination that such a duty indeed exists, the majority reasoned that this duty correlates with the right to participation as recognised in international human rights instruments.[235] As such, in the context of South Africa's constitutional democracy, it was acknowledged that ours is a democratic government that is partly representative and partly participatory.[236]

2.5.5 Constitutional democracy

What should be clear at this point is that South Africa's conception of democracy is multifaceted. The Constitution, as previously pointed out, recognises and embraces different conceptions of democracy while simultaneously holding democracy up as a central organising principle. For example, the importance attached to democracy in South Africa's constitutional project is discernible from its prominence in several provisions that can at best be said to be tangentially related such as the following: the Preamble; the Bill of Rights;[237] the limitation clause;[238] the interpretation clause;[239] the principles of co-operative governance;[240]and the provisions regulating legislative bodies and their procedures. Democracy is in many ways the central pillar around which our constitutional state is arranged, thus making South Africa a constitutional democracy. But what does it mean to be a constitutional democracy?

It has been pointed out that the term 'constitutional democracy' has no technical meaning nor does it have an underlying theory attached to it; it is said fundamentally to be a descriptive term.[241] As a descriptive term, constitutional democracy is used to describe a political system in which a particular political community's decisions are made in terms of a constitution. This constitution prescribes the terms and conditions under which such decisions may be made.[242] In our context, the term should be understood as something of a composite understanding of democracy that seeks to emphasise the **purpose or role** played by democracy in our constitutional system rather than its component parts. In other words, constitutional democracy seen as a whole is more than a sum of its parts as it comprises direct, representative, participatory, deliberative or majoritarian forms of democracy. The Constitution makes no claim to aspiring towards a particular form of democracy as representing a societal ideal. Instead, it posits a view of the type of democratic society that it seeks to build. The Constitution does this by trumpeting the important elements of this society, such as a supreme and justiciable Constitution, a culture of human rights and a commitment to a broad range of democratic ideals, non-racialism, multiculturalism and multilingualism. In practice, this means a democratic society that is not simply majoritarian in its orientation and practice and also one that accepts that judicial review is legitimate where it is employed to give effect to the Constitution. In terms of this conception, constitutional democracy must be viewed as a purposive concept. This means that democracy is not an end in itself but a means to achieve an end.[243]

234 *Doctors for Life* para 75.
235 *Doctors for Life* paras 106–8.
236 *Doctors for Life* para 116.
237 See s 7(1).
238 S 36(1).
239 S 39(1).
240 S 41.
241 Roux (2013) 10.18–10.19.
242 Roux (2013) 10.19.
243 Roux (2013) 10.19.

Indeed, the courts' use of the term can certainly be read as appealing to this purposive understanding of constitutional democracy. In *Doctors for Life*, Ngcobo J captures this idea when recognising that 'our constitutional democracy is not only representative but also contains participatory elements'.[244] In recognising this point, Ngcobo J does this within the context of discussing the Constitution's overarching vision, its goal, its values and its principles. In other words, these specific forms of democracy must be interpreted or viewed within the overall South African constitutional context that is closely attuned to South Africa's history of colonialism and apartheid.

SUMMARY

This chapter deals with the basic concepts of constitutional law which inform the more detailed discussion of the various aspects of the South African Constitution in subsequent chapters.

Constitutionalism is a multifaceted term and is concerned with the distribution and allocation of powers in an organised way within a given political community in which a government is established. It provides for the establishment of the institutions of governance, such as the legislature, the executive and the courts, as well as the allocation of powers, duties and functions to the various institutions of government which legitimise the exercise of power - within the limits set by the Constitution - of each of these institutions. Constitutionalism also plays an important role in determining the nature and basis of relations as they exist between institutions of government and those they govern.

The principle of the separation of powers deals with the division of governmental power across the three branches, namely the legislative branch (parliament), the executive branch (president/prime minister and cabinet) and the judicial branch (the courts). These branches ordinarily have separate functions and are staffed by different personnel. This allows the various branches to check the exercise of power of the other branches and thus ensures accountability. There are, however, several models of separation of powers and it is important to study these models and to understand the specific model adopted by the South African Constitution as well as the practical and legal consequences that flow from the adoption of this model.

The counter-majoritarian dilemma arises in a constitutional democracy (like that established in South Africa) in which the constitution rather than parliament is supreme and in which the judiciary is independent and empowered to review and set aside the actions of the other two branches of government. This is because the system affords the power of judicial review to courts. It thus permits an unelected and seemingly unaccountable judiciary to declare unconstitutional and invalid laws made and actions taken by democratically elected and accountable members of the legislature and executive. This can appear to be anti-democratic. It is important to engage with the arguments justifying the legitimacy of this system and attempting to resolve the counter-majoritarian difficulty.

The rule of law is a founding value of the South African Constitution and is based on the notion that the law is supreme. Hence, public power can only be exercised in terms of the authority conferred by law and in a non-arbitrary manner. Inherent in this concept is also the principle that everyone is equal before the law, the law must be applied equally to all persons irrespective of their status and all must be subject to the jurisdiction of the ordinary

244 *Doctors for Life* para 111.

courts. The rule of law can be conceptualised in formalistic terms or it can entail a more substantive notion.

The core idea at the heart of democracy is that decisions affecting the members of a political community should be taken by the members themselves or at least by elected representatives whose power to make decisions ultimately derives from the members. Different, and sometimes overlapping, forms of democracy can exist within a state: direct democracy; representative democracy; participatory democracy and constitutional democracy. It is important to be able to distinguish the various forms of democracy and to understand how these forms of democracy relate to one another.

Chapter 3

Separation of powers and the three branches of government

3.1 Introduction

A study of the different branches of government can best be done by using the separation of powers doctrine as a lens through which to look at how the three branches operate and how they relate to one another. In this chapter we therefore introduce the distinctly South African version of the doctrine of separation of powers. The judiciary is still developing this doctrine through the interpretation of the South African Constitution. In chapter 2 of this book we discussed the scope and content of the doctrine of separation of powers as it manifests in various constitutional systems in other parts of the world and, briefly, as it has thus far been developed in South Africa. In the next three chapters we focus more pertinently on the various branches of government established by the South African Constitution,[1] namely the legislature, the executive and the judiciary. We explore the composition, powers and functions of these branches of government and the nature of the relationship between the various branches with specific emphasis on the notion that these branches operate in accordance with a system of checks and balances. We also discuss the role, powers and functions of the National Prosecuting Authority (NPA).[2] This is an independent body created by the Constitution and tasked with overseeing the prosecution of accused persons.

The discussion of these separate branches of government and their relationship to each other takes place against the background of the particular South African context highlighted in chapter 1, most notably by what has been described as a 'surprise re-entry' and 'resurgence' of traditional leadership in South Africa in the post-apartheid era.[3] One of the most vexing constitutional questions in the democratic era relates to the role of traditional leaders and traditional governance structures, and where and how these structures fit into

1 See, generally, Chapters 4, 5 and 8 of the Constitution which detail the provisions pertaining to Parliament, the President and the national executive, and the judiciary respectively, read with Chapters 3 (co-operative government), 6 (the provinces), 7 (local government) and Schedules 4 and 5 that delineate areas of concurrent national and provincial, and exclusive provincial legislative competences.

2 See s 179 of the Constitution.

3 Oomen, B (2005) *Chiefs in South Africa, Law, Power and Culture in the Post-Apartheid Era* 11.

a scheme of separation of powers with its three branches of government.[4] We will address this question as we discuss the various branches of government. We do so as we contend that the resurgence of customary practices and leadership institutions in the democratic era is not as surprising as some commentators have argued. This is especially so given that 'South Africa is as rich in tenacious institutions with indigenous roots as other African countries' and that these institutions 'were entrenched (albeit in distorted ways) over many decades of segregationist and apartheid rule'.[5] Moreover, if viewed from a historical perspective, it is sometimes argued that traditional authorities in southern Africa 'have always engaged assertively with other sites of authority and forms of government'.[6] Current-day supporters of the maintenance and restoration of traditional governance institutions and customs have argued that traditional leaders have provided continuity of governance even though they are undoubtedly tainted by their association with segregation and apartheid. This is particularly so in rural areas where there were scant alternative governance structures and the influence of the institutions of the democratic state is at its weakest.[7] Others, however, see the resurgence of traditional governance institutions as a regressive step that undermines progress towards democratic consolidation in South Africa because traditional governance structures are inherently undemocratic, patriarchal and potentially oppressive.[8]

Whatever a person's view on traditional leadership and traditional governance institutions, it is nevertheless important to explore the powers and functions of the various branches of government and the relationship between these branches with reference to these institutions. To this end we also discuss the powers and functions of the National House of Traditional Leaders. Parliament created this institution via the National House of Traditional Leaders Act (the National House Act)[9] and pursuant to section 212(2)(*e*) of the Constitution. This section permits the promulgation of legislation to deal with matters relating to issues of traditional leadership.

Traditional descriptions of South African constitutional law ignore those aspects of the South African political and governance context that do not neatly reflect the Western-style constitutional structures established by the Constitution. In this book we focus on these structures but do so with an awareness that there are different centres of power in South Africa. One is centred around the formal institutions of the legislature, the executive and the judiciary, all of which are described and regulated in the Constitution. Another is centred around a more informal and ever-changing set of institutions such as traditional leadership institutions.

Apart from discussing the various branches of government with reference to the role played by traditional leaders, we will also discuss the various branches of government with reference to the role played by political parties in bringing the Constitution into operation.

---

4 Addressing this problem is made even more difficult by the fact that many traditional leaders were co-opted by the apartheid regime. At the time of writing there has been a resurgence of support for traditional leadership institutions and the role of African customary law. Evidence of the latter can be garnered from the promulgation of the Communal Land Rights Act 11 of 2004 (CLaRA) and the subsequent constitutional challenge to it in *Tongoane and Others v National Minister for Agriculture and Land Affairs and Others* (CCT100/09) [2010] ZACC 10; 2010 (6) SA 214 (CC); 2010 (8) BCLR 741 (CC) (11 May 2010). See also *Pilane and Another v Pilane and Another* (CCT 46/12) [2013] ZACC 3; 2013 (4) BCLR 431 (CC) (28 February 2013). For the leading commentary on CLaRA, traditional leadership and communal land, see Claassens, A and Cousins, B (eds) (2008) *Land, Power, and Custom: Controversies Generated by South Africa's Communal Land Rights Act*.

5 See Beall, J, Mkhize, S and Vawda, S (2005) Emergent democracy and 'resurgent' tradition: Institutions, chieftaincy and transition in KwaZulu-Natal *Journal of Southern African Studies* 31(4):755–71 at 756.

6 Beall et al (2005) 756.

7 Hobsbawm, E and Ranger, T (eds) (1983) *The Invention of Tradition* and Vail, L (ed) (1989) *The Creation of Tribalism in Southern Africa*.

8 See Beall et al (2005) fn 5.

9 Act 22 of 2009.

Power is centred in such political parties - especially the leadership of the most dominant political parties, the African National Congress (ANC) and the Democratic Alliance (DA). The internal culture of these parties and the leadership style of their leaders thus influence how especially the legislature and the executive operate within the doctrine of separation of powers.

Lastly, we consider the composition, powers and functions of various other constitutional institutions created to support constitutional democracy. These are sometimes referred to collectively as the Chapter 9 institutions. These constitutional bodies are required to play an oversight role over the legislature, the executive and the judiciary, and to deepen and safeguard democracy. However, we limit our discussion in this regard to the following institutions: the Public Protector;[10] the Auditor-General;[11] and the Electoral Commission.[12] In addition, we consider the Judicial Service Commission (JSC).[13]

In the following chapters we therefore deal with four interrelated issues relating to the structures of government as these operate within a system of separation of powers:

- The current chapter sets out and explains the framework within which the three branches of government operate and provides a brief overview of the historical origins of the doctrine of separation of powers and its influence on South Africa's new constitutional dispensation.
- Chapter 4 deals with the composition and functioning of the legislature and its relationship with the other branches of government.
- Chapter 5 deals with the composition and functioning of the executive and its relationship with the other branches of government.
- Chapter 6 deals with the composition and functioning of the judiciary and its independence from the other branches of government as well as the prosecuting authority.
- Chapter 7 considers the role of certain Chapter 9 institutions.

3.2 A new democratic constitutional dispensation within a system of separation of powers

The new constitutional dispensation established by the 1993 Constitution (the interim Constitution)[14] and later the 1996 Constitution is often said to serve as a bridge between a past that was characterised by the worst forms of political repression and inhumane treatment of masses of people, and a future that uncompromisingly commits the state to the values of human dignity, freedom and equality for all persons, irrespective of race or creed.[15]

10 S 181(1)(*a*) of the Constitution.

11 S 181(1)(*e*) of the Constitution.

12 S 181(1)(*f*) of the Constitution.

13 S 178 of the Constitution.

14 The Constitution of the Republic of South Africa 200 of 1993.

15 See s 1 read with s 7 of the Constitution. The metaphor of a bridge was first introduced into South Africa's constitutional lexicon by the postamble to the interim Constitution titled 'National Unity and Reconciliation'. It was popularised by Etienne Mureinik - see Mureinik, E (1994) A bridge to where? Introducing South Africa's interim Bill of Rights *SAJHR* 10:30. See also *S v Makwanyane and Another* (CCT3/94) [1995] ZACC 3; 1995 (6) BCLR 665; 1995 (3) SA 391; [1996] 2 CHRLD 164; 1995 (2) SACR 1 (6 June 1995) para 262 where Mohamed DP, quoting in part the postamble to the interim Constitution, said: 'The South African Constitution is different: it retains from the past only what is defensible and represents a decisive break from, and a ringing rejection of, that part of the past which is disgracefully racist, authoritarian, insular, and repressive and a vigorous identification of and commitment to a democratic, universalistic, caring and aspirationally egalitarian ethos, expressly articulated in the Constitution ... What the Constitution expressly aspires to do is to provide a transition from these grossly unacceptable features of the past to a conspicuously contrasting "future founded on the recognition of human rights, democracy and peaceful co-existence and development opportunities for all South Africans, irrespective of colour, race, class, belief or sex".'

As we have seen, when the interim Constitution was enacted, it signalled a dramatic change in the system of governance from one based on rule by Parliament to a constitutional state in which a supreme Constitution guarantees the rights of individuals. 'It also signalled a new dispensation, as it were, where rule by force would be replaced by democratic principles and a governmental system based on the precepts of equality and freedom.'[16]

But these dramatic changes were also reflected in necessary changes to the structures of government. The 1993 and 1996 Constitutions thus introduced significant changes to the composition and functioning of the legislative, executive and judicial branches of government as well as the composition and functioning of governance structures at the provincial and local level. At the heart of these changes we find a more decisive, if not entirely strict, division of power between the various branches of government and between different spheres of government at the national, provincial and local levels. In the following chapters we focus primarily on the national sphere of government and the institutions created by the Constitution to regulate and check the exercise of public power in this sphere. We then proceed to discuss the distribution of powers and functions between the national sphere of government and the other spheres in chapter 8 of this book.

The Constitution provides for the division of the national government into three separate branches:

- The national Parliament which consists of the National Assembly (NA) and the National Council of Provinces (NCOP). Its members are the people's representatives and it is the highest law-making authority.
- The national executive consists of the President and the Ministers who together form the Cabinet. The Ministers are the political heads of different government portfolios and perform executive functions.
- The judiciary exercises judicial review of government conduct. Section 165 of the Constitution vests judicial authority in the courts. The courts must be independent and are subject only to the law and the Constitution which they must apply without fear, favour or prejudice.[17]

The Constitution is structured in such a way that different chapters are dedicated to the different branches of government, namely the legislative authority, executive authority and judicial authority. Chapter 4 of the Constitution deals exclusively with the legislative authority in the national sphere of government, Chapter 5 deals with the executive authority in the national sphere of government, while Chapter 8 is dedicated to the judicial authority of the Republic. This means that the doctrine of separation of powers, although never directly mentioned in the document, is nevertheless firmly entrenched in the 1996 Constitution of South Africa. In *Glenister v President of the Republic of South Africa and Others* (*Glenister I*),[18] for example, Langa CJ, in reference to the separation of powers, stated that 'although not expressly mentioned in the text, it was "axiomatic" that it was part of the constitutional design'.[19] And in *Doctors for Life International v Speaker of the National*

16 *Makwanyane* para 220.

17 S 165(1) and (2).

18 (CCT 41/08) [2008] ZACC 19; 2009 (1) SA 287 (CC); 2009 (2) BCLR 136 (CC) (22 October 2008). This case is known as *Glenister I* as the Constitutional Court later handed down judgment in a similar matter in *Glenister v President of the Republic of South Africa and Others* (CCT 48/10) [2011] ZACC 6; 2011 (3) SA 347 (CC); 2011 (7) BCLR 651 (CC) (17 March 2011), known as *Glenister II*.

19 *Glenister I* paras 29–32.

Assembly and Others, Ngcobo J stated that 'the structure of the provisions entrusting and separating powers between the legislative, executive and judicial branches reflects the concept of separation of powers'.[20]

However, in at least one sense, the doctrine does not require a strict separation between the judiciary on the one hand and the legislature and executive on the other as it requires the judiciary to check whether the other branches comply with the law and exercise their authority in conformity with the Constitution.[21] This potentially places the judiciary in the firing line as the courts, which must ultimately interpret the Constitution and flesh out the notion of separation of powers and its limits, are the final arbiters of the supreme Constitution.[22] Because the Constitution is supreme and binding on all branches of government,[23] and because the courts must interpret and enforce the Constitution, it means that when the legislature or executive exercises its constitutionally mandated authority, it must act in accordance with, and within the limits of, the Constitution **as determined by the courts**. As the Court stated in *Doctors for Life*:

> **The supremacy of the Constitution requires that 'the obligations imposed by it must be fulfilled'. Courts are required by the Constitution 'to ensure that all branches of government act within the law' and fulfil their constitutional obligations. This Court 'has been given the responsibility of being the ultimate guardian of the Constitution and its values'. Section 167(4)(*e*), in particular, entrusts this Court with the power to ensure that Parliament fulfils its constitutional obligations. This section gives meaning to the supremacy clause, which requires that 'the obligations imposed by [the Constitution] must be fulfilled'. It would therefore require clear language of the Constitution to deprive this Court of its jurisdiction to enforce the Constitution.**[24]

The courts must exercise this vital task while at the same time remaining conscious of the limits on judicial authority and the Constitution's design and must leave certain matters to other branches of government. This means that the judiciary should not interfere in the processes of other branches of government unless to do so is mandated by the Constitution.[25] Accordingly, the division of powers is not strictly enforced if it appears, for example, that one sphere of government is failing to comply with its constitutional obligations. The courts can

---

20 (CCT12/05) [2006] ZACC 11; 2006 (12) BCLR 1399 (CC); 2006 (6) SA 416 (CC) (17 August 2006) para 37. See also *Certification of the Constitution of the Republic of South Africa, 1996* (CCT 23/96) [1996] ZACC 26; 1996 (4) SA 744 (CC); 1996 (10) BCLR 1253 (CC) (6 September 1996) paras 106–13 where the Court held that the provisions of the Constitution are structured in a way that makes provision for the separation of powers, and *South African Association of Personal Injury Lawyers v Heath and Others* (CCT27/00) [2000] ZACC 22; 2001 (1) SA 883; 2001 (1) BCLR 77 (28 November 2000) para 22.

21 See, for example, s 172(1) of the Constitution which provides that a court: '(*a*) must declare that any law or conduct that is inconsistent with the Constitution is invalid to the extent of its inconsistency; and (*b*) may make any order that is just and equitable, including: (i) an order limiting the retrospective effect of the declaration of invalidity; and (ii) an order suspending the declaration of invalidity for any period and on any conditions, to allow the competent authority to correct the defect'.

22 S 167(5) of the Constitution provides: 'The Constitutional Court makes the final decision whether an Act of Parliament, a provincial Act or conduct of the President is constitutional, and must confirm any order of invalidity made by the Supreme Court of Appeal, a High Court, or a court of similar status, before that order has any force.'

23 S1(*c*) read with s 8(1).

24 *Doctors for Life* para 38.

25 *Doctors for Life* para 37.

always intrude to check the other branches when they fail to comply with their constitutional obligations.[26]

In this regard, the judgment in *Glenister I* is apposite where the Court held that:

> **it is a necessary component of the doctrine of the separation of powers that courts have a constitutional obligation to ensure that the exercise of power by other branches of government occurs within constitutional bounds. But even in these circumstances, courts must observe the limits of their powers.**[27]

This is in accordance with the test formulated in *Doctors for Life* which provides that intervention by a court in the legislative process:

> **would only be appropriate if an applicant can show that there would be no effective remedy available ... once the legislative process is complete, as the unlawful conduct will have achieved its object in the course of the process. The applicant must show that the resultant harm will be material and irreversible.**[28]

PAUSE FOR REFLECTION

A dialogic model of the separation of powers doctrine

The separation of powers doctrine in a liberal democracy is said to enable the complex task of governance, law making and law enforcement to be performed by the institution best equipped to do so. It is also said to disperse power to avoid the overconcentration of power in one body or one person.[29] But as Liebenberg points out, the doctrine as it is traditionally envisaged in liberal thought 'has the potential to frustrate transformation when it assumes an idealised form of strictly demarcated separate spheres, instead of a functional and pragmatic device to facilitate responsive, accountable government'.[30] What is envisaged in the South African model of constitutional democracy is a relationship between the three branches that ensures accountability as well as responsiveness and openness on the part of the various branches. Liebenberg argues that in this model, which we shall call the 'post-liberal' model, the focus is not so much on whether one branch of government has transgressed the boundaries of the other, but rather on 'whether the branches all remain able to participate in the process of mutually defining their boundaries'.[31] This is also sometimes called a **dialogic model of the separation of powers** as it envisages an ongoing, structured, constitutional dialogue between the three branches of government. Although the dialogue will often

26 See *Minister of Health and Others v Treatment Action Campaign and Others (No 2)* (CCT8/02) [2002] ZACC 15; 2002 (5) SA 721; 2002 (10) BCLR 1033 (5 July 2002) para 99 where the Court stated: 'The primary duty of courts is to the Constitution and the law, "which they must apply impartially and without fear, favour or prejudice". The Constitution requires the state to "respect, protect, promote, and fulfil the rights in the Bill of Rights". Where state policy is challenged as inconsistent with the Constitution, courts have to consider whether in formulating and implementing such policy the state has given effect to its constitutional obligations. If it should hold in any given case that the state has failed to do so, it is obliged by the Constitution to say so. In so far as that constitutes an intrusion into the domain of the executive, that is an intrusion mandated by the Constitution itself.'

27 *Glenister I* para 33. See also *Mazibuko v Sisulu and Another* (CCT 115/12) [2013] ZACC 28; 2013 (6) SA 249 (CC); 2013 (11) BCLR 1297 (CC) (27 August 2013) para 31 where the Constitutional Court affirmed is reluctance to interfere in the power of the NA to determine its own internal arrangements, proceedings and procedures, and to make rules and orders concerning its business.

28 *Doctors for Life* para 44. This test applies equally to executive decision making and execution of law and policy.

29 *Glenister I* para 35. See also Liebenberg, S (2010) *Socio-Economic Rights Adjudication under a Transformative Constitution* 67.

30 Liebenberg (2010) 67.

31 Liebenberg (2010) 69, quoting Minow, M (1990) *Making All the Difference: Inclusion, Exclusion and American Law* 361.

be robust and although severe tensions may arise among the three branches of government, the three branches will remain engaged with one another on a formal level to test the limits of power exercised by each branch. Liebenberg contends that this fluid, dialogic model of separation of powers is best suited to promoting transformative jurisprudence.[32] When considering the appropriate role of the three branches of government in the South African context, it is therefore important to take into account the transformative nature of the South African Constitution.

In *Certification of the Constitution of the Republic of South Africa, 1996*, the Constitutional Court affirmed that there was no universal model of separation of powers. It claimed that in democratic systems of government in which checks and balances result in the imposition of restraints by one branch of government on another, there is no separation that is absolute. It continued:

> **[t]he principle of separation of powers, on the one hand, recognises the functional independence of branches of government. On the other hand, the principle of checks and balances focuses on the desirability of ensuring that the constitutional order, as a totality, prevents the branches of government from usurping power from one another. In this sense it anticipates the necessary or unavoidable intrusion of one branch on the terrain of another. No constitutional scheme can reflect a complete separation of powers: the scheme is always one of partial separation.[33]**

This means that courts will inevitably play an important role in regulating and safeguarding the separation of powers. However, it also means that the courts may be accused of intruding too far into the domain of the other two branches of government when they do so. This raises the counter-majoritarian problem highlighted in chapter 2. However, as the ultimate guardians of the Constitution, the courts not only have the right to intervene in order to prevent the violation of the Constitution, they also have the duty to do so.[34] This is because it is a necessary component of the doctrine of separation of powers that courts have a constitutional obligation to ensure that the exercise of power by other branches of government occurs within constitutional bounds. Courts must nevertheless observe the limits of their powers.

The converse question arises: can the legislature and the executive ever intrude on the terrain of the judiciary? For example, can the legislature impose limits on the power of the courts to sentence those convicted of criminal offences and, if so, to what extent?[35] Can the executive engage members of the judiciary in informal discussions,

32 Liebenberg (2010) 71.

33 (CCT 23/96) [1996] ZACC 26; 1996 (4) SA 744 (CC); 1996 (10) BCLR 1253 (CC) (6 September 1996) paras 108–9. See also *De Lange v Smuts NO and Others* (CCT26/97) [1998] ZACC 6; 1998 (3) SA 785; 1998 (7) BCLR 779 (28 May 1998) para 60 where Ackermann J stated: 'I have no doubt that over time our Courts will develop a distinctively South African model of separation of powers, one that fits the particular system of government provided for in the Constitution and that reflects a delicate balancing, informed both by South Africa's history and its new dispensation, between the need, on the one hand, to control government by separating powers and enforcing checks and balances and, on the other, to avoid diffusing power so completely that the government is unable to take timely measures in the public interest.'

34 *Doctors for Life* para 70.

35 In *S v Dodo* (CCT 1/01) [2001] ZACC 16; 2001 (3) SA 382 (CC); 2001 (5) BCLR 423 (CC) (5 April 2001), the Constitutional Court found that the legislative prescription requiring courts to impose mandatory minimum sentences in certain cases did not necessarily infringe on the separation of powers doctrine. As checks and balances constitute an integral part of the separation of powers principle and prevent one arm of the state from becoming too powerful in the exercise of the powers allocated to it, legislation on penal sentencing does not, *per se*, infringe the separation of powers principle between the legislature and the judiciary.

for example by creating 'appropriate mechanisms' in order 'to facilitate for [*sic*] regular interface between the three spheres of the State to enhance synergy and constructive engagement among them in pursuit of common transformative goals that are geared to benefit the society at large'?[36] These are complex questions, but in essence the answer is that as there is no absolute separation of powers, there is no absolute bar on the other two branches intruding on the terrain of the judiciary. However, there is one important caveat, namely that no intrusion can ever be allowed if such an intrusion will undermine the independence or impartiality of the judiciary. For this reason, it is unlikely that a court will ever approve of the creation of a mechanism to facilitate regular private discussions between the judiciary and the other branches of government to enhance synergy and constructive engagement among them in pursuit of common transformative goals.[37]

SUMMARY

The Constitution creates three branches of government – the legislature, the executive and the judiciary – and the study of each of these branches of government must be conducted with reference to the relationship between the branch being studied and the other two branches. It must also be understood with reference to the practices of traditional leadership and the culture within dominant political parties. Understanding the separation of powers doctrine is therefore pivotal for understanding how the various branches of government work and what the limits of the power of each branch are. In this regard, the judiciary must be treated as unique as it requires a high degree of independence from the other branches of government. The judiciary has the vital task of enforcing the provisions of the Constitution and of ensuring that the other branches of government act in accordance with its provisions. However, this format does not easily accommodate other structures of government such as traditional leadership or Chapter 9 institutions.

36 De Vos, P (2011, 24 November) Cabinet statement on transformation of judicial system *Constitutionally Speaking* available at http://constitutionallyspeaking.co.za/cabinet-statement-on-transformation-of-judicial-system/.

37 See Yacoob, Z (2012) 'The Dynamic Constitution', Keynote Address, University of Cape Town Constitution Week, 12 March 2012, available at http://constitutionallyspeaking.co.za/justice-zac-yacoob-on-the-dynamic-constitution/ where, in reference to the proposed Department of Justice's 'review' of the jurisprudence of South Africa's Constitutional Court and Supreme Court of Appeal and an evaluation of the contribution or lack thereof of jurisprudence to the transformation of society, the Justice stated: '... this cannot be intended to mean that the executive and the legislature should be able to discuss matters of importance with the judiciary directly and outside a court hearing, in an effort to influence it. If this is what is meant I would find it difficult to agree.'

Chapter 4

Separation of powers and the national legislature

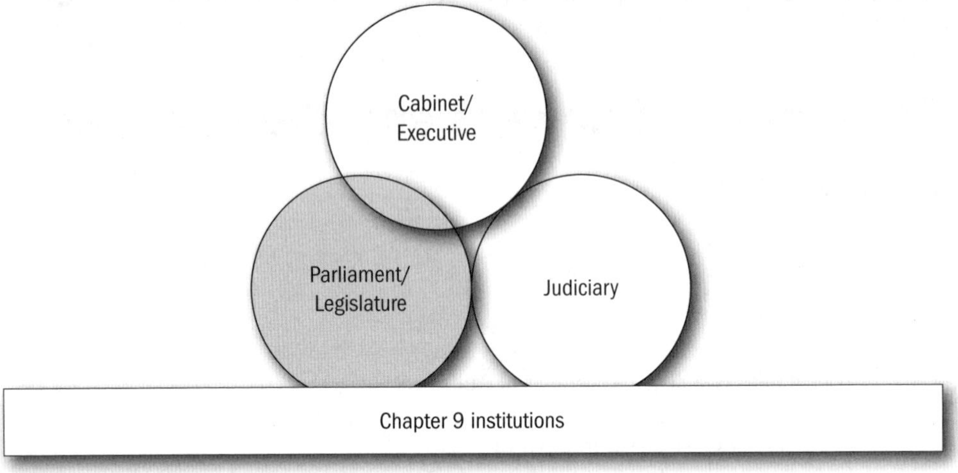

Figure 4.1 The separation of powers and the national legislature

4.1 Introduction

In this chapter, we focus on the national sphere of government and discuss the powers, functions and operation of the national legislature or **Parliament** as it is referred to in the Constitution. Parliament has the power to:

- consider, pass, amend or reject legislation on any subject that falls within its jurisdictional areas of competence
- ensure that all executive organs of state in the national sphere of government are accountable to it
- maintain oversight of the exercise of national executive authority, including the implementation of legislation
- maintain oversight of any organ of state.[1]

Apart from considering, passing, amending or rejecting legislation, therefore, Parliament has the power to check the exercise of power by the national executive and other organs of state and to ensure that the national executive and various other organs of state are held accountable for the manner in which they exercise their powers.

Parliament is a bicameral legislature. This means that it is divided into two Houses. The lower House of Parliament is called the **National Assembly (NA)** and the upper House of Parliament is called the **National Council of Provinces (NCOP)**.[2] Although legislative power is distributed between these two Houses, the NA is constitutionally and politically the dominant House. In essence, the idea behind **bicameralism** is that the two Houses of Parliament represent different interests and thus act as a check on one another.[3] Further, having two Houses is said to provide for better representation of the electorate in a heterogeneous society, to assist in alleviating Parliament's workload and to promote a thorough consideration of matters before Parliament.[4] We argue that the main justification for bicameralism is to ensure adequate democratic representation of different interests, namely

1 Ss 55 and 68 read with Schedules 4 and 5 of the Constitution.

2 See s 42(1) of the Constitution.

3 Currie, I and De Waal, J (2001) *The New Constitutional and Administrative Law, Vol 1 Constitutional Law* 133.

4 Rautenbach, IM and Malherbe, EFJ (2009) *Constitutional Law* 5th ed 122.

the interests of the electorate in general by the NA on the one hand, and the interests of the nine provinces by the NCOP on the other hand.[5]

In most bicameral legislatures, including the South African Parliament, the members of each House are elected or appointed in different ways. In the case of the NA, members are elected via their respective political parties in a national election. In the case of the NCOP, they are elected via the provincial legislatures. The members of each House are elected or appointed in different ways because they are supposed to represent different broad interests and to act as a check on the exercise of power by the other House. In South Africa, the NA is intended to represent the interests of all South Africans[6] while the NCOP is intended to represent the interests of provinces in the national legislature.[7]

Although legislative authority and other powers are distributed between the two Houses, the NA is the dominant and more powerful House of Parliament. This is because:

- the NA elects[8] and can also dismiss[9] the President
- with the exception of two members, all the other members of the executive must be selected from and remain members of the NA[10]
- the NA is explicitly tasked with the duty to hold all executive organs of state in the national sphere of government accountable to it and to maintain oversight of the exercise of national executive authority, including the implementation of legislation[11]
- the NA plays a decisive role in various other appointments.[12]

The NCOP has a less defined role in holding the executive to account and has no role in the appointment or dismissal of members of the executive. Unlike the executive, which has its seat in Pretoria, the seat of Parliament is in Cape Town.[13] However, an Act of Parliament can determine that the seat of Parliament is changed as long as the correct procedure is followed.[14] Sittings of the NA or the NCOP are permitted at places other than the seat of Parliament, but only on the grounds of public interest, security or convenience, and if provided for in the rules and orders of the NA[15] or the NCOP.[16]

It is important to note that, whether in the NA or the NCOP, the democratic link between voters and the legislature is mediated by political parties. This means in practice a person cannot become a member of one of the Houses of the national legislature unless the person is a member of a political party. The Constitution thus establishes not only a parliamentary system of government in which the majority party in the NA forms a government, but also a system of **party government**. This is because the system cannot function in the absence of political parties.[17]

Party government is usually defined as a system of government in which political parties have a decisive influence on the way in which the government is composed, on government

5 Currie and De Waal (2001) 133. See generally Ackerman, B (2000) The new separation of powers *Harvard Law Review* 113(3):633–729 at 682. According to Ackerman, the second House 'may enhance the deliberative character of political life'.
6 S 42(3) of the Constitution.
7 S 42(4) of the Constitution.
8 S 86 of the Constitution.
9 Ss 89 and 102 of the Constitution.
10 S 91(3) of the Constitution.
11 S 55(2) of the Constitution.
12 S 193(4) of the Constitution.
13 S 42(6) of the Constitution.
14 In terms of s 76(5) of the Constitution, an absolute majority of members of the NA – that is 200 or more of its members – is required to pass such legislation.
15 S 51(3) of the Constitution.
16 S 63(3) of the Constitution.
17 Currie and de Waal (2001) 131.

policy and on the actions of the elected representatives in the legislature.[18] Through a mixture of conventions and traditions inherited from British constitutional law and the effects of the **electoral system** employed to select members of the NA, political parties and their leaders are extremely powerful in South Africa and loom large in any discussion of the composition and functioning of the national legislature. Despite the important role played by political parties, the Constitution (as well as national legislation) provides little guidance as to the manner in which political parties must operate and about the specific relationship between the leadership of a political party (who might not serve in the legislature) and its representatives in the legislature or the executive.[19] Thus it is unclear to what extent political party leaders can 'micromanage' their members in the legislature and the executive and whether the extraparliamentary leadership of a political party can dictate to its members what they must say and how they should act in the legislature or executive.

CRITICAL THINKING

The rights of citizens as members of political parties

The relationship between political parties and their leaders, on the one hand, and the elected representatives of political parties serving in Parliament, on the other hand, is not clearly defined in the Constitution. However, in *Ramakatsa and Others v Magashule and Others*[20] the Constitutional Court affirmed the strong link between internal party democracy and the right of citizens to take part in the political process and to vote in elections. Thus Yacoob J stated that:

> the right to participate in the activities of a political party confers on every political party the duty to act lawfully and in accordance with its own constitution. This means that our Constitution gives every member of every political party the right to exact compliance with the constitution of a political party by the leadership of that party.[21]

Our democracy is founded on a multiparty system of government. However, unlike the electoral system in place in the United Kingdom and in South Africa before 1994 (based on geographical voting constituencies), the present electoral system for electing members of the NA and of the provincial legislatures must 'result, in general, in proportional representation'.[22] This means a person who intends to vote in national or provincial elections must vote for a political party registered for the purpose of contesting the elections and not for a candidate. It is the registered party that nominates candidates for the election on regional and national party lists. Political parties are therefore indispensable conduits for the enjoyment of the right to vote in elections.

If a person chooses to become a member of a political party and wants to take part in its internal elections, that person has a right to do so in accordance with the rules of

18 See Basson, DA and Viljoen, HP (1988) *South African Constitutional Law* 86–7.

19 It is true that s 1(*d*) of the Constitution states that the Republic of South Africa is a democratic state founded on, *inter alia*, a multiparty system of government and that several other provisions in the Constitution recognise the role of political parties in the legislative and executive process. However, the exact relationship between the representatives of political parties in the legislature and the executive on the one hand and the party leadership on the other hand is never defined. S 19 guarantees for everyone the rights to form a political party; to participate in the activities of, or recruit members for, a political party; and to campaign for a political party or cause. S 57(2)(*c*) states that the rules of the NA must provide for financial and administrative assistance to each party represented in the Assembly in proportion to its representation to enable the party and its leader to perform their functions in the NA effectively. S 57(2)(*d*) requires that the NA rules must recognise the leader of the largest opposition party in the Assembly as the Leader of the Opposition.

20 (CCT 109/12) [2012] ZACC 31; 2013 (2) BCLR 202 (CC) (18 December 2012).

21 *Ramakatsa* para 16.

22 S 46(1)(*d*) of the Constitution.

that party. The exercise of the right is protected not only against external interference but also against interference arising from within the party. Although it is left largely to political parties themselves to regulate how they deal with internal elections, political parties may not adopt constitutions which are inconsistent with the right of citizens to join political parties and to participate in their activities. This means that the constitution of a political party that limits or extinguishes the rights of members of that party freely and fairly to take part in its internal elections may well be declared invalid by a court as being in breach of section 19 of the Bill of Rights.

As we have seen, in practical terms political parties and their leaders hold enormous power over elected members of the legislature in South Africa. There are four interrelated reasons for this:

- First, we inherited our system of parliamentary government from Britain. In this system the support of the majority party in Parliament is required to form the government.[23] Thus, the executive requires the continued support of the majority of members of the legislature to survive. This provides a strong incentive to members of the legislature to 'toe the party line', regardless of any differences an individual member of the legislature may have with the decisions or actions of the political party leadership. If members of the governing party fail to respect party discipline and vote with opposition parties and against the majority party, and the government loses a vote in Parliament, this can erode the democratic legitimacy of the government and can even lead to the fall of that government.
- Second, we also inherited the convention of **strict party discipline** from the Westminster system associated with the system of parliamentary government.[24] This convention places severe restrictions on individual Members of Parliament (MPs) to disobey party leaders when they engage in legislative or executive action. The convention of strict party discipline was applied in pre-democratic South Africa in the Westminster Parliament as well as in the tricameral Parliament. When the new democratic system replaced the old system, the convention of strict party discipline was retained. Thus, this convention remains intact in democratic South Africa and forms part of the parliamentary culture.
- Third, the internal culture of South African political parties places great emphasis on internal party discipline. This type of internal culture values and rewards party members who demonstrate loyalty to the party and the decisions democratically arrived at by that party. It also values respect for the leadership of the party and rewards those who display such respect.[25] At its most extreme, such a culture can be said to be one of democratic centralism. This allows internal party debate on an issue until the party has made a decision on that issue. Once the decision has been taken, all members of the party are required to support the decision and are not allowed to criticise that decision or act in a way that would undermine the authority of the party and the decision taken.
- Last, the electoral system in South Africa assists party leaders to enforce strict discipline among members of the legislature. This is because, as we shall see, members of the legislature depend on the support of their various political parties to get elected to the legislature and can also easily be removed from the legislature by their respective political

23 See ss 86, 89 and especially 102 of the Constitution.

24 Hiebert, JL 'Constitutional experimentation: Rethinking how a Bill of Rights functions' in Ginsburg, T and Dixon, R (eds) (2011) *Comparative Constitutional Law* 307.

25 The disciplinary case lodged against former ANC Youth League leader, Julius Malema, and his ultimate expulsion from the ANC illustrates the governing party's insistence on party discipline. See Mthembu, J (2012, 4 February) ANC statement on the National Disciplinary Committee of appeal today available at http://www.anc.org.za/show.php?id=9363.

parties. Accordingly, members of the legislature are, to some extent, beholden to the leadership of their respective political parties and to the party machinery to retain their positions. This means that the members of the legislature are not free to act as they see fit in fulfilling their various duties as members of the NA or the NCOP. Once the political party to whom a legislator belongs has made a decision on a pertinent issue being considered by the legislature, the members of that party are usually bound by that decision and must follow it. For example, if a political party has decided to vote in favour of a **Bill** before Parliament and has instructed its legislators accordingly, they cannot refuse to vote for the Bill because for some reason or another they oppose the Bill. The members of that political party will usually be required to support the Bill and vote in favour of it even if a member disagrees with the position taken by his or her political party.[26] The situation is more fluid and complex in cases where the political party has not taken a final public stance on an issue being considered by the legislature or where members of the legislature are legally expected to fulfil their constitutional duty to consider and pass legislation, to hold the members of the executive accountable and to oversee the work of the executive in a diligent and responsible manner.

It is imperative to understand this delicate and sometimes complex relationship between members of the legislature, their respective political parties and the members of the executive in order to understand the practical day-to-day functioning of the legislature.

PAUSE FOR REFLECTION

Difficulties faced by MPs who must both fulfil their constitutional obligations while also toeing the party line

Section 5.4 of the Constitution of the African National Congress (ANC) states:

> **ANC members who hold elective office in any sphere of governance at national, provincial or local level are required to be members of the appropriate caucus, to function within its rules and to abide by its decisions under the general provisions of this Constitution and the constitutional structures of the ANC.**[27]

Members who fail to adhere to this injunction can be disciplined and punished, and such punishment could include suspension or expulsion from the party.[28] Many other political parties in South Africa have roughly similar provisions to assist the party to enforce its discipline on its elected members.

In 2011, when members of the NA were called on to vote on a controversial Bill, the Protection of State Information Bill, one ANC member of the NA abstained from voting and another left the chamber just as votes were being cast to avoid having to vote for a Bill which they did not support. The ANC then announced that it would institute disciplinary proceedings against these two MPs for 'ill-discipline'.[29] This move was not surprising as political parties in South Africa usually enforce strict party discipline and require MPs to support decisions taken by the parliamentary caucus of that political party, including decisions on whether to support a piece of legislation or not.

26 Requiring members to toe the party line on a particular vote on pain of sanction or disciplinary proceedings is often referred to as a 'three line whip'.

27 African National Congress Constitution, as amended and adopted at the 52nd National Conference, Polokwane, 2007 available at http://www.anc.org.za/show.php?id=207.

28 S 25.3 of the African National Congress Constitution.

29 See Malefane, M (2012, 1 April) Turok going juju route? *Sunday World* available at http://www.sundayworld.co.za/news/2012/04/01/turok-going-juju-route.

In another case in 2010, the chairperson of the NA Committee on Defence and Military Veterans was removed from his post by the governing party after insisting that the then Minister of Defence and Military Veterans should account to that committee for the work done in her department in a manner that displeased the Minister.[30]

These events illustrate the difficulties faced by individual MPs who must both fulfil their constitutional obligations to hold the executive to account and to pass constitutionally valid and appropriate legislation on the one hand while also being required to toe the party line on the other hand.

4.2 General rules regarding the operation of Parliament

4.2.1 Introduction

The NA and the NCOP have the power to determine and control their own internal arrangements, proceedings and procedures.[31] The Constitution authorises the NA and the NCOP to make joint rules and orders concerning the joint business of the two Houses.[32] The Constitution also authorises the two Houses to make rules separately regarding their own operations.[33] It also requires the NA and NCOP to make rules and orders to provide for the composition, powers and functioning of committees.[34] While Parliament can make such rules, these rules have to comply with and give effect to the provisions of the Constitution. Rules that clash with any section of the Constitution can therefore be declared invalid by a court of law.[35] Both Houses of Parliament and their committees have wide-ranging powers not dissimilar from a court of law and can summon any person, including the President and Cabinet Ministers, to appear before them to:

- give evidence under oath or affirmation, or to produce documents
- require any person or institution to report to it
- compel, in terms of national legislation or the rules and orders, any person or institution to comply with a summons or requirement to produce documents
- to receive petitions, representations or submissions from any interested persons or institutions.[36]

Usually, the relevant committee will request a witness to appear before it to answer questions and to produce any documents required, or institutions or individuals will request to make written and oral submissions to a committee. If a witness refuses to appear after being asked to do so by a committee, that witness can be summonsed to do so and can ultimately be compelled to appear and to answer questions. However, the Rules of the National Assembly[37]

30 Friedman, S (2012, 6 August) State secrecy is the real threat to our security *Business Day Live* available at http://www.businessday.co.za/articles/Content.aspx?id=128285.

31 Ss 57(1) and 70(1) of the Constitution.

32 S 45.

33 Ss 57 and 70.

34 Ss 57(2) and 70(2).

35 See generally *Oriani-Ambrosini, MP v Sisulu, MP Speaker of the National Assembly* (CCT 16/12) [2012] ZACC 27; 2012 (6) SA 588 (CC); 2013 (1) BCLR 14 (CC) (9 October 2012) and also *Mazibuko v Sisulu and Another* (CCT 115/12) [2013] ZACC 28; 2013 (6) SA 249 (CC); 2013 (11) BCLR 1297 (CC) (27 August 2013).

36 Ss 56 and 69 of the Constitution.

37 Parliament of the Republic of South Africa (2011, June) Rules of the National Assembly 7th ed available at http://www.pmg.org.za/files/doc/2012/NA%20Rules%207th%20edition-1.pdf.

make it clear that this power should be exercised sparingly and prohibits any committee from summonsing a witness without first having satisfied the Speaker that the evidence of such witness will be material to the enquiry.[38]

It is therefore clear that the two Houses of Parliament have wide powers to fulfil their mandates in the best way chosen by each of them. However, there are at least three distinct ways in which these powers are curtailed by the Constitution:

- First, both Houses are required to act in an open and transparent manner and cannot make Rules that would extinguish the constitutional requirement of openness.
- Second, members of both Houses as well as Cabinet members who appear before them enjoy certain privileges which cannot be curtailed by Parliament or anyone else.
- Third, both Houses are required to facilitate public involvement in their legislative and other processes.

4.2.2 Openness and transparency in Parliament

The Constitution requires both the NA and the NCOP to conduct their business in an open manner, and hold their sittings and those of their committees in public.[39] However, reasonable measures may be taken to regulate public access, including access of the media, to Parliament and its committees, and to provide for the searching of any person and, where appropriate, the refusal of entry to or the removal of any person.[40] The NA and the NCOP are further explicitly prohibited from excluding the public, including the media, from a sitting of a committee unless it is reasonable and justifiable to do so in an open and democratic society.[41] Rule 40 of the Rules of the NA further regulates the possible limits on the openness and transparency of the NA by stating:

> **[t]he power to admit strangers to the precincts of this House or an extended public committee or an appropriation committee of this House, and the places set apart for them in a Chamber, shall vest in the Speaker, subject to the provisions of the Constitution.**[42]

---

38 NA Rule 325(1). The Rules of the National Council of Provinces 9th ed (2008, March), available at http://www.pmg.org.za/parlinfo/ncoprules, do not contain a similar provision and merely state in Rule 103 that:

> **(1) For the purposes of performing its functions a committee may, subject to the Constitution, legislation, the other provisions of these Rules and resolutions of the Council –**
> **(*a*) summon any person to appear before it to give evidence on oath or affirmation, or to produce documents;**
> **(*b*) receive petitions, representations or submissions from interested persons or institutions;**
> **(*c*) conduct public hearings;**
> **(*d*) permit oral evidence, representations and submissions;**
> **(*e*) determine its own procedure;**
> **(*f*) meet at a venue determined by it, which may be a venue beyond the seat of Parliament if the Council is not in session.**

39 Ss 59(1)(*b*) and 72(1)(*b*).

40 Ss 59(1)(*b*) and 72(1)(*b*) of the Constitution.

41 Ss 59(2) and 72(2) of the Constitution.

42 The Rules of the NCOP also allow for certain limitations of public access to its committees. Rule 110(1) affirms that:

> **[m]eetings of committees and subcommittees are open to the public, including the media, and the member presiding may not exclude the public, including the media, from the meeting, except when:**
> **(*a*) legislation, these Rules or resolutions of the Council provide for the committee or subcommittee to meet in closed session; or**
> **(*b*) the committee or subcommittee is considering a matter which is –**
> **(i) of a private nature that is prejudicial to a particular person;**
> **(ii) protected under parliamentary privilege, or for any other reason privileged in terms of the law;**
> **(iii) confidential in terms of legislation; or**
> **(iv) of such a nature that its confidential treatment is for any other reason reasonable and justifiable in an open and democratic society.**

This means that normally it will not be allowed to hold a sitting of the NA or the NCOP or any of its committee meetings or other business of the NA or NCOP in secret or to prevent certain individuals from attending these events. These provisions entitle the public to access the proceedings of the NA and NCOP and their committees. In *Doctors for Life International v Speaker of the National Assembly and Others*, the Constitutional Court has hinted that non-compliance with these provisions 'would have grave implications for the validity of any conduct that passes a law. It is a manner and form provision equivalent to the provision for a quorum, and the number of votes required to take a decision'.[43] This means that where the media or ordinary members of the public are excluded from committees or from the plenary session of the NA while it is considering a particular Bill, the Court might well declare the passing of such a Bill unconstitutional.

PAUSE FOR REFLECTION

Access to Parliament is a right not a privilege

This is an extract from an opinion piece written by Mbete and February:

> While Parliament has many failings, its committees have always been open to the public. Yet it is easy to forget that the right the public has to attend committee meetings is granted by the Constitution and is not a privilege granted by Parliament, its presiding officers or its bureaucracy.
>
> Last week, Parliament took a retrogressive step when nine members of the Right2Know campaign were prevented from attending a meeting of the ad hoc committee on the Protection of Information Bill. The bill has been the subject of controversy as the civil society campaign against the bill and the, at times, flawed processes of the ad hoc committee gains momentum. The members were informed at access control that they were not allowed to enter Parliament as they were 'banned'. They were allowed into Parliament after nearly two hours, and the threat of court action, by which time the meeting had ended. The Speaker's office says it was a 'misunderstanding'.
>
> However, a press statement released by Parliament on March 31 cited the Right2Know silent protest (in which members of the campaign donned masks depicting State Security Minister Siyabonga Cwele) on February 15 as the reason the delegation was refused entry. The statement said 'security officials took precautionary security action by denying entry', ostensibly to prevent another protest. The statement does not deny the Right2Know campaign has been banned from entering Parliament.
>
> The Right2Know campaign is a coalition of 400 civil society organisations and 12 000 individuals. A ban of campaign members from Parliament is in effect a ban of civil society more generally. It is the arbitrariness of Parliament's action that should concern all who believe an open democracy is our right. Parliament has yet to provide details of who gave the security official the power to restrict access to the committee meeting. Who gave the instruction to 'ban' members

43 (CCT12/05) [2006] ZACC 11; 2006 (12) BCLR 1399 (CC); 2006 (6) SA 416 (CC) (17 August 2006) para 300 (per Yacoob J dissenting) speaking not about the 'public involvement' requirements common to ss 59, 72 and 118 of the Constitution and which were central to the matter before the court (at least in so far as s 118 was concerned), but rather about the 'public access' requirements common to the same sections.

from the committee meeting and on what grounds? Does a list exist of those 'banned' from Parliament? And if so, will those affected be granted access to such a list?[44]

After the writing of this piece the Right2Know campaigners were allowed back into the committee and the alleged 'ban' was therefore 'rescinded'. If the ban had not been rescinded, the legality of the passing of the Bill which was being discussed at the time may well have called into question. This incident illustrates that parliamentary officials must take care not to act in a way that may render the procedure for the passing of legislation unlawful.

4.2.3 The powers and privileges of Members of Parliament

The power of Parliament to determine its own procedures is not only limited or qualified by the constitutional requirements regarding openness, accountability and transparency as well as specific duties imposed on Parliament by the Constitution.[45] It is also limited by the provisions regarding the privileges enjoyed by Cabinet Ministers, Deputy Ministers and members of the NA and NCOP with regard to anything they say or do in the NA or the NCOP or one of its committees. Parliament and its members thus enjoy **parliamentary privilege** so that they are able to perform their functions without outside hindrance or interference.[46]

Parliamentary privilege is based on the notion that MPs need to be able to speak freely and uninhibitedly to be able to do their work and to expose wrongdoing without the fear of being held legally liable for what they say. Without this protection, MPs would be handicapped in performing their parliamentary duties. In addition, the authority of Parliament itself in confronting the executive and as a forum for expressing the anxieties of citizens would be correspondingly diminished.[47]

PAUSE FOR REFLECTION

Parliamentary privilege does not extend to personal matters

In *Dikoko v Mokhatla*,[48] the respondent, who was the municipal manager of the Southern District Municipality in the North West Province, sued the applicant, who was the mayor of the same municipality, for defamatory remarks the applicant had made while giving evidence to the Standing Committee on Public Accounts of the North West Provincial Legislature. In his defence, the applicant argued that he was protected by section 28 of the Local Government: Municipal Structures Act[49] which confers the same privileges and immunities on municipal councillors that the Constitution confers on MPs.

The Constitutional Court rejected this argument on the grounds that the defamatory statements made by the applicant did not form a part of the legitimate business of the Southern District Municipality, but rather a part of his own personal business. In arriving at this decision, however, the Court set out the purpose underlying the defence

44 Mbete, S and February, J (2011, 5 April) Access to Parliament is a right not a privilege *Business Day Live* available at http://www.bdlive.co.za/articles/2011/04/05/sthembile-mbete-and-judith-february-access-to-parliament-is-a-right-not-a-privilege;jsessionid=8485BDB17C0C6F9F61B042C08A00C41E.present1.bdfm.

45 *Mazibuko v Sisulu and Another* (CCT 115/12) [2013] ZACC 28; 2013 (6) SA 249 (CC); 2013 (11) BCLR 1297 (CC) (27 August 2013).

46 See Rautenbach and Malherbe (2009) 147.

47 Griffith, JAG and Ryle, M (1989) *Parliament: Functions, Practice and Procedures* 85.

48 (CCT62/05) [2006] ZACC 10; 2006 (6) SA 235 (CC); 2007 (1) BCLR 1 (CC) (3 August 2006).

of parliamentary privilege in a constitutional democracy. In this respect, the Court held that:

> [i]mmunising the conduct of members from criminal and civil liability during council deliberations is a bulwark of democracy. It promotes freedom of speech and expression. It encourages democracy and full and effective deliberation. It removes the fear of repercussion for what is said. This advances effective democratic government.[50]

Parliamentary privilege was developed in the British context to protect MPs from interference by the monarch. In the British context, parliamentary privileges are to be found chiefly in ancient practice, asserted by Parliament and accepted over time by the Crown and the courts as the law and custom of Parliament.[51] What the House of Commons originally claimed as customary rights in the course of repeated efforts to assert them eventually hardened into legally recognised privileges.[52] These privileges are now contained in the South African Constitution. Thus, Cabinet members, Deputy Ministers and members of the NA are guaranteed the freedom of speech in both the NA and the NCOP as well as in its committees, subject only to their rules and orders.[53] Members are also not liable to civil or criminal proceedings, arrest, imprisonment or damages for anything that they have said in, produced before or submitted to the NA or any of its committees, or anything revealed as a result of anything that they have said in, produced before or submitted to the NA or any of its committees.[54] Because the Constitution establishes a constitutional democracy and entrusts the judiciary with the power to enforce the Constitution, these privileges do not preclude the judiciary from enquiring into whether the procedures or limitations adopted by Parliament in this regard comply with the various provisions of the Constitution.

In South Africa, parliamentary privilege came under the spotlight in *Speaker of the National Assembly v De Lille MP and Another*.[55] The case arose from an incident in the NA in which one of the opposition members, Ms Patricia de Lille, stated that she had information that 12 members of the governing party had been spies for the apartheid government. When challenged, she mentioned eight names, some of which referred to people who were not members of the NA. The Speaker ruled that it was 'unparliamentary' to refer to some members of the NA as 'spies' and ordered her to withdraw her remarks, which she did.[56] An

---

49 Act 117 of 1998. S 28(1) of the Municipal Structures Act provides that:

> **[pr]ovincial legislation in terms of section 161 of the Constitution must provide at least –**
> **(*a*) that councillors have freedom of speech in a municipal council and in its committees, subject to the relevant council's rules and orders as envisaged in section 160(6) of the Constitution; and**
> **(*b*) that councillors are not liable to civil or criminal proceedings, arrest, imprisonment or damages for –**
> **(i) anything that they have said in, produced before or submitted to the council or any of its committees; or**
> **(ii) anything revealed as a result of anything that they have said in, produced before or submitted to the council or any of its committees'.**

S 28(2) goes on to provide that '[u]ntil provincial legislation contemplated in subsection (1) has been enacted the privileges referred to in paragraphs (*a*) and (*b*) of subsection (1) will apply to all municipal councils in the province concerned'.

50 *Dikoko* para 39.

51 Hatsell, J (1818) *Precedents of Proceedings in the House of Commons Vol 1* 2.

52 *R v Paty* (*Case of the Men of Aylesbury*) (1704) 2 Lord Raym 1105, 91 ER 817.

53 Ss 58(1)(*a*) and 71(1)(*a*) of the Constitution. See also NA Rule 44 and NCOP Rule 30.

54 Ss 58(1)(*b*) and 71(1)(*b*) of the Constitution read with NA Rule 44(2) and NCOP Rule 30(*b*).

55 (297/98) [1999] ZASCA 50; [1999] 4 All SA 241 (A) (26 August 1999).

56 *De Lille (SCA)* paras 2–3.

ad hoc committee of the NA recommended that Ms De Lille be directed to apologise and suspended for 15 parliamentary working days.[57] The NA adopted this recommendation.[58]

Ms De Lille had earlier successfully challenged the constitutionality of her suspension in the Cape High Court.[59] The Speaker argued that the NA had exercised its parliamentary privilege to control its own affairs and that the exercise of parliamentary privilege is not subject to judicial review. For this argument, the Speaker relied on section 5 of the Powers and Privileges of Parliament Act.[60] This section provides that a court shall stay proceedings before it if the Speaker issues a certificate to the effect that the matter in question is one which concerns the privilege of Parliament. The High Court held that, under a supreme Constitution, the exercise of parliamentary privilege is subject to judicial review. Hlophe J, as he then was, stated:

> **[T]he National Assembly is subject to the supremacy of the Constitution. It is an organ of state and therefore it is bound by the Bill of Rights. All its decisions and acts are subject to the Constitution and the Bill of Rights. Parliament can no longer claim supreme power subject to limitations imposed by the Constitution. It is subject in all respects to the provisions of our Constitution. It has only those powers vested in it by the Constitution expressly or by necessary implication or by other statutes which are not in conflict with the Constitution. It follows therefore that Parliament may not confer on itself or on any of its constituent parts, including the National Assembly, any powers not conferred on them by the Constitution expressly or by necessary implication.**[61]

The Judge concluded:

> **The nature and exercise of parliamentary privilege must be consonant with the Constitution. The exercise of parliamentary privilege, which is clearly a constitutional power, is not immune from judicial review. If a parliamentary privilege is exercised in breach of constitutional provisions, redress may be sought by an aggrieved party from law courts ...**[62]

The High Court held that Ms De Lille's suspension constituted an unjustified infringement of her constitutional rights to freedom of speech (section 16), administrative justice (section 33) and access to courts (section 34).[63]

The Supreme Court of Appeal upheld the decision of the Cape High Court, although on slightly narrower grounds.[64] Like Hlophe J, Mahomed CJ reasoned that section 58(1) of the Constitution expressly guarantees freedom of speech in the NA, subject only to its rules and orders. The threat that a member of the NA may be suspended for something said in the NA inhibits freedom of expression in the NA and must therefore adversely affect that guarantee.[65] Although section 58(2) states that other privileges and immunities of the NA may be

57 *De Lille (SCA)* para 8.

58 *De Lille (SCA)* para 9.

59 *De Lille and Another v Speaker of the National Assembly* 1998 (3) SA 430 (C).

60 Act 91 of 1963. This Act has been repealed and replaced with the Powers, Privileges and Immunities of Parliament and Provincial Legislatures Act 4 of 2004.

61 *De Lille (HC)* para 25.

62 *De Lille (HC)* para 33.

63 *De Lille (HC)* paras 37–8.

64 *De Lille SCA*. See also O'Regan, K (2005) Checks and balances: Reflections on the development of the doctrine of separation of powers under the South African Constitution *PER* 8(1):120–50 at 132–3.

65 *De Lille (SCA)* para 20.

prescribed by national legislation,[66] it must not be interpreted to detract from that guarantee of freedom of expression. What section 58(2) does is to authorise national legislation which will itself clearly and specifically articulate the 'privileges and the immunities' of the NA which affect the specific guarantee of free speech for members in the NA. There was furthermore nothing in the 'rules and orders' of the NA which qualified in any relevant way the right to freedom of speech in the NA guaranteed by section 58(1). Further, there is no constitutional authority for the NA to punish any member via suspension in this context.[67] As 'the right of free speech in the Assembly protected by section 58(1) is a fundamental right crucial to representative government in a democratic society ... [i]ts tenor and spirit must conform to all other provisions of the Constitution relevant to the conduct of proceedings in Parliament'.[68] The NA therefore had no constitutional authority to suspend Ms De Lille.[69] The Rules have since been amended to provide the Speaker or Deputy Speaker with the authority to suspend a member for a period of between five and 20 parliamentary working days.[70]

4.2.4 Public involvement in the legislative and other processes of the National Assembly and the National Council of Provinces

As we have seen, the South African Constitution establishes a democratic system of government with both representative and participatory elements. Part of the participatory aspect of democracy is the requirement that the NA and the NCOP should facilitate public involvement in the legislative and other processes of Parliament.[71] Parliament can therefore not pass legislation or engage in other important processes without considering the need to facilitate some form of public participation. Democracy can only function optimally if members of the public are informed about the activities of Parliament and if they are provided with an opportunity to get involved in some way or another in those activities. To this end, Parliament has taken steps to make its bodies and processes more accessible to the public, to build its profile as a key institution of democracy and to mobilise the media to provide information to the public about Parliament.[72]

In the negotiations leading to the establishment of the 1996 Constitution, it was clear that South Africa's democracy would emphasise active participation by the citizenry.[73] The Reconstruction and Development Programme, which was the lynchpin of government policy in the first few years after the advent of democracy, captured this new openness, stating:

> **Democracy for ordinary citizens must not end with formal rights and periodic one-person, one-vote elections. Without undermining the authority and responsibilities of elected representative bodies (Parliament, provincial legislatures, local government) the democratic order we envisage must foster a wide range of institutions of participatory democracy in partnership with civil society on the basis**

66 A similar provision regarding the NCOP can be found in s 71(2).
67 *De Lille (SCA)* para 17.
68 *De Lille (SCA)* para 29.
69 *De Lille (SCA)* para 29–30.
70 NA Rules 52–4.
71 Ss 59(1)(*a*) and 72(1)(*a*) of the Constitution.
72 Houston, G, Liebenberg, I and Dichaba, W 'The social dynamics of public participation in legislative processes in South Africa' in Houston, G (ed) (2001) *Public Participation in Democratic Governance in South Africa* 142.
73 See generally Hassen, E (1998) *The Soul of a Nation: Constitution-Making in South Africa* ch 7 on the inclusive and participatory process involved in the drafting of the 1996 Constitution. The process leading up to the adoption of the 1993 Constitution can hardly be said to have been inclusive and there was little attempt to ensure the participation of the general public in the constitutional negotiations at CODESA. See also Du Plessis, L and Corder, H (1994) *Understanding South Africa's Transitional Bill of Rights*.

> **of informed and empowered citizens and facilitate direct democracy ... social movements and community based organisations are a major asset in the effort to democratize and develop our society.**[74]

Participatory democracy simply means that individuals or institutions must be given an opportunity to take part in the making of decisions that affect them.[75] As such, public participation is a voluntary activity by which members of the public directly or indirectly engage with members of the legislature to provide input to the legislature during the law-making process.[76] The essence of public participation can be distilled by focusing on the various strategies that are the most important measures for public involvement in the legislative process. These include but are not limited to the following:

- Lobbying is used by organised groups in civil society to present well-reasoned arguments to targeted decision makers which may include detailed written representations outlining the group's views on a particular issue.
- Members of the public can raise issues at the constituency offices of their elected representatives, who then raise these issues in the legislature on their behalf.
- Petitions allow individuals or groups to raise issues in a formal way without having to go through a particular member of the legislature.
- Public hearings, which are normally convened by standing committees, afford the public the opportunity to make a written or oral submission on any matter for which a public hearing has been convened.[77]

In several cases[78] the Constitutional Court affirmed the principle that, in certain circumstances, where Parliament failed to take reasonable steps to facilitate public involvement in the law-making process, it would have failed to comply with section 59(1) or section 72(1) of the Constitution respectively,[79] and any law enacted in such a procedurally flawed way would then be null and void and of no effect.[80] The leading case on this point is the 2006 case of *Doctors for Life*.[81] This case dealt with the enactment by Parliament of four health statutes, among others, relating to the choice on termination of pregnancies. The applicants complained that during the legislative process, the NCOP and the provincial legislatures did not comply with their constitutional obligations to facilitate public involvement as required by section 72(1)(*a*) and 118(1)(*a*) respectively. Ngcobo J (for the majority) stated:

> **In the overall scheme of our Constitution, the representative and participatory elements of our democracy should not be seen as being in tension with each other**

74 Report of the Independent Panel Assessment of Parliament (Govender Report) 53 available at http://www.info.gov.za/view/DownloadFileAction?id=94365.

75 See Currie and De Waal (2001) 15 and Roux, T 'Democracy' in Woolman, S and Bishop, M (eds) (2013) *Constitutional Law of South Africa* 2nd ed rev service 5 10.14.

76 Houston et al (2001) 142.

77 Houston et al (2001) 149.

78 *Merafong Demarcation Forum and Others v President of the Republic of South Africa and Others* (CCT 41/07) [2008] ZACC 10; 2008 (5) SA 171 (CC); 2008 (10) BCLR 968 (CC) (13 June 2008); *Matatiele Municipality and Others v President of the Republic of South Africa and Others* (1) (CCT73/05) [2006] ZACC 2; 2006 (5) BCLR 622 (CC); 2006 (5) SA 47 (CC) (27 February 2006); *Matatiele Municipality and Others v President of the Republic of South Africa and Others* (2) (CCT73/05A) [2006] ZACC 12; 2007 (1) BCLR 47 (CC) (18 August 2006).

79 A similar provision in s 118(1)(*a*) of the Constitution deals with the need of provincial legislatures to facilitate public involvement in the law-making process.

80 See *Doctors for Life* para 209 where Ngcobo J for the majority held that '[t]he obligation to facilitate public involvement is a material part of the law-making process. It is a requirement of manner and form. Failure to comply with this obligation renders the resulting legislation invalid'.

81 *Doctors for Life* para 209.

> **as they are mutually supportive. General elections, the foundation of representative democracy, would be meaningless without massive participation by the voters. The participation by the public on a continuous basis provides vitality to the functioning of representative democracy. It encourages citizens of the country to be actively involved in public affairs, identify themselves with the institutions of government and become familiar with the laws as they are made. It enhances the civic dignity of those who participate by enabling their voices to be heard and taken account of. It promotes a spirit of democratic and pluralistic accommodation calculated to produce laws that are likely to be widely accepted and effective in practice. It strengthens the legitimacy of legislation in the eyes of the people. Finally, because of its open and public character it acts as a counterweight to secret lobbying and influence peddling. Participatory democracy is of special importance to those who are relatively disempowered in a country like ours where great disparities of wealth and influence exist.**[82]

The democratic government that is contemplated in the Constitution is thus both representative and participatory as discussed in chapter 2 of this book. It is also one which is accountable, responsive and transparent, and makes provision for the public to participate in the law-making process.[83] 'Our constitutional framework requires the achievement of a balanced relationship between representative and participatory elements in our democracy.'[84] Although 'the legislature will have considerable discretion in determining how best to achieve this balanced relationship',[85] this discretion is not unfettered. What is required will vary from case to case but the test will be whether the legislature had acted *reasonably* or not.[86] The Court stated that 'reasonableness is an objective standard which is sensitive to the facts and circumstances of a particular case'.[87] In other words, it is context specific. The factors that will be used to determine reasonableness are as follows:[88]

- 'The nature and importance of the legislation and the intensity of its impact on the public'.
- What is practically possible, with reference to time and expense, which relate to the efficiency of the law-making process. The Court noted, however, that 'the saving of money and time in itself does not justify inadequate opportunities for public involvement'.
- What Parliament itself considered 'to be appropriate public involvement in the light of the legislation's content, importance and urgency'.

---

82 *Doctors for Life* para 115.

83 *Doctors for Life* para 116 and para 227 where Sachs J (concurring) stated: 'Public involvement in our country has ancient origins and continues to be a strongly creative characteristic of our democracy. We have developed a rich culture of *imbizo, lekgotla, bosberaad,* and *indaba*. Hardly a day goes by without the holding of consultations and public participation involving all "stakeholders", "role-players" and "interested parties", whether in the public sector or the private sphere. The principle of consultation and involvement has become a distinctive part of our national ethos. It is this ethos that informs a well-defined normative constitutional structure in terms of which the present matter falls to be decided.'

84 *Doctors for Life* para 122.

85 *Doctors for Life* para 122.

86 *Doctors for Life* para 125.

87 *Doctors for Life* para 127. See also *Khosa and Others v Minister of Social Development and Others, Mahlaule and Another v Minister of Social Development* (CCT 13/03, CCT 12/03) [2004] ZACC 11; 2004 (6) SA 505 (CC); 2004 (6) BCLR 569 (CC) (4 March 2004) para 49 where the Court stated that '[i]n dealing with the issue of reasonableness, context is all important'.

88 *Doctors for Life* para 128.

This means Parliament has a duty, first, 'to provide meaningful opportunities for public participation in the law-making process' and, second, 'to take measures to ensure that people have the ability to take advantage of the opportunities provided'.[89] Parliament has a positive duty to take practical steps to facilitate public involvement for everyone from all spheres of life regardless of their socio-economic circumstances. 'They must provide notice of and information about the legislation under consideration and the opportunities for participation that are available'[90] to ensure citizens have an opportunity for effective participation in the process.

CRITICAL THINKING

The role of voters in the law-making process

In a minority decision in the *Doctors for Life* case, Yacoob J expressed a different understanding of the nature of the democracy established by the South African Constitution, focusing on the importance of political parties and the role of elected representatives in Parliament.[91] According to this view, MPs represent the people because they are chosen by the people. When MPs make decisions, therefore, they are not making decisions in their own interests but rather in the interests of the people. The decisions made by Parliament are not simply the decisions of the MPs, but rather the decisions of the people:

> In passing legislation or in conducting any other activity, members of provincial legislatures and the National Assembly do not act on their own whims but represent the people of this country. To undermine these representatives is to undermine the political will of the people and to negate their choice at free and fair elections. Provincial representatives on the NCOP are mandated by the provincial legislatures in their capacities as representatives of the people. They are therefore mandated by the people in the same way as the President is elected by the people when the National Assembly elects him. Constitutionally speaking, it is the people of our country who, through their elected representatives pass laws.[92]

Apart from the correctness of the various technical arguments raised by Justice Yacoob in favour of his interpretation of the Constitution, a broader question arises about the role of voters in the law-making process. This question is whether the view taken by Ngcobo J (for the majority) or that of Yacoob J (for the minority) would produce a more effective and more democratically accountable and responsive Parliament. On the one hand, it may be argued that MPs who belong to political parties, especially where the party has a majority that is not immediately threatened, may well be unresponsive to the views of the electorate and may not, in fact, pass laws supported by the electorate. On the other hand, it may be argued that voters have the right to vote for a different party if they disagree with the support of their preferred party for a specific law. Voters only lend their vote to a political party for five years at a time and can always vote for a different party if the MPs representing their former choice disappoint them. In this view, political parties play a pivotal role in our democracy and should not be undermined by placing constitutional obligations on their representatives to consult incessantly with voters between elections.

89 *Doctors for Life* para 129.
90 *Doctors for Life* para 131.
91 *Doctors for Life* para 278.
92 *Doctors for Life* para 292.

4.3 The National Assembly

4.3.1 The composition of the National Assembly

As noted above, the Constitution establishes a bicameral Parliament.[93] In terms of section 42(1) of the Constitution, Parliament consists of two Houses, namely the National Assembly (NA) and the National Council of Provinces (NCOP). The NA consists of between 350 and 400 members elected through an electoral system based on a national common voters roll that is designed to produce, in general, proportional representation.[94] Since the exact size of the NA has to be determined by an Act of Parliament,[95] Schedule 3 of the Electoral Act[96] has fixed this number at 400. Members of the NA are elected on the basis of 'universal adult suffrage, a national common voters roll, regular elections and a multi-party system of democratic government to ensure accountability, responsiveness and openness'.[97]

As we have seen, political parties play an important role in decisions about who serve as legislators in the NA. The manner in which decisions are made about how the millions of votes cast by voters are translated into seats for each political party in the legislature (and the role played by political parties in this process) is closely related to the electoral system adopted in a country. There are various forms of potential electoral systems through which citizens of a country can exercise their right to vote for political representatives.[98] According to Currie and De Waal:

> **[a]n electoral system sets out the rules for electing the political representatives. It consists of a body of rules concerning such matters as the franchise, the method of voting, the frequency of elections, the manner in which the number of votes is translated into the number of representatives [or seats] in the legislature, the qualification and nomination of candidates, and the determination and declaration of the results of an election.**[99]

Members of the NA are elected in terms of a closed list proportional representation electoral system.[100] This system requires each political party before an election to nominate a list of candidates, ranking them in order of preference. Parties submit their lists to the Electoral Commission when they register to take part in the election. Voters vote for a political party and not for individual candidates.[101] A political party will then be allocated the number of seats in the NA equal to the percentage of votes it received in the election. For example, if a party obtained 50% of the votes, it will be allocated 200 of the 400 seats in the NA and the first 200 names on the party's electoral list will become members of the NA. This means that the higher up on a political party's electoral list a person is ranked, the more likely it is that he or she will be elected to the NA.

---

93 S 42(1). See also Devenish, GE (2005) *The South African Constitution* 219 and Currie and De Waal (2001) 133.

94 S 46(1) of the Constitution.

95 S 46(1) and (2) of the Constitution.

96 Act 73 of 1998.

97 S 1(*d*) of the Constitution.

98 See Rautenbach and Malherbe (2009) 126. For a detailed look at electoral systems and choices, see generally Reynolds A (1999) *Electoral Systems and Democratisation in Southern Africa.*

99 Currie and De Waal (2001) 134.

100 For a brief history of why proportional representation was the electoral system of choice, see Klug, H (2010) *The Constitution of South Africa: A Contextual Analysis* 156–8. In particular, Klug notes at 158 that 'the option of proportional representation became a means to avoid the contentious task of immediate demarcation [into respective constituencies] and a way to guarantee the effective participation of small parties, including those with minority ethnic or racially based constituencies'.

101 See Rautenbach and Malherbe (2009) 127.

Decisions on who is ranked where on a political party's electoral list can be made democratically or party leaders can decide on this in an undemocratic manner.[102] Political parties have some discretion in making decisions about internal decision making and processes as political parties 'are best placed to determine how members would participate in internal activities'.[103] The constitution of each political party regulates how such decisions are taken. However, political parties may not adopt constitutions which are inconsistent with section 19 of the Constitution.[104] If the constitution of a political party fails to provide for the free participation of members in its activities, that constitution could be declared invalid.[105] Regardless of how political parties compile their electoral lists, it would be surprising if ambitious members of a political party do not manoeuvre to ensure placement high up on such an electoral list.

The closed list proportional representation electoral system has both advantages and disadvantages.[106] Advantages include the fact that it reflects the wishes of the voters more accurately than most other electoral systems. This is because the percentage of seats allocated to each party is proportional to the percentage of the votes cast for it and there are very few wasted votes.[107] This makes it much easier for smaller parties to be represented in the NA. In the 2009 general election, for example, a party needed to gain 44 092 votes or 0,25% of the total number of votes cast to obtain a seat in the NA. In addition, the proportional representation electoral system also eliminates the possibility of the artificial drawing of boundaries – so-called gerrymandering[108] – to dilute political support in certain constituencies.

Apart from the advantages set out above, closed list proportional representation systems usually produce more inclusive legislatures and ensure a relatively high representation for marginalised or previously discriminated groups such as women as well as for minorities. For example, after the 2009 election, more than 42% of the members of the NA were women, placing South Africa in the top 10 countries in the world as far as the representation of women is concerned.[109] A further advantage is the fact that the system limits 'pork-barrel' politics. Pork-barrel politics is a system of politics in which members of the legislature attempt to buy the support of voters in their constituencies by pressuring the legislature and the executive to spend public money in their constituencies on projects such as clinics,

---

102 For example, the Democratic Alliance (DA) provides for a complex selection process for members who stand for public office through an Electoral College, which is not necessarily a representative body. See Democratic Alliance (2010) Regulations for the Nomination of Candidates available at http://www.da.org.za/about.htm?action=view-page&category=469.

103 *Ramakatsa* para 73.

104 *Ramakatsa* para 74. S 19 of the Constitution states:

> (1) **Every citizen is free to make political choices, which includes the right –**
> > (*a*) **to form a political party;**
> > (*b*) **to participate in the activities of, or recruit members for, a political party; and**
> > (*c*) **to campaign for a political party or cause.**

105 *Ramakatsa* para 74.

106 See generally Norris, P (1997) Choosing electoral systems: Proportional, majoritarian and mixed systems *International Political Science Review* 18(3):297–312 at 302–4.

107 To gain a seat in the NA, a party has to obtain a minimum number of votes. The minimum number of votes per seat is determined by dividing the total number of votes cast by the number of seats plus one. The result plus one, disregarding fractions, then becomes the minimum number of votes per seat. In the 2009 elections, the minimum numbers of votes per seat was 44 092 votes (0,25%). An important consequence of the fact that a party had to obtain a minimum number of votes is that the votes cast for any party that does not obtain this minimum will be 'wasted'. The wastage, however, is far less than in a constituency-based system.

108 On the dangers of gerrymandering, see generally Issacharoff, S (2002) Gerrymandering and political cartels *Harvard Law Review* 116(2):593–648 at 593.

109 See the data compiled by the Inter-Parliamentary Union (2013) Women in national parliaments available at http://www.ipu.org/wmn-e/classif.htm.

roads, schools and so on irrespective of whether their constituents actually need these goods and services or not. In a closed list proportional representation system, the members of the legislature do not have constituencies and, consequently, will be less tempted to engage in pork-barrel politics. Finally, the system is also said to be simple and easy to administer.

Table 4.1 Representation of women in the NA[110]

Election year	Total seats	Women's seats	% women
2009	400	172	43
2004	400	131	32,75
1999	400	120	30
1994	400	111	27,74

However, there are also major disadvantages associated with the system:

- First, a closed list proportional representation electoral system does not create a strong link between voters and their elected representatives. This has the potential to lead to a lack of responsiveness to the concerns of voters by elected MPs. In this system the political party as a whole rather than individual MPs has to account to voters at the next election. Individual MPs do not lose their seats because of the anger of voters but because they have lost the support of the leaders of the political party they serve.[111]
- Second, the closed list proportional representation system potentially gives much power to the leaders of a party who may be able to determine who appears on electoral lists and where on those lists they are ranked. This means that the leaders of political parties may have disproportionate influence over the way in which individual MPs behave.
- Third, the system potentially produces a less effective and stable government, especially where one political party is not dominant. This is because a single party may not gain an overall majority in Parliament and will then have to form a **coalition government** with other parties. A coalition government may find it difficult to agree on all aspects of a joint programme of action.[112]

PAUSE FOR REFLECTION

The closed list proportional representation system versus the first-past-the-post system

The closed list proportional representation system that operates in South Africa in relation to the election of NA members is often contrasted with the first-past-the-post system, also known as the winner-take-all system or the plurality system.[113] This latter system is followed in the United Kingdom, the USA and was followed in South Africa

110 Hendricks, C 'Party strategy not popular prejudice: Electoral politics in South Africa' in Piper, L (ed) (2005) *South Africa's 2004 Election: The Quest for Democratic Consolidation, EISA Research Report No 12*, 66 at 82; Lowe Morna, C, Rama, K and Mtonga, L (2009, 15 July) Gender in the 2009 South African elections, Gender links for equality and justice, available at http://www.genderlinks.org.za/article/gender-in-the-2009-south-african-elections-2009-07-15.

111 De Vos, P 'South Africa's experience with proportional representation' in De Ville, J and Steytler, N (1996) *Voting in 1999: Choosing an Electoral System* 29–43.

112 Norris (1997) 306. See generally Matlosa, K (2004) Electoral systems, constitutionalism and conflict management in Southern Africa *African Journal on Conflict Resolution* 4(2):11–53 at 34.

113 See Currie and De Waal (2001) 134.

prior to 1994 during the colonial and apartheid eras. The aim of the system is to create a 'manufactured majority', that is, to exaggerate the share of seats for the leading party in order to produce an effective working parliamentary majority for the government. It simultaneously penalises minor parties, especially those whose support is spread out across the country and not concentrated in a specific area.

In the first-past-the-post system, the country is divided into geographical single-member constituencies.[114] Voters in each constituency cast a single ballot for the candidate of their choice. The candidate with the largest share of the vote in each constituency is returned to Parliament. All the other candidates of all the other political parties standing in that constituency are not elected, leading to the 'wasting' of all the votes cast for the non-winning candidates.[115]

The party with an overall majority of seats in the legislature forms the government. In this winner-takes-all model, the leading party receives a disproportionate number of seats in the legislature, often gaining large majorities even where far less than 50% of voters voted for that party. Smaller parties get meagre rewards. The focus is on effective governance, not representation of all minority views.[116]

For example, in constituencies where the vote splits almost equally three ways, the winning candidate may have only 35% of the vote, while the other contestants get 34% and 31% respectively. In such an election, 64% of the votes cast in that constituency would have been 'wasted'. Although two-thirds of voters supported other candidates, the plurality of votes is decisive. This makes this system less fair than the proportional representation system. Another potential problem with this system is the danger that the artificial drawing of constituency boundaries would lead to gerrymandering, or dilution or imbalance of political power or support in constituencies.[117]

However, because an individual may be voted into the legislature only because he or she is more popular than the party he or she represents, there is an incentive for individual members of the legislature to be responsive to the needs of voters in their constituency. They are thus - in theory at least - more accountable to voters than to the leadership of the political party they represent. Voters will be more likely to know the member of the legislature representing them and will be able to approach that person with their problems and concerns.

It is often contended that South Africa should change from the closed list proportional representation system and use the first-past-the-post system. Others argue that South Africa should move to a system that mixes the first-past-the-post and the proportional representation system. This could be done by allocating a large number of seats in the NA - say 300 of the 400 - based on a first-past-the-post model. The remaining 100 seats could be allocated from party lists to 'top up' the NA membership to achieve proportional representation of political parties in Parliament based on the percentage of votes received by each party. This, it is argued, will ensure a closer link between members of the NA and the voters they represent. It will also weaken the power of party

114 Currie and De Waal (2001) 134.
115 Currie and De Waal (2001) 134.
116 Matlosa (2004) 27.
117 Matlosa (2004) 27. See also Currie and De Waal (2001) 135. Gerrymandering is a practice that attempts to establish a political advantage for a particular party or group by manipulating geographical boundaries to create partisan or incumbent-protected districts. See *Britannica Academic Edition* available at http://www.britannica.com/EBchecked/topic/231865/gerrymandering.

leaders over individual MPs who will become more independent. However, it is unclear whether this will be the case in South Africa, especially if political party leaders retain the power to decide who would represent the party in an individual constituency. Because of the current dominance of one political party and because of the concentration of support for the main opposition party in certain geographical areas, most MPs elected in constituencies would have 'safe' seats and may well pay more attention to keeping the leaders of their political party happy than attending to the concerns of voters.[118]

Section 19(3) of the Constitution guarantees the right of every citizen to vote. Children are not allowed to vote and in terms of the Constitution only citizens who are above the age of 18 years qualify to vote.[119] In giving effect to the essence of the right to vote, the Constitution established the Electoral Commission (also colloquially called the *Independent* Electoral Commission) in terms of section 181(1)(*f*). The Commission is responsible for managing 'elections of national, provincial and municipal legislative bodies in accordance with national legislation', must 'ensure that those elections are free and fair', and must, in as a short a time as is reasonably possible, 'declare the results of those elections within a period that must be prescribed by national legislation'.[120]

The independence of the Electoral Commission is explicitly guaranteed in the Constitution.[121] The Constitutional Court pointed out in *Independent Electoral Commission v Langeberg Municipality*[122] that although the Electoral Commission is an organ of state as defined in section 239 of the Constitution, the requirement that it be independent from the government means that it cannot be said to be a department or an administration within the national sphere of government over which Cabinet exercises authority. The Electoral Commission – while a state institution – is not part of the government as independence of the institution refers to independence *from* the government.[123]

The independence of the Electoral Commission requires, first, financial independence. As the Constitutional Court stated in *New National Party v Government of the Republic of South Africa and Others*, 'This implies the ability to have access to funds reasonably required to enable the Commission to discharge the functions it is obliged to perform under the Constitution and the Electoral Commission Act.'[124] This requires Parliament to consider what is reasonably required by the Commission and deal with requests for funding rationally in the light of other national interests. Second, the Commission needs to enjoy administrative independence. This implies that there will be no control over those matters directly connected with the functions which the Commission has to perform under the Constitution and the Electoral Act. This means that the Department of Home Affairs cannot tell the Commission how to conduct registration and whom to employ. In short, the Commission cannot be part of the national government in any manner.[125]

118 See De Vos, P (2012, 14 August) Towards a parliament for the people *Constitutionally Speaking* available at http://constitutionallyspeaking.co.za/towards-a-parliament-for-the-people/.

119 See s 46(1)(*c*).

120 S 190(1)(*a*)-(*c*) of the Constitution. See also the relevant provisions of the Electoral Act 73 of 1998 and the Local Government: Municipal Electoral Act 27 of 2000.

121 S 181(2).

122 (CCT 49/00) [2001] ZACC 23; 2001 (3) SA 925 (CC); 2001 (9) BCLR 883 (CC) (7 June 2001).

123 *Langeberg Municipality* para 27.

124 (CCT9/99) [1999] ZACC 5; 1999 (3) SA 191; 1999 (5) BCLR 489 (13 April 1999) para 98.

125 *New National Party* paras 99–100.

In *August and Another v Electoral Commission and Others*,[126] the Constitutional Court pointed out that the right to vote in section 19(2) of the Constitution is unqualified. It therefore cannot be taken away from any citizen arbitrarily or in a way that is not reasonable and justifiable in an open and democratic society.[127] Sachs J declared that the vote of each and every citizen is a 'badge of dignity and personhood. Quite literally, it says that everybody counts'.[128] The Court held that the right to vote 'by its very nature imposes positive obligations upon the legislature and the executive... [and] ... [t]his clearly imposes an affirmative obligation on the Commission to take reasonable steps to ensure that eligible voters are registered'.[129] In the *August* case, the Court held that by omitting to take appropriate steps to ensure that prisoners were able to register and vote in the national election, the Commission had failed to comply with its obligations. The importance of the right to vote was reaffirmed in *New National Party* where Yacoob J stressed that the right to vote is fundamental to democracy and requires proper arrangements to be made for its effective exercise.[130]

CRITICAL THINKING

Limitations on the constitutional right to vote

As a result of the judgment in *August*, and shortly prior to the 2004 national elections, Parliament amended the Electoral Act. As a result of these amendments, prisoners who were serving a sentence of imprisonment without the option of a fine were prevented from registering as voters and from voting while in prison.[131] In other words, they were effectively disenfranchised.

The constitutionality of this amendment was questioned in *Minister of Home Affairs v National Institute for Crime Prevention and the Re-integration of Offenders (NICRO) and Others*.[132] The main issue in this case was whether the amendments to the Electoral Act constituted a justifiable limitation of the right to vote in terms of section 36 of the Constitution. Government argued that its rationale for the limitation of the right was to preserve the integrity of the voting process.[133] It was argued that voting at a polling station entailed the use of mobile voting facilities or special votes, both of which involved risks to the integrity of the vote and required special measures to counter these risks. The provision of these special arrangements, it was argued, placed a strain on the logistical and financial resources available to the Electoral Commission.[134] However,

---

126 (CCT8/99) [1999] ZACC 3; 1999 (3) SA 1; 1999 (4) BCLR 363 (1 April 1999).

127 *August* paras 3 and 20.

128 *August* para 17.

129 *August* para 16.

130 *New National Party* para 11.

131 The changes brought about by the amendment included ss 8(2)(*f*), and 24B(1) and (2) which read as follows:

> **8(2) The chief electoral officer may not register a person as a voter if that person–**
>
> ...
>
> **(f) is serving a sentence of imprisonment without the option of a fine.**
>
> ...
>
> **24B(1) In an election for the National Assembly or a provincial legislature, a person who on election day is in prison and not serving a sentence of imprisonment without the option of a fine and whose name appears on the voters' roll for another voting district, is deemed for that election day to have been registered by his or her name having been entered on the voters' roll for the voting district in which he or she is in prison.**
>
> **24B(2) A person who is in prison on election day may only vote if he or she is not serving a sentence of imprisonment without the option of a fine.**

132 (CCT 03/04) [2004] ZACC 10; 2005 (3) SA 280 (CC); 2004 (5) BCLR 445 (CC) (3 March 2004).

133 *NICRO* paras 39–46.

134 *NICRO* paras 39–46.

the Constitutional Court disposed of the logistics and costs leg of this argument on the basis that the state had failed to discharge its evidentiary burden in this regard.[135] In this regard, the Court indicated that:

> [i]n the present case, however, it is not necessary to take this issue further for the factual basis for the justification based on cost and the lack of resources has not been established. Arrangements for registering voters were made at all prisons to accommodate unsentenced prisoners and those serving sentences because they had not paid the fines imposed on them. Mobile voting stations are to be provided on election day for these prisoners to vote. There is nothing to suggest that expanding these arrangements to include prisoners sentenced without the option of a fine will in fact place an undue burden on the resources of the Commission. Apart from asserting that it would be costly to do so, no information as to the logistical problems or estimates of the costs involved were provided by Mr Gilder. The Commission abided by the decision of the Court. It lodged affidavits to explain its attitude to the Court, and was represented by counsel at the hearing. It did not place any information before the Court in regard to costs and logistics and did not suggest that it would be unable to make the arrangements necessary to enable all prisoners to vote.[136]

This judgment affirmed that while there may conceivably be situations in which a person could be deprived of his or her right to vote, such a limitation on the right to vote would have to be justified by the state. The state would have to show that the limitation was narrowly tailored to achieve an important purpose.

The Constitutional Court also considered whether South Africans living abroad have a right to vote. This was considered in *Richter v The Minister for Home Affairs and Others*[137] and *AParty and Another v The Minister for Home Affairs and Others, Moloko and Others v The Minister for Home Affairs and Another.*[138] The Court decided unanimously that South Africans living abroad have a right to vote if they are registered. The Court held that section 33 of the Electoral Act unfairly restricted the right to cast special votes while abroad to a very narrow class of citizens. This section was therefore declared unconstitutional and invalid.

The implication of this judgment for the elections which were to be held in April 2009 was that all citizens who were at that time registered voters, and who would be out of the country on the date of the elections, would be allowed to vote in the national, but not provincial, elections. This was 'provided they give notice of their intention to do so, in terms of the Election Regulations, on or before 27 March 2009 to the Chief Electoral Officer and identify the embassy, high commission or consulate where they intend to apply for the special vote'.[139]

Handing down the first of two separate judgments, O'Regan J held that the right to vote had a symbolic and democratic value and those who were registered should not be limited

135 *NICRO* paras 47–51.

136 *NICRO* para 49.

137 (CCT03/09, CCT 09/09) [2009] ZACC 3; 2009 (3) SA 615 (CC); 2009 (5) BCLR 448 (CC) (12 March 2009).

138 (CCT 06/09, CCT 10/09) [2009] ZACC 4; 2009 (3) SA 649 (CC); 2009 (6) BCLR 611 (CC) (12 March 2009).

139 *Richter* para 108.

by unconstitutional and invalid limitations in the Electoral Act.[140] However, a second judgment by Ngcobo J found that unregistered voters who were overseas could not vote.[141] This was due to the fact that the limitations of the right to vote of South Africans living abroad, who did not fall within certain categories, had been in effect since 2003 and the applicants had not explained why they had challenged these limitations so late. According to Ngcobo J:

> **... the applicants are the authors of their own misfortune; they created the urgency. The registration provisions of the Electoral Act have been in place since 2003. Voting by South African voters abroad in the 2004 elections was regulated by the amendment which was introduced in 2003. The applicants have known since then that they cannot vote. Their explanation for not approaching a court much earlier is utterly unsatisfactory.**[142]

The cases discussed above are an indication of the values of the new dispensation in ensuring the role of the electorate in relation to the corresponding responsibility of the state to create an environment that is conducive for everyone to ensure the advancement of the ideals of the new democratic order.

4.3.2 Eligibility for election to the National Assembly

Once elected, a member of the NA will normally serve for a full term of five years until the next election.[143] However, a person may lose membership of the NA if that person is no longer eligible to be a member of the NA. In terms of section 47 of the Constitution, a citizen who is qualified to vote for the NA is eligible to be a member of the NA, except for those citizens who are appointed by, or are in the service of, the state and receive remuneration for that appointment or service, other than:

- the President, Deputy President, Ministers and Deputy Ministers
- other office-bearers whose functions are compatible with the functions of a member of the NA and have been declared compatible with those functions by national legislation.

The following people are also not eligible to become or remain members of the NA:

- permanent delegates to the NCOP or members of a provincial legislature or a municipal council[144]
- unrehabilitated insolvents[145]
- anyone declared to be of unsound mind by a court of the Republic[146]
- anyone who, after the Constitution took effect, is convicted of an offence and sentenced to more than 12 months' imprisonment without the option of a fine, either in the Republic, or outside the Republic if the conduct constituting the offence would have been an offence in the Republic.[147]

---

140 *Richter* paras 52–4.
141 *AParty* paras 56–8.
142 *AParty* para 59.
143 S 49(1) of the Constitution.
144 S 47(1)(*b*) of the Constitution.
145 S 47(1)(*c*) of the Constitution.
146 S 47(1)(*d*) of the Constitution.
147 S 47(1)(*e*) of the Constitution.

Moreover, a member of the NA who is absent from the NA without permission in contravention of the rules of the NA (presumably more than 15 days),[148] or ceases to be a member of the party that nominated him or her,[149] will also automatically lose his or her seat in the NA.

4.3.3 Duration of the National Assembly, sittings and its dissolution

The NA is elected for a term of five years.[150] It will usually serve out this five-year term, but there are at least two situations in which an election could be held before the five-year term has elapsed:

- First, in terms of section 50(1) of the Constitution, the President 'must dissolve the NA if the Assembly has adopted a resolution to dissolve with a supporting vote of a majority of its members; and three years have passed since the Assembly was elected'. If this is done, 'the President, by proclamation, must call and set dates for an election, which must be held within 90 days of the date the Assembly was dissolved'.[151] This means that a majority party in Parliament may strategically adopt such a resolution to force a new national election to be held (without having to impose a **vote of no confidence** in the government) in the last two years of the life of the NA. They may wish to do so to ensure a political advantage for their party by timing the election to fall around a time when the party is particularly popular, say, after the national soccer team has won the African Cup of Nations tournament or after the successful staging of the Soccer World Cup.
- Second, in terms of section 50(2), where there is a vacancy in the Office of President because the President passed away, resigned or was removed from office by the NA in terms of section 89 or 102, and the NA then fails to elect a new President within 30 days after the vacancy occurred, the Acting President must dissolve the NA and new election must be called within 90 days.[152] This will occur in cases where no one party commands a majority of seats in the NA, the coalition of parties disintegrates and the parties cannot agree on forming a new coalition. Where one party commands more than 50% of the seats in the NA, it will be able to enforce party discipline to ensure that the majority party elects a new President before the 30-day period stipulated by the Constitution elapses.

After an election, the first sitting of the NA must take place not more than 14 days after the election results are finalised on a date determined by the Chief Justice.[153] The President will be elected from among the members elected to the NA at this sitting.[154] At the same sitting, the NA will also elect a Speaker and a Deputy Speaker from among its members.[155] The NA may otherwise determine the time and duration of its other sittings and its recess periods.[156] An exception is that the President may summons the NA to an extraordinary sitting at any

148 S 47(3)(*b*) of the Constitution read with NA Rule 20 which states: 'A member who wishes to absent himself or herself from sittings of this House, or of any other Parliamentary forum of which he or she is a member, for 15 or more consecutive days on which this House or such forum sits, shall, before so absenting himself or herself, obtain the leave of this House or of a committee of this House authorised to grant such leave.' A note states that this rule will have to be adapted in accordance with s 47(3)(*b*) of the Constitution, but this has not yet been done, leaving doubt about what consequences will follow if a person is absent for longer than 15 days without permission.

149 See s 47(3)(*c*) of the Constitution as amended by s 2 of the Constitution Fifteenth Amendment Act of 2008.

150 S 49(1) of the Constitution.

151 S 49(2) of the Constitution.

152 S 50(2) read with s 49(2) of the Constitution.

153 S 51(1) of the Constitution.

154 S 86(1) and (2) of the Constitution read with NA Rule 8.

155 S 52 of the Constitution read with NA Rules 9 and 13.

156 S 51(1) of the Constitution.

time to conduct special business.[157] Sittings of the NA are permitted at places other than the seat of Parliament, which is currently in Cape Town, only 'on the grounds of public interest, security or convenience, and if provided for in the rules and orders of the Assembly'.[158] NA Rule 24 requires the Speaker to consult the Leader of the Assembly and the Chief Whip of each party represented in the NA before directing that the Assembly sit somewhere other than in Cape Town.[159]

4.3.4 Powers and functioning of the National Assembly

The NA – unlike the NCOP representing the interests of separate provinces – is elected to represent the people of South Africa as a whole. According to section 42(3) of the Constitution, the NA has four main tasks:

- The NA elects the President.
- It serves as a national forum for public consideration of issues.
- It considers and passes legislation (along with the NCOP).
- It scrutinises and oversees executive action, holding the executive accountable.

In exercising its legislative power, the NA may consider, pass, amend or reject any legislation before the Assembly, and initiate or prepare legislation, except money Bills.[160] The NA must provide for mechanisms to ensure that all executive organs of state in the national sphere of government are accountable to it. The NA must also maintain oversight of the exercise of national executive authority, including the implementation of legislation, and any organ of state.[161] We shall return to the exercise of these powers below.[162]

Unless the Constitution specifically requires otherwise, section 59 of the Constitution controls quorum requirements for when the NA takes decisions. It distinguishes between Bills or amendments to Bills and 'any other question[s]' which may come before the NA for a vote. The NA may proceed with its business irrespective of the number of members present.[163] However, when the NA takes a vote on a Bill (that is, a piece of draft legislation), a majority of the members (at least 201 members) of the NA must be present.[164] At least one-third of the members (134 members) must be present before a vote may be taken on any other question before the NA.[165] If there is no prescribed quorum when a question is put for decision and if after an interval of five minutes, during which time the bells must be rung, there is still no quorum, the presiding officer (the Speaker or Deputy Speaker) may suspend the proceedings or postpone the decision of the question.[166]

157 S 51(2) of the Constitution.

158 S 51(3) of the Constitution. Sittings and recesses of the NA are covered generally in Ch 4 of the NA Rules.

159 NA Rule 24 states: 'Before directing under section 51(3) of the Constitution that this House shall sit at a place other than the Houses of Parliament in Cape Town, the Speaker shall consult the Leader of the House and the Chief Whip of each party represented in this House.'

160 In modern parliamentary systems, however, 'legislatures have limited responsibility for making laws. Instead, laws are usually prepared and drafted by the executive and presented to the legislature for approval. This inevitably means that relatively few laws will emanate from the legislature itself.' This is true of South Africa. See Nijzink, L and Murray, C (2002) *Building Representative Democracy: South Africa's Legislatures and the Constitution* 73. See also Klug (2010) 169.

161 S 55 of the Constitution.

162 See 4.5 below.

163 NA Rule 25(1).

164 S 53(1)(*a*) of the Constitution read with NA Rule 25(2)(*a*).

165 S 53(1)(*b*) of the Constitution read with NA Rule 25(2)(*b*).

166 NA Rule 26.

Most questions before the NA are determined 'by a majority of the votes cast' by the members present.[167] In certain circumstances, however, the quorum and voting requirements are set at a higher threshold. For example, the NA can only remove the President from office (impeachment) or amend provisions of the Constitution (other than section 1) with a 'supporting vote of at least two-thirds of its members'.[168] An amendment to section 1 of the Constitution requires a 'supporting vote of at least 75 per cent' of the members of the NA.[169]

The member of the NA presiding at a meeting of the NA, usually the Speaker or Deputy Speaker, has no deliberative vote, but is required to cast a deciding vote 'when there is an equal number of votes on each side of a question'.[170] The presiding member may cast a deliberative vote when a matter requiring a two-thirds majority to pass is before the NA.[171] Under section 54 of the Constitution, '[t]he President, and any member of the Cabinet or any Deputy Minister who is not a member of the National Assembly, may, subject to the rules and orders of the Assembly, attend and speak in the Assembly, but may not vote'.[172] The Constitution further requires the NA to provide for 'mechanisms to ensure that all executive organs of state in the national sphere of government are accountable to it; and to maintain oversight of the exercise of national executive authority, including the implementation of legislation; and any organ of state'.[173]

As far as the practical functioning of the NA is concerned, three important issues arise:

- First, under section 57(1)(*a*) and (*b*) of the Constitution, the NA 'may determine and control its internal arrangements, proceedings and procedures; and may make rules and orders concerning its business, with due regard to representative and participatory democracy, accountability, transparency and public involvement'. These powers of the NA are limited in the ways discussed above.
- Second, the Speaker or, in his or her absence, the Deputy Speaker, presides over the NA. The primary public role of the Speaker is to preside over debates in the NA. The Speaker is expected to be above party politics and to fulfil his or her role impartially, demonstrating the kind of impartiality expected of a judge.[174] The Speaker is required to keep discipline in the NA and must rule on any objections lodged by members against the conduct of other members. The Speaker is also (jointly with the Chair of the NCOP) the administrative head of Parliament. As the custodian of the rights and privileges of its members, the Speaker furthermore acts as the representative and spokesperson for the legislature and has the power to give an undertaking on behalf of the NA.[175]
- Third, members of the NA take part in public meetings of the NA where they may ask questions of members of the Cabinet. The NA also provides a platform for the President, members of Cabinet, party leaders and MPs to make speeches. In addition, it is an arena where the political parties debate the issues of the day. Finally, of course, members of the NA vote formally to pass legislation. However, most of the serious work of the NA is done in committees.

167 S 53(1)(*c*) of the Constitution.
168 Ss 74(2)(*a*) and 89(1) of the Constitution.
169 S 74(1)(*a*) of the Constitution.
170 S 53(2)(*a*) of the Constitution.
171 S 53(2)(*b*) of the Constitution.
172 This is confirmed by NA Rule 89(2).
173 S 55(2).
174 Currie and De Waal (2001) 142. See also *Gauteng Provincial Legislature v Killian and 29 Others* [562/98] [2000] ZASCA 75; 2001 (2) SA 68 (SCA); [2001] 1 All SA 463 (A) (29 Nov 2000) para 30.
175 See *Killian* para 26.

The establishment of committees is contemplated in section 57(2)(*a*) and (*b*) of the Constitution and their number, jurisdiction, membership and other details are fleshed out in the Rules of the Assembly.[176] The most important committees – the respective **portfolio committees** – are those set up to process legislation emanating from each Cabinet portfolio and to oversee the work done by the executive in each of these portfolios.[177] Section 57(2)(*b*) of the Constitution requires that the Rules of the Assembly provide for 'the participation in the proceedings of the Assembly and its committees of minority parties represented in the Assembly, in a manner consistent with democracy'. The Constitutional Court has not yet given clear guidance on what this might entail. However, a practice has developed in the NA that political parties are entitled to be represented in committees in substantially the same proportion as the proportion in which they are represented in the NA.[178] The majority party in the NA will therefore usually have a majority on each of the committees and will be able to outvote minority parties if disagreements arise about the handling of a particular matter or support for specific legislative provisions.

Political parties appoint the members of a committee to which they are entitled and advise the Speaker accordingly.[179] A committee must elect one of its members as the chairperson of the committee. With the exception of the Committee on Public Accounts, which has traditionally been chaired by a member of one of the opposition parties, the chairperson will be a member of the majority party earmarked for the position by the party leadership in the NA. The chairperson of a committee can also be removed as chairperson if the party to which he or she belongs deems it fit to do so. Members of a committee representing a specific political party can also be removed or changed by the political party that nominated the member. This means that the leadership of a political party has considerable influence over individual members of their party in the NA. Serving on some committees is deemed to be more desirable than serving on others. As the chairperson of a committee holds considerable power to arrange the affairs of a committee, members may act in a manner that would not detract from their chances of being allocated to desirable committees or – in the case of a majority party – being appointed as chairperson of a committee. As we shall see, committees of the NA have wide-ranging powers to assist them in fulfilling their various tasks, including the power to summons any person to appear before them.

4.4 The National Council of Provinces

4.4.1 The composition and functioning of the National Council of Provinces

The National Council of Provinces (NCOP) is the second chamber of the bicameral national Parliament. It was created to represent the provinces and 'to ensure that provincial interests are taken into account in the national sphere of government. It does this mainly by participating in the national legislative process and by providing a national forum for public consideration of issues affecting the provinces'.[180] Note that the NCOP should **not** be confused with the nine provincial legislatures that pass legislation for each province in the

176 See NA Rules Ch 12.
177 NA Rule 121.
178 NA Rule 125.
179 NA Rule 126.
180 S 42(4) of the Constitution.

functional areas exclusively or concurrently reserved for the provinces (see chapter 8).[181] The NCOP is the second chamber in the **national** Parliament, and thus **not** one of the provincial legislatures although it retains links with the respective provincial legislatures because of the way it is composed and operates. Naledi Pandor, then Chairperson of the NCOP, described the NCOP thus:

> **The NCOP acts at the national level of government in South Africa. It represents provincial and local government. It functions as a bridge between these three spheres of government. The NCOP is a linking mechanism that acts simultaneously to involve the provinces in national purposes and to ensure the responsiveness of national government to provincial interests. Through the NCOP, national government is sensitised to provincial interests and its processes are enriched accordingly. Equally, by engaging the provinces and provincial legislatures in the formulation of national policy, it avoids their becoming parochial.**[182]

In *Doctors for Life* the Constitutional Court stated:

> **The NCOP performs functions similar to the National Assembly but from the distinct vantage point of the provinces. Its role is both unique and fundamental to the basic structure of the government as it reflects one of the fundamental premises of the South African government, which sees national, provincial and local governments as 'spheres within a single whole', which are distinctive yet interdependent and interrelated. The NCOP ensures that national government is responsive to provincial interests while simultaneously engaging the provinces and provincial legislatures in the consideration of national policy. From this perspective, the NCOP plays a pivotal role 'as a linking mechanism that acts simultaneously to involve the provinces in national purposes and to ensure the responsiveness of national government to provincial interests'.**[183]

The NCOP is carefully designed as a key institution for ensuring co-operative government in law making and in overseeing the executive intergovernmental process. It plays a role both in the passage of national laws (both laws dealing with 'national' issues and laws that fall under the list of concurrent functions) and in overseeing the use of the extensive intervention powers vested in the national government and provinces.[184] As Murray and Simeon point out:

> **The NCOP is the quintessential institution of co-operative government, providing a forum for the representation of provincial interests in the national Parliament. Its role is to ensure that the institutional integrity and policy concerns of provinces are fully taken into account in the national legislative process. As a part of the national Parliament and as an (indirectly) elected body, it is designed to operate as an intergovernmental institution without the 'democratic deficit' which so often is part of intergovernmental relations.**[185]

181 S 104 of the Constitution.

182 Extract from a presentation at the Meeting of the World's Senates, 14 March 2000, Paris, cited in Nijzink and Murray (2002) 41.

183 *Doctors for Life* para 79. See generally Murray, C and Simeon, R (1999) From paper to practice: The National Council of Provinces after its first year *SA Public Law* 14(1):96–141 at 98–101 for a discussion on the role of the NCOP.

184 Murray, C and Simeon, R (2006) Tagging Bills in Parliament: Section 75 or section 76? *SALJ* 123(2):232–63 at 236.

185 Murray and Simeon (2006) 236.

PAUSE FOR REFLECTION

The NCOP resembles the German *Bundesrat*

In *Doctors for Life*, the Constitutional Court noted that the NCOP shares many of its structural characteristics with the German body known as the *Bundesrat* or Council of State Governments on which the NCOP was modelled.[186] Like the NCOP, the *Bundesrat* represents the interests of the *Länder* (the states) which, in the South African context, are equivalent to the nine provincial governments. The NA is similar to the second parliamentary body in Germany known as the *Bundestag* as the NA is elected to represent the interests of all the people of South Africa, not merely the interests of the citizens of an individual province. The members of the *Bundesrat* are members of the state governments and are appointed and subject to recall by the states - just like the members of the NCOP. They serve in the council as representatives of the *Länder*. Germany's Basic Law or Constitution[187] provides that the *Länder* shall participate, through the *Bundesrat*, in the national legislative process.[188] 'As constitutional partners, both the *Bund* or national government and the *Länder* have an obligation to consult, cooperate and communicate with each other, consistent with the principle of *Bundestreue*'[189] - this is how the Federal Constitutional Court of Germany[190] explained the constitutional obligation of trust and friendship that the *Bund* (national government) and the *Länder* (states) have towards each other.[191]

The NCOP consists of 90 members made up from delegations of 10 members from each of the nine provinces.[192] The nine provincial legislatures appoint the nine provincial delegations, one for each province. The individual delegation slots are allocated proportionally to the various parties in each provincial legislature in accordance with the relative strength of parties in each of the respective legislatures.[193] For example, if the ANC received 60% of the seats in the Gauteng legislature and the Democratic Alliance (DA) 30%, then the ANC would be entitled to six and the DA to three of the 10 delegates representing Gauteng in the NCOP.

186 *Doctors for Life* para 80. See also *Certification of the Constitution of the Republic of South Africa, 1996* (CCT 23/96) [1996] ZACC 26; 1996 (4) SA 744 (CC); 1996 (10) BCLR 1253 (CC) (6 September 1996) para 227; Malherbe, EFJ (1998) The South African National Council of Provinces: Trojan horse or white elephant? *TSAR* 1:77–96 at 82; Venter, F (2000) *Constitutional Comparison: Japan, Germany, Canada and South Africa as Constitutional States* 248.

187 Germany's Basic Law was drafted in 1949 and the drafters refrained from using the term 'constitution' because the Basic Law was drafted to govern a part of Germany for a transitional period that would last until reunification. On reunification, the Basic Law would cease to exist and a constitution for all German people would be adopted. On 3 October 1990, German unity was achieved within the framework of the Basic Law. The Basic Law is now thought of as an all-German Constitution despite the fact that it continues to go by the name of Basic Law and has come to 'assume the character of a document framed to last in perpetuity'. See Kommers, DP (1997) *The Constitutional Jurisprudence of the Federal Republic of Germany* 30 and Kommers, DP 'The Basic Law of the Federal Republic of Germany: An assessment after forty years' in Merkel, PH (ed) (1989) *The Federal Republic of Germany at Forty* 133 referring to the Basic Law as having taken on 'the status of a genuine Constitution'.

188 Art 50 of the Basic Law for the Federal Republic of Germany provides: 'The *Länder* participates through the *Bundesrat* in the legislation and administration of the Federation.'

189 *Doctors for Life* para 80 fn 61.

190 BVerfGE 1, 300.

191 See also De Villiers, B (1994) Intergovernmental relations: The duty to co-operate - A German perspective *SA Public Law* 9(1–2):430–7 at 432–3.

192 S 60 of the Constitution.

193 Each province is represented by a single delegation appointed in terms of a formula prescribed by the Determination of Delegates (National Council of Provinces) Act 69 of 1998 with the aim of ensuring the inclusion of all parties represented in a provincial legislature on the basis of proportional representation.

In addition, the members of each provincial delegation are classified as either special or permanent delegates.[194] There are four special delegates and six permanent delegates in each provincial delegation.[195] The four special delegates are composed of the Premier of a province together with three other delegates selected from among the members of that provincial legislature.[196] If the Premier is not available, he or she may delegate someone else to represent him or her.[197] The Premier or his or her delegate heads the delegation.[198] These four special delegates remain members of the provincial legislature: they are simultaneously members of the provincial Parliament and members of the national Parliament acting as special delegates to the NCOP. They are not appointed for a fixed term and the provincial legislature can change the composition of its special delegates 'from time to time'.[199] This means that a provincial legislature can send different members to the NCOP as special delegates to deal with different issues, for example on the basis that a delegate has special knowledge of a matter being considered by the NCOP.

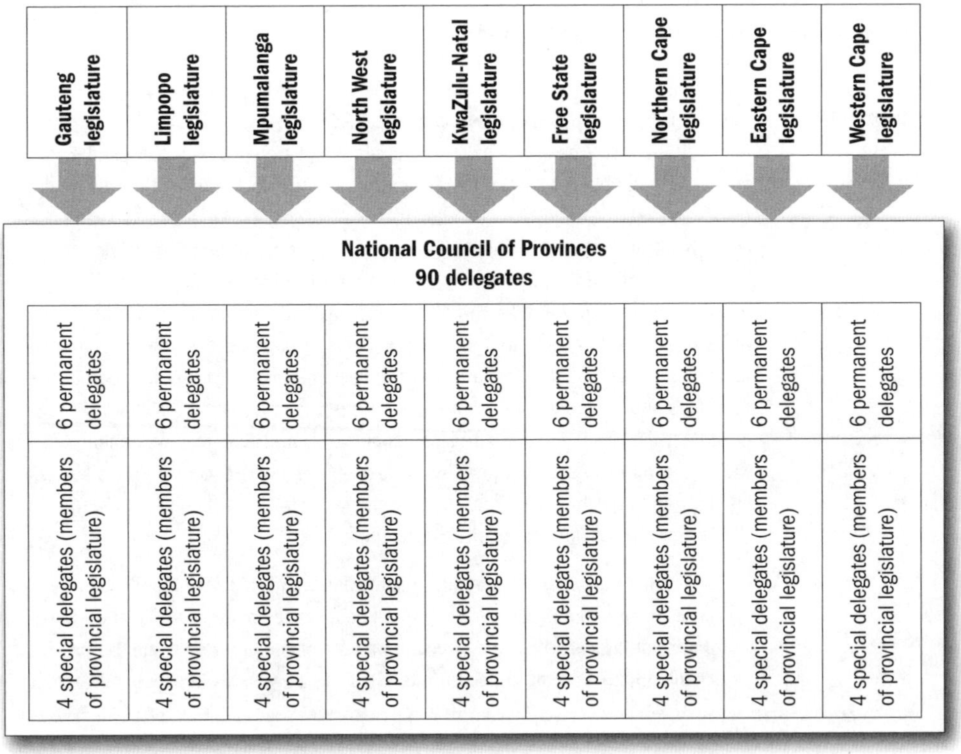

Figure 4.2 Composition of the National Council of Provinces

The provincial legislatures appoint the six permanent delegates of each provincial delegation on the basis of party affiliation to ensure the accurate proportional representation of each political party represented in the provincial legislature in the NCOP delegation. Permanent

194 S 60(2)(*a*) and (*b*) of the Constitution.
195 S 60(2)(*a*) and (*b*) of the Constitution.
196 S 60(2)(*a*)(i) and (ii) of the Constitution.
197 S 60(2)(*a*)(i) of the Constitution.
198 S 60(3) of the Constitution.
199 S 61(4) of the Constitution.

delegates cannot simultaneously be members of the provincial legislature and act as permanent delegates to the NCOP. They are either selected from among party members not elected to the provincial legislature or they are selected from among the members of the provincial legislature, in which case they automatically lose their seat in that House.[200] The permanent delegates perform an important function: they provide continuity and stability to the NCOP by providing a continuous political presence at the NCOP, ensuring that at least six of the 10 members of each provincial delegation to the NCOP are permanently stationed at Parliament in Cape Town.[201]

The provincial legislature may recall a permanent delegate if the delegate 'has lost the confidence of the provincial legislature and is recalled by the party that nominated that person'.[202] This will occur when the NCOP passes a vote of no confidence in the delegate, at which point the political party that nominated him or her acquires a right to recall that member.[203] The composition of the NCOP – with equal representation for small and large provinces – means that it is not a foregone conclusion that the political party who garners a majority in the NA will also do so in the NCOP.

PAUSE FOR REFLECTION

Factors influencing the operation of the NCOP

Although the NCOP perhaps has fewer powers than its predecessor, the Senate,[204] it seems to be a better collective representative of provincial interests. However, it may be wise to keep in mind that constitutional engineering is an imprecise science. The larger political context, the traditions and culture of political parties and the relative support of each political party in the system all influence the manner in which constitutional structures like the NCOP operate and whether they will fulfil their mandate. This also means that as the political landscape changes and as elections become more competitive, for example if one party were to win the election in five provinces and a coalition of other parties were to win a majority in the other four provinces, the dynamics around the functioning of the NCOP may well change. The NCOP may then come into its own as a true representative of the various provincial interests. The Constitutional Court reached the following conclusion in *Certification of the Constitution of The Republic Of South Africa, 1996*:

> **Although we are satisfied that the structure and the functioning of the NCOP as provided for in the [new Constitution] are better suited to the representation of provincial interests than the structure and functioning of the Senate, we are unable to say that the collective interest of the provinces will necessarily be**

200 S 62(2) and (4)of the Constitution.

201 Bishop, M and Raboshakga, N 'National legislative authority' in Woolman and Bishop (2013) 17.5.

202 S 62(4)(*c*) of the Constitution. In *Van Zyl v New National Party and Others* (2000/002) [2003] ZAWCHC 17; [2003] 3 All SA 737 (C) (22 May 2003) para 75, the Cape High Court found that the exercising of the authority to recall a permanent delegate to the NCOP in terms of s 62(4)(*c*) of the Constitution constitutes the exercising of a public power because such a decision has an influence on how the NCOP, the delegations of the respective provinces and the joint committees on which delegates may serve are constituted. Such a decision may affect the manner in which those bodies perform their functions and duties and this, in turn, may affect the interests of the community at provincial and national levels. Accordingly, the exercising of this authority has a strong public component.

203 *Van Zyl* para 90.

204 In *First Certification* para 328, the Constitutional Court held that in some respects the Senate has greater power than the Council; in other respects it has less. We disagree. While the collective power of the provinces may be enhanced by the new provisions relating to the appointment, structure and functioning of the Council, the Senate certainly had more constitutional power in the national legislative process than the Council.

> enhanced by the changes that have been made. We have found it extremely difficult to evaluate the overall impact of these changes. A number of variable and uncertain factors have to be taken into account. These include not only the differences in the powers of the two Houses which have been referred to, but also the method of appointing the members of the Houses, the contrast between direct and indirect representation, the different methods of voting, the different procedures to be followed, the influence of parties on voting patterns, and the possible impact of the anti-defection provisions on voting.[205]

The powers of the NCOP vary according to the impact of the legislation in question on provincial concerns and the nature of the legislation being considered. If the legislation does not directly affect the provinces, NCOP members usually each have an individual vote which they cast in accordance with the wishes of their respective political parties.[206] In all other cases - including when amending the Constitution or dealing with Bills affecting the provinces - each provincial delegation casts a single vote.[207] It does so under instruction, also called a mandate, from the provincial legislature of the province represented by the delegation.[208] As the Constitutional Court has explained in *Certification of the Amended Text of the Constitution of The Republic Of South Africa, 1996*, the NCOP 'is a council of provinces and not a chamber composed of elected representatives. Voting by delegation reflects accurately the support of the different provincial legislatures for a measure under consideration'.[209] 'In this manner the provincial legislatures are given a direct say in the national law-making process through the NCOP.'[210]

The various NCOP delegations have found it difficult to operate effectively, especially to obtain the requisite mandate from their respective provincial legislatures in the short time often provided for this task. There are a number of reasons for this. Because provincial legislative attention is so taken up with carrying out mandates imposed on them from above, and because they are far removed from the centre of political power in Parliament, they are ill equipped in terms of information and expertise to pass judgment on national legislation and to provide informed mandates to the respective NCOP delegations. This problem is exacerbated by poor communications between the NA and the NCOP and between NCOP delegations and their provincial legislatures. Draft Bills are often provided to the NCOP with little time for provinces to respond.[211]

In addition, NCOP members are supposed to provide a bridge between the national legislature and provincial legislatures, but their political links with both are often weak and ineffective. The technical and human resources for close communication are often lacking. Individual NCOP members, shuttling between Parliament in Cape Town and remote provincial capitals, are placed under enormous strain. It is highly unrealistic, and probably unnecessary, for provincial legislatures to pay the same attention to national legislation as

205 (CCT 23/96) [1996] ZACC 26; 1996 (4) SA 744 (CC); 1996 (10) BCLR 1253 (CC) (6 September 1996) paras 331–2.
206 S 75(2) of the Constitution.
207 S 75(1) of the Constitution.
208 S 65(2) of the Constitution. How such mandates are obtained is regulated by the Mandating Procedures of Provinces Act 52 of 2008.
209 (CCT37/96) [1996] ZACC 24; 1997 (1) BCLR 1; 1997 (2) SA 97 (4 December 1996) para 62. See also *Doctors for Life* para 84.
210 *Doctors for Life* para 84.
211 Simeon, R and Murray, C (2001) Multi-sphere governance in South Africa: An interim assessment *Publius: The Journal of Federalism* 31(4):65–92 at 78.

does the NA. It is far more important for them to come to grips with local issues and problems. However, it is critical that provinces are able to voice their opinions when legislation directly affects the economic or social interests of their region, and that they can ensure that national legislation they will be required to implement is workable. Another problem is that there is little linkage between the exchange of information and ideas that goes on within the processes of executive intergovernmental relations and exchanges at the parliamentary level through the NCOP. Indeed, provincial executives take little interest in NCOP matters. This differs greatly from the operation of the German *Bundesrat,* the members of which are themselves provincial executives, thus integrating legislative and executive intergovernmental relations.[212]

Because of these practical difficulties as well as the limited powers and functions formally bestowed on the NCOP, the NCOP, as the second House of the national Parliament, is often viewed as the less powerful and influential of the two chambers of the bicameral South African Parliament. This is so because almost all Cabinet Ministers will be members of the NA while NCOP members cannot serve as Cabinet Ministers. Although Cabinet Ministers and Deputy Ministers may attend and may speak in the NCOP, they may not vote in that chamber.[213] Moreover, unlike the NA, the NCOP is not given a clear mandate to hold members of the Cabinet accountable or to maintain oversight over the executive although the NCOP plays an important role in the passing of legislation.

Nevertheless, the NCOP and its committees are, under section 69 of the Constitution, given broad powers. They may 'summon any person to appear before it to give evidence on oath or affirmation or to produce documents; require any institution or person to report to it; compel, in terms of national legislation or the rules and orders, any person or institution to comply with a summons; and receive petitions, representations or submissions from any interested persons or institutions.'

CRITICAL THINKING

The role of strict party discipline in the effectiveness of the NCOP

The events which led to the Constitutional Court judgment in *Merafong Demarcation Forum and Others v President of the Republic of South Africa and Others*[214] illustrate the difficulties faced by NCOP delegations required to receive electoral mandates from their respective provinces. In this case the Gauteng legislature adopted a 'negotiating mandate' regarding proposed amendments to the Constitution to eradicate cross-border municipalities.[215] Its NCOP delegation would support the amendments on condition that the Merafong area would be retained in the Gauteng Province and would not be moved to the North West Province as the legislation proposed. It thus appeared to agree with the view expressed by the majority of the Merafong community at the public hearing that the phasing-out of cross-boundary municipalities had to be supported, but that the entire municipality of Merafong had to be located in Gauteng.

However, for technical reasons, the proposed constitutional amendment could not be changed and the NCOP had either to support the Bill, in which case it would be passed, or to reject the entire constitutional amendment, in which case it would not be adopted. Realising this, the NCOP delegation from Gauteng then changed its mind

212 Simeon and Murray (2001) 78.

213 S 66(1) of the Constitution.

214 (CCT 41/07) [2008] ZACC 10; 2008 (5) SA 171 (CC); 2008 (10) BCLR 968 (CC) (13 June 2008).

215 See s 5 of Schedule 1 of the Mandating Procedures of Provinces Act.

and voted in support of the Bill and it was passed. Challenging this decision, the applicants argued that the National Executive Committee (NEC) of the ANC had decided earlier that Merafong would go to North West and had instructed the NCOP to support the amendment. The majority of the Constitutional Court found that '[o]n the available evidence, it is not possible to determine whether and to what extent the final voting mandate and the debate in the NCOP [delegation] were directly or indirectly influenced by previously formulated policies of the ruling party'.[216]

Although there was not sufficient evidence to determine that the NCOP delegation changed its mandate because of instructions by the ANC NEC, the case demonstrates the potential problems of the system. Given the culture of political parties of strictly adhering to the discipline imposed by their leaders, and the fact that the governing party has the power to discipline the members of the provincial legislature as well as the NCOP delegation if they disobey leadership instructions, it is not far-fetched to imagine that provincial legislatures will provide NCOP delegations with mandates that align with the decisions of the party leadership and not necessarily with the interests of the province. In other words, the single factor most likely to determine to what extent the NCOP is able to represent the interest of the provinces in an effective manner is the degree to which political parties demand adherence to strict party discipline from their delegates. Where the majority party in the national Parliament is also in control of a majority of provincial legislatures, adherence to strict party discipline will mean that those provincial delegations controlled by the majority party will be reluctant to challenge the political consensus which emerges from the representatives of the majority party in the NA. This will be particularly true where a sensitive political issue is at stake. However, in more technical and politically less sensitive areas, strict party discipline will not necessarily emasculate the provincial delegations of the majority party in the NA.

4.4.2 Procedures, internal arrangements and committees of the National Council of Provinces

The Constitution requires the election of a Chairperson and two Deputy Chairpersons of the NCOP,[217] and provides for the NCOP to make its own internal arrangements and procedures.[218] The NCOP is also required to establish committees to oversee its work, which is done in terms of its rules.[219]

Because the NCOP is composed of a single delegation from each province, each province usually has one vote which must be cast on behalf of the province by the head of the delegation.[220] A majority is achieved when five delegations support a decision. However, when the NCOP has to pass legislation not affecting the provinces, each delegate in the NCOP has one vote and a majority of votes of delegates is required to pass a Bill.[221] An Act of Parliament 'must provide for a uniform procedure in terms of which provincial legislatures confer

216 *Merafong* para 50.

217 S 64(1) of the Constitution. While the Chairperson and one of the Deputy Chairpersons are elected from the permanent delegates for a term of five years unless their terms as delegates expire earlier (s 64(2)), the other Deputy Chairperson is elected for a term of one year and 'must be succeeded by a delegate from another province, so that every province is represented in turn' (s 64(3)).

218 S 70(1) of the Constitution. This provision mirrors the provision applicable to the NA – s 57(1).

219 S 70(2)(*a*) of the Constitution. S 57(2) contains identical provisions regarding the NA.

220 S 65(1) of the Constitution.

221 S 75(2) of the Constitution.

authority on their delegations to cast votes on their behalf'.[222] Pursuant to this, Parliament enacted the Mandating Procedures of Provinces Act.[223] However, despite the mechanisms that could be created for consensus building and consultation across party lines, in effect the majority party in the provincial legislature has the power to decide how the vote of the provincial delegation will be exercised. Except where the Constitution provides otherwise, questions before the NCOP are agreed when five of the nine provinces vote in favour of it.[224] In other words, an absolute majority is normally required.[225] These provisions recognise that the single delegation of a province in the NCOP normally acts as representative of the province.

However, as was noted above, sometimes the NCOP does not act in this capacity as representative of the province. For example, when Bills are considered which do not affect the provinces, in other words non-Schedule 4 and 5 Bills, the NCOP does not represent the provinces and the voting procedures described above do not apply. In respect of such matters, the Constitution provides that the delegates in the Council vote individually. A quorum of one-third of the delegates must be present and a decision must then be taken by a majority of those present.[226]

The Constitution further provides, consistent with this distinction, that when the NCOP acts as representative of the provinces, all the provinces must be allowed to participate in the 'proceedings in a manner consistent with democracy'.[227] However, when it comes to law making that does not affect the provinces, minority parties must be allowed to participate in law making.[228]

The NCOP may not be dissolved. In principle, it is a perpetual body without a fixed term. The tenure of the members of the NCOP is, however, far less secure. The terms of the permanent delegates are linked to the provincial legislature they represent and, as we stated above, they may be recalled. The position of the special delegates is even less secure. Because they are appointed from time to time, they will generally serve for short periods of time on the NCOP.

4.5 Functions of Parliament

4.5.1 Introduction

The main function of Parliament is to enact national legislation for the Republic of South Africa. However, the enactment of legislation is not the only function bestowed on Parliament by the Constitution. On a more symbolic level, Parliament also provides a national forum for public debate on issues of national importance. In this sense, Parliament provides a platform for representatives of political parties to present their views and debate each other.

While both Houses of Parliament play an integral role in the adoption of legislation, and while both provide platforms for debate about important issues, the Constitution confers additional powers on the NA that enable it to fulfil a special role as a 'check' on the executive authority. This special task is bestowed on the NA because of the fact that it appoints and can dismiss the President. It follows that the President and his or her Cabinet need to retain

222 S 65(2) of the Constitution.
223 Act 52 of 2008.
224 S 65(1) of the Constitution.
225 Since the whole delegation has only one vote, all the delegates do not have to be present and no quorum requirement is necessary.
226 S 75(2) of the Constitution.
227 S 70(2)(*b*).
228 S 70(2)(*c*) of the Constitution refers to s 75 Bills.

the confidence and hence the support of the NA to continue doing their job. Although the tasks of the two Houses are therefore not identical, the two Houses of Parliament can be said to fulfil four main functions. They must:

- provide a forum for debate on important issues[229]
- hold the executive organs of state in the national sphere of government accountable to Parliament[230]
- exercise an oversight function over the exercise of national authority and over other organs of state[231]
- pass national legislation.[232]

4.5.2 National forum for public consideration of issues

One of Parliament's most important functions may be described as fulfilling the role of 'national talk shop'.[233] Currie and De Waal argue that Parliament fulfils this role in two ways:

- First, Parliament is required to operate in a transparent and accountable manner.[234] The public, including the media, may not be excluded from a sitting of a committee unless it is reasonable and justifiable to do so in an open and democratic society.[235]
- Second, as we have seen, Parliament is required to operate in such a way as to give ordinary persons and affected individuals and institutions the opportunity to have access to its proceedings and to present their views on issues considered by Parliament in writing or by oral presentations.[236]

However, we contend that the two Houses of Parliament also fulfil this task by providing a platform for elected political representatives to deliver speeches and to engage in debates with one another and with the President about policy questions as well as issues of political importance. Because events in Parliament are relatively well reported by the print and electronic media, Parliament provides an important platform for the floating of new ideas and for elected politicians to 'perform' democracy by illustrating their willingness to debate important and often emotional issues with members from other political parties in a relatively rational and calm manner. Parliament, at its best, can therefore act as a body that educates citizens about the importance of embracing a participatory notion of democracy and the requirement to respect differences without having to agree with those who differ from oneself.

The Rules of the NA and the NCOP provide various mechanisms to achieve these goals.[237] For example, a member of the NA may propose a subject for discussion or a draft resolution for approval as a resolution of this House.[238] The Rules of the NA provide for an MP to request

---

229 S 42(3) of the Constitution states that the NA is able to represent the people and ensure democratic government by, among others, 'providing a national forum for public consideration of issues'. Similarly, under s 42(4), the NCOP does so by 'providing a national forum for public consideration of issues affecting the provinces'.

230 S 55(2)(*a*) read with s 92(2) of the Constitution.

231 S 55(2)(*b*) of the Constitution. The Constitution does not provide for similar powers for the NCOP. However, s 92 states that members of Cabinet are accountable to Parliament, which suggests that they are accountable to both Houses of Parliament.

232 S 42(3) read with ss 55(1) and 68 of the Constitution.

233 Currie and De Waal (2001) 159. See NA Rules 103–4 and NCOP Rules 83–5.

234 S 59(1)(*b*) of the Constitution for the NA and s 72(1)(*b*) for the NCOP. Business must be conducted in an open manner and sittings must be held in public, but reasonable measures may be taken to regulate public access, including access of the media, and to provide for the searching of any person and where appropriate, the refusal of entry to, or the removal of, any person.

235 S 59(2) of the Constitution for the NA and s 72(2) for the NCOP.

236 S 59(1)(*a*) of the Constitution for the NA and s 72(1)(*a*) for the NCOP.

237 NA Rules 58–72 determine the rules of debate.

238 NA Rule 94.

the Speaker to place a matter of public importance on the Order Paper for discussion.[239] The Rules also allow an MP to request the Speaker on any day the NA sits to allow a matter of urgent public importance to be discussed by the NA.[240]

The Rules of the NCOP allow its members too to request the Chairperson of the NCOP in writing to allow a matter of public importance to be discussed by the Council, but this request will only be granted if the matter affects the provinces or one or more of them.[241]

4.5.3 Holding the executive accountable to Parliament

As we have seen in the discussion about the separation of powers doctrine, the 1996 Constitution retains a form of parliamentary government which is similar but not identical to the Westminster model of government. The South African Constitution thus states that members of Cabinet are accountable to Parliament and must report to Parliament regularly.[242] Accountability is the hallmark of modern democratic governance and implies that members of the executive have to explain their actions to Parliament and its committees so that Parliament can play a role in checking the exercise of power by members of the executive. This power of Parliament to hold the executive accountable will only be effectively exercised where Parliament ultimately has the ability to sanction members of the executive who abuse their power or fail to fulfil their respective mandates. The power of Parliament to hold the executive accountable therefore, in essence, entails two distinct but interrelated aspects:

- First, it entails the powers of Parliament to call members of the executive and the public administration to account for their activities. This is aimed at enhancing the integrity of public governance to safeguard government against corruption, nepotism, abuse of power and other forms of inappropriate behaviour, and to assist in improving the performance of the Cabinet as well as the public administration. This kind of accountability also reflects a culture of transparency, responsiveness and answerability which is necessary to assure public confidence in government, to bridge the gap between the governed and the government, and to ensure public confidence in government. If used wisely and effectively, these accountability mechanisms enable the public to judge the performance of the government by the government giving account in public.[243]
- Second, accountability will arguably not be effective if it does not include the power of Parliament to take remedial action and even to dismiss members of the executive who fail to account properly for their actions. As such, accountability requires the establishment of institutional arrangements to effect democratic control over the executive as members of the executive, unlike the MPs, are not directly democratically elected.

As far as the first aspect is concerned, sections 56 and 69 of the Constitution respectively provide that the NA and the NCOP as well as any of their committees may 'summon any person to appear before it to give evidence on oath or affirmation, or to produce documents'. It may also require 'any person or institution to report to it'. Where anyone refuses to appear before Parliament or any of its committees, it can summons that person or institution and can compel such a person or institution to comply with the summons. The Rules of

239 NA Rule 103(1).

240 NA Rule 104(1).

241 NCOP Rule 84(1) and (2).

242 S 92(2).

243 See Parliament of the Republic of South Africa (2009) *Oversight and Accountability Model: Asserting Parliament's Oversight Role in Enhancing Democracy* 2.2.1 available at http://www.parliament.gov.za/content/Microsoft%20Word%20-%20OVAC%20Model%20-%20edited%20Word%20version%20-%20Replaced%20Diagrams,Chapter%20Upper%20case_27-Jan-09~1~1.pdf.

Parliament further provide for the powers of its committees to enable these committees to hold members of the executive accountable.[244] The Rules of the NA and the NCOP also provide for members of the NA to pose questions and receive oral answers from Ministers,[245] the Deputy President[246] and the President.[247]

As far as the second aspect is concerned, the NA has distinct powers (not given to the NCOP) to ensure democratic control over the executive. Although the Cabinet is accountable to both the NA and the NCOP, the Constitution clearly envisages a special role for the NA in this regard. Section 102(2) of the Constitution empowers the NA to pass a motion of no confidence in the President as long as such a motion is supported by a majority of its members. In this event, the President and the other members of the Cabinet and any Deputy Ministers must resign.[248] This power is a political power and the removal can thus be effected for purely political reasons. This provision means that the President and his or her Cabinet have a strong political incentive to retain the support of the majority party in the NA. In the South African political landscape, this means they also have a strong political incentive to retain the support of the leadership of the majority party outside Parliament. If a President loses the support of the majority party, he or she will have to resign. If he or she refuses to do so, he or she will be removed by a vote of no confidence in the NA as the majority party in the NA will instruct its members to support such a vote. If members of the NA refuse to support such a vote, the political party they represent will then be able to remove them from the NA.

Neither the majority party in the NA nor any of the minority parties are constitutionally allowed to block the tabling, discussion, consideration and voting on a motion of no confidence. In *Mazibuko v Sisulu and Another*,[249] the Constitutional Court confirmed this, declaring invalid Chapter 12 of the Rules of the NA that purported to do just that. The case arose after the Leader of the Opposition in the NA gave notice of a motion of no confidence in the President. The programme committee of the NA[250] met to consider the proposed motion of no confidence. However, its deliberations on the motion were deadlocked. Because there was an absence of consensus between the parties, the Speaker concluded that the motion could not be scheduled and could therefore not be debated or voted on.[251] The majority judgment (authored by Deputy Chief Justice Moseneke) found that the Constitution required the Rules of the NA to permit its members to deliberate and vote on a motion of no confidence in the President:

> **A motion of no confidence in the President is a vital tool to advance our democratic hygiene. It affords the Assembly a vital power and duty to scrutinise and oversee executive action ... The ever-present possibility of a motion of no confidence against the President and the Cabinet is meant to keep the President accountable to the Assembly which elects her or him. If a motion of no confidence in the President were to succeed, he or she and the incumbent Cabinet must resign. In effect, the people through their elected representatives in the Assembly would end the mandate they bestowed on an incumbent President.**[252]

244 NA Rule 138 and NCOP Rule 103.

245 NA Rule 109 and NCOP Rules 240–4.

246 NA Rule 110 and NCOP Rules 240–4.

247 NA Rule 111 and NCOP Rules 240–4.

248 See *Mazibuko v Sisulu and Another* (CCT 115/12) [2013] ZACC 28; 2013 (6) SA 249 (CC); 2013 (11) BCLR 1297 (CC) (27 August 2013).

249 (CCT 115/12) [2013] ZACC 28; 2013 (6) SA 249 (CC); 2013 (11) BCLR 1297 (CC) (27 August 2013).

250 NA Rules 187–90.

251 *Mazibuko* para 10.

252 *Mazibuko* para 43.

This right to have a motion of no confidence considered and voted on is central to the 'deliberative, multiparty democracy envisioned in the Constitution'.[253] The Court pointed out that it 'implicates the values of democracy, transparency, accountability and openness'.[254] It is for this reason that a 'motion of this kind is perhaps the most important mechanism that may be employed by Parliament to hold the executive to account, and to interrogate executive performance'.[255] The Rules of the NA may not 'deny, frustrate, unreasonably delay or postpone the exercise of the right'.[256] This means a decision whether a vote of no confidence is tabled, debated and voted on:

> **cannot be left to the whim of the majority or minority in the programme committee or any other committee of the Assembly. It would be inimical to the vital purpose of section 102(2) to accept that a motion of no confidence in the President may never reach the Assembly except with the generosity and concurrence of the majority in that committee. It is equally unacceptable that a minority within the Committee may render the motion stillborn when consensus is the decision-making norm.**[257]

Although the NA has the constitutional authority to 'determine and control its internal arrangements, proceedings and procedures',[258] such authority must be exercised in conformity with the Constitution. When a motion of no confidence is tabled, it 'must be accorded priority over other motions and business by being scheduled, debated and voted on within a reasonable time'.[259] The NA is therefore required to 'take prompt and reasonable steps to ensure that the motion is scheduled, debated and voted on without undue delay'.[260] This does not mean that when such a motion is tabled it will be passed. As long as the majority party in the NA retains confidence in the President and his or her Cabinet, there is little chance of the NA passing such a vote of no confidence. However, where the majority of members of the NA lose confidence in the President, such a vote will lead to the removal of the President. It is therefore not surprising that former President Thabo Mbeki resigned as President of the Republic after losing a leadership battle with his successor in the governing party and was consequently 'recalled' by the leadership of the party. If he had refused to resign, the ANC would in all likelihood have instructed its members in the NA to support a vote of no confidence in the President, something which would arguably have resulted in his removal.[261]

Section 89(1) of the Constitution also allows the NA to impeach the President by adopting a resolution with a supporting vote of at least two-thirds of its members to remove the President on the grounds of a serious violation of the Constitution or the law, serious misconduct or inability to perform the functions of office. This is not a purely political power, but a power to remove the President for objective reasons unrelated to the political support enjoyed by the President. Moreover, section 55(2)(*a*) of the Constitution commands the NA to devise mechanisms that will enable it to hold the executive organs of state accountable to Parliament. These provisions reiterate one of the fundamental principles of a traditional system of parliamentary government, namely that the President and his or her Cabinet must remain accountable to the democratically elected NA.[262]

253 *Mazibuko* para 44.
254 *Mazibuko* para 44.
255 *Mazibuko* para 44.
256 *Mazibuko* para 47.
257 *Mazibuko* para 57.
258 S 57(1)(*a*) of the Constitution.
259 *Mazibuko* para 66.
260 *Mazibuko* para 66.
261 S 102(2) of the Constitution.
262 See Currie and De Waal (2001) 160.

The extent to which the NA, and to a lesser extent the NCOP, are able to hold the executive accountable to Parliament depends on the traditions and practices that are developed in Parliament over time. This, in turn, depends on the attitude of the members of the majority party in Parliament, especially its leaders who serve in the government, towards the need for accountable government. It also depends on the way in which members of opposition parties fulfil their role in holding the executive to account. In this regard, the role of the portfolio committees discussed above is crucial. One of the most important ways in which Parliament holds the executive accountable is through the regular question-and-answer sessions in Parliament. During such question times, MPs have the opportunity to pose probing questions about the activities of the President, Deputy President and the Cabinet Ministers. Ministers are then obliged to provide statistics about different aspects of their departments, details of the expenditure on various items and to defend the policies they have adopted.[263]

CRITICAL THINKING

How accountable is the executive to Parliament?

Nash is critical of the notion of accountability built into the South African Constitution with its emphasis on the democratically elected Parliament and its role of holding the executive accountable. He argues that effective accountability practice - widely employed in the South African labour movement in the 1970s and 80s - does not 'depend on lawyers, bureaucrats or accountability experts or even a handbook. It depends on active participation in political life, informed by a shared ethical standard'.[264] This process of accountability, Nash argues, is important because it strengthens the capacity of oppressed and marginalised people to act collectively and consciously to take responsibility for their actions and those of their leaders. Where there is little or no active participation in the decision-making processes of Parliament or the executive by the electorate, and no real prospect of them recalling their leaders or changing their mandate, as happened in the earlier labour movement, the accountability remains no more than paper accountability with no or little practical effect for the oppressed.[265] This 'neoliberal' model of accountability 'can be understood largely as a way of providing the façade of democracy without the substance, ensuring that issues around which "factions of the majority" might unite against the interests of the propertied are taken out of the political arena and made the subject of bureaucratic procedure instead'.[266]

Nash's view is based on a more 'grassroots' understanding of democracy and accountability. It displays a scepticism towards the notion of representative democracy and the formal mechanisms put in place by the Constitution to ensure accountability. At its heart this view seems to be sceptical about the ability of the MPs - indirectly elected because of their standing in a political party and not directly accountable to any constituency - to hold the executive to account.

263 Kotzé, H (1997) *Take Us To Our Leaders: The South African National Assembly and Its Members* 18. See also Nijzink and Murray (2002) 91 where the authors argue that despite the important oversight functions of committees, we should not lose sight of the fact that the role of committees has often been at the expense of plenary sessions where committee reports could be more publicly aired and debated, the implementation of policy showcased and scrutinised, and question time be given more of a profile.

264 Nash, A 'Post-apartheid accountability: The transformation of a political idea' in Chirwa, DM and Nijzink, L (2012) *Accountable Government in Africa: Perspectives from Public Law and Political Studies* 21.

265 Nash (2012) 18–20.

266 Nash (2012) 24.

4.5.4 Maintaining oversight of the national executive authority and other organs of state

Oversight resembles, but is nevertheless to be distinguished from, accountability. It 'entails the informal and formal, watchful, strategic and structured scrutiny exercised by legislatures in respect of the implementation of laws, the application of the budget, and the strict observance of statutes and the Constitution'.[267] It requires the NA to oversee the day-to-day exercise of authority by the national executive and to oversee the actions of other organs of state. This task includes the task of overseeing the implementation of legislation.[268] 'In addition, and most importantly, it entails overseeing the effective management of government departments by individual members of Cabinet in pursuit of improved service delivery for the achievement of a better quality of life for all citizens. In terms of the provisions of the Constitution and the Joint Rules of Parliament, Parliament has the power to conduct oversight over all organs of state, including those at provincial and local government level.'[269] Organs of state are defined broadly in section 239 of the Constitution to include:

> **any department of state or administration in the national, provincial or local sphere of government; or any other functionary or institution exercising a power or performing a function in terms of the Constitution or a provincial constitution; or exercising a public power or performing a public function in terms of any legislation ...**

Parliament is therefore entitled to oversee the work of the more than 1 000 organs of state which include a wide array of institutions such as all public universities in South Africa, the Johannesburg Fresh Produce Market, the Public Protector, the Human Rights Commission, the Medical Research Council of South Africa, the National Gambling Board, the National Lotteries Board and the Natal Sharks Board, to name but a few. However, this does not include a court or a judicial officer, which means Parliament cannot fulfil an oversight role over the judiciary.[270]

The appropriate mechanism for Parliament to conduct oversight of these organs of state is through the various parliamentary committees, mostly the portfolio committees discussed above. 'In conducting oversight, the committee would either request a briefing from the organ of state [or Cabinet Minister] or visit the organ of state for fact-finding, depending on the purpose of the oversight ... One of the most important aspects of the oversight function is the consideration by committees of annual reports of organs of state and the Auditor-General's reports.'[271] The more independent, knowledgeable, hard-working and politically powerful the members of the committees are, the more rigorous the NA's oversight of the executive and other organs of state will be. Committees have the power to investigate and make recommendations on any matter relating to government departments, including budgets, rationalisation, restructuring, organisation, structure, function, personnel and policy formulation.[272]

The oversight role of the NCOP is more defined. The NCOP must review the intervention of the national executive in a province and the provincial executive in a municipality.[273] Both the NA and the NCOP must approve a decision by the Treasury to stop the transfer of funds

267 Parliament of South Africa 'Oversight and Accountability Model' 2.1.
268 S 55(2)(*b*) of the Constitution.
269 Parliament of South Africa 'Oversight and Accountability Model' 2.1.
270 S 239 of the Constitution.
271 Parliament of South Africa 'Oversight and Accountability Model' 2.1.
272 Kotzé (1997) 18.
273 Ss 100(1)(*b*) and 139(1)(*b*) of the Constitution respectively read with NCOP Rules 243–4.

to a province[274] or a decision by the President to declare a state of national defence.[275] Additionally, the NCOP resolves disputes concerning the administrative capacity of a province.[276]

CRITICAL THINKING

The relationship between the members of the executive and the ordinary members of parliamentary committees

Taljaard, speaking from a different ideological position than Nash quoted above, was intimately involved in overseeing the executive as a member of the NA's Public Accounts Committee (Scopa) during the so-called arms deal scandal. She provides the following perspective on the manner in which oversight occurred (or did not occur) in Parliament in the case of the arms deal:

> At the start of 2001 a concerted assault by the executive on the standing committee on public accounts (Scopa) and the auditor-general was about to commence with battle-like precision. I would look on with fascination, without realising that my party leader was about to hurl me right into the middle of the gladiatorial arena. On January 13, ministers Alec Erwin, Mosiuoa Lekota and Trevor Manuel opened with a salvo attacking Scopa's 'incompetence' and strongly defending the integrity of the arms acquisition process. Each minister defended his corner: Lekota, the procurement process itself; Manuel, the cost of the deal and its financing; and Erwin, the benefits of the offset or countertrade obligations for job creation. Despite this aggressive attack the ministers did commit themselves to full co-operation with the investigations, even though they complained bitterly that Scopa had not given them the opportunity to explain themselves before calling for a full probe - echoing the words of a cabinet statement the year before.
>
> ... The executive unleashed its strategy on Friday, January 19. This would bring half the cabinet, including the president, deputy president, minister of finance, minister of trade and industry, minister of public enterprises, minister of defence and minister of justice, into the fight between Parliament and the executive. But it was the president's turn to launch a broadside on the institution in the form of a public televised address. We knew that [then President Thabo] Mbeki was going to speak on the SABC on that day about the arms deal probe, and eagerly awaited his address. ... As we awaited his public broadcast, I was sitting in my office in the Marks Building when a fax came through from the office of Deputy President Jacob Zuma - in his capacity as leader of government business. It contained an explosive letter, attacking the integrity of Scopa and its chairman and calling into question its intentions in drafting the 14th report and in seeking a full-scale forensic probe of the arms deal (which the letter referred to as a 'fishing expedition'). I had never read such intemperate language - certainly not from a senior figure - and was amazed by the deputy president's opinions about the committee in view of his own attempts to enhance Parliament's oversight role in his capacity as leader of government business.

274 S 216(3)(*b*) of the Constitution.
275 S 203 of the Constitution.
276 S 125(4) of the Constitution.

> This was bad enough, but more was in store. As President Thabo Mbeki began his address on television I had the uncomfortable sensation of watching a concerted effort to frighten Scopa and the auditor-general by a sheer show of executive force. In his address Mbeki emphasised the government's efforts to fight corruption and its support for any probe, committed the government to upholding the rule of law, and emphasised that it would not break any contracts it had legally entered into. He complained bitterly about the fact that Scopa and the auditor-general had not communicated with the cabinet and cabinet subcommittees before coming to its conclusions about their decisions. This would be a recurring theme in the government's defence.[277]

Regardless of a person's ideological point of view, and whether he or she is broadly speaking a supporter of the governing party or an opposition party, and regardless of whether we agree with Taljaart's rendition of events, she does raise questions about the relationship between the members of the executive (who are usually also the leaders of the majority party in Parliament) and the ordinary members of parliamentary committees and the ability of such ordinary members to oversee the work done by more senior members of their party in government. It will indeed be very difficult for a member of a portfolio committee to hold the President and other members of the executive accountable and oversee their work in a vigorous manner for at least two reasons:

- First, it may well embarrass the government of the day if a member of the NA reveals damaging information about corruption or maladministration in the department of a Cabinet Minister. If this member embarrasses the government of the day, it would indirectly embarrass the political party of which this person may be a member. This may influence the electoral prospects of the member's party at the next election and may also endanger the member's political career as the member may lose his or her seat at the next election.
- Second, members of the NA are elected because they appear sufficiently high up on their political party's electoral list. If a member angers the party leadership, this member may well not be placed high enough on the electoral list to be re-elected to the NA, bringing an abrupt end to the member's political career.

4.5.5 Passing of legislation

The notion of co-operative government, enshrined in Chapter 3 of the Constitution, lies at the heart of the law-making process in the national Parliament. This is because the procedure for enacting legislation under the Constitution requires institutional co-operation and communication between national and provincial legislatures as well as between the executive and Parliament. However, the Constitution does not clearly define how this should occur. Such co-operation is necessary to implement the national legislative programme. It is important to note that this need for co-operation is intimately linked with the fact that the legislative process is based on the assumption that provincial interests (as defined in the Constitution) will be taken into account in the national law-making process whenever such

277 Taljaard, R (2012, 20 March) The day my idealism was extinguished *The Star* available at http://www.iol.co.za/the-star/the-day-my-idealism-was-extinguished-1.1260059#.UGxEGjkWHzI.

interests arise. As such, the NCOP plays an important role in institutionalising the principle of co-operation and communication by involving the nine provinces directly in the national legislative process and other national matters. As the Constitutional Court pointed out in *Doctors for Life*:

> **The local government is also involved indirectly in that local government may designate up to ten part-time, non-voting representatives to participate in the NCOP proceedings. Thus the NCOP represents the concerns and interests of the provinces and as well as those of local government in the formulation of national legislation.**[278]

The Court proceeded to note:

> **the principle of institutional co-operation and communication finds expression in the principle of co-operative government to which Chapter 3 of the Constitution is devoted. The role of the NCOP should be understood in the light of the constitutional principle of co-operative government, which shares similarities with the principle of *Bundestreue*. The basic structure of our government consists of a partnership between the national, provincial and local spheres of government which are distinctive, interdependent and interrelated. The principle of co-operative government requires each of the three spheres to perform their functions in a spirit of consultation and co-ordination with the other spheres.**[279]

It is important to note from the outset that the national Parliament (as opposed to the nine provincial legislatures) has the power to pass legislation on any topic, even those not explicitly listed in the Constitution, **unless** the Constitution provides otherwise. Thus Parliament may usually not pass legislation on the small number of topics reserved in Schedule 5 of the Constitution as areas for exclusive provincial legislative activity.[280] Parliament may pass legislation on any topic listed in Schedule 4 of the Constitution as this section sets out the concurrent powers on which **both** the national Parliament and the provincial Parliaments can legislate. However, where a conflict occurs between national legislation and provincial legislation dealing with a topic listed in Schedule 4, the provincial legislation will usually prevail over the national legislation unless one of the criteria listed in section 146 is present.[281] Section 44 of the Constitution further confers power on Parliament to amend the Constitution[282] while it also confers powers on the NA specifically 'to assign any of its legislative powers, except the power to amend the Constitution, to any legislative body in another sphere of government'.[283]

As indicated earlier, there is no absolute separation of the functions performed by the legislative and the executive branches of government. This is evident when we focus on the passing of legislation by Parliament, which is arguably the most important function of that body. Because of the political influence (we may even say dominance) of the executive in our system of government, draft legislation usually originates in the executive and is then tabled in and passed by Parliament. Individual members of the NA may initiate legislation[284]

278 *Doctors for Life* para 81.

279 *Doctors for Life* para 82.

280 S 44(1)(*a*)(ii) and 44(1)(*b*)(ii) of the Constitution. As we shall see, in certain very limited circumstances set out in s 44(2), Parliament may even legislate on those powers exclusively allocated to provincial legislatures.

281 The question of how to deal with conflicts between provincial and national legislation will be dealt with more fully in ch 5. On conflicts, see generally Bronstein, V 'Conflicts' in Woolman and Bishop (2013) 16.1–16.31.

282 S 44(1)(*a*)(i) and 44(1)(*b*)(i).

283 S 44(1)(*a*)(iii).

284 S 55(2) read with s 73(2) of the Constitution.

in the form of Bills called private members' Bills.[285] Committees of the NA may also initiate Bills.[286]

Section 73(2) of the Constitution allows any member of the NA to introduce a Bill in the NA if that member is not a Cabinet Minister and even if that member belongs to an opposition party. However, the previous Rules of the NA made it difficult for non-Cabinet members, especially from opposition parties, to initiate Bills. Until recently, the Rules of the NA stated that a member of the NA could only initiate and introduce a Bill into the NA if a majority of members of the NA had given 'permission' to an MP to initiate such legislation.[287] Members of opposition parties could attempt to initiate legislation by submitting legislative proposals to the Speaker. These proposals would set out the particulars of the proposed legislation, explain the objects of the proposed legislation and state whether the proposed legislation would have financial implications for the State.[288] The Speaker would then refer the member's memorandum to the Committee on Private Members' Legislative Proposals and Special Petitions. This Committee would then decide whether the proposal should proceed or not. In doing so, the Committee had to confine its consideration of the legislative proposal to whether it:

> **goes against the spirit, purport and object of the Constitution; seeks to initiate legislation beyond the legislative competence of the Assembly; duplicates existing legislation or legislation awaiting consideration by the Assembly or Council; pre-empts similar legislation soon to be introduced by the national executive; will result in a money bill; or is frivolous or vexatious.**[289]

Even if the Committee gave permission for the Bill to proceed, the majority party in the NA could still decide not to support the initiation of the Bill which meant that it would not be passed. In practice, this meant that members of the opposition could never introduce any Bills in the NA unless they were given permission by the majority party to do so. In *Oriani-Ambrosini, MP v Sisulu, MP Speaker of the National Assembly*,[290] the Constitutional Court invalidated the Rules of the NA which required a member of the NA to obtain permission from the NA to initiate and introduce Bills. The Court stated that South Africa's constitutional democracy 'is designed to ensure that the voiceless are heard', and is one in which the 'views of the marginalised or the powerless minorities cannot be suppressed'.[291] The Court approvingly quoted a passage from its earlier judgment in *Democratic Alliance and Another v Masondo NO and Another* to illustrate the principle that must apply to the evaluation of NA Rules giving effect to the constitutional provisions that empower members of the NA to take certain actions:

> **[T]he Constitution does not envisage a mathematical form of democracy, where the winner takes all until the next vote-counting exercise occurs. Rather, it contemplates a pluralistic democracy where continuous respect is given to the rights of all to be**

285 Until the Constitutional Court handed down judgment in *Oriani-Ambrosini, MP v Sisulu, MP Speaker of the National Assembly* (CCT 16/12) [2012] ZACC 27; 2012 (6) SA 588 (CC); 2013 (1) BCLR 14 (CC) (9 October 2012), the private members' Bills were regulated by the NA Rules 209–13 and 234–7.

286 NA Rules 238–40.

287 NA Rule 230 states: '(1) The Assembly initiates legislation through its committees and members acting with the permission of the Assembly in terms of these Rules. (2) Any committee or member of the Assembly may in terms of section 73(2) of the Constitution introduce a Bill in the Assembly that has been initiated in terms of Subrule (1).'

288 NA Rule 234.

289 NA Rule 235A.

290 (CCT 16/12) [2012] ZACC 27; 2012 (6) SA 588 (CC); 2013 (1) BCLR 14 (CC) (9 October 2012).

291 *Oriani-Ambrosini* para 43. See also *South African Transport and Allied Workers Union and Another v Garvas and Others* (CCT 112/11) [2012] ZACC 13; 2012 (8) BCLR 840 (CC); [2012] 10 BLLR 959 (CC); (2012) 33 ILJ 1593 (CC); 2013 (1) SA 83 (CC) (13 June 2012) para 61.

> **heard and have their views considered ... The open and deliberative nature of the process goes further than providing a dignified and meaningful role for all participants. It is calculated to produce better outcomes through subjecting laws and governmental action to the test of critical debate, rather than basing them on unilateral decision-making.[292]**

The provisions in the Constitution that allow individual MPs to initiate legislation and introduce Bills in the NA are important as these provide members of the NA with an opportunity 'to promote their legislative proposals so that they could be considered properly'.[293] The members of both the majority and minority parties in the NA will then be required 'to deliberate critically and seriously on legislative proposals and other matters of national importance'.[294] These deliberations take place in the relevant portfolio committee before the Bill is submitted to the NA for a vote. These provisions therefore allow for the accommodation of different views in a structured and formal manner during the consideration of legislative proposals. As the Constitutional Court pointed out:

> **South Africa's shameful history is one marked by authoritarianism, not only of the legal and physical kind, but also of an intellectual, ideological and philosophical nature. The apartheid regime sought to dominate all facets of human life. It was determined to suppress dissenting views, with the aim of imposing hegemonic control over thoughts and conduct, for the preservation of institutionalised injustice. It is this unjust system that South Africans, through their Constitution, so decisively seek to reverse by ensuring that this country fully belongs to all those who live in it.[295]**

This does not mean that the will of the majority party in the NA can ultimately be overridden. Once a legislative proposal has been initiated and tabled, the majority party can always vote against a Bill. This can only happen after the Bill initiated by an ordinary MP has been discussed and debated by the relevant portfolio committee. Some may say the right of opposition MPs to introduce their own Bills would therefore be of little more than ceremonial significance. However, as the Constitutional Court pointed out, this is not so as it will give opposition MPS the opportunity to go beyond an obstructionist oppositional role, allowing them to submit constructive proposals of their own about how to solve a particular legislative problem and allowing these proposals to be discussed seriously by the members of the NA.[296]

Despite the changes brought about by the *Oriani-Ambrosini* judgment, the large majority of Bills are still initiated and introduced by Cabinet members who are tasked with leading the legislative agenda of the elected government of the day. Ordinary members of the NA from the majority party usually defer to the legislative agenda set by Cabinet. This means a member of the executive, an individual Cabinet Minister, usually initiates legislation dealing with issues related to his or her portfolio before a Bill is introduced and adopted by Parliament. A Bill is the request submitted to Parliament for the approval of particular legislation in relation to a particular matter.

---

292 (CCT29/02) [2002] ZACC 28; 2003 (2) BCLR 128; 2003 (2) SA 413 (CC) (12 December 2002) paras 42–3. See *Oriani-Ambrosini* para 47.

293 *Oriani-Ambrosini* para 48.

294 *Oriani-Ambrosini* para 48.

295 *Oriani-Ambrosini* para 49.

296 *Oriani-Ambrosini* para 57.

PAUSE FOR REFLECTION

One small step for Parliament, one giant leap for Oriani-Ambrosini

One commentator welcomed the *Oriani-Ambrosini* judgment on the basis that it must be viewed in the context of the South African electoral system which disempowers voters and weakens the links between voters and the elected representatives in the NA. Writing on his blog, De Vos stated:

> Our electoral system – which requires us to vote for political parties and not for individual MPs – renders it difficult for voters to hold individual MPs accountable. Unless we join a political party and unless we actively take part in the election processes for the leadership of that party, we have little or no say in who represents us in Parliament and who is elected as our President. This diminishes transparency and accountability in the governance and law-making processes.
>
> Given these limitations, rules of the National Assembly which would make it impossible for individual MPs to have their alternative legislative proposals tabled and discussed by the Assembly diminishes our democracy and robs voters of the opportunity to judge whether they support the legislative proposals of the governing party or of any given opposition party.
>
> Chief Justice Mogoeng emphasised that providing such alternatives 'allows for a legislative proposal to be debated properly and in a manner that is open to the public, before its fate is decided'.[297] Furthermore:
>
>> public participation, so as to cultivate an 'active, informed and engaged citizenry', is also facilitated by rules that allow even minority party members, who are not ordinarily represented in Cabinet, to initiate or prepare legislation and introduce a Bill. This is because the public can only properly hold their elected representatives accountable if they are sufficiently informed of the relative merits of issues before the Assembly.[298]
>
> Of course, this does not mean, for example, that the majority party would have changed course and ditched the Secrecy Bill in favour of an alternative Bill proposed by Lindiwe Mazibuko. The majority party would remain entitled to make the final decision on which Bill to pass into law – no matter how unpopular that Bill might be with the electorate.
>
> But in the long run its MPs would have been forced to engage seriously with an alternative Bill proposed by the opposition. A failure to do so in a serious and competent manner would have run the risk of turning away more informed voters and would have eroded the voting majority of the dominant party. On the other hand, if the MPs of the majority party had managed to show up the Bill proposed by the opposition as frivolous, unworkable or unpopular, the party would have been able to gain more support from voters currently supporting an opposition party or not supporting any party at all. The judgment will not cure all the ills that beset our democratic Parliament. The culture within political parties, which requires strict party discipline and control of individual MPs by party leaders, is too strong for this. But it is a first small step towards making our democratic Parliament relevant once more.[299]

297 *Oriani-Ambrosini* para 64.

298 *Oriani-Ambrosini* para 64.

299 See De Vos, P (2012, 10 October) One small step for Parliament, one giant leap for Ambrosini *Constitutionally Speaking* available at http://constitutionallyspeaking.co.za/once-small-step-for-parliament-one-giant-leap-for-ambrosini/.

There are important structural and contextual reasons why legislation is usually initiated and prepared by the responsible Cabinet member and not by individual members of the NA or by a committee of the NA:[300]

- First, South Africa has been a one-party dominant political system since the dawn of democracy in 1994. Many of the leaders of the dominant party serve in Cabinet which, in turn, initiates legislation in accordance with the mandate of the majority party.[301]
- Second, members of the NA are elected via the closed list proportional representation system. They depend on their party's support to retain their seats, making it unlikely that members of the majority party will take an initiative not approved by the party leadership.[302]
- Third, the current governing party, the ANC, 'is a highly centralized organisation where power has become increasingly concentrated in the hands of the President ... and the party leadership'.[303]
- Fourth, the Speaker plays an important role in deciding which Bills are introduced and the Speaker is a member of the majority party in the NA.[304]
- Last, the political culture of the governing ANC is one in which internal debate flourishes but once a decision is taken, ordinary members tend to defer to the leadership who serve in Cabinet.[305]

Apart from these contextual reasons, there is also a practical reason for the dominance of the executive in the preparation and introduction of legislation. Legislation is usually introduced to give legislative effect to the political programme of action of the majority party which forms the government. In theory, the voters endorse this programme in an election. The party then has a democratic mandate to implement the policies for which it was elected as the governing party. However, no party can foresee all eventualities and therefore does not place its entire legislative programme before the electorate during an election. This is why - as we have seen - the Constitution requires Parliament to facilitate public involvement in the law-making process. Be that as it may, voters elected a party to lead the government and expect the leadership of the party to take the initiative and to formulate policies and eventually legislation to give effect to such policies.

The process of law making through the initiative of the executive, the normal way in which laws are passed, can be simplified as follows:

- Policy is formulated via various channels, including through Nedlac, through internal party discussions and Cabinet discussions which finally results in a draft Bill which is eventually approved by Cabinet.
- After Cabinet has approved the draft Bill, the Cabinet Minister responsible for the policy in question usually first introduces the Bill in the NA or, in some cases, the NCOP. This is referred to as the **first reading**.

---

300 Barkan, J (2005) Emerging legislature or rubber stamp? *The South African National Assembly after ten years of democracy* Working paper No 134, Centre for Social Science Research: Democracy in Africa Research Unit, University of Cape Town at 9-11, available at http://www.cssr.uct.ac.za/sites/cssr.uct.ac.za/files/pubs/wp134.pdf. A version of this paper has now been published in Barkan, JD (ed) (2009) *Legislative Power in Emerging African Democracies.*

301 Barkan (2005) 6.

302 Barkan (2005) 6.

303 Barkan (2005) 7. It is unclear whether this assertion is still correct. After the ousting of President Thabo Mbeki, power shifted from the Presidency back to the ANC leadership collective as represented by the Secretary General of the party.

304 Barkan (2005) 10.

305 Barkan (2005) 11.

- The Bill is then referred to the appropriate portfolio committee for review and amendment after facilitation of public involvement as discussed above. This is referred to as the **second reading** and the Bill is considered ready for passing.
- If the NA passes the Bill, it is forwarded to the upper House, the NCOP, for its assent. If the Bill was introduced in the NCOP and approved there, it is forwarded to the NA for its assent.[306]
- Once both Houses of Parliament have passed the Bill, it is presented to the President for signature. The President does not have a general right to veto Bills duly passed by Parliament but may refuse to sign the Bill if he or she has reservations about its constitutionality. In this case, the President must refer the Bill back to the NA for reconsideration.[307]

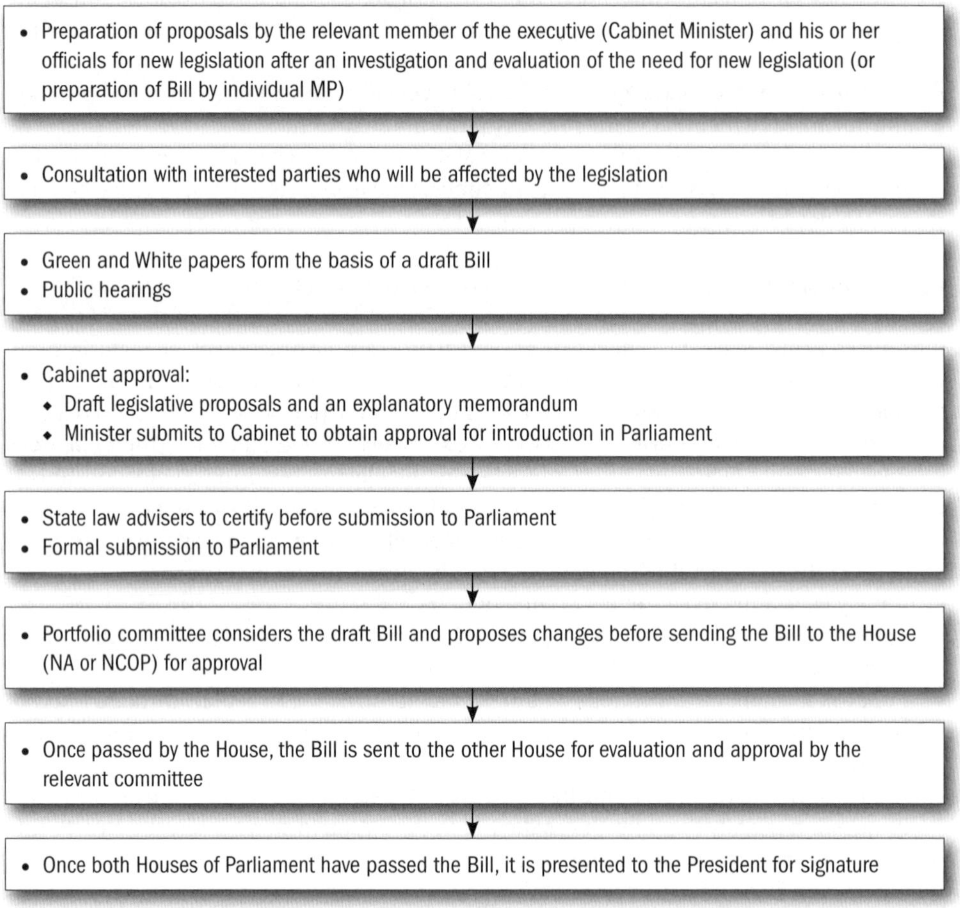

Figure 4.3 The law-making process

306 Barkan (2005) 13. Barken notes that Bills may be referred back to the committee for further amendment before a formal vote, including the amendments desired by the Minister. See also *Doctors for Life* para 40 where Ngcobo J pointed out that the first stage, the deliberative stage, takes place when Parliament is deliberating on a Bill before passing it; the second stage, the Presidential stage, occurs after the Bill has been passed by Parliament but while it is under consideration by the President; and the third stage is the period after the President has signed the Bill into law but before the enacted law comes into force.

307 S 79(1) of the Constitution. See also remarks by O'Regan J in *Executive Council of the Western Cape Legislature and Others v President of the Republic of South Africa and Others* (CCT27/95) [1995] ZACC 8; 1995 (10) BCLR 1289; 1995 (4) SA 877 (22 September 1995) para 7.

The Constitution regulates the manner in which Bills may be introduced in Parliament during the law-making process. The Constitution prescribes different procedures for Bills amending the Constitution,[308] ordinary Bills not affecting provinces,[309] ordinary Bills affecting provinces[310] and money Bills.[311] In *Tongoane and Others v National Minister for Agriculture and Land Affairs and Others*, the Constitutional Court stated that it is therefore important that a Bill must first be classified into or tagged as one of these four categories to determine which procedure should be followed in enacting the Bill.[312] Tagging is important because the procedures for the passing of the various kinds of Bills differ with some procedures being more onerous than others. The Joint Rules of Parliament establish the Joint Tagging Mechanism (JTM) which consists of the Speaker and Deputy Speaker of the NA and the Chairperson and Deputy Chairperson of the NCOP.[313] The function of the JTM is, among other things, to make final rulings as to the classification of Bills.[314]

The Constitutional Court clarified the test for tagging a Bill in *Tongoane*.[315] It is important to note that a distinction is drawn between the characterisation of a Bill for purposes of deciding whether the Bill affects the provinces or not (something we deal with in chapter 8 of this book) and its tagging. As the Constitutional Court pointed out, for the purposes of tagging, we do not enquire into the substance or the true purpose and effect of the Bill. Rather, what matters is whether the provisions of the Bill 'in substantial measure fall within a functional area' which the Constitution empowers provinces to legislate on. The test to be adopted when tagging Bills is therefore called the 'substantial measures test.[316] This test for classification or tagging is therefore different from that used by the Court to characterise a Bill in order to determine whether either the national or the provincial legislature has the legislative competence to enact the law (with which we deal in chapter 8 of this book). The latter test 'involves the determination of the subject-matter or the substance of the legislation, its essence, or true purpose and effect, that is, what the [legislation] is about'.[317] As the Court pointed out in *Tongoane*:

> **There is an important difference between the 'pith and substance' test and the 'substantial measure' test. Under the former, provisions of the legislation that fall outside of its substance are treated as incidental. By contrast, the tagging test is distinct from the question of legislative competence. It focuses on all the provisions of the Bill in order to determine the extent to which they substantially affect functional areas listed in Schedule 4 and not on whether any of its provisions are incidental to its substance. The test for tagging must be informed by its purpose. Tagging is not concerned with determining the sphere of government that has the competence to legislate on a matter. Nor is the process concerned with preventing interference in the legislative competence of another sphere of government. The process is concerned**

308 S 74.

309 S 75.

310 S 76.

311 S 77.

312 (CCT100/09) [2010] ZACC 10; 2010 (6) SA 214 (CC); 2010 (8) BCLR 741 (CC) (11 May 2010) para 45.

313 Joint Rules of Parliament (6th edition) (2011) Rule 151.

314 Joint Rule 151.

315 *Tongoane* para 45.

316 *Tongoane* para 58.

317 *Tongoane* para 58. See also *Ex Parte President of the Republic of South Africa: In re Constitutionality of the Liquor Bill* (CCT12/99) [1999] ZACC 15; 2000 (1) SA 732; 2000 (1) BCLR 1 (11 November 1999) paras 63–4; *Western Cape Provincial Government and Others In Re: DVB Behuising (Pty) Limited v North West Provincial Government and Another* (CCT22/99) [2000] ZACC 2; 2000 (4) BCLR 347; 2001 (1) SA 500 (2 March 2000) para 36; *In re: KwaZulu-Natal Amakhosi and Iziphakanyiswa Amendment Bill of 1995, In re: Payment of Salaries. Allowances and Other Privileges to the Ingonyama Bill of 1995* (CCT1/96, CCT6/96) [1996] ZACC 15; 1996 (7) BCLR 903; 1996 (4) SA 653 (5 July 1996) para 19.

> **with the question of how the Bill should be considered by the provinces and in the NCOP, and how a Bill must be considered by the provincial legislatures depends on whether it affects the provinces. The more it affects the interests, concerns and capacities of the provinces, the more say the provinces should have on its content.**[318]

The purpose of tagging is therefore to determine the nature and extent of the input of provinces (through the NCOP) on the contents of legislation affecting them. Tagging also determines whether the Bill should be passed with a simple majority or according to special procedures with super majority. Because the Constitution attaches considerable importance to the voice of the provinces in legislation affecting them, tagging is therefore pivotal. This is because – as we show elsewhere – depending how a Bill is tagged, the NCOP will either have more or less power in the passing of the Bill.

Tagging also reflects the fact that government under our Constitution 'is constituted as national, provincial and local spheres of government which are distinctive, interdependent and interrelated'.[319] As we shall see in chapter 8 of this book, legislative functions between the national and provincial spheres of government are not rigidly assigned to each sphere and many important functions are shared. This requires co-operation between the various spheres of government which 'include the requirement that each sphere of government must "respect the constitutional status, institutions, powers and functions of government in the other spheres" and "co-operate with one another in mutual trust and good faith by ... co-ordinating their actions and legislation with one another".'[320] As the NCOP helps to facilitate co-operative government in the law-making process, it should be accorded the requisite respect by ensuring that Bills are tagged in the correct manner.

As mentioned above, Bills can be tagged in at least four different ways after which different requirements apply to the passing of the Bill depending on how it was tagged.

First, a Bill can be tagged as a **section 74 Bill** because it is a Bill amending the Constitution. Section 74 Bills require special procedures to be adhered to. Special majorities are also required to pass the Bill to protect the Constitution from being amended too easily.

Section 1 – which contains the founding provisions of the Constitution – can only be changed with the support of 75% of the members of the NA and the support of at least six of the nine provincial delegations to the NCOP.[321]

Bills amending the Bill of Rights can only be changed with the support of two-thirds of the members of the NA and six of the nine provincial delegations in the NCOP.[322]

Any other provision of the Constitution may be amended by a Bill passed by the NA with a supporting vote of at least two-thirds of its members. The support of six of the provincial delegations to the NCOP is not required for these ordinary amendments to the Constitution unless the proposed amendment 'relates to a matter that affects the [NCOP]; or alters provincial boundaries, powers, functions or institutions; or amends a provision that deals specifically with a provincial matter'.[323]

To protect the powers and functions of individual provinces in the case of a Bill that concerns only a specific province or provinces, the NCOP may not pass the Bill or the relevant part unless it has been approved by the legislature or legislatures of the province or

318 *Tongoane* 59–60.
319 S 40(1).
320 *Tongoane* para 67, quoting from s 41(1)(*e*) and 41(1)(*h*)(iv) of the Constitution.
321 S 74(1) of the Constitution.
322 S 74(2) of the Constitution.
323 S 74(3) of the Constitution.

provinces concerned.[324] This means that a Bill that would amend the provincial boundary between, for example, Limpopo Province and Mpumalanga can only be passed with the approval of both the legislatures of Limpopo and Mpumalanga and only if, in addition to this, six of the nine provincial delegations support the amendment.

Second, Bills can be tagged as **section 75 Bills** or ordinary Bills that do not affect the Provinces. When a Bill is tagged as a section 75 Bill it can **only** be introduced in the NA (not in the NCOP).[325] Once passed by the NA, the NCOP must vote on the Bill, but in this case, members of the NCOP do not vote by delegation. Instead, in terms of section 75(2) of the Constitution, each delegate in a provincial delegation has one vote and the question is decided by a majority of votes cast subject to a quorum of one-third of the delegates being present.

The NCOP can pass the Bill, pass the Bill subject to amendments proposed by it or reject the Bill.[326] If the NCOP passes the Bill without proposing amendments, the Bill must be submitted to the President for assent.

If the NCOP rejects the Bill or passes it subject to amendments, the NA must reconsider the Bill, taking into account any amendment proposed by the NCOP. Because it is a section 75 Bill that does not affect the provinces, the NA has the power to override the NCOP amendments by passing the original Bill in the normal manner. In this case, the amendments made by the NCOP will fall away and the original Bill passed by the NA will be sent to the President for assent.

However, the NA may decide to endorse the amendments made by the NCOP by passing the same version passed by the NCOP. In this case, the Bill with the NCOP amendments will be sent to the President. Alternatively, the NA may decide not to proceed with the Bill at all. In this case, the Bill will lapse and will not become law.[327]

When considering these procedures it is important to note the differences between the legislative process to be followed when a Bill is tagged as a section 75 Bill and when it is tagged as a section 76 Bill and the relatively powerful role of the NA in the passing of the former compared to the latter. The most important difference is that a section 75 Bill can, in effect, be passed by the NA without support by the NCOP. This would become important if the majority party in the NA does not enjoy a majority in the NCOP, for example when less than 45 of the delegates in the NCOP are from the majority party. The second House could then conceivably try to obstruct the legislative programme of the majority party in the NA, something – as we shall see – that it may be able to do with section 76 Bills but not with section 75 Bills. This is because the NCOP represents the interest of the provinces in Parliament and will play a much more powerful role in the passing of legislation in cases where the draft legislation affects the provinces.

Third, Bills can be tagged as **section 76 Bills** or ordinary Bills affecting the provinces. A Bill will be tagged in this way if it falls within a functional area listed in Schedule 4 of the Constitution or provides for legislation envisaged in particular sections of the Constitution.[328] It will also be tagged as a section 76 Bill if it purports to intervene in Schedule 5 matters (in terms of section 44(2)) and other financial matters affecting the Provinces.[329] A Bill dealing with the seat of Parliament must be similarly tagged.[330] If the provisions of a Bill in

---

324 S 74(8) of the Constitution.

325 Ss 73(1) and 75(1) of the Constitution.

326 S 75(1) of the Constitution.

327 See s 75(1)(*a*)–(*d*) of the Constitution.

328 S 76(3) of the Constitution. These sections are ss 65(2), 163, 182, 195(3) and (4), 196 and 197.

329 S 76(4) of the Constitution.

330 S 76(5) of the Constitution.

substantial measure fall within the functional area listed in Schedule 4, it will be dealt with under section 76.[331]

Tagging a Bill as a section 76 Bill is important as this gives more weight to the position of the NCOP in the passing of the Bill. Unlike with a section 75 Bill, the Bill can be introduced in either the NA or the NCOP. Once the Bill has been passed in the House in which it was introduced, either the NA or the NCOP (the first House), it is sent to the other House (the second House) to pass, amend or reject it. If the second House passes the Bill without amendment, the Bill must be submitted to the President for assent. If the Bill is passed by the second House with amendments, it must be referred back to the first House which passed it. If that House passes the amended Bill, it must be submitted to the President for assent. However, if the second House which considers the Bill rejects the Bill, or if the first House which passed the Bill refuses to pass an amended Bill referred back to it, the Bill and, where applicable, also the amended Bill, must be referred to a Mediation Committee.[332]

The Mediation Committee is designed as a mechanism to try to reconcile differences between the two Houses of Parliament in line with the principle of co-operative government. It consists, first, of nine members of the NA elected by the NA. Each political party with seats in the Assembly is proportionally represented on the Committee. Second, there are another nine delegates – one from each provincial delegation in the NCOP. In effect, these delegates are from the political party with a majority of delegates in the NCOP delegation.[333]

The Mediation Committee can only make a decision if at least five of the representatives of the NA and at least five of the representatives of the NCOP agree to support it.[334] The Mediation Committee can agree to support the Bill as passed by the NA, the amended Bill as passed by the NCOP or its own version of the Bill.[335] If the Mediation Committee is unable to agree on any of these options within 30 days of the Bill's referral to it, the Bill will lapse unless the Bill was first passed by the NA and the NA again passes the original Bill, but with a supporting vote of at least two-thirds of its members.[336] This means that it is important whether the Bill was first introduced in the NA or the NCOP. Bills first introduced in the NCOP cannot ever be passed over the objections of the NCOP with a two-thirds majority in the NA as would be the case if a Bill was first introduced and passed in the NA.

If the Mediation Committee approves a version of the Bill first passed by the NA, it must be referred to the NCOP for approval. If it approves a version of the Bill first passed by the NCOP, it must be referred to the NA for approval. However, if the Mediation Committee agrees on its own version of the Bill, that version of the Bill must be referred to both the NA and the NCOP. If it is passed a second time by the NA and/or the NCOP in accordance with the procedure set out above, it must be submitted to the President for assent. Once again, the NA has an override power if it supports a Bill with a two-thirds majority in the event that the Bill was introduced in the NA and the NCOP has not supported the decision of the Mediation Committee. The NCOP does not have the same override power. In practice, it would be unlikely that the NA would be able to achieve a two-thirds majority to override the opposition of such a Bill in the NCOP. This means that as far as section 76 Bills are concerned, the NCOP is in a far more powerful position to influence or even block legislation supported

331 *Tongoane* para 56 *et seq*.
332 S 76(1) and (2) of the Constitution.
333 S 78(1) of the Constitution.
334 S 78(2) of the Constitution.
335 S 76(1)(*d*) and 76(2)(*d*) of the Constitution.
336 S 76(1)(*e*) and 76(2)(*e*) of the Constitution.

by the NA than is the case with section 75 Bills. This is because the NCOP represents the interest of the provinces in the national Parliament.

These rather complicated mechanisms are aimed at facilitating co-operation and seeking consensus between the two Houses of Parliament in line with the principle of co-operative government. They also ensure that the NA, with its 400 members representing the various political parties proportionally to their electoral strength, would not be able to ride roughshod over the NCOP whose delegates are equally divided between all provinces. In essence, this means that provincial delegations with fewer voters have the same power as provincial delegations of large provinces.

PAUSE FOR REFLECTION

What happens when the NA and NCOP are controlled by different majority parties?

The section 76 mechanism for passing ordinary legislation affecting the provinces will probably only become important in a case where one political party or a coalition of parties controls the NA while that party or coalition does not control the NCOP. This may happen if the majority party gains a substantial proportion of the votes in large provinces but loses its majority support in at least five provinces, which will then be governed by another political party or a coalition of political parties.

For example, the governing party could win 53% of the vote nationally. This will entitle it to 53% of the seats in the NA and its leader will be elected President. This President will appoint a Cabinet, usually from among the members of the winning party. However, if an opposition party wins 40% of the vote nationally, it will be entitled to only 40% of the seats in the NA. It may nevertheless have garnered a majority of support in five provinces, giving it control of five of the nine delegations to the NCOP. If a section 76 Bill is now proposed by the Cabinet and supported by the 53% of members of the majority party in the NA, it will not be passed into law unless the opposition party agrees to it as it would control five of the nine provincial delegation votes and would, in effect, be able to veto the Bill.

Fourth, **section 77** or **money Bills** require different procedures for their passing. These Bills deal with the imposition of taxes, levies, duties and surcharges to raise money for the state and with the allocation of the money raised in this way for a particular purpose, such as spending it on education, policing or health care.[337] The most important money Bill is the annual budget introduced by the Minister of Finance in the NA. Such a Bill will then be passed in accordance with the procedure laid down in section 75, as discussed above.

However, special procedures apply to the amendment of a money Bill by Parliament. As the Constitution stipulates,[338] these procedures are set down in the Money Bills Amendment Procedure and Related Matters Act.[339] The special procedures are necessary because the budget is a highly technical and complex Bill prepared in conjunction with the technical experts of the Treasury and it could create financial uncertainty and unintended consequences if Parliament were allowed to amend the budget in the same way as it is allowed to amend other pieces of legislation.

337 S 77(1) read with s 214 of the Constitution.
338 S 77(3).
339 Act 9 of 2009.

Once a Bill has been passed in the prescribed manner, either in terms of sections 74, 75, 76 or 77, the Bill must be sent to the President for his or her assent as envisaged in section 79 of the Constitution. In terms of section 79(1) of the Constitution, the President may refer a Bill back to the NA for reconsideration if he or she has reservations about its constitutionality. If the President has reservations about the constitutionality of the Bill, he or she must specify what these reservations are when he refers a Bill back to Parliament.[340] However, the President cannot refuse to sign the Bill because he or she does not support any aspect of the Bill for political reasons. In other words, the President does not have a general power to veto a Bill duly passed by Parliament because he or she does not agree politically with any provisions in the Bill or because his or her conscience would require him or her not to sign the Bill into law. As all constitutional obligations must be performed diligently and without delay,[341] the President is required to sign a Bill duly passed by Parliament within a reasonable time. If the President refers the Bill back to Parliament owing to concerns about its constitutionality, Parliament can address the President's concerns. If the reconsidered Bill fully accommodates the President's reservations, then he or she must sign it. If not, the President may, pursuant to section 79(4) of the Constitution, refer the Bill to the Constitutional Court for a decision on its constitutionality. The President is empowered to refer a matter to the Constitutional Court in terms of section 79 only if his or her reservations concerning the constitutionality of the Bill are not fully accommodated by Parliament. If the President has no reservations concerning the constitutionality of the Bill, or if his reservations have been fully accommodated by Parliament, the referral would be incompetent.[342] If the Constitutional Court decides that the Bill is constitutional, the President must assent to and sign it as envisaged in section 79(5).

In *Ex Parte President of the Republic of South Africa: In re Constitutionality of the Liquor Bill*,[343] the Constitutional Court spelled out, first, the circumstances under which the President is allowed to refer a Bill to the Constitutional Court, and, second, the scope of the Court's power to consider the constitutionality of the Bill. There were three main questions that the Constitutional Court had to consider in this judgment, namely:

- whether the Court was required to consider only the reservations that the President had expressed, or whether it can and should direct its attention more widely
- whether the Court, in determining the Bill's 'constitutionality', should examine every provision of the Bill so as to certify conclusively that in every part it accords with the Constitution
- whether the Court's finding regarding the Bill's constitutionality or otherwise precludes or restricts later constitutional adjudication regarding its provisions once enacted.[344]

The Constitutional Court found that it need only consider the reservation that the President has expressed when he or she refers to Bill to the Constitutional Court. Since the Constitutional Court need only consider reservations expressly specified by the President regarding the Bill's constitutionality, it does not have to consider the Bill in its entirety to determine its constitutionality by examining each and every provision. The Court also found that the decision regarding the constitutionality of the Bill does not preclude future constitutional adjudication regarding its provisions once enacted, except those provisions already

340 *Liquor Bill* para 12.

341 S 237 of the Constitution.

342 *Liquor Bill* para 13.

343 (CCT12/99) [1999] ZACC 15; 2000 (1) SA 732; 2000 (1) BCLR 1 (11 November 1999).

344 *Liquor Bill* para 11.

determined during the consideration of the President's reservation.[345] The Court left open whether it could in such proceedings consider the constitutionality of provisions not referred to by the President which are in obvious conflict with the Constitution.[346]

Even after a Bill has been duly passed by Parliament and signed into law by the President, after which the Bill becomes known as an Act of Parliament, the constitutionality of the Act can be challenged if a sufficient number of MPs applies to the Constitutional Court for an order declaring that all or part of an Act of Parliament is unconstitutional.[347] Such application can only be launched if it is supported by at least one-third of the members of the NA and if it is made within 30 days of the date on which the President assented to and signed the Act.[348] The Constitutional Court is given the power to stall the implementation of the Act referred to it in this manner and can order that all or part of an Act that is the subject of an application has no force until the Court has decided the application, but only if the interests of justice require this and the application has a reasonable prospect of success.[349]

Table 4.2 Bills passed by Parliament in 1999 and 2000[350]

Type of Bill	1999	2000
Section 76(1) Bills affecting provinces, introduced in the NA	5	8
Section 76(2) Bills affecting the provinces, introduced in the NCOP	14	12
Section 77 money Bills	6	6
Section 75 Bills not affecting provinces	33	44
Section 74(3) Bills amending the Constitution	2	0
Total	**60**	**70**

4.5.6 Delegation of legislative powers to executive or other legislatures

According to section 44(1)(*a*)(iii) of the Constitution, Parliament may assign its legislative authority, except the power to amend the Constitution, to any legislative body in another sphere of government. This power relates to the assignment of power to other legislative spheres of government. It is therefore explicitly provided in the Constitution that Parliament is allowed to assign its law-making power, except the power to amend the Constitution, to provincial legislative and municipal councils. Where the national Parliament is of the view that a certain issue may be better dealt with by provincial legislatures, it may therefore explicitly empower such legislatures to enact legislation on that topic even if the topic falls outside the exclusive or concurrent functional areas in which provincial legislatures have the competence to legislate.

A more difficult question arises where Parliament delegates its law-making powers to the executive. This kind of delegation is not unusual as Parliament is not always well

345 *Liquor Bill* paras 14 to 20.

346 See O'Regan J in *Executive Council of the Western Cape Legislature* para 151.

347 S 80(1) of the Constitution.

348 S 80(2) of the Constitution.

349 S 80(3) of the Constitution.

350 Annual Report of Parliament 1999 and 2000, available at http://www.pmg.org.za/minutes/20011018-sita-annual-report-19992000-briefing.

equipped to formulate detailed provisions regarding the implementation and regulation of laws. In *Executive Council of the Western Cape Legislature and Others v President of the Republic of South Africa and Others*, the Constitutional Court stated that in a modern state, Parliament cannot be expected to deal with all such matters itself and it is therefore necessary for effective law making to read this power delegating such legislative functions to other bodies into the Constitution.[351]

However, there are limits to what kind of law-making powers can be delegated and to whom.[352] In *Executive Council of the Western Cape Legislature*, the Constitutional Court stated that although there is nothing in the Constitution which prohibits Parliament from delegating subordinate regulatory authority to other bodies, there is 'a difference between delegating authority to make subordinate legislation within the framework of a statute under which the delegation is made, and assigning plenary legislative power to another body ...'[353] The question in each case would be whether, given the structure of the Constitution and the relevant empowering text, the Constitution permits a delegation of such law-making power or not. The Constitution uses a range of expressions when it confers legislative power on Parliament and the wording used will often give an indication of whether delegations would be permissible. As Ngcobo stated in *Executive Council of the Province of the Western Cape v Minister for Provincial Affairs and Constitutional Development and Another, Executive Council of KwaZulu-Natal v President of the Republic of South Africa and Others*:

> **Sometimes [the Constitution] states that 'national legislation must'; at other times it states that something will be dealt with 'as determined by national legislation'; and at other times it uses the formulation 'national legislation may'. Where one of the first two formulations is used, it seems to me to be a strong indication that the legislative power may not be delegated by the Legislature, although this will of course also depend upon context.**[354]

The text of the relevant empowering provision of the Constitution must be read in context and we should consider factors that flow from the nature of the Constitution, its structure and scheme. To this end, as stated by the Constitutional Court in *Justice Alliance of South Africa v President of Republic of South Africa and Others, Freedom Under Law v President of Republic of South Africa and Others, Centre for Applied Legal Studies and Another v President of Republic of South Africa and Others*, we must consider 'the nature and extent of the delegation'.[355]

We must keep in mind that the primary reason for delegation is to ensure that the legislature is not overwhelmed by the need to determine minor regulatory details. Delegation relieves Parliament from dealing with detailed provisions that are often required for the purpose of implementing and regulating laws and is necessary for effective law making. However, we must draw a distinction between delegation to make subordinate legislation

351 (CCT27/95) [1995] ZACC 8; 1995 (10) BCLR 1289; 1995 (4) SA 877 (22 September 1995) para 51.

352 *Executive Council of the Western Cape Legislature* para 51. See also *AAA Investments (Proprietary) Limited v Micro Finance Regulatory Council and Another* (CCT51/05) [2006] ZACC 9; 2006 (11) BCLR 1255 (CC); 2007 (1) SA 343 (CC) (28 July 2006) paras 49, 93 and 122–3; *Constitutionality of the Mpumalanga Petitions Bill, 2000* (CCT 11/01) [2001] ZACC 10; 2002 (1) SA 447 (CC); 2001 (11) BCLR 1126 (5 October 2001) para 19; *Executive Council of the Province of the Western Cape v Minister for Provincial Affairs and Constitutional Development and Another, Executive Council of KwaZulu-Natal v President of the Republic of South Africa and Others* (CCT15/99,CCT18/99) [1999] ZACC 13; 2000 (1) SA 661; 1999 (12) BCLR 1360 (15 October 1999) paras 123–4.

353 *Executive Council of the Western Cape Legislature* para 51.

354 (CCT15/99,CCT18/99) [1999] ZACC 13; 2000 (1) SA 661; 1999 (12) BCLR 1360 (15 October 1999) para 125.

355 (CCT 53/11, CCT 54/11, CCT 62/11) [2011] ZACC 23; 2011 (5) SA 388 (CC); 2011 (10) BCLR 1017 (CC) (29 July 2011) para 61.

within the framework of an empowering statute and 'assigning plenary legislative powers to another body'.[356] Where the doctrine of parliamentary sovereignty governs, Parliament may delegate as much power as it chooses. In a constitutional democracy, however, such as that operating in South Africa, Parliament may not ordinarily delegate its 'essential legislative functions' to the executive.[357] This means that Parliament can delegate some of its powers to the executive, most notably through delegating the power to make regulations in terms of legislation passed by Parliament to individual Ministers or to the President. However, Parliament may not delegate its plenary legislative power, that is, the power to make original legislation, to an executive authority such as the President or a Cabinet Minister as such a delegation will breach the separation of powers doctrine.[358] It may only delegate the power to make subordinate legislation such as proclamations and regulations.[359] This distinction between original and subordinate legislation is drawn from the fact that when Parliament makes legislation, it does so in accordance with the 'original' legislative powers conferred on it by the Constitution. However, the development of legislation, such as proclamations, by the executive refers to the law that is made by virtue of the power granted from a lawful source, such as the Constitution.[360] Thus, although the separation of powers doctrine does not allow one branch of government to exercise a power exclusively allocated to another branch of government, it can exercise powers delegated to it by another branch as long as this power is not exclusively reserved for the other branch of government.

The question whether Parliament can assign its law-making power to the executive was first answered in the case of *Executive Council of the Western Cape Legislature*. This case involved section 16A(1) of the Local Government Transition Act[361] that aimed to transform local government in line with the new constitutional dispensation. This section provided that 'the President may amend this Act and any schedule thereto by proclamation in the gazette'. This section therefore effectively conferred on the President, the head of the executive branch of government in the national sphere of government, the power to amend the Act by proclamation. The President used this power to transfer certain functions provided for in the Act from the provincial to the national sphere of government. The Executive Council of the Western Cape Legislature challenged the constitutionality of this section and the relevant proclamation on the basis that Parliament cannot delegate its law-making function to the executive. Chaskalson P, as he then was, held:

> **[t]he legislative authority vested in Parliament under section 37 of this [interim] Constitution is expressed in wide terms – 'to make laws for the Republic in accordance with this Constitution'. In a modern state, detailed provisions are often required for the purpose of implementing and regulating laws, and Parliament cannot be expected to deal with all such matters itself. There is nothing in the Constitution which prohibits Parliament from delegating subordinate regulatory authority to other bodies. The power to do so is necessary for effective law-making. It is implicit in the power to make law for the country and I have no doubt that under our Constitution Parliament can pass legislation delegating such legislative functions to other bodies. There is, however, a difference between delegating authority to make subordinate legislation within the framework of a statute under which the delegation**

356 *Executive Council of the Western Cape Legislature* para 51. See also *Justice Alliance* para 51.
357 *Justice Alliance* para 55.
358 *Justice Alliance* para 55.
359 See *Executive Council of the Western Cape Legislature* para 43.
360 See Hoexter, C (2007) *Administrative Law in South Africa* 50.
361 Act 209 of 1993.

> **is made, and assigning plenary legislative power to another body, including, as section 16A does, the power to amend the Act under which the assignment is made.**[362]

The Court then decided in this case that it was inconsistent with the doctrine of separation of powers for Parliament to delegate the power to amend its laws to the President as head of the executive.[363] It argued that although the need for assignment of subordinate legislative authority cannot be overemphasised, the assignment of plenary legislative powers is a different matter all together. This is not allowed under the new constitutional dispensation as it could give rise to a constitutional crisis. The Court indicated that the relevant constitutional provision which deals with legislative authority is not merely directive but is peremptory. It therefore cannot be said that the power to delegate primary legislative power is implied in the Constitution. Therefore, Parliament cannot delegate its original law-making power to the executive. It can only delegate the making of subordinate legislation such as presidential proclamations and ministerial regulations. The position is the same under the 1996 Constitution.[364]

PAUSE FOR REFLECTION

Parliament cannot delegate its plenary law-making power to the President

In *Justice Alliance*, the Constitutional Court confirmed the view that Parliament cannot delegate its **plenary law-making power** to the President. The Court stated that one should look at both textual and contextual indicators to determine whether such a drastic delegation would be permitted in terms of the separation of powers doctrine.

Section 176(1) of the Constitution states that the term of office for a Constitutional Court judge is normally 12 years 'except where an Act of Parliament extends the term of office of a Constitutional Court judge'. Parliament had passed section 8(*a*) of the Judges Remuneration and Condition of Employment Act[365] which permitted the further extension of the term of office of the Chief Justice if requested to do so by the President. The President had then relied on this section in an attempt to extend the term of office of the former Chief Justice, Sandile Ngcobo. The section on which the President relied was then challenged in Court which declared it unconstitutional. The Court confirmed that where the doctrine of parliamentary sovereignty governs, Parliament may delegate as much power as it chooses. However, in a constitutional democracy, Parliament may not ordinarily delegate its essential legislative functions, one of which would be to delegate the power to extend the term of office of the Chief Justice to the President.

The Court provided several reasons for this view. In this case, the power to extend the term of a Constitutional Court judge goes to the core of the tenure of the judicial office, judicial independence and the separation of powers. It was therefore deemed

362 *Executive Council of the Western Cape Legislature* para 51.
363 *Executive Council of the Western Cape Legislature* paras 106–13.
364 This basic principle was confirmed in a separate judgment in the same case by Mahommed DP (*Executive Council of the Western Cape Legislature* para 136), but for slightly different – more substantive – reasons. Mahommed said these things cannot be determined in the abstract but depend, *inter alia*, on 'the constitutional instrument in question, the powers of the legislature in terms of that instrument, the nature and ambit of the purported delegation, the subject-matter to which it relates, the degree of delegation, the control and supervision retained or exercisable by the delegator over the delegatee, the circumstances prevailing at the time when the delegation is made and when it is expected to be exercised, the identity of the delegatee and practical necessities generally'.
365 Act 47 of 2001.

to be an essential legislative function that could not be delegated.[366] The independence of its judges is given vigorous protection by means of detailed and specific provisions regulating their appointment. The Chief Justice is at the pinnacle of the judiciary and thus the protection of his or her independence is just as important.[367] Section 8(*a*) thus violated the requirement for judicial independence as well as violating the principle of separation of powers. This does not mean that the term of office of judges of the Constitutional Court could not be extended by Parliament in accordance with section 176(1). However, if Parliament wished to do so, it would have to pass legislation providing for such an extension that applied to all judges of the Constitutional Court.[368]

Apart from the legal point about the limits of the power of Parliament to delegate its legislative powers to the executive, this case also illustrates the need of members of the legislature and the executive to follow the correct legal route when they take action in terms of the Constitution and the law. Had Parliament passed a law extending the term of office of all Constitutional Court judges to 15 years, there would not have been a successful challenge to the move and the then Chief Justice would have been able to serve as Chief Justice for another three years.

4.6 National House of Traditional Leaders

The 1996 Constitution provides for the recognition of the 'institution, status and role of traditional leadership' in South Africa, provided that this is done subject to the other provisions in the Constitution.[369] It further provides for the establishment of a House of Traditional Leaders by the passing of national legislation. The Constitution envisages that this House of Traditional Leaders will deal with matters relating to traditional leadership, the role of traditional leaders, customary law and the customs of communities observing a system of customary law.[370] To this end, Parliament passed the National House of Traditional Leaders Act (NHTLA)[371] which establishes a House of Traditional Leaders who serve for a term of five years.[372]

The House is not democratically elected. Instead, the Act provides for the election of senior traditional leaders or headmen or women by the various provincial Houses of Traditional Leaders. If such Houses have not been established, leaders serving on traditional councils would serve in the National House of Traditional Leaders.[373] At least a third of the members of the House must normally consist of women. However, if the Minister is satisfied that there is an insufficient number of women to participate in the House, the Minister must, after consultation with the Premier of the province in question and the provincial House concerned, determine a lower threshold.[374]

Because the Constitution explicitly states that traditional leadership can only be recognised in a manner that complies with the other provisions of the Constitution, including the

366 *Justice Alliance* para 55.
367 *Justice Alliance* para 56.
368 *Justice Alliance* para 77.
369 S 211(1).
370 S 212(2)(*a*).
371 Act 22 of 2009.
372 S 2 of the NHTLA.
373 S 3(1) and 3(2) of the NHTLA.
374 S 3(4) of the NHTLA.

founding values of a democratic state that embody the values of 'universal adult suffrage ... regular elections and a multi-party system of government',[375] the role of the House of Traditional Leaders is advisory in nature. It does not have the power to veto legislation or to take part in a non-advisory role in the formal law-making processes prescribed in sections 74 to 77 of the Constitution. Instead, it is empowered to consider Parliamentary Bills referred to it by the Secretary to Parliament in terms of section 18 of the Traditional Leadership and Governance Framework Act (TLGFA).[376] These Bills are any Bills 'pertaining to customary law or customs of traditional communities'.[377] The National House of Traditional Leaders is then required, within 30 days, to make any comments about the Bill.[378]

The House of Traditional Leaders is also empowered to 'advise the national government' and to 'make recommendations' relating to policy and legislation regarding traditional leadership, the role of traditional leaders, customary law and the customs of communities observing a system of customary law.[379] The House of Traditional Leaders must also be consulted on 'national government development programmes that affect traditional communities'.[380]

The other powers bestowed on the House of Traditional Leaders are vague and of no binding consequence to the work of the national legislature. These include the powers and duties to co-operate with the provincial Houses of Traditional Leaders and to promote:

- the role of traditional leadership within a democratic constitutional dispensation
- nation building
- peace, stability and cohesiveness of communities
- the preservation of the moral fibre and regeneration of society
- the preservation of the culture and traditions of communities
- socio-economic development and service delivery
- the social well-being and welfare of communities
- the transformation and adaptation of customary law and custom so as to comply with the provisions of the Bill of Rights in the Constitution.[381]

The House of Traditional Leaders therefore does not have any direct legislative powers and cannot veto legislation passed by Parliament. It is, in essence, an advisory body aimed at ensuring that the interests of traditional leaders and the communities represented by traditional leaders are considered in the law-making process. Although the House of Traditional Leaders must therefore be consulted on issues affecting traditional communities, including the passing of legislation affecting traditional communities, the consultation process does not afford traditional leaders any powers to slow down or thwart the legislative programme of Parliament.

375 S 1(*d*) of the Constitution.
376 Act 41 of 2003.
377 S 18(1)(*a*) of the TLGFA.
378 S 18(2) of the TLGFA read with s 12(2)(*a*) of the NHTLA.
379 S 11(2)(*b*) of the NHTLA.
380 S 11(2)(*e*) of the NHTLA.
381 S 11(1)(*a*) of the NHTLA.

SUMMARY

The Constitution establishes a bicameral Parliament consisting of two Houses. The National Assembly (NA) is the directly elected House of Parliament representing the interests of all the people, to which MPs are elected in terms of a **pure proportional representation electoral system**. The National Council of Provinces (NCOP) is the indirectly selected House of Parliament representing the interests of the various provinces in the national Parliament. The NCOP comprises provincial delegations consisting of six permanent delegates appointed by each of the provincial legislatures and four special delegates nominated from among the members of each of the provincial legislatures.

The two Houses of Parliament together provide a forum for debate on important issues; hold the executive organs of state in the national sphere of government accountable to Parliament; exercise an oversight function over the exercise of national authority and over other organs of state; and pass national legislation. The NA is the more prominent and powerful of the two Houses because it is directly elected and because it elects and can also dismiss the President and the other members of the executive. The NA therefore has more power to hold the executive accountable than the NCOP.

Members of Parliament (MPs) enjoy important rights and privileges to protect their ability to take part in the various functions of Parliament without fear of legal sanction. MPs enjoy the right to freedom of expression in Parliament and in the various committees of Parliament and are insulated from the law of defamation.

The various committees of Parliament - especially the various portfolio committees that focus on the work associated with a specific government department - are seen as the engine room of Parliament. Although members of the NA and the NCOP can ask questions of members of the Executive and have a right to have their questions answered, either orally in each of the Houses or in written form, portfolio committees can call members of the executive and departmental officials to testify before them to oversee the work of the individual departments and to hold the members of the executive accountable.

Legislation is normally formulated by the relevant government department on the initiative of the Minister involved and then submitted to Parliament for consideration. MPs can also formulate Bills, but in the past this seldom happened. Even where members of opposition parties formulate and table Bills, such Bills have only a small chance of being adopted by Parliament because the majority party in Parliament will normally only support legislation in accordance with its own programme and policies. Without support from the majority party, Bills cannot be passed.

Once legislation is tabled in Parliament (after being approved by the Cabinet), discussions on the details of such Bills tabled in Parliament occur in portfolio committees who have the power to amend the draft legislation before it is sent to the NA and the NCOP for approval. During this process, members of the public have an important right to participate in the law-making process and can make written and sometimes oral submissions to the various portfolio committees about draft legislation.

Arguably, the most important power of Parliament is the power to pass legislation. Bills must be tagged by a Joint Tagging Mechanism to determine how Parliament will procedurally deal with the passing of the draft legislation. Once portfolio committees have processed Bills, each of the Houses of Parliament must consider and vote on a Bill. The Constitution prescribes different procedures to be followed for the passing of Bills that have been tagged as section 74, 75, 76 and 77 Bills. The Constitution also requires that Bills amending the Constitution can only be passed by enhanced majorities. Once both Houses of Parliament have passed the same version of a Bill, it is sent to the President for signature. The President can refer a Bill back to Parliament if he or she has reservations about the constitutionality of aspects of the Bill. If the reservations are not dealt with, the President can also refer the Bill to the Constitutional Court to determine whether the reservations about the constitutionality of the Bill are valid or not.

Chapter 5

Separation of powers and the national executive

5.1 Introduction

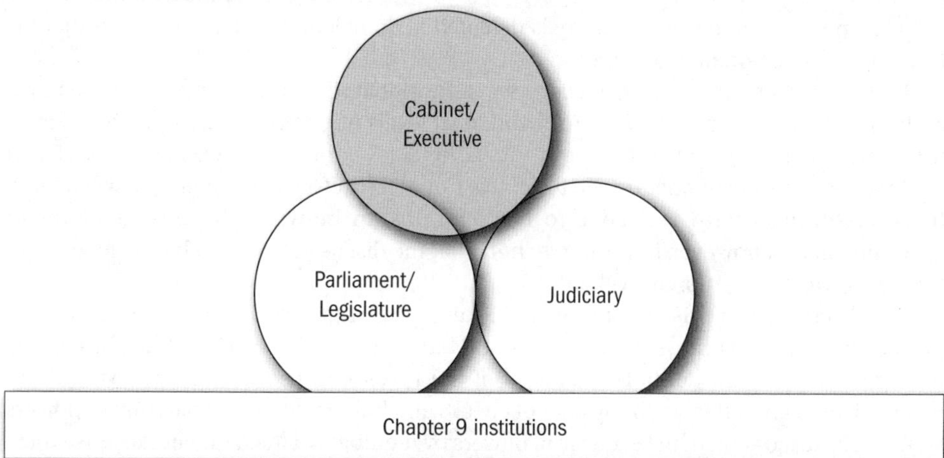

Figure 5.1 Separation of powers and the national executive

While Parliament is responsible for passing legislation and overseeing the exercise of national executive authority, the national executive is responsible for the day-to-day running of the country. The national executive consists of the President, the Deputy President and the members of the Cabinet. Parliament is made up of members of every political party which received enough votes in a general election to win at least one seat in the National Assembly (NA). The national executive, however, is usually made up only of the members - usually the leaders - of the majority party in the NA (or where no party has obtained a majority, the members of a coalition of parties).

It is important to distinguish between the executive, the public administration, public service and the state. When we refer to the executive, we mean the members who form the government of the day. A **government** is formed by the majority party (or parties who form a majority coalition[1]) in the NA for the limited duration of the life of the NA. This means governments come and go while the public administration, public service and the state - with all its permanent employees - stay the same even when the governing party loses an election and is replaced by another party. As the electoral fortunes of political parties wax and wane, they may find themselves either in government or in opposition. Although one political party can remain in government for many years because it remains popular and keeps winning elections, as has been the case with the ANC in democratic South Africa, that political party and the government it leads should not be conflated or confused with the public administration, public service and the state.

The **public administration** consists of the officials who do the core of the government's work and who implement the political decisions taken by the members of the executive.[2] These include all the employees of government departments, as well as the employees of other organs of state. A slightly narrower group is the members of the **public service** who are those persons who work for the national and provincial government departments.[3]

The government or the executive must also be distinguished from the state. The **state** is usually viewed as an organised political community occupying a certain territory and whose members live under the authority of a constitution. The state is therefore a far broader concept than the government: it does not change except in the case of a revolution in which the state itself is overthrown and replaced with a new constitutional order or other set of governing rules, or in which the state is recreated within new geographical boundaries, or both. Even when the governing party is defeated at an election and a new government is formed, the state remains the same.

In this chapter we discuss the executive authority at the national level. The executive authority is also exercised at provincial and local levels of government. At provincial level these structures largely mirror those at the national level: provincial executives consist of the Premier and the Members of the Executive Council (MECs). In chapter 8 we will refer to these institutions with reference to the relationship between the three spheres of government. It is, however, important to note that the discussion in this chapter focuses on the executive at the national level only.

The discussion in this chapter occurs against the larger canvas of the separation of powers doctrine and the system of **checks and balances** in this doctrine. When discussing the appointment and possible dismissal of the President, it must be understood as a mechanism to give effect to the system of checks and balances in the separation of powers system. The discussion of the exercise of powers by members of the national executive must

1 A coalition is formed if no party obtains at least 50% of the seats in the NA. Two or more parties who together have more than 50% of the seats in the NA will then agree to work together and form a government, based on agreed policies and principles.

2 *President of the Republic of South Africa and Others v South African Rugby Football Union and Others (SARFU II)* (CCT16/98) [1999] ZACC 9; 1999 (4) SA 147; 1999 (7) BCLR 725 (4 June 1999) para 138.

3 S 197(1) of the Constitution states: 'Within the public administration there is a public service for the Republic.' See also s 1 of the Public Service Act 103 of 1994 read with s 8 and Currie, I and De Waal, J (2001) *The New Constitutional and Administrative Law, Vol 1 Constitutional Law* 229.

also be considered with reference to the powers of the NA (discussed in chapter 4) to hold the members of the national executive accountable. It is therefore impossible to study the appointment, powers and the limits placed on the exercise of powers by members of the national executive without having regard to the powers and functions of Parliament. Neither is it possible to understand the way in which the executive's exercise of power is constrained without having regard to the role of the judiciary (discussed in chapter 6).

5.2 The President

5.2.1 Election and term of office

Unlike the previous 1983 tricameral Constitution, the 1996 Constitution does not provide for the election of a **State** President - it refers simply to the election of a **President**. The NA elects the President as both the Head of State and as the head of the national executive from among the members of the NA at its first sitting after a national general election or whenever a vacancy occurs in the office of the President.[4] The President, in turn, appoints the members of the Cabinet who will govern the country for the electoral term of the NA - usually five years. The election of the President must be held at a time and on a date determined by the Chief Justice, but not more than 30 days after a vacancy in the office of the President occurs.[5]

After his or her election, the President ceases to be a member of the NA. Within five days, the newly elected President must assume office by swearing or affirming faithfulness to the Republic and obedience to the Constitution in accordance with the oath of office contained in Schedule 2 of the Constitution.[6]

The President may not serve more than two full terms in office which will normally be 10 years. However, if the President is elected to fill a vacancy which has occurred between elections, the period he or she serves until the next election will not count as part of one of the two terms.[7] This means that a President who takes over the presidency halfway through the term of the NA, and then serves out that half term plus two full terms, could serve more than 10 years as President.

In light of the points set out above, it is clear that the President is not directly elected by the voters, but is indirectly elected by the members of the NA. Usually, the leader of the majority party in the NA, who was elected by representatives of the members of that political party at its national elective congress or conference, will be elected as President.[8] It follows, therefore, that the President is, in effect, elected by the delegates who are selected to attend the elective conference of the political party that wins the next general election and not directly by the voters. However, voters indirectly confirm the majority party's choice of leader, and therefore as President, by voting for that party in the general election that follows on the election of the party leader.

4 S 86(1) of the Constitution.

5 S 86(3) of the Constitution.

6 Section 87 of the Constitution. This means that the South African President will be elected to the NA, will take his or her seat, but will only remain a member of the NA for a few hours until such time as he or she is elected President, after which he or she ceases to be a member of the NA.

7 See s 88(2) of the Constitution.

8 For example, in terms of Rule 12.3 of the Constitution of the African National Congress (ANC), its national conference - held every five years - elects the President, the Deputy President, National Chairperson, the Secretary General, Deputy Secretary General, the Treasurer General and the remaining 80 additional members of the National Executive Committee (NEC) of the party. The NEC, as a whole, must consist of not less than 50% women. See African National Congress Constitution as amended and adopted at the 53nd National Conference, Mangaung, 2012, available at http://www.anc.org.za/show.php?id=10177.

On paper, the NA – the directly elected body – is more powerful than the President or his or her Cabinet as the NA has the power not only to elect the President, but also to remove him or her from office. In practice, the President and the other members of the executive remain the more powerful arm of government until such time as he or she loses the support of the majority party in the NA. This is because as long as the President enjoys the support of the members of the majority political party of which the President would usually be the leader, his or her position as party leader will provide him or her with enormous influence over ordinary members of the party in the NA.

The NA can remove the President from office in one of two ways. First, in terms of section 89(1) of the Constitution, the NA can remove the President from office if it adopts a resolution to that effect with a supporting vote of at least a two-thirds majority if they find that one of the specified grounds for the removal of the President exists. These grounds are a serious violation of the Constitution or the law, serious misconduct or inability to perform the functions of office.[9] These are objective grounds and the NA can only remove the President in this manner on the basis of a finding that one or more of these grounds is present.

The NA **cannot** remove the President from office in terms of section 89 merely because he or she has lost the support of the majority party in the NA. The power conferred on the NA does not provide a wide political discretion to members of the NA, but confers a power on its members related to safeguarding the nation against the abuse of power by the President. Removing the President in this manner, which is also called the impeachment of the President, has potentially serious consequences. Anyone who has been removed from the office of President because of a serious violation of the Constitution or the law, or for serious misconduct, is prohibited from receiving any benefits of that office, including a pension, and may not serve in any public office again.[10] A President who resigns, who retires after serving two full terms or whose party loses an election and is not re-elected as President is entitled to these benefits.

Second, the President can also be removed from office for purely political reasons in terms of section 102(2) of the Constitution, but only if the NA, by a vote supported by a simple majority of its members, passes a motion of no confidence in the President. Section 102 reflects the essentially parliamentary nature of our system of government as it signals that the President and his or her Cabinet are required at all times to retain the support of the majority of members of the NA.[11]

Where one political party has obtained more than 50% of the votes in the NA, this will in effect mean that the President is at all times required to retain the support of his or her party both inside and outside the NA. If the President loses the support of his or her party, a vote of no confidence can be instituted against the President after which he or she will have to resign. Following the Constitutional Court's judgment in *Mazibuko v Sisulu and Another*,[12] any member of the NA can now propose a motion of no confidence in the President and

---

9 S 89(1) of the Constitution.

10 S 89(2) of the Constitution.

11 The South African system is not a pure system of parliamentary government as the President is both Head of State and head of the executive, the President ceases to be a member of the NA once elected and, as we shall see, two members of Cabinet can be appointed from outside the NA. Nevertheless, as far as the constitutional structure is concerned, the South African system is essentially parliamentary in nature and not presidential in nature as the President is not directly elected by the people. See also Murray, C and Stacey, R 'The President and the national executive' in Woolman, S and Bishop, M (2013) *Constitutional Law of South Africa* 2nd ed rev service 5 18.3.

12 (CCT 115/12) [2013] ZACC 28; 2013 (6) SA 249 (CC); 2013 (11) BCLR 1297 (CC) (27 August 2013).

have it debated in the NA. It is, however, highly unlikely that such a motion will be passed unless the President has lost the support of his or her party.

South Africa has a closed list proportional representation electoral system in which political party leaders have influence over who represents the party in the NA. The practical effect of this system is that the President must retain the support of the majority party leadership to ensure that he or she is not 'recalled' by that leadership. If members of the majority party in the NA are instructed by the party leadership to support a vote of no confidence in the President, they would probably agree to do so as their failure to obey such an instruction may well lead to their removal from the NA and their replacement with members who will obey such an order. This is because the Constitution provides that a member of the NA ceases to be a member if he or she 'ceases to be a member the party that nominated that person as member of the Assembly'.[13] This means if a member of the NA refuses to follow instructions from party leaders to support a vote of no confidence in the President, he or she can be removed from the party for ill-discipline and replaced with a more docile member.

CRITICAL THINKING

The legality of the decision by the ANC NEC to 'recall' former President Mbeki from office

In his book, *Eight Days in September: The Removal of Thabo Mbeki*,[14] the Reverend Frank Chikane writes about the dramatic removal of then President Thabo Mbeki from office by the National Executive Committee (NEC) of the ANC. Members of the NEC were elected at Polokwane at the end of 2007 after a bitter struggle between Mbeki and his supporters and President Jacob Zuma and his supporters. Chikane writes as follows:

> It was after midnight of Friday, 19 September 2008 – to be precise, just before 1.00 a.m. on Saturday – when the first text messages began to come through: 'the NEC has decided to recall Mbeki as president of the country'. Another said that ANC officials had been appointed to visit Mbeki immediately, that night, to inform him of the NEC decision. Other text messages kept coming from NEC members in Esselen Park celebrating that they had won and that Mbeki was to be removed or else expressing concern over the consequences of the NEC decision ...
>
> Calls also began to come through from Mbeki's advisers asking what they should do. Advocate Mojanku Gumbi, the president's legal adviser, was among the first to call and we discussed what the presidency needed to do. Her second call concerned a message from the staff at Mahlamba Ndlopfu, saying that they had been asked to wake the president as a delegation from the ANC was coming to inform him about the NEC decision. Presumably the thinking was – as a matter of courtesy – that he should learn about the decision from the party, not from the media or third parties, but we believed he should not be woken. Advocate Gumbi and I would be at Mahlamba Ndlopfu early in the morning to inform him about the impending visit. We instructed the staff accordingly and made arrangements with the ANC to send their delegation at about 9.00 a.m., by which time we thought the president would be ready to start his day. Advocate Gumbi and I

13 S 47(3)(*c*).

14 Chikane, F (2012) *Eight Days in September: The Removal of Thabo Mbeki* 17–18.

agreed that she (together with the legal unit in the presidency) would review all the legal issues related to the decision and advise how the government would handle the matter – a procedure dependent on the nature of the decision, which we would only hear officially from the delegation later that morning.

Questions are asked (but not answered) in the book about the legality of the decision by the ANC NEC to 'recall' former President Mbeki from office and whether Mbeki was legally required to obey the 'recall' by the NEC. Constitutionally, former President Mbeki had no legal duty to obey the decision of the NEC to 'recall' him. He could have refused in the hope of garnering support from among the ANC members serving in the NA. However, if he had refused to heed the instruction by the NEC, serious consequences might have ensued. First, his refusal may have led to disciplinary charges being brought against him and he may eventually have been expelled from the ANC. Second, the ANC members of the NA would have been instructed to rely on section 102 of the Constitution to pass a vote of no confidence in Mbeki after which he would have had to resign. In these circumstances, the President had little choice but to resign, which he did in due course after addressing the nation.

This dramatic event in South Africa's history alerts us to the sometimes complex relationship between political parties (especially the governing party) and the elected officials in the legislature and the executive. Although the President and the members of the NA are constitutionally required to act in accordance with the Constitution, strict party discipline also requires them to obey the instructions of the political party to which they belong. In this context, the absence of more detailed provisions in the Constitution or legislation regulating the relationship between political parties and elected officials may be viewed as a weakness in our constitutional system.

Because the President fulfils a vital role in running the country as the Head of State and head of the executive, it is important that there should never be a vacancy in this position. Another office-bearer will act as President when:

- the President is absent from the Republic
- when the President is otherwise unable to fulfil the duties of President, for example due to illness
- there is a vacancy in the office of President that arises when the President resigns or dies while in office, a motion of no confidence is passed in the President or the President is removed from office.

The Deputy President will ordinarily fill this temporary vacancy but if he or she is unavailable, the following office-bearers will act as President in the following order:

- a Minister designated by the President, but if the President has not designated such a person
- a Minister designated by the other members of the Cabinet, but if the Cabinet has not designated such a person
- the Speaker of the NA until the NA designates one of its other members as acting President.[15]

15 S 90(1) of the Constitution.

This means that if the President falls ill, passes away or resigns, the Deputy President will usually act as President until a new President is elected or until the President can resume his or her duties. However, if the Deputy President is also unavailable because he or she has resigned or has also passed away, somebody else, in the order listed above, will be appointed as acting President to ensure that there is no power vacuum at the top of the executive.

An Acting President has all the responsibilities, powers and functions of the President.[16] Before assuming the responsibilities, powers and functions of the President, the Acting President must swear or affirm faithfulness to the Republic and obedience to the Constitution in accordance with the oath of office contained in Schedule 2 of the Constitution.[17] A person who as Acting President has sworn or affirmed faithfulness to the Republic need not repeat the swearing or affirming procedure for any subsequent term as Acting President during the period ending when the person next elected President assumes office.[18]

5.2.2 The President as Head of State and as head of the executive

The President is vested with powers that are conferred on him or her by the Constitution in his or her capacity as the Head of State as well as the head of the national executive.[19] The legal significance of this distinction is that as Head of State the President exercises his or her authority **alone** and usually need not consult the other members of the Cabinet.[20] When the President exercises head of the executive powers, he or she acts in consultation with his or her Cabinet.[21]

When the President acts as Head of State, he or she cannot 'abdicate' the exercise of such a power[22] by:

- unlawfully delegating that power conferred on him or her as Head of State[23]
- acting 'under dictation' by merely following the instructions of another without applying his or her mind to the matter at hand[24]
- 'passing the buck' by referring the decision to somebody else.[25]

This does not mean that when contemplating the exercise of this kind of Head of State power, the President should not (or does not have the right to) consult with and take the advice of Ministers and advisers as long as he or she takes the final decision.[26] The Constitutional Court can check on whether the Head of State powers are exercised in accordance with the

16 S 90(2) of the Constitution.

17 S 90(3) of the Constitution.

18 S 90(4) of the Constitution.

19 See s 83(*a*) of the Constitution.

20 *President of the Republic of South Africa and Another v Hugo* (CCT11/96) [1997] ZACC 4; 1997 (6) BCLR 708; 1997 (4) SA 1 (18 April 1997) para 14.

21 See s 85(2) of the Constitution, which states, 'The President exercises the executive authority, together with the other members of the Cabinet, ...', read with s 101(2): 'A written decision by the President must be countersigned by another Cabinet member if that decision concerns a function assigned to that other Cabinet member'. See also *President of the Republic of South Africa and Others v South African Rugby Football Union and Others (SARFU III)* (CCT16/98) [1999] ZACC 11; 2000 (1) SA 1; 1999 (10) BCLR 1059 (10 September 1999) para 38; and *Hugo* para 14.

22 See generally Baxter, L (1984) *Administrative Law* 434–4. See also *Hofmeyr v Minister of Justice and Another* 1992 (3) SA 108 (C) at 117 F–G.

23 *SARFU III* para 40: 'There can be no doubt that when the Constitution vests the power to appoint commissions of inquiry in the President, the President may not delegate that authority to a third party. The President himself must exercise the power. Any delegation to a third party would be invalid.'

24 *SARFU III* para 40:'cases where a functionary vested with a power does not of his or her own accord decide to exercise the power, but does so on the instructions of another'.

25 *SARFU III* para 40: '"passing the buck" contemplates a situation in which the functionary may refer the decision to someone else'.

26 *SARFU III* para 41.

Constitution and can confirm that such an exercise of power does not infringe on the Bill of Rights or breach the principle of legality. We deal with this check on the exercise of power by the President in more detail in the following section.

The Head of State powers are usually distinguished from the head of the executive powers by focusing on whether the President is required to exercise a political discretion on behalf of the government, in which case the President acts as the head of the executive, or whether the President is exercising a power as the Head of State, which implies an absence of a clear exercise of a political discretion. As Head of State, the President is representative of all the people, not only of the government formed by the majority party.[27] However, as Currie and De Waal point out, this distinction is difficult to uphold.[28]

A better distinction can be drawn between the exercise of the Head of State power and the head of the executive power by focusing on the historical emergence of the South African office of the President. For a large part of the twentieth century during most of the apartheid era, a prime minister headed the South African executive. At first, a Governor General and then, after 1961 when South Africa became a Republic, a State President fulfilled the more ceremonial role of Head of State. This mirrored the roles in the United Kingdom (UK) of the Prime Minister and the Queen. In this system, the Head of State (the Queen in the UK, the State President in South Africa) formally exercised the Head of State power but usually on the advice of his or her Prime Minister. Since 1983, the two positions have been joined in South Africa in the position of an executive State President, renamed President in 1994 with the advent of democracy. The former uncodified prerogative powers of the President, derived from the British system, were extinguished and were codified in section 84(2) of the Constitution.[29] In this system, the President therefore fulfils the duties of both the head of the executive, which are similar to the role of the Prime Minister in the UK, and the duties of the more ceremonial role of Head of State which is similar to the role of the Queen in the UK.

The Constitution provides some clarity on the distinction between Head of State and head of the executive powers by listing these powers in two separate sections. Section 84(2) of the Constitution lists the Head of State powers exercised by the President alone and states that the President exercises Head of State powers when he or she:

- assents to and signs Bills
- refers a Bill back to the NA for reconsideration of the Bill's constitutionality
- refers a Bill to the Constitutional Court for a decision on the Bill's constitutionality
- summons the NA, the NCOP or Parliament to an extraordinary sitting to conduct special business
- makes any appointments that the Constitution or legislation requires the President to make, other than as head of the national executive
- appoints commissions of enquiry
- calls a national referendum in terms of an Act of Parliament
- receives and recognises foreign diplomatic and consular representatives
- appoints ambassadors, plenipotentiaries, and diplomatic and consular representatives
- **pardons** or reprieves offenders and remits any fines, penalties or forfeitures
- confers honours.

---

27 *SARFU III* para 65.

28 Currie and De Waal (2001) 237.

29 For a discussion on prerogative powers and how these were replaced by enumerated powers by South Africa's democratic Constitution, see *Hugo* paras 5–10.

The President thus has the power to assent to Bills or to refer Bills back to Parliament because he or she 'has reservations about the constitutionality of a Bill'.[30] Unlike the President of the United States of America, the President of South Africa does not have the power to veto legislation merely because he or she opposes the legislation. However, section 79(1) of the Constitution places a duty on the President to refer a Bill back to the NA for reconsideration if the President has reservations about the constitutionality of specific sections of the Bill. In terms of section 79(4), the President must assent to and sign the Bill if, after reconsideration by the NA, a Bill fully accommodates the President's reservations. If it does not, the President must either assent to and sign the Bill or refer it to the Constitutional Court for a decision on its constitutionality. The Joint Rules of Parliament state that when the President refers a Bill back to the NA, the committee tasked with considering the President's constitutional objections 'must confine itself to the President's reservations'.[31] This means Parliament cannot reconsider the Bill in its entirety, but can only reconsider those sections identified by the President as being constitutionally problematic.[32]

Section 85(1) of the Constitution states that the executive authority of the Republic is vested in the President while section 85(2) confirms that the President exercises the executive authority together with the other members of the Cabinet. The President has the sole authority to appoint the Deputy President, Cabinet Ministers and Deputy Ministers and also has the power to dismiss the Deputy President, Cabinet Ministers and Deputy Ministers.[33] The President also has the sole authority to appoint the leader of government business in the NA from among the members of the NA.[34] The President exercises executive authority, together with the other members of the Cabinet, by:

- implementing national legislation except where the Constitution or an Act of Parliament provides otherwise
- developing and implementing national policy
- co-ordinating the functions of state departments and administrations
- preparing and initiating legislation
- performing any other executive function provided for in the Constitution or in national legislation, which includes the appointment of the National Director of Public Prosecutions,[35] the Military Command of the National Defence Force,[36] the National Commissioner of Police Service[37] and the heads of the intelligence services.[38]

CRITICAL THINKING

How the formal power of the President to appoint and dismiss is constrained by internal party political considerations

Although the President has the constitutional authority to appoint and dismiss the Deputy President and other members of the Cabinet, in practical terms this power is indirectly limited although not by any provision of the Constitution itself. As we have argued above,

30 S 79(1) of the Constitution.

31 Joint Rules of Parliament 203(2).

32 For a case where the President referred a Bill back to the NA, see *Ex Parte President of the Republic of South Africa: In re Constitutionality of the Liquor Bill* (CCT12/99) [1999] ZACC 15; 2000 (1) SA 732; 2000 (1) BCLR 1 (11 November 1999).

33 S 91(2) of the Constitution.

34 S 91(4) of the Constitution.

35 S 179(1)(*a*) of the Constitution.

36 S 202(1) of the Constitution.

37 S 207(1) of the Constitution.

38 S 209(2) of the Constitution.

a close relationship exists in the South African system between political parties on the one hand and the members of the legislature and the executive on the other. The reason for this is that members of the legislature are elected via their respective political parties and political parties insist that elected leaders adhere strictly to party discipline.

This means that when the President considers the appointment or dismissal of the Deputy President, Cabinet Ministers and Deputy Ministers, he or she will usually informally consult the leadership of the governing party before making an appointment or before dismissing a member of the Cabinet. This is despite the fact that constitutionally, the power to make these appointments is that of the President alone. When a President appoints or dismisses a Cabinet member, he or she needs to ensure support from his or her political party to retain the confidence of the political party of which he or she is the leader. The formal power to make these appointments may therefore be informally constrained by the demands of intraparty politics.

In June 2005, former President Thabo Mbeki 'relieved' then Deputy President Jacob Zuma from his position as Deputy President of the country after Zuma's financial adviser was convicted of soliciting a bribe on behalf of the then Deputy President. Mbeki stated that he had 'come to the conclusion that the circumstances dictate that in the interest of the Honourable Deputy President, the Government, our young democratic system, and our country, it would be best to release the Hon Jacob Zuma from his responsibilities as Deputy President of the Republic and Member of the Cabinet'.[39] This decision formed part of a series of events which culminated in the defeat of President Mbeki by Jacob Zuma as leader of the ANC at the ANC elective conference at Polokwane in December 2007. Some commentators – rightly or wrongly – have argued that the dismissal of the Deputy President by Mbeki, while constitutionally authorised and even admirable, contributed to the intensity of the leadership struggle between the two men and assisted Zuma in his efforts to build support inside the ANC in the run-up to the ANC conference. This illustrates the manner in which the formal power of the President to appoint and dismiss is constrained by internal party political considerations.[40]

The role, powers and administrative functions of the South African President have increased since 1994. When Nelson Mandela became President, the office of the President had been scaled down. Given the mammoth task facing the executive of transforming the country, it was important to enhance the capacity of the Presidency. To address this issue, Mr Mandela appointed a Commission of Enquiry Regarding the Transformation and Reform of the Public Service. This Presidential Review Commission aimed to assist with the transformation of the state and its principal executive arm to enable it to consolidate democracy and to ensure accountability, transparency and openness.[41] The Report argued that a radical reappraisal of the functions, structures, personnel and management of the Office of the President was required to ensure greater direction and co-ordination of government policy at all levels.[42]

39 Allen, J (2005, 14 June) South Africa: President Mbeki relieves Deputy President Zuma of post *AllAfrica* available at http://allafrica.com/stories/200506140114.html.

40 See Hartley, R (2008, 23 September) The five big mistakes that cost Mbeki the Presidency *TimesLive* available at http://blogs.timeslive.co.za/hartley/2008/09/23/the-five-big-mistakes-that-cost-mbeki-the-presidency/.

41 Report of the Presidential Review Commission on the Reform and Transformation of the Public Service in South Africa, Pretoria (1998) para 1.3 available at http://www.info.gov.za/otherdocs/1998/prc98/index.html. See also Klug, H (2010) *The Constitution of South Africa: A Contextual Analysis* 201.

42 Report of the Presidential Review Commission (1998) para 7.2.1.4.

Although not all the recommendations of the Review Commission were implemented, it did lead to a bolstering of the administrative capacity of the Office of the President and a greater centralisation of power in this Office. This tendency continued during the term of President Thabo Mbeki with some of his critics questioning what they called the 'excessive concentration of power' in the Office of the President.[43]

Another way of viewing this increased power of the Office of the President is to focus on the manner in which the executive has implemented the 1996 Constitution's provisions regarding the President and the national executive. This view argues that it gives effect to the structure intended by the drafters of the Constitution.[44] An alternative viewpoint with regard to the increased power of the Office of the President is to argue that the increased power of the Office of the President reflects the balance of political forces between the three branches of government. The power of the Office of the President has further increased under President Jacob Zuma who created two additional Ministries in his office – that of the National Planning Commission and that of the Minister of Performance and Evaluation.[45]

CRITICAL THINKING

Has the power of the Office of the President in fact increased during President Zuma's tenure?

In his book, *The Zuma Years: South Africa's Changing Face of Power*, Calland argues that compared to President Thabo Mbeki, President Jacob Zuma's Presidency is in some ways less influential and powerful. The reason for this is because of President Zuma's relatively lesser political standing and influence, and perhaps because of a deliberate move to water down the power of the President in relation to the governing party. Calland argues that to prevent a repeat of the 'imperial Mbeki presidency' in which the President was able to 'overcome' his Ministers through the sheer force of his organisational capacity, the 'kitchen cabinet' of influential advisers and Ministers has been smashed as part of the post-Polokwane reorganisation of government and the reassertion of the governing party over government. Calland states that:

> **The paradox of the Zuma years is this: the Presidency is less powerful because of who he is, but the Presidency is perhaps more so, because of structural changes. However, since so much of the Presidency's political and institutional heft is drawn directly from the president himself, his individual weaknesses, of which there are many, are exaggerated by the absence of a strong team around him. Zuma is afforded little protection from himself.[46]**

However, other commentators like Friedman have pointed out that President Zuma's Presidency must be viewed against the background of the increasing influence of Cabinet Ministers in the security cluster. Friedman claims President Zuma has staffed the security cluster with trusted allies which has led to an increased 'desire to operate in the dark'.[47]

---

43 Chothia, F and Jacobs, S 'Remaking the Presidency: The tension between co-ordination and centralisation' in Jacobs, S and Calland, R (eds) (2002) *Thabo Mbeki's World: The Politics and Ideology of the South African President* 150.

44 Klug (2010) 203.

45 See generally Calland, R (2013) *The Zuma Years: South Africa's Changing Face of Power* for a discussion of the way in which the Office of the Presidency has operated during President Jacob Zuma's tenure.

46 Calland (2013) 50.

47 Friedman, S (2012, 6 August) Secrecy Bill *Business Day Live* available at http://www.bdlive.co.za/articles/2011/11/22/steven-friedman-secrecy-bill.

The national Parliament is relatively weak due to the effects of the electoral system and strict party discipline. In addition, the President has so far always been the leader of the dominant party in Parliament. Given these facts, it was inevitable that the powers of the President and the executive would increase as they are mandated to give effect to the policies and programmes of the political party elected by the vast majority of South Africans to lead the country. However, given these practical political realities, it is important to focus on the constitutionally imposed limits of the powers of the President and his or her executive. As the powers of the Office of the President increase and as the electoral dominance of the majority party is extended, it is inevitable that the courts will be required to intervene and to check the exercise of power of the President and other members of the executive where they overstep their constitutionally granted authority.

5.2.3 The limits on the exercise of presidential power

As pointed out above, the President act as both Head of State and as head of the national executive and is granted wide powers to fulfil his or her duties in this regard. However, apart from the political constraints under which a President must exercise these powers, the powers of the President are also limited in other ways. It is important to establish the formal limits explicitly placed on the exercise of power by the President as well as the substantive limits placed on the exercise of power by the President. This is because of the requirement that the President must act in accordance with the provisions in the Bill of Rights and according to the principle of legality.

Several constitutional provisions place formal limits on the manner in which the President must exercise some of the Head of State and head of executive powers. For example, when appointing ordinary judges of the High Court, the President has no discretion and must appoint the candidates recommended to him or her by the Judicial Service Commission (JSC).[48] Similarly, when appointing the Public Protector, the Auditor-General and the members of the Human Rights Commission, the Commission for Gender Equality and the Electoral Commission, the President acts 'on the recommendation of the NA'.[49] The President therefore does not exercise an independent discretion but merely formally appoints the candidates selected by the NA. When appointing the head of the National Prosecuting Authority (NPA) in terms of section 179(1)(*a*) of the Constitution, read with section 9 of the National Prosecuting Authority Act,[50] the President can appoint only a fit and proper South African citizen with due regard for his or her experience, conscientiousness and integrity. Moreover, when appointing the Chief Justice and Deputy Chief Justice the President must first consult with the JSC and the leaders of opposition parties in the NA.[51] He or she must also consult the JSC before appointing the President and Deputy President of the Supreme Court of Appeal (SCA).[52] Failure to adhere to these requirements would render the appointments unlawful.[53]

In addition, a decision by the President must be in writing if it is taken in terms of legislation or has legal consequences.[54] Another Cabinet member must countersign a written

48 S 174(6) of the Constitution which states: 'The President must appoint the judges of all other courts on the advice of the Judicial Service Commission.'

49 S 193(4) of the Constitution.

50 Act 32 of 1998.

51 S 174(3) of the Constitution.

52 S 174(3) of the Constitution.

53 *Democratic Alliance v President of South Africa and Others* (CCT 122/11) [2012] ZACC 24; 2012 (12) BCLR 1297 (CC); 2013 (1) SA 248 (CC) (5 October 2012) paras 14–26.

54 S 101(1) of the Constitution.

decision by the President if that decision concerns a function assigned to that other Cabinet member.[55] For example, the decision by the President to appoint ambassadors would have to be countersigned by the Minister of International Relations.[56]

The Constitution also places more substantive limits on the exercise of power by the President. Courts can review the exercise of power by the President and set aside any decision by the President on certain substantive grounds. This conclusion necessarily flows from the fact that the Constitution is supreme[57] and that the rule of law (and the doctrine of legality that forms part of the rule of law) is a founding value of the Constitution. This means the exercise of the powers by the President must not infringe any provision of the Bill of Rights and, as is implicit in the Constitution, the President must act in **good faith** and must not misconstrue the powers.[58] These constraints would have no force and effect if they could not be enforced by the courts.

However, this invariably raises questions about the separation of powers doctrine and to what extent judicial officers should intervene in decisions taken by the President. On the one hand, the courts have to balance their duty to enforce the provisions of the Constitution and the principle of legality with, on the other hand, respect for the fact that the decisions of the President and the executive often contain a political component with which the courts should be slow to interfere. We contend that, as a general rule, the more directly political the discretion is that the President (or other members of the executive) exercises, the more hesitant the courts will be to intervene.

As implied above, many of these constraints also apply to other members of the executive exercising public power. This means the discussion below must be seen in a broader context and many of the principles set out below also apply to other members of the Cabinet or to provincial Premiers and MECs. There are at least three ways in which the exercise of power by the President and other members of the executive is constrained by the Constitution.

The exercise of power by the President is constrained in that such an exercise of power is, in principle, subject to the provisions contained in the Bill of Rights.[59] This means that when the President exercises any power, he or she is constitutionally bound by the provisions of the Bill of Rights and may not act (or cannot fail to act) in a manner that would impermissibly infringe on one or more of the rights protected in the Constitution. Thus, in *President of the Republic of South Africa and Another v Hugo*, the Constitutional Court stated:

> **In respect of most of the [Head of State] powers ... it is not difficult to conceive of cases (extreme and unlikely as they may be) where some provision of the Bill of Rights might be contravened, and especially the equality provisions contained in section 8 [now section 9]. One or another of the powers, for example, could be**

55 S 101(2) of the Constitution.

56 Currie and De Waal (2001) 241.

57 *Hugo* para 10.

58 *SARFU III* para 148. Even with regard to the interim Constitution, which did not contain an explicit provision about the rule of law, the Constitutional Court found in *Fedsure Life Assurance Ltd and Others v Greater Johannesburg Transitional Metropolitan Council and Others* (CCT7/98) [1998] ZACC 17; 1999 (1) SA 374; 1998 (12) BCLR 1458 (14 October 1998) paras 56–9 that the doctrine of legality, an incidence of the rule of law, was an implied provision of the interim Constitution. The Court stated at para 58, 'It seems central to the conception of our constitutional order that the legislature and executive in every sphere are constrained by the principle that they may exercise no power and perform no function beyond that conferred upon them by law. At least in this sense, then, the principle of legality is implied within the terms of the interim Constitution.'

59 *Hugo* para 10.

> **exercised in a manner which excluded from consideration persons of a particular religion or ethnic group ... the fact that the arbitrary exercise of the power to pardon may be a rarity is no ground for denying constitutional review.**[60]

However, as the Constitutional Court has pointed out, it may well be that, because of the nature of the power or the manner in which it is exercised by the President, the provisions of the Bill of Rights would provide no ground for an **effective** review of a presidential exercise of such a power.[61] (However, the exercise of power by the President can always still be reviewed under one of the other grounds explained below.) This does not mean the Court would not have the power to review any exercise of power by the President against the provisions of the Bill of Rights – it has the power to do so in each and every case. However, such an exercise may often not lead to an invalidation of the President's action because the Court could find that specific right cannot be effectively applied to test the President's exercise of power. For example, when the President exercises a purely political discretion that affects only one individual, and where that exercise of power is unconstrained by any constitutional or other legal requirements, it may not be possible for the Court successfully to review this exercise of power on the basis that it infringes on any of the rights guaranteed in the Bill of Rights. Thus in the *Hugo* case, the Constitutional Court argued that in cases where the President pardons or reprieves a single prisoner in terms of section 84 of the Constitution, it is difficult to conceive of a case where a constitutional attack could be mounted against such an exercise of the presidential power on the basis that it infringed any of the rights in the Bill of Rights.[62]

Another example would be cases where the President exercises his or her power to appoint or dismiss the Deputy President and other members of the Cabinet. The President is given a wide discretion to appoint the Deputy President and the members of the Cabinet.[63] He or she has to do so in a manner that complies with the Constitution. However, when he or she exercises this power, it would not often be possible to challenge the exercise of power on the basis that it infringes any of the rights in the Bill of Rights. The power to appoint Cabinet Ministers is a political discretion entrusted to the President to give effect to the mandate of the political party in government. It is thus difficult to see how a court would be able to invoke the right to equality in the Bill of Rights if the President fails to appoint a person to his or her Cabinet and that person is a women or if the President dismisses a Cabinet Minister and that Cabinet Minister has revealed his HIV positive status or that she is a lesbian. Such a move may be ethically problematic and some voters would refuse to vote for the party to which the President belongs if it is revealed that he or she harbours prejudices against people living with HIV or who are gay or lesbian. While the exercise of this power by the President may be tested on other grounds listed below, it is not easy to see how a court would be able to declare the decision invalid on the basis that it infringes the right not to be discriminated against.

In *Masetlha v President of the Republic of South Africa and Another*,[64] the decision of the President to dismiss the head of the National Intelligence Agency (NIA) was challenged. The

60 (CCT11/96) [1997] ZACC 4; 1997 (6) BCLR 708; 1997 (4) SA 1 (18 April 1997) para 15. The Court referred to judgments by the Bavarian and Hessen Constitutional Courts to support this claim. See BayVerfGHE NF 18 140 (1965) at 147; HessStGH NJW 1974, 791 at 793.

61 *Hugo* para 28.

62 *Hugo* para 29.

63 S 91(2) of the Constitution.

64 (CCT 01/07) [2007] ZACC 20; 2008 (1) SA 566 (CC); 2008 (1) BCLR 1 (3 October 2007).

basis of the challenge, among others, was that it was unfair to do so because the President did not afford Mr Masetlha an opportunity to be heard before the impending dismissal in contravention of the common law administrative law right (now codified in section 33 of the Bill of Rights). The Constitutional Court focused on the nature of the power of the President to appoint and dismiss the head of the NIA as set out in section 209(2) of the Constitution.[65] The Court dismissed the challenge, arguing that the dismissal constituted executive action rather than administrative action, particularly in this special category of appointments of members to the NIA. According to the Court, it would not be appropriate to constrain the exercise of executive power in the context of a dismissal of the head of the NIA by enforcing the constitutional requirements for procedural fairness. These powers to appoint and to dismiss are conferred specially on the President for the effective business of government and, in this particular case, for the effective pursuit of national security.[66] The Court quoted from its judgment in *Premier, Province of Mpumalanga and Another v Executive Committee of the Association of Governing Bodies of State Aided Schools: Eastern Transvaal*[67] where it cautioned that procedural fairness should not be made a requirement for the exercise of every decision by the executive (despite the fact that section 33 contains a specific administrative justice clause). The Court stated that:

> **In determining what constitutes procedural fairness in a given case, a court should be slow to impose obligations upon government which will inhibit its ability to make and implement policy effectively (a principle well recognised in our common law and that of other countries). As a young democracy facing immense challenges of transformation, we cannot deny the importance of the need to ensure the ability of the Executive to act efficiently and promptly.**[68]

Despite this warning, South African courts have consistently asserted the principle that all decisions by the President are **in principle** reviewable, if not on the basis that the decision contravenes the provisions of the Bill of Rights, then on other grounds that flow from the fact that the Constitution is supreme and that one of the founding values of the constitutional dispensation is respect for the rule of law.[69] The answer to the question of whether the exercise of power by the President in a particular case could be tested against the provisions of the Bill of Rights will be determined with reference to the nature of the power exercised and the context in which it is exercised. Where the President exercises a discretion in an individual case, affecting only one person, and where the power in terms of which the discretion is exercised is a Head of State power or a power conferred on the President as part of his or her political duties as head of the executive, it would be difficult to challenge that decision on the basis that it infringed one of the rights in the Bill of Rights. However, where the President exercises a general discretion affecting large numbers of people, the situation may well be different.

---

65 *Masetlha* para 77.

66 *Masetlha* para 77.

67 (CCT10/98) [1998] ZACC 20; 1999 (2) SA 91; 1999 (2) BCLR 151 (2 December 1998) para 41.

68 *Masetlha* para 77.

69 The actions of the President may also be found to infringe a constitutional right given effect to in legislation. In *President of the Republic of South Africa and Others v M & G Media Ltd* (CCT 03/11) [2011] ZACC 32; 2012 (2) BCLR 181 (CC); 2012 (2) SA 50 (CC) (29 November 2011), for example, the Constitutional Court had to decide whether the refusal by the President to hand over a Report commissioned by the President to the *Mail & Guardian* newspaper contravened the provisions of the Promotion of Access to Information Act 2 of 2000 which gives effect to s 32 of the Constitution.

PAUSE FOR REFLECTION

Limits placed by the Constitution on the exercise of Head of State powers

In *President of the Republic of South Africa and Others v South African Rugby Football Union and Others (SARFU III)*,[70] the decision by the President as Head of State to appoint a commission of enquiry to investigate the administration of rugby in South Africa was challenged on several grounds. One ground was that the President, when exercising the power to appoint a commission of enquiry, was obliged to afford those to be investigated with a hearing before appointing the commission.

The Constitutional Court overturned a High Court decision which had found that such a duty did indeed exist. The Constitutional Court pointed out that although the exercise of all public power is regulated by the Constitution, it is done in different ways. The Court further pointed out that the Head of State powers conferred by section 84(2) are original constitutional powers that must be distinguished from head of the executive powers. The Constitution places explicit limits on the exercise of some of these powers.

However, the remaining section 84(2) powers are discretionary powers conferred on the President which are not constrained in any express manner by the provisions of the Constitution. Their scope is narrow: the conferral of honours; the appointment of ambassadors; the reception and recognition of foreign diplomatic representatives; the calling of referenda; the appointment of commissions of enquiry and the pardoning of offenders. They are closely related to policy; none of them is concerned with the implementation of legislation. Several of these decisions result in little or no further action by the government, for example the conferral of honours, the appointment of ambassadors or the reception of foreign diplomats. When exercising these powers, the requirements of administrative law (enshrined in section 33 of the Constitution) could therefore not be applied to these Head of State powers. The Constitution therefore placed no obligation on the President to afford a hearing to those affected by the appointment of such a commission before he or she made the decision to appoint the commission. The Court then proceeded to remark as follows about the limits placed on the exercise of these Head of State powers by the President:

> In the case of the appointment of commissions of inquiry, it is well-established that the functions of a commission of inquiry are to determine facts and to advise the President through the making of recommendations. The President is bound neither to accept the commission's factual findings nor is he or she bound to follow its recommendations. A commission of inquiry is an adjunct to the policy formation responsibility of the President. It is a mechanism whereby he or she can obtain information and advice. When the President appointed the commission of inquiry into rugby he was not implementing legislation; he was exercising an original constitutional power vested in him alone. Neither the subject matter, nor the exercise of that power was administrative in character. The appointment of the commission did not, therefore, constitute administrative action within the meaning of section 33. ... It does not follow, of course, that because the President's conduct in exercising the power conferred upon him by section 84(2)(*f*) does not constitute administrative action, there are no constraints upon it. The constraints upon the President when exercising powers under section 84(2) are clear: the President is required to exercise the powers personally and any such

70 (CCT16/98) [1999] ZACC 11; 2000 (1) SA 1; 1999 (10) BCLR 1059 (10 September 1999).

> **exercise must be recorded in writing and signed; ... the exercise of the powers must not infringe any provision of the Bill of Rights; the exercise of the powers is also clearly constrained by the principle of legality and, as is implicit in the Constitution, the President must act in good faith and must not misconstrue the powers.[71]**

The *SARFU III* judgment therefore illustrates the fact that although the Constitution places limits on the exercise of the Head of State powers, these limits do not go as far as requiring the President always to consult those affected by a decision when he or she exercises this power or to adhere to the other requirements for just administrative action. As we shall see in the next section, the Constitutional Court later developed this point and added an important qualification to this general statement that the President was free to exercise the unqualified Head of State powers without consulting those affected.[72]

The exercise of power by the President (and other members of the executive) is further constrained by the requirement that such power must be duly authorised by the Constitution or some other constitutionally valid law. This means that whenever the President exercises his or her powers, this power must be sourced from the Constitution or legislation or must implicitly be derived from it. Put differently, the President cannot act lawfully unless he or she is authorised to exercise a specific power by the Constitution or by other valid law. The authority to act can be conferred explicitly or implicitly.

In *Masetlha* one of the legal questions which arose was whether the President was constitutionally authorised to dismiss the head of the NIA. Section 209 of the Constitution authorises the President, as head of the national executive, to 'appoint a woman or a man as head of each intelligence service'. However, the provision is silent on whether the President has the authority also to dismiss the head of each intelligence service. The Constitutional Court held that the power to dismiss in this case is necessary in order to exercise the power to appoint:

> **Without the competence to dismiss, the President would not be able to remove the head of the Agency without his or her consent before the end of the term of office, whatever the circumstances might be. That would indeed lead to an absurdity and severely undermine the constitutional pursuit of the security of this country and its people. That is why the power to dismiss is an essential corollary of the power to appoint and the power to dismiss must be read into section 209(2) of the Constitution.[73]**

When the President is authorised by an Act of Parliament to exercise a power, that authorisation is required to be constitutionally valid. Parliament cannot delegate a power to the President if that **delegation of legislative authority** itself is not authorised by the Constitution. For example, Parliament cannot delegate its own plenary legislative power conferred on it by the Constitution to another body or person, including the President. In

71 *SARFU III* paras 146–8.

72 See *Albutt v Centre for the Study of Violence and Reconciliation and Others* (CCT 54/09) [2010] ZACC 4; 2010 (3) SA 293 (CC); 2010 (2) SACR 101 (CC); 2010 (5) BCLR 391 (CC) (23 February 2010).

73 *Masetlha* para 68.

any given case, the question whether Parliament is entitled to delegate its own powers to the President must depend on whether the Constitution permits the delegation. This is so because the authority of Parliament to make laws, and so too to delegate that function, is subject to the Constitution. Thus, whether Parliament may delegate its law-making power or regulatory authority is a matter of constitutional interpretation dependent, in most part, on the language and context of the empowering constitutional provision.[74]

In *Executive Council of the Western Cape Legislature and Others v President of the Republic of South Africa and Others,* Chaskalson P stated that our 1993 and 1996 Constitutions represent a clear break from the past as the Constitution is now supreme and the Constitution provides law-making powers for the legislature, not the executive.[75] This does not mean that the power to issue subordinate legislation cannot be delegated to the executive. However, it does mean that usually the power of the legislature to delegate the power to amend or repeal legislation would not be permitted. This is because it would interfere with the 'manner and form' requirements in the Constitution which describe how laws are to be made.[76] Thus Parliament cannot delegate to the President an unrestricted power to amend legislation unless it is absolutely necessary, for example in a time of war or another exceptional situation. This is important because otherwise one would allow control over legislation to pass from Parliament to the executive. This could then be used to introduce contentious provisions in an Act, would undermine Parliament and would breach the separation of powers.[77]

As we have already noted in Chapter 4 of this book, in *Justice Alliance of South Africa v President of Republic of South Africa and Others, Freedom Under Law v President of Republic of South Africa and Others, Centre for Applied Legal Studies and Another v President of Republic of South Africa and Others,*[78] the President purported to extend the term of office of the then Chief Justice by relying on section 8(*a*) of the Judges' Remuneration and Conditions of Employment Act.[79] Section 8(*a*) granted the President the power to extend the term of office of the Chief Justice and reads as follows

> **A Chief Justice who becomes eligible for discharge from active service in terms of section 3(1)(a) or 4(1) or (2), may, at the request of the President, from the date on which he or she becomes so eligible for discharge from active service, continue to perform active service as Chief Justice of South Africa for a period determined by the President, which shall not extend beyond the date on which such Chief Justice attains the age of 75 years.**

74 *Justice Alliance of South Africa v President of Republic of South Africa and Others, Freedom Under Law v President of Republic of South Africa and Others, Centre for Applied Legal Studies and Another v President of Republic of South Africa and Others* (CCT 53/11, CCT 54/11, CCT 62/11) [2011] ZACC 23; 2011 (5) SA 388 (CC); 2011 (10) BCLR 1017 (CC) (29 July 2011) para 54. See also *Executive Council of the Province of the Western Cape v Minister for Provincial Affairs and Constitutional Development and Another, Executive Council of KwaZulu-Natal v President of the Republic of South Africa and Others* (CCT15/99,CCT18/99) [1999] ZACC 13; 2000 (1) SA 661; 1999 (12) BCLR 1360 (15 October 1999) para 54.

75 (CCT27/95) [1995] ZACC 8; 1995 (10) BCLR 1289; 1995 (4) SA 877 (22 September 1995) para 62.

76 *Executive Council of the Western Cape Legislature* para 62.

77 *Executive Council of the Western Cape Legislature* para 62. In a separate judgment in this case, Mahommed J confirmed this principle, but for slightly different – more substantive – reasons. Mahommed said at para 136 that these issues cannot be determined in the abstract but depend '*inter-alia* on the constitutional instrument in question, the powers of the legislature in terms of that instrument, the nature and ambit of the purported delegation, the subject-matter to which it relates, the degree of delegation, the control and supervision retained or exercisable by the delegator over the delegatee, the circumstances prevailing at the time when the delegation is made and when it is expected to be exercised, the identity of the delegatee and practical necessities generally'.

78 (CCT 53/11, CCT 54/11, CCT 62/11) [2011] ZACC 23; 2011 (5) SA 388 (CC); 2011 (10) BCLR 1017 (CC) (29 July 2011).

79 Act 47 of 2001.

However, section 176(1) of the Constitution states:

> **A Constitutional Court judge holds office for a non-renewable term of 12 years, or until he or she attains the age of 70, whichever occurs first, except where an Act of Parliament extends the term of office of a Constitutional Court judge.**

The Constitutional Court found that the power to extend the term of office is explicitly conferred on Parliament and not on the President. The Court stated that section 176(1) contains clear textual indicators that the Constitution does not empower Parliament to delegate the power to extend the term of service of a judge of the Constitutional Court as was purportedly done by section 8(*a*) of the Judges' Remuneration and Condition of Employment Act. The Court confirmed that where the doctrine of parliamentary sovereignty governs, Parliament may delegate as much power as it chooses. In a constitutional democracy, however, Parliament may not ordinarily delegate its essential legislative functions. In this case, the power to extend the term of a Constitutional Court judge goes to the core of the tenure of the judicial office, judicial independence and the separation of powers and was therefore deemed to be an essential legislative function that could not be delegated. As the Court stated:

> **The term or extension of the office of the highest judicial officer is a matter of great moment in our constitutional democracy .... The 2001 amendment requires an Act of Parliament to extend the term of office. It requires Parliament itself to set the term of office. ... Another important consideration in deciding whether section 8(*a*) is constitutionally compliant is the constitutional imperative of judicial independence. This Court is the highest court in all constitutional matters. The independence of its judges is given vigorous protection by means of detailed and specific provisions regulating their appointment. The Chief Justice is at the pinnacle of the judiciary and thus the protection of his or her independence is just as important. It is so that section 176(1) of the Constitution creates an exception to the requirement that a term of a Constitutional Court judge is fixed. That authority, however, vests in Parliament and nowhere else. It is notable that section 176(1) does not merely bestow a legislative power, but by doing so also marks out Parliament's significant role in the separation of powers and protection of judicial independence. The nature of this power cannot be overlooked, and the Constitution's delegation to Parliament must be restrictively construed to realise that protection. Accordingly, section 8(*a*) violates the principle of judicial independence. This kind of open-ended discretion may raise a reasonable apprehension or perception that the independence of the Chief Justice and by corollary the judiciary may be undermined by external interference of the Executive. The truth may be different, but it matters not. What matters is that the judiciary must be seen to be free from external interference.**[80]

One of the most important ways in which the exercise of power by the President is controlled is through the requirement that when exercising any duly authorised power, the President has to act rationally. This requirement stems from the principle that when the President (or other members of the executive) exercises power, he or she is constrained by the principle of legality in the sense that he or she is required to act rationally and in good faith.[81] The requirement that the President must act rationally when exercising his or her power 'is a

80 *Justice Alliance* paras 65–8.

81 See *Hugo* para 29. See also *SARFU III* para 148; *Fedsure Life* paras 56–8; *Masetlha* para 23; *Minister for Justice and Constitutional Development v Chonco and Others* (CCT 42/09) [2009] ZACC 25; 2010 (1) SACR 325 (CC); 2010 (2) BCLR 140 (CC); 2010 (4) SA 82 (CC) (30 September 2009) para 30; *Albutt* para 49; *Democratic Alliance* para 31.

minimum threshold requirement applicable to the exercise of all public power by members of the executive and other functionaries'.[82] Action that fails to pass this threshold is inconsistent with the requirements of our Constitution and therefore unlawful.

The rationality test must be distinguished from the test for reasonableness. The reasonableness standard asks whether the decision was one 'that a reasonable decision-maker could not reach'.[83] **Rationality** requires something different. In *Albutt v Centre for the Study of Violence and Reconciliation and Others*, the Constitutional Court explained the rationality standard as follows:

> **The Executive has a wide discretion in selecting the means to achieve its constitutionally permissible objectives. Courts may not interfere with the means selected simply because they do not like them, or because there are other more appropriate means that could have been selected. But, where the decision is challenged on the grounds of rationality, courts are obliged to examine the means selected to determine whether they are rationally related to the objective sought to be achieved. What must be stressed is that the purpose of the enquiry is to determine not whether there are other means that could have been used, but whether the means selected are rationally related to the objective sought to be achieved. And if, objectively speaking, they are not, they fall short of the standard demanded by the Constitution.**[84]

In *Democratic Alliance v President of South Africa and Others*, the Constitutional Court further explained that a:

> **rationality review is really concerned with the evaluation of a relationship between means and ends: the relationship, connection or link (as it is variously referred to) between the means employed to achieve a particular purpose on the one hand and the purpose or end itself. The aim of the evaluation of the relationship is not to determine whether some means will achieve the purpose better than others but only whether the means employed are rationally related to the purpose for which the power was conferred. Once there is a rational relationship, an executive decision of the kind with which we are here concerned is constitutional.**[85]

Rationality is a standard that will usually be easy for the President to meet. Where the courts test the actions of the President for rationality, they cannot substitute their opinions as to what is appropriate for the opinions of the President. They also cannot declare invalid an action of the President merely because they disagree with the wisdom of the presidential decision. As long as the purpose the President seeks to achieve by the exercise of public power is within his or her authority, and as long as the President's decision, viewed objectively, is rational, a court cannot interfere with the decision simply because it disagrees with it or considers that the power was exercised inappropriately.[86]

---

82 *Pharmaceutical Manufacturers Association of South Africa and Another: In re Ex Parte President of the Republic of South Africa and Others* (CCT31/99) [2000] ZACC 1; 2000 (2) SA 674; 2000 (3) BCLR 241 (25 February 2000) para 90; *Kruger v President of the Republic of South Africa and Others* (CCT 57/07) [2008] ZACC 17; 2009 (1) SA 417 (CC); 2009 (3) BCLR 268 (CC) (2 October 2008) para 99.

83 *Bato Star Fishing (Pty) Ltd v Minister of Environmental Affairs and Tourism and Others* (CCT 27/03) [2004] ZACC 15; 2004 (4) SA 490 (CC); 2004 (7) BCLR 687 (CC) (12 March 2004) para 44.

84 (CCT 54/09) [2010] ZACC 4; 2010 (3) SA 293 (CC); 2010 (2) SACR 101 (CC); 2010 (5) BCLR 391 (CC) (23 February 2010) para 51. See also *Democratic Alliance* para 30.

85 (CCT 122/11) [2012] ZACC 24; 2012 (12) BCLR 1297 (CC); 2013 (1) SA 248 (CC) (5 October 2012) para 32.

86 *Democratic Alliance* para 90. See also *Prinsloo v Van der Linde and Another* (CCT4/96) [1997] ZACC 5; 1997 (6) BCLR 759; 1997 (3) SA 1012 (18 April 1997) para 25; *Pharmaceutical Manufacturers* para 90.

The requirement that the President must act rationally means that there must be a rational relationship between the constitutionally permissible purpose the President seeks to achieve, on the one hand, and the manner in which the President exercises the power or the means used to achieve the purpose on the other hand. The President (and other members of the executive) usually has a wide discretion in selecting the means to achieve his or her constitutionally permissible objectives. Courts may not interfere with the means selected simply because they do not like them or because there are other more appropriate means that the President could have selected.

Furthermore, if the President were to abuse the power vested in him or her, a court would be able to review and set aside this exercise of power. For instance, a decision to grant a pardon in consideration for a bribe could no doubt be set aside by a court. This will also be the case if the President were to misconstrue his or her powers. This is so because the exercise of all public power - including the exercise of power by the President - must comply with the Constitution, which is the supreme law, and the doctrine of legality, which is part of the rule of law.[87] It follows further that the exercise of a power lawfully granted to the President must be rationally related to the purpose sought to be achieved by the exercise of it.[88]

In *Albutt*, the Constitutional Court affirmed the principle that to determine whether there is a **rational connection** between a legitimate purpose and the decision of the President, both the process by which the decision is made and the decision itself must be rational.[89] Where the purpose of the exercise of the President's power to pardon is to seek or achieve reconciliation, the means used to achieve this legitimate purpose will not be rationally related to the purpose if the procedure by which the decision was taken did not provide an opportunity for victims or their family members to be heard. One of the principles that underpinned the amnesty process was the participation of victims in seeking to achieve national unity and reconciliation. It is these principles and values that must underpin the special dispensation process.

The Constitutional Court further elaborated on this principle requiring both a rational decision and a rational process in *Democratic Alliance*. The Court found in this case that the purpose of appointing a National Director of Public Prosecutions (NDPP) was closely linked to the fact that the President was required to appoint a conscientiousness person of integrity to that post and that dishonesty was incompatible with this goal. Given the need for a rational relationship between achieving this purpose and the process used, the President should have initiated a further investigation for the purpose of determining whether the real and important questions which had been raised about the President's selected appointee to the post of NDPP rendered the appointment inappropriate. Where the President had ignored adverse findings as to the honesty of the appointee made by another body, there was no rational process followed.[90]

87 See *Affordable Medicines Trust and Others v Minister of Health and Another* (CCT27/04) [2005] ZACC 3; 2006 (3) SA 247 (CC); 2005 (6) BCLR 529 (CC) (11 March 2005) para 49; *Pharmaceutical Manufacturers* para 20; *SARFU III* para 38; *Fedsure Life* para 32.

88 *Albutt* para 49.

89 *Albutt* para 71.

90 *Democratic Alliance* para 89.

CRITICAL THINKING

Variable standards for the rationality review undermine respect for the rule of law

Du Plessis and Scott argue that the Constitutional Court judgments based on legality challenges use different levels of scrutiny and that in relation to the rationality review the standard 'varies depending on the circumstances of the particular case. In some instances the court will apply the test stringently, but in others the court takes a far more deferential approach'.[91] They complain that with variability comes uncertainty. 'A central and current problem with the variability of rationality review is the lack of guidance laid down by the Constitutional Court as to the standard's parameters and applicability.'[92] This, they claim, among other problems, undermines respect for the rule of law and justify this as follows:

> First, it causes problems for potential litigants who need to decide whether to challenge decisions or conduct that has affected them. Secondly, it creates difficulties for lawyers who have to advise these clients on their potential prospects of success. Due to the huge expense and far-reaching consequences of pursuing litigation for the litigants, lawyers should be able to do more than merely give vague statements about a litigant's prospects of success. With the increasingly variable nature of rationality review comes a concomitant decrease in the certainty with which legal representatives are able to advise clients who are contemplating a rationality challenge. While the goal is not rigid legal certainty, there must at least be some form of clarity or reasonable predictability on the approach that will be adopted by a court. Without this clarity comes the risk that the law is failing to meet the requirements clearly set out in the *Hugo* case. Finally, the lack of clear guidelines creates uncertainty for the High Courts that need direction on how to apply the rationality standard. Woolman neatly captures the problems associated with a lack of judicial guidelines: 'An approach to constitutional adjudication that makes it difficult for lower court judges, lawyers, government officials and citizens to discern, with some degree of certainty, how the basic law is going to be applied, and to know, with some degree of certainty, that the basic law is going to be applied equally, constitutes a paradigmatic violation of the rule of law.' These problems, relating to the confusion created by the lack of guidelines, are compounded by the importance of the safety-net function of the principle of legality, since a legality challenge may be an applicant's only available avenue to challenge conduct.[93]

The authors point out that this variable standard is even more problematic if one considers that in many instances the information necessary to determine whether there was a rational link between the purpose and the means used to achieve it, 'lies within the exclusive knowledge of the state body'.[94] In such situations it would be extremely difficult for the objector to discharge the burden of proof. They therefore suggest that in such cases if the objector makes a detailed written request to the state for the reasons and purpose of the conduct, and the state either fails to give any reasons for

91 Du Plessis, M and Scott, S (2013) The variable standard of rationality review: Suggestions for improved legality jurisprudence' *South African Law Journal* 130(3):597–620 at 597.

92 Du Plessis and Scott (2013) 598.

93 Du Plessis and Scott (2013) 608–9 (footnotes omitted).

94 Du Plessis and Scott (2013) 610.

the conduct or merely gives perfunctory reasons, then in these situations it is the government which ought to bear the onus of proving that the conduct was rational or suffer the consequences of the court drawing adverse conclusions as to the government's justification. Although the objection might be raised that this will place too much of a burden on the government, 'any increased burden is greatly tempered by the low standard the government has to meet in order to satisfy the test'.[95]

Although the exercise of power by the President is thus always in principle reviewable by the courts on the grounds set out above, at least two caveats must be raised. First, in *Minister of Home Affairs v Liebenberg,*[96] the Constitutional Court pointed out that when taking the President to court, it would be important to avoid imprecise and open-ended citing of the President in litigation. When asking a court to declare conduct of the President unconstitutional, it is necessary to indicate precisely which conduct is attributable to the President and falls foul of the Constitution.[97] As the Constitutional Court stated in *Von Abo v President of the Republic of South Africa*:

> **This requirement is important for at least two reasons. One important reason is that a concisely worded order would disclose the character of the conduct of the President in issue and thereby indicate whether the court concerned was properly clothed with jurisdiction to resolve the dispute. Also the President, as respondent is entitled to know which conduct has offended in order to decide whether to appeal or to correct the constitutionally recalcitrant conduct in issue.**[98]

A second caveat relating to the review of the exercise of power by the President is that when a court is required to do so it will not ordinarily require the President to give oral evidence in person. In *SARFU III*, the Constitutional Court found that this was a question 'of considerable constitutional significance going to the heart of the separation of powers under our Constitution'.[99] When making a decision on whether to call the President as a witness, courts will have to consider two competing considerations. First, courts are obliged to ensure that the status, dignity and efficiency of the Office of the President is protected. At the same time, however, the administration of justice cannot and should not be impeded by a court's desire to ensure that the dignity of the President is safeguarded.[100] As the Court explained in *SARFU III:*

> **We are of the view that there are two aspects of the public interest which might conflict in cases where a decision must be made as to whether the President ought to be ordered to give evidence. On the one hand, there is the public interest in ensuring that the dignity and status of the President is preserved and protected, that the efficiency of the executive is not impeded and that a robust and open discussion take place unhindered at meetings of the Cabinet when sensitive and important matters of policy are discussed. Careful consideration must therefore be given to a**

95 Du Plessis and Scott (2013) 617–8.

96 (CCT22/01) [2001] ZACC 3; 2001 (11) BCLR 1168; 2002 (1) SA 33 (CC) (8 October 2001).

97 *Liebenberg* para 15. See also *Von Abo v President of the Republic of South Africa* (CCT 67/08) [2009] ZACC 15; 2009 (10) BCLR 1052 (CC); 2009 (5) SA 345 (CC) (5 June 2009) para 45.

98 (CCT 67/08) [2009] ZACC 15; 2009 (10) BCLR 1052 (CC); 2009 (5) SA 345 (CC) (5 June 2009) para 45.

99 *SARFU III* para 240.

100 *SARFU III* para 242.

decision compelling the President to give evidence and such an order should not be made unless the interests of justice clearly demand that this be done. The judiciary must exercise appropriate restraint in such cases, sensitive to the status of the head of state and the integrity of the executive arm of government. On the other hand, there is the equally important need to ensure that courts are not impeded in the administration of justice.[101]

5.3 The Deputy President and the rest of the Cabinet

5.3.1 Appointment and removal

The Cabinet consists of the President, the Deputy President and other Cabinet Ministers.[102] The President appoints and may also dismiss the Deputy President as well as the other members of the Cabinet.[103] The Deputy President must be appointed from among the members of the NA.[104] All but two members of the Cabinet must similarly be appointed from among the members of the NA.[105] The requirement that all but two of the members of the Cabinet simultaneously have to serve as members of the NA affirms the principle of parliamentary government, mirroring to some degree the Westminster system. This, in theory, ensures that the executive is more directly accountable to the electorate because it allows the democratically elected NA to control the conduct of the executive.[106] This requirement waters down the strict separation between the legislature and the executive as almost all the members of the executive (except for the President and no more than two Cabinet Ministers) at all times also serve as members of the legislature.

This arrangement was challenged during the certification process of the Constitution on the ground that members of the Cabinet continue to be members of the legislature and, by virtue of their positions, are able to exercise a powerful influence over the decisions of the legislature. It was contended that this is inconsistent with the separation of powers doctrine as applied in the United States of America, France, Germany and the Netherlands. The Constitutional Court rejected this argument, noting that there is no universal model of separation of powers. In democratic systems of government in which checks and balances result in the imposition of restraints by one branch of government on another, there is no separation that is absolute.[107] The Court stated that:

The principle of separation of powers, on the one hand, recognises the functional independence of branches of government. On the other hand, the principle of checks and balances focuses on the desirability of ensuring that the constitutional order, as a totality, prevents the branches of government from usurping power from one another. In this sense it anticipates the necessary or unavoidable intrusion of one branch on the terrain of another. No constitutional scheme can reflect a complete separation of powers: the scheme is always one of partial separation.[108]

---

101 *SARFU III* para 243.
102 S 91(1) of the Constitution.
103 S 91(2) of the Constitution.
104 S 91(3)(*a*) of the Constitution.
105 S 91(3)(*b*) and (*c*) of the Constitution.
106 Currie and De Waal (2001) 254.
107 *Certification of the Constitution of the Republic of South Africa, 1996* (CCT 23/96) [1996] ZACC 26; 1996 (4) SA 744 (CC); 1996 (10) BCLR 1253 (CC) (6 September 1996) para 108.
108 *First Certification* para 109.

The fact that this overlap in personnel provides an important mechanism by which the legislature is able to check the exercise of power by the executive is emphasised by the provisions of section 92(2) of the Constitution. This section indicates that members of the Cabinet are 'accountable collectively and individually to Parliament for the performance of their functions', a point to which we shall return in the next section.

The provision that allows the President to appoint two members to the Cabinet who are not members of the NA creates the opportunity for the President to appoint members to the Cabinet with special skills or knowledge. This provision can be used to appoint members to the Cabinet who are not active members of the governing party or who are not politicians at all.

The President[109] or the NA[110] can remove the Deputy President and the other members of the Cabinet from office. The power of the President to dismiss members of his or her Cabinet is political in nature and will usually be exercised after consultations with the leadership of the majority party (although this is not a constitutional requirement). In a concurring judgment in *Masetlha*, Sachs J argued that there was a 'qualitative distinction' between the dismissal by the President of a Cabinet Minister or Deputy President, on the one hand, and his or her dismissal of other appointees like the head of the NIA, on the other. This is because the former appointees are 'purely political appointees placed in positions of governmental leadership'.[111] According to Sachs J, '[m]embers of Cabinet know that they are hired and can be fired at the will of the President; and if fired, they can mobilise politically, go to the press, even demonstrate outside Parliament, and hope to muster support for themselves at the next congress of their party'.[112] This suggests that when the President fires his or her Deputy President or another Cabinet Minister, the ordinary constitutional and legislative requirements relating to fair labour practice do not apply.[113]

In terms of section 102(1) of the Constitution, the NA can also pass a vote of no confidence with a simple majority vote in the Cabinet (excluding the President), after which the President must reconstitute the Cabinet. This means that where the NA retains confidence in the President but has lost confidence in one or more members of the President's Cabinet, it can force the President to fire the Cabinet Minister or Ministers in whom it has lost confidence. This is distinct from a motion of no confidence passed in terms of section 102(2) which would require the President and the Cabinet to resign.

In theory, section 102(1) of the Constitution provides the NA with a powerful tool to hold individual members of the Cabinet accountable. However, it is unlikely that the NA would pass a vote of no confidence in the Cabinet. This is because the President and his or her Cabinet are almost always members of the majority party in the NA and because most of the members of the majority party in the NA are more junior members of the same party as the President and the Cabinet, A vote of no confidence in the Cabinet would probably only happen if the elected leadership of the governing party instructs its members in the NA to pass such a vote of no confidence. This could happen if the party elects new leaders at its

109 S 91(2) of the Constitution.

110 S 102 of the Constitution.

111 *Masetlha* para 228, where Sachs stated: 'This suggests a qualitative distinction based on the fact that the three are not purely political appointees placed in positions of governmental leadership. Rather, they are important public officials with one foot in government and one in the public administration. Members of Cabinet know that they are hired and can be fired at the will of the President; and if fired, they can mobilise politically, go to the press, even demonstrate outside Parliament, and hope to muster support for themselves at the next congress of their party.'

112 *Masetlha* para 228.

113 See also Currie and De Waal (2001) 254 and *Mphele v Government of the Republic of South Africa* 1996 (7) BCLR 921 (CK) 954E.

elective conference while the President and the Cabinet are perceived to be loyal to the outgoing leadership. It could also happen if there is a coalition government and a majority of members in the NA are unhappy with the performance of one or more members of the coalition Cabinet.

PAUSE FOR REFLECTION

The actual power of party leadership on our system of government

In 2007 at its Polokwane conference, the ANC elected a new president, a new set of the 'top six' office-bearers of the party as well as a newly constituted National Executive Committee (NEC). President Thabo Mbeki and the candidates proposed by his supporters for leadership positions in the ANC were defeated at this conference, but at first President Mbeki and his Cabinet continued to serve in the executive undisturbed. As we have seen, the NEC eventually decided to 'recall' President Mbeki who then resigned as President of the country. The ANC NEC could also alternatively have decided, although it did not do so, to retain President Mbeki as President of the country while demanding that he reconstitute his Cabinet to appoint the newly elected members of the ANC top leadership to the Cabinet. If the President had then refused to do so, the NEC would have been able to rely on section 102(1) of the Constitution and could have instructed its members in the NA to adopt a vote of no confidence in the Cabinet (excluding the President). The President would then have been forced to implement the decision of the NEC. This imaginary scenario, unlikely as it may be, illustrates the actual power of the leadership of the governing party in our system of government even where members of that leadership are neither members of the executive nor members of the NA.

5.3.2 Powers of the Deputy President and the Cabinet

The Constitution does not list the powers of the Cabinet. As pointed out above, section 82(2) of the Constitution determines that executive authority is exercised by the President and his or her Cabinet and lists the various powers which the Cabinet has to exercise. In terms of section 85 of the Constitution the exercise of executive authority involves:

- the implementation of national legislation save where the Constitution or an Act of Parliament provides otherwise
- developing and implementing national policy
- co-ordinating the function of state departments and administrations
- preparing and initiating legislation
- carrying out any other executive function provided for in the Constitution or in national legislation.

To determine which powers and functions will be exercised by which Cabinet Minister, it is important to note that the President is the person who assigns powers and functions to the Deputy President as well as the rest of the Cabinet.[114] The Deputy President is required to assist the President in the execution of the functions of government.[115] This means that the powers of the Deputy President are not defined by the Constitution. Rather, the powers of the Deputy President are determined by the President. Depending on the relationship

114 S 91(2) of the Constitution.

115 S 91(5) of the Constitution.

between the President and the Deputy President and the relative influence and power of these two people in the governing party, the Deputy President could either fulfil a mostly ceremonial role or could emerge as a powerful *de facto* Prime Minister.[116]

The President similarly assigns the powers and functions to the various Ministers.[117] This means that the President must assign executive authority to his or her various Ministers in the Cabinet to enable them to exercise their powers and perform their functions. The President often assigns powers to Ministers by assigning different portfolios to different Cabinet Ministers and assigns the administration and implementation of specific pieces of legislation to individual Ministers. Ministers are then responsible for the exercise of power in terms of the legislation assigned to them.

Members of the Cabinet are accountable individually to the President and to the NA for the administration of their portfolios.[118] They are required to administer their portfolios in accordance with the policy determined by the Cabinet.[119] In a case that dealt with the relationship between Premiers and provincial MECs, but must equally apply to the Cabinet, the Eastern Cape High Court found that the President 'bears ultimate responsibility' for ensuring that the national government complies with the law and the other Cabinet members bear the responsibility for operations in their departments.[120]

Members of the Cabinet are also collectively and individually accountable to Parliament for the exercise of their powers and the performance of their functions.[121] They are correspondingly collectively accountable for the performance of the functions of the national government and for its policies.[122] This principle of Cabinet solidarity emphasises the fact that executive authority in South Africa is a collaborative venture and that members of the Cabinet must act together and must share responsibility for their actions.[123] This notion of Cabinet solidarity finds application in two different ways:

- First, as we have seen, the Constitution requires the Cabinet **as a collective** to retain the confidence of the NA, which can pass a vote of no confidence in the Cabinet (excluding the President) if the Cabinet fails to do so.

---

116 See Devenish, GE (1998) *A Commentary on the South African Constitution* 158. When President Thabo Mbeki served as Deputy President in the Cabinet of President Nelson Mandela he was widely regarded as playing the role of Prime Minister. See generally Gumede, WM (2008) *Thabo Mbeki and the Battle for the Soul of the ANC* 33–62.

117 S 91(2) of the Constitution.

118 S 92(1) and 92(2) of the Constitution.

119 This is the necessary implication of s 92(2) which states that members of the Cabinet are **collectively** responsible to Parliament.

120 See *Magidimisi v Premier of the Eastern Cape and Others* (2180/04, ECJ031/06) [2006] ZAECHC 20 (25 April 2006) paras 20–1:

> **The first respondent is the Premier of the province. The Constitution vests her with the ultimate executive authority of the province. The Premier and the Members of the Executive Council are responsible for the implementation of legislation in the province and for the performance of all other constitutional and statutory executive functions of the province. The Premier has taken an oath of office to 'obey, respect and uphold the Constitution and all other law of the Republic'. This includes the duties to uphold the rule of law.... As the ultimate executive authority in the province the Premier thus bears the ultimate responsibility to ensure that the provincial government honours and obeys all judgments of the courts against it. The second respondent, the Member of the Executive Council for Finance, bears the same general constitutional duties as those of the Premier, except that he does not bear the ultimate executive authority of the Premier. In addition, however, he bears responsibility for decisions of the provincial treasury. This would include decisions relating to the payment of judgments against the province for the payment of money.**

121 S 92(2) of the Constitution.

122 S 96(3) of the Constitution.

123 *SARFU II* para 41. See also Murray and Stacey (2013) 18.32.

- Second, section 85(2)[124] read with section 92(2) of the Constitution suggests that the Cabinet has a duty to act together as they are collectively accountable to Parliament for the decisions of the Cabinet. Cabinet members may disagree with one another when they debate an issue to decide the position of the Cabinet, but once such a decision has been taken, the members of the Cabinet have to take **collective accountability** for the decisions of the Cabinet. In theory, if an individual member of the Cabinet cannot tolerate or defend a decision of the Cabinet, he or she has the option to resign from the Cabinet.[125]

Ministers are not only collectively accountable for the decisions and actions of the Cabinet as a whole. Section 92(2) of the Constitution also holds the Cabinet individually accountable to Parliament. **Individual accountability** ensures that Parliament can identify the Cabinet member responsible for a particular issue and can take action to hold that Cabinet member accountable. As we have seen, the Constitution bestows wide powers on Parliament to enable it to hold the individual members of the Cabinet accountable. Moreover, in terms of section 92(3)(*b*) of the Constitution, Cabinet members are compelled to provide Parliament with full and regular reports concerning matters under their control. Collective ministerial accountability means that Cabinet members 'act in unison to the outside world and carry joint responsibility before Parliament for the way in which each member exercises or performs powers and functions'.[126] According to Rautenbach and Malherbe,[127] individual responsibility entails the following:
- a duty to explain to Parliament how the powers and duties under his or her control have been exercised and performed (the Constitution provides that members of the Cabinet must act in accordance with the Constitution and provide Parliament with full and regular reports concerning matters under their control)
- a duty to acknowledge that a mistake has been made and to promise to rectify the matter
- a duty to resign if personal responsibility has been accepted.[128]

Both the individual and collective responsibilities of Cabinet members are reinforced by section 96 of the Constitution which regulates their ethical conduct.[129] Section 96 provides that members of the Cabinet and Deputy Ministers must act in accordance with a code of ethics prescribed by legislation. They may not undertake any other paid work, act in a way that is inconsistent with their office, expose themselves to any situation involving the risk of a conflict between their official responsibilities and private interests, or enrich themselves or improperly benefit any other person.[130]

The other members of the Cabinet are constrained in a similar manner to that in which the President is constrained in the exercise of their duties. As we pointed out above, when

124 S 85(2) states: 'The President exercises the executive authority, together with the other members of the Cabinet ...'

125 See Murray and Stacey (2013) 18.32. They point out that this aspect requires confidentiality from members of the Cabinet and Cabinet members are usually not allowed to divulge information about debates within Cabinet. Although this rule is not encoded in the Constitution, it has been respected since the advent of the interim Constitution in 1994. The need for confidentiality has also been accepted by the Constitutional Court in *SARFU III* para 243.

126 See Rautenbach, IM and Malherbe, EFJ (2009) *Constitutional Law* 193.

127 Rautenbach and Malherbe (2009) 193.

128 See also Mafunisa, MJ (2008) The role of codes of conduct in promoting ethical conduct in the South African public service *South African Journal of Labour Relations* 32(1):81–92.

129 See also the Code of Conduct for Assembly and Permanent Council Members available at http://www.parliament.gov.za/live/content.php?Item_ID=235.

130 S 96(2) of the Constitution.

exercising public power in terms of the Constitution, the President as well as other members of the Cabinet are required to exercise their powers personally. In the case of Cabinet Ministers, these powers would have been delegated to them by the President or would derive from legislation whose administration the President had assigned to them in terms of sections 92(1), 98 or 99 of the Constitution.

Furthermore, the exercise of the powers by members of the Cabinet must not infringe any provision of the Bill of Rights. Lastly, the exercise of the powers by members of the Cabinet are also clearly constrained by the principle of legality and, as is implicit in the Constitution, the Cabinet members must act in good faith and must not misconstrue their powers. These significant constraints flow from the supremacy of the Constitution and the demands of the legality principle that is an incidence of the rule of law.

CRITICAL THINKING

The role of the Deputy President

The Constitution does not define the powers of the Deputy President. The Constitution merely states that the Deputy President 'must assist the President in the executions of the functions of government'.[131] The President therefore decides to what extent the Deputy President is involved in the day-to-day affairs of the government. The question is whether this leeway should be used to make a sharper distinction between the role of the President and the Deputy President, with the former playing a more ceremonial role above the fray of day-to-day politics while the latter in effect acts as a Prime Minister.

Some point to the French system as a possible model. In France, the President is directly elected by the French people every five years. The French Constitution declares the President Head of State and gives the President control over foreign policy and defence. After parliamentary elections, which are held every five years or sooner if the President calls them, the President appoints a Prime Minister. The appointment requires the approval of Parliament so the Prime Minister almost always comes from the party that controls the legislature. The Prime Minister serves as head of government and is in charge of domestic policy and day-to-day governing. The Prime Minister also recommends for presidential approval the other members of his or her Cabinet.

When the directly elected President represents a different party to that of the Prime Minister, a system of 'cohabitation' ensues. The President has to share power with a Prime Minister from a different party and this can lead to gridlock. In South Africa, such a situation will not arise as the President and the Deputy President will be from the same political party. The advantages of bestowing more power to deal with the domestic policy agenda on the Deputy President, acting as *de facto* Prime Minister as is the case in France, is that it allows the division of labour and could potentially improve the effectiveness of the government. The dangers of such a system are that two centres of power will develop and the conflict between the President and Deputy President will paralyse the government.

131 S 91(5).

SUMMARY

The national executive comprises the President, the Deputy President and the members of the Cabinet. The President is elected by the NA and the President and his or her Cabinet must retain the confidence of the majority of members of the NA to ensure the continued functioning of the government. The President acts as Head of State and as head of the executive, and in the latter case must act with the responsible member of Cabinet who must countersign decisions relating to his or her portfolio.

When the NA passes a vote of no confidence in the President in terms of section 102 of the Constitution, the President and his or her Cabinet must resign. The President can also be impeached by the NA in terms of section 89 of the Constitution for serious violations of the Constitution, for serious misconduct or for reasons of incapacity. In theory, this means the NA is more powerful than the President and his or her Cabinet as it elects the President and can also dismiss the President. However, because the President and his or her Cabinet are usually the leaders of the majority party and control the party, it would only be in exceptional cases where the NA would be able to assert its power over the executive branch of government. Members of the Cabinet can, however, be held accountable by the NA.

The exercise of powers by either the President or other members of the Cabinet is constrained. Because of the supremacy of the Constitution, the exercise of power by the President and the Cabinet must always be authorised by and conform to the requirements of the Constitution and ordinary legislation. This means that the power of the President and the Cabinet can be checked by the judiciary. The constraints on the executive when exercising power are several fold: they are required to exercise the powers personally and in accordance with the formal requirements set out by the Constitution; the exercise of the powers must not infringe any provision of the Bill of Rights; the exercise of the powers is also clearly constrained by the principle of legality which requires a rational exercise of power. As is implicit in the Constitution, this means the members of the executive must act in good faith and must not misconstrue their powers.

The President has the power to appoint and also to dismiss members of his or her Cabinet. The President also assigns tasks to members of his or her Cabinet. This power to compose the Cabinet and to determine its functions is constrained by larger political considerations. A dominant political party with a tradition of collective leadership will require the President to consult with the party leadership before making these decisions.

Members of the Cabinet are individually and collectively accountable to Parliament. While robust debate may occur within the Cabinet, once a decision is taken by Cabinet all members of the Cabinet are expected to support the decision regardless of whether they agree with the decision. Members of the Cabinet are both accountable to the President, who appoints and dismisses them, and to the NA which elects the President and can, in exceptional circumstances, also adopt a motion of no confidence in individual members of the Cabinet to force the President to reconstitute his or her Cabinet.

Chapter 6

Separation of powers and judicial authority

6.1 The historic legacy of parliamentary sovereignty and apartheid on the judiciary

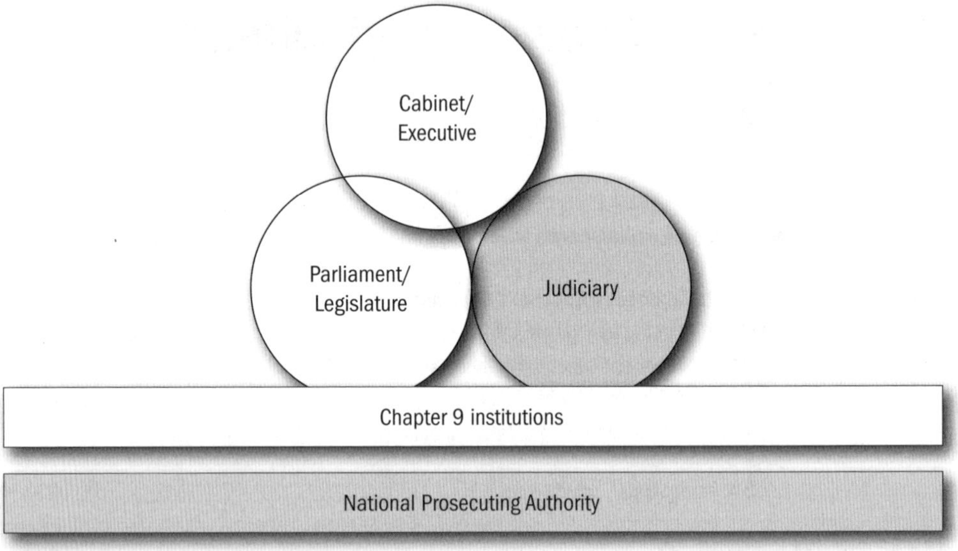

Figure 6.1 *Separation of powers and judicial authority*

In a constitutional democracy the **judiciary** is often referred to as the 'bastion of the legal order'.[1] This is because in a constitutional democracy with a supreme and enforceable constitution, an independent judiciary is free to interpret and apply the law impartially and without consideration of the wishes of politicians, powerful business interests or civil society groups. According to this theory, the system of separation of powers and checks and balances can only operate optimally if an independent and impartial judiciary is empowered to enforce the provisions of the Constitution. In such a system the judiciary acts as referee of the democratic process while also checking whether the two political branches of government, the legislature and the executive, act within the boundaries set out by the constitution and by legislation. The more dominant a political party is in government and the larger its majority in Parliament, the more likely it is that other role players will revert to the independent and impartial courts to check the exercise of powers of the legislature and executive, and to limit the potential abuse of power and breaches of the constitution, which some commentators associate with a prolonged period of political dominance by one political party.

As South Africa is, at the time of writing, viewed by many as a one-party dominant democracy,[2] these tendencies are also arising in the South African context. This places the judiciary in a difficult position. On the one hand, it is empowered by the Constitution to enforce its provisions and to declare invalid acts and omissions of the legislature and the executive that fail to comply with the obligations imposed by the Constitution.[3] The judiciary has a duty to enforce the provisions of the Constitution and the law, and to check the exercise of power by the legislature, executive and other powerful role players. From a purely

1 Van Zyl, D (2009) The judiciary as a bastion of the legal order in challenging times *Potchefstroom Electronic Law Journal* 12(2):1–13 at 2.

2 See Choudhry, S (2009) 'He had a mandate': The South African Constitutional Court and the African National Congress in a dominant party democracy *Constitutional Court Review* 2:1–86 at 1.

3 S 172(1)(*a*).

institutional and practical political perspective, the judiciary can appear to be relatively weak in relation to the other two branches of government. It may appear to lack the political clout and democratic legitimacy associated with the elected branches of government and is dependent on the other two branches of government for its funding and for ensuring that its decisions are adhered to. The truth is, as the Constitutional Court has pointed out, that the judiciary cannot function properly without the support and trust of the public.[4] As former Chief Justice Ismail Mahomed explained:

> **Unlike Parliament and the executive, however, judicial officers do not have the powers of the purse, the army, and the police to execute their will. All the courts put together in the country do not have a single soldier. They would be impotent to protect the Constitution or to execute the law if the agencies of the State which control the mighty physical and financial resources of the State, refused to command those resources to enforce the orders of the courts. The courts could then be reduced to paper tigers with a ferocious capacity to roar and to snarl but no teeth to bite and no sanctions to execute their judgments which could then simply be reduced to pieces of sterile scholarship, or futile exhibitions of toothless wisdom. The ultimate power of the courts must therefore rest on the esteem in which the judiciary is held within the psyche and soul of the nation and in the confidence it enjoys within the hearts and minds of potential litigants in search of justice. That esteem and that respect must substantially depend on the independence and integrity of judicial officers. No public figure anywhere, however otherwise popular, could afford to be seen to defy the order of a court which enjoys, within the nation, a perception of independence and integrity. His or her own future would then be in mortal jeopardy.**[5]

The way in which this tension can best be dealt with is by recognising that an independent and impartial judiciary is most effective when it respects the separation of powers doctrine and does not unnecessarily intrude on the domain of the legislature and the executive.

---

4 *S v Mamabolo* (CCT 44/00) [2001] ZACC 17; 2001 (3) SA 409 (CC); 2001 (5) BCLR 449 (CC) (11 April 2001) para 18:

> **Therefore courts have over the centuries developed a method of functioning, a self-discipline and a restraint which, although it differs from jurisdiction to jurisdiction, has a number of essential characteristics. The most important is that judges speak in court and only in court. They are not at liberty to defend or even debate their decisions in public. It requires little imagination to appreciate that the alternative would be chaotic. Moreover, as a matter of general policy judicial proceedings of any significance are conducted in open court, to which everybody has free access and can assess the merits of the dispute and can witness the process of its resolution. This process of resolution ought as a matter of principle to be analytical, rational and reasoned. The rules to be applied in resolving the dispute should either be known beforehand or be debated and determined openly. All decisions of judicial bodies are as a matter of course announced in public; and, as a matter of virtually invariable practice, reasons are automatically and publicly given for judicial decisions in contested matters. All courts of any consequence are obliged to maintain records of their proceedings and to retain them for subsequent scrutiny. Ordinarily the decisions of courts are subject to correction by other, higher tribunals, once again for reasons that are debated and made known publicly.**

5 Mahomed, I (1998) The role of the judiciary in a constitutional state *South African Law Journal* 115(1):111–15 at 112. See also *Mamabolo* para 16:

> **In our constitutional order the judiciary is an independent pillar of state, constitutionally mandated to exercise the judicial authority of the state fearlessly and impartially. Under the doctrine of separation of powers it stands on an equal footing with the executive and the legislative pillars of state; but in terms of political, financial or military power it cannot hope to compete. It is in these terms by far the weakest of the three pillars; yet its manifest independence and authority are essential. Having no constituency, no purse and no sword, the judiciary must rely on moral authority. Without such authority it cannot perform its vital function as the interpreter of the Constitution, the arbiter in disputes between organs of state and, ultimately, as the watchdog over the Constitution and its Bill of Rights – even against the state.**

However, this does not mean the courts must be timid in protecting and enforcing the Constitution. In *International Trade Administration Commission v SCAW South Africa (Pty) Ltd* the Constitutional Court thus said:

> **In our constitutional democracy all public power is subject to constitutional control. Each arm of the state must act within the boundaries set. However, in the end, courts must determine whether unauthorised trespassing by one arm of the state into the terrain of another has occurred. In that narrow sense, the courts are the ultimate guardians of the Constitution. They do not only have the right to intervene in order to prevent the violation of the Constitution, they also have the duty to do so. It is in the performance of this role that courts are more likely to confront the question of whether to venture into the domain of other branches of government and the extent of such intervention. It is a necessary component of the doctrine of separation of powers that courts have a constitutional obligation to ensure that the exercise of power by other branches of government occurs within constitutional bounds. But even in these circumstances, courts must observe the limits of their own power.**[6]

Courts must therefore act in a restrained but principled manner and must interpret and enforce the Constitution in a fearless way. This will help to ensure that the political process remains fair, democratic space remains open and political contestation remains robust while also playing a decisive role in protecting the vulnerable and marginalised in society.[7] When considering the role and functions of the judiciary, it is important to take note of this broader context within which the judiciary operates. This section of the chapter therefore focuses on the powers, functioning and composition of the judiciary in the light of the pressing need for the judiciary to retain the esteem and respect of the wider society while also scrupulously enforcing the Constitution and the law in an impartial and independent manner. This will be done against the background of the separation of powers doctrine.

Note from the outset that the judiciary was not left untainted by its role during South Africa's apartheid past.[8] There are many reasons why the judiciary cannot be said to have survived the apartheid era untainted. Before 1994, the doctrine of parliamentary supremacy was one of the cornerstones of South African constitutional law. This doctrine obviously limited the judiciary's capacity to enforce individual rights and freedoms. As Mtshaulana points out, because 'the rule of law was equated to rule by law, all arbitrary exercise of power, ... exercised in terms of a law enacted by correct procedures prescribed by Parliament was considered lawful and in accordance with the rule of law'.[9] Although some judges attempted to interpret and apply the law in such a way as to limit the harsh effects of apartheid laws, others diligently enforced apartheid laws. This meant that the judiciary lacked legitimacy in the eyes of the majority of people in South Africa.[10]

---

6 (CCT 59/09) [2010] ZACC 6; 2012 (4) SA 618 (CC); 2010 (5) BCLR 457 (CC) (9 March 2010) paras 92–3.

7 See generally Roux, T (2009) Principle and pragmatism on the Constitutional Court of South Africa *International Journal of Constitutional Law* 7(1):106–38.

8 For a discussion of the role of the judiciary during apartheid, see Forsyth, CF (1985) *In Danger for Their Talents: A Study of the Appellate Division of the Supreme Court of South Africa from 1950–1980*; Dyzenhaus, D (1991) *Hard Cases in Wicked Legal Systems: South African Law in the Perspective of Legal Philosophy*; Ellman, SJ (1992) *In a Time of Trouble: Law and Liberty in South Africa's State of Emergency*.

9 Mtshaulana, PM 'The history and role of the Constitutional Court in South Africa' in Andrews, P and Ellmann, S (2001) *The Post-Apartheid Constitutions: Perspectives on South Africa's Basic Law* 525.

10 See Klug, H (2010) *The Constitution of South Africa: A Contextual Analysis* 225–30. See also Dugard, J (1978) *Human Rights and the South African Legal Order*.

After anti-apartheid lawyers had won several important victories in the courts in the 1980s during the States of Emergency,[11] the Appellate Division overturned many of these judgments. This confirmed that the apartheid state had virtually unlimited power under the emergency provisions.[12] The outcome in these cases further confirmed the lack of impartiality and independence of the highest court and eroded whatever legitimacy the judiciary may still have enjoyed.

However, there is some disagreement about whether the timid approach of many judges during the apartheid years entirely destroyed the judiciary's credibility. On the one hand, Madala argues that 'the apartheid system created a society in which the majority came to regard the courts, judges and administration of justice with suspicion and anger'.[13] On the other hand, Ellmann argues that black South Africans surprisingly retained a significant degree of confidence in the legal system and the courts in particular.[14] Ellmann argues that this confidence lent a measure of legitimacy to the legal system. This, coupled with the history of anti-apartheid lawyering, 'might have encouraged South Africans to see virtue in the ideals of fearless advocacy, independent judging and the Rule of Law', offering the promise that these same ideals would be honoured in the post-apartheid South Africa.[15]

It is nevertheless clear that the institutionalisation of apartheid through law and legal regulation transformed the legal system and entrenched the political dominance of the minority over the majority through the operation of law enforced by the judiciary.[16] To this end, the judiciary 'was unable to resolve the impasse [of its subjugation] because it did not have the option to review and reverse unjust laws, rather the courts and all other institutions had to implement and administer such laws'.[17] Because the judiciary operated under the system of parliamentary supremacy, it meant that 'the judiciary during the apartheid period functioned as part of the apartheid legal order and contributed to legitimising and sustaining blatantly discriminatory and unjust legislation'.[18] Judges were regarded as mere mechanical interpreters of the law. Their function was seen by many – including by most judges and legal practitioners – merely to ascertain the intention of the apartheid legislature through the text of the legislation and then to give effect to that intention, no matter how obnoxious the intention might have been.[19] Most judges believed that they could employ only limited

11 Klug (2010) 226. See generally Haysom, N and Kahanovitz, S 'Courts and the State of Emergency' in Moss, G and Obery, I (eds) (1987) *South African Review 4* 192.

12 See Basson, D (1987) Judicial activism in a State of Emergency: An examination of recent decisions of the South African courts *South African Journal on Human Rights* 3(1):28–43 at 28.

13 See Madala, T (2001) Rule under apartheid and the fledgling democracy in post-apartheid South Africa: The role of the judiciary *North Carolina Journal of International Law and Commercial Regulation* 26(3):743–66 at 748. See also *Azanian Peoples Organization (AZAPO) and Others v President of the Republic of South Africa and Others* (CCT17/96) [1996] ZACC 16; 1996 (8) BCLR 1015; 1996 (4) SA 672 (25 July 1996) para 1 where Mahommed states: 'The legitimacy of law itself was deeply wounded as the country haemorrhaged dangerously in the face of this tragic conflict which had begun to traumatise the entire nation.'

14 Ellmann, S (1995) Law and legitimacy in South Africa *Law and Social Inquiry* 20(2):407–79 at 425.

15 Ellmann (1995) 409.

16 See Madala (2001) 745.

17 See Madala (2001) 748; Higginbotham, FM (1994) Sins from the past and lessons for the future: Eliminating apartheid in South African public accommodation and the challenge to an enlightened judiciary *Boston University International Law Journal* 12(1):1–56 at 1.

18 See the report by Gordon, A and Bruce, D (2006) Transformation and independence of the judiciary in South Africa, Centre for Study of Violence and Reconciliation (CSVR) 1–57 at 13.

19 See Dyzenhaus, D (1998) *Judging the Judges, Judging Ourselves: Truth, Reconciliation and the Apartheid Legal Order* 16, quoted in Gordon and Bruce (2006), indicating that this approach means that the 'judges hold that the judiciary duty when interpreting a statute is always to look to those parts of public record that make clear what the legislators as a matter of fact intended [and] in this way, the judges merely determined the law as it is, without permitting their substantive convictions about justice to interfere'.

interpretational aids in the event of ambiguity or inconsistency, or if adherence to the ordinary meaning of the text would result in absurdity.[20] They adhered to the notion that any modifications, corrections or additions to the text should be left to the legislature as the government branch responsible for making law. Value judgments of the content of a statute were irrelevant when interpreting and applying the legislation passed by the apartheid Parliament.[21] Corder draws the conclusion that:

> **The overall picture [of judicial attitudes] which emerges is one of a group of men who saw their dominant roles as the protectors of a stability ... The judges expressed it in terms of a positivistic acceptance of legislative sovereignty, despite a patently racist political structure, and a desire to preserve the existing order of legal relations, notwithstanding its basis in manifest social inequalities ...**[22]

These attitudes were amplified by the fact that the power of judges was constrained under the system of parliamentary supremacy.[23]

However, despite problems with the formalistic approach to the interpretation and application of unjust laws, there is widespread agreement that before the advent of democracy, the judiciary did exhibit many of the formal attributes of independence. Courtrooms were open to the general public and judges enjoyed security of tenure and of salary even though politics played a role in the promotion of judges to the Appellate Division. Judges served until the age of 70 and could be removed only by the State President at the request of the Houses of Parliament on the grounds of misbehaviour or incapacity. Moreover, the salaries of judges were legally guaranteed and could not be reduced during their term of office.[24]

Notwithstanding these features, the judiciary was not entirely free from indirect political influence through the process of appointment.[25] Before 1994, the State President appointed judges in terms of section 10 of the Supreme Court Act.[26] However, in practice, it was the Minister of Justice who made the appointments based on the recommendations of the Chief Justice or Judge President of the relevant division of the High Court.[27] The State President then merely formalised these appointments. The process of identifying potential candidates and their selection was also 'shrouded in secrecy' and 'political factors played a role in determining who secured appointment and who was promoted'.[28]

---

20 See Dugard (1978) 369.

21 See Govindjee, A and Olivier, M 'Finding the boundary: The role of the courts in giving effect to socio-economic rights in South Africa' in Osode, PC and Glover, G (eds) (2010) *Law and Transformative Justice in Post-Apartheid South Africa* 79.

22 Corder, H (2004) Judicial authority in a changing South Africa *Legal Studies* 24(2):253–74 at 255.

23 See *S v Makwanyane and Another* (CCT3/94) [1995] ZACC 3; 1995 (6) BCLR 665; 1995 (3) SA 391; [1996] 2 CHRLD 164; 1995 (2) SACR 1 (6 June 1995) para 301 where Mokgoro J stated that:

> **... due to the sovereignty of parliament, the supremacy of legislation and the absence of judicial review of parliamentary statutes, courts engaged in simple statutory interpretation, giving effect to the clear and unambiguous language of the legislative text – no matter how unjust the legislative provision.**

24 See Gordon and Bruce (2006) 11.

25 See Wesson, M and Du Plessis, M (2008) Fifteen years on: Central issues relating to the transformation of the South African judiciary *South African Journal on Human Rights* 24(2):187–213 at 190.

26 Act 59 of 1959.

27 Wesson and Du Plessis (2008) 190.

28 Wesson and Du Plessis (2008) 190. See also Cameron, E (1982) Legal chauvinism, executive-mindedness and justice: LC Steyn's impact on South African law *South African Law Journal* 99(1):38–75 at 40, detailing the 'meteoric' rise of LC Steyn to the position of Chief Justice, largely on the basis of his political affiliation.

Furthermore, in the pre-democratic era, the judiciary was composed almost entirely of white males, drawn from the elitist and privileged ranks of the ruling minority. Judicial appointees were drawn primarily from the ranks of senior counsel practising as advocates at the various bars in South Africa. Before 1990, only one white female had been appointed as a judge in South Africa while no black judges had been appointed.[29] The selection process was a confidential one which meant that candidates could be hand-picked based on whether their beliefs were sympathetic to the government of the day.[30] The first black male judge, Ismael Mahomed, was appointed in 1991.[31] When South Africa became a democracy in 1994, out of 166 judges, 161 were white men, two were white women, three were black men and there were no black women at all.[32]

Table 6.1 *Composition of the judiciary in 1994*[33]

Total	White male	Black male	White female	Black female
166	161	3	2	0

Before 1994, the Appellate Division of the Supreme Court (since renamed the Supreme Court of Appeal), with its seat in Bloemfontein, was the highest court in South Africa for all matters. The Appellate Division considered appeals from the various Provincial Divisions of the Supreme Court (since renamed High Courts), which had their seats in the main urban centres across South Africa. The Supreme Court (including the Appellate Division), together with a small number of other specialised courts created by legislation,[34] made up the superior courts.[35] The lower courts consisted primarily of the magistrates' courts which were divided into regional and district courts.

In 1927, a separate system of courts was also created for people classified as 'Africans' to interpret and enforce customary law.[36] This traditional judicial system, which was designed to deal with customary law through the institution of traditional leadership, was also subject to the control of first the Union government and then the apartheid government. The institution was controlled by native commissioners who included traditional leaders. They became state functionaries, exercising authority and constituting courts, no longer under the mandate of the people, but that of the government of the day.[37] Even though the traditional system of justice had elements of a democratic culture because of its consensual decision making, its values were fundamentally eroded by its transformation by colonial and apartheid rule.

29 See Madala (2001) 759.

30 Madala (2001) 759.

31 Mokgoro, Y (2010, December) Judicial appointments *Advocate* 43–8. See also Davis, DM (2010, December) Judicial appointments in South Africa *Advocate* 40–3.

32 Moerane, M (2003) The meaning of transformation of the judiciary in the new South African context *South African Law Journal* 120(4):708–18 at 712.

33 Moerane (2003) 712. See also Dugard, J (2007) Judging the judges: Towards an appropriate role for the role of the judiciary in South Africa's transformation *Leiden Journal of International Law* 20(4):965–81 at 968.

34 See, for example, the Income Tax Act 58 of 1962 which created a special court for hearing income tax appeals.

35 Currie, I and De Waal, J (2001) *The New Constitutional and Administrative Law, Vol 1 Constitutional Law* 273.

36 See generally the Black Administration Act 38 of 1927 (BAA).

37 Policy Framework on the Traditional Justice System under the Constitution, Department of Justice and Constitutional Development 10, available at http://www.pmg.org.za/policy-documents/2009/03/02/policy-framework-traditional-justice-system-under.

CRITICAL THINKING

How can the formation of new judicial structures that would truly deal responsibly with living customary law be achieved?

Vani argues that the colonial encounter fundamentally changed the way in which customary law was applied and developed in apartheid South Africa:

- Roman-Dutch and English law were given precedence over bodies of customary law and developed at the expense of customary law.
- Rules of evidence imported from a colonial legal system and imposed by statute and convention in court procedures resulted in the disappearance of customary law rules and principles.
- Strict criteria were imposed to prove the legal validity of customs. It had to be proved that customs had existed from time immemorial, and that they were invariable, continuous, certain, notorious, reasonable, peaceable and obligatory. Customs could not be immoral or opposed to an express enactment or to public policy.
- The **rule of *stare decisis*** ended the flexibility of customary law by preventing innovation to meet the changes in community opinion and sentiments. Modern legal machinery forced customary law to fall in line with national standards.[38]

Customary law was 'preserved, upgraded and frozen out of relevance to the flux of the [traditional community's] life'.[39] This was evidenced by cases such *Bhe and Others v Khayelitsha Magistrate and Others*[40] and *Shilubana and Others v Nwamitwa*,[41] which focused on the development of customary law through the lens of either the common law or the Constitution. Customary law thus 'became atrophied as a result of the rupture of its relationship with other sources of law'.[42]

Even the manner in which customary law was recorded changed. Before the colonial encounter, it 'was a body of orally transmitted precepts and precedents'.[43] Where disputes arose, 'solutions were sought to take the total situation of the parties into consideration'.[44] These basic features were eroded by the Union and apartheid administration and customary law:

> became a fixed body of law, indistinguishable from statute and case law. Opinions and evidence given by villagers on custom in courts were isolated from their contexts and utilized to describe a single transaction or an offence which gave rise to a sense of individual right not dependent on community opinion, enforced by courts even in opposition to community opinion.[45]

38 Vani, MS 'Customary law and modern governance of natural resources in India: Conflicts, prospects for accord and strategies' in Pradham, R (ed) (2002) *Legal Pluralism and Unofficial Law in Social, Economic and Political Development* 419.

39 Vani 419.

40 (CCT 49/03) [2004] ZACC 17; 2005 (1) SA 580 (CC); 2005 (1) BCLR 1 (CC) (15 October 2004).

41 (CCT 03/07) [2008] ZACC 9; 2008 (9) BCLR 914 (CC); 2009 (2) SA 66 (CC) (4 June 2008).

42 Vani 419.

43 Vani 419.

44 Vani 419.

45 Vani (2002) 419.

Moseneke J (as he then was) expressed a similar sentiment in *Daniels v Campbell and Others*:

> **True to their worldview, [which 'originates from the deep-rooted prejudice'] judges of the past displayed remarkable ethnocentric bias and arrogance at the expense of those they perceived different. They exalted their own and demeaned and excluded everything else.**[46]

Given these changes and the transformation during Union and apartheid rule of customary law and the institutions called on to develop and enforce it, it can be argued that the creation of new traditional courts that rely on the discredited structures of traditional leadership runs the risk of entrenching Union and apartheid forms of judicial governance instead of truly respecting age-old customary legal structures. But should the South African judiciary be restructured to enable the formation of new judicial structures that would truly deal responsibly with living customary law? If so, how could this be achieved? There are no easy answers to such questions as the debate which started in 2012 with proposals for the creation of new traditional courts illustrates.[47]

6.2 The judiciary in the new constitutional dispensation

6.2.1 The structure of the judiciary in the 1996 Constitution

In fulfilling the objectives of the new constitutional order, the change in government included the restructuring of the judicial system. The restructuring of the judicial system included changes to the hierarchical structure of the courts. Section 166 of the Constitution thus provides that the courts are:

> (*a*) **the Constitutional Court;**
> (*b*) **the Supreme Court of Appeal;**
> (*c*) **the High Courts, including any high court of appeal that may be established by an Act of Parliament to hear appeals from High Courts;**
> (*d*) **the Magistrates' Courts; and**
> (*e*) **any other court established or recognised in terms of an Act of Parliament, including any court of a status similar to either the High Courts or the Magistrates' Courts.**

One of the most significant changes is that a new Constitutional Court was created in the interim Constitution to serve as the final court in all constitutional and related matters. The Constitutional Court is headed by the Chief Justice who is also the head of the judiciary. The Chief Justice exercises responsibility over the establishment and monitoring of norms and

46 (CCT 40/ 03) [2004] ZACC 14; 2004 (5) SA 331 (CC); 2004 (7) BCLR 735 (CC) (11 March 2004) para 74.

47 See the Traditional Courts Bill B 1–2012 available at http://www.justice.gov.za/legislation/bills/2012-b01tradcourts.pdf. The Bill has been heavily criticised. See, for example, the submission made to Parliament by the Law, Race and Gender Institute, now the Centre for Law and Society, available at http://www.cls.uct.ac.za/usr/lrg/docs/TCB/2012/lrg_feb2012_ncopsubmission.pdf.

standards for the exercise of the judicial functions of all courts.[48] The Deputy Chief Justice serves as the deputy leader of the judiciary and must 'exercise such powers or perform such functions of the Chief Justice in terms of this or any other law as the Chief Justice may assign to him or her; and, in the absence of the Chief Justice, or if the office of Chief Justice is vacant, exercise the powers or perform the functions of the Chief Justice, as Acting Chief Justice'.[49]

The Constitutional Court has pointed out that the distinctive appointment process for the Chief Justice and Deputy Chief Justice (discussed below) indicates the high importance of their offices. They are required to 'represent the judiciary and to act on its behalf in dealings with the other arms of government'[50] and they may also be called on 'to perform ceremonial and administrative duties'.[51] As such, the Chief Justice and the Deputy Chief Justice 'are the most senior judges in the judicial arm of government, and their distinctive manner of appointment reflects the fact that they may be called upon to liaise and interact with the Executive and Parliament on behalf of the Judiciary'.[52]

Once they have been appointed, however, the Chief Justice and Deputy Chief Justice take their place alongside nine other judges of the Constitutional Court and have the same powers as any other judge of the Constitutional Court in as far as decisions about individual cases before the Court are concerned.[53]

The seat of the Constitutional Court is in Johannesburg, but the Chief Justice may allow the Court to sit elsewhere in the country if it is expedient or in the interests of justice to do so.[54]

The Appellate Division was renamed the Supreme Court of Appeal (SCA). Apart from the name change, the Appellate Division is no longer a division of the Supreme Court, but a fully fledged constitutional entity in its own right.[55] The SCA is headed by the President of the SCA who is assisted by a Deputy President of that Court.[56] In the absence of the President of the SCA or if the office of President of the SCA is vacant, the Deputy President perform the functions of the President of the SCA as Acting President of that Court.[57] The seat of the SCA is in Bloemfontein, but the President of the SCA may allow it to sit elsewhere in the country if it is expedient or in the interests of justice to do so.[58]

Both the Constitutional Court and the SCA have **jurisdiction** across the Republic. They do not, however, have jurisdiction over exactly the same subject matter. While the Constitutional Court has jurisdiction over all constitutional and non-constitutional matters, the SCA does not. This is because the SCA does not have jurisdiction over those matters that fall into the exclusive jurisdiction of the Constitutional Court.

---

48 S 167(1) read with s 165(6) of the Constitution as well as s 4(1) of the Superior Courts Act 10 of 2013. See also *Justice Alliance of South Africa v President of Republic of South Africa and Others, Freedom Under Law v President of Republic of South Africa and Others, Centre for Applied Legal Studies and Another v President of Republic of South Africa and Others* (CCT 53/11, CCT 54/11, CCT 62/11) [2011] ZACC 23; 2011 (5) SA 388 (CC); 2011 (10) BCLR 1017 (CC) (29 July 2011) para 78.

49 S 167(1) of the Constitution read with s 4(2) of the Superior Courts Act.

50 *Justice Alliance* para 78.

51 *Justice Alliance* para 78.

52 *Justice Alliance* para 78.

53 *Justice Alliance* para 79.

54 S 4(1)(*b*) of the Superior Courts Act.

55 S 166(*b*) of the Constitution. See also Currie and De Waal (2001) 278.

56 S 168(1) of the Constitution.

57 S 4(2)(*b*) of the Superior Courts Act.

58 S 5(1)(*b*) of the Superior Courts Act.

The Constitution also created a number of High Courts.[59] These were created from former provincial and local divisions of the Supreme Court and from the various superior courts of the former so-called 'independent' homelands. The different High Courts have now been replaced with a single High Court of South Africa. The High Court of South Africa, however, consists of the Divisions determined by an Act of Parliament.[60] The High Court functions as a superior court and acts both as a court of first instance and as a court hearing appeals from the lower courts. High Courts have geographically limited jurisdiction. Each Division of the High Court consists of a Judge President and one or more Deputy Judges President, each with specified headquarters within the area under the jurisdiction of that Division and so many other judges as may be determined in accordance with the prescribed criteria.[61] The Judge President leads his or her Division and is also responsible for the co-ordination of the judicial functions of all magistrates' courts falling within the jurisdiction of that Division.[62]

In 2013, Parliament passed legislation to streamline the High Court system to create separate Divisions of the High Court for each of South Africa's nine provinces.[63] The High Courts now consist of the following Divisions:

- Eastern Cape Division, with its main seat in Grahamstown
- Free State Division, with its main seat in Bloemfontein
- Gauteng Division, with its main seat in Pretoria
- KwaZulu-Natal Division, with its main seat in Pietermaritzburg
- Limpopo Division, with its main seat in Polokwane
- Mpumalanga Division, with its main seat in Nelspruit
- Northern Cape Division, with its main seat in Kimberley
- North West Division, with its main seat in Mahikeng
- Western Cape Division, with its main seat in Cape Town.

The magistrates' courts remain essentially unchanged. However, they have now become creatures of the Constitution and, to strengthen the independence of the judiciary, magistrates no longer fall within the ambit of the public service.[64] Magistrates' courts and all other courts are empowered in terms of section 170 of the Constitution to decide any matter determined by an Act of Parliament. Magistrates' courts may not enquire into or rule on the constitutionality of any legislation or conduct of the President. Although these courts are essential for the administration of justice, serving as the first port of call for most people who encounter the legal system, we will not focus on these courts because of their lack of constitutional jurisdiction.

Apart from the courts referred to in the Constitution, there are also several specialist courts created by statute. These specialist courts may be divided into superior specialist courts and inferior specialist courts.

The superior specialist courts include, but are not limited to, the following:

- The Labour Court was established in terms of section 151 of the Labour Relations Act[65] to deal with disputes between employers and employees.

---

59 S 169.
60 S 169(2) of the Constitution.
61 S 6(2) of the Superior Courts Act.
62 S 8(4)(*c*) of the Superior Courts Act.
63 S 6 of the Superior Courts Act. Most sections of the Act came into operation in August 2013.
64 See ss 10–16 of the Magistrates Act 90 of 1993.
65 Act 66 of 1995 as amended by Act 127 of 1998.

- The Land Claims Court was established in terms of section 22 of the Restitution of Land Rights Act[66] to resolve disputes that arise from land claims in relation to South Africa's land reform initiative. This initiative came about as a result of the legacy of apartheid that left many South Africans destitute after the apartheid government dispossessed them of their land.
- The Tax Court was established in terms of section 83(3) of the Income Tax Act.[67]

The inferior specialist courts include, but are not limited to, the following:
- The Children's Court was established to deal with matters related to children such as custody.[68]
- The Maintenance Courts were established in terms of the Maintenance Act[69] to deal with issues around maintenance.
- The Domestic Violence Courts were established in terms of the Domestic Violence Act.[70]

These specialist courts, which Berman refers to as 'problem-solving courts', are an important initiative seeking to provide a significant opportunity for using litigation as a transformative strategy in the promotion of constitutional values and principles.[71] However, apart from the Equality Courts, these courts do not usually play a direct role in the adjudication of constitutional issues.

6.2.2 Constitutional jurisdiction of the various courts

Jurisdiction refers to the power or competence of a court to hear and adjudicate on, and to determine and dispose of, a legal dispute. In civil matters, litigants must ensure that they approach the correct court with the requisite jurisdiction to hear the matter. In criminal matters, the National Prosecuting Authority (NPA) must ensure that a person is tried in the appropriate court with the power to consider his or her guilt and hand down the appropriate sentence. If we approach a court that does not have the jurisdiction to hear a matter or if we approach a court who has jurisdiction to hear similar matters but only on appeal, then the court will dismiss the application before hearing the merits of the case because it lacks jurisdiction to hear the case.

The rules of jurisdiction when constitutional issues are raised in a case differ in important ways from the rules of jurisdiction in non-constitutional matters. The reason for this is, in part, that in constitutional matters litigants have access to distinct remedies not usually available in non-constitutional matters. As jurisdictional issues are inextricably linked to questions of what remedy is being sought, there is a close relationship between constitutional jurisdiction and the remedy being sought in a particular constitutional matter. For example, constitutional cases often revolve around arguments about whether the law or the action of someone is unconstitutional and invalid, and whether it should be set aside. If a court does invalidate and set aside legislation or the acts of the President or other members of the executive, the court will be 'interfering' in the work of the democratically elected branches of government. The Constitution grants jurisdiction to certain courts only to award such remedies. There are also special rules relating to when these remedies may be granted and

66 Act 22 of 1994 as amended by Act 48 of 2003.
67 Act 58 of 1962.
68 Children's Act 38 of 2005.
69 Act 99 of 1998.
70 Act 116 of 1998.
71 Berman G, and Feinblatt, J (2001) Problem-solving courts: A brief primer *Law and Policy* 23(2):125–40 at 125.

when the ruling by a court on remedies is final or not. There will therefore always be a close relationship between the remedy that is sought and the question of whether a court has jurisdiction in a case so this section should be read with the section on constitutional remedies.[72]

In South Africa, the question of constitutional jurisdiction is further complicated by the fact that the interim and then the 1996 Constitutions created a new Constitutional Court which was welded onto the existing judicial system. In the interim Constitution, the Constitutional Court was initially placed in an equal position with the SCA, which retained its final jurisdiction over all non-constitutional matters but had no jurisdiction at all over constitutional issues.[73] In the 1996 Constitution this arrangement was changed and the SCA now also enjoys constitutional jurisdiction[74] although the Constitutional Court retained final jurisdiction over all constitutional matters.[75] To complicate matters further, the jurisdiction of the Constitutional Court was extended by the Constitution Seventeenth Amendment Act of 2012 (which came into effect in August 2013). When considering the various jurisdictional issues, it is therefore important to note this history and to understand that the system now provides for two distinct jurisdictional scenarios: first, in matters not raising any constitutional or related issue, and second, in matters raising constitutional issues. Given the fact that it is not always easy to determine whether a matter raises a constitutional issue or not, this division of jurisdictional turf is not without its problems.

6.2.2.1 Constitutional Court

Until August 2013, the Constitutional Court was a specialist court and not a court of general jurisdiction.[76] However, it is important to note that the Constitution Seventeenth Amendment Act has now drastically changed the jurisdiction of the Constitutional Court. The jurisdiction of the Constitutional Court before this change must be contrasted with the arrangement which came into effect in 2013. Previously, the Constitutional Court was the court of final instance in relation to constitutional matters 'and issues connected with a decision on a constitutional matter'.[77] This included any question that was not a constitutional matter but nevertheless had to be decided by the Court in order to reach a decision on a constitutional matter.[78] Constitutional matters include 'any issue involving the interpretation, protection or enforcement of the Constitution'.[79] Although the extension of the jurisdiction of the Constitutional Court beyond constitutional issues (which we discuss below) appears to be

---

72 See Currie and De Waal (2001) 279–80.

73 See Klug (2010) 237–8.

74 S 168(3).

75 S 167(3).

76 However, the Constitution Seventeenth Amendment Act, 2012, available at http://www.info.gov.za/view/DownloadFileAction?id=184794, changes this state of affairs.

77 See s 167(3) before it was amended.

78 S 167(3)(*b*) of the Constitution. See *Alexkor Ltd and Another v Richtersveld Community and Others* (CCT19/03) [2003] ZACC 18; 2004 (5) SA 460 (CC); 2003 (12) BCLR 1301 (CC) (14 October 2003) para 24 where the Court had to deal with the interpretation of the Restitution of Land Rights Act 22 of 1994 in dealing with questions about the Richtersveld community's rights to the land, but stated that it would also be necessary to deal with non-constitutional matters:

> **A more difficult question is to determine whether this Court has jurisdiction to deal with all issues bearing on or related to establishing the existence of these matters. For example, the question might be asked whether the issue concerning the existence of the Community's rights in land prior to the colonisation of the Cape, or the content or incidence of such rights, constitute in themselves 'constitutional matters'; the same might be asked concerning the continued existence of such rights after the British Crown's annexation of the Cape in 1806, or after the 1847 Proclamation or the subsequent statutory and other acts thereafter.**

79 S 167(7) of the Constitution.

a dramatic change, this change in jurisdiction may have less of an impact than we might think. This is because it is not always easy to distinguish between a constitutional matter and a non-constitutional matter. There are several reasons for this:

- First, in the important case, *Pharmaceutical Manufacturers Association of South Africa and Another: In re Ex parte President of the Republic of South Africa and Others*, the Constitutional Court stated that:

  > **I cannot accept this contention which treats the common law as a body of law separate and distinct from the Constitution. There are not two systems of law, each dealing with the same subject matter, each having similar requirements, each operating in its own field with its own highest court. There is only one system of law. It is shaped by the Constitution which is the supreme law, and all law, including the common law, derives its force from the Constitution and is subject to constitutional control.**[80]

  Read with section 39(2) of the Constitution, which states that '[w]hen interpreting legislation, and when **developing the common law** or customary law, every court, tribunal or forum must promote the **spirit, purport and objects of the Bill of Rights**', this means that any interpretation of legislation and any development of the common law or customary law will potentially raise constitutional issues. Legislation must be interpreted in line with the spirit, purport and object of the Bill of Rights if the words are reasonably capable of such an interpretation or are not unduly strained.[81] This makes such an interpretative exercise a constitutional matter. This is also called **reading down.**[82] Where 'the common law deviates from the spirit, purport and objects of the Bill of Rights the courts have an obligation to develop it by removing that deviation'.[83] This means that potentially any argument about the development of the common law or the interpretation of legislation could raise constitutional issues in an indirect manner.[84]
- Second, under the 1996 Constitution, '[t]he exercise of all public power must comply with the Constitution which is the supreme law, and the doctrine of legality which is part of that law'.[85] Any challenge to the exercise of public power is therefore a constitutional matter and is susceptible to the jurisdiction of the Constitutional Court. Public power is

80 (CCT31/99) [2000] ZACC 1; 2000 (2) SA 674; 2000 (3) BCLR 241 (25 February 2000) para 44.

81 *Investigating Directorate: Serious Economic Offences and Others v Hyundai Motor Distributors (Pty) Ltd and Others In re: Hyundai Motor Distributors (Pty) Ltd and Others v Smit NO and Others* (CCT1/00) [2000] ZACC 12; 2000 (10) BCLR 1079; 2001 (1) SA 545 (CC) (25 August 2000) para 24.

82 See Currie, I and De Waal, J (2005) *The Bill of Rights Handbook* 5th ed 66.

83 *Carmichele v Minister of Safety and Security* (CCT 48/00) [2001] ZACC 22; 2001 (4) SA 938 (CC); 2001 (10) BCLR 995 (CC) (16 August 2001) para 33; see also para 36. See also *Thebus and Another v S* (CCT36/02) [2003] ZACC 12; 2003 (6) SA 505 (CC); 2003 (10) BCLR 1100 (CC) (28 August 2003) para 25; *K v Minister of Safety and Security* (CCT52/04) [2005] ZACC 8; 2005 (6) SA 419 (CC); 2005 (9) BCLR 835 (CC); [2005] 8 BLLR 749 (CC) (13 June 2005) para 15; *Masiya v Director of Public Prosecutions Pretoria (The State) and Another* (CCT54/06) [2007] ZACC 9; 2007 (5) SA 30 (CC); 2007 (8) BCLR 827 (10 May 2007) para 33; *Barkhuizen v Napier* (CCT72/05) [2007] ZACC 5; 2007 (5) SA 323 (CC); 2007 (7) BCLR 691 (CC) (4 April 2007) para 35. Some commentators have wrongly taken issue with this interpretation, arguing that the Constitution accords the spirit, purport and object of the Bill of Rights only a secondary role to serve as a tie-breaker when the rights in the Bill of Rights, justice and the rules of the common law are indeterminate. See Fagan, A (2010) The secondary role of the spirit, purport and objects of the Bill of Rights in the common law's development *South African Law Journal* 127(4):611–27. Fagan has been criticised by Davis, who argues that the Constitution intended that the common law reflect the normative value system as found in a holistic reading of the text of the Constitution. This means that the trigger that propels judges to make the decision to develop the common law is to be found in a judicial engagement with the constitutional value system. See Davis, D (2012) How many positivist legal philosophers can be made to dance on the head of a pin? A reply to Professor Fagan *South African Law Journal* 129(1):59–72.

84 See *S v Boesak* (CCT25/00) [2000] ZACC 25; 2001 (1) BCLR 36; 2001 (1) SA 912 (1 December 2000) para 14.

85 *Pharmaceutical Manufacturers* para 20.

usually exercised by a public body or institution authorised by the Constitution or ordinary law to exercise that power. It includes power exercised by the President, Ministers, state officials and the courts.[86]

- Third, the Constitutional Court also has the jurisdiction to hear disputes as to whether any law or conduct is inconsistent with the Constitution and can declare such law or conduct unconstitutional and invalid.
- Fourth, the Constitutional Court can determine issues relating to the status, powers and functions of an organ of state.[87]
- Fifth, questions arising from the interpretation and application of ordinary legislation that has been enacted to give effect to constitutional rights or in compliance with the legislature's constitutional obligations are also constitutional matters.[88] For example, section 9(4) of the Constitution requires the legislature to enact legislation to prohibit unfair discrimination. The legislature consequently passed the Promotion of Equality and Prevention of Unfair Discrimination Act[89] to give effect to this injunction. Thus, any interpretation and application of this Act would give rise to a constitutional issue.[90]

Although the scope of what constitutes a constitutional issue is therefore potentially extraordinarily broad, this does not mean that all factual and legal questions can be turned into constitutional issues. However, the extension of the jurisdiction of the Constitutional Court in 2013 has now rendered this distinction less important as far as points of law are concerned. The amended section 167(3)(*a*) of the Constitution now makes clear that the Constitutional Court is the highest court of the Republic. Previously, this section stated that the Constitutional Court was the highest Court for all constitutional matters only. The 2013 amendments now determine that the Constitutional Court may decide constitutional matters and

> **any other matter, if the Constitutional Court grants leave to appeal on the grounds that the matter raises an arguable point of law of general public importance which ought to be considered by that Court.**[91]

The Constitutional Court itself has the power to make the final decision on whether a matter is within its jurisdiction.[92] These amendments mean that the Constitutional Court is no longer confined to hearing constitutional matters and matters that are connected with constitutional matters. The Court can now also consider non-constitutional matters. However, the Constitutional Court cannot hear appeals based solely on factual disputes. In cases where an appeal is lodged with the Constitutional Court that does not deal with a constitutional matter, the Constitutional Court has a relatively wide discretion to decide whether it will hear the appeal or not. In doing so, it will have to take two factors into consideration. First, it can only hear appeals on the grounds that the matter raises an

86 *Carmichele* para 54.

87 See ss 172(1) and 167(4)(*a*) of the Constitution. See also *Boesak* para 14.

88 *National Education Health & Allied Workers Union (NEHAWU) v University of Cape Town and Others* (CCT2/02) [2002] ZACC 27; 2003 (2) BCLR 154; 2003 (3) SA 1 (CC) (6 December 2002) para 14; *Alexkor* para 23; *Bato Star Fishing (Pty) Ltd v Minister of Environmental Affairs and Tourism and Others* (CCT 27/03) [2004] ZACC 15; 2004 (4) SA 490 (CC); 2004 (7) BCLR 687 (CC) (12 March 2004) para 25.

89 Act 4 of 2000.

90 *MEC for Education: Kwazulu-Natal and Others v Pillay* (CCT 51/06) [2007] ZACC 21; 2008 (1) SA 474 (CC); 2008 (2) BCLR 99 (CC) (5 October 2007).

91 S 167(3)(*b*) of the Constitution.

92 S 167(3)(*c*) of the Constitution.

arguable point of **law**. Second, this point of law must be of such general public importance that it is necessary for the Constitutional Court to hear the matter to give clarity on this point of law. As we shall see below, in certain cases the Constitutional Court has no choice and **must** consider a case before it. However, where an appeal is lodged with the Constitutional Court in a non-constitutional matter, the Constitutional Court itself can decide whether to hear the case **but** only if the two requirements set out above are met. Even if the two requirements are met, this does not mean the Constitutional Court must hear the appeal. It has a discretion to decide whether to hear it or not.

As pointed out above, matters that turn purely on questions of fact are not constitutional matters nor do they raise 'an arguable point of law'. This means such matters that raise only purely factual disputes cannot be heard by the Constitutional Court. Similarly, the Constitutional Court cannot hear matters involving the straightforward application of law that do not raise constitutional questions, do not require the Court to interpret or develop legislation, common law or customary law in line with the spirit, purport and objects of the Bill of Rights, and do not raise an arguable point of law.[93]

PAUSE FOR REFLECTION

The distinction between factual disputes and disputes about points of law

The Constitutional Court's judgment in *S v Boesak*[94] provides a helpful illustration of the distinction between factual disputes and disputes about points of law in the context of the pre-seventeenth amendment regime which still required a constitutional question to be raised for the Constitutional Court to hear the case. Boesak was convicted on a charge of fraud and three charges of theft in the High Court. On appeal, the SCA set aside the conviction on one of the theft charges but dismissed the appeal on the other charges. It nevertheless reduced the sentence to one of three years' imprisonment.[95]

Boesak approached the Constitutional Court to have the remaining convictions set aside, arguing that there was not sufficient evidence to support the findings of the SCA that his guilt had been proven beyond reasonable doubt. The SCA, Boesak argued, had interpreted the facts wrongly. This was a violation of the right to be presumed innocent guaranteed by section 35(3)(*h*) of the Bill of Rights.

The Constitutional Court found that, in essence, Boesak was arguing that the High Court and the SCA had got the facts wrong. It found that even if this were true, this would not raise a constitutional issue. The Court then went on to identify three broad principles informing the identification of constitutional issues:

(a) ***A challenge to a decision of the SCA on the basis only that it is wrong on the facts is not a constitutional matter.***
In the context of section 167(3) of the Constitution the question whether evidence is sufficient to justify a finding of guilt beyond reasonable doubt cannot in itself be a constitutional matter. Otherwise, all criminal cases would be constitutional matters, and the distinction drawn in the Constitution between the jurisdiction of this Court and that of the SCA would be illusory. There is a need for finality in criminal matters. The structure of the Constitution suggests clearly that finality should be achieved by the SCA unless a constitutional matter arises. Disagreement with the SCA's assessment of the facts is not sufficient to

93 *Boesak* para 15.
94 (CCT25/00) [2000] ZACC 25; 2001 (1) BCLR 36; 2001 (1) SA 912 (1 December 2000).
95 *S v Boesak* (105/99) [2000] ZASCA 24 (12 May 2000).

constitute a breach of the right to a fair trial. An applicant for leave to appeal against the decision of the SCA must necessarily have had an appeal or review as contemplated by section 35(3)(*o*) of the Constitution. Unless there is some separate constitutional issue raised therefore, no constitutional right is engaged when an appellant merely disputes the findings of fact made by the SCA.

(b) *The development of, or the failure to develop, a common-law rule by the SCA may constitute a constitutional matter.*
This may occur if the SCA developed, or failed to develop, the rule under circumstances inconsistent with its obligation under section 39(2) of the Constitution or with some other right or principle of the Constitution.

(c) *The application of a legal rule by the SCA may constitute a constitutional matter.*
This may occur if the application of a rule is inconsistent with some right or principle of the Constitution.[96]

The Constitutional Court's jurisdiction can be divided into concurrent jurisdiction and exclusive jurisdiction. Its concurrent jurisdiction is exercised concurrently with the High Courts and the SCA. On certain matters, only the Constitutional Court can decide, giving it exclusive jurisdiction on these issues.

The 1996 Constitution provides for the concurrent exercise of jurisdiction of the High Courts, the SCA and the Constitutional Court in respect of direct challenges to the constitutionality of all forms of legislation. This means that any challenge to a provision of an Act of Parliament, a provincial legislature or delegated legislation would usually first be lodged in the High Court. If the High Court or later the SCA declares the legislation invalid, the Constitutional Court must confirm this before such an order will have any force or effect.[97] This means all decisions by a High Court or the SCA declaring a legislative provision unconstitutional and invalid will always end up in the Constitutional Court as the Constitutional Court is required either to confirm the order of invalidity of the lower court or to reject that order. This is necessary because it would be untenable for a situation to arise where a High Court declares a legislative provision to be invalid and this provision is thus inoperable within the jurisdiction of that High Court while it remains in force in other jurisdictions. If a lower court does not declare the legislation invalid, an appeal can nevertheless be lodged against this decision with the Constitutional Court.

Jurisdiction on issues around the interpretation and application of legislation, common law or customary law are also shared between the High Courts, SCA and Constitutional Court. As we have seen, where a dispute arises on an arguable point of law of general public importance (even when this point of law is non-constitutional in nature), then the Constitutional Court also has concurrent jurisdiction with lower courts.

Over and above this concurrent jurisdiction, the Constitutional Court also has exclusive jurisdiction to hear cases dealing with a distinct set of issues. As the Constitutional Court explained in *Women's Legal Trust v President of the Republic of South Africa and Others*:

> **These exclusive competencies draw on the Court's political legitimacy. They reflect its special status as guardian of the Constitution, with exclusively constitutional functions and a specially determined composition. Any exercise of the judicial**

96 *Boesak* para 15.
97 S 167(5) of the Constitution.

> **function may cause tension with the other arms of government and trigger political contention. Hence the mere fact that a matter is or may become politically fraught does not of itself mean that only this Court has jurisdiction to deal with it. More is needed. Dispositive indications may lie in the nature of the obligation, whether its content can be clearly ascertained, whether it is stated unambiguously in the Constitution, how its content is determined, and whether it is capacity-defining or power-conferring.**[98]

Thus, the Constitutional Court has exclusive jurisdiction to decide disputes between organs of state in the national or provincial sphere concerning the constitutional status, powers or functions of any of those organs of state.[99] For example, where a dispute arises between a provincial government and the national government about their respective powers or between a provincial legislature and the national Parliament about the respective legislative powers of each, then only the Constitutional Court has jurisdiction to hear the case.

The Constitutional Court also has exclusive jurisdiction to decide on the constitutionality of any parliamentary or provincial Bill referred to it by the President or the relevant Premier in terms of section 79 or 121 of the Constitution when the President or the respective Premier has reservations about the constitutionality of a Bill.[100] In addition, the Constitutional Court has exclusive jurisdiction to decide on applications by members of the NA or provincial legislatures to declare invalid all or parts of an Act of Parliament or the provincial legislatures in terms of section 80 or 122 of the Constitution.[101] In terms of these sections, such an application can only be made if supported by at least one-third of the members of the NA[102] or at least 20% of the members of a provincial legislature.[103] Such an application must be made within 30 days of the date on which the President or the Premier assented to and signed the Act.[104] This provision allows opposition parties who believe that a newly passed Act is unconstitutional to refer the Act to the Constitutional Court before the Act is implemented.

The Constitutional Court has exclusive jurisdiction to decide on the constitutionality of any amendment to the Constitution.[105] Note, however, that in *United Democratic Movement v President of the Republic of South Africa and Others (No 2)*, the Court stated that amendments to the Constitution passed in accordance with the manner and form requirements of section 74 of the Constitution 'become part of the Constitution'.[106] Once part of the Constitution, amendments cannot be challenged on the grounds of inconsistency with other provisions of the Constitution. This means '[t]he Constitution, as amended, must be read as a whole and its provisions must be interpreted in harmony with one another. It follows that there is little if any scope for challenging the constitutionality of amendments that are passed in accordance with the prescribed procedures and majorities'.[107] Challenges to the constitutionality of amendments to the Constitution would therefore be based on whether

---

98 (CCT13/09) [2009] ZACC 20; 2009 (6) SA 94 (CC) (22 July 2009) para 15.
99 S 167(4)(*a*) of the Constitution.
100 S 167(4)(*b*) of the Constitution.
101 S 167(4)(*c*) of the Constitution.
102 S 80(2)(*a*) of the Constitution.
103 S 122(2)(*a*) of the Constitution.
104 Ss 80(2)(*b*) and 122(2)(*b*) of the Constitution.
105 S 167(4)(*d*) of the Constitution.
106 (CCT23/02) [2002] ZACC 21; 2003 (1) SA 495; 2002 (11) BCLR 1179 (4 October 2002) para 12.
107 *UDM* para 12.

the correct procedure was followed when passing the amendment. For example, if an amendment to the Constitution directly or indirectly amends section 1 of the Constitution, such an amendment must be passed with a 75% majority in the NA. If an amendment of any section of the Constitution would have the effect, say, of watering down the provision in section 1 regarding the supremacy of the Constitution and it is not passed with a 75% majority, the Court would be able to invalidate the amendment.

It is unclear whether a duly passed amendment of the 'basic structure' of the Constitution could be challenged in the Constitutional Court. In *Premier of KwaZulu-Natal and Others v President of the Republic of South Africa and Others*, Mahomed DP made the following *obiter* remarks about this matter:

> **There is a procedure which is prescribed for amendments to the Constitution and this procedure has to be followed. If that is properly done, the amendment is constitutionally unassailable. It may perhaps be that a purported amendment to the Constitution, following the formal procedures prescribed by the Constitution, but radically and fundamentally restructuring and reorganising the fundamental premises of the Constitution, might not qualify as an 'amendment' at all.**[108]

Given the fact that any radical restructuring of the fundamental premises of the Constitution would, in effect, constitute an amendment of section 1 of the Constitution which requires a 75% majority in the NA, it is difficult to see that the Constitutional Court would ever have the opportunity to develop this *obiter* statement.

The Constitutional Court has exclusive jurisdiction to decide that Parliament or the President has 'failed to fulfil a constitutional obligation'.[109] The words 'fulfil a constitutional obligation' must be given a narrow meaning.[110] This is because the words are part of a broader distribution of jurisdictional competence in the Constitution. We need to interpret the words narrowly to ensure that they do not clash with the provision in section 172(2)(*a*) that gives other courts jurisdiction over 'conduct of the President'. The same reasoning applies to obligations the Constitution imposes on Parliament as section 172(2)(*a*) also grants other courts jurisdiction over the validity of Acts of Parliament.[111] While the phrase 'failed to fulfil a constitutional obligation' in section 167(4)(*e*) must be narrowly construed, section 172(2)(*a*), which gives other courts competence to scrutinise the constitutionality of presidential and parliamentary acts, must be widely interpreted[112] to ensure that absurdities do not arise. Thus the Constitutional Court has held that it alone has jurisdiction to determine whether Parliament has fulfilled its obligation to facilitate public involvement in passing legislation.[113] Lastly, only the Constitutional Court has the jurisdiction to certify a provincial constitution in terms of section 144.[114]

---

108 (CCT36/95) [1995] ZACC 10; 1995 (12) BCLR 1561; 1996 (1) SA 769 (29 November 1995) para 47.

109 S 167(4)(*e*) of the Constitution.

110 *President of the Republic of South Africa and Others v South African Rugby Football Union and Others (SARFU I)* (CCT16/98) [1998] ZACC 21; 1999 (2) SA 14; 1999 (2) BCLR 175 (2 December 1998) para 25.

111 *Women's Legal Trust* para 11.

112 *Women's Legal Trust* para 12.

113 See generally *Doctors for Life International v Speaker of the National Assembly and Others* (CCT12/05) [2006] ZACC 11; 2006 (12) BCLR 1399 (CC); 2006 (6) SA 416 (CC) (17 August 2006).

114 See *Certification of the Kwazulu-Natal Constitution* (CCT15/96) [1996] ZACC 17; 1996 (11) BCLR 1419; 1996 (4) SA 1098 (6 September 1996); *Certification of the Constitution of the Western Cape, 1997* (CCT6/97) [1997] ZACC 8; 1997 (12) BCLR 1653; 1998 (1) SA 655 (2 September 1997); *Certification of the Amended Text of the Constitution of the Western Cape, 1997* (CCT29/97) [1997] ZACC 15; 1997 (12) BCLR 1653; 1998 (1) SA 655 (18 November 1997).

As pointed out above, in all matters not exclusively reserved for the jurisdiction of the Constitutional Court, the Constitutional Court ordinarily functions as a court of appeal, hearing cases that come to it after decisions by the High Courts and/or the SCA, or hearing cases in which it is required to consider whether to confirm an order of invalidity from lower courts. However, section 167(6) of the Constitution allows direct access to the Constitutional Court – even in cases where it does not have exclusive jurisdiction – when in the view of the Constitutional Court it is in the interest of justice to allow such direct access. This is an extraordinary procedure and the Court will only grant direct access to litigants on issues on which it has concurrent jurisdiction in the most exceptional cases. This means that 'compelling reasons are required to justify a different procedure and to persuade this Court that it should exercise its discretion to grant direct access'.[115] As a general rule, the Constitutional Court is reluctant to grant direct access as it would then have to decide the legal and factual issues without the benefit of the wisdom of one or more lower courts. It has ruled that the 'Court is placed at a grave disadvantage if it is required to deal with difficult questions of law, constitutional or otherwise ... virtually as a court of first instance'.[116] It is also not considered to be in the interest of justice for a court to sit as a court of first and last instance as the losing litigants will then have no chance of appealing against the decision given:

> **Experience shows that decisions are more likely to be correct if more than one court has been required to consider the issues raised. In such circumstances the losing party has an opportunity of challenging the reasoning on which the first judgment is based, and of reconsidering and refining arguments previously raised in the light of such judgment.**[117]

To decide whether it is in the interest of justice to grant direct access, the Court will ask whether the case is of such urgency that direct access should be granted.[118] This is because the Court has argued that it was normally important for a case first to be heard in the High Court (and perhaps the SCA) because of the 'benefits that may be derived from the judgments of other courts'.[119] Those courts should therefore not ordinarily be bypassed by

---

115 *Bruce and Another v Fleecytex Johannesburg CC and Others* (CCT1/98) [1998] ZACC 3; 1998 (2) SA 1143; 1998 (4) BCLR 415 (24 March 1998) para 9. See also *Van der Spuy v General Council of the Bar of South Africa* (CCT48/01) [2002] ZACC 17; 2002 (5) SA 392; 2002 (10) BCLR 1092 (18 July 2002) para 6; *National Gambling Board v Premier of KwaZulu-Natal and Others* (CCT32/01) [2001] ZACC 8; 2002 (2) BCLR 156; 2002 (2) SA 715 (21 December 2001) para 29; *Moseneke and Others v Master of the High Court* (CCT51/00) [2000] ZACC 27; 2001 (2) BCLR 103; 2001 (2) SA 18 (6 December 2000) paras 18–9; *Dormehl v Minister of Justice and Others* (CCT10/00) [2000] ZACC 4; 2000 (2) SA 825; 2000 (5) BCLR 471 (CC) (14 April 2000) para 5; *Christian Education South Africa v Minister of Education* (CCT13/98) [1998] ZACC 16; 1999 (2) SA 83; 1998 (12) BCLR 1449 (14 October 1998) paras 3–4; *Minister of Justice v Ntuli* (CCT15/97, CCT17/95) [1997] ZACC 7; 1997 (6) BCLR 677; 1997 (3) SA 772 (5 June 1997) para 4; *Transvaal Agricultural Union v Minister of Land Affairs and Another* (CCT21/96) [1996] ZACC 22; 1996 (12) BCLR 1573; 1997 (2) SA 621 (18 November 1996) para 16; *Brink v Kitshoff NO* (CCT15/95) [1996] ZACC 9; 1996 (4) SA 197; 1996 (6) BCLR 752 (15 May 1996) para 3; *Besserglik v Minister of Trade Industry and Tourism and Others (Minister of Justice intervening)* (CCT34/95) [1996] ZACC 8; 1996 (6) BCLR 745; 1996 (4) SA 331 (14 May 1996) paras 4–6; *Luitingh v Minister of Defence* (CCT29/95) [1996] ZACC 5; 1996 (4) BCLR 581; 1996 (2) SA 909 (4 April 1996) para 15; *S v Mbatha, S v Prinsloo* (CCT19/95, CCT35/95) [1996] ZACC 1; 1996 (3) BCLR 293; 1996 (2) SA 464 (9 February 1996) para 29; *Executive Council of the Western Cape Legislature and Others v President of the Republic of South Africa and Others* (CCT27/95) [1995] ZACC 8; 1995 (10) BCLR 1289; 1995 (4) SA 877 (22 September 1995) paras 15–7; *S v Zuma and Others* (CCT5/94) [1995] ZACC 1; 1995 (2) SA 642; 1995 (4) BCLR 401 (SA); 1995 (1) SACR 568; [1996] 2 CHRLD 244 (5 April 1995) para 11.

116 *S v Bequinot* (CCT24/95) [1996] ZACC 21; 1996 (12) BCLR 1588; 1997 (2) SA 887 (18 November 1996) para 15; See also *Carmichele* para 50.

117 *Bruce* para 8.

118 *Transvaal Agricultural Union* para 20.

119 *AParty and Another v The Minister for Home Affairs and Others, Moloko and Others v The Minister for Home Affairs and Another* (CCT 06/09, CCT 10/09) [2009] ZACC 4; 2009 (3) SA 649 (CC); 2009 (6) BCLR 611 (CC) (12 March 2009) para 30.

litigants who want to speed up the hearing of their case.[120] The Court first considered the provision relating to direct access in *Bruce and Another v Fleecytex Johannesburg CC and Others* where it set out the factors that are relevant to applications for direct access to it as follows:

> **Whilst the prospects of success are clearly relevant to applications for direct access to this Court, there are other considerations which are at least of equal importance. This Court is the highest Court on all constitutional matters. If, as a matter of course, constitutional matters could be brought directly to it, we could be called upon to deal with disputed facts on which evidence might be necessary, to decide constitutional issues which are not decisive of the litigation and which might prove to be purely academic, and to hear cases without the benefit of the views of other Courts having constitutional jurisdiction. These factors have been referred to in decisions given by this Court on applications for direct access under the interim Constitution, and are clearly relevant to the granting of direct access under the 1996 Constitution. It is, moreover, not ordinarily in the interests of justice for a court to sit as a court of first and last instance, in which matters are decided without there being any possibility of appealing against the decision given.[121]**

CRITICAL THINKING

Does the SCA still have a meaningful role to play?

As we have noted, the Constitution Seventeenth Amendment Act has changed the jurisdictional landscape. Among other things, this amendment effected changes to section 167(3)(*a*) of the Constitution to affirm the Constitutional Court as 'the highest court of the Republic'. This amendment thus turned the Constitutional Court into the court of final instance for all matters of points of legal doctrine (but not of factual disputes or disputes about the application of legal principles to factual disputes), whether these matters relate to the Constitution or not.

The SCA (discussed below) has therefore ceased to be the highest court for all non-constitutional matters. The proposed amendments have potentially far-reaching consequences, but these are ameliorated by amendments to section 167(3)(*b*) of the Constitution which states that the Constitutional Court may decide constitutional matters and 'any other matter', but only 'if the Constitutional Court grants leave to appeal on the grounds that the matter raises an arguable point of law of general public importance which ought to be considered by that Court'. The Constitutional Court retains the power to make the final decision on whether a matter is within its jurisdiction.[122] Section 167(3)(*b*) extends the jurisdiction of the Constitutional Court to all matters but allows the Court to manage its own docket by granting it the discretion to decide when to take on non-constitutional matters on the basis that these raise a point of law of general public importance.

Given the fact that section 39(2) of the Constitution already allows the Court to consider matters regarding the development of the common law and customary law and the interpretation of legislation in line with the spirit, purport and object of the Bill

120 *Bruce* para 9. See also *Van der Spuy* para 6; *National Gambling Board* para 29; *Moseneke* paras 18–19; *Dormehl* para 5; *Christian Education* paras 3–4; *Ntuli* para 4; *Transvaal Agricultural Union* para 16; *Brink* para 3; *Besserglik* paras 4–6; *Luitingh* para 15; *Mbatha, Prinsloo* para 29; *Executive Council of the Western Cape Legislature* paras 15–17; *Zuma* para 11.

121 (CCT1/98) [1998] ZACC 3; 1998 (2) SA 1143; 1998 (4) BCLR 415 (24 March 1998) paras 7–8. See also *Aparty* para29.

122 S 167(3)(*c*) of the Constitution.

of Rights, it is unclear to what extent the amendment will affect the case load of the Court. In effect, the answer to this question will depend on the rules developed by the Constitutional Court around when to consider a case that does not directly or indirectly raise any constitutional issue. However, arguably, the amendments lower the status and diminish the influence of the SCA as it no longer acts as the highest court in all non-constitutional matters. The question that can be posed is whether the SCA has not become superfluous. What meaningful role does the SCA still play, given that it no longer acts as the highest court in any matter apart from on disputes of fact?

6.2.2.2 Supreme Court of Appeal

As pointed out above, the interim Constitution established a seemingly clear division between the jurisdiction of the two appellate courts in relation to constitutional and non-constitutional issues.[123] The SCA was the court of final instance in non-constitutional matters while the Constitutional Court was the court of final instance in constitutional matters. In terms of the interim Constitution, the SCA had no jurisdiction to deal with constitutional matters.

The 1996 Constitution changed this arrangement and awarded the SCA jurisdiction to hear and decide constitutional matters as it is empowered to hear appeals 'in any matter arising from the High Court'.[124] Before the advent of the Constitution Seventeenth Amendment Act where a matter did not include a constitutional issue, the SCA was the court of final instance. Now the SCA may be the court of final instance in non-constitutional issues but only if the Constitutional Court decides not to hear an appeal from the SCA on the grounds that the matter raises an arguable point of law of general public importance which ought to be considered by the Constitutional Court. This means that the SCA will only be the truly final court for decisions relating to factual findings and ordinary appeals relating to the application of non-contested legal rules to sets of facts. When a case raises constitutional issues and does not deal with an issue on which the Constitutional Court has exclusive jurisdiction, the case is first heard by the High Court after which an appeal can be lodged with either the SCA or the Constitutional Court directly.

When the constitutional matter involved is one that turns on the direct application of the Constitution and does not involve the development of the common law or customary law, considerations of cost and time may make it desirable that the appeal be brought directly from the High Court to the Constitutional Court, circumventing the SCA.[125] The issue is different when the SCA is asked to develop the common law. The Constitutional Court will not ordinarily exercise its jurisdiction to develop the common law without the SCA having considered the matter first.[126] This is because the SCA is viewed as having a broad understanding and insight into the nature and scope of the common law. It will therefore arguably be able to make a valuable contribution to any debate on whether and to what extent the common law should be be developed.

123 Currie and De Waal (2005) 111.

124 S 168(3).

125 See *Islamic Unity Convention v Independent Broadcasting Authority and Others* (CCT13/99) [2000] ZACC 3; 2002 (4) SA 294 (CC) 2002 (5) BCLR 433 (11 April 2002) para 17; *De Reuck v Director of Public Prosecutions (Witwatersrand Local Division) and Others* (CCT5/03) [2003] ZACC 19; 2004 (1) SA 406 (CC); 2003 (12) BCLR 1333 (CC) (15 October 2003) para 4.

126 See *Amod v Multilateral Motor Vehicle Accidents Fund* (CCT4/98) [1998] ZACC 11; 1998 (4) SA 753; 1998 (10) BCLR 1207 (27 August 1998) para 33.

In *Masiya v Director of Public Prosecutions Pretoria (The State) and Another*, the Constitutional Court endorsed this important role of the SCA, holding that any constitutional issues that involve, for example, the development of the common law, should first be taken to the SCA because of its jurisdiction and expertise in the common law.[127] The same applies to matters involving the indirect application of the Bill of Rights to the interpretation of ordinary legislation. In such cases, the SCA would normally be required to deal with a case before it is considered by the Constitutional Court.[128] As the Constitutional Court stated in *Amod v Multilateral Motor Vehicle Accidents Fund*:

> **When a constitutional matter is one which turns on the direct application of the Constitution and which does not involve the development of the common law, considerations of costs and time may make it desirable that the appeal be brought directly to this Court. But when the constitutional matter involves the development of the common law, the position is different. The Supreme Court of Appeal has jurisdiction to develop the common law in all matters including constitutional matters. Because of the breadth of its jurisdiction and its expertise in the common law, its views as to whether the common law should or should not be developed in a 'constitutional matter' are of particular importance.**[129]

6.2.2.3 High Courts

The Constitution confers wide-ranging jurisdiction on the various High Courts in respect of constitutional matters as the High Courts may decide any constitutional matter except those matters exclusively reserved for the jurisdiction of the Constitutional Court or matters assigned by an Act of Parliament to another court of a similar status as a High Court.[130] This means that most cases raising constitutional issues will first be heard in one of the High Courts. However, as we noted above, where the High Court declares invalid any provisions of an Act of Parliament or a provincial legislature, such an order must be confirmed by the Constitutional Court before that order has any force.[131] In such cases, no appeal to the SCA is required and no leave for appeal need be sought from the Constitutional Court.

The situation is different where a High Court declines to find legislation inconsistent with the Constitution and does not declare the impugned provisions invalid. In this case, there will be no automatic referral to the Constitutional Court and an appeal will have to be lodged by the party seeking an order of invalidity.[132]

6.2.2.4 Magistrates' courts

Magistrates' courts do not have jurisdiction to hear constitutional matters. Section 170 of the Constitution states that magistrates' courts and all other courts may decide any matter determined by an Act of Parliament, but a court of a status lower than a High Court may not enquire into or rule on the constitutionality of any legislation or any conduct by the President. Section 110(1) of the Magistrates' Courts Act[133] confirms that magistrates' courts

---

127 (CCT54/06) [2007] ZACC 9; 2007 (5) SA 30 (CC); 2007 (8) BCLR 827 (10 May 2007) para 17.

128 *National Gambling Board* para 38; *Wallach v High Court of South Africa (Witwatersrand Local Division) and Others* (CCT2/03) [2003] ZACC 6; 2003 (5) SA 273 (CC) (4 April 2003) para 7.

129 (CCT4/98) [1998] ZACC 11; 1998 (4) SA 753; 1998 (10) BCLR 1207 (27 August 1998) para 33.

130 S 169(1)(*a*).

131 S 167(5) of the Constitution.

132 See Currie and De Waal (2005) 122.

133 Act 32 of 1944.

cannot pronounce on the validity of any law or conduct of the President. Section 110(2) states that when an allegation that a law or conduct by the President is unconstitutional and invalid is raised in a magistrates' court, the magistrate in question must continue and decide the matter on the assumption that the law or conduct in question is valid. If a litigant wishes to pursue the question, he or she will have to approach the High Court.

6.3 The independence of the superior courts

6.3.1 Introduction

South Africa's transition to an open and democratic society with a supreme Constitution relied heavily on the establishment of an independent and impartial judiciary. In the new system, the role of the judiciary was dramatically expanded to ensure the protection of fundamental rights and to ensure that government (as well as private institutions) remained within the bounds of the law and honoured the constitutional commitment to openness and democracy. Given the manner in which the judiciary was tainted during apartheid, it may be surprising that this institution was entrusted with such a crucial role in the transition to democracy, especially given the fact that in terms of the political settlement, it was the only branch that remained largely unchanged in the new democratic era.[134] As we have pointed out, when the new Constitution came into effect, the judiciary was still largely dominated by white men and tainted by its role in the interpretation and implementation of apartheid legislation.[135]

Despite this history, when South Africa became a democracy, no judges were relieved of their duties and the courts did not only retain their powers, but were given extended powers far exceeding those they had enjoyed under apartheid. The only change came in the form of the addition of the Constitutional Court to the existing court structure and changes to the manner in which judges are appointed. While the other courts and the judges who staffed these courts remained in place, the interim Constitution provided for the creation of a separate Constitutional Court to act as the final arbiter of all constitutional matters.

Against this background, the creation of the Constitutional Court is a significant development in South Africa's transition, representing a first step on the journey of transforming the legal system as a whole. It is difficult to imagine that the judiciary would have been awarded such an important role in the transition if a new Constitutional Court had not been put in place. It is also difficult to imagine that the judiciary would have been entrusted with the enforcement of a supreme Constitution in the absence of a newly created Constitutional Court. The decision to create the Constitutional Court was therefore partly a pragmatic political move and partly a principled move aimed at increasing the legitimacy of the judiciary. As the highest Court on constitutional matters and now also on other matters of legal doctrine, it was important that the Court be seen to be impartial and independent and not tainted by South Africa's apartheid past. Given the fact that the Court would also act as the ultimate guardian of the impartiality and independence of all other courts,[136] its creation could therefore be said to be the first step in restoring the independence of the South African

134 Wesson and Du Plessis (2008) 191.

135 See also O'Regan, K (2004) Human rights and democracy – a new global debate: Reflections on the first ten years of South Africa's Constitutional Court *International Journal of Legal Information* 32(2):200–16 at 202.

136 See *S and Others v Van Rooyen and Others (General Council of the Bar of South Africa Intervening)* (CCT21/01) [2002] ZACC 8; 2002 (5) SA 246; 2002 (8) BCLR 810 (11 June 2002) para 27.

judiciary. It also allowed the retention of the court structure and made it easier for the drafters of the interim and 1996 Constitutions to safeguard the tenure of judges appointed by the apartheid government before 1994.

CRITICAL THINKING

Should South Africa have followed the Kenyan model of vetting old-order judges?

When Kenya adopted a new Constitution in 2010, one of the most vexing questions faced by its drafters was how to deal with members of the judiciary, many of whom were widely believed to be corrupt or politically compromised. The Kenyan Constitution created a system of 'vetting' that required all judges to be vetted by an independent board of experts.[137] Only those judges who passed the vetting process retained their positions. Judges found to have been implicated in corruption or who had not shown the requisite diligence or impartiality required of members of an independent judiciary were not retained. The process was aimed at re-establishing the credibility and integrity of the Kenyan judiciary.

As we have seen, a similar process was not followed in South Africa and all judges appointed during the apartheid era retained their positions. Instead, section 174(1) of the South African Constitution merely states that 'any appropriately qualified woman or man who is a fit and proper person' may be appointed as a judicial officer while section 174(2) requires that the need for the judiciary to reflect broadly the racial and gender composition of South Africa must be considered when appointing new judicial officers. This decision ensured continuity in the judiciary while envisaging that a gradual transformation of the judiciary would take place through the appointment of new judges as old-order judges retired.

The question is whether this choice was a wise one or whether the Kenyan model would have been more appropriate. Given the need for the judiciary to enjoy legitimacy with the majority of South Africans, did the South African model place too much emphasis on the transformation of the judiciary through a gradual appointment of new-order judges?

The independence of the judiciary is a distinctive feature of a constitutional democracy. This independence refers to two ideals related to the functioning of the courts as it pertains to 'the relationship between the courts and other state organs, the organisation of the relationship between the courts themselves and the internal organisation of the courts as well as aspects regarding the legal position of individual members of the judiciary'.[138]

The first ideal is that individual judges should interpret and enforce the law impartially and without bias. This requires individual judges to approach a specific case with an open mind, without taking into account their own personal views, ideological commitments or

137 See Constitution of Kenya (2010) item 23 in Schedule 6, which states:

> **(1) Within one year after the effective date, Parliament shall enact legislation ... establishing mechanisms and procedures for vetting, within a timeframe to be determined in the legislation, the suitability of all judges and magistrates who were in office on the effective date to continue to serve in accordance with the values and principles set out in [the Constitution]...**
>
> **(2) A removal, or a process leading to the removal, of a judge, from office by virtue of the operation of legislation contemplated under subsection (1) shall not be subject to question in, or review by, any court.**

138 De Lange, R and Mevis, PAM (2007) Constitutional guarantees for the independence of the judiciary *Electronic Journal of Comparative Law* 11(1):1–17 at 7.

party political beliefs. Impartiality is a complex notion. At its most extreme, impartiality relates to the ability of each individual judge to apply the law without fear or favour in accordance with the law, oath of office and with his or her own sense of justice without submitting to any kind of pressure or being swayed by his or her own views on political, social and economic matters.[139] This extreme notion of impartiality presupposes that a judge can banish from his or her mind all personal views and prejudices and can interpret a legal text and apply it to a set of facts without being swayed by political or other personal commitments or culturally influenced values and assumptions. However, it is not clear whether a judge can always do so, especially as far as the interpretation of the rather open-ended and general language of the Constitution is concerned. Often a text – especially a text like the Constitution containing general language – will not have one objective meaning and a judge may be required to **interpret** that text. Interpretation requires a judge to refer to considerations outside the text itself to help give meaning to that text. In the first decision handed down by the Constitutional Court, Kentridge J signalled awareness of (but skirted) this issue when he remarked:

> **I am well aware of the fallacy of supposing that general language must have a single 'objective' meaning. Nor is it easy to avoid the influence of one's personal intellectual and moral preconceptions. But it cannot be too strongly stressed that the Constitution does not mean whatever we might wish it to mean.**[140]

On the one hand, the Court acknowledged the fact that the language of the Constitution does not necessarily yield one 'objective' meaning which the Court can discover in a mechanistic fashion. It thus recognised the need to refer to extra-textual factors – such as the South African context and history and comparable foreign case law[141] – when interpreting the provisions of the Constitution. On the other hand, the judgment resisted any move that would implicate the personal views, political commitments and philosophy of the judges themselves in the interpretative project in order to safeguard the (symbolic) boundary between the work done by judges when they interpret and apply the law and politics.[142]

In *S v Makwanyane and Another*,[143] several of the justices asserted the irrelevance of their personal, political or philosophical views when interpreting the Constitution. Impartiality, they claimed, required judges to ground their judgments in general human rights principles that are above controversy and cannot be related to the personal views of a judge.[144] At the same time, many of the justices tentatively acknowledged the open-ended nature of the language of the Constitution and the inherent need to refer to 'extra-legal' values and texts, including the South African political context and history, to justify their decisions.[145] The Constitutional Court has since often declared its commitment to the centrality of the constitutional text in constitutional interpretation. The judges of this court also acknowledge

---

139 See Ntlama, N (2009, 16–20 July) The Hlophe saga: the question for the institutional integrity of the judiciary, Paper presented at the Law Teachers Conference in Pietermaritzburg, available at http://wenku.baidu.com/view/6c6473f0fab069dc50220111.html.

140 *Zuma* para 17.

141 See also s 39(1)(*b*) and (*c*) of the Constitution which requires the court to take into account international law and allows the court to take into account foreign case law when interpreting the provisions of the Bill of Rights.

142 De Vos, P (2001) A bridge too far? History as context in the interpretation of the South African Constitution *South African Journal on Human Rights* 17(1):1–33 at 6.

143 (CCT3/94) [1995] ZACC 3; 1995 (6) BCLR 665; 1995 (3) SA 391; [1996] 2 CHRLD 164; 1995 (2) SACR 1 (6 June 1995).

144 Klare, K (1998) Legal culture and transformative constitutionalism *South African Journal on Human Rights* 14(1):146–88 at 173. See also *Makwanyane* para 207, per Kriegler J.

145 *Makwanyane* para 321, per O'Regan J; para 207, per Kriegler J; para 266, per Mahomed J; para 382, per Sachs J.

that any such interpretation can only be conducted with the assistance of objective or objectively determinable criteria, or, at the very least, criteria that are somehow distanced from the personal views, opinions and political philosophy of the presiding judge.[146] However, it is an open question whether judges can truly empty their minds of all their personal views and political commitments when they interpret the Constitution and apply it to a specific set of facts.

Despite these difficulties, the ideal of impartial adjudication remains a cornerstone of an independent judiciary which has often been affirmed by the Constitutional Court. Thus, the Constitutional Court in *President of the Republic of South Africa and Others v South African Rugby Football Union and Others - Judgment on recusal application (SARFU II)* stated that:

> **It must be assumed that they can disabuse their minds of any *irrelevant personal beliefs* or predispositions. They must take into account the fact that they have a duty to sit in any case in which they are not obliged to recuse themselves. At the same time, it must never be forgotten that an impartial judge is a fundamental prerequisite for a fair trial and a judicial officer should not hesitate to recuse herself or himself if there are reasonable grounds on the part of a litigant for apprehending that the judicial officer, for whatever reasons, was not or will not be impartial.[147]**

PAUSE FOR REFLECTION

The test for independence

In *S and Others v Van Rooyen and Others (General Council of the Bar of South Africa Intervening)*,[148] the Constitutional Court affirmed that **judicial independence** requires that individual judges must be able to hear and decide cases that come before them and that no outsider should be able to interfere with the way a judge conducts his or her case and makes his or her decision. This requires judges to act impartially and, at an institutional level, it requires structures to protect courts and judicial officers against external interference.[149]

At the same time, it is important to note that there are hierarchical differences between higher courts and lower courts and that the requirements for independence could be different for the two types of courts.[150] Just because they are treated differently does not mean that magistrates' courts are not independent. Lower courts are entitled to protection by higher courts if their independence is threatened so the greater the protection that is given to higher courts, the greater the protection is for lower courts. Moreover, lower courts do not have the power to deal with constitutional matters and the jurisdiction of the lower courts set out in the Constitution is much more restricted than that of the higher courts. This means that lower courts do not need the same kind of safeguards as the higher courts.

The test for independence is whether the court or tribunal 'from the objective standpoint of a reasonable and informed person, will be perceived as enjoying the essential conditions of independence'.[151] It is important that there is public confidence

146 See Klare (1998) 172–87 for examples of this kind of reasoning by the judges of the Constitutional Court.

147 (CCT16/98) [1999] ZACC 9; 1999 (4) SA 147; 1999 (7) BCLR 725 (4 June 1999) para 48.

148 (CCT21/01) [2002] ZACC 8; 2002 (5) SA 246; 2002 (8) BCLR 810 (11 June 2002).

149 *Van Rooyen* para 19. See also *De Lange v Smuts NO and Others* (CCT26/97) [1998] ZACC 6; 1998 (3) SA 785 (CC); 1998 (7) BCLR 779 (28 May 1998)(CC) para 71.

150 *Van Rooyen* para 22.

151 *Van Rooyen* para 32.

in the administration of justice. Without that confidence, the system cannot command the respect and acceptance that are essential to its effective operation. It is, therefore, important that a tribunal should be perceived as independent, as well as impartial, and that the test for independence should include that perception. This test is an objective one.[152] The apprehension of bias must be a reasonable one, held by reasonable and right-minded persons, applying themselves to the question and obtaining thereon the required information. We must ask what would an informed person conclude when viewing the matter realistically and practically, and having thought the matter through. The question is whether a reasonable, objective and informed person would on the correct facts reasonably apprehend that the judge has not or will not bring an impartial mind to bear on the adjudication of the case, that is a mind open to persuasion by the evidence and the submissions of counsel.

It is important to note that this objective test must be properly contextualised.[153] The perception that is relevant for such purposes is, however, a perception based on a balanced view of all the material information. We ask how things appear to the well-informed, thoughtful and objective observer, rather than the hypersensitive, cynical and suspicious person. Bearing in mind the diversity of our society, this cautionary injunction is of particular importance in assessing institutional independence. The well-informed, thoughtful and objective observer must be sensitive to the country's complex social realities, in touch with its evolving patterns of constitutional development, and guided by the Constitution, its values and the differentiation it makes between different levels of courts.

The *Van Rooyen* judgment provides a general test to establish whether a judge would be impartial and independent. We contend that when considering whether the appointments procedure and other structural safeguards intended to safeguard the impartiality and independence of judges are sufficient, this test must be used.

Judges may not always be able to be impartial (in the sense of being able to make decisions without taking into account factors that are legally irrelevant) and may not be able to act without fear or favour if the conditions under which the judicial function is exercised do not allow for this and if the judiciary is not created as an independent institution that functions separately from the other branches of government. Judges will only be able to rule impartially and to be truly independent (from pressure of both the state and private actors) if they are able to operate independently from the other branches of government. They must be free from potential direct and indirect pressures that could sway individual judges trying to act in as impartial a manner as is humanly possible.

Structural safeguards must therefore be put in place to ensure that judges are protected from the influence of and interference by other branches of government (as well as from private business interests).[154] This requirement for structural safeguards to guarantee the impartiality and independence of judges places an emphasis on the functional independence of the judiciary within the larger political system and its functional relationship with the

152 *Van Rooyen* para 33.

153 *Van Rooyen* para 32.

154 See by Lewis, C (2008, 14 October) The troubled state of South Africa's judiciary, Paper presented at the South African Institute of Race Relations, available at http://www.politicsweb.co.za/politicsweb/view/politicsweb/en/page71619?oid=106544&sn=Detail. See also Currie and De Waal (2001) 300.

other branches of government in South Africa. This second aspect of independence relates to:

> **the degree to which the judicial institution has a distinct and discrete role ... detached from the interests of the political system, the concerns of powerful social groups or the desires of the general public ... to regulate the legality of state acts, enact justice and determine general and constitutional and legal values.**[155]

This means that judicial independence is not meaningful if judges cannot exercise their judicial powers to check the arbitrary or unjust exercise of power by political and social actors in society. The courts (and the judges who staff the courts) must not be constrained by fear or by practical difficulties from carrying out the ideal judicial role. This implies that structures must be put in place to ensure that judges are insulated from political and financial pressures and incentives.[156] This fact was endorsed by Chaskalson CJ in *Van Rooyen* where he argued that:

> **the constitutional protection of the core values of judicial independence accorded to all courts by the South African Constitution means that all courts are entitled to and have the basic protection that is required ... implicit in this is recognition of the fact that the courts and their structure, with the hierarchical differences between higher courts and lower courts which then existed, are considered by the Constitution to be independent ... that involves an independence in the relationship between the courts and other arms of government.**[157]

To determine whether courts enjoy sufficient structural independence, several factors must be explored. We do so here with reference to the superior courts. As we have seen, magistrates do not exercise constitutional jurisdiction, which means we will leave aside the position of magistrates' courts.

6.3.2 Appointment of judges

As noted above, before 1994, political considerations often played a decisive role in the appointment of judges, thus potentially affecting the impartiality and independence of judges. The drafters of the interim and final Constitutions were faced with a difficult task in addressing this problem.

On the one hand, in the new constitutional dispensation, judges are given extensive additional powers. This includes the power to declare invalid acts of the democratically elected Parliament and acts of the executive, including the President. This means that the decisions of judges will often have political consequences. Judges are therefore potential actors in the political process as decisions of judges can have far-reaching political consequences.[158] The questions raised in chapter 2 about the counter-majoritarian dilemma therefore loom large. It was therefore felt that the appointment of judges could not be entirely insulated from the political process. This would potentially delegitimise the judiciary and

---

155 See Larkins, CM (1996) Judicial independence and democratization: A theoretical and conceptual analysis *American Journal of Comparative Law* 44(4):605–25 at 611.

156 Larkins (1996) 611.

157 *Van Rooyen* paras 22 and 31.

158 For example, after Judge Chris Nicholson found that there was political interference in the decision to charge Jacob Zuma for corruption in *Zuma v National Director of Public Prosecutions* (8652/08) [2008] ZAKZHC 71; [2009] 1 All SA 54 (N); 2009 (1) BCLR 62 (N) (12 September 2008), the NEC of the ANC decided to 'recall' then President Thabo Mbeki as President of South Africa. The judgment therefore had a profound and immediate effect on who headed up the executive and thus who governed the country.

make it more difficult for it to strike down legislation and the acts of members of the executive. On the other hand, it would be undesirable to leave the appointment of all judges in the hands of the President or other elected politicians. This could potentially lead to a perception that party political considerations are the sole criteria for the appointment of judges, thus affecting the independence and impartiality of the judiciary.[159]

As a compromise, the Constitution created the Judicial Service Commission (JSC) which is involved in the appointment of all superior court judges (although this involvement differs depending on who is appointed). The JSC was envisaged as playing a fundamental role in ensuring the independence of the judiciary. The creation of the JSC constituted the most radical break from the pre-constitutional procedure for the appointment of judges.[160] Section 178 of the Constitution as well as the Judicial Service Commission (JSC) Act[161] established and regulates this body.

The composition of the JSC is of some importance. The ANC favoured the establishment of a politically dominated body while, unsurprisingly, the judges and legal profession favoured a body in which the legal community would be in the majority.[162] The composition of the JSC reflects a compromise between these two positions. The JSC is normally composed of 23 members who are drawn from the judiciary, two branches (attorneys and advocates) of the legal profession, the two Houses of the national legislature, the executive, civil society and academia.[163] The chair is taken by the Chief Justice who also heads the Constitutional Court. Of the 23 members, 15 represent political interests, including the Minister of Justice, the six members of the NA (three members from minority parties), four members of the NCOP (representing the majority party) and four presidential nominees.[164]

When the members of the JSC discuss matters relating to a specific High Court, the Premier of the province together with the Judge President of the province also sit on the Commission.[165] Matters that affect a specific High Court include, for example, decisions about the appointment of judges to that High Court, as well as decisions about the possible disciplining or even removal of a judge of that High Court from office. If the Premier of the province is absent when the JSC makes a decision regarding either the appointment or the disciplining of a judge serving in that province, the decision of the JSC will be invalid.[166]

When vacancies occur in a court, the Chief Justice, as Chairperson of the JSC, calls for nominations after which shortlisted candidates are publicly interviewed. The JSC then makes recommendations to the President on whom to appoint. While the JSC conducts its interviews in public – a welcome departure from the secretive process followed during the apartheid years – there is little transparency exhibited in the criteria used for selection. The deliberations of the JSC are also kept confidential. This has led to criticism on the basis that

---

159 Wesson and Du Plessis (2008) 191.

160 Wesson and Du Plessis (2008) 192.

161 Act 9 of 1994.

162 See Malleson, K (1999) Assessing the performance of the Judicial Service Commission *South African Law Journal* 116(1):36–49 at 38.

163 S 178(1)(*a*)–(*j*) of the Constitution. See generally Davis (2010, December) 41 and Mgkoro (2010, December) 43.

164 For an extensive discussion about the political influence on the JSC, see Powell, C and Franco. J (2004) The meaning of institutional independence in *Van Rooyen v S South African Law Journal* 121(3):562–79 at 562.

165 S 178(1) of the Constitution.

166 *Acting Chairperson: Judicial Service Commission and Others v Premier of the Western Cape Province* (537/10) [2011] ZASCA 53; 2011 (3) SA 538 (SCA); [2011] 3 All SA 459 (SCA) (31 March 2011) para 12 where Harms AJ stated that:

> **it would be inconsistent and illogical for the Constitution to provide for a Premier to participate in the appointment of a high court judge – and, as I have said, the JSC agrees that a Premier is included for this purpose – but not in a decision to remove such a judge. Both affect the composition of the bench of a particular high court.**

the JSC's reasons for preferring one candidate are not always clear.[167] The JSC has also been criticised for the manner in which it interviews candidates. It is said that rarely are questions framed so as to afford a candidate an opportunity to explain his or her approach to adjudication and conception of the important constitutional values, and the candidate's general judicial philosophy and commitment to legal transformation.[168]

The role of the JSC in the appointment of judges differs depending on the nature of the appointment to be made. The President as head of the national executive has a relatively wide discretion when he or she appoints the Chief Justice and the Deputy Chief Justice who both also serve on the Constitutional Court. When making these appointments, the President, as head of the national executive, appoints the person of his or her choice **after consulting** the JSC and the leaders of parties represented in the NA.[169] The President must therefore consult the JSC, as well as the leaders of opposition parties in the NA, **before** deciding on a candidate for appointment, but the decision remains his or hers alone. Similarly, when appointing the President and Deputy President of the SCA, the President, as head of the national executive, appoints the person of his or her choice **after consulting** the JSC (but in such cases the President need not consult the leaders of parties represented in the NA).[170]

There has been some controversy around the nature of the consultation process required although, as stated, it is clear that consultation has to occur prior to the appointment. *Ex post facto* consultation after the President has made a final decision on an appointment is not acceptable. No matter how rigorous this consultation might have been, consultation requires more than informing the parties to be consulted of a decision. Although the Constitution does not define the notion of consultation, it has been argued that 'at least it must entail the good faith exchange of views, which must be taken seriously'.[171] However, it does not mean that the President must follow the advice of those consulted.

The President, as head of the national executive, appoints the other judges of the Constitutional Court after consulting the Chief Justice and the leaders of parties represented in the NA.[172] These appointments take place in accordance with a more complicated procedure in which the JSC plays a more important, but ultimately not decisive, role.

The JSC must prepare a list of nominees with three names more than the number of appointments to be made and submit the list to the President.[173] The President may make appointments from the list, but can also initially refuse to appoint someone from the list provided by the JSC. However, if the President refuses to appoint a judge from the list of names provided by the JSC, he or she must provide the JSC with reasons for the decision. If this happens, the JSC is required to supplement the list with further nominees and the President must make the remaining appointments from the supplemented list.[174] This means

167 Davis (2010, December) 41; Wesson and Du Plessis (2008) 193; Kentridge, S (2003) The highest court: Selecting the judges *Cambridge Law Journal* 62(1):55–71 at 55.

168 See, for example, McKaiser, E (2009, 6 August) Tragicomedy revealed more about JSC than about judges *Business Day* in which the author takes the JSC to task for its inability to probe any of these key questions when the JSC last year conducted interviews for four vacancies on the Constitutional Court. See also De Vos, P (2013, 21 January) Judicial appointments: The JSC's transformation problem *Constitutionally Speaking* available at http://constitutionallyspeaking.co.za/judicial-appointments-the-jscs-transformation-problem/.

169 S 174(3) of the Constitution.

170 S 174(3) of the Constitution.

171 See Gauntlett, J and Du Plessis, M (2011, 25 August) Ex Parte: Freedom under Law, In re: The Appointment of the Chief Justice Memorandum 10–11 *Constitutionally Speaking* available at http://constitutionallyspeaking.co.za/ful-proposes-changes-to-appointment-of-chief-justice/.

172 S 174(4) of the Constitution.

173 S 174(4)(*a*) of the Constitution.

174 S 174(4)(*b*) and (*c*) of the Constitution.

if there is one vacancy in the Constitutional Court, the JSC must send a list of four nominees to the President. The President will then appoint one of the four nominees unless he or she believes one or more of the nominees are not acceptable or that the list should include a wider selection of names. For example, if a vacancy occurs on the Constitutional Court and the JSC sends the names of four white male candidates to the President, the President may refuse to appoint one of the four nominees, asking for the list to be augmented with black and female candidates. When making decisions about the appointment of ordinary judges to the Constitutional Court, the JSC and the President must keep in mind the requirement that at least four members of the Constitutional Court must at any given time be persons who were judges at the time they were appointed to the Constitutional Court.[175]

The JSC plays a decisive role in the appointment of all other judges to the SCA, High Courts and other specialised courts. This includes the various Judge Presidents who serve as leaders of each of the High Courts. In the appointment of such ordinary judges, the JSC selects candidates to fill any vacancies and the President is then required to appoint the judges 'of all other courts on the advice of the Judicial Service Commission'.[176] Unlike with the appointment of the Constitutional Court judges and the leadership of the SCA and the Constitutional Court, in these cases the President has no discretion and is required to appoint the candidates selected by the JSC.

As we have seen, the JSC has not always been clear about the criteria used for the selection of judges for appointment. A starting point for an enquiry into the qualities a candidate should have for appointment to the bench is the text of the Constitution which spells out the formal criteria for selection as a judge.[177] Two essential criteria appear in section 174(1) of the Constitution. These criteria are that a person must be 'appropriately qualified' and 'a fit and proper person' to be appointed as a judge. A further criteria for a Constitutional Court judge is that the appointee must be a South African citizen. These criteria can be regarded as essential or necessary minimum criteria for appointment in the sense that a person who is not appropriately qualified or who is not a fit and proper person may not be appointed as a judicial officer.

However, the Constitution does not expressly detail the content of these criteria and we are therefore required to interpret them. The JSC itself has developed a set of criteria – over and above those mentioned in the Constitution – that it takes into account when considering appointments to the judiciary. These are as follows:

1. **Is the proposed appointee a person of integrity?**
2. **Is the proposed appointee a person with the necessary energy and motivation?**
3. **Is the proposed appointee a competent person? (a) Technically competent (b) Capacity to give expression to the values of the Constitution**
4. **Is the proposed appointee an experienced person? (a) Technically experienced (b) Experienced in regard to values and needs of the community**
5. **Does the proposed appointee possess appropriate potential?**
6. **Symbolism. What message is given to the community at large by a particular appointment?**[178]

175 S 174(5) of the Constitution.
176 S 174(6) of the Constitution.
177 S 174(1) and 174(2).
178 See Judicial Service Commission, Summary of the Criteria Used by the Judicial Service Commission when Considering Candidates for Judicial Appointments, available at http://constitutionallyspeaking.co.za/criteria-used-by-jsc-when-considering-judicial-appointments/.

Although somewhat vague, these criteria can serve as a starting point for a broader enquiry into the attributes of an ideal judge in South Africa's constitutional democracy. One way of engaging with this difficult question about the criteria for appointment is to take account of the characteristics of the ideal judge. In addition to the criteria formulated by the JSC, it has been argued that when considering the criteria for the appointment of the ideal judge, we should consider the nature of the judicial function and the powers that vest in judges.[179] The Constitution requires that the judiciary should be independent, must protect the Constitution and uphold rights, and must apply the law impartially and without fear, favour or prejudice.[180] Judicial nominees should display the qualities associated with these requirements for the judiciary. Chief Justice Mohamed made the following remarks about the qualities of an ideal judge:

> **'[S]ociety is ... entitled to demand from Judges fidelity to those qualities in the judicial temper which legitimize the exercise of judicial power. Many and subtle are the qualities which define that temper. Conspicuous among them are scholarship, experience, dignity, rationality, courage, forensic skill, capacity for articulation, diligence, intellectual integrity and energy. More difficult to articulate but arguably even more crucial to that temper, is that quality called wisdom, enriched as it must be by a substantial measure of humility, and by an instinctive moral ability to distinguish right from wrong and sometimes the more agonising ability to weigh two rights or two wrongs against each other which comes from the consciousness of our own imperfection.[181]**

More recently, the late Chief Justice Chaskalson described the qualities relevant to the appointment of a Chief Justice in the following terms:

> **Non-racism will not be an issue. Nor will commitment to transformation. (All will be committed to that.) The merits of the candidates, their qualities of leadership and institution-building, their commitment to the values of the Constitution, their independence and integrity, the impact their appointment might have on the standing of the Constitutional Court, and other relevant factors, will no doubt be considered.[182]**

We contend that the commitment of a candidate to the values enshrined in the Constitution is pivotal. These values include respect for human dignity, the achievement of equality and the advancement of human rights.[183] It has been argued that this commitment to the values in the Constitution be encapsulated in the requirement that candidates must be committed to the transformative goals of the Constitution. As Cowen argues:

> **Although the executive and legislative branches are the primary architects of social change, judges – as we have seen – are entrusted to protect rights and they have the power to halt and guide government action. It would thus seem legitimate for selectors to enquire whether candidates for judicial selection are committed to the process of social change as the Constitution mandates. That may either entail assessing whether a judge might seek to exercise judicial power with a view to preserving the status quo**

179 Cowen, S (2010) Judicial selection in South Africa, Democratic Governance Rights Unit (DGRU) Paper, available at http://www.dgru.uct.ac.za/usr/dgru/downloads/Judicial%20SelectionOct2010.pdf.

180 S 165(2).

181 In an address to the International Commission of Jurists in Cape Town on 21 July 1998 5.

182 Chaskalson, A (2009, 25 June) Does Hlophe approve of campaign on his behalf? *Cape Times*.

183 See section 1(*a*) of the Constitution.

> **(on the one hand) or by assuming the role of primary architect of social change (on the other). Either is arguably inimical to the values of the Constitution. While assessing commitment to constitutional values and the Constitution's transformative project is a legitimate exercise for selectors, selectors must be cautious not to venture beyond assessing values to assessing political commitments. It might at times be a difficult line to draw, but it is an important one if we are to preserve the principle of judicial independence. As foreshadowed above, an understanding of theories of adjudication might helpfully inform selectors' approach.[184]**

Apart from the personal values of judicial candidates, the JSC is also required to take into account another pivotal consideration, namely the need to transform the judiciary better to reflect the racial and gender composition of the broader South African community. These requirements are encapsulated by section 174(2) of the Constitution which states that:

> **The need for the judiciary to reflect broadly the racial and gender composition of South Africa must be considered when judicial officers are appointed.**

There are at least two reasons why this section is important. First, as pointed out above, at the time of the transition to democracy the South African judiciary was almost exclusively male and white, a situation that potentially affects the credibility and legitimacy of the judiciary.[185] Special measures are therefore required to increase diversity on the bench to ensure that the judiciary more fairly reflects the composition of the South African public whom it serves. It would be difficult, if not impossible, for the judiciary to retains its legitimacy in the eyes of the public if the overwhelming majority of judges remain white and male.

Second, South Africa has an egregious history of 300 years of racial and gender discrimination in society at large as well as in the legal profession, and there remain ongoing racial and gender prejudices in society and in the legal profession.[186] This provision is important as it redresses these racial and gender prejudices and provides a fair opportunity to groups who did not enjoy the same privileges and opportunities for professional advancement as white men did to be appointed to the bench. The requirement therefore addresses possible lingering racial and gender discrimination in the appointment of judges and is intended to ensure a fair appointment process. In short, it is necessary to consider the racial and gender composition of the bench to eradicate patterns of unfair discrimination in the appointment of judges.[187]

Finally, it is argued that diversity on the bench can also improve the quality of justice meted out by the courts. In a diverse society, judges from different racial backgrounds and

---

184 Cowen (2010) 47.

185 Forsyth, C (1991) Interpreting a bill of rights: The future task of a reformed judiciary *South African Journal on Human Rights* 7(1):1–23 at 15–17.

186 See generally Pruitt, LR (2002) No black names on the letterhead? Efficient discrimination and the South African legal profession *Michigan Journal of International Law* 23(3):545–676.

187 See, for example, Davis, RPB (1914) Women as advocates and attorneys *South African Law Journal* 31(4):383–86 at 384 for an example of early discriminatory attitudes towards women in the legal profession in South Africa:

> **We cannot but think the common law wise in excluding women from the profession of law ... the law of nature destines and qualifies the female sex for the bearing and nurture of children and our race and for the custody of the world ... all life-long callings of women, inconsistent with these radical and sacred duties of their sex, as is the profession of law, are departures from the order of nature and when voluntary treason against it. The cruel chances of life sometime baffle both sexes and may leave women free from peculiar duties of their sex ... but it is public policy to provide for the sex not for its superfluous members; and not to tempt women from the proper duties of their sex by opening to them duties peculiar to ours.**

different genders and sexual orientations will often bring different perspectives to bear. This can improve the quality of jurisprudence and strengthen the intellectual output of the judiciary.[188] As can be seen from Table 6.2 below,[189] the JSC has done relatively well in ensuring the creation of a non-racial judiciary. However, the same cannot be said of gender representation as illustrated in Table 6.3.[190] Similarly, the commitment to anti-discrimination on the grounds of sexual orientation is debatable.[191]

Table 6.2 *Statistics of judges per race group*

Black African	Coloured	Indian	White
74 (37%)	16 (8%)	19 (9%)	92 (46%)

Table 6.3 *Statistics as per gender composition*

Black African male	Black African female	Coloured male	Coloured female	Indian male	Indian female	White male	White female
59 (29,5%)	15 (7,5%)	10 (5%)	6 (3%)	11 (5,5%)	8 (4%)	79 (39%)	13 (6,5%)

There is some disagreement about the exact manner in which section 174(2) of the Constitution should be interpreted. Should considerations of racial and gender representation trump any other considerations for appointment as set out above, or should race and gender be important, but not always decisive, factors in making decisions about judicial appointments? It appears that from time to time the JSC commences its enquiry by an examination of the racial and gender composition of the particular court and the importance of the appointment in so far as the racial composition is concerned. In such cases, representativity then becomes the key determinant for an appointment.[192] Whether this approach is correct is vigorously debated in South Africa.[193] Given our apartheid history, it is difficult to argue against an appointment policy that would strive for a bench that is composed primarily of judges of African descent. However, this needs to be done without frustrating non-racialism and without perpetuating apartheid's offensive racial practices.[194] The appointment policy also needs to ensure the appointment of judges fully committed to the values enshrined in the Constitution. How to strike this balance without impeding the rapid transformation of the judiciary remains a vexing question.

The selection of judges by the JSC is subject to **judicial review**. The JSC is a body created by the Constitution. As such, the JSC exercises public power and is hence controlled by what is prescribed in the Constitution and the law. In the case of *Judicial Service Commission and*

188 See De Vos, P (2013, 11 April) The JSC must redefine merit to advance judicial transformation *Constitutionally Speaking* available at http://constitutionallyspeaking.co.za/the-jsc-must-redefine-merit-to-advance-judicial-transformation/.
189 See Lewis (2008, 14 October) 2.
190 See De Vos, P (2013, 21 January) Judicial appointments: The JSC's transformation problem *Constitutionally Speaking* available at http://constitutionallyspeaking.co.za/judicial-appointments-the-jscs-transformation-problem/.
191 Cowen (2010) 53.
192 Davis (2010, December) 42.
193 For divergent perspectives, see Mkhabela, M (2011, 19 August) Judiciary must be de-politicised *The Sowetan* available at http://www.sowetanlive.co.za/columnists/2011/08/19/judiciary-must-be-de-politicised; Hoffman, P (2011, 2 December) To judge the judgments *Mail & Guardian* available at http://mg.co.za/article/2011-12-02-to-judge-the-judgments.
194 Cowen (2010) 57.

Another v Cape Bar Council and Another,[195] the SCA affirmed that the decisions of the JSC – including decisions about the appointment or non-appointment of judges – could be reviewed by a court, based on the principle of legality and rationality.[196]

The judgment sets out the manner in which the members of the JSC ought to – but do not always – arrive at decisions about the appointment of judges. Apart from the requirement that the JSC can only make a valid decision if it is properly constituted,[197] the SCA also found that the JSC was obliged to provide reasons for a decision not to appoint a candidate. As the JSC is under a constitutional duty to exercise its powers in a way that is not irrational or arbitrary, and as the JSC is an organ of state, it is bound to the values of transparency and accountability. Without giving reasons, it would not be possible for the JSC to be held accountable and to act in a transparent manner.[198] The JSC is, therefore, as a general rule, obliged to give reasons for its decision not to recommend a particular candidate if properly called on to do so. Such reasons may not be restricted to a statement that the unsuccessful candidate failed to secure enough votes as this would amount to no reason at all.[199] However, the JSC is not under an obligation to give reasons under all circumstances for each and every one of the myriad potential decisions it has to take. It is, however, as a matter of general principle, obliged to give reasons for its decision not to appoint a candidate.

CRITICAL THINKING

How being black or female ought to influence the selection process in a specific case

In discussing the way in which section 174(2) of the Constitution should be applied, Cowen suggests how being black or female ought to influence the selection process in a specific case, arguing that:

> The easy case arises where two candidates who are similarly well-qualified are being considered for appointment. Subject to any special needs of a court, the appointment of a candidate to enhance racial or gender representativity would seem appropriate. The difficult case arises where two qualified candidates are being considered but the candidate who will not enhance racial or gender representativity is appreciably better qualified in an important respect. In that case, the consideration of the need for racial and gender representativity on the bench requires careful evaluation and cannot be the only relevant consideration. Importantly, whether the better qualified candidate should be appointed may depend on what qualities separate the two candidates and whether the qualities that stand out in the better qualified candidate are qualities that are needed to ensure a bench that is best able to perform the adjudicative functions entrusted to the judiciary by the Constitution. That evaluation cannot focus myopically on the relative merits of two candidates: rather, selectors require an appreciation of the overall needs of the judiciary and the court in question at the relevant time.

195 (818/2011) [2012] ZASCA 115; 2012 (11) BCLR 1239 (SCA); 2013 (1) SA 170 (SCA); [2013] 1 All SA 40 (SCA) (14 September 2012), affirming the decision of the Western Cape High Court in *Cape Bar Council v Judicial Service Commission and Others* (11897/2011) [2011] ZAWCHC 388; 2012 (4) BCLR 406 (WCC); [2012] 2 All SA 143 (WCC) (30 September 2011).

196 *Cape Bar Council* paras 20–2.

197 *Cape Bar Council* para 36.

198 *Cape Bar Council* paras 43–4.

199 *Cape Bar Council* para 45.

If that evaluation is to be conducted honestly and constructively, there is a real need to remove racist and sexist discourse from our discussions and to focus squarely on the detailed criteria for judicial selection. There is similarly a real need to be honest about mistakes we may have made in the past. The mistakes are many and will include engaging in discourse that assumes that more meritorious white candidates are being overlooked in favour of less meritorious black or female candidates. But they also include appointing judges for political favour or in circumstances where qualifications or fitness and propriety are in question. That much we know, at least, from our apartheid history.

In this regard, many express the view that being black, or being a woman, constitutes a valid criterion for judicial selection. This approach is misleading because the criteria for judicial selection are that a person be appropriately qualified and a fit and proper person. If a person is not appropriately qualified and is not a fit and proper person, it is irrelevant whether they are black or female. That person does not qualify for judicial office. It is also misleading because it encourages the thinking that being black or female somehow enhances a candidate's fitness and propriety for office. Yet, in a society committed to non-racialism and non-sexism, we should be vigilant not to assume that any qualities relevant to judging flow from membership of a group. As argued above in the context of the Sotomayor controversy, it may be that because a candidate is black or female, and has experienced discrimination, their capacity for empathy and compassion is enhanced, but that will depend on the person in question and does not flow automatically from their membership of a group. Similarly, a person's commitment to constitutional values or qualification to adjudicate questions of constitutional law does not flow from their race or gender, but from their humanity, what skills and experience they possess and how they have chosen to live their lives.

Finally, we ought not be too quick to assume that the legitimacy of the bench will be best enhanced if race and gender representativity is accelerated. We must obviously aim to meet the objective of racial and gender representativity with due expedition and treat it with priority, because the judiciary's legitimacy depends on it. But its legitimacy will ultimately depend on how well the judiciary is able to perform the functions the Constitution entrusts to it.[200]

6.3.3 The judicial oath of office

Before a South African judge takes office, he or she swears or affirms:

> **(to) be faithful to the Republic of South Africa, (to) uphold and protect the Constitution and the human rights entrenched in it, and (to) administer justice to all persons alike without fear, favour or prejudice, in accordance with the Constitution and the law.[201]**

200 Cowen (2010) 59–60.

201 S 174(8) of the Constitution states: 'Before judicial officers begin to perform their functions, they must take an oath or affirm, in accordance with Schedule 2, that they will uphold and protect the Constitution.'

This oath requires each judge to decide a case on its legal merits in accordance with the Constitution and the law and without showing either favour or disfavour to any of the litigants. The oath therefore requires judges to promise that they will, as far as it is humanly possible, always act impartially and uphold the law.[202] The requirement represents a further formal safeguard of the impartiality of judges and the independence of the judiciary.

6.3.4 Security of tenure

The independence of judges depends, in part, on a guarantee that judges will not be dismissed or face the threat of dismissal from office for making a decision adverse to the interest of the government of the day or of powerful business or other societal interests aligned with the government. This is why the security of tenure of judges is entrenched in the Constitution.[203] There are two aspects to this guarantee of security of tenure. First, judges are appointed for a fixed term or until they reach a fixed age of retirement. They cannot be forced to retire before their term ends or before they reach the prescribed age of retirement. Second, judges can only be removed from office before the end of their tenure after following a special procedure that entrenches their position. We deal with these two aspects in turn.

Section 176 of the Constitution states that Constitutional Court judges hold office for a non-renewable term of 12 years or until they attain the age of 70, whichever occurs first except where an Act of Parliament extends the term of office of a Constitutional Court judge.[204] Section 4 of the Judges' Remuneration and Conditions of Employment Act[205] extends this term to 15 years of active service. Active service includes service performed as a judge on any other court. However, regardless of the period of active service of a Constitutional Court judge, the judge must retire when he or she reaches the age of 75. This means that a Constitutional Court judge who has been in active service on a High Court or on the SCA for three or more years, will usually serve a fixed term of 12 years on the Constitutional Court. This is unless the judge turns 75 before completing the 12-year term, in which case the judge will retire when reaching the age of 75. However, a judge who has not served on any other court before appointment to the Constitutional Court will normally serve a fixed term of 15 years on that court, provided, again, that he or she does not reach the age of 75 before the end of this 15-year period.

The provision in section 176 of the Constitution that an Act of Parliament could extend the term of office of a Constitutional Court judge was effected by an amendment of the Constitution in 2001. The provisions of the Judges' Remuneration and Conditions of Employment Act then purported to give effect to the provisions of section 176. These provisions were subjected to sustained criticism[206] on the basis that they watered down the security of tenure provisions and could influence the independence of the judiciary.

This criticism was even more sustained in relation to the position of the Chief Justice and the President of the SCA. Section 8 of the Judges' Remuneration and Conditions of Employment Act authorised the President to request a Chief Justice or the President of the

202 Currie and De Waal (2001) 305.

203 See ss 176 and 177.

204 Section 176 was amended by the Constitution Sixth Amendment Act of 2001.

205 Act 47 of 2001.

206 The amendment was widely seen as a move to extend the term of office of then Chief Justice Arthur Chaskalson who was coming to the end of his term of office. See Du Bois, F (2002) Tenure on the Constitutional Court *South African Law Journal* 119(1):1–17 who criticised the amendment of section 176 of the Constitution as well as the provisions of the Judges' Remuneration and Conditions of Employment Act and referred to a submission made to Parliament at the time when it was debating this issue. The article also notes critical comments made by then Chief Justice Chaskalson about moves to extend his term.

SCA at the end of their term of service 'to continue to perform active service for a period determined by the President' on the condition that this extension could not go beyond the date on which the Chief Justice or President of the SCA turned 75 years of age. Section 8 therefore granted the power to extend the term of office of the Chief Justice and the President of the SCA to the President who could extend the term for any period and for as many times as he or she wished. The section was ostensibly passed in accordance with the amended section 176(1) of the Constitution, which, as we have seen, authorises Parliament to extend the term of office of a Constitutional Court judge.

When President Jacob Zuma attempted to extend the term of office of then Chief Justice Sandile Ngcobo, relying on section 8 of the Act, the constitutionality of section 8 was challenged in the Constitutional Court. In *Justice Alliance of South Africa v President of Republic of South Africa and Others, Freedom Under Law v President of Republic of South Africa and Others, Centre for Applied Legal Studies and Another v President of Republic of South Africa and Others,*[207] the Court declared invalid section 8(*a*) of the Judges' Remuneration and Conditions of Employment Act. The judgment affirmed and further elaborated on constitutional law principles relating to the independence of the judiciary, the rule of law and the separation of powers. The Court pointed out that section 8(*a*) was constitutionally problematic because it conferred on the President an executive discretion to decide whether to request a Chief Justice to continue to perform active service and, if he or she agrees, to set the period of the extension. The term of office could be extended if the President decided so and the Chief Justice acceded to the request. Deciding on the period of the extension was in the exclusive discretion of the President and was unfettered in the sense that the President was not required to consult anyone before extending the term of the Chief Justice.[208]

What made section 8(*a*) more problematic was that in its purported delegation, Parliament had not sought to furnish any, let alone adequate, guidelines for the exercise of the discretion by the President. The provision thus usurped the legislative power granted only to Parliament by section 176 of the Constitution and therefore constitutes an unlawful delegation of legislative power to the President.[209] In a constitutional democracy in which the separation of powers doctrine is respected, Parliament may not ordinarily delegate its essential legislative functions to the executive. Although section 176(1) of the Constitution creates an exception to the requirement that a term of a Constitutional Court judge is fixed, that authority, however, vests in Parliament and nowhere else. The Court noted that section 176(1) does not merely bestow a legislative power on Parliament, but by doing so also marks out Parliament's significant role in the separation of powers and protection of judicial independence.[210] As the Court stated:

> **Accordingly, section 8(*a*) violates the principle of judicial independence. This kind of open-ended discretion may raise a reasonable apprehension or perception that the independence of the Chief Justice and by corollary the judiciary may be undermined by external interference of the Executive. The truth may be different, but it matters not. What matters is that the judiciary must be seen to be free from external interference.**[211]

---

207 (CCT 53/11, CCT 54/11, CCT 62/11) [2011] ZACC 23; 2011 (5) SA 388 (CC); 2011 (10) BCLR 1017 (CC) (29 July 2011).
208 *Justice Alliance* para 50.
209 *Justice Alliance* para 51.
210 *Justice Alliance* para 57.
211 *Justice Alliance* para 58.

Focusing on the importance of a fixed term of office for judges to protect and safeguard the independence and impartiality of the judiciary, the Court stated:

> **It is well established on both foreign and local authority that a non-renewable term of office is a prime feature of independence. Indeed, non-renewability is the bedrock of security of tenure and a dyke against judicial favour in passing judgment. Section 176(1) gives strong warrant to this principle in providing that a Constitutional Court judge holds office for a non-renewable term. Non-renewability fosters public confidence in the institution of the judiciary as a whole, since its members function with neither threat that their terms will not be renewed nor any inducement to seek to secure renewal.**[212]

However, the Constitutional Court went further, finding that it would be impermissible for the legislature to single out the office of the Chief Justice for an extension of his or her term of office. Despite section 176(1), Parliament was therefore not authorised to pass legislation that would extend the term of office of only the Chief Justice:

> **In approaching this question it must be borne in mind that the extension of a term of office, particularly one conferred by the Executive or by Parliament, may be seen as a benefit. The judge or judges upon whom the benefit is conferred may be seen as favoured by it. While it is true, as counsel for the President emphasised, that the possibility of far-fetched perceptions should not dominate the interpretive process, it is not unreasonable for the public to assume that extension may operate as a favour that may influence those judges seeking it. The power of extension in section 176(1) must therefore, on general principle, be construed so far as possible to minimise the risk that its conferral could be seen as impairing the precious-won institutional attribute of impartiality and the public confidence that goes with it.**[213]

Although the Constitution specifically creates the office of the Chief Justice and that of Deputy Chief Justice, this does not allow for an extension of his or her term only. This is so because once appointed, the Chief Justice and Deputy Chief Justice take their place alongside nine other judges in constituting the membership of this Court. The Constitution provides that a matter before the Constitutional Court:

> **must be heard by at least eight judges ... Their high office and the extra-judicial duties they may be called upon to perform add nothing to the tally. ... Nor does their office count when this Court determines the cases and the matters before it. Their views count and their voices are heard equally with the respect and authority accorded every member of this Court.**[214]

Section 176(1) of the Constitution therefore did not allow Parliament to single out any individual Constitutional Court judge by name. It is also plain that no individual may be singled out on the basis of an irrelevant individual characteristic or feature. It follows that the term 'a Constitutional Court judge' in section 176(1) does not permit singling out any one Constitutional Court judge on the basis of his or her individual identity or position in the Court. It also follows that in exercising the power to extend the term of office of a Constitutional Court judge, Parliament may not single out the Chief Justice.

212 *Justice Alliance* para 73.
213 *Justice Alliance* para 75.
214 *Justice Alliance* paras 79–80.

It is important to note that the Court distinguished between section 8(*a*) and section 4 of the Judges' Remuneration and Conditions of Employment Act. It pointed out the amendment to section 8 differed from section 4 of the Act as section 4:

> **does not allow any member of the category of Constitutional Court judge to be singled out, whether on the basis of individual characteristic, idiosyncratic feature or the incumbency of office. Age is an indifferent criterion that may be applied in extending the term of office of a Constitutional Court judge. Age is an attribute that everyone attains. Previous judicial service is another criterion that may be indifferently applied to all the judges of this Court. The Act provides that a Constitutional Court judge whose 12-year term of office expires before he or she has completed 15 years' 'active service' as a judge must, subject to attaining the age of 75, serve for 15 years in this Court.**[215]

Ordinary judges (in other words, judges who do not serve on the Constitutional Court) hold office until they are discharged from active service in terms of an Act of Parliament.[216] Section 3(2) of the Judges' Remuneration and Conditions of Employment Act regulates this matter. This section states that other judges will normally hold office until the date on which they attain the age of 70 years if they have on that date completed a period of active service of not less than 10 years. If they have on that date not yet completed a period of 10 years' active service, the term of office will end after serving for 10 years. However, judges have a further discretion provided by section 4(4) of the Act. This section allows a judge who on attaining the age of 70 years has not yet completed 15 years' active service to continue to perform active service to the date on which he or she completes a period of 15 years' active service or attains the age of 75 years, whichever occurs first.

The requirement that the security of tenure of judges should be guaranteed has another important consequence: judges should only be removed from office as a last resort and then only for serious and objectively determinable reasons. Thus, section 177 of the Constitution determines that a judge may only be removed from office if the JSC finds that the judge:

- suffers from an incapacity
- is grossly incompetent
- is guilty of gross misconduct.

Once the JSC has made such a finding, this is not the end of the matter as the judge in question will only be removed from office if the NA calls for that judge to be removed by a resolution adopted with a supporting vote of at least two-thirds of its members. Once the NA has passed such a resolution, the President must remove the judge from office. The President has the power, on the advice of the JSC, to suspend a judge who is the subject of an investigation by the JSC to remove him or her from office.[217] Section 177 of the Constitution ensures that a judge cannot be arbitrarily removed from the bench for political or other reasons unrelated to the ability of that judge to perform his or her functions or the integrity of the judge.

The JSC Act determines the procedure to be followed by the JSC when dealing with complaints against judges. A Judicial Conduct Committee (a subcommittee of the JSC) is required to receive, consider and deal with complaints against judges. The Judicial Conduct

215 *Justice Alliance* para 91.

216 S 176(2) of the Constitution.

217 S 177(3) of the Constitution.

Committee comprises the Chief Justice, who is the Chairperson of the Committee, the Deputy Chief Justice and four judges, at least two of whom must be women, designated by the Chief Justice in consultation with the Minister.[218] The Committee can deal with both serious complaints, which may lead to the dismissal of a judge, or less serious complaints which will not lead to the dismissal of a judge. However, a lesser complaint can also be referred to the head of the court in which the judge complained of serves.[219]

A complaint must be dismissed if it is not of a serious nature or is solely related to the merits of a judgment or order, if it is frivolous or lacking in substance, or if it is hypothetical.[220] If the Chairperson of the Conduct Committee is satisfied that in the event of a valid complaint being established, it is likely to lead to a finding by the JSC that the judge being accused suffers from an incapacity, is grossly incompetent or is guilty of gross misconduct, the Chairperson must refer the complaint to the Conduct Committee. The Committee must then consider whether it should recommend to the JSC that the complaint should be investigated and reported on by a Judicial Conduct Tribunal. The Committee must also consider whether the complaint, if established, will *prima facie* indicate incapacity, gross incompetence or gross misconduct by the judge. Non-impeachable complaints can be dealt with by the Committee without referral to the Tribunal which will only be appointed in the case of impeachable offences.[221]

Impeachable offences **must** be referred to a Judicial Conduct Tribunal, which consists of two judges, one of whom must be designated by the Chief Justice as the Tribunal President, and one layperson.[222] The Tribunal will then, in effect, try the judge against whom a serious complaint had been lodged: witnesses will be called and those making the allegations as well as the judge being accused will be cross-examined. The Tribunal will then make the appropriate findings of fact, including the cogency and sufficiency of the evidence and the demeanour and credibility of any witness, as well as its findings as to the merits of the allegations in question. It will then submit a report to the JSC.[223] The JSC will decide whether to recommend impeachment of the judge to the NA. When considering a complaint against a judge, the JSC is obliged to decide the matter.

CRITICAL THINKING

The duty of the JSC when considering complaints against judges

In the case of *Freedom Under Law v Acting Chairperson: Judicial Service Commission and Others*,[224] the SCA declared invalid a decision of the JSC to dismiss a complaint lodged by the then judges of the Constitutional Court against Judge President John Hlophe. The SCA found that the JSC was required to investigate serious complaints and could not abdicate its constitutional duty to investigate the complaint properly. Such an abdication in this case was therefore unlawful and invalid.

The JSC had previously found that the evidence in respect of the complaint by the Constitutional Court against Judge President John Hlophe did not justify a finding that the Judge President was guilty of gross misconduct and that the matter accordingly be

218 S 8 of the JSC Act.

219 Ss 14 and 15 of the JSC Act.

220 S 15(2) of the JSC Act.

221 S 17 of the JSC Act.

222 S 22 of the JSC Act.

223 S 33 of the JSC Act.

224 (2011 (3) SA 549 (SCA); [2011] 3 All SA 513 (SCA)) [2011] ZASCA 59; 52/2011 (31 March 2011).

'treated as finalised'.[225] The JSC had assumed that because there were two versions of what happened - one presented by Hlophe and another presented by Justices Jafta and Nkabinde of the Constitutional Court - that cross-examination of the witnesses who presented these conflicting versions would serve no purpose. Hence, no further and proper investigation was required. The JSC had thus decided that because there were conflicting versions of events, they would not judge the merits of the case at all. The SCA rejected this argument, stating:

> **It cannot be in the interests of the judiciary, the legal system, the country or the public to sweep the allegation under the carpet because it is being denied by the accused judge, or because an investigation will be expensive, or because the matter has continued for a long time.[226]**

The SCA therefore found that the decision not to proceed with a full investigation was irrational.[227]

The problem for the JSC was that in the absence of cross-examination of the witnesses, its finding and reasons for the finding could not be justified. As the SCA pointed out, the JSC had applied the criminal standard applicable at the end of a criminal trial, namely proof beyond reasonable doubt, to dismiss the complaint at a stage when neither of the conflicting versions of the judges accusing Judge President Hlophe on the one hand and Hlophe JP on the other hand had been tested by cross-examination. Although the finding that it could not reject Hlophe JP's version was quite correct, this did not mean that no cross-examination was required:

> **By disallowing cross-examination that result was made inevitable. It would have been highly irregular to reject his evidence without having given him an opportunity to cross-examine his accusers. Utilising this procedure for the final resolution of a complaint of misconduct by a judge will always lead to a dismissal of the dispute where the conduct alleged by the accuser is disputed by the judge because the judge's version can never be rejected without having given him an opportunity to cross-examine his accusers. The procedure adopted was therefore not appropriate for the final determination of the complaint.[228]**

This case, read with the other SCA cases dealing with the procedure to be followed by the JSC when appointing and disciplining judges, suggests that the JSC does not only have an obligation to act rationally when it makes these decisions. It also has a duty to make some kind of decision and cannot decide not to make a decision at all in cases where a decision is required.

6.3.5 Financial security

The independence of the judiciary can be eroded if judges are not secure in making decisions without fear, favour or prejudice. This security can be threatened if judges are not financially secure and if they believe they can be 'punished' (or if, in fact, they can be punished) for making an unpopular decision by having their salaries and other benefits reduced by the

225 *Freedom Under Law* para 7.
226 *Freedom Under Law* para 63.
227 *Freedom Under Law* para 42.
228 *Freedom Under Law* para 45.

state. It is for this reason that the Constitution states that the 'salaries, allowances and benefits of judges may not be reduced'.[229] The conditions of service of judges are regulated by the Judges' Remuneration and Conditions of Employment Act. The Act provides that a judge shall be paid a monthly salary to be determined each year by the President by proclamation after taking into consideration the recommendations of the Independent Commission for the Remuneration of Public Office-bearers.[230] A proclamation setting out judges' salaries must be submitted to Parliament after its publication. Parliament may reject the proclamation or any provision of it, the effect of which will be to make the proclamation invalid. To emphasise that judges are not employees of the executive, judge's salaries are not included in the allocation of revenue to any government department, but are paid directly from the state revenue fund.[231]

6.3.6 Limitation of civil liability

By its very nature, the job of a judge is to make judgments about people. Such judgments – about the credibility of a witness or the guilt of an accused – can fundamentally affect the status and dignity of an individual. Such individuals wrongly impugned by a judge may therefore wish to revert to the law of defamation to claim damages from a judge who has impugned his or her reputation.

However, to carry out their functions, judges must be secure in the knowledge that they will not incur civil liability for what they say or do in the course of carrying out their duties.[232] Thus, in *Penrice v Dickenson*,[233] the Court held that delictual damages will not be awarded against a judicial officer, whether a judge or a magistrate, unless it is shown that he or she acted with malice. This common law rule was applied in *May v Udwin*[234] where it was held that a judicial officer can raise the defence of qualified privilege to a defamation action.

A judge or magistrate will therefore be liable for defamatory statements only if it can be proved that he or she made those statements out of personal spite, ill will or an improper, unlawful or ulterior motive. The reason for this rule is obvious. The judicial task would be made impossible if a judge could be sued for defamation every time in the course of giving judgment he or she expressed unfavourable views about a litigant or made an adverse finding regarding the credibility of a witness.[235] Without protection from defamation suits, judges could be exposed to endless litigation by disgruntled litigants, witnesses or accused persons.

Before the adoption of the Superior Courts Act,[236] section 25(1) of the Supreme Court Act afforded Supreme Court judges a further protection against defamation claims. The section prohibited the issuing of a civil summons or subpoena against a judge without the permission of the court out of which the process was to be served.[237] Currie and de Waal speculate that the reason why it was thought that this permission was needed may have been to protect judges from becoming the victims of frivolous proceedings or to prevent the disruption of the work of the court.[238]

---

229 S 176(3).
230 Established under s 2 of the Independent Commission for the Remuneration of Public Office-bearers Act 92 of 1997.
231 Ss 2(6) and 14 of the Judges' Remuneration and Conditions of Employment Act.
232 See generally Currie and De Waal (2001) 307.
233 1945 AD 6.
234 1981 (1) SA 1 (A).
235 Currie and De Waal (2001) 307.
236 Act 10 of 2013.
237 If it is sought to serve process out of a magistrates' court, then the litigant must obtain the prior permission of that division of the Supreme Court which has appeal jurisdiction over the magistrates' court in question.
238 Currie and De Waal (2001) 308.

A similar process was required in the case of judges of the Constitutional Court. The Supreme Court Act prohibited any civil proceedings from being instituted against or subpoena issued for the Chief Justice or other judges of the Constitutional Court without the consent of the Chief Justice. Again, where consent had been obtained, the date on which the judge was to appear had to be determined in consultation with the Chief Justice (in matters involving the President) or the President of the Court (in matters involving the other judges).[239] Similar provisions did not find their way into the Superior Courts Act.

6.4 Independence of the lower courts and traditional courts

6.4.1 The lower courts under the interim Constitution

Before 1993, the magistrates' courts in South Africa enjoyed little if any independence. In fact, judicial officers in lower courts had the status of ordinary public servants.[240] Magistrates and regional magistrates were employees of the Department of Justice and were usually promoted from the ranks of public prosecutors once they had passed the relevant examinations.[241] As Currie and De Waal point out, like other public servants, magistrates were subject to the disciplinary measures contained in the Public Service Act.[242] Following a departmental enquiry, they could be demoted or discharged on grounds of misconduct or inefficiency.[243] These factors exposed magistrates to being influenced by the executive and cast suspicion on their independence. This close relationship between magistrates and the executive was seen as incompatible with the doctrine of separation of powers.

The 1983 Hoexter Commission of Inquiry recommended legislative steps designed to shore up the independence of magistrates and to reduce the possibility of influence or control by the executive.[244] The independence of the magistrates' courts was then enhanced by the adoption in 1993 by the last apartheid Parliament of the Magistrates Act.[245] The Act removed magistrates from the ambit of the public service and created a Magistrates Commission to deal with the conditions of service, appointment and dismissal of magistrates. The Magistrates Act was passed prior to the adoption of the interim Constitution 'at a time when the great majority of the population of this country had no representation in Parliament' and when the 'power to appoint judges and magistrates was then vested in the executive'.[246] The Magistrates Act gave the Magistrates Commission an advisory function in the appointment of magistrates, but there was no obligation on the executive to consult any person or institution in respect of the appointment of judges. The Magistrates Commission was not a representative body and all but two of its members were designated by bodies controlled by white judicial officers and lawyers. The existence and functions of the Magistrates Commission were then constitutionalised by section 109 of the interim Constitution. According to section 109, the Commission had 'to ensure that the appointment, promotion, transfer or dismissal of, or disciplinary steps against magistrates take place

239 S 5 of the Constitutional Court Complementary Act 13 of 1995.
240 See generally Currie and De Waal (2001) 308–10.
241 See s 9(1)(*b*) of the Magistrates' Courts Act which sets out the necessary qualifications for appointment as a magistrate. See generally *Van Rooyen*.
242 Act 111 of 1984.
243 Currie and De Waal (2001) 308.
244 Hoexter Commission of Inquiry into the Structure and Functioning of the Courts (1983) RP 78/83 Part IV para 4.2.1 (g).
245 Act 90 of 1993.
246 *Van Rooyen* para 49.

without favour or prejudice ... and to ensure that no victimization or improper influencing of magistrates occurs'.

6.4.2 Independence of the lower courts under the 1996 Constitution

The 1996 Constitution vests **judicial authority** in the courts which, according to section 166(*d*), includes the magistrates' courts. Section 174(7) of the Constitution governs the appointment of magistrates. This section requires an Act of Parliament to be passed to 'ensure that the appointment, promotion, transfer or dismissal of, or disciplinary steps against, these judicial officers take place without favour or prejudice'. The 1996 Constitution does not explicitly mention that a Magistrates Commission should fulfil this task.

During the certification proceedings objection was made to the fact that there was no provision in the 1996 Constitution for a similar Magistrates Commission. There were also no express provisions governing the appointment, term of office, remuneration and removal from office of magistrates. The Constitutional Court held that it was sufficient that section 165 guaranteed the independence of the courts. The Act of Parliament governing the appointment of magistrates referred to in section 174(7) is subject to constitutional control. If the Act undermines the independence and impartiality of the courts specifically protected by section 165, it will not be valid.[247]

In 1996, changes were made to the composition of the Magistrates Commission. The change in the composition of the Magistrates Commission effected by the 1996 amendment brought the composition of that Commission closer to that of the JSC.[248] The Constitution itself recognises the JSC as a body appropriately constituted for the purpose of matters concerned with the appointment and impeachment of judges.[249]

The Constitutional Court held in the *Van Rooyen* case that the changes made in 1996 are consistent with and reflect the change that has taken place in our country since 1993 – a transformation required by the Constitution itself:

> **The Magistrates Commission is now more broadly representative of South African society as a whole. This was important particularly at this stage of our history. The overwhelming majority of the population is black and at least half the population is female. Yet the great majority of the legal profession and senior judicial officers are still white and male. In the light of our history and the commitment made in the Constitution to transform our society, these racial and gender disparities cannot be ignored. The recomposition of the Magistrates Commission viewed thus by an objective observer, could not fairly be seen as an attempt to exert executive control over the magistracy. There was a pressing need for the racial and gender disparities within the Commission to be changed, and for the Commission to be re-composed so as to become more representative of South African society. The changes made facilitated this, and that would have been understood by an objective observer taking a balanced view of all the relevant circumstances.**[250]

Currently, the Commission consists of a judge, six magistrates, four legal practitioners, a teacher of law, eight Members of Parliament and five nominees of the executive. In addition,

247 *Certification of the Constitution of the Republic of South Africa, 1996* (CCT 23/96) [1996] ZACC 26; 1996 (4) SA 744 (CC); 1996 (10) BCLR 1253 (CC) (6 September 1996) para 136.

248 See s 3 of the Magistrates Act.

249 *Van Rooyen* para 57.

250 *Van Rooyen* para 61.

the Minister and the head of Justice College are members of the Commission.[251] According to the Constitutional Court:

> **[o]n its face this is a diverse body of persons, nearly half of whom consist of members of the judiciary and the legal profession. The rest are nominees of Parliament and the executive. To some extent this is similar to the composition of the Judicial Service Commission which has a central role in the appointment of judges and the composition of which is dealt with in the Constitution itself.**[252]

In practice, the Commission does not conduct interviews but compiles a list of appointees who have undergone the required training and passed the examinations. The appointees are drawn from the ranks of public prosecutors. The same Commission that determines the salaries of judges also determines the remuneration of magistrates.

6.4.3 Independence of traditional courts

As the South African Law Commission (SALC) pointed out in its Report on Traditional Courts,[253] the administration of justice in rural South Africa is predominantly carried out by chiefs' courts. These courts administer justice largely on the basis of customary law and on the basis of authority granted by several apartheid-era laws.[254] Traditional courts gain their authority from sections 12 and 20 of the Black Administration Act (BAA),[255] read with section 16 of Schedule 6 of the Constitution.[256] This is seemingly authorised by Chapter 12 of the Constitution which requires the law to recognise the 'institution, status and role of traditional leadership according to customary law', but subject to other provisions in the Constitution.[257] The Constitution allows national legislation further to provide for this role.[258] It is surprising that traditional courts are still regulated by the BAA while most other provisions of this Act have been scrapped. The BAA has been described by the Constitutional Court as 'an egregious apartheid law which anachronistically has survived our transition to a non-racial democracy'.[259]

---

251 S 3(1)(*a*) of the Magistrates Act.

252 *Van Rooyen* para 48.

253 South African Law Commission (2003) *Customary Law: Report on Traditional Courts and the Judicial Function of Traditional Leaders* Project 90 1 available at http://www.justice.gov.za/salrc/reports/r_prj90_tradlead_2003jan.pdf (accessed on 25 January 2013).

254 See, for example, the Black Administration Act 38 of 1927, the Bophuthatswana Traditional Courts Act 29 of 1979, the KwaNdebele Traditional Authorities Act 8 of 1984, the Chiefs Courts Act 6 of 1993 (Transkei) and the KwaZulu Amakhosi and Iziphakanyiswa Act 9 of 1990.

255 Act 38 of 1927. Most sections of this law have been repealed, but these sections are some of the few that were retained and continue to be in operation.

256 Section 16 of Schedule 6 of the Constitution reads as follows:

> **Every court, including courts of traditional leaders, existing when the new Constitution took effect, continues to function and to exercise jurisdiction in terms of legislation applicable to it and anyone holding office as a judicial officer continues to hold office in terms of legislation applicable to that office, subject to any amendment or repeal of that legislation, and consistency with the new Constitution.**

257 S 211(1) states: 'The institution, status and role of traditional leadership, according to customary law, are recognised, subject to the Constitution.'

258 S 212(1).

259 *Western Cape Provincial Government and Others In Re: DVB Behuising (Pty) Limited v North West Provincial Government and Another* (CCT22/99) [2000] ZACC 2; 2000 (4) BCLR 347; 2001 (1) SA 500 (2 March 2000) para 1. See also *Moseneke* paras 20–1 where the Constitutional Court described the BAA as follows:

> **The Act systematised and enforced a colonial form of relationship between a dominant white minority who were to have rights of citizenship and a subordinate black majority who were to be administered. ... It is painful that the Act still survives at all. The concepts on which it was based, the memories it evokes, the language it continues to employ, and the division it still enforces, are antithetical to the society envisaged by the Constitution. It is an affront to all of us that people are still treated as 'blacks' rather than as ordinary persons seeking to wind up a deceased estate, and it is in conflict with the establishment of a non-racial society where rights and duties are no longer determined by origin or skin colour.**

The relevant sections of the BAA that apply here and are still in operation empower the Minister to confer civil and criminal jurisdiction on chiefs, headmen or chiefs' deputies. The BAA does not prescribe any hierarchy of customary courts and neither does it provide for appeals from the headman's court to a chief's court.[260] According to the SALC, in many traditional communities the practice is that claims or complaints start at the level of the family council. If a matter is not resolved at that level, it is taken to the headman who, together with his advisers, attempts to dispose of the matter. If it is still not resolved, the matter is taken on appeal to the chief. It is from the chief's court that the case is normally appealed to the magistrates' court.[261] As we have noted in a previous chapter, chiefs are not elected but obtain their positions on a hereditary basis.[262]

The BAA does not prescribe the composition of the chiefs' or customary courts. The Act merely provides for the conferment of jurisdiction on a chief, headman or chief's deputy to hear civil matters and to try certain criminal matters.[263] However, under customary law, the court formally consists of the chief and his councillors or the headman and his advisers (the chief or headman will very seldom be female). In most cases, the chief will not normally preside over the proceedings. Instead, a trusted councillor will be appointed to preside.[264] This situation differs from community to community. The flexible nature of customary law, along with its ability to develop to adapt to changing circumstances, means that it is not possible to identify a unified system according to which traditional courts operate. However, the Centre for Law and Society summarises the nature of traditional courts in South Africa as follows:

> **Customary courts are essentially non-professional institutions. Rather, they are community forums in which mature members of the community participate. The notion of a presiding officer who acts as a judge and is the single decision-maker has no real place in these forums as they are shared discussion spaces in which all present can participate in the hearing, questioning, deliberation and decision. Also, the variability between different communities (even within a single cultural group or locality) in the extent of the chief's participation in the court – ranging from non-participation to active participation – makes the notion of presiding officer an untenable notion to adopt and impose on all communities. The notion of a presiding officer, derived from western court systems, is misleading in the context of these forums. Several studies detail that, even where the chief formulates and pronounces the decision in a customary court, he is bound by what the council and/or community has found in hearing that case.**[265]

Because traditional leaders are also involved in the exercise of legislative and executive powers, it has been argued that traditional courts cannot be independent as required by the Constitution. However, different High Courts have reached different conclusions on this

260 S 12(4) of the BAA provides for appeals from judgments of a chief, headman or chief's deputy in a civil matter, while s 20(6) provides for appeals from a chief, headmen or chief's deputy in a criminal matter. In each case the appeal goes to the magistrates' court. See also Bennett, TW (2004) *Customary Law in South Africa* 127.

261 SALC (2003) *Report on Traditional Courts and the Judicial Function of Traditional Leaders* 5.

262 See s 28(1) of the Traditional Leadership and Governance Framework Act 41 of 2003 (TLGFA).

263 Ss 12 and 20 of the BAA.

264 SALC (2003) *Report on Traditional Courts and the Judicial Function of Traditional Leaders* 6.

265 See Law, Race and Gender Unit (now Centre for Law and Society) Submission on the Traditional Courts Bill (B1-2012) available at http://www.lrg.uct.ac.za/usr/lrg/docs/TCB/2012/lrg_feb2012_ncopsubmission.pdf17.

matter[266] and the Constitutional Court has not given its opinion on whether a system of traditional courts can be squared with the requirements of judicial independence.

We contend that it would be difficult to answer this question in the abstract as different customary courts operate differently and deal differently with disputes. Bennett also argues that a distinction should be drawn between traditional courts dealing with criminal matters and traditional courts dealing with civil matters. The requirements for independence would not arise as sharply in civil matters as in criminal matters where the presiding officer could also be the complainant, prosecutor and judge. Moreover, the question of whether traditional courts are compatible with the Constitution should be weighed against considerations of access to justice as those traditional courts that work well, provide immediate and effective access to justice for many citizens living in rural areas. Thus, argues Bennett, traditional courts should retain their civil jurisdiction, while not being awarded jurisdiction to try criminal matters.[267]

6.5 The National Prosecuting Authority

The 1996 Constitution established a single National Prosecuting Authority (NPA) for South Africa.[268] The NPA has the power to institute criminal proceedings on behalf of the state and to carry out any necessary functions incidental to instituting criminal proceedings.[269] One of the most vexing constitutional law issues is the question of where the NPA fits into the structure of government within the system of separation of powers. It is neither part of the legislature or the executive nor is it part of the judiciary. Yet, it is supposed to play a pivotal role in the effective and impartial functioning of the criminal justice system. Section 179 of the Constitution establishes the framework within which the NPA should operate, but requires the details of its structure to be provided for in an Act of Parliament.

The constitutional framework provides for a National Director of Public Prosecutions (the NDPP) to head the **prosecuting authority**,[270] a position that is equivalent to that of Attorney-General in most other Anglo-American dispensations. The President in his or her capacity as head of the national executive appoints the NDPP. The National Prosecuting Authority (NPA) Act[271] also provides for the removal of the NDPP by the President in certain circumscribed circumstances. Although the President has some discretion in who to appoint as NDPP, this discretion is not unfettered. The NPA Act prescribes objective criteria regarding the qualifications and abilities of the NDPP and a court can determine whether the President has complied with these criteria when selecting and appointing a new NDPP.[272] This is a necessary consequence of the wording of section 179 which requires that the NDPP must be appropriately qualified. The Constitution, read with the NPA Act, does not leave it open

266 S 165(2) of the Constitution. See Bennet (2004) 117. This argument was rejected in *Bangindawo v Head of the Nyanda Regional Authority; Hlantlalala v Head of the Western Tembuland Regional Authority* (1998) 3 BCLR 314 (Tk). However, in *Mhlekwa & Feni v Head of the Western Tembuland Regional Authority* 2000 (9) BCLR 979 (Tk) 1017–18, the Court held that the fact that there is a fusion of judicial and administrative functions does not necessarily denote an absence of judicial independence. Some of the functions performed by chiefs are such that they may potentially involve him or her in controversial public issues and may create a perception of an unduly close relationship with the executive branch of government. The Court implored the legislature to address this problem.

267 Bennet (2004) 128.

268 S 179(1).

269 S 179(2) of the Constitution.

270 S 179(1)(*a*) of the Constitution.

271 Act 32 of 1998.

272 *Democratic Alliance v President of South Africa and Others* (CCT 122/11) [2012] ZACC 24; 2012 (12) BCLR 1297 (CC); 2013 (1) SA 248 (CC) (5 October 2012) paras 14–26.

to the President to determine whether a candidate is appropriately qualified to be appointed as NDPP, but rather determines that the legislature must set out the criteria for appointment. The NPA Act thus requires the NDPP to possess legal qualifications that would entitle him or her to practise in all courts in the Republic, and must 'be a fit and proper person, with due regard to his or her experience, conscientiousness and integrity, to be entrusted with the responsibilities of the office concerned'.[273] The NDPP must also be a South African citizen.[274]

The NPA Act further states that the NDPP holds office for a non-renewable term of 10 years.[275] Although the NDPP serves a non-renewable term of 10 years and enjoys some security of tenure, this security is not absolute. The NPA Act also provides for the NDPP to be suspended and removed from office under certain circumstances. The President may provisionally suspend the NDPP from his or her office after instituting an enquiry into his or her fitness to hold office. This enquiry can be conducted by anyone appointed by the President,[276] but the enquiry must be aimed at determining whether the NDPP is guilty of misconduct, suffers from continued ill health, is incapable of carrying out his or her duties of office efficiently, or is no longer a fit and proper person to hold the office concerned. The NDPP can only be removed if the enquiry finds that, based on one or more of these objective criteria, there are reasons to dismiss him or her. Even then, the recommendation to dismiss the NDPP will only take effect if this is confirmed by the adoption of a motion to that effect in the NA.[277] These provisions relating to the appointment and the dismissal of the NDPP are all aimed at giving effect to the constitutional injunction in section 179(4) that requires the adoption of national legislation to ensure that the prosecuting authority exercises its functions without fear, favour or prejudice to ensure its independence. It provides a degree of protection to the NDPP to ensure his or her structural independence.

However, at first glance, this independence of the NPA and its head is not set out in as clear a manner in the Constitution as we would have thought necessary. Thus, section 179(6) of the Constitution states that the Cabinet member responsible for the administration of justice must exercise final responsibility over the prosecuting authority. Until recently, it was therefore unclear to what extent the NPA was truly independent from the executive and whether the Minister of Justice or the President could ever intervene in decisions taken by the NPA to prosecute or not to prosecute an accused. This is an important question that goes to the heart of the credibility and effectiveness of the NPA. Where the NPA has to decide on whether to prosecute or not to prosecute a politician or a politically well-connected individual or business leader, it is important that such a decision will be above suspicion and that a perception does not arise that the NPA makes decisions based on political or financial considerations.

However, in many Anglo-American countries there is no generally accepted rule that the prosecuting authority ought to be free from executive or political control. In many Anglo-American countries the Attorney-General (the equivalent of the NDPP) is a political appointee – often at ministerial level. Nevertheless, in most of these jurisdictions the

273 S 9(1).

274 S 9(2) of the NPA Act.

275 S 12(1).

276 This suggests that the President need not appoint a judge to head this enquiry although the appointment must be rational. Given the fact that the purpose of the appointment is to enquire into whether – objectively speaking – the NDPP is fit to continue with his or her work, it may well be that a court would declare invalid the appointment of a person to head this enquiry if that person is manifestly not capable of bringing an independent mind to bear on the enquiry.

277 S 12(6) and 12(7) of the NPA Act.

Attorney-General would be required by convention to make prosecutorial decisions without regard to political considerations and is not supposed to subject his or her discretionary authority to that of government. He or she is also usually not responsible to government to justify the exercise of his or her discretion because this political office has judicial attributes.[278]

In South Africa, the role of the Attorney-General in the pre-democratic era was not without controversy. The Union of South Africa Act, 1909 established the power of the Attorney-General to make prosecutorial decisions although he or she was always viewed as a civil servant. The position changed in 1926 when all powers, authorities and functions relating to the prosecution of crimes and offences were vested in the Minister of Justice despite the fact that the decision to prosecute or not to prosecute remained with the Attorneys-General. The Minister exercised an appeal or review function only. As from 1935, Attorneys-General had to exercise their authority and perform their functions under the relevant legislation[279] subject to the control and directions of the Minister who could reverse any decision.[280] As South Africa moved towards a democratic dispensation, this position was reversed and the independence of the Attorneys-General regarding prosecutorial decisions was reinstated in 1992. However, the Minister had to co-ordinate their functions and could request information from them or ask them to report on any matter, and they had to submit annual reports to the Minister.[281]

Until recently, the prosecution and prosecutorial authority did not receive much attention in South African constitutional jurisprudence. As pointed out above, this is important because if controversial prosecutions can be stopped before they reach the courts, even the most independent tribunal cannot guarantee equal treatment for all.[282] The independence of the NPA is therefore linked to that of the judicial system as a whole. Although at first there was some uncertainty about the nature of the independence of the NPA under the 1996 Constitution, the Constitutional Court and the SCA have since cleared up any confusion about the question.

Following precedent from the Namibian Supreme Court, the SCA found that the provision requiring that members of the NPA act without fear, favour or prejudice and the provision stating that the Minister of Justice must exercise final responsibility over the NPA are not incompatible.[283] A balance can be struck as follows. The Minister may not instruct the NPA to prosecute or to decline to prosecute or to terminate a pending prosecution, in other words interfere with individual prosecutorial decisions, because that would interfere with the independence of the NPA. However, the Minister is entitled to be kept informed in

---

278 See generally *National Director of Public Prosecutions v Zuma* (573/08) [2009] ZASCA 1; 2009 (2) SA 277 (SCA); 2009 (1) SACR 361 (SCA); 2009 (4) BCLR 393 (SCA); [2009] 2 All SA 243 (SCA) (12 January 2009) paras 28–30 for a history of the role of Attorneys-General in commonwealth countries. See also Scott, IG (1987) The role of the Attorney-General and the Charter of Rights *Criminal Law Quarterly* 29(2):187–99 at 187; Wade, ECS and Bradley, AW (1993) *Constitutional and Administrative Law* 11th ed 402–4; *Ex parte Attorney-General: In Re Constitutional Relationship between the Attorney-General and the Prosecutor-General* SA 7/93 [1995] NASC 1; 1995 (8) BCLR 1070 (Nm5) (13 July 1995); *Githunguri v Republic of Kenya* [1986] LRC (Const) 618 (HC); *Proulx v Quebec (Attorney-General)* 2001 SCC 66, [2001] 3 SCR 9. For the constitutional crisis about the independence of the Attorney-General in 1924 in the UK, see De Smith, SA (1981) *Constitutional and Administrative Law* 4th ed 380–1.

279 General Law Amendment Act 46 of 1935.

280 See *NDPP v Zuma* para 29.

281 See s 5 of the Attorney-General Act 92 of 1992.

282 See also Nicholson J in *Zuma v NDPP*.

283 *NDPP v Zuma* para 32. For the Namibian jurisprudence, see *Ex parte Attorney-General: In Re Constitutional Relationship between the Attorney- General and the Prosecutor-General* SA 7/93 [1995] NASC 1; 1995 (8) BCLR 1070 (Nm5) (13 July 1995).

respect of all prosecutions initiated or to be initiated which might arouse public interest or involve important aspects of legal or prosecutorial authority.[284]

The Constitutional Court has confirmed that the Constitution requires the NPA to act independently from the executive and, as such, the NDPP must be viewed as a 'non-political chief executive officer directly appointed by the President'.[285] This is significant as it underscores the fact that the office of the NDPP 'must be non-political and non-partisan', and that its role 'is closely related to the function of the judiciary'.[286] In affirming the need to appoint an independent NDPP in accordance with the Constitution and the NPA Act, the Constitutional Court set out a list of goals which the President must aim to achieve when he or she appoints the NDPP. The purpose of empowering the President to appoint the NDPP, stated the Court, is to ensure that the person appointed as NDPP is sufficiently conscientious and has the integrity required to be entrusted with the responsibilities of the office and, in particular, to ensure, among other things, that:[287]

- the prosecuting authority performs its functions honestly and without fear, favour or prejudice
- decisions to institute criminal prosecution are taken honestly, fairly and without fear, favour or prejudice
- any improper interference, hindrance or obstruction of the prosecuting authority by any organ of state is not tolerated.

CRITICAL THINKING

A critical analysis of the Ginwala Report on the dismissal of the NDPP, Vusi Pikoli

The former head of the NPA, Vusi Pikoli, was suspended from his job as NDPP and was then dismissed by the President on the basis of a report prepared by Frene Ginwala. This was after she had conducted the requisite enquiry mentioned above in accordance with the provisions of the NPA Act. It is unclear whether this removal from office was legally valid or not. De Vos provided the following critical analysis of the Ginwala Report:[288]

> At the heart of the Ginwala Commission of Enquiry Report and the decision by President Kgalema Motlanthe to recommend the removal from office of Vusi Pikoli, the National Director of Public Prosecutions, is a rather troubling interpretation of what is required to safeguard the constitutionally protected independence of the NPA. The Report correctly points out that the Constitutional Court had held that section 179(4) of the Constitution, providing that national legislation must ensure that the prosecuting authority exercises its functions 'without fear, favour

---

284 *NDPP v Zuma* para 32. This is made clear by the NPA Act. S 32(1)(*a*) of the NPA Act requires members of the prosecuting authority to serve 'impartially' and to exercise, carry out or perform their powers, duties and functions 'in good faith and without fear, favour or prejudice' and subject only to the Constitution and the law. S 32(1)(*b*) further provides that no one may interfere 'improperly' with the NPA in the performance of its duties and functions. S 33(2) reaffirms that the Minister must exercise final responsibility over the NPA and obliges the NDPP, at the request of the Minister, to furnish the latter with information or a report with regard to any case and to provide the Minister with reasons for any decision taken. S 22(2)(*c*) states that, in exercising the review power to prosecute or not to prosecute, the NDPP may advise the Minister 'on all matters relating to the administration of justice'. The SCA decision stands in sharp contrast to the decision of the High Court in the matter. In *Zuma v NDPP* para 89, Judge Nicholson stated that there must not be a hint of a relationship between the Minister of Justice and the NDPP.

285 *Democratic Alliance* para 16.

286 *Democratic Alliance* para 26.

287 *Democratic Alliance* para 49.

288 De Vos, P (2008, 8 December) National security, the last refuge of scoundrels? *Constitutionally Speaking* available at http://constitutionallyspeaking.co.za/national-security-the-last-refuge-of-scoundrels/.

or prejudice', amounted to 'a constitutional guarantee of independence'. It also points out that the Court had further noted that 'any legislation or executive action inconsistent therewith would be subject to constitutional control by the courts' and concludes that '[a]ny attempt by the Minister of Justice to influence prosecutorial discretion in individual cases would therefore be contrary to the Constitution'. But, the Report then states:

> Sufficient attention has not been paid to the requirement of democratic accountability of the prosecuting authority. In focusing only on independence from political interference they have erred in conflating freedom from control with freedom from accountability. Further, scant attention has been paid to the nature, content and ambit of the 'final responsibility' of the Minister, and even less to the relationship between this responsibility and the prosecutorial independence of the NDPP.

The Report then refers to Chapter 3 of the Constitution, which deals with the principle of co-operative government between the national, provincial and local spheres of government and all organs of state within those spheres. It argues that the NDPP has an extraordinarily onerous duty to co-operate with the President, the relevant Minister and other organs of state such as the South African Police Service.

If this interpretation is correct, it would place a very heavy burden on the NPA to co-operate with the executive when deciding to issue warrants for the arrest of high-ranking state officials or to prosecute them. In the case of Selebi, the Commission found that its own interpretation of the Constitution and the NPA Act required the NPA boss not only to have informed the Minister and the President *before* requesting that a warrant of arrest be issued for the National Police Commissioner, but also to have acquiesced to a request by the President not to proceed with executing the arrest until such time as the President had taken the steps he deemed necessary for what he deemed to be in the interest of 'national security'.

The interpretation of the NPA Act and the Constitution referred to seems controversial as the NPA Act does not explicitly require the NDPP to inform the Minister – let alone the President – of any actions to arrest anyone unless he or she explicitly asks for such information. It is not clear that the NPA's constitutional independence, safeguarded in the Constitution (as developed by the SCA and the Constitutional Court), can be squared with this interpretation that, in effect, gives the President a veto power over decisions to issue arrest warrants against high placed government officials merely because the President cites issues of 'national security'. It is also not clear that Chapter 3 of the Constitution applies to an independent body like the NPA as this Chapter deals with relations between the three spheres of government. It is my opinion that the heavy reliance placed by the Ginwala Commission on Chapter 3 of the Constitution completely misconstrues the nature of Chapter 3 as well as the constitutional requirements for an independent NPA. Her interpretation of the Constitution acknowledges the independence of the NPA on the one hand, then takes it away with the other. Moreover, there is a good reason that 'national security' is sometimes called the last refuge of scoundrels. It is such a vague concept that it would potentially give the President or the Minister extraordinary power to intervene in the decisions of the NDPP and may well place the NDPP in the untenable position of always having to worry whether his or her decision may be construed by the politicians as having national security implications on their say-so. Given the fact that Ginwala did not find that Pikoli's actions did indeed hold any threat for national security, the decision by the President to fire Pikoli seems like setting a dangerous precedent as a future President will now be able to pressure the NDPP when he or she embarks on a course of action not favoured by the President by making vague assertions of national security being at stake. It is also worrying that Ginwala expressed concern that Pikoli had not fully appreciated the sensitivities of the 'political environment' in which the NPA needs to operate and his responsibility to manage this environment. An appreciation of the 'political environment' does not seem to sit easily with a duty to exercise one's duties without fear, favour or prejudice.

Ginwala then continues:

> Adv Pikoli needs to always recognise the final responsibility of the Minister and should have proactively made her aware of all matters of a sensitive nature that the NPA became aware of in the course of its functions, and fully and regularly briefed her on the progress of high-profile investigations and prosecutions.

This obligation on the part of the NDPP is not found in the Constitution or the NPA Act and was invented by Ginwala. It stems from her view that the Minister has to exercise final responsibility over the NPA and that this means more than set out in the Act. If an NDPP could be fired for not informing the Minister of something she or he thought was important, the NDPP would be busy all day long writing reports to the Minister. This is not what the Act requires and, I would submit, it could not have been intended to require this as the Act must be read in the context of the Constitution that guarantees the independence of the NPA. Ginwala's interpretation would make the Act unconstitutional. The report does contain rather devastating findings although these findings are not followed to their logical conclusion. Thus, Ginwala analyses the letter signed by the then Minister of Justice a few days before Pikoli was suspended and states that:

> the letter conveys a meaning that Adv Pikoli was to stop any plan to arrest and prosecute the National Commissioner of Police until the Minister was satisfied that there was sufficient information and evidence to do so. The Minister has since on affidavit said that it was not her intention to stop Adv Pikoli from discharging his duties or performing his functions as the NDPP. Assuming this is correct, the conduct of the DG: Justice in drafting the document in the manner it reads was reckless to say the least. The DG: Justice should have been acutely aware of the constitutional protection afforded to the NPA to conduct its work without fear, favour or prejudice. The contents of the letter were tantamount to executive interference with the prosecutorial independence of the NPA, which is recognised as a serious offence in the Act.

So, Ginwala in effect found that there was an illegal and criminal order to Pikoli to stop the prosecution of Selebi. This order was drafted by the DG and signed by the Minister. Yet she also finds that there was no reason to believe that the President suspended Pikoli because of the prosecution of Selebi. What I wonder is: who decided that this letter had to be written? Was the President or his advisers involved? Would Ginwala have been forced to come to a different conclusion if the question was posed differently, namely whether the government wanted to fire Pikoli because he had issued an arrest warrant for Selebi? These questions are not answered in the Report. Could this be because the answers would not have favoured the man who appointed Ginwala and belonged to the same political party of which they are both disciplined members?

SUMMARY

The judiciary is the third, but distinct and most independent, branch of government within the system of separation of powers.

At the pinnacle of the superior courts is the Constitutional Court which now has the jurisdiction not only to hear any constitutional matter, but also any other matter that raises an arguable point of law of general importance which, in the opinion of the Constitutional Court, ought to be considered by it. The Constitutional Court ordinarily acts as a court of appeal, considering constitutional and other matters of legal doctrine on appeal from any of the High Courts or from the Supreme Court of Appeal (SCA). However, when a High Court declares invalid provisions of an Act of Parliament, the provisions of a provincial legislature or an act of the President, the matter automatically goes to the Constitutional Court which is required to confirm the order of invalidity before such an order has any force.

In addition, the Constitutional Court has exclusive jurisdiction to decide:

- on disputes between organs of state in the national or provincial sphere concerning the constitutional status, powers or functions of any of those organs of state
- on the constitutionality of any parliamentary or provincial Bill
- on the constitutionality of Bills referred to it by the NA or provincial legislatures
- on the constitutionality of any amendment to the Constitution
- that Parliament or the President has failed to fulfil a constitutional obligation
- or to certify a provincial constitution.

The SCA is an appeal court that can hear appeals from High Courts on any matter except matters exclusively reserved for the Constitutional Court. The SCA is the final court on matters relating to findings of fact and to the application of facts to law. The High Courts can hear constitutional matters, except those matters exclusively reserved for the Constitutional Court, and often sit as courts of first instance.

The judiciary (and, in South Africa, most pertinently the superior courts,) is tasked with interpreting and enforcing the Constitution and thus as acting as the referee to ensure that members of the other branches of government act in accordance with the Constitution. It is therefore important that special safeguards are put in place to secure its independence. During the apartheid era, the independence of the judiciary was not adequately guaranteed. With the advent of democracy, the Constitution created additional mechanisms to safeguard the independence of the judiciary.

The Judicial Service Commission (JSC), composed of a combination of lawyers, judges and politicians, now plays an important role in the appointment of all superior court judges. When the President appoints the Chief Justice or Deputy Chief Justice and the President and Deputy President of the SCA, this role of the JSC is only advisory. With all other High Court judges, the JSC selects the appointees who are then merely formally appointed by the President. There is much controversy about the criteria for the appointment of judges, but the need for the judiciary to reflect broadly the racial and gender composition of South Africa does play a pivotal role in the consideration of suitable candidates for appointment.

Apart from the appointment of impartial and independent judicial officers, the independence of the judiciary is formally guaranteed by requiring judges to take an oath of office, by safeguarding the security of tenure of judges, by protecting the financial security of judges and by limiting the civil liability of judges. Lower courts and traditional courts are less independent but it is assumed that the superior courts will protect these courts and will ensure that their decisions comply with the requisite impartiality and independence.

The National Prosecuting Authority (NPA) is neither part of government nor of the judiciary but it does play a pivotal role in the operation of the criminal justice system as it is tasked with making decisions on the prosecution of criminal suspects. The NPA has a duty to act without fear, favour or prejudice. This means that it must act independently from the government of the day although it is legally and constitutionally required to report to the Minister of Justice on its activities and decisions. The NPA is headed by the National Director of Public Prosecutions (NDPP) whose independence is safeguarded by the NPA Act. The President appoints the NDPP but the appointee must comply with the objective criteria set out in the NPA Act.

Chapter 7

Separation of powers and Chapter 9 institutions

7.1 Introduction

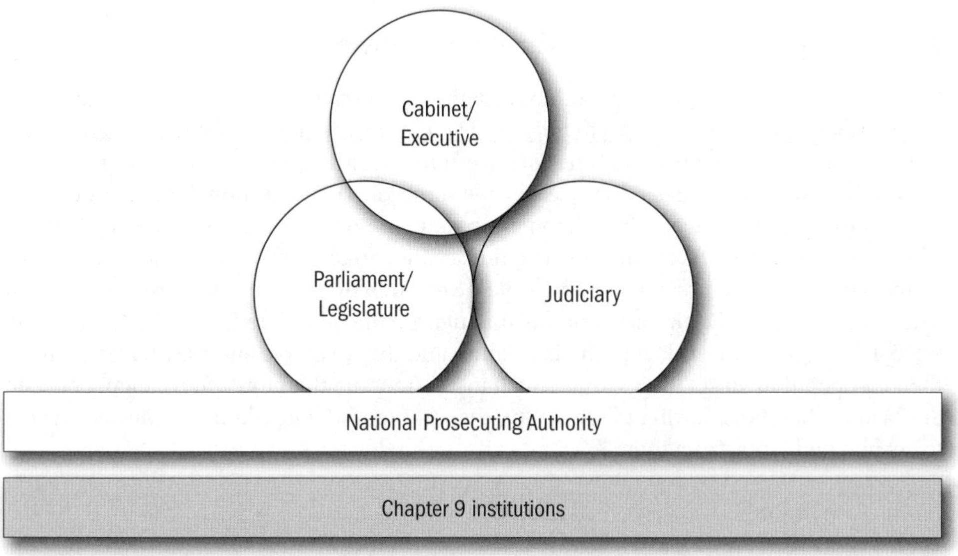

Figure 7.1 *Separation of powers and Chapter 9 institutions*

Chapter 9 of the Constitution establishes certain institutions that are designed to support and strengthen constitutional democracy. These institutions are:[1]

- the Public Protector
- the South African Human Rights Commission

1 S 181(1) of the Constitution.

- the Commission for the Promotion and Protection of the Rights of Cultural, Religious and Linguistic Communities
- the Commission for Gender Equality
- the Auditor-General
- the Electoral Commission.

Chapter 9 institutions 'share two roles: that of checking government (or, in the language of the Constitution, of contributing to accountable government or 'monitoring' government), and that of contributing to the transformation of South Africa into a society in which social justice prevails'.[2] These institutions are independent non-judicial institutions and do not play the same role as the judiciary in enforcing the Constitution. It is therefore not clear how these institutions fit into the traditional separation of powers model: while they are independent from the other branches of government,[3] they are also accountable to the National Assembly (NA), one of the other branches of government.[4] The institutions can make findings and recommendations but, unlike the judiciary, they do not have the power to review and set aside legislation or the actions of the executive. However, they are 'important tools to monitor the state's realisation of individuals' rights in terms of its constitutional obligations'.[5]

Regardless of this uncertain position in the separation of powers architecture, the role of these institutions is essential in the democracy emerging from a history of discrimination, oppression and lack of accountability as they assist the various organs of state to adhere to the values and principles of the new constitutional dispensation.[6] To fulfil this task, it is important that these institutions should enjoy a degree of independence.

7.2 Independence of Chapter 9 institutions

Institutions set up to safeguard and promote democracy (and the rights required to safeguard that democracy) can only do their work if they enjoy a certain level of independence from the legislative and executive branches of government.[7] However, these institutions are not judicial in nature and usually do not enjoy the same kind of institutional independence as that enjoyed by the judiciary in a democratic state. In South Africa – as elsewhere – these institutions therefore find themselves in a precarious situation. On the one hand, they have to act as watchdogs to prevent the abuse of power, often by state entities,[8] and are required to act in a scrupulously fair and impartial manner. On the other hand, these institutions are often also required to work with the legislature and the executive and may have to rely on their co-operation 'to get things done'. Such institutions are therefore often caught between Scylla and Charybdis, having to please the executive and the legislature while also having to act independently from them.[9]

---

2 Murray, C (2006) The Human Rights Commission et al: What is the role of South Africa's Chapter 9 institutions? *Potchefstroom Electronic Law Journal* 9(2):122–47 at 125.

3 S 181(2) of the Constitution.

4 S 181(5) of the Constitution.

5 See Holness, D and Vrancken, P 'Non-judicial enforcement of human rights' in Govindjee, A and Vrancken, P (eds) (2009) *Introduction to Human Rights Law* 240.

6 See Ntlama, N (2005) Unlocking the future: Monitoring court orders in respect of socio-economic rights *Tydskrif vir Hedendaags Romeins-Hollandse Reg* 68(1):81–9 at 83.

7 See generally De Vos, P 'Balancing independence and accountability: The role of Chapter 9 institutions in South Africa's constitutional democracy' in Chirwa, DM and Nijzink, L (eds) (2012) *Accountable Government in Africa: Perspectives from Public Law and Political Studies* 160–77.

8 The Human Rights Commission and the Public Protector are two such institutions.

9 De Vos (2009) 163.

This tension is reflected in the constitutional provisions regulating these institutions. The Constitution clearly guarantees the independence of these institutions and proclaims that they are independent and 'subject only to the Constitution and the law, and they must be impartial and must exercise their powers and perform their functions without fear, favour or prejudice'.[10] Moreover, section 181(3) of the Constitution requires other organs of state to 'assist and protect these institutions' to ensure their 'independence, impartiality, dignity and effectiveness'. Section 181(4) furthermore states that '[n]o person or organ of state may interfere with the functioning of these institutions'.[11] At the same time, section 181(5) of the Constitution states that these 'institutions are accountable to the National Assembly, and must report on their activities and the performance of their functions to the Assembly at least once a year'. It is therefore far from clear how the independence of these organisations can be squared with their responsibility to be accountable to the legislature.

In the two Constitutional Court judgments dealing directly with Chapter 9 institutions,[12] and another decision dealing with the concept of independence in more general terms,[13] the Constitutional Court provided some helpful guidelines for looking at the notion of independence of these institutions. We contend that an analysis of these judgments provides insight into the correct balance to be struck between the need for such institutions to account to the legislature on the one hand while safeguarding their independence on the other.

Because Chapter 9 institutions are required to account to the NA, this is sometimes wrongly taken to mean that they are subservient to the NA. However, if independence means anything, it means that the NA cannot interfere in the day-to-day running of the Chapter 9 institutions. This occurs where these institutions are viewed as part of the government instead of as independent institutions with their unique place in the separation of powers architecture set up by the Constitution.

The independence of institutions supporting and safeguarding democracy is often negatively affected by the fact that they are perceived and function in practice as institutions that form part of the government. Where, for example, the Human Rights Commission or the Electoral Commission is seen as being part of the government, this will place pressure on such institutions to co-operate with the government of the day and to align themselves with the interests of the government. This, in turn, means that it would become more difficult for such institutions to act without fear, favour or prejudice to hold the government accountable. Institutions called on to make findings against the government or to act against its interest will only be able to do so if they are really capable of acting impartially and independently. This becomes difficult where such institutions are seen as part of the very institution **from which** they have to be independent.

In principle, if not always in practice, Chapter 9 institutions in South Africa do enjoy constitutionally and legally protected independence from the government. The Constitutional

10 S 181(2).

11 The Constitution also guarantees the independence of other institutions such as the Public Service Commission (s 196(2)–(3)); the Broadcasting Authority (s 192) and the Financial and Fiscal Commission (s 220(2)). There is no explicit provision for the independence of the Pan South African Language Board which is established in s 6 of the Constitution. Furthermore, legislation that creates these institution also provides for further protection of the independence of these institutions. Thus, s 9(1)(*b*) of the Public Protector Act 23 of 1994 prohibits any person from insulting the Public Protector or the Deputy Public Protector and from doing anything in connection with an investigation 'which, if the said investigation had been proceeding in a court of law, would have constituted contempt of court'.

12 *Independent Electoral Commission v Langeberg Municipality* (CCT 49/00) [2001] ZACC 23; 2001 (3) SA 925 (CC); 2001 (9) BCLR 883 (CC) (7 June 2001) and *New National Party v Government of the Republic of South Africa and Others* (CCT9/99) [1999] ZACC 5; 1999 (3) SA 191; 1999 (5) BCLR 489 (13 April 1999).

13 *S and Others v Van Rooyen and Others (General Council of the Bar of South Africa Intervening)* (CCT21/01) [2002] ZACC 8; 2002 (5) SA 246; 2002 (8) BCLR 810 (11 June 2002).

Court pointed out in *Independent Electoral Commission v Langeberg Municipality*[14] that although a Chapter 9 institution such as the Electoral Commission is an organ of state as defined in section 239 of the Constitution,[15] these institutions cannot be said to be a department or an administration in the national sphere of government over which Cabinet exercises authority. These institutions are state institutions and are not part of the government. Independence of the institution refers to independence **from** the government. According to the Court, these institutions cannot be independent from the national government, yet be part of it.[16] The Court thus affirmed the institutional independence of these institutions. The logic of this view is that Chapter 9 institutions are **not** subject to the co-operative government provisions set out in Chapter 3 of the Constitution. These institutions perform their functions in terms of national legislation, but 'are not subject to national executive control'.[17] There is a need for these institutions to '**manifestly be seen to be outside government**'.[18]

The *Langeberg* case suggests that a clear and sharp distinction must be drawn between these institutions and the executive authority. Any action by the executive that would create an impression that the institution is not manifestly outside government would be constitutionally unacceptable. There is little room for manoeuvre here. More leeway exists regarding the relationship between Parliament and the Chapter 9 institutions because these institutions are accountable to the NA. As we shall see below, in practice, these institutions have not always operated at sufficient arms-length from either the executive or Parliament. This may have affected the effectiveness of these institutions in fulfilling their mandates.

Another aspect of independence can be found in section 181(3) of the Constitution. This section states that other organs of state, through legislative and other measures, must assist and protect these institutions to ensure their **independence, impartiality, dignity and effectiveness**. Section 181(4) states that no person or organ of state **may interfere** with the functioning of these institutions.

From these provisions we may draw a few conclusions. First, independence is not synonymous with impartiality. Just because a body is able to exercise its duties impartially does not mean that its independence has been safeguarded. Independence is, in essence, a more encompassing concept than impartiality. Second, other organs of state have a constitutional duty to ensure the dignity of the Chapter 9 institutions. In various judgments dealing with dignity in other contexts, the Constitutional Court has argued that dignity will be impaired when an action sends a signal that the institution is not worthy of respect.[19] Action by the legislature or executive that undermines respect for Chapter 9 institutions would thus

---

14 (CCT 49/00) [2001] ZACC 23; 2001 (3) SA 925 (CC); 2001 (9) BCLR 883 (CC) (7 June 2001).

15 S 239(2) defines an organ of state as follows:

(*a*) **any department of state or administration in the national, provincial or local sphere of government; or**

any other functionary or institution–

(*b*) **exercising a power or performing a function in terms of the Constitution or a provincial constitution; or exercising a public power or performing a public function in terms of any legislation, but does not include a court or a judicial officer.**

16 *Langeberg Municipality* paras 28–9.

17 *Langeberg Municipality* para 31. See also Parliament of the Republic of South Africa (2007) Report of the Ad Hoc Committee on the Review of Chapter 9 and Associated Institutions, A report to the National Assembly of the Parliament of South Africa, Cape Town, South Africa, 9 available at http://www.parliament.gov.za/content/chapter_9_report.pdf.

18 *Langeberg Municipality* para 31.

19 See generally *Dawood and Another v Minister of Home Affairs and Others; Shalabi and Another v Minister of Home Affairs and Others; Thomas and Another v Minister of Home Affairs and Others* (CCT35/99) [2000] ZACC 8; 2000 (3) SA 936; 2000 (8) BCLR 837 (7 June 2000).

be in contravention of the provisions mentioned above. This does not mean institutions should not and cannot be criticised and subjected to questioning, but such questioning should be done with due regard for the independence of these institutions. Lastly, organs of state have a duty to ensure the effectiveness of these institutions, which relates to accountability set out below.

The Constitutional Court affirmed the basic principle that Chapter 9 institutions must have some degree of financial independence to function independently and to be able to exercise their duties without fear, favour or prejudice. At the same time, the Constitutional Court made it clear that this does not mean that these institutions can set their own budgets. What is required is for Parliament to provide a reasonable amount of money that would enable the institutions to fulfil their constitutional and legal mandates. In discussing the financial independence of the Electoral Commission, the Constitutional Court explained in *New National Party v Government of the Republic of South Africa and Others*:

> **This implies the ability to have access to funds reasonably required to enable the Commission to discharge the functions it is obliged to perform under the Constitution and the Electoral Commission Act. This does not mean that it can set its own budget. Parliament does that. What it does mean, however, is that Parliament must consider what is reasonably required by the Commission and deal with requests for funding rationally, in the light of other national interests. It is for Parliament, and not the executive arm of government, to provide for funding reasonably sufficient to enable the Commission to carry out its constitutional mandate. The Commission must accordingly be afforded an adequate opportunity to defend its budgetary requirements before Parliament or its relevant committees.**[20]

It is important to note that this task is clearly one to be exercised by Parliament. The Court accepted that there inevitably would be a tension between the government/Parliament on the one side and the independent institution on the other about the reasonableness of the amount of money to be given to ensure the effective fulfilment of its constitutional mandate. It is incumbent on the parties to make every effort to resolve that tension and to reach an agreement by negotiation and good faith. This, according to the Constitutional Court, would no doubt entail considerable meaningful discussion, exchange of relevant information, a genuine attempt to understand the respective needs and constraints, and the mutual desire to reach a reasonable conclusion.[21] However, when Parliament engages in this process, it must deal with requests rationally in the light of other national interests. This means the institutions must be afforded an adequate opportunity to defend their budgetary requirements before Parliament or its relevant committees. Thus '[n]o member of the executive or the administration should have the power to stop transfers of money to any independent constitutional body without the existence of appropriate safeguards for the independence of that institution'.[22]

In addition, in *New National Party*, the Constitutional Court stated that the independent bodies supporting democracy require more than financial independence. For these institutions to operate independently and for them to fulfil their respective tasks without fear, favour or prejudice, the Constitutional Court said that the administrative independence of these institutions should be safeguarded.[23] This implies that these institutions must have

20 (CCT9/99) [1999] ZACC 5; 1999 (3) SA 191; 1999 (5) BCLR 489 (13 April 1999) para 98. See also *Langeberg* para 29.

21 *New National Party* para 97.

22 *New National Party* para 96.

23 *New National Party* para 99.

control over those matters directly connected with their functions under the Constitution and the relevant legislation. No matter what arrangements Parliament or the executive may make, it is important that the institutions must retain the ability to maintain operational control over their core business. What is required is that any arrangements must not interfere with the constitutional mandate of the bodies to perform their duties impartially. In *New National Party*, the Constitutional Court made it clear that section 181(3) of the Constitution requires the executive to engage with the bodies in a manner that would ensure that the efficient functioning of the Commission is not hampered.[24]

The Constitutional Court further indicated that a failure on the part of the executive to comply with such obligations 'may seriously impair the functioning and effectiveness of those State institutions supporting constitutional democracy and cannot be condoned'.[25] This means that Parliament or the executive cannot interfere directly in the day-to-day running of these institutions. They also cannot instruct the institutions on a micro level regarding their programmes and implementation thereof, and cannot get directly involved in the employment or management of staff. At the same time, Parliament and the executive have a duty to support these institutions. If institutional problems are of such magnitude or seriousness that they make it difficult or impossible for an institution to fulfil its constitutional and legislative tasks, Parliament can, and indeed must, assist such an institution to resolve these problems. Such assistance must not, however, have the effect of removing control over matters directly connected with an institution's functions and must not hamper the efficient functioning of an institution. In short, while Parliament and the executive can engage with these institutions to assist them to improve their performance, they cannot do so in a way that would remove final control over administration from the institutions or that results in interference in the efficient functioning of these institutions.

Thus, the Constitutional Court ruled that the Department of Home Affairs cannot tell the Electoral Commission how to conduct registration, whom to employ, and so on.[26] However, if the Commission asks the government to provide personnel to assist in the registration process, government must provide such assistance if it is able to do so. If not, the Commission must be provided with adequate funds to enable it to do what is necessary. As a general rule, there has been no direct interference by the executive with the day-to-day running of Chapter 9 institutions. Some may argue that this has not been necessary because the appointments process has been skewed in such a way as to ensure that those appointed to many of the Chapter 9 institutions would not be overtly critical of the executive or the legislature. While it is impossible to state categorically that this is indeed the case, it is important to investigate the appointments procedure of Chapter 9 bodies and it is to this which we now turn.

---

24 *New National Party* para 99:

> **The second factor, administrative independence, implies that there will be control over those matters directly connected with the functions which the Commission has to perform under the Constitution and the Act. The executive must provide the assistance that the Commission requires to ensure [its] independence, impartiality, dignity and effectiveness. The department cannot tell the Commission how to conduct registration, whom to employ, and so on; but if the Commission asks the government for assistance to provide personnel to take part in the registration process, government must provide such assistance if it is able to do so. If not, the Commission must be put in funds to enable it to do what is necessary.**

25 *New National Party* para 95.

26 *New National Party* para 99.

PAUSE FOR REFLECTION

The appointments procedure of Chapter 9 bodies

The independence of the various Chapter 9 bodies is further operationalised in legislation. If we take the Electoral Commission as an example, section 3 of the Electoral Commission Act[27] confirms that the Electoral Commission 'is independent and subject only to the Constitution and the law' and 'shall be impartial and shall exercise its powers and perform its functions without fear, favour or prejudice'.

Section 6 of the Electoral Commission Act helps to entrench the independence of the Commission by providing for a complicated appointments process. This section provides that the Commission shall consist of five members, one of whom shall be a judge, appointed by the President. However, the President has no discretion in the appointment. This is because section 6(2) also provides that no person can be appointed as a member of the Commission unless he or she:

- is a South African citizen
- does not at that stage have a high party-political profile
- has been recommended by the NA by a resolution by a majority of its members
- has been nominated by a committee of the NA from a list of recommended candidates submitted to it by an independent panel. This committee must consist of members of all of the parties represented in the NA in proportion to the number of seats they hold.

The independent panel is made up of the Chief Justice as chairperson, a representative of the Human Rights Commission, a representative of the Commission on Gender Equality and the Public Protector. It must submit a list of no fewer than eight recommended candidates to the committee of the NA and it must act in a transparent and open manner.[28]

Section 7(3) of the Electoral Commission Act entrenches the institutional independence of the Commission by providing some security of tenure for members of the Commission who serve for a period of seven years. This tenure of Commissioners is protected in that the section states that a commissioner may only be removed from office by the President:

- on the grounds of misconduct, incapacity or incompetence
- after a finding to that effect by a committee of the NA
- on the recommendation of the Electoral Court
- the adoption by a majority of the members of the NA of a resolution calling for that commissioner's removal from office.

This means that the process to remove a commissioner cannot be initiated by any politician. Only the Electoral Court can initiate the process of the removal of a Commissioner and only after the Electoral Court has made a finding as to the misconduct, incapacity or incompetence of a Commissioner and has referred the matter to the NA. It is only at this point that politicians get involved in the process.

27 Act 51 of 1996.
28 S 6(3)-(5) of the Electoral Commission Act.

The Public Protector and the Auditor-General are of great significance for the monitoring of the exercise of state authority. They play a fundamental role in the monitoring, investigation and reporting on government conduct.

7.3 The Public Protector

The Public Protector has the power to investigate any conduct of the government or administration that is alleged or suspected to be improper or to result in any impropriety or prejudice. It also has the power to report on that conduct and to take appropriate remedial action.[29] It is an independent and impartial institution.[30] It must report to the NA at least once a year.[31] This means that the Public Protector does not only report on public maladministration but also, indirectly, protects and enforces constitutional obligations as the government is required to act on the recommendations made although these recommendations are not binding. Then Chief Justice Sandile Ngcobo emphasised the importance of the Public Protector as he correctly pointed out that the role of the institution is critical particularly in countries emerging from the atrocities of the past because: 'good governance and the equitable distribution of resources is the only way for our people to enjoy the [benefits that are associated with the attainment of the democracy in 1994]'.[32]

The report released by the Public Protector on 'an investigation into complaints and allegations of maladministration, improper and unlawful conduct by the Department of Public Works and the South African Police Service relating to the leasing of office accommodation in Pretoria' attests to the significant role of the institution in curbing the abuse of state authority.[33] Without pronouncing on the merits of the investigation, the report fingered the National Commissioner of Police, Bheki Cele, for having abused his authority and failed to ensure that the signing of the lease was done in accordance with the requirements of the Constitution and other related legislation.[34]

7.4 The Auditor-General

The Auditor-General must audit and report on the accounts, financial statements and financial management of state departments and administrations.[35] He or she must submit audit reports to any legislature, such as Parliament or the provincial legislatures, which has a direct interest in the audit.[36] Like the Public Protector, the Auditor-General is an independent and impartial institution.[37] Conradie emphasises, 'the Auditor-General plays a crucial role in the public sector where the greatest number of stakeholders, the whole population in effect, is dependent on the Auditor to vigorously audit and report on accountability information as well as other functions of independence'.[38] It is, therefore,

29 S 182(1) of the Constitution.
30 S 182(2) of the Constitution.
31 S 182(5) of the Constitution.
32 See the report by Segalwe, O (2011, 16 March) Chief Justice Ngcobo highlights the importance of the Public Protector available at http://www.pprotect.org.
33 See Report No 33 (2010/2011) Against the rules available at http://www.pprotect.org.
34 Report No 33 (2010/2011) 85.
35 S 188(1) of the Constitution.
36 S 188(3) of the Constitution.
37 S 181(2) of the Constitution.
38 Conradie, J (2011, April) The evolution of accounting standards in the public sector, Unpublished paper available at http://www.accountancysa.org.za.

deduced from the powers vested in the Auditor-General that his or her primary purpose is to ensure the credibility of the flow of information in the accountability process.

SUMMARY

The Constitution creates a set of Chapter 9 institutions, including the Human Rights Commission, the Public Protector, the Auditor-General and the Electoral Commission, to promote and safeguard democracy. These institutions are not easily slotted into the traditional separation of powers model. While the institutions are independent and have their independence constitutionally guaranteed and further enhanced in legislation, they are also constitutionally required to report on their activities and the performance of their functions to the NA at least once a year and to account to the NA.

The Constitutional Court has nevertheless confirmed that these institutions are not part of government and enjoy both institutional and administrative independence from government. Although the institutions are independent, they are not in the same position as the judiciary as they do not usually make binding findings that can be enforced in a similar manner to that of the courts. They usually help to hold the government and officials accountable and make recommendations about remedial action.

Chapter 8

Multilevel government in South Africa

8.1 The division of powers between spheres of government: general principles

8.1.1 Introduction

An important characteristic of the Constitution is that it not only divides power vertically between the legislative, executive and judicial branches of government in terms of the separation of powers doctrine. It also divides power horizontally between the national, provincial and local spheres of government, thus establishing a quasi-federal system of government. Section 40(1) of the Constitution provides in this respect that '[i]n the Republic, government is constituted as national, provincial and local spheres of government which are distinctive, interdependent and interrelated'. In this chapter we deal with this horizontal division of power. We identify the exact powers allocated to each sphere of government, address the relationship between the different spheres of government and explore the constitutional management of conflicts between the various spheres of government.

It is important to understand that in a federal or quasi-federal system, the division of power between different spheres of government may be based either on a divided model of federalism or an integrated model of federalism.

In a **divided model of federalism**, the subject matters in respect of which policies and laws may be made are strictly divided between the different levels or spheres of government. Each level or sphere, therefore, has its own exclusive powers and there are very few, if any, concurrent or shared powers. In this model, the policies and laws made by each level or sphere will also be implemented and administered by their own separate civil services and departments of state. Australia, Canada and the United States are examples of a divided model of federalism.[1]

In an **integrated model of federalism**, some subject matters are allocated exclusively to one level or sphere of government, but most are concurrent or shared. The subject matters in respect of which policies and laws may be made, therefore, are not strictly divided between the different levels or spheres of government. In this model, the framework policies and laws made by the central level or sphere of government may be complemented by provincial or local policies and laws and must be implemented and administered by the provincial or local spheres of government. Germany and South Africa are examples of an integrated model of federalism.[2]

When we say that South Africa broadly adheres to an integrated model of federalism, we are not saying that South Africa is a fully fledged federal state. Throughout this chapter we will raise questions about the nature of the relationship between the three spheres of government. We contend that while the South African system displays several characteristics of a federal system, it could probably best be described as a **quasi-federal system**. In a quasi-federal system, the national government retains more power and influence over law making and policy formulation than is usually the case in a fully fledged federal system.

1 Huglin, TO and Fenna, A (2006) *Comparative Federalism: A Systematic Inquiry* 61.
2 Huglin and Fenna (2006) 61.

8.1.2 Historical background

Although we contend that South Africa could probably best be described as a quasi-federal state, it is important to note that the Constitution itself studiously avoids describing the system of governance in South Africa as federal or quasi-federal.[3] This is partly because there was profound antipathy towards the notion of a federal state among the African National Congress (ANC) and other liberation organisations and this manifested in positions assumed during the negotiations process.

The antipathy displayed by the ANC towards the notion of a federal state may be traced back, at least in part, to the 'grand design' of the apartheid government. This involved the fragmentation of the country into so-called 'self-governing' and later 'independent' entities based on ethnic, group or tribal affiliations. The ultimate goal of grand apartheid, therefore, was that black South Africans would be stripped of their South African citizenship and be afforded the citizenship of one of these 'independent' entities in which they would exercise their civil and political rights.[4]

The ANC and its allies were concerned that a federal system would result in the resurrection of the despised homeland system in a different guise. There were also concerns that a rigid division of powers between the national sphere of government and the various provincial spheres would inhibit and frustrate the developmental and egalitarian objectives of the new state seeking to the improve the quality of life of all.

During the process of negotiations, however, the ANC leadership started seeing the benefit and advantages of strong regional government for the delivery of services and the political empowerment of the citizens. It seems that exposure to models of federalism such as the German Constitution assisted in convincing the liberation organisations that effective regional government could be combined with strong central leadership and this was the model that was eventually adopted.[5]

Some of the political groups such as the predominantly Zulu party, the Inkatha Freedom Party (IFP), favoured a strong federal arrangement and advocated an asymmetrical arrangement with maximum devolution of original power to the Kwazulu-Natal (KZN) region. It was the inability to reach consensus on this and other issues that caused them to boycott the constitutional drafting process for the interim Constitution.[6]

---

3 Prior to 1994, South Africa had a unitary system of government. While provincial and local spheres of government existed, they were subservient to and subject to the control of a strong central government where all meaningful decisions were made. The constitutional system prior to 1994 was thus a unified one with little divergence in laws between the various provinces.

4 The National States Citizenship Act 26 of 1970 provided that every black person would become a citizen of the tribal entity to which he or she had a tribal or cultural affiliation and would simultaneously cease to be a citizen of South Africa. The fact that they did not live in that entity nor desired the new citizenship was irrelevant. The apartheid government described this as a process of internal decolonisation. In reality, it was nothing other than denationalisation. The homelands were impoverished parcels of land cobbled together to create 'independent states'. They were totally dependent on the South African state for their financial survival and were provided with monthly grants. Towards the end of the 1980s, most of the independent homelands had collapsed into military dictatorships and were dysfunctional. The apartheid grand design had unravelled even before formal negotiations began. See also ch 1.

5 Haysom, N 'Federal features of the final Constitution' in Andrews, P and Ellmann, S (eds) (2001) *The Post-Apartheid Constitutions: Perspectives on South Africa's Basic Law* 504.

6 See Woolman, S and Swanepoel, J 'Constitutional history' in Woolman, S and Bishop, M (eds) (2013) *Constitutional Law of South Africa* 2nd ed rev service 5 2.37. For a more detailed discussion of the approach adopted by the different political parties during the process of negotiations, see Spitz, R and Chaskalson, M (2000) *The Politics of Transition: A Hidden History of South Africa's Negotiated Settlement* 122.

PAUSE FOR REFLECTION

Should the number of provinces be reduced?

South Africa currently has a national government, nine provinces, six metropolitan councils together with a number of district and local municipalities. At the time of the transition, the provincial system allowed parties which had strong regional support but limited national support to participate meaningfully in the political process. This contributed to the stabilisation of the democratic order.

The IFP boycotted the initial constitutional drafting process in the run-up to the 1994 elections, but eventually participated in the elections and was the dominant party in the KZN provincial legislature for about 10 years. This contributed to the ending of the civil strife in the province as the IFP, despite their limited national support, played an important role in the provincial legislature. In this sense, the system accommodated diverse political aspirations.

There is now some thinking, particularly within the ANC, that we should reduce the number of provinces and emphasise strong national and local governments.[7] Part of the argument is that the costs do not justify the benefits derived from having nine provincial governments. In addition, there are concerns about whether all the regions possess the capacity to function effectively and to implement wide-ranging policies devised by the national sphere of government. On the other hand, the argument is that provincial government has the potential to secure a closer link between voters and their democratically elected representatives. If all decisions are taken in Cape Town or Pretoria, the quality of democracy would suffer. However, the question remains: should the number of provinces be reduced, say, from nine to five? If this is reduced, will it enhance the efficiency and democratic accountability of government?

8.1.3 The constitutional principles

As we saw in chapter 2, the transition to democracy in South Africa took place in two stages. An important aspect of this two-stage process was that the final Constitution had to be consistent with 34 Constitutional Principles agreed to by the various parties at the multiparty negotiating process and enshrined in Schedule 4 of the interim Constitution. A significant number of these principles dealt with the structure of government. They provided in this respect that:

- government shall be structured at national, provincial and local levels[8]
- the powers and functions of the various spheres had to be defined in the final Constitution and that they could not be substantially less or substantially inferior to those provided for in the interim Constitution[9]
- the functions of the national and provincial levels of government had to include exclusive and concurrent powers[10]
- the allocation of a competence to either the national or provincial spheres had to be in accordance with listed criteria[11]

7 African National Congress 53rd National Conference Resolutions 4. Legislature and Governance 4.2.1 28 available at http://www.anc.org.za/docs/res/2013/resolutions53r.pdf.

8 Principle XVI of Schedule 4 of the interim Constitution.

9 Principle XVIII.

10 Principle XIX.

11 Principle XXI.

- the national sphere was precluded from exercising its powers so as to encroach on the geographical, functional and institutional integrity of the provinces[12]
- disputes concerning legislative powers allocated by the Constitution concurrently to the national and provincial spheres had to be resolved by a court of law.[13]

A framework dealing with powers, function and structures of local government also had to be set out in the Constitution.[14] In addition, every sphere of government had to be guaranteed an equitable share of revenue collected nationally to ensure that provinces and local government were able to provide basic services and execute the functions allocated to them.[15]

In *Certification of the Constitution of the Republic of South Africa, 1996*, the Constitutional Court held that the question of whether the powers and functions allocated to the provinces were substantially less or substantially inferior to those provided for in the interim Constitution was the most difficult question it had to deal with.[16] After evaluating the allocation of the powers to various spheres of government and assessing the breadth of the override clause that allows for national legislation to prevail over provincial legislation in certain instances, the Court concluded that the diminution in provincial power was substantial and that this was inconsistent with Constitutional Principle XVIII.[17] This required the drafters to reorder the arrangements, afford more powers to the provinces and restrict the scope of the override clause before it met the approval of the Court. In *Certification of the Amended Text of the Constitution of The Republic Of South Africa, 1996*, the Constitutional Court found that the revised override clause (section 146) was more stringently drafted and removed any presumption in favour of national legislation.[18] This, together with the adjustment of the allocation of powers to the provinces, satisfied the Court that the amended text complied with Constitutional Principle XVIII.

We discuss the exact allocation of powers to the various spheres of government and the override clauses applying when there is a conflict between the spheres of government in detail below.

8.1.4 The principles of co-operative government

As we noted in the introduction to this chapter, an important characteristic of the Constitution is that it not only divides power vertically between the legislative, executive and judicial branches of government, but also horizontally between the national, provincial and local spheres of government and that this horizontal division of power follows an integrated model.[19]

An important consequence of the integrated model adopted by the drafters of the Constitution is that mechanisms must be put in place to regulate the overlap of power between the various spheres of government. The principle of co-operative government plays an important role in regulating the overlap of power between the various spheres of government.

12 Principle XXII.
13 Principle XXIII.
14 Principle XXIV.
15 Principle XXVI.
16 (CCT 23/96) [1996] ZACC 26; 1996 (4) SA 744 (CC); 1996 (10) BCLR 1253 (CC) (6 September 1996) para 472.
17 *First Certification* paras 480–1.
18 (CCT37/96) [1996] ZACC 24; 1997 (1) BCLR 1; 1997 (2) SA 97 (4 December 1996) paras 109–10.
19 It has been argued that the description of the various facets as spheres as opposed to levels was meant to convey the notion of parity of esteem and responsibility between the different spheres. See Woolman, S and Roux, T 'Co-operative government and intergovernmental relations' in Woolman and Bishop (2013) 14.1ff.

To understand fully this principle of co-operative government, it is necessary to set out the basic structure according to which power is divided beween the three spheres of government. It is to this basic structure that we now turn.

First, the nine provincial governments share the power to make laws on a wide range of important matters with the national government. Schedule 4 of the Constitution sets out these shared or concurrent matters that include important matters such as education, the environment, health, housing and policing.[20]

Second, in so far as the concurrent powers of the national and provincial governments are concerned, the national and provincial governments have equal law-making powers. If the laws made by the national and provincial governments conflict with each other, the national law will override the provincial law, but only if the national law satisfies the criteria set out in section 146 of the Constitution.[21]

Third, apart from their concurrent powers, provincial governments also have the exclusive power to make laws on the matters set out in Schedule 5 of the Constitution. These exclusive powers deal with relatively unimportant matters such as abattoirs, ambulance services and libraries other than national libraries. Despite the fact that these Schedule 5 powers have been exclusively reserved for provinces, section 44(2) of the Constitution provides that the national government may intervene and pass a law on a Schedule 5 matter if it is necessary to achieve the objectives set out in section 44(2) itself.

Fourth, local government has been given the authority to make by-laws for the effective administration of the matters they have the power to administer. These local government matters are set out in Part B of Schedule 4 and Part B of Schedule 5. By-laws which conflict with national or provincial laws are invalid.[22]

Fifth, the laws that are made by the national government and that fall into the broad areas of concurrent competence must be implemented and administered by provincial and local governments. The primary role of provincial and local governments, therefore, is the implementation and administration of national laws.[23]

Last, the national government has the plenary power to pass laws and administer laws on any other topic or subject matter not mentioned in either Schedule 4 or 5. This means that the powers of provinces are explicitly restricted to those functional areas set out in either Schedule 4 or 5, while the powers of the national government are not restricted and can encompass any matter not mentioned in Schedule 4 or 5.

PAUSE FOR REFLECTION

When the principles of co-operative government become pivotal

This system that allocates important service delivery powers to both the national sphere and the provincial spheres of government can create governance challenges. For example, the national government department is required to oversee the basic education system and to ensure the smooth running of schooling in the country. However, each of the nine provincial departments of education has to implement the broad policy objectives set out by the national department and the national South African Schools Act.[24] But what happens if a provincial department of education fails

20 Freedman, DW 'Constitutional law: Structures of government' in Joubert, WA (ed) (2012) *Law of South Africa* 2nd ed Vol 5 Part 4 para 57.

21 Freedman (2012) para 57.

22 Freedman (2012) para 57.

23 Freedman (2012) para 57.

24 Act 84 of 1996.

to implement these broad policy objectives? What can a national Minister of Education do if a provincial education department fails to deliver textbooks to schools on time or when it fails to spend its capital budget to eradicate mud schools and pit latrines which still exist in many schools in South Africa?

As we shall see, in extreme cases, the national government can take over the running of a provincial department if it fails to fulfil its constitutional and legal obligations.[25] But short of this, it is not clear how much power the national Minister and his or her department will have to ensure that the money allocated for basic education to each province is spent effectively and in accordance with the broad policy directives set out by the national department. It is for this reason that the principles of co-operative government set out in Chapter 3 of the Constitution become pivotal as they require the national government department and the provincial government departments to meet regularly and to co-operate with one another. Even when different political parties govern nationally and in some of the provinces, these governments at national and provincial level are required by these provisions to co-operate with one another to ensure the effective implementation of national policies.

Given the overlap between the legislative and executive authority of the national, provincial and local spheres of government, the Constitution makes provision for a system of intergovernmental co-ordination to manage any potential conflict between the various spheres exercising concurrent competences. This forms the heart of the system of co-operative government. The most important rules governing this system are set out in Chapter 3 of the Constitution. Chapter 3 of the Constitution entrenches the notion of co-operative government which recognises the distinctiveness, interdependence and interrelatedness of the national, provincial and local spheres of government.[26]

All spheres of government – national, provincial and local – are required to observe and adhere to the principles of co-operative government set out in Chapter 3 of the Constitution.[27] Particularly important in this context are the principles set out in section 41. This section provides, *inter alia*, that '[a]ll spheres of government and all organs of state within each sphere' must:

- respect the constitutional status, institutions, powers and functions of government in the other spheres[28]
- not assume any power or function except those conferred on them in terms of the Constitution[29]
- exercise their powers and perform their functions in a manner that does not encroach on the geographical, functional or institutional integrity of government in another sphere[30]
- co-operate with each other in mutual trust and good faith.[31]

25 S 100 of the Constitution. See *Centre for Child Law and Others v Minister of Basic Education and Others* (1749/2012) [2012] ZAECGHC 60; [2012] 4 All SA 35 (ECG); 2013 (3) SA 183 (ECG) (3 July 2012).

26 S 40(1).

27 S 40(2).

28 S 41(1)(*e*) of the Constitution.

29 S 41(1)(*f*) of the Constitution.

30 S 41(1)(*g*) of the Constitution.

31 S 41(1)(*h*) of the Constitution.

In addition, Chapter 3 of the Constitution also provides that an organ of state involved in an intergovernmental dispute must make every reasonable effort to settle the dispute by means of mechanisms and procedures provided for that purpose, and must exhaust all remedies before approaching a court of law to settle the dispute.[32] There has been some confusion about which bodies are bound by these provisions. Do they apply only to those organs of state that exercise legislative and executive power in the national, provincial and local spheres of government or do they also apply to those organs of state that are supposed to be independent such as the Electoral Commission, the National Prosecuting Authority (NPA) and the South African Human Rights Commission (SAHRC)?

After some ambivalence, there is now relative certainty as to the bodies bound by Chapter 3. In *Independent Electoral Commission v Langeberg Municipality*,[33] the Constitutional Court held that the Independent Electoral Commission (IEC) is an organ of state as defined in section 239 of the Constitution. However, it is not part of government as it is not an organ of state in the national sphere of government. Chapter 9 entrenches the independence of the institutions identified in this Chapter and hence these institutions cannot simultaneously be independent of and yet part of government.[34] Thus, a dispute between a Chapter 9 institution and an organ of government cannot be regarded as an intergovernmental dispute requiring compliance with Chapter 3. The Court stated that while it is preferable for organs of state not to litigate against each other readily, there was no obligation on Chapter 9 institutions to follow the prescripts of Chapter 3.[35]

In *Uthukela District Municipality and Others v President of the Republic of South Africa and Others*, the Constitutional Court confirmed that municipalities are organs of state in the local sphere of government while the President and the national Ministers are organs of state in the national sphere.[36] Thus, a dispute involving these spheres would, prior to being referred to court, have to comply with Chapter 3. For these purposes, the provincial executive cannot be distinguished from the national executive and the provincial executive will be regarded as an organ of state in the provincial sphere.

The essence of Chapter 3 was described by the Constitutional Court as requiring that disputes 'where possible be resolved at a political level rather than through adversarial litigation'.[37] In *Uthukela*, the Court held that it will rarely decide an intergovernmental dispute 'unless the organs of State involved in the dispute have made every reasonable effort to resolve it at a political level.'[38] The Court held that the duty to avoid legal proceedings placed a two-fold obligation on all organs of state. They had to make every reasonable effort to settle the dispute through the mechanisms provided and to exhaust all other remedies before they approached the courts.[39] The Court will decline to hear the matter if there is a failure to comply with this obligation. In effect, the matter will be referred back to the parties to comply with their obligations in terms of Chapter 3.

8.1.5 Intergovernmental co-ordination

To avoid conflicts between the national, provincial and local spheres of government, especially in so far as their concurrent powers are concerned, the Constitution establishes

32 S 41(3).
33 (CCT 49/00) [2001] ZACC 23; 2001 (3) SA 925 (CC); 2001 (9) BCLR 883 (CC) (7 June 2001).
34 *Langeberg* paras 27–9.
35 *Langeberg* para 31.
36 (CCT7/02) [2002] ZACC 11; 2002 (11) BCLR 1220; 2003 (1) SA 678 (CC) (12 June 2002) para 18.
37 *First Certification* para 291.
38 *Uthukela* para 14.
39 *Uthukela* para 13.

or provides for the establishment of co-ordinating bodies. Some of these bodies are responsible for co-ordinating the **legislative activities** of the three spheres of government and others for co-ordinating the **executive activities** of government.

The responsibility for co-ordinating the legislative activities of the different spheres of government has been vested in the National Council of Provinces (NCOP). This is because each province, as well as organised local government, is represented in the NCOP. Given that we have already discussed the NCOP, however, we will not dwell on the manner in which it co-ordinates the legislative activities of the three spheres of government here. Instead, we will focus on those bodies that have been established by the Intergovernmental Relations Framework Act (IGRFA)[40] to co-ordinate the executive activities of the different spheres of government.

The IGRFA was passed to establish structures to promote and facilitate intergovernmental relations and to provide mechanisms to settle intergovernmental disputes. The provisions of the IGRFA do not apply to conflicts between the national and provincial legislatures.[41] These conflicts have to be resolved in accordance with section 146 of the Constitution. As a consequence of the *Langeberg* case, all Chapter 9 institutions and other independent institutions fall outside the scope of the Act. Finally, as the courts are independent, they too are not bound by the provisions of the IGRFA.

The purpose of the IGRFA is to provide a framework for the various spheres of government and organs of state within those spheres to facilitate co-ordination in the implementation of policy and legislation.[42] These include the provision of coherent government, the effective provision of services, the monitoring of implementation of policy and the realisation of national priorities.[43] To help achieve this purpose, the IGRFA creates a number of co-ordinating forums. Among the most important of these are the President's Co-ordinating Council,[44] National Intergovernmental Forums,[45] the Premiers' Intergovernmental Forum[46] and District Intergovernmental Forums.[47]

PAUSE FOR REFLECTION

Co-operative intergovernmental relations or coercive intergovernmental relations?

Steytler draws a distinction between co-operative intergovernmental relations and coercive intergovernmental relations.[48] He argues that while the Constitution envisages a system of co-operative intergovernmental relations, statutes such as the IGRFA lean more in the direction of a system of coercive intergovernmental relations dominated by the national sphere of government. This leads him to the conclusion that South Africa currently operates as an integrated federal state that utilises a coercive form of intergovernmental relations. In other words, while the national sphere is obliged to co-operate with the other spheres, it also dominates them.

40 Act 13 of 2005.
41 S 2 of the IGRFA.
42 S 4 of the IGRFA.
43 S 4(*a*)-(*d*) of the IGRFA.
44 S 6 of the IGRFA.
45 S 9 of the IGRFA.
46 S 18 of the IGRFA.
47 S 24 of the IGRFA.
48 See Steytler, N 'Co-operative and coercive models of intergovernmental relations: A South African case study' in Courchene, TJ and Allen, JR (eds) (2011) *The Federal Idea: Essays in Honour of Ronald L. Watts* 413–28.

In some instances, organs of state have to act in conjunction with other organs of state to carry out their statutory and constitutional responsibilities or to provide effective service delivery. The IGRFA requires that in these instances, implementation protocols must be agreed on by the various participating organs of state.[49] Among various objectives, the implementation protocols must:

- identify the roles and responsibilities of each organ of state in implementing policy and carrying out its statutory functions
- provide for aims and objectives of the project
- determine indicators to measure the attainment of the objectives
- provide for monitoring and evaluation mechanisms
- provide for dispute-resolving procedures
- determine the duration of the protocol.[50]

One of the most important objectives of the IGRFA is to set in place mechanisms to deal with intergovernmental disputes. The IGRFA does not apply to disputes concerning interventions in terms of sections 100 and 139 of the Constitution.[51] Any intervention in terms of these sections must satisfy the procedural and substantive constraints built into these sections.

An intergovernmental dispute is defined as a dispute between different spheres of government or between organs of state from different spheres concerning matters arising from statutory powers or functions assigned to them or from an agreement between the parties regarding the implementation of their statutory powers. In addition, the issue must be justiciable in a court of law.[52]

The definition is wide and covers disputes that arise as a consequence of the various parties exercising their statutory power. This would include disputes about which party is responsible for paying for the services provided and which party should provide particular services. In addition, disputes may arise as a consequence of an agreement entered into by the parties in furtherance of a joint mandate. The IGRFA imposes a direct duty to avoid intergovernmental disputes.[53] This duty involves taking reasonable steps both to avoid intergovernmental disputes and to settle intergovernmental disputes that arise without resorting to judicial proceedings. The IGRFA prescribes various steps which must be followed as a prerequisite to taking legal proceedings.

As a first step, the parties must try to settle the dispute through direct negotiations or through an intermediary. If this is unsuccessful, then one of the parties may declare a formal intergovernmental dispute by notifying the other party of this in writing.[54]

After a formal intergovernmental dispute has been declared, the parties are obliged to convene a meeting to determine the precise issues that are in dispute, the material issues that are not in dispute and any mechanisms and procedures, other than judicial proceedings, that are in place and which can resolve the dispute. The parties are also required to agree on appropriate mechanisms to settle the dispute and to designate a person to act as a facilitator.[55]

49 S 35.
50 S 35(3) of the IGRFA.
51 S 39(1)(*b*) of the IGRFA.
52 S 1 of the IGRFA.
53 S 40 of the IGRFA.
54 S 41 of the IGRFA.
55 S 42 of the IGRFA.

If the meeting is not convened and if the dispute involves a national organ of state, the Minister responsible for provincial and local government must convene the meeting.[56] Similar responsibilities rest on the MEC for local government in respect of disputes involving provincial organs of state and local government or municipal organs of state.

The IGRFA assigns specific responsibilities to the facilitator.[57] The main mandate is to settle the dispute in any manner necessary and to provide progress reports to the relevant parties. The attempts to settle and the contents of the progress reports are deemed to be privileged documents and may not be used in judicial proceedings. Importantly, no organ of state may institute proceedings to settle an intergovernmental dispute unless it has been declared a formal intergovernmental dispute and efforts made to settle the dispute have proved to be unsuccessful.

8.2 The division of legislative and executive power between the national and provincial spheres of governments

8.2.1 Introduction

The division of legislative and executive authority between the three spheres of government is one of the key features of the system of multisphere government adopted in the Constitution. In this part of the chapter, we discuss the division of legislative and executive authority between the national and provincial spheres of government. Although there is a large overlap between the matters over which each sphere has, first, legislative authority and, second, executive authority, these matters are not necessarily identical. For example, additional administrative powers may be delegated to provincial executives by the national legislature.[58] This would empower provincial executives to exercise administrative powers in terms of such legislation even though the provincial legislatures may not be empowered to legislate on that matter. Nevertheless, to a large degree, provincial executives have authority over the same subject matter as provincial legislatures. Unless indicated otherwise, we will deal with these matters as if they overlap. Before discussing this further, however, it will be helpful to discuss briefly the objectives and structure of provincial government.

8.2.2 The objectives and structure of provincial government

South Africa is divided into nine provinces, namely the Eastern Cape, Free State, Gauteng, KwaZulu-Natal, Mpumalanga, Northern Cape, Northern Province, North West and Western Cape.[59] The Constitution regulates the governance of the provinces in Chapter 6 and sets out the structure, powers and functions of the provincial legislatures[60] as well as the provincial executive authorities.[61] Judging from the structure and powers bestowed by the Constitution on the nine provinces, provinces are required to fulfil at least three important interrelated but distinct functions:

- First, provinces provide a close link between voters and their government to ensure that the government addresses the particular concerns and unique challenges and needs of discrete geographical areas.

56 S 42(3) of the IGRFA.
57 S 43 of the IGRFA.
58 S 125(2)(*c*) of the Constitution.
59 S 103(1) of the Constitution.
60 Ss 104–124.
61 Ss 125–141.

- Second, provinces are required to implement national policies and plans relating to important service delivery areas such as housing, health care, policing and education.
- Third, provinces must oversee the smooth running of the local sphere of government within the boundaries of the province.

To a large extent the structures and functions of the nine provinces mirror one another. Each province is entitled to pass a provincial constitution,[62] and the Western Cape Province has indeed done so.[63] However, such a constitution cannot bestow substantially more powers on a province or deviate from the basic structure of governance of the province as set out in the national Constitution.[64] The constitution-making power is not a power to constitute a province with powers, functions or attributes in conflict with the overall constitutional framework established by the national Constitution. The provinces remain creatures of the national Constitution and cannot, through their provincial constitution-making power, alter their character or their relationship with the other levels of government.[65] When discussing the structure and functioning of provinces, we shall therefore focus on the provisions of the 1996 Constitution only.

The legislative authority of each province is vested in its provincial legislature. The provincial legislature has the legislative power to pass a provincial constitution and to pass legislation for its province with regard to any matter:

- within a functional area listed in Schedule 4[66]
- within a functional area listed in Schedule 5[67]
- outside those functional areas and that is 'expressly assigned' to the province by national legislation[68]
- for which a provision of the Constitution 'envisages' the enactment of provincial legislation.[69]

A provincial legislature may also assign any of its legislative powers to a municipal council in that province.[70] In addition, the legislature of a province may change the name of that province by adopting a resolution with a supporting vote of at least two-thirds of its members, requesting Parliament to change the name of that province.[71]

Apart from the legislative powers set out above, the Constitution also provides that provincial legislation with regard to any matter that is reasonably necessary for, or incidental to, the effective exercise of a power concerning any matter listed in Schedule 4, is for all purposes legislation with regard to a matter listed in Schedule 4.[72]

The members of provincial legislatures are elected in accordance with the same electoral system that applies to the election of members of the National Assembly (NA). The size of each of the legislatures is determined in terms of a formula prescribed by national legislation

62 S 142 of the Constitution.
63 Constitution of the Western Cape of 1998.
64 See *Certification of the Kwazulu-Natal Constitution* (CCT15/96) [1996] ZACC 17; 1996 (11) BCLR 1419; 1996 (4) SA 1098 (6 September 1996).
65 *Certification of the Kwazulu-Natal Constitution* para 8. See also *Certification of the Constitution of the Western Cape, 1997* (CCT6/97) [1997] ZACC 8; 1997 (12) BCLR 1653; 1998 (1) SA 655 (2 September 1997) para 8.
66 S 104(1)(*b*)(i) of the Constitution.
67 S 104(1)(*b*)(ii) of the Constitution.
68 S 104(1)(*b*)(iii) of the Constitution.
69 S 104(1)(*b*)(iv) of the Constitution.
70 S 104(1)(*c*) of the Constitution.
71 S 104(2) of the Constitution.
72 S 104(4).

relating to the population size of that province, but cannot be smaller than 30 and no larger than 80 members.[73] The Western Cape legislature's size is determined by the Western Cape Constitution.[74] The requirements for membership of provincial legislatures, as well as the loss of membership, are identical to those prescribed for the NA.[75] Provincial legislatures are also elected for a term of five years and can be dissolved before the expiry of that term for exactly the same reasons as those that apply to the NA.[76]

As we may recall, a province's permanent delegates to the NCOP are not members of the provincial legislature. However, such permanent delegates to the NCOP may attend and may speak in their provincial legislature and its committees, but may not vote. The legislature may require a permanent delegate to attend the legislature or its committees.[77] The rules regarding the functioning of provincial legislatures also mirror those prescribed for the NA.

The executive authority of a province is vested in the Premier of that province, whose role mirrors that of the President at national level. Obviously, though, Premiers do not enjoy the head of state powers bestowed on the President by section 84 of the Constitution. The Premier exercises executive authority, together with the other members of the Executive Council, by:

- implementing provincial legislation in the province
- implementing all national legislation in the functional areas listed in Schedule 4 or 5 except where the Constitution or an Act of Parliament provides otherwise
- administering in the province national legislation outside the functional areas listed in Schedules 4 and 5, the administration of which has been assigned to the provincial executive in terms of an Act of Parliament
- developing and implementing provincial policy
- co-ordinating the functions of the provincial administration and its departments
- preparing and initiating provincial legislation
- performing any other function assigned to the provincial executive in terms of the Constitution or an Act of Parliament.[78]

Over and above the explicit powers bestowed on the Premier and his or her executive, they also enjoy any additional powers that have been bestowed on them by the national legislature.

A province has executive authority in terms of those functional areas listed in Schedules 4 and 5 of the Constitution, but 'only to the extent that the province has the administrative capacity to assume effective responsibility'.[79] The Constitution enjoins the national government to assist provinces to develop the administrative capacity required for the effective exercise of their powers and performance of their functions through legislative and other measures.[80] Any dispute concerning the administrative capacity of a province in regard to any function must be referred to the NCOP for resolution within 30 days of the date of the referral to the Executive Council.[81] A member of the Executive Council of a province may

73 S 105(2) of the Constitution. The legislation referred to in s 105(2) is the Electoral Act 73 of 1998. The formula for determining the number of members of each provincial legislature is set out in Schedule 3 of the Electoral Act.

74 S 13 of the Constitution of the Western Cape determines the size to be 42.

75 S 106 of the Constitution.

76 S 109 of the Constitution.

77 S 113 of the Constitution.

78 S 125(2) of the Constitution.

79 S 125(3) of the Constitution.

80 S 125(3) of the Constitution.

81 S 125(4) of the Constitution.

assign any power or function that is to be exercised or performed in terms of an Act of Parliament or a provincial Act to a municipal council. An assignment must be in terms of an agreement between the relevant Executive Council member and the municipal council. It must be consistent with the Act in terms of which the relevant power or function is exercised or performed, and it takes effect on proclamation by the Premier.[82]

Premiers are elected by the provincial legislature.[83] Premiers can also be removed in two ways:

- First, Premiers can be impeached in terms of section 130(3) of the Constitution for a serious violation of the Constitution or the law, serious misconduct or inability to perform the functions of office.
- Second, in terms of section 141 of the Constitution, a provincial legislature may remove a Premier for purely political reasons by instituting a motion of no confidence in the Premier.

PAUSE FOR REFLECTION

The division and demarcation of legislative competences between the national and provincial spheres

Unlike Parliament, which has plenary legislative powers, the provincial legislatures have limited legislative powers. The limited nature of the provincial legislatures' legislative powers was highlighted by the Constitutional Court in its judgment in *Premier: Limpopo Province v Speaker of the Limpopo Provincial Legislature and Others*.[84]

The facts of this case were as follows. In 2009, the Limpopo Provincial Legislature passed the Financial Management of the Limpopo Provincial Legislature Bill, 2009. The purpose of this Bill was to regulate the financial management of the Limpopo Provincial Legislature itself. After the Limpopo Provincial Legislature had passed this Bill, it was referred to the Premier of Limpopo for his assent and signature. The Premier, however, had reservations about the constitutional validity of the Bill and refused to assent to it. Acting in terms of section 121 of the Constitution, the Premier referred the Bill back to the Provincial Legislature and, after the Provincial Legislature had failed to address his concerns, to the Constitutional Court for a decision on its constitutional validity.[85]

The Premier's reservations were based on the fact that the financial management of a provincial legislature is not listed as a functional area in either Schedule 4 or Schedule 5 of the Constitution. This meant he argued that the Bill fell outside the Provincial Legislature's legislative competence.

The Provincial Legislature accepted that financial management of a provincial legislature is not listed as a functional area in either Schedule 4 or Schedule 5. It argued, however, that the Bill did fall into its legislative competence because the power to pass legislation regulating the financial management of a provincial legislature has been 'expressly assigned' to the provinces by the Financial Management of Parliament

82 S 126 of the Constitution.

83 S 128 of the Constitution.

84 (CCT 94/10) [2011] ZACC 25; 2011 (11) BCLR 1181 (CC); 2011 (6) SA 396 (CC) (11 August 2011).

85 S 121 of the Constitution enables the Premier of a province to refer a Bill back to the provincial legislature if he or she has misgivings about the constitutionality of the Bill. The section goes on to provide that if the reservations are not adequately addressed by the provincial legislature, the Premier may refer the Bill to the Constitutional Court for a decision.

Act.[86] In addition, the Provincial Legislature argued further, the power to pass legislation regulating the financial management of a provincial legislature was 'envisaged' by sections 195, 215 and 216 the Constitution.[87] Section 195 deals with the basic values and principles governing public administration. Section 215 deals with the national, provincial and municipal budgets and section 216 indicates the nature of treasury controls that must be implemented.

A majority of the Constitutional Court rejected both these arguments and came to the conclusion that the Bill did not fall into the legislative competence of the Limpopo Provincial Legislature. It was, therefore, unconstitutional and invalid.

In arriving at this conclusion, the Constitutional Court pointed out that the defining feature of our constitutional scheme for the allocation of legislative powers between Parliament and the provinces is that the legislative powers of the provinces are enumerated and clearly defined, while those of Parliament are not.[88] The plenary power that resides in Parliament is therefore contrasted with the limited powers that have been given to provincial legislatures.[89] An important consequence of this feature, the Constitutional Court pointed out further, is that a provincial legislature may pass legislation only on:

- those matters set out in Schedule 4
- those matters set out in Schedule 5
- those that have been 'expressly assigned' to the provinces by national legislation
- those in respect of which a provision of the Constitution 'envisages' the enactment of provincial legislation.[90]

The general scheme of the Constitution, the Constitutional Court went on to point out, was aimed at ensuring that the legislative authority of the provinces is clearly identified.[91] In addition to the competences directly articulated in Schedules 4 and 5, the Constitution specifically requires that additional competences are 'expressly assigned' by national legislation to the provinces or are 'envisaged' by a provision of the Constitution.[92]

After setting out these principles, the Constitutional Court turned to consider whether the Financial Management of Parliament Act has expressly assigned the financial management of a provincial legislature to the provinces. In this respect, the Constitutional Court noted that the word 'expressly' must be interpreted as part of the objective to ensure that provincial competences are clearly identified. This meant, the Court noted further, that the national legislation assigning the additional powers must leave no doubt of its intent and must clearly stipulate the nature and scope of the

86 Act 10 of 2009. S 104(1)(*b*)(iii) of the Constitution provides that each provincial legislature has the power 'to pass legislation for its province with regard to any matter outside (the functional areas listed in Schedules 4 and 5), and that is expressly assigned to the province by national legislation'.

87 S 104(1)(*b*)(iv) of the Constitution provides that each provincial legislature has the power 'to pass legislation for its province with regard to any matter for which a provision of the Constitution envisages the enactment of provincial legislation'.

88 *Premier: Limpopo Province* para 24.

89 *Premier: Limpopo Province* para 24.

90 *Premier: Limpopo Province* para 21.

91 *Premier: Limpopo Province* para 23.

92 *Premier: Limpopo Province* paras 34–9.

powers assigned. The reason why the national legislation assigning the additional powers must leave no doubt of its intent, the Constitutional Court went on to note, is because it will provide reasonable certainty as to the areas of competence of the provincial legislatures.[93]

Clarity as to the nature and extent of the power assigned will advance co-operative government which has, as one of its guiding principles, that no sphere will assume any power or function except those conferred in terms of the Constitution. This clarity, the Constitutional Court also held, would prevent disputes and inform the public as to which sphere has competence over the particular matter.[94]

The Court suggested that the preamble and the objectives of the enabling legislation should make the intent clear and unequivocal.[95] The Court concluded that if the assignment is merely implied as opposed to express, it will fail to comply with the requirements of the Constitution regarding the assignment of legislative authority.[96]

Having found that the Financial Management of Parliament Act did not expressly assign the financial management of a provincial legislature to the provinces, the Constitutional Court turned to consider whether the power to pass legislation regulating the financial management of a provincial legislature was 'envisaged' by sections 195, 215 and 216 of the Constitution.[97] In keeping with the theme of maximum clarity in respect of the allocation of legislative powers to the various spheres, the Constitutional Court also adopted a restrictive approach to this argument. It held that only those provisions of the Constitution which in clear, unequivocal and express terms sanctioned the enactment of provincial legislation fell under this section.[98] The Constitutional Court stated that the power had to be expressly assigned and not merely implied. To do otherwise would, in the view of the Court, undermine the principle of certainty and adversely affect the constitutional scheme.[99] The Court identified section 155(5) of the Constitution as an example of such express assignment. This section provides that provincial legislation must determine the different types of municipalities to be established in the province.[100] On the facts, the Constitutional Court concluded that the sections of the Constitution relied on by the provincial legislature did not in clear and unmistakeable terms envisage the enactment by the provincial legislature of this law.[101]

In their dissenting judgments, the minority of the Constitutional Court disagreed with the manner in which the majority interpreted the word 'envisages'. The word 'envisages', the minority reasoned, must mean something different from the phrase 'expressly assigned'.[102] If they meant the same thing, the drafters of the Constitution would not have used different words. The word 'envisages', the minority reasoned further, means something less than 'expressly assigned', but not much less.[103] 'It must appear

93 *Premier: Limpopo Province* para 36.
94 *Premier: Limpopo Province* para 37.
95 *Premier: Limpopo Province* para 38.
96 *Premier: Limpopo Province* para 39.
97 *Premier: Limpopo Province* para 40.
98 *Premier: Limpopo Province* para 41.
99 *Premier: Limpopo Province* para 41.
100 *Premier: Limpopo Province* para 53.
101 *Premier: Limpopo Province* para 60.
102 *Premier: Limpopo Province* para 85.
103 *Premier: Limpopo Province* para 85.

that the relevant provisions of the Constitution read in context lead to no conclusion but that the Constitution contemplates the exercise of the power by the provincial legislature and that the Constitution could mean nothing else'.[104] After setting out these principles, the minority turned to apply them to the facts and found that the power to pass legislation regulating the financial management of a provincial legislature was 'envisaged' by sections 195, 215 and 216 of the Constitution.[105]

The case represents an attempt to have reasonable certainty in respect of the division and demarcation of legislative competences between the national and provincial spheres. The constitutional scheme vests the residual legislative powers in the national sphere and makes specified allocations to the provincial legislatures. The Court did not permit the boundaries to be blurred and insisted that the provinces can only legislate in respect of functional areas falling within Schedules 4 and 5, or if national laws clearly assign further function to the provinces, or if the Constitution expressly assigns power to the provinces to legislate on specified matters.[106]

8.2.3 Determining legislative competence

As we have already seen, the legislative powers bestowed on Parliament overlap to some degree with the legislative powers bestowed on provincial legislatures. One of the more difficult questions of South African constitutional law is the exact relationship between the legislative powers of the national Parliament in relation to the legislative powers of the provincial legislatures. There are two distinct issues at play here:

- First, when dealing with concurrent competences listed in Schedule 4, both the national legislature and the provincial legislatures are empowered to pass legislation on a particular topic. When both the national legislature and a provincial legislature have passed legislation on a particular concurrent competence set out in Schedule 4, both the national and the provincial legislation will have been validly passed. However, as we shall see, where there is a direct conflict between the provisions of national legislation and provincial legislation, the provisions of the provincial legislation will prevail unless one or more of the requirements of section 146 of the Constitution is met in which case the national legislation will prevail.[107] We shall deal with the rules relating to such clashes below.
- Second, usually only provincial legislatures can pass legislation dealing with one or more of the exclusive competences listed in Schedule 5. However, in exceptional cases set out in section 44(2) of the Constitution, the national Parliament may intervene and pass legislation listed in Schedule 5. We shall deal with this below.

At this point it is important to note that the division of legislative authority between the national, provincial and local spheres of government imposes important federalist limits on the power of each sphere of government to legislate. At the heart of these limits lies the principle that each sphere may not adopt legislation that falls outside its legislative

104 *Premier: Limpopo Province* para 85.
105 *Premier: Limpopo Province* para 92.
106 For a critical discussion of this judgment, see Steytler, N and Williams, RF (2012) Squeezing out provinces' legislative competence in *Premier: Limpopo Province v Speaker: Limpopo Provincial Legislative and Others I and II South African Law Journal* 129(4):621–37.
107 S 146(5) of the Constitution.

authority. Legislation passed by a legislature in a particular sphere, therefore, may be challenged on the ground that it does not fall into the legislature's authority. Whenever a person challenges legislation on the ground that it does not fall into a legislature's authority, a court will have to determine whether the legislature in question was competent to pass the legislation. There are two distinct questions that arise whenever there is uncertainty whether the legislature of one sphere of government is competent to pass legislation on a specific topic:

- First, there is a need to decide whether the impugned legislation deals with a topic listed in Schedule 4 or Schedule 5. Our courts have developed a special test for this which we will discuss below.
- Second, once we have determined whether the legislation falls within Schedule 4 or 5, we must ask whether the relevant legislature was authorised to pass the legislation as a matter of course or in terms of section 44(2) or section 146 of the Constitution.

The Constitutional Court considered the manner in which a court must determine whether a piece of legislation has been competently enacted by either the national legislature or by one of the provincial parliaments (or both) in several cases, including in *Ex Parte President of the Republic of South Africa: In re Constitutionality of the Liquor Bill.*[108]

In this case, the national legislature passed the Liquor Bill which sought to regulate comprehensively the liquor industry. The Bill divided the economic activity of the liquor industry into three categories: manufacture, distribution and retail sales. The Bill treated manufacture and distribution as national issues and retail sales as provincial issues to be dealt with by provincial liquor authorities. However, even in respect of retail sales, the Bill prescribed detailed mechanisms as to how the provincial legislatures should establish their retail licensing systems.

The Western Cape government, then controlled by the New National Party, challenged the constitutionality of the Bill by arguing that it exhaustively regulated issues concerning manufacture and distribution and that even in the retail sphere, it relegated the provinces to the role of funders and administrators. Parliament contended that the Bill primarily dealt with trade, economic and social welfare issues, which are concurrent competences. The Western Cape provincial government argued that the Bill dealt with liquor licences, an exclusive competence of the province in terms of Schedule 5. The Bill, in fact, affected both concurrent and exclusive provincial competencies.

The Constitutional Court emphasised that under the post-apartheid constitutional developments, governmental power is not located in the national sphere alone.[109] Legislative authority is vested in Parliament for the national sphere, in the provincial legislature for the provincial sphere and in municipal councils for the local sphere.[110] Any interpretation must recognise and promote the philosophy of co-operative government at various levels.[111] However, given the breadth of the competencies listed in the various Schedules, their parameters of operation will, of necessity, overlap.[112]

The Constitutional Court pointed out (as we have done above) that the Constitution allows for provincial exclusivity in respect of matters falling within Schedule 5, subject to an

---

108 (CCT12/99) [1999] ZACC 15; 2000 (1) SA 732; 2000 (1) BCLR 1 (11 November 1999).
109 *Liquor Bill* para 55.
110 *Liquor Bill* para 39.
111 *Liquor Bill* para 39.
112 *Liquor Bill* para 46.

intervention by the central sphere that is justified in terms of section 44(2) of the Constitution. This, argued the Court, meant that the functional competencies in Schedule 4 should be interpreted as being distinct from, and excluding, Schedule 5 competencies.[113] The Court found that the primary purpose of Schedule 4 is to enable the national government to regulate various issues interprovincially (between all the provinces).[114] Conversely, the provinces, whose jurisdiction is confined to their geographical territory, are accorded exclusive powers in respect of matters that may be regulated intraprovincially (exclusively within the province).[115]

The main substance and character of the legislation determines the field of competence in which it falls. A single piece of legislation may have various parts and more than one substantive character.[116] According to this reasoning, the Court concluded that the national sphere has the power to regulate the liquor trade in all respects other than liquor licensing. The manufacture and distribution segments of the legislation affect interprovincial as opposed to intraprovincial competencies.[117] This would suggest that the competence of liquor licensing in Schedule 5 was not intended to encompass the manufacturing and distribution of liquor.[118] In any event, the Court was prepared to conclude that even if the provincial competence in respect of liquor licences extends to licensing, production and distribution, 'its (the central spheres) interest in maintaining economic unity authorises it to intervene under section 44(2) of the Constitution'.[119]

However, the Court adopted a much stricter approach to the national regulation in respect of retail sales. A relatively uniform approach to liquor licensing in the country may be desirable but this did not amount to a necessity that justified an intrusion into the exclusive provincial competence. Thus, the Court deemed those aspects of the law that regulated the manufacture and distribution of liquor constitutional and the segment of the national law regulating the retail industry unconstitutional.[120]

CRITICAL THINKING

The substantial measure test versus the pith and substance test for Bills

It is important to recall what we stated in chapter 3, namely that there is a distinction between the test to determine whether a Bill should be tagged and then passed as a section 75 Bill not affecting provinces or a section 76 Bill affecting provinces, and the test to determine whether a Bill deals with a concurrent competence in terms of Schedule 4 or an exclusive provincial competence in terms of Schedule 5. There is an important difference between the substantial measure test used to decide how to tag a Bill and the pith and substance test used to determine whether the subject matter of a Bill falls within Schedule 4 or Schedule 5.

In terms of the pith and substance test, those provisions of a Bill that fall outside its substance are treated as incidental. In contrast, the tagging test is distinct from the question of legislative competence. It focuses on all the provisions of the Bill to determine the extent to which they substantially affect functional areas listed in

113 *Liquor Bill* para 47.
114 *Liquor Bill* para 50.
115 *Liquor Bill* para 51.
116 *Liquor Bill* para 61.
117 *Liquor Bill* para 73.
118 *Liquor Bill* para 75.
119 *Liquor Bill* para 76.
120 *Liquor Bill* para 86.

Schedule 4 and not on whether any of its provisions are incidental to its substance. The more it affects the interests, concerns and capacities of the provinces, the more say the provinces should have on its content.[121]

Importantly, the Court endeavoured to remain faithful to the structure of the Constitution. Had the Court interpreted the competence of 'trade' very broadly, this would have provided an opportunity for the national legislature to intervene in a variety of matters that fall under Schedule 5 such as liquor licensing, control of undertakings that sell liquor, licensing and control of undertakings that sell food to the public, markets and street trading. By demarcating the boundary by reference to intra- and interprovincial activities, the Court ensured that national intervention in respect of Schedule 5 matters that apply intraprovincially must comply with section 44(2) of the Constitution. A broad interpretation of the competences listed in Schedule 4 would have ultimately negated the exclusive competence of the provinces to legislate in respect of matters listed in Schedule 5.[122]

Given that subject matter or the substance of legislation determines the field of competence in which it falls, it is important to be able to identify the subject matter or the substance of a law. The Constitutional Court discussed the manner in which this may be done in *Abahlali Basemjondolo Movement SA and Another v Premier of the Province of Kwazulu-Natal and Others*.[123]

In this case, the applicants, an association representing residents of informal settlements, applied for an order declaring the Elimination and Prevention of the Re-emergence of Slums Act,[124] which had been passed by the KZN Provincial Legislature, to be unconstitutional and invalid. They based their application on a number of grounds, one of which was that the KZN Provincial Legislature lacked the competence to pass this law. The KZN Provincial Legislature lacked the competence to pass the Act, the applicants argued, because it did not deal with housing. Housing is a functional area of concurrent national and provincial competences listed in Schedule 4. They argued that the Act dealt with land tenure and access to land which, in terms of section 25 of the Constitution, is a functional area of exclusive national competence.[125]

The key question the Constitutional Court had to determine, therefore, was whether the subject matter or substance of the Act was housing, in which case it would fall into the legislative competence of the KZN Provincial Legislature, or whether it was land tenure and access to land, in which case it would not fall into the legislative competence of the KZN Provincial Legislature. When it comes to determining the subject matter or substance of a law, the Constitutional Court held that two important principles must be taken into account:

- First, the substance of the law does not depend on its form, but rather on the true purpose, effect and essence of what the law is about.
- Second, no national or provincial legislative competence is watertight and it is therefore important to determine the main substance of the legislation in order to ascertain whether the provincial legislature has legislative competence.[126]

121 *Liquor Bill* paras 59–60.
122 *Liquor Bill* para 76.
123 (CCT12/09) [2009] ZACC 31; 2010 (2) BCLR 99 (CC) (14 October 2009).
124 Act 6 of 2007.
125 *Abahlali* para 20.
126 *Abahlali* para 21.

After setting out these principles, the Constitutional Court applied them to the facts. In this respect, the Court held that in determining the substance of the Act it had to be considered as a whole.[127] The preamble of the Act identified the purpose of the legislation as being to eliminate and prevent the re-emergence of slums in a manner that protects and promotes the housing construction programmes of provincial and local governments.[128] The Court found that the overall strategy of the Act was to eliminate slums and to make provision for the progressive realisation of adequate housing by improving service delivery and by generally improving the conditions under which people are housed. It was not simply about eviction with no regard for the consequences of rendering people homeless.[129]

The Court concluded that the Act was primarily about improving the housing conditions of those living in slums in KZN.[130] It was therefore about housing and fell within the legislative competence of the province.[131] However, the majority of the court found that section 16 of the Elimination and Prevention of the Re-emergence of Slums Act obliged owners to institute eviction proceedings when directed to do so by the MEC even if to do so would not be in accordance with the Prevention of Illegal Eviction from and Unlawful Occupation of Land Act (PIE Act).[132] The majority found this to be inconsistent with section 25 of the Constitution which seeks to provide greater security of tenure to communities whose tenure is legally insecure as a result of past racially discriminatory laws.[133]

Thus, a full and complete appraisal of the law is required to determine the substance of the legislation. This, in turn, assists with assessing whether the law deals with a matter that falls under Schedule 4 or 5 or within the exclusive competence of Parliament. Once this determination has been made, then clarity can be obtained as to which legislative body has competence over the matter.

8.2.4 The resolution of conflicts between the national and provincial spheres

8.2.4.1 Conflicts related to concurrent competences set out in Schedule 4

As stated earlier, both the national and provincial legislatures possess power to legislate concurrently over the functional areas contained in Schedule 4. Affording concurrent legislative responsibilities over the same functional areas to different legislatures can lead to conflicting laws being enacted over the same subject matter. For instance, education is a concurrent function and thus both the national and provincial legislatures have jurisdiction to pass laws in respect of this competence. Provisions of a law passed by the national legislature on education may conflict with provisions of a law passed by a provincial legislature on the same subject matter. It is thus imperative for the Constitution to anticipate such conflicts and to include provisions that seek to resolve conflicts between laws dealing with the same subject matter and which are passed by the different legislatures. Section 146 of the Constitution provides a framework in terms of which these conflicts are to be resolved.

---

127 *Abahlali* para 26.
128 *Abahlali* para 29.
129 *Abahlali* para 30.
130 *Abahlali* para 37.
131 *Abahlali* para 40.
132 Act 19 of 1998.
133 *Abahlali* para 92.

It has been suggested that conflicts between central and provincial laws are dealt with by reference to the following enquiries:[134]

- Does the central legislature have the legislative competence to pass its law?
- Does the provincial legislature have the legislative competence to pass its law?
- If both legislatures have the legal competence to pass the laws, then the issue would be whether the different laws can be reconciled.
- If there is an irreconcilable conflict, then the central law will prevail if the provisions of section 146 of the Constitution are satisfied.
- If the provisions of section 146 of the Constitution are not met, then the provincial law will prevail.

Thus, the first question is whether the legislative body possesses the constitutional power to legislate over the matter. If the response is that the provincial legislature, as in the case of the *Premier: Limpopo*, or Parliament, as in *Executive Council of the Western Cape Legislature and Others v President of the Republic of South Africa and Others*,[135] does not possess the authority to legislate, then that is the end of the enquiry. The legislative body lacking the power cannot constitutionally legislate and therefore there is no need to determine whether national law should prevail or provincial law or vice versa. It is only if both national and provincial legislatures have the power to legislate and do so that attempts must be made to reconcile the laws. If the laws cannot be reconciled, section 146 of the Constitution must then be applied to determine which law should prevail.

If any one of the criteria listed in section 146 is met, the national law will prevail.[136] The provisions of section 146 can only be resorted to in respect of conflicting laws dealing with a functional area listed in Schedule 4.[137] Criteria permitting the central override are divided into two categories. If one of the criteria listed either in section 146(2) or 146(3) is satisfied, then the conflicting provincial law is rendered inoperative for the period of the conflict.[138] If, for some reason, the conflicting national law is repealed, the provincial law that had been rendered inoperative as a result of the application of section 146 will again be operative. All the criteria listed in section 146(2) are subject to the additional requirement that the central legislation must apply uniformly to the country as a whole. Thus, a national law that targets a particular province will not prevail in terms of section 146(2).

In terms of section 146(2), central law will prevail if any one of the following three conditions is established:

- The central legislation deals with a matter that cannot be regulated effectively by legislation enacted by the respective provinces individually.[139]
- The central legislation deals with a matter that, to be dealt with effectively, requires uniformity across the nation, and national legislation provides that uniformity by establishing norms and standards, frameworks or national policies.[140]

---

134 See *In re: KwaZulu-Natal Amakhosi and Iziphakanyiswa Amendment Bill of 1995, In re: Payment of Salaries. Allowances and Other privileges to the Ingonyama Bill of 1995* (CCT1/96, CCT6/96) [1996] ZACC 15; 1996 (7) BCLR 903; 1996 (4) SA 653 (5 July 1996). See also Bronstein, V 'Conflicts' in Woolman and Bishop (2013) 16.4.

135 (CCT27/95) [1995] ZACC 8; 1995 (10) BCLR 1289; 1995 (4) SA 877 (22 September 1995).

136 Klaaren, J 'Federalism' in Chaskalson, M et al (eds) (1999) *Constitutional Law of South Africa* 1st ed 5-12.

137 S 146(1) of the Constitution.

138 S 149 of the Constitution.

139 S 146(2)(*a*) of the Constitution.

140 S 146(2)(*b*) of the Constitution.

- The central legislation is necessary for the maintenance of national security; the maintenance of economic unity; the protection of the common market in respect of the mobility of goods, services, capital and labour; the promotion of economic activities across provincial boundaries; the promotion of equal opportunities or equal access to government services; or the protection of the environment.[141]

In *Mashavha v President of the Republic of South Africa and Others*,[142] the Constitutional Court had to consider the constitutionality of the President assigning to the provinces the administration of the Social Assistance Act[143] in its entirety. In terms of the interim Constitution, the President could only assign the administration of the Act to the provinces if the provisions of section 126(3) of the interim Constitution[144] were not applicable.

The Court found that the assignment was invalid as the administration dealt with a matter that could not be regulated effectively by separate provincial legislation. For the administration of social welfare grants to be administered fairly and equitably, it needed to be regulated or co-ordinated by uniform norms or standards that applied throughout the Republic.[145] To achieve equity and effectiveness, it was necessary to set minimum standards across the nation.[146] The primary objection of the Court was that if Gauteng, the richest province in the country, paid a higher old-age pension than Limpopo, then the dignity of people in Limpopo would be offended as different classes of citizenship would be created.[147] Thus, to prevent inequality and unfairness in the provision of social assistance to people in need, uniform norms and standards had to be applicable throughout the country.[148]

In terms of section 146(3) of the Constitution, national law will prevail over provincial law if it is aimed at preventing unreasonable action by a province that is prejudicial to the economic, health or security interests of another province or the country as a whole, or impedes the implementation of national economic policy.

PAUSE FOR REFLECTION

When is section 146 invoked?

It is important to note that conflicts only arise and section 146 will only be invoked when one or more of the specific legal provisions in a provincial Act cannot be obeyed at the same time as one or more of the provisions in a national Act. It is also important to remember that as both the national and provincial spheres have legislative competence over these matters, the provisions that conflict do not become invalid. All that happens is that section 146 is used to decide whether the provisions of the provincial Act will prevail or whether the conflicting provisions of the national Act will prevail. The provisions of the Act that do not prevail will remain in limbo. If the conflicting provisions of the Act that prevails are scrapped, the provisions of the conflicting Act will be 'resurrected', so to speak, and will again become operational.

141 S 146 (2)(*c*) of the Constitution.
142 (CCT 67/03) [2004] ZACC 6; 2005 (2) SA 476 (CC); 2004 (12) BCLR 1243 (CC) (6 September 2004).
143 Act 59 of 1992.
144 This was the predecessor of s 146 of the final Constitution.
145 *Mashavha* para 57.
146 Bronstein (2013) 16.19.
147 *Mashavha* para 51.
148 *Mashavha* para 57.

For example, if both the national Parliament and the Western Cape Provincial Parliament pass legislation dealing with the regulation of the use of blue-light brigades by politicians, both will have the legislative power to pass such legislation as Schedule 4 states that road traffic regulation is a concurrent competence. If there is a direct clash between the provisions of the Western Cape law and the provisions of the national law, say the national law allows all politicians to use blue-light convoys while the Western Cape law prohibits this, then a court may have to decide whether the national legislation prevails in terms of section 146 of the Constitution. If the court finds that section 146 is indeed applicable and that the provisions of the national law would prevail, the prohibition contained in the provincial law would become inoperable until such time as the national law is amended or scrapped. If the court finds that section 146 is not applicable, then the prohibition contained in the provincial law against the use of blue-light convoys by politicians will prevail, but only in the Western Cape.

8.2.4.2 Conflicts related to exclusive provincial competences in Schedule 5

Section 44(2) of the Constitution states that even though provincial legislatures have the exclusive powers to pass legislation on one of the functional areas listed in Schedule 5 of the Constitution, the national Parliament may nevertheless intervene in areas listed in Schedule 5, but only when it is necessary:

- to maintain national security
- to maintain economic unity
- to maintain essential national standards
- to establish minimum standards required for the rendering of services
- to prevent unreasonable action taken by a province which is prejudicial to the interests of another province or to the country as a whole.

If Parliament does intervene and validly passes legislation on one of the functional areas listed in Schedule 5, a conflict may arise between national legislation and provincial legislation with respect to the matters listed in Schedule 5. A conflict between national legislation and provincial legislation with respect to these matters must be resolved in terms of section 147(2) of the Constitution. This section provides that national legislation referred to in section 44(2) of the Constitution prevails over provincial legislation that falls with the functional areas listed in Schedule 5.

8.3 The division of legislative and executive power between the national and provincial and local spheres of government

8.3.1 Introduction

As we have already seen, an important aspect of the Constitution is that it distributes legislative and executive authority between the national, provincial and local spheres of government. In the first part of this chapter, we discussed the division of legislative and executive authority between the national sphere of government, on the one hand, and the provincial spheres of government, on the other. In this part of the chapter, we discuss the division of legislative and executive authority between the national and provincial spheres of government, on the one hand, and the local sphere of government, on the other. Before doing so, however, it will be helpful to discuss briefly the objectives and structure of local government.

8.3.2 The objectives of local government

The objectives of local government are set out in section 152(1) of the Constitution. This section provides that the objectives of local government are:

- to provide democratic and accountable local government for local communities
- to ensure the provision of services to communities in a sustainable manner
- to promote social and economic development
- to promote a safe and healthy environment
- to encourage the involvement of communities and community organisations in the matters of local government.

In addition, section 153 of the Constitution also provides that a municipality must:

- structure and manage its administration and budgeting and planning processes to give priority to the basic needs of the community
- structure and manage its administration and budgeting and planning processes to promote the social and economic development of the community
- participate in national and provincial development programmes.

Despite the fact that these sections impose a wide range of obligations on local government, the Constitutional Court held in *Joseph and Others v City of Johannesburg and Others* that one of the most important objectives of local government is to meet the basic needs of all of the inhabitants of South Africa.[149]

To achieve this objective, the Constitutional Court held further that sections 152 and 153 of the Constitution, read together with the Local Government: Municipal Systems Act,[150] impose an obligation on every municipality to provide basic municipal services to their inhabitants, such as water and electricity, irrespective of whether or not they entered in a contract for the supply of these services with the municipality.[151]

PAUSE FOR REFLECTION

Municipalities derive their power from the Constitution

The constitutional status of local government today is radically different from what it was prior to the transition to democracy in 1994. Prior to 1994, municipalities were at the bottom of a hierarchy of law-making powers. This is because they derived their existence and their powers from provincial ordinances which, in turn, derived their existence and powers from Acts of Parliament. An important consequence of this fact is that municipalities were not recognised or protected by the pre-1994 Constitution. Instead, they were classified as mere administrative agencies exercising delegated or subordinate powers. The institution of elected local government could, therefore, have been terminated at any time and its functions entrusted to administrators appointed by the central or provincial governments.

149 (CCT 43/09) [2009] ZACC 30; 2010 (3) BCLR 212 (CC); 2010 (4) SA 55 (CC) (9 October 2009) para 34.
150 Act 32 of 2000.
151 *Joseph* para 39.

Today, however, as the Constitutional Court pointed out in *City of Cape Town and Other v Robertson and Other*,[152] the Constitution has moved away from this hierarchical division of governmental power. It has ushered in a new vision of government in which the sphere of local government is interdependent, 'inviolable and possesses the constitutional latitude within which to define and express its unique character' subject to constraints permissible under our Constitution.[153]

This means, the Constitutional Court pointed out further, that:

> [a] municipality under the Constitution is not a mere creature of statute otherwise moribund save if imbued with power by provincial or national legislation. A municipality enjoys 'original' and constitutionally entrenched powers, functions, rights and duties that may be qualified or constrained by law and only to the extent the Constitution permits. Now the conduct of a municipality is not always invalid only for the reason that no legislation authorises it. Its power may derive from the Constitution or from legislation of a competent authority or from its own laws.[154]

8.3.3 The structure of local government

Section 155 of the Constitution distinguishes between three different categories of municipalities, namely category A municipalities, category B municipalities and category C municipalities:

- A category A municipality has exclusive municipal executive and legislative authority in its area and is referred to as a metropolitan municipality in section 1 of the Local Government: Municipal Structures Act.[155]
- A category B municipality shares its municipal executive and legislative authority in its area with a category C municipality and is referred to as a local municipality in section 1 of the Municipal Structures Act.
- A category C municipality has municipal executive and legislative authority in an area which includes more than one municipality and is referred to as a district municipality in section 1 of the Municipal Structures Act.

Apart from distinguishing between category A (metropolitan), category B (local) and category C (district) municipalities, section 155 of the Constitution also provides that national legislation must establish the criteria for determining when an area should have a single category A municipality or when it should have municipalities of both category B and category C. The national legislation referred to in this section is the Municipal Structures Act. Section 2 of this Act provides that metropolitan municipalities must be established in metropolitan areas, and section 3 provides that local and district municipalities must be established in all other areas.

A metropolitan area is defined in section 1 of the Municipal Structures Act as any area which reasonably can be regarded as a conurbation featuring areas of high population

152 (CCT 19/04) [2004] ZACC 21; 2005 (2) SA 323 (CC) (29 November 2004). See also *Fedsure Life Assurance Ltd and Others v Greater Johannesburg Transitional Metropolitan Council and Others* (CCT7/98) [1998] ZACC 17; 1999 (1) SA 374; 1998 (12) BCLR 1458 (14 October 1998) para 38 and *CDA Boerdery (Edms) Bpk en Andere v Nelson Mandela Metropolitan Municipality* (526/05) [2007] ZASCA 1; [2007] SCA 1 (RSA) (6 February 2007) para 33.

153 *City of Cape Town* para 60.

154 *City of Cape Town* para 60.

155 Act 117 of 1998.

density, intense movement of people, goods and services, extensive development, multiple business districts and a number of industrial areas. In addition, the social and economic linkages between the constituent units should be strong.[156] The power to determine whether an area satisfies criteria and should therefore be classified as a metropolitan area with a metropolitan municipality is vested in an independent body known as the Municipal Demarcation Board. The Municipal Demarcation Board is responsible for determining and re-determining the boundaries of municipalities. Its powers and functions as well as the procedure it must follow when it exercises it powers and carries out its functions are set out in the Local Government: Municipal Demarcation Act.[157]

PAUSE FOR REFLECTION

Why an independent authority must carry out the task of determining municipal boundaries

Section 155(3)(*b*) of the Constitution declares that national legislation must establish criteria and procedures for the determination of municipal boundaries by an independent authority. The independent authority referred to in this section is the Municipal Demarcation Board. The Constitutional Court highlighted the reasons why an independent authority must carry out the task of determining municipal boundaries in its judgment in *Matatiele Municipality and Others v President of the Republic of South Africa and Others*.[158]

In 2005, Parliament passed the Constitution Twelfth Amendment Act and the Cross-Boundary Municipalities Laws Repeal and Related Matters Act.[159] In terms of these laws, the boundary between KwaZulu-Natal and the Eastern Cape was altered so that the area in which the Matatiele Municipality was located was transferred from KwaZulu-Natal to the Eastern Cape and new municipal boundaries were created.

The applicants then applied for an order declaring the Constitution Twelfth Amendment Act to be unconstitutional and invalid on the grounds that it violated section 155(3)(*b*) of the Constitution. They argued that the new boundaries of the Matatiele Municipality had been determined by Parliament and not by an independent authority, namely the Municipal Demarcation Board.

The Constitutional Court rejected this argument and refused to grant the order. In arriving at this decision, however, it set out some of the reasons why section 155(3)(*b*) of the Constitution provides that the Municipal Demarcation Board must be an independent body. In this respect, the Constitutional Court pointed out that the 'purpose of section 155(3)(*b*) is to guard against political interference in the process of creating new municipalities',[160] This is because, the Constitutional Court pointed out further, if municipalities were established along political lines or if there was political interference in the establishment of new municipalities, our system of multiparty democratic government would be undermined.[161] A deliberate decision, the Constitutional Court went on to conclude, was therefore made to confer the power to establish municipal areas on an independent authority.[162]

156 Steytler, N and De Visser, J 'Local government' in Woolman and Bishop (2013) 22.20.
157 Act 27 of 1998.
158 (1) (CCT73/05) [2006] ZACC 2; 2006 (5) BCLR 622 (CC); 2006 (5) SA 47 (CC) (27 February 2006).
159 Act 23 of 2005.
160 *Matatiele Municipality* para 41.
161 *Matatiele Municipality* para 41.
162 *Matatiele Municipality* para 41.

The different types of municipalities that may be established within each category of municipality are also set out in the Municipal Structures Act. The Act begins in this respect by distinguishing between three 'executive systems' of municipal government and two 'participatory systems'.[163] The three executive systems are the collective executive system, the mayoral executive system and the plenary executive system:

- A collective executive system is one in which the executive authority of the municipality is exercised by an executive committee. In this system, the leadership of the municipality is therefore collectively vested in the executive committee.
- A mayoral executive system is one in which the executive authority of the municipality is exercised by an executive mayor assisted by a mayoral committee. In this system, the leadership of the municipality is vested in an executive mayor.
- A plenary executive committee is one in which executive authority is exercised by the municipal council itself. In this system, the leadership of the municipality is vested in the municipal council.

The two participatory systems are the subcouncil participatory system and the ward participatory system:

- A subcouncil participatory system is one which allows for delegated powers to be exercised by subcouncils established for parts of the municipality.
- A ward participatory system is one which allows for matters of local concern to wards to be dealt with by committees established for wards.

After distinguishing between these different systems of municipal government, the Municipal Structures Act goes on to provide that:

- a metropolitan council must have either a collective or mayoral executive system and may combine its executive system with a subcouncil participatory system or a ward participatory system or both[164]
- a local council may have a collective, mayoral or plenary executive system and may combine its executive system with a ward participatory system but not with a subcouncil participatory system[165]
- a district council may have a collective, mayoral or plenary executive system but may not combine its executive system with a subcouncil or ward participatory system.[166]

The articulation of the type of municipality is important to determine three issues:

- first, the institutional relationship between the municipality's executive and legislative functions
- second, whether a metropolitan or local municipality is permitted to establish ward committees
- third, whether a metropolitan municipality is permitted to establish subcouncils that exercise delegated powers for parts of the municipality.

Finally, it is important to note that section 155 of the Constitution also provides that national legislation must make provision for an appropriate division of powers and functions

163 S 7 of the Municipal Structures Act.
164 S 8 of the Municipal Structures Act.
165 S 9 of the Municipal Structures Act.
166 S 10 of the Municipal Structures Act.

between local and district municipalities. A division of powers and functions between a local and a district municipality, however, does not have to be symmetrical, but must constantly ensure that the need to provide municipal services in an equitable and sustainable manner is being upheld.[167] The national legislation referred to in this section is the Municipal Structures Act.

8.3.4 Municipal powers

As we have already seen, municipalities are no longer simply creatures of statute. Instead, they derive at least some of their executive and legislative powers directly from the Constitution itself.[168] The executive and legislative powers of a municipality are set out in section 156 of the Constitution. This section provides that a municipality has executive authority in respect of and has the right to administer:

- the local government matters listed in Part B of Schedule 4 and Part B of Schedule 5[169]
- any other matter assigned to it by national or provincial legislation.[170]

In addition, section 156 of the Constitution also provides that a municipality may make and administer by-laws for the effective administration of the matters which it has the right to administer.[171] A careful examination of this section shows that it distinguishes between two types of powers:

- those powers that are derived directly from the Constitution and that may be referred to as original powers
- those powers that are assigned to municipalities in terms of national or provincial legislation and that may be referred to as assigned powers.

Apart from those powers that are derived directly from the Constitution or that are assigned to it in terms of national or provincial legislation, section 156(5) of the Constitution also provides that a municipality has the right to exercise any power concerning a matter reasonably necessary for, or incidental to, the effective performance of its functions.[172]

8.3.4.1 Original municipal powers

Section 156(1)(*a*) of the Constitution provides that a municipality has executive and legislative authority in respect of the local government matters listed in Part B of Schedule 4 and in Part B of Schedule 5. In addition, section 156(5) of the Constitution also provides that a municipality has the right to exercise any power concerning a matter reasonably necessary for or incidental to the effective performance of its Schedule 4 Part B and Schedule 5 Part B functions. Given that these powers can only be altered or withdrawn if the Constitution itself is amended, they form the most significant source of municipal powers and are a fundamental feature of local government's institutional integrity.[173]

167 S 155(4) of the Constitution.
168 *City of Cape Town* para 55.
169 S 156(1)(*a*) of the Constitution.
170 S 156(1)(*b*) of the Constitution.
171 S 156(2).
172 A municipality also has those powers that have been granted to it by its own by-laws.
173 See Steytler and De Visser (2013) 22.47.

PAUSE FOR REFLECTION

Using the bottom-up method to determine the scope and ambit of the matters set out in Schedule 4 and Schedule 5

In both the *Liquor Bill* case and in *City of Johannesburg Metropolitan Municipality v Gauteng Development Tribunal and Others*,[174] the Constitutional Court held that the scope and ambit of the matters set out in Schedule 4 and Schedule 5 of the Constitution must be interpreted in light of the model of government adopted by the Constitution and the manner in which the Constitution allocates power to the different spheres of government.

Besides these principles, the Constitutional Court also held in *Gauteng Development Tribunal* that where two or more matters appear to overlap with each other, they should be interpreted in a bottom-up manner.[175] A bottom-up method of interpretation is one in which the more specific matter is defined first and all residual areas are left for the much broader matter.[176]

In the *Gauteng Development Tribunal* case, for example, one of the key questions the Constitutional Court had to answer was whether the power to approve applications for the rezoning of land and the establishment of townships fell into the broad matter of urban and rural development, which is listed in Schedule 4A, or into the specific matter of municipal planning, which is listed in Schedule 4B. In accordance with the bottom-up method of interpretation, the Constitutional Court began its analysis, not with an examination of the scope and ambit of the broad matter of urban and rural development, but rather with an examination of the scope and ambit of the specific matter of municipal planning.

In so far as the scope and ambit of municipal planning was concerned, the Constitutional Court began by noting that although the term is not defined in the Constitution, it has a particular and well known meaning, which includes the zoning of land and the establishment of townships.[177] In addition, the Constitutional Court noted further, there is nothing in the Constitution which indicates that the term 'municipal planning' should be given a meaning which is different from its common meaning.[178] The power to approve applications for the rezoning of land and the establishment of townships did, therefore, fall into the area of municipal planning listed in Schedule 4B.[179]

After coming to this conclusion, the Constitutional Court turned to consider whether the same powers also fell into the broad matter of urban and rural development. The Court held that they did not. In arriving at this conclusion, the Constitutional Court began by noting that the term 'urban and rural development' could not be interpreted in a way that included the power to approve applications for the rezoning of land and the establishment of townships. This is because, the Constitutional Court noted further, such an interpretation would infringe the principles of co-operative government which provide that each sphere of government must respect the functions of the other spheres

174 (CCT89/09) [2010] ZACC 11; 2010 (6) SA 182 (CC); 2010 (9) BCLR 859 (CC) (18 June 2010). See also *Maccsand (Pty) Ltd v City of Cape Town and Others* (CCT103/11) (CC) [2012] ZACC 7; 2012 (4) SA 181 (CC); 2012 (7) BCLR 690 (CC) (12 April 2012).

175 See also Steytler and De Visser (2013) 22.21–22.22.

176 Steytler and De Visser (2013) 22.21–22.22.

177 *Gauteng Development Tribunal* para 57.

178 *Gauteng Development Tribunal* para 57.

179 *Gauteng Development Tribunal* para 57.

and must not assume any functions or powers not conferred on them by the Constitution or encroach on the functional integrity of the other spheres.[180] An important consequence of this approach, the Court went on to note, was that the term 'urban and rural development' should be interpreted narrowly so that each sphere of government could exercise its powers without interference by another sphere of government.[181]

Having found that the term 'urban and rural development' was not broad enough to include the powers that form a part of municipal planning, the Constitutional Court then concluded that it was not necessary to go any further and define exactly what the scope of the functional area of urban and rural development was.[182]

The Constitution confers the authority on municipalities to pass laws in respect of the matters listed in Part B of Schedule 4 and Part B of Schedule 5. However, it is important to note that the authority to pass laws on the matters listed in Schedule 4B and Schedule 5B has also been conferred on the national[183] and provincial governments.[184] The authority conferred on the national and provincial governments to pass laws on the matters listed in Schedule 4B, however, is limited by section 155(6)(*a*) and 155(7) of the Constitution.[185] The authority conferred on the provincial governments to pass laws on the matters listed in Schedule 5B is limited by section 155(6)(*a*) and 155(7) of the Constitution.[186]

Section 155(6)(*a*) of the Constitution provides in this respect that '[e]ach provincial government ... by legislative and other measures, must provide for the monitoring and support of local government in the province'. Section 155(7) of the Constitution provides that:

> **[t]he national government, subject to section 44, and the provincial governments have the legislative and executive authority to see to the effective performance by municipalities of their functions in respect of matters listed in Schedule 4 and 5, by regulating the exercise by municipalities of their executive authority referred to in section 156(1).**

In the *Gauteng Development Tribunal* case, the Constitutional Court held that an important consequence of section 155(7) of the Constitution is that neither the national nor the provincial spheres of government can, by legislation, give themselves the power to exercise executive municipal powers or the right to administer municipal affairs.[187] This is because, the Constitutional Court held further, the mandate of these two spheres is ordinarily limited to regulating the exercise of executive municipal powers and the administration of municipal affairs by municipalities.[188] In other words, while the national and provincial spheres of government are entitled to pass laws regulating the local government matters set out in Schedule 4B and Schedule 5B, they are not entitled to pass laws giving themselves the power to administer or implement those laws. The municipalities themselves must exercise the power to administer or implement those laws.

---

180 *Gauteng Development Tribunal* para 58.
181 *Gauteng Development Tribunal* para 63.
182 *Gauteng Development Tribunal* para 63.
183 S 44(1) of the Constitution.
184 S 104(1) of the Constitution.
185 Schedule 4 of the Constitution.
186 Schedule 5 of the Constitution.
187 *Gauteng Development Tribunal* para 43.
188 *Gauteng Development Tribunal* para 59.

8.3.4.2 Assigned municipal powers

Sections 44(1)(*a*)(iii) and 104(1)(*c*) of the Constitution provide that both the national and provincial governments may increase the legislative powers of specific municipalities or municipalities in general by assigning any of their legislative powers to a specific municipality or to municipalities in general. Apart from sections 44(1)(*a*)(iii) and 104(1)(*c*), sections 99 and 126 of the Constitution provide that a national or provincial Minister may increase the executive powers of a specific municipality by assigning their executive powers to the municipal council of that municipality. The assignment must, however, be consistent with the Act in terms of which the relevant power is exercised or performed.[189] Finally, it is also important to note that section 156(4) of the Constitution provides that the national and provincial governments must assign the administration of a matter listed in Part A of Schedule 4 or Part A of Schedule 5 to a municipal council if certain conditions are met. These conditions are as follows:

- First, the matter necessarily relates to local government.
- Second, the matter would most effectively be administered locally.
- Third, the municipality has the capacity to administer the matter.
- Fourth, the municipal council agrees to the assignment.

A key difference between section 156(4) of the Constitution and sections 99 and 126 is that while section 156(4) is mandatory, sections 99 and 126 are discretionary. Section 156(4) thus reinforces the principle of subsidiarity, which requires that the exercise of public power takes place at a level as close as possible to the citizenry.

PAUSE FOR REFLECTION

The assignment of legislative and executive powers

It is not entirely clear how section 156(4) of the Constitution relates to the assignment of legislative powers in terms of sections 44(1)(*a*)(iii) and 104(1)(c) and the assignment of executive powers in terms of sections 99 and 126. On the one hand, it may be argued that section 156(4) of the Constitution is an additional basis for the assignment of both legislative and executive powers to a municipality. This is because it refers to the national and provincial 'governments' and not simply the national and provincial legislatures. On the other hand, it may be argued that section 156(4) of the Constitution simply sets out the circumstances under which the assignment of executive powers in terms of sections 99 and 126 becomes compulsory. This is because it refers to the assignment of the 'administration' of the matters listed in Schedules 4A and 5A in terms of an 'agreement' to a 'specific municipality'.

Steytler and De Visser argue that the terms 'administration', 'agreement' and 'specific municipality' in section 156(4) of the Constitution all point towards assignments that have their basis in sections 99 and 126 of the Constitution. This means, they argue further, that section 156(4) is not an additional basis for assignment, but rather a principle that sets out the circumstances under which an assignment of executive powers in terms of section 99 or 126 becomes compulsory.[190]

189 This mode of assignment only takes effect upon a proclamation by the President or the Premier.
190 See Steytler and De Visser (2013) 22.61.

An assigning agent may set the parameters for the exercise of the assigned authority in the legislative act of assignment. The assignment is intended to be a complete transfer of the function and it entails the final decision-making power in individual matters. Accordingly, the assignment must conform to the requirements of section 151(4) of the Constitution. The assignment of powers and functions to municipalities by legislation or by an executive act or by agreement is regulated by the Local Government: Municipal Systems Act.

8.3.4.3 Incidental municipal powers

Section 156(5) of the Constitution provides that a municipality has the right to exercise any power concerning a matter that is reasonably necessary for or incidental to the effective performance of its functions. This power is sometimes referred to as the **incidental power**. The incidental power refers to those powers that strictly speaking fall outside the matters over which a municipality has legislative and executive authority, but are so closely connected to the effective performance of its functions that they are considered to be a part of the matters over which a municipality has authority. While they are not intended to create new functional areas of legislative and executive authority, the incidental powers do broaden a municipality's existing functional areas of legislative and executive authority.

PAUSE FOR REFLECTION

Determining the subject matter of a law

The matters over which a municipality has legislative and executive authority may be divided into three categories:

- first, those set out in Schedules 4B and 5B of the Constitution
- second, those that have been assigned to a municipality by the national or provincial government
- third, those that are reasonably necessary for or incidental to the effective performance of its functions.

As the judgment in *Le Sueur and Another v Ethekwini Municipality and Others*[191] illustrates, a municipality may base its power to pass legislation on a particular subject matter on any one or all three of these categories. The facts of this case were as follows. In 2010, the eThekwini Municipal Council adopted a resolution amending its town planning scheme to introduce the Durban Open Space System (D-MOSS). This system is aimed at protecting areas that have a high biodiversity value in Durban by creating a system of open spaces that will link them together. To achieve this goal, the system provides that land which falls within a D-MOSS area may not be developed without first obtaining an environmental authorisation. Even then, it may only be developed subject to strict controls aimed at protecting the ecological goods and services the land provides.

After the Municipal Council had adopted this resolution, the applicant, who owned land located in the eThekwini Municipality, applied for an order declaring the resolution to be unconstitutional and invalid. He based his application, among others, on the grounds that the subject matter of the resolution was the environment, that this matter is listed in Schedule 4A as a functional area of national and provincial legislative competence and, consequently, that the resolution fell outside the legislative authority of the Municipal Council.

191 (9714/11) [2013] ZAKZPHC 6 (30 January 2013).

The High Court rejected this argument. In arriving at this decision, the Court noted that the functional area of municipal planning which is set out in Schedule 4B must be interpreted in the light of section 24 of the Constitution.[192] This section provides that '[e]veryone has a right to an environment that is not harmful to their health or well-being'. In addition, section 152(1)(*d*) of the Constitution provides that one of the objectives of local government is to 'promote a safe and healthy environment'. These sections clearly indicate that the functional area of municipal planning includes responsibility over environmental affairs.[193]

The Court noted further that it is clear that legislative and executive authority over environmental matters as a part of municipal planning has been assigned to municipalities by national and provincial legislation.[194] Section 23(1)(*c*) of the Municipal Systems Act, which deals with integrated development planning at a municipal level, for example, recognises that there is an obligation on municipalities together with other organs of state to contribute to the progressive realisation of the fundamental rights contained in section 24 of the Constitution.[195]

Apart from the grounds set out above, the Court also appears to have accepted that the environment may be classified as a matter that is reasonably necessary for or incidental to the effective performance of a municipality's municipal planning function. This is because municipalities have traditionally been involved in regulating environmental matters at the local level and it is inconceivable that the drafters of the Constitution intended to exclude municipalities from legislating in this area.[196]

While the decision appears to be correct, it highlights the fact that it may not always be easy to determine whether the subject matter of a law falls into one of the functional areas set out in Schedules 4B and 5B, or into the incidental powers set out in section 156(5) of the Constitution.

8.3.5 Conflicting national, provincial and municipal laws

Given that Parliament, the provincial legislatures and the municipal councils all have the power to pass laws in respect of the matters listed in Schedules 4B and 5B, it is inevitable that these laws will on occasion conflict with one another. Conflicts between national and provincial laws and municipal laws are resolved in terms of section 156(3) of the Constitution. This section provides simply that, subject to section 151(4), a by-law that conflicts with national or provincial legislation is invalid. An important consequence of this provision is that a municipality must exercise its legislative and executive authority within the parameters set by national or provincial legislation. In the absence of any national or provincial law regulating a local government matter, however, a municipality is free to determine the content of its legislative and executive decisions.

192 *Le Sueur* para 19.
193 *Le Sueur* para 19.
194 *Le Sueur* para 22.
195 *Le Sueur* para 25.
196 *Le Sueur* para 39.

PAUSE FOR REFLECTION

National and/or provincial legislation does not always prevail over municipal law

There is a common misconception that national and/or provincial legislation always prevails over municipal law. An example illustrating that this is not the case is section 29(1) of the National Building Regulations and Building Standards Act[197] which provides that 'the provisions of any law applicable to any local authority are hereby repealed in so far as they confer a power to make building regulations or by-laws regarding any matter provided for in this Act'. However, the Constitution grants original legislative and executive authority to local government over building regulations in Schedule 4B. Local government power therefore prevails in this situation.

8.3.6 Supervision of local government

Although the Constitution confers legislative and executive powers on local government, it also recognises that local government is the weakest of the three spheres of government and often lacks the capacity to exercise these powers.

The Constitution, therefore, also provides that the manner in which local government exercises its legislative and executive powers must be supervised by the national and provincial spheres of governments. These supervisory powers may be divided into four different categories:

- the power to monitor local government
- the power to support local government
- the power to regulate local government
- the power to intervene in local government.[198]

The power to monitor local government is set out in section 155(6) of the Constitution. This section provides that each provincial government must, by legislative or other measures, provide for the monitoring and support of local government in the province. Provincial governments must also promote the development of local government capacity to enable municipalities to perform their functions and to manage their own affairs. In the *First Certification* judgment, the Constitutional Court held that this power grants the provincial governments the authority to 'observe' or 'keep under review' the manner in which a municipality manages its affairs. It does not, however, confer on provincial government the authority to control the affairs of a municipality. It is accordingly the least intrusive of all the supervisory powers.[199]

The power to support local government is set out in section 154(1) of the Constitution. This section provides that the national and provincial governments, by legislative and other measures, must support and strengthen the capacity of municipalities to manage their own affairs, to exercise their powers and to perform their functions.[200] In the *First Certification* judgment, the Constitutional Court held that this power grants both the national and provincial governments the authority to strengthen a municipality's ability to manage its affairs. It may also be used by national and provincial governments to prevent a decline or

197 Act 103 of 1977.

198 Freedman (2012) para 231–5.

199 *First Certification* para 372.

200 S 155(6) of the Constitution also provides that each provincial government must, by legislative or other measures, provide for the monitoring and support of local government in the province and promote the development of local government capacity to enable municipalities to perform their functions and to manage their own affairs.

degeneration in a municipality's existing structures, powers and functions.[201] It is, therefore, more intrusive than the power to monitor local government, but not as intrusive as the power to regulate or intervene.[202]

The power to regulate local government is set out in section 155(7) of the Constitution. This section provides that both the national and provincial governments have the legislative and executive authority to see to the effective performance by municipalities of their functions in respect of the matters listed in Schedules 4 and 5 by regulating the exercise by municipalities of their executive authority. In the *First Certification* judgment, the Constitutional Court held that this power grants the national and provincial governments the authority to 'control' the manner in which a municipality manages its affairs.[203] It does not, however, confer on the national and provincial governments the authority to exercise municipal powers or perform municipal functions.[204] It simply authorises the national and provincial governments to establish a framework within which a municipality must perform.[205] It is a 'hands-off' and not a 'hands-on' power.

Section 139(1) of the Constitution provides that when a municipality cannot or does not fulfil an executive obligation in terms of the Constitution or legislation, the relevant provincial executive may intervene by taking any appropriate steps to ensure the fulfilment of that obligation. The appropriate steps which the provincial executive may take include measures such as issuing a directive, assuming responsibility and dissolving a municipal council.[206] The power to intervene in terms of section 139(1) of the Constitution is commonly referred to as a **regular intervention**. Apart from regular interventions, section 139 of the Constitution also provides for budgetary interventions and financial crises interventions.

Section 139(4) of the Constitution governs budgetary interventions. This section provides that if a municipality cannot or does not fulfil an obligation in terms of the Constitution or legislation to approve a budget or any revenue-raising measures necessary to give effect to the budget, the national or relevant provincial executive must intervene by taking any appropriate steps to ensure that the budget or those revenue-raising measures are approved. The appropriate steps which the national or provincial executive may take include measures such as the mandatory dissolution of the municipal council and the adoption of a temporary budget or revenue-raising measures.[207]

Section 139(5) of the Constitution governs financial crises interventions. This section provides that if a municipality, as a result of a crisis in its financial affairs, is in serious or persistent material breach of its obligations to provide basic services or to meet its financial commitments, or admits that it is unable to meet its obligations or financial commitments, the national or relevant provincial executive must impose a financial recovery plan, dissolve the municipal council, or assume responsibility for the implementation of a recovery plan.

In the *First Certification* judgment, the Constitutional Court explained that the power to intervene gives the provincial government the authority to intrude on the functional terrain of local government.[208] In other words, it does confer on provincial government the authority

201 *First Certification* para 371.
202 *First Certification* para 371.
203 *First Certification* para 372.
204 *First Certification* para 373.
205 *First Certification* para 375.
206 See *Mnquma Local Municipality and Another v Premier of the Eastern Cape and Others* (231/2009) [2009] ZAECBHC 14 (5 August 2009).
207 See *Premier of the Western Cape and Others v Overberg District Municipality and Others* (801/201) [2011] ZASCA 23; 2011 (4) SA 441 (SCA); [2011] 3 All SA 385 (SCA) (18 March 2011).
208 *First Certification* para 376.

to exercise municipal powers and perform municipal functions. It is a 'hands-on' power. It is, accordingly, the most intrusive power.[209] Given its intrusive nature, the circumstances under which a provincial government can exercise this power are not only restricted, but are also subject to various procedural requirements.

8.4 Financial affairs

8.4.1 Introduction

Apart from dividing legislative and executive power between the national, provincial and local spheres of government, the Constitution also divides fiscal powers - the power to collect and spend public funds - between the three spheres of government. Chapter 13 of the Constitution sets out the constitutional provisions regulating fiscal powers. Chapter 13 is sometimes referred to as the financial constitution. Apart from regulating the power to collect and spend public funds, Chapter 13 of the Constitution also establishes two important regulatory bodies, namely the central bank and the Fiscal and Financial Commission (FFC).

CRITICAL THINKING

The power of the purse

Murray and Simeon argue that:

> [I]n multilevel systems of government, fiscal federalism, or the division of revenues and expenditures among central and provincial governments, may say as much, if not more, about how power and influence are distributed than the constitutional text. Constitutional competencies are meaningless without an accompanying fiscal competence (not to mention other dimensions of competence such as administrative capacity). Financial sticks and carrots in a centralized financial system give the centre power to influence provincial actions and priorities well beyond the formal allocation of authority.[210]

After reading Chapter 13 of the Constitution and after assessing the financial powers of each sphere of government, it is easier to determine which sphere of government has been provided with more decisive powers. From such a study, it becomes apparent that the provincial sphere of government is less powerful than the other spheres.

8.4.2 The division of fiscal powers

The division of fiscal powers between different spheres of government gives rise to a number of difficult questions. Among these are the following:

- First, whether the power to raise revenue should be distributed between the different spheres of government or centralised in the national sphere. In a competitive or divided system of federalism, for example in Canada, the power to impose taxes is usually distributed between the different spheres of government. In a co-operative or integrated system of federalism, such as South Africa, the power to impose taxes is usually centralised in the national sphere of government.[211]

209 *First Certification* para 370.

210 Murray, C and Simeon, R (2000) South Africa's financial Constitution: Towards better delivery? *SA Public Law* 15(2):477–504 at 477.

211 Murray and Simeon (2000) 479.

- Second, if the power to impose taxes is centralised in the national sphere of government, the next question that arises is how the revenue that has been raised by the national sphere of government should be distributed, not only between the different spheres of government, but also within each sphere. Insofar as this question is concerned, there are a number of different approaches that may be adopted. The transfer of funds could, for example, take the form of conditional grants, on the one hand, or unconditional grants, on the other.[212]
- Finally, there is also the question of how the decision to divide national revenue between the different spheres of government and within each sphere of government should be made and by whom. Should it be made by the national sphere of government alone or should the other spheres have a say? What about third parties? Should they be given a role to play?[213]

8.4.3 The collection of revenue

As Kriel and Monadjem point out, the power to collect revenue is vested primarily in the national sphere of government.[214] This is because Chapter 13 of the Constitution restricts the power of the provincial and local spheres of government to impose taxes. In so far as the provincial sphere of government is concerned, section 228(1) of the Constitution provides that a provincial legislature may impose:

- taxes, levies and duties other than income tax, value-added tax, general sales tax, rates on property or customs duties
- flat-rate surcharges on any tax, levy or duty, other than corporate income tax, value-added tax, rates on property or customs duty.

An important consequence of these provisions is that the main sources of revenue such as income tax, value-added tax, general sales tax, and rates and customs duties have been expressly removed from the jurisdiction of the provinces.

PAUSE FOR REFLECTION

The reason for the decision to restrict the power of the provincial legislatures to impose taxes

Although the power to impose taxes promotes the principles of accountability and transparency in government, the drafters of the Constitution decided to restrict the power of the provincial legislatures to impose taxes. This is partly because the drafters of the Constitution believed that the economic disparities that already exist between the provinces would have been exacerbated if significant taxing powers were given in the provinces.

Apart from the provisions set out above, section 228(2) of the Constitution also provides that a provincial legislature's power to impose taxes, levies, duties and surcharges may not be exercised in a way that materially and unreasonably prejudices national economic policies, economic activities across provincial boundaries, or the mobility of goods, services, capital

212 Murray and Simeon (2000) 479. A conditional grant is one in which the money that has been transferred must be used for a specific purpose and not for any other purpose. An unconditional grant is one in which the money can be used by the recipient for any purpose.

213 Murray and Simeon (2000) 480.

214 Kriel, R and Monadjem, M 'Public finance' in Woolman and Bishop (2013) 27.8.

or labour. In addition, a provincial legislature's power to impose taxes must be regulated by an Act of Parliament which may be passed only after any recommendations made by the FFC have been considered.[215] The Act of Parliament referred to in this section is the Provincial Tax Regulation Process Act.[216]

The Provincial Tax Regulation Process Act restricts a provincial legislature's power to introduce a new provincial tax. This is because it essentially provides that if a province wishes to introduce a new provincial tax, it must first submit a proposal to the Minister of Finance who, after consulting the Budget Council, must introduce a Bill into the NA to regulate the new provincial tax. Given the restrictions imposed by this Act, it is not surprising that no new provincial taxes have ever been introduced.

In so far as municipalities are concerned, section 229(1) of the Constitution provides that a municipality may impose:

- rates on property and surcharges on fees for services provided by or on behalf of the municipality
- if authorised by national legislation, other taxes, levies and duties appropriate to local government or to the category of local government into which the municipality falls.

Like the provincial legislatures, however, municipalities may not impose income tax, value-added tax, general sales tax or customs duty. Apart from the provisions set out above, section 229(2) of the Constitution also provides that a municipality's power to impose rates on property, surcharges on fees or other taxes, levies or duties may not be exercised in a way that materially and unreasonably prejudices national economic policies, economic activities across provincial boundaries, or the mobility of goods, services, capital or labour.

In addition, a municipality's power to impose rates on property, surcharges on fees or other taxes, levies or duties may be regulated by national legislation which may be passed only after organised local government and the FFC have been consulted and any recommendations made by the FFC have been considered.[217] The national legislation referred to in this section is the Local Government: Municipal Property Rates Act[218] and the Municipal Fiscal Powers and Functions Act.[219] The Municipal Property Rates Act regulates the municipalities' power to levy property rates and the Municipal Fiscal Powers and Functions Act regulates their power to levy surcharges on fees.

PAUSE FOR REFLECTION

Determining when property is state property

Section 3(3)(*a*) of the Rating of State Property Act[220] (Rating Act) provides that a municipality may not impose rates on state property that is held by the state in trust for the inhabitants of an area that falls into the jurisdiction of a municipality. In *Ingonyama Trust v eThekwini Municipality*,[221] the Supreme Court of Appeal (SCA) had to decide whether land owned by the Ingonyama Trust fell into section 3 of the Rating Act and was therefore exempt from paying property rates to the eThekwini Municipality.

215 S 228(2) of the Constitution.
216 Act 53 of 2001.
217 S 229(2) of the Constitution.
218 Act 6 of 2004.
219 Act 12 of 2007.
220 Act 79 of 1984.
221 (149/2011) [2012] ZASCA 104; 2013 (1) SA 564 (SCA) (1 June 2012).

The Ingonyama Trust was established in terms of the KwaZulu Ingonyama Trust Act.[222] It owns all the land that was previously owned by the government of KwaZulu and is administered by a board made up of the Ingonyama and eight other members appointed by the Minister of Land Affairs.

The key issue that the SCA had to decide was whether the land owned by the Ingonyama Trust could be classified as state property. The Court held that it could and, consequently, that the Trust was exempt from paying rates in terms of section 3 of the Rating Act.[223]

In arriving at this decision, the SCA noted that the land owned by the Ingonyama Trust could be defined as state property because the Trust itself could be said to be a part of the state.[224] The SCA gave the following reasons why the Trust could be said to be a part of the state:

- First, eight of the nine trustees were appointed by the Minister of Land Affairs who also had the power to make regulations governing the affairs of the Trust.[225]
- Second, the cost of administering the Trust had to be paid by the Department of Land Affairs.[226]
- Third, the financial statements of the Trust had to be audited by the Auditor-General.
- Fourth, an annual report on the activities of the Trust had to be submitted to the Minister of Land Affairs by the accounting authority of the Trust.[227]
- Last, the land owned by the Trust was defined as state land by Parliament in a number of other statutes, for example the National Veld and Forest Fire Act,[228] the National Forests Act[229] and the South African Schools Act.[230]

8.4.4 The distribution of revenue

Although the Constitution restricts the power of the provincial and local spheres of government to impose taxes and thus to raise revenue, it compensates them for this loss by granting them a right to an equitable share of revenue collected nationally. Section 214(1) of the Constitution provides in this respect that an Act of Parliament must provide for:

- the equitable division of revenue raised nationally between the national, provincial and local spheres of government
- the determination of each province's equitable share of the provincial share of that revenue
- any other allocations to provinces, local government or municipalities from the national government's share of that revenue, and any conditions on which those allocations may be made.

The Act referred to in section 214(1) of the Constitution is the annual Division of Revenue Act (DORA). Section 214(2) of the Constitution provides that the DORA may be passed only

222 Act 3 of 1994.
223 *Ingonyama Trust* para 11.
224 *Ingonyama Trust* para 11.
225 *Ingonyama Trust* para 8.
226 *Ingonyama Trust* para 8.
227 *Ingonyama Trust* para 8.
228 Act 101 of 1998.
229 Act 84 of 1998.
230 *Ingonyama Trust* para 10; Act 84 of 1996.

after the provincial governments, organised local government and the FFC have been consulted and any recommendations made by the FFC have been considered. In addition, section 214(2) of the Constitution also provides that the DORA is required to take into account:

> (*a*) **the national interest;**
> (*b*) **any provision that must be made in respect of the national debt and other national obligations;**
> (*c*) **the needs and interests of the national government, determined by objective criteria;**
> (*d*) **the need to ensure that the provinces and municipalities are able to provide basic services and perform the functions allocated to them;**
> (*e*) **the fiscal capacity and efficiency of the provinces and the municipalities;**
> (*f*) **developmental and other needs of provinces, local government and municipalities;**
> (*g*) **economic disparities within and among the provinces;**
> (*h*) **obligations of the provinces in terms of national and provincial legislation;**
> (*i*) **the desirability of stable and predictable allocations of revenue shares; and**
> (*j*) **the need for flexibility in responding to emergencies or other temporary needs, and other factors based on similar objective criteria.**

While regard must be had for the need of the provinces to be able to provide basic services and carry out their developmental objectives, the criteria set out in section 214(2) place a heavy emphasis on the importance of national objectives and priorities. The listing appears to suggest that the other criteria will be evaluated through the prism of national objectives. The process preceding the adoption of the DORA is set out in the Intergovernmental Fiscal Relations Act.[231]

At least 10 months before the start of each financial year, the FFC must submit recommendations for an equitable division of revenue raised nationally between the three spheres of government as well as each province's share of the provincial share of national revenue to the Minister of Finance, Parliament and the provincial legislatures.[232] After receiving the FFC's recommendations, the Minister of Finance must consult with the FFC itself, the provinces, either in the Budget Council or in some other way, and organised local government, either in the Budget Forum or in some other way.[233] The Budget Council and the Budget Forum are statutory bodies established by the Intergovernmental Fiscal Relations Act to facilitate intergovernmental consultation with respect to fiscal matters.[234] Once these consultations have taken place, the Minister of Finance must introduce the annual Division of Revenue Bill in the NA at the same time that the annual budget is introduced. The equitable share allocated to each sphere of government as well as each province's share of the provincial share of national revenue must be set out in this Bill.[235]

The DORA begins by dividing the revenue raised nationally between the three spheres of government. It then goes on to divide the provincial share of revenue raised nationally

---

231 Act 97 of 1997.

232 S 9(1) of the Intergovernmental Fiscal Relations Act.

233 S 10(3) of the Intergovernmental Fiscal Relations Act.

234 Ss 2 and 5 of the Intergovernmental Fiscal Relations Act. The Budget Council consists of the Minister of Finance and the MEC for Finance in each province, while the Budget Forum consists of the Minister of Finance, the MEC for Finance in each province, five representatives from the national body representing organised local government and one representative from each of the provincial bodies representing organised local government.

235 S 10(1) of the Intergovernmental Fiscal Relations Act.

between the provinces and finally it divides the municipal share of revenue raised nationally between the municipalities. The amounts allocated to each province and each municipality are based on different formulae. These formulae are made up of a number of different components.[236]

Finally, it is important to note that although the equitable share of national revenue is supposed to be an unconditional grant, there are some restraints on the manner in which the provinces may spend this money. Section 227 of the Constitution, for example, states that 'each province is entitled to an equitable share ... to enable it to provide basic services and perform the functions allocated to it'. Provinces, therefore, must use the equitable share to provide basic services and perform the functions allocated to them.

8.4.5 The budgetary process

Section 215(1) of the Constitution provides that the national, provincial and municipal budgetary processes must promote transparency, accountability and the effective financial management of the economy, debt and the public sector. In addition, section 215(2) of the Constitution provides that national legislation must prescribe the form of national, provincial and municipal budgets; when national and provincial budgets must be tabled; and that budgets in each sphere of government must show the sources of revenue and the way in which proposed expenditure will comply with national legislation. Budgets in each sphere of government must also contain:

- estimates of revenue and expenditure, differentiating between capital and current expenditure
- proposals for financing any anticipated deficit for the period to which they apply
- an indication of the intentions regarding borrowing and other forms of public liability that will increase public debt during the ensuing year.[237]

As the Constitutional Court pointed out in the *Premier: Limpopo Province* case,[238] the Public Finance Management Act (PFMA)[239] deals with public finance. To help achieve the objects of section 215 of the Constitution, section 27(1) of the PFMA provides that the Minister of Finance must table the annual budget for the financial year before the start of that financial year. In addition, the MEC for Finance in each province must table an annual provincial budget within two weeks of the Minister's budget speech unless an extension has been granted by the Minister of Finance.[240] Section 27(3) provides that, among other factors, the annual budget must contain:

- estimates of all revenue expected to be raised during the financial year
- estimates for the current expenditure for that financial year
- estimates of interest and debt servicing charges
- any repayments on loans
- estimates of capital expenditure for that financial year and projected financial implications of that expenditure for future financial years

236 The provincial government equitable formula consists of six components: an education component, a health component, a basic share component, an institutional component, a poverty component and an economic output component. The local government equitable formula consists of five components: a basic services component, an institutional support component, a development component, a revenue-raising capacity correction and a correction and stabilisation factor (see the Explanatory Memorandum to the Division of Revenue Bill 2013).

237 S 215(3) of the Constitution.

238 *Premier: Limpopo Province* para 26.

239 Act 1 of 1999.

240 S 27(2) of the PFMA.

- estimates of all direct charges against the relevant revenue fund and standing appropriations for that financial year
- proposals for financing any anticipated deficit in that financial year.

Apart from helping to achieve the objects of section 215 of the Constitution, the PFMA is also aimed at fulfilling the obligations imposed on Parliament by section 216 of the Constitution. Section 216 provides that national legislation must establish a national treasury and prescribes measures to ensure both transparency and expenditure control in each sphere of government by introducing generally recognised accounting practices, uniform expenditure classifications and uniform treasury norms and standards.

Although section 216 of the Constitution imposes an obligation on Parliament to establish a national treasury and not provincial treasuries, the PFMA makes provision not only for a national treasury, but also for a provincial treasury in each province. The Minister of Finance heads the National Treasury which comprises those departments that are responsible for financial and fiscal matters.[241] The main functions of the National Treasury are to:

- promote the national government's fiscal policy framework
- co-ordinate macroeconomic policies
- co-ordinate intergovernmental financial and fiscal relations
- manage the budget preparation process
- exercise control over the implementation of the annual budget
- facilitate the implementation of the annual DORA
- monitor the implementation of the provincial budget
- promote and enforce transparency and effective management in respect of revenue, expenditure, assets and liabilities of departments, public entities and constitutional institutions.[242]

In terms of section 11 of the PFMA, the National Treasury is also in charge of the National Revenue Fund. The National Revenue Fund is established in terms of section 213 of the Constitution. This section provides that all money received by the national government, except money excluded by an Act of Parliament, must be paid into the fund. In addition, it also provides that money may be withdrawn from the National Revenue Fund only in terms of an appropriation by an Act of Parliament or a direct charge against the National Revenue Fund when it is provided for in the Constitution or an Act of Parliament. A province's equitable share of national revenue is a direct charge against the National Revenue Fund.

The provincial treasury for each province is headed by the MEC for Finance in the province and the provincial department responsible for financial matters in each province.[243] The main functions of each provincial treasury are to:

- prepare a provincial budget
- exercise control over the implementation of the provincial budget
- promote the transparent and effective management in respect of revenue, expenditure, assets and liabilities of the provincial departments and provincial public entities
- ensure that its fiscal policies do not materially and unreasonably prejudice national economic policies.[244]

---

241 S 5 of the PFMA.
242 S 6 of the PFMA.
243 S 17 of the PFMA.
244 S 18 of the PFMA.

In terms of section 21 of the PFMA, each provincial treasury is in charge of the Provincial Revenue Fund for its province. Provincial Revenue Funds are established in terms of section 226 of the Constitution. This section provides that all money received by a provincial government, except money excluded by an Act of Parliament, must be paid into the Provincial Revenue Fund. In addition, it also provides that money may be withdrawn from a Provincial Revenue Fund only in terms of an appropriation by a provincial Act or a direct charge against the Provincial Revenue Fund when it is provided for in the Constitution or a provincial Act. Revenue allocated to local government in terms of section 214 of the Constitution is a direct charge against a Provincial Revenue Fund.

8.4.6 The central bank

Section 223 of the Constitution provides that the Reserve Bank is the central bank of the Republic and that it must be regulated in terms of an Act of Parliament. The Act referred to in this section is the South African Reserve Bank Act.[245] In terms of section 224(2) of the Constitution, the 'primary objective of the South African Reserve Bank is to protect the value of the currency in the interest of balanced and sustainable economic growth'. In addition, section 224(2) also provides that the bank is obliged to function independently and without fear, favour or prejudice, but must consult regularly with the Minister of Finance. The Reserve Bank plays a key role in the management of the money and banking system. The Reserve Bank describes this role as follows:

- **The formulation and implementation of monetary policy:** Monetary policy refers to the measures taken to influence the quantity of money and the rate of interest in the country. This assists is ensuring stability of prices and seeks to promote employment and economic growth. The Reserve Bank sets the interest rates at which other banks can borrow money and this ultimately determines the interest that consumers pay in respect of their debts such as mortgage bonds.
- **The provision of liquidity to banks:** When banks face a liquidity problem as a result of a temporary shortage of cash, the Reserve Bank provides liquidity to these banks on a conditional and temporary basis. The main purpose of this assistance is to prevent banks going into bankruptcy and people losing their savings and deposits that they invested in the banks.
- **Bank notes and coins:** The Reserve Bank has the exclusive authority to issue and destroy bank notes and coins in the country.
- **Banker of other banks:** The Reserve Bank is the custodian of the cash reserves that banks are legally required to hold.[246]

The Reserve Bank thus plays a vital role in the formulation and implementation of economic policies. Its decisions have a direct impact on the lives of people. Importantly, the policy decisions of the Reserve Bank and the government in power may not always coincide and it is for this reason that the independence of the Bank is entrenched. The Reserve Bank is meant to act is the best interests of the economy of the country and to be shielded from having to act in accordance with the popular will.

245 Act 90 of 1989.

246 The Role and Functions of the South African Reserve Bank available at http://www.resbank.co.za/AboutUs/Functions/Pages/default.aspx.

8.4.7 Procurement

8.4.7.1 Introduction

Section 217 of the Constitution makes it imperative for an organ of state in the national, provincial or local sphere to contract for goods and services in a manner that is fair, equitable, transparent, competitive and cost-effective. However, organs of state are not prevented from implementing a procurement policy providing for categories of preferences in the allocation of contracts and the protection or advancement of persons or categories of persons previously disadvantaged by unfair discrimination.[247] The section goes on to require national legislation to be enacted to prescribe a framework to implement the policy of preference to previously disadvantaged persons. The Preferential Procurement Policy Framework Act (PPPFA)[248] is the empowering legislation that seeks to achieve this objective.

In *Millennium Waste Management (Pty) Ltd. v Chairperson of the Tender Board: Limpopo Province and Others,*[249] the SCA required tenders to be evaluated in a manner that advances the five constitutional values identified in section 217 of the Constitution. In this case, the appellant had submitted its tender which met all the specifications of the advertisement. However, the appellant had inadvertently omitted to sign the declaration of interest, but had inserted the name of the relevant person and had filled in the relevant information. A tender committee on behalf of the Limpopo Department of Health and Social Development disqualified the applicant and finally awarded the tender to a consortium called TTP. A particularly concerning aspect was that TTP's bid for the removal, treatment and disposal of hospital waste was R3 600 000 per month which was significantly more than appellant's tender which would have cost the Department R400 000 per month.

The Tender Board argued that the signing of the declaration of interest was peremptory and as the appellant had not signed it, the Tender Board was obliged to disqualify the appellant.

The SCA held that the decision to award the tender was administrative action and had to comply with the provisions of the Promotion of Administrative Justice Act (PAJA),[250] with section 217 of the Constitution and with the PPPFA.[251] Interpreting the regulations in terms of which the Tender Board was acting, the SCA held that the Tender Board had the power to condone non-compliance with procedural defects in the application.[252] However, the SCA went on to hold that 'our law permits condonation of non-compliance with peremptory requirements in cases where condonation is not incompatible with public interest and if such condonation is granted by the body in whose benefit the provision was enacted'.[253] The SCA stated further that the condonation of the failure to sign would have been in the public interest as it would have facilitated competitiveness.[254] A condonation in this instance would have served the broader constitutional values of fairness, competiveness and cost-effectiveness.[255]

---

247 S 217(2) of the Constitution.

248 Act 5 of 2000.

249 (31/2007) [2007] ZASCA 165; [2007] SCA 165 (RSA); [2008] 2 All SA 145; 2008 (2) SA 481; 2008 (5) BCLR 508; 2008 (2) SA 481 (SCA) (29 November 2007).

250 Act 3 of 2000.

251 *Millennium Waste Management* para 21.

252 *Millennium Waste Management* para 16.

253 *Millennium Waste Management* para 17.

254 *Millennium Waste Management* para 17.

255 *Millennium Waste Management* para 17.

Importantly, the SCA held that whether the appellant's tender constituted an acceptable tender in terms of the PPPFA must be construed in the context of a system that is fair, equitable, transparent, competitive and cost-effective.[256] In other words, the constitutional values must be the prism through which the enabling legislation must be interpreted. The SCA held the term 'tender' must be given a relatively narrow meaning and cannot mean that the tender must comply with conditions which are immaterial, unreasonable or unconstitutional.[257] The SCA concluded that by insisting on disqualifying the appellant for an innocent omission, the Tender Board had acted unreasonably.[258] The SCA set aside the decision of the Tender Board and ordered the Tender Board to reconsider and adjudicate on the bids submitted by the appellant and TTP afresh. The Court thus assessed the entire tender process against the five values identified in the Constitution and not just the final evaluation process of the shortlisted candidates.

PAUSE FOR REFLECTION

When is condonation permissible?

Assume that the price differential was not as stark and assume that tenderer B had submitted their tender a day after the date stipulated in the advertisement. Tenderer B tendered to remove hospital waste for R400 000 per month and the successful tenderer (Tenderer A) quoted R1 million per month. In all other respects, the tenders are similar. Does the *Millennium Waste Management* case allow a tender board to entertain the late submission of the tender by tenderer B? Alternatively, could such an option not be used to overlook all sorts of non-compliance and in the final analysis be contrary to the values in the Constitution?

In *Minister of Social Development and Others v Phoenix Cash & Carry Pmb CC*,[259] the SCA once again reiterated that the five principles of fairness, equitable treatment, transparency, competitiveness and cost-effectiveness must inform all aspects of the tender process. In a frank judgment, the SCA directly questioned the legitimacy of the process that led to the appellants being denied the tender and in a damning indictment indicated that from its experience drawn from matters before the Court, the values of section 217 are more honoured in the breach than in the observance.[260]

The facts of this case were as follows. Bids were invited to supply food hampers to indigent families in KwaZulu-Natal and in the Eastern Cape. The price of the bid submitted by Phoenix was approximately 40% less than that submitted by the successful tenderer. In response to a request for reasons, the department indicated that it had evaluated the bids and that Phoenix was unsuccessful. Subsequently, the department attempted to supplement their reasons by stating that Phoenix had not complied with certain prerequisites.

The SCA found that the department in excluding the bid by Phoenix had elevated form above substance.[261] Had it properly appraised the documents submitted, it would have concluded that the material issues dealing with financial viability had been dealt with even

256 *Millennium Waste Management* para 18.
257 *Millennium Waste Management* para 19.
258 *Millennium Waste Management* para 21.
259 (189/06, 244/06) [2007] ZASCA 26; [2007] SCA 26 (RSA); [2007] 3 All SA 115 (SCA) (27 March 2007).
260 *Phoenix Cash & Carry* para 1.
261 *Phoenix Cash & Carry* para 2.

though no audited statements were submitted.[262] Accordingly, the SCA held that the process was fundamentally flawed and set aside the decision. In an effort to prevent such a fundamentally flawed process from being repeated, the Court laid down the following principles:

- It is against the principle of fairness for the tender process to be evaluated on the basis of uncertain criteria which could have the effect of meritorious applicants being excluded.
- A process that emphasises form over substance could have the effect of facilitating corrupt practices by providing an excuse not to consider meritorious tenders and by excluding them on technicalities. This is often inimical to fairness, competitiveness and cost-effectiveness.
- The tender board can prescribe formalities, provided the requirements are made clear and the consequences of non-compliance spelt out.[263]

The SCA cautioned against unreasonably elevating matters of subsidiary importance to a level of primary importance and then deeming non-compliance to be fatal to the bid.[264]

Section 217 of the Constitution must be read with section 5 of the PAJA which requires a functionary to provide adequate reasons for administrative decisions which materially and adversely affect rights if requested. Once reasons are provided, the decision can be appraised against the constitutional criteria in section 217. In the *Phoenix Cash & Carry* case, the reasons supplied were woefully inadequate and the supplementary reasons confirmed that, at best, an unreasonable and irrational decision had been made. The tenor of the judgment appears to suggest that the irrationality bordered on improper conduct.

What is apparent from these decisions is that while price may not be the decisive factor, massive disparities in pricing will weigh with the court when determining whether a public body has discharged its ultimate mandate of acting in the public good. It would be advisable therefore that if the successful tenderer's contract price is much more expensive than the unsuccessful tenderer, that the reasons provided deal with the disparity in price and justify the decision to award the tender despite the price differential.

PAUSE FOR REFLECTION

Dealing with disparities in price

When a tender is awarded to a body that did not submit the lowest tender, the state is paying more for a service or product. Assume that Cleaners Incorporated, a group of female cleaners who have been cleaning the officers of the KZN Provincial Administration for the last five years, form a consortium and bid for a new provincial government cleaning contract against their previous employers, Sparkling Clean CC. Most members of Cleaners Incorporated are African female and many of them are sole breadwinners. Their bid is R10 000 more a month to clean the buildings than the corresponding offer by Sparkling Clean, which is a national company. Should the government procurement policy be used to bridge the economic disparity in our society or should government attempt to obtain the maximum value for its rands given the demands on a limited budget?

262 *Phoenix Cash & Carry* para 17.
263 *Phoenix Cash & Carry* para 2.
264 *Phoenix Cash & Carry* para 2.

8.4.7.2 The Preferential Procurement Policy Framework Act 5 of 2000

While section 217(1) of the Constitution imposes an obligation to act in terms of a system that accords with the five principles, section 217(2) permits public bodies to implement a preferential procurement policy. The PPPFA requires organs of state to determine a preferential procurement policy and to implement it.[265]

The process envisaged by the PPPFA is that:

- persons are invited to tender in respect of a formal tender proposal
- all applications are assessed in terms of evaluation criteria specifically identified in the tender proposal
- the various bids are ranked in terms of each evaluation criteria.[266]

Section 2 of the PPPFA draws a distinction between contracts above the prescribed amount[267] and contracts below the prescribed amount. In respect of contracts above the prescribed amount, a maximum of 10 points may be allocated for the specific goals identified in the PPPFA while in respect of contracts below the prescribed amount a maximum of 20 points may be allocated for the specific goals. The specific goals relate to contracting with people who were historically disadvantaged by unfair discrimination on the basis of race, gender, sex or disability or for the purposes of implementing the Reconstruction and Development Programme. Thus, a maximum of 10 points or 20 points, depending on the contract price, may be assigned to historically disadvantaged individuals. In terms of the regulations,[268] a maximum of 90 or 80 points must be assigned for price. The points allocated must be out of 100 and the person scoring the highest points must be allocated the tender. Thus, the PPPFA and the regulations adopt a fairly rigid system to ensure that price is allocated the overwhelming segment of the points, but that equity issues are not ignored.

SUMMARY

The Constitution does not only divide power vertically, but also horizontally between the national, provincial and local spheres of government. This horizontal division of power establishes a quasi-federal system of government. Power is divided largely according to an integrated model of federalism in which the subject matters in respect of which policies and laws may be made are not strictly divided between the different levels or spheres of government but are shared between them. To ensure that this system works optimally, the Constitution also establishes the principle of co-operative government, requiring the various spheres of government to work together regardless of the political party in power nationally, provincially or at local government level. The National Council of Provinces (NCOP), the second House of the national legislature, plays an important role in co-ordinating the legislative activities of the three spheres of government.

The structures of government for the nine provinces largely mirror that of the national sphere. A Premier elected by the provincial legislature heads the provincial executive and can also be removed by the provincial legislature. A province has executive authority in terms of those functional areas listed in Schedules 4 (concurrent powers shared with the national executive) and 5 (exclusive powers) of the Constitution. Provincial legislatures operate largely in the same manner and according to the same principles as the national legislature.

265 S 2 of the PPPFA.

266 See the discussion by Penfold, G and Reyburn, P 'Public procurement' in Woolman and Bishop (2013) 25.16.

267 The prescribed amount at the time of writing is R1 000 000.

268 GN R502, *GG* 34350, 8 June 2011.

However, provincial legislatures only have one House and not two although their interests are represented in the NCOP at national level. When both the national legislature and the provincial legislature pass legislation on one of the areas listed in Schedule 4, the provincial legislation shall prevail except if one of the criteria set out in section 146 of the Constitution is present in which case the national legislation shall prevail. It will only be permissible in exceptional circumstances for the national legislature to pass legislation relating to one of the areas exclusively reserved for provinces in Schedule 5 if this is authorised by section 44(2) of the Constitution. When determining whether the subject matter of a Bill falls within Schedule 4 or Schedule 5, we must apply the pith and substance test. This test must be distinguished from the substantial measure test used to decide how to tag a national Bill to decide on the procedure to be used to pass it.

In the constitutional dispensation, local government fulfils an important role. Municipalities thus enjoy original and constitutionally entrenched powers, functions, rights and duties that may be qualified or constrained by law and only to the extent to which these are set out in section 152(1) of the Constitution. Section 155 of the Constitution distinguishes between three different categories of municipalities, namely:

- category A municipalities with exclusive municipal executive and legislative authority in their area and which are referred to as metropolitan municipalities
- category B municipalities which share their municipal executive and legislative authority in their area with a category C municipality and which are referred to as local municipalities
- category C municipalities with municipal executive and legislative authority in an area which includes more than one municipality and which are referred to as district municipalities.

The Constitution determines that a municipality has executive authority in respect of and has the right to administer the local government matters listed in Part B of Schedule 4 and Part B of Schedule 5 and any other matter assigned to it by national or provincial legislation. In addition, municipalities may make and administer by-laws for the effective administration of the matters which they have the right to administer. Conflicts between national and provincial laws and municipal laws are resolved in terms of section 156(3) of the Constitution. This section provides simply that, subject to section 151(4), a by-law that conflicts with national or provincial legislation is invalid. An important consequence of this provision is that a municipality must exercise its legislative and executive authority within the parameters set by national or provincial legislation. In the absence of any national or provincial law regulating a local government matter, however, a municipality is free to determine the content of its legislative and executive decisions.

The financial arrangements in the Constitution tilt power decisively in favour of the national sphere of government as the power to collect revenue is vested primarily in the national sphere of government. This is because Chapter 13 of the Constitution restricts the power of the provincial and local spheres of government to impose taxes. Although the Constitution restricts the power of the provincial and local spheres of government to impose taxes and thus to raise revenue, it compensates them for this loss by granting them a right to an equitable share of revenue collected nationally. Section 215(1) of the Constitution provides that the national, provincial and municipal budgetary processes must promote transparency, accountability and the effective financial management of the economy, debt and the public sector. Section 217 of the Constitution also makes it imperative for an organ of state in the national, provincial or local sphere to contract for goods and services in a manner that is fair, equitable, transparent, competitive and cost-effective.

PART TWO

The Bill of Rights and the enforcement of the Constitution

Chapter 9

Introduction to and application of the Bill of Rights

9.1 Introduction

The South African Bill of Rights – constructed in a manner to give effect to the transformative vision of the Constitution – sets out a unique human rights vision. Its breadth of application – to both the state and, in many cases, to private parties – and the range of rights protected in it, establishes the Bill of Rights as a post-liberal text aimed at facilitating the social and economic transformation of South Africa while protecting the human dignity of all. However, before we look at the various rights protected by the Bill of Rights, it is necessary to deal with several important technical issues regarding Bill of Rights adjudication. This is because the structure of Bill of Rights litigation differs from litigation dealing with other alleged breaches of the Constitution.

When confronted with the question of whether law or conduct is in breach of the Bill of Rights, several preliminary questions arise. First, a court must ask whether the person or organisation which claims that their rights have been infringed is entitled to the protection provided by the Bill of Rights and whether the person or organisation which wishes to approach the court has **standing** to bring the case. While most of the rights in the Bill of Rights are granted to everyone, including non-citizens, some are specifically restricted. There are also complicated rules to determine whether **juristic persons** can claim the protection of the Bill of Rights.

Once the court has established that the person or organisation which claims that their rights have been infringed is covered by the Bill of Rights, it must ask whether the person or organisation which is alleged to have infringed the rights is bound by the Bill of Rights. The South African Bill of Rights does not bind only the state but, when applicable in accordance with complicated provisions in the Constitution, also private individuals and organisations.

After the court has established that the rights of a natural or juristic person have been infringed, it has to determine whether the infringement is justifiable in terms of the limitation clause set out in section 36. If the court finds that the limitation is justifiable, the infringement is 'saved' and the law or conduct is constitutionally valid. However, if the court finds that the limitation is not justifiable, then an infringement cannot be saved and the law or conduct is unconstitutional and invalid.

Law or conduct which unjustifiably infringes the Bill of Rights must be declared invalid. Apart from a declaration of invalidity, however, there are a number of other constitutional remedies a court may issue. Among these are declaratory orders, prohibitory interdicts, mandatory interdicts, structural interdicts, constitutional damages and meaningful engagement.

This chapter, as well as chapters 10 and 11, deal with the technical questions relating to Bill of Rights adjudication. While we will discuss the substantive scope and content of the various rights in subsequent chapters, it is important first to answer the relevant preliminary questions about the manner in which Bill of Rights adjudication should proceed. These questions include the following:

- Who can claim the rights protected in the Bill of Rights and who is bound to respect the same rights?
- Can the rights be claimed only by people or also by organisations, and if the latter, when?
- Are the rights only binding on the state or are private parties also bound to respect the rights?
- To what extent and how can rights be legally limited and in which situations?
- If there is an infringement of a right, how can that infringement be remedied to ensure that the person whose rights have been infringed can be assisted?

9.2 The structure of Bill of Rights litigation

When a person alleges that the state or another person has infringed a fundamental right, the process that a court must follow to determine whether this allegation is valid or not is usually divided into three stages, namely an application stage, a limitation stage and a remedies stage:[1]

- During the **application stage**, the court has to answer a number of questions. The two most important are:
    - Can X go to court to claim his or her right was infringed?
    - Is the person who allegedly infringed X's rights bound by the duties imposed by the right?[2]

1 Currie, I and De Waal, J (2013) *The Bill of Rights Handbook* 6th ed 24.

2 Currie and De Waal (2013) 24.

- During the **limitation stage**, the court also has to answer a number of questions. The two most important are:
  - What is the scope of the right and does the law or conduct infringe the right?
  - If it does, is the infringement justifiable in terms of the limitation clause set out in section 36 of the Constitution?[3]
- During the **remedies stage**, the court has to decide what the most appropriate remedy would be. It is important to note, however, that this stage arises only in those cases in which the court has found that law or conduct unjustifiably infringes a fundamental right or does not promote the values in the Bill of Rights.[4]

1. **Procedural stage**
   - Can X go to court to claim his or her right was infringed?
   - Is the person or organisation who allegedly infringed X's rights bound by the duties imposed by the right?

↓

2. **Substantive stage**
   - What is the scope of the right and does the law or conduct infringe on the right?
   - If it does, is the infringement justifiable in terms of the limitation clause set out in section 36 of the Constitution?

↓

3. **Remedy stage**
   If there is an unjustifiable infringement of the right, what order must the court give to remedy the problem?

Figure 9.1 The three stages of Bill of Rights adjudication

The constitutional provisions that regulate these questions are set out in the **operational provisions of the Bill of Rights.** Unlike the substantive provisions dealing with specific rights, the operational provisions do not regulate the substance of the fundamental freedoms and rights that are guaranteed in the Bill of Rights. Instead, they regulate the manner in which the Bill of Rights operates and the manner in which it can be enforced by the courts.[5]

The operational provisions are:

- **section 7:** the state's duty to respect, protect, promote and fulfil the rights in the Bill of Rights
- **section 8:** who the right binds
- **section 36:** the **limitation of rights**
- **section 37:** the suspension of rights in a state of emergency
- **section 38:** who has standing to enforce the rights
- **section 39:** the interpretation of rights.

Apart from these operational provisions, sections 167 and 172 of the Constitution also regulate the enforcement of the Bill of Rights. These provisions deal with the jurisdiction of the courts, especially in constitutional matters, and the remedies that the courts may grant when a provision of the Bill of Rights has been unjustifiably infringed.

3 Currie and De Waal (2013) 26.
4 Currie and De Waal (2013) 26–7.
5 Freedman, DW 'Constitutional law: Bill of Rights' in Joubert, WA (ed) (2012) *Law of South Africa* 2nd ed *Vol 5 Part 4* para 2.

PAUSE FOR REFLECTION

Classifying rights

As we have already seen, the **substantive provisions of the Bill of Rights** are those provisions that regulate the actual substance of the rights that are entrenched and protected in the Bill of Rights. These rights may be classified in a number of different ways and some rights may fall into more than one category.

One of the most widely used methods of classifying rights is to draw a distinction between civil and political rights, on the one hand, and social and economic rights on the other hand. This classification is based on the distinction drawn between the rights protected in the International Covenant on Civil and Political Rights (ICCPR)[6] and the rights protected in the International Covenant on Economic, Social and Cultural Rights (ICESCR).[7]

Civil and political rights are aimed at protecting people from unlawful interference by the state, private organisations and individuals and at guaranteeing the ability of everyone to participate fully in the civil and political life of the state. Civil and political rights include the right to equality, the right to freedom of expression, the right to a fair trial, the right to freedom of assembly and the right to elections and to vote.[8]

Social and economic rights include the right to education, the right to housing, the right to health and the right to social security. They impose an obligation on the state not to interfere with the existing enjoyment of these rights and, where applicable, to take positive steps to provide people with the resources and the services they need to live a decent, fulfilling and minimally good life.[9]

Another common method of classifying human rights is to draw a distinction between first generation, second generation and third generation rights. This classification is based on the historical development of human rights.

First generation rights are the oldest. They arose in the eighteenth century and were included in the American Bill of Rights (1789–1791) and the French Declaration of the Rights of Man and Citizen (1789). First generation rights consist largely of traditional civil and political rights. Sometimes they are also referred to as **blue rights.**[10]

Second generation rights arose at the end of the nineteenth century and the beginning of the twentieth century. They were included in the 1931 Constitution of Spain and the 1936 Constitution of the Union of Soviet Socialist Republics. Second generation rights consist largely of social and economic rights. Sometimes they are also referred to as **red rights.**[11]

Third generation rights are the most recent and arose towards the end of the twentieth century. Third generation rights include the right to self-determination, the right to development and the right to a healthy environment. Sometimes they are also referred to as **green rights.**[12]

While the classifications set out above provide us with some insights into the history and nature of the rights protected in the Bill of Rights, it is important to note that the Bill of Rights itself does not classify or categorise rights in any of these ways. Although

6 United Nations (1996) International Covenant on Civil and Political Rights available at http://www.ohchr.org/en/professionalinterest/pages/ccpr.aspx.

7 United Nations (1996) International Covenant on Economic, Social and Cultural Rights available at http://www.ohchr.org/en/professionalinterest/pages/CESCR.aspx.

8 Dlamini, CRM (1995) *Human Rights in Africa: Which way South Africa?* 5–6.

9 Dlamini (1995) 5–6.

10 Du Plessis, LM (1999) *An Introduction to Law* 3rd ed 168–9.

11 Du Plessis (1999) 168–9.

12 Du Plessis (1999) 168–9.

the Bill of Rights contains examples of the different categories or generations of rights, it does not distinguish in any way between the various rights.

Implicit, therefore, in the Bill of Rights is the idea that our Constitution does not create a hierarchy of rights.[13] Rather than drawing hard and fast distinctions between the rights, the courts have been mindful to show the rights in the Bill of Rights as being interrelated, interdependent and mutually supporting.

9.3 The application of the Bill of Rights

During the application stage a court has to decide who is entitled to claim the right in question and who is bound by the right in question.[14] In addition, it also has to decide whether the Bill of Rights applies directly or indirectly to the dispute before it.[15]

When the Bill of Rights applies **directly**, the purpose is to determine whether the ordinary rules of law (legislation, common law and customary law) are consistent with the Bill of Rights. If they are not, the Bill of Rights overrides the ordinary rules of law. In these cases, the Bill of Rights also generates its own set of special remedies, for example declaratory orders, structural interdicts, constitutional damages and meaningful engagement.[16]

When the Bill of Rights applies **indirectly**, the purpose is to determine whether the ordinary rules of law promote the values of the Bill of Rights. If they do not, the Bill of Rights does not override the ordinary law nor does it generate it own special remedies. Instead, the court uses the Bill of Rights to develop the rules and remedies of the ordinary law to avoid any inconsistency between the ordinary law and the Bill of Rights.[17]

We consider each of these issues in turn in the next sections.

9.3.1 Who is entitled to claim the rights in the Bill of Rights?

9.3.1.1 Introduction

In most cases, 'everyone' can claim the rights contained in the Bill of Rights. This includes everyone present in South Africa as well as non-citizens. A limited number of rights are qualified in that only 'citizens',[18] 'children'[19] or 'detained' persons can claim them.[20] When a specific provision states that 'everyone' can claim the right, it usually means that **natural persons**[21] can claim the right and, in some cases, also juristic persons.[22] However, as we shall see, not all rights can be claimed by juristic persons.

13 See *Certification of the Constitution of the Republic of South Africa, 1996* (CCT 23/96) [1996] ZACC 26; 1996 (4) SA 744 (CC); 1996 (10) BCLR 1253 (CC) (6 September 1996) paras 77–8 where the Court held that socio-economic rights are no less justiciable than civil and political right, nor would a court adjudicating on them necessarily lead to a breach of the separation of powers.

14 See Currie and De Waal (2013) 24 and 29.

15 See Currie, I and De Waal, J (2001) *The New Constitutional and Administrative Law, Vol 1 Constitutional Law* 321.

16 Currie and De Waal (2001) 321.

17 Currie and De Waal (2001) 321.

18 Ss 19, 20 and 22 of the Constitution.

19 S 28 of the Constitution.

20 S 35 of the Constitution.

21 In law, a natural person is a real human being as opposed to a legal person which may be a private (business entity) or public (government) organisation.

22 A juristic person is an artificial entity through which the law allows a group of natural persons to act as if it were a single composite individual for certain purposes. This legal fiction does not mean these entities are human beings, but rather that the law recognises them and allows them to act as natural persons for some purposes, most commonly in lawsuits, property ownership and contracts. For example, a company or a club will act as a juristic person.

9.3.1.2 Natural persons

Most of the rights in the Bill of Rights are for the benefit of 'everyone'. Section 9(1), for example, provides that '**everyone** is equal before the law and has the right to equal protection and benefit of the law'; section 11 that '**everyone** has the right to life'; and section 13 that '**no one** may be subjected to slavery, servitude and forced labour'.

The courts have interpreted the reference to everyone to refer not only to South African citizens, but also to various categories of immigrants, be they permanent residents[23] or persons present in South Africa on the basis of a temporary permit such as a work permit or a study permit.[24] Even foreigners who have yet to be lawfully admitted into South Africa have been recognised as being beneficiaries of the rights guaranteed in the Bill of Rights.[25] The term 'everyone', however, does not include a foetus.[26]

While most of the rights in the Bill of Rights are for the benefit of 'everyone', some are for the benefit of a narrower category of persons only. Section 19(1)(*a*), for example, provides that 'every **citizen** is free to make political choices, which includes the right to form a political party'; section 23(2)(*a*) that 'every **worker** has the right to form and join a trade union'; and section 28(1)(*a*) that 'every **child** has the right to a name and a nationality from birth'. Only those natural persons who fall into the definition of the category in question may claim these rights.[27]

To determine whether a particular person may claim such a right, the courts will have to interpret the scope of the category in question. In *South African National Defence Union v Minister of Defence*,[28] for example, members of the South African National Defence Force claimed that they were entitled to form and join a trade union in terms of section 23(2)(*a*) of the Constitution. To decide whether this claim was valid, the Constitutional Court had to establish whether the word 'worker' was wide enough to include members of the armed forces. In its judgment, the Constitutional Court found that the word 'worker' was indeed wide enough to include members of the armed forces. The Court based its decision on the fact that members of the armed forces receive many of the same benefits as other employees, for example a salary.[29] In addition, the International Labour Organisation considers members of the armed forces to be workers for the purposes of the Convention on the Freedom of Association and Protection of the Right to Organise 87 of 1948 and the Convention on the Right to Organise and Collective Bargaining 98 of 1949, both of which South Africa has signed and ratified.[30]

9.3.1.3 Juristic persons

It seems self-evident that individual human beings are entitled to the protection provided by the rights in the Bill of Rights. But what about other non-human bodies? Can a big corporation claim to have a right to free speech? Can a religious group claim the right to

---

23 *Khosa and Others v Minister of Social Development and Others, Mahlaule and Another v Minister of Social Development* (CCT 13/03, CCT 12/03) [2004] ZACC 11; 2004 (6) SA 505 (CC); 2004 (6) BCLR 569 (CC) (4 March 2004) para 47.

24 *Dawood and Another v Minister of Home Affairs and Others; Shalabi and Another v Minister of Home Affairs and Others; Thomas and Another v Minister of Home Affairs and Others* (CCT35/99) [2000] ZACC 8; 2000 (3) SA 936; 2000 (8) BCLR 837 (7 June 2000) para 37.

25 *Lawyers for Human Rights and Other v Minister of Home Affairs and Other* (CCT 18/03) [2004] ZACC 12; 2004 (4) SA 125 (CC); 2004 (7) BCLR 775 (CC) (9 March 2004) para 27.

26 *Christian Lawyers Association of SA v Minister of Health* 1998 (11) BCLR 1434 (T) 1441.

27 *Christian Lawyers Association* 1441.

28 (CCT27/98) [1999] ZACC 7; 1999 (4) SA 469; 1999 (6) BCLR 615 (26 May 1999).

29 *South African National Defence Union* para 23.

30 *South African National Defence Union* para 26.

bodily integrity. Can the human dignity of a tennis club be infringed? Can a trade union claim it has a right not to be discriminated against?

In terms of the Constitution, apart from natural persons, juristic persons, such as churches, companies, trade unions and universities that have legal personality, may also claim some of the rights in the Bill of Rights in certain circumscribed circumstances. It is, however, important to note that unlike human beings, these juristic persons will not always be able to claim protection of a right. Section 8(4) of the Constitution provides in this respect that '[a] juristic person is entitled to the rights in the Bill of Rights to the extent required by the nature of the rights and the nature of that juristic person'.

This provision, while recognising juristic persons as bearers of rights, suggests that the rights that juristic persons can claim will be the subject of interpretation by the courts. To determine whether a juristic person can claim a particular right, therefore, the courts have to take into account at least two factors, namely:

- the nature of the right being invoked
- the nature of the juristic person in question.

In so far as the first factor is concerned, it is quite clear that there are some rights which by their very nature cannot be claimed by juristic persons, for example the right to life (section 11), the right to vote (section 19) and the right to health care, food and social security (section 27). This is because juristic persons cannot enjoy these rights as the rights are peculiarly related to individual human beings. Juristic persons are not alive, they cannot vote and they do not require health care, food or social security.[31] There are, however, other rights which juristic persons may claim, for example the rights to equality (section 9); privacy (section 14); freedom of expression (section 16); freedom of association (section 18); property (section 25); access to information (section 32); just administrative action (section 33); and access to courts (section 34). There is nothing in the nature of these rights which prevents juristic persons from enjoying them.[32]

In so far as the second factor is concerned, a distinction may be drawn between those juristic persons which can claim the rights in the Bill of Rights and those which cannot. This distinction is based on the aim or purpose of the juristic person in question.[33] If natural persons established the juristic person to help them achieve their rights, the juristic person may be entitled to claim the rights in the Bill of Rights. For example, a church or a media company which has legal personality may be entitled to claim the right to religious freedom or the right to freedom of expression. This is because natural persons established the church or the media company to help them achieve those particular rights.[34]

If, however, the juristic person was not created by natural persons to help them achieve their human rights, it may not be entitled to claim the rights in the Bill of Rights. For example, organs of state such as Parliament or the President may not be entitled to claim any rights in the Bill of Rights. This is because their purpose is to exercise the powers that have been given to them in a way that promotes and protects the rights of the people. They are not, therefore, entitled to the rights in the Bill of Rights. Instead, they are bound by them.[35]

31 Govindjee, A and Vrancken, P (eds) (2009) *Introduction to Human Rights Law* 41.
32 Govindjee and Vrancken (2009) 41.
33 Govindjee and Vrancken (2009) 41.
34 Govindjee and Vrancken (2009) 41.
35 Govindjee and Vrancken (2009) 41.

COUNTER POINT

Controversy about the entitlement of juristic persons to some of the rights in the Bill of Rights

The fact that juristic persons are entitled to claim the benefit of some of the rights in the Bill of Rights has caused much controversy. This is because juristic persons frequently want to claim these rights simply to promote their business interests and to make a profit. The debate about whether such juristic persons can claim rights is often ideological and pro-business supporters of the free market system often support wider protection for juristic persons. This was illustrated during the United States presidential campaign in 2012 when the Republican candidate, Mitt Romney, said at a campaign stop: 'Corporations are people, my friend.'[36]

The fact that section 8(4) of the Constitution allows juristic persons to claim the benefits of some of the rights in the Bill of Rights was, therefore, challenged in *Certification of the Constitution of the Republic of South Africa, 1996.*[37] In this case, the challengers argued that by allowing juristic persons to claim some of the rights in the Bill of Rights, section 8(4) reduced the protection the Bill of Rights gave to natural persons.

The Constitutional Court, however, rejected this argument on the grounds that natural persons often come together and form a juristic person to help them achieve and protect their fundamental rights. For example, natural persons may establish a media company to achieve and protect the right to freedom of expression. That media company must, therefore, have the power to claim the benefits and protection of the rights in the Bill of Rights.[38]

9.3.1.4 Standing to enforce rights

It is important to note that the requirements set out in section 8(4) of the Constitution have not played a significant role in practice. This is because the Constitution has adopted a generous approach towards legal standing. Section 38 of the Constitution provides in this respect that:

> **Anyone listed in this section has the right to approach a competent court, alleging that a right in the Bill of Rights has been infringed or threatened, and the court may grant appropriate relief, including a declaration of rights. The persons who may approach a court are:**
> **(*a*) anyone acting in their own interest;**
> **(*b*) anyone acting on behalf of another person who cannot act in their own name;**
> **(*c*) anyone acting as a member of, or in the interest of, a group or class of persons;**
> **(*d*) anyone acting in the public interest;**
> **(*e*) an association acting in the interest of its members.**

36 See Rucker, P (2011, 11 August) Mitt Romney says 'corporations are people' at Iowa State Fair *Washington Post* available at http://articles.washingtonpost.com/2011-08-11/politics/35270239_1_romney-supporters-mitt-romney-private-sector-experience.

37 (CCT 23/96) [1996] ZACC 26; 1996 (4) SA 744 (CC); 1996 (10) BCLR 1253 (CC) (6 September 1996).

38 *First Certification* paras 57–8.

The Constitutional Court has considered the scope and ambit of section 38 on a number of occasions.[39] In these cases, the Court has held that a complainant does not have to show that he or she has a 'direct and personal interest' in the relief claimed.[40] Instead, a complainant simply has to:

- allege that one of the fundamental rights set out in the Bill of Rights has been infringed or threatened
- show that one of the categories of persons listed in section 38 of the Constitution has a 'sufficient interest' in obtaining a remedy.[41]

An important consequence of this approach is that an applicant does not have to allege that a particular person's fundamental right has been infringed or threatened. An applicant simply has to allege that a fundamental right has been infringed or threatened.[42]

It is important to note, however, that it is not enough simply to allege that a fundamental right has been infringed or threatened. In addition, a complainant must also show that one of the categories of persons listed in paragraphs (*a*) to (*e*) of section 38 of the Constitution has a sufficient interest in the remedy the complainant is seeking.[43] For example, if a complainant approaches a court in terms of section 38(*a*) of the Constitution, the complainant must show that he or she has a sufficient interest. If a complainant approaches the court in terms of section 38(*d*) of the Constitution, the complainant must show that the public has a sufficient interest.

Although the Constitutional Court has adopted a generous approach to standing, in *Giant Concerts CC v Rinaldo Investments (Pty) Ltd and Others* it held that this does not mean that litigants, and especially own-interest litigants, have a broad and unqualified capacity to litigate against illegalities.[44] An own-interest litigant must still show that he or she has a 'sufficient interest' in the relief he or she is applying for.

In this case, the Constitutional Court held that when it comes to deciding whether a litigant does have a sufficient own-interest, a court must assume that the act or decision being challenged is, in fact, unlawful. This is because the question of standing is a point ***in limine*** which has to be decided before the merits of the case. The merits of the case, therefore, must be separated from the issue of standing.[45]

The separation of the merits of the case from the question of standing, the Constitutional Court held further, has two important consequences for an own-interest litigant:

- First, simply because the act or decision being challenged is unlawful does not mean that the applicant has legal standing. To have standing, an applicant must also have a sufficient interest in the lawfulness of the act or decision in question.[46]

39 See, for example, *Ferreira v Levin NO and Others; Vryenhoek and Others v Powell NO and Others* (CCT5/95) [1995] ZACC 13; 1996 (1) SA 984 (CC); 1996 (1) BCLR 1 (6 December 1995); *Minister of Home Affairs v Eisenberg & Associates In re: Eisenberg & Associates v Minister of Home Affairs and Others* (CCT15/03) [2003] ZACC 10; 2003 (8) BCLR 838; 2003 (5) SA 281 (CC) (27 June 2003); *Kruger v President of the Republic of South Africa and Others* (CCT 57/07) [2008] ZACC 17; 2009 (1) SA 417 (CC); 2009 (3) BCLR 268 (CC) (2 October 2008); *Viking Pony Africa Pumps (Pty) Ltd t/a Tricom Africa v Hidro-Tech Systems (Pty) Ltd and Another* (CCT 34/10) [2010] ZACC 21; 2011 (1) SA 327 (CC); 2011 (2) BCLR 207 (CC) (23 November 2010); *Tulip Diamonds FZE v Minister for Justice and Constitutional Development and Others* (CCT 93/12) [2013] ZACC 19; 2013 (10) BCLR 1180 (CC); 2013 (2) SACR 443 (CC) (13 June 2013).

40 *Kruger* para 21.

41 *Kruger* para 90.

42 See Currie and De Waal (2013) 77.

43 Currie and De Waal (2013) 77.

44 (CCT 25/12) [2012] ZACC 28; 2013 (3) BCLR 251 (CC) (29 November 2012) para 23.

45 *Giant Concerts* para 32.

46 *Giant Concerts* para 33.

- Second, if an own-interest litigant does not have a sufficient interest, he or she will be denied legal standing even though the result could be that an unlawful act or decision stands.[47]

When a litigant acts solely in his or her own interest, therefore, there is no broad or unqualified capacity to litigate against illegalities. Something more must be shown.[48] How much more, the Constitutional Court went on to hold, has been set out in several of its previous judgments, especially *Ferreira v Levin NO and Others; Vryenhoek and Others v Powell NO and Others;*[49] *Minister of Home Affairs v Eisenberg & Associates In re: Eisenberg & Associates v Minister of Home Affairs and Others;*[50] and *Kruger v President of the Republic of South Africa and Others.*[51] A careful examination of these judgments, the Constitutional Court noted, shows the following:

> **1. To establish own-interest standing under the Constitution a litigant need not show the same 'sufficient personal and direct interest' that the common law requires, but must still show that a contested law or decision directly affects his or her rights or interests, or potential rights or interests.**
> **2. This requirement must be broadly and generously interpreted to accord with constitutional goals.**
> **3. The interest must, however, be real and not hypothetical or academic.**
> **4. Even under the requirements for common law standing, the interest need not be capable of monetary valuation, but in a challenge to legislation purely financial self-interest may not be enough – the interests of justice must also favour affording standing.**
> **5. Standing is not a technical or strictly-defined concept. And there is no magical formula for conferring it. It is a tool a court employs to determine whether a litigant is entitled to claim its time, and to put the opposing litigant to trouble.**
> **6. Each case depends on its own facts. There can be no general rule covering all cases. In each case, an applicant must show that he or she has the necessary interest in an infringement or a threatened infringement.**[52]

Apart from the requirements that must be satisfied when a person approaches a court in his or her own interest, the Constitutional Court has also considered the requirements a person must satisfy when he or she approaches a court in the public interest.

In her minority judgment in *Ferreira; Vryenhoek*, O'Regan J held that a person will be granted standing to act in the public interest only if he or she is genuinely acting in the public interest.[53] To determine whether a person is genuinely acting in the public interest, the following factors must be taken into account:

- whether there is another reasonable and effective manner in which the challenge can be brought
- the nature of the relief sought and the extent to which it is of general and prospective application

47 *Giant Concerts* para 34.
48 *Giant Concerts* para 35.
49 (CCT5/95) [1995] ZACC 13; 1996 (1) SA 984 (CC); 1996 (1) BCLR 1 (6 December 1995).
50 (CCT15/03) [2003] ZACC 10; 2003 (8) BCLR 838; 2003 (5) SA 281 (CC) (27 June 2003).
51 (CCT 57/07) [2008] ZACC 17; 2009 (1) SA 417 (CC); 2009 (3) BCLR 268 (CC) (2 October 2008).
52 *Giant Concerts* para 41.
53 *Ferreira; Vryenhoek* para 234.

- the range of persons or groups who may be directly or indirectly affected by any order made by the court and the opportunity that those persons or groups have had to present evidence and argument to the court.[54]

Despite the fact that the approach set out above formed a part of O'Regan J's minority judgment, it was referred to with approval by the Constitutional Court in its subsequent judgment in *Lawyers for Human Rights and Other v Minister of Home Affairs and Other*.[55] In this case, the Court held that even though the approach adopted by O'Regan J formed a part of her minority judgment, it was not inconsistent with anything said in the majority judgment on the issue of standing. This is because the majority in *Ferreira; Vryenhoek* found that the applicants were acting in their own interests and, consequently, that it was not necessary also to consider whether they had standing to act in the public interest.[56]

Besides referring to the approach adopted by O'Regan J with approval, the Court in *Lawyers for Human Rights* also held that the list of relevant factors is not closed. Other factors that should be taken into account include the degree of vulnerability of the people affected, the nature of the right said to be infringed and the consequences of the infringement of the right.[57]

9.3.2 Who is bound by the rights in the Bill of Rights?

9.3.2.1 Introduction

Once a court has determined who can claim rights in terms of the Bill of Rights, it has to ask a second question, namely against whom can these rights be claimed. In other words, the court has to ask who is bound to respect the rights claimed by either a natural or juristic person. Although 'everyone' is entitled to claim the benefit of the rights (or at least most of the rights) in the Bill of Rights, not everyone is bound by every right contained in the Bill of Rights. This is because while the Bill of Rights is always binding on the state, it is not always binding on private persons.

When it comes to the question of who is bound by the Bill of Rights, it is important to distinguish between the direct application of the Bill of Rights and the indirect application of the Bill of Rights:

- When the Bill of Rights **applies directly**, the purpose is to determine whether the ordinary rules of law (legislation, common law and customary law) are consistent with the Bill of Rights. If they are not, the Bill of Rights overrides the ordinary rules of law. When the Bill of Rights applies directly, it also generates its own set of special remedies, for example **reading down** or **reading in**.[58]
- When the Bill of Rights **applies indirectly**, the purpose is to determine whether the ordinary rules of law promote the values of the Bill of Rights. If they do not, the Bill of Rights does not override the ordinary law or generate its own special remedies. Instead, the Bill of Rights is used to develop the rules and remedies of the ordinary law to avoid any inconsistency between the ordinary law and the Bill of Rights.[59]

---

54 *Ferreira; Vryenhoek* para 234.

55 (CCT 18/03) [2004] ZACC 12; 2004 (4) SA 125 (CC); 2004 (7) BCLR 775 (CC) (9 March 2004).

56 *Lawyers for Human Rights* para 17.

57 *Lawyers for Human Rights* para 18. In his minority judgment in *Lawyers for Human Rights*, Madala J held that another important factor to be taken into account when determining whether a party has standing to act in the public interest is 'the egregiousness of the conduct complained of' (para 73).

58 Currie and De Waal (2001) 321.

59 Currie and De Waal (2001) 321.

Apart from distinguishing between the direct and indirect application of the Bill of Rights, it is also important to distinguish between the vertical application of the Bill of Rights and the horizontal application of the Bill of Rights:

- When the Bill of Rights **applies vertically**, it confers rights on private persons and imposes obligations on the state to respect, protect, promote and fulfil the rights in the Bill of Rights. It does not impose these obligations on private persons. In other words, when the Bill of Rights applies vertically, only the state is bound by the Bill of Rights. An important consequence of this approach is that the Bill of Rights may be applied directly to a legal dispute only if one of the parties to that dispute is the state. We refer to a dispute in which one of the parties is the state as a **vertical dispute**.[60]
- When the Bill of Rights **applies horizontally**, it not only confers rights on private persons, but also imposes obligations on them to respect the rights in the Bill of Rights, at least in certain circumstances. In other words, when the Bill of Rights applies horizontally, both the state and private persons are bound by the Bill of Rights. An important consequence of this approach is that the Bill of Rights may be applied directly to a legal dispute even if both of the parties to that dispute are private persons. We refer to a dispute in which neither of the parties is the state as a **horizontal dispute**.[61]

In South Africa, unlike in most other constitutional democracies, the Bill of Rights applies not only directly and indirectly, but also vertically and sometimes horizontally. Section 8(1) of the Constitution governs the direct vertical application of the Bill of Rights while section 8(2) governs the direct horizontal application. Section 39(2) of the Constitution governs the indirect vertical and horizontal application of the Bill of Rights.

COUNTER POINT

When fundamental rights are abused by private persons

In the many constitutional democracies such as the United States, the Bill of Rights applies vertically and not horizontally. This is because the state is considered to be in a unique position to abuse or threaten the fundamental rights of private persons. The reason why the state is considered to be in a unique position to abuse or threaten the fundamental rights of private persons is because political or state authority is vested in the state. This means that the state is more powerful than private persons and that the relationship between them is always an unequal or vertical one.

Unfortunately, this argument overlooks the fact that fundamental rights may be abused or threatened not only by the state but also by private persons. This is because even though none of the parties in a private relationship can be said to have political or state authority, it does not necessarily follow that the relationship between private persons is always an equal or horizontal one. Some private organisations wield enormous power and can use this power to infringe the rights of others. As a result of factors such as the free market system and the privatisation of state functions, it is quite clear that some private persons are more powerful than others, for example banks, insurance companies and those companies that provide important services such as electricity and water.

Hutchinson, for example, argues that it is corporations and not governments that pose the greatest threat to individuals because they make the most crucial decisions about human and economic resources. 'There is no choice,' he argues, 'in dealing with

60 Currie and De Waal (2013) 41.

61 Currie and De Waal (2013) 41.

corporations, for their activities pervade the lives of every citizen. How we put food on the table, what food we put on the table, what we pay to put food on the table, and what food we think we should put on the table are all questions that are deeply shaped by the actions of corporations and the life-images that they project.'[62]

Given that fundamental rights may be abused by private persons, most constitutional scholars and human rights activists have welcomed as a progressive step the fact that the South African Bill of Rights 'binds a natural or a juristic person if, and to the extent that, it is applicable'.[63]

9.3.2.2 The direct vertical application of the Bill of Rights

9.3.2.2.1 Introduction

Section 8(1) of the Constitution governs the direct vertical application of the Bill of Rights. This section stipulates in unqualified terms that '[t]he Bill of Rights applies to all law, and binds the legislature, the executive, the judiciary and all organs of state'.

Despite the fact that section 8(1) of the Constitution provides that the Bill of Rights applies directly to 'all law', the Constitutional Court has held that section 8(1) does not regulate the direct application of the Bill of Rights to disputes between private persons that are governed by the common law or customary law. This is because section 8(2) of the Constitution regulates the direct application of the Bill of Rights to these horizontal disputes.[64]

For the same reasons, section 8(1) does not regulate the direct application of the Bill of Rights to the judiciary when it is called on to resolve a dispute between private parties that is governed by the common law or customary law. This is because section 8(2) of the Constitution also regulates the direct application of the Bill of Rights to the judiciary in these horizontal disputes.[65]

The fact that section 8(2) rather than section 8(1) regulates the direct application of the Bill of Rights to horizontal disputes was confirmed by the Constitutional Court in its judgment in *Khumalo and Others v Holomisa*.[66]

The facts of this case were as follows. The respondent, who was a prominent politician, sued the appellants, who were the publishers of a newspaper, for defamation. The appellants, however, raised an exception to the respondent's claim. The exception was that the common law rules of defamation infringed the constitutional right to freedom of expression guaranteed in section 16 of the Constitution because they did not impose an obligation on the plaintiff to prove that the defamatory statements were false. Instead, they imposed an obligation on the defendant to prove that they were true.

---

62 Hutchinson, AC (1990) Mice under a chair: Democracy, courts and the administrative state *University of Toronto Law Journal* 40(3):374–404 at 380.

63 S 8(2).

64 *Khumalo and Others v Holomisa* (CCT53/01) [2002] ZACC 12; 2002 (5) SA 401; 2002 (8) BCLR 771 (14 June 2002) para 31. S 8(2) of the Constitution stipulates that '[a] provision in the Bill of Rights binds a natural or juristic person if, and to the extent that, it is applicable, taking into account the nature of the right and the nature of the duty imposed by the right'. S 8(3) goes on to stipulate that '[w]hen applying a provision of the Bill of Rights to a natural or juristic person in terms of subsection (2), a court: (*a*) in order to give effect to a right in the Bill, must apply, or if necessary develop, the common law to the extent that legislation does not give effect to that right; and (*b*) may develop rules of the common law to limit the right, provided the limitation is in accordance with section 36(1)'.

65 *Khumalo* para 31.

66 (CCT53/01) [2002] ZACC 12; 2002 (5) SA 401; 2002 (8) BCLR 771 (14 June 2002).

The Constitutional Court dismissed the exception. In arriving at this decision, however, the Constitutional Court had to answer a number of questions. One of these was whether section 16 of the Constitution applied directly to the dispute even though it was governed by the common law and neither of the parties was an organ of state.

To answer this question, the Constitutional Court stated it had to deal with two issues:

- first, whether section 8(1) or section 8(2) of the Constitution governed the direct horizontal application of the Bill of Rights
- second, if section 8(2) governed the direct horizontal application of the Bill of Rights, whether section 16 satisfied the requirements of section 8(2).[67]

In so far as the first issue was concerned, the Constitutional Court held that section 8(2) and not section 8(1) governed the direct horizontal application of the Bill of Rights. In arriving at its conclusion, the Constitutional Court began by noting that sections 8(1) and 8(2) of the Constitution distinguish between two categories of persons and institutions bound by the Bill of Rights. Section 8(1) binds the legislature, executive, judiciary and all organs of state without qualification, while section 8(2) provides that natural and juristic persons are bound by the provisions of the Bill of Rights, but only 'to the extent that it is applicable, taking into account the nature of the right and the nature of the duty imposed by the right'.[68]

Once a court has determined that a natural person is bound by a particular provision of the Bill of Rights, the Constitutional Court noted further, section 8(3) of the Constitution provides that the court must apply and if necessary develop the common law to the extent that legislation does not give effect to the right. In addition, it also provides that the rules of the common law may be developed so as to limit a right as long as the limitation is consistent with the provisions of section 8(3)(*b*).[69]

If section 8(1) of the Constitution governed the direct application of the Bill of Rights to a horizontal dispute, the Constitutional Court went on to note, the Bill of Rights would apply directly to horizontal disputes in all circumstances and section 8(2) read together with section 8(3) would have no purpose. To avoid such an absurd result, the direct application of the Bill of Rights to horizontal disputes had to be governed by section 8(2) and not by section 8(1).[70]

In so far as the second issue was concerned, the Constitutional Court noted that the appellants were members of the media who were expressly identified as bearers of constitutional rights to freedom of expression and that there could be no doubt that the law of defamation does affect the right to freedom of expression. The Constitutional Court noted further:

> **Given the intensity of the constitutional right in question, coupled with the potential invasion of that right which could be occasioned by persons other than the state or organs of state, it is clear that the right to freedom of expression is of direct horizontal application in this case as contemplated by section 8(2) of the Constitution.**[71]

Apart from these exceptions, section 8(1) of the Bill of Rights regulates the direct application of the Bill of Rights:

- to disputes between the state and private parties that are governed by legislation, the common law or customary law ('all law')

67 *Khumalo* paras 30–4.
68 *Khumalo* para 31.
69 *Khumalo* para 31.
70 *Khumalo* para 32.
71 *Khumalo* para 33.

- to disputes between private parties that are governed by legislation, but not by the common law or customary law.

COUNTER POINT

An interpretation of the *Khumalo* judgment

Following the Constitutional Court's judgment in *Khumalo*, it seems to be fairly clear that section 8(2) of the Constitution regulates the direct application of the Bill of Rights to disputes between private parties that are governed by the **common law or customary law**. It is not entirely clear, however, whether section 8(1) or section 8(2) regulates the direct application of the Bill of Rights to disputes between private parties that are governed by **legislation**.

Although the judgment in *Khumalo* deals with the common law of defamation, Woolman argues that the Constitutional Court held, by implication, that section 8(2) regulates the direct application of the Bill of Rights to disputes between private parties that are governed not only by the common law or customary law, but also by legislation. In other words, section 8(2) regulates the direct application of the Bill of Rights to **all** disputes between private persons.[72]

If this interpretation of the judgment in *Khumalo* is correct, he goes on to argue, then certain criticisms may be levelled against it. Among these are the following:

- First, it defers - and potentially suppresses - the direct application of the Bill of Rights to disputes between private parties, irrespective of whether the dispute is governed by legislation, the common law or customary law.[73]
- Second, less law is subject to the direct application of the Bill of Rights under the *Khumalo* Court's reading of the Constitution than it was under the Court's reading of the interim Constitution in *Du Plessis and Others v De Klerk and Another*.[74] This is because it was generally accepted that the Bill of Rights in the interim Constitution did apply directly to disputes between private persons governed by legislation.[75]
- Third, while the provisions of a statute or regulation may not necessarily be subject to the direct application of the Bill of Rights if the dispute was between two private parties, they would automatically be subject to the direct application of the Bill of Rights if the dispute was between a private party and the state. This distinction is absurd because it infringes the **doctrine of objective unconstitutionality**. This doctrine provides, *inter alia*, that constitutional cases, and thus the constitutionality of laws, cannot be distinguished on the basis of the parties before the court.[76]

Given the important obligations the Bill of Rights imposes on the bodies and institutions that are bound by it, it is important to determine which bodies and institutions fall within the scope of the words 'legislature', 'executive', 'judiciary' and 'all organs of state'. While the Constitution itself defines what is meant by the term 'organ of state', it does not define what is meant by the words 'legislature', 'executive' and 'judiciary'. This is because the meaning

72 See Woolman, S 'Application' in Woolman, S and Bishop, M (eds) (2013) *Constitutional Law of South Africa* 2nd ed rev service 5 31.6.
73 Woolman (2013) 31.7.
74 (CCT8/95) [1996] ZACC 10; 1996 (3) SA 850; 1996 (5) BCLR 658 (15 May 1996).
75 Woolman (2013) 31.8.
76 Woolman (2013) 31.8.

of these words may be discerned from the provisions of the Constitution. Given that we have already discussed what is meant by the words 'legislature', 'executive' and 'judiciary' in Part I of this book, we are only going to consider what is meant by the term 'organ of state' here.

9.3.2.2.2 All organs of state

Recall that section 8(1) of the Constitution states that the rights in the Bill of Rights bind all organs of state. In so far as the term 'organ of state' is concerned, section 239 of the Constitution provides that 'organ of state' means:

> **(*a*) any department of state or administration in the national, provincial or local sphere of government; or**
> **(*b*) any other functionary or institution**
> **(*i*) exercising a power or performing a function in terms of the Constitution or a provincial constitution; or**
> **(*ii*) exercising a public power or performing a public function in terms of any legislation,**
> **but does not include a court or a judicial officer.**

In terms of this definition, all organs of state may be divided into three categories:

- first, any department of state or administration in the national, provincial or local spheres of government
- second, any functionary or institution exercising a power or performing a function in terms of the Constitution or a provincial constitution
- third, any functionary or institution exercising a public power or performing a public function in terms of any legislation.[77]

While it is usually easy to identify those bodies or institutions that fall into the first two categories, it is not always easy to identify those bodies or institutions that fall into the third category. This is because it is not always clear whether a body or institution is exercising a public power or performing a public function in terms of any legislation. Is the University of Cape Town, for example, an organ of state? What about state-owned companies such as Eskom, SAA or Telkom? What about state institutions that have been privatised such as Iscor or, as it is called today, Mittalsteel South Africa Ltd?

The manner in which a court should go about determining whether a body or institution is exercising a public power or performing a public function was considered by the Supreme Court of Appeal (SCA) in *Calibre Clinical Consultants (Pty) Ltd and Another v National Bargaining Council for the Road Freight Industry and Another*.[78]

The facts of this case were as follows. In 2007, the respondent decided to establish an antiretroviral programme for HIV-positive employees in the road freight industry. The respondent, however, did not want to manage and implement the programme itself and invited interested parties to submit written proposals for the provision of these services.

The appellant submitted a written proposal and was then invited to present its proposal to an interview panel. After the presentation, the appellant was told that the respondent had decided in principle to award it the tender, but that a due diligence review still had to be performed.

---

77 Freedman (2012) para 7.

78 (410/09) [2010] ZASCA 94; 2010 (5) SA 457 (SCA); [2010] 4 All SA 561 (SCA) (19 July 2010).

Unfortunately, the due diligence review revealed a number of problems with the appellant's financial status. Following a long and complicated process, during which the appellant attempted, but failed, to address its financial problems, the respondent rejected the appellant's proposal and awarded the tender to another party.

The appellant then applied to the South Gauteng High Court: Johannesburg for an order reviewing and setting aside the respondent's decision not to award the tender to it. It based its application on the grounds that the respondent's decision infringed the right to procedural fairness guaranteed in the Promotion of Administrative Justice Act (the PAJA).[79]

The High Court dismissed the application and the appellant then appealed to the SCA which dismissed the appeal. In arriving at this decision, the SCA began by pointing out that a decision can only be reviewed in terms of the PAJA if it is an administrative act. A decision will only be classified as an administrative act if, *inter alia*, it is made by an organ of state as defined in section 239 of the Constitution.[80]

Given that the respondent was not 'exercising a power or performing a function in terms of the Constitution or a provincial constitution',[81] the key question that had to be answered, therefore, was whether it was 'exercising a public power or performing a public function in terms of any legislation'.[82]

In so far as this question was concerned, the SCA observed that while there is no single test to determine whether a power or function is of a public nature, the courts both in South Africa and in foreign comparable jurisdictions have usually taken into account the extent to which the power or function may be described as 'governmental' in nature. The more governmental in nature a power or function is, therefore, the more it may be said to be public in nature.[83]

The sorts of factors that courts will take into account to determine whether a power or function is of a public nature, therefore, include the extent to which the powers or functions are 'woven into a system of governmental control', or are 'integrated into a system of statutory regulation', or are 'regulated, supervised and inspected' by government, or are 'linked to the functions and powers of government', or are 'publicly funded' and so on.[84]

This approach, the SCA observed further, is a useful one because it asks whether the person or body which is exercising the power or performing the function is accountable to the public for the way in which the person or body has exercised the power or performed the function. It is about accountability to those with whom the functionary or body has no special relationship other than that they are affected by its conduct. The question in each case will be whether the person or body can properly be said to be accountable, notwithstanding the absence of any such special relationship.[85]

After setting out these principles, the SCA turned to apply them to the facts. In this respect, the Court found that even though the Labour Relations Act[86] regulates the establishment and powers of bargaining councils, they are essentially voluntary associations created by agreement to perform functions in the interests and for the benefit of their members. They are, therefore, not accountable to the public for the procurement of services

79 Act 3 of 2000.
80 *Calibre Clinical Consultants* para 20.
81 S 239(*b*)(i) of the Constitution.
82 S 239(*b*)(ii) of the Constitution; *Calibre Clinical Consultants* para 19.
83 *Calibre Clinical Consultants* para 24.
84 *Calibre Clinical Consultants* para 38.
85 *Calibre Clinical Consultants* para 40.
86 Act 66 of 1995.

for projects that are implemented for the benefit of their members. Consequently, bargaining councils cannot be said to be exercising public powers or performing public functions.[87]

In light of this judgment, therefore, it can be said that the exercise of a power or the performance of a function may be classified as public if the body or institution that has exercised the power or performed the function is accountable to the public for the manner in which it has exercised that power or performed that function.

9.3.2.3 The direct horizontal application of the Bill of Rights

While section 8(1) of the Constitution governs the direct vertical application of the Bill of Rights, section 8(2) governs the direct horizontal application of the Bill of Rights. Section 8(2) provides in this respect that '[a] provision in the Bill of Rights binds a natural or a juristic person if, and to the extent that, it is applicable, taking into account the nature of the right and the nature of any duty imposed by the right'.

PAUSE FOR REFLECTION

The Bill of Rights in the interim Constitution did not apply directly to horizontal disputes

The fact that the Bill of Rights may be applied directly to a horizontal dispute if the requirements of section 8(2) have been satisfied is one of the most significant differences between the Constitution and the interim Constitution. Section 7 regulated the application of the Bill of Rights in the interim Constitution, stating simply that '[the Bill of Rights] shall bind all legislative and executive organs of state at all levels of government'.

In *Du Plessis* the Constitutional Court held that the fact that section 7 did not refer to 'all law' and 'the judiciary' meant that the Bill of Rights in the interim Constitution did not apply directly to horizontal disputes. It only applied directly to vertical disputes.[88]

In light of this judgment and in an attempt to ensure that the Bill of Rights in the Constitution would apply directly to horizontal disputes, the Constitutional Assembly made two important changes:

- First, it added the words 'all law' and 'the judiciary' to the application clause. Section 8(1) thus provides that '[t]he Bill of Rights applies to all law and binds the legislature, the executive, the judiciary and all organs of state'.
- Second, it added an entirely new clause imposing an obligation to apply the Bill of Rights directly to horizontal disputes, at least in some cases. Section 8(2) thus provides that '[a] provision in the Bill of Rights binds a natural or juristic person if, and to the extent that, it is applicable, taking into account the nature of the right and the nature of any duty imposed by the right'.

87 *Calibre Clinical Consultants* para 41.

88 *Du Plessis* para 129. Although the Bill of Rights in the interim Constitution did not apply directly to horizontal disputes, it did apply indirectly. S 35(3) of the interim Constitution thus provided that '[i]n the interpretation of any law and the application and development of the common law and customary law, a court shall have due regard to the spirit, purport and objects of [the Bill of Rights]'. The approach adopted by the Constitutional Court in *Du Plessis* resulted in much academic debate and criticism. See, for example, Woolman, S and Davis, D (1996) The last laugh: *Du Plessis v De Klerk*, classical liberalism, Creole liberalism and the application of fundamental rights under the interim and final Constitutions *South African Journal on Human Rights* 12(2):361–404 at 361 and Sprigman, C and Osborne, M (1999) Du Plessis is *not* dead: South Africa's 1996 Constitution and the application of the Bill of Rights to private disputes *South African Journal on Human Rights* 15(1):25–51 at 25.

Unlike section 8(1) of the Constitution, which is not subject to any qualifications, section 8(2) is subject to an important qualification, namely that a fundamental right only applies directly to a horizontal relation 'if, and to the extent that, it is applicable, taking into account the nature of the right and the nature of the duty imposed by the right'.

Since the Bill of Rights does not apply directly to every horizontal dispute, but only to those in which 'it is applicable, taking into account the nature of the right and the nature of the duty imposed by the right', it is important to know what these words mean. Unfortunately, it is not easy to say exactly what they mean. This is partly because they are quite vague and partly because the Constitutional Court has only considered section 8(2) in two cases, namely *Khumalo* and *Governing Body of the Juma Musjid Primary School & Others v Essay NO and Others*.[89]

The Constitutional Court's judgment in *Juma Musjid* does, however, provide us with some useful guidelines on the manner in which section 8(2) should be interpreted and applied. In this case, the Court had to determine whether the right to a basic education guaranteed in section 29(1) of the Constitution applied directly to the common law principles governing evictions, despite the fact that none of the parties was the state or an organ of state.

The Constitutional Court found that it did. In arriving at this decision, the Constitutional Court began by stating that when it comes to determining whether a right in the Bill of Rights applies directly to a horizontal dispute governed by the common law, a court must take into account the purpose of section 8(2). This purpose 'is not to obstruct private autonomy or to impose on a private party the duties of the state in protecting the Bill of Rights. It is rather to require private parties not to interfere with or diminish the enjoyment of a right'.[90]

Apart from the purpose of section 8(2) of the Constitution, the Constitutional Court stated further that when it comes to determining whether a right in the Bill of Rights applies directly to a horizontal dispute governed by the common law, a court must also take into account the factors highlighted in *Khumalo*, namely 'the intensity of the constitutional right in question, coupled with the potential invasion of that right which could be occasioned by persons other than the state or organs of state'.[91]

Given these principles, the Constitutional Court went on to state, it may be said that the right to a basic education does apply directly to a horizontal dispute governed by the common law, but only in the sense that it imposes a negative obligation on private parties not to use their common law powers to interfere with or diminish the enjoyment of that right. It does not impose a positive obligation on private parties to take steps to provide basic education to learners.[92]

In light of this judgment, the following is in summary the current state of affairs:

- First, the courts may not interpret section 8(2) of the Constitution in a manner that imposes positive socio-economic obligations directly on natural or juristic persons.
- Second, the courts may interpret section 8(2) of the Constitution in a manner that does impose at least some negative socio-economic obligations directly on natural or juristic persons.
- Third, to determine which socio-economic negative obligations section 8(2) of the Constitution imposes directly on natural or juristic persons, the courts must take into

89 (CCT 29/10) [2011] ZACC 13; 2011 (8) BCLR 761 (CC) (11 April 2011).

90 *Juma Musjid* para 58.

91 *Juma Musjid* para 58. See also *Khumalo* para 33.

92 *Juma Musjid* para 60.

account the 'intensity of the constitutional right in question' and the extent to which the right could potentially be invaded by persons other than the state or organs of the state.[93] Unfortunately, it is not entirely clear what is meant by the 'intensity of the constitutional right in question'.[94]

9.3.2.4 The indirect application of the Bill of Rights

9.3.2.4.1 Introduction

In some cases the Bill of Rights will not apply directly to law and a court will not be asked to measure the law against the specific right and then to declare invalid the provision of the law. Instead, the Bill of Rights will indirectly influence the way in which the court interprets the law, but they will not declare the law unconstitutional. While sections 8(1) and 8(2) of the Constitution govern the direct vertical and horizontal application of the Bill of Rights, section 39(2) of the Constitution governs the indirect vertical and horizontal application of the Bill of Rights. Section 39(2) provides that '[w]hen interpreting any legislation, and when developing the common law or customary law, every court, tribunal or forum must promote the spirit, purport and objects of the Bill of Rights'.

When the Bill of Rights applies indirectly, the relationship between the Bill of Rights and the ordinary law is not governed by the principles and rules set out in the Bill of Rights. Instead, it is governed by the principles and rules set out in the ordinary law (legislation, common law and customary law). The manner in which the courts interpret legislation or develop the common law and customary law, however, must promote the values in the Bill of Rights.

Unlike the direct application of the Bill of Rights, therefore, the indirect application of the Bill of Rights is not based on an enquiry as to whether the law is in direct conflict with an identifiable right. Instead, the court has to invoke the values that underlie the Bill of Rights and ask whether it should interpret or develop the law to bring it in line with these values.

COUNTER POINT

Has the principle of avoidance or subsidiarity followed by the Constitutional Court undermined the rule of law?

Section 39(2) of the Constitution does not specify when the courts should apply the Bill of Rights indirectly in terms of section 39(2) rather than directly in terms of section 8(1) and (2). However, the Constitutional Court has stated on a number of occasions that where it is possible to decide a case without applying the Bill of Rights directly, then this is the approach the courts should adopt.[95] This approach is referred to as the **principle of avoidance or the principle of subsidiarity.**

In practice, this approach means that when a court is confronted with a statutory provision, it should first attempt to interpret the provision in accordance with the values that underlie the Bill of Rights before it tests the validity of the provision against a

93 *Juma Musjid* para 58.

94 Freedman (2012) para 9.

95 *S v Mhlungu and Others* (CCT25/94) [1995] ZACC 4; 1995 (3) SA 867; 1995 (7) BCLR 793 (CC) (8 June 1995) para 59; *Zantsi v Council of State, Ciskei and Others* (CCT24/94) [1995] ZACC 9; 1995 (10) BCLR 1424; 1995 (4) SA 615 (22 September 1995) paras 2–5; *Ferreira; Vryenhoek* para 199; *S v Bequinot* (CCT24/95) [1996] ZACC 21; 1996 (12) BCLR 1588; 1997 (2) SA 887 (18 November 1996) paras 12–13; *National Coalition for Gay and Lesbian Equality and Another v Minister of Justice and Others* (CCT11/98) [1998] ZACC 15; 1999 (1) SA 6; 1998 (12) BCLR 1517 (9 October 1998) para 21.

specific provision of the Bill of Rights. Similarly, when a court is confronted with a common or customary law rule, it should first attempt to develop the rule in accordance with the values underlying the Bill of Rights before it tests the validity of the rule against a specific provision of the Bill of Rights.

Woolman has criticised the fact that the Constitutional Court favours the indirect application of the Bill of Rights over the direct application. He argues that the problem with this approach is that:

- it has freed the Constitutional Court almost entirely from the text and has thus granted it the licence to decide each case as it likes
- it has relieved the Constitutional Court of the obligation to give content to the specific rights guaranteed in the Bill of Rights and to engage in the nuanced process of justification required by the limitation clause
- it has undermined the rule of law by making it difficult for lower court judges, lawyers, government officials and citizens to discern, with some degree of certainty, how the basic law is going to be applied.

In other words, the indirect application of the Bill of Rights has grown to assume such a central space in the Constitutional Court's approach to Bill of Rights matters that it seems to have reduced the relevance and space for the direct application of the Bill of Rights to a bare minimum.[96]

9.3.2.4.2 The indirect application of the Bill of Rights to legislation

Section 39(2) of the Constitution governs the indirect application of the Bill of Rights to legislation. This section provides that 'when interpreting any legislation ... every court, tribunal or forum must promote the spirit, purport and objects of the Bill of Rights'. To achieve this objective, the courts have held that section 39(2) of the Constitution imposes an obligation on judicial officers to examine the objects and purport of an Act and to read the provisions of legislation, so far as possible, 'in conformity' with the Bill of Rights.[97]

The principle of **reading in conformity** with the Bill of Rights means that the courts must prefer interpretations that fall within the boundaries of the Bill of Rights over those that do not, provided that such an interpretation can be reasonably ascribed to the section.[98] The process of interpreting legislation in conformity with the Bill of Rights, therefore, is limited to what the texts of the provisions in question are reasonably capable of meaning.[99] The interpretation 'must not be fanciful or far-fetched but one that reasonably arises from the challenged text without unwarranted strain, distortion or violence to the language'.[100]

The application of these principles and rules, however, is subject to certain limits. On the one hand, it is the duty of the judicial officer to interpret legislation in conformity with the

96 See Woolman, S (2007) The amazing vanishing Bill of Rights *South African Law Journal* 124(4):762–94 at 762.

97 See *Investigating Directorate: Serious Economic Offences and Others v Hyundai Motor Distributors (Pty) Ltd and Others In re: Hyundai Motor Distributors (Pty) Ltd and Others v Smit NO and Others* (CCT1/00) [2000] ZACC 12; 2000 (10) BCLR 1079; 2001 (1) SA 545 (CC) (25 August 2000) para 22.

98 *Hyundai* para 23.

99 See *South African Police Service v Police and Prisons Civil Rights Union and Another* (CCT 89/10) [2011] ZACC 21; [2011] 9 BLLR 831 (CC); 2011 (9) BCLR 992 (CC); 2011 (6) SA 1 (CC); (2011) 32 ILJ 1603 (CC) (9 June 2011) para 29.

100 *Daniels v Campbell and Others* (CCT 40/ 03) [2004] ZACC 14; 2004 (5) SA 331 (CC); 2004 (7) BCLR 735 (CC) (11 March 2004) para 83.

Constitution so far as this is reasonably possible. On the other hand, the legislature is under a duty to pass legislation that is reasonably clear and precise, enabling citizens and officials to understand what is expected of them.[101]

A balançe will have to be struck, therefore, to resolve this tension. There will be occasions when a judicial officer will find that the legislation, although open to a meaning which would be unconstitutional, is reasonably capable of being read 'in conformity with the Constitution'.[102] Such an interpretation should not, however, be unduly strained.[103]

COUNTER POINT

Benefits and drawbacks of an expansive approach to the principle of reading in conformity with the Bill of Rights

In some cases the Constitutional Court has adopted an expansive approach to the principle of reading in conformity with the Bill of Rights and has strayed quite far from the actual words used in a statutory provision in order to give it a constitutional meaning.

In *Bertie Van Zyl (Pty) Ltd and Another v Minister for Safety and Security and Others*,[104] for example, the applicant applied for an order declaring section 20(1)(*a*) of the Private Security Industry Regulation Act[105] to be unconstitutional and invalid on the grounds that it was overbroad or vague and therefore irrational. Section 20(1)(*a*) of the Act was overbroad, the applicant argued, because if read together with the definition of a 'security service' in section 1 of the Act, it applied not only to people who provided security services in the true sense, but to also to countless other people, including, for example, childminders, doctors and teachers, all of whom protect and safeguard people in the course of their work.

Section 20(1)(*a*) of this Act provided in part that '[n]o person, except a security service contemplated in section 199 of the Constitution (Act No. 108 of 1996), may in any manner render a security service for remuneration, reward, a fee or benefit, unless such person is registered as a security service provider in terms of this Act' and section 1(*a*) provided in part that 'security service means ... protecting or safeguarding a person or property in any manner'.

A majority of the Constitutional Court rejected this argument. In arriving at this decision, however, the Court held that the words 'security service' must be read down to mean 'the protection or safeguarding of persons or property from unlawful physical harm, including injury, physical damage, theft, or kidnapping caused by another person. This must be so because the security of persons and property is central to what the Act aims to protect ... [T]he Act is not intended to regulate the response to hazards from nature or harm from animals'.[106]

To uphold the constitutional validity of section 1(*a*) of the Act, therefore, the majority of the Constitutional Court essentially rewrote it by cutting the words 'in any manner' from the section and adding the words 'from unlawful physical harm, including injury, physical damage, theft, or kidnapping caused by another person' to it.

101 *Daniels* para 24.
102 *Hyundai* para 22.
103 *Daniels* para 24.
104 (CCT 77/08) [2009] ZACC 11; 2010 (2) SA 181 (CC); 2009 (10) BCLR 978 (CC) (7 May 2009).
105 Act 56 of 2001.
106 *Bertie Van Zyl* para 40.

As Bishop and Brickhill have pointed out, this expansive approach has both advantages and disadvantages. On the one hand, 'it allows courts to avoid declaring legislation unconstitutional and thus, in some sense at least, respect the separation of powers. It also avoids the recurrent difficulties and delays that often follow declarations of invalidity until new legislation is passed'.[107] On the other hand, 'government officials who have to apply the section will not be able to tell from reading it what its proper meaning is. They will have to know about (and read) the court decision in order to do their jobs'.[108]

In addition, they point out further:

> because High Court interpretations that avoid a finding of unconstitutionality need not be confirmed by the Constitutional Court, they will occasion much greater uncertainty than declarations of invalidity. It is also possible that different High Courts may reach different interpretations, none of which could be ascertained merely by reading the section.[109]

Finally, they conclude:

> the supposed separation of powers benefits that accrued through interpretation are largely illusory, as the degree of interference in the legislature's sphere of operation occasioned by interpretations that exceed the ordinary meaning of the words is the same as an order of invalidity accompanied by orders of reading in or severance. The Constitutional Court has developed a detailed jurisprudence about how to accommodate separation of powers concerns when making those orders, a jurisprudence that seems to be largely ignored in the current approach to interpretation. This massive power in effect permits courts - and not only the Constitutional Court - to legislate about what the legislation is meant to achieve.[110]

Apart from the points set out above, the courts have also held that it is important to distinguish between interpreting legislation in a manner that promotes the spirit, purport and objects of the Bill of Rights, sometimes called reading down, and the process of reading words into or severing them from a statutory provision under section 172(1)(*b*) of the Constitution following on a declaration of constitutional invalidity under section 172(1)(*a*) of the Constitution.[111]

The first process is an interpretative one and is limited to what the text is reasonably capable of meaning. The second process is a remedial one and can only take place after the statutory provision in question has been found to be constitutionally invalid.[112] It follows that where a legislative provision is reasonably capable of a meaning that places it within constitutional bounds, it should be preserved. Only if this is not possible should courts resort to the remedy of reading in or notional severance.[113]

107 Bishop, M and Brickhill, J (2010) 'Constitutional Law' *Juta's Annual Survey of South African Law* 224.
108 Bishop and Brickhill (2010) para 224.
109 Bishop and Brickhill (2010) para 224.
110 Bishop and Brickhill (2010) para 225.
111 Bishop and Brickhill (2010) para 225.
112 Bishop and Brickhill (2010) para 225.
113 Bishop and Brickhill (2010) para 225.

9.3.2.4.3 The indirect application of the Bill of Rights to the common law and customary law

Section 39(2) of the Constitution also governs the indirect application of the Bill of Rights to the common law and customary law. This section provides that '... when developing the common law or customary law, every court, tribunal or forum must promote the spirit, purport and objects of the Bill of Rights'.

The Constitutional Court has considered the circumstances in which the courts must develop the common law on a number of occasions.[114] In these cases, the Court has held that while the courts are under a general obligation to develop the common law, they do not have to carry out this exercise in each and every case that comes before them.

In *Carmichele v Minister of Safety and Security*, for example, the Constitutional Court held that:

> **the obligation of courts to develop the common law, in the context of section 39(2) objectives, is not purely discretionary. On the contrary, it is implicit in section 39(2) read with section 173 that where the common law as it stands is deficient in promoting the section 39(2) objectives, the courts are under a general obligation to develop it appropriately.**[115]

This general obligation, the Constitutional Court held further, does not mean:

> **that a court must, in each and every case where the common law is involved, embark on an independent exercise as to whether the common law is in need of development and, if so, how it is to be developed under section 39(2). At the same time there might be circumstances where a court is obliged to raise the matter on its own and require full argument from the parties.**[116]

The obligation imposed on the courts to develop the common law, therefore, is an extensive one. It requires the courts to be alert to the normative framework of the Constitution not only when some startling new development of the common law is in issue, but in all cases where the incremental development of the rule is in issue.[117]

PAUSE FOR REFLECTION

Differing interpretations of section 39(2)

There has been considerable academic debate about the nature of the horizontal application of the Bill of Rights and whether the courts are obliged to develop the common law in each case or not.[118] Fagan argues that contrary to decisions of the Constitutional Court in *Carmichele*, the Constitution does not regard the spirit, purport and objects of the Bill of Rights as providing an independent reason for developing the common law. According to Fagan, the phrase, 'spirit, purport and objects of the Bill of Rights', as

---

114 See, for example, *Du Plessis*; *Amod v Multilateral Motor Vehicle Accidents Fund* (CCT4/98) [1998] ZACC 11; 1998 (4) SA 753; 1998 (10) BCLR 1207 (27 August 1998).

115 (CCT 48/00) [2001] ZACC 22; 2001 (4) SA 938 (CC); 2001 (10) BCLR 995 (CC) (16 August 2001) para 39.

116 *Carmichele* para 39.

117 See *K v Minister of Safety and Security* (CCT52/04) [2005] ZACC 8; 2005 (6) SA 419 (CC); 2005 (9) BCLR 835 (CC); [2005] 8 BLLR 749 (CC) (13 June 2005) para 17.

118 For an interesting and lively debate on this topic, see Fagan, A (2010) The secondary role of the spirit, purport and objects of the Bill of Rights in the common law's development *South African Law Journal* 127(3):611–27; Davis, DM (2012) How many positivist legal philosophers can be made to dance on the head of a pin? A reply to Professor Fagan *South African Law Journal* 129(1):59–72; Fagan, A (2012) A straw man, three red herrings, and a closet rule-worshipper: A rejoinder to Davis JP *South African Law Journal* 129(3):788–98; Davis, DM (2013) The importance of reading: A rebuttal to the jurisprudence of Anton Fagan *South African Law Journal* 130(1):52–9.

contained in section 39(2) of the Constitution, constitutes a set of reasons for choosing between different ways of developing the common law. However, this choice can only be made after adopting a **prior** decision based on an **independent** reason for developing the common law. There is a distinction to be drawn between a justification provided by a constitutionally entrenched right and one provided by the objects of the Bill of Rights. The wording of section 39(2) does not imply an obligation to develop the common law. If there is an obligation to develop the common law, it must be found in independent reasons; that is, reasons other than those sourced in the objects of the Bill of Rights.

Davis took issue with this line of reasoning, arguing that the interpretation was too formalistic, that it 'ignores the intricacies of adjudication and its relationship to justice' and continues:

> On this line of argument, the demands of a post-constitutional jurisprudence require a re-examination of legal thinking, a deep reflection on the consequences of the past in order that we do not reproduce its shibboleths, but rather its reflective power, in order in turn to meet the conception of justice which is set out in the Constitution, in the form of a normative framework for a future South Africa. In other words, the Constitution, read as a whole, provides a concept of justice which, if implemented, would result in the attainment of a journey from apartheid to the democratic society envisaged in the Constitution. Admittedly, this is a difficult task and not one that is met easily by way of a grand narrative which can be grasped immediately.[119]

In essence, Davis argues that in order for the Constitution to play its role in transforming the private law, section 39(2) requires the courts to develop the common law in each case to bring it in line with the spirit, purport and objects of the Bill of Rights. An argument that limits the ability of the courts to do so is therefore essentially in opposition to the transformation of the private law in accordance with the precepts of justice.

Apart from the circumstances in which the courts are obliged to develop the common law, the Constitutional Court has also dealt with the manner in which the courts must carry out this exercise. In *Thebus and Another v S*, for example, the Constitutional Court explained that the Constitution embodies an 'objective normative value system'.[120] It is within the matrix of this objective normative value system that the common law must be developed. This means, the Court explained further, that 'under section 39(2) of the Constitution, concepts which are reflective of, or premised upon, a given value system might well have to be replaced, or supplemented and enriched by the appropriate norms of the objective value system embodied in the Constitution'.[121]

After making these points, the Constitutional Court went on to explain that the need to develop the common law under section 39(2) of the Constitution could arise in two circumstances:

> **The first would be when a rule of the common law is inconsistent with a constitutional provision. Repugnancy of this kind would compel an adaptation of the common law to resolve the inconsistency. The second possibility arises even when a rule of the common**

119 Davis (2012) 67–8.
120 (CCT36/02) [2003] ZACC 12; 2003 (6) SA 505 (CC); 2003 (10) BCLR 1100 (CC) (28 August 2003) para 27.
121 *Thebus* para 27.

> **law is not inconsistent with a specific constitutional provision but may fall short of its spirit, purport and objects. Then, the common law must be adapted so that it grows in harmony with the 'objective normative value system' found in the Constitution.**[122]

In those cases in which a common law rule is alleged to be inconsistent with a constitutional provision, a court is obliged to carry out a two-stage enquiry. First, it must determine whether or not the common law rule does in fact limit an entrenched right. If it does, the court must move onto the second stage and determine whether the limitation is reasonable and justifiable. If the limitation is not reasonable and justifiable, the court itself is obliged to adapt or develop the common law rule in order to harmonise it with the constitutional norm.[123]

In those cases in which a common law rule falls short of the spirit, purport and objects of the Bill of Rights, a court is also obliged to undertake a two-stage enquiry. First, it must ask itself whether, given the objectives of section 39(2) of the Constitution, the common law should be developed beyond existing precedent. If the answer to this question is a negative one, then this should be the end of the enquiry. If not, the next enquiry should be how the development should occur and which court should embark on this exercise.[124]

In *K v Minister of Safety and Security*,[125] the Constitutional Court also set out some of the ways in which the common law can be developed. In this respect, the Court stated that the common law can be developed by, for example, introducing a new rule or significantly changing an existing one. It can also be developed by extending the ambit of a rule to include a new set of facts or limiting the ambit to exclude those facts.[126]

PAUSE FOR REFLECTION

The development of customary law

The indirect application of the Bill of Rights, which leads to the development of the law, is often thought of only in terms of the development of the common law. However, as section 39 clearly states, it is not only the common law that must be developed but also the customary law. In *Mayelane v Ngwenyama and Another*, the Constitutional Court summarised its approach to the development of customary law as follows:

> This Court has, in a number of decisions, explained what this resurrection of customary law to its rightful place as one of the primary sources of law under the Constitution means. This includes that:
>
> a) customary law must be understood in its own terms, and not through the lens of the common law;
> b) so understood, customary law is nevertheless subject to the Constitution and has to be interpreted in the light of its values;
> c) customary law is a system of law that is practised in the community, has its own values and norms, is practised from generation to generation and evolves and develops to meet the changing needs of the community;
> d) customary law is not a fixed body of formally classified and easily ascertainable rules. By its very nature it evolves as the people who live by its norms change their patterns of life;

122 *Thebus* para 28.
123 *Thebus* para 32.
124 *Thebus* para 26.
125 (CCT52/04) [2005] ZACC 8; 2005 (6) SA 419 (CC); 2005 (9) BCLR 835 (CC); [2005] 8 BLLR 749 (CC) (13 June 2005).
126 *K* para 16.

e) customary law will continue to evolve within the context of its values and norms consistently with the Constitution;
f) the inherent flexibility of customary law provides room for consensus-seeking and the prevention and resolution, in family and clan meetings, of disputes and disagreements; and
g) these aspects provide a setting which contributes to the unity of family structures and the fostering of co-operation, a sense of responsibility and belonging in its members, as well as the nurturing of healthy communitarian traditions like *ubuntu*.[127]

SUMMARY

This chapter deals with some of the technical questions relating to Bill of Rights adjudication. The application of the Bill of Rights gives rise to a number of difficult questions. The two most important, however, are who is entitled to claim the right in question and who is bound by the right in question?

The rights guaranteed in the Bill of Rights may be claimed by both natural and, in certain circumstances, juristic persons. In so far as natural persons are concerned, the majority of rights state that they can be claimed by 'everyone'. The use of the word 'everyone' refers to South African citizens as well as any other person who is physically present in the country, irrespective of whether they are here legally or illegally.

Although the majority of rights state that they can be claimed by 'everyone', certain rights state that they may be claimed only by a narrower category of natural persons, for example citizens, children or detained persons. These rights may be claimed only by those natural persons who fall into the definition of the relevant category.

In so far as juristic persons are concerned, section 8(4) of the Constitution provides that '[a] juristic person is entitled to the rights in the Bill of Rights to the extent required by the nature of the rights and the nature of the juristic person'. To determine whether a juristic person can claim a particular right, therefore, two factors must be taken into account: whether the juristic person is capable of exercising the right in question and whether the juristic person is entitled to exercise the right in question.

Once a court has determined who can claim rights in terms of the Bill of Rights, it has to ask a second question, namely, against whom can these rights be claimed? In other words, the court has to ask who is bound to respect the rights claimed by either a natural or juristic person. Although 'everyone' is entitled to claim the benefit of the rights (or at least most of the rights) in the Bill of Rights, not everyone is bound by every right contained in the Bill of Rights. This is because while the Bill of Rights is always binding on the state, it is not always binding on private persons.

When it comes to the question of who is bound by the Bill of Rights, it is important to distinguish between the direct application of the Bill of Rights and the indirect application

127 (CCT 57/12) [2013] ZACC 14; 2013 (4) SA 415 (CC); 2013 (8) BCLR 918 (CC) (30 May 2013) para 24. See also *Gumede (born Shange) v President of the Republic of South Africa and Others* (CCT 50/08) [2008] ZACC 23; 2009 (3) BCLR 243 (CC); 2009 (3) SA 152 (CC) (8 December 2008) para 22; *Alexkor Ltd and Another v Richtersveld Community and Others* (CCT19/03) [2003] ZACC 18; 2004 (5) SA 460 (CC); 2003 (12) BCLR 1301 (CC) (14 October 2003); *Bhe and Others v Khayelitsha Magistrate and Others* (CCT 49/03) [2004] ZACC 17; 2005 (1) SA 580 (CC); 2005 (1) BCLR 1 (CC) (15 October 2004) para 41; *First Certification* para 197.

of the Bill of Rights as well as between the vertical and horizontal application of the Bill of Rights. This is because in South Africa the Bill of Rights applies not only directly and indirectly, but also vertically and sometimes horizontally. Section 8(1) of the Constitution governs the direct vertical application of the Bill of Rights while section 8(2) governs the direct horizontal application. Section 39(2) of the Constitution governs the indirect vertical and horizontal application of the Bill of Rights.

Chapter 10

The limitation of rights

10.1 Introduction

Rights are not absolute and can, in certain circumstances, be limited. Section 36 of the Bill of Rights contains a limitation clause that allows for the constitutionally valid limitation of rights in certain instances. Once a court has established that a law infringes on one or more of the rights guaranteed in the Bill of Rights, the court must ask whether this infringement, also called a limitation, is justifiable. This means that somebody who claims that a legal provision has limited his or her rights will not automatically win the case simply because his or her rights have been limited. The person will only win if the court finds that the limitation is not justifiable in terms of the limitation clause set out in section 36 of the Bill of Rights.

Determining whether a limitation of rights is justified or not is difficult and rightly so. It is difficult on a number of levels. First, South Africa is a country emerging from a historical period during which individuals' fundamental rights and freedoms were systematically and routinely violated, first under colonialism and then apartheid, often under the colour of law. South Africa has now committed itself to a system of constitutional democracy.[1] This new political dispensation requires all arms of government[2] and, in certain circumstances, private actors,[3] to respect and protect the basic, fundamental rights contained in our Bill of Rights. In this constitutional order, any limitation of these basic rights will understandably and necessarily be a difficult and, at times, painful exercise.

Second, the commitment to a rights-based constitutional order means that society's political, social, economic and historical controversies are often resolved using the language and the logic of rights. At times, this requires courts to address these pressing and complex issues, some of which invoke age-old questions that go to the heart of how society and government should be structured and should function, using contested empirical bases. This sometimes places courts in a difficult position in relation to the other arms of government, namely the legislature and the executive, as well as the public at large. The commitment to individual rights means that courts may also have to make decisions that go against public opinion.[4] This, in essence, is the cost of 'taking rights seriously'.[5]

Apart from the difficulties identified above, there is another sense in which the limitation of rights is a difficult exercise. It is often difficult for people to understand the approach adopted by the Constitutional Court (and to a far lesser extent the Constitution's drafters) towards the limitation of rights. The inaccessibility of the limitation clause is problematic in a number of respects. First and foremost, it makes it difficult for other branches of government to bring their conduct into line with what the Bill of Rights expects and demands. As the Court itself noted in *S v Mhlungu and Others*, constitutional interpretation should take the form of 'a principled judicial dialogue, in the first place between members of this Court, then between our Court and other courts, the legal profession, law schools, Parliament, and, indirectly, with the public at large'.[6] The problem with the Court's current approach to rights limitation is that aspects of its approach are often lost in translation.[7]

---

1 S 1(*c*) of the Constitution states that South Africa is a sovereign, democratic state founded on, *inter alia*, '[the] supremacy of the Constitution and the rule of law'. Further, s 7 states: 'This Bill of Rights is a cornerstone of democracy in South Africa. It enshrines the rights of all people in our country and affirms the democratic values of human dignity, equality and freedom.'

2 S 8(1) of the Constitution states: 'The Bill of Rights applies to all law, and binds the legislature, the executive, the judiciary and all organs of state.'

3 For example, s 9(4) of the Constitution prohibits horizontal discrimination, stating: 'No person may unfairly discriminate directly or indirectly against anyone on one or more [prohibited] grounds.'

4 For a fairly negative assessment of public support for the Constitutional Court, see Gibson, JL and Caldeira, GA (2003) Defenders of democracy? Legitimacy, popular acceptance, and the South African Constitutional Court *Journal of Politics* 65(1):1–30 at 1. Du Plessis argues that the Constitutional Court must go a step further by not only engaging with public opinion, but where necessary changing it by 'edify[ing] the South African public about their ethical identity under the Constitution'. See Du Plessis, M (2002) Between apology and utopia: The Constitutional Court and public opinion *South African Journal on Human Rights* 18(1):1–40 at 1.

5 See Dworkin, RM (1978) *Taking Rights Seriously* 184.

6 (CCT25/94) [1995] ZACC 4; 1995 (3) SA 867; 1995 (7) BCLR 793 (CC) (8 June 1995) para 129.

7 Even if the test can be conceptually pinned down, it is problematic by the use of language alone. In *Prince v President of the Law Society of the Cape of Good Hope* (CCT36/00) [2002] ZACC 1; 2002 (2) SA 794; 2002 (3) BCLR 231 (25 January 2002) para 151, Sachs J, for example, attempts to bring the abstract enquiry down to the ground by noting that 'the weighing of the respective interests at stake does not take place on weightless scales of pure logic pivoted on a friction-free fulcrum of abstract rationality'. This description is not easy to comprehend.

Second, in its current form, the limitation clause, as well as the Court's jurisprudence in respect of the clause, is difficult for students to understand.

Although some level of complexity is inevitable, this chapter tries to simplify the process of limiting rights under the Constitution. To do so, we begin by discussing the shift from the structured, sequential limitation enquiry required by section 33 of the interim Constitution to a unified, balancing limitation enquiry required by section 36 of the Constitution.[8] Next, we consider the two stages of the limitation analysis: the threshold stage and the justification stage. At the threshold stage, we draw attention to the different approaches taken by the Constitutional Court. The justification stage is further divided into its two sub-components, namely the law of general application requirement and the reasonable and justifiable requirement. Crucial to understanding the latter is a reconsideration of the notion of **proportionality** that has come to dominate the understanding and misunderstanding of how section 36 works. In the final part of the chapter we discuss the limitation of rights outside section 36(1).

10.2 The evolution of the limitation clause

It is now trite to say – as we indicated right at the outset in this chapter – that rights are not absolute.[9] Rather, they can be limited by the rights of others as well as competing social interests. In providing for the limitation of rights, the drafters of the interim Constitution were faced with three options. The first was merely to set out the various protected rights without any formal limitation device. This is the approach adopted in the United States Constitution, 'as a result of which courts in that country have been obliged to find limits to constitutional rights through a narrow interpretation of the rights themselves'.[10] The second was to include rights-specific limitation clauses such as those found in regional and international human rights instruments like the European Convention for the Protection of Human Rights and Fundamental Freedoms (1950).[11] The third was to include a general limitation clause applicable to all the rights protected under the Constitution, such as that found in Canada's Charter of Rights and Freedoms.[12]

Under both the interim and final Constitution the drafters opted for a general limitation clause. Section 33(1) of the interim Constitution delineated a staged process for the limitation of rights. This allowed for the rights entrenched in Chapter 3 to be limited by a law of general application, 'provided that such limitation (*a*) shall be permissible only to the extent that it is (i) reasonable; (ii) justifiable in an open and democratic society based on freedom and equality; and (*b*) shall not negate the essential content of the right in

---

8 This evolution will form the basis of the reconsideration of the notion of proportionality below.

9 In *De Reuck v Director of Public Prosecutions (Witwatersrand Local Division) and Others* 2003 (3) SA 389 (W) 425G, the High Court noted:

> **I reiterate that the rights contained in the Bill of Rights are not absolute. Rights have to be exercised with due regard and respect for the rights of others. Organised society can only operate on the basis of rights being exercised harmoniously with the rights of others. Of course, the rights exercised by an individual may come into conflict with the rights exercised by another, and where rights come into conflict, a balancing process is required.**

10 *S v Makwanyane and Another* (CCT3/94) [1995] ZACC 3; 1995 (6) BCLR 665; 1995 (3) SA 391; [1996] 2 CHRLD 164; 1995 (2) SACR 1 (6 June 1995) para 100.

11 See *Makwanyane* para 104.

12 Art 1 of the Canadian Charter of Rights and Freedoms in Part 1 of the Constitution Act (1982) states: 'The Canadian Charter of Rights and Freedoms guarantees the rights and freedoms set out in it subject only to such reasonable limits prescribed by law as can be demonstrably justified in a free and democratic society.'

question …'[13] Further, it provided that the limitation of certain entrenched rights[14] must also be necessary.[15]

The drafters of section 33 of the interim Constitution were clearly influenced by the limitation clause contained in the Canadian Charter of Rights and Freedoms and, to a lesser extent, the German limitation clause which is similarly structured.[16] Given this, it was widely expected that when it came to interpreting section 33, the Constitutional Court would follow the approach adopted by the Canadian Supreme Court in *R v Oakes*.[17] In this case, Dickson CJC stated that there are three important components to the proportionality test:

> **First, the measures adopted must be carefully designed to achieve the objective in question. They must not be arbitrary, unfair or based on irrational considerations. In short, they must be rationally connected to the objective. Secondly, the means, even if rationally connected to the objective in the first sense, should impair 'as little as possible' the right or freedom in question. … Thirdly, there must be a proportionality between the effects of the measures which are responsible for limiting the Charter right or freedom, and the objective which has been identified as of 'sufficient importance'.[18]**

Instead of following the structured and sequential test adopted by the Canadian Courts in *Oakes*, however, the Constitutional Court in *S v Makwanyane and Another* opted to adopt a singular **global** approach in which it considers a list of factors together in a kind of balancing test.[19] This approached conflated the two requirements of reasonableness and necessity, omitted justifiability and introduced the notion of **proportionality** 'which calls for the balancing of different interests'.[20] In his judgment, Chaskalson P thus stated the following:

> **The limitation of constitutional rights for a purpose that is reasonable and necessary in a democratic society involves the weighing up of competing values, and ultimately an assessment based on proportionality. This is implicit in the provisions of s 33(1). The fact that different rights have different implications for democracy and, in the case of our Constitution, for 'an open and democratic society based on freedom and**

13 S 33(1) of the interim Constitution. Regarding the evolution of s 33(1), Woolman and Botha note: 'The basic form of the interim Constitution's limitations clause did not change over the course of the 12 reports generated by the Multi-Party Negotiating Forum's Technical Committee on Fundamental Rights. In its second report, the Committee identified what it believed to be the primary features of a limitations clause: (a) a 'law of general application' threshold test; (b) a reasonableness requirement; (c) a necessity requirement; (d) a 'justifiable in a free, open and democratic society' requirement; (e) a proportionality or balancing approach; (f) a 'non-derogation from the essential content of the right' requirement; and (g) an immunisation of select rights from any limitation at all. With the exception of the last characteristic, all of these attributes appear in one form or another in the 12th and final version of the interim Constitution's limitations clause.' See Woolman, S and Botha, H 'Limitation' in Woolman, S and Bishop, M (eds) (2013) *Constitutional Law of South Africa* 2nd ed rev service 5 34.10–34.11. For a discussion of the limitations clause in s 33 of the interim Constitution, see White, J 'Constitutional litigation and interpretation, and fundamental rights' (1994) *Juta's Annual Survey of South African Law* 35–66.

14 Entrenched rights were listed in s 33(1) (*b*)(*aa*) and (*bb*) of the interim Constitution as ss 10, 11, 12, 14(1), 21, 25 or 30(1) (*d*), 30(1)(*e*) or 30(2) and ss 15, 16, 17, 18, 23, or 24 in so far as such rights relate to free and fair political activity.

15 For a more detailed discussion of the evolution of s 33(1), see Woolman and Botha (2013).

16 In *Makwanyane* para 108, the German test was described by the Constitutional Court as follows:

> **It has regard to the purpose of the limiting legislation, whether the legislation in fact achieves that purpose, whether it is necessary therefor, and whether a proper balance has been achieved between the value enhanced by the limitation, and the fundamental right that has been limited.**

17 [1986] 1 SCR 103. This judgment was also favourably quoted in *Makwanyane* para 105.

18 *R v Oakes* [1986] 1 SCR 103 para 74.

19 (CCT3/94) [1995] ZACC 3; 1995 (6) BCLR 665; 1995 (3) SA 391; [1996] 2 CHRLD 164; 1995 (2) SACR 1 (6 June 1995).

20 *Makwanyane* para 104.

> **equality', means that there is no absolute standard which can be laid down for determining reasonableness and necessity. Principles can be established, but the application of those principles to particular circumstances can only be done on a case-by-case basis. This is inherent in the requirement of proportionality, which calls for the balancing of different interests.**[21]

CRITICAL THINKING

Is the limitation of rights an assessment based on proportionality?

We could question the finding that it is implicit in the language of section 33(1) of the interim Constitution that the limitation of rights is 'ultimately an assessment based on proportionality'.[22] The language of section 33(1), which spoke of justifiability, implied that the enquiry will **at times** involve the weighing up of competing values (balancing) and their proportionality. This might be the ultimate leg of the staged process **should it get to that point**. However, to reduce section 33 and the process of limiting of rights generally to **only** being about proportionality is difficult to reconcile with the text of section 33(1). What is more, it is confusing as it makes the whole endeavour about a metaphorical formulation of proportionality and balancing.[23] However, it is difficult to know exactly what must be balanced against what else and whether the various interests at play in any limitation clause enquiry can indeed be balanced against each other at all.

Regardless of the merits of the Court's approach in *Makwanyane*, it clearly had an effect on the drafters of section 36(1) of the final Constitution which states:

> **The rights in the Bill of Rights may be limited only in terms of law of general application to the extent that the limitation is reasonable and justifiable in an open and democratic society based on human dignity, equality and freedom, taking into account all relevant factors, including–**
> **(*a*) the nature of the right;**
> **(*b*) the importance of the purpose of the limitation;**
> **(*c*) the nature and extent of the limitation;**
> **(*d*) the relation between the limitation and its purpose; and**
> **(*e*) less restrictive means to achieve the purpose.**

---

21 *Makwanyane* para 104. The reformulation was, it must be noted, welcomed by some commentators at the time. See Bronstein, V and Robinson, K 'Constitutional jurisprudence and the Bill of Rights' (1996) *Juta's Annual Survey of South African Law* 53: 'Here the court acknowledges one's intuitive sense that the effect of the proportionality test used in analysing rights and their limitations does not depend on the wording of the limitation clause in an individual case. The best interpretation of the statement quoted above is that the rights in the Bill of Rights are not weakened by the omission of the word "necessary". The implication is that it does not make a difference whether the operative words in the limitation clause are "necessary" or "reasonable and justifiable". This pronouncement should be interpretively important in the future.' Such an early departure from the wording of s 36 – by academics no less – was a sign of things to come.

22 *Makwanyane* para 104.

23 In doing so, the Constitutional Court took its lead from the German Constitutional Court which, Chaskalson J remarked in *Makwanyane* para 108, 'also has a provision similar to section 33(1)(*b*) of our Constitution, but the Court apparently avoids making use of this provision, preferring to deal with extreme limitations of rights through the proportionality test'.

The most notable difference between the limitation clauses of the interim and final Constitutions is that the drafters of the final Constitution elected to abandon the sequential, structured approach in which a series of specific questions were addressed.[24] Instead, they favoured *Makwanyane's* singular, global approach in which certain factors are considered. However, the drafters did not go so far as to adopt the language of balancing and proportionality. They chose rather the phrase 'reasonable and justifiable'.[25] This left open the possibility that some of the structure of the interim Constitution might survive, but that window was quickly closed by the Court. The Constitution also included the factors listed by *Makwanyane* as relevant to balancing[26] and added another one: less restrictive means.[27]

PAUSE FOR REFLECTION

The absence of reasons for the the Constitutional Court's adjudicative approach to rights limitation

The reasons for the Constitutional Court's deliberate move away from a structured, criteria-based approach to the limitation of rights - such as that found in the interim Constitution and *Oakes* - towards a global, unstructured test that turns almost entirely on the problematic metaphor of balancing are not easily identified. One possible explanation is that it is a reaction (or perhaps an overreaction) to the formalistic, positivist legal culture that was pervasive under apartheid. As Lenta notes:

> It is widely recognised that the radical divorce decreed by modernity under the guise of legal positivism, between law and ethics, legality and morality, justice as process and justice as substance was in large measure responsible for the complicity of the legal system with the apartheid regime. Positivism has

24 Under the text of the interim Constitution's limitation clause, courts must first ask if a limitation is reasonable. Only if it is deemed to be reasonable, will they move on to the second question as to whether it is justifiable, at which point the courts would be required to balance competing interests.

25 At the time of its drafting, the exact phraseology was contested and confused. As noted at the time: 'While the section in the Working Draft on the limitation of rights was replete with alternative constructions providing that a right may be limited only to the extent that it is "reasonable/reasonable and justifiable/reasonable and necessary/necessary/justifiable" (s 35(1)(*a*), Working Draft), in the end the Constitutional Assembly settled for the reasonable and justifiable formulation [s 36(1) in the final Constitution] despite some rather puerile debate in which it seemed as if the constitutional experts did not really seem to have an opinion as to whether there was any significant point to the different formulations. This particular debate created some confusion in a public already well rehearsed in the promise that the "draft text has been written in plain language so that everyone can read and understand it".' See *Annual Survey of South African Law.*

26 In *Makwanyane* para 104, the Court also introduced factors to be considered in the balancing process, noting: 'In the balancing process the relevant considerations will include the nature of the right that is limited and its importance to an open and democratic society based on freedom and equality; the purpose for which the right is limited and the importance of that purpose to such a society; the extent of the limitation, its efficacy and, particularly where the limitation has to be necessary, whether the desired ends could reasonably be achieved through other means less damaging to the right in question.'

27 While these factors added some substance to an otherwise fairly abstract process, this value was offset by the exclusion of two features of s 33 of the interim Constitution that could potentially have narrowed down the 'universe of possibility' presented by the open-ended nature of the balancing test. The first was the requirement in s 33(1)(*b*) of the interim Constitution that limitations must not 'negate the essential content of the right in question'. The second was the requirement that, in respect of certain entrenched rights, the limitation must pass the additional test of being necessary. See Woolman, S 'Application' in Woolman and Bishop (2013) 31.145. While these will no doubt have presented their own problems, they would have brought some clarity to the process of limiting rights. Notably, there was an objection raised in the *First Certification* judgment regarding the omission of 'necessary' but that was quickly dismissed. See *Certification of the Constitution of the Republic of South Africa, 1996* (CCT 23/96) [1996] ZACC 26; 1996 (4) SA 744 (CC); 1996 (10) BCLR 1253 (CC) (6 September 1996) para 90.

> **accordingly and rightly been rejected by the judiciary and many in the legal academy.**[28]

However, this may be too simplistic an explanation that, in any event, is difficult to reconcile with the Court's decision to resort to formalism at other times in its jurisprudence.[29] As Roux notes, 'none of the mainstream theories of adjudication adequately explains the [Constitutional Court's] record'.[30]

In the absence of a theory that explains the Court's adjudicative approach generally, let alone rights limitation in particular, Roux submits that the Court's decision-making process can best be understood as a form of 'tactical adjudication'.[31] Leaning on political sciences approaches to the understanding of law and courts, he argues that the Court is 'a political actor pursuing a determinate strategic objective: the establishment of constitutional democracy'.[32] The pursuit of that objective requires that the Court use the available legal materials - including section 36 - 'to give meaningful effect to the Constitution whilst building its institutional legitimacy, either directly or indirectly, by creating doctrinal space for itself in later judgments to hand down context-sensitive judgments'.[33] This 'mix of principle and pragmatism', Roux argues elsewhere, 'seems likely to provide the best way for a constitutional court in a new democracy to build its legal legitimacy without sacrificing its institutional security'.[34]

Of the five 'adjudicative devices' Roux identifies as being employed by the Court to create this 'doctrinal space', one has particular relevance to section 36.[35] This adjudicative device is the conversion of conceptual distinctions into 'multi-factor balancing tests' or 'discretionary standards'.[36] Referring to the case of *First National Bank of SA Limited t/a Wesbank v Commissioner for the South African Revenue Services and Another; First National Bank of SA Limited t/a Wesbank v Minister of Finance*,[37] Roux argues:

> **In a decision that says much about its general approach to constitutional adjudication, the [Court] ... cut through all of [section 25's] conceptual distinctions and reduced the constitutional property clause inquiry to a single, multi-factor balancing test.**[38]

According to the Court, this test requires consideration of 'a complexity of relationships' that must be scrutinised under a review standard that will vary between **rationality** and

28 Lenta, P (2001) Just gaming? The case for postmodernism in South African legal theory *South African Journal on Human Rights* 17(2):173–209 at 175–6.

29 See, for example, the equality test in *Harksen v Lane NO and Others* (CCT9/97) [1997] ZACC 12; 1997 (11) BCLR 1489; 1998 (1) SA 300 (7 October 1997).

30 Roux, T (2007) Tactical adjudication: How the Constitutional Court of South Africa survived its first decade 29, available at http://www.saifac.org.za/docs/2007/Tactical%20Adjudication.pdf.

31 Roux (2007) 30.

32 Roux (2007) 30.

33 Roux (2007) 30.

34 Roux, T (2009) Principle and pragmatism on the Constitutional Court of South Africa *International Journal of Constitutional Law* 7(1):106–38 at 108.

35 Roux (2009) 135.

36 Roux (2009) 135.

37 (CCT19/01) [2002] ZACC 5; 2002 (4) SA 768; 2002 (7) BCLR 702 (16 May 2002).

38 Roux (2009) 134–5.

proportionality depending 'on all the relevant facts of each particular case'.[39] Rather than being 'unconscious or whimsical', Roux argues persuasively that these adjudicative approaches are part of a deliberate strategy on the part of the CCSA to make its leading doctrines more context-sensitive.[40]

Although Roux does not cite the Court's approach to section 36 as evidence of tactical adjudication, there are a number of reasons to include it as a good, if not better, example than those he does include. While employing adjudicative devices that create the necessary doctrinal space in specific cases might be useful in future cases of a similar nature, doing so in respect of the limitation clause would create such space systemically. Further, if the Court is employing such devices in order to manage its relationship with the executive and legislature, and to protect its institutional security, then there is no better place to do so than section 36: the lynchpin of that relationship.

10.3 The two-stage approach to the limitation of rights

Since the Constitutional Court's very first case under the interim Constitution, the Court has advocated a 'two-stage approach' to the limitation of rights.[41] Since the adoption of the final Constitution, the Court has for the most part followed this two-stage approach. In terms of this approach: 'The first question to be asked is whether the provision in question infringes the rights protected by the substantive clauses of the Bill of Rights. If it does, the next question that arises will be whether that infringement is justifiable'.[42]

In *Ex Parte Minister of Safety and Security and Others: In Re S v Walters and Another*, the Constitutional Court set out this two-stage approach in more detail, noting:

> **First, there is the threshold enquiry aimed at determining whether or not the enactment in question constitutes a limitation on one or other guaranteed right. This entails examining (a) the content and scope of the relevant protected right(s) and (b) the meaning and effect of the impugned enactment to see whether there is any limitation of (a) by (b). Subsections (1) and (2) of s 39 of the Constitution give guidance as to the interpretation of both the rights and the enactment, essentially requiring them to be interpreted so as to promote the value system of an open and democratic society based on human dignity, equality and freedom. If upon such analysis no limitation is found, that is the end of the matter. The constitutional challenge is dismissed there and then. If there is indeed a limitation, however, the second stage ensues. This is ordinarily called the limitations exercise. In essence this**

39 *First National Bank* para 100.

40 Roux (2009) 136.

41 *S v Zuma and Others* (CCT5/94) [1995] ZACC 1; 1995 (2) SA 642; 1995 (4) BCLR 401 (SA); 1995 (1) SACR 568; [1996] 2 CHRLD 244 (5 April 1995) para 21. Kentridge AJ added: 'First, has there been a contravention of a guaranteed right? If so, is it justified under the limitation clause?' See also *S v Williams and Others* (CCT20/94) [1995] ZACC 6; 1995 (3) SA 632; 1995 (7) BCLR 861 (CC) (9 June 1995) para 54; *Makwanyane* paras 100–02, 208. However, Sachs J emerged in opposition to this, noting in *Coetzee v Government of the Republic of South Africa; Matiso and Others v Commanding Officer Port Elizabeth Prison and Others* (CCT19/94, CCT22/94) [1995] ZACC 7; 1995 (10) BCLR 1382; 1995 (4) SA 631 (22 September 1995) para 46 that 'faithfulness to the Constitution is best achieved by locating the two-stage balancing process within a holistic, value-based and case-oriented framework'.

42 *South African National Defence Union v Minister of Defence* (CCT27/98) [1999] ZACC 7; 1999 (4) SA 469; 1999 (6) BCLR 615 (26 May 1999) para 18.

> **requires a weighing-up of the nature and importance of the right(s) that are limited together with the extent of the limitation as against the importance and purpose of the limiting enactment. Section 36(1) of the Constitution spells out these factors that have to be put into the scales in making a proportional evaluation of all the counterpoised rights and interests involved.**[43]

The two-stage approach therefore requires a court first to focus on the substantive rights, for example the right to equality, the right to vote or the right of detained persons, to determine whether the right was infringed or limited. It then secondly requires the court to ask whether the infringement or limitation is justifiable in terms of section 36.

COUNTER POINT

Exceptions to the two-stage enquiry

We contend that the Court has at times strayed (explicitly and implicitly) from the two-stage approach. In *Christian Education South Africa v Minister of Education*,[44] the Court went straight into the justification of the infringement of the rights implicated by the measure without considering whether they were, in fact, infringed. The Court merely assumed - without ever deciding - that the relevant rights might have been infringed. More disturbingly, the Court has on one occasion failed to consider the second stage of the limitation enquiry at all.[45] We assume that these cases are exceptions and that they do not suggest a new departure for the Court. We therefore assume that the Court is required in each case to follow the two-stage approach to limitation analysis.

10.4 The threshold enquiry: does the measure limit a protected right?

We deal with the threshold enquiry as it relates to each of the rights in more detail in the chapters that follow. However, to understand the two-stage approach, it is important to make some preliminary remarks about the threshold enquiry. The Constitutional Court noted in *Walters* that the threshold enquiry 'entails examining (a) the content and scope of the relevant protected right(s) and (b) the meaning and effect of the impugned enactment to see whether there is any limitation of (a) by (b)'.[46]

Two differing approaches have emerged to the threshold enquiry in the jurisprudence of the Constitutional Court. The first is to give a comprehensive consideration to the scope and content of the right in question before considering whether (and later on to what extent) the limiting measure infringes on the content of the right as set out. The alternative approach

43 (CCT28/01) [2002] ZACC 6; 2002 (4) SA 613; 2002 (7) BCLR 663 (21 May 2002) paras 26–7.

44 (CCT13/98) [1998] ZACC 16; 1999 (2) SA 83; 1998 (12) BCLR 1449 (14 October 1998) para 27: 'For the purposes of this judgment, I shall adopt the approach most favourable to the appellant and assume without deciding that appellant's religious rights under sections 15 and 31(1) are both in issue. I shall also assume, again without deciding, that corporal punishment as practised by the appellant's members is not "inconsistent with any provision of the Bill of Rights" as contemplated by section 31(2). I assume therefore that section 10 of the Schools Act limits the parents' religious rights both under section 31 and section 15.'

45 *Veldman v Director of Public Prosecutions (Witwatersrand Local Division)* (CCT19/05) [2005] ZACC 22; 2007 (3) SA 210 (CC); 2007 (8) BCLR 827 (CC) (5 December 2005).

46 *Walters* paras 26–7.

is to accept notionally[47] or even hypothetically[48] that a right has been limited and then to proceed to the second phase of the limitation analysis without much analytical rigour. Unfortunately, the Constitutional Court has vacillated between these two approaches to the threshold enquiry of the limitation clause.

PAUSE FOR REFLECTION

Advantages of a substantive, value-based approach to the threshold enquiry

While there is nothing wrong in principle with adopting a notional approach to the threshold enquiry, there are some factors that weigh in favour of adopting a more substantive, value-based approach. As Woolman and Botha explain, among these are the following:

> First, it is consistent with the text's admonition that the provisions of the Bill of Rights be interpreted in light of the values which underlie an open and democratic society based on human dignity, equality and freedom. The Final Constitution was not meant to protect certain forms of behaviour and a value-based approach permits us to screen out those forms of behaviour which do not merit constitutional protection.
>
> Secondly, high value-based barriers for the first stage of analysis mean that only genuine and serious violations of a constitutional right make it through to FC s 36. If only serious infringements make it through, then the court can take a fairly rigorous approach with respect to the justification for the impairment. It could then be fairly confident that when it nullified law or conduct there would be something worth protecting.
>
> Thirdly, the value-based approach is consistent with the notion that a 'unity of values' underlies both the rights-infringement determination and the limitation-justification analysis. The language of the interpretation clause and the limitation clause strongly suggests that both enquiries are driven by a desire to serve the five values underlying our entire constitutional enterprise: openness, democracy, human dignity, freedom, and equality.[49]

47 See *Beinash and Another v Ernst & Young and Others* (CCT12/98) [1998] ZACC 19; 1999 (2) SA 91; 1999 (2) BCLR 125 (2 December 1998).

48 In *Mistry v Interim National Medical and Dental Council and Others* (CCT13/97) [1998] ZACC 10; 1998 (4) SA 1127; 1998 (7) BCLR 880 (29 May 1998) para 28, Sachs J found the periodic inspection of health professionals' business premises would have 'entailed only the most minimal and easily justifiable invasions of privacy, **if they had qualified as invasions of privacy at all**' (our emphasis). This approach was followed by Ngcobo J in *S v Jordan and Others (Sex Workers Education and Advocacy Task Force and Others as Amici Curiae* (CCT31/01) [2002] ZACC 22; 2002 (6) SA 642; 2002 (11) BCLR 1117 (9 October 2002) paras 28–9. Ngcobo J held: '...even if the right to privacy is implicated, [h]aving regard to the legitimate State interest in proscribing prostitution and brothel-keeping, viewed against the scope of the limitation on the right of the prostitute and brothel-keeper to earn a living, I conclude that if there be a limitation of the right to privacy, the limitation is justified'. See Woolman and Botha (2013) 34.4, fn1. See *South African Broadcasting Corporation Limited v National Director of Public Prosecutions and Others* (CCT58/06) [2006] ZACC 15; 2007 (1) SA 523 (CC); 2007 (2) BCLR 167 (CC); [2006] JOL 18339 (CC) (21 September 2006).

49 See Woolman and Botha (2013) 34.17–34.18.

10.4.1 The content and scope of the relevant protected right

At a general level, the following two comments are relevant to determining the content and scope of a right at the threshold enquiry. First, it is governed by the general interpretation clause in section 39 of the Constitution. In *Walters*, the Constitutional Court held that 'both the rights and the enactment ... must be interpreted so as to promote the value system of an open and democratic society based on human dignity, equality and freedom'.[50] In this regard, certain values will play a greater role in the interpretation of particular rights than others.[51] In addition, the Constitutional Court has on several occasions stated that rights must be interpreted contextually.[52] Finally, international human rights law may be relevant to the content of certain rights.[53]

Second, in a two-stage limitation process it is crucial not to restrict the right unnecessarily by adopting an excessively narrow interpretation of the right as this would result in the premature termination of the enquiry at the expense of the litigant. However, too generous or insufficiently discerning an interpretation would render the two-stage approach redundant as all the work would be left to the limitation enquiry and the value of the substantive approach to this stage of the enquiry would be undercut. Kentridge AJ noted as much early on in the Constitutional Court's jurisprudence: 'The two-stage approach may call for a broader interpretation of the fundamental right, qualified only at the second stage.'[54] An example of this approach can be seen in *De Reuck v Director of Public Prosecutions (Witwatersrand Local Division) and Others* where the Constitutional Court was faced with the question of whether or not child pornography amounts to protected speech.[55] The State asked the Court to follow the approach of the US Supreme Court where certain categories of expression are unprotected forms of speech. The basis for this is that 'such materials do not serve any of the values traditionally considered as underlying freedom of expression, namely, truth-seeking, free political activity and self-fulfillment'.[56] The Court rejected this argument, noting:

> **[O]ur Constitution is different from that of the United States of America. Limitations of rights are dealt with under section 36 of the Constitution and not at the threshold level. Section 16(1) expressly protects the freedom of expression in a manner that does not warrant a narrow reading. Any restriction upon artistic creativity must satisfy the rigours of the limitation analysis.**[57]

---

50 *Walters* para 26.

51 As Woolman and Botha note: 'For each right there are specific values that can be said to have led to its constitutionalisation.' As a result, the 'specific values that animate each right' will play particular roles in interpreting those rights. See Woolman and Botha (2013) 34.17.

52 In *Bernstein and Others v Bester NO and Others* (CCT23/95) [1996] ZACC 2; 1996 (4) BCLR 449; 1996 (2) SA 751 (27 March 1996) para 79, Ackermann J noted in the context of the right to privacy:

> **The two-stage approach requires, as the first step, a definition of the scope of the relevant right. At this stage already ... it is necessary to recognize that the content of the right is crystallized by mutual limitation. Its scope is already delimited by the rights of the community as a whole (including its members).**

53 See *South African National Defence Union* paras 25–7 where O'Regan J considered the recommendations and conventions of the International Labour Organization in setting out the content of the right to work.

54 *Zuma* para 21. Further, in *Makwanyane* para 100: 'Our Constitution ... calls for a "two-step" approach, in which a broad rather than a narrow interpretation is given to the fundamental rights enshrined in Chapter 3 and limitations have to be justified through the application of section 33.'

55 (CCT5/03) [2003] ZACC 19; 2004 (1) SA 406 (CC); 2003 (12) BCLR 1333 (CC) (15 October 2003).

56 *De Reuck* para 48.

57 *De Reuck* para 48.

The dangers of failing to observe this approach can be seen in *New National Party v Government of the Republic of South Africa and Others*.[58] In this case, the majority found that '[t]he requirement that only those persons whose names appear on the national voters roll may vote' was a 'constitutional requirement of the right to vote, and **not a limitation of the right**' (our emphasis).[59] As such, the question the Court had to answer was whether there was a 'rational relationship between the [electoral] scheme ... and the achievement of a legitimate governmental purpose'.[60] The question was not whether the right to vote was justifiably limited under section 36(1) by the electoral scheme.[61] As Roux notes, 'apart from a few perfunctory remarks about the "importance of the right to vote", the majority made no effort to develop a principled understanding of the right in its constitutional and political context'.[62]

Aside from these general observations, specific rights may also contain features relevant to delineating their scope and content. Here a distinction must be drawn between those rights written in 'unqualified terms',[63] and those that contain so-called internal modifiers. These internal modifiers may either restrict the scope of the right or provide conditions for its operation. In so far as the second category is concerned, two broad varieties can be distinguished:

- First, there are internal modifiers that qualify the scope of the right either by explicitly excluding certain practices from its protection or by conditioning its application more subtly.
- Second, there are internal modifiers that modify or supplant the limitation of specific rights.

Internal modifiers that restrict or enumerate the scope and content of rights are relevant at this stage of the enquiry, while internal modifiers that relate to the limitation of rights are relevant at the limitation stage.

The high-water mark of the Constitutional Court's approach to the scope and content of a right at this stage of the limitation analysis is the right to privacy guaranteed in section 14 of the Constitution. Although section 14 does include internal modifiers which enumerate certain aspects of the right, including the right not to have one's person, home or property searched, possessions seized or the privacy of communications infringed, its full scope and content was left up to courts to decide.

In *Bernstein and Others v Bester NO and Others*, Ackermann J set out a complex formulation of the right, noting:

> **The truism that no right is to be considered absolute, implies that from the outset of interpretation each right is always already limited by every other right accruing to another citizen. In the context of privacy this would mean that it is only the inner sanctum of a person, such as his/her family life, sexual preference and home environment, which is shielded from erosion by conflicting rights of the community. This implies that community rights and the rights of fellow members place a corresponding obligation on a citizen, thereby shaping the abstract notion of**

58 (CCT9/99) [1999] ZACC 5; 1999 (3) SA 191; 1999 (5) BCLR 489 (13 April 1999).
59 *New National Party* para 15.
60 *New National Party* para 19.
61 *New National Party* para 24.
62 Roux (2009) 127. See, however, the dissenting opinion of O'Regan J.
63 *Williams* para 21.

individualism towards identifying a concrete member of civil society. Privacy is acknowledged in the truly personal realm, but as a person moves into communal relations and activities such as business and social interaction, the scope of personal space shrinks accordingly.[64]

A similar approach can be seen in respect of the right to freedom of expression guaranteed in section 16 of the Constitution. Unlike the right to privacy, the right to freedom of expression contains three internal modifiers.[65] These internal modifiers are unique in that they are definitional: they neither enumerate nor contract the scope of the right in general terms. Rather, they specifically exclude certain forms of expression, namely, propaganda for war, incitement to violence and hate speech, from the right's ambit.[66] As a result, if a form of expression is considered to be one of these three excluded forms, then the limitation of that expression will not affect a right and the matter will end there. As for the content of the right, in *De Reuck*, the Court employed a similar core/periphery construction of the right to freedom of expression.

As noted above, these examples reflect the high-water mark of the jurisprudence on this stage of the limitation enquiry.[67] In a number of other cases, the Court has failed to undertake a rigorous, meaningful analysis of the scope and content of the impugned right. Instead, it has pushed the work to the second stage and left behind little in the way of content for subsequent cases involving the same right.

10.4.2 Is the right infringed by the measure?

Once the scope and content of the right in question has been determined, the next question to be asked is whether the limiting measure infringes the right as it is defined. According to the Constitutional Court, this involves determining 'the meaning and effect of the impugned enactment' to see whether it limits the relevant protected right.[68] Often this question is addressed simultaneously with that of scope and content, but it is conceptually distinct.

This aspect of the threshold enquiry is often a fact-specific exercise and turns mainly on the nature and breadth of the particular limiting measure. Even when the content and scope of the right are clearly set out, this is a complex enquiry. By way of illustration, in *S v Jordan and Others (Sex Workers Education and Advocacy Task Force and Others as Amici Curiae)*,[69] Sachs and O'Regan JJ, in their minority judgment, faced the problem of where to place

---

64 (CCT23/95) [1996] ZACC 2; 1996 (4) BCLR 449; 1996 (2) SA 751 (27 March 1996) para 67.

65 *Magajane v Chairperson, North West Gambling Board* (CCT49/05) [2006] ZACC 8; 2006 (10) BCLR 1133 (CC); 2006 (5) SA 250; 2006 (2) SACR 447 (8 June 2006) para 59 fn 73.

66 In *Islamic Unity Convention v Independent Broadcasting Authority and Others* (CCT36/01) [2002] ZACC 3; 2002 (4) SA 294; 2002 (5) BCLR 433 (11 April 2002) para 30:

> **How is section 16(2) to be interpreted? The words 'the right in subsection (1) does not extend to ...' imply that the categories of expression enumerated in section 16(2) are not to be regarded as constitutionally protected speech. Section 16(2) therefore defines the boundary beyond which the right to freedom of expression does not extend. In that sense, the subsection is definitional. Implicit in its provisions is an acknowledgment that certain expression does not deserve constitutional protection because, among other things, it has the potential to impinge adversely on the dignity of others and cause harm. Our Constitution is founded on the principles of dignity, equal worth and freedom, and these objectives should be given effect to.**

67 See further *Zealand v Minister for Justice and Constitutional Development and Another* (CCT54/07) [2008] ZACC 3; 2008 (6) BCLR 601 (CC); 2008 (2) SACR 1 (CC); 2008 (4) SA 458 (CC) (11 March 2008) para 34 (right to freedom and security).

68 *Walters* paras 26–7.

69 (CCT31/01) [2002] ZACC 22; 2002 (6) SA 642; 2002 (11) BCLR 1117 (9 October 2002).

commercial sex on *Bernstein's* privacy continuum in order to determine whether the prohibition thereof infringed the right to privacy. In concluding that it did infringe the right to privacy, they noted:

> **[I]t is necessary to realise that there are a range of factors relevant to distinguishing the core of privacy from its penumbra. One of the considerations is the nature of the relationship concerned: an invasion of the relationship between partners, or parent and child, or other intimate, meaningful and intensely personal relationships will be a strong indication of a violation close to the core of privacy. Another consideration is the extent to which the body of a person is invaded: physical searches or examinations are often invasive of privacy as section 13 of the interim Constitution suggests. As we observed before, the constitutional commitment to human dignity invests a significant value in the inviolability and worth of the human body. The right to privacy, therefore, serves to protect and foster that dignity. Commercial sex involves the most intimate of activity taking place in the most impersonal and public of realms, the market place; it is simultaneously all about sex and all about money. Selling sex represents an opportunity for women to earn money but within the framework of deeply structured sexist and patriarchal patterns of social life. A prohibition on commercial sex, therefore, will not ordinarily encroach upon intimate or meaningful human relationships. Yet it will intrude upon the intensely personal sphere of sexual intercourse, albeit intercourse for reward.**[70]

10.5 The justification stage: is the limiting measure in terms of a law of general application and reasonable and justifiable?

Once a court has determined that a particular measure limits a protected right, it turns its attention to the second stage of the limitation analysis where it must consider whether the limitation of the right can be justified. If the court finds that the limitation is justified, the measure has passed the test of constitutionality. If the court finds that the limitation is not justified, then the legal provision will be unconstitutional and hence invalid. At this stage, there are two independent requirements that must be met to justify the limitation of a right:
- The limitation must be 'in terms of law of general application'.[71]
- The limitation must be 'reasonable and justifiable in an open and democratic society based on equality, freedom and human dignity'.[72]

10.5.1 Law of general application

The first hurdle to be cleared at the justification stage of the enquiry is that the limiting measure must be 'sourced'[73] in a law of general application. This means that the limitation of a right by some means other than a law of general application will always be unconstitutional. However, a limitation done in terms of a law of general application may be saved from unconstitutionality by the limitation clause. The two most common rationales advanced

70 *Jordan* para 80–1. Sachs and O'Regan JJ later qualified their finding by noting at para 86 that the limiting measure did 'not reach into the core of privacy, but only [touched] its penumbra'.
71 S 36(1) of the Constitution.
72 S 36(1) of the Constitution.
73 Woolman and Botha (2013) 34.48.

for this requirement are specifically to prevent the legislature from singling out an individual or group for punishment without a trial and to respect the principle of the rule of law more generally.[74] What exactly is required by this stage of enquiry is unclear as the Constitutional Court has yet to articulate a general set of requirements that must be met. Rather, it has dealt with this requirement episodically and without much fervour. What is clear is that this requirement makes demands of both the **form** and the **content** of the source of the limiting measure.

First and foremost, the limiting measure must be in terms of something the Court recognises as law.[75] A decision by the Cabinet which is not authorised or mandated by law or the decision of a big corporation would therefore not constitute a law of general application. Similarly, the Electoral Commission made a decision not to facilitate the registration of prisoners for the elections prior to the country's 1999 general elections. This decision denied prisoners the right to vote afforded all adult citizens over 18 years of age. The Constitutional Court thus found that the decision was an administrative decision which was not sourced in a law of general application.[76] In such cases, where there is no law to speak of, the operation of this requirement is fairly straightforward. The question of which of the multitude of exercises of power **will** qualify as law for these purposes is more complex. Less controversially, the term includes legislation,[77] common law[78] and customary law.[79] In addition to legislation, common law and customary law, the Court has considered other exercises of government power to amount to law, including subordinate legislation,[80] municipal by-laws,[81] domesticated international conventions[82] and rules of court.[83]

In *President of the Republic of South Africa and Another v Hugo*,[84] Mokgoro and Kriegler JJ addressed the question of whether or not the powers vested in the President as Head of State would qualify as law for the purposes of section 36(1) in their separate dissenting opinions. (The majority did not address the issue as it found that the measure in question effectively did not limit the right to equality.) For her part, Mokgoro J held that '[a]lthough the Presidential Act is not conventional legislation, in my view, it satisfies [the law of general application] ... precondition'.[85]

Conversely, Kriegler J held:

> **The exercise by the President of the powers afforded by s 82(1)(*k*) – even in the general manner he chose in this instance – does not make 'law', nor can it be said to be 'of general application'. The exercise of such power is non-recurrent and specific,**

---

74 Woolman and Botha (2013) 34.48.

75 The Court has not yet considered the relationship that must exist between the law and the limiting measure, and more specifically what the phrase 'in terms of' means.

76 The Electoral Act 73 of 1998 – which governed the Commission's operation – made no provision for the disqualification of voters.

77 See Woolman and Botha (2013) 34.34 fn 2.

78 See Woolman and Botha (2013) 34.52 fn 1.

79 See Woolman and Botha (2013) 34.52 fn 2.

80 *Larbi-Odam and Others v Member of the Executive Council for Education (North-West Province) and Another* (CCT2/97) [1997] ZACC 16; 1997 (12) BCLR 1655; 1998 (1) SA 745 (26 November 1997) para 27.

81 *Du Toit v Minister of Transport* (CCT22/04) [2005] ZACC 9; 2005 (11) BCLR 1053 (CC); 2006 (1) SA 297 (CC) (8 September 2005).

82 *Sonderup v Tondelli and Another* (CCT53/00) [2000] ZACC 26; 2001 (2) BCLR 152; 2001 (1) SA 1171 (4 December 2000).

83 *Ingledew v Financial Services Board* (CCT6/02) [2003] ZACC 8; 2003 (8) BCLR 825; 2003 (4) SA 584 (CC) (13 May 2003) para 19.

84 (CCT11/96) [1997] ZACC 4; 1997 (6) BCLR 708; 1997 (4) SA 1 (18 April 1997).

85 *Hugo* para 96.

> **intended to benefit particular persons or classes of persons, to do so once only, and is given effect by an executive order directed to specific state officials.**[86]

As far as the content of such laws is concerned, the Constitution makes no explicit demands of the impugned law in this regard beyond that it must be of general application. To date, the Court has not grappled with the nature of the general application requirement in great detail. In her dissenting opinion in *Hugo*, Mokgoro J considered the correlative 'prescribed by law' requirement in the European Convention and Canadian Charter of Rights, noting:

> **It can be seen then that several concerns underlie the interpretation of 'prescribed by law'. The need for accessibility, precision and general application flows from the concept of the rule of law. A person should be able to know of the law, and be able to conform his or her conduct to the law. Further, laws should apply generally, rather than targeting specific individuals.**[87]

Here, in addition to the law of general application requirement, Mokgoro J placed two additional requirements on the content of the law: precision and accessibility. Similarly, in *Dawood and Another v Minister of Home Affairs and Others; Shalabi and Another v Minister of Home Affairs and Others; Thomas and Another v Minister of Home Affairs and Others*, the Constitutional Court held:

> **It is an important principle of the rule of law that rules be stated in a clear and accessible manner. It is because of this principle that section 36 requires that limitations of rights may be justifiable only if they are authorised by a law of general application.**[88]

These three demands – general application, accessibility and precision (clarity) – can be said to reflect the minimalist position on what this precondition demands of the content of the law in question. Some academic commentators go further, setting out additional requirements to be met by the content of the law in question in order to pass constitutional muster under section 36(1).[89] As far as which approach should be preferred when it comes to the demands on content, the point could be made that these broader concerns are best left to the next phase of the enquiry.[90]

---

86 *Hugo* para 76 fn 7.

87 *Hugo* para 102. In doing so she relied, *inter alia*, on the decision of the European Court of Human Rights in *Sunday Times v the United Kingdom* (1979–80) 2 EHRR 245 Eur Crt of HR 1979-04-26 para 49 where it noted:

> **In the Court's opinion, the following are two of the requirements that flow from the expression "prescribed by law". First, the law must be adequately accessible: the citizen must be able to have an indication that is adequate in the circumstances of the legal rules applicable to a given case. Secondly, a norm cannot be regarded as a "law" unless it is formulated with sufficient precision to enable the citizen to regulate his conduct: he must be able – if need be with appropriate advice – to foresee, to a degree that is reasonable in the circumstances, the consequences which a given action may entail.**

88 (CCT35/99) [2000] ZACC 8; 2000 (3) SA 936; 2000 (8) BCLR 837 (7 June 2000) para 47.

89 Woolman and Botha (2013) 34.61.

90 However, Woolman and Botha suggest that the movement should be the other way, in other words, content-specific questions should be considered under the rubric of law of general application rather than during the justification stage. See Woolman and Botha (2013) 34.62–34.63.

10.5.2 Reasonable and justifiable in an open and democratic society based on human dignity, equality and freedom

10.5.2.1 Reconsidering the role of proportionality in the justification enquiry

From the outset, the Constitutional Court's jurisprudence on the limitation of rights has turned almost entirely on the notion of proportionality or balancing. This is notwithstanding the fact that proportionality does not feature in the text of section 36 of the Constitution. An important criticism is that it is unclear what exactly proportionality requires and how it drives the limitation enquiry. This confusion was not necessarily inevitable as both reasonableness and justifiability are capable of greater textual certainty. However, the phrase, 'reasonable and justifiable', is generally understood conjunctively as shorthand for the notion of proportionality or balancing. Academics have not simplified matters, often accepting the conclusion of proportionality without unpacking the term. This is not surprising as the term's flexibility lends itself to morally appealing but legally inexact analysis.

However, neither the confusing nature of proportionality nor high-minded theoretical critiques are sufficient to warrant a departure from this metaphorical test that has been held to be the centrepiece of the limitation enquiry by the Constitutional Court. Rather, the primary reason for reconsidering the proportionality enquiry here is to make it simpler to understand without changing its substance. By identifying those aspects of the limitation enquiry that implicate proportionality and those that do not, it is hoped that this section will not only demystify the process of limiting rights, but also makes it clearer how proportionality actually works.

The first step in reconsidering the justificatory enquiry is to separate into different questions the factors the Court considers when undertaking a section 36 limitation analysis. Under the interim Constitution, certain criteria had to be met by the limiting measure.[91] As noted above, had the Court chosen to follow the *Oakes* formulation, these criteria would have been further divided into more specific questions.[92] In the end, the Constitutional Court and the drafters of the Constitution opted to move in form in the other direction altogether: from a structured, sequential enquiry with set criteria to be met to a global singular enquiry with factors to be considered.[93]

Despite this, the first two questions in the *Oakes* formulation are present in all the Constitutional Court's limitation jurisprudence without exception. These two questions are the following:

- Does the limiting measure serve a legitimate purpose (in an open and democratic society based on equality, freedom and human dignity)?
- Is there a rational connection between the limiting measure and its stated purpose?

---

91 S 33(1) of the interim Constitution provided that '[t]he rights entrenched in this Chapter may be limited by law of general application, provided that such limitation (*a*) shall be permissible only to the extent that it is (i) reasonable; and (ii) justifiable in an open and democratic society based on freedom and equality; and (*b*) shall not negate the essential content of the right in question ...' Further, it provided that the limitation of certain entrenched rights must also be necessary.

92 Paraphrased by Woolman and Botha as 'first, whether the limitation serves a sufficiently important objective; second, whether the limitation is rationally connected to the said objective; third, whether the limitation impairs the right as little as possible; and fourth, whether the actual benefits of the limitation are proportionate to its deleterious consequences for the rights-holder'. See Woolman, S and Botha, H 'Limitations: Shared constitutional interpretation, an appropriate normative framework and hard choices' in Woolman, S and Bishop, M (eds) (2008) *Constitutional Conversations* 155.

93 There is a difference: the *Makwanyane* formulation does not separate them but has them considered globally with proportionality as a device. Factors do not suffice as they are all to be considered under proportionality and often conflate threshold and proportionality questions. We might note a difference between factors that may be considered and threshold questions that must be met.

What is more, these two questions find loose and partial expression in the factors contained in sections 36(1)(*b*)[94] and 36(1)(*d*).[95] Conceptually, these are threshold tests[96] that are the starting point of limitation analysis both logically and legally. These threshold tests are logically the starting point as we cannot go on to balance competing rights and interests without first quantifying them. The tests are legally the starting point in that if a measure fails the two questions, then it can never justifiably limit a right.

Crucially, these two questions have nothing to do with proportionality or balancing. That is to say, they are not relative to other factors in the section 36 analysis and can be answered in isolation from the other factors by using conventional legal reasoning.[97] As a result, when it comes to answering these two threshold questions, we do not have to choose between 'formal or categorical reasoning' and 'balancing and proportionality'.[98] Having isolated the threshold questions, what remains of the section 36 factors makes up the proportionality enquiry proper.[99] By unpacking section 36 in this manner, the point is not to deny the significance of proportionality, but rather to place it in its proper context and, it is hoped, make the term easier to understand.[100]

The next question to be asked is how these different enquiries or factors interact. There is no sequence suggested in the text of section 36(1). Rather, the balancing metaphor suggests that they should be considered simultaneously. As noted above, this distinguishes section 36 from the interim Constitution and *Oakes*. Under the interim Constitution, the limitation process was structured into separate questions. In addition, these questions were sequenced. This meant that if the enquiry failed at one of the stages, the Court would not proceed to the next phase. However, under section 36 even when the Court separates the factors into different constituents - and generally considers the threshold questions first - it does not sequence them but sometimes, ironically, considers them mechanically.[101] Having done so, the Court then balances all the factors, notwithstanding the difference between threshold

94 As discussed further below, the **importance of the purpose of the limitation factor** is made up of two sub-parts: first, the purpose of the limitation and second, its importance. The latter is relevant to the limiting measure side of the proportionality scale.

95 The **relationship between the limitation and its purpose** is similarly complex. At this stage of the justification enquiry, the relationship requires at a minimum a rational connection between the purpose and the limitation, what courts have labelled the **rational connection requirement**. Labelling them as factors is, in a sense, misleading as it gives them an optional feel, whereas unlike other section 36 factors, these threshold questions are imperative to any limitations enquiry.

96 Iles, K (2007) A fresh look at limitations: Unpacking section 36 *South African Journal on Human Rights* 23(1):68–92 at 68.

97 We could consider steps one and two - which deal with the internal aspects of the limiting measure - as addressing the question of reasonableness, while the latter two - which address the relationship between the limiting measure and externalities - address the issue of justifiability.

98 As Sachs J noted in *Prince* para 155: 'Limitations analysis under our Constitution is based not on formal or categorical reasoning but on processes of balancing and proportionality as required by section 36.'

99 These remaining section 36 factors are also, broadly speaking, captured in stages three and four of the *Oakes* formulation. The third step in *Oakes* - whether the limitation impairs the right as little as possible - is similar to the less restrictive means factor in s 36(1)(*e*), but is perhaps more appropriately compared to the phrase 'to the extent that'. The fourth and final step under the *Oakes* formulation - whether the actual benefits of the limitation are proportionate to its deleterious consequences for the rights-holder - is proportionality in a limited sense. On this score, section 36 is more comprehensive. What remains of section 36 factors collectively ask if the legitimate, rationally based measure constitutes a proportionate limitation on the right in question, taking into account the degree of infringement, the nature of the right, the breadth of the measure and the social good it achieves.

100 With apologies to Iles who used the phrase in respect of his scaled-down approach to s 36. Iles (2007) 68.

101 It was never intended that the section 36 factors would be applied sequentially. Nor, for that matter, are they logically sequenced although the Constitutional Court has remarkably on a few occasions applied them mechanically (See *Magajane*).

questions and those relating to proportionality proper.[102] Even when the Court effectively terminates the enquiry after the threshold, it does so using the language of balancing.[103]

This is a clear, if confounding, rejection of the *Oakes* formulation and one that took many by surprise.[104] Aside from general critiques of the balancing exercise, the all-at-once approach raises specific problems in so far as the threshold questions are concerned:

- First, the all-at-once approach is illogical as it can never be that a measure that does not seek a constitutionally acceptable objective or does not achieve that objective will pass the requirement of proportionality.
- Second, and related to this, the all-at-once approach makes for extra work as the Court could just as well stop after the threshold question is failed.
- Third, the all-at-once approach is less analytically sound. Questions that are initially addressed separately are often lumped together and resolved using the all-inclusive language of proportionality, glossing over the nuances of the decision-making process.
- Fourth, the all-at-once approach reduces precedential value by making the balance struck too case-specific.

PAUSE FOR REFLECTION

Concerns regarding the all-at-once approach

The fact that the Constitutional Court glosses over the nuances of the decision-making process by using the all-inclusive language of proportionality to lump together and resolve questions that were initially addressed separately is clearly illustrated in its judgment in *Makwanyane*.

After first having considered retribution, prevention and deterrence separately, the Constitutional Court went on to conclude that:

> **[i]n the balancing process the principal factors that have to be weighed are on the one hand the destruction of life and dignity that is a consequence of the**

---

102 There have been occasions when certain judges have recognised the intuitive difference between the section 36 factors and tried to re-introduce some structure into the limitation clause by applying 'reasonable and justifiable' separately. However, these are few and are between. In his dissenting judgment in *Prince* para 81, Ngocbo J held:

> **I accept that the goal of the impugned provisions is to prevent the abuse of dependence-producing drugs and trafficking in those drugs. I also accept that it is a legitimate goal. The question is whether the means employed to achieve that goal are reasonable. In my view, they are not. The fundamental reason why they are not is because they are overbroad ... On that score they are unreasonable and they fall at the first hurdle. This renders it unnecessary to consider whether they are justifiable.**

Similarly, in *Engelbrecht v Road Accident Fund and Another* (CCT57/06) [2007] ZACC 1; 2007 (6) SA 96 (CC); 2007 (5) BCLR 457 (CC) (6 March 2007), Kondile AJ employed reasonable and justifiable disjunctively. Having found that the measure '[did] not meet the threshold test of reasonableness' (para 40), he went on to 'consider whether the regulation is justifiable, on the assumption that it may still be necessary, despite the manifest unreasonableness referred to above' (para 41), citing *Makwanyane* paras 209–10.

103 In *S v Bhulwana, S v Gwadiso* (CCT12/95, CCT11/95) [1995] ZACC 11; 1996 (1) SA 388; 1995 (12) BCLR 1579 (29 November 1995) para 24, O'Regan J held:

> **In my view, section 21(1)(*a*)(i) of the Act cannot be justified in terms of section 33(1) of the Constitution. Although the need to suppress illicit drug trafficking is an urgent and pressing one, it is not clear how, if at all, the presumption furthers such an objective. In addition, there appears to be no logical connection between the fact proved (possession of 115g) and the fact presumed (dealing). On the other hand, the presumption gives rise to an infringement of the right entrenched in section 25(3)(*c*), which is a pillar of our system of criminal justice. Section 21(1)(*a*)(i) of the Act is an unconstitutional infringement of the right entrenched in section 25(3)(*c*) which is not reasonable, justifiable or necessary as contemplated by section 33.**

104 As Woolman and Botha note: 'Prior to the judgment in *Makwanyane*, it was widely expected that the Court would model its analysis of the reasonableness and justifiability of fundamental-rights limitations on the approach adopted by the Canadian Supreme Court in *R v Oakes*. However, the approach of the *Makwanyane* Court represents a significant departure from the Oakes test.' See Woolman and Botha (2008) 155.

> implementation of the death sentence, the elements of arbitrariness and the possibility of error in the enforcement of capital punishment, and the existence of a severe alternative punishment (life imprisonment) and, on the other, the claim that the death sentence is a greater deterrent to murder, and will more effectively prevent its commission, than would a sentence of life imprisonment, and that there is a public demand for retributive justice to be imposed on murderers, which only the death sentence can meet ... Retribution cannot be accorded the same weight under our Constitution as the rights to life and dignity, which are the most important of all the rights in Chapter Three. It has not been shown that the death sentence would be materially more effective to deter or prevent murder than the alternative sentence of life imprisonment would be. Taking these factors into account, as well as the elements of arbitrariness and the possibility of error in enforcing the death penalty, the clear and convincing case that is required to justify the death sentence as a penalty for murder, has not been made out. The requirements of section 33(1) have accordingly not been satisfied ...[105]

In this regard, Woolman and Botha note:

> The balancer is inclined to restrict her finding to the case at hand, as the next case may, ostensibly, require that a different balance be struck. While there may be advantages to such a judicious approach, ... there is a growing concern within the academy that the case-by-case approach to constitutional analysis, in general, and limitations analysis, in particular, blunts the transformative potential of the Final Constitution.[106]

This is not just a problem with threshold questions and proportionality questions. It also conflates different aspects of the proportionality enquiry such as less restrictive, over-broad and reasonable accommodation.

In discussing the justification enquiry, we follow the approach set out below:

- What is the purpose of the limiting measure (not importance yet)? Is it legitimate in an open and democratic society based on equality, freedom and human dignity?
- What is the relationship between the limiting measure and its stated purpose? More specifically, are they rationally connected?
- Are there clear, alternative means available that are less restrictive on the full enjoyment of the right?
- Is the legitimate, rationally based limiting measure a proportionate limitation on the right in question, taking into account the degree of infringement, the nature of the right, the breadth of the measure and the social good it achieves? This is balancing and proportionality proper.

105 *Makwanyane* paras 145–6.
106 Woolman and Botha (2008) 161.

In Figure 10.1, the question that the diagram seeks to answer is whether an infringement of a fundamental right satisfies the various requirements of the limitation clause. If it does, then the infringement is constitutionally valid and the law authorising the infringement will be upheld by the courts.

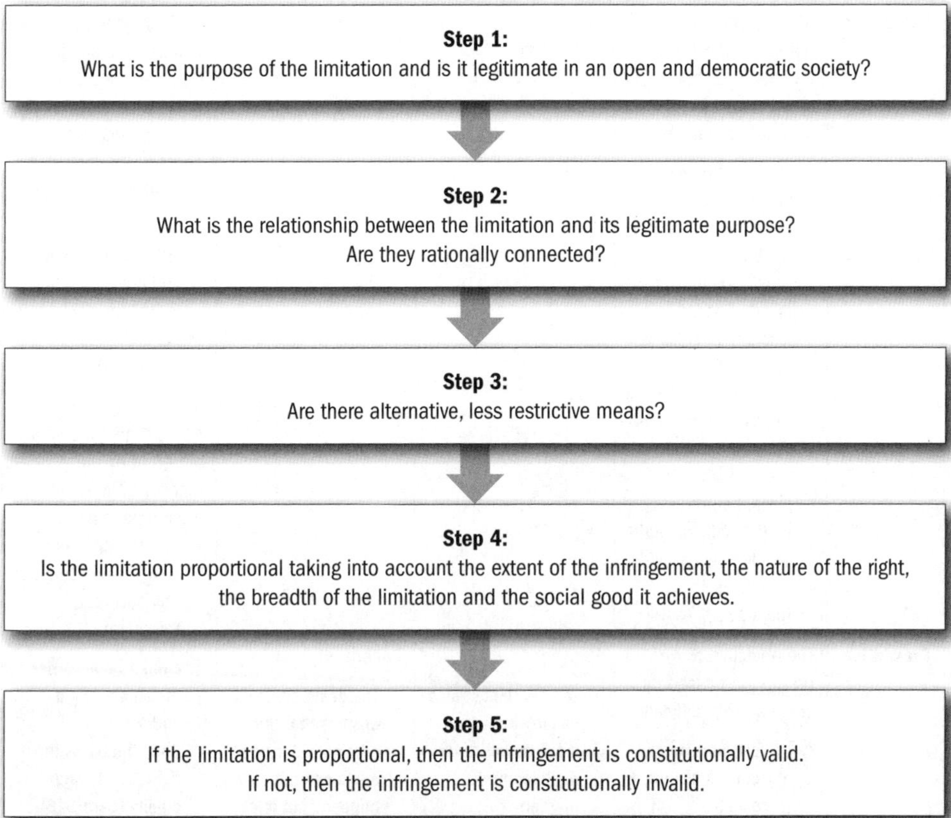

Figure 10.1 *The steps in the justification enquiry*

The aim of reconsidering proportionality is not substantively to alter the enquiry. The aim is rather to make proportionality more accessible by providing a simplified lens through which to view the numerous decisions involving limitation and to understand the different types of limitation analyses undertaken by the courts. We discuss at each point the jurisprudence that illustrates how courts have followed a particular enquiry. As a brief example, Table 10.1 illustrates how, in *Makwanyane*, the Court applied the threshold questions to the three objectives sought by the death penalty, namely retribution, prevention and deterrence, before concluding with the proportionality assessment. In the process, the differences between the stages are well illustrated.

Table 10.1 Applying the threshold questions and the proportionality assessment in Makwanyane

Purpose of limiting measure	Stage 1: Constitutionally valid objective	Stage 2: Rational connection test	Stage 3: Less restrictive means	Stage 4: Proportionality
Retribution	Although the Court did not state so clearly, retribution all but failed this basic threshold requirement: **The Constitution is premised on the assumption that ours will be a constitutional state founded on the recognition of human rights ... To be consistent with the value of *ubuntu* ours should be a society that 'wishes to prevent crime ... [not] to kill criminals simply to get even with them (para 131).**			On balancing the different factors, the Court reached the conclusion that the death penalty was not constitutionally justifiable by upgrading the rights in question: **[t]he rights to life and dignity are the most important of all human rights ... (para 144)** and systematically downgrading the goods aimed at by the measure. The Court argued as follows: • Retribution was not a valid constitutional objective and therefore: **cannot be accorded the same weight under our Constitution as the rights to life and dignity (para 146).** • Prevention could be achieved by life imprisonment (less restrictive means). • Deterrence is less weighty in the balancing process as: **[i]t has not been shown that the death sentence would be materially more effective to deter or prevent murder than the alternative sentence of life imprisonment would be (paras 146 and 127).**
Prevention	The objective of prevention passed this stage without difficulty: **Prevention is another object of punishment (para 128).**	Passed: **The death sentence ensures that the criminal will never again commit murders (para 128).**	Failed: **The death sentence ensures that the criminal will never again commit murders, but it is not the only way of doing so, and life imprisonment also serves this purpose (para 128).**	
Deterrence	Deterrence passed without difficulty: **The need for a strong deterrent to violent crime is an end the validity of which is not open to question. The state is clearly entitled, indeed obliged, to take action to protect human life against violation by others (para 117).**	Passed (with some reservations).	Failed: **It has not been shown that the death sentence would be materially more effective to deter or prevent murder than the alternative sentence of life imprisonment would be (para 146).**	

COUNTER POINT

A critique of the balancing process

Woolman and Botha critique the balancing process on a number of theoretical grounds:

- First, they point out that people value things differently in qualitative and not solely quantitative terms (**pluralism**). The things that we value are not always (or often) commensurate with one another (incommensurability). As a result, balancing 'requires substantially more than the invocation of such pat metaphors as the "scales of justice" (complexity)'.[107]
- Second, they argue that 'the Final Constitution - like most constitutional texts - provides little or no guidance as to how a court should determine the relative weight to be attached to conflicting rights and interests. One possible result is that the weighting and the ranking of interests are not grounded in constitutional interpretation ... but are based, instead, on the subjective preferences of individual judges. This enables judges to skirt the demands that attach to difficult and controversial value-choices by employing the ostensibly neutral, objective or scientific language of balancing'.[108]
- Third, they point out that the balancing approach has historically been associated with conservative and incrementalist approaches to adjudication. As a result, the context or case-specific nature of the balancing approach 'blunts the transformative potential of the Final Constitution'.[109]
- Fourth, balancing can lead judges to employ 'scientific' language and concepts, such as cost-benefit analysis, Woolman and Botha argue, which 'invites a new type of formalism which, like all formalist doctrines, tends to eschew dialogue about important moral and political issues'.[110]

10.5.2.2 Section 36 in practice

10.5.2.2.1 The purpose of the limiting measure

One of the factors listed in section 36 is 'the importance of the purpose of the limitation'. This factor is made up of two separate subcomponents: first, the purpose of the limiting measure, and second, its importance in an open and democratic society.[111] At this stage of the enquiry the focus is on the purpose of the limiting measure. The limiting measure (the aim it is designed to meet) must pursue a legitimate constitutional purpose.[112] In determining whether or not a particular limiting measure is legitimate, courts must be mindful not to overstep their role and enter the realm of policy making.

There are no hard-and-fast rules for determining whether the purpose will be considered constitutionally legitimate. Broadly speaking, the constitutional values of openness, democracy, freedom, equality and dignity will play a role in determining what a legitimate purpose is. Furthermore, if the purpose of the limiting measure is to comply with an

107 Woolman and Botha (2008) 159.
108 Woolman and Botha (2008) 160.
109 Woolman and Botha (2008) 161.
110 Woolman and Botha (2008) 161.
111 S 36(1)(*b*) of the Constitution.
112 *Jordan* para 15.

obligation laid out in the Constitution or is closely connected to the fulfilment of a right contained in Chapter 2, then this requirement will clearly be met.[113]

Examples of purposes that have been held to be legitimate include:

- creating and maintaining a disciplined military force[114]
- preventing the use and proliferation of harmful substances[115]
- maintaining discipline in schools[116]
- administering the recovery of debts[117]
- regulating of the gambling industry[118]
- regulating public broadcasting[119]
- preventing and punishing commercial sex (prostitution)[120]
- the general administration of justice[121]
- protecting the privacy and dignity of people involved in divorce proceedings, in particular children.[122]

One example of a purpose that failed at this point of the enquiry is the enforcement of 'private moral views'. In *National Coalition for Gay and Lesbian Equality and Another v Minister of Justice and Others*, Ackermann J stated:

> **The enforcement of the private moral views of a section of the community, which are based to a large extent on nothing more than prejudice, cannot qualify as such a legitimate purpose. There is accordingly nothing, in the proportionality enquiry, to weigh against the extent of the limitation and its harmful impact on gays. It would therefore seem that there is no justification for the limitation.**[123]

As noted above, the Court in *Makwanyane* considered the imposition of the death penalty as a means to achieve not one but three purposes: retribution, prevention and deterrence. Although the Court did not go so far as to reject deterrence as a constitutionally acceptable purpose outright, it did note that '[t]o be consistent with the value of *ubuntu* ours should be a society that "wishes to prevent crime ... [not] to kill criminals simply to get even with them"'.[124]

---

113 See, for example, *South African National Defence Union* where the aim was to comply with s 200(1) of the 1996 Constitution which provides that the South African National Defence Force (SANDF) must be structured and managed as a disciplined military force.

114 *South African National Defence Union* para 11.

115 *Bhulwana* para 20; *Prince* para 35.

116 *Christian Education* paras 39–41.

117 *Jaftha v Schoeman and Others, Van Rooyen v Stoltz and Others* (CCT74/03) [2004] ZACC 25; 2005 (2) SA 140 (CC); 2005 (1) BCLR 78 (CC) (8 October 2004) para 37.

118 *Magajane* para 81.

119 *Islamic Unity Convention* para 45.

120 *Jordan* para 15.

121 *Moise v Greater Germiston Transitional Local Council* (CCT 54/00) [2001] ZACC 21; 2001 (4) SA 491 (CC); 2001 (8) BCLR 765 (CC) (4 July 2001).

122 *Johncom Media Investments Limited v M and Others* (CCT 08/08) [2009] ZACC 5; 2009 (4) SA 7 (CC); 2009 (8) BCLR 751 (CC) (17 March 2009) para 29.

123 (CCT11/98) [1998] ZACC 15; 1999 (1) SA 6; 1998 (12) bclr 1517 (9 October 1998) para 37. Although not all were framed as section 36 enquiries, the same logic has been persuasive in a number of subsequent cases that purged the discriminatory preferences against individuals in homosexual relationships from our law. See *Du Toit and Another v Minister of Welfare and Population Development and Others* (CCT40/01) [2002] ZACC 20; 2002 (10) BCLR 1006; 2003 (2) SA 198 (CC) (10 September 2002); *Satchwell v President of the Republic of South Africa and Another* (CCT48/02) [2003] ZACC 2; 2003 (4) SA 266 (CC); 2004 (1) BCLR 1 (CC) (17 March 2003); *J and Another v Director General, Department of Home Affairs and Others* (CCT46/02) [2003] ZACC 3; 2003 (5) BCLR 463; 2003 (5) SA 621 (CC) (28 March 2003); *Minister of Home Affairs and Another v Fourie and Another* (CCT 60/04) [2005] ZACC 19; 2006 (3) BCLR 355 (CC); 2006 (1) SA 524 (CC) (1 December 2005).

124 *Makwanyane* para 131.

Once a court is satisfied that the limiting measure pursues a constitutionally legitimate purpose, the focus turns to the relationship between that purpose and the means chosen to achieve it.

10.5.2.2.2 The rational connection requirement

The first basic question to be asked is whether the means chosen achieves its accepted purpose.[125] This threshold stage of the analysis focuses narrowly on whether there is a rational connection between the limiting measure and the purpose it seeks to achieve. At this stage, the enquiry is not concerned with whether the means chosen is the optimum means of achieving the measure nor whether there are more appropriate means of doing so. It is not often that a measure will fail this leg of the test although there are some examples of it doing so.

In *South African National Defence Union v Minister of Defence*,[126] the Constitutional Court first determined that maintaining a disciplined military (required under section 200(1) of the Constitution) was clearly a constitutionally legitimate objective. The Court then held that the blanket ban on soldiers forming and joining trade unions was not rationally connected to that objective.[127]

Further, the Court held in *S v Bhulwana, S v Gwadiso*:

> **In my view, section 21(1)(*a*)(i) of the Act cannot be justified in terms of section 33(1) of the Constitution. Although the need to suppress illicit drug trafficking is an urgent and pressing one, it is not clear how, if at all, the presumption furthers such an objective. In addition, there appears to be no logical connection between the fact proved (possession of 115 g) and the fact presumed (dealing).**[128]

In addition, there are other examples of limiting measures that have failed this basic level of scrutiny.[129] As noted above, it makes little sense to undertake a complex consideration of the balance to be struck between a right and a limiting measure which bears no rational relationship to its aim.[130]

10.5.2.2.3 Less restrictive, alternative means of achieving the end

Having established that the reason for limiting the right in question is constitutionally acceptable and that the measure in question rationally achieves that end, the Court may

---

125 If the court is satisfied, then it will turn its attention to considering the limiting measure in more detail, as well as any other less restrictive means of achieving that end.

126 (CCT27/98) [1999] ZACC 7; 1999 (4) SA 469; 1999 (6) BCLR 615 (26 May 1999).

127 O'Regan J held at para 35 in *South African National Defence Union*:

> **There can be no doubt of the constitutional imperative of maintaining a disciplined and effective Defence Force. I am not persuaded, however, that permitting members of the Permanent Force to join a trade union, no matter how its activities are circumscribed, will undermine the discipline and efficiency of the Defence Force. Indeed, it may well be that in permitting members to join trade unions and in establishing proper channels for grievances and complaints, discipline may be enhanced rather than diminished. Whether this proves to be the case will depend, of course, on a variety of factors including the nature of the grievance procedures established, the permitted activities of trade unions in the Defence Force, the nature of the grievances themselves and the attitudes and conduct of those involved.**

128 (CCT12/95, CCT11/95) [1995] ZACC 11; 1996 (1) SA 388; 1995 (12) BCLR 1579 (29 November 1995) para 24.

129 *S v Dodo* (CCT 1/01) [2001] ZACC 16; 2001 (3) SA 382 (CC); 2001 (5) BCLR 423 (CC) (5 April 2001); *Lesapo v North West Agricultural Bank and Another* (CCT23/99) [1999] ZACC 16; 2000 (1) SA 409; 1999 (12) BCLR 1420 (16 November 1999) para 26.

130 This has not prevented the Constitutional Court from doing so however.

consider the availability of a less restrictive means.[131] This requirement was the only addition the drafters of the Constitution made to the *Makwanyane* factors. Often, the question of the availability of less restrictive means is conceptually or practically conflated, in both the literature and jurisprudence, with the related notion of overbreadth. For example, the majority in *Prince v President of the Law Society of the Cape of Good Hope* stated:

> **A challenge to the constitutionality of legislation on the grounds that it is overbroad is in essence a challenge based on the contention that the legitimate government purpose served by the legislation could be achieved by less restrictive means.**[132]

However, there are in fact two conceptually different enquiries at play here. The one we are concerned with here considers the possibility of a hypothetical, alternative measure that is less restrictive of the right. We may refer to this as the less restrictive alternative means enquiry. The other considers whether the chosen measure – considering all the circumstances and not merely the effect on the right – is well-tailored in light of all the relevant circumstances.[133] We may refer to this as the well-tailored enquiry. This second enquiry can only be addressed as part of the proportionality enquiry when all the relevant factors are considered and not merely the measure's effect on the right.

When the global proportionality approach is taken, it may seem superfluous to separate them, especially since the Court so often conflates the two. However, there are a number of reasons for, first, maintaining the distinction between these two related but distinct enquiries and, second, considering the least restrictive, alternative means enquiry before considering the well-tailored enquiry.

First, maintaining the distinction addresses the difficult question of how far the Court should go in considering less restrictive means. Means that are less restrictive will always be possible to identify but might not – on balance – be proportionate when considering all the factors at play, for example cost and other rights. In this sense, a means may not be less restrictive, but may still be proportional. While the Constitutional Court has stated that it is not its job to find the least restrictive means, it is rightly far less deferential when considering whether the means chosen by the legislature are well tailored (proportionate) to their purpose in light of all the relevant section 36 factors.

Second, maintaining the distinction assists in the proper formulation of the notion of reasonable accommodation. This notion, discussed in more detail below, is often understood as a question of whether there are less restrictive means available. However, it is better understood as a reverse proportionality enquiry. In other words, the question is not whether the state has gone too far in restricting the enjoyment of the right (negative protection), but rather whether the state should have gone further by taking positive steps to prevent the effective limitation of the right (positive protection).[134] This broader enquiry can only be undertaken at the proportionality stage of the enquiry when all the relevant factors are considered and not merely the possible impact on the right.

Understanding it through the lens of less restrictive means leads to the problem, discussed above, that there are generally always less restrictive means. This in turn means

131 Although this factor is sequentially last, it makes little sense to consider it after making the proposed means run the gauntlet of the proportionality enquiry although the Constitutional Court has done so on occasion.

132 (CCT36/00) [2002] ZACC 1; 2002 (2) SA 794; 2002 (3) BCLR 231 (25 January 2002) para 114.

133 As was noted by O'Regan J in *South African National Defence Union* para 18, 'the use of the term "overbreadth" can be confusing, particularly as the phrase has different connotations in different constitutional contexts', adding '[c]are should therefore be taken when employing the term'.

134 Although the Constitutional Court has equated this with the less restrictive means requirement, for the reasons set out above, this is better placed under the notion of proportionality.

that a reasonable accommodation is always notionally possible. However, when considered as a reverse proportionality enquiry, the question is not whether less restrictive means can be found, but rather whether they should be employed, taking into consideration all the factors including the cost to society. Here, too, the Court must be careful not to transform its role into that of policy making.

Finally, if the distinction is maintained, then the less restrictive alternative enquiry can be viewed as a gentle enticement to the courts, as well as the executive and the legislature, to look for an alternative means before resorting to the difficult task of trying to balance two hard ends. It is an invitation to consider alternative means that are less restrictive of the right as a factor in the limitation process. Naturally, this minimalist approach makes the most sense when considered before undertaking a full-blown proportionality enquiry.

Admittedly, if this narrow construction of this factor is adopted, the number of examples of limiting measures failing this leg of the test is significantly diminished. Also, they become more difficult to identify given the tendency to elide this with aspects of the proportionality enquiry. Nevertheless, there are some examples of the Court favouring less restrictive alternative means. In *S v Williams and Others*, for example, Langa J rejected the suggestion that whipping was justified (under the limitation clause) as a superior alternative to a custodial sentence on the ground that more humane sentencing options were available.[135] Further, in a number of cases the Constitutional Court has refused to justify reverse-onus presumptions as limitations on the right to be presumed innocent on the basis that there are less restrictive means available to achieve the end, namely evidentiary burdens.[136]

10.5.2.2.4 Balancing and proportionality proper

Once it has been determined that the end is legitimate, that the means meet the end and that the court has declined to raise alternative, less restrictive means, then at this point we have something worth balancing. This stage involves balancing or proportionality which turns intimately on the facts. In broad terms, this stage involves the balancing of competing goods: the right and the limiting measure that serves a constitutionally acceptable purpose. Returning to the quote in *Walters*:

> **In essence this requires a weighing-up of the nature and importance of the right(s) that are limited together with the extent of the limitation as against the importance and purpose of the limiting enactment. Section 36(1) of the Constitution spells out these factors that have to be put into the scales in making a proportional evaluation of all the counterpoised rights and interests involved.**[137]

Before considering how this balancing process might unfold, there are a few general comments to be made about how the right and the limitation influence the proportionality process generally.

As far as stacking the rights side of the balancing scales is concerned, there are two elements to be considered. The first is the relative importance of the right under the scheme of rights/interests protected by the Constitution. The question of hierarchy is controversial

135 (CCT20/94) [1995] ZACC 6; 1995 (3) SA 632; 1995 (7) BCLR 861 (CC) (9 June 1995) para 62.

136 See *Zuma*; *Bhulwana*; *S v Mbatha*, *S v Prinsloo* (CCT19/95, CCT35/95) [1996] ZACC 1; 1996 (3) BCLR 293; 1996 (2) SA 464 (9 February 1996); *S v Julies* (CCT7/96) [1996] ZACC 14; 1996 (7) BCLR 899; 1996 (4) SA 313 (11 June 1996); *S v Coetzee and Others* (CCT50/95) [1997] ZACC 2; 1997 (4) BCLR 437; 1997 (3) SA 527 (6 March 1997); *S v Ntsele* (CCT25/97) [1997] ZACC 14; 1997 (11) BCLR 1543 (14 October 1997); *S v Mello* (CCT5/98) [1998] ZACC 7; 1998 (3) SA 712; 1998 (7) BCLR 908 (28 May 1998); *S v Singo* (CCT49/01) [2002] ZACC 10; 2002 (4) SA 858; 2002 (8) BCLR 793 (12 June 2002).

137 *Walters* paras 26–7.

and subject to contradictory judicial pronouncements. There is no formal hierarchy of rights under the Constitution[138] and the Constitutional Court has on a number of occasions denied any such hierarchy.[139] However, when it comes to the process of limiting certain rights, the Court has on a number of occasions suggested that there is, in fact, some form of hierarchy under the Constitution. The Court noted in *National Coalition for Gay and Lesbian Equality* that '[a]lthough section 36(1) does not expressly mention the importance of the right, **this is a factor which must of necessity be taken into account in any proportionality evaluation**' (our emphasis).[140] In *Makwanyane*, the Court stated that '[t]he rights to life and dignity are the most important of all human rights ...'[141] More recently, in its limitation analysis in *Bhe and Others v Khayelitsha Magistrate and Others*, the Court noted:

> **The rights violated are important rights, particularly in the South African context. The rights to equality and dignity are of the most valuable of rights in any open and democratic state. They assume special importance in South Africa because of our past history of inequality and hurtful discrimination on grounds that include race and gender.**[142]

At other times, the Court has held that certain rights are not paramount, implying some form of hierarchy.[143] Similarly, our courts have noted that we do not place the same premium on privacy as other countries.[144] If there is some hierarchy, logically those rights which are **directly** based on the founding constitutional values of dignity, freedom and equality are likely to receive greater attention than others.

The second and more difficult element of stacking the rights side of the scale is determining which portion of the right the limiting measure strikes at. Does it strike at the core of the right or its periphery (or penumbra[145])? This is the section 36 factor referred to as the 'extent of the limitation'.[146] However, it has as much to do with the nature of the right as it does the limitation (not every right is capable of part-infringement). If the threshold enquiry is comprehensive, then the groundwork for this aspect of the enquiry will already have been covered in that the nature and scope of the right in question will have been covered in some detail. What is left then is to locate the impact of the limiting measure on the right and assign it a nominal value to be balanced against the competing value of the limiting measure. Unfortunately, as part of a more general reluctance to give rights content,[147]

138 Notably, under the interim Constitution there was a hierarchy of rights. This is because s 33 listed a number of entrenched rights which were harder to limit, but this feature was dropped from the final Constitution.

139 Recently, in *Johncom* para 19, the Constitutional Court categorically stated that the Constitution does not 'accord **hierarchical precedence** to any particular right entrenched in the Bill of Rights over other rights referred to therein' (our emphasis).

140 *National Coalition for Gay and Lesbian Equality* para 34.

141 *Makwanyane* para 144. Although *Makwanyane* was decided under the interim Constitution, no reference was made to the formal hierarchy of rights by the Court when it described these rights as 'the most important of all human rights'.

142 (CCT 49/03) [2004] ZACC 17; 2005 (1) SA 580 (CC); 2005 (1) BCLR 1 (CC) (15 October 2004) para 71.

143 As Moseneke J held in *Laugh It Off Promotions CC v South African Breweries International (Finance) BV t/a Sabmark International and Another* (CCT42/04) [2005] ZACC 7; 2006 (1) SA 144 (CC); 2005 (8) BCLR 743 (CC) (27 May 2005) para 47: 'Plainly, the right to free expression in our Constitution is neither paramount over other guaranteed rights nor limitless.' As Kriegler J held in *S v Mamabolo* (CCT 44/00) [2001] ZACC 17; 2001 (3) SA 409 (CC); 2001 (5) BCLR 449 (CC) (11 April 2001) para 41: 'With us it is not a pre-eminent freedom ranking above all others. It is not even an unqualified right.'

144 See *Bernstein* para 79.

145 *Jordan* paras 80 and 86.

146 S 36(1)(*c*) of the Constitution.

147 See Woolman, S (2007) The amazing, vanishing Bill of Rights *South African Law Journal* 124(4):762–94 at 762.

the Constitutional Court has refused to undertake a detailed analysis of the core and periphery of each right on a number of occasions.[148]

Notably, when it comes to proportionality exercises, it is the impact of the measure on the right that will set the bar to be met by the justification.[149] In other words, the point of reference is the right itself. As a general rule, the greater the impact is, the more justification is required. In *S v Manamela and Another (Director-General of Justice Intervening)*, the Constitutional Court stated:

> **As a general rule, the more serious the impact of the measure on the right, the more persuasive or compelling the justification must be. Ultimately, the question is one of degree to be assessed in the concrete legislative and social setting of the measure, paying due regard to the means which are realistically available in our country at this stage, but without losing sight of the ultimate values to be protected.**[150]

Once the importance of the right and the extent of the limitation are stacked on one end of the balancing scale, the opposing end is to be filled with the limiting measure. As noted above, there is little point in undertaking a balancing process in respect of a limiting measure that has been found either not to be **rationally connected** to a constitutionally acceptable **purpose**, or which can be reached through other, less restrictive means (although this has not stopped the Constitutional Court from doing so). Therefore, a proper balancing exercise involves a limiting measure that meets this minimum, **internal** threshold. What is left to consider are the external aspects of the limitation: a more thorough consideration of its objectives and aims in an open and democratic society based on freedom, equality and dignity.

At this point, the analysis can become complicated by the influence of other rights implicated by the measure or, more specifically, its purpose. In *Christian Education*, the limiting measure – the ban on corporal punishment in schools – was designed to protect the dignity of children.[151] Further, in considering the weight to be assigned to the limiting measure and the interest it seeks to achieve or protect, the Court has at times looked to the relevant practice of other 'open and democratic' societies. As O'Regan and Sachs JJ noted in their dissent in *Jordan*: 'In approaching the question of proportionality, the Court is obliged to apply the standards of an open and democratic society.'[152] The Court has

---

148 As an aside, there is some debate over whether some rights have an unlimitable core. In *Williams* paras 55–6, the Constitutional Court raised but left open the question whether there are rights that, despite the apparent universality of the limitation clause, cannot be limited. Similarly, in *Bernstein* para 77, Ackermann J spoke of 'a final untouchable sphere of human freedom that is beyond interference from any public authority. So much so that, in regard to this most intimate core of privacy, no justifiable limitation thereof can take place'.

149 Du Plessis, M and Penfold, G 'Bill of Rights jurisprudence: Operational provisions of the Bill of Rights' (2008) *Juta's Annual Survey of South African Law* 50.

150 (CCT25/99) [2000] ZACC 5; 2000 (3) SA 1; 2000 (5) BCLR 491 (14 April 2000) para 32. The same was held to be the case under the interim Constitution. In *Bhulwana; Gwadiso* para 18, the Court held: '[T]he court places the purpose, effects and importance of the infringing legislation on one side of the scales and the nature and effect of the infringement caused by the legislation on the other. The more substantial the inroad into fundamental rights, the more persuasive the grounds of justification must be.'

151 *Christian Education* para 43. For example, in *Islamic Unity Convention* paras 42–3, the Constitutional Court considered whether a legislative provision which prohibited the broadcasting of any material 'likely to prejudice relations between sections of the population' was a justifiable limitation on the right to freedom of expression, among others. In its defence of the provision, the *amicus curiae* (Jewish Board of Deputies) raised a number of arguments that invoked interests that were protected by the provision, namely that 'the interests of human dignity and equality, which are founding values of the Constitution, and national unity, which is an important and legitimate state objective'.

152 *Jordan* para 90. Concluding at para 91:

> **[A]lthough nearly all open and democratic societies condemn commercialised sex, they differ vastly in the way in which they regulate it. These are matters appropriately left to deliberation by the democratically elected bodies of each country.**

undertaken such reviews in a number of important cases, including *National Coalition for Gay and Lesbian Equality*[153] and *Prince.*[154]

Once the Court has weighed the right and the limiting measure in their fullest sense and has taken into account the implications for other rights, then it is left to resolve the conflicting ends using the balancing and proportionality metaphors. When it comes to this stage, there are broadly two possible arguments available to the Court:

- First, the Court may conclude that the limitation is justifiable because its effect on the right is proportionate.[155] This, in practice, often involves a finding that the measure strikes the periphery of the right, making its limitation easier to justify.
- Alternatively, the Court may decide that the limitation is not justifiable, in other words the right must prevail. The reason may be because:
    - the effect on the right is disproportionate to the good achieved by the measure
    - the means chosen is disproportionate in the sense that it is not well tailored to the purpose.[156]

When the measure is held to be reasonable and justifiable, or proportionate to the impact on the right and its importance, this is balancing in its purest sense: where 'one right (or interest or value) will simply "outweigh" another right (or interest or value)'.[157] The Court has been reluctant to make a hard choice of one fixed, compellingly important 'good' (in this case the limiting measure) over another (the right). Rather, it has tended (at times simultaneously) to devalue the rights side of the scale, most often by minimising the impact of the limiting measure on the right. Alternatively, it has elevated the limitation side, often by underlining the social good achieved by the measure. For example, in reaching the conclusion that the limitation of the right to freedom of expression occasioned by the prohibition on the possession of child pornography was reasonable and justifiable, the Constitutional Court in *De Reuck* focused on the impact of the limiting measure on the right. It noted that pornography 'does not implicate the core values of the right'.[158] Rather it is an 'expression of little value which is found on the periphery of the right'.[159] Against this, it weighed the compelling interest of protecting children, as well as the dignity of society as a whole,[160] and concluded that the peripheral infringement of the right was outweighed by the interests protected by the limiting measure.[161]

153 In *National Coalition for Gay and Lesbian Equality* para 57, Ackermann J noted:

> **A number of open and democratic societies have turned their backs on the criminalisation of sodomy in private between adult consenting males, despite the fact that sexual orientation is not expressly protected in the equality provisions of their constitutions. Their reasons for doing so ... fortify the conclusion which I have reached that the limitation in question in our law regarding such criminalisation cannot be justified under section 36(1) of the 1996 Constitution.**

154 See *Prince* paras 119–27 where the majority undertook a thorough review of how foreign courts have dealt with the question of allowing special exemptions for the use of prohibited substances.

155 This is proportionality with a capital 'P'.

156 These are often employed in concert.

157 Woolman and Botha (2008) 159.

158 *De Reuck* para 59.

159 *De Reuck* para 59.

160 *De Reuck* para 67.

161 *De Reuck* para 70.

PAUSE FOR REFLECTION

How should the Constitutional Court handle hard choices?

Woolman and Botha set out the complexities of making hard choices as follows:

> How should the Court handle hard choices? First, the Court must be candid and recognise that there will be situations in which constitutional goods will urge independent and irreconcilable claims upon us: In such situations, we will have to choose between incommensurable goods. Second, the Court must acknowledge that it lacks a set of second-order rules which might tell us how to reconcile competing goods with one another. Most importantly, the Court must not view the choice of one good over another good in hard cases as arbitrary. Instead, it must be candid about the reasons for its choices and hope that its candour about the reasons for its choices ultimately reflects the exercise of good judgment: for only such candour will allow the litigants to become full citizens through their participation in the process of giving the basic law meaning. This recognition, in turn, holds out the promise that the basic law will come to possess the normative legitimacy associated with a just legal order.[162]

When the limiting measure is found to be unjustifiable and the right prevails, this too is often because the effect on the right is deemed disproportionate or unjustifiable in light of the good achieved by the measure. It may also be because the right is too important and the effect on it too great and/or because the good achieved by the measure is not sufficiently meritorious.

An example of this can be seen in *Islamic Unity Convention v Independent Broadcasting Authority and Others.*[163] In this case, the Constitutional Court struck down the legislative provision prohibiting the broadcasting of any material 'likely to prejudice relations between sections of the population'.[164] The Court found that '[t]he inroads on the right to freedom of expression made by the prohibition on which the complaint is based are far too extensive and outweigh the factors considered by the Board as ameliorating their impact'.[165]

Similarly, in *Potgieter v Lid van die Uitvoerende Raad: Gesondheid Provinsiale Regering Gauteng en Andere*, the Constitutional Court found section 68(4) of the Mental Health Act,[166] which provided a three-month prescription period for legal proceedings to be brought against any person in respect of acts performed under the Act, to be an unjustifiable limitation on the right to access courts.[167] The Court stated that this was 'particularly outrageous and drastic, having regard to the category of persons it strikes'.[168]

It is often the case that the limiting measure will fail not as a result of the proportionality of the end it seeks to achieve in relation to the impact on the right, in other words failing the balancing test, but rather because the means chosen to achieve that end is not well tailored to its purpose.

162 Woolman and Botha (2008) 159–60.

163 (CCT36/01) [2002] ZACC 3; 2002 (4) SA 294; 2002 (5) BCLR 433 (11 April 2002).

164 Schedule 1 Clause 2(*a*) of the Code of Conduct for Broadcasting Services in the Independent Broadcasting Authority Act 153 of 1993.

165 *Islamic Unity Convention* para 49. The Court also held the provision to be overbroad.

166 Act 18 of 1973.

167 (CCT 26/01) [2001] ZACC 4; 2001 (11) BCLR 1175 (8 October 2001).

168 *Potgieter* para 7.

In *Islamic Unity Convention*, the Constitutional Court noted that '[i]t has ... not been shown that the very real need to protect dignity, equality and the development of national unity could not be adequately served by the enactment of a provision which is appropriately tailored and more narrowly focused'.[169] In *South African National Defence Union*, the Constitutional Court found that a legislative provision[170] that limited the right to freedom of expression by prohibiting members of the SANDF from performing any 'act of public protest' was not reasonable and justifiable as it 'goes far further than is necessary to ensure [its] end'.[171] In *Coetzee v Government of the Republic of South Africa; Matiso and Others v Commanding Officer Port Elizabeth Prison and Others*, the Court held that 'although [the] objective of enforcing judgment debts was legitimate and reasonable, the means chosen were not reasonable ... because the provisions were overbroad, catching not only those who would not pay, but also those who could not'.[172]

Finally, the notion of reasonable accommodation requires special consideration. At the heart of this notion lies the right to be different. In *Christian Education*, the Constitutional Court summed up the question as follows:

> **The underlying problem in any open and democratic society based on human dignity, equality and freedom in which conscience and religious freedom has [*sic*] to be regarded with appropriate seriousness, is how far such democracy can and must go in allowing members of religious communities to define for themselves which laws they will obey and which not. Such a society can cohere only if all its participants accept that certain basic norms and standards are binding. Accordingly, believers cannot claim an automatic right to be exempted by their beliefs from the laws of the land. At the same time, the state should, wherever reasonably possible, seek to avoid putting believers to extremely painful and intensely burdensome choices of either being true to their faith or else respectful of the law.**[173]

Conceptually, the reasonable accommodation notion is unique in that it is an exercise in reverse proportionality. This is done by shifting the focus of the enquiry from the justifiability of the limiting measure to the justifiability of the **effect** of that measure on a particular group or individual. As Sachs J noted in *Christian Education*:

> **In the present matter it is clear that what is in issue is not so much whether a general prohibition on corporal punishment in schools can be justified, but whether the impact of such a prohibition on the religious beliefs and practices of the members of the appellant can be justified under the limitations test of section 36. More precisely, the proportionality exercise has to relate to whether the failure to accommodate the appellant's religious belief and practice by means of the**

---

169 *Islamic Unity Convention* para 49.

170 S 126B(4) of the Defence Act 44 of 1957.

171 *South African National Defence Union* para 11.

172 (CCT19/94, CCT22/94) [1995] ZACC 7; 1995 (10) BCLR 1382; 1995 (4) SA 631 (22 September 1995) paras 13–4.

173 *Christian Education* para 35. Further, in *MEC for Education: Kwazulu-Natal and Others v Pillay* (CCT 51/06) [2007] ZACC 21; 2008 (1) SA 474 (CC); 2008 (2) BCLR 99 (CC) (5 October 2007) para 73, Langa CJ noted the following regarding the concept:

> **At its core is the notion that sometimes the community, whether it is the State, an employer or a school, must take positive measures and possibly incur additional hardship or expense in order to allow all people to participate and enjoy their rights equally. It ensures that we do not relegate people to the margins of society because they do not and cannot conform to certain social norms.**

> **exemption for which the appellant asked, can be accepted as reasonable and justifiable in an open and democratic society based on human dignity, freedom and equality.**[174]

Similarly, in *Prince*, the Constitutional Court phrased its task as deciding whether or not 'the failure to provide an exception in respect of the use of cannabis for religious purposes by Rastafari infringed their religious rights under the Constitution'.[175] The question the Court must address is not whether the state has gone too far in restricting the enjoyment of a right (negative protection), but rather whether the state should have gone further by taking positive steps to prevent effective limitation of a right (positive protection).[176] It is about the failure of the state to act in light of the proportional effect on the right, not the measures already taken.[177]

It is difficult to draw lines around how the reasonable accommodation test works in practice. However, the Court set out some ground rules in *MEC for Education: Kwazulu-Natal and Others v Pillay*.[178] The Court had to decide whether a school was required reasonably to accommodate a learner's desire to wear a nose stud in pursuit of her rights to religion and culture. It considered first the importance of the practice to the learner and second, the 'hardship that permitting her to wear the stud would cause the school'.[179] In respect of the importance of the practice to the learner, the Court found that '[p]reventing her from wearing it for several hours of each school day would undermine the practice and therefore constitute a significant infringement of her religious and cultural identity'.[180] In respect of the effect on the school of permitting the learner to wear the nose stud, the Court found that accommodating the practice would not impose 'an undue burden upon the school'.[181] As a result, the balance was tipped in favour of the learner being allowed to wear the nose stud. The Court ordered the school to make a 'reasonable accommodation' of this practice.[182]

Clearly, in addressing the notion of reasonable accommodation, courts must be mindful of the separation of powers. As Sachs J noted in *Prince*:

> **The search for an appropriate accommodation in this frontier legal territory accordingly imposes a particularly heavy responsibility on the courts to be sensitive to considerations of institutional competence and the separation of powers. Undue judicial adventurism can be as damaging as excessive judicial timidity.**[183]

---

174 *Christian Education* para 32.

175 *Prince* para 94.

176 As noted above, although the Constitutional Court has equated this with the less restrictive means requirement, for the reasons set out above, this is better placed under the notion of proportionality.

177 *Prince* para 139: 'The use made of cannabis by Rastafari cannot in the circumstances be sanctioned without impairing the state's ability to enforce its legislation in the interests of the public at large and to honour its international obligation to do so. The failure to make provision for an exemption in respect of the possession and use of cannabis by Rastafari is thus reasonable and justifiable under our Constitution.'

178 (CCT 51/06) [2007] ZACC 21; 2008 (1) SA 474 (CC); 2008 (2) BCLR 99 (CC) (5 October 2007).

179 *Pillay* para 79.

180 *Pillay* para 85.

181 *Pillay* para 112.

182 *Pillay* para 162. It was a hollow victory in light of the fact that the student had matriculated by the time judgment was handed down.

183 *Prince* para 156.

PAUSE FOR REFLECTION

Applying the notion of reasonable accommodation

The notion of reasonable accommodation applies in two distinct contexts. First, it can apply in cases where a court has to decide whether discrimination is either fair or unfair and hence in breach of section 9 of the Constitution or the relevant section of the Promotion of Equality and Prevention of Unfair Discrimination Act (PEPUDA).[184] Second, it can apply when dealing with the justificatory stage to determine whether the limitation was justifiable or not.

In the second context, the question focuses on whether the state has done enough to accommodate the interests of the person or group who claim that their rights have been infringed. Put differently, where a law of general application infringes on a right, the question is whether this infringement is justifiable because the law has reasonably accommodated the interests of those whose rights are being infringed by the legislative provision. In such cases, the burden of proof, discussed in the next section, becomes important.

10.6 The burden of justification

The jurisprudence of the Constitutional Court on the question of whether there is a **burden of proof or justification** on the party seeking to rely on the limiting measure to justify it under section 36 is complex. The general principle was set out in *Makwanyane* as follows: 'It is for the legislature, or the party relying on the legislation, to establish this justification, and not for the party challenging it to show that it was not justified.'[185] This has been repeated in a number of subsequent cases.

The difficulty arises when the government or private actor seeking to rely on the limiting measure makes an unsatisfactory attempt at justifying it under section 36 or none at all. If the burden of justification was applied strictly, in other words as an onus in the proper sense, then in such instances the limitation would fail. However, the Court has pointed out on a number of occasions that this is a unique form of onus, an 'onus of a special type'.[186]

What is required under this special type of onus is less clear. The Court in *Moise v Greater Germiston Transitional Local Council* noted:

> **It is also no longer doubted that, once a limitation has been found to exist, the burden of justification under s 36(1) rests on the party asserting that the limitation is saved by the application of the provisions of the section. The weighing up exercise is ultimately concerned with the proportional assessment of competing interests but, to the extent that justification rests on factual and/or policy considerations, the party contending for justification must put such material before the Court. It is for this reason that the government functionary responsible for legislation that is being challenged on constitutional grounds must be cited as a party. If the government wishes to defend the particular enactment, it then has the opportunity – indeed an obligation – to do so. The obligation includes not only the submission of legal argument but the placing**

184 Act 4 of 2000.

185 *Makwanyane* para 102.

186 In *Minister of Home Affairs v National Institute for Crime Prevention and the Re-Integration of Offenders (NICRO) and Others* (CCT 03/04) [2004] ZACC 10; 2005 (3) SA 280 (CC); 2004 (5) BCLR 445 (CC) (3 March 2004) para 34, the Court noted: 'It is not the conventional onus of proof as it is understood in civil and criminal trials where disputes of fact have to be resolved. It is rather a burden to justify a limitation where that becomes an issue in a section 36 analysis.'

> **before Court of the requisite factual material and policy considerations. Therefore, although the burden of justification under s 36 is no ordinary onus, failure by government to submit such data and argument may in appropriate cases tip the scales against it and result in the invalidation of the challenged enactment.[187]**

Further, in *Minister of Home Affairs v National Institute for Crime Prevention and the Re-Integration of Offenders (NICRO) and Others*, the Court laid down the general principles:

> **Where justification depends on factual material, the party relying on justification must establish the facts on which the justification depends. Justification may, however, depend not on disputed facts but on policies directed to legitimate governmental concerns. If that be the case, the party relying on justification should place sufficient information before the court as to the policy that is being furthered, the reasons for that policy, and why it is considered reasonable in pursuit of that policy to limit a constitutional right. That is important, for if this is not done the court may be unable to discern what the policy is, and the party making the constitutional challenge does not have the opportunity of rebutting the contention through countervailing factual material or expert opinion. A failure to place such information before the court, or to spell out the reasons for the limitation, may be fatal to the justification claim. There may however be cases where despite the absence of such information on the record, a court is nonetheless able to uphold a claim of justification based on common sense and judicial knowledge.[188]**

From this we can distil three species of justification arguments: factual arguments, policy-based arguments and legal arguments. The Court appears to suggest that the onus that will be applied will differ depending on which form (or forms) of argument are being applied. Although the Court will at times come to the assistance of the state or the individual trying to justify the limitation, it can only do so in terms of arguments and not in terms of facts.[189] Similarly, when it comes to policy-based arguments, the Court must be wary of its role and that of the executive under the separation of powers doctrine. However, when there is scope for the Court to come to the assistance of an ailing justificatory argument, it has been willing to do so with varying levels of enthusiasm.

On a number of other occasions the Court has come to the assistance of the government when it comes to justifying limiting measures. In *National Coalition for Gay and Lesbian Equality*, it held that 'even if the respondent makes no attempt to discharge its "burden of justification", the court must nevertheless consider the possibility that a limitation of rights is justifiable'.[190] In *Phillips and Another v Director of Public Prosecutions and Others*, Yacoob J noted that 'the absence of evidence and argument from the state does not exempt the court

187 (CCT 54/00) [2001] ZACC 21; 2001 (4) SA 491 (CC); 2001 (8) BCLR 765 (CC) (4 July 2001) para 18.

188 (CCT 03/04) [2004] ZACC 10; 2005 (3) SA 280 (CC); 2004 (5) BCLR 445 (CC) (3 March 2004) para 36.

189 For example, in *S v Steyn* (CCT19/00) [2000] ZACC 24; 2001 (1) BCLR 52; 2001 (1) SA 1146; 2001 (1) SACR 16 (29 November 2000), the Court found that the imposition of a leave to appeal requirement on all criminal appeals from the magistrates' courts violated the right to appeal contained in s 35 of the Constitution. The Court was then faced with the difficulty that the State had made little to no attempt at a justification argument. In finding that the measure had failed the justification test, the court held at para 32:

> **The State has failed to adduce any evidence on the clogging of appeal rolls, the impact of unmeritorious appeals, and the existence of any resource-related problems or other relevant considerations that could justify the existence of the procedure introduced by ss 309B and 309C. Clearly it was incumbent on the State to establish factors that justify these limitations of the right of appeal ... In the present case the State produced no such data, nor did it refer to any objectively determinable factors that could be considered in justification of the challenged provisions.**

190 Currie, I and De Waal, J (2005) *The Bill of Rights Handbook* 5th ed 237–38.

from the obligation to conduct the justification analysis and to apply [the limitation clause]'.[191] More recently, in *Johncom Media Investments Limited v M and Others*, Jafta AJ noted that even though '[n]o party contended that the section 36 justification requirements were met ... [i]t is nevertheless necessary to deal with the question of justification briefly'.[192] Conversely, in *Centre for Child Law v Minister for Justice and Constitutional Development and Others*, Cameron J, having criticised the government's attempts at justification, found that 'no maintainable justification has been advanced' for including children in the minimum sentencing regime for certain offences.[193]

10.7 Internal limitations

As noted above, a number of rights are subject to internal modifiers or internal limitations which, broadly speaking, modify the scope and content of the right or the manner in which it is limited. These internal limitations limit the scope and content of the right and must be considered before considering the section 36 limitation clause. This means a court first looks at the internal limitation to determine the scope and content of the right and the outer limits of that right. If there is still an infringement of the right despite the fact that the right is internally limited, then the court has regard to the limitation clause.

Sections 9, 15, 24, 25, 26, 27, 29, 30, 31 and 32 of the Constitution all contain some form of internal limitation provisions. The relationship between these provisions and section 36 is complex. The Court has generally chosen to undertake, at times mechanically, section 36 analyses in conjunction with these internal limitation provisions. Beyond this, it has avoided adopting a general approach to managing this relationship. As such, each of the internal limitations must be considered in the context of the relevant right.[194] However, two examples deserve further mention as they illustrate the difficulties associated with simultaneously applying internal limitations provisions and section 36.

In respect of the right to equality, section 9 of the Constitution includes the right not to be subject to unfair discrimination by the state or private individuals.[195] In *Harksen v Lane NO and Others*, the Constitutional Court set out a complex test for determining first whether discrimination has taken place and second whether such discrimination is unfair.[196] This second test contains a number of factors that are similar to those considered under section 36.[197] This has led some to argue that the section 9 *Harksen* 'enquiry into unfair

191 (CCT20/02) [2003] ZACC 1; 2003 (3) SA 345; 2003 (4) BCLR 357 (11 March 2003) para 20.

192 (CCT 08/08) [2009] ZACC 5; 2009 (4) SA 7 (CC); 2009 (8) BCLR 751 (CC) (17 March 2009) para 25.

193 (CCT98/08) [2009] ZACC 18; 2009 (2) SACR 477 (CC); 2009 (6) SA 632 (CC); 2009 (11) BCLR 1105 (CC) (15 July 2009) para 63.

194 See chs 12–16.

195 S 9(3) states: 'The state may not unfairly discriminate directly or indirectly against anyone on one or more grounds, including race, gender, sex, pregnancy, marital status, ethnic or social origin, colour, sexual orientation, age, disability, religion, conscience, belief, culture, language and birth.' S 9(4) states: 'No person may unfairly discriminate directly or indirectly against anyone on one or more grounds in terms of subsection (3). National legislation must be enacted to prevent or prohibit unfair discrimination.'

196 (CCT9/97) [1997] ZACC 12; 1997 (11) BCLR 1489; 1998 (1) SA 300 (7 October 1997) para 48. See also *Prinsloo v Van der Linde and Another* (CCT4/96) [1997] ZACC 5; 1997 (6) BCLR 759; 1997 (3) SA 1012 (18 April 1997).

197 In *Hugo* paras 41–3, the Constitutional Court held that:

> **Each case, therefore, will require a careful and thorough understanding of the impact of the discriminatory action upon the particular people concerned to determine whether its overall impact is one which furthers the constitutional goal of equality or not. A classification which is unfair in one context may not necessarily be unfair in a different context ... To determine whether that impact was unfair it is necessary to look not only at the group who has been disadvantaged but at the nature of the power in terms of which the discrimination was effected and also at the nature of the interests which have been affected by the discrimination.**

discrimination ... exhausts a meaningful enquiry into the justification for any such violations - whether it occurs in terms of law or conduct'.[198] However, in each case where the Court has applied this test, it has continued to apply section 36 independently.[199] That being said, the Court has yet to find that an act that amounts to unfair discrimination is a justifiable limitation of the right to equality under section 36.

Similarly, the Court's complex approach to section 25(1) has called into question the usefulness of section 36.[200] In *First National Bank*, the Court developed a complex test for determining whether property had been arbitrarily deprived in violation of section 25(1) of the Constitution.[201] The Court then went on to consider the relationship between this internal limitation and section 36. It acknowledged the 'circularity' of applying section 36 in such circumstances,[202] but noted that '[n]either the text nor the purpose of section 36 suggests that any right in the Bill of Rights is excluded from limitation under its provisions'.[203] Having set out the difficulty, the Court then noted:

> **In view of the conclusion ultimately reached on this part of the case, it is not necessary to decide this question finally here. It will be assumed, without deciding, that an infringement of section 25(1) of the Constitution is subject to the provisions of section 36.**[204]

The argument of circularity is even stronger in the case of section 25(1) as the Constitutional Court's formulation closely approximates, to the extent of specifically referencing,[205] the proportionality test in section 36. Woolman and Botha note:

> **[The section 25] test for arbitrary deprivation of property consciously incorporates a sliding scale proportionality assessment - the *sine qua non* of limitations enquiries - into the rights stage of the analysis. Little, if any, space remains for additional forms of justification to be offered under [section 36].**[206]

---

198 Woolman and Botha (2013) 34.6. Similarly, Currie and De Waal (2005) 237–8:

> **In the case of the right to equality it is difficult to apply the usual two-stage analysis of a right and its limitation. Indeed, it is far from clear whether s 36 has any meaningful application to s 9. This is because it is, for instance, difficult to see how any discrimination that has already been characterized as "unfair" (because it is based on attributes and characteristics which have the potential to impair the fundamental human dignity of persons as human beings) can ever be acceptable in an open and democratic society based on human dignity, freedom and equality. Similarly, it is difficult to see how one could justify as "reasonable" a law which differentiates for reasons not rationally related to a legitimate government purpose, and which is therefore arbitrary.**

199 In *Bhe* para 68 the Constitutional Court concluded that it was unfair discrimination but still applied section 36: 'The only question that remains to be considered is whether the discrimination occasioned by section 23 and its regulations is capable of justification in terms of section 36 of our Constitution.' See also *Geldenhuys v National Director of Public Prosecutions and Others* (CCT 26/08) [2008] ZACC 21; 2009 (2) SA 310 (CC); 2009 (1) SACR 231 (CC); 2009 (5) BCLR 435 (CC) (26 November 2008). The same approach was adopted under the interim Constitution. See *Larbi-Odam* para 18.

200 In *First National Bank* paras 47–70, Ackermann J set out the operation of s 25 in detail.

201 *First National Bank* para 100.

202 *First National Bank* para 110: 'It might be contended that once the deprivation has been adjudged to be arbitrary, no scope remains for justification under section 36.'

203 *First National Bank* para 110.

204 *First National Bank* para 110.

205 The *First National Bank* para 100 test includes as a consideration: 'Depending on such interplay between variable means and ends, the nature of the property in question and the extent of its deprivation, there may be circumstances when sufficient reason is established by, in effect, no more than a mere rational relationship between means and ends; **in others this might only be established by a proportionality evaluation closer to that required by section 36(1) of the Constitution**. (our emphasis)'

206 Woolman and Botha (2008) 149.

Nevertheless, the Court continues to apply internal limitations provisions and section 36 conjunctively, but generally to no practical effect.

PAUSE FOR REFLECTION

The interaction between legislation giving effect to certain rights and the limitation clause

A number of provisions in the Bill of Rights require the legislature to enact specific legislation to give effect to certain rights. See, for example, section 9(4) and section 33. Although they will be dealt with in more detail in the relevant chapters, brief mention must be made of the interaction between such legislation and the limitation clause. The general principle governing the relationship between such legislation and the right it seeks to give effect to is that 'courts must assume that the [legislation] is consistent with the Constitution and claims must be decided within its margins'.[207] The upshot of this is that 'a litigant cannot circumvent legislation enacted to give effect to a constitutional right by attempting to rely directly on the constitutional right',[208] but must challenge the legislation in its entirety if they are not happy with it.

Although the limitation aspect is given less attention, logically both the application and the limitation of a right must be addressed within the margins of the relevant piece of legislation. As a result, aspects of the section 36 enquiry are often incorporated in substance in provisions of such legislation. For example, under the Promotion of Administrative Justice Act (PAJA),[209] 'the requirements of fair administrative procedure contemplated in s 3(2) may be departed from where it is reasonable and justifiable to do so',[210] taking into account, among others, the object of the empowering provision and the nature and the purpose of the decision. Here the Court uses section 36 in substance to interpret a provision of PAJA, a piece of legislation. Similarly, section 14 of the PEPUDA set outs the requirements for determining whether discrimination is unfair. This closely maps the questions asked under section 36, including the notion of reasonable accommodation.

This approach does not mean that the right falls away entirely. Rather, it will remain relevant, whether expressly or by implication, to the interpretation of the legislation in question. As the Court held in *National Education Health & Allied Workers Union (NEHAWU) v University of Cape Town and Others* in the context of the Labour Relations Act (LRA):[211]

> **[T]he LRA gives content to section 23 of the Constitution and must therefore be construed and applied consistently with that purpose. Section 3(*b*) of the LRA underscores this by requiring that the provisions of the LRA must be interpreted 'in compliance with the Constitution'.**[212]

This opens up the possibility of section 36 having an interpretative influence on the correlative limitations provisions of the legislation in question. For example, in *MEC: Department of Agriculture, Conservation and Environment and Another v HTF*

207 *Pillay* para 40.
208 *Pillay* para 40.
209 Act 3 of 2000.
210 S 4 of the PAJA.
211 Act 66 of 1995.
212 (CCT2/02) [2002] ZACC 27; 2003 (2) BCLR 154; 2003 (3) SA 1 (CC) (6 December 2002) para 14.

Developers (Pty) Limited, one of the few Constitutional Court cases that deal with section 24, Ngcobo J wrote:

> Of course procedural fairness as envisaged in s 33 of PAJA is flexible. In the case of s 33, the right to just administrative action may be limited under s 36(1). In the case of PAJA, the requirements of fair administrative procedure contemplated in s 3(2) may be departed from where it is reasonable and justifiable to do so. Factors that are relevant to the question whether there should be a departure include the objects of the empowering provision; the nature and the purpose of the decision; and the urgency of taking the decision or the urgency of the matter.[213]

10.8 The limitation of rights apart from section 36(1)

Section 36(2) provides that no law may limit any right entrenched in the Bill of Rights except as provided for in subsection (1) or 'in any other provision of the Constitution'. An example of such a provision can be found in the amnesty provision contained in the epilogue of the interim Constitution.[214] In *Azanian Peoples Organization (AZAPO) and Others v President of the Republic of South Africa and Others*, the Constitutional Court found that this amnesty provision condoned any possible violation of the right to access court of victims of apartheid crimes and their relatives by the granting of civil and criminal amnesty by the TRC.[215]

The more difficult question is how to justify rights violations based indirectly on provisions of the Constitution. The Court has dealt with the possibility of the violation of rights by section 173 of the Constitution on two separate occasions without clarifying the textual basis for doing so.[216] In *South African Broadcasting Corporation Limited v National Director of Public Prosecutions and Others*, the majority applied a proportionality test in determining whether the violation of rights by section 173 of the Constitution was justifiable without relying expressly on section 36(1) or 36(2).[217] Likewise, the minority (per Moseneke DCJ, Mokgoro J concurring) drew a distinction between the limitation of a right by 'relying only on the power to regulate procedure under s 173 [of the Constitution]' and the limitation of rights by relying 'on a law of general application that confers a discretion to limit an entrenched right'.[218] They implied that the test to be applied was different from that in

213 (CCT 32/07) [2007] ZACC 25; 2008 (2) SA 319 (CC); 2008 (4) BCLR 417 (CC) (6 December 2007) para 76.

214 The relevant part of this provision reads: 'In order to advance such reconciliation and reconstruction, amnesty shall be granted in respect of acts, omissions and offences associated with political objectives and committed in the course of the conflicts of the past.'

215 (CCT17/96) [1996] ZACC 16; 1996 (8) BCLR 1015; 1996 (4) SA 672 (25 July 1996) para 38:

> **In the result I am satisfied that section 20(7) [of the Promotion of National Unity and Reconciliation Act 34 of 1995] is not open to constitutional challenge on the ground that it invades the right of a victim or his or her dependant to recover damages from a wrongdoer for unlawful acts perpetrated during the conflicts of the past. If there is any such invasion it is authorised and contemplated by the relevant parts of the epilogue.**

216 S 173 of the Constitution states: 'The Constitutional Court, Supreme Court of Appeal and High Courts have the inherent power to protect and regulate their own process, and to develop the common law, taking into account the interests of justice.'

217 (CCT58/06) [2006] ZACC 15; 2007 (1) SA 523 (CC); 2007 (2) BCLR 167 (CC); [2006] JOL 18339 (CC) (21 September 2006) para 42. The majority concluded at para 46 that, in the circumstances of the case, the SCA had struck 'an appropriate relationship of proportionality between the right to freedom of expression and the court's obligation to ensure that the proceedings before it are fair'.

218 *South African Broadcasting Corporation* para 92.

section 36. However, the Court went on to insist that 'at a bare minimum, the limitation must, in substance, fall within the bounds imposed by section 36(1)'.[219]

Then, in *Independent Newspapers (Pty) Ltd v Minister for Intelligence Services (Freedom of Expression Institute as Amicus Curiae) In re: Masetlha v President of the Republic of South Africa and Another*, the Court again (this time per Moseneke DCJ) used section 173 and proportionality rather than 'a statute or other law of general application as the basis for restricting the disclosure of the material'.[220]

It is not clear what the textual basis for the Court's proportionality assessment is. In this regard, Du Plessis and Penfold note:

> **[T]he majority used section 173 as the basis for limiting the right to open justice. It is surprising that Moseneke DCJ should adopt such a position, given that he appears previously to have rejected the approach of using section 173 as a self-standing basis for limiting fundamental rights [in *South African Broadcasting Corporation*] ... It seems to us that the application of this reasoning in *Independent Newspapers* would mean that a limitation on the right to open justice, occasioned by a court directing that certain parts of the record are not to be made publicly available, is required to pass the limitations test in section 36(1). This requires the limitation to be in terms of law of general application, and to be reasonable and justifiable. We would have thought that section 173 is capable of fulfilling the law of general application requirement, with the remaining question being whether the limitation is reasonable and justifiable.**[221]

The use of proportionality by the Court in both these cases suggests it is applying section 36(1). However, it seems unwilling to do so formally. The difficulty with the Court's approach is that it grants courts considerable power to infringe rights under section 173 without comparable protection. As Yacoob J noted in his dissent in *Independent Newspapers*, '[i]t is difficult to justify a regime in which a court can limit rights more easily than a legislature can'.[222]

SUMMARY

When a person challenges a law on the grounds that it infringes one or more of the rights guaranteed in the Bill of Rights, a court has to perform two tasks. The court must first determine whether the law being challenged limits any of the rights protected by the substantive clauses of the Bill of Rights. If it does, the court then has to go on to determine whether that limitation is justifiable. A limitation will be justifiable if it satisfies the requirements of section 36(1) of the Constitution (the limitation clause).

When it came to interpreting the limitation clause, most commentators expected the Constitutional Court to follow the sequential structured approach, in which a series of specific questions are addressed, adopted by the Canadian Supreme Court in *Oakes*. In *Makwanyane*, however, the Constitutional Court rejected this approach and adopted a singular global approach in which certain factors are considered. This singular global approach is usually referred to as a balancing or proportionality test.

219 *South African Broadcasting Corporation* para 92.
220 (CCT38/07) [2008] ZACC 6; 2008 (5) SA 31 (CC); 2008 (8) BCLR 771 (CC) (22 May 2008) para 55.
221 Du Plessis and Penfold (2008) 70–1.
222 *Independent Newspapers* para 83.

Unfortunately, it is not always clear what this balancing or proportionality test requires or how it drives the limitation enquiry. To make it simpler to understand this test, we divided the factors listed in section 36(1) into four different questions. These questions are as follows:

- What is the purpose of the limiting measure? Is it legitimate in an open and democratic society based on equality, freedom and human dignity?
- What is the relationship between the limiting measure and its stated purpose? More specifically, are they rationally connected?
- Are there clear, alternative means available that are less restrictive on the full enjoyment of the right?
- Is the legitimate, rationally based limiting measure a proportionate limitation on the right in question, taking into account the degree of infringement, the nature of the right, the breadth of the measure and the social good it achieves? This is balancing and proportionality proper.

The aim of this reconsideration is not to alter substantively the justification enquiry. Instead, it is to make proportionality more accessible by providing a simplified lens through which to view the numerous decisions involving limitation and to understand the different types of limitation analysis undertaken by the courts.

Chapter 11

Constitutional remedies

11.1 Introduction

One of the most important characteristics of a judicially enforceable Constitution is that courts are empowered to hand down orders that address infringements of the Constitution in a manner that assists litigants and those in a similar situation to the litigants. In those cases where a court has found that law or conduct unjustifiably infringes a fundamental right or does not promote the values in the Bill of Rights, it therefore has to decide what the most appropriate remedy would be to resolve the problem. It is important when litigating constitutional matters that litigants know from the outset what remedy they want the court to provide. Courts are reluctant to grant remedies that are impractical, that would not cure the constitutional defect or that would tread too drastically on the powers of the other branches of government. Most of this chapter deals with the ways in which the courts try to limit the impact of declaring law or conduct unconstitutional.

A remedy is defined as 'a process of legal redress embracing all the legal procedures that a person has to follow to redress the violation of their rights'.[1] It can also be understood in a narrower sense of the order made by a court in response to a proven violation of a person's rights.[2]

As these definitions indicate, a remedy is the mechanism used to repair an infringement of rights once a court has interpreted the right and found the conduct of a government department or a private individual to be lacking. To a significant extent, therefore, the enforcement of rights and remedies determines what a right means in practice in the lives of the parties.[3]

Given its function as a mechanism used to repair an infringement of rights, it is not surprising that an important principle of the law of constitutional remedies is that successful litigants should obtain the relief they seek to vindicate their rights. In *S v Bhulwana, S v Gwadiso*, for example, the Constitutional Court held that '[c]entral to a consideration of the interests of justice in a particular case is that successful litigants should obtain the relief they seek'.[4] When a court determines what the appropriate remedy in a case will be, it engages in a profoundly practical exercise. It has to consider the consequences of granting or not granting a particular remedy, both for the litigant who brought the case and for the state and society at large.

CRITICAL THINKING

When relief cannot be afforded to successful litigants

Although it is generally accepted that a successful litigant should be afforded the relief he or she seeks, there are some exceptions to the principle. These exceptions are:

- where the relief cannot properly be tailored by a court[5]
- where even though a litigant would otherwise be successful, other interests or matters preclude an order in his or her favour[6]
- where an order would otherwise produce such disorder or administrative difficulties that the interests of justice served by an order in favour of a successful litigant are outweighed by the social dislocation such an order might occasion.[7]

In these circumstances, the broad issue of the administration of justice is taken into account in the determination of just and equitable remedies. This means that the granting of remedies by a court, while guided by legal principles, is also based partly on pragmatism and with a keen eye to the potentially disruptive effects of granting the 'wrong' remedy.

1 Zakrzewski, R (2005) *Remedies Reclassified* 13.

2 Mbazira, C (2008) You are the 'weakest link' in realizing socio-economic rights: Goodbye – Strategies for effective implementation of court orders in South Africa, Socio-economic Rights Project, Community Law Centre, available at http://www.escr-net.org/usr_doc/Mbazira,_Weakest_Link_in_Realising_Socio-Economic_Rights.pdf.

3 Klare, K (2008) Legal subsidiarity and constitutional rights: A reply to AJ van der Walt *Constitutional Court Review* 1:129–40 at 140.

4 (CCT12/95, CCT11/95) [1995] ZACC 11; 1996 (1) SA 388; 1995 (12) BCLR 1579 (29 November 1995) para 32.

5 See *Dawood and Another v Minister of Home Affairs and Others; Shalabi and Another v Minister of Home Affairs and Others; Thomas and Another v Minister of Home Affairs and Others* (CCT35/99) [2000] ZACC 8; 2000 (3) SA 936; 2000 (8) BCLR 837 (7 June 2000) paras 63–4; *Fraser v Naude and Another (Fraser II)* (CCT14/98) [1998] ZACC 13; 1999 (1) SA 1; 1998 (11) BCLR 1357 (23 September 1998) paras 9–10.

6 *Fraser (II)* paras 9–10.

7 *Tsotetsi v Mutual and Federal Insurance Company Ltd* (CCT16/95) [1996] ZACC 19; 1996 (11) BCLR 1439; 1997 (1) SA 585 (12 September 1996) para 10.

These points are clearly illustrated in *AllPay Consolidated Investment Holdings (Pty) Ltd and Others v CEO of the South African Social Security Agency and Others*.[8]

In this case the appellant applied for an order setting aside a multibillion rand tender that had been granted to a company called Cash Paymaster Services (Pty) Ltd by the South African Social Security Agency (SASSA). The tender was for the payment of social grants. The appellant, which was one of the losing bidders, based its application on the grounds that the tender process infringed section 217(1) of the Constitution because it was unfair. Section 217(1) provides that 'when an organ of state ... contracts for goods and services, it must do so in accordance with a system which is fair, equitable, transparent, competitive and cost-effective'.

The Supreme Court of Appeal (SCA) rejected the appellant's argument and refused to set the tender aside. In arriving at this conclusion, however, the Court held that even if the tender process had been unfair it would not have granted an order setting the tender aside. This is because such an order would have significantly disrupted the payment of social grants and this would have had serious consequences not only for Cash Paymaster Services itself, which was completely innocent, but also for the millions of poor South Africans who receive social grants every month. In so far as the recipients of social grants are concerned, the Court stated that:

> **We need no evidence to know the immense disruption that would be caused, with dire consequences to millions of elderly, children and the poor, if this contract were to be summarily set aside. The prospect of that occurring has prompted the Centre for Child Law to intervene as amicus curiae in the case. We value the contribution they have made but they had no cause for concern. It is unthinkable that that should occur.**[9]

The kinds of remedies a court may grant depend on the manner in which the Bill of Rights applies to a dispute. In this respect a distinction may be drawn between:

- the direct vertical application of the Bill of Rights
- the direct horizontal application of the Bill of Rights
- the indirect vertical and horizontal application of the Bill of Rights.

In those cases where the Bill of Rights applies directly and vertically, sections 38 and 172(1) of the Constitution govern the kinds of remedies a court may grant. In those cases where the Bill of Rights applies directly and horizontally, sections 8(2) and 8(3) of the Constitution govern the kinds of remedies a court may grant. In those cases where the Bill of Rights applies indirectly, section 39(2) of the Constitution governs the kinds of remedies a court may grant.

This distinction is important because sections 38 and 172(1) of the Constitution confer on the courts the power to apply and develop unique constitutional law remedies such as declarations of invalidity, constitutional damages and meaningful engagement. Sections 8(2), 8(3) and 39(2) of the Constitution simply provide, however, that the courts must use and develop the common law and statutory remedies. For the purposes of this

8 (678/12) [2013] ZASCA 29; [2013] 2 All SA 501 (SCA); 2013 (4) SA 557 (SCA) (27 March 2013).

9 *AllPay* para 99.

chapter, therefore, we are going to focus only on the kinds of remedies a court may grant when the Bill of Rights applies directly and vertically.

When it comes to identifying the kinds of remedies a court may grant when the Bill of Rights applies directly and vertically, it is helpful to start with section 172(1)(*a*) of the Constitution. This section provides that '[w]hen deciding a constitutional matter a court must declare that any law or conduct that it is inconsistent with the Constitution is invalid to the extent of its inconsistency'.

Apart from issuing a declaration of invalidity, section 172(1)(*b*) of the Constitution also provides that when deciding a constitutional matter, a court may make any order that is 'just and equitable'. The Constitutional Court has used this power to develop a number of mechanisms aimed at regulating the impact of a declaration of invalidity. Among these are severance, notional severance, reading in, controlling the retrospective effect of a declaration of invalidity and temporarily suspending a declaration of invalidity.

Unlike severance, notional severance and reading in, the power to control the retrospective effect of a declaration of invalidity is expressly referred to in section 172(1)(*b*)(i) and to suspend temporarily a declaration of invalidity is expressly referred to in section 172(1)(*b*)(ii) of the Constitution.[10]

The constitutional remedies referred to in sections 172(1)(*a*) and (*b*) of the Constitution must also be read together with section 38. This section provides that a court may grant 'appropriate relief, including a declaration of rights' whenever a right in the Bill of Rights has been violated or threatened. The Constitutional Court has used this power to develop a number of additional remedies. Among these are interdicts, constitutional damages and meaningful engagement.

Table 11.1 The remedies available for different breaches of the Constitution

Direct vertical application	Sections 38 and 172(1)	• Declaration of invalidity • Declaration of rights • An interdict • Constitutional damages • Meaningful engagement
Direct horizontal application	Sections 8(2) and 8(3)	• Remedies contained in legislation that give effect to the Bill of Rights • Develop the common law to give effect to the Bill of Rights
Indirect vertical and horizontal application	Section 39(2)	• Common law remedies • Customary law remedies

10 S 172(1)(*b*)(i) provides that '[w]hen deciding a constitutional matter within its power a court may make any order that is just and equitable, including an order limiting the retrospective effect of the declaration of invalidity'. S 172(1)(*b*)(ii) provides that '[w]hen deciding a constitutional matter within its power a court may make any order that is just and equitable, including an order suspending the declaration of invalidity for any period and on any conditions, to allow the competent authority to correct the defect'.

PAUSE FOR REFLECTION

The nature of constitutional remedies

In those cases where a court finds that law or conduct has unjustifiably infringed a right guaranteed in the Bill of Rights, it must determine what the most appropriate remedy would be. In this respect, it is important to note that a constitutional remedy is one that focuses not only on the harm to the complainant, but also on the harm to the constitutional goal of creating a just and fair society. A constitutional remedy must, therefore, vindicate the Constitution and deter future infringement.

In *Fose v Minister of Safety and Security*, for example, Kriegler J stated that:

> **[t]he harm caused by violating the Constitution is a harm to the society as a whole, even where the direct implications of the violation are highly parochial. The rights violator not only harms the particular person, but impedes the further realisation of our constitutional promise.[11]**

The constitutional promise will therefore only be upheld if suitable remedies may be invoked in the event of a breach of the Constitution and obviously if those remedies are subsequently enforced. However, the challenge with respect to determining an appropriate remedy is that to ensure its effective enforcement, the remedy must be extremely detailed and specific. If the remedy is not detailed and specific, the violator could argue that he or she is unable to comply with the order due to its vagueness.

This reaffirms the fact that constitutional remedies are forward-looking, community-orientated and structural as opposed to backward-looking, individualistic and corrective or retributive. At all times, the remedy must operate generally to deter future infringements and eradicate inconsistencies between law or conduct and the Constitution.

11.2 Declarations of invalidity

11.2.1 Introduction

As we have seen, section 172(1)(*a*) of the Constitution states that when deciding a constitutional matter within its power, a court 'must declare that any law or conduct that is inconsistent with the Constitution is invalid to the extent of the inconsistency'. Section 172(1)(*a*) does not confer a discretion on the courts. Where a law or provision conflicts with the Constitution, a court is obliged to declare the law or provision invalid to the extent of the inconsistency.[12] The same applies to the conduct of a person or institution bound by the Constitution.[13]

The obligation to declare law or conduct that is inconsistent with the Constitution to be invalid flows logically from the fact that the Constitution is supreme. It is not surprising, therefore, that section 2 of the Constitution expressly provides that '[t]his Constitution is the

11 (CCT14/96) [1997] ZACC 6; 1997 (7) BCLR 851; 1997 (3) SA 786 (5 June 1997) para 95.

12 See *Dawood* para 59, where the Court stated:

> **It is clear from this provision that a court is obliged, once it is has concluded that a provision of a statute is unconstitutional, to declare that provision to be invalid to the extent of its inconsistency with the Constitution. In addition, the court may also make any order that it considers just and equitable including an order suspending the declaration of invalidity for some time.**

13 S 2 read with s 172(1) of the Constitution.

supreme law of the Republic; law or conduct inconsistent with it is invalid, and the obligations imposed by it must be fulfilled'.

An important consequence of the supremacy of the Constitution is that any law or conduct in conflict with the Constitution is invalid from the moment that the conflict arises. This is the so-called **doctrine of objective invalidity**. Although the invalidity will only have legal effect once a court has confirmed that there is a conflict between the Constitution and legislation or the actions of an individual, the invalidity does not only arise at the moment when it is affirmed by the court.[14] This means that an order of invalidity usually has retrospective effect as the court merely confirms that the legislation or the actions of an individual were invalid from the moment the conflict with the Constitution arose.

The Constitutional Court adopted the doctrine of objective invalidity in its judgment in *Ferreira v Levin NO and Others; Vryenhoek and Others v Powell NO and Others*.[15] In this case, the Court held as follows:

> **The Court's order does not invalidate the law; it merely declares it to be invalid. It is very seldom patent, and in most cases is disputed, that pre-constitutional laws are inconsistent with the provisions of the Constitution. It is one of this Court's functions to determine and pronounce on the invalidity of laws, including Acts of Parliament.[16]**

This does not detract from the reality that pre-existing laws either remained valid or became invalid upon the provisions of the Constitution coming into operation. In this sense, laws are objectively valid or invalid depending on whether they are or are not inconsistent with the Constitution. The fact that a dispute concerning inconsistency may only be decided years afterwards does not affect the objective nature of the invalidity. The issue of whether a law is invalid or not does not in theory, therefore, depend on whether, at the moment when the issue is being considered, a particular person's rights are threatened or infringed by the offending law or not.[17]

When a person alleges that a statutory provision is constitutionally invalid, a court must first attempt to interpret the impugned provision in a way that would render it constitutionally valid. This is called reading down. If this is not possible, however, the court must declare the law invalid. Instead of simply declaring the law to be completely invalid, however, a court should attempt to limit the substantive impact of the declaration by severing the offending words or reading in new words to cure the constitutional defect.[18] It may also be necessary to limit the potentially disruptive impact of the order by suspending the order of invalidity[19] or limiting its retrospective effect. We will deal with each one of these situations in turn.

---

14 *Ferreira v Levin NO and Others; Vryenhoek and Others v Powell NO and Others* (CCT5/95) [1995] ZACC 13; 1996 (1) SA 984 (CC); 1996 (1) BCLR 1 (6 December 1995) paras 26, 27 and 158; *Fose* para 94.

15 (CCT5/95) [1995] ZACC 13; 1996 (1) SA 984 (CC); 1996 (1) BCLR 1 (6 December 1995).

16 *Ferreira; Vryenhoek* para 27.

17 *Ferreira; Vryenhoek* para 27.

18 See *S and Others v Van Rooyen and Others (General Council of the Bar of South Africa Intervening)* (CCT21/01) [2002] ZACC 8; 2002 (5) SA 246; 2002 (8) BCLR 810 (11 June 2002) para 88:

> **[L]egislation must be construed consistently with the Constitution and thus, where possible, interpreted so as to exclude a construction that would be inconsistent with [the Constitution]. If held to be unconstitutional, the appropriate remedy ought, if possible, to be in the form of a notional or actual severance, or reading in, so as to bring the law within acceptable constitutional standards. Only if this is not possible, must a declaration of complete invalidity of the section or subsection be made.**

See also Bishop, M 'Remedies' in Woolman, S and Bishop, M (eds) (2013) *Constitutional Law of South Africa* 2nd ed rev service 5 9.86.

19 *J and Another v Director General, Department of Home Affairs and Others* (CCT46/02) [2003] ZACC 3; 2003 (5) BCLR 463; 2003 (5) SA 621 (CC) (28 March 2003) para 22.

However, as we consider all the permutations for remedies, it is important to keep in mind that the overarching consideration taken into account by the courts is the interests of justice and equity. What is required is to vindicate the rights and interests of the successful litigant and to provide effective relief with the least amount of disruption. In *Fose*, decided under the interim Constitution, Ackermann J held:

> **Given the historical context in which the interim Constitution was adopted and the extensive violation of fundamental rights which had preceded it, I have no doubt that this Court has a particular duty to ensure that, within the bounds of the Constitution, effective relief be granted for the infringement of any of the rights entrenched in it. In our context an appropriate remedy must mean an effective remedy, for without effective remedies for breach, the values underlying and the rights entrenched in the Constitution cannot properly be upheld or enhanced.**[20]

Although a court therefore has a general obligation to grant a remedy that is just and equitable to litigants who successfully raise a constitutional complaint, there are exceptions to this rule. For example, where a court cannot properly tailor the relief while still providing an effective remedy, the court may have to revert to other remedies that are less effective or it may even decline to hear the appeal.[21] In some cases, other interests or matters, for example the best interest of the child over whom litigation is being conducted, would preclude an order in favour of a successful litigant.[22]

Where an order would otherwise produce such disorder or administrative difficulties that the interests of justice served by such an order in favour of a successful litigant are outweighed by the social dislocation such an order may occasion, the court may also decline to provide an effective remedy.[23] However, there are several ways in which the court can fashion its remedies to avoid these problems while still providing effective relief. We now turn to the various ways in which the court minimises the disruptive effect of an order of invalidity while providing effective relief to the successful litigant.

11.2.2 Reading down

Reading down occurs when the words in a specific provision of a statute can be interpreted in different ways: one construction is constitutional while the other directly violates a constitutional provision. A court faced with this situation must choose the interpretation that would render the provision constitutionally valid over the unconstitutional interpretation.[24] The Constitutional Court has explained reading down as follows:

> **[J]udicial officers must prefer interpretations of legislation that fall within constitutional bounds over those that do not, provided that such an interpretation can be reasonably ascribed to the section.**[25]

Reading down is therefore not strictly speaking a remedy, but rather a mandatory rule of interpretation used to avoid the invalidation of a legal provision.

20 *Fose* para 69.

21 *Dawood* paras 63–4; *Fraser (II)* paras 9–10; *Minister of Home Affairs and Another v Fourie and Another* (CCT 60/04) [2005] ZACC 19; 2006 (3) BCLR 355 (CC); 2006 (1) SA 524 (CC) (1 December 2005) para 170.

22 *Fraser (II)* paras 9–10.

23 *Tsotetsi* para 10.

24 See Bishop (2013) 9.87.

25 *Investigating Directorate: Serious Economic Offences and Others v Hyundai Motor Distributors (Pty) Ltd and Others In re: Hyundai Motor Distributors (Pty) Ltd and Others v Smit NO and Others* (CCT1/00) [2000] ZACC 12; 2000 (10) BCLR 1079; 2001 (1) SA 545 (CC) (25 August 2000) para 23.

Reading down must therefore be distinguished from reading in which is discussed below. Reading in is applied only once the court has made a finding of invalidity. With reading down, the finding of invalidity is avoided precisely by reading down the impugned provision. Reading down can only occur when the impugned provision- on one reading of it - actually conflicts with the Constitution. The court then prefers another reading to avoid making an order of invalidity. Reading down is not always possible: the court can only read down a legislative provision if that provision is reasonably capable of the constitutional interpretation.[26] If it is not reasonably capable of that meaning, then the court must sever or read in words to the statute.[27] As the Constitutional Court explained:

> **On the one hand, it is the duty of a judicial officer to interpret legislation in conformity with the Constitution so far as this is reasonably possible. On the other hand, the Legislature is under a duty to pass legislation that is reasonably clear and precise, enabling citizens and officials to understand what is expected of them. A balance will often have to be struck as to how this tension is to be resolved when considering the constitutionality of legislation. There will be occasions when a judicial officer will find that the legislation, though open to a meaning which would be unconstitutional, is reasonably capable of being read 'in conformity with the Constitution'. Such an interpretation should not, however, be unduly strained.[28]**

Whether the wording of an impugned legislative provision is reasonably capable of a specific interpretation is not always obvious.[29] Thus, the Constitutional Court has provided different interpretations of the word 'spouse' in two different contexts. The Court found in one case that the word 'spouse' was incapable of being interpreted as including couples in permanent same-sex relationships[30] while finding that it was capable of being interpreted as including the partners who had entered into a Muslim marriage.[31]

11.2.3 Severance

Section 172(1)(*a*) requires a court to declare law or conduct invalid to the extent of its inconsistency with the Constitution.[32] A court therefore does not have to declare invalid a complete section of the legislation if it is possible to cut the bad parts out of the provision and retain those parts that are not unconstitutional. This is called **severance**. The court will then strike down a particular section, subsection or individual words in a subsection of a law but leave the rest of the law intact.

The test for severance is whether 'the good is not dependent on the bad'[33] and whether the good can be separated from the bad. The question to ask is whether it is possible to give effect to the good part of the provision that remains after the severance of the bad part. In other words, after the exercise in severance in which the bad part is declared invalid, will the good part still give effect to the main objective of the statute? 'The test has two parts: first,

26 See, for example, *Bhulwana; Gwadiso* para 29; *National Coalition for Gay and Lesbian Equality and Others v Minister of Home Affairs and Others* (CCT10/99) [1999] ZACC 17; 2000 (2) SA 1; 2000 (1) BCLR 39 (2 December 1999) paras 25–6.

27 See *Fourie* para 33.

28 *Hyundai Motor Distributors* para 24.

29 See, for example, *Wary Holdings (Pty) Ltd v Stalwo (Pty) Ltd and Another* (CCT78/07) [2008] ZACC 12; 2009 (1) SA 337 (CC); 2008 (11) BCLR 1123 (CC) (25 July 2008) where the judges on the Constitutional Court differed about this question.

30 *National Coalition for Gay and Lesbian Equality v Minister of Home Affairs* paras 25–6.

31 *Daniels v Campbell and Others* (CCT 40/ 03) [2004] ZACC 14; 2004 (5) SA 331 (CC); 2004 (7) BCLR 735 (CC) (11 March 2004) paras 19–25.

32 Currie, I and De Waal, J (2001) *The New Constitutional and Administrative Law, Vol 1 Constitutional Law* 290.

33 See *Coetzee v Government of the Republic of South Africa; Matiso and Others v Commanding Officer Port Elizabeth Prison and Others* (CCT19/94, CCT22/94) [1995] ZACC 7; 1995 (10) BCLR 1382; 1995 (4) SA 631 (22 September 1995) para 16.

is it possible to sever the invalid provisions and second, if so, does what remains give effect to the purpose of the legislative scheme?'[34]

It is not always possible to sever the good from the bad while still giving effect to the purpose of an impugned provision. In such case, the court has to declare the provision as a whole invalid.[35] The court will be circumspect because of concerns about overstepping the separation of powers. It is usually the legislature - and not the judiciary - that should draft and amend legislation. Where an offending legislative provision is so overbroad that the blame for the constitutional invalidity of the section 'cannot be laid at the door of any one word, or group of words, but rather permeates the entire text', then severance would not be appropriate.[36]

In *Case and Another v Minister of Safety and Security and Others, Curtis v Minister of Safety and Security and Others*,[37] for example, the Constitutional Court had to consider the constitutionality of a censorship provision enacted during the apartheid years that was so overbroad that it clearly infringed on the right to freedom of expression. Because the section was so overbroad, the Court could not sever the good from the bad and had to strike down the provision as a whole. In arriving at this conclusion, the Court held that if it had to:

> **apply a blue pencil to each and every noun form and transitive verb that presents overbreadth problems, we effectively would write a new provision that bears only accidental resemblance to that enacted by Parliament. If, as appears to be the case, the scheme behind the statute was to impose a comprehensive scheme of censorship to give effect to a particular moral, cultural and political world-view, it hardly does justice to the 'main object' thereof for this Court to pare it down to prohibit only that discrete set of sexually-oriented expressions that this Court believes may constitutionally be restricted. For this Court to attempt that textual surgery would entail it departing fundamentally from its assigned role under our Constitution. It is trite but true that our role is to review, rather than to re-draft, legislation. This Court has already had occasion to caution against judicial arrogation of an essentially legislative function in the guise of severance.**[38]

11.2.4 Notional severance

Notional severance is often confused with reading down and is not an easy remedy to understand. Like severance it allows for certain parts of the law or provision to be left intact while removing the constitutionally offending parts. Unlike severance, however, the words are not actually struck out of the impugned section. Instead, the impugned section is given a particular meaning in the sense that the court instructs those who apply it that the section can apply only to certain cases or in certain circumstances.

Notional severance differs from reading down in that the words in the impugned legislation cannot reasonably be interpreted in the manner provided by the court. If words can reasonably be interpreted in a manner that would ensure that the impugned provision in the legislation is constitutionally valid, the court is required to read down that section to

---

34 *Coetzee; Matiso* para 16.

35 See Bishop (2013) 9.99.

36 *Case and Another v Minister of Safety and Security and Others, Curtis v Minister of Safety and Security and Others* (CCT20/95, CCT21/95) [1996] ZACC 7; 1996 (3) SA 617; 1996 (5) BCLR 608 (9 May 1996) para 71.

37 (CCT20/95, CCT21/95) [1996] ZACC 7; 1996 (3) SA 617; 1996 (5) BCLR 608 (9 May 1996).

38 *Case, Curtis* paras 72–3.

do so. With notional severance, the court instructs others how to interpret and apply the section even when the words cannot reasonably be said to encapsulate this instruction.[39]

Notional severance is usually deployed if other remedies would leave an impermissible gap in the law. Thus, in *Islamic Unity Convention v Independent Broadcasting Authority and Others*,[40] the Constitutional Court found that a regulation which prohibited the broadcasting of material that was 'likely to prejudice relations between sections of the population'[41] was overbroad. The regulation thus limited the right to freedom of expression in the Bill of Rights. However, the Court declined to strike down the relevant portion quoted above because 'a dangerous gap would result' and 'it would be neither just and equitable nor in the public interest to allow such a gap to exist'.[42]

The Constitutional Court therefore decided that notional severance was the only just and equitable remedy available. The Court wanted to ensure that the relevant part of the impugned regulation would be 'rendered ineffective in its application to protected expression, but that a prohibition [would be] left in place to prevent the broadcasting of unprotected expression' like hate speech.[43] The Court therefore declared the impugned regulation to be inconsistent with section 16 of the Constitution and invalid to the extent that it prohibits the broadcasting of material that is:

> **likely to prejudice relations between sections of the population; provided that this order does not apply to (i) propaganda for war; (ii) incitement of imminent violence; or (iii) advocacy of hatred that is based on race, ethnicity, gender or religion, and that constitutes incitement to cause harm.**[44]

Finally, it is important to note that a court will not always be able to use notional severance. In *National Coalition for Gay and Lesbian Equality and Others v Minister of Home Affairs and Others*, for example, the Constitutional Court pointed out that where:

> **the invalidity of a statutory provision results from an *omission*, it is not possible, ... to achieve notional severance by using words such as 'invalid to the extent that', or other expressions indicating notional severance. An omission cannot, notionally, be cured by severance .... The only logical equivalent to severance, in the case of invalidity caused by omission, is the device of reading in.**[45]

11.2.5 Reading in

When the court employs the remedy of **reading in**, it literally read words into an unconstitutional legislative provision to cure that provision of its unconstitutionality. As such, it is exactly the opposite of severance where the court strikes out words from an unconstitutional provision to cure it of its unconstitutionality.[46] It follows that reading in is used in cases where a legislative provision is unconstitutional because of the omission of certain words and

39 See Bishop (2013) 9.102.

40 (CCT36/01) [2002] ZACC 3; 2002 (4) SA 294; 2002 (5) BCLR 433 (11 April 2002).

41 Schedule 1 Clause 2(*a*) of the Code of Conduct for Broadcasting Services in the Independent Broadcasting Authority Act 153 of 1993.

42 *Islamic Unity Convention* para 54.

43 *Islamic Unity Convention* para 55.

44 *Islamic Unity Convention* para 58. See also *Ferreira; Vryenhoek*.

45 (CCT10/99) [1999] ZACC 17; 2000 (2) SA 1; 2000 (1) BCLR 39 (2 December 1999) para 64.

46 *National Coalition for Gay and Lesbian Equality v Minister of Home Affairs* para 74; *Lawyers for Human Rights and Other v Minister of Home Affairs and Other* (CCT 18/03) [2004] ZACC 12; 2004 (4) SA 125 (CC); 2004 (7) BCLR 775 (CC) (9 March 2004) paras 45–7.

phrases.[47] However, the courts have also read words into a provision to narrow the reach of the provision that 'is unduly invasive of a right'.[48] The court then orders that certain words or phrases should be read into the provision to render it constitutionally valid.

It is important to note that reading in occurs only after the court has established that a legislative provision is in conflict with the Constitution and has declared the provision invalid. As such, reading in must be distinguished from reading down which is a technique used to avoid an order of invalidity altogether. Reading down is a method of statutory interpretation required by section 39(2) of the Constitution and occurs to avoid a finding of constitutional invalidity. Reading in, however, is a remedy that is granted by the court after it has declared invalid an impugned provision of legislation to cure the provision of its unconstitutionality.[49]

Reading in is an invasive remedy and raises separation of powers concerns.[50] However, the Constitutional Court held in *National Coalition for Gay and Lesbian Equality v Minister of Home Affairs* that there is in principle no difference between severance and reading in. In both cases, legislation enacted by parliament 'is being altered by the order of a court. In the one case by excision and in the other by addition'.[51] The Court has argued that reading in is justified, particularly if we embrace the view of separation of powers as a structured dialogue between the three branches of government. Reading in does not give the judiciary the final word on how legislative provisions should be formulated:

> **It should also be borne in mind that whether the remedy a court grants is one striking down, wholly or in part; or reading into or extending the text, its choice is not final. Legislatures are able, within constitutional limits, to amend the remedy, whether by re-enacting equal benefits, further extending benefits, reducing them, amending them, 'fine-tuning' them or abolishing them. Thus they can exercise final control over the nature and extent of the benefits.**[52]

Before reading words into a statute a court has to ensure, first, that the newly created provision to which words have been added is consistent with the Constitution and its fundamental values and, second, that the result achieved would interfere with the laws adopted by the legislature as little as possible. As long as there are still many provisions on the statute books from the pre-constitutional era, 'the first consideration will in those cases often weigh more heavily than the second'.[53]

However, it will not always be appropriate to read words into an impugned provision to cure its unconstitutionality. As the Constitutional Court stated in *National Coalition for Gay and Lesbian Equality v Minister of Home Affairs*:

> **... it will not be appropriate to read words in, unless in so doing a court can define with sufficient precision how the statute ought to be extended in order to comply with the Constitution. Moreover, when reading in (as when severing) a court should**

47 *National Coalition for Gay and Lesbian Equality v Minister of Home Affairs* para 74.

48 *S v Manamela and Another (Director-General of Justice Intervening)* (CCT25/99) [2000] ZACC 5; 2000 (3) SA 1; 2000 (5) BCLR 491 (14 April 2000) para 57.

49 In *Zuma v National Director of Public Prosecutions* (8652/08) [2008] ZAKZHC 71; [2009] 1 All SA 54 (N); 2009 (1) BCLR 62 (N) (12 September 2008) paras 23–5, Nicholson J wrongly used reading in as an interpretative strategy without having declared invalid the relevant section of the National Prosecuting Authority Act 32 of 1998 into which words were read. See generally Bishop (2013) 9.104–9.111.

50 *National Coalition for Gay and Lesbian Equality v Minister of Home Affairs* para 66.

51 *National Coalition for Gay and Lesbian Equality v Minister of Home Affairs* para 67. The Constitutional Court partly relied on the Canadian Supreme Court judgment in *Schachter v Canada* (1992) 93 DLR (4th) 1 para 69 to justify its use of the reading in remedy.

52 *National Coalition for Gay and Lesbian Equality v Minister of Home Affairs* para 76.

53 *National Coalition for Gay and Lesbian Equality v Minister of Home Affairs* para 74.

> **endeavour to be as faithful as possible to the legislative scheme within the constraints of the Constitution. Even where the remedy of reading in is otherwise justified, it ought not to be granted where it would result in an unsupportable budgetary intrusion. In determining the scope of the budgetary intrusion, it will be necessary to consider the relative size of the group which the reading in would add to the group already enjoying the benefits. Where reading in would, by expanding the group of persons protected, sustain a policy of long standing or one that is constitutionally encouraged, it should be preferred to one removing the protection completely.**[54]

Despite the warning to avoid reading in where it would result in an unsupportable budgetary intrusion, the Court has read words into a statute even where it did have budgetary implications.[55]

CRITICAL THINKING

How radical a constitutional remedy is reading in?

Reading in can appear to be a rather radical remedy. This is because it implicates the separation of powers doctrine as the court - and not the legislature - in effect rewrites a section of the law by reading words into the statute. It is usually the legislature and not the judiciary that has to formulate the wording of specific legal provisions and reading in seems to come close to breaching this principle. It is for this reason that the criteria set out above must be adhered to.

However, remember that when a court performs a reading in, it does not necessarily provide a final and definitive determination of the law. The legislature is free to amend the law in which words were read in by the court. When the legislature does this, it engages in the kind of constitutional dialogue which we discussed in chapter 2 on the separation of powers. The legislature therefore potentially has the final say on the exact wording of the impugned provision.

As long as any amendments to the law conform to the Constitution, the court will not be able to interfere with the determination of the wording made by the legislature. In this sense, reading in is perhaps less radical than it may at first appear. Lawyers must be aware, however, that reading in may mean that the provisions of a statute as passed by Parliament do not always accurately reflect its true meaning as the Constitutional Court may have read words into that statute.

11.3 Limiting the retrospective effect of an order of invalidity

As we have seen, the constitutional supremacy clause automatically makes any unconstitutional law or conduct a nullity from the moment the inconsistency occurred.[56] It is not only the legislation in conflict with the Constitution that is nullified: any actions performed under the ostensible authority of the legislation will also be invalid. Obviously, the **retrospective invalidation of legislation** and any actions taken in good faith under the authority of ostensibly valid legislation could have disruptive results. As is always the case

54 *National Coalition for Gay and Lesbian Equality v Minister of Home Affairs* para 75.

55 See *Khosa and Others v Minister of Social Development and Others, Mahlaule and Another v Minister of Social Development* (CCT 13/03, CCT 12/03) [2004] ZACC 11; 2004 (6) SA 505 (CC); 2004 (6) BCLR 569 (CC) (4 March 2004) para 88.

56 *Fose* para 94. See also *National Coalition for Gay and Lesbian Equality and Another v Minister of Justice and Others* (CCT11/98) [1998] ZACC 15; 1999 (1) SA 6; 1998 (12) BCLR 1517 (9 October 1998) paras 93–6.

with the granting of remedies, the question to ask is whether consideration of the interests of justice in a particular case justifies the granting of an order.

As far as the retrospective effect of orders of invalidity is concerned, we must ask if it is in the interests of justice that successful litigants obtain the relief they seek:

> **It is only when the interests of good government outweigh the interests of the individual litigants that the court will not grant relief to successful litigants ... the litigants before the court should not be singled out for the grant of relief, but relief should be afforded to all people who are in the same situation as the litigants ... [but the court should] be circumspect in exercising [its powers in this regard].**[57]

For example, when a court invalidates the provisions of a law that authorise the Department of Home Affairs to grant refugee status to qualifying applicants, the previous granting of refugee status to individual applicants in terms of the now nullified law would also normally be invalid. Accordingly, the court must consider in every case whether the interests of justice and equity justify limiting the retrospective effect of a declaration of invalidity.

The Constitutional Court has identified the following five factors as relevant to such a consideration:[58]

- The 'interest of individuals must be weighed against the interest of avoiding dislocation to the administration of justice and the desirability of a smooth transition from the old to the new' and the interest of avoiding 'the dislocation and inconvenience of undoing transactions, decisions or actions taken under [the] statute'.[59]
- 'Central to a consideration of the interests of justice in a particular case is that successful litigants should obtain the relief they seek. It is only when the interests of good government outweigh the interests of the individual litigants that the Court will not grant relief to successful litigants. In principle too, the litigants before the Court should not be singled out for the grant of relief, but relief should be afforded to all people who are in the same situation as the litigants.'[60]
- 'As a general principle ... an order of invalidity should have no effect on cases which have been finalised prior to the date of the order of invalidity.'[61]
- 'No one, not criminal defendants, not the judicial system, not society as a whole is benefited by a judgment providing a man shall tentatively go to jail today, but tomorrow and everyday thereafter his continued incarceration shall be subject to fresh litigation on issues already resolved.'[62]
- The Constitutional Court has expressed doubt as to whether section 98(6) of the interim Constitution (section 172(1)(*b*)(i) of the final Constitution) may be used by a court to direct that actions are constitutionally valid despite having been taken in terms of any proclamation issued under a law declared to be invalid.[63]

---

57 *Bhulwana, Gwadiso* para 32.

58 See *S v Ntsele* (CCT25/97) [1997] ZACC 14; 1997 (11) BCLR 1543 (14 October 1997) para 14 and *Bhulwana, Gwadiso* para 32.

59 *S v Zuma and Others* (CCT5/94) [1995] ZACC 1; 1995 (2) SA 642; 1995 (4) BCLR 401 (SA); 1995 (1) SACR 568; [1996] 2 CHRLD 244 (5 April 1995) para 43.

60 *Bhulwana, Gwadiso* para 32.

61 *Bhulwana, Gwadiso* para 32.

62 *Mackey v US* 401 US 667 (1971) at 691 quoted with approval in *Bhulwana, Gwadiso* para 32.

63 *Executive Council of the Western Cape Legislature and Others v President of the Republic of South Africa and Others* (CCT27/95) [1995] ZACC 8; 1995 (10) BCLR 1289; 1995 (4) SA 877 (22 September 1995) para 105. In this case the President sought to invoke the interim Constitution's equivalent of s 172(1)(*b*)(i) to validate proclamations which had the effect of amending an Act of Parliament. The Court found this to be 'logically inconsistent' since the reason why the amendments were invalid in the first place was that they should have been passed by Parliament and not the President.

Usually, where the Constitutional Court decides to vary the retrospective effect of its declaration of invalidity, it does so by invalidating a statute prospectively in the sense that it may no longer be applied from the date of the order in unresolved matters. At the same time, its order operates retrospectively in the limited sense that where appeal or review is still pending or the time for the noting of an appeal has not yet expired, the unconstitutionality of the statute may be raised on appeal.[64]

PAUSE FOR REFLECTION

Using a qualified retrospective order

In *National Coalition for Gay and Lesbian Equality and Another v Minister of Justice and Others*,[65] the Constitutional Court declared invalid the common law rule that criminalised sodomy between adult men, even where this occurred consensually and in private. A crucial question that had to be answered was whether the retrospective effect of this invalidation should be curtailed.

The Court argued that it would be 'manifestly and grossly unjust and inequitable that such convictions should not be capable of being set aside as people have been convicted of an offence which – because of the principle of objective constitutional invalidity – had ceased to exists as an offence when the interim Constitution came into force on 27 April 1994'.[66] However, an unqualified retrospective order may have had undesirable consequences as the provision was used to convict and punish not only consensual acts between adults but also acts of male rape. The Constitutional Court therefore found that:

> The least disruptive way of giving relief to persons in respect of past convictions for consensual sodomy is through the established court structures. On the strength of the order of constitutional invalidity such persons could note an appeal against their convictions for consensual sodomy, where the period for noting such appeal has not yet expired or, where it has, could bring an application for condonation of the late noting of an appeal or the late application for leave to appeal to a court of competent jurisdiction. In this way effective judicial control can be exercised. Although this might result in cases having to be reopened, it will in all probability not cause dislocation of the administration of justice of any moment. We should, however, limit the retrospective effect of the order declaring the offence of sodomy to be constitutionally invalid to cases of consensual sodomy. In respect of all other cases of sodomy, the order should be limited to one which takes effect from the date of this judgment. This is essential, in my view, to prevent persons convicted of sodomy which amount to 'male rape' from having their past convictions set aside. To permit this would be neither just nor equitable. In the absence of such a limitation confusion might arise, upon a conviction being set aside in such cases, as to whether a conviction of indecent assault or assault with intent to do grievous bodily harm, could validly be substituted.[67]

64 The order in *Bhulwana, Gwadiso* is a representative example.
65 (CCT11/98) [1998] ZACC 15; 1999 (1) SA 6; 1998 (12) BCLR 1517 (9 October 1998).
66 *National Coalition for Gay and Lesbian Equality v Minister of Justice* para 96.
67 *National Coalition for Gay and Lesbian Equality v Minister of Justice* paras 97–8.

11.4 Suspension of an order of invalidity

Where a court declares legislation or conduct invalid, this order will normally have immediate effect. However, section 172(1)(*b*)(ii) of the Constitution allows a court temporarily to suspend the effect of a declaration of invalidity in the interests of justice and equity after finding the law to be inconsistent with the Constitution. When the court suspends its order of invalidity, the invalid legislative provision remains operative on condition that Parliament corrects the defect within a prescribed period of time. If the matter is rectified, the declaration falls away and what was done in terms of the law is given validity. If not, the declaration of invalidity takes place at the expiry of the prescribed period and the normal consequences attaching to such a declaration ensue.[68]

A **suspension of an order of invalidity** is used sparingly as it will have the effect of not providing immediate and effective relief to the successful litigant. Where the invalidity arises in a complex case in which 'multifarious and nuanced legislative responses ... might be available to the legislature' to resolve the problem, the court may suspend its order of invalidity and provide Parliament with a grace period to resolve the problem.[69] A suspension of an order of invalidity is also appropriate where a lacuna or gap would be left in the law if the impugned provision is declared invalid. As the Constitutional Court explained in *J and Another v Director General, Department of Home Affairs and Others*:

> **The suspension of an order is appropriate in cases where the striking down of a statute would, in the absence of a suspension order, leave a lacuna. In such cases, the Court must consider, on the one hand, the interests of the successful litigant in obtaining immediate constitutional relief and, on the other, the potential disruption of the administration of justice that would be caused by the lacuna. If the Court is persuaded upon a consideration of these conflicting concerns that it is appropriate to suspend the order made, it will do so in order to afford the legislature an opportunity 'to correct the defect'. It will also seek to tailor relief in the interim to provide temporary constitutional relief to successful litigants.[70]**

The Court may also suspend an order of invalidity where the defect in the impugned legislation is purely procedural, for example in cases where Parliament has failed to facilitate adequate public involvement in the law-making process.[71] The time provided to Parliament to resolve the problem depends on the 'complexity and variety of the statutory and policy alternatives' available to Parliament.[72] Sometimes, proper legislation passed by Parliament is the only appropriate manner with which to deal with a constitutional defect in legislation.[73] It would also not be appropriate to invalidate legislation where such an order would be 'chaotic and prejudicial to the interests of justice and good government'.[74] The Court is more likely to exercise its powers to suspend the invalidity of pre-constitutional legislation than

---

68 *Executive Council of the Western Cape Legislature* para 106.

69 *Fraser v Children's Court Pretoria North and Others* (CCT31/96) [1997] ZACC 1; 1996 (8) BCLR 1085; 1997 (2) SA 218 (5 February 1997) (*Fraser I*) para 50. See also *Dawood* para 63; *South African National Defence Union v Minister of Defence and Others* (CCT65/06) [2007] ZACC 10; 2007 (5) SA 400; 2007 (8) BCLR 863 (CC); [2007] 9 BLLR 785 (CC); (2007) 28 ILJ 1909 (CC) (30 May 2007).

70 (CCT46/02) [2003] ZACC 3; 2003 (5) BCLR 463; 2003 (5) SA 621 (CC) (28 March 2003) para 21.

71 *Doctors for Life International v Speaker of the National Assembly and Others* (CCT12/05) [2006] ZACC 11; 2006 (12) BCLR 1399 (CC); 2006 (6) SA 416 (CC) (17 August 2006) para 114.

72 *Fraser I* para 51.

73 *Fraser I* para 50.

74 *Fraser I* para 51.

post-constitutional legislation.[75] When it declares invalid post-constitutional legislation, it would only suspend the order 'where the result of invalidating everything done under such legislation is disproportional to the harm which would result from giving the legislation temporary validity'.[76]

A court looks at the precise circumstances of each case to determine whether the order of invalidity should be suspended.[77] The court does not normally suspend an order of invalidity if the provisions are so 'clearly inconsistent' with a fundamental right and 'manifestly indefensible' under the general limitation clause that there is 'no warrant for its retention, not even temporarily'.[78] This means that there have to be persuasive reasons to exercise the power to suspend before a court will do so.[79]

In cases where the legislation limits a right of heightened importance - such as the right to non-discrimination guaranteed in section 9 of the Constitution - the Constitutional Court has found that:

> **those subject to the impugned provisions should not be made to wait much longer to be relieved of the burden of inequality and unfair discrimination ... [as] ... that would mean that the benefits of the Constitution would continue to be withheld from those who have been deprived of them for so long.[80]**

This places a burden on a litigant seeking a suspension of an order of invalidity (usually the State) to persuade the court to exercise its powers in terms of section 172(1)(*b*)(ii) of the Constitution in the interests of justice and equity.[81] It is important that all relevant information is placed before the Court when it is asked to suspend an order of invalidity. The information must relate to the consequences of an order of invalidity and the time that will be needed to remedy the defect in the legislation.[82]

A suspension of an order of invalidity can be seen as a technique used by the Constitutional Court to negotiate separation of powers tensions that may arise from invalidating legislation. As such, it can be seen as part of the constitutional dialogue between the three branches of government mentioned above. A consequence of this is that the power of Parliament is only partly circumscribed by the suspended order of invalidity. As long as the legislature amends the law to bring it into harmony with the Constitution, it has a wide discretion to choose the means to achieve this goal.

While Parliament (or any other legislature) may choose to correct the defect in the invalidated law within the period specified, it need not do so. If it chooses not to correct the defect in the period provided, the suspension will fall away and the law or provision will become invalid. The legislature may also take other steps to address the effect of the declaration of invalidity. In the latter two situations, the declaration of invalidity will come into effect on the specified date.[83]

---

75 *Executive Council of the Western Cape Legislature* para 108.

76 *Executive Council of the Western Cape Legislature* para 107.

77 *Fourie* para 135.

78 *Coetzee; Matiso* para 18; *S v Mbatha, S v Prinsloo* (CCT19/95, CCT35/95) [1996] ZACC 1; 1996 (3) BCLR 293; 1996 (2) SA 464 (9 February 1996) para 30.

79 *Bhulwana, Gwadiso* para 30; *Brink v Kitshoff NO* (CCT15/95) [1996] ZACC 9; 1996 (4) SA 197; 1996 (6) BCLR 752 (15 May 1996) para 51.

80 *Bhe and Others v Khayelitsha Magistrate and Others* (CCT 49/03) [2004] ZACC 17; 2005 (1) SA 580 (CC); 2005 (1) BCLR 1 (CC) (15 October 2004) para 108.

81 See Currie and De Waal (2001) 295.

82 See *Minister of Justice v Ntuli* (CCT15/97, CCT17/95) [1997] ZACC 7; 1997 (6) BCLR 677; 1997 (3) SA 772 (5 June 1997) para 41.

83 *Executive Council of the Western Cape Legislature* para 113.

CRITICAL THINKING

Suspending an order of invalidity

In *Minister of Home Affairs and Another v Fourie and Another*,[84] the Constitutional Court declared invalid the common law definition of marriage (as well as an omission in the Marriage Act[85]) because it did not permit same-sex couples to enjoy the status and the benefits it accords to heterosexual couples. However, the majority (per Sachs J) suspended this order for 12 months from the date of the judgment to allow Parliament to correct the defects. The Court ruled further that if Parliament did not correct the defects within this period, the order of invalidity would take effect.[86] The majority in effect argued that for pragmatic political reasons relating to the acceptance and legitimacy of the ruling, a suspension would be required to allow Parliament to resolve the problem:

> This is a matter involving status that requires a remedy that is secure. To achieve security it needs to be firmly located within the broad context of an extended search for emancipation of a section of society that has known protracted and bitter oppression. The circumstances of the present matter call out for enduring and stable legislative appreciation. A temporary remedial measure would be far less likely to achieve the enjoyment of equality as promised by the Constitution than would lasting legislative action compliant with the Constitution. The claim by the applicants in *Fourie* of the right to get married should, in my view, be seen as part of a comprehensive wish to be able to live openly and freely as lesbian women emancipated from all the legal taboos that historically have kept them from enjoying life in the mainstream of society. The right to celebrate their union accordingly signifies far more than a right to enter into a legal arrangement with many attendant and significant consequences, important though they may be. It represents a major symbolical milestone in their long walk to equality and dignity. The greater and more secure the institutional imprimatur for their union, the more solidly will it and other such unions be rescued from legal oblivion, and the more tranquil and enduring will such unions ultimately turn out to be.[87]

In a minority judgment O'Regan J disagreed, pointing out that the 'effect of this order is that gay and lesbian couples will not be permitted to marry during this period'.[88] O'Regan J stated that this case concerned the development of the common law by the courts, a responsibility that lies, in the first place, with the courts and not with the legislature.[89] This is why the Court ought to have developed the common law with immediate effect to permit gays and lesbians to be married by civil marriage officers.[90] The doctrine of the separation of powers cannot be used 'to avoid the obligation of a court to provide appropriate relief that is just and equitable to litigants who successfully raise a constitutional complaint'.[91] According to O'Regan J, the power

84 (CCT 60/04) [2005] ZACC 19; 2006 (3) BCLR 355 (CC); 2006 (1) SA 524 (CC) (1 December 2005).
85 Act 25 of 1961.
86 *Fourie* paras 132 and 162.
87 *Fourie* paras 136–7.
88 *Fourie* para 165.
89 *Fourie* para 167.
90 *Fourie* para 169.
91 *Fourie* para 170.

and duty to protect constitutional rights is conferred on the courts. This means the:

> courts should not shrink from that duty. The legitimacy of an order made by the Court does not flow from the status of the institution itself, but from the fact that it gives effect to the provisions of our Constitution. Time and again, there will be those in our broader community who do not wish to see constitutional rights protected, but that can never be a reason for a court not to protect those rights.[92]

Given the Constitutional Court's previous judgments in which it held that where the right implicated is of specific importance, a suspension would not ordinarily be granted, and in the absence of technical impediments to an immediate invalidation of the impugned provisions, it appears as if O'Regan J's view is more consistent with precedent.

11.5 A declaration of rights

Section 38 of the Constitution provides that when a right in the Bill of Rights has been infringed or threatened, a competent court may grant appropriate relief, including a **declaration of rights**. In *Rail Commuters Action Group v Transnet Ltd t/a Metrorail*, the Constitutional Court explained that 'declaratory relief is of particular value in a constitutional democracy which enables courts to declare the law, on the one hand, but leave to the other arms of government, the executive and the legislature, the decision as to how best the law, once stated, should be observed'.[93]

It is important to distinguish between a declaration of rights and a declaration of invalidity. This is because a declaration of rights is aimed only at resolving a dispute between specific parties and may be given even when no law or conduct has been found to be inconsistent with the Bill of Rights.[94] In addition, a declaration of rights, unlike a declaration of invalidity, is also a discretionary remedy in the sense that the claim lodged by an interested party for such an order does not in itself oblige the court handling the matter to respond to the question which it poses.[95]

Declaratory orders are routinely used alongside structural interdicts whereby a court declares the aspects in which the state has fallen short of its constitutional obligations and then requires compliance by way of a structural interdict. This enables the court to assert its role in performing the 'watchdog' function by proclaiming what a right in the Constitution entails and how it should be interpreted. It then further allows the court to retain jurisdiction over the case through the structural interdict.

11.6 An interdict

Interdicts are usually directed at future events and compel a defendant (or any party to the litigation) to perform a task or to refrain from undertaking a specific course of action. Apart from mandatory interdicts and prohibitory interdicts, the Constitutional Court has held that

---

92 *Fourie* para 171.

93 (CCT 56/03) [2004] ZACC 20; 2005 (2) SA 359 (CC); 2005 (4) BCLR 301 (CC) (26 November 2004) para 108.

94 See *National Director of Public Prosecutions v Mohamed NO and Others* (CCT44/02) [2003] ZACC 4; 2003 (1) SACR 561; 2003 (5) BCLR 476; 2003 (4) SA 1 (CC) (3 April 2003) para 58.

95 See *JT Publishing (Pty) Ltd and Another v Minister of Safety and Security and Others* (CCT49/95) [1996] ZACC 23; 1996 (12) BCLR 1599; 1997 (3) SA 514 (21 November 1996) para 15.

a structural interdict may be an appropriate remedy when a right in the Bill of Rights has been unjustifiably infringed.

A **structural interdict** is also referred to as a supervisory interdict. A structural interdict is a type of injunction which 'requires the government to report back to the court at regular intervals about the steps taken to comply with the Constitution'.[96] Essentially, this interdict compels the violator to rectify the breach of fundament rights under court supervision. This is usually achieved by requiring the official to report to the court on his or her efforts to comply with the order. This allows the courts to exercise a monitoring role over the administration of the order in cases that affect individual rights. Structural interdicts are often used when the courts are faced with any form of recalcitrant or incompetent official behaviour.

As the points set out above indicate, a structural interdict is an invasive remedy. This is because it allows the courts to inspect proposed plans and to ensure that they are not constitutionally suspect.[97] Despite its invasive nature, this remedy is used to avoid violating the separation of powers doctrine since the courts defer to the authority and expertise of the executive arm of government by allowing the relevant government department to formulate plans to give effect to the Constitution.

The Constitutional Court initially seldom issued structural interdicts. However, as we shall see when we discuss social and economic rights enforcement in chapter 16, the Court has issued several supervision and engagement orders in eviction cases.[98] The first time the Court issued a structural interdict was in the case of *August and Another v Electoral Commission and Others*[99] where the Electoral Commission was found to have violated prisoners' rights to vote. Recognising that it is the Electoral Commission's mandate to regulate the election process according to the applicable legislation, the Court directed the Electoral Commission to rectify the violation of constitutional rights. The approach taken by the Court was to require the Electoral Commission to furnish it with an affidavit within two weeks setting out exactly how the Commission would comply with the order.

The Constitutional Court issued its second structural interdict in the case of *Sibiya and Others v Director of Public Prosecutions: Johannesburg High Court and Others (Sibiya I)*.[100] This case arose as a result of the 1995 case of *S v Makwanyane and Another*[101] where the Court declared the death penalty to be inconsistent with the interim Constitution and ordered the substitution of lawful punishments for prisoners who had been sentenced to death. However, a decade later, finding that '[t]he process of the substitution of sentences has taken far too long',[102] the Court issued a structural interdict so that it could supervise the sentence-conversion process. The order required government to report by not later than 15 August 2005 to the Court on the enforcement of the order.[103] Once a comprehensive plan

96 Roach, K 'Crafting remedies for violations of economic, social and cultural rights' in Squires, J, Langford, M and Thiele, B (eds) (2005) *The Road to a Remedy: Current Issues in the Litigation of Economic, Social and Cultural Rights* 113.

97 Ebadolahi, M (2008) Using structural interdicts and the South African Human Rights Commission to achieve judicial enforcement of economic and social rights in South Africa *New York University Law Review* 83(5):1565–1606 at 1596.

98 See *Occupiers of 51 Olivia Road, Berea Township and 197 Main Street Johannesburg v City of Johannesburg and Others* (24/07) [2008] ZACC 1; 2008 (3) SA 208 (CC); 2008 (5) BCLR 475 (CC) (19 February 2008) para 14 and *Schubart Park Residents' Association and Others v City of Tshwane Metropolitan Municipality and Another* (CCT 23/12) [2012] ZACC 26; 2013 (1) SA 323 (CC); 2013 (1) BCLR 68 (CC) (9 October 2012).

99 (CCT8/99) [1999] ZACC 3; 1999 (3) SA 1; 1999 (4) BCLR 363 (1 April 1999).

100 (CCT45/04) [2005] ZACC 6; 2005 (5) SA 315 (CC); 2005 (8) BCLR 812 (CC); 2006 (1) SACR 220 (CC); [2005] JOL 14514 (CC) (25 May 2005).

101 (CCT3/94) [1995] ZACC 3; 1995 (6) BCLR 665; 1995 (3) SA 391; [1996] 2 CHRLD 164; 1995 (2) SACR 1 (6 June 1995).

102 *Sibiya I* para 59.

103 *Sibiya I* para 63.

had been formulated, a final judgment was handed down and the resolution of the matter was achieved.[104] This was notwithstanding that government had to make an application for an extension of the timeframe for compliance with the order.[105]

In *Residents of Joe Slovo Community, Western Cape v Thubelisha Homes and Others,*[106] the Constitutional Court granted an order for the eviction of residents of the Joe Slovo Informal Settlement in Cape Town. However, the Court required the applicants and the respondents, through their respective representatives, to engage meaningfully with each other with a view to reaching agreement on how the eviction should occur. The Court further directed the parties to report back to the Court on the implementation of its order as well as the allocation of permanent housing opportunities to those affected by the order. It further instructed that in the event of the order not being complied with by any party, or in the event of unforeseen difficulties, any party would have the right to approach the Court for an amendment, supplementation or variation of its order.

Structural interdicts usually take the form of a series of steps in pursuit of achieving the mutually acceptable and achievable implementation of a plan which provides for constitutional entitlements. The steps are as follows:

- The starting point is a declaration by the court that the conduct is not consonant with the provisions and duties stipulated in the Constitution.
- Thereafter, the court prescribes the conduct which is expected to bring the deficient conduct into conformity with the constitutional imperatives.
- The process is not a dictatorial, top-down process. The court invites the government department that has failed to perform its constitutional obligations to submit a comprehensive plan. This plan must rectify the incompatibility between the constitutional provisions and the conduct (or omission) that is being complained of.
- The responsible government department draws up the plan, taking cognisance of the department's budgetary and human resource constraints. The department must also take into account the sustainability of the plan in terms of the timeframe set for its implementation. In this regard, the department should set a series of achievable deadlines so that progress can consistently be monitored.
- Once the department has drawn up the plan, it presents the plan to the court. At this stage, the court invites comment by the plaintiff and any other interested parties to the litigation.
- The court then incorporates any constructive comments into the plan. The plan then becomes a binding order of court which the department must implement strictly in accordance with the deadlines and achievable targets set out in the plan.

CRITICAL THINKING

When the state fails to obey court orders

If the responsible government department does not draw up and submit a plan to the court, the court will reluctantly draw up its own plan which the government department will then have to implement. In such a case, the court may rely on the assistance of any other parties to the litigation who express an interest in assisting the court to craft the

104 *Sibiya and Others v Director of Public Prosecutions (Sibiya III)* (CCT45/04B) [2006] ZACC 22; 2006 (2) BCLR 293 (CC) (30 November 2006) paras 22–3.

105 *Sibiya and Others v Director of Public Prosecutions: Johannesburg High Court and Others (Sibiya II)* (CCT 45/04) [2005] ZACC 16; 2006 (2) BCLR 293 (CC); [2005] JOL 15699 (CC) (7 October 2005).

106 (CCT 22/08) [2009] ZACC 16; 2009 (9) BCLR 847 (CC); 2010 (3) SA 454 (CC) (10 June 2009) para 7.

plan. The consequence of this is that the judiciary then appears to intrude into the domain of the executive in the formulation of policy choices and the methods of implementation.

However, this argument can be countered with reference to the rule of law which is a founding value of our constitutional democracy. In South Africa, many people do not have the financial or other resources to approach a court to have legal duties owed to them enforced. When an order is handed down by a court, the rule of law is seriously threatened if the state fails to obey court orders.

The provisions of section 34, read with sections 165 and 173 of the Constitution, place positive duties on the state to ensure respect for the rule of law and adherence to the law by providing citizens with effective mechanisms for resolving disputes between themselves or between themselves and the state. Failure to comply with court orders then represents an attack on the effectiveness of the legal system and the right to have legal duties enforced by the state.

Apart from drawing up and submitting a comprehensive plan to the court, the responsible government department must also provide continuous feedback to the court on the status and success of the implementation of the plan according to the deadlines contained in the plan. In some instances, independent bodies, such as the South African Human Rights Commission, may be appointed to monitor the implementation of the plan.

When the matter is heard in court, the defendant, the monitoring body and other interested parties are entitled to address the court on the progress achieved in implementing the plan. The nature of a structural interdict entails that if the plan is seen to be deficient or unachievable, it may be amended and the amended plan then becomes the order of court. This is repeated until such time as the constitutional norms have been achieved.

11.7 Constitutional damages

Damages is a concept that is usually associated with private law relationships. **Damages** refers to a sum of money paid to a person to compensate him or her for harm that was caused to him or her either by the state or by another individual. Damages can also be paid to mitigate future loss suffered as a result of the wrongful conduct of an individual or the state.

The private law concept of damages is not designed to vindicate the values underlying the Constitution nor to deter and prevent future infringements. However, the Constitutional Court has accepted that where these objects can be achieved through the payment of compensation, it may be appropriate to issue an order awarding the complainant **constitutional damages**.

The Constitutional Court discussed the concept of constitutional damages for the first time in its judgment in *Fose*. In this case the Constitutional Court held as follows:

- Where the violation of human rights entails the commission of a delict, the award of constitutional damages in addition to damages available under the common law will seldom be available. This is because it would amount to awarding punitive damages against the state.
- Even when delictual damages are not available, constitutional damages will not always be granted.[107]

107 *Fose* para 58.

In *Fose*, Fose alleged that he had been assaulted and tortured by the police and claimed R130 000 in delictual damages for pain and suffering, loss of amenities of life and infringement of his dignity. In addition, he also claimed R200 000 in constitutional damages for the infringement of his constitutional rights to human dignity, freedom, security of the person and privacy.

In so far as his claim for constitutional damages was concerned, Fose argued that a private law action for damages seeks to provide compensation for harm caused to one private party by the wrongful action of another private party. However, a constitutional action for damages seeks to:

- vindicate the fundamental right itself
- deter and prevent future infringements of the fundamental right by organs of state
- punish those organs of state whose officials have infringed fundamental rights in an egregious manner.[108]

The Constitutional Court dismissed Fose's claim for constitutional damages on the grounds that he had already been awarded delictual damages and a person cannot benefit twice from the harm he or she has suffered.

In arriving at this decision, the Constitutional Court began by stating that there is:

> **no reason in principle why appropriate relief should not include an award of damages, where such an award is necessary to protect and enforce [the rights in the Bill of Rights]. Such awards are made to compensate persons who have suffered loss as a result of the breach of a statutory right if, on a proper construction of the statute in question, it was the legislature's intention that such damages should be payable, and it would be strange if damages could not be claimed for, at least, loss occasioned by the breach of a right vested in the claimant by the supreme law.**[109]

After finding that appropriate relief does include an award of constitutional damages where such an award is required to enforce or protect the rights in the Bill of Rights, the Constitutional Court turned to consider whether constitutional damages could also be claimed to deter or punish organs of state whose officials have infringed fundamental rights.

In this respect, the Constitutional Court began by stating that even though punitive constitutional damages are awarded in some comparative foreign jurisdictions such as the United States, serious criticisms have been levelled against this practice. These criticisms include the following:

- There is no evidence that punitive damages do have a deterrent effect.
- Punitive damages provide the plaintiff with an unjustifiable windfall.
- Punitive damages exact punishment without the protection which the criminal law affords.
- In those cases where punitive damages are awarded against the government, the cost involved is almost inevitably shifted to the public at large.[110]

Having set out these principles, the Constitutional Court went on to apply them to the facts. In this respect, the Court first dealt with Fose's claim for damages to vindicate his constitutional rights and then with his claim for damages to deter or punish the police for infringing his constitutional rights.

108 *Fose* para 17.
109 *Fose* para 60.
110 *Fose* para 65

In so far as the claim for vindicatory damages was concerned, the Constitutional Court began by stating that in the case at hand it was not necessary to award constitutional damages to vindicate the plaintiff's constitutional rights. This was because if Fose succeeded in proving that he had been assaulted by the police, he would be awarded substantial delictual damages and that would be enough to vindicate his constitutional rights.[111]

In addition, the Constitutional Court stated further, it is doubtful whether, even in the case of the infringement of a right which does not cause damage to a plaintiff, an award of constitutional damages to vindicate the right would be appropriate. This is because a declaratory order combined with a suitable order as to costs would be a sufficiently appropriate remedy to vindicate a plaintiff's rights even in the absence of an award of damages.[112]

In so far as the claim for punitive damages was concerned, the Constitutional Court began by stating that it was not persuaded that awarding punitive damages against the government would effectively deter the police from torturing suspects. This is because nothing in our own recent history, where substantial awards for death or brutality in detention were awarded or agreed to, suggested that they had any preventative effect.[113]

In addition, the Constitutional Court stated further, in a country where there is a great demand on scarce public resources, it would be inappropriate to use them to pay punitive damages to plaintiffs who had already been compensated by delictual damages for the injuries caused to them. The funds could be better employed in structural and systemic ways to eliminate or substantially reduce the causes of infringements.[114]

Having made these points, the Constitutional Court went on to dismiss the claim for constitutional damages.

Unlike in the case of *Fose*, constitutional damages were awarded in the case of *President of the Republic of South Africa and Another v Modderklip Boerdery (Pty) Ltd.*[115] This case concerned the positive obligations on the state to assist Modderklip to remove what had become approximately 80 000 trespassers from a portion of its farm.

After a High Court interdict for the eviction of the occupiers had not been complied with, a writ of execution was issued at Modderklip's instance. The sheriff of Benoni insisted on a deposit of R1,8 million to secure the costs of the eviction occasioned by the need to engage the services of a security firm to facilitate the removals. Even the police would not help Modderklip except to secure the peace during the eviction.

Having no other alternative, Modderklip approached the High Court. The High Court found that Modderklip's section 25 rights to property had been violated by the trespassing of the occupiers. In addition, the state had failed to realise its obligations under section 26 of the Constitution to seek, within its available resources, to achieve the realisation of the occupiers' right of access to adequate housing and land.

On appeal, the SCA agreed with the High Court's judgment and expended its energies on determining an appropriate remedy. In the circumstances, the SCA awarded compensation to the owner of the illegally occupied property. It determined the amount of such compensation with reference to section 12 of the Expropriation Act.[116]

111 *Fose* para 67.
112 *Fose* para 68.
113 *Fose* para 71.
114 *Fose* para 72.
115 (CCT20/04) [2005] ZACC 5; 2005 (5) SA 3 (CC); 2005 (8) BCLR 786 (CC) (13 May 2005).
116 Act 63 of 1975.

The Constitutional Court endorsed the SCA's judgment and held that the SCA had referred to a number of advantages which other forms of relief did not have. The award compensated Modderklip for the unlawful occupation of its property in violation of its rights. It also ensured that the unlawful occupiers would continue to have accommodation until suitable alternatives were found and it relieved the state of the urgent task of having to find such alternatives.[117]

The award for damages was further endorsed by the fact that the Constitutional Court was acutely aware of the fact that Modderklip had been forced into a dead-end by the unlawful occupation of its land and the recalcitrant behaviour of the state in assisting it to enforce the interdict to have the settlers removed. However, the *Modderklip* case is certainly not authority for the proposition that constitutional damages are always available.[118]

Although the cases where constitutional damages have been granted are not numerous, Currie and De Waal argue that such damages are necessary for at least two reasons:

- First, constitutional damages may be awarded where any other form of relief will not vindicate the right or deter future infringements. This may occur especially when the victim has missed a unique opportunity to exercise a fundamental right, such as voting, attending a religious ceremony or participating in an organised protest.
- Second, constitutional damages may be necessary to encourage victims to come forward and report on human rights violation, thus vindicating the Constitution.[119]

CRITICAL THINKING

Social assistance grants as a form of constitutional damages

Currie and De Waal argue that various judgments in which the courts have awarded social assistance grants to litigants may be seen as a form of constitutional damages. Referring to a slew of cases that arose in the mid-1990s, in which many grant holders successfully challenged the unlawfulness of the termination of their grants, but the reinstatement of grants or the payment of moneys owed was delayed, the authors argue as follows:

> **Faced with increasing numbers of applicants for welfare grants, the [provincial governments] soon started to fall behind with the processing of applications. This generated a second phase of litigation.**[120]

Rather than granting the usual mandamus remedy where there was a delay, the courts started to substitute their own decisions for those of government on a wide scale. If a decision was not made within a reasonable time, the High Courts were prepared, as a form of 'constitutional relief', to approve social assistance grants themselves, in addition ordering government to make available back-payment and interest. To an extent, the courts became an alternative forum for the processing of social grants.

117 *Modderklip* para 58.

118 *City of Johannesburg Metropolitan Municipality v Blue Moonlight Properties 39 (Pty) Ltd and Another* (CC) [2011] ZACC 33; 2012 (2) BCLR 150 (CC); 2012 (2) SA 104 (CC) (1 December 2011).

119 Currie and De Waal (2005) 219.

120 Currie and De Waal (2005) 223–4.

11.8 Meaningful engagement

Some remedies are aimed at directing role players to act in a manner more in accordance with the notion of participatory democracy. Courts can use these remedies to help deepen democracy and empower citizens who can easily feel alienated from the bureaucratic state. One such a remedy is the remedy of **meaningful engagement**. This remedy is similar in effect to the structural interdict.[121] The Constitutional Court granted this remedy for the first time in its judgment in *Occupiers of 51 Olivia Road, Berea Township and 197 Main Street Johannesburg v City of Johannesburg and Others.*[122]

In this case the Constitutional Court held that it would be unconstitutional for a municipality to evict unlawful occupiers without first engaging with them, individually and collectively, in a meaningful manner. In arriving at this decision, the Constitutional Court stated that the City:

> **must respect, protect, promote and fulfil the rights in the Bill of Rights. The most important of these rights for present purposes is the right to human dignity and the right to life. In light of these constitutional provisions a municipality that ejects people from their homes without first meaningfully engaging with them acts in a manner that is broadly at odds with the spirit and purpose of the constitutional obligations set out in this paragraph taken together.**[123]

Apart from the constitutional provisions referred to above, the Constitutional Court also stated that the duty to engage meaningfully with people who may be rendered homeless after being evicted is squarely grounded in section 26(2) of the Constitution. This is because section 26(2) imposes an obligation on every sphere of government to take reasonable legislative and other measures, within its available resources, to achieve the progressive realisation of the right of access to adequate housing.[124]

The test for reasonableness, the Constitutional Court went on to state, does not only impose an obligation on the City to engage meaningfully with potentially homeless persons, but also to respond to the concerns they raise during that process in a reasonable manner. This means that in some cases it may be reasonable to make permanent housing available and, in others, to provide no housing at all. The possibilities between these extremes are almost endless. As long as the response of the municipality in the engagement process is reasonable, however, that response complies with section 26(2).[125]

In the same judgment, the Constitutional Court also stated that engagement is a two-way process in which the City and those about to become homeless would talk to each other meaningfully in order to achieve certain objectives. While there is no closed list of objectives,

---

121 The High Court had previously adopted a similar method of insisting on constructive dialogue between the parties before handing down its order. In *Lingwood and Another v The Unlawful Occupiers of R/E of Erf 9 Highlands* 2008 (3) BCLR 325 (W) para 33, the Court refused an eviction order until such time as the parties had attempted to achieve a mutually acceptable solution. This case, along with the cases of *Sailing Queen Investments v The Occupants La Colleen Court* 2008 (6) BCLR 666 (W) and *Blue Moonlight Properties 39 (Pty) Ltd v Occupiers of Saratoga Avenue and Another* 2009 (1) SA 470 (W), established the trend towards the creation of meaningful engagement as a remedy.

122 (24/07) [2008] ZACC 1; 2008 (3) SA 208 (CC); 2008 (5) BCLR 475 (CC) (19 February 2008). See also *Port Elizabeth Municipality v Various Occupiers* (CCT 53/03) [2004] ZACC 7; 2005 (1) SA 217 (CC); 2004 (12) BCLR 1268 (CC) (1 October 2004) para 39 and *Residents of Joe Slovo Community*. See also Chenwi, L (2009) A new approach to remedies in socio-economic rights adjudication: *Occupiers of 51 Olivia Road and Others v City of Johannesburg and Others Constitutional Court Review* 2:371–93 at 373.

123 *Occupiers of 51 Olivia Road* para 16.

124 *Occupiers of 51 Olivia Road* para 17.

125 *Occupiers of 51 Olivia Road* para 18.

the Court explained further, the sorts of objectives that ought to be achieved when a city wishes to evict people who may be rendered homeless as a result of the eviction are as follows:

> (a) **what the consequences of the eviction might be;**
> (b) **whether the city could help in alleviating those dire consequences;**
> (c) **whether it was possible to render the buildings concerned relatively safe and conducive to health for an interim period;**
> (d) **whether the city had any obligations to the occupiers in the prevailing circumstances; and**
> (e) **when and how the city could or would fulfil these obligations'.**[126]

The order granted by the Constitutional Court thus provided as follows:

> 1. **The City of Johannesburg and the applicants are required to engage with each other meaningfully and as soon as it is possible for them to do so in an effort to resolve the differences and difficulties aired in this application in the light of the values of the Constitution, the constitutional and statutory duties of the municipality and the rights and duties of citizens concerned.**
> 2. **The City of Johannesburg and the applicants must also engage with each other in an effort to alleviate the plight of the applicants who live in the two buildings concerned in this application by making the buildings safe and as conducive to health as is reasonably practicable.**
> 3. **The City of Johannesburg and the applicants must file affidavits before this Court on or before 3 October 2007 reporting on the results of the engagement between the parties as at 27 September 2007.**[127]

The agreement reached between the parties contained interim measures to secure the safety of the building and to provide the occupiers with alternative accommodation in the inner City of Johannesburg. These interim measures included the provision, at the City's expense, of toilets, potable water, waste disposal services, fire extinguishers and a once-off operation to clean and sanitise the properties. The City and the occupiers also agreed that the alternative accommodation would consist of security against eviction, access to sanitation, access to potable water, and access to electricity for heating, lighting and cooking. Agreement was furthermore reached that the City would decide on the nature and location of permanent housing in consultation with the occupiers.

CRITICAL THINKING

Meaningful engagement as a means of enhancing participatory democracy

It has been convincingly argued that the remedy of meaningful engagement is 'a progressive and effective remedy capable of promoting social transformation and enhancing participatory democracy and transparency and accountability'.[128]

According to Chenwi, meaningful engagement recognises the core importance of fostering participation, especially by those confronted with the prospect of eviction. She states that 'the remedy fits into the Constitutional Court's vision of the kind of democracy the South African Constitution establishes'.[129]

126 *Occupiers of 51 Olivia Road* para 14.
127 *Occupiers of 51 Olivia Road* para 5.
128 Chenwi (2009) 373.
129 Chenwi (2009) 381.

Support for this view is the well known case of *Doctors for Life International v The Speaker of the National Assembly and Others*[130] where the Court held that our constitutional democracy contemplates both representative as well as participatory democracy.

SUMMARY

In every case of a *prima facie* violation (or threatened violation) of rights or the perceived contravention of the Constitution, one of the first questions the legal representative will ask is, 'What remedy do we want in order to vindicate the clients' right?' The remedy being sought will usually inform how the case is structured and argued. This is in accordance with the Latin maxim ***ubi ius ubi remedium*** – where there is a right, there is a remedy. This is the defining principle of the South African legal order with respect to the enforcement of the Constitution. It would be nonsensical for the Constitution to prescribe a comprehensive set of rights if there were no mechanisms created to uphold those rights. Therefore, with regard to the effectiveness of courts in awarding appropriate and enforceable remedies, it is appropriate to quote the late Chief Justice Mahomed when he said:

> **Unlike Parliament or the executive, the courts do not have the power of the purse or the army or the police to execute their will. The highest courts in constitutional democracies do not have a single solider at their command. They would be impotent to protect the Constitution if the agencies of the state that control the massive financial and physical resources refuse to command those resources to enforce the orders of the courts. The courts could easily be reduced to paper tigers with ferocious capacity to snarl and to roar but no teeth with which to bite and no sinews to execute their judgments which may be reduced to pieces of sterile scholarship, toothless wisdom or pious poetry. As already happened many times, the potentially awesome theoretical power of the judiciary in the Constitution could, in those circumstances, implode into nothingness. Judges in such circumstances would visibly be demeaned. But much, much worse, human rights could irreversibly be impaired and civilisation itself dangerously imperilled.**[131]

Invalidating legislation can have drastic consequences. Courts use various techniques to limit the drastic consequences of orders of invalidity, including suspending an order of invalidity to give Parliament a chance to remedy the defect, severing the bad parts of a provision from the good without invalidating an entire section and reading words into the statute to render it constitutionally valid.

130 (CCT12/05) [2006] ZACC 11; 2006 (12) BCLR 1399 (CC); 2006 (6) SA 416 (CC) (17 August 2006) paras 111 and 116.
131 Mahomed, I (1998) The independence of the judiciary *South African Law Journal* 115(4):658–67 at 658.

Chapter 12

Equality, human dignity and privacy rights

12.1 Introduction

The value of dignity is a central value underlying the Constitution and we could even say it is the cornerstone of the Constitution and the rights protected in it.[1] This is made clear by section 1(*a*) of the Constitution, which states that the Republic of South Africa is founded on the values of human dignity, the achievement of equality and the advancement of human rights and freedoms.[2] When considering the scope and content of the various rights in the Bill of Rights, it is important to understand that human dignity informs constitutional adjudication and interpretation and is 'a value that informs the interpretation of many, possibly all, other rights'.[3] It is a 'motif which links and unites equality and privacy', and which 'runs right through the protections offered by the Bill of Rights'.[4] The value of dignity permeates the Bill of Rights to contradict South Africa's apartheid past 'in which human dignity for black South Africans was routinely and cruelly denied'.[5]

As we shall see, dignity is not only a value that permeates the Bill of Rights and the Constitution as a whole; it is also a justiciable and enforceable right. In many cases where the value of human dignity is offended, the primary constitutional breach occasioned may be of a more specific right. Arguably, the most important of these rights in the South African context - given its history of discrimination - is the right to equality.[6] As we shall see, there is a strong link between the **value** of dignity and the enforcement of the right to equality and non-discrimination. The truth is that the value of dignity also undergirds most, if not all, of the other rights contained in the Bill of Rights.

It is not easy to pin down the content of the value of human dignity.[7] The Constitutional Court has recognised that, in the context of Bill of Rights adjudication, this value of human dignity recognises the inherent worth of all individuals as members of our society, as well as the value of the choices that they make. It comprises the 'deeply personal understanding we have of ourselves, our worth as individuals and our worth in our material and social context'.[8] The value of dignity asserts that every human being counts; that every human being has infinite value, regardless of his or her personal circumstances or actions. Given that every human being counts, every human being is entitled to be treated **as** a human being and to be valued. As we discuss the various rights in the Bill of Rights, it will be important to keep in mind that this notion of human dignity informs the approach taken by the Constitutional Court in interpreting and applying the various substantive rights.

---

1 See *S v Makwanyane* (CCT3/94) [1995] ZACC 3; 1995 (6) BCLR 665; 1995 (3) SA 391; [1996] 2 CHRLD 164; 1995 (2) SACR 1 (6 June 1995) para 329; *Teddy Bear Clinic for Abused Children and Another v Minister of Justice and Constitutional Development and Another* (CCT 12/13) [2013] ZACC 35; 2013 (12) BCLR 1429 (CC) (3 October 2013) para 52.

2 See Currie, I and De Waal, J (2013) *The Bill of Rights Handbook* 6th ed 250.

3 *Dawood and Another v Minister of Home Affairs and Others; Shalabi and Another v Minister of Home Affairs and Others; Thomas and Another v Minister of Home Affairs and Others* (CCT35/99) [2000] ZACC 8; 2000 (3) SA 936; 2000 (8) BCLR 837 (7 June 2000) para 35.

4 *National Coalition for Gay and Lesbian Equality and Another v Minister of Justice and Others* (CCT11/98) [1998] ZACC 15; 1999 (1) SA 6; 1998 (12) BCLR 1517 (CC) (9 October 1998) para 120.

5 *Dawood* para 35.

6 *Dawood* para 35.

7 For an admirable book-length attempt to do so, see Ackermann, L (2012) *Human Dignity: Lodestar for Equality in South Africa*.

8 *Teddy Bear Clinic* para 52. See also *Khumalo and Others v Holomisa* (CCT53/01) [2002] ZACC 12; 2002 (5) SA 401; 2002 (8) BCLR 771 (14 June 2002) para 27. See also Cameron, E (2012) Dignity and disgrace: Moral citizenship and constitutional protection, lecture delivered at the University of Oxford's Understanding Human Dignity Conference (26–29 June 2012) (as yet unpublished) at 10.

In this chapter we focus on the right to equality, the right to dignity and the right to privacy, the denial of which can arguably be said to have resulted in some of the most egregious forms of injustice during the apartheid era and continue to rob many people of respect and concern. The denial of these rights has drastic direct and personal effects on individuals, but it would be a mistake to view these rights only in such individualistic terms. Often, the manner in which society is structured, the cultural assumptions deeply embedded in society and the vast inequalities between rich and poor have a direct and lasting effect on the denial of these rights. It is therefore impossible not to consider these rights against the backdrop of the broader social, economic and political context and to remain mindful of how the broader context influences our understanding of the operation of these rights. It would therefore be a mistake to analyse these rights and the jurisprudence of the Constitutional Court relating to these rights (or any other rights protected in the Bill of Rights for that matter) in an a-contextual or overtly formalistic manner. It must always be remembered that rights are aimed at protecting individual human beings and at promoting their well-being and ability to make meaningful life choices. This means that the actual lived reality of individuals and the effects of impugned actions or omissions by both the state and private parties will always be centre stage when considering breaches of the rights in the Bill of Rights.[9]

PAUSE FOR REFLECTION

The broader context within which rights adjudication takes place

The social and economic realities of South Africa (including deep inequality and an uneven distribution of social and economic privileges), some cultural beliefs and practices as well as sometimes deeply entrenched prejudices and harmful beliefs all potentially affect the ability of individuals to live lives of dignity and respect. The provisions in the Bill of Rights cannot on their own eradicate these factors which hamper the realisation of the rights in the Bill of Rights. While human rights can be invoked to help facilitate the South African transformation, more systemic problems require concerted action from other important role players, including the government of the day, civil society groups, religious institutions, unions, political parties, business and individual citizens.

However, by taking account of the broader context in South Africa within which rights adjudication takes place, the Constitutional Court acknowledges that the full harm of the denial of human rights cannot be identified and addressed by merely looking in a formalistic and a-contextual manner at individual litigants and asking whether that litigant was harmed. This approach recognises that South Africa's colonial and apartheid history created a society that is profoundly unfair and unjust. It also acknowledges that deeply entrenched forms of patriarchy, homophobia as well as a long history of political oppression, have not fostered a culture of respect for diversity and for democratic values of openness, tolerance and broadmindedness. When interpreting rights in the Bill of Rights and when deciding whether rights are being infringed, these realities can therefore not be denied.

9 See *Sanderson v Attorney-General, Eastern Cape* (CCT10/97) [1997] ZACC 18; 1997 (12) BCLR 1675; 1998 (2) SA 38 (2 December 1997) para 23.

12.2 The right to equality and non-discrimination

12.2.1 Introduction: substantive equality versus formal equality

Apartheid systematically discriminated against black South Africans in all aspects of economic and social life. As the Constitutional Court has pointed out:

> **Black people were prevented from becoming owners of property or even residing in areas classified as 'white', which constituted nearly 90% of the landmass of South Africa; senior jobs and access to established schools and universities were denied to them; civic amenities, including transport systems, public parks, libraries and many shops were also closed to black people. Instead, separate and inferior facilities were provided. The deep scars of this appalling programme are still visible in our society. It is in the light of that history and the enduring legacy that it bequeathed that the equality clause needs to be interpreted.**[10]

But it is not only black people who have suffered and sometimes continue to suffer from discrimination. Women, gay men and lesbians, people with disabilities, HIV-positive people, foreigners, religious minorities and many individuals with distinctive attributes or characteristics have also suffered marginalisation and exclusion and to some extent still do. When considering the scope and content of the right to equality, it is important to have regard to these realities.

No two people in the world are identical in terms of their attributes, characteristics, intelligence or other talents. Nor do people enjoy identical benefits and opportunities as they grow up. This is particularly true in South Africa, a country in which vast discrepancies in wealth, educational opportunities and access to resources led to an unequal distribution of opportunities. Race, class and gender differences have also had an impact and perpetuate the subordination of black people, women, gay men, lesbians and the poor. A person's inborn talents, predisposition and the status accorded to him or her based on irrelevant considerations such as race, gender or sexual orientation, as well as other factors such as the quality of education he or she receives, the access he or she has to financial and other resources, and the opportunities and support parents or caregivers are capable of providing, influence the extent to which he or she manages to live a rich and fulfilled life. Through no fault of their own, different people from different backgrounds have an unequal chance to reach their goals in life.

The right to equality is guaranteed in section 9 of the Bill of Rights. Section 9 reads as follows:

> **(1) Everyone is equal before the law and has the right to protection and benefit of the law.**
>
> **(2) Equality includes the full and equal enjoyment of all rights and freedoms. To promote the achievement of equality, legislative and other measures designed to protect or advance persons, or categories of persons, disadvantaged by unfair discrimination may be taken.**
>
> **(3) The state may not unfairly discriminate directly or indirectly against anyone on one or more grounds, including race, gender, sex, pregnancy, marital status, ethnic or social origin, colour, sexual orientation, age, disability, religion, conscience, belief, culture, language and birth.**

10 *Brink v Kitshoff NO* (CCT15/95) [1996] ZACC 9; 1996 (4) SA 197; 1996 (6) BCLR 752 (15 May 1996) para 40.

(4) No person may unfairly discriminate directly or indirectly against anyone on one or more grounds in terms of subsection (3). National legislation must be enacted to prevent or prohibit unfair discrimination.

(5) Discrimination on one or more of the grounds listed in subsection (3) is unfair unless it is established that the discrimination is fair.

Section 9 thus aims to address some of the unfairness inherent in this state of affairs while also providing a legal framework to prevent unfair treatment of individuals based on their race, sex, gender, sexual orientation, disability and other personal characteristics or attributes. As such, the right to equality is an essential component of the transformative Constitution. The reason for this is that the right to equality encapsulates the aspiration of eventually achieving a society in which all enjoy equal access to the resources and amenities of life, and are able to develop their full human potential.[11]

Two important consequences flow from this conception of the right to equality:

- First, the right to equality cannot entail a guarantee that all people should be treated identically at all times, regardless of their personal attributes or characteristics, social or economic status. The right should therefore be viewed as entailing more than a formal prohibition against discrimination.
- Second, the right to equality must guarantee more than equality before the law and must focus on the **effects or impact** of legal rules or other differentiating treatment on individuals. The right to equality cannot therefore focus merely on whether two people have been treated in an identical manner by the legal rule or by the institution or individual concerned. The idea of **substantive equality** best captures this approach to equality jurisprudence.

We can contrast substantive equality with the traditional, liberal idea of **formal equality**.[12] Underlying formal equality is the belief that inequality is irrational and arbitrary, that people are all born free and equal, and that the harm of discrimination is situated in the failure of a government to treat all people as equally free.[13] Formal equality focuses on the formal way in which the law treat individuals or groups. It explicitly denies the need to take into account the social and economic context or the differences in power, status and opportunities between individuals or groups of individuals when judging whether the equality injunction has been breached or not. Formal equality demands that all people should be treated in the same manner, regardless of their personal circumstances, their history, their social and economic status, and whether they have been discriminated against in the past or still face discrimination in the present.[14] Formal equality demands neutrality and does not accommodate different treatment of people who are socially and economically different from one another.

The concept of formal equality is often criticised because this neutral approach to equality masks forms of bias. It ignores the fact that neutral standards often embody the interests and experiences of socially privileged groups whose views and attitudes are so dominant that they have become invisible and appear to be neutral. Formal equality is also

11 Langa, P (2006) Transformative constitutionalism *Stellenbosch Law Review* 17(3):351–60 at 352–3. See also Albertyn, C and Goldblatt, B 'Equality' in Woolman, S and Bishop, M (eds) (2013) *Constitutional Law of South Africa* 2nd ed rev service 5 35.5.

12 Currie and De Waal (2013) 213.

13 See De Vos, P (2000) Equality for all? A critical analysis of the equality jurisprudence of the Constitutional Court *Tydskrif vir Hedendaagse Romeins-Hollandse Reg* 63(1):62–75 at 65; Albertyn and Goldblatt (2013) 35.6.

14 De Vos (2000) 65.

said to ignore the actual social and economic differences between people, how this affects people's chances in life and the different power wielded by different individuals and groups in society. As such, an insistence on the formal equal treatment of all people – regardless of their social and economic status – may exacerbate the inequality of socially and economically marginalised and vulnerable groups. It does this by ignoring the actual inequality between the dominant or privileged groups and marginalised and vulnerable groups and the ways in which seemingly neutral rules continue to advantage the privileged and dominant in society.[15]

Substantive equality, however, proceeds from the understanding that there are structural or systemic reasons why not all individuals enjoy equal opportunities to reach their full life potential. Substantive equality focuses on the actual economic, social and political conditions of groups and individuals in society. As the Constitutional Court pointed out:

> **Particularly in a country such as South Africa, persons belonging to certain categories have suffered considerable unfair discrimination in the past. It is insufficient for the Constitution merely to ensure, through its Bill of Rights, that statutory provisions which have caused such unfair discrimination in the past are eliminated. Past unfair discrimination frequently has ongoing negative consequences, the continuation of which is not halted immediately when the initial causes thereof are eliminated, and unless remedied, may continue for a substantial time and even indefinitely. Like justice, equality delayed is equality denied.**[16]

Substantive equality asks what impact differentiating legal rules or other differentiating treatment will have on groups or individuals, given differences in the social and economic status of such groups or individuals, and given the way in which existing 'neutral' legal rules privilege the economically and culturally dominant and powerful in society. A legal commitment to substantive equality therefore entails attention to the context. This context includes the social and economic inequalities in society, the effects of past and ongoing prejudice and discrimination on the basis of race, sex, gender, sexual orientation, disability, economic status and other grounds on the life opportunities of individuals. The context also includes the manner in which private relationships, such as marriage and child-rearing duties, continue to be structured in ways that produce or perpetuate disadvantage and subordination. The focus is on the impact of the treatment instead of the treatment itself. Substantive equality is remedial in nature and aims to overcome the effects of past and ongoing prejudice and discrimination as well as the broader structural reasons for the disempowerment and economic disadvantage faced by some individuals or groups in society.

The South African Constitutional Court has embraced the notion of substantive equality, stating in *Minister of Finance and Other v Van Heerden* that:

> **This substantive notion of equality recognises that besides uneven race, class and gender attributes of our society, there are other levels and forms of social differentiation and systematic under-privilege, which still persist. The Constitution enjoins us to dismantle them and to prevent the creation of new patterns of disadvantage. It is therefore incumbent on courts to scrutinise in each equality claim**

15 Albertyn and Goldblatt (2013) 35.6. See also Albertyn, C and Goldblatt, B (1998) Facing the challenge of transformation: Difficulties in the development of an indigenous jurisprudence of equality *South African Journal on Human Rights* 14(2):248–76 at 152–3.

16 *National Coalition for Gay and Lesbian Equality v Minister of Justice* para 60.

> **the situation of the complainants in society; their history and vulnerability; the history, nature and purpose of the discriminatory practice and whether it ameliorates or adds to group disadvantage in real life context, in order to determine its fairness or otherwise in the light of the values of our Constitution. In the assessment of fairness or otherwise a flexible but 'situation-sensitive' approach is indispensable because of shifting patterns of hurtful discrimination and stereotypical response in our evolving democratic society. The unfair discrimination enquiry requires several stages.**[17]

It is clear from this approach that the context within which a court must judge an equality case is of primary importance to determine whether there was a breach of section 9. This context in which the court must judge an equality case is formed, first, by the constitutional text in its entirety. Second, the court must take into account the country's recent history, particularly the systematic discrimination suffered by black people under apartheid[18] as well as systematic patterns of discrimination on grounds other than race that have caused, and may continue to cause, considerable harm.[19] Any consideration of whether a legally relevant differentiation actually constitutes a breach of section 9 must therefore take into account the history of the impugned provision as well as the history of the group or groups to which the complainant belongs. Taking this context into account, the court determines whether the legally relevant differentiation aims to create or perpetuate patterns of group disadvantage, or whether it aims to break down these structural inequalities and thus reach for true or substantive equality. If the latter is the case, the court will be reluctant to declare the measures unconstitutional or unlawful.[20]

Because the court's approach requires **a contextual analysis**, it may thus take into account the ongoing structural inequality in society when deciding on the unfairness of the discrimination.[21] The court's contextual or remedial approach acknowledges that inequality results from complex power relations in society. It appears to view the law as having an important role in reordering these power relations in ways which strive to ensure that all individuals are treated as if they have the same moral worth. Disadvantage here, then, is not equated with different treatment of individuals who are born free and equal. Disadvantage is rather equated with some harmful impact, whether direct or indirect, that the differentiation between groups might have on a set of complainants within the historical context of South Africa.[22]

As mentioned above, the focus is on the impact of the treatment instead of the treatment itself. Substantive equality is remedial in nature and aims to overcome the effects of past and ongoing prejudice and discrimination. It requires a retreat from legal formalism and a

---

17 (CCT 63/03) [2004] ZACC 3; 2004 (6) SA 121 (CC); 2004 (11) BCLR 1125 (CC); [2004] 12 BLLR 1181 (CC) (29 July 2004) para 27. See also *Brink* para 40; *President of the Republic of South Africa and Another v Hugo* (CCT11/96) [1997] ZACC 4; 1997 (6) BCLR 708; 1997 (4) SA 1 (18 April 1997) para 41; *Prinsloo v Van der Linde and Another* (CCT4/96) [1997] ZACC 5; 1997 (6) BCLR 759; 1997 (3) SA 1012 (18 April 1997) para 31; *City Council of Pretoria v Walker* (CCT8/97) [1998] ZACC 1; 1998 (2) SA 363; 1998 (3) BCLR 257 (17 February 1998) para 46; *Hoffmann v South African Airways* (CCT17/00) [2000] ZACC 17; 2001 (1) SA 1; 2000 (11) BCLR 1235; [2000] 12 BLLR 1365 (CC) (28 September 2000).

18 *Brink* para 40. See also *Walker* para 26 where Langa DP stated that the assessment of discrimination cannot be undertaken in a vacuum, 'but should be based both on the wording of the section and in the constitutional and historical context of the developments in South Africa'.

19 *Brink* para 41.

20 *Brink* para 41.

21 See, for example, *Harksen v Lane NO and Others* (CCT9/97) [1997] ZACC 12; 1997 (11) BCLR 1489; 1998 (1) SA 300 (7 October 1997) para 51(b).

22 See De Vos (2000) 66.

focus on the underlying purpose of the right to equality – what harm it seeks to address – as well as the values underlying equality. The harm to be addressed rests on at least three pillars:

- the culturally constructed ideology of differences based on the belief in the superiority of dominant groups and the inferiority of non-dominant groups
- the economic exploitation and disempowerment of those without power because of their race, sex, gender, sexual orientation or other attributes
- in the South African context, also the previous political disenfranchisement of black South Africans.[23]

PAUSE FOR REFLECTION

Distinguishing between formal equality and substantive equality

To distinguish between formal equality and substantive equality, it may be helpful to focus on a specific example. Where a guesthouse catering to gay and lesbian tourists refuses to accommodate any heterosexual clients, that guesthouse would be treating people differently based on their sexual orientation. A heterosexual couple who are denied accommodation at the guesthouse may feel that they have been discriminated against on the basis of their sexual orientation as they have been denied accommodation purely because they are heterosexual. A court that adheres to a formal notion of equality may have to find in favour of the heterosexual couple on the basis that the guesthouse treats gay men and lesbians differently from heterosexuals to the detriment of the latter group. Formally, the guesthouse rule denies the heterosexual couple a benefit that is not denied to gay men and lesbians.

A court that embraces a substantive notion of equality may look at the larger social and economic context. The court may acknowledge that gay men and lesbians continue to suffer from prejudice, stigmatisation and discrimination. They may therefore feel vulnerable and exposed in situations where they are required to book into a guesthouse along with heterosexual clients. In an ordinary guesthouse, gay and lesbian couples may fear being subjected to the prejudices (presumed or real) of non-homosexual clients. This may inhibit them from showing affection for one another and may detract from their enjoyment of their stay.

The guesthouse in our example aims to provide a safe space for gay men and lesbians where couples can openly express physical affection for one another and interact in loving and intimate ways with each other as heterosexual couples do every day in public. They can do so in a manner in which they may not be able to do when they fear the judgment of heterosexuals staying at the establishment.

The court embracing substantive equality may find that this different treatment is not in breach of the equality guarantee. Heterosexual couples will have no problem in finding alternative accommodation because there is no widespread discrimination against them in society. The guesthouse rule will not send a signal that heterosexuals are somehow less worthy of concern and respect than gay men and lesbians. The court will take into account the broader context. This context includes the fact that heterosexuals are not generally believed to be marginalised or suffering from patterns of discrimination, disadvantage or harm. In addition, different treatment will not establish

23 Botha, H (2009) Equality, plurality and structural power *South African Journal on Human Rights* 25(1):1–37 at 7.

new patterns of discrimination, disadvantage and harm by a powerful group over a disempowered and vulnerable group. The court may therefore well dismiss a complaint of discrimination brought by a heterosexual couple.[24] For exactly the same reasons, the court will find a guesthouse that prohibits black people from staying at its establishment guilty of discrimination as such an exclusion will perpetuate long-standing patterns of discrimination and prejudice.

In the following sections we first set out the basic assumptions underlying the substantive approach to equality as well as the values implied by the right to equality. We then focus on two distinct situations in which the right to equality arises:

- cases where individuals are treated differently but where this different treatment does not explicitly address the effects of past and ongoing prejudice and discrimination
- cases where the different treatment is explicitly justified on the grounds that it addresses the effects of past and ongoing prejudice and discrimination (so-called affirmative action measures or better referred to as redress measures).

We also discuss the Promotion of Equality and Prevention of Unfair Discrimination Act (PEPUDA).[25] The PEPUDA gives legislative effect to section 9 of the Constitution and is often relied on instead of section 9 itself.

12.2.2 Differentiation and discrimination

The idea of differentiation lies at the heart of South Africa's equality jurisprudence.[26] Not all forms of differentiation are constitutionally problematic: relatively benign forms of differentiation between people or groups of people permeate human relations in a modern society and the Constitution does not usually prohibit the law from making such distinctions. A modern state is required to regulate the affairs of its inhabitants extensively. It is impossible to do so without differentiation and without classifications that treat people differently and which affect people differently.[27]

Moreover, private individuals or institutions differentiate daily between individuals in many ways. These numerous forms of differentiation are seldom problematic from a constitutional law perspective and the vast majority of cases in which people or groups of people are treated differently from one another are legally benign.

However, some forms of differentiation by the state or by private parties do infringe on the right to equality guaranteed in section 9 of the Constitution. As we shall see, the Constitutional Court draws a sharp distinction between **mere differentiation** dealt with in terms of section 9(1) of the Constitution and discrimination dealt with in terms of section 9(3) of the Constitution.

The consequence of this distinction between mere differentiation and discrimination is that questions around discrimination dominate the Constitutional Court's approach to

24 For a real-life example, see Kassiem, A (2006, 26 June) Guest houses can be for gay men only available at http://www.iol.co.za/news/south-africa/guest-houses-can-be-for-gay-men-only-1.283071.

25 Act 4 of 2000.

26 *Prinsloo* para 23.

27 *Prinsloo* para 24.

equality.[28] It is clear that for a claimant to succeed with an equality challenge, it will usually (but not in every case) be necessary to frame a claim about a breach of section 9 of the Constitution as one of discrimination rather than in terms of a general claim to equality or a claim of differentiation. The Constitutional Court has chosen to focus its equality jurisprudence on the notion of discrimination rather than on the more 'complex', 'elusive' and 'empty'[29] notion of equality or on all cases of differentiation. This choice stems from a need to provide a suitably 'structured' and 'focused' legal framework that will provide an effective and easy-to-apply legal test to determine whether the equality guarantee has been breached.[30]

The Constitutional Court views the concept of non-discrimination as providing the legal mechanism that will deal effectively with egregious forms of inequality and different treatment while avoiding the opening of the litigation floodgates. By focusing on targeted forms of discrimination instead of on the more general equality guarantee dealing with all forms of differentiation, the Court aims to discourage well-resourced litigants in the private sector from challenging every conceivable form of legal differentiation. The Constitutional Court therefore focuses on the importance of non-discrimination and sees it as a safe and more or less predictable way of dealing with the difficult issues of equality with which it has been, and no doubt will continue to be, confronted.[31]

12.2.3 Values underlying the right to equality: human dignity and equality

The judges of the Constitutional Court have unanimously embraced the idea that at its core, the equality guarantee protects individuals' human dignity. The centrality of the value of human dignity for equality jurisprudence was first established in *President of the Republic of South Africa and Another v Hugo* where the Court placed human dignity at the heart of its equality enquiry.[32] The Court stated:

> **The prohibition on unfair discrimination in the interim Constitution seeks not only to avoid discrimination against people who are members of disadvantaged groups. It seeks more than that. At the heart of the prohibition of unfair discrimination lies a recognition that the purpose of our new constitutional and democratic order is the establishment of a society in which all human beings will be accorded equal dignity and respect regardless of their membership of particular groups (our emphasis).**[33]

28 *Brink*; *Prinsloo*; *Hugo*; *Harksen*; *Larbi-Odam and Others v Member of the Eexecutive Council for Education (North-West Province) and Another* (CCT2/97) [1997] ZACC 16; 1997 (12) BCLR 1655; 1998 (1) SA 745 (26 November 1997); *Walker*; *National Coalition for Gay and Lesbian Equality v Minister of Justice*; *Hoffmann*; *Moseneke and Others v Master of the High Court* (CCT51/00) [2000] ZACC 27; 2001 (2) BCLR 103; 2001 (2) SA 18 (6 December 2000); *Satchwell v President of Republic of South Africa and Another* (CCT45/01) [2002] ZACC 18; 2002 (6) SA 1; 2002 (9) BCLR 986 (25 July 2002); *J and Another v Director General, Department of Home Affairs and Others* (CCT46/02) [2003] ZACC 3; 2003 (5) BCLR 463; 2003 (5) SA 621 (CC) (28 March 2003); *Du Toit and Another v Minister of Welfare and Population Development and Others* (CCT40/01) [2002] ZACC 20; 2002 (10) BCLR 1006; 2003 (2) SA 198 (CC) (10 September 2002); *Bhe and Others v Khayelitsha Magistrate and Others* (CCT 49/03) [2004] ZACC 17; 2005 (1) SA 580 (CC); 2005 (1) BCLR 1 (CC) (15 October 2004); *Volks NO v Robinson and Others* (CCT12/04) [2005] ZACC 2; 2005 (5) BCLR 446 (CC) (21 February 2005); *Minister of Home Affairs and Another v Fourie and Another* (CCT 60/04) [2005] ZACC 19; 2006 (3) BCLR 355 (CC); 2006 (1) SA 524 (CC) (1 December 2005); *Gory v Kolver NO and Others* (CCT28/06) [2006] ZACC 20; 2007 (4) SA 97 (CC); 2007 (3) BCLR 249 (CC) (23 November 2006). See also Pretorius, JL (2010) Fairness in transformation: A critique of the Constitutional Court's affirmative action jurisprudence *South African Journal on Human Rights* 26(3):536–70.

29 See generally Fagan, A (1998) Dignity and unfair discrimination: A value misplaced and a right misunderstood *South African Journal on Human Rights* 14(2):220–47 at 220; and Westen, P (1982) The empty idea of equality *Harvard Law Review* 95(3):537–96 at 537.

30 *National Coalition for Gay and Lesbian Equality v Minister of Justice* para 122.

31 De Vos (2000) 64.

32 (CCT11/96) [1997] ZACC 4; 1997 (6) BCLR 708; 1997 (4) SA 1 (18 April 1997).

33 *Hugo* para 41.

The Court accepts that the equality guarantee protects individuals from differentiation based on one of the specified grounds in section 9(3) or similar forms of differentiation that have the potential to infringe on a person's fundamental human dignity. Conversely, where differentiation is not based on one of the specified grounds and where it does not have the potential to infringe on a person's fundamental human dignity, there will be no unfair discrimination in terms of section 9(3) of the Constitution.

The Constitutional Court has provided quite a broad and expansive definition of human dignity. It has stated that human dignity will be impaired whenever a legally relevant differentiation treats people as 'second-class citizens', 'demeans them', 'treats them as less capable for no good reason', otherwise offends 'fundamental human dignity' or where it violates an individual's self-esteem and personal integrity.[34] This idea of dignity is based on the notion that all human beings have an equal moral worth - the right to be treated with equal concern and respect - and derives from the work of Immanuel Kant.[35]

This view of equality as inextricably linked to the concept of dignity has been reiterated in subsequent Constitutional Court judgments[36] and has further been elaborated on, most notably in *Prinsloo v Van der Linde and Another*.[37] However, in this case, the Court gave an even more expansive interpretation of when treatment will be discriminatory. It added that not only an infringement of human dignity, but also 'other forms of differentiation, which in some other way affect persons adversely in a comparably serious manner', could constitute a harm prohibited by the non-discrimination provisions of the Constitution.[38] Where legal provisions deny this equal moral worth, the Court will find that there has been an impairment of human dignity or that the complainant has been adversely affected in a comparably serious manner. This is a confirmation of Malherbe's proposition that 'equality without dignity is inhuman'.[39]

CRITICAL THINKING

Does South African dignity-based equality jurisprudence narrow the understanding of the right to equality?

Some academics have criticised the South African dignity-based equality jurisprudence on the basis that it can narrow the understanding of the right to equality to an abstract and individualised notion about the personal feelings of a litigant who feels hurt by prejudice and misrecognition.[40] The fear is that the reliance on the value of dignity would focus equality jurisprudence on the individual harm caused by prejudice as well as on the narrow need to address such harms. This narrow focus on the individual and the harm suffered by him or her, so the argument goes, runs the risk of ignoring the larger social and economic disadvantages as well as the systemic nature of inequality in South African society.

For example, some people argue that a dignity-based approach to equality can powerfully address issues of discrimination against gay men, lesbians and other sexual

34 *Hugo* para 41. See also Albertyn and Goldblatt (1998) 257.

35 See Woolman, S 'Dignity' in Woolman and Bishop (2013) 36.3.

36 *Hugo* para 41; *Prinsloo* paras 31–3; *Harksen* para 50.

37 (CCT4/96) [1997] ZACC 5; 1997 (6) BCLR 759; 1997 (3) SA 1012 (18 April 1997).

38 *Prinsloo* para 33. See also *Harksen* para 50: 'Whether or not there is discrimination will depend upon whether, objectively, the ground is based on attributes and characteristics which have the potential to impair the fundamental human dignity of persons as human beings or to affect them adversely in a comparably serious manner.'

39 Malherbe, R (2007) Some thoughts on unity, diversity and human dignity in the new South Africa *Tydskrif vir die Suid Afrikaanse Reg/Journal of South African Law* 70(1):127–33 at 132.

40 Albertyn and Goldblatt (1998) 256–60.

minorities. The reason for this is that such discrimination is rooted in moral disapproval and results directly in an affront to their dignity and identity.[41] By contrast, the fear is that discrimination against women or black people can often not be captured fully in terms of a dignity-based analysis. Such discrimination results from a complex mix of superficially neutral laws, entrenched structural inequality and cultural stereotypes.[42] South Africa has a sexist, racist and homophobic past. Prejudices based on race, gender and sexual orientation continue to linger in our society. Discrimination faced by many women, black people and to a lesser extent gay men and lesbians, thus also has an economic component. This component cannot easily be captured with reference to an infringement of a person's dignity.

However, the Constitutional Court's contextual approach to equality has allowed it to move beyond a narrow, individualised notion of equality focused on individual personal autonomy, psychology and self-worth. This contextual approach has permitted a systematic understanding of individual, group-based, civil, political and material inequalities. Dignity is thus linked to the achievement of a world in which the basic needs of all people will be met.[43] In *Khosa and Others v Minister of Social Development and Others, Mahlaule and Another v Minister of Social Development*,[44] the Constitutional Court recognised that the dignity of individuals will not be respected if the material conditions do not exist to allow for such a respect for dignity. It also suggested that dignity is a group-based concept involving a collective concern for the well-being of others and that the allocation of resources is important for considering equality concerns:

> **Sharing responsibility for the problems and consequences of poverty equally as a community represents the extent to which wealthier members of the community view the minimal well-being of the poor as connected with their personal well-being and the well-being of the community as a whole. In other words, decisions about the allocation of public benefits represent the extent to which poor people are treated as equal members of society.**[45]

Apart from the value of dignity, the Constitutional Court has also affirmed that the value of equality is relevant for any understanding of section 9 of the Constitution especially when dealing with the restitutionary aspects of equality. In *Van Heerden*, the Constitutional Court affirmed the Constitution's commitment to strive for a society based on social justice. Equality thus requires more than equal protection before the law and non-discrimination, 'but also the start of a credible and abiding process of **reparation** for past exclusion, dispossession, and indignity within the discipline of our constitutional framework'.[46] As the Court per Moseneke DCJ argued:

> **What is clear is that our Constitution and in particular section 9 thereof, read as a whole, embraces for good reason a substantive conception of equality inclusive of**

41 Botha (2009) 8.
42 Botha (2009) 9.
43 Albertyn and Goldblatt (2013) 35.10. See, for example, *Government of the Republic of South Africa and Others v Grootboom and Others* (CCT11/00) [2000] ZACC 19; 2001 (1) SA 46; 2000 (11) BCLR 1169 (4 October 2000) para 23.
44 (CCT 13/03, CCT 12/03) [2004] ZACC 11; 2004 (6) SA 505 (CC); 2004 (6) BCLR 569 (CC) (4 March 2004).
45 *Khosa* para 74.
46 *Van Heerden* para 25.

measures to redress existing inequality. Absent a positive commitment progressively to eradicate socially constructed barriers to equality and to root out systematic or institutionalised underprivilege, the constitutional promise of equality before the law and its equal protection and benefit must, in the context of our country, ring hollow.[47]

12.2.4 Attacking the constitutionality of a legislative provision: section 9 of the Constitution

12.2.4.1 Introduction

Different legal tests apply to different situations in which an equality complaint is lodged. First, where a distinction between different people stems from a legislative provision and the litigant asks a court to declare that legislative provision invalid, the court has to rely directly on sections 9(1), 9(2) or 9(3) of the Constitution. These three sections apply in different situations and, as we shall see, require the court to apply a different legal test in each case. It is important to identify whether a set of facts dealing with a complaint about different treatment between people or groups of people fits under section 9(1), 9(2) or 9(3). The court then applies the relevant test applicable to that set of facts. When attacking the constitutionality of a legislative provision, it is therefore important, at the outset, to determine whether the attack will be based on section 9(1), 9(2) or (9(3). A direct reliance on section 9 is required in such cases because legislation can only be invalidated by invoking the Constitution itself. This is because the Constitution is supreme and therefore superior to the legislative provision under attack.

Second, where a litigant attacks the actions of a public official or private entity on equality grounds but this attack does not relate to the possible invalidation of a legislative provision, the litigant will have to rely on the relevant provisions of the PEPUDA. This is because the principle of subsidiarity requires a litigant who claims that one of his or her constitutional rights has been infringed must rely on legislation adopted to protect that right. The litigant may thus not rely on the underlying constitutional provision directly. Unless the litigant wants to attack the constitutionality of the legislative provision itself, he or she cannot rely on section 9 as the PEPUDA gives effect to section 9 and will be the first port of call.[48] Given that the PEPUDA gives effect to section 9 of the Constitution, it must be interpreted in the light of the Constitutional Court's jurisprudence on section 9. We therefore first discuss the Constitutional Court's jurisprudence regarding section 9 before turning to the PEPUDA as the general principles discussed when dealing with section 9 apply in the interpretation of the PEPUDA.

As noted above, section 9 deals with three distinct situations. First, section 9(1) applies in cases where the legislative provision differentiates between people or groups of people, but this differentiation is not based, either directly or indirectly, on one of the grounds listed

---

47 *Van Heerden* para 31.

48 *South African National Defence Union v Minister of Defence and Others* (CCT65/06) [2007] ZACC 10; 2007 (5) SA 400; 2007 (8) BCLR 863 (CC); [2007] 9 BLLR 785 (CC); (2007) 28 ILJ 1909 (CC) (30 May 2007) paras 51–2; *MEC for Education: Kwazulu-Natal and Others v Pillay* (CCT 51/06) [2007] ZACC 21; 2008 (1) SA 474 (CC); 2008 (2) BCLR 99 (CC) (5 October 2007) paras 39–40; *Walele v City of Cape Town and Others* (CCT 64/07) [2008] ZACC 11; 2008 (6) SA 129 (CC); 2008 (11) BCLR 1067 (CC) (13 June 2008) paras 29–30; *Nokotyana and Others v Ekurhuleni Metropolitan Municipality and Others* (CCT 31/09) [2009] ZACC 33; 2010 (4) BCLR 312 (CC) (19 November 2009) paras 47–9. See also Van der Walt, AJ (2008) Normative pluralism and anarchy: Reflections on the 2007 term *Constitutional Court Review* 1:77–128 at 100–03.

in section 9(3) or on an **analogous ground** that is similar to the grounds explicitly listed in section 9(3). We refer to such cases as cases of mere differentiation.[49]

In *Prinsloo*, the Court explained that it would be impossible to govern a modern country like South Africa efficiently and to harmonise the interests of all its people for the common good without differentiation and classifications which treat people differently and affect them differently. Such differentiations which are necessary to regulate the affairs of a country, or mere differentiations, will, according to the Court, rarely constitute discrimination in and of themselves.[50] Mere differentiation therefore refers to the many distinctions that the law makes that have nothing to do with the kind of discrimination based on race, sex, gender or other grounds listed in or similar to those listed in section 9(3) of the Constitution. For example, where the legislative provision makes a distinction between lawyers and doctors, a litigant attacking that provision will have to rely on section 9(1) as section 9(3) does not explicitly prohibit discrimination against a group of people who are identified as doctors or lawyers.

Second, section 9(2) applies to cases where the legislative provision explicitly aims to give effect to restitutionary measures. These measures are also popularly known as affirmative action measures. If a legislative provision aims to implement a restitutionary measure, the court first tests the constitutionality of that provision under section 9(2). If the restitutionary measure complies with section 9(2), that is the end of the enquiry. The provision is constitutionally valid and cannot be tested against section 9(3).[51] As we shall see, this is important as the onus of proving or disproving an infringement of section 9 may differ depending on whether a litigant relies on section 9(2) or section 9(3). However, if the legislative provision does not comply with section 9(2), the court can still test it against section 9(3). In other words, the court uses section 9(2) to test legislative provisions that implement affirmative action measures. However, when it finds that such measures do not comply with section 9(2), the court can test their constitutionality against section 9(3).

The third instance is whenever the different treatment is based either directly or indirectly on one or more of the grounds listed in section 9(3) or on a ground that the Court has found to be sufficiently similar to the grounds listed in section 9(3) to be considered under that section. Also, the different treatment should not form part of an affirmative action programme or policy. Here, the court must test the provision against section 9(3). In the case of listed grounds or grounds sufficiently similar to the grounds listed in section 9(3), it is not necessary to invoke section 9(1) first. The litigant complaining of discrimination as opposed to complaining about mere differentiation may directly invoke section 9(3).[52] As noted, this situation is distinguished from mere differentiation as it relates to different treatment on the basis of race, sex, gender, sexual orientation or one of the other problematic distinctions and is referred to as discrimination.

In the sections that follow, we deal with the test to be applied to the three situations:

- differentiation that amounts to mere differentiation (section 9(1))
- different treatment mandated to advance an affirmative action policy (section 9(2))
- differentiation that amounts to discrimination but is not part of an affirmative action policy (section 9(3)).

---

49 *Prinsloo* para 25.
50 *Prinsloo* paras 23–4.
51 *Van Heerden* para 33.
52 *National Coalition for Gay and Lesbian Equality v Minister of Justice* para 18.

Although the Constitutional Court stated that it would be neither desirable nor feasible to separate sections 9(1) and 9(3) into watertight compartments, it nevertheless focused on section 9(1) as dealing with mere differentiation while section 9(3) was earmarked as dealing with unfair discrimination.[53]

Table 12.1 Framework for challenging different treatment

Legal nature of differentiation	Example	Legal provision relied on
Legislative provision constituting mere differentiation	A legal provision that requires cigarette products but not alcohol products to carry warning labels	Section 9(1) of the Constitution
Legislative provision introducing an affirmative action programme	Employment Equity Act (EEA)[54] provisions requiring certain employers to institute affirmative action policies	Section 9(2) of the Constitution
Legislative provision that distinguishes directly or indirectly between groups based on grounds listed in section 9(3) or analogous grounds	A legislative provision that grants women but not men the right to a certain number of days of pregnancy leave	Section 9(3) of the Constitution
An act by a private or public body or person that distinguishes directly or indirectly between groups of people based on grounds set out in section 9(3) or analogous grounds	A holiday resort which allows only Christians to visit or an affirmative action policy of a small company	Section 14 of the PEPUDA

12.2.4.2 Mere differentiation: section 9(1)

Given the Constitutional Court's focus on discrimination when dealing with equality claims, it is not surprising that cases of mere differentiation are not easy to prove. Recall that cases of mere differentiation are dealt with in terms of section 9(1) which states: 'Everyone is equal before the law and has the right to equal protection and benefit of the law.' According to the Constitutional Court, this section means:

- first, that everybody is entitled, at the very least, to equal treatment by our courts of law
- second, that none should be above or beneath the law and that all are subject to law impartially applied and administered.[55]

Examples of mere differentiation include distinctions between different types of prisoners or distinctions between different classes of taxpayers. Impugned provisions involving mere differentiation will fall foul of both aspects of section 9(1)[56] if a litigant can show that the

53 *Prinsloo* para 22.
54 Act 55 of 1998.
55 *Prinsloo* para 22, quoting, in part, Didcott in *S v Ntuli* (CCT17/95) [1995] ZACC 14; 1996 (1) BCLR 141; 1996 (1) SA 1207 (8 December 1995) para 18. See also *Walker* para 27.
56 *Prinsloo* para 25 and *Walker* para 27.

state did not act in a **rational manner** when differentiating between individuals or groups of individuals. This means that the state 'should not regulate in an arbitrary manner or manifest "naked preferences" that serve to legitimise governmental purpose'.[57] What is required is that the state functions 'in a rational manner'[58] and that it does not distinguish between people or groups of people in a way that is irrational.

This requirement of **rationality** has emerged as an extremely stringent test which is very difficult for any plaintiff alleging mere differentiation to overcome.[59] This requirement is made even more apparent by the Constitutional Court's insistence that there is no need for the state or other relevant actors to prove that the objective could not have been achieved in a better or different way in such a case.[60] As long as any rational relationship, in other words, the absence of arbitrariness,[61] is demonstrated between the purpose sought to be achieved by the impugned provision and the means chosen by the provision, the Court will find that the differentiation does not infringe section 9(1) of the Constitution.[62]

Rationality is part of accountability and justification in a democratic state. It is important in a rationality enquiry 'to identify and examine the specific government object sought to be achieved by the impugned rule of law or provision' and a court will not rely on a generic general purpose identified.[63] However, all the state has to show is that the purpose was neither arbitrary nor irrational. It does not have to show that the purpose pursued was a wise one or one with which the Court agrees.[64]

Where there is no discernible purpose for the differentiation, the Court will find the legislative provision to be in breach of section 9(1). For example, in *Ngewu and Another v Post Office Retirement Fund and Others*,[65] the Court declared certain sections of the Post Office Act[66] unconstitutional as they breached section 9(1) of the Constitution. This was because the impugned provisions treated divorced spouses of employees of the Post Office differently from other divorced spouses whose treatment is regulated by other legislation. The Constitutional Court found that this differentiation was irrational as it had no basis. The different treatment was an anomaly that could not be explained in a rational manner.[67] As the different treatment was not based on a ground like race or sex or gender, but on whether a person worked for the Post Office or another employer, the Court relied on section 9(1) to invalidate the provisions of the Post Office Act. However, because the rationality test is

---

57 *Prinsloo* para 25.

58 *Prinsloo* para 25.

59 See Mendes, E 'The crucible of the Charter' in Beaudoin, GA and Mendes, E (eds) (1996) *The Canadian Charter of Rights and Freedoms* 3.20; Tribe, LH (1988) *American Constitutional Law* 2nd ed 1442–3.

60 *Prinsloo* para 35.

61 *Harksen* para 43.

62 *Prinsloo* paras 24–6.

63 *Van der Merwe v Road Accident Fund and Another* (CCT48/05) [2006] ZACC 4; 2006 (4) SA 230 (CC); 2006 (6) BCLR 682 (CC) (30 March 2006) para 33. See also *Jooste v Score Supermarket Trading (Pty) Ltd (Minister of Labour intervening)* (CCT15/98) [1998] ZACC 18; 1999 (2) SA 1; 1999 (2) BCLR 139 (27 November 1998).

64 In *Jooste* para 16 the Constitutional Court explained this as follows:

> **It is clear that the only purpose of rationality review is an inquiry into whether the differentiation is arbitrary or irrational, or manifests naked preference and it is irrelevant to this inquiry whether the scheme chosen by the legislature could be improved in one respect or another. Whether an employee ought to have retained the common law right to claim damages, either over and above or as an alternative to the advantages conferred by the Compensation Act, represents a highly debatable, controversial and complex matter of policy. It involves a policy choice which the legislature and not a court must make. The contention represents an invitation to this Court to make a policy choice under the guise of rationality review; an invitation which is firmly declined.**

65 (CCT 117/11) [2013] ZACC 4; 2013 (4) BCLR 421 (CC) (7 March 2013).

66 Act 44 of 1958.

67 *Ngewu* para 17.

applied relatively strictly, the Court does not often invalidate legislation because it breaches section 9(1) of the Constitution.

12.2.4.3 Redress measures (affirmative action): section 9(2)

12.2.4.3.1 Basic approach

The question of the exact scope of constitutionally permissible redress measures (affirmative action) is one of the most hotly debated and, for some, most controversial, constitutional law issues. Disagreement on this issue can be traced back to different views about the extent to which the harmful consequences of racism and racial discrimination which were imposed by the apartheid government continue to render present-day South Africa a fundamentally unfair place for many (if not all) black South Africans. If we accept that the harmful effects of past racial discrimination stubbornly persist in society and that racism continues to disadvantage black South Africans, the need for redress measures to overcome this will be apparent. For those who deny these facts, however, redress measures - especially redress measures based on race - represent a form of reverse discrimination. As we shall see, however, the Constitutional Court has clearly rejected the latter view in favour of the first. Section 9(2) states:

> **Equality includes the full and equal enjoyment of all rights and freedoms. To promote the achievement of equality, legislative and other measures designed to protect or advance persons, or categories of persons, disadvantaged by unfair discrimination may be taken.**

This section recognises that the achievement of equality requires the state and other powerful institutions in society to take positive steps to address the deep social and economic inequalities in society. In addition, the state and other powerful institutions must also address the structures and systems in society that help to perpetuate this inequality. These structures and systems prevent individuals from enjoying equal opportunities and benefits that will allow them to flourish because opportunities and benefits are available to some people but not to others in society.[68]

This recognition lies at the heart of the notion of substantive equality discussed above. As indicated above, the substantive notion of equality recognises that there are uneven race, class and gender levels and forms of social and systemic differentiation. This type of differentiation continues to persist in South African society and requires positive action to dismantle it and to prevent the creation of new **patterns of disadvantage.**[69] As the Constitutional Court stated in *Van Heerden*, the precedent-setting case on section 9(2), corrective or restitutionary measures are mandated by section 9(2) as part of a 'credible and abiding process of reparation for past exclusion, dispossession, and indignity within the discipline of our constitutional framework'.[70]

The United States anti-discrimination approach regards restitutionary measures as an exception to the general equality and non-discrimination guarantee. By contrast, the South African equality jurisprudence does not view such measures as a deviation from or invasion of the right to equality guaranteed by the Constitution. These measures are not reverse

68 *Brink* para 42. See generally *Walker*.

69 *Van Heerden* para 27.

70 *Van Heerden* para 25.

discrimination or positive discrimination.[71] Instead, corrective or restitutionary measures are an integral part of our equality guarantee. They aim to eradicate a system that perpetuates inequality and to address social and economic inequality to achieve equality in the long term. South Africa is a country in transition from a society based on inequality to one based on equality.[72] Thus, the constitutional order is committed to the transformation of our society from a grossly unequal society to one in which there is equality between men and women and people of all races. In this fundamental way, our Constitution differs from other constitutions which assume that all are equal and in so doing simply entrench existing inequalities. This constitutionally mandated transformation is part of an ongoing process. It is not an end in itself but a means to an end: the achievement of equality in the long term.[73]

Of course, there are profound difficulties that will have to be confronted in giving effect to the constitutional commitment of achieving equality. This is because the measures that bring about transformation will inevitably adversely affect some members of our society, particularly those people coming from previously advantaged communities. However, as we shall see, the interests of those people negatively affected by such remedial measures must be balanced against the interests of those people who suffered discrimination in the past and may very well continue to suffer from discrimination today. This is why section 9(2) mandates positive measures. This means section 9(2) 'imposes a positive duty on all organs of state to protect and promote the achievement of equality - a duty which binds the judiciary too'.[74] In the absence of 'a positive commitment progressively to eradicate socially constructed barriers to equality and to root out systematic or institutionalised under-privilege, the constitutional promise of equality before the law and its equal protection and benefit must, in the context of our country, ring hollow'.[75]

A constitutional challenge to restitutionary measures - even based on any of the grounds of discrimination listed in section 9(3) - must be tested against section 9(2). Once a court has determined that the measures comply with the requirements of section 9(2), they cannot be presumed to be unfairly discriminatory and cannot be tested against section 9(3).[76] This means that if it is shown that measures comply with section 9(2), this is a complete defence against any charge that the measures unfairly discriminate against anyone.

The onus for an enquiry into the constitutionality of restitutionary measures differs from the onus in cases where it is alleged that a person has been unfairly discriminated against on one of the grounds listed in section 9(3) in a situation where the discrimination was not part of a set of restitutionary measures. In the latter case, once a court has established that there was indeed discrimination on one of the grounds listed in section 9(3), the onus of showing that the discrimination is not unfair rests with the party defending the different

71 See the debate on the nature of these measures in Currie and De Waal (2013) 241–2; Gutto, S (2001) *Equality and Non-Discrimination in South Africa: The Political Economy of Law and Law Making* 204–5. See also Du Plessis, L and Corder, H (1994) *Understanding South Africa's Transitional Bill of Rights* 144–5; Pretorius, JL (2001) Constitutional standards for affirmative action in South Africa: A comparative overview *Heidelberg Journal of International Law* 61(8):403–57 at 403; Van Reenen, TP (1997) Equality, discrimination and affirmative action: An analysis of section 9 of the Constitution of the Republic of South Africa *SA Publiekreg/Public Law* 12(1):151–65 at 151; Dupper, O (2004) In defence of affirmative action *South African Law Journal* 121(1):187–215; Dupper, O, MacEwan, M and Louw, A (2006) Employment equity in the tertiary sector in the Western Cape *International Journal of Discrimination and the Law* 8(3):191–212; De Vos, P (2012) The past is unpredictable: Race, redress and remembrance in the South African Constitution *South African Law Journal* 129(1):73–103.

72 *Van Heerden* para 73.

73 *Van Heerden* para 75.

74 *Van Heerden* para 24.

75 *Van Heerden* para 31.

76 *Van Heerden* para 33.

treatment. However, in cases where the constitutionality of restitutionary measures is attacked, the onus rests with the party who alleges that the measures are unconstitutional. Legislative and other measures, which properly fall within the provision of section 9(2), do not attract a presumption of unfairness.[77]

CRITICAL THINKING

The aim of redress measures: equality of opportunity or equality of outcomes?

When considering the aim of redress measures (as with all measures aimed at achieving substantive equality), the question arises as to the exact end goal of such measures. Are we striving to achieve equality of opportunity or equality of outcomes? Fargher presents the following thoughtful argument for the equality of outcomes:

> If you lean just enough against the window of your business class seat to discomfort yourself, you can see the shanty towns as you come into land at Cape Town International Airport. South Africa is unequal. And we know it. In fact, we are told in multiple headlines that South Africa is the most unequal country in the world. But what we aren't told is what that means, why it matters and what we should do to respond.
>
> Inequality, as most people think of it, is simply the existence of both rich and poor. In other words, there is some inequality in the outcome of people's lives. If we interrogate ourselves, I think many people would find that it is not inequality of outcomes that is so problematic. If I choose not to work and live a modest, subsistence lifestyle, I don't think many people would think I deserve to earn as much as a teacher or doctor that works many hours a day. Really, what many people find inherently objectionable is inequality of opportunity.
>
> Many libertarians will tell you this and I am sure a couple of CEOs are nodding their head in agreement, thinking to themselves, "That's right. It's not about taxing my income anymore, it's about fixing education so that everyone has the opportunity to work as hard as I have for my money." But in reality, there still seems to be something so unsettling about driving from Alexandra township through to Sandton. There seems to be something so wrong with the inequality of outcomes in South Africa that must prompt us to look past inequality of opportunity and focus on the sheer inequality of outcomes. And there is.
>
> I would argue that there are three primary reasons why South Africa needs to address inequality of outcomes. First, the extreme spectrum of wealth in South Africa means the very poor simply do not have sufficient means to lead a dignified and humane life. We have a responsibility to provide a minimum standard of life to our fellow human beings. Second, South Africa is not a society where inequality of outcomes has arisen as the result of chance.
>
> Instead, we can identify the unjust acts under apartheid and colonialism that specifically engineered the repression and robbery of black people in our society. While most of the laws may be gone, there remains the obligation to ensure corrective justice. This raises difficult questions of blame, guilt and how one practically ensures restitution in the face of intergenerational injustice.

77 *Van Heerden* paras 34–5.

These two questions of basic standards of living and restitution, whether land or money, have been debated at length. I, however, think there is a third, more nuanced reason that demands our consideration. The third reason is that inequality of outcomes fundamentally obscures our conception of what it means to have equal opportunity and thus hinders our ability to deliver a society in which we maximize equality of opportunity.

Even a society with perfect equality of opportunity suffers from the fact that unequal outcomes result in unequal power distribution. This power is used to favour elites. At first, I am sure your thoughts turned to business deals going to the politically connected or corporates colluding for illegitimate profits. Rather turn your thoughts to the more subtle and morally ambiguous ways in which society operates.

What about the inheritance you received or plan to leave? What about places in top schools for children of alumni, large donors or simply those whose parents can afford it? Or the jobs and internships you gave to the son of a friend or the daughter of a colleague?

Even well intentioned power brokers that explicitly work to create a society truly characterized by equality of opportunity are necessarily required to decide what the concept of opportunity means and what the barriers to equality of opportunity are. And extreme inequality of outcomes means that those in power may not know what the barriers to opportunities are. In South Africa's case, this is at an extreme.

The result of apartheid is a society that is starkly segregated in such a way that private power, economic class, culture, geography and race are largely divided along the same lines. The result is that white middle-class South Africans can live their lives in such a way that they rarely have to interact on the terms of the average, poor black South African. Sure, increasingly there are instances where the `best friend' might be black but he is likely to have interacted on the terms of white South Africans: he's middle class, he attended his model C school and forked out the R50 to go watch movies at the mall.

This is a dangerous situation where the influential in society – and here I mean us: the white professionals, professors, business leaders – do not understand the extent and nature of the inequality of opportunities. In fact, without structures to ensure a proliferation of views of what the conception of equal opportunity is, it is difficult to even know what needs to be done to ensure it ....

Furthermore, at the many interviews I have done in my life, almost every company says they want a candidate who will get on with the team, fit into the company's "culture" or who the boss will enjoy spending 10 hours a day working with. How can that person be a poor black person if the rest of the team are white, middle-class men who have never engaged on the terms of the average black South African?

Similarly, it's often asked why Africans rarely turn entrepreneurs and seize the opportunities that BEE has offered. But the decision of striking it out on your own is heavily influenced by your attitude toward risk, your role models and your community's expectations. Can you even understand the barriers to equal opportunity in entrepreneurship that community and personal mentalities impose on someone who's grown up in a society characterized by generational destitution versus someone who's been surrounded by successful business people?

What this argument should illustrate is that there exists an inherent tension between equality of opportunity and equality of outcomes. Being aware that inequality of outcomes limits our ability to ensure a society that strives for equality of opportunity, we may need to adopt policies that prima facie work against equality of opportunity.

For example, we need AA appointments in companies so that that person will one day be in management and able to say, "These are the difficulties people growing up in the townships of Eldorado Park face. I understand them and so I am not adverse to the person who offers me a soft handshake and I love talking with her about memories of shisa nyama on Sundays".

To what extent we need to make that trade-off depends on how well we understand the lives of our fellow countrymen. Unfortunately in South Africa, there are few public spaces we all interact in, few public goods we all share and cross race, class and cultural understanding must be one of the poorest in the world.

This reality needs to inform our discussions of policy in general. When we consider policies like a year of compulsory community service for school-leavers, most of the debate surrounds the economic impact but what about the role such a policy would have in creating a space where the poor and the rich, black and white, interact? Or should all school-goers learn an African language?

While personally I thought it was a terrible idea, with little to no direct economic benefit, I have come to realise that perhaps in the context of allowing our future power brokers to interact and understand South Africa on the average South African's term, it could be immensely valuable.

Alexis de Tocqueville, a French philosopher, remarked when he arrived in America that he'd never seen a country so free and equally led. He wasn't amazed by the fact that everyone earned the same, but that the equality meant that leaders governed whilst fully cognizant of the circumstances of their fellow men.

Inequality, of both outcomes and opportunity, is so problematic in South Africa because we have opportunities being ever suppressed for the poor and a corporate and government leadership that is becoming ever more out of touch with those realities.[78]

78 Fargher, M (2013, 5 October) White-washed equality Politicsweb available at http://www.politicsweb.co.za/politicsweb/view/politicsweb/en/page71619?oid=412294&sn=Detail&pid=71616.

12.2.4.3.2 The test for redress (affirmative action) measures in terms of section 9(2)

To determine whether a set of corrective measures complies with section 9(2) and is therefore constitutionally valid, a court will focus on three distinct questions:

- Do the measures target persons or categories of persons who have been disadvantaged by unfair discrimination?
- Are the measures designed to protect or advance such persons or categories of persons?
- Do the measures promote the achievement of equality in the long term?

a) Do the measures target persons or categories of persons who have been disadvantaged by unfair discrimination?

The first question focuses on the group that is being targeted for advancement because it was previously subjected to unfair discrimination and continues to suffer from the effects of that discrimination. With section 9(3), the focus is on the effect of non-restitutionary discriminatory measures on those people complaining of discrimination. By contrast, this requirement asks whether the right group was targeted for advancement or whether undeserving groups or individuals will benefit from the restitutionary measures. A court asks **whether the programme of redress is designed to protect and advance a disadvantaged class**. This means that the measures of redress chosen must favour a group or category designated in section 9(2). The beneficiaries, either individuals or categories of persons who belong to an identifiable class defined by their race, sex, gender, disability or sexual orientation, must be shown to have been disadvantaged by unfair discrimination. Because the test focuses on whether the group has been disadvantaged in the past by unfair discrimination, such groups include black (rather than white) citizens; women (rather than men); gay men and lesbians (rather than heterosexuals); people living with disabilities (rather than able-bodied people); and people living with HIV (rather than HIV-negative people).

The Constitutional Court has acknowledged the fact that it would be difficult, impractical or undesirable always to devise a legislative scheme or programme that 'purely' or precisely targets the affected classes. 'Within each class, favoured or otherwise, there may indeed be exceptional or "hard cases" or windfall beneficiaries'.[79] The Court thus acknowledges that not all the members of a class targeted to benefit from restitutionary measures may themselves have suffered from unfair discrimination or may have been disadvantaged because of the effects of past discrimination. However, we contend that as long as patterns of racism, sexism, homophobia or other prejudices exist in society, even those members of a class who may be economically privileged would normally still suffer from the effects of past unfair discrimination. Nevertheless, not every single person who benefits from a restitutionary programme needs to have been disadvantaged by unfair discrimination. What is required is that an 'overwhelming majority of members of the favoured class are persons designated as disadvantaged by unfair exclusion'.[80]

CRITICAL THINKING

Is the programme of redress designed to protect and advance a disadvantaged class?

The case of *Van Heerden* revolved around a remedial programme that targeted individuals who became Members of Parliament (MPs) in 1994 by providing such members with more advantageous pension benefits for a period of five years. The programme

79 *Van Heerden* para 39.
80 *Van Heerden* para 40.

excluded individuals who were Members of the apartheid Parliament and continued to serve in Parliament after 1994. The majority judgment found that this remedial programme did indeed meet this first requirement.

The minority judgment of Mokgoro J in *Van Heerden* disagreed with the approach taken by the majority about the precision with which a targeted class had to be defined. Mokgoro J pointed out that in this case many beneficiaries who became MPs in 1994 were not black but indeed white. There were 251 members elected to the national legislature for the first time in 1994. Of these, 53 were white. This means that only 79% of the beneficiaries of the higher rate were black. For the minority this meant that the restitutionary measures were not tailored sufficiently narrowly to pass the first leg of the section 9(2) test. At the heart of this disagreement was a disagreement about the level of scrutiny that the Court should impose on such measures.[81] Mokgoro justified her view as follows:

> **[S]ection 9(2) must be used only in appropriate cases and with great circumspection. The vision of substantive equality and the need for transformation cannot be underestimated. For that reason section 9(2), as an instrument for transformation and the creation of a truly equal society, is powerful and unapologetic. It would therefore be improper and unfortunate for section 9(2) to be used in circumstances for which it was not intended. If used in circumstances where a measure does not in fact advance those previously targeted for disadvantage, the effect will be to render constitutionally compliant a measure which has the potential to discriminate unfairly. This cannot be what section 9(2) envisages.[82]**

A possible reason for the majority's application of this requirement in a relatively permissive manner may be its recognition that for measures to fit snugly into the first requirement set out above, the measures may well explicitly have to target a group that has been unfairly discriminated against. As Sachs J pointed out, in the present case this was not done. Instead of race, the measures distinguished between members of the legislature who became members in 1994 and others who were members of the non-democratic Parliament, avoiding any mention of race. As Sachs J stated, 'For the new scheme to have distinguished on grounds of race or previous political affiliation between individual persons in this large and diverse new generation of members of Parliament, would have been divisive and invidious.'[83] By using other criteria as a proxy for race (or sex or sexual orientation), those who craft a remedial scheme may choose not to rely on the very categories used in the past to exclude and oppress people. This is an attempt to signal that we should not accept these categories uncritically and that it is not advisable in the long term to entrench such categories in law.

However, commentators have pointed out that race remains relevant in South Africa. As De Vos wrote:

> **But race hovers not far from the surface in private or other everyday settings: as an unspoken presence, a (wrongly) perceived absence or as a painful, confusing, liberating or oppressive reality in social, economic or other – more intimate**

81 Albertyn and Goldblatt (2013) 35.35.
82 *Van Heerden* para 87.
83 *Van Heerden* para 155.

– interactions between individuals or between groups of individuals. In South Africa we cannot escape the fact that – despite the best efforts of many – race insinuates itself into our responses to situations and people. Even when we claim that we have escaped the perceived shackles of race, we are merely confirming its presence by our stated yearning for its absence. And escaping poverty and joining the middle class does not – as some have argued – free 'black' South Africans from the effects of racial identity and race-based thinking. When I sit at a restaurant with my companion and the waiter presents me, and not him, with the wine list or the bill, should I not assume that this is done because I am 'white' and he is 'black'? (I hasten to add that this has happened to me on many occasions, regardless of the race of the waiter or, it must be said, regardless of whether my companion is an actuary earning at least double my academic salary, or a relatively impecunious graduate student.) When I see a young man walking a dog through the streets of the posh, overwhelmingly 'white', and affluent suburb of Bantry Bay in Cape Town (as often happens in the morning when I drive to work), will the story I make up about that man not differ depending on whether he is 'white'or 'black'– even if, after a second or two, I will be startled by the deeply problematic racial assumptions to which I might have fallen prey, and will try to correct myself?[84]

b) Are the measures designed to protect or advance such persons or categories of persons?

The second requirement for a valid restitutionary programme is that the measure must be designed to protect or advance those disadvantaged by unfair discrimination. In essence, the remedial measures are directed at an envisaged future outcome and must be designed to achieve that outcome. The outcome could be to eradicate social and economic inequality between groups as well as to eradicate the structures of advantage and privilege that help to perpetuate such inequality. However, a court will not require the defenders of the scheme to show that the measures are necessary to achieve this goal. Nor will the court require the defenders to show that the measures will definitely achieve the intended goals.

Instead, what is required is that the measures 'must be reasonably capable of attaining the desired outcome' of addressing the effects of past unfair discrimination.[85] 'If the remedial measures are arbitrary, capricious or display naked preference, they can hardly be said to be designed to achieve the constitutionally authorised end.'[86] If it is clear that these measures are not reasonably likely to achieve the end of advancing or benefitting the interests of those who have been disadvantaged by unfair discrimination, they would not constitute measures contemplated by section 9(2).

It is also not required to show that the remedial measures are a necessity to disfavour one class in order to uplift another. 'They are not predicated on a necessity or purpose to prejudice or penalise others, and so require supporters of the measure to establish that there is no less onerous way in which the remedial objective may be achieved. The prejudice that may arise is incidental to but certainly not the target of remedial legislative choice.'[87] It is

84 De Vos (2012) 77–8.

85 *Van Heerden* para 41.

86 *Van Heerden* para 41. See also *Prinsloo* paras 24–6 and 36; *Jooste* para 16.

87 *Van Heerden* para 43.

important to note that the onus here rests on the party trying to convince the court that the remedial measures are unconstitutional and do not comply with section 9(2). The person or institution attacking the remedial measures will have to show that the measures are not reasonably capable of achieving the stated redress goals. It is possible to do this if it can be shown that the measures are arbitrary or 'display a naked preference'.[88]

c) Do the measures promote the achievement of equality in the long term?

The third requirement for a valid remedial programme is probably the most difficult and complex to grapple with but it is pivotal for determining the constitutionality of the scheme. Whether a remedial scheme meets the requirements of section 9(2) may well hinge on whether this last requirement is met. We contend that this third requirement requires a value judgment. A court would have to make this value judgment in the light of all the circumstances. These circumstances include the history of marginalisation and oppression of people based on race, sex, sexual orientation and other grounds, the current social and economic status of various groups previously unfairly discriminated against, as well as the prevalence of racism, sexism, homophobia and other forms of misrecognition still prevalent in society.

This third requirement asks whether the remedial measures **promote the achievement of equality in the long term**. What is required is a balancing of different interests: the interests of those people suffering from the effects of past or ongoing unfair discrimination on the one hand, and the interests of those people who benefitted from past unfair discrimination or continue to benefit from the lingering effects of that discrimination on the other hand. In his concurring judgment in the *Van Heerden* case, Sachs J explained how to balance these interests as follows:

> **Courts must be reluctant to interfere with [remedial] measures, and exercise due restraint when tempted to interpose themselves as arbiters as to whether the measure could have been proceeded with in a better or less onerous way. At the same time, if the measure at issue is manifestly overbalanced in ignoring or trampling on the interests of members of the advantaged section of the community, and gratuitously and flagrantly imposes disproportionate burdens on them, the courts have a duty to interfere. Given our historical circumstances and the massive inequalities that plague our society, the balance when determining whether a measure that promotes equality is fair will be heavily weighted in favour of opening up opportunities for the disadvantaged. That is what promoting equality (section 9(2)) and fairness (section 9(3)) require. Yet some degree of proportionality, based on the particular context and circumstances of each case, can never be ruled out.**[89]

In other words, a court will be slow to strike down remedial measures targeting black South Africans, women, people with disabilities, gay men and lesbians or other groups who have suffered from unfair discrimination in the past. However, the court will not automatically find that such measures comply with section 9(2). The court will have to look at the effect that a measure has on the advantaged section of the community (white citizens, men, able-bodied individuals, heterosexuals or other groups who benefitted from past unfair discrimination). The court has to consider the effect of the measure on those excluded by the measure in the context of our broader society. The court may find that measures that

88 *Van Heerden* para 41.
89 *Van Heerden* para 152.

completely exclude or are aimed purely at punishing those people who belong to a group that benefitted in the past disproportionately burden the previous beneficiaries of discrimination. However, this does not mean that measures may not have the effect of disadvantaging those who benefitted from the past system of discrimination. As Justice Moseneke explained in *Van Heerden*:

> It must be accepted that the achievement of this goal may often come at a price for those who were previously advantaged. Action needs to be taken to advance the position of those who have suffered unfair discrimination in the past. [...] However, it is also clear that the long-term goal of our society is a non-racial, non-sexist society in which each person will be recognised and treated as a human being of equal worth and dignity. Central to this vision is the recognition that ours is a diverse society, comprised of people of different races, different language groups, different religions and both sexes. This diversity, and our equality as citizens within it, is something our Constitution celebrates and protects. In assessing therefore whether a measure will in the long term promote equality, we must bear in mind this constitutional vision. In particular, a measure should not constitute an abuse of power or impose such substantial and undue harm on those excluded from its benefits that our long-term constitutional goal would be threatened (our emphasis).[90]

A court must therefore look at the effect the remedial measures will have on the group or groups who may be negatively affected or who may not be targeted by the measures. In this regard, there appear to be similarities between this third requirement of the test and the test for unfair discrimination in terms of section 9(3) discussed below.[91] For example, a programme aimed at addressing the effects of past racial discrimination may negatively affect white South Africans. Employment equity legislation or rules designed to accommodate more black students or women at a university may affect some white applicants for jobs or university places who may not be appointed or may be denied a place to study at the university because of the remedial programme. This in itself will not invalidate the programme. However, where the measures taken are so extreme that they send a signal that the equal dignity of white applicants is not respected, the programme may be invalidated. Thus, where an admissions policy takes race into account and the effect of that policy is to exclude the vast majority or all of the white applicants, the programme would probably not pass constitutional muster.[92] In effect, this is a value judgment importing an internal fairness requirement into the test for a valid remedial programme.[93]

PAUSE FOR REFLECTION

Fairness and proportionality considerations when applying section 9(2)

The question whether the test for remedial measures as set out by Moseneke J in the *Van Heerden* case acquires 'bite' from the third requirement set out above has elicited some debate in academic circles. Pretorius argues that it is unclear whether this requirement goes 'beyond mere rationality testing', saying that this depends on our interpretation of the Moseneke judgment and especially the third requirement

90 *Van Heerden* para 44.

91 This view is bolstered by the concurrent decisions of Sachs J in the *Van Heerden* judgment (para 146), in which he emphasises the substantive nature of equality and affirms that s 9(2) must be applied within this framework.

92 De Vos (2012) 93–4.

93 Pretorius (2010) 564.

postulated by him.[94] According to Pretorius, the third requirement as explained by Moseneke J and discussed above:

> can be understood narrowly or broadly. If the 'promotion of equality' in this context is understood narrowly, i.e. as synonymous with remedial or restitutive equality, it will in effect not add anything additional to the previous two rationality requirements and cumulatively the s 9(2) conditions for the constitutional validity of affirmative action will stay within the confines of a rationality inquiry ... The equation is also unequivocally implicit in the observation that 'it would be inimical to the pursuit of substantive equality if the State was required to show that each restitutionary measure that it enacted was fair, as would be required by s 9(3)'. Affirmative action measures ought therefore to be judged solely in terms of whether they serve the goal of 'advancing those previously disadvantaged'. If on the other hand the phrase 'to promote the achievement of equality' in s 9(2) is understood more broadly and *inclusively*, i.e. recognising and balancing the equality aspirations of all, then considerations regarding the fairness and proportionality of the impact of affirmative action measures will inevitably surface. This can be illustrated with reference to the majority opinion itself. ... Moseneke J in his actual application of the third s 9(2) criterion – and contrary to his initial starting point – leaned towards the broader interpretation. The realisation of the remedial objective is balanced with reference to the ideal of the promotion of an inclusive 'non-racial, non-sexist society in which each person will be recognised and treated as a human being of equal worth and dignity'. Mindful of this 'constitutional vision', remedial measures should therefore 'not constitute an abuse of power or impose such substantial and undue harm on those excluded from its benefits that our long-term constitutional goal would be threatened'. That fairness and proportionality considerations are invariably brought to the fore once this direction is taken, is clearly evidenced by Justice Moseneke's application of the third requirement to the facts of the case. In his consideration of the question whether the evidence revealed an abuse of power or the existence of such a degree of substantial and undue harm that could be construed as a threat to the realisation of the long-term goal of equality, he referred to factors normally at issue when the fairness of discriminatory measures is examined. He considered the question 'whether the *adverse impact* of the employer contribution scheme on [the sub-class that the complainant belonged to] is such as to render it *unfairly discriminatory*'. He also specifically noted the relevance of the fact that the complainant did not claim that the aggrieved class of parliamentarians is in any sense vulnerable or marginalised or that in the past these parliamentarians were unfairly excluded or discriminated against, or that the impugned pension scheme could be considered as invasive of their dignity.[95]

We contend that this third requirement does require a balancing of interests and therefore does import the fairness requirement in a different guise into the section 9(2) analysis. This does not mean that a court will easily invalidate an affirmative action policy, but where the policy overburdens the excluded group, it will have the constitutional duty to do so.

94 Pretorius (2010) 562.

95 Pretorius (2010) 562–3.

12.2.4.4 Unfair discrimination: section 9(3)

In some situations a legislative provision differentiates between people or groups of people on one or more of the grounds listed in section 9(3) or on analogous grounds (discussed below) and therefore discriminates against an individual or a group of people. Where this discrimination does not comply with the requirements for a remedial programme in section 9(2), a court will rely on section 9(3) to determine whether the discrimination is unfair and hence in conflict with the equality provisions of the Constitution. In some cases there may well be a rational relationship between the differentiation in question and the governmental purpose which is proffered to validate it and the requirements of section 9(1) are met. In other cases the measures may purport to give effect to an affirmative action or remedial programme but do not meet the requirements of section 9(2). In these cases, the court has to ask whether the differentiation may still constitute unfair discrimination as envisaged by section 9(3).[96]

In *Harksen v Lane NO and Others*, the Constitutional Court stated that a determination of whether differentiation amounts to unfair discrimination in terms of section 9(3) requires a two-stage analysis:

- First, the court has to determine whether the differentiation in fact amounts to discrimination.
- Second, if it does, the court has to determine whether the discrimination amounts to unfair discrimination.[97]

The Court thus distinguished between discrimination and unfair discrimination, arguing that not all forms of discrimination are unfair. Where discrimination can be proven not to be unfair, the legislative provision thus does not fall foul of section 9(3).[98]

In the first of the two stages of analysis, a court must determine whether the differentiation in fact constitutes discrimination. In *Harksen*, Goldstone J further subdivided the enquiry following the arguments first set out in *Prinsloo*. He stated that section 9(3) contemplates two categories of discrimination and that courts should deal with each one in a different way.[99] The first category is differentiation based on one or more of the sixteen grounds specified in section 9(3), in other words, grounds such as race, sex, gender and sexual orientation. The second category is differentiation on a ground not specified in section 9(3) but analogous to such grounds.[100] The Court in *Harksen* summarised the steps as follows:

> **(b)(i) Firstly, does the differentiation amount to 'discrimination'? If it is on a specified ground, then discrimination will have been established. If it is not on a specified ground, then whether or not there is discrimination will depend upon whether, objectively, the ground is based on attributes and characteristics which have the potential to impair the fundamental human dignity of persons as human beings or to affect them adversely in a comparably serious manner.**

---

96 In *National Coalition for Gay and Lesbian Equality v Minister of Justice* para 18, the Court stressed that the two enquiries need not follow one from the other. The rational connection enquiry would be clearly unnecessary in a case in which a court holds that the discrimination is unfair and unjustifiable.

97 (CCT9/97) [1997] ZACC 12; 1997 (11) BCLR 1489; 1998 (1) SA 300 (7 October 1997) para 44.

98 *Harksen* para 44. This distinction and the concomitant two-stage analysis were not employed in the cases preceding *Harksen*. In *Prinsloo*, for example, the Court combined the two stages or, at least, did not identify the two stages (paras 30–1). See Currie and De Waal (2013) 223.

99 *Prinsloo* para 29.

100 *Harksen* para 46.

(b)(ii) If the differentiation amounts to 'discrimination', does it amount to 'unfair discrimination'? If it has been found to have been on a specified ground, then unfairness will be presumed. If on an unspecified ground, unfairness will have to be established by the complainant. The test of unfairness focuses primarily on the impact of the discrimination on the complainant and others in his or her situation.[101]

12.2.4.4.1 Does the differentiation amount to discrimination?

The text of section 9(3) prohibits unfair discrimination. This means that discrimination can be either fair and hence constitutionally permissible, or unfair and hence constitutionally impermissible. Although the term, 'discrimination', carries a pejorative meaning in general language, section 9(3) - in line with the substantive notion of equality - does not prohibit all forms of discrimination but only impermissible or unfair forms of discrimination.[102]

The starting point of this enquiry is the text of section 9(3) which sets out no less than 16 prohibited grounds of discrimination, namely race, gender, sex, pregnancy, marital status, ethnic or social origin, colour, sexual orientation, age, disability, religion, conscience, belief, culture, language and birth. When a legislative provision differentiates against anyone or any group on any of these grounds, a court will find that the differentiation amounts to discrimination. The court must determine **objectively** whether differentiation has occurred on a specified or an unspecified ground.[103] This means that the intention of the alleged discriminator is not relevant to the enquiry as to whether discrimination occurred. (However, intention may be relevant to determine whether the discrimination was fair or unfair.[104]) The court has to decide whether the differentiation is based on one of the specified grounds listed in section 9(3), for example whether the legislative provision distinguishes between individuals who are black or white; male or female; gay or straight; able-bodied or disabled. Once the court has established that the distinction is indeed based on one of these 16 listed grounds, it will assume that the differentiation is discriminatory. However, the party seeking to uphold the validity of the legislative provision can still show that the discrimination is not unfair. This is so because section 9(5) explicitly states that '[d]iscrimination on one or more of the grounds listed in subsection (3) is unfair unless it is established that the discrimination is fair'.[105] This means that a finding that there was discrimination will never end the enquiry as one of the parties then has to try to convince the court that the discrimination is fair or unfair as the case may be.

It is important to note that section 9(3) does not only prohibit unfair discrimination on the grounds specifically listed in that section. Section 9(3) also prohibits unfair

101 *Harksen* para 50(b).

102 See Albertyn and Goldblatt (2013) 35.43.

103 *Harksen* para 47.

104 *Walker* para 43.

105 *Walker* para 43. Albertyn and Goldblatt (1998) 268 criticise this view and argue that it 'denudes discrimination of its prejudicial connotations by not requiring that such prejudice be demonstrated'. They find support for this view from the dissenting opinion of Sachs J in *Walker* paras 105–6 who argued that there can only be a finding of discrimination (the first stage of the analysis) if the claimant can prove that he or she had been prejudiced - that there had been 'actual negative impact' associated with a specified ground - by the differentiation which was based on one of the specified grounds. He concludes:

> **The core of my argument at this stage is that the complainant has not made out a case of having suffered *prima facie* discrimination at all. In order to invoke the presumption of unfairness contained in s 8(4) [now s 9(5)] some element of actual or potential prejudice must be immanent in the differentiation, otherwise there is no "discrimination" to be evaluated, and the need to establish fairness or unfairness has no subject matter.**

This view was, however, explicitly rejected in the same case by the majority judgment of Langa DP as contrary to the previous equality decisions of the Court (para 33).

discrimination against anyone on one or more grounds, '**including**' those listed in section 9(3). The word 'including' suggests that the list set out in section 9(3) is not a closed list and that distinctions made between people or groups of people on the basis of other grounds not listed may also amount to discrimination. Such grounds are called **analogous grounds**. This allows the court to discover new forms of discrimination not explicitly recognised by the drafters of the Constitution.

A court is required to make an objective assessment about two important questions to determine whether discrimination has occurred on an analogous ground:

- First, the court must determine whether the differentiation relates to the unequal treatment of people based on other 'attributes and characteristics attaching to them' which are not related to the specified grounds but are nevertheless comparable to them.[106]
- Second, the court has to determine whether this differentiation has the effect of treating persons differently in a way which 'impairs their fundamental dignity as human beings, who are inherently equal in dignity' or affects a person adversely in 'a comparably serious manner'.[107]

Regarding the first aspect of this enquiry, in *Harksen* the Constitutional Court cautioned against a narrow definition of these attributes and characteristics. The Court stated that when a court is called on to make such a determination, it must look at whether the differentiation is based on attributes and characteristics comparable in some way or another with those specified grounds:

> **What the specified grounds have in common is that they have been used (or misused) in the past (both in South Africa and elsewhere) to categorise, marginalise and often oppress persons who have had, or who have been associated with, these attributes or characteristics. These grounds have the potential, when manipulated, to demean persons in their inherent humanity and dignity.**[108]

The second aspect of this enquiry is the impairment of human dignity or a comparably serious disadvantage. It seems as if the Constitutional Court has in mind an open-ended process in which it may discover, over time, more differentiations which are not based on specified grounds but which, in its opinion, are based on grounds similar to those specified. From the decided cases it does seem, however, as though it will not be too difficult for complainants who belong to a marginalised or vulnerable group to prove that a differentiation was based on a characteristic which has the potential to impair their fundamental human dignity or to affect them adversely in a comparably serious manner. What is required is to show that the ground on which a complainant is treated differently from others has the same characteristics as those listed in section 9(3). In *Hoffmann v South African Airways*,[109] the Constitutional Court found that where HIV-positive individuals are treated differently on the basis of their HIV status, this constitutes discrimination on the analogous ground of HIV status. The Court justified its reasoning as follows:

> **People who are living with HIV constitute a minority. Society has responded to their plight with intense prejudice. They have been subjected to systemic disadvantage**

106 *Harksen* para 46.
107 *Harksen* para 46.
108 *Harksen* para 47.
109 (CCT17/00) [2000] ZACC 17; 2001 (1) SA 1; 2000 (11) BCLR 1235; [2000] 12 BLLR 1365 (CC) (28 September 2000).

and discrimination. They have been stigmatised and marginalised. As the present case demonstrates, they have been denied employment because of their HIV positive status without regard to their ability to perform the duties of the position from which they have been excluded. Society's response to them has forced many of them not to reveal their HIV status for fear of prejudice. This in turn has deprived them of the help they would otherwise have received. People who are living with HIV/AIDS are one of the most vulnerable groups in our society. Notwithstanding the availability of compelling medical evidence as to how this disease is transmitted, the prejudices and stereotypes against HIV positive people still persist. In view of the prevailing prejudice against HIV positive people, any discrimination against them can, to my mind, be interpreted as a fresh instance of stigmatisation and I consider this to be an assault on their dignity. The impact of discrimination on HIV positive people is devastating. It is even more so when it occurs in the context of employment. It denies them the right to earn a living. For this reason, they enjoy special protection in our law.[110]

PAUSE FOR REFLECTION

What other grounds of often invisible prejudice exist in society?

At present the Constitutional Court has recognised that apart from HIV status, differentiation on the basis of not being a South African citizen also constitutes an analogous ground of discrimination.[111] But what about other kinds of distinctions that people generally make? Consider the following extract from an article on the manner in which people generally discriminate in favour of tall and attractive people:

> We can't all be Brad Pitt or Angelina Jolie, or sculpted like a 6 foot 5 inch Olympic athlete, but what we may lack in looks, we can make up in intelligence or personality. Or so the common argument goes, which may be more myth than fact.
>
> The British National Child Development study conducted by Daniel Nettle of the Open University shows that the taller men are, the less likely they were to be single or childless, concluding that taller men are deemed more sexually attractive and more likely to find a mate. "In choosing a husband, size matters," Dr. Nettle argues, echoing a well-known phrase. A study by researchers at the University of Florida, the University of North Carolina and the University of Pittsburgh found tall people earned considerably more money throughout their careers than shorter workers. Not that all men who are successful are necessarily tall or attractive. For example, Bill Gates is 5 foot 9 inches; Jack Welch at 5 feet 8 inches and billionaire Jim Pattison at barely 5 feet 7 inches. Most male movie stars such as Tom Cruise and Jack Nicholson are well below the average male height ...
>
> According to Dr. Gordon Patzer, who has concluded 3 decades of research on physical attractiveness, human beings are hard-wired to respond more favorably to attractive people: "Good-looking men and women are generally regarded to be more talented, kind, honest and intelligent than their less attractive counterparts." Patzer contends, "controlled studies show people go out of their way to help

110 *Hoffmann* para 28.
111 *Larbi-Odam* para 19.

> **attractive people – of the same sex and opposite sex – because they want to be liked and accepted by good-looking people." Even studies of babies show they will look more intently and longer at attractive faces, Patzer argues.[112]**

A university study conducted in the USA further found that unattractive employees are more likely the subject of rude, uncivil and even cruel treatment by their co-workers.[113] Does this mean that how a person looks should become an analogous ground on which discrimination could be alleged? What other grounds of often invisible prejudice exist in society and are taken for granted by all? Should we develop the South African jurisprudence to take cognisance of the various ways in which people are treated badly not through any fault of their own, but because they have attributes and characteristics that many people implicitly or explicitly use to judge them more harshly?

The prohibition on discrimination applies to both direct and indirect discrimination. This must not be confused with listed and analogous grounds of discrimination discussed above. **Direct discrimination** occurs where a provision specifically differentiates on the basis of either a listed or an unlisted ground. For example, a legislative provision that differentiates between men and women or between HIV-positive and HIV-negative people discriminates directly. Thus, the previous common law definition of marriage as being between a man and a woman explicitly excluded same-sex couples from the definition and hence directly discriminated against gay men and lesbians on the basis of sexual orientation.[114]

Indirect discrimination occurs where certain requirements, conditions or practices, while appearing neutral, actually have an effect or result that is unequal or that disproportionately affects a group defined in terms of a listed or analogous ground. For example, in the South African context with its deeply entrenched racialised residential patterns, a measure that treats people in one geographical area differently from people living in another geographical area may constitute indirect racial discrimination. This was the case in *City Council of Pretoria v Walker*[115] where the Constitutional Court pointed out that it was necessary to include indirect discrimination in the ambit of section 9(3) to ensure that we focus on the consequences rather than the form of conduct. This is necessary because conduct which may appear to be neutral and non-discriminatory may nonetheless result in discrimination.[116]

PAUSE FOR REFLECTION

The problem of hidden forms of discrimination

In *S v Jordan and Others (Sex Workers Education and Advocacy Task Force and Others as Amici Curiae*,[117] the majority of judges of the Constitutional Court rejected an argument that a legislative provision that criminalised the conduct of sex workers but not the clients of sex workers discriminated indirectly against women. The relevant section made a distinction between the prostitute and the customer. It was argued that

112 Williams, RB (2012, 18 August) Wired for success *Psychology Today* available at http://www.psychologytoday.com/blog/wired-success/201208/im-successful-because-im-beautiful-how-we-discriminate-in-favor-attractive.

113 DiSalvo, D (2013, 17 July) Study: Unattractive people are targets for cruelty at work *Forbes* available at http://www.forbes.com/sites/daviddisalvo/2013/07/17/study-unattractive-people-are-targets-for-cruelty-at-work/.

114 See *Fourie*.

115 (CCT8/97) [1998] ZACC 1; 1998 (2) SA 363; 1998 (3) BCLR 257 (17 February 1998).

116 *Walker* para 31.

117 (CCT31/01) [2002] ZACC 22; 2002 (6) SA 642; 2002 (11) BCLR 1117 (9 October 2002).

although the section targeted all sex workers and was therefore gender neutral, it nevertheless discriminated on the basis of gender because it had a more severe impact on women as the vast majority of sex workers are women and the vast majority of clients of sex workers are men. The majority held that the sex worker is engaged in the business of commercial sex and that one of the ways of curbing commercial sex is to strike at the 'merchant' by means of criminal sanctions. The differentiation between the dealer and customer was a common distinction that is made in a number of statutes and therefore could not be said to constitute indirect discrimination.[118] The minority judgment disagreed with this view. The judgment by O'Regan J and Sachs J explains their position as follows:

> **Prostitutes and their customers engage in sexual activity, which is one of the constitutive elements of the relationship between men and women in all societies. As partners in sexual intercourse, they both consent to and participate in the action which lies at the heart of the criminal prohibition. There are only three differences between them. The first is that the one pays and the other is paid. The second is that in general the one is female and the other is male. The third is that the one's actions are rendered criminal by [the impugned provision] but the other's actions are not. Moreover, the effect of making the prostitute the primary offender directly reinforces a pattern of sexual stereotyping which is itself in conflict with the principle of gender equality. The differential impact between prostitute and client is therefore directly linked to a pattern of gender disadvantage which our Constitution is committed to eradicating. In all these circumstances, we are satisfied that, as in *Walker's* case, this is a case where an apparently neutral differentiating criterion producing a markedly differential impact on a listed ground results in indirect discrimination on that ground.[119]**

The importance of prohibiting indirect discrimination is that often discrimination is hidden or disguised by those who wish to discriminate: they utilise seemingly neutral criteria to deny members of a certain group access to goods and benefits in the hope that this discrimination will not be detected. If indirect discrimination is not prohibited, it would therefore make it very difficult to address the problem of these hidden forms of discrimination. Whenever a club or bar refuses a patron entry to that club or bar (as still happens)[120] based on his or her dress, for example, and that patron happens to be black, the excluded patron would be able to show that indirect discrimination had occurred if he or she could show that other white patrons who were dressed in a similar manner were admitted to the bar or club.

12.2.4.4.2 Is the discrimination unfair?

Because the aim of section 9 of the Constitution is the pursuit of substantive equality, not all forms of discrimination will be found to be unconstitutional. Once it is shown that the differentiation constitutes discrimination – either on a ground listed in section 9(3) or on an analogous ground and whether direct or indirect – the enquiry moves to the question of

118 *Jordan* para 10.
119 *Jordan* para 60.
120 See Kassiem, A (2004, 11 February) Gay nightclub admits to discrimination *Independent Online* available at http://www.iol.co.za/news/south-africa/gay-nightclub-admits-to-racial-discrimination-1.122764.

whether the discrimination is fair or unfair. As we have seen, when discrimination occurs on a listed ground, it is presumed, in accordance with section 9(5), that the discrimination is unfair and hence unconstitutional.

However, it is possible to rebut the presumption and establish that the discrimination is not unfair.[121] In other words, the complainant must establish that the differentiation is based on one or more of the specified grounds in order for the (rebuttable) presumption of unfair discrimination to be of effect. Once this has been established, it then becomes the duty of the other party to rebut the presumption of unfairness and, instead, to show that the discrimination is in fact fair. If the discrimination is on a ground not listed in section 9(3), the onus to prove that the discrimination is unfair remains with the party attacking the constitutionality of the legislative provision. Either way, one of the parties has to engage with the requirements for fair versus unfair discrimination. The question of how to determine whether discrimination is fair or unfair therefore remains relevant, regardless of whether the discrimination is on a listed or unlisted ground.

According to the Constitutional Court, the relevant party will be able to prove the unfairness of the discrimination with reference to the fact that at the heart of the prohibition of unfair discrimination lies a recognition that the purpose of the Constitution is the establishment of a society in which all people are accorded equal dignity and respect regardless of their membership of particular groups. As the Court remarked in *Harksen*, the prohibition on unfair discrimination 'provides a bulwark against invasions which impair human dignity or which affect people adversely in a comparably serious manner'.[122] This remark seems to imply that any determination of the unfairness of the discrimination depends on whether the human dignity of the complainant has been impaired.[123] The Court therefore stressed that what is important is that the enquiry focus on the impact of the discrimination on the victim.[124] To determine whether the discriminatory provision has had an unfair impact on a complainant, a court must consider various factors. Although there is no closed list of factors, the Constitutional Court in the *Harksen* case highlighted the following factors to guide this enquiry:[125]

(a) '[T]he position of the complainants in society, whether they have suffered in the past from patterns of disadvantage, whether the discrimination in the case under consideration is on a specified ground or not': The examination is often backward looking so as to establish the historical factors that led to patterns of group disadvantage and harm.[126] A group of complainants can be vulnerable for a range of often interrelated reasons. They can belong to a group that is economically marginalised[127] and/or suffers from stigmatisation, marginalisation or prejudice, for instance because of racism, sexism, homophobia or HIV stigmatisation,[128] and/or political minority status.[129] It is more difficult to show that discrimination against those who have suffered from past or ongoing discrimination is fair than it is to show that discrimination against those who

121 *Harksen* para 44.

122 *Harksen* para 49.

123 Such an interpretation would mean that human dignity is employed by the court in both step 1 and step 2 in cases where the differentiation is based on one of the unspecified grounds. This would make the process somewhat strange and at least one of the two steps completely superfluous.

124 *Harksen* para 49: 'In the final analysis it is the impact of the discrimination on the complainant that is the determining factor regarding the unfairness of the discrimination.'

125 *Harksen* para 50.

126 *Brink* para 27. See also Albertyn and Goldblatt (2013) 35.76.

127 *Khosa* para 76.

128 See *Hoffmann*.

129 *Khosa* para 71.

have benefitted from past discrimination is unfair. Therefore, discrimination against white people, men, heterosexuals and able-bodied individuals is easier to justify as fair than discrimination against black people, women, gay men and lesbians and disabled individuals.

(b) '[T]he nature of the provision or power and the purpose sought to be achieved by it': If the purpose of the provision is not directed at impairing the complainants' human dignity, but is aimed at achieving a worthy goal such as, for example, the furthering of the achievement of substantive equality or some other important societal or legislative goal, this may tip the scales in favour of a finding that the discrimination is fair. For example, a legislative provision that prohibits blind people from acquiring a driver's licence discriminates against a group on the basis of disability. However, this discrimination may well be found to be fair because the discrimination is aimed at achieving an important purpose, namely to ensure road safety. The more important and pressing the purpose of the discrimination is, the more likely that a court will find the discrimination to be fair.

(c) With due regard to the factors mentioned above as well as any other relevant factors, a court must then ask to what extent 'the discrimination has affected the rights or interests of the complainants and whether it has led to an impairment of their fundamental human dignity or constitutes an impairment of a comparably serious nature': The more invasive the nature of the discrimination is, the more likely the discrimination will be held to be unfair. For example, in *National Coalition for Gay and Lesbian Equality and Others v Minister of Home Affairs and Others*, the Constitutional Court found that the discrimination against gays and lesbians was 'severe' since 'no concern, let alone anything approaching equal concern' was shown towards the group.[130] In other words, a court must ask whether, given the factors above, it would be fair to discriminate against a group. It will not be fair if the discrimination fundamentally affects the human dignity of the group of complainants.

This contextual test is aimed at protecting all individuals in society without hampering the achievement of substantive equality which provides that individuals belonging to different groups may have to be treated differently in certain circumstances.

This analysis acknowledges the fact that a determination of unfair discrimination cannot be made in the abstract. The determination must take into account South Africa's particular history as well as the structural inequality in our society which promotes and perpetuates the subordination of certain individuals and groups.[131] Both the social and economic effects of past discrimination as well as the continuing prejudice and stigmatisation of people belonging to disfavoured groups frame this contextual enquiry into the fairness or unfairness of the discrimination.

PAUSE FOR REFLECTION

An example of indirect discrimination

It will be helpful to consider an example to understand the application of section 9(3). Imagine the South African Police Service Act[132] is amended to regulate the employment of police officers in the South African Police Service (SAPS). A new section of the Act

130 (CCT10/99) [1999] ZACC 17; 2000 (2) SA 1; 2000 (1) BCLR 39 (2 December 1999) para 54.

131 See *National Coalition for Gay and Lesbian Equality v Minister of Justice* para 22 where Ackermann J further stressed that the harm of discrimination is structural in nature.

132 Act 68 of 1995.

determines that no one shall be appointed to the SAPS unless that person is at least 1,79 m tall and weighs at least 75 kg. The Minister argues that these requirements are necessary because members of the SAPS encounter many strong and violent individuals. Police officers therefore need to have the physical strength to subdue suspects.

A constitutional attack on the provision could be launched on the basis that the section indirectly discriminates against women. This is because a disproportionate number of women compared to men are shorter than 1,79 m. Although the provision does not directly exclude women from employment, the effect of the provision would be to exclude most women from employment in the SAPS. When considering whether this discrimination is unfair, a court will have regard to the fact that there is a long history of discrimination against women, also in the employment field, which would weigh heavily in favour of a finding of unfair discrimination. Given the fact that the purpose of the provision, although seemingly rational, is not pressing because women officers will be armed and could be partnered with physically stronger male colleagues, and given the severe impact of the provision on women, a court may well find that the discrimination is unfair.

12.2.5 Non-statutory imposed discrimination: the Promotion of Equality and Prevention of Unfair Discrimination Act 4 of 2000

As we have seen, a litigant may only rely on section 9 of the Constitution when attacking the constitutionality of legislative provisions. In cases where a litigant alleges that discrimination has occurred on the basis of conduct by a public official, organ of state or private individual or institution, he or she has to rely on the Promotion of Equality and Prevention of Unfair Discrimination Act (PEPUDA).[133] The PEPUDA was passed in fulfilment of section 9(4) of the Constitution which states: 'No person may unfairly discriminate directly or indirectly against anyone on one or more grounds in terms of subsection (3). National legislation must be enacted to prevent or prohibit unfair discrimination.' This section affirms the horizontal application of section 9 to ensure that not only discrimination by the state but also discrimination by private individuals or institutions is prohibited.

Because of the principle of subsidiarity, litigants who claim that they have been discriminated against but who do not wish to attack the constitutionality of legislation must rely on the provisions of the PEPUDA.[134] In the absence of a direct challenge to the PEPUDA, courts must assume that the PEPUDA is consistent with the Constitution and must decide claims within its parameters.[135] For example, a policy by a bar or restaurant to reserve its facilities for white people only, a policy by a school not to admit Rastafarian learners, and a decision by a Minister to employ only male officials in his department potentially constitute invalid unfair discrimination. However, these policies or decisions will have to be attacked by relying on the provisions of the PEPUDA.

The general principles regarding the application of section 9 of the Constitution, set out above, remain relevant as the courts must interpret the PEPUDA in the light of the general principles developed by the Constitutional Court regarding the enforcement of section 9. The enquiry into unfair discrimination set out in the PEPUDA includes factors normally taken

133 Act 4 of 2000.

134 *Minister of Health and Another v New Clicks South Africa (Pty) Ltd and Others* (CCT 59/2004) [2005] ZACC 14; 2006 (8) BCLR 872 (CC); 2006 (2) SA 311 (CC) (30 September 2005) paras 96 (Chaskalson CJ) and 434–7 (Ngcobo J).

135 *Pillay* para 40.

into consideration when dealing with section 9 as well as factors normally taken into account when dealing with section 36, the limitation clause.[136] This is because the PEPUDA deals with non-statutory instances of alleged discrimination not based on a law of general application.

Section 1 of the PEPUDA defines discrimination as:

> **any act or omission, including a policy, law, rule, practice, condition or situation which directly or indirectly:**
> **(*a*) imposes burdens, obligations or disadvantage on; or**
> **(*b*) withholds benefits, opportunities or advantages from,**
> **any person on one or more of the prohibited grounds.**

Prohibited grounds listed in section 1 of the PEPUDA include the 16 grounds listed in section 9(3) of the Constitution as well as:

> **(*b*) any other ground where discrimination based on that other ground –**
> **(i) causes or perpetuates systemic disadvantage;**
> **(ii) undermines human dignity; or**
> **(iii) adversely affects the equal enjoyment of a person's rights and freedoms in a serious manner that is comparable to discrimination on one of the listed grounds'.**

In other words, the PEPUDA prohibits discrimination on both listed and analogous grounds, just like section 9(3). Mirroring the section 9 jurisprudence, the onus of proving or disproving unfair discrimination differs depending on whether the discrimination is on a listed or on an analogous ground.[137] The onus thus rests on the respondents to prove that discrimination on a listed ground is fair.

Section 14 of the PEPUDA deals with the determination of fairness or unfairness. The section states:

> **(1) It is not unfair discrimination to take measures designed to protect or advance persons or categories of persons disadvantaged by unfair discrimination or the members of such groups or categories of persons.**
> **(2) In determining whether the respondent has proved that the discrimination is fair, the following must be taken into account:**
> **(*a*) The context;**
> **(*b*) the factors referred to in subsection (3);**
> **(*c*) whether the discrimination reasonably and justifiably differentiates between persons according to objectively determinable criteria, intrinsic to the activity concerned.**
> **(3) The factors referred to in subsection (2)(*b*) include the following:**
> **(*a*) Whether the discrimination impairs or is likely to impair human dignity;**
> **(*b*) the impact or likely impact of the discrimination on the complainant;**
> **(*c*) the position of the complainant in society and whether he or she suffers from patterns of disadvantage or belongs to a group that suffers from such patterns of disadvantage;**
> **(*d*) the nature and extent of the discrimination;**
> **(*e*) whether the discrimination is systemic in nature;**
> **(*f*) whether the discrimination has a legitimate purpose;**

136 *Pillay* para 70.
137 S 13 of the PEPUDA.

(*g*) **whether and to what extent the discrimination achieves its purpose;**

(*h*) **whether there are less restrictive and less disadvantageous means to achieve the purpose;**

(*i*) **whether and to what extent the respondent has taken such steps as being reasonable in the circumstances to–**

(i) **address the disadvantage which arises from or is related to one or more of the prohibited grounds; or**

(ii) **accommodate diversity.**

What is clear is that the PEPUDA allows a court to take into account a wider range of factors than those set out in the *Harksen* case relating to section 9(3) of the Constitution to determine whether discrimination is fair or unfair. Some of the factors mentioned in section 14 of the PEPUDA mirror those relied on by the Constitutional Court in section 9(3) cases. Other factors seem to track more closely questions raised during a section 9(2) enquiry, while yet other factors track the limitation clause enquiry. The Constitutional Court has not provided an expansive interpretation of this section so we must assume that its section 36 and sections 9(2) and 9(3) analyses are all relevant when applying section 14 of the PEPUDA.

A contextual enquiry remains at the heart of a section 14 enquiry. Such a contextual enquiry takes account of the history of the complainants and their position in society as well as the need for remedial measures to address the effects of past and ongoing unfair discrimination. This is in order to advance the value of human dignity for all. Courts have a discretion to consider all the relevant factors listed in section 14 and then to decide whether the discrimination is fair or unfair in the light of these factors. All relevant factors relating to a specific case must be considered as part of a proportionality analysis to make an overall assessment of whether the discrimination is fair or unfair. Not all factors listed in section 14 will be relevant in every case – it will always depend on the facts of the specific case.

An innovation of section 14 can be found in section 14(2)(*c*) which requires a court to ask 'whether the discrimination reasonably and justifiably differentiates between persons according to objectively determinable criteria, intrinsic to the activity concerned'. This section recognises that activities require individuals to possess inherent attributes or characteristics not shared by everyone. Arguably, only a black man can play Othello in the Shakespeare play while only a white man can play AWB leader Eugene Terreblanche in a movie about South Africa's transition to democracy. Considering only members of a certain race for one of these parts would discriminate on the basis of race, but, it could be argued, the differentiation is based on attributes intrinsic to the playing of that part.

One aspect of the section 14 enquiry, which has elicited some discussion by the Constitutional Court, is the requirement that a court must have regard to 'whether and to what extent the respondent has taken such steps as being reasonable in the circumstances to ... accommodate diversity'.[138] This factor is generally known as the requirement for **reasonable accommodation**.

In *MEC for Education: Kwazulu-Natal and Others v Pillay*,[139] the Constitutional Court had to decide whether the failure of a school disciplinary code to take into account the religious or cultural practices of a Hindu learner unfairly discriminated against her. Ms Pillay wanted to wear a nose stud to school as this formed part of her religious and cultural beliefs, but the school's disciplinary code prohibited this. At the heart of the case was whether the school had reasonably accommodated the minority's religious and cultural practices.

138 *Pillay* para 69.

139 (CCT 51/06) [2007] ZACC 21; 2008 (1) SA 474 (CC); 2008 (2) BCLR 99 (CC) (5 October 2007).

The Court explained that reasonable accommodation required institutions to 'take positive measures and possibly incur additional hardship or expense in order to allow all people to participate and enjoy all their rights equally'.[140] The aim is to ensure that groups are not relegated to the margins of society because they do not or cannot conform to certain social norms.[141] At the heart of this principle is the need positively to accommodate diversity. 'Those steps might be as simple as granting and regulating an exemption from a general rule or they may require that the rules or practices be changed or even that buildings be altered or monetary loss incurred.'[142] The extent to which an institution or community should reasonably accommodate the cultural and religious beliefs and practices of others is a difficult question. However, the Constitutional Court has argued that this must be answered with reference to the specific context. As such, reasonable accommodation is 'an exercise in proportionality that will depend intimately on the facts' of each case.[143]

When considering whether discrimination as defined by the PEPUDA is reasonable or not, 'reasonable accommodation will always be an important factor'.[144] However, it would be wrong to reduce the test for fairness to a test for reasonable accommodation. As the Constitutional Court explained in *Pillay*:

> **There may be circumstances where fairness requires a reasonable accommodation, while in other circumstances it may require more or less, or something completely different. It will depend on the nature of the case and the nature of the interests involved. Two factors seem particularly relevant. First, reasonable accommodation is most appropriate where, as in this case, discrimination arises from a rule or practice that is neutral on its face and is designed to serve a valuable purpose, but which nevertheless has a marginalising effect on certain portions of society. Second, the principle is particularly appropriate in specific localised contexts, such as an individual workplace or school, where a reasonable balance between conflicting interests may more easily be struck. Even where fairness requires a reasonable accommodation, the other factors listed in section 14 will always remain relevant.**[145]

What is clear is that when determining whether discrimination is fair or unfair, a court has to balance the various interests and has to make a value judgment, guided by the factors set out in section 14 of the PEPUDA. Thus, an institution may discriminate against a group who previously benefitted from unfair discrimination in order to address the effects of past and ongoing unfair discrimination. In other words, the institution institutes affirmative action measures. This may well weigh heavily in favour of finding the discrimination to be fair unless the considerations set out by the Constitutional Court when it applied section 9(2) mitigates against such a finding. Similarly, where discrimination entrenches the privileges of those who benefitted from past unfair discrimination or perpetuates the stigmatisation and marginalisation of disfavoured groups, it would be difficult for a court to find that the discrimination was fair. It is therefore important when applying the section 14 criteria to have regard for the Constitutional Court's jurisprudence on the various subsections of section 9 of the Constitution.

---

140 *Pillay* para 73.
141 *Pillay* para 73.
142 *Pillay* para 75.
143 *Pillay* para 76.
144 *Pillay* para 77.
145 *Pillay* para 78.

PAUSE FOR REFLECTION

The principle of reasonable accommodation as it applies in the disability field

In *Pillay*, Ngcobo J explained the principle of reasonable accommodation as it applies in the disability field in the following manner:

> Disabled people are often unable to access or participate in public or private life because the means to do so are designed for able-bodied people. The result is that disabled people can, without any positive action, easily be pushed to the margins of society:
>
> > Exclusion from the mainstream of society results from the construction of a society based solely on 'mainstream' attributes to which disabled persons will never be able to gain access. Whether it is the impossibility of success at a written test for a blind person, or the need for ramp access to a library, the discrimination does not lie in the attribution of untrue characteristics to the disabled individual. The blind person cannot see and the person in a wheelchair needs a ramp. Rather, it is the failure to make reasonable accommodation, to fine-tune society so that its structures and assumptions do not result in the relegation and banishment of disabled persons from participation, which results in discrimination against them.[146]

The notion of reasonable accommodation is therefore a powerful tool to disturb often invisible norms which prevail because these norms are shared by the majority or by economically and culturally powerful groups. For example, municipal regulations that prohibit the slaughtering of animals in residential areas are based on the cultural beliefs and practices of the white minority who do not generally slaughter animals during major celebrations. The neutral rule prohibiting the slaughtering of animals is based on a seemingly rational assumption that it is unhygienic to allow the slaughtering of animals in residential areas. This rule can arguably be said to fail reasonably to accommodate the cultural beliefs and practices of many black South Africans. Once this is accepted, the question is not whether such cultural practices of the majority should be accommodated, but rather how to accommodate such practices while not negating the seemingly rational aims of such regulations.

12.3 The right to human dignity

12.3.1 Introduction

As we indicated at the beginning of this chapter, dignity is one of the founding **values** of the Constitution and permeates many aspects of the Constitution.[147] As we have seen, the value of dignity is used to interpret the equality guarantees in section 9 of the Constitution. Dignity also permeates the interpretation of other rights in the Bill of Rights, including social and economic rights.[148]

However, dignity is not only one of the founding values of the Constitution, it is also an independent, self-standing, enforceable **right**. Section 10 of the Constitution states that

146 *Pillay* para 74, quoting from Canadian Supreme Court judgment *Eaton v Brant County Board of Education* [1997] 1 SCR 241 para 67.

147 S 1(*a*). See also s 36. See also *Teddy Bear Clinic* para 52.

148 *Grootboom* para 23.

everyone has inherent dignity and the right to have their dignity respected and protected. The right therefore implies an expectation to be protected from conditions or treatment which offends the subject's sense of his or her worth in society. In particular, treatment which is abusive, degrading, humiliating or demeaning is a violation of this right.[149] Moreover, conduct which treats the subject as non-human or less than human or as an object is intolerable and contrary to section 10 of the Constitution.[150]

At the heart of the right to dignity is the assumption that each human being has incalculable human worth, regardless of circumstances, and should be treated accordingly. This idea or value is 'at the inner heartland of our rights culture'.[151] Dignity can be viewed narrowly as a personal right associated with a person's identity,[152] autonomy and moral agency.[153] According to Sachs J, the right to dignity necessarily entails that everyone has the same moral worth[154] as dignity entails an acknowledgement of 'the intrinsic worth of human beings' and the recognition that 'human beings are entitled to be treated as worthy of respect and concern'.[155] Moreover, human dignity demands that people be treated as unique individuals rather than as representatives of a group.

South African courts have developed a comprehensive meaning of the right to human dignity. In light of the fact that the Constitution permits reference to foreign law to interpret the right in the Bill of Rights, our courts have invoked the jurisprudence of foreign jurisdictions to clarify the meaning of the concept of human dignity. Specifically, former Chief Justice Chaskalson referred to the case of *Law v Canada (Minister of Employment and Immigration)*[156] in his academic paper concerning the meaning of the right to human dignity.[157] In the *Law v Canada* case, the Canadian Supreme Court explained human dignity as follows:

> **Human dignity means that an individual or group feels self-respect and self-worth. It is concerned with physical and psychological integrity and empowerment. Human dignity is harmed by unfair treatment premised upon personal traits or circumstances which do not relate to individual needs, capacities, or merits. It is enhanced by laws which are sensitive to the needs, capacities and merits of different individuals, taking into account the context of their differences. Human dignity is harmed when individuals and groups are marginalised, ignored, or devalued, and is enhanced when laws recognise the full place of all individuals and groups within society.**[158]

However, dignity can be viewed as including more than the individualised personal well-being of the bearers of rights. Understood more broadly, dignity aims to create the

149 In the case of *S v Williams and Others* (CCT20/94) [1995] ZACC 6; 1995 (3) SA 632; 1995 (7) BCLR 861 (CC) (9 June 1995), which concerned corporal punishment, the Court held at para 45 that 'the fact that the adult is stripped naked [for purposes of the whipping] merely accentuates the degradation and humiliation. The whipping of both is, in itself, a severe affront to the dignity as a human being'.

150 Haysom, N 'Dignity' in Cheadle, H, Davis, D and Haysom, N (eds) (2002) *South African Constitutional Law: The Bill of Rights* 131. For further reading on dignity generally, see Davis, DM (1999) Equality: The majesty of legoland jurisprudence *South African Law Journal* 116:398–414 at 414; Cowen, S (2001) Can dignity guide South Africa's equality jurisprudence? *South African Journal on Human Rights* 17(1):34–58 at 34; Fagan (1998) 220.

151 *Masetlha v President of the Republic of South Africa and Another* (CCT 01/07) [2007] ZACC 20; 2008 (1) SA 566 (CC); 2008 (1) BCLR 1 (3 October 2007) para 98.

152 See generally the case of *Pillay*.

153 Woolman, S 'The widening gyre of dignity' in Woolman, S and Bishop M (eds) (2008) *Constitutional Conversations* 197.

154 *Walker* para 113.

155 *Makwanyane* para 28 as per O'Regan J.

156 1 SCR 497 (1999).

157 See Chaskalson, A (2000) The Third Bram Fischer Lecture: Human dignity as a foundational value of our Constitutional order *South African Journal on Human Rights* 16(2):193–205.

158 *Law v Canada (Minister of Employment and Immigration)* 1 SCR 497 (1999) para 53.

opportunity for every individual to reach his or her full potential and to experience complete freedom. In terms of this more encompassing view, 'dignity, properly understood, secures the space for self-actualisation'.[159] If we view dignity as the conduit to achieve the more expansive notion of human freedom, it addresses the entire set of factors – including social and economic factors – that may limit an individual's agency. Ackermann J's dictum in the case of *Ferreira v Levin NO and Others; Vryenhoek and Others v Powell NO and Others* is telling when he states:

> **Human dignity cannot be fully valued or respected unless individuals are able to develop their humanity, their 'humanness' to the full extent of its potential. Each human being is uniquely talented. Part of the dignity of every human being is the fact and awareness of this uniqueness. An individual's human dignity cannot be fully respected or valued unless the individual is permitted to develop his or her unique talents optimally. Human dignity has little value without freedom; for without freedom personal development and fulfilment are not possible. Without freedom, human dignity is little more than an abstraction. Freedom and dignity are inseparably linked. To deny people their freedom is to deny them their dignity.**[160]

In the following sections we discuss the manner in which dignity as a **value** differs from dignity as a protected **right**. We also explore the ways in which the Constitutional Court has used the right to dignity as a catch-all right to be invoked in cases where none of the other rights are applicable.

12.3.2 Human dignity as a right and as a value

It is important to distinguish between dignity as a value invoked to interpret other rights in the Bill of Rights and dignity as a free-standing right that can be relied on. *Dawood and Another v Minister of Home Affairs and Others; Shalabi and Another v Minister of Home Affairs and Others; Thomas and Another v Minister of Home Affairs and Others*[161] is an important case for the purpose of illustrating the fact that dignity operates as both a right and a value in our constitutional sphere. This case concerned the right of spouses, dependent children and destitute, aged or infirm family members to remain in the country pending an application for permanent residence status while all other family members were required to leave the country.

In light of the fact that s 25(9)(*b*) of the Aliens Control Act 96 of 1991 stipulated that such applications had to be considered on their merits, these provisions necessarily authorised immigration officials and the Director General to refuse to issue or extend such temporary permits. In the event that an application was rejected, the consequence was that a South African married to a foreign spouse had to choose between going abroad with his or her partner while the application was considered, or remaining in South Africa, thereby infringing on the marital right to cohabit. This limitation on the right to cohabit was deemed to be an infringement of the right to dignity and accordingly, s 25(9)(*b*) of the Aliens Control Act was found to be unjustifiable and invalid.

However, the Bill of Rights does not contain an explicit right to marry or to have a person's family life protected. For this reason, the Court relied on the right to human dignity to

159 Woolman (2008) 202.
160 (CCT5/95) [1995] ZACC 13; 1996 (1) SA 984 (CC); 1996 (1) BCLR 1 (6 December 1995) para 49.
161 (CCT35/99) [2000] ZACC 8; 2000 (3) SA 936; 2000 (8) BCLR 837 (7 June 2000).

invalidate the impugned legal provisions. In the process of doing so, O'Regan J explained the importance of the **value** of human dignity in the following terms:

> **The value of dignity in our Constitutional framework cannot ... be doubted. The Constitution asserts dignity to contradict our past in which human dignity for black South Africans was routinely and cruelly denied. It asserts it too to inform the future, to invest in our democracy respect for the intrinsic worth of all human beings. Human dignity therefore informs constitutional adjudication and interpretation at a range of levels. It is a value that informs the interpretation of many, possibly all, other rights. This Court has already acknowledged the importance of the constitutional value of dignity in interpreting rights such as the right to equality, the right not to be punished in a cruel, inhuman or degrading way, and the right to life. Human dignity is also a constitutional value that is of central significance in the limitations analysis.**[162]

Human dignity as a value has therefore been invoked in many different settings. For example, when dealing with discrimination on the basis of sexual orientation, the Constitutional Court invoked dignity as a powerful value underlying its analysis. In *National Coalition for Gay and Lesbian Equality and Another v Minister of Justice and Others*,[163] the Court held that the common law criminalisation of sodomy was a violation of the right not only of equality but also of dignity. The reason for this decision was that as a result of the criminal offence, gay men were at risk of arrest, prosecution and conviction of the offence of sodomy simply because they sought to engage in sexual conduct which was part of their experience of being human. The criminalisation of sodomy had the effect of degrading and devaluing gay men which was an invasion of their dignity. More recently, in the case of *Minister of Home Affairs and Another v Fourie and Another*, the Constitutional Court declared that the denial of the right of homosexual persons to marry 'represented a harsh if oblique statement by the law that same-sex couples are outsiders, and that their need for affirmation and protection of their intimate relations as human beings is somehow less than that of heterosexual couples'.[164] The inference was that same-sex couples were not worthy of the same rights and protection as heterosexual couples. To remedy this indignity, the Court declared the common law definition of marriage inconsistent with the Constitution and invalid to the extent that it did not permit same-sex couples to enjoy the status and benefits coupled with responsibilities it accorded to heterosexual couples.

The value of human dignity has also been invoked in socio-economic rights interpretation. As we shall see, when determining whether the state has acted reasonably to give effect to various social and economic rights, the notion of dignity is often invoked. Thus in *Government of the Republic of South Africa and Others v Grootboom and Others*, the Court held that the foundational values of the Constitution, those of human dignity, freedom and equality, are denied to those who have no food, clothing or shelter.[165] A similar move occurred in *Minister of Health and Others v Treatment Action Campaign and Others (No 2)*, in which the Court held with reference to the right of access to health care that '[n]o one should be condemned to a life below the basic level of dignified human existence'.[166] As Liebenberg points out, the value of dignity is here used in its expansive form, implying that the dignity of human beings can only be safeguarded if they live in conditions that enable

162 *Dawood* para 35.
163 (CCT11/98) [1998] ZACC 15; 1999 (1) SA 6; 1998 (12) BCLR 1517 (9 October 1998).
164 (CCT 60/04) [2005] ZACC 19; 2006 (3) BCLR 355 (CC); 2006 (1) SA 524 (CC) (1 December 2005) para 71.
165 (CCT11/00) [2000] ZACC 19; 2001 (1) SA 46; 2000 (11) BCLR 1169 (4 October 2000) para 34.
166 (CCT8/02) [2002] ZACC 15; 2002 (5) SA 721; 2002 (10) BCLR 1033 (5 July 2002) para 28.

them to develop their capabilities, to participate as agents in the shaping of their society.[167] As Liebenberg suggests, the reliance on the value of dignity in social and economic rights cases affirms that dignity 'does not or should not confine us to individual personality issues but can focus our gaze on material conditions of advantage and disadvantage in society'.[168]

Dignity was further defined in *Occupiers of 51 Olivia Road, Berea Township and 197 Main Street Johannesburg v City of Johannesburg and Others*, concerning access to adequate shelter, where the Court held as follows:

> **It is fundamental to an evaluation of the reasonableness of State action that account be taken of the inherent dignity of human beings. The Constitution will be worth infinitely less than its paper if the reasonableness of State action concerned with housing is determined without regard to the fundamental constitutional value of human dignity. Section 26, read in the context of the Bill of Rights as a whole, must mean that the respondents have a right to reasonable action by the State in all circumstances and with particular regard to human dignity. In short, I emphasise that human beings are required to be treated as human beings. This is the backdrop against which the conduct of the [State] must be seen.**[169]

However, the Court pointed out that section 10 of the Bill of Rights makes it plain that dignity is not only a **value** fundamental to our Constitution, it is also a justiciable and enforceable **right** that must be respected and protected. Because the value of dignity informs the interpretation of many if not all rights contained in the Bill of Rights, in most cases where the value of human dignity is offended, 'the primary constitutional breach occasioned may be of a more specific right'.[170] This leaves a limited but pivotal role for the right (as opposed to the value) to human dignity. The right to dignity will usually only be relied on where none of the other rights will specifically protect the interest at stake.[171] In *Dawood*, the Constitutional Court relied on the right to dignity precisely because no other right in the Bill of Rights explicitly guarantees the right to marry and family life for individuals. The Court argued that because there was not a more specific right available 'that protects individuals who wish to enter into and sustain permanent intimate relationships',[172] it was required to rely on section 10:

> **The decision to enter into a marriage relationship and to sustain such a relationship is a matter of defining significance for many if not most people and to prohibit the establishment of such a relationship impairs the ability of the individual to achieve personal fulfilment in an aspect of life that is of central significance. In my view, such legislation would clearly constitute an infringement of the right to dignity. It is not only legislation that prohibits the right to form a marriage relationship that will constitute an infringement of the right to dignity, but any legislation that significantly impairs the ability of spouses to honour their obligations to one another would also limit that right. A central aspect of marriage is cohabitation, the right (and duty) to live together, and legislation that significantly impairs the ability of spouses to honour that obligation would also constitute a limitation of the right to dignity.**[173]

---

167 Liebenberg, S (2005) The value of human dignity in interpreting socio-economic rights *South African Journal on Human Rights* 21(1):1–31.
168 Liebenberg (2005) 5.
169 (24/07) [2008] ZACC 1; 2008 (3) SA 208 (CC); 2008 (5) BCLR 475 (CC) (19 February 2008) para 10.
170 *Dawood* para 35.
171 *Dawood* para 35.
172 *Dawood* para 36.
173 *Dawood* para 37.

This means that the right to dignity has the potential to be used by the courts to deal with human rights infringements not specifically addressed by other rights explicitly included in the Bill of Rights. It may well be that as society evolves and as we recognise new forms of indignity not captured by the text of the Bill of Rights, the Constitutional Court may interpret the right to human dignity to provide protection to individuals affected by these affronts to their dignity. This turns the right to human dignity into a potentially powerful tool to ensure that the Bill of Rights addresses evolving human rights concerns.

PAUSE FOR REFLECTION

New forms of indignity not captured by the text of the Bill of Rights

In *Teddy Bear Clinic for Abused Children and Another v Minister of Justice and Constitutional Development and Another*,[174] the Constitutional Court also invoked the right to human dignity to declare invalid sections 15 and 16 of the Sexual Offences and Related Matters Amendment Act.[175] The impugned sections criminalised consensual sexual intercourse between adolescents (between 12 and 16 years of age) as well as other forms of physical contact between adolescents including petting, kissing and hugging. The Act stated that in such cases both of the adolescents involved had to be prosecuted. The Act provided for a 'close-in-age' defence to an adolescent who is charged with petting, kissing and hugging, but not to an adolescent who is charged with sexual intercourse with another adolescent. This means that where both the adolescents were children 'and the age difference between them was not more than two years at the time of the alleged commission of the offence'[176] they could not be prosecuted, but only in cases of petting, kissing and other non-intercourse related sexual contact.

In coming to the conclusion that sections 15 and 16 of the Act unconstitutionally infringed the right to human dignity, the Constitutional Court stated:

> It cannot be doubted that the criminalisation of consensual sexual conduct is a form of stigmatisation which is degrading and invasive. In the circumstances of this case, the human dignity of the adolescents targeted by the impugned provisions is clearly infringed. If one's consensual sexual choices are not respected by society, but are criminalised, one's innate sense of self-worth will inevitably be diminished. Even when such criminal provisions are rarely enforced, their symbolic impact has a severe effect on the social lives and dignity of those targeted. It must be borne in mind that sections 15 and 16 criminalise a wide range of consensual sexual conduct between children: the categories of prohibited activity are so broad that they include much of what constitutes activity undertaken in the course of adolescents' normal development. There can also be no doubt that the existence of a statutory provision that punishes forms of sexual expression that are developmentally normal degrades and inflicts a state of disgrace on adolescents. To my mind, therefore, the stigma attached to adolescents by the impugned provisions is manifest. The limitation of section 10 of the Constitution is obvious and undeniable.[177]

174 (CCT 12/13) [2013] ZACC 35; 2013 (12) BCLR 1429 (CC) (3 October 2013).

175 Act 32 of 2007.

176 S 56(2)(*b*) of the Sexual Offences and Related Matters Amendment Act.

177 *Teddy Bear Clinic* para 55.

12.4 The right to privacy

12.4.1 Introduction

One of the most notorious legislative provisions in place during the apartheid era was section 16 of the Immorality Act.[178] This section criminalised all extramarital sexual relations between a white male and a non-white female, or vice versa. (Interracial marriages were prohibited by the Prohibition of Mixed Marriages Act.[179]) The Immorality Act authorised police officers to invade people's private homes in order to catch couples in the act of breaking this law, thus infringing on their privacy. The playwright Athol Fugard wrote a play, which opened in 1972, entitled *Statements After an Arrest Under the Immorality Act*, to dramatise the absurdity, the heartache and the pain caused by this provision. A short summary of the play illustrates the effects of section 16:

> **Set in apartheid South Africa, where relationships across the colour bar were a criminal offence, two lovers - a black man and white woman meet secretly in the library where the woman works to make love and share their hopes and fears. An observant neighbour reports them to the police who secretly photograph them from the informant's backyard and eventually break in and arrest the couple under the then inhuman and universally pilloried Immorality Act. The play is a compelling and deeply moving love story in which the physically and emotionally naked lovers expose not only their bodies but also their deepest longings for personal and emotional freedom.**[180]

Given this history, it is no surprise that section 14 of the Constitution provides that '[e]veryone has the right to privacy', which includes the right not to have their person or home searched; their property searched; their possessions seized; or the privacy of their communications infringed. Section 14 therefore contains a general right to privacy as well as specifically enumerated infringements of privacy.[181] These enumerated areas of protection form part of the general right to privacy.

12.4.2 Scope and content of the right to privacy

Privacy recognises that we all have a right to a sphere of private intimacy and autonomy. By protecting this private and intimate sphere, we are allowed 'to establish and nurture human relationships without interference from the outside community'.[182] The scope of a person's privacy extends only to those aspects 'in regard to which a legitimate expectation of privacy can be harboured'.[183] There are two distinct components to this expectation: first, 'a *subjective expectation* of privacy' and second, an expectation that the society has recognised as '*objectively reasonable*'.[184] A person cannot have a subjective expectation of privacy in cases where he or she has willingly consented to waive that privacy.[185] The second component

178 Act 23 of 1957, later renamed the Sexual Offences Act.

179 Act 55 of 1949.

180 See http://www.capetownmagazine.com/events/statements-after-an-arrest-under-the-immorality-act/11_37_54253.

181 Currie and De Waal (2013) 294.

182 *National Coalition for Gay and Lesbian Equality v Minister of Justice* para 32.

183 *Bernstein and Others v Bester NO and Others* (CCT23/95) [1996] ZACC 2; 1996 (4) BCLR 449; 1996 (2) SA 751 (27 March 1996) para 75.

184 *Bernstein* para 75.

185 This is why participants in a reality television show such as *Big Brother* - in which contestants are filmed 24 hours a day in a secluded house - would not be able to claim that their right to privacy had been infringed.

does not focus on the subjective expectations of the claimant based on his or her explicit or implicit consent to waive his or her privacy. Rather, the second component focuses on a determination by a court on whether the person claiming that his or her privacy was infringed could reasonably expect his or her privacy to be protected in the particular circumstances.

The decision whether, reasonably speaking, a person has a legitimate expectation to privacy may depend at least partly on whether the interference was of the 'inner sanctum' of personhood or not. As the Constitutional Court pointed out in *Bernstein and Others v Bester NO and Others*:

> **The truism that no right is to be considered absolute, implies that from the outset of interpretation each right is always already limited by every other right accruing to another citizen. In the context of privacy this would mean that it is only the inner sanctum of a person, such as his/her family life, sexual preference and home environment, which is shielded from erosion by conflicting rights of the community. This implies that community rights and the rights of fellow members place a corresponding obligation on a citizen, thereby shaping the abstract notion of individualism towards identifying a concrete member of civil society. Privacy is acknowledged in the truly personal realm, but as a person moves into communal relations and activities such as business and social interaction, the scope of personal space shrinks accordingly.**[186]

The effect of this view regarding privacy is that in the 'inner sanctum' of a person's life, in his or her 'truly personal realm' like his or her home or bedroom, there would be a far greater likelihood that a person's expectation of having his or her privacy respected is reasonable. Privacy is therefore viewed as a continuum with more intense protection at its core and less intense protection on the periphery. Privacy becomes more intense the closer it moves to the intimate personal sphere of life of human beings and less intense as it moves away from that core.[187] Privacy and dignity are therefore closely related.[188] This is so because where a person's privacy is breached, that person will often not be treated with concern and respect.

There is a range of factors relevant to distinguishing the core of privacy from its penumbra. One of the considerations is the nature of the relationship concerned. For example, in *Jordan*, the minority judgment of the Constitutional Court found with regard to the regulation of sex work that:

> **One of the considerations is the nature of the relationship concerned: an invasion of the relationship between partners, or parent and child, or other intimate, meaningful and intensely personal relationships will be a strong indication of a violation close to the core of privacy.**[189]

Following this reasoning, the minority in the *Jordan* case concluded that the commercial nature of the conduct under consideration removed it from the inner sanctum of privacy. The majority in this case, controversially, came to the same conclusion, holding that if the

186 (CCT23/95) [1996] ZACC 2; 1996 (4) BCLR 449; 1996 (2) SA 751 (27 March 1996) para 67.

187 *Investigating Directorate: Serious Economic Offences and Others v Hyundai Motor Distributors (Pty) Ltd and Others In re: Hyundai Motor Distributors (Pty) Ltd and Others v Smit NO and Others* (CCT1/00) [2000] ZACC 12; 2000 (10) BCLR 1079; 2001 (1) SA 545 (CC) (25 August 2000) para 18.

188 Currie and De Waal (2013) 30.

189 *Jordan* para 80.

right to privacy is implicated at all in a case where sex work is regulated, 'it lies at the periphery and not at its inner core'.[190]

For the same reason the Constitutional Court found in *Investigating Directorate: Serious Economic Offences and Others v Hyundai Motor Distributors (Pty) Ltd and Others In re: Hyundai Motor Distributors (Pty) Ltd and Others v Smit NO and Others*[191] that the privacy rights of a juristic person would be less intense than those of a human being. Although juristic persons like big companies also enjoy the protection of the privacy right, this protection would be weaker than for an ordinary human being:

> **As we have seen, privacy is a right which becomes more intense the closer it moves to the intimate personal sphere of the life of human beings, and less intense as it moves away from that core. This understanding of the right flows, as was said in *Bernstein*, from the value placed on human dignity by the Constitution. Juristic persons are not the bearers of human dignity. Their privacy rights, therefore, can never be as intense as those of human beings. However, this does not mean that juristic persons are not protected by the right to privacy. Exclusion of juristic persons would lead to the possibility of grave violations of privacy in our society, with serious implications for the conduct of affairs. The state might, for instance, have free licence to search and seize material from any non-profit organisation or corporate entity at will. This would obviously lead to grave disruptions and would undermine the very fabric of our democratic state. Juristic persons therefore do enjoy the right to privacy, although not to the same extent as natural persons. The level of justification for any particular limitation of the right will have to be judged in the light of the circumstances of each case. Relevant circumstances would include whether the subject of the limitation is a natural person or a juristic person as well as the nature and effect of the invasion of privacy.[192]**

12.4.3 Privacy regarding sexual intimacy

Few aspects of a person's life can be said to be more intimate and private than his or her consensual sexual conduct conducted in private. The way in which we give expression to our sexuality is therefore at the core of the protection afforded by the right to private intimacy.[193] Whenever a person expresses his or her sexuality consensually and without harming another, invasion of that precinct will be a breach of that person's privacy.[194] Where legislation aims to regulate consensual adult sexual intimacy it will therefore strike at the heart of the right to privacy. However, it has been argued that where such regulation discriminates against a targeted group - like gay men, lesbians and transgendered individuals - it would be inappropriate to invoke the right to privacy, instead of the right against non-discrimination, as this would not capture the true obnoxious nature of the discrimination. As Cameron had previously argued in the context of the regulation of same-sex sexual desire:

> **[T]he privacy argument has detrimental effects on the search for a society which is truly non-stigmatizing as far as sexual orientation is concerned. On the one hand, the privacy argument suggests that discrimination against gays and lesbians is**

190 *Jordan* para 29.
191 (CCT1/00) [2000] ZACC 12; 2000 (10) BCLR 1079; 2001 (1) SA 545 (CC) (25 August 2000).
192 *Hyundai Motor Distributors* para 18.
193 *National Coalition for Gay and Lesbian Equality v Minister of Justice* para 32.
194 *National Coalition for Gay and Lesbian Equality v Minister of Justice* para 32.

> **confined to prohibiting conduct between adults in the privacy of the bedroom. This is manifestly not so. On the other hand, the privacy argument may subtly reinforce the idea that homosexual intimacy is shameful or improper: that it is tolerable so long as it is confined to the bedroom — but that its implications cannot be countenanced outside. Privacy as a rationale for constitutional protection therefore goes insufficiently far, and has appreciable drawbacks even on its own terms.[195]**

However, in *National Coalition for Gay and Lesbian Equality v Minister of Justice*, the Constitutional Court rejected this argument. The Court pointed out that rights should not be construed absolutely or individualistically in ways which denied that all individuals are members of a broader community and are defined in significant ways by that membership.[196] The regulation of sexual conduct can infringe both the right to equality and the right to privacy. Emphasising the breach of both these rights could highlight 'just how egregious the invasion of the constitutional rights' are. When recognising the breach of privacy in such a setting, it can strengthen the conclusion that the discrimination inherent in the breach of privacy also constitutes unfair discrimination.[197]

In *Teddy Bear Clinic*, the Constitutional Court affirmed that the right to privacy in sexual matters is not only enjoyed by adults but also by adolescents. Where legislation criminalises the consensual sexual conduct of adolescents, it applies to the most 'intimate sphere of personal relationships and therefore inevitably implicate[s] the constitutional right to privacy'.[198] 'The offences allow police officers, prosecutors and judicial officers to scrutinise and assume control of the intimate relationships of adolescents, thereby intruding into a deeply personal realm of their lives.'[199]

SUMMARY

This chapter deals with the right to equality and the right to dignity. Section 9 of the Constitution guarantees the right to equality. A litigant invokes section 9 in cases where he or she wishes to attack the constitutionality of a legislative provision because the litigant believes that the provision impermissibly differentiates between people or groups of people. The courts rely on section 9(1), section 9(2) or section 9(3), depending on the nature of the differentiation complained of, to decide the case.

The courts rely on section 9(1) where a legislative provision differentiates between groups of people on grounds other than those listed in section 9(3) or analogous to those listed in section 9(3). This so-called mere differentiation includes the many distinctions made in legislation that are not related to the personal attributes and characteristics of groups of people. A section 9(1) challenge has to be based on the question of whether the differentiation (mere differentiation) was rational or arbitrary.

The courts rely on section 9(2) where the legislative provision being challenged differentiates between groups of people on one of the grounds listed in section 9(3) or on grounds analogous to those listed in this section, for example race, sex or sexual orientation. However, in this case, the legislation differentiates between groups of people with the aim

195 Cameron, E (1993) Sexual orientation and the Constitution: A test case for human rights *South African Journal on Human Rights* 110(3):450–72 at 464.

196 *National Coalition for Gay and Lesbian Equality v Minister of Justice* para 30.

197 *National Coalition for Gay and Lesbian Equality v Minister of Justice* para 32.

198 *Teddy Bear Clinic* para 60.

199 *Teddy Bear Clinic* para 60.

of correcting the effects of past unfair discrimination (affirmative action). When testing an affirmative action provision against section 9(2), the court asks:

- whether the affirmative action scheme devised by the legislature targets a group who was unfairly discriminated against in the past
- whether the scheme is designed to achieve its redress goal, in other words, whether it is reasonably capable of doing so
- whether the scheme will achieve the long-term goal of equality, which would not be the case if the scheme gratuitously and flagrantly imposes disproportionate burdens on the excluded group.

Section 9(3) deals with unfair discrimination. This is discrimination on one or more of the grounds listed in that section or analogous to those grounds, but only when the differentiation was not done with the aim of implementing an affirmative action policy. When deciding whether discrimination is fair or unfair for purposes of section 9(3), the court follows a contextual approach. This means that the court considers:

- whether the complainant belongs to a group previously discriminated against
- whether the discrimination pursues an important purpose
- how severe the impact of the discrimination is on the group.

The courts must deal with allegations of discrimination by private individuals, public officials or institutions, in other words, allegations of non-statutory forms of discrimination, in terms of the Promotion of Equality and Prevention of Unfair Discrimination Act (PEPUDA). The PEPUDA was passed in accordance with section 9(4) of the Constitution to ensure the horizontal application of the prohibition on discrimination. When applying the provisions of the PEPUDA, the concept of reasonable accommodation is important but not always decisive. The PEPUDA requires a court to consider many of the same considerations relevant to a section 9(2) or a section 9(3) enquiry, as well as considerations relevant to a limitations clause enquiry in terms of section 36, when it decides whether the discrimination is fair or unfair.

Section 10 of the Constitution protects the right to dignity. The right to dignity must be distinguished from the value of dignity that permeates the Constitution and underlies the interpretation of many, if not all, the other rights in the Bill of Rights. The courts usually rely on the right to dignity if the dignity interest is not adequately protected by any of the other rights in the Bill of Rights.

Section 14 of the Constitution protects the right to privacy. This right is viewed as having a core which is more rigorously protected than its penumbra. While both individuals and juristic persons can rely on this right, the level of protection will differ depending on the nature of the situation. Courts ask whether privacy protection could reasonably be expected, given the nature of the relationship that is being protected. In this schema, it goes without saying that consensual intimate sexual relationships go to the heart of the right to privacy.

Chapter 13

Diversity rights

13.1 Introduction

South Africa is a **heterogeneous** society in which individuals with diverse religious affiliations, cultural beliefs and practices, and languages must coexist. Given the heterogeneous nature of South Africa, it is important for the law to respect and protect the beliefs, practices and languages of the diverse groups that make up South Africa's population. This is because in a society in which **diversity** is not respected or protected, the law will normally reflect the beliefs, practices and languages of the majority or of the culturally or economically dominant group, and will marginalise the beliefs, practices and languages of discrete groups. When the beliefs, practices and languages of discrete groups are marginalised, this not only diminishes the constitutional goal of establishing a diverse society, but may also cause harm to members of a marginalised group. This is especially so in those cases where the group in question is economically or politically vulnerable.

This state of affairs could arise, for example, where the law recognises and endorses the views of some sections of society (inspired by their particular religious beliefs) that homosexuality is wrong and that gay men and lesbians do not deserve to be treated with equal concern and respect. This would be extremely harmful to gay men and lesbians who would be marginalised and discriminated against and who may even face threats to their physical well-being. Similarly, if the law recognises and endorses the views of some sections of society that certain cultural practices, such as male circumcision, were harmful to all boys, the concomitant ban on male circumcision would limit the rights of those sections of society whose cultural beliefs demand that all young men should undergo circumcision. Again, if the law endorses the view that English should be the only medium of communication in South Africa, this would marginalise many South Africans whose mother tongue is not English.

While it is important to respect the beliefs, practices and languages of diverse groups, it is also important to recognise that there is an inevitable tension between doing so and preventing those beliefs, practices and languages from marginalising, excluding and oppressing other people in society. This is so because some individual beliefs, practices and languages are potentially harmful to other people. Also, they can exclude other people from certain benefits or from access to physical spaces or certain opportunities. To protect individuals from such exclusion, the Constitution must balance the interests of people who hold or practise certain beliefs or who wish to associate with members of the group they feel closest to with the interests of others in society. Other people may be excluded by those beliefs and practices and may, consequently, be harmed by those beliefs and practices because they are denied opportunities or benefits. This requires limiting the associational rights of diverse cultural, religious and other groups in specific situations.

Striking the correct balance is not always easy. Sometimes the interests of some groups have to yield to the interests of other groups. It is impossible for the law to accommodate all the diverse beliefs, practices and attitudes of all people living in South Africa in an absolute manner while also protecting individuals against discrimination, marginalisation and exclusion.

In this chapter we discuss some of the rights where the problem of accommodating diversity arises most acutely. These rights include the right to freedom of association, freedom of religion, the rights of cultural and religious communities, and language rights. It is impossible to do so without keeping in mind the scope and content of the right to equality, human dignity and privacy discussed in chapter 12 of this book. This is because the cultural and religious beliefs and practices of some groups are often in direct conflict with the demands not to discriminate unfairly against others and to respect the human dignity of all. Although we discuss the scope and content of the various rights in detail, we do so against the background of the broader question regarding the manner in which the law can respect and protect cultural and religious diversity without negating the rights of other groups who do not share the same beliefs and who do not engage in the same practices.

13.2 Freedom of association

13.2.1 Introduction

Section 18 of the Constitution provides that '[e]veryone has the right to freedom of association'. Freedom of association is often said to be a foundational right for any flourishing democracy. A right to associate freely with others 'makes participatory politics meaningful and genuinely representative politics possible'.[1] This right also allows individuals to make choices about how they want to arrange their lives and about their identities as people in relationships with others in a given society, thus advancing respect for and protecting diversity.[2] The right to freedom of association guarantees a degree of **autonomy** that allows individuals to make both overtly political and more intimate choices about who to associate with. These are choices that may affect their lives and their identities by giving them expression in community with others.

At the heart of the right to freedom of association lies the recognition of the communal nature of people[3] and the need for people to exercise some of their rights as individuals 'in association with others of like disposition'.[4] It is based on an understanding that people live in communities with others. Also, people develop their full potential only by relating to other people either individually or collectively. In addition, people can often only engage in meaningful political action in association with others. In other words, the right to freedom of association 'protects the rights of collective self-determination'.[5] In *MEC for Education: Kwazulu-Natal and Others v Pillay*, the Constitutional Court linked this notion with the concept of *ubuntu*, stating:

> **The notion that 'we are not islands unto ourselves' is central to the understanding of the individual in African thought. It is often expressed in the phrase *umuntu ngumuntu ngabantu* which emphasises 'communality and the inter-dependence of the members of a community' and that every individual is an extension of others. According to Gyekye, 'an individual human person cannot develop and achieve the fullness of his/her potential without the concrete act of relating to other individual persons'. This thinking emphasises the importance of community to individual identity and hence to human dignity. Dignity and identity are inseparably linked as one's sense of self-worth is defined by one's identity. Cultural identity is one of the most important parts of a person's identity precisely because it flows from belonging**

1 Woolman, S 'Freedom of association' in Woolman, S and Bishop, M (eds) (2013) *Constitutional Law of South Africa* 2nd ed rev service 5 44.6.

2 *MEC for Education: Kwazulu-Natal and Others v Pillay* (CCT 51/06) [2007] ZACC 21; 2008 (1) SA 474 (CC); 2008 (2) BCLR 99 (CC) (5 October 2007) para 150.

3 Ackermann, L (2012) *Human Dignity: Lodestar for Equality in South Africa* 109.

4 *Certification of the Amended Text of the Constitution of The Republic Of South Africa, 1996* (CCT37/96) [1996] ZACC 24; 1997 (1) BCLR 1; 1997 (2) SA 97 (4 December 1996) para 24.

5 *Second Certification* para 26.

> **to a community and not from personal choice or achievement. And belonging involves more than simple association; it includes participation and expression of the community's practices and traditions.**[6]

Associational rights are often instrumental in nature as they enable the individuals who form the associations to protect better and to assert more robustly other constitutional rights.[7] No wonder, then, that De Toqueville is quoted as saying that 'no legislator can attack [the right to freedom of association] without impairing the very foundations of society'.[8] What De Toqueville suggests is that the right to freedom of association supports and underpins many other important rights. These include the right to make political choices, the right to form a political party, the right to participate in the activities of that party by recruiting, organising and campaigning on its behalf, and the right to campaign for a political party or cause. These rights are described as political rights in the Constitution and are the very essence of a vibrant constitutional democracy.

Even though the right to freedom of association has a communal aspect, it is important to note that it is primarily a right that belongs to the individual rather than the association that has been established to give better effect to the protection of the rights of the individual.[9] In other words, associational rights do not protect groups **as groups**: these rights remain individual rights that protect the right of individuals to associate or not to associate with others or groups of others. As Summers points out:

> **Although commonly asserted by the organisation, freedom of association is not simply a collective right vested in the organisation for its benefit. Freedom of Association is an individual right vested in the individual to enable him [*sic*] to enlarge his [*sic*] personal freedom. Its function is not merely to grant power to groups, but to enrich the individual's participation in the democratic process by his [*sic*] acting through those groups.**[10]

The Constitutional Court affirmed this point in *Pillay* where O'Regan J stated that associative rights such as the right to belong to cultural, religious and linguistic communities are exercised by the individual person.[11] They are not rights that attach to the group. This does not mean that the right is not related to the need for individuals to belong to organised or informal organisations or groupings. To advance their political, social, cultural, religious, recreational, charitable, educational and other interests or objectives, individuals band together in organisations. This is because individual interests are often better served if they are advanced by associations of like-minded persons. However, it is not the right of the organisation that is protected. Nor is the right of the group who belongs to the organisation protected. Rather, the right of the individual to belong to that organisation is protected. This is so because the right recognises the autonomy of the individual to advance his or her interests in concert with others in this manner.

---

6 (CCT 51/06) [2007] ZACC 21; 2008 (1) SA 474 (CC); 2008 (2) BCLR 99 (CC) (5 October 2007) para 53.

7 Currie, I and De Waal, J (2013) *Bill of Rights Handbook* 6th ed 397.

8 Quoted by Woolman (2013) 44.1.

9 The Canadian Supreme Court approved of this analysis in *Alberta Union of Provincial Employees v Alberta* (AG) (1987), 28 C.R.R. 305. (SCA).

10 Summers, CW (1964) Freedom of association and compulsory unionism in Sweden and the United States *University of Pennsylvania Law Review* 112(5):674–96 at 674 as quoted in *Alberta Union of Provincial Employees v Alberta* (AG) (1987), 28 C.R.R. 305. (SCA).

11 *Pillay* para 150.

As suggested above, the right to freedom of association is closely related to and sometimes overlaps with other rights such as the right to human dignity and the right to privacy.[12] In the previous chapter we noted that the Constitutional Court has recognised that the right to human dignity contains an associational element at least as far as intimate relationships, such as marriage, are concerned. Thus, in *Dawood and Another v Minister of Home Affairs and Others; Shalabi and Another v Minister of Home Affairs and Others; Thomas and Another v Minister of Home Affairs and Others*, the Constitutional Court held that a 'decision to enter into a marriage relationship and to sustain such a relationship is a matter of defining significance for many if not most people' and to limit this right would clearly constitute an infringement of the right to dignity.[13]

However, because of problems related to the accommodation of diversity raised in the introduction to this chapter, it must be noted that difficult questions arise about the scope and content of the right to freedom of association. This is because the need to respect this right sometimes clashes directly with the need to respect other important rights such as the right to human dignity, the right not to be unfairly discriminated against and the right to free dom of movement. Associational rights can be used to exclude and marginalise others. Many seemingly private institutions or bodies are powerful because they provide access to goods, services, benefits and opportunities. Their actions can therefore have a detrimental effect on the well-being of those individuals whom they exclude, marginalise or discriminate against.

The more powerful the body is and the more serious the potential harmful effect of that body's actions on others is, the less likely it is that the members of that body will be allowed to exercise their right to freedom of association in an untrammelled manner. This is because seemingly private bodies created to ensure that individuals can exercise their right of association in conjunction with others of like mind may well exclude and marginalise certain people. The actions of these bodies may send a signal that the people whom they exclude or marginalise are less worthy of constitutional concern and respect. Their actions can also deny certain individuals access to benefits and opportunities in a manner that is discriminatory.

The problem is particularly acute where so-called private bodies provide a service to the public. The owner of a holiday resort catering for white Afrikaans, Christian holiday makers, for example, may wish to restrict access to that holiday resort to white, heterosexual visitors. Given that the holiday resort provides a benefit and a service to the public, those people who are excluded from enjoying the benefit are harmed as they will never be able to enjoy the same privileges as the people accommodated by the holiday resort. The question arises whether the holiday resort is entitled to invoke the right to freedom of association to justify its discrimination against black South Africans or against gay and lesbian South Africans. When a holiday resort excludes a person because of his or her race or sexual orientation, this can send a powerful signal to that person and the group to whom he or she belongs that he or she is not equally valued in society and cannot access the same benefits and services provided by the ostensibly 'private' body that others can access.

In the following sections we explore the scope and content of the right to freedom of association with reference to this dichotomy. As we will see, the conundrum the courts often face is to balance the rights of individuals in the association asserting their autonomy with those of others seeking access to the association.

12 See *National Coalition for Gay and Lesbian Equality and Another v Minister of Justice and Others* (CCT11/98) [1998] ZACC 15; 1999 (1) SA 6; 1998 (12) BCLR 1517 (9 October 1998) para 32, for example, where the Constitutional Court held that 'privacy recognises that we all have a right to a sphere of private intimacy and autonomy which allows us to establish and nurture human relationships'.

13 (CCT35/99) [2000] ZACC 8; 2000 (3) SA 936; 2000 (8) BCLR 837 (7 June 2000) para 37.

PAUSE FOR REFLECTION

Examples of issues raised by the accommodation of diversity within the framework of associational rights

The following examples illustrate the issues raised by the accommodation of diversity within the framework of associational rights.

The Afrikaanse Taal en Kultuur Vereeniging (ATKV) is a cultural organisation that promotes Afrikaans culture and Christianity. It owns a number of holiday resorts in various parts of the country. These resorts are open to all who can pay the entrance fee and the costs of hiring the bungalows. However, members of the ATKV are entitled to a 20% discount if they visit the resorts. To be admitted as members, applicants have to commit to advancing the Afrikaans culture and Christianity.

Mr Mohamed and Mr Omar regard themselves as 'Afrikaners' and have no difficulty committing to advancing Afrikaans cultural interests. However, as they are Muslims, they delete the part of the application form calling for a commitment to advancing Christianity. As a consequence of this, their application to join the ATKV is turned down.

Say that Mr Mohamed and Mr Omar were to challenge the rules for joining the ATKV on the basis that these rules unfairly discriminated against them on the basis of their religion. The ATKV would then probably argue that Christians have a right to freedom of association and that this right should trump the right against unfair discrimination.

In determining whether the ATKV acted lawfully by excluding the Muslim applicants, a court will have to decide which of the rights should prevail in the particular circumstance. The answer the court gives will probably depend on the importance it attaches to the right to non-discrimination in relation to the right to freedom of association. As we continue the discussion of freedom of association, it would be helpful to keep in mind this example.

Now imagine that the body that is discriminating against Muslims is not the ATKV providing a public service in the form of access to various holiday resorts, but a private book club. Mr Van der Merwe hosts the book club in the privacy of his own home in Waterkloof or Sandton. Mr Van der Merwe started the book club with the specific aim of creating a safe environment where he and his likeminded friends could discuss books with a Christian theme (provided to the club by CUM Books), which they have all eagerly read. Most people would probably instinctively think that - unlike the ATKV - Mr Van der Merwe should be allowed to discriminate against non-Christians. As the nature of the benefit denied to others is limited and as the association is of an extremely private nature, this view would almost certainly conform to the legal position. As we continue discussing this issue, it would be helpful to reflect on what basis such a determination would be made.

13.2.2 The scope and content of the right to freedom of association: general principles

The right to freedom of association protects the right of individuals:

- to associate with whom they wish
- to disassociate from whom they wish
- to form intimate bonds or relationships with others with whom they share common interests or cultural or religious attitudes and beliefs
- to protect those relationships from untoward infringement by the state or other powerful role players.

Importantly, the right to freedom of association supports the right to form religious, cultural and linguistic associations to give greater expression to the protection of cultural liberties. As such, freedom of association safeguards the liberty of individuals to decide for themselves how they want to live and with whom they want to associate in the private sphere. In the United States context, Brennan J affirmed this point in *Roberts v United States Jaycees* where he stated:

> **The Court has long recognized that, because the [United States] Bill of Rights is designed to secure individual liberty, it must afford the formation and preservation of certain kinds of highly personal relationships a substantial measure of sanctuary from unjustified interference by the State.[14]**

The constitutional shelter afforded such relationships reflects the realisation that individuals draw much of their emotional enrichment from close ties with others. Providing a degree of protection to these relationships from unwarranted interference by the state and by powerful private bodies therefore safeguards the ability of a person to define independently his or her identity that is central to any concept of liberty.

Examples of intensely private relationships protected by this right include the institution of marriage, the raising of children and cohabiting with a person's partner.[15] In *Roberts v United States Jaycees*, Brennan J distinguished those associations that have an intrinsic element of personal liberty from associations situated at the other end of the continuum such as large business enterprises. He correctly argued that the constitutional constraints on the state's power to regulate private intimate associations were greater than the constraints on its power to regulate business enterprises. The state's power to control the selection of a person's partner in an intimate relationship is severely curtailed but not so in respect of decisions to select employees.[16]

As a general rule, the more public the activity is and the further removed the activity is from the intimate activities of an individual, the less likely it is that the right to freedom of association will protect an activity and prevent intrusion into or regulation of that activity. This is especially so where the activity excludes others or is harmful to others. So, the state cannot force a person to marry somebody of the opposite sex or of a different racial identity as these activities are deeply personal and close to the core of the individual's private beliefs and attitudes. However, the state may well prohibit a large company from discriminating against homosexuals or against black people when employing staff or when deciding whether to provide a service to them.

Between these two extremes lies a large number of voluntary, semi-private associations that contribute towards the enrichment and happiness of individuals in different ways. These associations are semi-private because they fulfil some public function or provide a service or benefit to the public. However, these semi-private associations constitute a grey area where it will not always be easy to decide whether intrusion by the state or others would be constitutionally warranted or not. The state's reach into these organisations depends on the nature of the organisation, the impact it has on the public, the extent to which it regulates economic and social mobility, and the constitutional right that the association furthers and protects. According to Brennan J, the size, purpose, policies, selectivity, congeniality and

14 468 US 609 (1984) 618.

15 See generally *Dawood*.

16 468 US 609 (1984) 620.

other characteristics of an association may be pertinent in determining whether it should be subject to state regulation.[17]

When a court has to make a determination as to the constitutionality of exclusionary practices, it will consider the nature of the constitutional right a party seeks to enforce as well as the potentially negative effect this has on the other party whose right the association seeks to enforce. Thus, if, on the one hand, the association has been formed for commercial activities, thus affecting the right to choose a trade, occupation and profession, the state may have greater latitude in reaching into the domains of these associations. If, on the other hand, the constitutional rights that the association seeks to protect, promote and enhance relate to religion, culture and language, then the reach of the state may be more circumscribed. Similarly, if the state seeks to invade the associational rights of an organisation in a manner that poses a real risk to the organisation's members or if such an intrusion would have a detrimental effect on individuals joining the organisation or association, then courts may well attempt to protect such rights in a robust fashion.

PAUSE FOR REFLECTION

The right to freedom of association indispensable where a group holds dissident beliefs

The National Association for the Advancement of Coloured People (NAACP) is a civil rights non-governmental organisation that seeks to ensure that black people in the United States are accorded their constitutional rights. In the 1950s and 60s, they engaged in protest action and litigation in many states in the south of the USA where legally sanctioned racial discrimination was rife. In *NAACP v Alabama*,[18] the state of Alabama demanded the names and addresses of all the NAACP members in Alabama. This would have enabled the state to see who was contributing effort and funds to the organisation. The US Supreme Court held that the compulsory disclosure of membership lists would violate the associational rights of members and that 'privacy in group association may in many circumstances be indispensable to preservation of freedom of association, particularly where a group espouses dissident beliefs'.[19]

Apart from safeguarding the liberty of individuals to decide for themselves how they want to live and with whom they want to associate, associational rights are also protected to prevent 'capture'.[20] Associations require their members to expend time, energy and funds on building the organisation. Members readily volunteer because of their commitment to the cause. The right to freedom of association allows the organisation to adopt policies to prevent persons with aims that are inimical to the objectives of the organisation from 'capturing' the organisation and subverting its objectives. Thus in *Royal Society for the Prevention of Cruelty to Animals (RSPCA) v Attorney-General*,[21] the English Court upheld exclusionary policies of the RSPCA designed to remove and exclude members who wished to change the society's policy on hunting and blood sports. Given the RSPCA's commitment to the humane treatment of animals, policy changes favouring hunting and blood sports would effectively result in the 'capture' of the society and change its focus and emphasis.

17 *Roberts v United States Jaycees* 468 US 609 (1984) 620.
18 357 U.S. 449 (1958).
19 *NAACP v Alabama* 357 U.S. 449 (1958) para 462.
20 Woolman (2013) 44.9.
21 [2002] 1 WLR 448.

The Court held that the RSPCA's exclusionary policies were consistent with the Human Rights Act of 1998. The close nexus between the objectives and the exclusionary policies and the limited impact on the rights of the people denied admission or excluded from the organisation adequately justified the policy of the organisation and rendered it permissible.[22]

A corollary of the right to associate is the right to dissociate. Thus, in *Hurley v Irish-American Gay, Lesbian and Bisexual Group of Boston*,[23] the US Supreme Court held that the right to dissociate included the right to exclude unwanted members and unwanted messages. The organisers of a St Patrick's Day parade were willing to allow gay men and lesbians to participate in the parade, but refused to allow them to march as a unit under their own banners. The Court held that the parade organisers had a right to refuse to endorse a message supporting gay rights which would be conveyed by permitting the banners. The Court held that 'it boils down to the choice of a speaker not to propound a particular point of view, and the choice is presumed to lie beyond the government's power to control'.[24]

13.2.3 Societal interests overriding association rights

The right to freedom of association is not an unqualified right. As discussed in the introduction to this chapter, a tension may arise between the right to associate and the important interests of others and of the broader society. Sometimes the state may therefore wish to interfere with the right to freedom of association to secure the safety of society, to protect the dignity of all citizens and to facilitate greater political participation.[25] For example, the state may ban criminal associations to protect society against the dangers of organised crime. The state may also interfere with the right to freedom of association to ensure that certain groups open themselves up to a wider potential membership because such organisations control access to important social goods. The extent to which the function being fulfilled by the association fulfils a public function will also play an important role in deciding on whether the association could be limited. The more the public goods distributed by an association or the more public its function, the more likely it is to be subject to legitimate state intervention.[26] The state may therefore interfere with the freedom of association in certain contexts. We discuss examples of this in the sections that follow.

13.2.3.1 Equality

Certain associations may be required to 'open themselves up to a wider potential membership because they control access to important social goods'.[27] One way in which this is mandated in the South African context is by the Promotion of Equality and Prevention of Unfair Discrimination Act (PEPUDA).[28] The PEPUDA asserts the primary importance of equality concerns and presents a challenge to the right to freedom of association. This is especially so because the PEPUDA seems to challenge control over membership policies and the internal affairs of every private organisation and institution in the country. As membership policies and the organisation of internal affairs are often critical to an association's identity, the PEPUDA could, in effect, force a change in these policies. The PEPUDA therefore represents a severe limitation on the general right to freedom of association.[29]

22 *Royal Society for the Prevention of Cruelty to Animals (RSPCA) v Attorney-General* [2002] 1 WLR 448 para 37.
23 515 US 557 (1995).
24 515 US 557 (1995) para 21.
25 Woolman (2013) 44.32.
26 Currie and De Waal (2013) 403.
27 Currie and De Waal (2013) 404.
28 Act 4 of 2000, discussed in detail in Chapter 12.
29 Woolman (2013) 44.35.

Section 6 of the PEPUDA states that '[n]either the State nor any person may unfairly discriminate against any person'. As we have seen in chapter 12, when a private individual or organisation discriminates against an individual, say by excluding that person from membership of the organisation on the basis of his or her race, gender or sexual orientation, the onus is on the party who discriminated to prove that the discrimination was not unfair but rather that it was fair. Sections 14(2) and (3) of the PEPUDA set out the factors a court must take into account when determining whether the respondent has proven the discrimination to be fair. These factors are:

- the context
- whether the discrimination reasonably and justifiably differentiates between persons according to objectively determinable criteria intrinsic to the activity concerned
- whether the discrimination impairs or is likely to impair human dignity
- the impact or likely impact of the discrimination on the complainant
- the position of the complainant in society and whether he or she suffers from patterns of disadvantage or belongs to a group that suffers from such patterns of disadvantage
- the nature and extent of the discrimination
- whether the discrimination is systemic in nature
- whether the discrimination has a legitimate purpose
- whether and to what extent the discrimination achieves its purpose
- whether there are less restrictive and less disadvantageous means to achieve the purpose
- whether and to what extent the respondent has taken such steps as are reasonable in the circumstances to address the disadvantage which arises from or is related to one or more of the prohibited grounds or to accommodate diversity.

A private organisation whose policies regarding admission discriminate against an individual based on his or her sexual orientation, for example, would have to argue that the exclusion is 'intrinsic to the activity' of that organisation and that it is not based merely on prejudice or irrelevant attitudes that fuel discrimination.[30] The organisation may also argue that the discrimination has a legitimate purpose and, as such, can be justified. In each case, a court has to determine whether the discrimination is intrinsic to the nature of the organisation and its purpose in the manner discussed in chapter 12. In each case the association claiming a right to association in potential conflict with the PEPUDA will have the burden of showing that its associational interests trump the interests to equality. This will not always be easy to do.

13.2.3.2 Democracy

The state may also interfere in the right to freedom of association in the furtherance of the goals of democracy. This may require organisations in certain contexts to structure their internal affairs in a more democratic and egalitarian fashion.[31] In each case the question would be to what extent the state's interest in the integrity of a democratic process and in the maintenance and protection of a democratic society justifies the limitation on the association's right to order its affairs as it wishes and to pursue the goals it was set up to pursue. The freedom of political parties to arrange their internal affairs as they wish and to

30 See *Hoffmann v South African Airways* (CCT17/00) [2000] ZACC 17; 2001 (1) SA 1; 2000 (11) BCLR 1235; [2000] 12 BLLR 1365 (CC) (28 September 2000) para 37 where the Constitutional Court stated: 'Prejudice can never justify unfair discrimination.'

31 Currie and De Waal (2013) 404.

pursue the ends they were set up to pursue will potentially be acutely affected by the need to safeguard democracy. This will be less evident if we start from the premise that political parties and other associations are largely private entities created to pursue private ends.[32] However, if our premise is that political parties and other associations are essential for a functioning representative democracy, a more onerous burden will fall on political parties to be structured along democratic lines and not to pursue undemocratic ends.

In Germany, for example, the German Constitutional Court banned the Socialist Reich Party (SRP) in 1952 and the Communist Party of Germany (KPD) in 1956. According to article 21, paragraph 2 of the German Basic Law, parties which, by reason of their aims or the behaviour of their members, seek to impair or destroy the free democratic order or to endanger the existence of the Federal Republic of Germany are unconstitutional.[33] Thus, legislation may attempt to force political organisations to structure themselves in a more democratic and egalitarian way.

In the United States, in *Buckley v Valeo*,[34] the US Supreme Court confirmed the constitutionality of laws requiring compulsory disclosure of the source of campaign contributions over $10 and in respect of political contributions of more than $100 per annum. The applicants in this case argued that the laws violated the associational rights of minor parties and small contributors. The Court held that associational rights were infringed. However, the countervailing state interests were sufficiently important to outweigh the limitation on the right to freedom of association.[35] The societal interests identified in this case were the need to help the electorate evaluate the candidates standing for office by disclosing the identity of their supporters, the need to avoid corruption and the appearance of corruption, and the need to gather data required to enforce the contribution limits set down in other laws.[36]

In *Institute for Democracy in South Africa and Others v African National Congress and Others*,[37] the High Court adopted a different approach. In this case, the Institute for Democracy in South Africa (IDASA) brought an application in terms of the Promotion of Access to Information Act (PAIA)[38] against all the major political parties for access to their donation records regarding the date of donation, name of the donor, amount or value of the donation and the conditions, if any, on which the donation was made or received. In the main, the African National Congress (ANC) resisted the application on the basis that there should be comprehensive legislation on this issue as opposed to having to disclose information on an ad hoc basis.

The Court was of the opinion that the political parties for the purposes of this application were to be regarded as private bodies. In terms of the PAIA, an applicant had to demonstrate that they required the information from the private body for the exercise or protection of any rights.[39] One of the arguments made by the applicants was that they required the records to assist citizens to make more accurate political choices and to choose between the various parties. Disclosure of financial benefactors would place citizens in a better position to make

32 Currie and De Waal (2013) 404.

33 See McWhinney, E (1957) The German Federal Constitutional Court and the Communist Party decision *Indiana Law Journal* 32(3):295–312 at 295.

34 424 U.S. 1 (1976).

35 *Buckley v Valeo* 424 U.S. 1 (1976) para 17.

36 *Buckley v Valeo* 424 U.S. 1 (1976) para 18.

37 (9828/03) [2005] ZAWCHC 30; 2005 (5) SA 39 (C) [2005] 3 All SA 45 (C) (20 April 2005).

38 Act 2 of 2000.

39 *IDASA* para 33.

these decisions. The Court was of the view that this did not adequately demonstrate 'how the donation records would assist them in exercising or protecting any of the rights on which they rely or why, in the absence of these donation records, they are unable to exercise those rights'.[40] It went on to hold:

> **On the face of it, section 19(1) prevents any restrictions being imposed on a citizen's right of making political choices, such as forming a political party, participating in the activities of and recruiting members for a party, and campaigning for a political cause. Similarly, the right to 'free, fair and regular elections' enshrined in section 19(2) does not impose a duty on political parties to disclose funding sources, nor does it afford citizens a right to gain access to such records. The emphasis in section 19(2) lies upon the elections and the nature of the electoral process and not so much upon the persons or parties participating in those elections.**[41]

The application was unsuccessful. This interpretation of section 19 is narrower than that required to develop a constitutional democracy. The right to vote must include the right to make properly informed political choices. Knowing the identity of the financial benefactors of political parties would enable the electorate to know potential sources of influence in that party and hence whether it is deserving of their vote. This information would enable them to exercise their right in a more effective manner. Given these arguments, the Court ought to have found that the information was required for the exercise or protection of rights and then determined whether the parties could refuse disclosure in terms of the exceptions listed in the PAIA.

In *Ramakatsa and Others v Magashule and Others*, the Constitutional Court found that the Constitution requires political parties to act lawfully.[42] In the context of section 19 of the Constitution, which guarantees for every citizen the right to participate freely in the activities of a political party, the Court found that there was a duty on every political party 'to act lawfully and in accordance with its own constitution'.[43] This means that the Constitution gives every member of every political party the right to exact compliance with the constitution of a political party by the leadership of that party. Courts can therefore scrutinise a political party's constitution to establish whether that party has acted in accordance with its own constitution and may set aside decisions of that party where the party has failed to adhere to its own constitution.[44] The Court emphasised that in the South African system of democracy, political parties 'occupy the centre stage and play a vital part in facilitating the exercise of political rights'.[45] Therefore, political parties are indispensible conduits for the enjoyment of some of the rights included in the Bill of Rights.[46]

Arguably, the implication of this judgment is that political parties must operate in an essentially democratic manner and that political parties cannot pursue policies that, at their core, are aimed at destroying the constitutional democracy established by the Constitution. However, the Constitutional Court has not provided a definitive answer on how to approach the question of political parties whose aim is to overthrow our constitutional democracy.

40 *IDASA* para 71.
41 *IDASA* para 71.
42 (CCT 109/12) [2012] ZACC 31; 2013 (2) BCLR 202 (CC) (18 December 2012) para 16.
43 *Ramakatsa* para 16.
44 *Ramakatsa* para 16.
45 *Ramakatsa* para 65.
46 *Ramakatsa* para 68.

CRITICAL THINKING

Is the infringement of the right to freedom of association justifiable in the interests of preserving constitutional democracy in South Africa?

As we have seen, some political parties exercise significant power in South Africa. In 2013, after Mr Julius Malema was expelled from the ANC, he came together with other interested individuals and formed a new political formation called the Economic Freedom Fighters (EFF). The Constitution of the EFF sets out its aims as follows:

1. ECONOMIC FREEDOM FIGHTERS (EFF) is a Political organization styled as a Political Party which seeks to act in the interests of all South Africans striving for ECONOMIC EMANCIPATION IN OUR LIFE TIME.
2. The EFF is anti-capitalist, anti-racist, anti-sexist and anti-imperialist in its world outlook and is driven by sound democratic socialist values where the leadership is accountable to the membership which elected it.
3. The basic programme of the EFF is the complete overthrow of the neo liberal anti-black state as well as the bourgeoisie and all other exploiting classes; the establishment of the dictatorship of the people in place of the dictatorship of the bourgeoisie and the triumph of socialism over capitalism. The ultimate aim of the EFF is the realization of socialism through people's power and the establishment of a state that responds to the needs of its people.
4. The EFF is a vigorous vanguard organization leading the revolutionary masses in the fight against the class enemy.
5. The EFF takes socialism as the theoretical basis guiding its thinking and development of its political line and in this respect identifies itself as a MARXIST, LENINIST, and FANONIAN organisation.
6. Members of EFF, who dedicate their lives to the struggle for socialism must be resolute, fearless and surmount every difficulty to win victory![47]

The EFF Constitution thus states that one of its aims is the overthrow of the current state and replacing it with a 'dictatorship of the people'. Any move to prohibit the EFF from participating in elections or from operating in South Africa in line with these goals will be met by arguments regarding freedom of association. If the EFF is banned and individuals are prohibited from belonging to the party, it will infringe on the right of freedom of association of everyone as well as the right of every citizen to form a political party and to take part in its activities guaranteed in section 19 of the Constitution. The question that will face a court in such an event is whether the infringement of the rights is justifiable in the interests of preserving constitutional democracy in South Africa.

13.2.4 Balancing rights

It is not uncommon for the right to freedom of association to clash with other rights and the adjudicating body then has to strike an appropriate balance between the competing rights. In *Forum for Black Journalists v Katy Katopodis*,[48] the Appeal Committee of the South African Human Rights Commission (SAHRC) had to consider whether a group of black journalists

47 Economic Freedom Fighters Constitution, adopted on 27 July 2013, available at http://effighters.org.za/documents/constitution/.

48 Case ref no.: GP/2008/0161/L BIOS available at at http://cdn.bizcommunity.com/f/0902/Katy%20Katopodis%20vs%20%20FBJ%20findings.pdf.

could constitutionally exclude white journalists from a meeting of their organisation. The primary objective of the Forum for Black Journalists (FBJ) is the 'upliftment of black journalists in general and the African in particular'.[49] FBJ organised an *imbizo* which was addressed by Mr Jacob Zuma, the President of the ANC, as part of its relaunch. This was before Mr Zuma became President of South Africa. The FBJ directed invitations exclusively to black journalists, but these invitations were not restricted to members of the organisation. White journalists who attempted to attend the *imbizo* were either denied entry or requested to leave.

The FBJ argued that the right to associate, especially of a private body, includes the right to dissociate. All the FBJ had to demonstrate was a rational connection between the discriminatory policy and the association's ends. It justified its closed membership by pointing to the legitimate objective of preventing the dilution of its voice in its pursuit of substantive equality. The white journalists contended that excluding them from the meeting solely on account of their race amounted to unfair discrimination on the basis of race.

The Appeal Committee of the SAHRC found that the FBJ could not be described as an intimate or private association as its membership was open to all black journalists in the country.[50] It lay on the continuum between an intimate or private organisation and an overtly public organisation.[51] The more public an organisation is, the more difficult it is to justify exclusions in furtherance of the freedom of association.[52] The Appeal Committee found that the purpose of uplifting black journalists in general and Africans in particular was a legitimate objective.[53] In defence of its racially exclusive admissions policy, the FBJ relied heavily on their right to freedom of association. The Committee reasoned as follows:

> **The issue before us is whether the FBJ acted in a constitutionally impermissible fashion when it decided to exclude white journalists from its membership and prevented them from attending the Imbizo. The assertion by the respondent is that the rights to dignity and not to be subjected to unfair discrimination on the basis of race have been infringed by the policies and practices of the appellant.**
>
> **Not admitting white journalists on the basis of their race to the Imbizo and excluding them from membership of the FBJ on the same basis is clearly invasive of their right to dignity. The issue is whether the benefits that accrue to the organisation justifies [*sic*] this intrusion ...**
>
> **..., the Supreme Court of Appeal in *Midi Television (Pty) Limited t/a e-tv v Director of Public Prosecutions*[54] had to reconcile and balance the freedom of expression and the right to a fair trial. The following was stated:**
>
> > **Where the constitutional rights themselves have the potential to be mutually limiting – in that the full enjoyment of one necessarily curtails the full enjoyment of another and vice versa – a court must necessarily reconcile them. They cannot be reconciled by purporting to weigh the value of one right against the value of another and then preferring the right that is considered to be more valued, and**

49 *Forum for Black Journalists* [2009] 2 All SA 499 (SAHRC) 510.
50 *Forum for Black Journalists* 511.
51 *Forum for Black Journalists* 512.
52 *Forum for Black Journalists* 511.
53 *Forum for Black Journalists* 511.
54 (100/06) [2007] ZASCA 56; [2007] SCA 56 (RSA); [2007] 3 All SA 318 (SCA) (18 May 2007).

> **jettisoning the other, because all protected rights have equal value. They are rather to be reconciled by recognising a limitation upon the exercise of one right to the extent that it is necessary to do so in order to accommodate the exercise of the other (or in some cases, by recognising an appropriate limitation upon the exercise of both rights) according to what is required by the particular circumstances and within the constraints that are imposed by Section 36.**[55]

The judgment of the Appeal Committee of the SAHRC goes on to state:

> **In determining the extent to which the full exercise of one right to the other or both of them might need to be curtailed in order to reconcile them what needs to be compared with one another are the 'extent of the limitation' that is placed upon the particular right, on the one hand, and the 'purpose, importance and effect of the intrusion', on the other hand. To the extent that anything needs to be weighed in making that evaluation it is not the relative values of the rights themselves that are weighed (I have said that all protected rights have equal value) but it is rather the benefit that flows from allowing the intrusion that is to be weighed against the loss that the intrusion will entail. It is only if the particular loss is outweighed by the particular benefit, to an extent that meets the standard that is set by section 36, that the law will recognise the validity of the intrusion.**
>
> **Thus the submission by the appellant that it can adopt a racially exclusive membership policy provided that it demonstrates a rational connection between its discriminatory policy and the association's ends is inconsistent with comments made in the VA report and with the dicta from Midi Television quoted above. The FBJ has the right to form an association to uplift black journalists and exclude persons whose objectives are inimical to its founding values. FBJ used race as the criterion and formed the view that all white journalists should be excluded from their organisation. No argument has been made as to why the less intrusive admission policy which required a full commitment to the values and goals of the organisation would not have been sufficient to protect its distinct 'voice' and identity. The imprecise and blunt instrument of racial exclusivity was relied upon notwithstanding the egregious impact of exclusions upon people who may have supported the broader objectives of the organisation. There is nothing before us which leads us to conclude that the racially exclusive membership policies and practices bring a legitimate benefit to the FBJ which justifies the infringement of the right to dignity of the persons excluded on the basis of race. In the circumstances, we find that the exclusion of the white journalists both from the Imbizo and from membership of the FBJ is not justified in terms of section 36 of the Constitution.**[56]

The Appeal Committee of the SAHRC thus found against the FBJ in this case. As will be apparent from the above, it is necessary to determine what benefit accrues as a consequence of the exclusion. The benefit must then be weighed against the cost occasioned by such exclusion. The courts will sanction the exclusion if the benefit outweighs the cost of the exclusion and is a reasonable and proportionate response.

55 *Midi Television* para 9 on page 519 of *Forum for Black Journalists.*
56 *Forum for Black Journalists* 520.

CRITICAL THINKING

When can the right to freedom of association justifiably be used to exclude others from associating with the organisation?

This question is a source of great jurisprudential and moral anxiety, partly because the ability to associate holds potential financial and social benefits. Excluding some from these benefits on the basis of personal attributes or characteristics may therefore harm those who are excluded.

White suggests certain rules to deal with this difficult question.[57] The first rule or guideline White suggests is that an exclusionary rule is presumptively legitimate if it is **purpose-protecting**. In other words, if an exclusionary rule is aimed at protecting the very purpose for which the association was created, it will be presumed to be legitimate.[58]

However, White suggests a second rule, namely that if an exclusionary rule is **opportunity-depriving**, the rule must presumptively be viewed as not being legitimate. In other words, if by excluding individuals from the association they are potentially deprived of opportunities, it will be difficult to justify the exclusion.[59]

A third rule is that the presumption of legitimate exclusion is especially strong if the rule is **integrity-protecting**. In other words, where the formation of an association is particularly important to allow an individual to exercise his or her liberties of **conscience** or expression, then there will be a strong assumption that the exclusionary rule that safeguards this associational space should be held as being legitimate.[60]

Of course, it will be clear that these three rules could easily be in tension with one another. An exclusionary rule that is purpose-protecting as well as integrity-protecting can be so drastically opportunity-depriving that it would not be held to be valid. For example, a rule that allows a religious school to exclude female learners on the grounds that male and female learners must be taught separately may be both purpose-protecting and integrity-protecting. But where that school offers a high-quality education and provides its graduates with opportunities in life that are not easily provided to others in the same community, the rule may also be opportunity-depriving. This is because female learners will be deprived in a drastic manner of some of the opportunities that are available to male learners. Consequently, it is far from clear whether such a rule conforms with the right to freedom of association.

13.3 Freedom of religion, belief and opinion

13.3.1 Introduction

Freedom of religion and conscience – the freedom to hold views about religious and other moral issues and the freedom to practice those beliefs – goes to the heart of what it means to be human in a modern democracy. In the open and democratic society contemplated by the Constitution, both the religious beliefs held by the great majority of South Africans as

57 White, S (1997) Freedom of association and the right to exclude *The Journal of Political Philosophy* 5(4):373–91 at 373.
58 White (1997) 380.
59 White (1997) 380.
60 White (1997) 381.

well as the beliefs of non-believers and minority faiths must be fully respected.[61] As the Constitutional Court pointed out in *Minister of Home Affairs and Another v Fourie and Another*:

> **For many believers, their relationship with God or creation is central to all their activities. It concerns their capacity to relate in an intensely meaningful fashion to their sense of themselves, their community and their universe. For millions in all walks of life, religion provides support and nurture and a framework for individual and social stability and growth. Religious belief has the capacity to awaken concepts of self-worth and human dignity which form the cornerstone of human rights. Such belief affects the believer's view of society and founds a distinction between right and wrong. It expresses itself in the affirmation and continuity of powerful traditions that frequently have an ancient character transcending historical epochs and national boundaries. For believers, then, what is at stake is not merely a question of convenience or comfort, but an intensely held sense about what constitutes the good and proper life and their place in creation.**[62]

However, non-believers may hold similarly strong and profound views about the meaning of their lives not based on religious beliefs. This means that religious beliefs or the absence of such beliefs - however honestly and sincerely held - 'cannot influence what the Constitution dictates'.[63] This conundrum highlights the fact that freedom of religion and conscience is a right that demands serious engagement with the notion of diversity: how to accommodate different and often diametrically opposed beliefs and views about the world, while respecting and accommodating these diverse beliefs and views.

To accommodate diversity in the realm of belief, section 15(1) of the Bill of Rights guarantees the right of everyone to 'freedom of conscience, religion, thought, belief and opinion' while section 15(2) deals with the circumstances under which religious observance may be conducted in state or state-aided institutions. In a heterogeneous and multicultural society like South Africa, the protection of the right to freedom of conscience, religion, thought, belief and opinion takes on a special significance. It signals the Constitution's unique concern with the protection of people with diverse beliefs and opinions. It recognises the importance of accommodating the views, opinions and practices of people with diverse world views and religious beliefs that will often be in conflict with one another. This right contained in section 15 is therefore an important right through which we accommodate and carefully manage diversity in our society.

In this regard, the grouping together of the freedom of conscience, religion, thought, belief and opinion is significant. The deliberate clustering of these rights signifies the protection of the right to hold the religious beliefs of a person's choice, together with the right to entertain agnostic or atheistic views and other beliefs. It thus protects the right to believe in a particular God or Gods and the religious teachings associated with a belief in that God or Gods; the right to remain uncertain about believing in a God or Gods and the religious teachings associated with a belief in that God or Gods; as well as the right not to believe in any God at all. In other words, the fact that the right protects freedom of

61 *Minister of Home Affairs and Another v Fourie and Another* (CCT 60/04) [2005] ZACC 19; 2006 (3) BCLR 355 (CC); 2006 (1) SA 524 (CC) (1 December 2005) para 89.

62 *Fourie* para 89. See also *Christian Education South Africa v Minister of Education* (CCT4/00) [2000] ZACC 11; 2000 (4) SA 757; 2000 (10) BCLR 1051 (18 August 2000) para 36.

63 *National Coalition for Gay and Lesbian Equality v Minister of Justice* para 38.

PAUSE FOR REFLECTION

How religious are South Africans?

South Africans are truly diverse as far as their beliefs are concerned. Although statistics differ widely depending on who measures them, a 2011 survey found that the number of people in South Africa who consider themselves religious has dropped by 19%. According to the poll, released by the Win-Gallup International Religiosity and Atheism Index which measures global self-perceptions on belief, religious South Africans dropped from 83% in 2005 to 64% in 2012.[64] Official figures from the South African census are different regarding religious adherence. Table 13.1 contains the latest available figures from the census and provides a breakdown of those who adhere to various religious beliefs in South Africa.

Table 13.1 Census statistics regarding adherents of religious beliefs

Religion	Adherents	%	Adherents	%
	2001[65]		2007[66]	
Christianity	35 750 641	79,77	29 684 861	73,52
Non-religious	6 767 165	15,10	3 262 428	8,08
Other	283 815	0,63		
Buddhism/Chinese folk			12 113	0,03
Islam	654 064	1,46	985 460	1,45
Undetermined	610 974	1,36		
Hinduism	551 668	1,23	504 707	1,25
African traditional belief	125 898	0,28	6 056 487	15,00
Judaism	75 549	0,17	68 640	0,17

conscience, religion, thought, belief and opinion indicates that the scope of its protection journeys beyond protecting the right to believe in a supreme being.[67]

However, it is not only the right **to believe** or **not to believe** that is protected by section 15 of the Bill of Rights. Section 15 also protects the right **to act** in accordance with those beliefs or non-beliefs and for a person to organise his or her life in a manner that demonstrates allegiance to the particular chosen belief system. As pointed out by Sachs J in the Constitutional Court judgment in *Christian Education South Africa v Minister of Education*, the right of an individual to act or not to act in accordance with his or her beliefs is one of the key ingredients of a person's human dignity.[68] For many people, their relationship with their

64 The survey, conducted during November 2011 to January 2012, was based on interviews with 52 000 men and women from 57 countries in five continents. See Fewer religious people in SA – Survey available at http://www.news24.com/SouthAfrica/News/Fewer-religious-people-in-SA-survey-20120810.

65 Statistics South Africa (2001) Census 2001 by province, gender, religion recode (derived) and population group.

66 Country Profile: South Africa (2007–8) Religious Intelligence.

67 See Farlam, P 'Freedom of religion, belief and opinion' in Woolman and Bishop (2013) 41.13.

68 (CCT4/00) [2000] ZACC 11; 2000 (4) SA 757; 2000 (10) BCLR 1051 (18 August 2000) para 36.

God or creator is central to their being and often influences much of their interaction both with their sectarian peers and with secular society.[69] For others, their rejection of the idea of a higher being or creator is central to their personality.

The persecution of people because of their religious beliefs or their refusal to believe has been the cause of intense conflict, upheaval and strife. Such strife is often caused when the state treats one religion more favourably than other religions or when the state treats religion or non-religion in a more favourable manner. In this regard, the manner in which the state treated religion during the apartheid era is significant. Prior to 1994, the state officially endorsed a certain version of Christianity and the state was often described as a Christian Nationalist state.[70] The apartheid state passed several laws to promote a specific conception of the Christian religion, giving credence to the perception that the state favoured a certain narrow form of Christianity above other religions and above non-religion.[71] Primary and secondary education in public schools reserved for white children was based on the principle of Christian national education while education in schools reserved for black children had to have a Christian character.[72] The pre-democratic state also refused to recognise the validity of marriages that did not conform to the Christian prototype.[73] The judiciary, too, was not free from demonstrating a preference for Christianity. In 1917, a South African judge even identified Christianity with what he called 'civilized peoples'.[74]

This history of preferential treatment for a certain version of Christianity above other religions and non-religion does not mean that Christianity should not be respected and protected as the dominant religion in South Africa in the post-apartheid era. In fact, although the Constitutional Court has insisted that the rights of non-believers and minority faiths must be fully respected, it has also emphasised the need to respect the religious beliefs held by the majority of South Africans.[75] The Constitutional Court has pointed out that while religion is an intensely personal issue, it would nevertheless not be appropriate in all cases to relegate religious practices and observance to the private sphere.[76] Religious bodies play a large and important part in public life through schools, hospitals and poverty relief programmes. In addition, religious bodies 'command ethical behaviour from their members and bear witness to the exercise of power by state and private agencies'.[77] Religious bodies also 'promote music, art and theatre' and 'provide halls for community activities'.[78] As such, they form part of the very fabric of society.[79] However, the Court also warned that while this role must be recognised, it must be done in a manner that does not infringe on the rights of those who do not share the beliefs of the majority religion as '**[m]ajoritarian opinion can**

69 *Christian Education South Africa* para 36.

70 See generally Dubow, S (1992) Afrikaner nationalism, apartheid and the conceptualization of race *Journal of African History* 33(2):209–37.

71 Van der Vyver, JD 'Religion' in Joubert, WA (ed) (2009) *Law of South Africa* 2nd ed Vol 23 197. See also *S v Lawrence, S v Negal; S v Solberg* (CCT38/96, CCT39/96, CCT40/96) [1997] ZACC 11; 1997 (10) BCLR 1348; 1997 (4) SA 1176 (6 October 1997) para 149. Van der Vyver points out that the Publications Act 42 of 1974 'seemingly subject[ed] the entire censorship system to the dictates of Christian morality'.

72 *Lawrence* para 149.

73 *Lawrence* para 151. See also, generally, Sinclair, J (1996) *The Law of Marriage* volume 1 164–5.

74 *Seedat's Executors v The Master (Natal)* 1917 AD 302 at 307 (per Innes CJ). See also *Ismail v Ismail* 1983 (1) SA 1006 (A) 1026; Kerr, AJ (1984) Back to the problems of a hundred or more years ago: Public policy concerning contracts relating to marriages that are potentially or actually polygamous *South African Law Journal* 101(3):445–56 at 445.

75 *Fourie* para 89.

76 *Fourie* para 89.

77 *Fourie* para 90.

78 *Fourie* para 90.

79 *Fourie* para 90.

often be harsh to minorities that exist outside the mainstream' (our emphasis).[80] What is needed is to strike a balance between recognising and respecting the religious beliefs of the majority and protecting those people and groups whose views do not conform to that of the majority. The Court stated:

> **In the open and democratic society contemplated by the Constitution there must be mutually respectful co-existence between the secular and the sacred. The function of the Court is to recognise the sphere which each inhabits, not to force the one into the sphere of the other. Provided there is no prejudice to the fundamental rights of any person or group, the law will legitimately acknowledge a diversity of strongly-held opinions on matters of great public controversy. I stress the qualification that there must be no prejudice to basic rights.[81]**

By recognising the need to accommodate both the secular and the sacred within the framework of managing a diverse society, section 15 of the Constitution does not require a strict separation between the state on the one hand and religious institutions and organisations on the other. In the following sections we discuss the scope and content of the right to freedom of conscience and religion. We explore the ways in which the religious beliefs of the majority can be respected and recognised within the constitutional framework while also providing protection for those people who adhere to minority beliefs and those people who are not religious at all.

PAUSE FOR REFLECTION

The nuanced relationship between the secular and the sectarian spheres of our society

The Constitutional Court considered the nuanced relationship between the secular and the sectarian spheres of our society in *Fourie*, a case that dealt with the recognition of same-sex marriage. The Court had to determine whether the non-recognition of same-sex marriages was inconsistent with the Constitution. If so, the Court had then to determine what needed to be done to remedy the situation.

One of the arguments made was that if the law was under-inclusive by not recognising same-sex unions, the situation should be remedied by providing an appropriate alternative form of recognition to same-sex unions and not by accommodating these unions within the existing institution of marriage. This argument was premised on the religious belief of some that the institution of marriage is restricted to the union of one man and one woman and thus cannot be extended to include same-sex unions. To extend the definition of marriage would, according to this submission, amount to a significant infringement of the right to freedom of religion of those people who believed in the religious texts that defined marriage as the union of one man and one women.

The Court recognised the broad and important role that religion plays in the life of society through the provision of schools and hospitals, by poverty alleviation programmes and other initiatives that enrich people's lives.[82] According to the Court, these activities form part of the fabric of a diversified society and must be recognised

80 *Fourie* para 94.
81 *Fourie* para 94.
82 *Fourie* para 90.

as such.[83] However, the Court reasoned that this did not mean that religious texts must be used to interpret the Constitution. There had to be a mutually respectful coexistence between the secular and the sacred.[84] The state should not intervene in the spiritual or sacred sphere by pronouncing on religious texts or by insisting that all religions solemnise same-sex marriages. Similarly, when the state affords same-sex couples the same status, entitlements and responsibilities as heterosexual couples, it does not impinge on the right of religious organisations that do not wish to solemnise same-sex marriages.[85] By doing so, it is simply functioning within the secular sphere over which the Constitution is supreme.[86] Thus, the rights of the religious groups functioning within their spiritual sphere will not be affected by the recognition of same-sex unions by the law.[87]

Subsequent to the *Fourie* judgment, Parliament passed the Civil Union Act.[88] This Act recognises same-sex unions which can now be described as marriages. In the view of Parliament, having an alternative such as a civil union for same-sex couples would amount to segregation and would continue to reinforce negative stereotypes. Hence, Parliament made the decision that parties could refer to these unions as marriages should they choose to do so. However, the Civil Union Act also allows religious denominations to opt out of solemnising same-sex marriages. The Act allows such religious denominations to adhere to their particular views on the nature of marriage while accommodating the need to respect the right to equality of gay men and lesbians.

13.3.2 The scope and content of section 15(1) of the Constitution

It is far from clear what the Constitutional Court's understanding is of the exact scope and content of the right to freedom of religion protected in section 15(1). This is because a divided Constitutional Court differed sharply on the scope and content of the right when it first had to decide on its meaning in the case of *S v Lawrence; S v Negal; S v Solberg*.[89]

The starting point for understanding the scope and content of the right to freedom of religion - agreed on by all the judges of the Constitutional Court - is that our Constitution does not require a strict separation between the state and religious bodies.[90] This approach differs markedly from that required by the United States (US) Constitution. The US Constitution prohibits the state from setting up a church or passing laws which aid one religion, aid all religions or prefer one religion over another. In the US it is assumed that the US constitutional clause against the establishment of a religion by law was intended to erect 'a wall of separation between church and State'.[91] As Chaskalson J explained in the *Lawrence* case, the right to freedom of religion in the South African Constitution - unlike the US - does not include an 'establishment clause'.[92] The US view that a wall of separation should be

83 *Fourie* para 90.
84 *Fourie* para 94.
85 *Fourie* para 96.
86 *Fourie* para 94.
87 *Fourie* para 108.
88 Act 17 of 2006.
89 (CCT38/96, CCT39/96, CCT40/96) [1997] ZACC 11; 1997 (10) BCLR 1348; 1997 (4) SA 1176 (6 October 1997).
90 *Lawrence* para 119.
91 *Everson v Board of Education of the Township of Ewing* [1947] USSC 44; 330 US 1, 15-6 (1947) para 11.
92 *Lawrence* para 100.

erected between religion and the state is not applicable here.[93] To read such a requirement into section 15:

> **would have far reaching implications beyond the apparent scope and purpose of section 14 [now 15]. If such obligations on the part of the state are to be read into section 14 [now section 15] does this mean that Christmas Day and Easter Friday can no longer be public holidays, that 'Family Day' is suspect because it falls on Easter Monday, that the SABC as public broadcaster cannot broadcast church services (as it does regularly on Sunday mornings, though it does not regularly broadcast Muslim services on Fridays or Jewish services on Saturdays or Hindu services on any particular day of the week), that its daily religious programmes must be cancelled, and that state subsidies to denominational schools are prohibited? These examples can be multiplied by reference to the extremely complex United States law which has developed around the 'establishment clause'.**[94]

The reason for the rejection of the US view can be found in section 15(2) of the Constitution (discussed below) which allows for religious observances to be conducted at state or state-aided institutions. This means that in the South African context, the right to freedom of religion will **not** automatically be infringed every time the state provides any benefit to a specific religion or all religions in relation to non-religious groups. The state is thus allowed to provide specific benefits to a religious institution and to engage in activities that demonstrate reverence or respect for religion in general.

It is within this broader context that the scope and content of the South African guarantee of freedom of religion must be understood. Drawing on the jurisprudence of the Canadian Supreme Court, all the judges of the Constitutional Court also agreed that the essence of the right to freedom of religion involves:[95]

- 'the right to entertain such religious beliefs as a person chooses': In other words, people have the right to choose their religious beliefs freely and openly. Thus, an individual must be free from direct or indirect pressure by the state or other sources when choosing religious beliefs. Religious organisations cannot prevent people from leaving their fold and converting to other religions. Preferring persons of a particular religion when employing for state positions could amount to both unfair discrimination on the basis of religion and an infringement of the right to freedom of religion.
- 'the right to declare religious beliefs openly and without fear of hindrance or reprisal': In other words, people have the freedom to express their beliefs in public. People should never be compelled to worship in private and the right to do so in public is an acknowledgment that the broader society recognises and endorses this right. In a democracy such as ours that celebrates diversity, worshippers should be able to manifest their religious beliefs and practices publically.
- 'the right to manifest religious belief by worship and practice by teaching and dissemination': In other words, people have the freedom to engage in all the practices associated with their religion. For example, members of the Muslim and Jewish faiths believe in the circumcision of baby boys as part of practising their religion. Moreover, some Hindus walk on a bed of burning coal as a form of penance and in worship of the goddess Draupathi who they believe had to walk on burning coal to prove her fidelity. Although

93 *Lawrence* para 118.
94 *Lawrence* para 101.
95 *Lawrence* para 92.

minorities engage in these practices, they are protected as they are an important part of the manifestation of their religious beliefs. This is despite the majority disapproving or even questioning the rationality of the practice.

In short, all the justices of the Constitutional Court agreed that the right to freedom of religion is protected if there is an 'absence of coercion or constraint' on a particular religious belief or practice.[96] Freedom of religion will 'be impaired by measures that force people to act or refrain from acting in a manner contrary to their religious [and, we assume, other non-religious] beliefs'.[97] Subsequent Constitutional Court judgments essentially endorsed this view of the scope of the right to freedom of religion.[98] The Court also noted that the right to freedom of religion would not only be infringed by acts of direct coercion. Actions by the state could also run the risk of indirectly coercing individuals into certain religious beliefs and practices. This was a particular danger when the power, prestige and financial support of government were placed behind a particular religious belief as it would place indirect coercive pressure on religious minorities to conform to the prevailing officially approved religion.[99]

A far more difficult question that arose in the *Lawrence* case was whether the state was required to treat all religions in a fair and **equitable** manner. It is on this issue that the judges of the Constitutional Court differed. Chaskalson J, writing for four justices of the Constitutional Court, rejected the notion that the right to freedom of religion required the state to act in an even-handed or equitable manner towards all religions.[100] O'Regan J, writing for three justices of the Constitutional Court, however, argued that the right to freedom of religion required more than the absence of direct or indirect coercion to be fully and effectively protected.[101] This additional requirement of fairness or equity, argued O'Regan J, reflected 'an important component of the conception of freedom of religion contained in our Constitution'.[102] She stated:

> **Our society possesses a rich and diverse range of religions. Although the state is permitted to allow religious observances, it is not permitted to act inequitably. In determining what is meant by inequity in this context, it must be remembered that the question of voluntary participation is a consideration separately identified in section 14(2) [now section 15(2)]. The requirement of equity must therefore be something in addition to the requirement of voluntariness. It seems to me that, at the least, the requirement of equity demands the state act even-handedly in relation to different religions.[103]**

96 *Lawrence* para 92.

97 *Prince v President of the Law Society of the Cape of Good Hope* (CCT36/00) [2002] ZACC 1; 2002 (2) SA 794; 2002 (3) BCLR 231 (25 January 2002) para 38, where Ngcobo stated that:

> **The Court has on two occasions [in *Lawrence and Christian Education*] considered the right to freedom of religion. On each occasion, it is accepted that the right to freedom of religion at least comprehends: (a) the right to entertain the religious beliefs that one chooses to entertain; (b) the right to announce one's religious beliefs publicly and without fear of reprisals; and (c) the right to manifest such beliefs by worship and practice, teaching and dissemination. Implicit in the right to freedom of religion is the 'absence of coercion or restraint'. Thus freedom of religion may be impaired by measures that force people to act or refrain from acting in a manner contrary to their religious beliefs.**

See also *Christian Education* para 18.

98 *Prince* para 38.

99 *Lawrence* para 120, quoting from the US Supreme Court judgment of *Engel v Vitale:* [1962] USSC 116; 370 US 421 (1962) 431.

100 *Lawrence* para 102.

101 *Lawrence* para 122.

102 *Lawrence* para 121.

103 *Lawrence* paras 121–2.

This did not mean complete neutrality but did require that observances should not favour one religion over another.[104] This judgment went on to state that the purpose of the right was a rejection of past practices when Christianity was deemed to be the favoured religion.[105] Endorsement by the state of any one religion would not be permitted as it would result in indirect coercion and would amount to a threat to those wishing to exercise other religious beliefs.[106] O'Regan J concluded by holding that it is not sufficient that there is no direct coercion of religious beliefs. In addition, there had to be no inequitable or unfair preference of one religion over others.[107]

In a separate judgment, Sachs J appeared to agree with the approach adopted by O'Regan J when he held that the right to religious freedom does not only prohibit the state from forcing people to act or refrain from acting in a manner contrary to their religious beliefs, but also from endorsing or favouring one particular faith, for example Christianity, over all others:

> **By endorsing a particular faith as a direct and sectarian source of values for legislation binding on the whole nation, [the State] exceeds the competence granted to it by the Constitution. Even if there is no compulsory requirement to observe or not to observe a particular religious practice, the effect is to divide the nation into insiders who belong, and outsiders who are tolerated. This is impermissible in the multi-faith, heterodox society contemplated by our Constitution.**[108]

The difference between these positions is important and could lead to different results in a particular case. Insisting on the requirement of equity would require the state to act in a more even-handed manner regarding the various religions. For example, the state officially recognises certain Christian religious holidays, such as Easter and Christmas for example, but refrains from officially recognising religious holidays of other religions. It could be argued that the state is not treating the various religions in an equitable manner as it is endorsing or favouring the Christian religion over other religions and over non-religion.

PAUSE FOR REFLECTION

Defining the right to freedom of religion

In *Lawrence*, the applicants, who were supermarket owners, sought to challenge certain sections of the Liquor Act[109] which prohibited the sale of alcohol on closed days. These days were defined as Sundays, Good Friday and Christmas. They argued that the prohibition on the sale of alcohol on the closed days infringed the religious beliefs of non-Christians by forcing them to observe Christian beliefs.

Chaskalson P, writing for himself and three other justices, and applying the more restrictive definition of the right to freedom of religion discussed above, held that a Sunday had become a day of rest for most South Africans and was not solely a Christian holiday.[110] He held that the supermarket owners were able to ply their trade on Sundays and were only prohibited from selling wine.[111] Chaskalson P held that the

104 *Lawrence* para 122.
105 *Lawrence* para 123.
106 *Lawrence* para 123.
107 *Lawrence* para 123.
108 *Lawrence* para 179.
109 Act 27 of 1989.
110 *Lawrence* para 131.
111 *Lawrence* para 75.

applicants did not satisfy the court that this limited restriction amounted to a violation of the right to freedom of religion because the impugned law did not, in fact, coerce anyone into observing or not observing a particular religious belief or practice.[112]

In Chaskalson P's opinion, the right to freedom of religion cannot be read as obliging the state to abstain from any action that may advance or inhibit religion.[113] However, he went on to hold that in some circumstances, the advancement or endorsement of a particular religion would have the effect of coercing a person, either directly or indirectly, to observe or abide by the practices of that religion.[114] If such coercion is established, it would amount to an infringement of the right to freedom of religion.[115] This judgment found that on the facts there was too tenuous a connection between restrictions on the sale of wines on Sundays and the Christian religion for this to be deemed to be advancing Christianity and thus coercive as far as non-Christians were concerned. Hence, he came to the conclusion that the right to freedom of religion was not infringed.[116]

As we have noted, O'Regan J framed the scope and content of the right to freedom of religion more broadly.[117] While acknowledging that the Constitution does not require a strict separation between the state and religious institutions, this judgment held that apart from being non-coercive, legislation may not favour one religion over others. This is because fairness and even-handedness in relation to diverse religions is a necessary component of the right to freedom of religion. Applying these principles to the facts, O'Regan J found that the prohibition on the sale of wine on days that are important to Christians endorsed Christianity and thus infringed the right to freedom of religion. In addition, O'Regan J found that this infringement was not justifiable. The Liquor Act, therefore, was unconstitutional and invalid.

In his separate judgment, Sachs J also found that the Liquor Act infringed the right to freedom of religion because it clearly endorsed Christianity. Unlike O'Regan J, however, he went on to find that this infringement was justifiable and, consequently, that the Liquor Act was constitutionally valid.[118] Sachs J, therefore, agreed with the order issued by Chaskalson P.

Apart from the points set out above, it is also important to note that religious activities often take place in a communal context. In recognition of this fact, section 31 of the Constitution adds to the scope and content of the right to freedom of religion. Section 31 of the Constitution deals with the right of religious communities to practise their religion together with other members of their community. The right can only be optimally exercised if people of similar beliefs or faiths can assemble, jointly express their beliefs, advance their religion and regulate their affairs. The right to religious freedom, therefore, also includes the right to interact with fellow believers to advance their religion and to regulate the religious affairs of their organisations. This means an individual religious denomination must have the right – to

112 *Lawrence* para 148.
113 *Lawrence* para 148.
114 *Lawrence* para 152.
115 *Lawrence* para 152.
116 *Lawrence* para 173.
117 *Lawrence* paras 118–25.
118 *Lawrence* para 179.

the extent that other rights do not limit this right – to decide for itself on the rules for membership as well as the rules about the behaviour of all members of the religious denomination. A fuller discussion of the association rights contained in section 31 follows later in the chapter.

In the context of section 15, it is unnecessary to focus on whether a specific belief is religious in nature or not as the section not only protects the right to freedom of religion, but also to the right to freedom of conscience, thought, belief and opinion. Nevertheless, it has been suggested that to qualify as a 'religious belief system' a religion should have some of the following features: 'belief in a supreme being, belief in transcendent reality, a moral code, a world view accounting for people's role in the universe, sacred rituals, worship and prayers, a sacred text, and membership in a social organisation'.[119]

In the US context, it was held that the test should not be whether the belief is objectively reasonable, but rather whether it forms part of the practices and beliefs of that religion and whether persons belonging to that religion genuinely and sincerely embrace the practice. The courts are generally reluctant to question the genuineness of the belief if there is evidence to suggest that the belief is sincerely held by the applicant. In addition, the courts are generally reluctant to make determinations as to whether the practice being restricted is central or foundational to the religious beliefs. It is not the function of the court to interpret religious texts or dogma. As O'Connor J, a former justice of the US Supreme Court, put it:

> **The dissent offers us the prospect of this court holding that some sincerely held religious beliefs and practices are not 'central' to certain religions, despite the protestations to the contrary from religious observers who brought the lawsuit. In other words, the dissent's approach would require us to rule that some religious adherents misunderstand their own religious beliefs. We think that such an approach cannot be squared with the Constitution or with our precedents, and that it would cast the judiciary in a role that we never intended to play.**[120]

Ngcobo J expressed similar sentiments in his dissenting judgment in *Prince v President of the Law Society of the Cape of Good Hope*.[121] In this case, the issue was whether the Drugs and Drug Trafficking Act[122] and section 22A of the Medicines and Related Substances Control Act[123] were inconsistent with the Constitution in that they did not grant an exemption to Rastafarians to possess and use dagga for religious purposes. Ngcobo J cautioned against being overly concerned with whether a particular practice is central to the religion, stating that:

> **Apart from this, as a general matter, the Court should not be concerned with questions whether, as a matter of religious doctrine, a particular practice is central to the religion. Religion is a matter of faith and belief. The beliefs that believers hold sacred and thus central to their religious faith may strike non-believers as bizarre, illogical or irrational. Human beings may freely believe in what they cannot prove. Yet, that their beliefs are bizarre, illogical or irrational to others or are incapable of scientific proof, does not detract from the fact that these are religious beliefs for the purposes of enjoying the protection guaranteed by the right to freedom of religion.**

119 Freeman, GC (1983) The misguided search for the constitutional definition of religion *Georgetown Law Journal* 71(6):1519–66 quoted in Stone, GR (ed) (1996) *Constitutional Law* 3rd ed 1546.

120 *Lyng v Northwest Indian Cemetery* 485 US 439 para 457.

121 (CCT36/00) [2002] ZACC 1; 2002 (2) SA 794; 2002 (3) BCLR 231 (25 January 2002). Although Ngcobo J dissented, these remarks are not inconsistent with the reasoning of the majority.

122 Act 140 of 1992.

123 Act 101 of 1965.

The believers should not be put to the proof of their beliefs or faith. For this reason, it is undesirable for courts to enter into the debate whether a particular practice is central to a religion unless there is a genuine dispute as to the centrality of the practice.[124]

PAUSE FOR REFLECTION

Determining whether a specific belief is religious or not

The fact that it is very difficult to determine whether a specific belief is religious or not is clearly illustrated by the example set out below.

> A 'church' whose central tenet is the right to file-share has been formally recognised by the Swedish government.
>
> The Church of Kopimism claims that 'kopyacting' – sharing information through copying – is akin to a religious service.
>
> The 'spiritual leader' of the church said recognition was a 'large step'. But others were less enthusiastic and said the church would do little to halt the global crackdown on piracy.
>
> The Swedish government agency Kammarkollegiet finally registered the Church of Kopimism as a religious organisation shortly before Christmas, the group said.
>
> 'We had to apply three times,' said Gustav Nipe, chairman of the organisation.
>
> The church, which holds CTRL+C and CTRL+V (shortcuts for copy and paste) as sacred symbols, does not directly promote illegal file sharing, focusing instead on the open distribution of knowledge to all.
>
> It was founded by 19-year-old philosophy student and leader Isak Gerson. He hopes that file-sharing will now be given religious protection.
>
> 'For the Church of Kopimism, information is holy and copying is a sacrament. Information holds a value, in itself and in what it contains and the value multiplies through copying. Therefore copying is central for the organisation and its members,' he said in a statement.
>
> 'Being recognised by the state of Sweden is a large step for all of Kopimi. Hopefully this is one step towards the day when we can live out our faith without fear of persecution,' he added'.[125]

In most constitutional democracies, issues concerning the right to freedom of religion arise when legislation is passed or other governmental action undertaken which aims to achieve a societal objective, but which simultaneously is perceived as adversely affecting religious beliefs. Superficially neutral laws may sometimes adversely affect the religious rights of individuals. Thus, the aspect of the right that enables believers to give expression to and manifest their beliefs in public and to engage in practices associated with the religious beliefs

124 *Prince* para 42. See also *Taylor v Kurstag NO and Others* 2005 (1) SA 362 (W); 2005 (7) BCLR 705 (W); [2004] 4 All SA 317 (W).

125 Sweden recognises new file-sharing religion Kopimism (2012, 5 January) available at http://www.bbc.co.uk/news/technology-16424659.

of an individual is the component most likely to be affected by state regulation. In addition to clashes with state objectives, the exercise of the freedom of religion may clash with the constitutional rights of others, including the right not to be unfairly discriminated against. The courts generally attempt to balance the competing imperatives.[126] However, difficult issues arise when the right to freedom of religion collides with the right not to be unfairly discriminated against on the basis of, for example, gender and sexual orientation.

This question arose in the case of *Strydom v Nederduitse Gereformeerde Gemeente Moreleta Park.*[127] The Moreleta Park Dutch Reformed Church appointed a music teacher, Mr Strydom, to teach music to the learners who participated in the arts academy it had established. When the church discovered that Strydom was in a same-sex relationship, it dismissed him from his job. Strydom took the case to the equality courts established under the PEPUDA. The church argued that its right to freedom of religion should trump the right of Mr Strydom to non-discrimination on the basis of sexual orientation. The Court found that unfair discrimination had indeed taken place on grounds of sexual orientation. As Bilchitz explains:

> **On the facts, the Court found that Strydom's work 'involved no religious responsibilities at all' and that he had performed excellently in his job until then. Strydom was not a member of the church and he was teaching as an independent contractor. As such, he did not hold himself out to be a role model to the students in their religious lives. Consequently, Basson J found that the impact on the church's freedom of religion of keeping Strydom in employment was 'minimal'. On the other hand, there was an enormous impact on Strydom's right to equality and dignity. Strydom was also affected in a material way, suffering from depression, unemployment and being forced to sell his piano and house. Consequently, the church did not succeed in discharging its onus of proving that the discrimination was not unfair. The case thus demonstrates clearly that the protections against unfair discrimination in the Constitution and the Equality Act may restrict the autonomy of a religious association to refuse to employ or dismiss individuals whom it deems unsuitable if such a decision is based on grounds upon which discrimination is prohibited.**[128]

CRITICAL THINKING

Where to draw the line between a church's core activities and its other activities

In terms of the doctrines of the Catholic Church only men can be ordained as priests. The prohibition on women priests clearly discriminates against women on the basis of sex and gender. Equally, however, the right of the church to arrange its affairs in accordance with its own beliefs and doctrines requires it to be able to discriminate against women.

If a specific woman ever wished to challenge the practice of the Catholic Church in South Africa, she may want to invoke the precedent created by the High Court in the *Strydom* judgment. However, a court would almost certainly distinguish such a case from the *Strydom* case. It would probably argue that the right to freedom of religion in this particular case should trump the right of women not to be discriminated against.

126 See generally Bilchitz, D (2011) Should religious organisations be entitled to discriminate? *South African Journal on Human Rights* 27(2):219–48; Lenta, P (2012) The right of religious associations to discriminate *South African Journal on Human Rights* 28(2):231–57; Woolman, S (2012) Seek justice elsewhere: An egalitarian pluralist's reply to David Bilchitz on the distinction between differentiation and domination *South African Journal on Human Rights* 28(2):273–95.

127 (26926/05) [2008] ZAEQC 1; (2009) 30 ILJ 868 (EqC) (27 August 2008).

128 Bilchitz (2011) 221.

This is because in *Strydom* the church employed the music teacher as an independent contractor. The task of teaching music was far removed from the core functions of the church.

Assume, however, that Strydom had not been a music teacher but a *dominee* and that the Dutch Reformed Church had adopted policies which precluded a gay man or lesbian from becoming *dominees*. Then the Court would almost certainly have found that the freedom of religion of the church and those who belonged to it should trump the rights of the individual *dominee*. Similarly, in a case where a women challenges the male-only rule for the ordination of priests in the Catholic Church, the courts would almost certainly find in favour of the Catholic Church.

As these examples demonstrate, the line between activities so closely associated with the core doctrines of a church and its other activities may not always be easy to draw in an individual case. This suggests that courts may find it difficult to know how to deal with the accommodation of diversity in a particular case.

13.3.3 The reasonable accommodation of religious beliefs and practices

Issues of religious freedom often arise in contexts where seemingly neutral and universal rules that reflect a particular religious orientation or belief system are applied in a manner that may have the effect of marginalising or negating the beliefs and practices of people from minority religions or people who do not embrace any form of religion at all. For example, where a school imposes a particular dress code or a particular disciplinary code that applies equally to everyone, the code may nevertheless fail to accommodate the practices of minority beliefs and religions. Thus, a school dress code which prohibits all girls from wearing scarves or hats may discriminate against Muslim learners and may thus infringe on the religious freedom of such learners. Similarly, a disciplinary code which requires all boys in a school to wear their hair in a short style may discriminate against Rastafarian learners who are required to wear dreadlocks. In such cases, the right to freedom of religion and the right not to be unfairly discriminated against on the basis of a person's belief or religion intersect. The manner in which the law deals with such cases is to require the institution reasonably to accommodate the beliefs and practices of all, regardless of their beliefs or religious affiliations.

At its core, **reasonable accommodation** is the notion that sometimes the community, whether it is the state, an employer or a school, must take positive measures and possibly incur additional hardship or expense to allow all people to participate and enjoy all their rights - including the right to freedom of belief - equally. It ensures that we do not relegate people to the margins of society because they do not or cannot conform to certain social norms.[129] In *Christian Education*, in the context of accommodating religious belief in society, a unanimous Court identified the underlying motivation of the concept as follows:

> **The underlying problem in any open and democratic society based on human dignity, equality and freedom in which conscientious and religious freedom has to be regarded with appropriate seriousness, is how far such democracy can and must go in allowing members of religious communities to define for themselves which laws they will obey and which not. Such a society can cohere only if all its participants accept that certain basic norms and standards are binding. Accordingly, believers**

129 *Pillay* para 73.

> **cannot claim an automatic right to be exempted by their beliefs from the laws of the land. At the same time, the State should, wherever reasonably possible, seek to avoid putting believers to extremely painful and intensely burdensome choices of either being true to their faith or else respectful of the law.**[130]

The notion of reasonable accommodation has arisen **directly** only in cases such as *Pillay*, in which the litigant alleged that he or she was being discriminated against on the basis of his or her religion. However, the notion of reasonable accommodation also finds application **indirectly** in cases where the freedom of religion of a litigant has been infringed and the court has had to decide whether this infringement was justifiable in terms of the limitation clause (discussed in chapter 10). Because the outcome of most freedom of religion cases turns on the application of the limitation clause, it is important to note how the notion of reasonable accommodation indirectly affects the application of the limitation analysis in freedom of religion cases. This notion can be illustrated by two cases in which the Constitutional Court found (or assumed) that a breach of section 15 had occurred. The Court then had to decide whether the limitation was justifiable or not in terms of the limitation clause. The Court did not directly invoke the concept of reasonable accommodation in either of these cases. However, we contend that the cases turned on whether the law reasonably accommodated the religious beliefs and practices of the relevant group and hence whether the limitation of the group's religious freedom was, in fact, justifiable.

In *Christian Education*, the applicants challenged section 10 of the South African Schools Act (SASA)[131] which prohibited corporal punishment in all schools, including independent parochial schools.[132] The applicants were an umbrella body of 196 independent Christian schools. The schools were originally established to promote evangelical Christian education. The applicants argued that section 10 was unconstitutional as it infringed their rights to freedom of religion and to cultural life. They referred to various verses in the Christian Bible which countenance and, in some instances, prescribe corporal punishment as an appropriate means of disciplining children. For instance, Proverbs 22:15 provides: 'Foolishness is bound in the heart of a child, but the rod of correction shall drive it far from him.' Proverbs 23:13 and 14 provide: 'Do not withhold discipline from a child, if you punish with a rod he will not die. Punish him with a rod and save his soul from death.' The applicants contended that corporal punishment was therefore a vital aspect of the Christian religion. They argued that by prohibiting its use when parents had consented to it, the state was unjustifiably interfering with their freedom of religion.

The Constitutional Court had no doubt that the parents sincerely believed that their religious rights were being infringed by the law.[133] The Court held that freedom of religion may be 'impaired by measures that coerce persons into acting or refraining from acting in a manner contrary to their beliefs'.[134] The Court went further and recognised that religious practices involve interaction with fellow believers and thus section 31 of the Constitution makes provision for the practice of religion in community with others.[135] The Court 'assumed without deciding' that section 10 of the SASA limited the parents' religious rights under sections 15 and 31 of the Constitution.[136] Having made these assumptions, the Court turned

130 *Christian Education* para 35.
131 Act 84 of 1996.
132 *Christian Education* para 35.
133 *Christian Education* para 37.
134 *Christian Education* para 19.
135 *Christian Education* para 23.
136 *Christian Education* para 27.

to the issue of whether it was reasonable and justifiable in an open and democratic society for the state to limit these rights in terms of section 36 of the Constitution.

The key question in this case, therefore, was whether the failure of the law to accommodate the applicants' religious beliefs by means of an appropriate exemption was reasonable and justifiable. The main purpose of the SASA was to create uniform norms and standards for all schools. The main objective of section 10 of SASA was to reduce the level of violence in our schools and to protect children from maltreatment, abuse or degradation. The blanket ban on corporal punishment was meant to convey a principled stance affirming the dignity of learners. Granting an exemption to the applicant would detract from this and would be difficult to administer. The infringement, according to the Court, did not oblige parents to make 'an absolute and strenuous choice between obeying the law of the land or following their conscience'.[137] Except for not being able to authorise educators to administer corporal punishment, the schools were not prevented from fully exercising their religious beliefs. Thus, the law was achieving an important objective while the intrusion on the religious rights of the applicants was limited.[138]

The Court concluded that making an exception would detract from the symbolic, moral and pedagogical purpose of reducing the level of violence in schools.[139] In the circumstances, the Court concluded that the law was reasonable and justifiable and hence not unconstitutional.[140] In this case, the limited infraction of the freedom of religion was outweighed by the important objectives that the law was designed to achieve. The flexibility of the limitation clause enables the courts to engage in these balancing exercises.

In *Prince*, the Law Society formed the view that the applicant was not a fit and proper person and refused to register his articles as a candidate attorney. The Society reached this conclusion because the applicant had two previous convictions for the possession of dagga. The applicant had also indicated that he intended to continue using dagga as part of his religious practices.

The Constitutional Court held that Rastafarianism is a religion although it does not have a centralised organisational structure.[141] The use of dagga is one of the ways in which believers of this religion manifest their belief.[142] Thus, the statutory limitation on the use of dagga is an infringement of the applicant's right to freedom of religion.[143] However, the Court was sharply divided on whether the law, which made an exception only for the medical use of the drug, was justifiable in terms of the limitation clause. The majority upheld the law and found against the applicant on the basis that it would not be administratively feasible to make a religious exception for the users of dagga as it would be difficult to police and oversee.[144] According to the majority, it would be difficult to police a private activity of this nature in the absence of a formally organised religious structure, stating that:

> **There is no objective way in which a law enforcement official could distinguish between the use of cannabis for religious purposes and the use of cannabis for recreation. It would be even more difficult, if not impossible, to distinguish objectively between the possession of cannabis for the one or the other of the above purposes.**

137 *Christian Education* para 51.
138 *Christian Education* para 51.
139 *Christian Education* para 51.
140 *Christian Education* para 51.
141 *Prince* para 135.
142 *Prince* para 129.
143 *Prince* para 129.
144 *Prince* para 130.

> **Nor is there any objective way in which a law enforcement official could determine whether a person found in possession of cannabis, who says that it is possessed for religious purposes, is genuine or not. Indeed, in the absence of a carefully controlled chain of permitted supply, it is difficult to imagine how the island of legitimate acquisition and use by Rastafari for the purpose of practising their religion could be distinguished from the surrounding ocean of illicit trafficking and use.[145]**

The minority were of the view that the statute was overbroad and not carefully tailored to 'constitute a minimal intrusion upon the right to freedom of religion'.[146] The law, according to the minority, was unconstitutional as it did not allow for the religious use of cannabis that was not necessarily harmful and which could be controlled more effectively.[147]

The inherent flexibility of the limitation clause allows the courts to assess whether the law that infringes aspects of the right to freedom of religion is proportionate. As the *Prince* case demonstrates, even the judges of the highest court may differ in their determination of what is reasonable in the circumstances. In essence, the state must identify a societal objective which the governmental action advances, the attainment of which justifies the right being infringed. The courts then ask the additional question of whether the societal objective could reasonably be achieved by a less intrusive limitation of the right. The governmental conduct limiting the right will only pass constitutional muster if the courts are satisfied that the importance of the societal objective sought to be achieved outweighs the adverse effects of the limitation on the right to freedom of religion. Ultimately, both the prohibition on corporal punishment and the prohibition on the use of dagga except for medicinal reasons were upheld even though both measures infringed aspects of the right to freedom of religion.

PAUSE FOR REFLECTION

An example of reasonable accommodation

The requirement that various religious beliefs and practices have to be accommodated in a reasonable manner can be illustrated with reference to a specific example. Imagine that Claremont High School in Cape Town has been besieged by ill-discipline and in some instances learners have attacked educators. Imagine further that in a specific incident a grade 12 learner stabbed an educator who had reprimanded the learner for being drunk at a sports event hosted by the school.

Now, it would not be surprising if the school, in an effort to improve the teaching and learning environment, adopted a code of conduct after consultation with the learners, the parents and educators. Such a code could, among others, expressly forbid learners from bringing to school knives, daggers or other weapons or instruments that could cause harm to the learner, other learners or staff at the school.

On the face of it, such a rule would seem to be eminently reasonable. However, the rule would have a disproportionate impact on Sikh learners. This is because according to the *Reht Maryada*, the official Sikh Code of Conduct, a Sikh must at all times carry five items, including a kirpan, on his person. According to this code, a kirpan is a dagger that represents the power of truth to cut through untruth. A Sikh learner would therefore be able to argue that the seemingly neutral code of conduct infringed on his right to freedom of religion, read with his right not to be discriminated against on the basis of

145 *Prince* para 130.
146 *Prince* para 83.
147 *Prince* para 77.

his religion, because it would prohibit him from wearing the kirpan to school. In deciding whether the code should make an exception for Sikh learners, the court would have to employ the principle of reasonable accommodation.[148]

13.3.4 The right not to believe in any God

As we noted above, section 15 of the Constitution protects both the right to freedom of religion and the right to freedom of other beliefs and conscience. As such, it also protects a person's right not to believe in a God and not to have to participate in any religious practices such as prayers and the singing of hymns. In *Torcaso v Watkins*,[149] the US Supreme Court invalidated a state law which required all public office holders to declare that they believed in God prior to assuming public office. The Court held that the free exercise clause prevented government from either awarding benefits or imposing burdens based on a person's religious beliefs or lack of religious belief.[150] Our courts have held that this free exercise in the US Constitution is similar to the right to freedom of religion and conscience protected by section 15 of the South African Constitution. Similar sentiments were expressed by Sachs J in *Lawrence* when he held:

> **South Africa is an open and democratic society with a non-sectarian state that guarantees freedom of worship; is respectful of all and accommodatory towards, rather than hostile to or walled-off from, religion; acknowledges the multi-faith and multi-belief nature of the country; does not favour one religious creed or doctrinal truth above another; accepts the intensely personal nature of individual conscience and affirms the intrinsically voluntary and non-coerced character of belief; respects the rights of non-believers; and does not impose orthodoxies of thought or require conformity of conduct in terms of a particular world-view.**[151]

The breadth of section 15 signifies that our society must not act punitively towards non-believers by withholding benefits or imposing burdens on them because of their non-belief. However, it is probable that if a non-believer is discriminated against, he or she will rely on the right not to be unfairly discriminated against on the basis of conscience and belief rather than the right to freedom of religion, belief and conscience.

13.3.5 Conducting religious observances at state institutions: section 15(2) of the Constitution

As we noted above, the South African Constitution - unlike its US counterpart - does not require a complete separation between the state and religion. The South African Constitution does allow some entanglement between the state and religion. Section 15(2) of the Constitution makes this clear when it states that religious observances may be conducted at state or state-aided institutions on condition that:

- these observances follow rules made by appropriate public authorities
- they are conducted on an equitable basis
- attendance at these observances is free and voluntary.

148 This example is based loosely on the facts in *Multani v Commission Scolaire Marguerite - Bourgeoys* [2006] 1 SCR 256. In this case, the Canadian Supreme Court struck down a school board's decision that prohibited a Sikh child from wearing a kirpan to school on the grounds that it infringed the right to freedom of religion guaranteed in section 2(*a*) of the Canadian Charter of Rights and Freedoms.

149 *Torcaso v Watkins* 367 U.S. 488.

150 *Torcaso v Watkins* 367 U.S. 488 para 489.

151 *Lawrence* para 148.

Religious observance must be distinguished from religious education.[152] **Religious observance** refers to the acts or rituals of a religious character usually conducted at public events such as at school assemblies, at the opening of Parliament or at the start of a soccer match. **Religious education** refers to education that occurs inside the classroom about the beliefs and teachings of various religions. It is only religious observances that have to comply with the conditions listed in section 15(2) if the observances are to be held at state or state-aided institutions. The primary purpose of this provision is to regulate equitably the conducting of prayers at school. In *Lawrence*, the Constitutional Court held that equitable treatment does not require equal treatment of all religious affiliations and beliefs in a public institution and held:

> **In the context of a school community and the pervasive peer pressure that is often present in such communities, voluntary school prayers could also amount to the coercion of pupils to participate in the prayers of the favoured religion. To guard against this, and at the same time to permit school prayers, S14(2) [section 15(2) in the final Constitution] makes clear that there should be no coercion. It is in this context that it requires the regulation of school prayers to be carried out on an equitable basis. I doubt whether this means that a school must make provision for prayers for as many denominations as there may be within the pupil body; rather it seems to me to require education authorities to allow schools to offer prayers that may be most appropriate for a particular school, to have that decision taken in an equitable manner applicable to all schools, and to oblige them to do so in a way which does not give rise to indirect coercion of the 'non-believer'.**[153]

According to this judgment, a state or state-aided institution would not be required to provide for religious observance to be conducted in a manner that would accommodate every single form of religion, as well as all forms of non-religion, in such an institution. So, say 90% of the pupils at a school profess to be Christian, 9% profess to be Muslim and the other 1% profess other religions or no religion at all. The school would then probably have to accommodate both Christian and Muslim observance in proportion to the number of pupils adhering to these religions. However, the school would not have to provide for religious observance for the remaining 1% of pupils as long as everyone is given a free choice to attend or not to attend such occasions where religious observance is conducted. This is because the observance must be equitable. The requirement that the observance must be equitable does not require absolutely equal treatment of all religious beliefs. Mureinik argues that equitable refers to the observances being fair and just.[154] Excusing learners from minority religious groups from attending prayers of the majority religion may satisfy the requirement of being free and voluntary. However, it may not satisfy the requirement that it also be just and equitable especially in cases where minority religions are adhered to by at least a sizable number of members of that institution.[155]

It appears that this would require the schools to accommodate reasonably all those religions that have a sizeable number of adherents among the learners. It would not be permissible to determine the religion of the majority of learners and accommodate only that particular religion. Much more is required than merely giving expression to majoritarian sentiments. The overt endorsement of a particular religion by a public school, given the age

152 *Wittmann v Deutscher Schulverein* 1998 (4) SA 423 (T).
153 *Lawrence* para 103.
154 Quoted by Farlam (2013) 41.51.
155 See the earlier discussion in this chapter on the issue of coercion versus even-handedness.

and impressionability of learners, will probably be unduly coercive and a violation of the right to freedom of religion of those learners belonging to other religions.

State-aided institutions refer to those institutions, including educational institutions, which the state funds extensively and regulates heavily.[156] Thus, the Court in *Wittmann v Deutscher Schulverein* did not regard private or independent schools as state-aided institutions for the purposes of section 15(2) even though they are recipients of state funding.[157] This must be correct. It would be incongruent to permit institutions to set up their religion-based schools at their own expense in terms of section 29(3) of the Constitution and then also to oblige them to conduct religious observances in an equitable, free and voluntary manner. The purpose of section 29(3) is to enable religious organisations to set up parochial schools and propagate their religion. They thus cannot be compelled to act in the manner required by section 15(2) of the Constitution. However, all public schools are bound by section 15(2) and cannot have a preferred or favoured religion.

13.3.6 Legislation recognising religious and traditional marriages: section 15(3)(*a*)(i) of the Constitution

In terms of the common law, marriage was defined as the union of one man and one woman to the exclusion of all others. This common law definition applies to marriages concluded in terms of the Marriage Act.[158] Couples married under Muslim, Hindu and customary law could not use the Marriage Act to conclude a valid marriage in terms of the common law. This means that the state did not officially recognise, in the same manner as common law marriages solemnised in terms of the Marriage Act, marriages of couples that were concluded in accordance with Muslim, Hindu or customary law and who did not also conclude a marriage in terms of the Marriage Act. This obviously constituted a form of discrimination on the basis of religion or custom. In *Ismail v Ismail*,[159] for example, the appellate division refused to recognise a Muslim marriage on the basis that it was potentially polygamous. Thus any claim based on the polygamous union was also regarded as void and unenforceable.

However, section 15(3)(*a*)(i) of the Constitution states that the guarantee of freedom of religion and the requirements for equitable treatment of religions as far as observance in state and state-aided institutions is concerned 'does not prevent legislation recognising marriages concluded under any tradition, or a system of religious, personal or family law'. This subsection therefore allows for legislation to be drafted which recognises marriages concluded under traditional or other religious systems such as Hinduism and Islam. It permits legislative intervention to rid our law of some of the chauvinistic attitudes of the common law as exemplified in the judgment in *Ismail*.

The wording of section 15(3)(*a*)(i) is curious.[160] The premise on which section 15(3) is based is that laws recognising traditional forms of marriage may infringe on the guarantee in section 15(1). It is difficult to see how the state recognition of marriages recognised by religious, personal or family law would violate the religious rights of others in society. This is so because a law recognising different forms of marriage will not coerce individuals who do not intend to conclude such marriages to believe or not believe anything or to enter or not enter forms of marriage that conflict with their religious beliefs. The only reasonable explanation is that the Christian definition of marriage of one man and one woman may be

156 Currie and De Waal (2013) 330.
157 1998 (4) SA 423 (T) para 449.
158 Act 25 of 1961.
159 1983 (1) SA 1006 (A).
160 Farlam (2013) 41.54.

offended by laws recognising polygamous marriages. However, it is unclear whether this section was necessary at all. This is illustrated by the case of *Fourie* where it was contended that allowing the institution of marriage to be extended to include same-sex couples would fundamentally infringe deeply held religious beliefs. However, the Constitutional Court held that the Constitution allowed an accommodation of both the secular and the sacred:

> **The function of the Court is to recognise the sphere which each inhabits, not to force the one into the sphere of the other. Provided there is no prejudice to the fundamental rights of any person or group, the law will legitimately acknowledge a diversity of strongly-held opinions on matters of great public controversy. I stress the qualification that there must be no prejudice to basic rights. Majoritarian opinion can often be harsh to minorities that exist outside the mainstream. It is precisely the function of the Constitution and the law to step in and counteract rather than reinforce unfair discrimination against a minority. The test, whether majoritarian or minority positions are involved, must always be whether the measure under scrutiny promotes or retards the achievement of human dignity, equality and freedom.[161]**

Given this requirement of coexistence, the Court found that recognising the rights of gay men and lesbians to marry did not mean that religions that believed that marriage was the union of one man and one woman had to solemnise gay and lesbian marriages. They could refuse to solemnise gay and lesbian marriages if doing so would run counter to their belief and creed.[162] However, recognition by the state would not result in a violation of the right to freedom of religion of those religions that were opposed to gay and lesbian marriages.[163]

It is important to note that any laws passed in terms of section 15(3) must be consistent with other provisions of the Constitution. Thus, section 15(3) would not sanction a law which unfairly discriminates against women in the marital relationship even if the law gave expression to a particular traditional or religious belief. The challenge facing Parliament when drafting laws recognising marriages consecrated in terms of religious or traditional law is to interfere as little as possible with the tenets of the religion concerned. In addition, these laws must also provide effective security and stability to the parties in a manner which accords with the Constitution.

To give effect to traditional cultural beliefs, Parliament passed the Recognition of Customary Marriages Act (RCMA).[164] The RCMA represents 'a belated but welcome and ambitious legislative effort to remedy the historical humiliation and exclusion meted out to spouses in marriages which were entered into in accordance with the law and culture of the indigenous African people of this country'.[165] The RCMA was passed to deal specifically with customary law. It was inspired by the dignity and equality rights as well as the normative value system of the Constitution.[166] Section 1 of the RCMA defines customary law as 'customs and usages traditionally observed among the indigenous African peoples of South Africa and which form part of the cultures of those peoples'. The RCMA defines a customary marriage as 'a marriage concluded in accordance with customary law'.[167]

161 *Fourie* para 94.
162 *Fourie* para 96.
163 *Fourie* para 98.
164 Act 120 of 1998.
165 *Gumede (born Shange) v President of Republic of South Africa and Others* (CCT 50/08) [2008] ZACC 23; 2009 (3) BCLR 243 (CC); 2009 (3) SA 152 (CC) (8 December 2008) para 16. See also *Mayelane v Ngwenyama and Another* (CCT 57/12) [2013] ZACC 14; 2013 (4) SA 415 (CC); 2013 (8) BCLR 918 (CC) (30 May 2013) para 26.
166 *Gumede* para 21 and *Mayelane* para 26.
167 S 1.

Insofar as customary marriages are concerned, it is important to note that most of the customary law systems that apply in South Africa differentiate between men and women. This is because men may marry more than one woman while women may not marry more than one man. Unfortunately, it is not clear whether this differentiation is constitutionally valid or not.[168] On the one hand, it could be argued that polygamous marriages unfairly discriminate against women and that section 15(3), therefore, should not authorise the recognition of such marriages. On the other hand, it could be argued that the RCMA prevents the most egregious forms of discrimination against women, among others, by requiring the consent of the first wife before a husband may conclude a subsequent **polygynous marriage**. In addition, section 6 of the RCMA also states that:

> **A wife in a customary marriage has, on the basis of equality with her husband and subject to the matrimonial property system governing the marriage, full status and capacity, including the capacity to acquire assets and to dispose of them, to enter into contracts and to litigate, in addition to any rights and powers that she might have at customary law.**

Section 7(6) goes on to provide that:

> **A husband in a customary marriage who wishes to enter into a further customary marriage with another woman after the commencement of this Act must make an application to the court to approve a written contract which will regulate the future matrimonial property system of his marriages.**

PAUSE FOR REFLECTION

Do the customary principles and rules that govern polygamous marriages pass constitutional muster?

The discussion on polygamous marriages illustrates that constitutional issues cannot always be solved with reference to a single section of the Bill of Rights. When considering whether the principles and rules of customary law that govern polygamous marriages are constitutionally valid, it would not be sufficient to invoke section 15(3) to arrive at an answer. We would also have to refer to the right to equality guaranteed in section 9 of the Constitution and would specifically have to engage with the Constitutional Court's jurisprudence around the meaning of section 9(3) to arrive at the correct constitutional answer to this problem.

Given these complexities, it remains an open question whether the customary principles and rules that govern polygamous marriages would pass constitutional muster. Despite the provisions of the RCMA which go a long way towards protecting women in polygamous marriages, in most customary law systems women are not allowed to enter such marriages. This raises serious questions about whether the customary law principles and rules that govern customary marriages show proper respect for the equal dignity of women. Given these serious questions was it correct for Parliament to pass a law recognising polygamous marriages simply on the basis that a number of communities in South Africa engage in and endorse this practice on the basis that it accords with their cultural or religious beliefs? Polygamy allows a man to take multiple wives - does this unfairly discriminate against women?

168 *Mayelane* para 70.

13.4 The rights of cultural and religious communities

13.4.1 The individual nature of these rights and how other rights both qualify and enhance them

Section 30 of the Constitution guarantees everyone the right to use the language and participate in the cultural life of their choice. Section 31 guarantees every person belonging to a cultural, religious or linguistic community the right, together with other members of that community, to enjoy their culture, practise their religion and use their language, and to form, join and maintain cultural, religious and linguistic associations and other organs of civil society. Both these sections, however, provide explicitly that these rights may not be exercised in a manner that is inconsistent with any of the other provisions of the Bill of Rights.

The rights guaranteed in sections 30 and 31 lie at the heart of the protection of diversity. As the Constitutional Court has pointed out, these rights 'underline the constitutional value of acknowledging diversity and **pluralism** in our society'.[169] They stem from the recognition that we are different in the sense that we do not all share the same language, religion or history and do not embrace the same cultural practices and assumptions. As such, these rights acknowledge that South Africa is a diverse society of many languages, cultures and religions and they affirm, embrace and celebrate this diversity.

The rights guaranteed in sections 30 and 31 of the Constitution are also enhanced by some of the other provisions of the Bill of Rights. Section 9(3), for example, prohibits unfair discrimination on the basis of, among others, religion, culture and language and section 15(1) provides that everyone has the right to freedom of religion. Section 29(2) provides that '[e]veryone has the right to receive education in the official language or languages of their choice in public educational institutions where that education is reasonably practicable'. Apart from these provisions, the rights guaranteed in sections 30 and 31 are also enhanced by section 6 of the Constitution. Although it does not form a part of the Bill of Rights, section 6 requires the state proactively to advance the use of official languages that were previously neglected and to treat various languages with 'parity of esteem'.[170]

Like the right to freedom of association, the rights guaranteed in sections 30 and 31 of the Constitution are not group rights. Instead, they are primarily rights that belong to the individual. The Constitution does not protect the rights of groups at all. It protects only the rights of individuals who may best exercise their rights in association with others. As Sachs J pointed out in *Christian Education*:

> **The protection of diversity is not effected through giving legal personality to groups as such. It is achieved indirectly through the double mechanism of positively enabling individuals to join with other individuals of their community, and negatively enjoining the state not to deny them the rights collectively to profess and practise their own religion (as well as enjoy their culture and use their language).**[171]

The rights guaranteed in sections 30 and 31, therefore, allow **individuals** to assert their rights to advance the objectives of specific cultural, religious or linguistic organisations or institutions as well as their own rights as members of such bodies.[172] Despite their decidedly

169 *Christian Education* para 24.
170 S 6(4) of the Constitution.
171 *Christian Education* para 23.
172 Currie and De Waal (2013) 626–7.

individual character, cultural, religious and linguistic rights are usually best exercised in association with others and these rights are therefore sometimes described as **associational individual rights**. The hybrid scope of these rights complicates their application. This is because the interests of individuals to associate with other individuals and to express their identity as members of a cultural, religious or linguistic group may lead to restrictions on the rights of others to participate in the life of that community. An individual's interests protected by sections 30 and 31 may therefore clash with the interests of other individuals who could be excluded from participating in communal life by the exercise of this right.[173]

The challenge facing the drafters of the Constitution was to protect these rights in a manner that was consistent with a non-racial democracy based on majority rule and which protects individual rights. This is exactly why the exercise of these rights is explicitly made subject to the other rights protected in the Bill of Rights, including to the right not to be unfairly discriminated against in section 9. An individual therefore cannot exercise his or her right to associate with other members of a linguistic or cultural community in a manner that would unfairly discriminate against others.

Given that other rights could qualify and limit the rights guaranteed in sections 30 and 31 of the Constitution, they must be interpreted and applied in conjunction with the other rights in the Bill of Rights. In addition, the rights guaranteed in sections 30 and 31 are also partly advanced in an indirect manner through the exercise of other rights. The right not to be unfairly discriminated against on the basis of race, ethnic or social origin, colour, religion, belief, culture and language in section 9(3), for example, indirectly advances these rights. Other examples include section 16(2) which deems hate speech based on race, ethnicity, gender or religion to be unprotected speech and section 29(3) which protects the rights of everyone to establish and maintain, at their own expense, independent institutions that do not discriminate on the basis of race, are registered with the state and maintain appropriate standards.

13.4.2 The international protection of cultural liberties

The rights protected in sections 29(3), 30 and 31 are sometimes referred to as **cultural liberties**.[174] The cultural liberties they are seeking to protect are a vital part of human development. As a United Nations report stated:

> **Cultural liberty is a vital part of human development because being able to choose one's identity – who one is – without losing the respect of others or being excluded from other choices is important in leading a full life. People want freedom to practice their religion openly, to speak their language, to celebrate their ethnicity or religious heritage without fear or ridicule or punishment or diminished opportunity. People want the freedom to participate in society without having to slip off their chosen cultural moorings.**[175]

Human beings are social creatures who derive satisfaction when interacting with people who share their values, aspirations and concerns. Language, cultural and religious associations afford people the opportunity to engage in activities that are immensely important to them. Society as a whole benefits from this, hence the constitutional protection of these activities.

---

173 Currie and De Waal (2013) 627.

174 South African Human Rights Commission (2006) *The Exclusionary Policies of Voluntary Associates: Constitutional Considerations.*

175 South African Human Rights Commission (2006) 15.

A religious or cultural organisation that is established, funded and operated to promote a particular culture, religion or language should be able to protect the financial and other investments of its members. If the law is to protect cultural liberties, then it must provide the means for cultural, religious and linguistic organisations, in pursuit of constitutionally permissible goals, to avoid capture.

At an international level, various treaties protect these cultural liberties:

- Article 22 of the International Covenant on Civil and Political Rights (ICCPR)[176] protects the right to freedom of association with others.
- Article 10 of the African Charter on Human and People's Rights[177] protects the right of every individual to free association, provided he or she abides by the law.[178]
- Article 27 of the ICCPR protects the rights of ethnic, religious and linguistic minorities, in a community with other members of their group, to enjoy their own culture, to profess and practise their own religion and to use their language.
- Article 2 of the Declaration of Rights of Persons Belonging to National or Ethnic, Religious and Linguistic Minorities[179] obliges states to protect the national or ethnic, cultural, religious and linguistic identity of minorities as well as their existence. States are required to encourage conditions for the promotion of that identity. Article 2(2) entrenches the right of people belonging to minorities to establish and maintain their own associations.

To safeguard further these cultural liberties and to provide institutional state support, section 185 of the Constitution provides for the establishment of the Commission for the Promotion and Protection of the Rights of Cultural, Religious and Linguistic Communities (CRL Commission). The primary purpose of this Commission is to promote respect for the rights of cultural, religious and linguistic communities. The CLR Commission is empowered to carry out a number of responsibilities including:

- conducting educational programmes to promote respect for and further the protection of cultural, religious and linguistic rights
- monitoring, investigating and researching issues
- educating, lobbying, advising and facilitating the resolution of friction between cultural, religious and linguistic communities.[180]

The CLR Commission, like other institutions protected in Chapter 9 of the Constitution, is independent and is accountable to the National Assembly (NA). All organs of state are obliged to assist and protect all Chapter 9 institutions to ensure their independence, impartiality, dignity and effectiveness. Finally, there is a constitutional obligation on these Chapter 9 institutions to be impartial and to exercise their powers and perform their functions without fear, favour or prejudice.[181]

---

176 Adopted by the General Assembly of the UN, Resolution 2200(xxi) of 16 December 1966.

177 Adopted by the Organisation of African Unity at the 18th Conference of the Heads of State and Government on 27 June 1981, Nairobi, Kenya. The treaty entered into force on 21 October 1986.

178 In *Amnesty International and Others v. Sudan*, African Commission on Human and Peoples' Rights, Comm. No. 48/90, 50/91, 52/91, 89/93 (1999) para 82, the Commission appears to be advocating that restrictions on the freedom of association must be proportionate and appropriate to the objectives of the law.

179 Adopted by General Assembly Resolution 47/135 of 18 December 1992.

180 S 5 of the Commission for the Promotion and Protection of the Rights of Cultural, Religious and Linguistic Communities Act 19 of 2002.

181 S 181 of the Constitution.

13.4.3 An analysis of the scope and content of sections 30 and 31 of the Constitution

The Constitutional Court has described these rights as 'associational individual rights, namely those rights which cannot be fully or properly exercised by individuals otherwise than in association with others of like disposition'.[182] It is apparent that sections 30 and 31 draw heavily from article 27 of the ICCPR. There are also some differences between the wording of the two provisions. In *Christian Education*, the Constitutional Court made the following general observations about sections 30 and 31:

- Sections 30 and 31 do not refer to 'minorities' unlike article 27 of the ICCPR.
- Sections 30 and 31 effectively protect the rights of individuals to practise their religion, speak their language and enjoy their culture with others in communities which they constitute.
- Individuals are best able to exercise these rights within the context of the community. Individual rights to make choices about whether they want to associate with some and not others therefore lie at the heart of these rights.
- Most open and democratic societies are tolerant and accepting of cultural pluralism. These rights acknowledge the respect for diversity and give greater content to the generic right to freedom of association. People can be who they are without the need to conform to the practices and expectations of the majority. These rights permit the right to be different.
- These rights are protected through the double mechanism of enabling individuals to associate with others of their community and by preventing the state from denying them the right collectively to exercise their cultural, religious and linguistic rights. Thus, section 30 is positively phrased and gives everyone the right to use the language and participate in the cultural life of their choice. In contrast, section 31 is phrased in the negative and provides that persons may not be denied the right with other members of their community to enjoy their culture, practise their religion and use their language.
- The state provides institutional support in the form of the CLR Commission to assist in the better enjoyment of these rights.
- Given their numbers, majority communities often have more effective access to the political process. Minority communities engaging in practices that the majority may regard as bizarre or unusual may not as easily have access to the legislative and policy-making processes. The Constitution manifests its respect for diversity by having these various measures to protect the cultural, religious and linguistic rights of communities.[183]

These cultural liberties are rights which individuals exercise most effectively in associations formed to advance their interests. It is thus proper to afford people the protected space in which to give expression to their preferences, to prevent the state from unreasonably interfering in their affairs, to provide institutional support to resolve disputes and to provide assistance to some communities that lack capacity.

It is often easier to identify and verify a religious as opposed to a cultural practice or belief. Cultural practices evolve and change, often in an incremental and imperceptible manner. While organised religious bodies usually regulate religious practices, there is a lack of similar supervisory bodies that exercise oversight over the divergent cultural activities. Because of the difficulties associated with objective verification, it is sometimes difficult to

182 *Second Certification* para 24.
183 *Christian Education* para 23.

determine whether the asserted practice is a genuine cultural activity that the law should protect. Culture is not static and can change. Moreover, different individuals who associate with a specific cultural group or practice may have different views about what the exact nature of the cultural belief or practice might be.

The Constitutional Court in *Pillay* provided some guidance as to what amounts to a cultural belief. The Court contrasted the South African approach to the approach adopted by English courts. The English courts have offered a definition of what constitutes an 'ethnic group',[184] stating that such a group must have a long shared history and cultural tradition of their own.[185] Other relevant factors include common geographical origin, a common language, a common literature peculiar to the group and a common religion different from that of neighbouring groups. Thus it is a combination of religion, language, geographical origin, ethnicity and artistic traditions which determines the culture of a person. The Court in *Pillay* was of the view that this definition was too restrictive and said a wider definition should be adopted. However, the Court pointed out that if too wide a meaning is given to culture, 'the category becomes so broad as to be rather useless for understanding differences among identity groups'.[186]

As it was unnecessary to resolve the question of what exactly constitutes a protected cultural belief or practice in the context of this case, the Court did not provide any workable definition for it. It merely found that the applicant in the case was part of the South Indian Tamil cultural group which, in any event, fell within the narrow definition of culture.[187] A cultural practice is enjoyed in association with others and therefore the factors suggested by the English courts provide a useful starting point to assess any assertion of a cultural practice. It is apparent that the Constitutional Court was inclined to afford a significant measure of latitude as to what would qualify as a cultural belief. A very wide interpretation could lead to personal predilections or preference being elevated to cultural practices to claim constitutional protection.

It is also clearly undesirable for the courts to have to determine whether the practice is an appropriate manifestation of that particular culture. The greater the number is of people who engage in the practice in the particular cultural community, the more likely it is to be deemed a genuinely held cultural belief. If the belief or practice is highly contested in the cultural community itself, the Court is more likely to require clearer proof from a person asserting the belief to demonstrate that it is a genuinely held cultural belief.

As pointed out above, these religious, cultural and linguistic rights contain a so-called internal qualifier as the enjoyment of these rights is made subject to the other rights protected in the Bill of Rights. In other words, unlike other rights in the Bill of Rights, both section 30 and section 31 are qualified by the proviso that the rights may not be exercised in a manner inconsistent with any provision of the Bill of Rights. This does not mean that other rights will always trump a section 30 or 31 right whenever there is a clash between any of those other rights and sections 30 and 31, no matter how trivial the inconsistency. Often, issues of inconsistency arise when an association refuses admission to an individual or where an individual who was a member of the association is expelled or denied some of the benefits or privileges that he or she previously enjoyed. For example, a cultural group may believe that it is wrong to be gay or lesbian. If the group now discovers that a member is secretly gay and expels that member, they discriminate against him on the basis of sexual

184 *Mandla and Another v Dowell Lee and Another* [1983] 1 All ER 1062 (HL).
185 *Pillay* para 48.
186 *Pillay* para 49.
187 *Pillay* para 50.

orientation which is prohibited by section 9(3) of the Constitution. In such a case, given the importance afforded by the Constitutional Court to the right against non-discrimination and given the harmful effect on gays and lesbians, the rights in sections 30 and 31 may have to give way to the right against unfair discrimination.

PAUSE FOR REFLECTION

A clash between rights

The clash between the right to cultural association versus the right not to be unfairly discriminated against is illustrated in the online news report set out below:

> "Kleinfontein – There are no signs that say "Whites Only." There are, though, men in military fatigues who log the license plates of vehicles approved to enter Kleinfontein, a rural enclave that is home to about 1 000 Afrikaner whites. And there is a bust of Hendrik Verwoerd, the former South African leader who spearheaded white racist rule.
>
> This exercise in separate, self-sufficient living near the South African capital, Pretoria, is more than just a throwback to the apartheid era that ended with the country's first all-race elections in 1994. In recent days, Kleinfontein and its campaign to be formally recognized as a township have become a touchstone for fresh debate about law, freedom and the kind of "rainbow nation" that South Africa is trying to be.
>
> Kleinfontein, which is all private property, requires its residents to be Afrikaners, descendants of settlers who arrived from Europe centuries ago and speak Dutch-based Afrikaans, the idiom of South Africa's former overseers. That brings accusations of racism in a nation whose population of over 50 million is mostly black, but the community skirts race references in its manifesto. Descendants of British settlers, for example, would not be welcome to live here.
>
> The community is not organized "on the basis of race," said Jan Groenewald, chairman of the board of directors of Kleinfontein, which means "Little Fountain" in Afrikaans. Instead, he said, the goal is to preserve a cultural bedrock that stretches back to the lore of the hardy Voortrekker settlers.
>
> The dig-in mindset at the austere settlement echoes that of its ancestors, who drew ox wagons into a defensive circle, a tactic that helped them defeat a much bigger Zulu force at the Dec. 16, 1838 Battle of Blood River. The date has near-mystical import for staunch Afrikaners, though the vast majority of whites accepted South Africa's new, multi-racial order in 1994 as part of a negotiated settlement.
>
> "We are here to stay," read Afrikaans-language signs outside modest brick-and-tile homes linked by dirt roads in Kleinfontein.
>
> Residents don't pay taxes on municipal services because they don't receive them. They draw water from a spring and are building a sewage system. There is a cafe, a primary school and a care centre for the elderly. Zebra, antelope and wildebeest roam in one part of the fenced, 721-hectare (1,780-acre) property. Residents buy many of their goods from outside the fence.

"If I was a racist, we wouldn't speak to a black. We wouldn't do business with them," said Annatjie Oncke, a 49-year-old house cleaner living in a caravan park. She and other poor residents do the kind of menial labour reserved for blacks in the era when whites were in charge. Kleinfontein also has engineers and other skilled workers, as well as retirees.

In the past, small bands of Afrikaners have sought to establish enclaves elsewhere in South Africa, notably in the Northern Cape community of Orania, founded in 1990. Nelson Mandela, South Africa's first black president, travelled to Orania in 1995 and had coffee there with Verwoerd's widow in a show of racial reconciliation. Verwoerd was assassinated in 1966.

Kleinfontein has been around almost as long as Orania, but is now under scrutiny in part because it wants local authorities to recognize it as an entity with the right to run its own affairs. *The Times*, a South African newspaper, reported that provincial lawmakers were informed last year that black police officers were barred from entering the enclave.

Last week, members of the Democratic Alliance, a political party, protested outside Kleinfontein.

"By creating a 'whites-only' area, this community is saying that it has no respect for people who are different from them. It is saying that it fears people who are different," said Mbali Ntuli, the party's youth leader.

On Wednesday, Kgosientso Ramokgopa, the mayor of Pretoria and surrounding areas, visited Kleinfontein as part of an inquiry into its alleged failure to comply with municipal planning laws. Delegations of the two sides met in a hall with a corrugated iron roof, a church bell mounted outside in a scaffold.

Ramokgopa noted the right of every citizen to "reside in any part of the country," while Groenewald, Kleinfontein's chairman, spoke of the right to "self-determination."

The mood was diplomatic and jovial at times. Ramokgopa joked about "koeksusters," a fried, sugary snack favoured by his Afrikaner hosts. Groenewald referred to Mandela's leadership, but also hinted at his resolve with a mention of Koos de la Rey, a general in the 1899-1902 Anglo-Boer war who did not want conflict but fought hard when it began.

South Africa's national flag does not fly in Kleinfontein, though some residents were seen recently with the "Vierkleur" ("Four-color"), the flag of the Transvaal republic, which in the 19th century formed part of what is now South Africa. A community member handed out a declaration that complained of betrayal and persecution of the "Boer-Afrikaner nation," and described South African democracy as a sham.

"We find ourselves exiles in our own fatherland," the statement said. "We experience this new dispensation not as a democracy, but as the dictatorship of an alien majority."[188]

188 See Kleinfontein raises old race questions (2013, 31 May) available at http://www.iol.co.za/news/politics/kleinfontein-raises-old-race-questions-1.1525543

In *Christian Education*, the Constitutional Court held that section 31(2) was intended to ensure that practices offensive to the Bill of Rights were not shielded by the protection afforded by section 31(1):

> **It should be observed, further, that special care has been taken expressly to acknowledge the supremacy of the Constitution and the Bill of Rights. Section 31(2) ensures that the concept of rights of members of communities that associate on the basis of language, culture and religion, cannot be used to shield practices which offend the Bill of Rights. These explicit qualifications may be seen as serving a double purpose. The first is to prevent protected associational rights of members of communities from being used to 'privatise' constitutionally offensive group practices and thereby immunise them from external legislative regulation or judicial control. This will be particularly important in relation to practices previously associated with the abuse of the notion of pluralism to achieve exclusivity, privilege and domination. The second relates to oppressive features of internal relationships primarily within the communities concerned, where section 8, which regulates the horizontal application of the Bill of Rights, might be specially relevant.**[189]

Despite the provisos in sections 30 and 31, the associational rights are not presumptively inferior and of less weight than the rights to equality, dignity and other rights.

A 'constitutionally offensive group practice' in this context means any exclusionary policies, rules or conduct adopted or applied by a religious, linguistic or cultural organisation and which are not permitted by the Constitution. The issue is whether the rules or conduct of the communities are consistent with the Constitution. In deciding whether these policies, rules or conduct are permitted, regard must be had to whether the rule or conduct is reasonable and justifiable. This involves a balancing of the rights of the individual being denied access against the purpose that the rule or conduct is seeking to achieve. In addition, an assessment needs to be made as to whether the rule or conduct is proportionate. Thus, the rights of the organisation or community have to be weighed and balanced against the infraction of the individual rights.

Clearly, the impact on the complainant is of central importance in this deliberation. The more egregious the violation is, the less likely it is that it will be deemed fair. In *Lovelace v Canada*,[190] the applicant challenged a Canadian federal statute, the Indian Act 1970. This Act provided that a Canadian Indian woman who married a non-Indian could not be registered as an Indian. Ms Lovelace married a non-Indian. As a consequence of the law, she was denied the right to return to her native home in the Tobique Reservation in Canada. She argued that the law excluded her from living her life as an Indian. In addition, it specifically resulted in her losing the cultural benefits of living in an Indian community and of having emotional ties to her home, family, friends and neighbours. The United Nations Human Rights Committee upheld the complaint as the exclusion of Lovelace from the tribe meant that she was not able to enjoy her cultural rights as an Indian. This drastic intrusion was not reasonable and necessary to preserve the identity of the tribe.

Ms Lovelace simply had no other forum or association, other than the tribal area, within which to exercise and enjoy her cultural rights. Her exclusion thus meant an eradication of

---

189 *Christian Education* para 26.

190 *Lovelace v Canada* CCPR/C/13/D/24/1977, United Nations International Covenant on Civil and Political Rights Communications No 24/1977, 30 July 1981.

her right to enjoy her culture. This was impermissible given the fact that article 27 of the ICCPR protects the right to cultural associations. The cost that she had to bear was disproportionate and excessive when compared to the potential benefit that would accrue to the tribe as a consequence of the law. Section 31 of the Constitution is materially similar and it is likely that a similar outcome would have been reached through an application of the limitation clause.

The manner in which the rights of the organisation or community must be weighed and balanced against the infraction of the individual rights is also illustrated in the case of *Taylor v Kurtstag NO and Others*.[191] The applicant and his wife had voluntarily submitted to the jurisdiction of the ad hoc Beth Din (Jewish Ecclesiastical Tribunal) and requested that it arbitrate on the custody of their children and on the maintenance to be paid. The applicant did not comply with the findings and was effectively excommunicated. The applicant sought to set aside the edict of the Beth Din that effectively excommunicated him from Jewish society for failing to comply with its decision. He argued that the edict[192] conflicted with his individual rights to religion and to cultural association. The edict, according to the community, was the only means available to it to ensure compliance with the rulings of the Beth Din.

The Court enquired into whether the limitation of the applicant's rights could be justified by reference to the associational rights of the community. The Court concluded that the limitation on the applicant's rights was reasonable and justifiable as a failure to enforce the Beth Din's rulings would result in the Jewish faith not being able to protect the integrity of Jewish law.[193] The associational rights of the organisation took precedence over the personal rights of the individual.[194] In reaching its conclusion, the Court assessed the full extent of the limitation on the rights of the applicant and weighed this against the associational rights of the organisation.[195] Malan J concluded:

> **At the core of this dispute is a matter of religious doctrine: in all religions there are rules entailing consequences if the rules are broken. It does not follow that a contravention of the rules will invariably lead to the conclusion that, because the member's rights of dignity have been infringed, the infringement is unconstitutional. Were this the position, it would be impossible for voluntary organisations, particularly religious communities, to require conformity with particular values and to impose sanctions for the contraventions.**[196]

The Court went on to hold that the purpose of the edict was to punish, to maintain standards and to encourage the dissenter to return by complying with the ruling.[197] In the circumstances, the Court held that the community had not acted in a constitutionally offensive manner and upheld the edict.[198]

As stated earlier, the courts have to balance the rights of the individual who has been shut out of the organisation or community and the rights of the community or organisation to protect its identity. Where an individual asserts that his or her constitutional right has been infringed by another private person or entity and that the other entity seeks to justify

191 2005 (1) SA 362 (W); 2005 (7) BCLR 705 (W); [2004] 4 All SA 317 (W).
192 The edict is referred to as *Cherem* in Jewish law.
193 *Taylor v Kurtstag* para 58.
194 *Taylor v Kurtstag* para 23.
195 *Taylor v Kurtstag* para 26.
196 *Taylor v Kurtstag* para 58.
197 *Taylor v Kurtstag* para 58.
198 *Taylor v Kurtstag* para 58.

the limitation by reference to his or her own rights, then sections 8(2) and (3) of the Constitution have application. Section 8(2)provides:

> **A provision of the Bill of Rights binds a natural or a juristic person if, and to the extent that, it is applicable, taking into account the nature of the right and the nature of any duty imposed by the right.**

Section 8(3) provides:

> **When applying a provision of the Bill of Rights to a natural or juristic person in terms of subsection (2), a court –**
> (*a*) **in order to give effect to a right in the Bill, must apply, or if necessary develop, the common law to the extent that legislation does not give effect to that right; and**
> (*b*) **may develop rules of the common law to limit the right, provided that the limitation is in accordance with section 36(1).**

In terms of sections 8(2) and 8(3), an individual can rely on a right in the Bill of Rights against another natural or juristic person. Where both sides are asserting rights in support of their positions, the courts will use the limitation clause enquiry to determine whether the limitation of the rights is reasonable and justifiable. The relationship between natural and juristic persons in so far as it pertains to cultural, religious and linguistic relationships is most likely to be regulated by the common law or by customary law. The directive contained in section 8(3) enables the courts to reshape and develop the common law by balancing the conflicting rights.

In *Lovelace v Canada*, the law completely cut off the applicant from her community and she was not able to practise her culture outside that community. The law which was designed to protect this community was disproportionate and excessive in the sanction it visited on those who married persons outside the tribe. In contrast, in the case of *Taylor v Kurstag*, the Court was of the view that the punishment was required to ensure that the edicts of the Beth Din were respected. In any event, the applicant would be readmitted if he complied with the edict.

The possibility of readmission to the community if there was compliance with the edict distinguishes *Taylor* from *Lovelace*. The choice facing Lovelace was stark and unpalatable. She had to choose between her marriage and her community. The law should never require persons to make such painful choices. By way of contrast, the applicant in *Taylor* had to abide by the decision of a process to which he had voluntarily subjected himself and he would have been readmitted to the community. Thus, what was being asked of him was not particularly onerous and the community required compliance with rulings of its religious tribunal. This resulted in the Court's conclusion that the community in *Taylor* had acted reasonably and justifiably.

The Constitutional Court adopted a similar approach in *Bhe and Others v Khayelitsha Magistrate and Others.*[199] In this case, the Court had to consider inconsistencies between aspects of customary law and the right not to be unfairly discriminated against on the basis of sex and birth. Ms Bhe and the deceased lived together and two children were born of the relationship. The deceased applied for and obtained state housing. At the time, the Black Administration Act (BAA)[200] regulated intestate succession of black people. The BAA read

199 (CCT 49/03) [2004] ZACC 17; 2005 (1) SA 580 (CC); 2005 (1) BCLR 1 (CC) (15 October 2004).
200 Act 38 of 1927.

with the regulations provided that intestate succession had to be implemented in accordance with customary law. Customary law provided that the eldest male who is related to the deceased qualified as heir while women were not permitted to participate in intestate succession. This is referred to as the **rule of primogeniture**. When the deceased died, his father, who resided in the Eastern Cape, was appointed sole heir. The father wanted to sell the house to defray the funeral expenses. The effect of this was that the two minor children would have been rendered homeless. The applicants, on behalf of the minor children, contended that the primogeniture rule violated their right to human dignity and equality.

The Court held that in the past, customary law was interpreted through the prism of the common law and its content was ascertained from an analysis of the codes and from the views of experts. This resulted in it becoming stagnant and incapable of development and growth.[201] The Constitutional Court affirmed that customary law is now an integral part of our law. Courts must now analyse and interpret customary law in accordance with the Constitution and make adjustments to bring its provisions into line with the spirit, purport and objects of the Bill of Rights.[202]

The Court assessed the primogeniture rule in context. It found that the heir succeeded not just to the assets, but also had to take responsibility for the preservation and perpetuation of the family unit. As property was collectively owned, the family head held it for the entire unit.[203] However, circumstances had changed significantly and nuclear families have replaced extended families as the principal family unit. Now the male heir would acquire the assets but not necessarily the responsibility to provide support and maintenance as was required in the past.[204] Thus, applying the rule in the context where the applicants lived in the Western Cape and the heir to the estate resided in the Eastern Cape would not accord with the original objectives of the law.[205] The Court emphasised that customary law had to evolve and develop to keep pace with changed circumstances.[206] It found that the exclusion of women from inheritance was a clear violation of section 9(3) of the Constitution.[207] It found further that this exclusion violated the right to human dignity as it was premised on the belief that women are not fit to administer and own property. As such, the limitation that the rule imposes on rights was not reasonable and justifiable in an open and democratic society.[208]

The Court was of the view that the legislature was in the best position to intervene and safeguard the rights of those violated by the primogeniture rule.[209] However, in the interim and pending the promulgation of the remedial law, relief had to be afforded to those whose rights were being violated by the rule. In this case, the victims were among the most vulnerable in the society.[210] As an interim measure, the Court held that the Intestate Succession Act[211] was also to apply to all intestate deceased estates that were formerly governed by the BAA.[212]

201 *Bhe* para 43.
202 *Bhe* para 44.
203 *Bhe* para 76.
204 *Bhe* para 80.
205 *Bhe* para 15.
206 *Bhe* para 81.
207 *Bhe* para 91.
208 *Bhe* para 92.
209 *Bhe* para 115.
210 *Bhe* para 116.
211 Act 81 of 1987.
212 *Bhe* para 117.

The approach adopted by the Court was to test the primogeniture rule against constitutional rights. Having found that the rule infringed various rights, the Court determined that the infringements were not reasonable and justifiable. This meant weighing the rights that were infringed against the purpose or objective of the rule. In this case, the rule had had relevance and importance at a time when the extended family system was the norm for African people. However, the rule had much less relevance in the current situation. In effect, the rule was no longer achieving a laudable societal objective that justified the infringements of constitutional rights. Customary rules, notwithstanding their antiquity, can now be tested against constitutional provisions and could be changed if found to be inconsistent with the Constitution. The courts now have the power in terms of section 8(3) to effect these changes to bring principles of the common law and customary law in line with the Constitution.

In *Gumede (born Shange) v President of the Republic of South Africa and Others*, the Constitutional Court also effected changes to customary law to bring it into line with the Constitution.[213] The RCMA provides that customary marriages concluded after the year 2000 are deemed to be in community of property. Marriages concluded before that date had to be regulated by customary law. Mrs Gumede was married prior to 2000 and her husband instituted divorce proceedings. In terms of the customary law, as codified by the KwaZulu Act on the Code of Zulu Law[214] and the Natal Code of Zulu Law,[215] the husband was deemed to the head of the family and the owner of all the property. The consequence of this was that in respect of a customary law marriage concluded before 2000, a wife was not entitled to any of the matrimonial property on dissolution and was subject to the marital power of the husband.

In *Gumede*, the Constitutional Court held that these provisions of customary law discriminated, among others, on the basis of gender. These unequal proprietary consequences applied only to women in customary marriages concluded before 2000.[216] The Court held that the presumption of unfair discrimination was not rebutted and there was no justification for this rule.[217] The Court found that the section of the RCMA which distinguished between marriages concluded before 2000 and those concluded after that date was also unconstitutional.[218] The net effect was that all customary marriages are to be deemed to be in community of property.

In both the *Bhe* and *Gumede* cases, customary law provisions were found to offend against the right not to be unfairly discriminated against on the basis of gender. In both instances the Court materially changed the substance of the law to bring it into line with the Constitution. It may be advisable for the custodians of customary law such as the House of Traditional Leaders proactively to reappraise those aspects of customary law that may violate the Constitution and develop them in a way that accords with the Constitution. In this way, they remain the main role players in the development of this area of the law. It will afford them the opportunity to make customary law more relevant and more applicable to current circumstances. Failure to do so will leave the courts with no alternative but to develop customary law as they did in these cases. It is also important to emphasise that the Court did not simply make declarations of invalidity and leave it to the vagaries of the legislative and political process to fashion a remedy. In both cases, the law was changed to provide

213 (CCT 50/08) [2008] ZACC 23; 2009 (3) BCLR 243 (CC); 2009 (3) SA 152 (CC) (8 December 2008).

214 Act 16 of 1985.

215 Proclamation R151 of 1987.

216 *Gumede* para 10.

217 *Gumede* para 13.

218 *Gumede* para 14.

effective relief to the successful applicants. Clearly, if the legislature is not satisfied with the changes made by the Court to the law, it is at liberty to legislate differently provided it does so in a manner that is consistent with the Constitution.

13.5 Language rights

13.5.1 Introduction

One of the factors that triggered the Soweto student uprisings in 1976 was the insistence by the education authorities that Afrikaans and English be the dual mediums of instruction in black schools in the area. Prior to this decree, English was the sole medium of instruction. At the time, English and Afrikaans were the only official languages. The apartheid government perceived the implementation of Afrikaans as the medium of instruction in schools as a method of entrenching and extending its dominance. The perception that the language of the oppressor was being imposed on black children fuelled the revolt against the apartheid government.

The uprising occurred against the backdrop of the mistreatment of indigenous languages under apartheid. Such indigenous languages, even though spoken by millions of people, were not afforded official recognition in South Africa in the pre-democratic era. The message conveyed by this non-recognition was that these languages were less important than English and Afrikaans and had a lower status than the two languages then officially recognised by the apartheid state.

To affirm the dignity of communities using the various languages and to signal a decisive break with past thinking in this regard, section 6 of the Constitution recognises Sepedi, Sesotho, Setswana, siSwati, Tshivenda, Xitsonga, Afrikaans, English, isiNdebele, isiXhosa and isiZulu as official languages of the Republic. Section 6(4) requires all official languages to be treated equitably and to enjoy parity of esteem. Recognising that some indigenous languages had been systematically disadvantaged, the Constitution imposes an obligation on the state to take positive measures to advance the status of these languages.[219] The establishment of the Pan South African Language Board is one of the initiatives that aims to foster respect for all languages. The challenge facing those seeking to foster parity of esteem is to deal with the dominance of English as the international language of commerce, science, the law and technology.

CRITICAL THINKING

Achieving parity of esteem for languages

The University of KwaZulu-Natal announced in 2013 that it would become compulsory in 2014 for all first-year undergraduate students to complete a course in isiZulu. The language of instruction would remain English.

Critics of this move have argued that scientists, lawyers, entrepreneurs, politicians, pilots and many others are required to have a fluency in English to function and to succeed at a global level. Although it would be good if more South Africans learnt to speak other South African languages, this should not be made compulsory.

However, supporters of the move point to section 6 of the Constitution which requires that all languages be treated with parity of esteem. They also note that almost 60% of

219 S 6(2) of the Constitution.

registered students at the University of KwaZulu-Natal are first-language isiZulu speakers. They therefore argue that the move is long overdue.

Consider the language policy at your own university. Do you think all the dominant regional languages spoken in the region in which your institution is situated treat indigenous languages with parity of esteem? If not, how could this practically be achieved?

Section 30 of the Constitution provides that everyone has the right to use their language while section 31 protects the right to do so with other members of that community. As we have noted, sections 30 and 31 are supported and buttressed by other rights. These rights include the right not to be unfairly discriminated against on the basis of language in section 9(3) and the qualified right to be educated in the official language of a person's choice in public educational institutions in section 29(2). People cannot exercise these rights in a manner that unreasonably and unjustifiably limits the rights of others. A decision by a governing body of an outstanding school to retain Afrikaans as the sole medium of instruction may adversely affect the rights of non-Afrikaans speaking learners in the region to an effective and proper education.[220] As in other instances, competing rights may have to be appropriately balanced.

PAUSE FOR REFLECTION

Balancing language rights with competing rights

In *Head of Department: Mpumalanga Department of Education and Another v Hoërskool Ermelo and Another*, the Constitutional Court sketched the context within which such questions should be considered, pointing out that apartheid has created a 'vast discrepancy in access to public and private resources'.[221] It is important always to keep this context in mind when evaluating the scope and content of the appropriate rights. The quote below illustrates how this context and the mutually enforcing and interdependent rights give rise to specific constitutional obligations. The Court continued that the 'fault line of our past oppression ran along race, class and gender' and that the apartheid system 'authorised a hierarchy of privilege and disadvantage'.[222] It then proceeded to remark:

> Unequal access to opportunity prevailed in every domain. Access to private or public education was no exception. While much remedial work has been done since the advent of constitutional democracy, sadly deep social disparities and resultant social inequity are still with us. It is so that white public schools were hugely better resourced than black schools. They were lavishly treated by the apartheid government. It is also true that they served and were shored up by relatively affluent white communities. On the other hand, formerly black public schools have been and by and large remain scantily resourced. They were deliberately funded stingily by the apartheid government. Also, they served in the main and were supported by relatively deprived black communities. That is why perhaps the most abiding and debilitating legacy of our past is an unequal distribution of skills and competencies acquired through education. In an unconcealed design, the Constitution ardently demands that this social

220 See *Head of Department : Mpumalanga Department of Education and Another v Hoërskool Ermelo and Another* (CCT40/09) [2009] ZACC 32; 2010 (2) SA 415 (CC); 2010 (3) BCLR 177 (CC) (14 October 2009).

221 (CCT40/09) [2009] ZACC 32; 2010 (2) SA 415 (CC); 2010 (3) BCLR 177 (CC) (14 October 2009) para 45.

222 *Hoërskool Ermelo (CC)* para 45.

unevenness be addressed by a radical transformation of society as a whole and of public education in particular. This the Constitution does in a cluster of warranties. I cite only a handful. Section 1(*a*) entrenches respect for human dignity, achievement of equality and freedom. Section 6(1) read with section 6(2) warrants and widens the span of our official languages from a partisan pair to include nine indigenous languages which for long have jostled for space and equal worth. Sections 9(1) and (2) entitle everyone to formal and substantive equality. Section 9(3) precludes and inhibits unfair discrimination on the grounds of, amongst others, race and language or social origin. Section 31(1) promises a collective right to enjoy and use one's language and culture. And even more importantly, section 29(1) entrenches the right to basic education and a right to further education which, through reasonable measures, the state must make progressively accessible and available to everyone.

... Of course, vital parts of the 'patrimony of the whole' are indigenous languages which, but for the provisions of section 6 of the Constitution, languished in obscurity and underdevelopment with the result that at high school level, none of these languages have acquired their legitimate roles as effective media of instruction and vehicles for expressing cultural identity.

And that perhaps is the collateral irony of this case. Learners whose mother tongue is not English but rather one of our indigenous languages, together with their parents, have made a choice to be taught in a language other than their mother tongue. This occurs even though it is now well settled that, especially in the early years of formal teaching, mother tongue instruction is the foremost and the most effective medium of imparting education. Ample literature indicates that in Africa the former colonial languages have become the dominant medium of teaching. Professor Kwessi Kwaa Prah describes this as the 'language of instruction conundrum in Africa'. However, I need say no more about this irony because the matter does not arise for adjudication.[223]

According to the *Oxford Dictionary*, language 'is the method of human communication either spoken or written consisting of the use of words in a structured and conventional way'.[224] Given the nature of this right, people can exercise it meaningfully only with other members of that linguistic group. Language in this context is not restricted to the list of 11 official languages and protects the rights of individuals generally to use the language of their choice. The right to use the language of a person's choice is integrally related to the right to enjoy a person's culture and to practise a person's religion. The Constitution seeks the dual objective of protecting the specific rights of the speakers of a language and promoting respect for diversity. As Sachs J put it:

> **Its [the Afrikaans language] protection and development is therefore the concern not only of its speakers but of the whole South African nation. In approaching the future of the Afrikaans language, then, the issue should not be regarded as simply one of satisfying the self-centred wishes, legitimate or otherwise, of a particular**

223 *Hoërskool Ermelo (CC)* paras 45–9.

224 *Online Oxford English Dictionary* available at http://www.oxford dictionaries.com/definition/english/language.

> **group, but as a question of promoting the rich development of an integral part of the variegated South African national character. ... Stripped of its association with race and political dominance, cultural diversity becomes an enriching force which merits constitutional protection, thereby enabling the specific contribution of each to become part of the patrimony of the whole.**[225]

In some instances states have prohibited the use of specific languages in public places. The Turkish Anti-Terror Act[226] made it an offence to use the Kurdish language in public places.[227] Some international instruments, such as article 7 of the Treaty between the Allied Powers and Poland, affirm the right of minorities to use their language by providing that 'no restriction shall be imposed on the free use by any Polish national of any language in private intercourse, in commerce, in religion, in the press or in publications of any kind or at public meetings'.

Laws such as the Turkish Anti-Terror Act would be an infringement of section 31 of the Constitution. As the South African Bill of Rights is, in certain circumstances, of horizontal application, this right may be enforceable against natural or juristic persons. Thus, private schools and employee organisations that prohibit the use of certain languages are acting contrary to section 31. There is now a general acceptance that respect for diversity includes allowing communities actively to pursue their culture, use their language and practise their religion even if it is different from that of the majority and provided it is not constitutionally offensive to do so.

13.5.2 The right not to be unfairly discriminated against on the basis of language

In addition, the right to use and communicate in the language of choice is protected directly and indirectly in a number of provisions. Section 9(3) of the Constitution prohibits the state from unfairly discriminating directly or indirectly against anyone on the various grounds including language. Section 9(4) of the Constitution extends this prohibition and provides that no person may unfairly discriminate on any of the prohibited grounds. The prohibition therefore operates on both a horizontal and vertical level.

As we noted in chapter 10, the Promotion of Equality and Prevention of Unfair Discrimination Act (PEPUDA) was enacted to give further effect to these constitutional rights. It defines discrimination as any act or omission which imposes burdens, obligations and disadvantages or withholds benefits, opportunities or advantages from any person on one or more of the prohibited grounds.[228] There must be some link or nexus between the disadvantage suffered and an identified prohibited ground such as language. Section 6 of the PEPUDA provides that neither the state nor any person may unfairly discriminate against any person on any of the prohibited grounds including language. However, what is prohibited is unfair discrimination and not simply discrimination. Once a person makes out a *prima facie* case of discrimination, a presumption of unfairness effectively arises which the respondent needs to rebut. In determining unfairness, the court will have regard for the impact of the discrimination on the complainant, whether it is reasonable and justifiable,

225 *Gauteng Provincial Legislature In re: Gauteng School Education Bill of 1995* (CCT39/95) [1996] ZACC 4; 1996 (4) BCLR 537; 1996 (3) SA 165 (4 April 1996) para 49.

226 Act 3713 of 1991.

227 Example quoted in Woolman, S 'Community rights: Language, culture and religion' in Woolman and Bishop (2013) 58.44.

228 S 1 of the PEPUDA.

and whether the respondent has taken reasonable steps to address the disadvantage and accommodate diversity. These issues are discussed more fully under the right to equality.

13.5.3 The right to receive education in the official language of choice

The language provisions set out above must be read in conjunction with section 29(2) of the Constitution. This section protects the right to receive education in the official language of choice in public institutions where that education is reasonably practicable. Section 29(2) goes on to provide that:

> **to ensure the effective access to, and implementation of, this right, the state must consider all reasonable educational alternatives, including single medium institutions, taking into account**
> (a) **equity;**
> (b) **practicability; and**
> (c) **the need to redress the results of past racially discriminatory laws and practices.**

The right of Afrikaans medium public schools to continue to be single medium schools was one of the most contentious issues in the constitutional negotiation process. The depth of sentiment felt by some communities about their language of choice was demonstrated by the protracted legal battles by some schools to retain Afrikaans as sole medium of instruction.[229] These cases - adjudicated in the context set out above - pose difficult questions about the accommodation of diversity in the language field in cases where the dominant language of instruction at a school may have the effect of excluding pupils who have suffered unfair discrimination in the past.

In *Minister of Education (Western Cape) v Mikro Primary School Governing Body*,[230] the Supreme Court of Appeal (SCA) had to consider the legality of a directive issued by the Department of Education directing the governing body of an Afrikaans medium school to convert the school to a parallel medium school. The department wanted the school to admit learners and provide tuition for them in English. The school, which was historically an Afrikaans medium school, refused various requests by the department to convert it to a parallel medium school. The department then issued the directive.

The Court held that it is the function of the governing body of a public school to determine the language policy of the school subject to the Constitution and applicable law.[231] In this instance, the governing body had acted lawfully. If the governing body had acted unreasonably in the adoption of its language policy, the department could challenge it in terms of the Promotion of Administrative Justice Act (PAJA).[232] Alternatively, the head of the Department of Education could, in terms of the South African Schools Act (SASA), replace the governing body if he or she formed the view that it had ceased to perform the functions allocated to it.[233] The Court held that by not following either of these options and by instructing the principal to admit learners contrary to the admission and language policies

229 See *Governing Body of the Rivonia Primary School and Another v MEC for Education: Gauteng Province and Others* (11/08340) [2011] ZAGPJHC 182; [2012] 1 All SA 576 (GSJ); 2012 (5) BCLR 537 (GSJ) (7 December 2011); *Governing Body of the Rivonia Primary School and Another v MEC for Education: Gauteng Province and Others* (161/12) [2012] ZASCA 194; 2013 (1) SA 632 (SCA); [2013] 1 All SA 633 (SCA) (30 November 2012); *Hoërskool Ermelo (CC)* and *Minister of Education (Western Cape) v Mikro Primary School Governing Body* (140/2005) [2005] ZASCA 66; [2005] 3 All SA 436 (SCA) (27 June 2005).

230 (140/2005) [2005] ZASCA 66; [2005] 3 All SA 436 (SCA) (27 June 2005).

231 *Mikro Primary School* paras 29 and 32.

232 Act 3 of 2000. See *Mikro Primary School* para 36.

233 *Mikro Primary School* para 37.

of the school, the Department of Education had acted unlawfully.[234] According to the Court, the Department did not have the power to determine the language or admission policy of the school.[235] The directive to the school was seeking to do just that and was therefore declared unlawful and invalid.[236] The school was thus permitted to continue being a single medium school and allowed to determine its language preferences.[237]

Subsequently, the SCA overruled parts of the *obiter dictum* in *Mikro* in *Hoërskool Ermelo*. The head of the Department of Education took the view that the governing body was acting unreasonably in not changing the school from an Afrikaans medium school to a parallel medium school and disbanded it. He then appointed an interim committee to determine the language policy of the school. The interim committee decided to change the language policy to that of a parallel medium school. The school challenged all these decisions and the SCA had to determine whether the department had acted legally.

The SCA held that the SASA vests the governance of the school in the governing body.[238] Importantly, the governing body has the authority to determine the language policy of the school subject to complying with the Constitution and applicable law.[239] The governing body comprising parents, learners, educators, members of staff and the principal is representative of the school community and is thus in a position to make an informed decision on behalf of the school community.[240] The SCA held:

> **Language is a sensitive issue. Great care is taken in the Act [SASA] to establish a governing body that is representative of the community served by a school and to allocate to it the function of determining the language policy. The Act only authorises the governing body to determine the language policy of an existing school, and nobody else. As nobody else is empowered to exercise that function, it is inconceivable that section 22 was intended to give the head of department the power to withdraw that function, albeit on reasonable grounds, and appoint somebody else to perform it, without saying so explicitly.[241]**

The head of the Department of Education could not do indirectly that which he was prohibited from doing directly. He could not change the language policy of the school as this power was vested in the governing body. The SCA held, after interpreting the SASA, that he could not achieve that objective by disbanding the governing body and by appointing an interim body to change the policy. The Court thus held that the *obiter* in *Mikro* indicating otherwise was incorrect.[242]

The Mpumalanga Department of Education then appealed this decision to the Constitutional Court.[243] Hoërskool Ermelo had been in existence for some 98 years and had a reputation for excellence. The Department contended that the school had excess capacity and hence its insistence that it operate as a parallel medium school. In addition, the number of learners attending the school had steadily diminished over the years. All the English medium schools in the immediate vicinity of the school were filled to capacity.

---

234 *Mikro Primary School* para 1.

235 *Mikro Primary School* para 5.

236 *Mikro Primary School* para 43.

237 *Mikro Primary School* para 43.

238 *Hoërskool Ermelo and Another v Head of Department of Education: Mpumalanga and Others* (219/2008) [2009] ZASCA 22; 2009 (3) SA 422 (SCA); [2009] 3 All SA 386 (SCA) (27 March 2009) para 32.

239 *Hoërskool Ermelo (SCA)* para 59.

240 *Hoërskool Ermelo (SCA)* para 74.

241 *Hoërskool Ermelo (SCA)* para 21.

242 *Hoërskool Ermelo (SCA)* paras 23–4.

243 *Hoërskool Ermelo (CC)*.

The Constitutional Court took the view that while this was a case about legality, it was also about whether it was unreasonable for a school to preserve its Afrikaans-only language policy in the face of dwindling numbers and greater demand for tuition in English.[244] The broader description of the issue meant that social imperatives to redress past disadvantages had to be taken into account together with the need to act lawfully.[245] The Court held that one of the broader visions of the Constitution is that 'social unevenness be addressed by a radical transformation of society as a whole and of public education in particular'.[246]

The Court, with this in mind, interpreted section 29(2) of the Constitution. The Court held that the section comprised two parts. The first part protects the right to receive public education in the language of choice. However, this right is modified by the requirement that it accrues where reasonably practicable. What is reasonable will depend on the circumstances of the particular case. This would include availability of and accessibility to public schools, their enrolment levels, the medium of instruction adopted by the governing body, language choices of the parents and learners, and the curriculum options.[247] Further, the Court held that this aspect of the right means that if a learner already enjoys the right to be educated in the language of choice, the state has a negative duty not to diminish the right without adequate justification.[248]

According to the Court, the second part of section 29(2) refers to the manner in which the state must ensure access to the right to be taught in the language of choice. In deciding on the preferred option, whether it be a single medium school, parallel or dual medium school, the 'state must take into account what is fair, feasible, and satisfies the need to remedy the results of past racially discriminatory laws and practices'.[249] The main purpose of the SASA was to create a system that would redress past injustices in the provision of education and provide education of a progressively high quality to learners. According to the Court, the SASA devolved to the governing body the power to determine the language of instruction of the school.[250] However, the exercise of this power must be in accordance with the Constitution. The Court interpreted this to mean that the policy adopted must fit with the ethos of the Constitution.[251] The Constitution requires the language policy to assist in making education progressively available to everyone, to take into account what is fair and practicable, and to enhance historical redress. Thus, the school must have regard to making education accessible to all in the area and cannot restrict its consideration to the interests of the learners attending the school.[252]

The Constitutional Court took the view that the authority of the head of the Department of Education to revoke the functions of a governing body was a broad one and it related to any function conferred on the governing body by law, including the power to determine the medium of instruction.[253] Thus, the Court affirmed the reasoning in *Mikro* that the head of the Department of Education may, on reasonable grounds, withdraw a school's language policy.[254]

---

244 *Hoërskool Ermelo (CC)* para 38.
245 *Hoërskool Ermelo (CC)* para 40.
246 *Hoërskool Ermelo (CC)* para 47.
247 *Hoërskool Ermelo (CC)* para 52.
248 *Hoërskool Ermelo (CC)* para 40.
249 *Hoërskool Ermelo (CC)* para 53.
250 *Hoërskool Ermelo (CC)* para 57.
251 *Hoërskool Ermelo (CC)* para 59.
252 *Hoërskool Ermelo (CC)* para 51.
253 *Hoërskool Ermelo (CC)* para 58.
254 *Hoërskool Ermelo (CC)* para 72.

The Court also indicated that in determining whether the head of the Department of Education has acted reasonably, regard must be had to the nature of the function, the purpose for which it is revoked in the light of the best interest of learners, including potential learners, the views of the governing body, the nature of the power sought to be withdrawn and the well-being of the school, its learners, parents and educators.[255] Importantly, the Court held that section 29(2) of the Constitution imposes a duty on the state to respect the right to be taught in a language of choice. It also imposes the additional responsibility on the state of ensuring that there are adequate school places for all children in the province and that admission to schools is fair.[256] A finding that language policies vest exclusively in the governing body could frustrate the broader objectives of the Constitution and the SASA which is to provide an effective education for all.[257]

The Court concluded that the Department of Education was entitled to intervene and revoke the exercise of any function exercised by the governing body if reasonable grounds exist.[258] The Constitutional Court thus overruled the SCA. However, the Court concluded that legally once a power is revoked, it vests in the head of the Department of Education and he or she then needs to exercise that power. In this case, the head of the Department erred by revoking the power and then transferring it to an interim committee. He was not permitted to do so and hence the decision of the interim committee was set aside.[259]

Section 31 entrenches the right of people belonging to a particular linguistic community to use their language when interacting with members of their community. Finally, every accused person has the right to be tried in a language that he or he understands. If this is not practicable, the accused has the right to have the proceedings interpreted in that language.

PAUSE FOR REFLECTION

The implications of the expansive interpretation of section 29(2) by the Constitutional Court

The issue of single medium schools proved highly contentious during the constitutional negotiations. The National Party robustly argued for the right of schools to determine the medium of instruction to protect the right of single medium Afrikaans schools to continue to exist. The ANC and its allies equally forcefully opposed this as they were concerned that this would permit segregated education to continue. As a compromise, the negotiating parties agreed on the somewhat convoluted provisions of section 29(3).

It can be argued that the expansive interpretation of section 29(2) by the Constitutional Court in *Hoërskool Ermelo* effectively emasculates the right to be educated in Afrikaans single medium educational institutions. Given South Africa's history of racial discrimination and exclusion, it would be unconscionable if language provisions were used to exclude black learners from a school and in effect to deny black learners access to well resourced schools. The Constitutional Court, alive to these dangers, provided an expansive interpretation of section 29(2) of the Constitution in an effort to prevent the section from being used to exclude black learners from access to well resourced schools on the basis of language rights.

255 *Hoërskool Ermelo (CC)* para 74.
256 *Hoërskool Ermelo (CC)* para 76.
257 *Hoërskool Ermelo (CC)* para 77.
258 *Hoërskool Ermelo (CC)* para 78.
259 *Hoërskool Ermelo (CC)* para 88.

13.5.4 Languages: section 6 of the Constitution

Section 6(1) provides that there are 11 official languages in the Republic. These are Sepedi, Sesotho, Setswana, siSwati, Tshivenda, Xitsonga, Afrikaans, English, isiNdebele, isiXhosa and isiZulu. The Constitution recognises that many of the indigenous languages were neglected and historically diminished. There is therefore a need to take practical steps to elevate their status and enhance their usage.[260] Other languages spoken by minorities in South Africa, such as Hindi and Greek, were not listed as official languages. They are spoken in other parts of the world and their survival does not depend on usage and growth in South Africa.

Section 6(3) allows the national and provincial governments to use any particular official languages for governance purposes after having regard to usage, practicality, expense, regional circumstances and preferences of the population as a whole or in the province concerned. At the very least, the national government and each provincial government must use two official languages. All official languages must enjoy parity of esteem and must be treated equitably.[261] The duty to act equitably does not necessitate equal treatment but requires that the state act even-handedly and fairly towards the various languages.[262] However, the requirement that the state be even-handed in its treatment of the various languages is subject to the requirement that the state must take practical measures to elevate the status and advance the use of indigenous languages which in the past had a diminished use and status.

The Constitution also provides for the establishment of the Pan South African Language Board. This Language Board has a constitutional mandate to promote and create conditions for the development of all official languages together with the Khoi, Nama, San and sign languages. In addition, it is required to promote and ensure respect for various other languages spoken by communities in South Africa.

PAUSE FOR REFLECTION

Should Tamil be one of South Africa's official languages?

Although the Constitution officially recognises 11 languages, many more languages are spoken in South Africa. In a memorable exchange between Mohamed J and Mr B Naidoo during the hearings in *Certification of the Constitution of the Republic of South Africa, 1996*,[263] the issue was whether the drafters of the Constitution had acted contrary to the constitutional principles by not recognising Tamil as one of the official languages. The Constitutional Court rejected this argument.

Mr Naidoo argued that Tamil, like the indigenous languages, was discriminated against under apartheid and should also have been afforded recognition as an official language. Tamil is a language spoken by a section of the Indian community and is one of the oldest languages in the world. Mohamed J responded that unlike the indigenous languages, Tamil is spoken by millions outside South Africa and will survive and flourish whatever happens in this country. This is not the case with the indigenous languages and hence there is a need to provide the additional protection of official recognition for them. Provisions in the Constitution prohibit unfair discrimination

260 S 6(2) of the Constitution.
261 S 6(4) of the Constitution.
262 See the comments of O'Regan J when considering the meaning of equitable in the context of s 15(2) in *Lawrence* para 122.
263 (CCT 23/96) [1996] ZACC 26; 1996 (4) SA 744 (CC); 1996 (10) BCLR 1253 (CC) (6 September 1996)

against Tamil speakers and protect their rights to enjoy and use their language and culture. Their language rights are thus adequately protected by other provisions of the Constitution.[264]

Are you convinced by Mohamed J's reasoning as to why it was permissible for Tamil not to be recognised as an official language given the necessity, from a symbolic perspective, for previously disadvantaged languages to be recognised and affirmed?

13.5.5 The Pan South African Language Board

The Pan South African Language Board Act[265] was passed to provide for the recognition, implementation and furtherance of multiculturalism in South Africa and to promote the development of previously marginalised languages. An independent Board with defined statutory powers was created to realise and achieve the mandate. Some of the objectives of the Board are to:

- create conditions for the development and the promotion of the equal use and enjoyment of all the official South African languages
- prevent the use of any language for the purposes of exploitation, domination or division
- promote multilingualism and translation and interpretation facilities
- foster respect for languages spoken in the Republic
- further the development of the official languages
- promote respect for and the development of other languages used by communities in South Africa.[266]

The Board has various functions including:

- making recommendations with regard to any proposed or existing legislation, practice and policy dealing with language matters
- advising an organ of state on the implementation of any proposed or existing legislation, policy or practice that relates to language matters
- investigating any complaint alleging a violation of a language right, language policy and language practice
- initiating studies and research aimed at promoting and creating conditions for the development and use of the various languages.

Any person acting on his or her own behalf or on behalf of another person may lodge a complaint about an alleged violation or threatened violation of a language right with the Board.[267] The complaint must be in writing and must specify details of the violation. The Board is required to render its assistance free of charge. The Board, on receipt of the written complaint, is required to investigate the alleged violation of any language right, policy or practice. The Board has the power to subpoena persons to appear before it and give evidence and produce relevant documents and records.

If, after investigation, the Board is of the opinion that there is substance to the complaint, it will endeavour by mediation or conciliation to resolve the issue or rectify any act or omission. If the Board is unsuccessful in mediating the matter and it is of the view that there

264 *First Certification* para 209.
265 Act 59 of 1995.
266 S 3 of the Pan SA Language Board Act.
267 S 11 of the Pan SA Language Board Act deals with the procedure regarding complaints lodged with the Board.

are good reasons to address the matter, it shall assist the complainant further. It may make a recommendation to an organ of state against which the complaint is lodged recommending that financial or other assistance be provided as redress. The Board may provide the complainant with financial or other assistance to redress any damage. Alternatively, the Board may provide the complainant with financial or other assistance to enable him or her to obtain relief from any other organ of state or a court of law.

At the time of writing, Parliament has not passed the act required by the Constitution to regulate and monitor the use of official languages by the national and provincial governments. An application was successfully brought in the High Court compelling the government to comply with its constitutional obligations.

SUMMARY

It will always be difficult to accommodate the beliefs and practices of individuals who belong to different cultures, who have different religious beliefs and who speak different languages. In a heterogeneous society like South Africa, this challenge becomes even more pronounced. In this chapter we look at the various rights that protect these diverse interests and ask how these interests should be accommodated to prevent the beliefs or actions of some from harming others in society.

To this end we look at the scope and content of freedom of association and show how this right is often instrumental in helping to protect other rights including political rights. We also ask when the right to freedom of association will be trumped by other rights, including the right not to be discriminated against. We point out that the right to freedom of religion, belief and conscience does not only guarantee the right to believe in a God and to practise those beliefs, but also the right not to believe in any God at all. We ask when justifiable limits can be placed on the exercise of religious beliefs and practices, pointing out that some beliefs and practices are so harmful to others while not sufficiently closely associated with the core aspects of that religion that these beliefs and practices will not be protected by the Constitution.

Finally, we engage with the manner in which all associational rights protect individuals while acknowledging that these rights are often exercised more effectively in conjunction with others or when individuals belong to institutions where these rights are exercised collectively. However, we note that the Constitution does not protect group rights, but only the rights of individuals who belong to specific cultural, language or religious or groups.

Chapter 14

Political and process rights

14.1 The right to freedom of expression

14.1.1 Introduction

In the pre-democratic era, the apartheid state enforced severe forms of censorship to limit the range of political speech as well as the range of artistic expression allowed in the country. It was a criminal offence to quote the words of former President Nelson Mandela or any other member of the banned liberation movements. The Film and Publications Board also regularly banned movies and books because of their political or sexual content. Banning made it a criminal offence to possess, read or watch these products of artistic expression. During the various states of emergency which were in place for long periods in the 1980s, the ability of newspapers to report on the actions of the police and the military were severely limited by law.

Thus, in this pre-Internet era, the dark pall of censorship hung over South Africa. These restrictions did not only constitute a denial of democracy. They also exacerbated the impact of the systemic violations of other fundamental human rights in South Africa.[1]

PAUSE FOR REFLECTION

Black Wednesday

On 12 September 1977, Steve Bantu Biko - who espoused the idea of black consciousness - died at the hands of the apartheid police while in detention. Biko's funeral was attended by about 20 000 people. Partly in response to these events, on the morning of 19 October 1977, scores of Black Consciousness activists were arrested and detained under section 10 of the Internal Security Act.[2]

In addition to the scores of people detained, about 18 organisations were banned and three newspapers - *The World*, *Weekend World* and *Pro Veritate* - were also 'banned'. Journalists were detained, including Mr Percy Qoboza, then editor of *The World*, as well as a former editor of the *Sowetan*, Mr Aggrey Klaaste. The Chairman of the Committee of Ten, Dr Nthato Motlana, and some executive committee members of the Teachers' Action Committee were also detained.

This day came to be known as Black Wednesday. In South Africa today, 19 October is still commemorated with the aim of celebrating media freedom and to protest against real or perceived threats to the freedom of the media.

Censorship is incompatible with South Africa's present commitment to a society based on a 'constitutionally protected culture of openness and democracy and universal human rights for South Africans of all ages, classes and colours'.[3] To prevent a recurrence of censorship, section 16 of the Constitution explicitly guarantees the right to freedom of expression for everyone. Section 16(1) states that this right includes:

- freedom of the press and other media
- freedom to receive or impart information or ideas
- freedom of artistic creativity
- academic freedom and freedom of scientific research.

1 See *S v Mamabolo* (CCT 44/00) [2001] ZACC 17; 2001 (3) SA 409 (CC); 2001 (5) BCLR 449 (CC) (11 April 2001) para 28; *Islamic Unity Convention v Independent Broadcasting Authority and Others* (CCT36/01) [2002] ZACC 3; 2002 (4) SA 294; 2002 (5) BCLR 433 (11 April 2002) para 25.

2 Act 74 of 1982.

3 *Shabalala and Others v Attorney-General of the Transvaal and Another* (CCT23/94) [1995] ZACC 12; 1995 (12) BCLR 1593; 1996 (1) SA 725 (29 November 1995) para 26.

However, section 16 does not protect all forms of expression. Section 16(2) lists several forms of speech explicitly excluded from the protections contained in section 16(1). Thus, propaganda for war, incitement of imminent violence and advocacy of hatred that is based on race, ethnicity, gender or religion, and that constitutes incitement to cause harm are not constitutionally protected speech. Section 16(2) therefore 'defines the boundaries beyond which the right to freedom of expression does not extend', representing an 'acknowledgment that certain expression does not deserve constitutional protection because, among other things, it has the potential to impinge adversely on the dignity of others and cause harm'.[4]

The right to freedom of expression is one of a 'web of mutually supporting rights' in the Constitution.[5] It is closely related to freedom of religion, belief and opinion, the right to dignity, the right to freedom of association, the right to vote and to stand for public office, and the right to assembly. The Constitutional Court has considered the purpose behind the right to freedom of expression in a number of cases.[6] At the heart of the guarantee of freedom of expression is the recognition of the importance, 'both for a democratic society and for individuals personally, of the ability to form and express opinions, whether individually or collectively, even where those views are controversial'.[7]

Freedom of expression is therefore important for two reasons. First, freedom of expression contributes to the goal of establishing a democratic society. Second, freedom of expression constitutes an important aspect of what it is to be human - it empowers individuals, bestows a certain agency on us, and helps us to make informed and hopefully wise life choices and to decide for ourselves who we are and how we want to live our lives. O'Regan J referred to these two goals in her judgment in *South African National Defence Union v Minister of Defence*, where she held that:

> **[f]reedom of expression lies at the heart of democracy. It is valuable for many reasons, including its instrumental function as a guarantor of democracy, its implicit recognition and protection of the moral agency of individuals in our society and its facilitation of the search for truth by individuals and society generally. The Constitution recognizes that individuals in our society need to be able to hear, form and express opinions and views freely on a wide range of matters.**[8]

Given South Africa's oppressive past, it is not surprising that the Constitutional Court has emphasised the important role freedom of expression plays in promoting democracy. In *S v Mamabolo*, for example, Kriegler J held that:

> **[h]aving regard to our recent past of thought control, censorship and enforced conformity to governmental theories, freedom of expression - the free and open exchange of ideas - is no less important than it is in the United States of America. It could actually be contended with much force that the public interest in the open market-place of ideas is all the more important to us in this country because our democracy is not yet firmly established and must feel its way.**[9]

4 *Islamic Unity Convention* para 30.

5 *South African National Defence Union v Minister of Defence* (CCT27/98) [1999] ZACC 7; 1999 (4) SA 469; 1999 (6) BCLR 615 (26 May 1999) para 8.

6 See *Shabalala; South African National Defence Union; Islamic Unity Convention; Mamabolo.*

7 *South African National Defence Union* para 8.

8 (CCT27/98) [1999] ZACC 7; 1999 (4) SA 469; 1999 (6) BCLR 615 (26 May 1999) para 7.

9 (CCT 44/00) [2001] ZACC 17; 2001 (3) SA 409 (CC); 2001 (5) BCLR 449 (CC) (11 April 2001) para 37.

In the absence of freedom of expression, individuals will not be able to take part in the democratic process in a free and informed manner. Democracy only functions well in a society in which it is possible for an individual to change his or her mind. This is only possible when individuals are free to report on events without fear, to express their opinions and beliefs, and to receive such communication from others. This view of freedom of expression is commonly related to the search for truth, which is said to be best facilitated in an 'open market-place of ideas'.[10] Where there is a free competition of ideas, so it is said, the best ideas, or the truth whatever that may be, will eventually triumph. However, as the Constitutional Court pointed out, '[t]hat obviously presupposes that both the supply and the demand side of the market will be unfettered'.[11] In a deeply unequal society in which not everyone has equal access to information and in which the voices of some may be privileged and may carry more weight than others, it is unclear whether such a free marketplace of ideas can ever exist.

CRITICAL THINKING

Is there truly a free marketplace of ideas?

It is often said that in a society in which freedom of expression is vigorously protected, the search for the truth in the free marketplace of ideas will allow the best ideas to rise to the top and the worst and most dangerous ideas to be rejected by society. However, consider this: no citizen has access to all the media sources available in the country, nor to all the books, films and other forms of artistic expression. Nor would most citizens be able to make their voices heard outside their immediate circle of friends – even in the age of Twitter and other forms of social media. It can be argued that a person's level of education, command of the English language, race, gender and sexual orientation, and relative wealth partly determine to what extent this person would have the opportunity to make his or her voice heard in the public sphere. Even on talk radio stations, only those people who have access to a telephone and, in the case of cell phones, to airtime, will be able to call a phone-in programme. Power, so the argument goes, is unevenly distributed and even in a democracy in which free speech is guaranteed, the mass media in particular contribute to the manufacturing of a consensus in which the voices of the marginalised are drowned and the interests of the powerful are promoted.

In their book, *Manufacturing Consent: A Propaganda Model*, Herman and Chomsky argue that it is the function of the mass media to amuse, entertain and inform, 'and to inculcate individuals with the values, beliefs, and codes of behaviour that will integrate them into the institutional structures of the larger society'.[12] To fulfil this role requires systematic propaganda. They continue:

> **In countries where the levers of power are in the hands of a state bureaucracy, the monopolistic control over the media, often supplemented by official censorship, makes it clear that the media serve the ends of a dominant elite. It is much more difficult to see a propaganda system at work where the media are private and formal censorship is absent. This is especially true where the media**

10 *Mamabolo* para 37.
11 *Case and Another v Minister of Safety and Security and Others, Curtis v Minister of Safety and Security and Others* (CCT20/95, CCT21/95) [1996] ZACC 7; 1996 (3) SA 617; 1996 (5) BCLR 608 (9 May 1996) para 26.
12 Herman, ES and Chomsky, N (1988) *Manufacturing Consent: The Political Economy of the Mass Media* 306.

actively compete, periodically attack and expose corporate and governmental malfeasance, and aggressively portray themselves as spokesmen for free speech and the general community interest. What is not evident (and remains undiscussed in the media) is the limited nature of such critiques, as well as the huge inequality in command of resources, and its effect both on access to a private media system and on its behavior and performance. A propaganda model focuses on this inequality of wealth and power and its multilevel effects on mass-media interests and choices. It traces the routes by which money and power are able to filter out the news fit to print, marginalize dissent, and allow the government and dominant private interests to get their messages across to the public. The essential ingredients of our propaganda model, or set of news 'filters', fall under the following headings: (1) the size, concentrated ownership, owner wealth, and profit orientation of the dominant mass-media firms; (2) advertising as the primary income source of the mass media; (3) the reliance of the media on information provided by government, business, and 'experts' funded and approved by these primary sources and agents of power; (4) 'flak' as a means of disciplining the media; and (5) 'anticommunism' as a national religion and control mechanism. These elements interact with and reinforce one another. The raw material of news must pass through successive filters, leaving only the cleansed residue fit to print. They fix the premises of discourse and interpretation, and the definition of what is newsworthy in the first place, and they explain the basis and operations of what amount to propaganda campaigns. The elite domination of the media and marginalization of dissidents that results from the operation of these filters occurs so naturally that media news people, frequently operating with complete integrity and goodwill, are able to convince themselves that they choose and interpret the news 'objectively' and on the basis of professional news values. Within the limits of the filter constraints they often are objective; the constraints are so powerful, and are built into the system in such a fundamental way, that alternative bases of news choices are hardly imaginable.[13]

Freedom of expression is not only of pivotal importance for the healthy functioning of a democracy. As pointed out above, the Constitutional Court has also emphasised a second goal of freedom of expression – to safeguard the moral agency of individuals. Dealing with this aspect of freedom of expression, the Court held that:

> **[F]reedom of speech is a *sine qua non* for every person's right to realise his or her full potential as a human being, free from the imposition of heteronomous power. Viewed in that light, the right to receive others' expression has more than merely instrumental utility, as a predicate for the addressee's meaningful exercise of his or her own rights of free expression. It is also foundational to each individual's empowerment to autonomous self-development.[14]**

13 Herman and Chomsky (1988) 306.

14 *Case* para 26.

PAUSE FOR REFLECTION

Greater latitude for political speech

Although the Constitutional Court has accepted that the right to freedom of expression serves both democracy-promoting and human dignity-reinforcing goals, it has tended to favour political speech over other forms of expression, especially at the limitation stage of analysis. In *Khumalo and Others v Holomisa*, for example, the Court held that when it comes to determining the reasonableness of a publication, 'greater latitude is usually allowed in respect of political discussion'.[15] In *Thint Holdings (Southern Africa) (Pty) Ltd and Another v National Director of Public Prosecutions, Zuma v National Director of Public Prosecutions*, the Court held that where its jurisprudence touches on the status of political information, 'it tends towards permitting greater dissemination rather than the restriction of it'.[16]

14.1.2 Scope and ambit of the right to freedom of expression

Unlike the First Amendment of the United States Constitution,[17] section 16 does not protect the right to freedom of speech, but rather the right to freedom of expression. The term 'expression' is much broader than the term 'speech'. It thus includes not only words, but also expressive activities such as symbolic acts, for example burning a flag, wearing items of clothing, for example wearing a party-political T-shirt, and physical gestures, for example raising a fist or gesturing with a finger.

The Constitutional Court confirmed the fact that the term 'expression' includes not only words but also expressive activities in its judgment in *Phillips and Another v Director of Public Prosecutions and Others*.[18] In this case the Court held that a statutory provision that prohibited any person from appearing or performing naked or semi-naked at a venue that was licensed to sell alcohol infringed the right to freedom of expression. This was because freedom of expression included freedom of artistic creativity and the freedom to receive and impart information.[19] In principle, a work of art, for example a naked painting of the President of the country, would also constitute expression and would also be protected by section 16.

Apart from expressive activities, the Constitutional Court has also held that the right to freedom of expression includes not only information or ideas that are favourably received or regarded as inoffensive or as a matter of indifference, but also includes those ideas that offend, shock or disturb.[20] Even false speech is, in principle, protected. However, false speech may be more easily limited as justification thereof may be more difficult in terms of the provisions of the limitation clause.[21]

Although the Constitutional Court has interpreted the term 'expression' broadly, it is important to note that the right to freedom of expression does not encompass every form of expression. This is because section 16(2) of the Constitution expressly excludes certain forms

15 (CCT53/01) [2002] ZACC 12; 2002 (5) SA 401; 2002 (8) BCLR 771 (14 June 2002) para 18.

16 (CCT 90/07, CCT 92/07) [2008] ZACC 14; 2008 (2) SACR 557 (CC); 2009 (1) SA 141 (CC); 2009 (3) BCLR 309 (CC) (31 July 2008) para 52. See also *Mthembi-Mahanyele v Mail & Guardian Ltd and Another* (054/2003) [2004] ZASCA 67; [2004] 3 All SA 511 (SCA) (2 August 2004) para 41.

17 The First Amendment reads as follows: 'Congress shall make no law respecting an establishment of religion, or prohibiting the free exercise thereof; or abridging the freedom of speech, or of the press; or of the right of the people peaceably to assemble, and to petition the Government for a redress of grievances'.

18 (CCT20/02) [2003] ZACC 1; 2003 (3) SA 345; 2003 (4) BCLR 357 (11 March 2003).

19 *Phillips* para 15.

20 *Islamic United Convention* paras 28–9.

21 *Hamata and Another v Chairman, Peninsula Technikon Internal Disciplinary Committee and Others* 2000 (4) SA 621 (C) para 32.

of expression from the scope and ambit of the right, namely propaganda for war, incitement of imminent violence and advocacy of hatred that is based on one or other of the listed grounds, namely race, ethnicity, gender or religion and that amounts to 'incitement to cause harm'. Although the Constitution does not itself ban these forms of expression, it does not protect these forms of expression because the 'pluralism and broadmindedness that is central to an open and democratic society' can be undermined by such forms of speech 'which seriously threatens democratic pluralism itself'.[22] Section 16(2) recognises the fact that some forms of expression have the potential to impair the exercise and enjoyment of other important rights, such as the right to dignity, as well as state interests, such as the pursuit of national unity and reconciliation.[23] The Constitution therefore recognises that the state has a particular interest in regulating this type of expression:

> **because of the harm it may pose to the constitutionally mandated objective of building the non-racial and non-sexist society based on human dignity and the achievement of equality. There is accordingly no bar to the enactment of legislation that prohibits such expression. Any regulation of expression that falls within the categories enumerated in section 16(2) would not be a limitation of the right in section 16.**[24]

We will discuss these provisions in more detail below with specific reference to the question of hate speech.

While the forms of expression listed in section 16(2) of the Constitution are not protected by the right to freedom of expression guaranteed in section 16(1), the Constitutional Court has held that all other forms of expression are protected. This means that any restrictions that are imposed by the state, as well as, where appropriate, private institutions, on any form of expression that falls outside section 16(2) will amount to an infringement of the right to freedom of expression. It will accordingly have to be justified in terms of the limitation clause if the limitation was imposed in terms of a law of general application.

In *Laugh It Off Promotions CC v South African Breweries International (Finance) BV t/a Sabmark International and Another*, for example, the Constitutional Court held that:

> **[w]e are obliged to delineate the bounds of the constitutional guarantee of free expression generously. Section 16 is in two parts: the first subsection sets out expression protected under the Constitution. It indeed has an expansive reach which encompasses freedom of the press and other media, freedom to receive or impart information or ideas, freedom of artistic creativity, academic freedom and freedom of scientific research. The second part contains three categories of expression which are expressly excluded from constitutional protection. It follows clearly that unless an expressive act is excluded by s 16(2) it is protected expression. Plainly, the right to free expression in our Constitution is neither paramount over other guaranteed rights nor limitless. As Kriegler K in *S v Mamabolo* puts it: 'With us it is not a pre-eminent freedom ranking above all others. It is not even an unqualified right. In appropriate circumstances authorised by the Constitution itself, a law of general application may limit freedom of expression.' (our emphasis)**[25]

An important consequence of this approach is that section 16(1) of the Constitution includes certain forms of expression that are often excluded in other jurisdictions, such as pornography,

22 *Islamic Unity Convention* para 27.
23 *Islamic Unity Convention* para 28.
24 *Islamic Unity Convention* para 31.
25 (CCT42/04) [2005] ZACC 7; 2006 (1) SA 144 (CC); 2005 (8) BCLR 743 (CC) (27 May 2005) para 47.

child pornography and commercial speech.[26] Although these forms of expression are included in section 16(1), the Constitutional Court attaches less weight to them and has found in specific cases that they are easily outweighed by countervailing interests, such as the rights of women and children. Instead of determining the weight that should be attached to a particular form of expression at the first stage of the two-stage limitation analysis, therefore, the Court carries this task out at the second stage.

This approach is clearly illustrated in the Constitutional Court's judgment in *De Reuck v Director of Public Prosecutions (Witwatersrand Local Division) and Others*.[27] Mr De Reuck, who was a film producer, was found in possession of child pornography and was charged in the regional magistrates' court with contravening section 27(1) of the Film and Publications Act.[28] This section provided that a person would be guilty of an offence if he or she created, produced, imported or possessed any publication or film which contains child pornography. Section 1 of the Act defined child pornography as including any image, real or simulated, however created, depicting a person who is or who is shown as being under the age of 18 years, engaged in sexual conduct or a display of genitals which amounts to sexual exploitation, or participating in, or assisting another person to engage in sexual conduct which amounts to sexual exploitation or degradation of children.

The Constitutional Court dismissed an appeal of Mr De Reuck and found that section 27(1) of the Film and Publications Act was constitutionally valid. In arriving at this conclusion, the Court explained that it first had to decide whether section 27(1) of the Act infringed section 16(1) of the Constitution and if it did, whether that infringement was reasonable and justifiable in an open and democratic society based on human dignity, equality and freedom.[29] In so far as the first issue was concerned, the NDPP argued that section 27(1) of the Act did not infringe the right to freedom of expression because child pornography, as defined in the Act, could not be classified as expression, but rather as a form of unprotected speech. This is because, the NDPP argued further, child pornography does not serve any of the values that underlie the right, namely truth seeking, free political activity and self-fulfilment.[30]

Although child pornography was classified as unprotected speech in other jurisdictions such as the United States, the Constitutional Court held that the same approach could not be adopted in South Africa. This is because in South Africa all forms of expression except for those listed in section 16(2) are protected by section 16(1). Child pornography, therefore, did fall into the scope and ambit of the right to freedom of expression. The constitutional validity of section 27(1) of the Act had to be decided not at the first stage of the two-stage limitation analysis, but rather at the second stage, namely the limitation stage.[31]

After setting out these principles, the Constitutional Court turned to consider whether section 27(1) of the Film and Publications Act was a reasonable and justifiable limitation of the right to freedom of expression. The Constitutional Court found that it was for the following reasons:

- First, the limitation of the right to freedom of expression by prohibiting the possession of child pornography was not particularly serious. This is because child pornography is a form of expression that has very little value, it is found on the periphery of the right and

26 See *De Reuck v Director of Public Prosecutions (Witwatersrand Local Division) and Others* (CCT5/03) [2003] ZACC 19; 2004 (1) SA 406 (CC); 2003 (12) BCLR 1333 (CC) (15 October 2003) para 48.
27 (CCT5/03) [2003] ZACC 19; 2004 (1) SA 406 (CC); 2003 (12) BCLR 1333 (CC) (15 October 2003).
28 Act 65 of 1996.
29 *De Reuck* paras 46–7.
30 *De Reuck* para 48.
31 *De Reuck* para 48.

is a form of expression that is not protected as part of the freedom of expression in many democratic societies.[32]

- Second, the purpose of section 27(1) of the Film and Publications Act was extremely important. This is because it was aimed at curbing child pornography which not only undermines the dignity of all children, but is also harmful to those children who are used in its production. In addition, child pornography can be used to groom children for sex, to reinforce the belief that sex with children is normal and to fuel the fantasies of paedophiles before they commit acts of abuse. It is regarded as evil in all democratic societies.[33]
- Third, while section 27(1) of the Film and Publications Act did not create a defence for researchers and documentary film makers who possess child pornography as 'raw material' for their legitimate academic or documentary projects, section 22 of the Act created a process in terms of which a person who wishes to possess or otherwise deal with child pornography could apply to an executive committee of the Film and Publications Board to do so. This meant that section 27(1) did not impose a blanket prohibition on the possession of child pornography and could not, therefore, be described as overbroad.[34]

CRITICAL THINKING

Can the findings in the *De Reuck* case be applied to legislation that limits other forms of pornographic expression?

In the *De Reuck* judgment, the Constitutional Court found that child pornography had little value. Taking into account the fact that freedom of expression was guaranteed to help secure democracy and to protect the moral agency of individuals, there was clearly little or no link between the production, possession or consumption of child pornography and the promotion of these goals.

However, it has been argued that there is a clear distinction between child pornography - which harms children - and other forms of pornography produced and consumed by consenting adults. Adult pornography, so it is argued, can play an important role in protecting the moral agency of individuals who can be empowered by pornography to make important life choices about their true sexual orientation. For example, in the United States context, Lucas[35] argues in favour of the value of specifically gay pornography for gay men struggling with their sexual identities as 'gay porn can act to liberate as well as educate a historically closeted segment of society' and 'can validate homosexuality and create community. It can be an outlet, perhaps the only outlet, for one's desires - desires that are generally suppressed if not condemned by society as a whole'.[36] It might therefore not be possible to apply the findings in the *De Reuck* case to legislation that limits other forms of pornographic expression because the harm, if any, of adult pornography would be far more difficult to quantify or prove. Also, for some segments of society at least, it might play an important educative and liberating role.

32 *De Reuck* para 59.
33 *De Reuck* para 64–5.
34 *De Reuck* paras 71–9.
35 Lucas, M (2006) On gay porn *Yale Journal of Law and Feminism* 18(1):299–302 at 299.
36 Lucas (2006) 299. See also Sherman, JG(1995) Love speech: The social utility of pornography *Stanford Law Review* 47(4):661–706 at 702–3, where he argues that 'gay male pornography is a necessary tool in gay men's struggle to attain sexual integrity', and asserts that '[t]he relative importance of pornography in the gay male imagination results from the suppression of other forms of gay expression: not only artistic expression but lived interpersonal expression'.

14.1.3 Freedom of the press and other media

14.1.3.1 Introduction

Apart from the general right to freedom of expression, section 16(1) of the Constitution lists certain specific forms of protected expression. These are:

> (*a*) **freedom of the press and other media;**
> (*b*) **freedom to receive or impart information or ideas;**
> (*c*) **freedom of artistic creativity; and**
> (*d*) **academic freedom and freedom of scientific research.**

Of these four specific forms of protected expression, the right to freedom of the press and other media has received the most attention from the courts and commentators. For the purposes of this book, therefore, we are going to focus on this aspect of the right only.

14.1.3.2 The role of the press

The mere fact that the right to freedom of the press and other media has been expressly included in section 16(1) of the Constitution confirms the important role that the press and other media play in a democratic society. The Constitutional Court has referred to this role in a number of cases.[37] In these cases, the Court has held that the right of every citizen to receive information and ideas depends largely on the freedom of the press and other media. The press and other media, therefore, are key agents in ensuring that this aspect of the right to freedom of expression is respected. Freedom of the media also plays a pivotal role in securing the enjoyment of other rights. This is in line with the Constitutional Court's assertion (discussed above) that freedom of expression forms part of a web of mutually supporting rights that underpin democracy.

Apart from ensuring that the right to receive information and ideas is respected, the Constitutional Court has also held that the press and other media play a key role in ensuring that government is open, responsive and accountable to the people. This is because:

> **[i]t is the function of the press and other media to ferret out corruption, dishonesty and graft wherever it may occur and to expose its perpetrators. The press must reveal dishonest mal- and inept administration. ... It must advance the communication between the governed and those who govern.**[38]

In light of these responsibilities, it is important to note that the press and other media are not simply bearers of the right to freedom of expression, but are also bearers of constitutional obligations with respect to freedom of expression. In *Khumalo*, the Constitutional Court summed up the rights and obligations of the media as follows:

> **In a democratic society, then, the mass media play a role of undeniable importance. They bear an obligation to provide citizens both with information and with a platform for the exchange of ideas which is crucial to the development of a democratic culture. As primary agents of the dissemination of information and ideas, they are, inevitably, extremely powerful institutions in a democracy and have a**

37 *Khumalo* paras 22–4; *South African Broadcasting Corporation Limited v National Director of Public Prosecutions and Others* (CCT58/06) [2006] ZACC 15; 2007 (1) SA 523 (CC); 2007 (2) BCLR 167 (CC); [2006] JOL 18339 (CC) (21 September 2006) para 24; *Print Media South Africa and Another v Minister of Home Affairs and Another* (CCT 113/11) [2012] ZACC 22; 2012 (6) SA 443 (CC); 2012 (12) BCLR 1346 (CC) (28 September 2012) para 54.

38 *Government of the Republic of South Africa v Sunday Times Newspaper and Another* 1995 (2) SA 221 (T) 227H–228A.

constitutional duty to act with vigour, courage, integrity and responsibility. The manner in which the media carry out their constitutional mandate will have a significant impact on the development of our democratic society. If the media are scrupulous and reliable in the performance of their constitutional obligations, they will invigorate and strengthen our fledgling democracy. If they vacillate in the performance of their duties, the constitutional goals will be imperilled. The Constitution thus asserts and protects the media in the performance of their obligations to the broader society, principally through the provisions of section 16.[39]

PAUSE FOR REFLECTION

The impact of the Secrecy Bill on the role of the press and other media in a democracy

It can be argued that the role of the press and other media 'to ferret out corruption, dishonesty and graft wherever it may occur and to expose its perpetrators'[40] is threatened by legislative attempts to limit the free flow of information and to prevent the media from reporting on matters of public concern. In this regard, the adoption of the Protection of State Information Bill[41] ('the Secrecy Bill') by Parliament has been heavily criticised by its opponents. This so-called Secrecy Bill was sent back to Parliament by President Jacob Zuma in September 2013 to correct potential unconstitutional aspects of the Bill.

The Secrecy Bill is ostensibly aimed at protecting the national security of the country by empowering members of the Cabinet, the various security services, including the police and the military, and those bodies overseeing the security services to classify information as confidential, secret or top secret.[42] The Minister of State Security is further empowered to grant the power to classify documents to any organ of state or part thereof although this power cannot be granted to municipalities.[43]

This means that the Minister of State Security has wide powers to authorise other bodies - after approval by Parliament - to classify information. If the Minister (and the majority party in Parliament) wishes to, he or she could empower any department of state or administration in the national or provincial sphere of government, any other functionary or institution exercising a public power or performing a public function in terms of any legislation and any owner of a facility or installation declared as a National Key Point to classify information.[44]

Although information can only be classified to protect 'national security', the Bill defines national security in a manner that is indeterminate and open-ended. The Bill thus states that 'national security *includes*', but is not limited to, threats against the Republic based on terrorism and sabotage and acts directed at undermining the capacity of the Republic to respond to the use of, or the threat of the use of, force and the carrying out of the Republic's responsibilities to any foreign country.[45]

Because the definition is open-ended, it is conceivable that an authorised classifier could interpret national security in a far broader manner than the examples mentioned

39 *Khumalo* para 24.
40 *Sunday Times* 227H–228A.
41 Bill B1.4 of 2010.
42 S 1.1.
43 S 1.1 of the Secrecy Bill.
44 S 1.1 of the Secrecy Bill.
45 1.1.

in the definition of national security contained in the Bill. This means that the Secrecy Bill potentially empowers many people at various levels of government (and many organs of state) to censor information in the name of protecting national security. This therefore potentially imposes drastic limits on the right to freedom of expression and the right of access to information. It does so in two interrelated but distinct ways:

- First, when information is classified, anyone who leaks or holds or publishes the information commits a criminal offence.[46] This means that whistle-blowers in possession of incriminating evidence of maladministration, 'dirty tricks' by members of the security forces, evidence of corruption or of criminal activities will think twice before leaking such information to the media for fear of being sent to jail for up to 25 years.[47]
- Second, journalists and editors will be fearful of receiving any such information and of publishing it for fear of being sent to jail for long periods of time. The potential 'chilling effect' of this law is therefore real.

To pass constitutional muster, it will have to be shown that these restrictions on the right to freedom of expression and information are justifiable. It will have to be demonstrated that the law struck the appropriate balance between the need to protect national security, on the one hand, and the need to protect the rights of citizens to the free flow of information, on the other hand. It will also have to be shown whether less restrictive means could not have been used to protect national security in an appropriate manner.

Section 8 of the Bill purports to limit the potentially broad scope of the Bill by stating that classification of state information is justifiable only when it is 'necessary to protect national security'. It states further that classification may not under any circumstances be used to conceal corruption or any other unlawful act, to avoid criticism, or to prevent embarrassment to a person, organisation or organ of state or agency. The section also includes other guidelines which, if meticulously and honestly followed by the classifier, would substantially narrow the scope of the Bill.

Section 45 of the Bill criminalises the wrongful classification of information while section 46 further determines that a 'head of an organ of state or an official of such organ of state who wilfully or in a grossly negligent manner fails to comply with the provisions' of the Bill could be sentenced to two years' imprisonment. These safeguards would go some way to deter abuse of the Bill, but only if an independent body existed to investigate and to prosecute those who wrongfully classify documents to hide corruption or avoid embarrassment.

Those who defend the constitutionality of the Bill will rely heavily on section 41 of the Bill to argue that it limits the rights no more than is necessary. This is so because the section provides a defence to those charged and prosecuted for disclosing even wrongly classified or corruptly classified information in a limited number of cases. This includes cases where the disclosure of the information is authorised by other legislation and where the classified information reveals criminal activity, including any criminal activity in terms of section 45 of the Bill.

46 S 32 of the Secrecy Bill.
47 S 32 of the Secrecy Bill.

Section 41 indeed provides an important safeguard for potential whistle-blowers. Whistle-blowers and journalists who are exceedingly brave (or just plain stupid or reckless about their own freedom and well-being) may well be prepared to take their chances in the hope that it could be shown that the leaked or published classified information in fact reveals criminal activity.

However, how this defence would work in practice is unclear. In terms of our Constitution, every person is presumed to be innocent by a court of law until proven guilty. It is therefore unclear whether this defence in section 41 would be available to a whistle-blower or a journalist who receives or publishes classified information that reveals criminal activity if those involved in the criminal activity have not actually been convicted of a crime. How will a whistle-blower or a journalist be able to convince a court that the information reveals criminal activity if the criminal activity has not been successfully prosecuted? And how will the criminal activity be successfully prosecuted when the information revealing that criminal activity remains classified? This defence may therefore well turn out to be illusory.

The Secrecy Bill also provides for a Review Panel to review classifications of information but the panel is appointed by the majority party in Parliament and is therefore not independent.[48] A person can appeal the classification of information, but as it is a criminal offence to be in possession of classified documents, it is unclear how the person can appeal the classification of documents he or she is not allowed to know about and that the person is not allowed to have in his or her possession.[49]

Although the press and media have an important role to fulfil in a democracy, this does not mean that the press and other media have a different and superior status in the Constitution. This is because the right to a free press and other media is designed to serve the interests that all citizens have in the free flow of information and not the specific interests of the press and other media. When the state infringes the right to a free press and other media, therefore, it infringes the rights of all citizens and not merely the rights of the press itself.[50]

14.1.3.3 Access to and broadcasting of court proceedings

Courts often consider matters of public importance. Courts often also consider matters that are of interest to the public without being matters of public interest. The extent to which the press and other media may access and broadcast such court proceedings has therefore become contested. The courts considered this vexing question in *South African Broadcasting Corporation Ltd v National Director of Public Prosecutions and Others*.[51] The case dealt with a request by the SABC for permission to broadcast live on radio and television a high-profile criminal appeal with potential political consequences being argued before the Supreme

---

48 S 22.

49 De Vos, P (2011, 31 May) Let me tell you a secret ... *Constitutionally Speaking* available at http://constitutionallyspeaking.co.za/let-me-tell-you-a-secret/. For further criticism on the Bill, see generally Donnelly, L (2011, 23 June) Secrecy bill extension welcomed - concerns remain *Mail & Guardian* Newspapers available at http://mg.co.za/article/2011-06-23-secrecy-bill-extension-welcomed-concerns-remain.

50 See *Holomisa v Argus Newspaper* 1996 (2) SA 588 (W) 855–56; *Midi Television (Pty) Ltd v Director of Public Prosecutions (Western Cape)* (100/06) [2007] ZASCA 56; [2007] SCA 56 (RSA); [2007] 3 All SA 318 (SCA) (18 May 2007) para 6; *South African Broadcasting Corporation* para 42; *Johncom Media Investments Limited v M and Others* (CCT 08/08) [2009] ZACC 5; 2009 (4) SA 7 (CC); 2009 (8) BCLR 751 (CC) (17 March 2009) para 28.

51 (CCT58/06) [2006] ZACC 15; 2007 (1) SA 523 (CC); 2007 (2) BCLR 167 (CC); [2006] JOL 18339 (CC) (21 September 2006).

Court of Appeal (SCA). The case dealt with an appeal of Mr Schabir Shaik who had been convicted on several counts of corruption in respect of payments he had made to the then Deputy-President of the Republic, Mr Jacob Zuma.

The SABC based its application on the grounds that the live radio and television broadcasts were necessary to enable it to fulfil its constitutional and statutory obligations to inform the public and that the broadcasts would play an important educational role given the intense public interest the case had generated. In addition, the SABC also argued that the broadcasts would not disrupt the conduct of the hearing.

A majority of the Constitutional Court dismissed these claims. The Court explained that while the accused's right to a fair trial and the SABC's right to freedom of expression were obviously important, the key issue in the case was not about those rights, but rather about the public's right to be informed about the manner in which one of the three arms of government, namely the judiciary, operates.[52]

The public's right to be informed about the manner in which the judiciary operates, the Constitutional Court explained, means that courts should be open and accessible. This principle of open justice is important not only because it promotes the public's right to be informed about the manner in which the courts operate. It is important also because it can prevent the courts from abusing their power by, for example, following unfair procedures. Open justice is, accordingly, an intrinsic part of the right to a fair trial and should be welcomed by the courts.[53]

However, despite the demands for open justice (linking the right of freedom of expression to the right to a fair trial and to the need to safeguard an independent judiciary), the Constitutional Court explained that it would not interfere with the manner in which the SCA exercised its discretion simply because it disagreed with the SCA. Instead, it would only interfere with the manner in which the SCA exercised its discretion if the SCA had abused its discretion by failing to act judicially, or by applying the wrong principles of law, or by misdirecting itself on the material facts.[54] The Court therefore declined to interfere with the decision of the SCA 'that live or recorded sound broadcasting should not be allowed unless the Court is satisfied that justice will not be inhibited'.[55] This decision struck a proportionate balance between the SABC's right to freedom of expression and the SCA's obligation to ensure that appeal proceedings before it are fair.[56]

The Court affirmed the notion of open justice in subsequent cases. Thus, in *Independent Newspapers (Pty) Ltd v Minister for Intelligence Services (Freedom of Expression Institute as Amicus Curiae) In re: Masetlha v President of the Republic of South Africa and Another*, the Constitutional Court affirmed the constitutional imperative of dispensing justice in the open.[57] It stated further:

> **This systemic requirement of openness in our society flows from the very founding values of our Constitution, which enjoin our society to establish democratic government under the sway of constitutional supremacy and the rule of law in order, amongst other things, to ensure transparency, accountability and responsiveness in the way courts and all organs of state function. From the right to open justice flows**

52 *SABC* para 29

53 *SABC* para 30.

54 *SABC* para 41.

55 *SABC* para 11.

56 *SABC* para 42. See also generally *S v Shinga (Society of Advocates (Pietermaritzburg)) as Amicus Curiae), S v O'Connell and Others* (CCT56/06, CCT80/06) [2007] ZACC 3; 2007 (5) BCLR 474 (CC); 2007 (2) SACR 28 (CC) (8 March 2007).

57 (CCT38/07) [2008] ZACC 6; 2008 (5) SA 31 (CC); 2008 (8) BCLR 771 (CC) (22 May 2008) para 39.

> **the media's right to gain access to, observe and report on, the administration of justice and the right to have access to papers and written arguments which are an integral part of court proceedings subject to such limitations as may be warranted on a case-by-case basis in order to ensure a fair trial.**[58]

However, the Court found that a restriction placed on public access to court proceedings is not only permissible as an exceptional occurrence[59] as the cluster of rights that guarantees open justice is not absolute. These rights may be limited by a law of general application provided the limitation is reasonable and justifiable:[60]

> **There may be instances where the interests of justice in a court hearing dictate that oral evidence of a minor or of certain classes of rape survivors or confidential material related to police crime investigation methods or to national security be heard in camera. In each case, the court will have to weigh the competing rights or interests carefully with the view to ensuring that the limitation it places on open justice is properly tailored and proportionate to the end it seeks to attain. In the end, the contours of our constitutional rights are shaped by the justifiable limitation that the context presents and the law permits.**[61]

14.1.3.4 Access to divorce proceedings

The Constitutional Court discussed the extent to which the press and other media may access and report on divorce proceedings in *Johncom Media Investments Limited v M and Others*[62] in which the constitutionality of section 12 of the Divorce Act[63] was attacked. This kind of case presents difficult issues about the tension between the right to privacy and dignity of individuals involved in often traumatic divorce proceedings and especially the need to protect the best interests of the child on the one hand, and the right to freedom of the press on the other.

To protect the dignity and privacy of divorcing parties and their children, section 12 provided that no person could publish any information that came to light during a divorce action except for the names of the parties, the fact that they were getting divorced and the judgment of the divorce court.

The Constitutional Court found that section 12 did not fall within any of the exceptions set out in section 16(2) of the Constitution and that the section therefore infringed on the freedom of the media. The key question that had to be answered, therefore, was whether the infringement satisfied the requirements of the limitation clause.[64] The requirements of the limitation clause were not satisfied for two reasons:

- First, section 12 was too broad. This is because it prohibited the publication of any information that came to light during a divorce action even if that information did not affect the dignity and privacy of the divorcing parties and their children and did not, therefore, require protection. It was also contrary to the principle of open justice.[65]

---

58 *Independent Newspapers* paras 40–1.
59 *Independent Newspapers* para 43.
60 *Independent Newspapers* para 44.
61 *Independent Newspapers* para 45.
62 (CCT 08/08) [2009] ZACC 5; 2009 (4) SA 7 (CC); 2009 (8) BCLR 751 (CC) (17 March 2009).
63 70 of 1979.
64 *Johncom Media Investments* para 23.
65 *Johncom Media Investments* para 29.

- Second, section 12 did not achieve its purpose. This is because even though it prohibited the publication of any information that came to light during a divorce action, it did not prohibit the publication of the names of the divorcing parties and their children. A much more effective method of protecting the dignity and privacy of the divorcing parties and their children was simply to prohibit the publication of their identities.[66]

After finding that section 12 of the Divorce Act was unconstitutional and invalid, the Constitutional Court turned to consider what would be the most appropriate remedy. In this respect, the Court held that apart from declaring section 12 to be invalid, it would be appropriate to issue an order prohibiting the publication of the identities of divorcing parties and their children and any information that could reveal their identities.[67]

14.1.3.5 Prior restraints

Prior restraints refers to cases where a publication is prohibited or stopped from publishing information or where the law requires the publication to seek approval from a person or body before it is allowed to publish information. The Constitutional Court considered the question of when and to what extent Parliament could impose prior restraints on the publication of material by the press and other media in *Print Media South Africa and Another v Minister of Home Affairs and Another*.[68]

In this case, the Constitutional Court found that section 16(2)(*a*) of the Film and Publications Act was unconstitutional and invalid on the grounds that it infringed the right to freedom of expression. Section 16(2)(*a*) of the Act provided that, except for the publisher of a registered newspaper, any person who intended to 'create, produce, publish or advertise' a publication 'containing sexual conduct which violates or shows disrespect for the right to human dignity of any person, degrades a person, or constitutes incitement to cause harm' had to submit that publication to the Film and Publications Board for classification before it was distributed. Depending on the way in which it was classified by the Film and Publications Board, a publication containing the sexual conduct referred to in section 16(2)(*a*) could be banned, distributed subject to certain restrictions or freely distributed. In addition, the Act also provided that a publisher who failed to submit a publication containing the sexual conduct referred to in section 16(2)(*a*) to the Film and Publications Board for classification before publishing it, irrespective of how it would have been classified, committed a criminal offence and could be sentenced to a fine or imprisonment of up to five years or both.

In declaring this section invalid, the Constitutional Court explained that section 16(2)(*a*) imposed a system of 'administrative prior consent' for the publication of information on sexual conduct.[69] The Film and Publications Act was aimed at achieving important goals: to provide consumers with advice, to protect children from exposure to harmful or age-inappropriate material, and to ban child pornography. While banning child pornography and protecting children from exposure to harmful or age-inappropriate material were obviously important goals, providing adults with more complete information about a publication's content was also important. This is because it enhanced a consumer's ability to make informed choices about what he or she consumed or what he or she exposed others to through his or her consumption.[70]

---

66 *Johncom Media Investments* para 30.
67 *Johncom Media Investments* para 42.
68 (CCT 113/11) [2012] ZACC 22; 2012 (6) SA 443 (CC); 2012 (12) BCLR 1346 (CC) (28 September 2012).
69 *Print Media South Africa* para 20.
70 *Print Media South Africa* para 27.

However, in this case, the prior constraint limited the right to freedom of expression in a severe fashion. This is because the system of 'administrative prior consent' created by the Act transferred control over the decision to publish material from the person in whom the right to freedom of expression is vested to an administrative body.[71] The problem with this type of system is that administrative bodies are much more likely to restrict publications when they have to classify them upfront rather than when they have to take punitive or restrictive action after publication. In addition, this type of system often leads to delays which may prevent important information from reaching the public or which may result in information being redundant by the time it is published.[72]

After examining the importance of the purpose of the limitation and the nature and extent of the limitation, the Constitutional Court turned to balance all the competing factors. In this respect, the Court held that the extent of the limitation appeared to outweigh the importance of the purpose of the limitation. This is because the system of 'administrative prior consent' would inevitably delay or restrict the flow of information that people were lawfully entitled to receive.[73] This would undermine the autonomy of the individual to formulate an opinion about information received which would in turn undermine the moral agency of the individual. The limitation would only satisfy the requirements of the limitation clause, therefore, if there was no other less restrictive means of achieving the goals of the Act.[74] Unfortunately for the Minister and the Film and Publications Board, the Constitutional Court went on to conclude, there were other less restrictive means of achieving the goals of the Act such as applying for an interdict or voluntarily submitting the publication for classification.[75]

PAUSE FOR REFLECTION

Applying for an interdict to prevent the publication of a story

The members of the South African Press Council (which include almost all the print media in South Africa) voluntarily subject themselves to a form of independent self-regulation through the Press Ombudsman. The Ombudsman aims to provide impartial, expeditious and cost-effective adjudication to settle disputes between newspapers and magazines, on the one hand, and members of the public, on the other, over the editorial content of publications. The Council has adopted the South African Press Code to guide journalists in their daily practice of gathering and distributing news and opinion and to guide the work of the Ombudsman. Section 2.5 of the Code states that:

> A publication shall seek the views of the subject of critical reportage in advance of publication; provided that this need not be done where the publication has reasonable grounds for believing that by doing so it would be prevented from publishing the report or where evidence might be destroyed or sources intimidated. Reasonable time should be afforded the subject for a response. If the publication is unable to obtain such comment, this shall be stated in the report.

This provision aims to protect newspapers and magazines from attempts to muzzle them while protecting the rights of people on whom the press reports in a critical fashion.

71 *Print Media South Africa* para 17.
72 *Print Media South Africa* para 60.
73 *Print Media South Africa* para 98.
74 *Print Media South Africa* para 55.
75 *Print Media South Africa* para 56.

On occasion, courts have granted urgent interdicts against newspapers that were about to publish news stories critical of individuals. This occurred after the newspaper had sought comment from the affected person and that person had then approached the court to stop the publication of the critical story. The granting of such an interdict is a classic form of prior restraint. However, in the light of the Constitutional Court judgment in *Print Media South Africa*, it will arguably be difficult for an affected party to convince a court to grant such an interim interdict. The Press Code nevertheless seeks to protect newspapers from such forms of prior restraint by waiving the requirement to seek comment from the subject of critical reportage in limited circumstances.

14.1.3.6 The regulation of broadcasting

As broadcasting is a particularly powerful form of expression and as there are limited frequencies available in some areas and in respect of some forms of broadcasting, control is necessary to ensure that diverse views are broadcast. Section 192 of the Constitution thus provides that '[n]ational legislation must establish an independent authority to regulate broadcasting in the public interest, and to ensure fairness and diversity of views broadly representing South African society'. The independent authority referred to in section 192 is the Independent Communications Authority of South Africa (ICASA).[76]

In addition to the regulatory function of ICASA, the Broadcasting Complaints Commission of South Africa (BCCSA) is tasked with ensuring that broadcasting is in accordance with the Broadcasting Code. The BBCSA can be called on to investigate broadcasts that are not in accordance with the provisions of the Code.[77]

14.1.4 Hate speech

14.1.4.1 Introduction

The Constitution is founded on the principles of dignity, equal worth and freedom, and these principles should be given effect to. For this reason, certain forms of expression do not deserve constitutional protection since they have the potential to impugn the dignity of others and to cause harm.[78] As we pointed out above, section 16(2) of the Constitution deals with expression that is specifically excluded from the protection of the right to freedom of expression. While section 16(2)(*a*) and (*b*) are concerned with 'propaganda for war' and 'incitement of imminent violence', section 16(2)(*c*) is concerned with what is commonly referred to as 'hate speech'. Out of these three forms of excluded expression, hate speech has received the most attention from the courts and commentators. For the purposes of this book, therefore, we are going to focus on this form of excluded expression only.

Hate speech at a social level is said to be prohibited for one or more of the following four reasons:

1. **To prevent disruption to public order and social peace stemming from retaliation by victims.**

---

76 ICASA was created by the Independent Communications Authority of South Africa Act 13 of 2000. For a discussion on the role of the regulation of the public broadcaster, see Tomaselli, KG (2008) Exogenous and endogenous democracy: South African politics and media *International Journal of Press/ Politics* 13(2):171–80 at 171.

77 There are therefore similarities between the regulation of electronic broadcasters and that of the print media although different bodies deal with complaints relating to these categories of the media in terms of different Codes.

78 *Islamic United Convention* para 10.

2. **To prevent psychological harm to targeted groups that would effectively impair their ability to positively participate in the community and contribute to society.**
3. **To prevent both visible exclusion of minority groups that would deny them equal opportunities and benefits of ... society and invisibly exclude their acceptance as equals.**
4. **To prevent social conflagration and political disintegration.**[79]

14.1.4.2 The scope and extent of hate speech

The exact scope and content of hate speech is contested, but the jurisprudence confirms that it would be impossible to judge whether a specific statement constitutes hate speech without reference to the broader context within which the statement was made. As we noted above, section 16(2)(*c*) excludes certain forms of hate speech from constitutional protection. The clause excludes advocacy of hatred based on race, ethnicity, gender and religion that amounts to the incitement to cause harm from the protection of the right to freedom of expression. The list of grounds is a closed list which means that other forms of hate speech such as homophobic and xenophobic speech are not included under section 16(2) and do not automatically fall outside the protection of the freedom of expression guarantee contained in section 16(1). Before an expression can be considered as hate speech, the expression must constitute advocacy of hatred on one of the listed grounds and the advocacy must constitute the incitement to cause harm. Therefore, irrespective of how offensive advocacy of hatred may be, it does not qualify to be classified as hate speech unless the second element, namely incitement to cause harm, is present.[80]

It is important to remember that section 16(2) is definitional in that it merely defines certain forms of speech to which the protection of the right to freedom of expression does not extend. The Constitution does not prohibit any speech. Legislation may be enacted that prohibits the forms of unprotected speech. A general prohibition on hate speech was enacted in section 10 of the Promotion of Equality and Prevention of Unfair Discrimination Act (PEPUDA).[81] The grounds in the PEPUDA are not confined to the three grounds listed in section 16(2).[82] Section 10 (read with section 12) does indeed place limits on several kinds of speech. This section provides that:

> **no person may publish, propagate, advocate or communicate words based on one or more of the prohibited grounds, against any person, that could reasonably be construed to demonstrate a clear intention to:**
> (*a*) **be hurtful;**
> (*b*) **be harmful or incite harm;**
> (*c*) **promote or propagate hatred.**

The **prohibition** on hate speech in the PEPUDA is more far reaching than the **description** of hate speech in section 16(2)(*c*) of the Constitution. As the constitutionality of this section

79 *Afri-Forum and Another v Malema and Others* (20968/2010) [2011] ZAEQC 2; 2011 (6) SA 240 (EqC); [2011] 4 All SA 293 (EqC); 2011 (12) BCLR 1289 (EqC) (12 September 2011) para 29, citing Braun, S (2004) *Democracy Off Balance: Freedom of Expression and Hate Propaganda Law in Canada* 62.

80 See also Govindjee, A 'Freedom of expression' in Govindjee, A and Vrancken, P (2009) *Introduction to Human Rights Law* 122.

81 Act 4 of 2000.

82 S 1 of the PEPUDA defines prohibited grounds as 'race, gender, sex, pregnancy. marital status, ethnic or social origin, colour, sexual orientation, age, disability, religion, conscience, belief, culture, language and birth' or any other ground where discrimination causes or perpetuates systemic disadvantage or undermines human dignity or adversely affects the equal enjoyment of a person's rights and freedoms in a serious manner that is comparable to discrimination on a listed ground.

has not yet been challenged, we will assume that the extended prohibition of hate speech in section 10 of the PEPUDA is constitutionally valid. The prohibition is far reaching as it relates to words based on all prohibited grounds, not only on the basis of race, ethnicity, gender and religion as is the case in section 16(2)(*c*). These grounds include race, gender, sex, pregnancy, marital status, ethnic or social origin, colour, sexual orientation, age, disability, religion, conscience, belief, culture, language and birth, or any other similar ground such as HIV status. It is important to note that speech will **not** constitute hate speech merely because it is offensive or because it offends a certain section of the population. The threshold test is that the speech must be aimed at one of the defined groups. Offending speech targeting all lawyers or all journalists would therefore never constitute hate speech because it does not target a person on the basis of one of the listed or associated grounds.

Once it is determined that the speech targets a person based on one of the listed or similar grounds, the question will be asked whether the speech could reasonably be construed to demonstrate a clear intention to be hurtful, harmful or to propagate hatred. An Equality Court need not find that the speaker actually had the intention to be hurtful or to incite harm. The question is whether the words of the speaker could reasonably be construed thus. The subjective question (the intention of the speaker) must be determined by using an objective test (what a reasonable person would have thought).[83] To decide this question, we would need to look at who the speaker is, in what context the words were uttered and, given this context, how a reasonable person would have interpreted the words. We would assume that such a reasonable person would be someone who is imbued with the values of the Constitution and who understands the importance of freedom of speech and robust debate in a democracy. He or she will not be hypersensitive and will not assume that the speaker had the intention to be hurtful or to incite harm merely because the words may have offended the person targeted. It would not be sufficient to show that members of the targeted group were hurt by the speech or believed that the speech incited harm against them. What is required is to determine whether a reasonable person could have believed that the speaker had the intention to hurt the targeted group or to incite harm against that group.

In *Sonke Gender Justice Network v Malema*, Mr Julius Malema was accused of hate speech in contravention of section 10 of the PEPUDA for stating the following:

> **When a woman didn't enjoy it, she leaves early in the morning. Those who had a nice time will wait until the sun comes out, request breakfast and taxi money. In the morning that lady requested breakfast and taxi money. You don't ask for taxi money from someone who has raped you.[84]**

The Court in this case held that the quoted words constituted hate speech as per the definitions found in the framework of the PEPUDA. The Court held that the utterances could reasonably be construed as hurtful, harmful and demeaning to women.[85] The utterances were made in general terms and then applied to the complainant in the Zuma rape trial. This judgment has been criticised for not engaging in a serious manner with the requirement that a reasonable person needed to have construed Mr Malema as having the intention to be hurtful to a class of people, namely women:

> **Given the fact that these – admittedly sexist – statements were made by Malema in defence of President Zuma (and in response to a question at an election rally) and**

83 See De Vos, P (2010) *On 'Shoot the Boer', hate speech and the banning of struggle songs* 11.
84 (2010 (7) BCLR 729 (EqC)) [2010] ZAEQC 2; 02/2009 (15 March 2010) para 2.
85 *Sonke Gender Justice Network* para 17(*b*)(x).

> **came after Zuma was acquitted on the rape charge, I am far from convinced that a reasonable person would have construed his statements as intending to be hurtful to the rape accused or to women in general. One may well argue that a reasonable person would have concluded that Malema was motivated not by hate but by disbelief about the charges of rape levelled against President Zuma - a disbelief actually endorsed by the court who acquitted Zuma of the charge of rape. As the expert witnesses pointed out, such utterances were gender insensitive and trivialised rape. It perpetuated male sexual entitlement and was obviously sexist and would have upset many South Africans - including the survivors of rape. However ... Malema's words could reasonably be construed to be intended to make the point that the judgment of the High Court, which acquitted Zuma's of rape, was the correct judgment.[86]**

Mr Julius Malema faced another hate speech charge in *Afri-Forum and Another v Malema and Others*.[87] In this case the Equality Court considered whether Mr Malema had engaged in hate speech when he sang the song, '*Awudubula (i) bhulu ... Dubula amabhunu baya raypha*' (translated as '*Shoot the Boer/farmer ... Shoot the Boers/farmers they are rapists/ robbers*'). The Court found that Mr Malema had engaged in hate speech and ordered that both Mr Malema and the ANC be interdicted and restrained from singing the song known as *Dubula Ibhunu* at any public or private meeting held or conducted by them.[88] In coming to this decision, the Court relied on the SCA judgment in *Le Roux and Others v Dey* to cast light on the requirement that the words should reasonably have been construed as having the intention to be hateful:[89]

> **It may be accepted that the reasonable person must be contextualised and that one is not concerned with a purely abstract exercise. One must have regard to the nature of the audience. In this case the main target was the school children at the particular school, but it also included at least teachers.[90]**

The Court thus argued that some South Africans, who would largely, but not exclusively, be black, would not reasonably construe the song to have had the intention of being hurtful to whites. However, others, who would largely, but not exclusively, be white, would indeed do so. The Court stated:

> **each meaning must be considered and be accepted as a meaning .... If the words mean different things to different portions of society then each meaning, for the reasonable listener in each portion of society, must be considered as being the appropriate meaning.[91]**

In this way, the judgment avoided dealing with a difficult legal problem, namely that the song would be viewed differently depending on the audience.

86 De Vos (2010) 12.

87 (20968/2010) [2011] ZAEQC 2; 2011 (6) SA 240 (EqC); [2011] 4 All SA 293 (EqC); 2011 (12) BCLR 1289 (EqC) (12 September 2011).

88 *Afri-Forum* paras 109–11.

89 *Afri-Forum* para 93.

90 (44/2009) [2010] ZASCA 41; 2010 (4) SA 210 (SCA); [2010] 3 All SA 497 (SCA) (30 March 2010) para 7.

91 *Afri-Forum* paras 7–8.

CRITICAL THINKING

A critique of the *Afri-Forum* judgment

The judgment in *Afri-Forum* was criticised for the manner in which it dealt with race and racial politics in South Africa. De Vos argued:

> Judge Lamont divided South Africa into the majority and a minority and suggested that minorities (defined as white South Africans or as white Afrikaners) are therefore in particular need of protection from words that could be construed as having the intention to be hurtful to that minority. Hinting that white people might well in the future be in danger of facing a genocide, Judge Lamont stated that:
>
>> It must not however be forgotten that minority groups are particularly vulnerable. It is precisely the individuals who are members of such minorities who are vulnerable to discriminatory treatment and who in a very special sense must look to the Bill of Rights for protection. The Court has a clear duty to come to the assistance of such affected people.
>>
>> Minorities have no legislative or executive powers and are compelled to approach the Court to protect their rights. They are particularly at risk due to the expense involved in such approaches. The fact that they are minorities and experience such difficulties frequently results in them being driven to protect their identity by invoking and enforcing within their group, customs practices and conventions which are believed to be appropriate. In addition, they are fragile in that they are readily assumed by the mass and lose their identity. A Court which hears a matter must, while balancing the rights in question, take into account in the construction of what hate speech is the fact that it is directed at a minority.[92]
>
> This means that religious and sexual minorities, say, might be entitled to special protection in terms of this Act and that a court should take note of the sensibilities of such groups when they judge whether a reasonable homosexual or a reasonable Muslim would have viewed a specific communication as having the intention to be hurtful to them as Muslims or as homosexuals. Almost any cartoon that depicts the prophet Mohammed, say, might therefore constitute hate speech. Statements by a pastor that homosexuals are perverts that will burn in hell would also, most probably, constitute hate speech if this line of reasoning is followed. I am also fearful that if I were to call devout Christians "bigots" because of their views on homosexuality, I might be found to have had the intention (judged by these religious fundamentalists) to be hurtful to them and hence that I am guilty of hate speech.
>
> This rather essentialistic and simplistic division of South Africans into different race groups could be viewed as problematic. Instead of dealing with South Africans *as South Africans* and instead of demonstrating a blindness to race (as required by opponents of affirmative action), the court relied on racial assumptions and stereotypes to justify its finding. One would assume that all the critics of race-based affirmative action would be quick to condemn this judgment on the basis that it invokes apartheid era race categories and assumes that one

92 *Afri-forum* paras 35–6.

would have a different reaction to words depending on one's race and/or the language that one speaks. Surely the principled DA supporters who complain about affirmative action will have to reject this judgment because of its purported unholy valorisation of race?[93]

Finally, it is important to note that the prohibition of hate speech in section 10(1) of the PEPUDA overlaps with the prohibition of the publication of information that unfairly discriminates in section 12 (the proviso to this section also applies to section 10). Section 12 of the PEPUDA provides that:

> **[n]o person may:**
> **(a) disseminate or broadcast any information;**
> **(b) publish or display any advertisement or notice,**
>
> **that could reasonably be construed or reasonably be understood to demonstrate a clear intention to unfairly discriminate against any person: Provided that *bona fide* engagement in artistic creativity, academic and scientific inquiry, fair and accurate reporting in the public interest or publication of any information, advertisement or notice in accordance with section 16 of the Constitution, is not precluded by this section.**

14.2 The rights to freedom of assembly, demonstration, picket and petition

14.2.1 Introduction

One of the most powerful ways in which individuals can express their views on political and social issues is by coming together and protesting peacefully. The freedom to assemble, demonstrate, picket and petition therefore forms an integral part of the democratic rights of citizens in a democracy. When a large crowd of people assemble in the street to express their views on issues of the day, this can be viewed as a form of participatory democracy.

In the apartheid era, rallies and demonstrations protesting against the policies of the apartheid regime or aimed at popularising the ideas of anti-apartheid organisations such as the United Democratic Front (UDF), Azanian People's Organisation (AZAPO), the African National Congress (ANC) or the Pan Africanist Congress (PAC) were often banned by the government. In one of the most famous incidents early in September 1989, peaceful protest marchers in support of liberation, bearing placards proclaiming 'the people shall govern' were sprayed with purple dye by the police. A spirited activist seized the initiative and the nozzle from the police and painted Cape Town purple, while an inspired graffitist put the writing on the wall: 'The purple shall govern!'[94]

93 De Vos, P (2011, 12 September) Malema judgment: A re-think on hate speech needed *Constitutionally Speaking* available at http://constitutionallyspeaking.co.za/malema-judgment-a-re-think-on-hate-speech-needed. See also Modiri, J (2013) Race, realism and critique: The politics of race and *Afri-forum v Malema* in the Equality Court *South African Law Journal* 130(2):274–93; Brown, J (2012) Judges' history: On the use of history in the *Malema* judgment *South African Journal on Human Rights* 28(2):316–27.

94 Smuts, D and Westcott, S (eds) (1999) *The Purple Shall Govern: A South African A to Z of Nonviolent Action*.

In post-apartheid South Africa, the right to assemble and demonstrate cannot legally be curtailed in the same manner. This is because section 17 of the Constitution guarantees the right to freedom of assembly, demonstration, picket and petition. This section provides that '[e]veryone has the right, peacefully and unarmed, to assemble, to demonstrate, to picket and to present petitions'.

Democracy entails more than the right to vote in regular free and fair elections. As we have seen in the first part of this book, democracy also requires citizens actively to participate in public affairs. For this reason, the right to freedom of assembly plays an important role in a democratic society. Assemblies, demonstrations, pickets and petitions allow groups, whose influence on political parties or the political process would otherwise be minimal, to raise issues that are important to them, to draw attention to these issues and to engage with their fellow citizens and representatives about these issues.

Citizens also use such events to enforce their rights outside the formal legal process because they can place pressure on the legislature and the executive to ensure that these bodies do not infringe on the rights of individuals. Such events can also help civil society groups to build support for their causes and to mobilise voters in order to ensure more responsive and accountable government from those who were elected to serve the people. Often, such activities precede or go hand-in-hand with court action.[95]

CRITICAL THINKING

Using political mobilisation with litigation to achieve human rights

Berger and Kapczynski discuss the manner in which the Treatment Action Campaign (TAC) used both social mobilisation and litigation in its struggle to ensure access by all HIV-positive South Africans to life-saving antiretroviral drugs. They argue that human rights are not always best won or defended in courtrooms, but often require sustained political mobilisation. This political mobilisation requires the freedom to assemble and to demonstrate. Without the right to freedom of assembly and to demonstrate, it would be difficult to mobilise politically or to ensure that battles won through litigation are translated into real changes in the lives of people. In their discussion of the battle to ensure that all HIV-positive pregnant women have free access to medication that diminishes the risk of transmitting HIV to their newborn babies, these authors wrote as follows:

> Little has been written about how the case came into being or the impact it has had on the life options and experiences of people living with and affected by HIV in South Africa. Consider here three facts: the *TAC* case was brought only after four years of sustained lobbying and organizing efforts demanding PMTCT programs in South Africa. The suit itself was framed by carefully orchestrated advocacy work and mass demonstrations that caused dramatic change in the government's policy even during the litigation. Years after the stunning victory in the *TAC* case, and despite claims by some that the government 'quickly implemented the orders of the Constitutional Court', reliable estimates indicate that only about thirty percent of women in South Africa who need medicine to

95 See Berger, JM (2001) Litigation strategies to gain access to treatment for HIV/AIDS: The case of South Africa's Treatment Action Campaign *Wisconsin International Law Journal* 20:595–614 at 596; Berger, JM and Kapczynski, A 'The story of the TAC case: The potential and limits of socio-economic rights litigation in South Africa' in Hurwitz, DR and Satterthwaite, ML (eds) (2009) *Human Rights Advocacy Stories.*

prevent the transmission of HIV to their children are receiving it. These facts alone demonstrate that to describe the *TAC* case in terms that focus on courts or legal texts alone is to miss the true story of the case. That story is less about a judgment or a doctrine than it is about a movement. More specifically, it is about the power that an organized movement can have if it makes strategic use of constitutionally entrenched and justiciable human rights, lays the groundwork necessary to give those abstract guarantees meaning, and energetically builds broad public support for its cause. TAC did the political and technical work to make the Constitutional Court's judgment seem both legally obvious and morally necessary, and thereby created a precedent that helped bring real improvements in access to PMTCT services in South Africa, and that was also likely central to the establishment of a public sector HIV treatment program for the country. But the ultimate promise of the case – that all women in South Africa have access to quality medicines and services to prevent the transmission of HIV to their children – still awaits fulfillment. The judgment alone could not guarantee the result that it declared constitutionally required. For that, it needed a movement. And unfortunately, the Court very likely overestimated the work that the movement in question could do to implement the Court's judgment. That too is part of the legacy of the *TAC* case. In the end, then, the story of the *TAC* case is less a story about the power and limits of courts than it is a story about the power and limits of the Treatment Action Campaign.[96]

The Constitutional Court highlighted the goals of the right to freedom of assembly in *South African Transport and Allied Workers Union and Another v Garvas and Others (SATAWU)* where it stated that:

> **The right to freedom of assembly is central to our constitutional democracy. It exists primarily to give a voice to the powerless. This includes groups that do not have political or economic power, and other vulnerable persons. It provides an outlet for their frustrations. This right will, in many cases, be the only mechanism available to them to express their legitimate concerns. Indeed, it is one of the principal means by which ordinary people can meaningfully contribute to the constitutional objective of advancing human rights and freedoms. This is only too evident from the brutal denial of this right and all the consequences flowing therefrom under apartheid. In assessing the nature and importance of the right, we cannot therefore ignore its foundational relevance to the exercise and achievement of all other rights.**[97]

Apart from promoting participation in political processes, the right to freedom of assembly, demonstration, picket and petition also fulfils a number of other goals. Perhaps the most important of these is the development of each individual's unique personality. This is because our personalities do not develop in isolation. Instead, they develop in the context of groups. Assemblies for cultural, educational, religious, sport and recreational purposes, therefore, may be as important as assemblies for political purposes.

96 Berger and Kapczynski (2009) 4.

97 (CCT 112/11) [2012] ZACC 13; 2012 (8) BCLR 840 (CC); [2012] 10 BLLR 959 (CC); (2012) 33 ILJ 1593 (CC); 2013 (1) SA 83 (CC) (13 June 2012) para 61.

PAUSE FOR REFLECTION

To what sort of assemblies does the right to freedom of assembly refer?

Although the right to freedom of assembly exists primarily to give voice to the powerless, section 17 itself does not expressly restrict the scope and ambit of the right to assemblies that are aimed at promoting political participation. It may, therefore, also include assemblies that are aimed at promoting cultural, economic and social activities such as religious, sports and entertainment gatherings.

However, Woolman argues that the scope and ambit of section 17 may plausibly be restricted to those assemblies that have some connection to the political process. This is because if the right is defined too widely, it may weaken our commitment to assembly as a form of political participation.[98] Of course, if we agree with this view, the difficulty that will arise is how to determine whether a specific protest has some connection to the political process. People may wish to assemble to protest against the Film and Publications Board's banning of a movie which they believe contains child pornography. This may at first not appear to be linked to the political process. However, if politics is defined broadly, then questions about whether citizens should be allowed to see works of artistic merit that depict uncomfortable realities may well form part of the political process. It is therefore unclear how we would be able to draw this distinction.

14.2.2 Scope and ambit of the right to assembly

As the words of section 17 indicate, the right to assembly applies only to those assemblies that are peaceful and unarmed. Assemblies that are not peaceful or that are armed are thus excluded from the scope and ambit of section 17. The requirement that a protected assembly must be peaceful and unarmed thus serves as an internal modifier limiting the scope of the right itself.

PAUSE FOR REFLECTION

Peaceful Assemblies

Like section 17 of the Constitution, Article 8(1) of the German Constitution provides that 'all Germans' have the right to 'assemble peacefully and unarmed without prior notification or permission'.

In the *Brokdorf Demonstration* case,[99] a number of non-governmental organisations announced that they were planning to hold a large demonstration against plans to build a nuclear power plant in Brokdorf. Following this announcement, the relevant authorities banned any demonstrations against the nuclear power plant in an area covering 210 km^2 around the site. The relevant authorities based their decision on the grounds that they believed that 50 000 people would attend the demonstration and that some of the demonstrators intended to engage in acts of violence.

In dealing with this case, the Federal Constitutional Court discussed the scope and ambit of the right to assemble and, in particular, the requirements that the right applies only to those assemblies that are peaceful. The Court held that an assembly will be classified as non-peaceful only if acts of physical violence against persons or property are committed or threatened.[100] In addition, the Court also held that where the

98 Woolman, S 'Assembly, demonstration and petition' in Currie, I and De Waal, J (2013) *The Bill of Rights Handbook* 6th ed 377.
99 BVerfGE 73, 206.
100 BVerfGE 73, 206 at 360.

organisers and participants in a demonstration do not plan to engage in acts of physical violence, that demonstration may not be prohibited or broken up if a small minority of demonstrators or counter-demonstrators plan to engage in acts of violence. In these sorts of cases, the Court went on to hold, the authorities must act against the violent minority and not against the demonstration as a whole. The demonstration as a whole remains protected by Article 8.[101]

14.2.3 Distinguishing between assemblies, demonstrations, pickets and petitions

14.2.3.1 Assemblies and demonstrations

The Constitution does not define the word 'assembly'. It appears, however, to apply to those situations where people intend to meet together, either in public or in private, and remain together for some or other collective purpose. The fact that the participants must intend to meet together distinguishes a protected assembly from a coincidental gathering of people, for example at the site of a road accident. The Constitution does not protect this sort of gathering.[102]

The Constitution also does not prescribe the purposes of a protected assembly. It may, therefore, be for a political purpose or for an economic, social or cultural purpose. In addition, Rautenbach and Malherbe suggest that it is also not limited to the communication of ideas or the discussion of matters. This is because the right to assemble is not simply a part of the right to freedom of expression. The right also applies to assemblies where no opinions are formed or expressed, such as a concert or soccer match.[103]

Demonstrations and pickets are manifestations of assemblies and are usually aimed at expressing support for a particular point of view in public. The Regulation of Gatherings Act (Gatherings Act)[104] distinguishes between demonstrations and gatherings. It defines a demonstration as 'any demonstration by one or more persons, but not more than 15 persons, for or against any person, cause, action or failure to take action'.[105] It defines a gathering as 'any assembly, concourse or procession of more than 15 people in or on any public road as defined in the Road Traffic Act ..., or any other public place or premises wholly or partly open to the air ...'.[106] The Regulation of Gatherings Act thus distinguishes demonstrations from gatherings on the basis of their size.

The reason for distinguishing between demonstrations and gatherings is that demonstrations, given their small size, are not perceived to be a threat to public order while gatherings are. The organisers of a demonstration are thus not required to provide prior notification of the intent to demonstrate, while the organisers of a gathering are.[107]

In light of the fact that size is a somewhat arbitrary basis on which to define the statutory concept of a demonstration, it is unlikely that this criterion will be used to define the constitutional concept of a demonstration.

101 BVerfGE 73, 206 at 361.
102 Rautenbach, IM and Malherbe, EFJ (2012) *Constitutional Law* 6th ed 376.
103 Rautenbach and Malherbe (2012) 376.
104 Act 205 of 1993.
105 S 1 of the Regulation of Gatherings Act.
106 S 1 of the Regulation of Gatherings Act.
107 Woolman (2013) 386.

14.2.3.2 Pickets

Picketing is a common feature in labour disputes. The Labour Relations Act (LRA)[108] protects the right of trade unions and their members to picket. Section 69(1) of the LRA, for example, provides that '[a] registered trade union may authorize a picket by its members and supporters for the purposes of peacefully demonstrating (*a*) in support of any protected strike; or (*b*) in opposition to any lock-out'.

Section 69(2) of the LRA goes on to provide that '[d]espite any law regulating the right to assembly, a picket authorised in terms of subsection (1), may be held (*a*) in any place to which the public has access but outside the premises of an employer; or (*b*) with the permission of the employer, inside the employer's premises'. The permission referred to in this section may not be unreasonably withheld.[109] The sorts of places referred to in section 69(2) include shopping malls and waterfronts.

PAUSE FOR REFLECTION

Balancing striking workers' right to picket against a landowner's right to the peaceful use and enjoyment of property

When striking workers picket, they often sing, shout, ululate, bang instruments and blow whistles. These noises can interfere with a landowner's right to use and enjoy his or her property. A difficult issue which arises in these sorts of cases is how to balance striking workers' right to picket against a landowner's right to the peaceful use and enjoyment of his or her property. The KwaZulu-Natal High Court: Durban considered this issue in *Growthpoint Properties Ltd v South Africa Commercial Catering and Allied Workers Union (SACCAWU) and Others*.[110]

The facts of this case were as follows. The applicant owned the La Lucia Shopping Mall in Durban. One of the tenants in this mall was Dis-Chem Pharmacies (Pty) Ltd. Towards the end of May 2010, the employees of Dis-Chem embarked on a strike and, as a part of this strike, they picketed in the basement parking entrance of the Mall. While they were picketing, the strikers blew whistles, sang, shouted and ululated. Unfortunately, these noises disturbed members of the public and disrupted normal business activities in the Mall. The applicant then claimed that the noise amounted to a nuisance and applied to the High Court for an interdict to prevent the nuisance.

The High Court granted the interdict. In arriving at this decision, the Court began by stating that the key challenge it had to address was how to balance the striking workers' constitutional right to picket against the landowner's constitutional right to property, to trade and to a healthy environment.[111] Before turning to this task, however, it would be helpful to summarise the nature and purpose of picketing.

In labour law, the High Court explained further, picketing is commonly understood as an organised effort of people carrying placards in a public place at or near a business premises. The act of picketing involves an element of physical presence which, in turn, incorporates an expressive component. Its purposes are usually twofold: first, to convey information about a labour dispute to gain support for the cause from other workers, clients of the struck employer or the general public, and second, to put social

108 Act 66 of 1995.

109 S 69(3) of the LRA.

110 (6467/2010) [2010] ZAKZDHC 38; 2011 (1) BCLR 81 (KZD); [2011] 1 All SA 537 (KZD); (2010) 31 ILJ 2539 (KZD) (3 September 2010).

111 *Growthpoint Properties* para 46.

and economic pressure on the employer, and often, by extension, on its suppliers and clients.[112]

After summarising the nature and purpose of picketing, the High Court turned to balance the conflicting constitutional rights. In this respect, the High Court started by explaining that like all other rights, the right to picket is not unlimited and absolute. Inevitably in the nature of pickets, non-parties to the labour dispute are inconvenienced and sometimes even prejudiced.[113] Although protests and demonstrations are part of the fabric of everyday life and non-parties to the disputes have to develop some tolerance to withstand the disruption caused by picketers, such tolerance has its limits.[114]

In this case, the High Court explained further, tolerance levels were exceeded when the applicant and its tenants could not conduct their business and suffered a loss of revenue as the public took their business elsewhere. In addition, the evidence given by experts employed by the applicant showed that the level of noise was unacceptably high. It exceeded the legal limit of 85 decibels set by the regulations governing noise-induced hearing loss. The noise made by the strikers thus created an unhealthy environment and prevented the applicant and its tenants from using their property.[115]

In light of these findings, the High Court went on to conclude that the strikers could exercise their rights reasonably without interfering with the applicant, its tenants and the general public. The fact that the noise made by the strikers caused the applicant and its tenants to lose business was an unacceptable and unjustifiable limitation on their right to property, to trade and to a healthy environment.[116]

The strikers were, therefore, ordered to lower their noise level, but not to stop demonstrating, picketing, carrying placards or singing and chanting softly.[117]

14.2.3.3 Petitions

The right to petition protects the right to make direct submissions to the relevant person or institution.[118] The right to petition in terms of section 17 should be read together with sections 56 and 115 of the Constitution which provide that the National Assembly (NA) and the provincial legislatures are obliged to 'receive petitions, representations or submissions from any interested persons or institutions'.

To give effect to these rights and obligations, all the provincial legislatures, with the exception of the Eastern Cape Provincial Legislature, have enacted Petitions Acts.[119] Section 1 of the KwaZulu-Natal Petitions Act defines a petition as:

> **a complaint, request, representation or submission addressed by a petitioner to the Committee, and may take the form of:**
>
> **(*a*) a single petition, which is an individual submission from a single petitioner concerning a particular complaint or request;**

112 *Growthpoint Properties* paras 47–8.

113 *Growthpoint Properties* para 57.

114 *Growthpoint Properties* para 58

115 *Growthpoint Properties* para 59.

116 *Growthpoint Properties* para 60

117 *Growthpoint Properties* para 61.

118 Rautenbach and Malherbe (2012) 377.

119 See Free State Petitions Act 2 of 2008; Gauteng Petitions Act 5 of 2002; KwaZulu-Natal Petitions Act 4 of 2003; Limpopo Petitions Act 4 of 2003; Mpumalanga Petitions Act 6 of 2000; Northern Cape Petitions Act 8 of 2009; North West Petitions Act 2 of 2010.

(*b*) a collective petition, which is a collection of signatures from a number of petitioners concerning a particular complaint or request;

(*c*) a group petition, made up of individual or group submissions from a number of petitioners concerning the same or substantially similar complaints or requests;

(*d*) an association petition, which is an individual submission from an association, or an individual mandated by an association, concerning a particular complaint or request.

14.2.4 The Regulation of Gatherings Act 205 of 1993

During the apartheid era a number of repressive laws were enacted to prohibit assemblies and demonstrations and to suppress dissent. Among the most notorious of these laws were the Riotous Assemblies Act[120] and the Internal Security Act.[121] In terms of the Internal Security Act, the Minister issued an annual notice in terms of which all outdoor gatherings were declared illegal - except gatherings for *bona fide* religious and sporting events - unless a magistrate granted permission to hold a gathering.

A constructive attempt to reconcile the rights of assemblers with the state's interest in maintaining public order was advanced through the Regulation of Gatherings Act (Gatherings Act). The Gatherings Act includes the view of demonstrations as a right. However, the right is subject to notification to the local authorities and police seven days in advance.[122] The Act represents a compromise between the old and the new order. Many of the provisions are not libertarian in essence and seem to favour authority rather than the realisation of the right to freedom of assembly. The seven-day notice period could, in effect, put on ice many passionate pleas.[123] A further factor that may chill the collective efforts of demonstrators is the imposition of civil liability on the members of the demonstration.[124] However, the basic premise underlying the Gatherings Act remains that everyone has the right to assemble and protest peacefully and that authorities have a duty to facilitate this through negotiations with organisers of such an event if necessary.

Given that the right to protest is fundamental to the proper functioning of a democracy, the Gatherings Act assumes that gatherings and protests will almost always be allowed and that technicalities will not be used to ban protests that would make the powers-that-be uncomfortable. Although the provisions in the Act assume that notification will be given, the absence of giving notice does not automatically render a gathering illegal. Thus, the Gatherings Act requires the relevant police officers to try to identify organisers of protests and gatherings and then to engage with those organisers even if no notice was given of the protest or gathering by its organisers.[125] The Act further places a legal duty on the responsible officer to engage with organisers of a gathering or protest to try to reach agreement about how the gathering or protest should be conducted.[126]

To ensure the facilitation of peaceful gatherings, the Gatherings Act allows the responsible officer to impose certain conditions on the gathering or protest if there are

120 Act 17 of 1956.

121 Act 74 of 1982.

122 For a comprehensive discussion of the operation of the Regulation of Gatherings Act, see Currie and De Waal (2013) 381–3.

123 S 9(2)(*e*) of the Gatherings Act. See also Memeza, M (2006) A critical review of the implementation of the Regulation of Gatherings Act 205 of 1993: A local government and civil society perspective available at http://www.fxi.org.za.

124 De Vos, P (2009) Freedom of assembly and its limits *Constitutional Court: Without Prejudice* 9(8):4–5.

125 S 3(5)(*c*).

126 S 4(1).

reasonable grounds to do so to minimise traffic disruptions, to ensure continued access for others to their places of work and property, to prevent injury to any person and to prevent the destruction of property.[127] When an officer imposes such conditions, he or she is required by law to give written reasons for this.[128] The Gatherings Act makes it clear that a gathering or protest may only be prohibited in extreme cases. Section 5 states that:

> **When credible information on oath is brought to the attention of a responsible officer that there is a threat that a proposed gathering will result in serious disruption of vehicular or pedestrian traffic, injury to participants in the gathering or other persons, or extensive damage to property, and that the Police and the traffic officers in question will not be able to contain this threat, he shall forthwith meet or, if time does not allow it, consult with the convener and the authorized member, if possible, and any other person with whom, he believes, he should meet or consult, including the representatives of any police community consultative forum in order to consider the prohibition of the gathering.**

Only after such a meeting would a responsible officer be able to prohibit a gathering if he or she is convinced on reasonable grounds that no amendment to the conditions of the gathering would prevent serious disruptions or extensive damage to property.

CRITICAL THINKING

A balancing act gone awry

The police have a duty to keep the peace. They must also protect the interests of all parties and must protect the safety of individuals as well as their property. At the same time, in doing so, the police cannot infringe on the right of others to protest peacefully. When a protest takes place without the necessary notice having been given, the police officer in charge cannot automatically prohibit such a gathering or disperse those who have gathered to take part in a protest. The individual police officers must exercise a discretion, guided by the Gatherings Act and informed by section 17 of the Constitution. In doing so, they must carefully balance the various interests.

In August 2012 – after several incidents of violence in the preceding days – the police opened fire and killed 34 mineworkers at Marikana. After this massacre, the President appointed a Commission of Inquiry to look into the circumstances that led to this disaster. However, in the wake of the massacre, various institutions prohibited gatherings around Marikana as this news report explains:

> In the wake of the [Marikana] massacre, activists alleged a crackdown on dissent, especially in the platinum belt, but certainly not confined to it. In September, the Rustenburg Local Municipality prohibited the Wonderkop Community Development Association from organising a protest against police violence after a councillor, Paulinah Masutlho, was shot dead, allegedly by the police.
>
> Another protest, to be held by the Marikana Support Campaign outside the Farlam Commission, was also prohibited. In Makause on the East Rand of Gauteng, the police thwarted criticism of their own by blocking attempted protests against police violence.

127 S 4(4)(*b*).

128 S 4(4)(*c*) of the Gatherings Act.

> Then it emerged that before the massacre, the Bafokeng Landbuyers' Association had also attempted to hold protests on mining rights, the demolition of houses, and the Protection of State Information Bill, but their attempts were repeatedly thwarted by the Rustenburg Municipality, which banned their protests on what they claimed to be spurious grounds. They have also claimed that the Municipality is placing a myriad obstacles in the way of their and others' right to protest, to protect powerful mining interests and to stifle dissent against their practices in the platinum belt.[129]
>
> Can these prohibitions on gatherings in the wake of the Marikana massacre be justified?

14.2.5 Liability for damage caused during a gathering

Apart from imposing an obligation on the organisers of a gathering to provide notice to the local authority and police seven days prior to the gathering,[130] the Gatherings Act also imposes joint and several liability on the organisers of a demonstration or gathering for riot damage caused by the participants in the demonstration or gathering.[131]

Section 11(2) of the Gatherings Act goes on to provide, however, that an organiser can avoid liability if it can prove:

> (*a*) **that it did not permit or connive at the act or omission which caused the damage in question;**
>
> (*b*) **that the act or omission in question did not fall within the scope of the objectives of the demonstration or gathering in question and was not reasonably foreseeable; and**
>
> (*c*) **that it took all reasonable steps within its power to prevent the act or omission in question.**

The constitutional validity of these provisions was challenged in *SATAWU*.

The facts of this case were as follows. SATAWU organised a large gathering in the centre of Cape Town as part of a strike by its members in the security industry. In preparation for the gathering, SATAWU complied with all the procedural requirements of the Gatherings Act. In addition, it appointed approximately 500 marshals and advised its members to refrain from unlawful and violent behaviour. It also asked the municipality to clear the roads of vehicles and to erect barriers along the route.

Despite the precautions carried out by SATAWU, the respondents' shops were looted and their vehicles damaged during the gathering. The respondents then sued SATAWU for damages in terms of section 11(1) of the Gatherings Act. In response, SATAWU denied that it was liable and applied for an order declaring section 11(2) of the Act to be unconstitutional and invalid on the grounds that it was irrational.

SATAWU argued that section 11(2) of the Gatherings Act was irrational because it required the organisers of a gathering to take all reasonable steps to prevent the act or omission in question even when that act or omission was not reasonably foreseeable. Apart from being irrational, SATAWU argued in the alternative that section 11(2) also limited the right to freedom of assembly and that this limitation was not reasonable or justifiable.

---

129 Inside Rustenburg's banned protests (2013, 7 March) available at http://www.ru.ac.za/facultyofhumanities/latestnews/name,79323,en.html.

130 S 3(2)

131 S 11(1).

A majority of the Constitutional Court rejected both these arguments and found that section 11(2) was constitutionally valid. In arriving at this decision, the Constitutional Court began by noting that it was obliged – to the extent that this was possible – to interpret section 11(2) in a manner that gave it a rational meaning and preserved its validity so that the purpose for which it was enacted could be realised.[132] The Court then remarked that:

> **Gatherings, by their very nature, do not always lend themselves to easy management. They call for extraordinary measures to curb potential harm. The approach adopted by Parliament appears to be that, except in the limited circumstances defined [in section 11(2)], organisations must live with the consequences of their actions, with the result that harm triggered by their decision to organise a gathering would be placed at their doorsteps.**[133]

After making these points, the Constitutional Court then turned to examine section 11(2). In this respect, the Court began by noting that the purpose of the section was:
(a) to provide for the statutory liability of organisations
(b) to afford the organiser a tighter defence by allowing it to rely on the absence of reasonable foreseeability and the taking of reasonable steps
(c) to place the onus on the organiser to prove this defence instead of requiring the plaintiff to prove the organiser's unlawfulness and negligence.[134]

There is a interrelationship, the Constitutional Court noted further, between the steps that an organiser takes on the one hand and what is reasonably foreseeable on the other. Section 11(2) requires that the organiser take reasonable steps within its power to prevent the act or omission that is reasonably foreseeable. The real link between the foreseeability and the steps taken is that the steps must have been reasonable to prevent what was foreseeable. If the steps taken at the time of planning the gathering were indeed reasonable to prevent what was foreseeable, the taking of those preventative steps would render the act or omission that subsequently caused the riot damage reasonably unforeseeable.[135]

It must be emphasised, however, that the Constitutional Court went on to note:

> **that organisations are required to be alive to the possibility of damage and to cater for it from the beginning of the planning of the protest action until the end of the protest action. At every stage in the process of planning, and during the gathering, organisers must always be satisfied of two things: that an act or omission causing damage is not reasonably foreseeable and that reasonable steps are continuously taken to ensure that the act or omission that becomes reasonably foreseeable is prevented. This is the only way in which organisers can create a situation where acts or omissions causing damage remain unforeseeable. In such a case, the requirement of taking reasonable steps is not met simply by guarding against the occurrence of the damage-causing act or omission. The inquiry whether the steps taken were sufficient to render the act or omission in question no longer reasonably foreseeable might be very exacting. An important qualification is that the steps that the organisers are required to take must be within their power.**[136]

132 *SATAWU* para 37.
133 *SATAWU* para 38.
134 *SATAWU* para 39.
135 *SATAWU* para 43.
136 *SATAWU* paras 4–5.

Although section 11(2) therefore provided a viable defence to the organisers of a demonstration or gathering, the majority judgment found that this nevertheless limited the right to freedom of assembly guaranteed in section 17 of the Constitution. This is because compliance with the requirements of section 11(2) of the Gatherings Act significantly increased the cost of organising protest action. It may also well be that poorly resourced organisations that wish to organise protest action about controversial causes that are nonetheless vital to society could be inhibited from doing so. Both of these factors amounted to a limitation of the right to assemble and to demonstrate.[137]

The Court nevertheless found the limitation to be reasonable and justifiable in terms of the limitation clause set out in section 36 of the Constitution. This is because, the Constitutional Court found, the limitation served an important purpose of protecting members of society, including those who do not have the resources or capability to identify and pursue the perpetrators of the riot damage for which they seek compensation. When a gathering imperils the physical integrity, the lives and the sources of livelihood of the vulnerable, the organisations that are responsible for setting in motion the events that gave rise to the suffered loss must bear liability for damages arising therefrom.[138]

14.3 Political rights

14.3.1 Introduction

Before 1994, the majority of South Africans were prohibited from voting in elections based solely on their race. The oppressive and undemocratic state curtailed much of extra-parliamentary political activity. Liberation movements such as AZAPO, the ANC, the PAC and the South African Communist Party (SACP) were prohibited from operating in the country. Police harassed and at times detained, tortured and even killed activists who belonged to organisations such as the UDF - which was established in 1983 to spearhead resistance against apartheid - and the End Conscription Campaign (ECC). In short, the majority of South Africans who opposed the apartheid regime enjoyed little or no political rights.

The drafters of the Constitution therefore included a wide range of political rights in the Constitution. Section 19(1) of the Constitution thus states that '[e]very citizen is free to make political choices'. This includes the right:
- to form a political party
- to participate in the activities of, or recruit members for, a political party
- to campaign for a political party or cause.

Section 19(2) states that '[e]every citizen has the right to free, fair and regular elections for any legislative body established in terms of this Constitution' while section 19(3) confirms that '[e]very adult citizen' has the right:
- to vote in elections for any legislative body established in terms of this Constitution and to do so in secret
- to stand for public office and, if elected, to hold office.

137 *SATAWU* paras 51–9.
138 *SATAWU* paras 34 and 94.

The Constitutional Court has considered the purpose behind the political rights guaranteed in section 19 of the Constitution in a number of cases.[139] In these cases, the Court has held that these rights are important for two reasons. First, the rights are important because they are aimed at preventing a recurrence of the wholesale denial of political rights that took place during the apartheid era. Deputy Chief Justice Moseneke eloquently explained this in *Ramakatsa and Others v Magashule and Others* where he held that:

> **[d]uring the apartheid order, the majority of people in our country were denied political rights that were enjoyed by a minority. The majority of black people could not form or join political parties of their choice. Nor could they vote for those who were eligible to be members of Parliament. Differently put, they were not only disenfranchised but were also excluded from all decision-making processes undertaken by the government of the day, including those affecting them ... The purpose of section 19 is to prevent the wholesale denial of political rights to citizens of the county from ever happening again.[140]**

A second reason why these rights are important is that they aim to give effect to a system of representative democracy. In *Ramakatsa*, Moseneke DCJ explained this by affirming that section 19 has to be interpreted against the background of the Constitution as a whole, especially the role afforded in the Constitution to political parties:

> **In our system of constitutional democracy political parties occupy the centre stage and play a vital part in facilitating the exercise of political rights. This fact is affirmed by section 1 of the Constitution which proclaims that '[u]niversal adult suffrage, a national common voters roll, regular elections and a multi-party system of democratic government, to ensure accountability, responsiveness and openness' are some of the values on which our State is founded.[141]**

In contrast to most of the rights set out in the Bill of Rights that attach to 'every person', the rights contained in section 19 of the Constitution are available only to citizens.[142] It can therefore be observed that the Constitution distinguishes between citizens who are the bearers of political rights and 'everyone' else, including, for example, foreign nationals, who are not entitled to participate in the exercise of political rights. While foreign nationals enjoy almost all the other rights contained in the Bill of Rights, only citizens can invoke the political rights set out in section 19.

---

139 *New National Party v Government of the Republic of South Africa and Others* (CCT9/99) [1999] ZACC 5; 1999 (3) SA 191; 1999 (5) BCLR 489 (CC) (13 April 1999) para 10; *Minister of Home Affairs v National Institute for Crime Prevention and the Re-Integration of Offenders (NICRO) and Others* (CCT 03/04) [2004] ZACC 10; 2005 (3) SA 280; 2004 (5) BCLR 445 (CC) (3 March 2004) para 47; *Ramakatsa and Others v Magashule and Others* (CCT 109/12) [2012] ZACC 31; 2013 (2) BCLR 202 (CC) (18 December 2012) para 64.

140 (CCT 109/12) [2012] ZACC 31; 2013 (2) BCLR 202 (CC) (18 December 2012) para 64.

141 *Ramakatsa* para 65.

142 In *Richter v The Minister for Home Affairs and Others* (CCT03/09, CCT 09/09) [2009] ZACC 3; 2009 (3) SA 615 (CC); 2009 (5) BCLR 448 (CC) (12 March 2009) and *AParty and Another v The Minister for Home Affairs and Others, Moloko and Others v The Minister for Home Affairs and Another* (CCT 06/09, CCT 10/09) [2009] ZACC 4; 2009 (3) SA 649 (CC); 2009 (6) BCLR 611 (CC) (12 March 2009), the Constitutional Court was called on to determine the voting rights of non-resident citizens.

PAUSE FOR REFLECTION

Does section 19 restrict the political activities of non-citizens?

Rautenbach and Malherbe argue that the political activities guaranteed in section 19 of the Constitution should be restricted to those activities that form a part of the formal democratic process such as participation in elections and the appointment and functioning of institutions provided for in the Constitution and legislation. This is because only citizens are the bearers of the rights guaranteed in section 19. If the concept of political activities was interpreted broadly to include all actions associated with holding or expressing political views or engaging in political activities, then the rights of non-citizens to freedom of opinion, expression, assembly and association, which are guaranteed for everyone, would be drastically restricted.[143]

However, section 19 itself does not restrict the rights of non-citizens. It merely reserves the enjoyment of these rights for citizens. If the legislature or other sections of the Constitution place restrictions on the rights of non-citizens to take part in the activities of a political party, such restrictions would not fall foul of section 19. However, if such restrictions also limit the rights to freedom of expression, assembly and association of non-citizens, non-citizens will be able to invoke the latter rights to challenge the restricting provisions. A court will then have to decide whether such restrictions are justifiable or not in terms of the limitation clause. In other words, it is important to remember that rights are interdependent and that a legislative provision (or other action) can infringe on more than one right at the same time.

14.3.2 The right to make political choices and the role of political parties

14.3.2.1 Introduction

Political parties lie at the heart of South Africa's constitutional democracy. The Constitution does not regulate the internal affairs of political parties. Nor does it contain extensive provisions on the appropriate constitutional relationship between political parties and constitutional structures such as legislatures and executives. Note too that the right to make political choices goes beyond the involvement of citizens in party politics: the involvement of some citizens in social movements, citizen activism and other civil society organs is also pivotal for the proper functioning of a democracy. The rights to freedom of expression, assembly and association ensure that these political activities not associated directly with political parties are adequately protected by the Constitution.

However, section 19(1) of the Constitution, which guarantees for all citizens the right to form, participate in the activities of and campaign for political parties, affirms that such participation lies at the heart of the right to make political choices. Section 19(1) thus primarily guarantees the freedom to make a choice with regard to a political party and once that choice has been made, it safeguards a member's free and fair participation in the activities of the party concerned.[144]

These provisions have a number of important consequences. Among these are the following:

- First, members of a political party have a constitutional right to participate in the activities of their party.

143 Rautenbach and Malherbe (2012) 382.

144 *Ramakatsa* para 71. S 197(3) of the Constitution provides that no employee of the public service may be favoured or prejudiced because he or she supports a particular political party or cause.

- Second, this constitutional right can be enforced not only against external interference, but against interference arising from within the party itself.[145] The constitutions and rules of political parties must, therefore, be consistent with the Constitution.[146]

Although the constitutions and rules of political parties must be consistent with the Constitution, it is important to note that section 19(1) does not spell out how members of a political party should exercise their right to participate in the activities of their party. Instead, it is left to political parties themselves to determine how their members should participate in their activities. This is because these activities are internal matters of each political party and they are best placed to determine how members should participate. The constitutions of political parties are the instruments which facilitate and regulate participation by members in the activities of a political party.[147]

CRITICAL THINKING

Enforcing internal party discipline without negatively affecting internal party democracy

In 2012, the then President of the ANC Youth League, Mr Julius Malema, was expelled from the ANC after he was found guilty of contravening what were then rules 25.5(c) and (i) of the ANC Constitution. Section 25.5(c) - since amended - stated that '[b]ehavior which brings the organisation into disrepute or which manifests a flagrant violation of the moral integrity expected of members and public representatives or conduct unbecoming that of a member or public representative' shall constitute misconduct by a member of the ANC. Section 25.5(i) stated that '[b]ehaving in such a way as to provoke serious divisions or a break-down of unity in the organization' would similarly constitute misconduct. A disciplinary committee of the ANC relied on these provisions to expel Mr Malema for expressing his personal views at a press conference of the ANC Youth League 'which sought to portray the ANC government and its leadership under President [Jacob] Zuma in a negative light in relation to the African agenda and which had the potential to sow division and disunity in the ANC, and for expressing his personal views on Botswana which contravened ANC policy'.[148]

Assuming that the various disciplinary committees were properly constituted and that they provided Mr Malema a fair hearing, the expulsion of Mr Malema would probably be found to pass constitutional muster. However, Mr Malema and his allies argued at the time that the action against him was motivated by political considerations. They also argued that such actions would have a chilling effect on robust debate within the internal structures of the ANC.

This case thus provides evidence of the difficult constitutional and broader ethical issues that arise when a political party wishes to discipline its members. On the one hand, no organisation - especially not a political party - can allow ill-discipline of its members. On the other hand, where members of a party are disciplined for asking critical questions about the leadership of their political party, internal party democracy may suffer and may even be extinguished.

---

145 *Ramakatsa* para 71.

146 *Ramakatsa* para 72.

147 *Ramakatsa* para 73.

148 ANC National Disciplinary Committee: Press Statement (2012, February) Public Announcement on the Disciplinary Hearings of F Shivambu, J Malema and S Magaqa available at http://www.anc.org.za/show.php?id=9414.

Two pertinent issues arise. Would vague and general disciplinary rules that prohibit members of a political party from bringing that party into disrepute and of sowing divisions in that party pass constitutional muster? If not, how could a political party formulate its disciplinary rules to ensure that party discipline is enforced without snuffing out internal debate in the party?

14.3.2.2 The regulation of political parties

As pointed out above, political parties play an important role in South Africa's system of representative democracy. However, there are no significant constitutional or legislative provisions that regulate the internal affairs of political parties such as the manner in which they select their candidates for elections or the manner in which they discipline members who have allegedly breached their rules.[149]

The legal relationship between a party and its members, therefore, is largely based on the common law principles that govern voluntary associations. In terms of the common law, a voluntary association is taken to have been created by agreement as it is not a body established by statute. A political party's constitution together with its rules collectively comprise the terms of the agreement entered into by its members. It is, however, regarded as a unique agreement.

Although there are no significant constitutional or legislative provisions regulating the internal affairs of political parties, the Electoral Act[150] and the Electoral Commission Act[151] do regulate the manner in which political parties may participate in elections. These Acts provide, *inter alia,* that political parties who wish to contest an election must register,[152] submit a list of candidates[153] and pay a deposit which is forfeited in the event of the party not securing a seat in the elections. Every political party and every participating candidate must also subscribe to the code of conduct.[154] Finally, it is important to note that the Electoral Commission may not accept the late submission of candidate lists by parties.[155]

PAUSE FOR REFLECTION

A generous interpretation of sections 14 and 17 of the Municipal Electoral Act

In *African Christian Democratic Party v Electoral Commission and Others*, the Constitutional Court held that the reason why political parties are required to pay a deposit before they can contest an election is to ensure that their participation in the election in question is not frivolous.[156]

In this case, the applicant decided to contest the 2006 local government elections in the Cape Town Metro. After taking this decision, it lodged a notice of intention to contest the elections together with a list of candidates at the Electoral Commission's office in

149 There are several references to political parties in the Constitution. For example, s 47(3)(*c*) states that a member of the NA who 'ceases to be a member of the party that nominated that person as a member of the Assembly' will lose his or her membership of the Assembly. S 57(2)(*b*) similarly allows minority parties to participate in the proceedings of the NA in a manner consistent with democracy.

150 Act 73 of 1998.

151 Act 51 of 1996.

152 Ss 15, 16 and 17 of the Electoral Commission Act as well as ss 26–31 of the Electoral Act.

153 Ss 26(*b*) and 27 of the Electoral Act.

154 S 99 of the Electoral Act.

155 *Liberal Party v The Electoral Commission and Others* (CCT 10/04) [2004] ZACC 1; 2004 (8) BCLR 810 (CC) (5 April 2004).

156 (CCT 10/06) [2006] ZACC 1; 2006(3) SA 305 (CC); 2006(5) BCLR 579 (CC) (24 February 2006) para 31.

Cape Town. Unfortunately, it did not pay a deposit at the Commission's Cape Town office as required by sections 14 and 17 of the Local Government: Municipal Electoral Act.[157]

When the applicant was informed of this fact, it asked the Electoral Commission to take the deposit from the surplus funds it had deposited at the Electoral Commission's head office in Pretoria. The Electoral Commission, however, refused to do so and disqualified the applicant from contesting the elections in Cape Town. The applicant then applied unsuccessfully to the Electoral Court for an order overturning the Commission's decision. After the Electoral Court dismissed the application, the applicant appealed to the Constitutional Court. The Constitutional Court upheld the appeal and found in favour of the applicant.

In arriving at this decision, the Constitutional Court began by noting that even though sections 14 and 17 of the Municipal Electoral Act specifically stated that the deposit should be paid at the Electoral Commission's local offices and not at its head office, these sections should not be interpreted in a way that prohibited deposits being paid at the head office. This is because the central purpose of sections 14 and 17 was to make sure that political parties who have notified the Commission that they intend to contest the election are being serious. There was no central purpose attached to the precise place where the deposit was paid.[158]

In addition, the Constitutional Court explained further, interpreting sections 14 and 17 of the Municipal Electoral Act in a manner that allowed the deposits to be paid at the Electoral Commission's head office facilitated participation in the elections rather than exclusion. This interpretation was also consistent with section 1(*d*) of the Constitution which provides that '[t]he Republic of South Africa is one sovereign, democratic state founded on the following values: Universal adult suffrage, a national common voters roll, regular elections and a multi-party system of democratic government to ensure accountability, responsiveness and openness'.[159]

Apart from the reasons set out above, the Constitutional Court also held that no other candidates or parties would be harmed by a generous interpretation of sections 14 and 17 of the Municipal Electoral Act.[160]

14.3.3 State funding of political parties

Political parties can only operate effectively if they have access to funds. However, this need for funds is a source of anxiety in many democracies. Where political parties are reliant on private donors and big corporations for their funds, this often distorts the policies and programmes of political parties to the detriment of those voters who cannot influence the policies and programmes in a similar fashion. Money, so it is said, can corrupt democratic policies and those with money will often try to do so. Section 236 of the Constitution therefore states that 'to enhance multi-party democracy, national legislation must provide for the funding of political parties participating in national and provincial legislatures on an equitable and proportional basis'. The national legislation referred to in this section is the Public Funding of Represented Political Parties Act.[161]

157 Act 27 of 2000.
158 *African Christian Democratic Party* para 27.
159 *African Christian Democratic Party* para 21.
160 *African Christian Democratic Party* para 33.
161 Act 103 of 1997.

This Act establishes a fund which is managed by the Electoral Commission. Money is allocated from this fund to the parties represented in the national and provincial legislatures from time to time. The amount each party is allocated depends on two factors: first, each party's proportional number of seats, and second, the principle of equity. The principle of equity provides that each party must at least receive a fixed minimum amount. This means larger parties will receive more funds than smaller parties. New parties entering the political space will receive no funds as they will have no seats in Parliament. The money allocated to each party must be used for purposes that are compatible with the functioning of a political party in a democratic society.

PAUSE FOR REFLECTION

Proportional national funding provides an unfair advantage to incumbent parties

Lowry suggests that instead of adopting a system of proportional national funding of political parties it would be better to adopt an egalitarian model similar to those employed in the United Kingdom and Canada. In terms of this approach, spending caps are imposed on political parties and greater transparency of funding and in particular private financing is required.[162] Where funding is allocated on the basis of the proportional support the party received in the previous election, so the argument goes, it makes it very difficult for smaller parties to compete fairly in elections. The more money to which a party has access, the better it can run an election campaign. The converse is also true. Thus, the system is often criticised because it provides an unfair advantage to incumbent parties.

Apart from the money allocated to political parties represented in the national and provincial legislatures, each political party is free to raise its own funds through private donations. Unlike the approach adopted in a number of other constitutional democracies, however, there is limited regulation of private funding in South Africa.[163]

In *Institute for Democracy in South Africa and Others v African National Congress and Others*, the High Court held that the Promotion of Access to Information Act (PAIA)[164] does not impose an obligation on political parties represented in the national and provincial legislatures to provide members of the public with information about the private donations they have received.[165] In arriving at this decision, the High Court held that for the purpose of their private donation records, political parties should not be classified as public bodies, but rather as private bodies. This meant, the High Court held further, that the applicant was entitled to be granted access to the respondents' private donation records only if it could show that this information was 'required for the exercise or protection of any right'.[166]

---

162 Lowry, MP (2008) Legitimizing elections through the regulation of campaign financing: A comparative constitutional analysis and hope for South Africa *Boston College International and Comparative Law Review* 31(2):185–212 at 185.

163 Steytler, N 'The legislative framework governing party funding in South Africa' in Matlosa, K (2004) *The Politics of State Resources: Party Funding in South Africa* 59 and 64. For a discussion regarding the funding of political parties, see generally Tshitereke, C (2002) Securing democracy: Party finance and party donations – the South African challenge *Institute for Security Studies* 63:1–12.

164 Act 2 of 2000.

165 (9828/03) [2005] ZAWCHC 30; 2005 (5) SA 39 (C) [2005] 3 All SA 45 (C) (20 April 2005) para 50.

166 *IDASA* para 53. S 50(1)(*a*) of the PAIA provides that '[a] requester must be given access to any record of a private body if: (*a*) that record is required for the exercise or protection of any right; (*b*) that person complies with the procedural requirements in this Act relating to a request for access to that record; and (*c*) access to that record is not refused in terms of any ground for refusal contemplated in Chapter 4 of this Part'.

Although the applicant argued that the donor records were required for the exercise or protection of the rights set out in section 19 of the Constitution, the High Court went on to hold, they did not explain how the respondent's donation records would assist them in exercising or protecting those rights or why, in the absence of those donation records, they would be unable to exercise them.[167]

On the face of it, the High Court concluded, section 19(1) prevents any restrictions from being imposed on a citizen's right to make political choices, such as forming a political party, participating in the activities of and recruiting members for a party, and campaigning for a political cause. Similarly, the right to 'free, fair and regular elections' enshrined in section 19(2) does not impose a duty on political parties to disclose funding sources nor does it afford citizens a right to gain access to such records. The emphasis in section 19(2) lies on the elections and the nature of the electoral process and not so much on the persons or parties participating in those elections.[168]

CRITICAL THINKING

The debate about the disclosure of sources of campaign funds

Lowry suggests that one way of ensuring public confidence in elections would be to compel political parties to disclose the sources of their campaign funds to public scrutiny.[169] However, in South Africa there has been little enthusiasm for this proposal from both the majority party and from minority parties.

Smaller parties argue that the majority party is entrenched and attracts large state funding and private funding as a result. Smaller parties are left to scrounge for private donations to fund the greater part of their expenses. Such donations, so the argument goes, may be difficult to obtain as donors may fear retaliation from the governing party if it becomes known that they have made donations to opposition parties.[170]

In the absence of legislation that compels all political parties to disclose all sources of their funding, it will be impossible to hold political parties accountable and to prevent the powerful and wealthy from attempting to buy influence by donating money to political parties.

14.3.4 The right to free, fair and regular elections

Apart from the right to make political choices guaranteed in section 19(1) of the Constitution, section 19(2) provides that '[e]very citizen has the right to free, fair and regular elections for any legislative body established in terms of this Constitution'.

As the Constitutional Court pointed out in *New National Party v Government of the Republic of South Africa and Others,*[171] this right to free and fair elections is closely related to the right to vote. This is because 'the right to vote is indispensable to, and empty without, the right to free and fair elections; the latter gives content and meaning to the former'.[172]

167 *IDASA* para 71.
168 *IDASA* para 71.
169 Lowry (2008) 189.
170 In this regard, see Sarakinsky, I (2007) Political party finance in South Africa: Disclosure versus secrecy *Democratization* 14(1):111–28 at 120–1.
171 (CCT9/99) [1999] ZACC 5; 1999 (3) SA 191; 1999 (5) BCLR 489 (13 April 1999).
172 *New National Party* para 12. In the same case the Constitutional Court also held that unlike the right to vote, all South African citizens irrespective of their age have a right to free, fair and regular elections (para 12).

Most rights contained in the Constitution merely require the state not to interfere with the exercise of the right. By contrast, the right to free, fair and regular elections imposes positive obligations on the state to ensure that it is fulfilled.[173] For example, a date for elections has to be promulgated, the secrecy of the ballot ensured and the process of elections must be managed. The results of an election also have to be declared.[174]

To ensure that these positive obligations are carried out in a free and fair manner, the Constitutional Court has held that the power to organise and manage elections must be vested in an independent institution.[175] Sections 181 and 190 of the Constitution read together with the Electoral Commission Act fulfil this requirement by establishing an independent Electoral Commission (a so-called Chapter 9 institution) and then conferring the power to organise and manage elections on this institution.

Together with the other Chapter 9 institutions, section 181(2) of the Constitution expressly refers to the independence of the Electoral Commission. Section 181(2) provides that '[the Chapter 9 institutions] are independent, and subject only to the Constitution and the law, and that they must be impartial and must exercise their powers and perform their functions without fear, favour or prejudice'.[176]

In the *New National Party* case, the Constitutional Court held that the independence of the Electoral Commission encompasses at least two aspects: financial independence and administrative independence.

Financial independence means that the Electoral Commission must have access to funds reasonably required to enable it to carry out its functions. An important consequence of this principle is that while Parliament has the authority to set a budget for the Commission, it must consider what is reasonably required by the Commission and deal with its requests for funding in a rational manner. In addition, it also means that Parliament rather than the executive must allocate the funds required by the Commission.[177]

Administrative independence means that the Electoral Commission must have control over those matters directly connected with the functions the Commission has to carry out. An important consequence of this principle is that while the executive is obliged to provide the Commission with any assistance it requires 'to ensure its independence, impartiality, dignity and effectiveness', the executive may not tell the Commission how to conduct registration, whom to employ, and so on.[178]

The main functions of the Electoral Commission are set out in section 190(1) of the Constitution. This section provides as follows:

> **1. The Electoral Commission must:**
>
> **(*a*) manage elections of national, provincial and municipal legislative bodies in accordance with national legislation;**

---

173 *New National Party* para 118 where O'Regan stated: 'Unlike some of the other rights in chapter 2 of the Constitution, the primary obligation which section 19(2) and (3) impose upon government is not a negative one, requiring government to refrain from conduct which could cause an infringement of the right, but a positive one, requiring government to take positive steps to ensure that the right is fulfilled.'

174 See *New National Party* paras 13–14; *August and Another v Electoral Commission and Others* (CCT8/99) [1999] ZACC 3; 1999 (3) SA 1; 1999 (4) BCLR 363 (1 April 1999) para 16; *NICRO* para 28; *Richter* para 54.

175 *New National Party* para 16.

176 S 181(3) provides that '[o]ther organs of state, through legislative and other measures, must assist and protect [the Chapter Nine Institutions] to ensure the independence, impartiality, dignity and effectiveness of these institutions' and s 181(4) provides that '[n]o person or organ of state may interfere with the functioning of [the Chapter Nine Institutions]'. The Electoral Commission is also accountable to the NA, and must report on its activities and the performance of its functions at least once a year (s 181(5)).

177 *New National Party* para 98.

178 *New National Party* para 99.

(*b*) ensure that those elections are free and fair; and

(*c*) declare the results of those elections within a period that must be prescribed by national legislation and that is as short as reasonably possible.

Besides vesting the power to organise and manage elections in an independent institution, the Constitutional Court has also held that an election will only be fair if the following two requirements are satisfied: first, each citizen entitled to do so must not be allowed to vote more than once in an election, and second, any person who is not entitled to vote should not be allowed to do so. This means that the regulation of the exercise of the right to vote is necessary so that any deviations from these requirements can be eliminated or restricted to ensure the proper implementation of the right to vote.[179]

The duty that rests on the state to realise effectively an individual's political rights is aptly demonstrated in the matter of *August and Another v Electoral Commission and Others.*[180] In this case the Constitutional Court was required to determine whether the right of prisoners to vote had been infringed in so far as the Commission had not taken the necessary steps to ensure that prisoners could register and therefore vote. One of the functions of the Commission is to compile and maintain a voters roll.[181] The Commission decided primarily for budgetary and administrative requirements that it would not take any steps to allow prisoners to vote in the 1999 elections. The Court held that the Commission had a duty to ensure the registration of these prisoners so as to enable them to exercise their political rights.[182]

Note that the freeness and fairness of elections do not depend solely on the Electoral Commission. Where some political parties are not treated fairly by the media (including the state media), or where the ability of political parties to campaign is restricted by the state, the freeness and fairness of the election will be questioned. Similarly, where state institutions or the members of powerful political parties are allowed to intimidate voters, the freeness and fairness of the election would similarly be compromised. Section 18 of the Electoral Commission Act establishes an Electoral Court to prevent such abuses from occurring. Section 96 of the Electoral Act empowers the Electoral Court to enforce the various provisions in that Act aimed at preventing just such abuses.

14.3.5 The right to vote

14.3.5.1 Introduction

Section 19(3) of the Constitution provides that '[e]very adult citizen has the right: (*a*) to vote in elections for any legislative body established in terms of this Constitution and to do so in secret; and (*b*) to stand for public office and, if elected, to hold office'.

The Constitutional Court highlighted the significance of the right to vote (and its intimate relationship with the value of human dignity that permeates the Bill of Rights) in *August.* The Court held that '[t]he vote of each and every citizen is a badge of dignity and of personhood. Quite literally, it says that everybody counts'.[183] The right to vote, therefore, is symbolic of our citizenship and represents a practical manifestation of how the Constitution

179 *New National Party* para 12.

180 (CCT8/99) [1999] ZACC 3; 1999 (3) SA 1; 1999 (4) BCLR 363 (1 April 1999).

181 S 5(1)(*e*) of the Electoral Commission Act.

182 *August* para 33.

183 *August* para 17.

recognises and protects the dignity of every citizen. Given South Africa's history in which the dignity of black South Africans was systematically denied by the state - in part by denying black South Africans the right to vote - this right and its protection is of profound importance for every citizen. As O'Regan J stated in the *New National Party* judgment:

> **The obligation to afford citizens the right to vote in regular, free and fair elections is important not only because of the relative youth of our constitutional democracy but also because of the emphatic denial of democracy in the past. Many of the injustices of the past flowed directly from the denial of the right to vote on the basis of race to the majority of South Africans. The denial of the right to vote entrenched political power in the hands of white South Africans.**[184]

Apart from its symbolic role of affirming the dignity of all, the Constitutional Court held in *Richter v The Minister for Home Affairs and Others* that the right to vote is also a crucial working part of our democracy:

> **Without voters who want to vote, who will take the trouble to register, and to stand in queues, as millions patiently and unforgettably did in April 1994, democracy itself will be imperilled. Each vote strengthens and invigorates our democracy. In marking their ballots, citizens remind those elected that their position is based on the will of the people and will remain subject to that will. The moment of voting reminds us that both electors and the elected bear civic responsibilities arising out of our democratic Constitution and its values.**[185]

To put this differently, voting reminds us that those elected to govern the country do so by invitation of the voters who lend their vote to a specific political party for a maximum period of five years. After five years, voters have a right to re-evaluate this choice. If they are unhappy with how the political party of their choice has served them, they can decide to lend their vote to another party again for a limited period of no more than five years.

Section 1 of the Electoral Act defines a voter as a South African citizen who is 18 years or older and whose name appears on the voters roll. As this definition indicates, a citizen who is 18 years or older may vote only if his or her name appears on the voters roll.[186]

A citizen's name will appear on the voters roll only if he or she has registered to vote in terms of section 6 of the Electoral Act. In *New National Party*, the Constitutional Court held that the requirement in section 1 of the Constitution that voting must occur in terms of a common voters role means that registering to vote is an inherent requirement for the exercise of the right to vote. The legislation that requires registration and prevents unregistered voters from voting can therefore not be classified as an infringement of the right to vote. It is a requirement for exercising the right not an infringement of it.[187]

---

184 *New National Party* para 120.

185 (CCT03/09, CCT 09/09) [2009] ZACC 3; 2009 (3) SA 615 (CC); 2009 (5) BCLR 448 (CC) (12 March 2009) para 53.

186 In *New National Party* para 6, the Constitutional Court held that these three requirements are derived from s 19(3) of the Constitution read together with s 46(1)(*b*) and 46(1)(*c*). S 46(1)(*b*) provides that 'the National Assembly consists of no fewer than 350 and no more than 400 women and men elected as members in terms of an electoral system that is based on the national common voters roll' and s 46(1)(*c*) provides that 'the National Assembly consists of no fewer than 350 and no more than 400 women and men elected as members in terms of an electoral system that provides for a minimum voting age of 18 years'.

187 *New National Party* para 15.

PAUSE FOR REFLECTION

Is the requirement of registration for exercising the right to vote a limitation on the right to vote?

Rautenbach and Malherbe have criticised the approach adopted by the Constitutional Court in *New National Party*. They argue that the requirement that citizens must register before they can vote should not be classified as an inherent part of the right to vote, but rather as a limitation of the right to vote that needs to be justified in terms of the limitation clause. This is because the national voters roll could have been compiled simply by transferring the names on the population register to the national voters roll.[188] This argument assumes that only the names of those 18 years and older could be placed on such a voters role. It also assumes that the population register is up to date and accurate.

The opposite view is that while voting is a right, it is not unreasonable to say that it imposes certain duties on citizens in order to exercise this right. One of these duties is to take the trouble to register to vote. Voters who do not bother to register on the voters role may also be less concerned and informed about politics and about issues of the day and would arguably be far less likely to cast their votes.

Despite the fact that section 19(3) of the Constitution provides that every adult citizen has the right to vote, section 8 of the Electoral Act excludes certain categories of adult citizens from voting by providing that they may not be registered as voters. Section 8 of the Act provides in this respect that:

> **The chief electoral officer may not register a person as a voter if that person:**
> **(*a*) has applied for registration fraudulently or otherwise than in the prescribed manner;**
> **(*b*) has been declared by the High Court to be of unsound mind or mentally disordered;**
> **(*c*) is detained under the Mental Health Act 18 of 1973; or**
> **(*d*) is serving a sentence of imprisonment without the option of a fine.**[189]

These limitations are subject to the limitation clause as set out in section 36 of the Constitution and the courts could be called on to determine the constitutionality of these exclusions. Apart from the right to vote, section 19(3) also provides that every citizen has the right to vote in secret.[190]

14.3.5.2 Regulating the right to vote

Like all other rights guaranteed in the Bill of Rights, Parliament may pass legislation that regulates the manner in which the right to vote may be exercised. The Constitutional Court set out the test that must be used to determine whether legislation that regulates the right to vote is constitutionally valid in *New National Party*.

---

188 Rautenbach and Malherbe (2012) 89 fn 56.

189 The fact that prisoners who were serving life sentences without the option of a fine were excluded from voting was declared unconstitutional by the Constitutional Court in *NICRO*.

190 The rendering of assistance by electoral officials at the request of a voter is also subject to the secrecy of the vote. S 39 of the Electoral Act provides that assistance may be given to voters who are unable to read, are blind or visually impaired. For a discussion of the plight of the visually impaired, see generally Maseko, TW (2009) The right of blind and visually impaired citizens to vote in secret: Is there a duty to do more? *SA Public Law* 24(2):623–39.

At issue in this case was the fact that before a citizen may register as a voter, he or she has to fulfil the registration requirements set out in section 6 of the Electoral Act. One of these requirements is that he or she must be in possession of a green bar-coded identity document.[191] This document replaced the old, much larger, blue identity document which did not contain a bar code in 1986. In *New National Party*, a majority of the Constitutional Court held that this requirement was constitutionally valid because it was rationally related to a legitimate governmental purpose. At the time when the case was brought, several older voters (especially white voters) had not replaced the old blue identity document with the new green document. According to statistics accepted by the Constitutional Court, approximately 80% of eligible voters had bar-coded IDs, 10% had no IDs at all and 10% were in possession of valid IDs that were not bar-coded. The 10% of eligible voters who were in possession of valid IDs that were not bar-coded amounted to approximately 2,5 million people.

In rejecting the argument that the requirement that a person could only register if he or she were in possession of a green bar-coded identity book was unconstitutional, the Constitutional Court affirmed that Parliament had the authority to determine the way in which voters must identify themselves. It nevertheless stated that Parliament does not have a free hand to do so. This is because the Constitution imposes important limits on the manner in which Parliament may exercise its powers.

First, the method that Parliament adopts for voters to identify themselves must not infringe the principle of the rule of law.[192] This will be the case if the measures are not rationally related to a legitimate governmental objective. This is because arbitrariness is inconsistent with the rule of law which is a core value of the Constitution.[193] The majority held that requiring the bar-coded identity book for voter registration was rational because:

> **[t]he bar-code on the document facilitates quick, easy and reliable verification of the fact that the name of the person has been entered on the population register. In addition, it is much easier for officers charged with the verification of the necessary particulars at the point of registration and voting to perform this task if they are to do so consistently by reference to a single type of identity document. Recognition of a multiplicity of documents for this purpose could be potentially confusing, give rise to error and slow down the process.**[194]

Second, the measures must not unjustifiably infringe the right to vote guaranteed in section 19(3) of the Constitution.[195] In this regard, the Constitutional Court held that the method Parliament adopts for voters to identify themselves will infringe the right to vote if, at the time the method was adopted by Parliament, an eligible voter who wanted to vote would not be able to do so even though he or she took reasonable steps in pursuit of his or her right to vote. This is because any method which was not sufficiently flexible to be reasonably capable of achieving the goal of ensuring that people who wanted to vote would be able to do so if they acted reasonably in pursuit of the right, had the potential to infringe the right.[196]

191 S 6(1) of the Electoral Act provides that '[a]ny South African citizen in possession of an identity document may apply for registration as a voter' and s 1 of the Act defines an identity document as a bar-coded identity card issued in terms of the Identification Act 68 of 1997 or a temporary identification certificate issued in terms of the Identification Act.

192 *New National Party* para 19.

193 *New National Party* para 24.

194 *New National Party* para 26.

195 *New National Party* para 20.

196 *New National Party* para 23.

Given this test, the majority found that the bar-coded ID requirement did not infringe the right to vote. This is because even though the Electoral Act had been promulgated only nine months before the general election, there was no evidence to show that at the time Parliament passed the Electoral Act the Department of Home Affairs would be unable to issue a bar-coded ID to any eligible voter who applied for one before the voter registration process closed. Any eligible voter who took reasonable steps to obtain a bar-coded ID and to register as a voter, therefore, would be able to vote.[197]

CRITICAL THINKING

Was the rationality standard used by the majority in the *New National Party* case correct?

In her minority judgment in the *New National Party* case, O'Regan J disagreed with the application of a rationality standard to this issue. Given the role played by voting in determining who should exercise political power, the right to vote is 'worthy of particular scrutiny by a court to ensure that fair participation in the political process is afforded'.[198] According to O'Regan J, the majority's approach would be appropriate in relation to determining whether legislation giving rise to differential treatment is constitutional, but it would be:

> far too deferential a standard for determining whether legislation enacted by Parliament to enable citizens to exercise their right to vote gives rise to an infringement of the right to vote.
>
> In my view, it is quite appropriate to require Parliament to act reasonably. The right to vote is foundational to a democratic system. Without it, there can be no democracy at all. What is more the right cannot be exercised in the absence of a legislative framework. That framework should seek to enhance democracy not limit it. To do so, it needs to draw all citizens into the political process. Regulation, which falls short of prohibiting voting by a specified class of voters, but which nevertheless has the effect of limiting the number of eligible voters needs to be in reasonable pursuance of an appropriate government purpose. For a court to require such a level of justification, is not to trample on the terrain of Parliament, but to provide protection for a right which is fundamental to democracy and which cannot be exercised at all unless Parliament enacts an appropriate legislative framework.[199]

The difference between the majority judgment and the minority judgment is therefore quite stark. The majority used a rationality standard and hence found that the impugned provisions requiring bar-coded identity books to register to vote was in compliance with the right to vote. O'Regan J in her minority decision, using a reasonableness standard, held the very opposite. Given South Africa's history, in which the vast majority of citizens were denied the right to vote, it is surprising that the majority employed the rationality standard, which is easy to meet, rather than the more searching standard of reasonableness which O'Regan J supported.

197 *New National Party* para 43.
198 *New National Party* para 122.
199 *New National Party* para 122.

14.3.5.3 Exclusions from the right to vote

14.3.5.3.1 Introduction

Besides regulating the right to vote, Parliament has also excluded certain categories of citizens from the right to vote. Among these are prisoners and citizens living abroad. The Constitutional Court has considered the constitutional validity of these exclusions in a number of cases.[200]

14.3.5.3.2 Prisoners

Apart from *August* which is discussed above, the Constitutional Court has considered the exclusion of prisoners from the right to vote in *Minister of Home Affairs v National Institute for Crime Prevention and the Re-integration of Offenders (NICRO) and Others.*[201] Unlike in *August*, this case dealt with a legislative provision purporting to limit the rights of prisoners to vote.[202] The provisions effectively disenfranchised convicted prisoners serving sentences of imprisonment without the option of a fine by prohibiting them from registering as voters and from voting while in prison.[203] Unsentenced prisoners and prisoners incarcerated because of their failure to pay their fines retained the right to register and vote.

After the provisions of the Electoral Laws Amendment Act[204] came into operation, the respondents applied for an order declaring them to be unconstitutional and invalid on the grounds that they unjustifiably infringed the right to vote. A majority of the Constitutional Court agreed with the respondents and granted the order.

The Constitutional Court accepted (and this was conceded by all parties) that these provisions, which prevented most prisoners from voting, infringed on their right to vote which is guaranteed in section 19(3)(*a*) of the Constitution. The only question was whether such a limitation of the right was justifiable in terms of the limitation clause or not. The majority of the court (per Chief Justice Chaskalson) held that the limitation was not justifiable and hence was unconstitutional.[205]

The Court rejected the argument that special arrangements would have to made for the prisoners in question to vote and that these special arrangements could put the integrity of the voting process at risk. Special measures, therefore, would have to be put in place and this would put a strain on the Electoral Commission's financial and logistical resources. The factual basis for this justification had not been established. The Electoral Commission had made arrangements for registering unsentenced prisoners and prisoners incarcerated because of their failure to pay their fines. There was nothing to suggest that extending these arrangements to include convicted prisoners serving sentences of imprisonment without the option of a fine would place an undue burden on the Electoral Commission's financial and logistical resources. Apart from saying that it would be costly to do so, the Minister provided no information about the logistical problems or estimates of the costs involved.[206]

---

200 See *August*; *NICRO*; *Richter*; *AParty*.

201 (CCT 03/04) [2004] ZACC 10; 2005 (3) SA 280 (CC); 2004 (5) BCLR 445 (CC) (3 March 2004).

202 The amendments to the Electoral Act effecting these limitations were made shortly before the 2004 general election when Parliament passed the Electoral Laws Amendment Act 34 of 2003.

203 S 8(2)(*f*) of the Electoral Act prohibited convicted prisoners who were 'serving a sentence of imprisonment without the option of a fine' from registering as voters and s 24B(2) prohibited convicted prisoners who were 'serving a sentence of imprisonment without the option of a fine' and who were already on the voters roll from voting if they were in prison on the day of the election.

204 Act 34 of 2003.

205 *NICRO* para 16.

206 *NICRO* para 49.

The Court also grappled with the argument advanced by the government that it was important for the government to denounce crime and to communicate to the public that the rights that citizens have, such as the right to vote, are related to fulfilling their duties and obligations as citizens. The Court pointed out that a majority of the Canadian Supreme Court had rejected a similar argument in *Sauve v Canada (Chief Electoral Officer)*[207] despite the fact that the Canadian government had presented a great deal of evidence to justify the law in question.[208] Unlike the Canadian government, the Court held further, the Minister had presented almost no evidence to justify the Amendment Act other than simply saying that the 'government did not want to be seen to be soft on crime and that it would be unfair to others who cannot vote to allow prisoners to vote'.[209] These statements, the Court went on to conclude, could not hope to justify the Amendment Act which applied to both serious and relatively minor crimes and even to prisoners whose convictions and sentences were still under appeal.[210]

PAUSE FOR REFLECTION

Why the government lost the *NICRO* case

The *NICRO* case must be understood with reference to the discussion on the limitation clause enquiry in chapter 10. The government lost the case because it failed to provide evidence to justify its legislative choices. It did not put any evidence before the Court as to why the particular category of prisoners (all convicted prisoners serving sentences of imprisonment without the option of a fine) had to be distinguished from other categories of prisoners and why it was important to disenfranchise them. If the law had only disenfranchised prisoners convicted of the most serious crimes and if the government had provided evidence on how the legislation effectively targeted the most dangerous and morally reprehensible criminals, the limited disenfranchisement might have been found to be justifiable.

14.3.5.3.3 Citizens working abroad

It is widely believed that a sizeable number of South African citizens live abroad although exact figures are not available. Legislation did not provide for citizens living abroad (who have not emigrated and thus remain citizens of the country) to vote in South African elections.

In 2009, the Constitutional Court declared invalid the legal provisions which excluded South Africans living abroad from voting in *Richter*. The applicant was a South African citizen who was a registered voter and who was working in the United Kingdom as a teacher. Although he wanted to vote in the 2009 general elections, he was unable to do so because section 33(1)(*e*) of the Electoral Act only made provision for South Africans who were temporarily absent from the Republic for business, holiday, educational and sporting purposes to cast special votes. It made no provision for South Africans who were absent for employment or other purposes to cast special votes.

The Constitutional Court affirmed that the right to vote also imposes burdens on citizens. First, they have to register in good time. Then, on polling day, they may have to journey some

207 2002 SCC 68.
208 *NICRO* para 58.
209 *NICRO* para 66.
210 *NICRO* para 67.

distance to a voting station. They have to be in possession of a bar-coded identity document and they may have to stand in a long queue to vote.[211] To determine whether the burdens placed on a voter who wishes to exercise his or her right to vote are inconsistent with the Constitution, the Court held further, it must apply the test adopted in *New National Party*. This test provides that a statutory provision will infringe the right to vote if it prevents an eligible voter who wishes to vote and who has taken reasonable steps in pursuit of the right to vote from voting.[212] Note that reasonableness here does not relate to the test developed by O'Regan J for the minority in *New National Party*. That test asked whether **Parliament** had acted reasonably. In this case, the Court asked whether arrangements to vote would have made it impossible for a **voter** who had acted reasonably to exercise his or her vote.

The Constitutional Court noted that apart from travelling back to South Africa from the United Kingdom to be present on polling day, there were no steps that the applicant in the position of Mr Richter could take to vote in the 2009 general elections. Requiring the applicant and other citizens in his position to travel thousands of kilometres across the globe to be in their voting districts on voting day, the Court held further, was not reasonable. This was especially so in light of the fact that section 33(1)(*b*) of the Electoral Act provided that those citizens who were working abroad on government service did not have to return home to vote but could vote at South African embassies, high commissions and consulates.[213]

In addition, the Court went on to hold, it was important to note that we live in a global economy and that more and more South Africans are working abroad. The fact that these citizens want to exercise their civic responsibilities and vote should be encouraged.[214]

After finding that section 33(1)(*e*) of the Electoral Act infringed the right to vote, the Constitutional Court turned to consider whether this infringement satisfied the requirements of the limitation clause. The Court held that it did not. In arriving at this decision, the Court began by pointing out that in terms of section 33(1)(*b*) those citizens who are working abroad for the government on voting day are permitted to vote while they are abroad.[215] In addition, the Court pointed out further, many other open and democratic societies allow citizens who are abroad on voting day to vote while they are abroad.[216] Finally, the Minister was unable to point to any legitimate governmental purpose that would be served by preventing citizens who are abroad from voting.[217]

14.3.6 The right to stand for and hold office

Political rights do not only include the right to vote and to participate as a citizen voter in free and fair elections. Section 19(3)(*b*) of the Constitution also guarantees for every adult citizen the right to 'stand for public office and, if elected, to hold office'. As we pointed out in chapter 4 in this book, sections 47(1) and 106(1) specifically state that some citizens are not eligible to become a member of the national Parliament or the provincial legislatures. Similarly, sections 47(3) and 106(3) provide for incidences where a citizen elected to the national Parliament or the provincial legislatures as a member of a specific political party would lose his or her membership. As we have already discussed these matters, we will not deal with them again here.

---

211 *Richter* para 56.
212 *Richter* para 57.
213 *Richter* para 68.
214 *Richter* para 69.
215 *Richter* para 76.
216 *Richter* para 77.
217 *Richter* para 78.

SUMMARY

Given that the majority of South Africa's citizens were denied political rights prior to 1994, it is not surprising that section 19 of the Constitution protects a wide range of political rights. Among these are the right to make political choices; the right to free, fair and regular elections and the right to vote in secret and to stand for public office. These rights are important not only because they are aimed at preventing the wholesale denial of political rights from ever taking place again, but also because they are aimed at giving effect to the system of representative democracy enshrined in the Constitution.

In so far as the rights guaranteed in section 19 of the Constitution are concerned, however, it is important to note that, unlike most of the other rights set out in the Bill of Rights, these rights are available only to citizens. The Constitution, therefore, distinguishes between citizens who are the bearers of political rights and 'everyone' else, including, for example, foreign nationals, who are not entitled to participate in the exercise of political rights. While foreign nationals enjoy almost all of the other rights contained in the Bill of Rights, only citizens can invoke the political rights set out in section 19.

The political rights protected in section 19 of the Constitution must be read together with the right to freedom of expression guaranteed in section 16 and the right to freedom of assembly, demonstration, picket and petition guaranteed in section 18. This is because democracy entails more than simply being able to vote. It must also give people an opportunity to form their own views and to express them by coming together and protesting peacefully. This allows people whose influence on political parties would otherwise be minimal to raise issues that are important to them, to draw attention to these issues and to engage with their fellow citizens and representatives about these issues.

Apart from participation in the political process, the rights to freedom of expression and assembly, demonstration, picket and petition also promote a number of other goals. The right to freedom of expression, for example, recognises and protects the moral agency of individuals in our society and facilitates the search for truth. The right to freedom of assembly, demonstration, picket and petition promotes the development of each individual's unique personality. This is because our personalities do not develop in isolation, but rather in the context of groups. Cultural, education and religious assemblies may, therefore, be as important as political assemblies.

Finally, it is important to note that both of these rights have internal modifiers. The right to freedom of expression, therefore, does not include the right to promote war, incite imminent violence or advocate hatred that is based on race, ethnicity, gender or religion, and that constitutes incitement to cause harm. The right to freedom of assembly, demonstration, picket and petition does not include the right to assemble, demonstrate, picket or petition in a violent or armed manner. Although these sorts of activities are not prohibited by the Constitution, they are also not protected by the Constitution. This means that they may be prohibited by legislation. The Promotion of Equality and Prevention of Unfair Discrimination Act (PEPUDA) thus prohibits hate speech and the Regulation of Gatherings Act prohibits armed and violent assemblies, demonstrations and pickets.

Chapter 15

Administrative justice, access to information, access to courts and labour rights

15.1 Introduction

Certain rights are of particular importance because they enhance the quality of a democracy and the conditions under which people live in that democracy. Although these rights are not political rights *per se*, they create conditions within which individuals can exercise many of their other rights in an effective manner. Such rights are closely aligned with the value of human dignity. This is because they take as their starting point the idea that the individual human dignity of each person can be effectively protected only if legal rules and regulations enhance the ability of each individual to make important life choices despite the fact that they may not hold as much power as the state or private bodies. These rights therefore aim to equal the playing field by requiring the powerful to adhere to pre-announced rules, to act in a relatively transparent manner, to share information and to provide individuals with access to courts. This access to courts will assist individuals to enforce these rights as well as the other rights needed to promote their well-being and for their dignity to be fully respected. In this chapter we discuss some of these rights, including the right to fair administrative action, the right of access to information, the right of access to courts and labour rights.

15.2 The right to just administrative action

15.2.1 Introduction

In most modern societies the law confers a wide range of discretionary powers on public officials. These discretionary powers allow public officials, for example, to grant a person a pension, a social grant, a tender or a tax exemption. They also give public officials the power to issue building permits, fishing licences, passports and so on.

While these sorts of discretionary powers have to be granted to government officials to ensure that modern government works effectively, the exercise of such powers may also be abused to the detriment of ordinary people who rely on the state to deal fairly with such matters. To prevent abuse, the right to administrative justice guaranteed in section 33 of the Constitution provides that these powers must be exercised in a manner that is lawful, reasonable and procedurally fair.

This right must be viewed against the context of South Africa's apartheid past. During the apartheid era, government officials routinely abused their discretionary powers. These discretionary powers were constantly expanded by legislation, especially in the latter years of the apartheid regime. At the same time, the court's common law authority to review the exercise of these powers was often restricted or ousted.[1] Even where the courts' jurisdiction was not ousted, apartheid-era courts sometimes appeared reluctant to exercise their power of administrative review.[2]

The Constitution seeks to prevent a recurrence of this abuse of power. It therefore includes a right to just administrative action in section 33 of the Bill of Rights. The primary purpose of the right to administrative justice is to ensure that the administrative powers given to public officials are exercised in a **procedurally fair** manner and that the outcome of the decision is **lawful** and **reasonable**. It is thus a right which seeks to ensure proper processes are followed before administrative decisions are made and that those decisions are lawful and reasonable.

Apart from granting courts the power to review and set side decisions that are unreasonable, unlawful and procedurally unfair, the right to administrative justice also requires public officials to provide reasons for administrative decisions that adversely affect rights. The duty to supply reasons is intended to ensure that public officials properly apply their minds before making a decision. This particular provision of the right contributes to better decision making.

Baxter divides administrative law into general and particular aspects. **Specific administrative law** refers to the principles of law that are applicable to discrete areas of administration, for example education, the environment, the police, the revenue service and so on. In most instances, an enabling Act regulates these areas, as well as regulations promulgated in terms of the Act and decisions interpreting the Act and the regulations. **General administrative law** refers to the principles of law that are applicable to all administrative entities. Most textbooks deal with the general principles of administrative law that are applicable to the entire administration.[3]

Prior to 1994, the legal principles that were applicable to all administrative entities, in other words, general administrative law, were drawn largely from the common law. The common law afforded the courts the inherent power to set aside decisions that were

1 Currie, I and De Waal, J (2013) *The Bill of Rights Handbook* 6th ed 645.

2 See, for example, Dyzenhaus, D (1991) *Hard Cases in Wicked Legal Systems: South African Law in the Perspective of Legal Philosophy*.

3 Baxter, L (1984) *Administrative Law* 3.

procedurally unfair, that failed to comply with the requirements of the enabling statute or that were so grossly unreasonable that some irregularity could be inferred. One of the major shortcomings of the common law, however, was that it imposed no general obligation on the public official to provide reasons for his or her decision.

In 1994, momentous changes occurred with the promulgation of the interim Constitution. Section 24 of the interim Constitution entrenched the right to administrative justice. It afforded every person the right to lawful and procedurally fair administrative action in certain circumstances. In addition, there was an obligation to provide reasons when rights or interests were affected. Apart from these rights, 'every person' was also given the right to 'administrative action which is **justifiable** in relation to the reasons given for it where any of his or her rights is affected or threatened' (our emphasis).[4]

The final Constitution retained an administrative justice clause in section 33 of the Bill of Rights, but the wording of the section is slightly different from the wording in section 24 in the interim Constitution. Section 33 of the Constitution specifically protects four categories of administrative justice rights. It protects the right to lawful, reasonable and procedurally fair administrative action[5] and affords everyone whose rights have been adversely affected by administrative action the right to be given written reasons.[6]

PAUSE FOR REFLECTION

The law of administrative justice a hybrid of the old and the new

Kohn and Corder explain the context within which the law of administrative justice must be understood by explaining that the South African law is a 'curious hybrid of the old and the new'.[7] Despite its common law roots which predate the 1994 Constitution, it is a field of law that epitomises the negotiated constitutional 'revolution'.[8] Chaskalson P explained the implications of this transformation as follows in the decision of *Pharmaceutical Manufacturers Association of South Africa and Another: In re Ex parte President of the Republic of South Africa and Others*:

> [A]dministrative law ... occupies a special place in our jurisprudence ... It is built on constitutional principles ... Prior to the coming into force of the interim Constitution, the common law was "the main crucible" for the development of these principles of constitutional law. The interim Constitution ... was a legal watershed. It shifted constitutionalism, and with it all aspects of public law, from the realm of the common law to the prescripts of a written constitution which is the supreme law.[9]

4 S 24 of the interim Constitution provided that

> **[e]very person shall have the right to –**
> **(*a*) lawful administrative action where any of his or her rights or interests is affected or threatened;**
> **(*b*) procedurally fair administrative action where any of his or her legitimate expectations is affected or threatened;**
> **(*c*) be furnished with reasons in writing for administrative action which affects any of his or her rights or interests unless the reasons for such action have been made public; and**
> **(*d*) administrative action which is justifiable in relation to the reasons given for it where any of his or her rights is affected or threatened.**

5 S 33(1) of the Constitution.

6 S 33(2) of the Constitution.

7 Kohn, L and Corder, H (2013) 'Judicial regulation of administrative action' *International Encyclopaedia of Laws* available at http://www.ielaws.com/index.htm.

8 Currie, I and De Waal, J (2001) *The New Constitutional and Administrative Law, Vol 1 Constitutional Law* 37.

9 (CCT31/99) [2000] ZACC 1; 2000 (2) SA 674; 2000 (3) BCLR 241 (25 February 2000) para 45.

As Kohn and Corder point out, prior to this shift, South African administrative law was entirely based on the common law and bore all the hallmarks of its parent English system.

> In particular, thanks in large part to the influence of the English constitutional lawyer, Albert Venn Dicey, it rested upon the twin pillars of parliamentary sovereignty and the rule of law with its obverse facet, the *ultra vires* doctrine, which operated as the organising rationale of administrative law. Along with this Westminster inheritance, came a deep distrust of government and discretionary power and a concomitantly heavy reliance on judicial review of administrative action as the principal means of checking this power. Unfortunately, transplanted into the South African context, these two key organising principles of English constitutional law failed to complement one another. Under apartheid, parliamentary sovereignty came to be associated with rule *by* law, rather than a substantive notion of the rule *of* law pursuant to which law is insulated from politics and judges serve as impartial and independent guardians of human rights. The separation of powers did not exist as a practical reality and as a result, parliamentary sovereignty came to be coupled with judicial timidity as the hamstrung courts struggled to find ways of controlling public power, which was largely abused for racial ends.[10]

Because of this context, the role of administrative law during apartheid is ambiguous. While it was 'underdeveloped and functioned in an undemocratic system that was antagonistic to fundamental rights, was secretive and unaccountable',[11] it was also used by lawyers in certain cases to challenge the unbridled exercise of power by the authoritarian state.

Apart from the four categories of administrative justice rights, the right to lawful, reasonable and procedurally fair administrative action and the right to be given written reasons for a decision, section 33 also provides that national legislation has to be enacted to give effect to the right to administrative justice and that this legislation has to achieve three objectives:

- It has to ensure and provide for the review of administrative action by a court or other independent tribunal.
- It has to impose a duty on the state to give effect to the rights.
- It has to promote an efficient administration.[12]

The primary purpose of the third objective is to ensure that an appropriate balance is maintained so that the state is not unduly burdened by administrative requirements which could seriously inhibit its core functions.

Unlike most of the other rights in the Bill of Rights, section 33 did not come into operation when the rest of the Constitution did on 3 February 1997. This is because the transitional provisions in section 23 of Schedule 6 provided that Parliament had to enact the national legislation referred to in section 33(3) within three years of the commencement of the

10 Kohn and Corder (2013).

11 Plasket, C (2007) Post-1994 administrative law in South Africa: The Constitution, the Promotion of Administrative Justice Act 3 of 2000 and the common law *Speculum Juris* 21(1):25–40 at 25.

12 S 33(3) of the Constitution.

Constitution, namely by 3 February 2000. In addition, it also provided that during this period, section 33 would be suspended and the right to administrative justice guaranteed in section 24 of the interim Constitution (slightly reworded) would remain in force.

The national legislation referred to in section 33(3) is the Promotion of Administrative Justice Act (PAJA).[13] This Act was passed on 3 February 2000 and, with the exceptions of section 4 and section 10, it came into operation on 30 November 2000. Sections 4 and 10 came into operation on 31 July 2002.

15.2.2 The relationship between the Constitution, the Promotion of Administrative Justice Act 3 of 2000 and the common law

Prior to the transition to democracy, the judicial review of administrative action was governed largely by common law principles and rules. When the interim Constitution and later the Constitution came into operation, however, these common law rules and principles were incorporated into the Constitution.

The Constitutional Court referred to this process in the *Pharmaceutical Manufacturers* case, when it held that:

> **[t]he common law principles that previously provided the grounds for judicial review of public power have been subsumed under the Constitution and, insofar as they might continue to be relevant to judicial review, they gain their force from the Constitution. In the judicial review of public power, the two are intertwined and do not constitute separate concepts.**[14]

An important consequence of the incorporation of the common law principles and rules governing judicial review of administrative action is that they no longer have a separate existence. Instead, these common law principles and rules have become a part of constitutional law. As stated by the Constitutional Court:

> **There are not two systems of law ... [but] only one ... which is shaped by the Constitution ... and all law, including the common law, derives its force from the Constitution and is subject to constitutional control.**[15]

The constitutionalisation of administrative law meant that before the PAJA came into operation, challenges to the validity of administrative action involved the direct application of the right to administrative justice first in terms of the interim Constitution and subsequently in terms of the Constitution. It is important to note, however, that after the Constitution was enacted but before the PAJA came into operation, the directly enforceable right to administrative justice was not section 33, but rather the rights contained in section 23(2)(*b*) of Schedule 6 of the Constitution.

When the PAJA was finally enacted in 2000, section 33 became operative. Section 33 of the Constitution provides as follows:

> (1) **Everyone has the right to administrative action that is lawful, reasonable and procedurally fair;**
> (2) **Everyone whose rights have been adversely affected by administrative action has the right to be given written reasons.**

13 Act 3 of 2000.
14 *Pharmaceutical Manufacturers* para 33.
15 *Pharmaceutical Manufacturers* para 44.

(3) National legislation must be enacted to give effect to these rights, and must –
- **(*a*) provide for the review of administrative action by a court or, where appropriate, an independent and impartial tribunal;**
- **(*b*) impose a duty on the state to give effect to the rights in subsections (1) and (2); and**
- **(*c*) promote an efficient administration.**

In terms of the principle of subsidiarity, however, a litigant challenging the validity of administrative action first has to turn to the provisions of the PAJA and would not normally be able to rely directly on the Constitution. The fact that the PAJA is now the primary mechanism for asserting administrative justice rights was confirmed by the Constitutional Court in its judgment in *Minister of Health and Another v New Clicks South Africa (Pty) Ltd and Others.*[16]

In this case, Chaskalson CJ held that:

> **PAJA is the national legislation that was passed to give effect to the rights contained in section 33. It was clearly intended to be, and in substance is, a codification of these rights. It was required to cover the field and it purports to do so. A litigant cannot avoid the provisions of PAJA by going behind it, and seeking to rely on s 33(1) of the Constitution or the common law. That would defeat the purpose of the Constitution in requiring the rights contained in s 33 to be given effect by means of national legislation.**[17]

Despite Chaskalson CJ's statement that '[a] litigatant cannot avoid the provisions of PAJA by going behind it, and seeking to rely on s 33(1) of the Constitution or the common law', section 33 is not entirely irrelevant. This is because section 33 still exists as a free-standing constitutional right and can be relied on in certain exceptional cases,[18] namely to challenge the validity of the provisions of the PAJA itself; to challenge legislation that is alleged to infringe the right to just administrative action; and, indirectly, to interpret the provisions of the PAJA.[19]

In much the same way that section 33 is not entirely irrelevant, neither is the common law. This is because the common law continues to have **direct** application in cases where neither the Constitution nor the PAJA apply, for example when a private association such as a club, a church or a political party exercises disciplinary powers over its members.[20] These sorts of cases fall outside the PAJA's scope because it applies only to the exercise of public power and not to the exercise of private power.[21] In addition, the common law principles of administrative law, developed over many centuries, have an **indirect** influence on administrative law in that they are used as a source informing the interpretation of the various provisions of both the PAJA and section 33.[22]

---

16 (CCT 59/2004) [2005] ZACC 14; 2006 (8) BCLR 872 (CC); 2006 (2) SA 311 (CC) (30 September 2005) paras 96–6. See also *Bato Star Fishing (Pty) Ltd v Minister of Environmental Affairs and Tourism and Others* (CCT 27/03) [2004] ZACC 15; 2004 (4) SA 490 (CC); 2004 (7) BCLR 687 (CC) (12 March 2004) para 22; *Walele v City of Cape Town* (CCT 64/07) [2008] ZACC 11; 2008 (6) SA 129 (CC); 2008 (11) BCLR 1067 (CC) (13 June 2008) para 29.

17 *New Clicks SA* paras 95–6.

18 Currie and De Waal (2013) 649.

19 Currie and De Waal (2013) 650–1.

20 See, for example, *Ismail v New National Party in the Western Cape and Others* (2001) JOL 8206 (C).

21 See Currie and De Waal (2013) 651.

22 See, for example, *Bato Star Fishing* para 22 where O'Regan stated that:

> **The common law informs the provisions of PAJA and the Constitution, and derives its force from the latter. The extent to which the common law remains relevant to administrative review will have to be developed on a case-by-case basis as the courts interpret and apply the provisions of PAJA and the Constitution.**

PAUSE FOR REFLECTION

The principle of subsidiarity

There are similarities between the relationship between section 9 of the Constitution and the Promotion of Equality and Prevention of Unfair Discrimination Act (PEPUDA),[23] discussed in chapter 12, on the one hand, and the relationship between section 33 and the provisions of the PAJA, on the other. In both cases, the principle of subsidiarity requires a litigant to rely on the legislation and not on the constitutional right directly unless the litigant is challenging the constitutionality of the subsidiary Act or other legislation or using the Constitution to help interpret the Act.

However, in the case of section 33 and the PAJA, the situation is complicated further by the fact that before 1994, administrative law was largely a part of the common law developed by the judiciary. These common law principles may assist courts to interpret the provisions of the PAJA. There are no similar common law principles of equality that predate the Constitution and it is therefore arguably less complicated to interpret the PEPUDA than it is to interpret the PAJA.

Whenever considering an administrative law issue, we must first ask whether the PAJA is applicable and if so, how it must be interpreted having regard to the Constitution and to common law principles. If the PAJA is not applicable and if section 33 is not invoked to challenge the constitutionality of legislation, this does not mean that the non-administrative exercise of public power cannot be reviewed by a court. The courts can still review such exercises of power under the principle of legality as part of a section 1 analysis.

15.2.3 Legislative, executive and judicial actions

Today, every exercise of public power is to some extent justiciable under the Constitution even if it does not entail administrative action as defined by the PAJA.[24] However, the nature of the legal principles that apply to the review of the exercise of public power will differ depending on the nature of the public power. Administrative action - as defined in the PAJA - will be reviewed under a different standard than the exercise of power that is not classified as administrative action. It is therefore important to understand what constitutes administrative action and to distinguish it from other forms of the exercise of power.

In this regard, it is important to note that the exercise of public power can be divided into three categories, namely legislative actions, executive actions and judicial actions. This division is based on the separation of powers. When the President assents to and signs an Act of Parliament, for example, he or she is performing a legislative action.[25] When the President appoints the members of his or her Cabinet, however, he or she is not performing a legislative action, but rather an executive action.[26] Similarly, when a judge imposes a sentence on a convicted person, he or she is performing a judicial action.[27] When a judge

23 Act 4 of 2000.

24 *Kaunda and Others v President of the Republic of South Africa* (CCT 23/04) [2004] ZACC 5; 2005 (4) SA 235 (CC); 2004 (10) BCLR 1009 (CC) (4 August 2004) para 244.

25 S 79(1) of the Constitution provides that '[t]he President must either assent to and sign a Bill passed in terms of this Chapter or, if the President has reservations about the constitutionality of the Bill, refer it back to the National Assembly for reconsideration'.

26 S 91(2) of the Constitution provides that '[t]he President appoints the Deputy President and Ministers, assigns their powers and functions, and may dismiss them'.

27 *S v Dodo* CCT 1/01) [2001] ZACC 16; 2001 (3) SA 382 (CC); 2001 (5) BCLR 423 (CC) (5 April 2001).

presides over the election of the President, however, he or she is not performing a judicial action, but rather a legislative action.[28]

Executive actions may also be divided into those executive actions that are administrative actions and those executive actions that are not. When the President exercises his or her power under the Constitution to appoint a commission of enquiry, for example, he or she is performing an executive action.[29] When, however, the President exercises his or her powers under the Commissions Act[30] to confer on a commission the power to summon and question witnesses, he or she is performing an administrative action.[31]

It is important to distinguish administrative actions from all other exercises of public power. This is because section 33 of the Constitution applies only to administrative actions and not to any of the other exercises of public power listed above. Unfortunately, it is not always easy to draw this distinction. This is because there is no clear line demarcating administrative actions from all other exercises of public power. The Constitutional Court, however, has identified certain criteria that must be taken into account when making this decision. The Court identified some of these criteria in its judgment in *President of the Republic of South Africa and Others v South African Rugby Football Union and Others (SARFU III)*.[32]

In this case the President appointed a commission of enquiry in terms of section 84(2)(*f*) of the Constitution to investigate the administrative and financial affairs of the South African Rugby Football Union (SARFU). SARFU then applied for an order setting aside the President's decision on the grounds that it was an administrative action and that in terms of the right to administrative justice, he had to follow a fair procedure and give SARFU a hearing before he made his decision to appoint the commission. SARFU argued that the President did not give them a hearing before he made his decision and his decision, therefore, was unconstitutional and invalid. The Constitutional Court rejected this argument.

In arriving at its decision, the Constitutional Court stated that the key issue it had to determine was whether the President's decision to appoint a commission of enquiry was, in fact, an administrative action. In this respect, the Constitutional Court began by stating that the Constitution confers a variety of functions on the executive, including the responsibility for preparing and initiating legislation, for developing policy, for implementing legislation and for implementing policy. The Court emphasised that the test for determining whether conduct constitutes administrative action must not focus on whether the action concerned is performed by a member of the executive arm of government:

> **What matters is not so much the functionary as the function. The question is whether the task itself is administrative or not. ... The focus of the enquiry as to whether conduct is 'administrative action' is not on the arm of government to which the relevant actor belongs, but on the nature of the power he or she is exercising.**[33]

Where the President and Cabinet members in the national sphere (and Premiers and Members of Executive Councils in the provincial sphere) ensure the implementation of

28 S 86(2) of the Constitution provides that '[t]he Chief Justice must preside over the election of the President or designate another judge to do so. The procedure set out in Part A of Schedule 3 applies to the election of the President'.

29 S 84(2)(*f*) of the Constitution provides that '[t]he President is responsible for appointing commissions of enquiry'. See also *President of the Republic of South Africa and Others v South African Rugby Football Union and Others (SARFU III)* (CCT16/98) [1999] ZACC 11; 2000 (1) SA 1; 1999 (10) BCLR 1059 (10 September 1999).

30 Act 8 of 1947.

31 S 1(1)(*a*) of the Commissions Act. See also *SARFU III*.

32 (CCT16/98) [1999] ZACC 11; 2000 (1) SA 1; 1999 (10) BCLR 1059 (10 September 1999).

33 *SARFU III* para 141.

legislation, they are exercising an administrative function which is justiciable. This will ordinarily constitute administrative action within the meaning of section 33. However, Cabinet members also have other constitutional responsibilities such as the responsibility for developing policy and initiating legislation. When they do so, they are not engaged in administrative action as encompassed by section 33 of the Constitution.[34] The closer the power is to the implementation of legislation, the more likely it is to be classified as administrative action. The closer the power is to the formulation of policy, the less likely it is to be classified as administrative action. As the Constitutional Court explained:

> **A series of considerations may be relevant to deciding on which side of the line a particular action falls. The source of the power, though not necessarily decisive, is a relevant factor. So too is the nature of the power, its subject matter, whether it involves the exercise of a public duty, and how closely it is related on the one hand to policy matters, which are not administrative, and on the other to the implementation of legislation, which is. While the subject matter of a power is not relevant to determine whether constitutional review is appropriate, it is relevant to determine whether the exercise of the power constitutes administrative action for the purposes of section 33. Difficult boundaries may have to be drawn in deciding what should and what should not be characterised as administrative action for the purposes of section 33. These will need to be drawn carefully in the light of the provisions of the Constitution and the overall constitutional purpose of an efficient, equitable and ethical public administration. This can best be done on a case by case basis.**[35]

Applying these principles, the Constitutional Court concluded that the appointment of a commission of enquiry was an aid to policy formulation as it enables the President to obtain advice and information. It was not the implementation of legislation but was the exercise of a constitutional power. Hence, the decision to appoint the commission of enquiry was not administrative action and was therefore not challengeable under the deemed section 33 of the Constitution.[36]

Importantly, however, the Constitutional Court went on to state that simply because the President's conduct did not constitute administrative action, this did not mean that there are no constraints on the President when he or she exercises a public power. Instead, the Court stated further, the Constitution imposes significant constraints on the President. Among these are the requirements that the President must exercise his or her powers personally, that any such exercise must be recorded in writing and signed, and that the President must act in good faith and must not misconstrue his or her powers. In addition, the President must not infringe any provision of the Bill of Rights or the principle of legality which is implicit in the rule of law.[37]

Following this judgment, the **principle of legality** has become an alternative means of challenging any exercise of public power that cannot be classified as administrative action. We have already touched on this principle and its application to the exercise of power by the President in chapter 5 of this book. To recap, in these judgments, the Constitutional Court has held that the principle of legality provides that a functionary must act within his or her

34 *SARFU III* para 142.
35 *SARFU III* para 143.
36 *SARFU III* para 147.
37 *SARFU III* para 148.

power. This is known as the **principle of authority**. In addition, any decision taken by the functionary must, from an objective perspective, be rationally related to the purpose for which the power is given. This is known as the **principle of rationality**.

15.2.4 The principle of legality

As discussed above, the principle of legality, which forms a part of the rule of law, has become an alternative means of challenging any exercise of public power that cannot be classified as administrative action. In *Democratic Alliance v eThekwini Municipality*,[38] the Supreme Court of Appeal (SCA) set out the scope and ambit of the principle of legality. In this case, the SCA held that:

> **[t]he fundamental principle, deriving from the rule of law itself, is that the exercise of all public power, be it legislative, executive or administrative, is only legitimate when lawful (see eg *Fedsure* para 56). This tenet of constitutional law which admits of no exception, has become known as the principle of legality (see eg Cora Hoexter *Administrative Law in South Africa* 117). Moreover, the principle of legality not only requires that the decision must satisfy all legal requirements, it also means that the decision should not be arbitrary or irrational (see eg *Pharmaceutical Manufacturers of South Africa and Another: In re Ex parte President of the Republic of South Africa and Others* 2000 ZACC 1 (2) SA 674 (CC) at para 85; *Affordable Medicines Trust and Others v Minister of Health and Another* 2005 ZACC 3; 2006 (3) SA 247 (CC) at paras 73–75).**[39]

It is important to distinguish between the rules applicable to the judicial review of the exercise of public power under the principle of legality and judicial review of the exercise of public power deemed to be administrative action. As the rules set out above clearly indicate, the constraints imposed on the exercise of public power by the principle of legality are not as rigorous as those imposed on administrative actions by the right to administrative justice. The most significant differences are that the right to administrative justice provides that administrative actions must be reasonable and procedurally fair, while the principle of legality simply provides that all other exercises of public power must rational. In other words, the principle of legality does not provide that all other exercises of public power have to be reasonable or procedurally fair.

There are a number of reasons why the constraints imposed on legislative, executive and judicial actions by the principle of legality are not nearly as rigorous as those imposed on administrative actions by the right to administrative justice. One of these reasons is that legislative and executive decisions are usually made by democratically elected representatives and are based on political considerations. Given their political nature, the courts are reluctant to overstep their authority by subjecting these decisions to invasive standards of review.

In *Democratic Alliance v President of South Africa and Others*, for example, the Constitutional Court held that:

> **[t[he rule that executive decisions may be set aside only if they are irrational and may not ordinarily be set aside because they are merely unreasonable or procedurally unfair has been adopted precisely to ensure that the principle of the**

38 (887/2010) [2011] ZASCA 221; 2012 (2) SA 151 (SCA); [2012] 1 All SA 412 (SCA) (30 November 2011).

39 *Democratic Alliance v eThekwini Municipality* para 21.

separation of powers is respected and given full effect. If executive decisions are too easily set aside, the danger of courts crossing the boundaries into the executive sphere would loom large. As O'Regan J helpfully explained:

> A central principle of the United States jurisprudence has been to impose different levels of scrutiny on different categories of legislative classification. The most stringent level of scrutiny is reserved for classifications based on race or nationality, or those that invade fundamental rights. Such classifications are almost inevitably considered to be a breach of the Fourteenth Amendment. An intermediate level of scrutiny is applied to classifications concerning gender or socio-economic rights. The third level of scrutiny requires merely that a classification be shown to have a rational relationship to the legislative purpose.

It is evident that a rationality standard by its very nature prescribes the lowest possible threshold for the validity of executive decisions: it has been described by this Court as the 'minimum threshold requirement applicable to the exercise of all public power by members of the Executive and other functionaries'. And the rationale for this test is 'to achieve a proper balance between the role of the legislature on the one hand, and the role of the courts on the other'.[40]

PAUSE FOR REFLECTION

Applying the principles of legality and rationality

The Constitutional Court accepted the fact that the principle of legality does not provide that the exercise of public power must follow a fair procedure in its judgment in *Masetlha v President of the Republic of South Africa and Another*.[41] In this case, the President dismissed the applicant who was the Head of the National Intelligence Agency (NIA) after it was revealed that the NIA had been unlawfully spying on a member of the ANC's National Executive Committee.

The applicant then applied for an order setting aside the President's decision. He based his application on a number of grounds, one of which was that the President's decision to dismiss him was an administrative action. In terms of the right to administrative justice, the President was obliged to follow a fair procedure and give him a hearing before making the decision to dismiss him. It was argued that as the President had not done so, his decision was unconstitutional and invalid.

The Constitutional Court rejected this argument. In arriving at this decision, a majority of the Court stated that the key issue it had to decide was whether the President's decision to dismiss the applicant was, in fact, an administrative action.

In this respect, the Constitutional Court held that the power to appoint and to dismiss the Head of the NIA arose out of the special legal relationship that existed between the President and the Head of the NIA. The Constitution conferred this special legal relationship on the President to promote the security of the nation. Given these factors, the power to dismiss the Head of the NIA could not be classified as an administrative action.[42]

---

40 (CCT 122/11) [2012] ZACC 24; 2012 (12) BCLR 1297 (CC); 2013 (1) SA 248 (CC) (5 October 2012) paras 41–2. The quote from O'Regan J is from *Brink v Kitshoff NO* (CCT15/95) [1996] ZACC 9; 1996 (4) SA 197; 1996 (6) BCLR 752 (15 May 1996) para 35.

41 (CCT 01/07) [2007] ZACC 20; 2008 (1) SA 566 (CC); 2008 (1) BCLR 1 (3 October 2007).

42 *Masetlha* para 77.

However, the Constitutional Court stated further, simply because the President's decision did not constitute administrative action, this did not mean that he could exercise his power in any way that he chose. This is because every exercise of public power, including the power to dismiss the Head of the NIA, is subject to the principle of legality.[43]

While the principle of legality imposes an obligation on the President to act in a rational way, it does not impose an obligation on the President to follow a fair procedure. This is because such a requirement would restrict the President's ability to act in an efficient and prompt manner. The only requirement the President's decision to dismiss the applicant had to comply with, therefore, was the principle of rationality.[44]

Although the Constitutional Court held in the *Masethla* case that the **principle of legality** does not impose an obligation on the President to follow a fair procedure and give the affected parties a hearing when he or she exercises a public power, it held in *Albutt v Centre for the Study of Violence and Reconciliation and Others*[45] that the **principle of rationality** may impose such an obligation on the President, at least in certain exceptional cases.

In *Albutt*, the Constitutional Court set aside a decision of the President, based on the recommendations of the Pardon Reference Group, to pardon persons who did not participate in the Truth and Reconciliation Commission (TRC) process. The objective of the TRC process was to achieve national unity and reconciliation. Given this objective, the Court held that it was irrational and unconstitutional to prevent the victims from making representations to the Pardon Reference Group and on this basis set aside the decisions to pardon.[46]

Apart from finding that the principle of rationality may impose an obligation to follow a fair procedure, at least in certain exceptional cases, in *Democratic Alliance v President of South Africa*, the Constitutional Court also held that the principle of rationality applies not only to the merits of a decision made by the President, but also to the process by which such a decision is made.[47] This is because, the Constitutional Court held further, the test for rationality asks whether the means chosen to achieve a particular purpose are rationally related to the purpose for which the power was conferred and everything that is done in the process of exercising that power forms a part of the relevant 'means'. In other words, the relevant means includes not only the decision taken to achieve the purpose, but also everything done in the process of taking that decision.[48]

In addition, the Court went on to hold, when it comes to determining whether the means (which encompass both the decision itself and the decision-making process) are rationally related to the ends, the courts may consider whether the decision-maker failed to take relevant considerations into account. If the decision-maker did fail to do so and that failure rendered the entire process irrational, then the decision itself will be irrational and thus constitutionally invalid.[49]

43 *Masetlha* para 81.

44 *Masetlha* para 77.

45 (CCT 54/09) [2010] ZACC 4; 2010 (3) SA 293 (CC); 2010 (2) SACR 101 (CC); 2010 (5) BCLR 391 (CC) (23 February 2010).

46 *Albutt* para 69.

47 *Democratic Alliance v President of South Africa* para 34.

48 *Democratic Alliance v President of South Africa* para 36.

49 *Democratic Alliance v President of South Africa* para 39.

In *Democratic Alliance v President of South Africa* the Constitutional Court set aside a decision of the President to appoint Mr Menzi Simelane as the head of the National Director of Public Prosecutions (NDPP) on the following grounds: first, that a person could be appointed as the NDPP only if he or she was 'a fit and proper person'; second, that a report issued by the Ginwala Commission of Enquiry raised serious concerns about Mr Simelane's honesty, integrity and conscientiousness; third, that the President had failed to take the concerns raised by the report into account before he appointed Mr Simelane as the NDPP; and, finally, that the President's failure to take the concerns raised by the report into account rendered the entire decision-making process irrational.

As Price points out, the judgments in *Albutt* and *Democratic Alliance v President of South Africa* appear to be in tension with the judgment in *Masethla*. One way to resolve this apparent tension, he argues, is to draw a distinction between procedural fairness and procedural rationality:

> On this approach, while procedural fairness is not a general requirement of the principle of legality (as established in *Masethla* in the context of executive functions) procedural fairness is *sometimes* required by the narrower principle of rationality, depending on the "means" and "ends" under consideration (as established in *Albutt* and confirmed in *Democratic Alliance* in the context of presidential powers). This solution is attractive because it creates a degree of flexibility: the executive and president need not always act with procedural fairness, but must do so if it would be irrational not to ... On the other hand, one wonders whether such a fine distinction - between procedural fairness and procedural rationality - can be maintained. Professor Cora Hoexter[50] is surely correct to emphasise the "tremendous scope for the further development of procedural fairness as a requirement of the principle of legality and rationality" in future.[51]

No doubt the concept of legality is an evolving one and its full impact will be incrementally felt. At present, the standard of review under legality is that of rationality whereas the more exacting standard of reasonableness can be used in terms of the PAJA when reviewing administrative action.

The current position, therefore, is that administrative action is reviewable under the PAJA while the exercise of public power that cannot be classified as administrative action can be reviewed under the principle of legality. Table 15.1 below illustrates the differences between the principle of legality and the right to just administrative action. We thus have parallel tracks to review the exercise of public power. It may be argued that it would be more effective if the definition of administrative action in the PAJA was either omitted or broadened to cover some executive action. Litigants could then rely on the PAJA for the review of decisions by members of the executive even when these decisions constitute executive action and not administrative action.

50 Hoexter, C 'The rule of law and the principle of legality in South African administrative law today' in Carnelley, M and Hoctor, S (eds) (2011) *Law, Order and Liberty: Essays in Honour of Tony Matthews* 61.

51 Price, A (2013) The evolution of the rule of law *South African Law Journal* 130:649 at 654–5.

However, this argument may be problematic. Some exercises of public powers by the executive are inherently more political than other decisions. They may also require that the members of the executive have a wider discretion when they exercise these powers. When the President wishes to fire the head of the intelligence service, for example, or when he or she wishes to appoint a commission of enquiry into a recent catastrophic event such as the shooting of a large number of citizens by the police, it would be impractical and would hinder effective government if the President was required to follow all the requirements of fair process associated with administrative action. It may take weeks or even months to comply with all the fair procedures required by the PAJA while the executive decision may require much swifter action to ensure good governance.

Table 15.1 *The differences between the principle of legality and the right to just administrative action*

The exercise of public power must be:	**The principle of legality (section 1)**	**The right to just administrative action (section 33)**	**The Promotion of Administrative Justice Act**
Lawful	Yes	Yes	Yes (section 6(2)(*a*), (*b*), (*d*), (*e*) and (*i*))
Rational	Yes	Yes	Yes (section 6(2)(*f*))
Reasonable	No	Yes	Yes (section 6(2)(*h*))
Procedurally fair	No	Yes	Yes (section 3)
Written reasons must be given	Yes	Yes	Yes (section 5)

15.2.5 The main provisions of the PAJA

15.2.5.1 What constitutes administrative action

As we have seen, a litigant would normally have to rely on the provisions of the PAJA when he or she wishes to challenge the validity of administrative actions. The PAJA is the national legislation enacted to give effect to section 33 of the Constitution. The first step in determining whether the PAJA will apply is to determine whether the exercise of power qualifies as administrative action as defined in the PAJA.

Section 1 of the PAJA defines administrative action in an overly complicated manner and the layers of qualification have presented some difficulties in interpreting this section and reconciling it with other sections in the Act. Section 1 distinguishes between administrative decisions made by an organ of state and administrative decisions made by a natural or juristic person.

In so far as organs of state are concerned, section 1 of the PAJA provides that:

> **administrative action means any decision taken, or any failure to take a decision, by an organ of state, when exercising a power in terms of the Constitution or a provincial**

> **constitution, or exercising a public power or performing a public function in terms of any legislation, which adversely affects the rights of any person and which has a direct, external legal effect, but does not include [the powers and functions listed in paragraphs *(aa)* to *(ii)* of the section].**[52]

This definition may be broken down into the following components:
- a decision taken or any failure to take a decision
- made by an organ of state
- when exercising a public power or performing a public function in terms of the Constitution, a provincial constitution or any legislation
- which adversely affects rights
- which has a direct external legal effect
- which has not been specifically excluded from the definition.

In so far as natural and juristic persons are concerned, section 1 of the PAJA provides that:

> **administrative action means any decision taken, or any failure to take a decision, by a natural or juristic person, other than an organ of state, when exercising a public power or performing a public function in terms of an empowering provision, which adversely affects the rights of any person and which has a direct, external legal effect, but does not include [the powers and functions listed in paragraphs *(aa)* to *(ii)* of the section].**

This definition may be broken down into the following components:
- a decision taken or any failure to take a decision
- made by a natural or juristic person
- when exercising a public power or performing a public function in terms of an empowering provision
- which adversely affects rights
- which has a direct external legal effect
- which has not been specifically excluded from the definition.

Thus, it is not the description of the decision maker but the nature of the decision that is the critical starting point in determining whether the decision constitutes administrative action

52 The powers and functions referred to in paras (*aa*) to (*ii*) are as follows:

(*aa*) **the executive powers or functions of the National Executive, including the powers or functions referred to in section 79(1) and (4), 84(2)(*a*), (*b*), (*c*), (*d*), (*f*), (*g*), (*h*), (*i*) and (*k*), 85(2)(*b*), (*c*), (*d*) and (*e*), 91(2), (3), (4) and (5), 92(3), 93, 97, 98, 99 and 100 of the Constitution;**

(*bb*) **the executive powers or functions of the Provincial Executive, including the powers or functions referred to in section 121(1) and (2), 125(2)(*d*), (*e*) and (*f*), 126, 127(2), 132(2), 133(3)(*b*), 137, 138, 139 and 145(1) of the Constitution;**

(*cc*) **the executive powers or functions of a municipal council;**

(*dd*) **the legislative functions of Parliament, a provincial legislature or a municipal council;**

(*ee*) **the judicial functions of a judicial officer of a court referred to in section 166 of the Constitution or of a Special Tribunal established under section 2 of the Special Investigating Units and Special Tribunals Act, 1996 (Act No. 74 of 1996), and the judicial functions of a traditional leader under customary law or any other law;**

(*ff*) **a decision to institute or continue a prosecution;**

(*gg*) **a decision relating to any aspect regarding the nomination, selection, or appointment of a judicial officer or any other person, by the Judicial Service Commission in terms of any law;**

(*hh*) **any decision taken, or failure to take a decision, in terms of any provision of the Promotion of Access to Information Act, 2000; or**

(*ii*) **any decision taken, or failure to take a decision, in terms of section 4(1).**

under the PAJA and can thus be reviewed.[53] A decision made by a juristic person is as susceptible to a challenge under the PAJA as a decision of an organ of state. The issue is whether the decision is of an administrative nature and involves the exercise of a public power or the performance of a public function. A decision by a private institution not exercising a public power or performing a public function in terms of 'an empowering provision' would not constitute administrative action.

However, the notion of an 'empowering provision' is broadly defined in the PAJA to mean a 'law, a rule of common law, customary law, or an agreement, instrument or other document in terms of which administrative action was purportedly taken'.[54] This is a broad definition and means that the PAJA potentially allows the review of many different kinds of decisions taken by private institutions. For example, if a municipality invites an accounting and auditing company to run the process of inviting and awarding tenders for the supply of services to it, the decision to award the tender is an exercise of public power and will be administrative action even though the decision was taken by a private company and not by an organ of state.[55]

The Constitution defines an organ of state as any department of state or administration in the national, provincial or local sphere of governance.[56] This refers to all the various departments of government such as the department of housing, education and social development. The definition goes further and includes any other functionary or institution exercising a power or performing a function in terms of the Constitution, a provincial constitution or those exercising a public power or performing a public function in term of legislation.

Thus, it is likely that a body such as the South African Human Rights Commission, which exercises power in terms of the Constitution, will be regarded as an organ of state. In *Independent Electoral Commission v Langeberg Municipality*, the Constitutional Court held that the Independent Electoral Commission was exercising a public power or performing a public function in terms of the Constitution and was hence an organ of state.[57] However, it was not part of government and was therefore not obliged to follow the provisions regarding

53 The concept of a decision is defined in s 1 of the PAJA as follows:

'decision' means any decision of an administrative nature made, proposed to be made made, or required to be made, as the case may be, under an empowering provision, including a decision relating to:

(*a*) **making, suspending, revoking or refusing to make an order, award or determination;**
(*b*) **giving, suspending, revoking or refusing to give a certificate, direction, approval, consent or permission;**
(*c*) **issuing, suspending, revoking or refusing to issue a licence, authority or other instrument;**
(*d*) **imposing a condition or restriction;**
(*e*) **making a declaration, demand or requirement;**
(*f*) **retaining, or refusing to deliver up, an article; or**
(*g*) **doing or refusing to do any other act or thing of an administrative nature, and a reference to a failure to take a decision must be construed accordingly.**

54 S 1.

55 *AAA Investments (Proprietary) Limited v Micro Finance Regulatory Council and Another* (CCT51/05) [2006] ZACC 9; 2006 (11) BCLR 1255 (CC); 2007 (1) SA 343 (CC) (28 July 2006) para 40.

56 S 239 of the Constitution states:

(2) **'organ of state' means –**
  (*a*) **any department of state or administration in the national, provincial or local sphere of government; or**
  (*b*) **any other functionary or institution –**
    (i) **exercising a power or performing a function in terms of the Constitution or a provincial constitution; or**
    (ii) **exercising a public power or performing a public function in terms of any legislation,**
  but does not include a court or a judicial officer.

57 (CCT 49/00) [2001] ZACC 23; 2001 (3) SA 925 (CC); 2001 (9) BCLR 883 (CC) (7 June 2001) para 22.

co-operative governance which are binding on government and intergovernmental bodies.[58] In addition, a whole plethora of regulatory bodies such as the Law Society and the Health Professionals Council will be deemed organs of state as they exercise public power or perform public functions in terms of legislation.

The definition of administrative action in section 1 of the PAJA gives rise to a number of difficult questions. One of the most controversial of these is what is meant by the requirement that administrative action must have a 'direct external legal effect'. Another is what is meant by materially and adversely affects rights. The Constitutional Court discussed these issues in its judgment in *Joseph and Others v City of Johannesburg and Others*.[59] In this case, the Court laid down three important principles:

- First, the phrase, 'direct external legal effect', in section 1 of the PAJA does not play a particularly important role. This is because a finding that a right has been materially and adversely affected means that there has been a direct, external affect.[60]
- Second, the phrase, 'materially and adversely affected', in section 3 of the PAJA does not mean that the right in question has to be breached or infringed. Instead, it simply means that the right has to be affected in a significant way.[61]
- Third, the term, 'right', in section 3 of the PAJA does not refer only to common law rights, but also to constitutional and statutory rights.[62]

In this case the applicants rented apartments in a building which was owned by a certain Mr Nel and which was supplied with electricity by the City of Johannesburg. As a part of their lease agreements, each applicant paid the amount he or she owed for electricity to Mr Nel. Unfortunately, Mr Nel failed to pay this money over to the City and the City terminated the supply of electricity to the building without first notifying the applicants.

After the City had disconnected the supply of electricity to the building, the applicants applied for an order setting aside the City's decision. The applicants based their application on the following grounds:

- The City's decision was an administrative action.
- This administrative action materially and adversely affected their rights.
- In terms of section 3 of the PAJA, the City should have followed a fair procedure and given them notice before it terminated the supply of electricity even though there was no contract and therefore no contractual rights between the applicants and the City.

Section 3 of the PAJA states that '[a]dministrative action which materially and adversely affects the rights or legitimate expectations of any person must be procedurally fair'. The key questions the Constitutional Court had to answer, therefore, were as follows:

- First, was the City's decision to terminate the supply of electricity an administrative action?
- Second, if the decision was an administrative action, did the City's decision materially and adversely affect any of the applicants' rights?

58 *Langeberg Municipality* para 27.

59 (CCT 43/09) [2009] ZACC 30; 2010 (3) BCLR 212 (CC); 2010 (4) SA 55 (CC) (9 October 2009).

60 *Joseph* para 26. See also the SCA judgment in *Grey's Marine Hout Bay (Pty) Ltd and Others v Minister of Public Works and Others* [2005] ZASCA 43; 2005 (6) SA 313 (SCA) para 23.

61 *Joseph* para 31.

62 *Joseph* para 42. See also *Premier, Province of Mpumalanga and Another v Executive Committee of the Association of Governing Bodies of State Aided Schools: Eastern Transvaal* (CCT10/98) [1998] ZACC 20; 1999 (2) SA 91; 1999 (2) BCLR 151 (2 December 1998) para 41.

- Third, if the decision did materially and adversely affect any of the applicants' rights, was the City required to give the applicants notice before it terminated the supply?

In so far as the first issue was concerned, the Constitutional Court began its analysis by stating that the City had argued that its decision could not be classified as an administrative action because it did not have a 'direct, external effect'. To determine whether the City's decision was an administrative action, therefore, the Court had to determine what is meant by the phrase, 'direct, external effect'. This phrase, according to the Constitutional Court, must be interpreted broadly and 'serves to emphasise that administrative action impacts directly and immediately on individuals'.[63] This means that:

> **a finding that the rights of the applicants were materially and adversely affected for the purposes of section 3 of PAJA would necessarily imply that the decision had a 'direct, external legal effect' on the applicants. Conversely, a finding that the rights of the applicants were not materially and adversely affected would have the result that section 3 of PAJA would not apply.**[64]

After finding that the City's decision would have a direct, external effect if it materially and adversely affected any of the applicants' rights, the Constitutional Court turned to consider the second issue, namely whether the City's decision did, in fact, materially and adversely affect any of the applicants' rights.

In so far as the second issue was concerned, the Constitutional Court began by stating that the City had argued that while its decision may have materially and adversely affected Mr Nel's rights, it did not materially and adversely affect any of the applicants' rights because there was no contract between the City and the applicants. To determine whether the City's decision materially and adversely affected the applicants' rights, therefore, the Court had to determine whether the applicants had any rights they could enforce against the City.

The Constitutional Court stated that it was true that the applicants did not have any contractual rights which they could enforce against the City. However, a careful examination of the Constitution and the Local Government: Municipal Systems Act[65] showed that every municipality was obliged to provide basic services to their inhabitants irrespective of whether or not they had a contractual relationship with the relevant service provider. In addition, one of the most important basic services every municipality was obliged to provide was electricity.[66]

The key question that then arose, the Constitutional Court stated further, was whether the constitutional and statutory right to receive electricity as a basic municipal service was the kind of right referred to in section 3 of the PAJA. Adopting a purposive approach, the Constitutional Court held that it was. This is because the rights referred to in section 3 of the PAJA 'include not only vested, private law rights but also legal entitlements that have their basis in the constitutional and statutory obligations of government':

> **In my view, proper regard to the import of the right to administrative justice in our constitutional democracy confirms the need for an interpretation of rights under section 3(1) of PAJA that makes clear that the notion of 'rights' includes not only vested, private law rights but also legal entitlements that have their basis in the**

63 *Joseph* para 26.
64 *Joseph* para 26.
65 Act 32 of 2000.
66 *Joseph* paras 33–9.

> **constitutional and statutory obligations of government. The Preamble of PAJA gives expression to the role of administrative justice and provides that the objectives of PAJA are, inter alia, to 'promote an efficient administration and good governance' and to 'create a culture of accountability, openness and transparency in the public administration or in the exercise of public power or the performance of a public function'. These objectives give expression to the founding values in section 1 of the Constitution, namely that South Africa is founded on the rule of law and on principles of democratic government to ensure accountability, responsiveness and openness.**[67]

After setting out these principles, the Constitutional Court turned to apply them to the facts. In this respect, the Court found that the applicants had a constitutional and statutory right to receive electricity as a basic municipal service from the City. This constitutional and statutory right was the sort of right referred to in section 3 of the PAJA. When the City terminated the supply of electricity to the building, this action materially and adversely affected the constitutional and statutory right of the applicants living in it. Therefore, the City should have followed a fair procedure.[68]

In arriving at this decision, the Constitutional Court also stated that the phrase, 'materially and adversely affects' a right in section 3(1) of the PAJA, does not mean that a fair procedure has to be followed only when a right is breached by the administrative action in question. Instead, it means that a fair procedure must be followed whenever a right is affected in a significant and not a trivial way by the administrative action in question.[69]

Having found that the City should have followed a fair procedure before it terminated the supply of electricity, the Constitutional Court turned to consider the third issue, namely whether the City was required to give the applicants notice before it terminated the supply of electricity to their building. In so far as this issue was concerned, the Constitutional Court began by stating that the applicants had argued that in terms of section 3(2) of the PAJA, the City was required to provide them with adequate notice before it terminated the supply of electricity. In addition, they had argued further, this requirement could be satisfied simply by posting a written notice in a prominent place in the building they occupied and that such a notice would not place an undue burden on the City.[70]

The Constitutional Court accepted this argument and held that the City had to provide the applicants with a pre-termination notice. This notice had to contain all relevant information including the date and time of the proposed termination and the place where the affected parties could challenge the termination. Approximately 14 days' pre-termination notice would be adequate and appropriate.[71]

Given that the City had failed to do so, the Constitutional Court concluded that the termination of the electricity supply was unlawful and ordered the City to reconnect the electricity supply to the building the applicants occupied. The provisions of the PAJA were therefore successfully invoked to have a decision by the City Council set aside that would have had serious effects on the economic and social well-being of the inhabitants of the building.

---

67 *Joseph* para 42.
68 *Joseph* para 46.
69 *Joseph* para 30.
70 *Joseph* para 59.
71 *Joseph* para 60.

PAUSE FOR REFLECTION

Using other rights apart from social and economic rights to advance the interests of the marginalised and vulnerable

In the last chapter of this book, we will discuss the Court's role in the realisation of social and economic rights in more detail. However, what the *Joseph* judgment illustrates is that other rights apart from social and economic rights - including the right to fair administrative action guaranteed in section 33 and given effect to by the PAJA - can be used to advance the social and economic interests of the marginalised and vulnerable in society.

15.2.5.2 The key obligations imposed by the PAJA

15.2.5.2.1 Introduction

After an applicant has managed to show that the exercise of public power in question falls into the definition of an administrative action, he or she is entitled to claim the administrative rights set out in the PAJA. Among the most important of these administrative rights are the following:

- the right to lawful administrative action
- the right to reasonable administrative action
- the right to procedural fairness
- the right to be given reasons for an administrative decision.

In so far as these rights are concerned, however, it is important to note that section 2 of the PAJA provides that the Minister of Justice may, by notice in the *Government Gazette*, if it is reasonable and justifiable in the circumstances, exempt an administrative action or a group or class of administrative actions from either of the first two rights. Parliament must approve such an exemption before it is published in the *Gazette*.

The Minister's power to exempt administrative actions from the first two rights is therefore subject to two constraints:

- First, the exemption must be reasonable and justifiable.
- Second, Parliament must approve the exemption.

15.2.5.2.2 Lawful administrative action

a) Introduction

Lawfulness lies at the very heart of just administrative action and provides that an administrator - somebody who exercises public power that amounts to administrative action - must act in terms of and in accordance with the terms of an empowering statute. The right to lawful administrative justice, therefore, prohibits administrators from taking decisions that are not authorised by law or from ignoring any statutory requirements that are attached to the exercise of the power in question. An administrator who fails to comply with these requirements, therefore, is said to be acting ***ultra vires***.[72]

The right to lawful administrative action, however, goes beyond simply providing that an administrator must act in terms of and in accordance with the terms of an empowering statute and includes a number of other grounds of review. Where an administrator acts, for example, in bad faith, for an ulterior purpose, takes into account irrelevant considerations

72 Hoexter, C (2007) *Administrative Law* 224.

or fails to take into account relevant considerations, or makes an error of law, he or she acts beyond his or her powers.[73]

These different grounds of review may be divided into three categories:

- the requirement of authority, which provides that administrators may only exercise the powers that have been conferred on them by the law and may not unlawfully delegate them
- the concept of jurisdiction, which provides that administrators must remain within the procedural and substantive bounds of their power and may not misconstrue them
- the umbrella ground of abuse of discretion.[74]

Many, if not most, of the different grounds of review that fall under each of these categories have been included in section 6(2) of the PAJA. Section 6(2) provides as follows:

> **(2) A court or tribunal has the power to judicially review an administrative action if:**
> **(*a*) the administrator who took it:**
> **(i) was not authorised to do so by the empowering provision;**
> **(ii) acted under a delegation of power which was not authorised by the empowering provision; or**
> **(iii) was biased or reasonably suspected of bias;**
> **(*b*) a mandatory and material procedure or condition prescribed by an empowering provision was not complied with;**
> **(*c*) the action was procedurally unfair;**
> **(*d*) the action was materially influenced by an error of law;**
> **(*e*) the action was taken:**
> **(i) for a reason not authorised by the empowering provision;**
> **(ii) for an ulterior purpose or motive;**
> **(iii) because irrelevant considerations were taken into account or relevant considerations were not considered;**
> **(iv) because of the unauthorised or unwarranted dictates of another person or body;**
> **(v) in bad faith; or**
> **(vi) arbitrarily or capriciously;**
> **(*f*) the action itself:**
> **(i) contravenes a law or is not authorised by the empowering provision; or**
> **(ii) is not rationally connected to:**
> **(*aa*) the purpose for which it was taken;**
> **(*bb*) the purpose of the empowering provision;**
> **(*cc*) the information before the administrator; or**
> **(*dd*) the reasons given for it by the administrator;**
> **(*g*) the action concerned consists of a failure to take a decision;**
> **(*h*) the exercise of the power or the performance of the function authorised by the empowering provision, in pursuance of which the administrative action was purportedly taken, is so unreasonable that no reasonable person could have so exercised the power or performed the function; or**
> **(*i*) the action is otherwise unconstitutional or unlawful.**

73 Klaaren, J and Penflod, G 'Just administrative action' in Woolman, S and Bishop, M (eds) (2013) *Constitutional Law of South Africa* 2nd ed rev service 5 63.77.

74 Klaaren and Penflod (2013) 63.77.

b) The requirement of authority

As mentioned above, the requirement of authority provides that administrators may only exercise the powers that have been conferred on them by the law and may not unlawfully delegate them. This requirement is given expression in section 6(2)(*a*) of the PAJA which focuses on the administrator who took the decision. The requirement states that a decision may be reviewed and set aside if the person exercising the power lacked the authority to do so, or had power delegated to him or her in an unauthorised manner, or was biased or was reasonably suspected of being biased.

In *SARFU III*, the Constitutional Court pointed out that the circumstances in which a functionary has unlawfully abdicated the power vested in him or her may be divided into three categories:

- first, where the functionary unlawfully delegates the power to someone else
- second, where the functionary acts on the instructions of someone else
- third, where the functionary refers the decision to someone else.[75]

In *SARFU III*, the Constitutional Court explained the three categories of abdication as occurring:

> **where a functionary in whom the power has been vested delegates that power to someone else. Whether such delegation is valid depends upon whether the recipient of the power is lawfully entitled to delegate that power to someone else. There can be no doubt that when the Constitution vests power to appoint commissions of inquiry in the President, the President may not delegate that authority to a third party. The President himself must exercise that power. Any delegation to a third party would be invalid. The second category referred to by Baxter deals with cases when a functionary vested with a power does not of his or her own accord decide to exercise the power, but does so on the instructions of another. The third category, passing the buck, contemplates a situation in which a functionary may refer the decision to someone else.**[76]

If there is an unlawful abdication of power, the decision will be set aside on review. However, note that section 238(*a*) of the Constitution contemplates the inevitability that powers will be delegated as a necessity for the 'daily practice of governance', stating that:

> **An executive organ of state in any sphere of government may –**
>
> > **delegate any power or function that is to be exercised or performed in terms of legislation to any other executive organ of state, provided the delegation is consistent with the legislation in terms of which the power is exercised or the function is performed.**

In each case a court will have to determine whether a delegation is lawful or unlawful. In the case of *AAA Investments (Proprietary) Limited v Micro Finance Regulatory Council and Another*, the Constitutional Court set out some criteria to determine whether a delegation is acceptable, stating that:

> **Criteria relevant to determining whether a delegation of a delegated power is acceptable include the following: the character of the original delegation; the extent**

75 *SARFU III* para 40.

76 *SARFU III* para 40.

of the delegation of the delegated power; the extent to which the original delegee continues to review the exercise of the delegated power; considerations of practicality and effectiveness; and the identity of the institutions or persons by whom and to whom power is delegated.[77]

The exercise of an administrative power in terms of delegated authority will only be impermissible and unlawful if that delegation does not comply with the criteria set out above.

PAUSE FOR REFLECTION

Determining whether an administrator has unlawfully abdicated his or her power to make a decision

It will not always be easy to determine whether an administrator has unlawfully abdicated his or her power to make a decision. In a modern state, an administrator may rely on other functionaries to assist him or her to make a sound decision. When the decision of an administrator, who is authorised to make a decision, is informed by the advice of others, this will not necessarily be unlawful. In complex matters of a technical nature the administrator may not necessarily have the requisite expertise to make a proper decision. In such cases, it will not necessarily be unlawful for that administrator to take advice from others.

The situation will be different where the authorised administrator fails to exercise his or her discretion at all and, instead, rubberstamps the decision of somebody who is not authorised to make the decision at all. For example, say a departmental official is authorised to make a decision on whether or not to grant a fishing licence. The decision is based, *inter alia*, on a technical assessment of whether the granting of such a licence would threaten the sustainability of fishing in a particular area. If that departmental official is not a marine biologist with expertise about the effects of fishing in an area on the fish stock in that area, there would arguably be nothing wrong with that official consulting a marine biologist for advice. However, the situation will be different when, say, that official grants a fishing licence to someone after having been instructed to do so by a politician who is not authorised to make a decision on the granting of fishing licences.

Apart from the points set out above, the requirement of authority also provides that the administrator must comply with any statutory requirements or preconditions attached to the exercise of the power in question. It is not surprising, therefore, that section 6(2)(*b*) of the PAJA allows for administrative action to be reviewed and set aside if there is no compliance with a mandatory or material procedure or condition.

c) The concept of jurisdiction

An administrator is required to remain within the substantive and procedural bounds of his or her powers and may not misconstrue these. If he or she fails to do so, the decision could be reviewed on the basis that he or she lacks jurisdiction to exercise that power. The concept of jurisdiction may be divided into two separate elements, namely a material mistake of law - where the legal provision on which the decision is based is wrongly

77 (CCT51/05) [2006] ZACC 9; 2006 (11) BCLR 1255 (CC); 2007 (1) SA 343 (CC) (28 July 2006) para 127.

interpreted – and, more controversially, a material mistake of fact. A **material mistake of law** occurs when an administrator misinterprets the law. As a result of this misinterpretation, the administrator misunderstands the nature of his or her power and, therefore, exercises it improperly.[78]

This ground of review is referred to in section 6(2)(*d*) of the PAJA which simply states that a court may review an administrative action if the action was materially influenced by an error of law. In so far as this provision is concerned, it is important to note that it is only decisions based on material errors of law that will be set aside. Materiality has been defined as follows:

> **If, for instance, the facts found by the tribunal are such as to justify its decision even on a correct interpretation of the statutory criterion, then normally (ie: in the absence of some other review ground) there would be no ground for interference.**[79]

Thus, if the same conclusion would have been reached had the decision maker not erred, the decision will not be set aside as the error is not material.

A **material mistake of fact** occurs when an administrator fails to follow a prescribed procedure or makes a decision in breach of a substantive condition the administrator was required to fulfil before making the decision. A material mistake of fact can enable an administrator to inflate his or her jurisdiction by accumulating powers beyond those that the empowering legislation confers on him or her. Although this ground is not explicitly referred to in the PAJA, it is recognised as a ground for judicial review.[80]

d) Abuse of discretion

This ground – which tends to overlap with the requirement of reasonableness – is dealt with in some detail in the PAJA. Section 6(2)(*e*) thus provides that administrative action may be reviewed on the grounds that it was taken:

- for a reason not authorised by the empowering provision
- for an ulterior purpose
- because irrelevant considerations were taken into account and relevant considerations were not
- because of the unauthorised or unwarranted dictates of another person or body
- in bad faith or arbitrarily or capriciously.

When a power is granted for one purpose, it cannot be exercised for any ulterior purpose or objective. As the Constitutional Court held in the *Pharmaceutical Manufacturers* case:

> **Powers are not conferred in the abstract. They are intended to serve a particular purpose. That purpose can be discerned from the legislation that is the source of the power and this ordinarily places limits upon the manner in which it is exercised. If those limits are transgressed a court is entitled to intervene and set aside the decision.**[81]

An example of a power being exercised for a purpose for which it was not granted can be found in the pre-constitutional judgment of *Van Eck NO and Van Rensburg NO v Etna*

78 See Kohn and Corder (2013).

79 *Hira and Another v Booysens and Another* 1992 (4) SA 69 (A) 70E.

80 See *Pepcor Retirement Fund v Financial Services Board* 2003 (6) SA 38 (SCA) as well as, generally, Kohn and Corder (2013).

81 *Pharmaceutical Manufacturers* para 76.

Stores.[82] This case dealt with wartime regulations permitting the administrator to seize food in order to obtain evidence of suspected violations of the regulations. The administrator acting in terms of these regulations seized bags of rice as part of a food distribution scheme and not to obtain evidence of contravention of the regulations. As the administrator had acted for an improper purpose, the decision was set aside.

15.2.5.2.3 Reasonable administrative action

The notion that an administrative decision can be reviewed and set aside on the basis that the decision was not reasonable, remains a contentious one in our law.[83] This is so because administrative review is not normally seen as focusing on the correctness or wisdom of an administrative decision. Given the constraints placed on courts by the separation of powers doctrine, it is generally thought that it would not normally be appropriate for a court to review and set aside an administrative decision merely because the court believes the decision was not the best possible decision to be made in the circumstances. Administrative decisions deal with the review of decisions, not with the appeal of such decisions on the merits of the decision. Reasonableness review is controversial because it draws the courts into the awkward space between review and appeal by necessitating an assessment of the merits of an administrative decision. This is something that is usually associated with the appeal of a decision, not with its review in terms of administrative law grounds.[84]

Nevertheless, reasonableness review does form part of South African law. In the pre-constitutional era, the Appellate Division in *Johannesburg Stock Exchange and Another v Witwatersrand Nigel Ltd and Another* held that in terms of the common law, an administrative decision could be reviewed and set aside if 'the decision ... was so grossly unreasonable as to warrant the inference that he had failed to apply his mind to the matter in the manner aforestated'.[85] However, the pre-constitutional jurisprudence failed to establish reasonableness as a free-standing ground of review.[86] Unreasonableness was only considered to be a ground of review to the extent that it could be shown that a decision was so unreasonable as to lead to a conclusion that the official had failed to apply his or her mind to the decision.[87]

Section 33(1) of the Constitution now states that everyone has the right to administrative action, *inter alia*, that is 'lawful, reasonable and procedurally fair'. The reasonableness aspect is purportedly given effect to by section 6(2)(*h*) of the PAJA which states that the court can review an administrative action if:

> **the exercise of the power or the performance of the function authorised by the empowering provision, in pursuance of which the administrative action was purportedly taken, is so unreasonable that no reasonable person could have so exercised the power or performed the function.**

---

82 1947 (2) SA 984 (A).

83 Hoexter (2007) 293.

84 See Kohn and Corder (2013) 8. See also Hoexter, C (2004) The principle of legality in South African administrative law *Macquarie Law Journal* 3(4):165–86 at 172.

85 1988 (3) SA 132 (A) 152A–D.

86 *Union Government (Minister of Mines and Industries) v Union Steel Corporation (South Africa) Ltd* 1928 AD 220 at 236; *National Transport Commission and Another v Chetty's Motor Transport (Pty) Ltd* 1972 (3) SA 726 (A) 735; *The Administrator, Transvaal and The Firs Investments (Pty) Ltd v Johannesburg City Council* 1971 (1) SA 56 (A) 79–80; *Johannesburg City Council v The Administrator, Transvaal and Mayofis* 1971 (1) SA 87 (A) 96A–D. See, however, the minority judgment of Jansen JA in *Theron en Andere v Ring van Wellington van die NG Sendingkerk in Suid-Afrika en Andere* 1976 (2) SA 1 (A) 14–21.

87 *Bato Star Fishing* para 43.

This seems like a rather clumsy formulation. However, in *Bato Star Fishing (Pty) Ltd v Minister of Environmental Affairs and Tourism and Others*[88] the Constitutional Court interpreted this provision in the light of section 33 of the Constitution. The Court said that even if it may be thought that the language of section 6(2)(*h*) of the PAJA, if taken literally, might set a standard which would rarely if ever lead to a finding that a decision was unreasonable, 'that is not the proper constitutional meaning' of the subsection. Instead, section 6(2)(*h*) should be 'understood to require a simple test, namely, that an administrative decision will be reviewable if ... it is one that a reasonable decision-maker could not reach'.[89]

> **What will constitute a reasonable decision will depend on the circumstances of each case, much as what will constitute a fair procedure will depend on the circumstances of each case. Factors relevant to determining whether a decision is reasonable or not will include the nature of the decision, the identity and expertise of the decision-maker, the range of factors relevant to the decision, the reasons given for the decision, the nature of the competing interests involved and the impact of the decision on the lives and well-being of those affected. Although the review functions of the court now have a substantive as well as a procedural ingredient, the distinction between appeals and reviews continues to be significant. The court should take care not to usurp the functions of administrative agencies. Its task is to ensure that the decisions taken by administrative agencies fall within the bounds of reasonableness as required by the Constitution.**[90]

PAUSE FOR REFLECTION

A substantive element in the administrative review process

As the Constitutional Court admitted in *Bato Star Fishing*, the fact that an administrative decision can be reviewed and set aside on the basis of reasonableness infuses a substantive element into the administrative review process. However, it is important to note that this does not mean that the Court can set aside an administrative decision because it believes that the decision is unwise or wrong. Administrative review must not be confused with an appeal that attacks the merits of a decision on the basis that it infringes one of the other rights in the Constitution.

The distinction between these two types of review can be explained with the help of an example. When an administrative body decides to refuse to grant permission to an organisation to hold a protest march, this decision can be attacked on substantive grounds by invoking the right to freedom of assembly guaranteed by section 17 of the Bill of Rights. This appeal of the decision will not be based on administrative law. However, in principle, the administrative decision itself could also be reviewed in terms of section 6(2)(*h*) of the PAJA on the basis that the decision was unreasonable because no reasonable decision maker could have made the decision.

---

88 (CCT 27/03) [2004] ZACC 15; 2004 (4) SA 490 (CC); 2004 (7) BCLR 687 (CC) (12 March 2004).

89 *Bato Star Fishing* para 44.

90 *Bato Star Fishing* para 45.

15.2.5.2.4 Procedurally fair administrative action

a) Introduction

The requirement that an administrative decision must be procedurally fair places context at the heart of the enquiry. This means that a determination on whether the administrative decision was procedurally fair will depend on the facts of the individual case. A court must therefore interpret and apply the relevant provisions of the PAJA with reference to the factual matrix within which the administrative decision was made. The right to procedural fairness in administrative decisions is set out in section 3 of the PAJA.[91] Section 3 provides as follows:

> **(1) Administrative action which materially and adversely affects the rights or legitimate expectations of any person must be procedurally fair.**
>
> **(2) (*a*) A fair administrative procedure depends on the circumstances of each case.**
>
> **(*b*) In order to give effect to the right to procedurally fair administrative action, an administrator, subject to subsection (4), must give a person referred to in subsection (1):**
>
> **(i) adequate notice of the nature and purpose of the proposed administrative action;**
>
> **(ii) a reasonable opportunity to make representations;**
>
> **(iii) a clear statement of the administrative action;**
>
> **(iv) adequate notice of any right of review or internal appeal, where applicable; and**
>
> **(v) adequate notice of the right to request reasons in terms of section 5.**
>
> **(3) In order to give effect to the right to procedurally fair administrative action, an administrator may, in his or her or its discretion, also give a person referred to in subsection (1) an opportunity to:**
>
> **(*a*) obtain assistance and, in serious or complex cases, legal representation;**
>
> **(*b*) present and dispute information and arguments; and**
>
> **(*c*) appear in person.**
>
> **(4) (*a*) If it is reasonable and justifiable in the circumstances, an administrator may depart from any of the requirements referred to in subsection (2).**
>
> **(*b*) In determining whether a departure as contemplated in paragraph (*a*) is reasonable and justifiable, an administrator must take into account all relevant factors, including:**
>
> **(i) the objects of the empowering provision;**
>
> **(ii) the nature and purpose of, and the need to take, the administrative action;**
>
> **(iii) the likely effect of the administrative action;**
>
> **(iv) the urgency of taking the administrative action or the urgency of the matter; and**
>
> **(v) the need to promote an efficient administration and good governance.**
>
> **(5) Where an administrator is empowered by an empowering provision to follow a procedure which is fair but different from the provisions of subsection (2), the administrator must act in accordance with that different procedure.**

91 For a discussion on procedural fairness that precedes the adoption of the PAJA, see the Constitutional Court judgments in *Bel Porto School Governing Body and Others v Premier of the Western Cape Province and Another* (CCT58/00) [2002] ZACC 2; 2002 (3) SA 265; 2002 (9) BCLR 891 (21 February 2002); *Premier, Mpumalanga.*

Unfortunately, the formulation of section 3 is not a model of clarity. It is necessary to understand the complex interplay of its various subsections to determine its scope and meaning. It is also necessary to reconcile the section with the definition of administrative action set out in section 1 of the Act.[92] As the provisions set out above indicate, section 3 is divided into five subsections. Subsection 3(1) lists the requirements that must be met before the right to procedural fairness can be asserted. Subsection 3(2) reaffirms the flexibility of the concept and identifies five requirements as being core features of procedural fairness. Subsection 3(3) recognises that in certain circumstances a trial-type hearing may be required for the process to be procedurally fair. Subsection 3(4) allows the administrator to depart from the requirement of subsection 3(2) if it is reasonable and justifiable to do so and lists the factors that need to be considered. Finally, subsection 3(5) is an enabling section which allows an administrator to follow an alternative procedure provided it is fair. Before turning to consider these subsections, however, it will be helpful to discuss briefly what is meant by the concept of procedural fairness.

b) The concept of procedural fairness

The concept of procedural fairness is inherently flexible and its content depends on the circumstances to which it is applied. Fairness of process – which we discuss here – must be distinguished from the correctness of the outcome. When we talk of procedural fairness we are not, in the first instance, focusing on the outcome, but rather on the quality of the process which led to the outcome. As De Smith, Woolf and Jowell point out, the concept 'ranges from mere consultation at the lower level, upward through an entitlement to make written representation, to make oral representations, to a fully-fledged hearing at the other extreme with most of the characteristics of a judicial trial'.[93]

What is required in any particular case is incapable of definition in abstract terms. As Lord Bridge put it:

> **the so called rules of natural justice are not engraved on tablets of stone. To use the phrase which better expresses the underlying concept, what the requirement of fairness demands when anybody, domestic, administrative or judicial, has to make a decision which will affect the rights of individuals depends on the character of the decision-making body, the kind of decision it has to make and the statutory or other framework in which it operates.**[94]

Because of the flexibility of the concept, the administrator has to make a determination of what is procedurally fair in the specific circumstances. It is not necessary in every case to afford a person a trial-type hearing before making a decision that affects that person. In some instances, consultation or the opportunity to make written representations will suffice. In *Doody v Secretary of State for the Home Department and other Appeals*,[95] the House of Lords accurately captured the legal principles regarding procedural fairness.[96] These principles are as follows:

- Where an Act of Parliament confers an administrative power, there is a presumption that it will be exercised in a manner which is fair in all circumstances.
- The standards of fairness are not immutable. They may change with the passage of time, both in general and in their application to decisions of a particular type.

92 See Currie and De Waal (2013) 675.

93 De Smith, SA, Woolf, H and Jowell, JL (1995) *Judicial Review of Administrative Action* 431.

94 *Lloyd v Mcmahon* [1987] AC 625 at 702.

95 [1993] 3 All Er 92 (HL) at 106.

96 These comments have been quoted with approval by our courts in *Du Preez and Another v Truth and Reconciliation Commission* 1997 (3) SA 204 (A) and *Chairman: Board of Tariffs and Trade and Others v Brenco Incorporated* (285/99) [2001] ZASCA 67 (25 May 2001).

- The principles of fairness are not applied by rote and are not identical in every situation. What fairness demands is dependent on the context of the decision and this is to be taken into account in all its aspects.
- An essential feature of the context is the statute which creates the discretion as regards both its language and the shape of the legal and administrative system within which the decision is taken.
- Fairness often requires that a person who may be adversely affected by the decision has an opportunity to make representations on his or her own behalf either before the decision is taken with a view to producing a favourable result or after it is taken with a view to procuring its modification, or both.
- Since the person affected usually cannot make worthwhile representations without knowing what factors may weigh against his or her interests, fairness often requires that the person is informed of the gist of the case which he or she has to answer.

One of the major concerns about having multiple processes is that it may impede effective and expeditious decision making. If a regulator has to afford three sets of hearings to parties at various stages in the decision-making process, the taking of the ultimate decision will be delayed. This delay may adversely affect the implementation of policy and cause frustration.

PAUSE FOR REFLECTION

The tension between strict enforcement of fair procedures and the efficient running of the country

O'Regan J highlighted the flexible nature of the concept of procedural fairness in her judgment in *Premier, Province of Mpumalanga and Another v Executive Committee of the Association of Governing Bodies of State Aided Schools: Eastern Transvaal.*[97]

In this case, the Member of the Executive Council (MEC) responsible for education in Mpumalanga decided on 31 August 1995 that bursaries paid to former state-aided schools (so-called Model C schools) to assist poor students with their fees, transport and accommodation costs would be terminated with effect from 1 July 1995.

After the MEC had made this decision, the respondent applied for an order setting aside the MEC's decision on the ground that it violated the right to procedural fairness guaranteed in section 24(*b*) of the interim Constitution. Section 24(*b*) provides that '[e]very person shall have the right to procedurally fair administrative action where any of his or her rights or legitimate expectations are affected or threatened'.

In determining whether the MEC had followed a fair procedure before he decided to terminate bursaries, the Constitutional Court pointed out that while section 24(*b*) of the interim Constitution required that administrative action which affected or threatened legitimate expectations must be procedurally fair, this did not mean that a hearing would be required in all circumstances. 'It is well-established in our legal system and in others that what will constitute fairness in a particular case will depend on the circumstances of the case.'[98] The Court pointed out further that:

> **[i]n determining what constitutes procedural fairness in a given case, a court should be slow to impose obligations upon government which will inhibit its ability to make and implement policy effectively (a principle well recognised in our**

97 (CCT10/98) [1998] ZACC 20; 1999 (2) SA 91; 1999 (2) BCLR 151 (2 December 1998).

98 *Premier, Mpumalanga* para 39.

> common law and that of other countries). As a young democracy facing immense challenges of transformation, we cannot deny the importance of the need to ensure the ability of the executive to act efficiently and promptly. On the other hand, to permit the implementation of retroactive decisions without, for example, affording parties an effective opportunity to make representations would flout another important principle, that of procedural fairness. ... Citizens are entitled to expect that government policy will ordinarily not be altered in ways which would threaten or harm their rights or legitimate expectations without their being given reasonable notice of the proposed change or an opportunity to make representations to the decision-maker.[99]

This passage is significant for two reasons. First, it affirms that the common law notion of procedural fairness is now essentially encapsulated by section 33 of the Constitution (in this case, section 24 of the interim Constitution) which is given effect to by section 3 of the PAJA. Second, it affirms that there will sometimes be a tension between strict enforcement of fair procedures and the efficient running of the country. As is so often the case in the adjudication of constitutional disputes, the broader context will be pivotal in deciding whether a hearing is required or not. In this case, the Court found that the MEC had neither given the recipients reasonable notice of the impending termination nor were they given an opportunity to make representations to the decision maker. In the circumstances of this case, this amounted to a failure of procedural fairness and a violation of constitutional rights. The Court ordered the provincial government to pay the subsidies for that year.

c) Rights and legitimate expectations

In terms of section 3 of the PAJA, a person can claim the right to be treated procedurally fairly if either his or her rights or his or her legitimate expectations are materially and adversely affected. It is consequently important to understand what is meant by the concept of a right and the concept of a legitimate expectation. There seems to be a conflict between the definition of administrative action set out in section 1 which applies to action that adversely affects **rights** and section 3 which applies to administrative action that adversely affects **rights or legitimate expectations.**[100] Can the conflict between these two provisions be solved?

As we have already seen, the Constitutional Court interpreted the concept of a right broadly in *Joseph* to 'include not only vested, private law rights but also legal entitlements that have their basis in the constitutional and statutory obligations of government'.[101] However, even when a right is defined in this manner, it does not encompass a legitimate expectation.

A legitimate expectation arises either from an express promise made by a public authority or as a consequence of a regular practice of a public authority which the claimant can reasonably expect to continue.[102] If either of these criteria is established, then the expectation is legitimate and will, depending on the circumstances of the case, give rise to a right to a hearing before the decision is taken.

---

99 *Premier, Mpumalanga* para 41.
100 This conflict has been said to have been caused by a drafting error. See Currie and De Waal (2013) 675.
101 *Joseph* para 42.
102 *Council of Civil Service Unions and Others v Minister for the Civil Service* [1984] 3 All ER 935 (HL).

Thus, an expectation is something that is broader than a right. It has been described as a benefit, an advantage or a privilege. In *South African Veterinary Council and Another v Szymanski*, the Supreme Court of Appeal (SCA) held that it is not whether the expectation exists in the mind of the litigant, but whether objectively such expectation exists in a legal sense.[103] In *Walele v City of Cape Town and Others*, the Constitutional Court confirmed that the enquiry is essentially a factual one and that there is a two-stage process.[104] In this case the Constitutional Court dealt with the anomaly between the definition in section 1 and the inclusion of legitimate expectation in section 3 as follows:

> **But the difficulty is that administrative action is defined in section 1 of PAJA as a decision which adversely affects the rights of another person. In the definition no reference is made to a decision affecting legitimate expectations. Yet section 3 refers to administrative action that affects legitimate expectations. Applying the definition to the interpretation of section 3 will lead to absurdity. Therefore, I am willing not to apply it and to assume that section 3 of PAJA confers the right to procedural fairness also on persons whose legitimate expectations are materially and adversely affected by an administrative decision. In the context of section 3, administrative action cannot mean what was intended in the definition section.**[105]

The Court also stated that the applicant has to establish objectively that the facts give rise to an expectation. If the applicant succeeds in establishing this, the enquiry moves to the second stage which is whether in the circumstances of the case, procedural fairness requires a pre-decision hearing.[106] Thus, if a municipality regularly invited interested parties to inspect the plans and to make representations when considering applications for the approval of plans for the erection of buildings, then a legitimate expectation would arise as a consequence of this regular practice. A person who is affected by the development could argue that they have a legitimate expectation, that they should be treated procedurally fairly and be given the opportunity to make representations. In *Walele*, the Court held that the fact that the City had afforded a hearing in one application does not constitute a legitimate expectation.

Once the applicant has established that either a right or a legitimate expectation has been materially and adversely affected, he or she thus has the right to be treated procedurally fairly. The content of this right is flexible and will depend on the circumstances of the case. The following are the core obligations that must be met for the functionary to act procedurally fairly.

d) Procedural fairness of administrative action that affects any person: section 3 of the PAJA

Section 3(2)(*b*) of the PAJA sets out five compulsory elements of any procedurally fair administrative action that affects the rights and, as we saw above, the legitimate expectations, of any person. The five core requirements can be divided into two parts, namely the pre-hearing and post-hearing requirements.

The pre-hearing requirements oblige first that the affected person be given adequate notice of the nature and purpose of the proposed administrative action and a reasonable opportunity to make representations. Thus, the applicant must be given adequate time to

103 (79/2001) [2003] ZASCA 11 (14 March 2003) para 20.
104 (CCT 64/07) [2008] ZACC 11; 2008 (6) SA 129 (CC); 2008 (11) BCLR 1067 (CC) (13 June 2008) para 14.
105 *Walele* para 37.
106 *Walele* para 38.

prepare a response and sufficient information to know the case he or she has to meet and to be aware of the consequences of the proposed administrative action.

Second, there must be a reasonable opportunity to make representations. What is reasonable will depend on the circumstances of each case. Section 3(2)(*b*)(ii) requires that a reasonable opportunity be given to make representations. This is less exacting than the requirement in section 3(3)(*c*) which requires that in certain circumstances an opportunity be given to appear in person. It is clear that section 3(2)(*b*)(ii) permits written representations and is an attempt to prevent the proceedings from becoming too formal.[107] However, what is appropriate will depend on a variety of factors including whether the affected person is able to communicate in writing.

Once the functionary has made the decision, he or she must, third, provide a clear statement of the administrative action. As Hoexter indicates, the statement should detail 'what has been decided, when, by whom and on what legal and factual basis'.[108] Fourth, the functionary must provide adequate notice of any right of review or internal appeal. In many instances, enabling laws allow an appeal from the decision of the functionary to an internal appeal tribunal. Notices of this internal appeal must be provided to the affected person. Finally, the functionary is obliged to inform the affected person of his or her right to request reasons in terms of section 5 of the PAJA.

However, section 3(4)(*a*) of the PAJA provides that if it is 'reasonable and justifiable in the circumstances', the requirements set out above need not be complied with. Section 3(4)(*b*) lists the following factors to be taken into account when making such a determination:

> **(i) the objects of the empowering provision;**
> **(ii) the nature and purpose of, and the need to take, the administrative action;**
> **(iii) the likely effect of the administrative action;**
> **(iv) the urgency of taking the administrative action or the urgency of the matter; and**
> **(v) the need to promote an efficient administration and good governance.**

This means these 'compulsory' requirements for a procedurally fair administrative action are not, in fact, compulsory in all cases. The PAJA therefore aims to prevent the imposition of duties on the administrator that are so onerous that it would make effective administration difficult or even impossible.

PAUSE FOR REFLECTION

The 'compulsory' requirements for a procedurally fair administrative action

Currie and De Waal argue that the compulsory nature of these five requirements set out in section 3(2)(*b*) of the PAJA can be deceptive:

> First, the elements are always subject to interpretation informed by a circumstance-based understanding of procedural fairness. Their content will thus tend to vary from case to case. Secondly, in several elements the score for variation is increased by the use of inherently flexible standards ... Thirdly, the Constitutional Court has held that s 3(2)(*a*) must be read as giving courts the discretion in enforcing the minimum requirements under s 3(2)(*b*) even when s 3(4) is not invoked. In other words, the court is not bound to enforce even the

107 Hoexter (2007) 334.
108 Hoexter (2007) 337.

compulsory requirements, and an administrator may be able to depart from them without relying on s 3(4).[109]

In *Joseph*, the Constitutional Court had to decide whether a fair administrative process had been followed when the City decided to terminate the electricity supply to a block of flats. The Court enforced the requirement that a pre-termination notice had to be given to all tenants in the block of flats. However, noting its decision in *Premier, Mpumalanga* that in 'determining what constitutes procedural fairness in a given case, a court should be slow to impose obligations upon government which will inhibit its ability to make and implement policy effectively',[110] the Court declined to impose a duty on the City to receive and process representations from tenants in every case.[111]

Section 3(3) recognises that in certain circumstances a further layer of procedural formalities is necessary. Thus, in certain circumstances it may be necessary for the affected persons to be permitted legal representation, to be permitted to be present and to dispute information and argument and to appeal in person. In *Hamata and Another v Chairperson, Peninsula Technikon Internal Disciplinary Committee and Others*,[112] the applicant requested to be legally represented at a disciplinary hearing. The Court held that while there was no right to legal representation in administrative proceedings, there was a right to have the request for legal representation considered. Thus, the presiding officer must have discretion to determine whether to allow legal representation. In making this decision, regard must be had to the following factors:

- the degree of legal and factual complexity of the matter
- the potential seriousness of the consequences for the relevant parties of an adverse finding
- whether the opposing party is legally represented.

Should the administration wish to depart from the requirements of the section, it may do so provided it establishes that it is reasonable and justifiable to do so. In making this decision, the administrator must have regard to all the criteria listed in section 3(4) of the PAJA.

CRITICAL THINKING

An example of the contextual approach to procedural fairness

The contextual approach to procedural fairness can be applied with reference to the following set of facts. Assume that the Department of Mineral Resources has to follow a two-stage process before issuing a licence to mine. The first stage is a preliminary stage during which the applicant requests permission to conduct an initial feasibility study and viability assessment. The second stage is when an application is formally considered for the licence to be granted.

Assume further that an application is made to mine the banks of the Vaal River. The Department indicates that all parties will be given an opportunity to participate during

109 Currie and De Waal (2013) 677.
110 *Premier, Mpumalanga* para 41.
111 *Joseph* paras 62–3.
112 (1) (384/2000) [2002] ZASCA 44 (17 May 2002).

the second phase of the process when the merits of the applications will be fully considered. However, it declines to give an association of residents the opportunity to make representations at the first phase on the basis that it would unnecessarily hinder and slow down the process.

Do you think the Department is obliged to give the residents the opportunity to make representations during both phases? If not, why not?

e) Procedural fairness of administrative action that affects the public: section 4 of the PAJA

It is not only when an administrative action affects an individual person that the action may have to be procedurally fair. Section 4(1) of the PAJA places certain obligations on an administrator where the administrative action 'materially and adversely affects the rights of the public'. The two procedures outlined in section 4 are a notice and comment procedure and a public enquiry procedure.[113] Section 4 states that:

> **(1) In cases where an administrative action materially and adversely affects the rights of the public, an administrator, in order to give effect to the right to procedurally fair administrative action, must decide whether –**
> **(*a*) to hold a public inquiry in terms of subsection (2);**
> **(*b*) to follow a notice and comment procedure in terms of subsection (3);**
> **(*c*) to follow the procedures in both subsections (2) and (3);**
> **(*d*) where the administrator is empowered by any empowering provision to follow a procedure which is fair but different, to follow that procedure; or**
> **(*e*) to follow another appropriate procedure which gives effect to section 3.**
>
> **2) If an administrator decides to hold a public inquiry –**
> **(*a*) the administrator must conduct the public inquiry or appoint a suitably qualified person or panel of persons to do so; and**
> **(*b*) the administrator or the person or panel referred to in paragraph (*a*) must –**
> **(i) determine the procedure for the public inquiry, which must –**
> **(*aa*) include a public hearing; and**
> **(*bb*) comply with the procedures to be followed in connection with public inquiries, as prescribed;**
> **(ii) conduct the inquiry in accordance with that procedure;**
> **(iii) compile a written report on the inquiry and give reasons for any administrative action taken or recommended; and**
> **(iv) as soon as possible thereafter –**
> **(*aa*) publish in English and in at least one of the other official languages in the *Gazette* or relevant provincial *Gazette* a notice containing a concise summary of any report and the particulars of the places and times at which the report may be inspected and copied; and**
> **(*bb*) convey by such other means of communication which the administrator considers effective, the information referred to in item (*aa*) to the public concerned.**

113 Currie and De Waal (2013) 680.

(3) If an administrator decides to follow a notice and comment procedure, the administrator must –

(*a*) take appropriate steps to communicate the administrative action to those likely to be materially and adversely affected by it and call for comments from them;

(*b*) consider any comments received;

(*c*) decide whether or not to take the administrative action, with or without changes; and

(*d*) comply with the procedures to be followed in connection with notice and comment procedures, as prescribed.

(4) (*a*) If it is reasonable and justifiable in the circumstances, an administrator may depart from the requirements referred to in subsections (1)(*a*) to (*e*), (2) and (3).

(*b*) In determining whether a departure as contemplated in paragraph (*a*) is reasonable and justifiable, an administrator must take into account all relevant factors, including –

(i) the objects of the empowering provision;

(ii) the nature and purpose of, and the need to take, the administrative action;

(iii) the likely effect of the administrative action;

(iv) the urgency of taking the administrative action or the urgency of the matter; and

(v) the need to promote an efficient administration and good governance.

This section only applies to 'cases where an administrative action materially and adversely affects the rights of the public'. It can be distinguished from section 3 as it does not apply to 'legitimate expectations' but only to cases where the rights of the public are adversely affected. Also, it does not apply to cases where one or more **individuals** are concerned but rather to cases where the rights of members of the public are concerned. In other words, the section applies to administrative actions that have an adverse impact of a general kind where the rights of members of the public are at issue and where the impact is not trivial.[114] For example, say a decision is taken to declare certain national roads toll roads where tolls will be levied via e-toll tags. The administrative decision will apply to the general public, will affect the rights of the public to use national roads and will have some impact on everyone who wishes to use such roads. These provisions may then potentially be imposed on the administrator who makes the decision.

As can be seen from the text of section 4, it has a fairly 'straightforward structure'.[115] It details the procedures to be followed in cases where notice and comment procedures are required and where a public enquiry is required and sets out departures from these obligations.

114 Currie and De Waal (2013) 681.

115 Currie and De Waal (2013) 681.

15.2.5.2.5 The right to be given reasons for an administrative action

a) Introduction

In our law it is assumed that there will often be great value in giving reasons for an administrative action. A duty to give reasons entails a duty to **rationalise** the decision. As Baxter argues: 'Reasons therefore help to structure the exercise of discretion, and the necessity of explaining *why* a decision is reached requires one to address one's mind to the decisional referents which ought to be taken into account.'[116] Giving reasons also satisfies an important desire on the part of the affected individual to know why a decision was reached. According to Baxter, 'This is not only fair: it is also conducive to public confidence in the administrative decision-making process.'[117] The most important reason for having to give reasons is that it allows for rational criticism of a decision. It thus subjects the administration to public scrutiny and it also provides an important basis for appeal or review. Lastly, where reasons are provided, this 'may serve a genuine educative purpose, for example where an applicant has been refused on grounds which he is able to correct for the purpose of future applications'.[118]

The right to be given reasons for an administrative action is set out in section 5 of the PAJA. Section 5 provides as follows:

> **(1) Any person whose rights have been materially and adversely affected by administrative action and who has not been given reasons for the action may, within 90 days after the date on which that person became aware of the action or might reasonably have been expected to have become aware of the action, request that the administrator concerned furnish written reasons for the action.**
>
> **(2) The administrator to whom the request is made must, within 90 days after receiving the request, give that person adequate reasons in writing for the administrative action.**
>
> **(3) If an administrator fails to furnish adequate reasons for an administrative action it must, subject to subsection (4) and in the absence of proof to the contrary, be presumed in any proceedings for judicial review that the administrative action was taken without good reason.**
>
> **(4) (*a*) An administrator may depart from the requirement to furnish adequate reasons if it is reasonable and justifiable in the circumstances, and must forthwith inform the person making the request of such departure.**
>
> **(*b*) In determining whether a departure as contemplated in paragraph (*a*) is reasonable and justifiable, an administrator must take into account all relevant factors, including:**
>
> **(i) the objects of the empowering provision;**
>
> **(ii) the nature, purpose and likely effect of the administrative action concerned;**
>
> **(iii) the nature and the extent of the departure;**
>
> **(iv) the relation between the departure and its purpose;**
>
> **(v) the importance of the purpose of the departure; and**
>
> **(vi) the need to promote an efficient administration and good governance.**

116 Baxter (1984) 228.

117 Baxter (1984) 228.

118 Baxter (1984) 228. See also *Transnet Ltd. v Goodman Brothers (Pty) Ltd* (373/98) [2000] ZASCA 62; 2001 (1) SA 853 (SCA) (9 November 2000) para 5.

(5) Where an administrator is empowered by any empowering provision to follow a procedure which is fair but different from the provisions of subsection (2), the administrator may act in accordance with that different procedure.

(6) (*a*) In order to promote an efficient administration, the Minister may, at the request of an administrator, by notice in the *Gazette* publish a list specifying any administrative action or a group or class of administrative actions in respect of which the administrator concerned will automatically furnish reasons to a person whose rights are adversely affected by such actions, without such person having to request reasons in terms of this section.

(*b*) The Minister must, within 14 days after the receipt of a request referred to in paragraph *(a)* and at the cost of the relevant administrator, publish such list, as contemplated in that paragraph.

Section 5 is divided into six subsections. Subsection 1 confers a right to request reasons within 90 days on any person whose rights have been materially and adversely affected by an administrative act. This right is activated on request. If no such request has been made, no reasons need to be given unless the Minister, acting in terms of subsection 6, has designated the administrative action as one for which reasons must automatically be given. Subsection 2 provides that adequate and written reasons must be given within 90 days after a request has been made. Subsection 3 sets out some of the consequences that arise if an administrator fails to provide adequate and written reasons. The circumstances in which an administrator can depart from the requirement to furnish reasons are set out in subsection 4. Finally, subsection 5 allows an administrator to follow an alternative procedure provided it is fair.

b) Rights and legitimate expectations

Like the right to procedural fairness, a person can claim the right to be given reasons if his or her rights or legitimate expectations have been materially and adversely affected by administrative action. While it is quite clear that section 5 applies to a person who already has a right or a legitimate expectation, it is not so clear whether it applies to a person who does not already have such a right or expectation. For example, does this right apply to a person who is applying for a benefit or a licence they do not already have?

In *Transnet Ltd. v Goodman Brothers (Pty) Ltd*,[119] the SCA had to consider whether a tenderer had a right to reasons under the interim Constitution for their tender being unsuccessful. This case was decided before the PAJA came into effect. Clearly, a person who tenders for a contract does not have a right to the contract. Transnet argued that the tenderer was 'a stranger to the tender process' and thus not granting the tender to Goodman Brothers did not adversely affect their rights.[120] As a consequence, there was no obligation to provide reasons for the decision not to award Goodman Brothers the tender.[121]

The SCA focused not on the right to the contract, but rather on the right to lawful and procedurally fair administrative justice. The Court took the view that if Goodman Brothers were not given reasons, their rights to lawful and fair administrative action would be adversely affected as there would be no way of knowing whether these rights had been

119 (373/98) [2000] ZASCA 62; 2001 (1) SA 853 (SCA) (9 November 2000).
120 *Goodman Brothers* para 9.
121 *Goodman Brothers* para 10.

violated. Finding that their rights were affected, the Court directed Transnet to provide reasons for not awarding the tender to Goodman Brothers.[122]

A case that deals much more directly with the issue is *Wessels v Minister for Justice and Constitutional Development and Others*.[123] The applicant was a regional court magistrate who applied for the post of President of the Regional Court. The Magistrates Commission found four candidates including the applicant to be appointable and sent this recommendation to the then Minister of Justice. The Minister appointed magistrate B to the post and provided no response when the applicant asked for reasons.

The Court rejected the Minister's contention that the appointment of magistrates was an executive and not an administrative action. The Minister argued that as the applicant had applied for a post and was unsuccessful, no rights were adversely affected and hence there was no obligation to provide reasons in terms of section 5 of the PAJA. The High Court held that this would mean that there would be no obligation to provide reasons for any 'application cases'.[124]

In rejecting this argument, the Court held that the obligation to provide reasons would then arise only in narrow and limited circumstances and would not give effect to the constitutional right to just administrative action. Such an interpretation, according to the Court, must be avoided.[125] The Court referred to *dicta* of Kondile AJ in *Union of Refugee Women and Others v Director, Private Security Industry Regulatory Authority and Others*,[126] where the Constitutional Court held that a refusal to register a private security company had an adverse effect on their rights. This was held in *Wessels* to mean that a decision to refuse an applicant a licence or a benefit adversely affects the rights of the applicant. As a consequence, reasons must be provided.[127]

In this case, the Court held that the Minister was obliged to provide reasons and as the Minister did not provide reasons, the Court, acting in terms of section 5(5) of the PAJA, concluded that the decision was taken without good reason.[128] The consequence of this was that the Court set aside the appointment of magistrate B.

While reasons must be submitted for both deprivation and determination cases, the nature, quality and quantity of the reasons submitted may differ depending on whether a person's rights are being determined or diminished.

PAUSE FOR REFLECTION

Is the requirement to provide reasons an excessive burden?

On the basis of *Wessels*, a public body must provide reasons to applicants who are unsuccessful in applying for positions or benefits. Do you think that this imposes an excessive burden on public bodies that could detract from the performance of their core function? Alternatively, do you think that it would be a healthy exercise if government gets into the habit of supplying reasons?

---

122 *Goodman Brothers* para 5.

123 (594/09) [2009] ZAGPPHC 81; 2010 (1) SA 128 (GNP) (2 June 2009).

124 *Wessels* para 10.

125 *Wessels* para 27.

126 (CCT 39/06) [2006] ZACC 23; 2007 (4) BCLR 339 (CC); (2007) 28 ILJ 537 (CC) (12 December 2006).

127 *Wessels* 15.

128 *Wessels* 26.

c) The meaning of adequate reasons

Once the right to be provided with reasons arises, the administrator is obliged to provide adequate reasons. It is probable that administrators will submit reasons and the issue will then be whether the reasons provided are adequate. Summarising the law in the United Kingdom, De Smith, Woolf and Jowell state that the 'reasons must show that the decision maker successfully came to grips with the main contentions advanced by the parties' and must 'tell the parties in broad terms why they lost or, as the case may be, won'.[129]

In a similar vein, in *Minister of Environmental Affairs and Tourism and Others v Phambili Fisheries (Pty) Ltd and Another*,[130] Schultz JA approvingly quoted an extract from a judgment of the Federal Court of Australia[131] where that Court said adequate reasons had to be given to enable:

> **the decision-maker to explain his decision in a way which will enable a person aggrieved to say, in effect: 'Even though I may not agree with it, I now understand why the decision went against me. I am now in a position to decide whether that decision has involved an unwarranted finding of fact, or an error of law, which is worth challenging.' This requires that the decision-maker should set out his understanding of the relevant law, any findings of fact on which his conclusions depend (especially if those facts have been in dispute), and the reasoning processes which led him to those conclusions. He should do so in clear and unambiguous language, not in vague generalities or the formal language of legislation. The appropriate length of the statement covering such matters will depend upon considerations such as the nature and importance of the decision, its complexity and the time available to formulate the statement. Often those factors may suggest a brief statement of one or two pages only.**[132]

In summary, De Ville submits that the determination of adequacy should be made by having regard to the consequences of the action taken, whether the application involves a benefit or a deprivation of a right, the nature of the right that is adversely affected, the nature of the proceedings preceding the actions taken, the nature and complexity of the decision, the nature of the authority taking the decision, the time available to formulate the reasons and the need to ensure administrative efficiency.[133]

If the administrator fails to provide adequate reasons, then in the absence of proof to the contrary, it will be presumed that the administrative action was taken without good reason and, as a consequence, could be reviewed and set aside. The administrator may depart from the requirement to provide adequate reasons if it is reasonable and justifiable to do so taking into account all the relevant factors listed in section 5(4)(*b*) of the PAJA.

The duty to provide reasons will ensure that proper decisions are made at source and that the administrators are both responsive and accountable to those who are affected by the decisions.

---

129 De Smith, Woolf and Jowell (1995) 354.

130 (32/2003, 40/2003) [2003] ZASCA 46; [2003] 2 All SA 616 (SCA) (16 May 2003).

131 *Ansett Transport Industries (Operations) Pty Ltd and Another v Wraith and Others* (1983) 48 ALR 500 at 507 (lines 23–41).

132 *Phambili Fisheries* para 40.

133 De Ville, J (2005) *Judicial Review of Administrative Action in South Africa* 294.

15.3 The right of access to information

15.3.1 Introduction

Section 1 of the Constitution establishes the principle that the South African system of government is based on several values, including a multiparty system of government 'to ensure accountability, responsiveness and openness'.[134] The right of access to information partly gives effect to this norm by establishing for everyone the right of access to information that may potentially affect them. The right of access to information is therefore one of the most important rights (along with freedom of expression and the right to vote) contained in the Constitution to ensure the establishment of the ideal government postulated in the founding values set out in section 1 of the Constitution. In the apartheid era, the state was secretive and often withheld information from people - something which was, of course, easier to do in the pre-Internet era. The secretiveness of the apartheid state was often aimed at keeping citizens in the dark about aspects of its policies and actions and was therefore profoundly undemocratic.

PAUSE FOR REFLECTION

The importance of the right of access to information

In 1975, the apartheid government decided to intervene militarily in the civil war which had erupted in Angola after the withdrawal of the Portuguese from their erstwhile colony. At first, the South African government denied that South African troops were present in Angola despite the fact that the troops were at the outskirts of Luanda. This information was kept secret from the South African public. The apartheid regime saw nothing wrong with lying to the country about the Defence Force involvement in Angola.

South Africans only received confirmation of this invasion when it was revealed in the whites-only Parliament by Frederick van Zyl Slabbert, a member of the opposition Progressive Federal party, who later became the Leader of the Opposition before leaving Parliament because he felt that participating in it no longer served any purpose. Van Zyl Slabbert had to reveal the information in Parliament where he was protected by parliamentary privilege in order to evade the strict secrecy legislation in place at the time.

Our Constitution now requires the President to inform Parliament promptly whenever the Defence Force is deployed to prevent the government from misleading the public again in such a flagrant manner. As the deployment of South African troops in a war situation is a radical step, and as the President is accountable to Parliament and to the voters for taking such a step, the President cannot deploy troops in secret to avoid accountability for his or her actions. The events of 1975 vividly illustrate how important it was for the drafters of the Constitution to include the right of access to information in the Bill of Rights.

Section 32 of the Bill of Rights states:

> **(1) Everyone has the right of access to -**
> **(*a*) any information held by the state; and**
> **(*b*) any information that is held by another person and that is required for the exercise or protection of any rights.**

134 S 1(*d*).

(2) National legislation must be enacted to give effect to this right, and may provide for reasonable measures to alleviate the administrative and financial burden on the state.

The right of access to information has a political dimension in that an open and free democratic society requires that government be accountable for its actions. These actions should be informed by rational reasons that government can explain to those affected by such decisions. It is impossible to hold accountable a government that operates in secrecy.[135] Access to information is fundamental to encouraging transparency and accountability in government operations. First, transparency aims to promote accountability in government and second, to promote greater public participation. It is further an important tool in the fight against corruption.[136]

Besides the political dimension of the right of access to information, the right is also closely connected to the realisation of other rights such as the right to freedom of expression, the right to privacy and the right to vote. This is because the right of access to information is closely related to the right to **receive** information. In addition, the right of access to information is grounded, in part, on the principle that an individual should be allowed access to information that is specifically about him or her or, in more general terms, information that the state uses to make decisions that may affect an individual. The right of access to information is also crucial in allowing an accused person adequate facilities with which to prepare a defence.[137] In a democratic society, the effective exercise of the right to vote also depends on the right of access to information. Without access to information, the ability of citizens to make responsible political decisions and to participate meaningfully in public life is undermined.[138]

In *Brümmer v Minister for Social Development and Others*, the Constitutional Court explained the importance of the right of access to information in a country founded on 'values of accountability, responsiveness and openness' as follows:

> **To give effect to these founding values, the public must have access to information held by the state. Indeed one of the basic values and principles governing public administration is transparency. And the Constitution demands that transparency "must be fostered by providing the public with timely, accessible and accurate information." Apart from this, access to information is fundamental to the realisation of the rights guaranteed in the Bill of Rights. For example, access to information is crucial to the right to freedom of expression which includes freedom of the press and other media and freedom to receive or impart information or ideas ... The role of the media in a democratic society cannot be gainsaid. Its role includes informing the public about how our government is run, and this information may very well have a bearing on elections. The media therefore has a significant influence in a democratic state. This carries with it the responsibility to report accurately. The consequences of inaccurate reporting may be devastating. Access to information is crucial to accurate reporting and thus to imparting accurate information to the public.**[139]

135 *President of the Republic of South Africa and Others v M & G Media Ltd* (CCT 03/11) [2011] ZACC 32; 2012 (2) BCLR 181 (CC); 2012 (2) SA 50 (CC) (29 November 2011) para 10.

136 Currie and De Waal (2013) 692.

137 Currie and De Waal (2013) 692.

138 *M & G Media Ltd* para 10.

139 (CCT 25/09) [2009] ZACC 21; 2009 (6) SA 323 (CC); 2009 (11) BCLR 1075 (CC) (13 August 2009) paras 62–3.

The right of access to information is in stark contrast with the 'culture of secrecy' which, as noted above, prevailed in the apartheid state.[140] It is therefore not surprising that the right of access to information was included in the interim Constitution. Section 23 of the interim Constitution provided that:

> **Every person shall have the right of access to all information held by the state or any of its organs at any level of government in so far as such information is required for the exercise or protection of any of his or her rights.**

Constitutional Principle IX further required that the final Constitution make provision for 'freedom of information so that there can be open and accountable administration at all levels of government'. To give effect to this Constitutional Principle, the 1996 Constitution expanded the right beyond the scope of of the right protected in the interim Constitution. The right in the final Constitution expanded the scope of the right to apply to information held by a private person or institution. This extension recognises the fact that private institutions, such as large corporations, may exercise enormous power in a society. The information these private institutions hold could easily be used to the detriment of individuals or could be required by individuals to exercise their other rights, including their rights as consumers not to be exploited for profit.

However, for practical purposes, the most important difference between the interim Constitution and the final Constitution is that the final Constitution extends the right of access to information by placing a duty on the state to enact supplementary legislation to give effect to the right. The Constitution required this legislation to be adopted within a period of three years after the commencement of the 1996 Constitution. The Promotion of Access to Information Act (PAIA)[141] was enacted in 2000 to give effect to section 32 of the Constitution. The PAIA is the principal legal source defining the right of access to information and the promotion of access to information in South Africa is now almost entirely regulated by the PAIA.[142] This is because of the principle of subsidiarity which states that:

> **Where ... the Constitution requires Parliament to enact legislation to give effect to the constitutional rights guaranteed in the Constitution, and Parliament enacts such legislation, it will ordinarily be impermissible for a litigant to found a cause of action directly on the Constitution without alleging that the statute in question is deficient in the remedies that it provides. Legislation enacted by Parliament to give effect to a constitutional right ought not to be ignored. And where a litigant founds a cause of action on such legislation, it is equally impermissible for a court to bypass the legislation and to decide the matter on the basis of the constitutional provision that is being given effect to by the legislation in question.**[143]

A litigant who wishes to gain access to information held by the state or by a private institution will therefore have to follow the procedures set out in the PAIA and will usually only have the right to gain access to that information if the PAIA allows this.

---

140 Truth and Reconciliation Commission of South Africa (1998) *Report: Volume 1 Chapter 8 The Destruction of Records* para 24; *Volume 2 Chapter 2 The State Outside SA Between 1960 and 1990* paras 10–19.

141 Act 2 of 2000.

142 For an overview of the application of the PAIA, see Holness, D 'The right of access to information' in Govindjee, A and Vrancken, P (2009) *Introduction to Human Rights Law* 192–6.

143 *New Clicks SA* para 437; *Walele* para 29.

15.3.2 Interpretation of the Promotion of Access to Information Act 2 of 2000

15.3.2.1 The purpose of the PAIA

It is important to note when interpreting the provisions of the PAIA that the Act was passed with the intention of giving effect to the right of access to information.[144] This means the PAIA is meant to elaborate on section 32 of the Constitution, to make the section effective in a practical manner and to promote the right set out in the Bill of Rights.[145] This means the courts must interpret the PAIA generously and purposively and with the necessary attention to the context.[146] When interpreting the PAIA, it is important to understand that legislation cannot be precisely drafted to anticipate every eventuality. Courts should keep in mind the broad purpose of the PAIA when confronted with the need to interpret the Act to decide if and how it applies to a unique set of circumstances. The first step in understanding the PAIA is therefore to identify the various purposes of the Act.[147]

Section 9 of the PAIA states:

> **The objects of this Act are –**
>
> **(*a*) to give effect to the constitutional right of access to:**
>
> **(i) any information held by the State; and**
>
> **(ii) any information that is held by another person and that is required for the exercise or protection of any rights;**
>
> **(*b*) to give effect to that right:**
>
> **(i) subject to justifiable limitations, including, but not limited to, limitations aimed at the reasonable protection of privacy, commercial confidentiality and effective, efficient and good governance; and**
>
> **(ii) in a manner which balances that right with any other rights, including the rights in the Bill of Rights in Chapter 2 of the Constitution;**
>
> **(*c*) to give effect to the constitutional obligations of the State of promoting a human rights culture and social justice, by including public bodies in the definition of "requester", allowing them, amongst others, to access information from private bodies upon compliance with the four requirements in this Act, including an additional obligation for certain public bodies in certain instances to act in the public interest;**
>
> **(*d*) to establish voluntary and mandatory mechanisms or procedures to give effect to that right in a manner which enables persons to obtain access to records of public and private bodies as swiftly, inexpensively and effortlessly as reasonably possible; and**
>
> **(*e*) generally, to promote transparency, accountability and effective governance of all public and private bodies by, including, but not limited to, empowering and educating everyone:**
>
> **(i) to understand their rights in terms of this Act in order to exercise their rights in relation to public and private bodies;**
>
> **(ii) to understand the functions and operation of public bodies; and**
>
> **(iii) to effectively scrutinise, and participate in, decision-making by public bodies that affects their rights.**

144 See s 9 of the PAIA.
145 Currie and De Waal (2013) 696.
146 Currie and De Waal (2013) 696.
147 Currie and De Waal (2013) 697.

It is clear from section 9 that the PAIA must be understood and interpreted with reference to the purposes for which section 32 was included in the Bill of Rights as the provisions of the PAIA are aimed at giving effect to the constitutional right of access to any information held by the state.

Section 11 of the PAIA underscores the rights-based focus of the Act as it casts the duty on those bound by the PAIA to provide information in peremptory terms – the requester 'must' be given access to the report so long as the request complies with the procedures outlined in the PAIA and the record requested is not protected from disclosure by one of the exemptions set out in the Act. Under our law, therefore, the disclosure of information is the rule and exemption from disclosure is the exception.[148]

As a general rule, a requester must be given access to a record held by a public body[149] if:

- the requester complies with all the procedural requirements set out in the PAIA relating to a request for access to that record
- access to that record is not refused in terms of any ground for refusal as set out in the PAIA.[150]

As a a general rule, a requester must be given access to records held by a private body[151] if:

- that record is required for the exercise or protection of any rights
- that person complies with the procedural requirements set out in the PAIA relating to a request for access to that record
- access to that record is not refused in terms of any ground for refusal set out in the PAIA.[152]

The PAIA should be interpreted by keeping in mind that the Act envisages that the granting of access to information should be the default position. Note that the right of access to information from a private body is more limited than the right of access to information from a public body. It is only when the record is required 'for the exercise or protection of any rights' that a private body is obliged to provide access to that information to a requester. When assessing whether access to information is actually **required**, the requester of information from a private body will have to show the private body that the information requested would be of assistance to him or her.[153] The existence of alternative remedies under the common law would be a factor to be taken into account. The requester of

148 *M & G Media Ltd* para 9.

149 S 1 of the PAIA defines a public body as:

> **(*a*) any department of state or administration in the national or provincial sphere of government or any municipality in the local sphere of government; or**
> **(*b*) any other functionary or institution when –**
> **(i) exercising a power or performing a duty in terms of the Constitution or a provincial constitution; or**
> **(ii) exercising a public power or performing a public function in terms of any legislation.**

150 S 11(1) of the PAIA.

151 S 1 of the PAIA defines a private body as:

> **(*a*) a natural person who carries or has carried on any trade, business or profession, but only in such capacity;**
> **(*b*) a partnership which carries or has carried on any trade, business or profession; or**
> **(*c*) any former or existing juristic person, but excludes a public body.**

152 S 50 of the PAIA.

153 *Unitas Hospital v Van Wyk and Another* (231/05) [2006] ZASCA 34; 2006 (4) SA 436 (SCA); [2006] 4 All SA 231 (SCA) (27 March 2006) para 17 where the SCA stated:

> **The threshold requirement of 'assistance' has thus been established. If the requester cannot show that the information will be of assistance for the stated purpose, access to that information will be denied. Self-evidently, however, mere compliance with the threshold requirement of 'assistance' will not be enough.**

information from a private body will also have to show that a 'substantial advantage' will be gained from access to the information or will have to show an 'element of need' for the information.[154]

It is unclear whether the requester of information from a private body must show that the record is required for the exercise of a fundamental right protected in the Constitution or whether the PAIA envisages a broader application of the right to gain access to information held by a private body by also covering records required to exercise non-constitutional rights. These rights would include private law rights arising from contractual or delictual obligations. Currie and De Waal argue that the purposes of the PAIA are best served by a narrower reading of rights. They argue that a requester will only be entitled to a record held by a private body if the record is required to prevent harm to fundamental rights, including rights protected in the Bill of Rights and other rights derived from the Bill of Rights protected in common law.[155]

PAUSE FOR REFLECTION

The vast majority of requests for access to information in terms of the PAIA to various public institutions go unanswered

The obligations in the PAIA to provide access to information held by the state and private bodies are extensive. In legal terms, the heart of the PAIA centres around the various exceptions set out in the Act that would allow refusal to grant access to records. However, one of the most problematic aspects of the PAIA relates to something entirely different, namely the refusal or inability of record holders to respond to access to information requests at all. A 2010 Report reveals that the vast majority of requests for access to information in terms of the PAIA to various public institutions went unanswered as illustrated in Figure 15.1.[156]

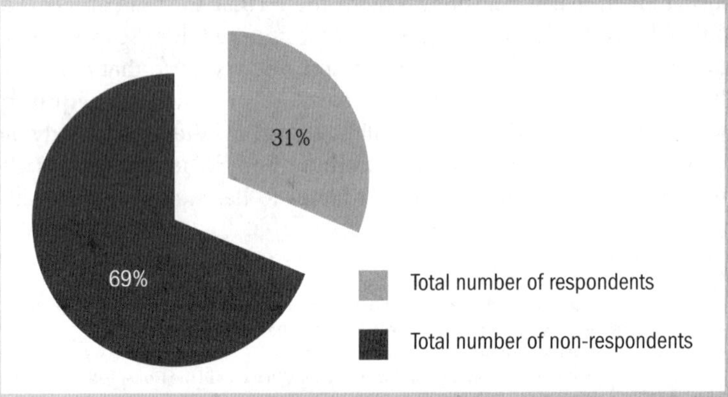

***Figure 15.1** Results of 82 institutions sampled in 2010*

This Report was compiled after a total number of 82 institutions were sampled in 2010.

154 *Clutchco (Pty) Ltd v Davis* (035/04) [2005] ZASCA 16; [2005] 2 All SA 225 (SCA); 2005 (3) SA 486 (SCA) (24 March 2005) para 13.

155 Currie and De Waal (2013) 705.

156 South African Human Rights Commission (2010) *Golden Key Awards Report on Access to Information in South Africa* (with the Open Democracy Advice Centre) available at http://www.opendemocracy.org.za/wp-content/uploads/2010/10/2010-GKA-REPORT.pdf.

Only 26 institutions responded to the requests for access to information. As the Report explains:

> **8 institutions out of 23 responded in the national department category, 9 out of 25 institutions responded on the provincial level, while 8 out of 34 municipalities responded at the local government level. The 2010 31% result is a cause for concern as it is significantly lower than the 2009 and the 2008 results where we recorded a response of 40% and 39% respectively from the sampled institutions.**[157]

These statistic do not deal with whether access to information requests were refused. Rather, the statistics deal with whether access to information requests were responded to **at all**. Accurate statistics about whether requests are correctly refused are not available. As we shall see in the next section, the PAIA contains several exceptions which allow a public or private body to refuse to grant an access to information request. Unless officials are trained and understand what these exceptions entail, there will be a danger that they will rely wrongly on one or more of these exceptions to deny a request for access to information.

15.3.2.2 The regulation of access to information by the PAIA

Although non-disclosure of information ought to be the exception, this does not mean that the PAIA does not place limitations on the right of access to information. It does this by stipulating procedures that need to be followed for making a valid access to information request. The PAIA also exempts certain information from disclosure as it may be necessary to place 'reasonable and justifiable' limitations on the right of access to information, even in an open and democratic society, to protect other rights or interests.[158] Although the default position in the PAIA is to give access to information to those who request it, at the heart of the Act are the grounds for justifying a refusal to grant access to information.

In so far as these grounds are concerned, the PAIA provides that the information officer of a public or a private body must refuse a request for access to records of that body:

- if its disclosure would involve the unreasonable disclosure of personal information about a third party,[159] including a deceased individual
- if the record contains information which was obtained or is held by the South African Revenue Service for the purposes of enforcing legislation concerning the collection of revenue[160]
- if the record contains trade secrets of a third party; financial, commercial, scientific or technical information other than trade secrets of a third party, the disclosure of which would be likely to cause harm to the commercial or financial interests of that third party; or information supplied in confidence by a third party, the disclosure of which could reasonably be expected to put that third party at a disadvantage in contractual or other negotiations or to prejudice that third party in commercial competition[161]

---

157 *Golden Key Awards Report* 9 South African Human Rights Commission (2010).

158 *Clutchco* para 11.

159 S 34 (public bodies) and s 63 (private bodies) of the PAIA. The sections contain exceptions which provide mandatory protection of privacy of third parties and which would prevent a body from granting access to the requested information.

160 S 35 of the PAIA.

161 S 36 (public bodies) and s 64 (private bodies) of the PAIA. These sections contain exceptions which provide mandatory protection of commercial information of third parties and which would prevent a body from granting access to the requested information.

- if the disclosure of the record would constitute an action for breach of a duty of confidence owed to a third party in terms of an agreement;[162] and a public body may refuse a request for access to a record of the body if the record consists of information that was supplied in confidence by a third party, the disclosure of which could reasonably be expected to prejudice the future supply of similar information or information from the same source; and if it is in the public interest that similar information or information from the same source should continue to be supplied
- if its disclosure could reasonably be expected to endanger the life or physical safety of an individual; if its disclosure would be likely to prejudice or impair the security of a building, structure or system, including, but not limited to, a computer or communication system; a means of transport; any other property; methods, systems, plans or procedures for the protection of an individual in accordance with a witness protection scheme; the safety of the public or any part of the public; or the security of property as contemplated above[163]
- if the record is privileged from production in legal proceedings unless the person entitled to the privilege has waived the privilege.[164]

In addition, public body must also refuse to grant access to information:

- if its disclosure could reasonably be expected to cause prejudice to the defence of the Republic; the security of the Republic; the international relations of the Republic; would reveal information supplied in confidence by or on behalf of another state or an international organisation; supplied by or on behalf of the Republic to another state or an international organisation in terms of an arrangement or international agreement with that state or organisation which requires the information to be held in confidence; or required to be held in confidence by an international agreement or customary international law
- if its disclosure would be likely to materially jeopardise the economic interests or financial welfare of the Republic or the ability of the government to manage the economy of the Republic effectively in the best interests of the Republic.[165]

Despite these provisions, the PAIA contains a general public interest override for requests of most of the records which bodies are granted the power to deny in the Act.[166] In such cases, the public or private body will have to grant access to the information – despite the information falling within one of the exceptions set out in the Act – if the disclosure of the record would reveal evidence of:

- a substantial contravention of, or failure to comply with, the law
- an imminent and serious public safety or environmental risk
- the public interest in the disclosure of the record clearly outweighs the harm contemplated in the provision in question.

Note that this public interest override is narrow in scope as it does not cover cases where records would show maladministration that does not rise to the level of an unlawful act.

162 S 37 (public body) and s 65 (private body) of the PAIA.
163 S 38 (public body) and s 66 (private body) of the PAIA.
164 S 40 (public body) and s 67 (private body) of the PAIA.
165 S 42 of the PAIA.
166 S 46 (public body) and s 70 (private body) of the PAIA.

15.3.2.3 The question of a 'judicial peek' at refused records

In cases where a body refuses to grant access to records, it will be very difficult for a litigant to establish whether the refusal was done properly in terms of one of the exceptions set out above or whether the refusal was unlawful. The PAIA empowers courts to review independently the record in order to assess the validity of the exemptions claimed and provides legislative recognition that, through no fault of their own, the parties may be constrained in their abilities to present and refute evidence. If a person who requested access to a record is denied access and wishes to appeal the decision to deny him or her access, the PAIA allows the court to have a 'judicial peek' at the requested record to determine whether the refusal was lawfully granted or not. Section 80 – the so-called 'judicial peek' provision of the PAIA – states:

> **(1) Despite this Act and any other law, any court hearing an application, or an appeal against a decision on that application, may examine any record of a public or private body to which this Act applies, and no such record may be withheld from the court on any grounds.**
>
> **(2) Any court contemplated in subsection (1) may not disclose to any person, including the parties to the proceedings concerned, other than the public or private body referred to in subsection (1) –**
>
> **(*a*) any record of a public or private body which, on a request for access, may or must be refused in terms of this Act; or**
>
> **(*b*) if the information officer of a public body, or the relevant authority of that body on internal appeal, in refusing to grant access to a record in terms of section 39(3) or 41(4), refuses to confirm or deny the existence or non-existence of the record, any information as to whether the record exists.**
>
> **(3) Any court contemplated in subsection (1) may –**
>
> **(*a*) receive representations *ex parte*; conduct hearings in camera; and prohibit the publication of such information in relation to the proceedings as the court determines, including information in relation to the parties to the proceedings and the contents of orders made by the court in the proceedings.**

In *President of the Republic of South Africa and Others v M & G Media Ltd,*[167] the Constitutional Court was required to determine when to apply this provision. A majority of the Court (per Ngcobo CJ) emphasised that the court has a duty to exercise its power to have a judicial peek at confidential documents in a responsible manner.[168] A judicial peek facilitates the exercise of the judicial function where courts may be lacking the material necessary to determine responsibly whether the record falls within the exemption claimed. A difficulty arises for courts when they apply section 80 as the section does not spell out the circumstances under which the power to examine the record may be exercised. The majority argued that the discretionary power they are granted by section 80 must 'be exercised judiciously, with due regard to the constitutional right of access to information and the difficulties the parties face in presenting and refuting evidence'.[169] The majority set out the following test:

> **Courts should exercise their discretion to call for additional evidence in the form of the contested record only where there is the potential for injustice as a result of the**

167 (CCT 03/11) [2011] ZACC 32; 2012 (2) BCLR 181 (CC); 2012 (2) SA 50 (CC) (29 November 2011).

168 *M & G Media Ltd* para 41.

169 *M & G Media Ltd* para 42.

unique constraints placed upon the parties in access to information disputes. This injustice, as I have pointed out above, may arise because either the requester or the holder of information is prevented by factors beyond its control from presenting the evidence necessary to make its case.

As a discretionary power afforded to the courts to prevent injustice, the standard for assessing whether a court should properly invoke section 80 in a given case is whether it would be in the interests of justice for it to do so.

...

... It will generally be in the interests of justice to invoke section 80 where there is doubt, emerging from the unique limitations parties in access to information disputes face in presenting and refuting evidence, as to whether an exemption is rightly claimed. This may be the case where, through no fault of the state, the evidence put forth by it is insufficient to allow the court to responsibly determine whether the exemptions claimed are valid, or where the validity of the exemptions claimed cannot responsibly be evaluated without reference to the information sought to be protected.

It may also be in the interests of justice to invoke section 80 where the probabilities are evenly balanced. Ordinarily, where the probabilities are evenly balanced, the rules of civil procedure would require a court to find against the holder of information as the bearer of the burden of proof. Where, however, a court is faced with a record that it acknowledges may or may not be protected, in whole or in part, from disclosure, and the doubt as to the validity of the exemptions claimed can be explained in terms of the limitations placed upon the parties in access to information disputes in presenting and refuting evidence, it would be in the interests of justice for the court to invoke section 80 in order to responsibly decide the merits on the basis of the additional evidence provided by the record.[170]

CRITICAL THINKING

A cautious approach to the invoking of section 80

In the minority decisions of the Constitutional Court in *M & G Media Ltd*, Cameron J cautioned courts against the exercise of their powers in terms of section 80 of the PAIA. This case dealt with an access to information request by the *Mail & Guardian* newspaper. The request related to a report on the conduct of the 2002 presidential election in Zimbabwe compiled by judges who had been sent to the country by then President Thabo Mbeki. In his separate judgment, Cameron J disputed the finding of the majority that when remitting the case to the High Court, that Court could invoke section 80 of the PAIA to have a judicial peek at the document. This was because the provision 'should be invoked with care' and 'should be resorted to only in exceptional circumstances'.[171] The minority proffered two reasons for this:

> First, a cautious approach to section 80 accords with the structure of the statute. The Constitution creates an entitlement to information held by government, which the statute has limited under the Bill of Rights. The structure of PAIA is to stipulate

170 *M & G Media Ltd* paras 44–7.
171 *M & G Media Ltd* para 124.

the process required to claim access, and to enumerate the instances where it may be refused. The statute creates an over-riding judicial power to examine the record, but goes on to provide explicitly that the burden of establishing that an exemption is properly invoked lies on the party claiming it. If the object of the statute were to create a novel form of proceeding in access disputes, and invest courts with inquisitorial powers for ready use in disputes, its provisions would not have included so plain an imposition of the burden on the holder of information.[172]

...

Second, the very provisions of section 80 make it plain that the power it confers should be of rare recourse. The provision makes the court a party to the secrecy claimed, and prohibits it from disclosing the disputed record to any person, "including the parties to the proceedings concerned". In effect, two fundamental principles of the administration of justice are here upended: first, the adversary nature of the parties' dispute, in which the court is a disinterested arbiter, is suspended; and, second, the indispensable attribute of the administration of justice, its openness, is shrouded. These are consequences that we should be reluctant to countenance too readily.[173]

15.4 The right of access to the courts

15.4.1 Introduction

The right of access to court is a fundamental component of the rule of a law in a constitutional democracy.[174] Thus section 34 of the Bill of Rights states that '[e]veryone has the right to have any dispute that can be resolved by the application of law decided in a fair public hearing before a court or, where appropriate, another independent and impartial tribunal or forum'.

The inclusion of this section in the Bill of Rights must be seen against the background of the apartheid-era practice of ousting the jurisdiction of the courts to enquire into the legal validity of certain laws or conduct. This practice was in breach of the rule of law which establishes the principle, *inter alia,* that anyone may challenge the legality of any law or conduct.[175] However, it would only be meaningful to challenge such law or conduct if this could be done in front of an independent and impartial body like a court otherwise the right to challenge the legality of law or conduct would be illusory. Section 34 is therefore closely related to upholding the rule of law. As the Constitutional Court stated in *Lesapo v North West Agricultural Bank and Another,* section 34:

> **and the access to courts it guarantees for the adjudication of disputes are a manifestation of a deeper principle; one that underlies our democratic order. The effect of this underlying principle on the provision of s 34 is that any constraint upon a person or property shall be exercised by another only after recourse to a court**

172 *M & G Media Ltd* para 125.
173 *M & G Media Ltd* para 128.
174 Currie and De Waal (2013) 711.
175 *De Lange v Smuts NO and Others* (CCT26/97) [1998] ZACC 6; 1998 (3) SA 785; 1998 (7) BCLR 779 (28 May 1998) paras 46–7.

recognised in terms of the law of the land. ... Respect for the rule of law is crucial for a defensible and sustainable democracy. In a modern constitutional State like ours, there is no room for legislation which, as in this case, is inimical to a fundamental principle such as that against self help. This is particularly so when the tendency for aggrieved persons to take the law into their own hands is a constant threat.[176]

Section 34 creates the right of access to courts or another tribunal or forum but such other tribunal or forum other than a court must be independent and impartial. It also creates a due process right that requires a fair and a public hearing. However, it is important to note that there is a threshold that must be met before this right can be applied, namely that the dispute at issue can, in fact, be resolved by the application of law.

15.4.2 Threshold question: can the dispute in question be resolved by the application of law?

Section 34 is clear: the right does not apply to all people who wish to have a dispute between them resolved by a court or independent tribunal. Some disputes, for example disputes of a purely moral or religious nature, cannot be resolved by the application of law and individuals with such disputes cannot rely on section 34 to gain access to a court for the purposes of the court resolving their dispute.[177] It would also sometimes be difficult to resolve disputes of a purely political nature in the courts.[178]

The distinction between moral, religious and political disputes on the one hand and legal disputes on the other is, however, not that easy to draw. For example, in *Ramakatsa and Others v Magashule and Others*,[179] the Constitutional Court considered the arguments by the applicants which, to some extent, were of a political nature. The appellants in the case were all members of the African National Congress (ANC) in the Free State province. They approached the Court with a view to 'setting aside as invalid the Free State Provincial Conference of the ANC and all its outcomes on the basis that there were irregularities in many of the branch meetings that elected delegates to the Provincial Conference'.[180] The Court had to hear the case because section 19 of the Bill of Rights grants every citizen the right to participate in the activities of a political party. The Court found that it could therefore look into whether a political party had followed the procedures prescribed by its own constitution.

Other disputes may well be capable of being resolved by the application of law but will nevertheless not fall within the ambit of section 34. Thus, section 34 does not apply to those aspects of criminal proceedings regulated exhaustively by section 35 of the Constitution.[181] Currie and De Waal argue that the same applies to section 33 which regulates the conduct of administrative action.[182]

---

176 (CCT23/99) [1999] ZACC 16; 2000 (1) SA 409; 1999 (12) BCLR 1420 (16 November 1999) paras 16–17.

177 Currie and De Waal (2013) 712.

178 *National Director of Public Prosecutions v Zuma* (573/08) [2009] ZASCA 1; 2009 (2) SA 277 (SCA); 2009 (1) SACR 361 (SCA); 2009 (4) BCLR 393 (SCA); [2009] 2 All SA 243 (SCA) (12 January 2009) para 18.

179 (CCT 109/12) [2012] ZACC 31; 2013 (2) BCLR 202 (CC) (18 December 2012).

180 *Ramakatsa* para 6.

181 *Thint (Pty) Ltd v National Director of Public Prosecutions and Others, Zuma and Another v National Director of Public Prosecutions and Others* (CCT 89/07, CCT 91/07) [2008] ZACC 13; 2008 (2) SACR 421 (CC); 2009 (1) SA 1 (CC); 2008 (12) BCLR 1197 (CC) (31 July 2008) paras 60–2; *President of the Republic of South Africa and Others v South African Rugby Football Union and Others - Judgment on recusal application (SARFU II)* (CCT16/98) [1999] ZACC 9; 1999 (4) SA 147; 1999 (7) BCLR 725 (4 June 1999) para 29.

182 Currie and De Waal (2013) 713.

CRITICAL THINKING

The difficulties faced by courts when dealing with issues of a political nature

In *Mazibuko Leader of the Opposition in the National Assembly v Sisulu MP Speaker of the National Assembly and Others*,[183] the Western Cape High Court considered whether the National Assembly and its Speaker had erred in not scheduling a debate on a vote of no confidence in the President of the country which had been tabled by the official opposition. The Court remarked in general about the difficulties faced by a court when litigants approach a court to resolve disputes of an essentially political nature.

> Courts do not run the country, nor were they intended to govern the country. Courts exist to police the constitutional boundaries, as I have sketched them. Where the constitutional boundaries are breached or transgressed, courts have a clear and express role; and must then act without fear or favour. There is a danger in South Africa, however, of the politicisation of the judiciary, drawing the judiciary into every political dispute as if there is no other forum to deal with a political impasse relating to policy or disputes which clearly carry polycentric consequences beyond the scope of adjudication. In the context of this dispute, judges cannot be expected to dictate to parliament when and how it should arrange its precise order of business matters. What courts can do, however, is to say to parliament: 'you must operate within a constitutionally compatible framework; you must give content to s 102 of the Constitution; you cannot subvert this expressly formulated idea of a motion of no confidence; however, how you allow that right to be vindicated is for you to do, not for the courts to so determine'. I regret the need to emphasise this point but it appears to me to be vital to the future integrity of the judicial institution. An overreach of the powers of judges – their intrusion into issues which are beyond their competence or intended jurisdiction – which have been deliberately and carefully constructed legally so as to ensure that the other arms of the state deal with these matters, can only result in jeopardy for our constitutional democracy. In this dispute I am not prepared to create a juristocracy, and thus do more than that which I am mandated to do in terms of our constitutional model.[184]

This passage should not be interpreted to mean that the right in section 34 to approach a court with a dispute about any breach of the Constitution or ordinary law will evaporate when the legal dispute – despite its political overtones – remains a dispute that is capable of being resolved by the application of law. If anybody, including the legislature or any member of the executive, fails to comply with a constitutional duty, the court will have the responsibility to hear the dispute that may arise from such a failure. The passage, however, serves as a warning for especially political parties to be circumspect and to think carefully before approaching a court with a dispute that – while capable of legal resolution – is highly politicised.

15.4.3 Access to courts and other forums

Once the threshold set out above has been met, the right in section 34 comes into operation and protects individuals from both direct and more subtle attempts by the state to prevent

183 (21990/2012) [2012] ZAWCHC 189; 2013 (4) SA 243 (WCC) (22 November 2012).

184 *Mazibuko* 256E–H.

their accessing courts to have their legal disputes resolved. This right contains both a negative obligation and a positive obligation which, in accordance with section 7(2) of the Constitution, place a duty on the state to 'respect, protect, promote and fulfil' all the rights in the Bill of Rights. Where the state places stumbling blocks in the path of a potential litigant that makes it more difficult or even impossible for the potential litigant to access courts, the right will be infringed. Similarly, where the state fails to take positive steps to create, maintain and finance the court system, it will be potentially infringing its positive obligation to protect, promote and fulfil this right.

However, note that section 34 does not entitle a potential litigant to approach any court he or she chooses: a litigant cannot normally, for example, directly approach the Constitutional Court.[185] The rules of jurisdiction in civil proceedings are therefore not an obstacle to access to courts as long as these rules allow the potential litigant to approach **some** court which has the requisite jurisdiction.[186] Section 34 does not create a right to a specific decision by the court either.[187]

15.4.3.1 A positive obligation on the state

The question arises whether the state has a positive duty not only to create, maintain and finance courts and tribunals, but also whether the state has the duty to provide individuals with the means that would allow them to access courts and other tribunals. Given the limited state resources, it is not clear whether the Constitutional Court would make such a finding. However, the North Gauteng High Court found in *Magidiwana and Another v President of the Republic of South Africa and Others*,[188] in the context of that specific case, that such a duty could arise even though the case dealt with a commission of enquiry.

What is clear is that the state does have a positive duty to enhance access to justice through legislative and other measures. Thus, the legislature is mandated to ensure the impartiality and efficiency of the courts and their accessibility via legislative measures. Where the legislature and the executive fail to take measures, legislative or otherwise, to ensure that the orders of a court are obeyed, for example, this may constitute a failure on the state to respect its positive duties in relation to access to courts. The state is also required to take heed of orders made by courts and to change the manner in which it deals with issues if instructed to do so.[189]

15.4.3.2 The prohibition of self-help

One of the reasons why access to courts is so important is that such access provides a structured mechanism though which disputes can be resolved and helps to prevent lawlessness and self-help which is anathema to the rule of law. In *Lesapo*, the Constitutional

---

185 *S v Zuma and Others* (CCT5/94) [1995] ZACC 1; 1995 (2) SA 642; 1995 (4) BCLR 401 (SA); 1995 (1) SACR 568; [1996] 2 CHRLD 244 (5 April 1995) para 11; *Executive Council of the Western Cape Legislature and Others v President of the Republic of South Africa and Others* (CCT27/95) [1995] ZACC 8; 1995 (10) BCLR 1289; 1995 (4) SA 877 (22 September 1995) paras 15–17; *Ferreira v Levin NO and Others; Vryenhoek and Others v Powell NO and Others* (CCT5/95) [1995] ZACC 13; 1996 (1) SA 984 (CC); 1996 (1) BCLR 1 (6 December 1995) para 10; *S v Mbatha, S v Prinsloo* (CCT19/95, CCT35/95) [1996] ZACC 1; 1996 (3) BCLR 293; 1996 (2) SA 464 (9 February 1996) para 29; *Dormehl v Minister of Justice and Others* (CCT10/00) [2000] ZACC 4; 2000 (2) SA 825; 2000 (5) BCLR 471 (CC) (14 April 2000) para 4.

186 *Besserglik v Minister of Trade Industry and Tourism and Others (Minister of Justice intervening)* (CCT34/95) [1996] ZACC 8; 1996 (6) BCLR 745; 1996 (4) SA 331 (14 May 1996).

187 *Van der Walt v Metcash Trading Limited* (CCT37/01) [2002] ZACC 4; 2002 (4) SA 317; 2002 (5) BCLR 454 (11 April 2002) para 4.

188 (37904/2013) [2013] ZAGPPHC 292 (14 October 2013).

189 *Nyathi v Member of the Executive Council for the Department of Health Gauteng and Another* (CCT 19/07) [2008] ZACC 8; 2008 (5) SA 94 (CC); 2008 (9) BCLR 865 (CC) (2 June 2008) para 84.

Court stressed the need for this institutionalising of the resolution of disputes and preventing remedies being sought through self-help. A trial or hearing before a court or tribunal is therefore not an end in itself. It is a means of determining whether a legal obligation exists and whether the coercive power of the state can be invoked to enforce an obligation or to prevent an unlawful act being committed. No one is entitled to take the law into his or her own hands. Self-help, in this sense, is inimical to a society in which the rule of law prevails. Taking the law into one's own hands is thus inconsistent with the fundamental principles of our law.[190] It is in this context that the rule against self-help and its importance come into focus. As the Constitutional Court stated in *Lesapo*:

> **This rule against self-help is necessary for the protection of the individual against arbitrary and subjective decisions and conduct of an adversary. It is a guarantee against partiality and the consequent injustice that may arise. ... It is to emphasise and protect generally, but also specifically for the protection of the individual, the separation of powers, particularly the separation of the Judiciary from the other arms of the State. ... [B]y ensuring that the courts and other fora which settle justiciable disputes are independent and impartial [it achieves these goals]. It is a provision fundamental to the upholding of the rule of law, the constitutional State, the 'regstaat idee' ...**[191]

15.4.3.3 Does a commission of enquiry constitute an independent and impartial tribunal?

Section 34 provides for the right to have any dispute that can be resolved by the application of the law decided in a fair public hearing before a court or, where appropriate, another independent and impartial tribunal or forum. It is unclear whether judicial commissions of enquiry could be considered to constitute independent or impartial tribunals and whether the term 'dispute' applies to matters considered by such commissions of enquiry.

It may be considered that commissions of enquiry are fact-finding tribunals. As such, they do not concern themselves with justiciable matters where their adjudication may bring an end to a dispute. According to this view, a 'commission is merely investigative in nature with a view to making recommendations to the President'.[192] If we agree with this view, section 34 would not find application to commissions of enquiry.[193]

In *Magidiwana*, the North Gauteng High Court had to determine whether the affected surviving miners were entitled to legal representation at state expense before the commission of enquiry into the Marikana massacre in which 34 miners were killed by the police. The Court held that the commission of enquiry fell within the scope of section 34 despite the fact that the commission was not of a judicial or quasi-judicial nature:

> **At conceptual level, the general proposition that the proceedings of commissions of inquiry fall outside the scope of s 34 at the outset, is, to my mind, an over-simplification of a complex situation involving constitutional rights and a distinct possibility of those rights being adversely affected by the outcome of the commission. A preferable view is that the right to legal representation at commissions is not an**

---

190 *Lesapo* para 11; *Bon Quelle (Edms) Bpk v Munisipaliteit van Otavi* 1989 (1) SA 508 (A) 511H–512A; *Nino Bonino v De Lange* 1906 TS 120 at 122.

191 *Lesapho* para 18.

192 *Magidiwana* paras 27–8.

193 *Magidiwana* paras 27–8.

absolute one, but depends on the context. Counsel for Ledingoane family asserted that the right arises in the following circumstances:

(a) when the nature and type of inquiry demands that some or all interested parties be legally represented;

(b) when the interests of justice and the rule of law would be undermined by a failure to uphold the right;

(c) when the constitutional rights of parties or witnesses appearing before a commission are implicated or potentially threatened.[194]

15.5 Labour relations

15.5.1 Introduction

The relationship between an employer and an employee is based on a contract of employment which has traditionally been regulated by the common law. Unfortunately, the common law principles governing employment contracts do not recognise the unequal power relations that exist between employers and employees and the fact that they are not in an equal bargaining position. This is, in fact, also the case when individuals enter into contracts with economically powerful institutions, be it banks, cell phone companies or furniture stores. In addition, these common law principles also do not recognise the relationships brought about by the rise of trade unions nor do they facilitate the acquisition of rights through collective bargaining.[195]

To address these shortcomings, Parliament has intervened on numerous occasions and passed legislation aimed at establishing basic conditions of employment, introducing principles of equity and fairness, and promoting collective bargaining. As a result of these interventions, the employment relationship today is regulated largely by legislation and the rights and obligations acquired through collective bargaining.

Among the most important statutes regulating the employment relationship are the Labour Relations Act (LRA),[196] the Basic Conditions of Employment Act (BCEA)[197] and the Employment Equity Act (EEA).[198] These Acts all aim to give effect to various aspects of the rights guaranteed in section 23 of the Constitution which provides that:

(1) Everyone has the right to fair labour practices.

(2) Every worker has the right –
- **(*a*) to form and join a trade union;**
- **(*b*) to participate in the activities and programmes of a trade union; and**
- **(*c*) to strike.**

(3) Every employer has the right –
- **(*a*) to form and join an employers' organization; and**
- **(*b*) to participate in the activities and programmes of an employers' organization.**

(4) Every trade union and every employers' organization has the right –
- **(*a*) to determine its own administration, programmes and activities;**
- **(*b*) to organize; and**
- **(*c*) to form and join a federation.**

---

194 *Magidiwana* para 37.

195 Le Roux, R 'Employment' in Du Bois, F (ed) (2007) *Wille's Principles of South African Law* 9th ed 924–5.

196 Act 66 of 1995.

197 Act 75 of 1997.

198 Act 55 of 1998.

(5) **Every trade union, employers' organization and employer has the right to engage in collective bargaining. National legislation may be enacted to regulate collective bargaining. To the extent that the legislation may limit a right in this Chapter, the limitation must comply with section 36(1).**

(6) **National legislation may recognize union security arrangements contained in collective agreements. To the extent that the legislation may limit a right in this Chapter, the limitation must comply with section 36(1).**

As is the case with other rights, the principle of subsidiarity requires that litigants rely first on the provisions of the various Acts that give effect to the rights contained in the Constitution before they can rely on the rights contained in the Constitution itself.

PAUSE FOR REFLECTION

Regulating the unequal power relationship between employers and employees

The LRA is the national legislation referred to in sections 23(5) and (6) of the Constitution. The stated purpose of the LRA is to advance economic development and social justice, to maintain industrial peace, to regulate the work environment and to provide processes to deal with disputes that arise. At the heart of the LRA is an assumption that employment relationships contain an inherently unequal power relationship between employers and employees. These relationships require special legal regulation to protect usually weaker employees and to provide them with an easy and cheap mechanism to enforce their rights. In essence, achieving fairness in employment relationships is the ultimate aim of the LRA.

According to Grogan, the main features of the LRA are as follows:

- The LRA encourages collective bargaining and the settlement of disputes by enhancing the powers of the forums that have been set up to achieve these objects.
- The broad definition of an unfair labour practice in the 1956 Labour Relations Act has been replaced with specific rules and rights, all of which are justiciable in the Commission for Conciliation, Arbitration and Mediation (CCMA).
- The CCMA has both mediation and arbitration functions. All labour disputes must be processed through it unless the parties are subject to a collective agreement which makes provision for private arbitration.
- Disputes which cannot be settled by mediation are referred to arbitration either by a commission, an arbitrator or a judge of the Labour Court depending on the nature of the proceedings.
- Arbitration proceedings are meant to be expeditious and subsequently reviewable and not appealable.
- The LRA affords employees the freedom to strike if they comply with the requirements of the Act.
- Trade unions are given specific rights to organise.
- The LRA regulates bargaining councils whose key function is to facilitate the collective bargaining process. Collective bargaining refers to the negotiations and interactions between employers and workers aimed at preventing or settling disputes.[199]

199 Grogan, J (2009) *Workplace Law* 10th ed 6.

In *National Union of Metal Workers of South Africa and Others v Bader Bop (Pty) Ltd and Another*, the Constitutional Court held that the rights guaranteed in section 23 of the Constitution are aimed at creating a 'fair industrial relations environment' and that collective bargaining between employers and workers is one of the key mechanisms for achieving this goal.[200] The Court stated that:

> **In section 23, the Constitution recognises the importance of ensuring fair labour relations. The entrenchment of the right of workers to form and join trade unions and to engage in strike action, as well as the right of trade unions, employers and employer organisations to engage in collective bargaining, illustrates that the Constitution contemplates that collective bargaining between employers and workers is key to a fair industrial relations environment. This case concerns the right to strike. That right is both of historical and contemporaneous significance. In the first place, it is of importance for the dignity of workers who in our constitutional order may not be treated as coerced employees. Secondly, it is through industrial action that workers are able to assert bargaining power in industrial relations. The right to strike is an important component of a successful collective bargaining system. In interpreting the rights in section 23, therefore, the importance of those rights in promoting a fair working environment must be understood. It is also important to comprehend the dynamic nature of the wage-work bargain and the context within which it takes place. Care must be taken to avoid setting in constitutional concrete, principles governing that bargain which may become obsolete or inappropriate as social and economic conditions change.**[201]

This paragraph provides a succinct description of the context within which the labour relations regime must be judged and the considerations which animate the proper operation of this regime. As is the case with other aspects of the interpretation of the provisions of the Bill of Rights, the Court emphasised the fact that such an interpretation and application occurs in a specific (and potentially changing) context. This means that it is not always easy to set down hard-and-fast rules.

15.5.2 The scope and ambit of section 23 of the Constitution

Although the right to fair labour practices guaranteed in section 23(1) of the Constitution applies to 'everyone', the other provisions of section 23 apply to a much narrower category of persons, namely 'workers', 'employers', 'trade unions' and 'employers' organisations'.

CRITICAL THINKING

The meaning of 'everyone' in the right to fair labour practices

Despite the fact that the right to fair labour practices guaranteed in section 23(1) of the Constitution applies to 'everyone', Cheadle argues that – like the rights guaranteed in sections 23(2) to (5) – it applies only to workers, employers and their respective organisations. This is because, he argues further, section 23(1) applies only to those persons who are engaged in a 'labour practice'. A labour practice is one that arises from the relationship between workers, employers and their respective organisations.

200 (CCT14/02) [2002] ZACC 30; 2003 (2) BCLR 182; 2003 (3) SA 513 (CC); [2003] 2 BLLR 103 (CC) (13 December 2002) para 13.

201 *NUMSA* para 13.

The right to a fair labour practice should not be read as extending the class of persons beyond those classes envisaged by the section as a whole.[202]

It is also important to note that the reference to 'everyone' in section 23(1) of the Constitution includes both workers and employers. In *National Education Health & Allied Workers Union (NEHAWU) v University of Cape Town and Others*,[203] the applicant argued that the right to fair labour practices applied to workers only because the term 'everyone' referred to human beings and not to juristic persons. The Constitutional Court, however, rejected this argument. In arriving at its conclusion, the Court held that:

> Where the rights in the section are guaranteed to workers or employers or trade unions or employers' organisations as the case may be, the Constitution says so explicitly. If the rights in s 23(1) were to be guaranteed to workers only, the Constitution would have said so. The basic flaw in the applicant's submission is that it assumes that all employers are juristic persons. That is not so. In addition section 23(1) must apply either to all employers or none. It should make no difference whether they are natural or juristic persons.[204]

While it is fairly clear what is meant by the terms 'employer', 'trade union' and 'employers organisation', it is less clear what is meant by the term 'worker'. The Constitutional Court, however, considered the meaning of the term in its judgment in *South African National Defence Union v Minister of Defence*.[205]

In this case, the applicant applied for an order declaring section 126B(1) of the Defence Act[206] to be unconstitutional and invalid on the grounds that it infringed section 23(2) of the Constitution. Section 126B(1) of the Defence Act prohibited permanent members of the South African National Defence Force (SANDF) from joining or becoming members of a trade union. Section 23(2) of the Constitution provides that that '[e]very worker has the right (*a*) to form and join a trade union; (*b*) to participate in the activities and programmes of a trade union, and (*c*) to strike'.

Given that section 23(2) of the Constitution applies only to workers, the first issue the Constitutional Court had to consider was whether the word 'worker' was wide enough to include permanent members of the SANDF. The Court held that it was.

In arriving at this decision, the Constitutional Court began by explaining that permanent members of the SANDF receive many of the same benefits as other employees, for example a salary, leave, medical and transport benefits, and certain mess expenses.[207] In addition, the Constitutional Court explained further, the International Labour Organisation considers members of the armed forces to be workers for the purposes of the Convention on the Freedom of Association and Protection of the Right to Organise 87 of 1948 and the Convention on the Right to Organise and Collective Bargaining 98 of 1949, both of which South Africa has ratified.[208]

---

202 Cheadle, H 'Labour relations' in Cheadle, MH, Davis, DM and Haysom, NRL (2013) *South African Constitutional Law: The Bill of Rights* 2nd ed 18.4–18.10.

203 (CCT2/02) [2002] ZACC 27; 2003 (2) BCLR 154; 2003 (3) SA 1 (CC) (6 December 2002).

204 *NEHAWU* para 39.

205 (CCT27/98) [1999] ZACC 7; 1999 (4) SA 469; 1999 (6) BCLR 615 (26 May 1999).

206 Act 44 of 1957.

207 *South African National Defence Union* paras 23–4.

208 *South African National Defence Union* paras 26–7.

Even though permanent members of the SANDF are not employees in the full contractual sense of the word, the Constitutional Court went on to conclude, the factors set out above indicated that the relationship between permanent members of the SANDF and the SANDF itself was 'akin to an employment relationship' and 'in many respects mirrors those of people employed under a contract of employment'.[209] Although members of the SANDF may be thought to be in a special kind of situation because there is a requirement that members of the armed forces must adhere to strict discipline,[210] the term 'worker' nevertheless had to be given a generous interpretation. The need for strict discipline will not necessarily be undermined by holding that members of the SANDF constitute 'workers' for the purpose of section 23(2) 'because in appropriate circumstances rights may be limited'.[211] After coming to the conclusion that the word 'worker' was wide enough to include permanent members of the SANDF, the Constitutional Court went on to find that section 126B(1) of the Defence Act did infringe section 23(2) of the Constitution.

A number of important consequences flow from the approach adopted by the Constitutional Court in this case. Among these are the following:

- First, section 23 of the Constitution does not apply only to persons who are in an employment relationship, but also to persons who are in a relationship that is 'akin' to an employment relationship. This means that neither the existence of a contract nor the category of contract is strictly necessary for a person who is performing work for another person to be defined as a 'worker' for the purposes of section 23 of the Constitution.
- Second, the extension of labour rights beyond the limits of a contract of employment is in keeping with the different forms of employment that may be found in a modern economy. Among these are part-time employees, temporary employees, casual employees, persons employed through employment agencies, home workers and so on. These sorts of employees are often vulnerable to exploitation because the nature of their employment makes it difficult for them to form and join trade unions and to bargain collectively.
- Third, while section 23 of the Constitution applies to persons who are in an employment relationship or a relationship akin to an employment relationship, it does not apply to everyone who works. This is because not everyone who works is an employee or is akin to an employee. People who own or work in their own businesses, such as independent contractors, partners and self-employed people, for example, are not employees nor are they akin to employees.

CRITICAL THINKING

What should be the defining characteristic of a worker for the purposes of section 23 of the Constitution?

Given that the concept of a worker in section 23 of the Constitution is wider than the concept of an employee under a contract of employment, but not as wide as the concept of a person who owns and works in his or her own business, the question arises as to who should be protected by section 23. Cheadle argues in this respect that the defining characteristic for deciding whether a person is a worker for the purposes of section 23 should not be whether the person has entered into a contract

209 *South African National Defence Union* paras 24 and 28.

210 See, for example, *R v Genereux* (1992) 88 DLR (4th) 110 (SCC) 156–7 where a minority of the Canadian Supreme Court advanced this argument against the inclusion of members of armed forces in the protection of labour rights.

211 *South African National Defence Union v Minister of Defence* para 29.

of employment or a contract for services, but rather whether the person has entered into a personal and dependent work relationship or is genuinely running his or her own business. In other words, if a person has entered into a personal and dependent work relationship, he or she should be classified as a worker for the purposes of section 23 of the Constitution, but not if he or she is genuinely running his or her own business.[212]

The personal and dependent nature of the work relationship rather than the existence of a contract of employment, he argues further, should be the defining characteristic of a worker for the purposes of section 23 of the Constitution for the following reasons:

- First, the provision of personal and dependent work need not take the form of a contract of employment but may be cast in the form of a contract of service.
- Second, a person who has entered into a personal and dependent work relationship is more vulnerable to exploitation than a person who genuinely owns and works in his or her own business.
- Third, the purpose underlying section 23 of the Constitution is to protect vulnerable workers from being exploited in a way that is unfair.[213]

The personal and dependent nature of the work relationship, Cheadle goes on to concede, may not always provide a clear answer as to who is a worker for the purposes of section 23 of the Constitution. This is because there are certain categories of employees who are neither dependent nor in need of protection, for example executive directors, professional employees or employees with special skills. It is consequently not clear whether these categories of employees should be defined as workers for the purposes of section 23 of the Constitution or not.[214]

While section 23 of the Constitution applies only to those persons who are in an employment relationship or in a relationship akin to an employment relationship, it is important to note that it does not apply only to those persons who are in a **lawful** employment relationship. Instead, it also applies to those persons who are in an unlawful employment relationship, for example sex workers employed by a brothel.

---

212 Cheadle (2013) 18.10.

213 Cheadle (2013) 18.10.

214 Cheadle (2013) 18.4–18.10. S 200A(1) of the LRA provides that

> **until the contrary is proved, a person who works for, or renders services to, any other person is presumed, regardless of the form of the contract, to be an *employee*, if any one or more of the following factors are present:**
> **(*a*) the manner in which the person works is subject to the control or direction of another person;**
> **(*b*) the person's hours of work are subject to the control or direction of another person;**
> **(*c*) in the case of a person who works for an organisation, the person forms part of that organisation;**
> **(*d*) the person has worked for that other person for an average of at least 40 hours per month over the last three months;**
> **(*e*) the person is economically dependent on the other person for whom he or she works or renders services;**
> **(*f*) the person is provided with tools of trade or work equipment by the other person; or**
> **(*g*) the person only works for or renders services to one person.**

Section 200A(2) goes on to provide that subsection (1) does not apply to any person who earns in excess of the amount determined by the Minister in terms of section 6(3) of the BCEA.

PAUSE FOR REFLECTION

Applying section 23 to those persons who are in an unlawful employment relationship

In *Kylie v Commission for Conciliation, Mediation and Arbitration*,[215] the appellant, who was a sex worker, was dismissed by the owner of the massage parlour where she worked without a prior hearing. After she was dismissed, she referred her dismissal to the CCMA for arbitration. Before any evidence was heard, however, the Commissioner dismissed her application on the grounds that the CCMA did not have jurisdiction to arbitrate this matter because the appellant was engaged in an illegal activity. In South African law, engaging in sex work as either a client or as a sex worker is a criminal offence.

Kylie then applied to the Labour Court for an order reviewing and setting aside the Commissioner's decision. The Labour Court, however, dismissed her appeal on the grounds that by accepting jurisdiction, the Commissioner would be sanctioning or encouraging illegal activities. In addition, the Labour Court also held that the primary remedy for an unfair dismissal is reinstatement and it would be untenable for a court to order reinstatement to an activity that was proscribed by law.

The appellant then appealed successfully to the Labour Appeal Court. In arriving at its decision, the Labour Appeal Court began by pointing out that the right to fair labour practices guaranteed in section 23(1) of the Constitution vests not only in those persons who are engaged in lawful activities, but also those persons who are engaged in unlawful activities such as sex workers.

This is because, the Labour Appeal Court pointed out further, the reference to 'everyone' in section 23(1) of the Constitution indicated that the scope of the right to fair labour practices should be interpreted broadly. In addition, it also indicated that the right to fair labour practices applied to persons in employment relationships as well as to persons in relationships that are akin to employment relationships.[216]

It was also important to note, the Labour Appeal Court went on to point out, that sex workers are not stripped of their right to be treated with dignity by their employers simply because they are engaged in illegal activities. Given that section 23 of the Constitution, at its core, aims to protect the dignity of those in employment relationships or relationships akin to employment relationships, it follows that section 23 must also apply to sex workers.[217]

Having found that the right to fair labour practices guaranteed in section 23 of the Constitution vested in the appellant, the Labour Appeal Court turned to consider the question of a remedy.

In this respect, the Labour Appeal Court began by explaining that where a person has performed in terms of an illegal contract, the common law provides that he or she is not allowed to recover his or her performance using an enrichment-based remedy. This is known as the ***par delictum rule***. To prevent an injustice from occurring, however, the courts have been given the power to relax the *par delictum* rule and to allow a person to recover his or her performance using an enrichment remedy.[218]

---

215 2010 (4) SA 383 (LAC).
216 *Kylie* paras 16–22.
217 *Kylie* paras 25–7.
218 *Kylie* paras 32–7.

Given the flexible approach that the courts have adopted towards illegal contracts in terms of the common law, the Labour Appeal Court explained further, there is no reason in principle why the courts cannot adopt a flexible approach towards illegal contracts in terms of section 23 of the Constitution and the LRA. Courts should thus be able to grant a remedy or some other form of protection, especially in those cases where one of the parties forms part of a vulnerable group, such as a sex worker.[219]

Although there is no reason in principle why the courts cannot grant a remedy or some other form of protection in terms of section 23 of the Constitution and the LRA where one of the parties to an illegal contract forms part of a vulnerable group, the Labour Appeal Court went on to explain, this does not mean that a court can grant the full range of remedies available in terms of the LRA. An order reinstating a sex worker, for example, would violate the criminal prohibition on prostitution. In these sorts of cases it would be more appropriate to award the sex worker compensation in the form of money.[220] In light of these considerations, the Labour Appeal Court concluded, there is no doubt that the CCMA did have the jurisdiction to consider the matter.

The approach in the *Kylie* case can be contrasted with the more moralistic approach towards sex workers taken by the majority of the Constitutional Court in *S v Jordan and Others (Sex Workers Education and Advocacy Task Force and Others as Amici Curiae*[221] discussed in chapter 6. In that judgment the Constitutional Court in fact stated that the 'stigma that attaches to prostitutes attaches to them not by virtue of their gender, but by virtue of the conduct they engage in' and declined to recognise the law's discriminatory effect on women.[222]

15.5.3 The right to fair labour practices

15.5.3.1 Introduction

Section 23(1) of the Constitution provides that '[e]veryone has a right to fair labour practices'. The concept of a fair labour practice may be traced back to the Wiehahn Commission. This Commission was appointed to report on and make recommendations about existing labour legislation and published its report in1979.[223] The government accepted the report and amended the 1956 Labour Relations Act[224] to give effect to the Commission's recommendations. The most significant of these amendments was the extension of trade union rights to black employees, the introduction of the concept of unfair labour practices and the establishment of a new court to deal with labour disputes, namely the Industrial Court.

The 1956 Labour Relations Act defined the concept of an unfair labour practice widely as 'any labour practice which in the opinion of the Industrial Court is an unfair labour

219 *Kylie* paras 40–6.
220 *Kylie* paras 52–3.
221 (CCT31/01) [2002] ZACC 22; 2002 (6) SA 642; 2002 (11) BCLR 1117 (9 October 2002).
222 *Jordan* para 16.
223 South Africa Commission of Inquiry into Labour Legislation Wiehahn, NE (1980) *Report of the Commission of Inquiry into Labour Legislation* Republic of South Africa, Department of Manpower Utilisation.
224 Act 28 of 1956.

practice'.[225] This definition was amended in 1982 to introduce a greater degree of specificity. It thus provided that:

> **Unfair labour practice means any act or omission, other than a strike or lock-out, which has the effect that –**
>
> **(i) any employee or class of employees is or may be unfairly affected or that his or their employment opportunities, work security is or may be prejudiced or jeopardised thereby;**
>
> **(ii) the business of any employer or class of employers is or may be unfairly affected or disrupted thereby;**
>
> **(iii) labour unrest is or may be created or promoted thereby;**
>
> **(iv) the labour relationship between employer and employee is or may be detrimentally affected thereby.**[226]

These definitions allowed the Industrial Court to ask not only whether a decision was lawful or not, but also whether a lawful decision was inequitable or unfair. They therefore conferred an equitable jurisdiction on the Industrial Court. In other words, the Industrial Court could act not simply as a court of law, but also as a court of equity. It could judge on a case-by-case basis whether employees had been treated inequitably or unfairly.

Many of the practices that the Industrial Court identified as unfair labour practices were related to dismissals. In this respect, the Industrial Court found, for example, that a decision to dismiss a worker that was substantively unfair was an unfair labour practice and so was a decision to dismiss a worker after following an unfair procedure.[227]

Apart from these practices, the Industrial Court also found that a failure to renew a fixed-term contract, the dismissal of strikers during a lawful strike, selective re-employment and the victimisation of workers who engaged in trade union activities were unfair labour practices.[228]

When the 1956 Labour Relations Act was repealed by the 1995 LRA, the definition contained in the 1956 Act was replaced with a number of provisions that codified some of the practices the Industrial Court had identified as unfair labour practices. Among the most important of these codified provisions are those that regulate dismissals.

15.5.3.2 Unfair dismissals in terms of the Labour Relations Act 66 of 1995

In so far as dismissals[229] are concerned, the LRA provides that a dismissal is unfair if the employer fails to prove on a balance of probabilities that the reason for the dismissal is a fair

---

225 S 1 of the 1956 LRA.

226 S 1 of the 1956 LRA.

227 Van Niekerk, A (2012) *Law@Work* 2nd ed 39.

228 Van Niekerk, A (2012) *Law@Work* 2nd ed 39.

229 S 186(1) of the LRA provides that

> **[d]ismissal means that –**
>
> **(*a*) an employer has terminated a contract of employment with or without notice;**
>
> **(*b*) an employee reasonably expected the employer to renew a fixed term contract of employment on the same or similar terms but the employer offered to renew it on less favourable terms, or did not renew it;**
>
> **(*c*) an employer refused to allow an employee to resume work after she –**
>
> **(i) took maternity leave in terms of any law, collective agreement or her contract of employment;**
>
> **(*d*) an employer who dismissed a number of employees for the same or similar reasons has offered to re-employ one or more of them but has refused to re-employ another; or**
>
> **(*e*) an employee terminated a contract of employment with or without notice because the employer made continued employment intolerable for the employee; or**
>
> **(*f*) an employee terminated a contract of employment with or without notice because the new employer, after a transfer in terms of section 197 or section 197A, provided the employee with conditions or circumstances at work that are substantially less favourable to the employee than those provided by the old employer.**

one and is related to the employee's conduct or capacity, or is based on the employer's operational requirements, and that the dismissal was effected in accordance with a fair procedure.[230] An important consequence of this approach is that, in effect, the LRA allows an employee to be dismissed only on the grounds of misconduct, incapacity or for operational reasons.

Misconduct occurs when an employee breaches a rule of employment. Most collective agreements incorporate codes of conduct which are binding on the parties to the agreement. If a party to the collective agreement breaches a provision of the code of conduct, he or she will be guilty of misconduct. In addition, Schedule 8 of the LRA provides for a Code of Good Practice: Dismissal. Item 2 of this Code provides that a dismissal will be unfair if it is not effected for a fair reason and in accordance with a fair procedure even if it complies with a notice period stipulated in a contract.

The LRA deems certain dismissals to be automatically unfair. Section 187 of the LRA provides in this respect that a dismissal is automatically unfair if the reason for the dismissal is:

> **(i) that the employee participated in a protected strike;**
> **(ii) that the employee is pregnant or intends to fall pregnant; or**
> **(iii) that the employer unfairly discriminated against the employee, directly or indirectly, on any arbitrary ground, including, but not limited to, race, gender, sex, ethnic or social origin, colour, sexual orientation, age, disability, religion, conscience, belief, political opinion, culture, language, marital status or family responsibility.**

Dismissal for incapacity relates to an inability to perform the functions of the job. The Code of Good Practice: Dismissals draws a distinction between a dismissal for poor work performance[231] and a dismissal because of ill health or injury.[232]

A dismissal for poor work performance will be fair if the employee fails to meet the standard set by the employer and was aware or could reasonably be expected to be aware of the standard. In addition, the employer must give the employee a fair opportunity to meet the standard and dismissal must be an appropriate sanction.

In respect of dismissal because of ill health or injury, the employer must make a determination as to whether it is temporary or permanent. The employer must also determine the length of time that the employee is likely to be incapacitated and must investigate possible alternatives, short of dismissal. Relevant factors to consider in determining whether alternatives to dismissal are feasible include the nature of the job, the period of absence, the seriousness of the illness or injury, and the possibility of securing a temporary replacement for the ill or injured employee.[233]

Operational requirements relate to the economic, technological, structural or similar needs of the employer. If the business has to be restructured and the staff complement reduced as a consequence of an economic downturn, then the employer may dismiss employees for operational reasons. The Code of Good Practice issued in terms of the LRA[234] categorises this as a 'no fault dismissal'. The Code obliges employers to consider all possible

230 S 188(1) of the LRA.
231 Items 8 and 9 of the Code of Good Practice: Dismissals.
232 Items 10 and 11 of the Code of Good Practice: Dismissals.
233 Items 10 and 11 of the Code of Good Practice: Dismissals.
234 GN 1517 in *Government Gazette* 20254 of 16 July 1999.

alternatives to dismissal. The employer is also obliged to consult with the workers in good faith.

The employer must adopt fair criteria in determining who is to be dismissed and generally the last in first out principle must be used. Employees dismissed on the basis of operational reasons are entitled to severance pay of at least one week's remuneration for each year of continuous service. Employees dismissed for operational reasons must be given preference if the employer hires employees again.

Apart from the requirements set out above, all dismissals must be carried out in accordance with a fair procedure.[235] This is an independent requirement and a dismissal that is procedurally unfair will be deemed to be an unfair dismissal even if there are good reasons for the dismissal. The requirements of procedural fairness depend on the circumstances of the case. The seriousness of the consequences for the affected employee and the nature of the matter will determine the nature of the process to be followed.

Finally, it is important to note that the employer must give timely notice of the pending disciplinary hearing and must provide sufficient detail of the gist of the case against the employee in a form that the employee understands. The employee must be permitted to be represented by a co-worker or union representative. The employee must be given a reasonable opportunity to dispute the case against him or her and be allowed to put his or her version before an independent person. This includes challenging witnesses and calling witnesses on his or her behalf. Finally, the person making the decision must provide reasons for his or her conclusion.[236]

15.5.3.3 Unfair labour practices in terms of the LRA

Apart from codifying some of the practices that the Industrial Court had identified as unfair labour practices, the 1995 LRA also contains a general definition of an unfair labour practice. Section 186(2) of the LRA provides in this respect that:

> **Unfair labour practice means any unfair act or omission that arises between an employer and an employee involving –**
>
> **(*a*) unfair conduct by the employer relating to the promotion, demotion, probation (excluding disputes about dismissals for a reason relating to probation) or training of an employee or relating to the provision of benefits to an employee;**
>
> **(*b*) the unfair suspension of an employee or any other unfair disciplinary action short of dismissal in respect of an employee;**
>
> **(*c*) a failure or refusal by an employer to reinstate or re-employ a former employee in terms of any agreement; and**
>
> **(*d*) an occupational detriment, other than dismissal, in contravention of the Protected Disclosures Act, 2000 (Act 26 of 2000), on account of the employee having made a protected disclosure defined in that Act.**

The act or omission complained of must be between an employee and his or her employer and must not extend beyond the employment relationship. It regulates the most important facets of the employment relationship such as promotion, training, provision of benefits, suspensions, disciplinary action, failure to reinstate in accordance with an agreement and actions in contravention of the Protected Disclosures Act. Thus, an employee alleging that

---

235 S 188(1)(*b*) of the LRA.

236 Du Toit, D et al (2006) *Labour Relations Law: A Comprehensive Guide* 5th ed 403–6.

he or she has been treated in a manner that contravenes section 186(2) can use the procedures prescribed in the LRA to seek relief.

15.5.3.4 Unfair labour practices in terms of section 23(1) of the Constitution

Given that the LRA deals extensively with the right to fair labour practices, it is unlikely that the parties to a labour dispute will rely on the constitutional right to institute a claim for an unfair labour practice. Despite this fact, the Constitutional Court has discussed the scope and ambit of section 23(1) of the Constitution on more than one occasion. While the Labour Appeal Court and the Labour Court are responsible for overseeing the interpretation and application of the LRA, this does not mean the Constitutional Court has no role to play in the determination of fair labour practices. 'Indeed,' said the Court, 'it has a crucial role in ensuring that the rights guaranteed in section 23(1) are honoured.'[237]

Thus in *NEHAWU*, for example, the Constitutional Court held that when it comes to determining what amounts to a fair labour practice regard must be had to what is fair to both sides.[238] In addition, the Court held further there must also be an appreciation of the inherent tensions in the employee/employer relationship and an attempt must be made to accommodate these differing concerns appropriately.[239]

The focus of section 23(1) is, broadly speaking, the relationship between the worker and the employer and the continuation of that relationship on terms that are fair to both. In giving content to that right, it is important to bear in mind the tension between the interests of the workers and the interests of the employers which is inherent in labour relations. Care must therefore be taken to accommodate, where possible, these interests so as to arrive at the balance required by the concept of fair labour practices.

The approach adopted in *NEHAWU* was confirmed in *Sidumo and Another v Rustenburg Platinum Mines Ltd and Others*.[240] In this case, the Court decided that a commissioner did not have to defer to an employer's decision on sanctions. In arriving at this decision, the Court said:

> **Neither the Constitution nor the LRA affords any preferential status to the employer's view of the fairness of the dismissal. It is against constitutional norms and against the right to fair labour practices to give pre-eminence to the views of either party to a dispute. Dismissal disputes are often emotionally charged. It is therefore all the more important that a scrupulous even-handedness be maintained. The approach of the Supreme Court of Appeal tilts the balance against employees.**[241]

In *NEHAWU*, the Constitutional Court also recognised that fairness is incapable of precise definition, especially in light of the tension that exists between the interests of workers and the interests of employers. It is accordingly a value judgment which depends on the circumstances of each case.

Our Constitution is unique in constitutionalising the right to fair labour practice. However, the concept is not defined in the Constitution. The concept of fair labour practice is incapable of precise definition. This problem is confounded by the tension between the interests of the workers and the interests of the employers that is inherent in labour relations. Indeed, what

---

237 *NEHAWU* para 35.

238 *NEHAWU* para 38.

239 *NEHAWU* para 40.

240 (CCT 85/06) [2007] ZACC 22; [2007] 12 BLLR 1097 (CC); 2008 (2) SA 24 (CC); (2007) 28 ILJ 2405 (CC); 2008 (2) BCLR 158 (CC) (5 October 2007).

241 *Sidumo* para 74.

is fair depends on the circumstances of a particular case and essentially involves a value judgment. It is therefore neither necessary nor desirable to define the concept.[242]

15.5.4 The right of every worker to form and join a trade union

Given the unequal power of individual workers/employees on the one hand and employers on the other hand, the right of workers to form trade unions that can protect the interests of individual workers is a pivotal aspect of a fair labour relations regime. Section 23(2)(*a*) of the Constitution provides that '[e]very worker has the right (*a*) to form and join a trade union'. Taken together with section 23(3)(*a*) of the Constitution, which provides that '[e]very employer has the right to form and join an employers' organisation', this right gives effect to the right to freedom of association in a labour context.

PAUSE FOR REFLECTION

Was the Constitutional Court correct when it held that the total ban on trade unions in the SANDF was unconstitutional and invalid?

As we have already seen in *South African National Defence Union*, the Constitutional Court found that section 126B(1) of the Defence Act, which prohibited members of the SANDF from joining or becoming members of a trade union, infringed the right to join a trade union guaranteed in section 23(2) of the Constitution. After coming to this conclusion, the Constitutional Court had to consider whether the infringement was reasonable and justifiable in terms of the limitation clause.

In this respect, the Minister argued that section 126B(1) of the Defence Act was necessary to maintain a disciplined military force. If soldiers were allowed to join a union, bargain collectively and subsequently to strike, the Minister argued further, military discipline would be seriously and adversely affected and this would have grave consequences for the security of the country.[243]

In response, the applicant argued that granting permanent members of the SANDF the right to join a union would not affect military discipline and weaken the combat readiness of the SANDF because it was not claiming the right to strike, but simply the right to join or form a trade union and to bargain collectively. A trade union, the applicant argued further, could function and further the interests of its members without participating in strike action.[244]

The Constitutional Court pointed out that while the state is clearly entitled to take steps to achieve the legitimate constitutional goal of maintaining a disciplined and effective defence force, there is no evidence to suggest that permitting permanent members of the SANDF to join a trade union, no matter how its activities are circumscribed, will undermine the discipline and efficiency of the SANDF.[245]

Given this conclusion, the Court found that the total ban on trade unions in the SANDF went beyond what is reasonable and justifiable to achieve the legitimate state objective of a disciplined and effective military force. Such a ban could not therefore be justified in terms of the limitation clause and section 126B(1) of the Defence Act had to be declared unconstitutional and invalid.[246]

---

242 *Sidumo* paras 38 and 65.
243 *South African National Defence Union* para 32.
244 *South African National Defence Union* para 33.
245 *South African National Defence Union* para 35.
246 *South African National Defence Union* para 36.

The mere fact that trade unions are entitled to operate in the SANDF does not mean, however, the Constitutional Court also observed, that they should enjoy the same rights and powers as all other trade unions. A trade union operating in the SANDF may be subject to controls and restrictions aimed at achieving military discipline and efficiency provided these controls and restrictions satisfy the requirements of the limitation clause.[247]

In 2009, approximately 1 000 disgruntled members of the SANDF participated in an illegal march on the Union Buildings in Pretoria demanding better salaries. Unfortunately, the march turned violent and the police had to use water cannon, rubber bullets and teargas to disperse the soldiers. The following day, the Minister of Defence, Ms Lindiwe Sisulu called the march 'a serious and immediate threat to national security'.[248] The Minister's comments were premised on the idea that the existence of a trade union in the defence force was by its very nature problematic and potentially threatened the national security of the country.

The question arises whether the Constitutional Court was correct when it held that the total ban on trade unions in the SANDF was unconstitutional and invalid. Did the Court err when it made this decision or is there is a distinction between the general principle - that trade unions should be allowed in the armed forces - and the specific rogue actions of the soldiers involved in the incident described above?

A trade union is defined in the LRA as 'an association of employees whose principle purpose is to regulate relations between employees and employers, including any employers' organisation'.[249] Chapter II of the LRA regulates the right of every worker to form and join a trade union. Section 2 of the LRA provides in this respect as follows:

> **(1) Every employee has the right -**
> **(*a*) to participate in forming a trade union or federation of trade unions; and**
> **(*b*) to join a trade union, subject to its constitution.**
> **(2) Every member of a trade union has the right, subject to the constitution of that trade union -**
> **(*a*) to participate in its lawful activities;**
> **(*b*) to participate in the election of any of its office-bearers, officials or trade union representatives;**
> **(*c*) to stand for election and be eligible for appointment as an office-bearer or official and, if elected or appointed, to hold office; and**
> **(*d*) to stand for election and be eligible for appointment as a trade union representative and, if elected or appointed, to carry out the functions of a trade union representative in terms of this Act or any collective agreement.**

247 *South African National Defence Union* para 36.

248 South African Government News Agency (2009, August) Address by Defence and Military Veterans Minister, Lindiwe Sisulu, on the Illegal March by SANDF Members to the Union Buildings available at http://www.sanews.gov.sa/south-africa/address-defence-and-military-veterans-minister-lindiwe-sisulu-illegal-march-sandu.

249 S 213 of the LRA.

> **(3) Every member of a trade union that is a member of a federation of trade unions has the right, subject to the constitution of that federation –**
> **(*a*) to participate in its lawful activities;**
> **(*b*) to participate in the election of any of its office-bearers or officials; and**
> **(*c*) to stand for election and be eligible for appointment as an office-bearer or official and, if elected or appointed to hold office.**

Section 5 of the LRA protects the individual rights conferred on employees by the Act.[250] Chapter 2 of the LRA also confers somewhat similar rights on employers. Section 6 provides in this respect as follows:

> **(1) Every employer has the right –**
> **(*a*) to participate in forming an employers' organisation or federation of employers' organisations; and**
> **(*b*) to join an employers' organisation, subject to its constitution.**
> **(2) Every member of an employers' organisation has the right, subject to the constitution of that employers' organisation –**
> **(*a*) to participate in its lawful activities;**
> **(*b*) to participate in the election of any of its office-bearers or officials; and**
> **(*c*) if –**
> **(i) a natural person, to stand for election and be eligible for appointment as an office-bearer or official and, if elected or appointed, to hold office;**
> **(ii) if a juristic person, to have a representative stand for election, and be eligible for appointment, as an office-bearer or official and, if elected or appointed, to hold office.**

---

250 S 5 of the LRA provides that:

> **(1) No person may discriminate against an employee for exercising any right conferred by this Act.**
> **(2) Without limiting the general protection conferred by subsection (1), no person may do, or threaten to do, any of the following –**
> **(*a*) require an employee or a person seeking employment –**
> **(i) not to be a member of a trade union or workplace forum;**
> **(ii) not to become a member of a trade union or workplace forum; or**
> **(iii) to give up membership of a trade union or workplace forum;**
> **(*b*) prevent an employee or a person seeking employment from exercising any right conferred by this Act or from participating in any proceedings in terms of this Act; or**
> **(*c*) prejudice an employee or a person seeking employment because of past, present or anticipated –**
> **(i) membership of a trade union or workplace forum;**
> **(ii) participation in forming a trade union or federation of trade unions or establishing a workplace forum;**
> **(iii) participation in the lawful activities of a trade union, federation of trade unions or workplace forum;**
> **(iv) failure or refusal to do something that an employer may not lawfully permit or require an employee to do;**
> **(v) disclosure of information that the employee is lawfully entitled or required to give to another person;**
> **(vi) exercise of any right conferred by this Act; or**
> **(vii) participation in any proceedings in terms of this Act.**
> **(3) No person may advantage, or promise to advantage, an employee or a person seeking employment in exchange for that person not exercising any right conferred by this Act or not participating in any proceedings in terms of this Act. However, nothing in this section precludes the parties to a dispute from concluding an agreement to settle that dispute.**
> **(4) A provision in any contract, whether entered into before or after the commencement of this Act, that directly or indirectly contradicts or limits any provision of section 4, or this section, is invalid, unless the contractual provision is permitted by this Act.**

(3) Every member of an employers' organisation that is a member of a federation of employers' organisations has the right, subject to the constitution of that federation –

(*a*) to participate in its lawful activities;

(*b*) to participate in the election of any of its office-bearers or officials; and

(*c*) if –

(i) a natural person, to stand for election and be eligible for appointment as an office-bearer or official and, if elected or appointed, to hold office; or

(ii) if a juristic person, to have a representative stand for election, and be eligible for appointment, as an office-bearer or official and, if elected or appointed, to hold office.

Section 7 of the LRA protects the individual rights conferred on employers by the Act.[251]

PAUSE FOR REFLECTION

Do closed shop and agency shop agreements infringe the right to freedom of association?

Sections 25 and 26 of the LRA make provision for so-called closed shop and agency shop agreements. A closed shop agreement is a collective agreement entered into by a majority union and an employer or employers organisation. The agreement provides that all employees covered by the agreement must become members of the majority trade union. An employee who refuses to join the majority union or who is refused membership may be dismissed.[252] An agency shop agreement is a collective agreement entered into by a majority union and an employer or employers organisation. This

---

251 S 7 of the LRA provides that:

7. (1) No person may discriminate against an employer for exercising any right conferred by this Act.

(2) Without limiting the general protection conferred by subsection (1), no person may do, or threaten to do, any of the following –

(*a*) require an employer –

(i) not to be a member of an employers' organisation;

(ii) not to become a member of an employers' organisation; or

(iii) to give up membership of an employers' organisation;

(*b*) prevent an employer from exercising any right conferred by this Act or from participating in any proceedings in terms of this Act; or

(*c*) prejudice an employer because of past, present or anticipated –

(i) membership of an employers' organisation;

(ii) participation in forming an employers' organisation or a federation of employers' organisations;

(iii) participation in the lawful activities of an employers' organisation or a federation of employers' organisations;

(iv) disclosure of information that the employer is lawfully entitled or required to give to another person;

(v) exercise of any right conferred by this Act; or

(vi) participation in any proceedings in terms of this Act.

(3) No person may advantage, or promise to advantage, an employer in exchange for that employer not exercising any right conferred by this Act or not participating in any proceedings in terms of this Act. However, nothing in this section precludes the parties to a dispute from concluding an agreement to settle that dispute.

(4) A provision in any contract, whether entered into before or after the commencement of this Act, that directly or indirectly contradicts or limits any provision of section 6, or this section, is invalid, unless the contractual provision is permitted by this Act.

252 S 26(1) of the LRA. S 26 contains a number of safeguards aimed at promoting its constitutional validity.

agreement does not compel all employees to become members of the majority union, but does require non-members to contribute an agency fee to the majority union as a condition of employment.[253]

A difficult question that arises in respect of these agreements is whether they infringe the right to freedom of association and, in particular, the right not to associate guaranteed in section 23(2)(*a*) of the Constitution and section 4 of the LRA. To answer this question, Du Toit suggests that a two-stage enquiry should be adopted:

> The first question is whether, in fact, the closed shop provision does limit the right to freedom of association in a constitutional sense. This involves examining whether any formal limitation of the above rights by a closed shop agreement is outweighed by its promotion of other basic rights contained in the Constitution, notably the right of trade unions to engage in collective bargaining. Through 'internal balancing' of these related rights, it may be concluded that section 26 in a substantive sense reinforces rather than limits those rights. If, on the other hand, it is found to be a limitation, the second question is whether it can be justified in terms of section 36 of the Constitution.[254]

15.5.5 The right of every worker to participate in the activities and programmes of a trade union

Section 23(2)(*b*) provides that '[e]very worker has the right to participate in the activities and programmes of a trade union'. Taken together with section 23(3)(*b*), which provides that '[e]very employer has the right to participate in the activities and programmes of an employers' organization', these rights give effect to the right to organise. Organisational rights make it possible for trade unions to recruit members, to interact and engage with them in the workplace, to elect union representatives, to access certain information for the purposes of collective bargaining, to maintain financial stability, and thus ultimately to promote the system of collective bargaining.[255] The LRA grants unions several organisational rights designed to ensure that they are able to compete for members, remain financially stable and perform their day-to-day functions. These organisational rights contained in the LRA therefore aim to give substance to the general rights conferred on unions by the Constitution.[256]

Chapter 3 of the LRA regulates the organisational rights of trade unions. These organisational rights may be divided into five categories, namely:

- trade union access to the workplace[257]
- deductions of trade union subscriptions[258]
- election of trade union representatives[259]
- leave for trade union activities[260]
- disclosure of information.[261]

---

253 S 25(1) of the LRA. Like s 26, s 25 also contains a number of safeguards aimed at promoting its constitutional validity.
254 Du Toit (2006) 191.
255 Van Niekerk (2012) 349.
256 Currie and De Waal (2013) 486.
257 S 12 of the LRA.
258 S 13 of the LRA.
259 S 14 of the LRA.
260 S 15 of the LRA.
261 S 16 of the LRA.

As its name suggests, the right of trade union access to the workplace provides that trade union officials may have access to an employer's premises for purposes of recruiting members, communicating with them or for holding meetings outside working hours.

The right to deductions of trade union subscriptions provides that members of trade unions may authorise their employers to deduct their trade union subscriptions from their salaries and remit the subscriptions to the trade unions.

The right to elect trade union representatives provides for the recognition of elected shop stewards for certain purposes, most importantly, perhaps, to represent trade union members in grievance and disciplinary proceedings.

The right to leave for trade union activities provides that employees who are union office bearers are entitled to reasonable amounts of time off during working hours to attend to union business.

The right to disclosure of information provides that a union may require the disclosure of certain information.

PAUSE FOR REFLECTION

Is a minority union entitled to take lawful strike action?

Section 11 of the LRA provides that a trade union may only claim the organisational rights set out in sections 12, 13 and 15 of the Act if it is 'sufficiently representative' of the employees employed by an employer in a workplace. Sections 14(1) and 16(1) provide that a trade union may only claim the organisational rights set out in sections 14 and 16 respectively if it has as members a majority of the employees employed by an employer in a workplace. This means the LRA only confers organisational rights on unions which can demonstrate at least the minimum threshold of support. This does not mean that minority unions will never acquire these rights. They can do so with the employer's support or by demonstrating support through strike action. This was confirmed in *NUMSA*.

In this case, the Constitutional Court held that while the organisational rights set out in sections 12 to 16 of the LRA may be claimed as a right only by a representative trade union, there is nothing to prevent other trade unions from obtaining organisational rights through other means, including industrial action. In doing so, the Court relied on international law precedent and identified two important principles:

- First, the Court said that organisational rights are closely associated with the right to freedom of association, which is ordinarily interpreted to afford unions the right to recruit members and to represent those members at least in individual workplace grievances. Also, unions should have the right to strike to enforce collective bargaining demands.
- Second, it must be assumed that unions have the right to take industrial action to pursue their demands.[262]

In this case, the key issue the Constitutional Court had to decide was whether a minority union and its members were entitled to take lawful strike action to persuade an employer to recognise its shop stewards. The Court held that they were.

262 *NUMSA* paras 34–5.

15.5.6 The right of every worker to strike

Section 23(2)(*c*) of the Constitution provides that '[e]very worker has the right to strike'. The right to strike occurs when workers withhold their labour in an effort to pressurise an employer to accede to their demands. It is recognised that the right to strike addresses the power imbalances and allows for effective collective bargaining.

In *NUMSA*, the Constitutional Court held that the right to strike is important for two reasons:

- First, the right to strike protects the dignity of workers who, in our constitutional order, may not be treated as coerced employees.
- Second, this right is an important component of a successful collective bargaining system. This is because it is through industrial action that workers are able to assert bargaining power in industrial relations.[263]

Section 213 of the LRA defines a strike as follows:

> **Strike means the partial or complete concerted refusal to work, or the retardation or obstruction of work, by persons who are or have been employed by the same employer or by different employers, for the purpose of remedying a grievance or resolving a dispute in respect of any matter of mutual interest between employer and employee, and every reference to 'work' in this definition includes overtime work, whether it is voluntary or compulsory.**

The LRA regulates the right of every worker to strike. This section prescribes the procedural and substantive requirements that must be met for a strike to be lawful and protected. In so far as the procedural requirements are concerned, section 64(1) of the LRA provides that every employee has the right to strike and every employer has the recourse to lock-out if:

- the issue has been referred for conciliation either to a bargaining council or to the CCMA and a certificate indicating that the parties are unable to resolve the issues has been issued
- the employer, the Bargaining Council or the employers' organisation has been given at least 48 hours' notice of the commencement of the strike, in writing
- the employees, the trade union or the Bargaining Council has been given at least 48 hours' notice of the commencement of the lock-out, in writing.

In those cases in which the state is the employer, at least seven days' notice of the commencement of the strike or lock-out must be given.[264]

Section 64 also prescribes the circumstances when it is permissible to depart from the statutory requirements listed above. These include cases in which:

- the parties to the dispute are members of a bargaining council and the dispute has been dealt with by that council
- the strike conforms to procedures in a collective agreement
- the strike is in response to an unlawful lock-out by the employer.

---

263 *NUMSA* para 13.

264 S 64(1)(*d*) of the LRA.

PAUSE FOR REFLECTION

Who is required to give notice of the commencement of a strike?

Although section 64 of the LRA provides that an employer must be given at least 48 hours' notice of the commencement of a strike in writing, it does not say who should give this notice. The question of who is required to give such a notice was considered by the Constitutional Court in its judgment in *South African Transport and Allied Workers Union (SATAWU) and Others v Moloto NO and Another.*[265]

In this case, a company called Equity Aviation (Pty) Ltd (Equity) employed 1 157 people. Of these employees, 725 were members of the South African Transport and Allied Workers Union (SATAWU). SATAWU was, therefore, the majority union at Equity. On 13 November 2003, SATAWU referred a wage dispute to the CCMA for conciliation. Unfortunately, this attempt at conciliation failed and on 15 December 2003 the CCMA issued a certificate to that effect. On the same day, SATAWU issued a strike notice to Equity in accordance with section 64(1)(*b*) of the LRA.

When the strike action commenced, however, members not only of SATAWU but also of the other minority unions represented at Equity joined the strike even though they had not issued a strike notice in accordance with section 64(1)(*b*). Given this failure, Equity warned the non-SATAWU employees to return to work because it considered their participation in the strike to be unlawful. When they refused to return to work, Equity dismissed them for unauthorised absence from work during the strike. Section 64(1)(*b*) states that striking employees are protected and cannot be fired if certain procedural requirements are met, including the requirement that 'at least 48 hours' notice of the commencement of the strike, in writing, has been given to the employer'.

For the majority, the starting point of the enquiry was the Constitution which protects the right to strike as a fundamental right without expressly limiting this right. The majority affirmed that constitutional rights conferred without express limitation should not be cut down by interpreting ambiguous legislative provisions as imposing implicit limitations on them.[266]

As section 64(1)(*b*) contains no express requirement that every employee who intends to participate in a protected strike must personally or through a representative give notice of the commencement of the intended strike, nor that the notice must indicate who will take part in the strike, it was sufficient that SATAWU had given notice that it would strike. As the majority stated:

> **The point of departure in interpreting section 64(1) is that we should not restrict the right to strike more than is expressly required by the language of the provision, unless the purposes of the Act and the section on 'a proper interpretation of the statute ... imports them.' The relevance of a restrictive approach is to raise a cautionary flag against restricting the right more than is expressly provided for. Intrusion into the right should only be as much as is necessary to achieve the purpose of the provision and this requires sensitivity to the constraints of the language used.**[267]

265 (CCT128/11) [2012] ZACC 19; 2012 (6) SA 249 (CC); 2012 (11) BCLR 1177 (CC); [2012] 12 BLLR 1193 (CC); (2012) 33 ILJ 2549 (CC) (21 September 2012).

266 *SATAWU* paras 10–11.

267 *SATAWU* para 54.

It is an accepted interpretative principle in our constitutional jurisprudence that if there is more than one interpretation of a statutory provision that is constitutionally compliant, the interpretation that best conforms with the spirit, purport and objects of the Bill of Rights should be preferred. In this case, the interpretation not requiring every non-unionised member to give notice of their intention to take part in a strike organised by a union best conforms to the spirit, purport and object of the Bill of Rights.[268]

This becomes even more evident if we recall that the right to strike is protected in the Constitution at least partly in recognition of the fact that there are disparities in the social and economic power held by employers and employees. Employers have far more power than individual employees and to redress the inequality in social and economic power in employer/employee relations, employees are granted the right to strike to even out the playing field. To require individual employees to give detailed information of not only when they will strike, but how many of them will strike, 'would run counter to the underlying purpose of the right to strike in our Constitution – to level the playing fields of economic and social power already generally tilted in favour of employers'.[269] As the majority pointed out:

> **to hold otherwise would place a greater restriction on the right to strike of non-unionised employees and minority union employees than on majority union employees. It is these employees, much more than those who are unionised or represented by a majority union, who will feel the lash of a more onerous requirement. There is no warrant for that where they were already denied the right to bargain collectively on their own behalf in the preceding process.**[270]

The minority judgment took a more restrictive view of the rights of strikers and is more closely aligned with the interests of employers than with those of employees. Focusing on the objects of the LRA instead of on the relevant section in the Bill of Rights which guarantees employees the right to strike, the minority found that employers would be negatively affected if not all employees were required either individually or through their representatives to give notice to employers that they were going to embark on a strike.[271]

In contrast to the majority view, which focused on the imbalances in power between striking workers and their employers, the minority seemed to assume that employers were powerless in the face of a strike. Accordingly, the minority claimed:

> **if a notice gives an employer no indication of which of its employees might strike, it is nigh impossible to conceive how the employer will prepare properly for the impending power play. How will it make an informed decision as to whether or not to yield to the employees' demands? And, if it resists, how will it take proper steps to protect its business, the employees and the public and engage meaningfully in pre-strike regulatory discussions regarding issues such as picketing rules?**[272]

268 *SATAWU* para 53.
269 *SATAWU* para 86.
270 *SATAWU* para 92.
271 *SATAWU* para 17.
272 *SATAWU* para 27.

The minority would therefore have reinterpreted the relevant section of the LRA so as to require that employees provide an employer with a notice:

> **that makes it possible for the employer to reasonably identify the employees that may strike. And whilst this requirement may well place a burden on the exercise of the right to strike, the constitutionality of the provisions is not in the balance and it is therefore unnecessary to resolve the question.**[273]

The two judgments therefore seem to reflect rather stark ideological differences between the judges on the Constitutional Court as well as differences in how to view the relationship between the provisions of the Bill of Rights, on the one hand, and provisions of legislation giving effect to those rights on the other.

The majority seems to be decidedly more progressive by assuming that the right to strike contained in the Bill of Rights should be limited as little as possible to ensure the levelling of the playing field between employers and employees. They would therefore oppose an interpretation of the legislation that would impose limitations on this right unless such limitations are expressly stated in the LRA itself.

The minority seems to be rather more sympathetic to employers and less enthusiastic about protecting the rights of striking workers. They are also more eager to interfere in the work of the democratically elected Parliament by reinterpreting legislation passed by that Parliament in such a manner that it would limit the rights of workers even if that was perhaps not what the democratically elected Parliament intended to do.[274]

In so far as the substantive requirements that must be met for a strike to be lawful are concerned, the LRA draws a distinction between disputes of rights and disputes of interests.

Rights disputes revolve around the interpretation and application of existing rights and are generally arbitrable through the bargaining councils or through the labour courts.

Disputes of interest relate to proposed new terms and conditions of employment. These disputes can be the subject of industrial action as parties use either strike action or lock-out in an attempt to strengthen their bargaining positions.

15.5.7 The right to engage in collective bargaining

15.5.7.1 Introduction

The right to strike, as well as the organisational rights of unions, must be viewed in the light of the broader aims of unions and their members, namely to engage in collective bargaining to improve the working conditions of workers. The assumption is that workers will be more powerful if they bargain collectively than if they bargain as individuals, thus levelling the playing field. Section 23(5) of the Constitution provides that '[e]very trade union, employers' organization and employer has the right to engage in collective bargaining. National legislation may be enacted to regulate collective bargaining. To the extent that the legislation may limit a right in this Chapter, the limitation must comply with section 36(1)'.

---

273 *SATAWU* para 34.

274 See De Vos, P (2012, 25 September) Sharp divisions on the Constitutional Court about the right to strike *Constitutionally Speaking* available at http://constitutionallyspeaking.co.za/sharp-divisions-on-the-constitutional-court-about-the-right-to-strike/.

Grogan describes collective bargaining as the process:

> **by which employers and organised groups of employees seek to reconcile their conflicting goals through mutual accommodation. The dynamic of collective bargaining is demand and concession; its objective is agreement. Unlike mere consultation, therefore, collective bargaining assumes willingness on each side not only to listen and to consider the representations of the other but also to abandon fixed positions where possible in order to find common ground.**[275]

Collective bargaining works best when the parties have relatively equal bargaining power and when this happens in an atmosphere of mutual trust and respect.

15.5.7.2 The right to engage in collective bargaining and the LRA

The LRA does not impose a legally enforceable obligation on employers and employees to engage in collective bargaining. However, it does seek to promote and facilitate collective bargaining in terms of which employee organisations and employers and employer organisations negotiate on matters of mutual interest that concern their sector. The main purpose of these negotiations is to preserve industrial peace. Much of these negotiations occur in bargaining councils created for the various sectors and areas. Thus there is a bargaining council for the local government sector as there is for the metal and engineering industries, the motor industry and the building industry. Bargaining councils have to be registered in terms of the LRA.[276]

PAUSE FOR REFLECTION

The exclusion of a duty to bargain from the LRA

Prior to the enactment of the LRA in 1995, the Industrial Court held that employers were legally required to recognise representative trade unions and bargain with them in certain circumstances. This duty to bargain, however, was not absolute and arose only in those cases in which an employer's refusal to bargain could be classified as an unfair labour practice. To determine whether an employer's refusal to bargain was an unfair labour practice, the Industrial Court took various factors into account, such as the interests of the employer and the interests of the employees.[277]

The drafters of the LRA, however, decided to adopt a different approach and deliberately excluded any mention of a duty to bargain from the definition of an unfair labour practice. The reasons behind this decision are set out in the Explanatory Memorandum to the Labour Relations Bill. The Memorandum states that '[a] notable feature of the draft Bill is the absence of any statutory duty to bargain. In its deliberations on a revised system of collective bargaining, the Task Team gave consideration to three competing models'.[278]

The first of these models, the Memorandum states further:

> **is a system of statutory compulsion, in which a duty to bargain is underpinned by a statutory determination of the levels at which bargaining should take place and the issues over which parties are compelled to bargain. The second model is not**

275 Grogan (2009) 343.
276 S 29 of the LRA.
277 Van Niekerk (2012) 370.
278 Ministerial Legal Task Team (1995, January) Explanatory Memorandum *Industrial Law Journal* 16(2):278–336 at 292.

> dissimilar though more flexible. It relies on intervention by the judiciary to determine appropriate levels of bargaining and bargaining topics. The third model, unanimously adopted by the Task Team, is one that allows the parties, through the exercise of power, to determine their own arrangements.
>
> ...
>
> The exercise of power, or indeed persuasion, is given statutory impetus by the draft Bill's provision for organisational rights and a protected right to strike.[279]

As Van Niekerk points out, the approach adopted by the Task Team involves a trade-off. On the one hand, there is a voluntary system of collective bargaining, while on the other hand there is a strong set of organisational rights for registered trade unions, coupled with a right to strike over recognition and bargaining demands.[280]

The functions of bargaining councils include the conclusion of collective agreements, the enforcement of these collective agreements and the prevention and resolution of labour disputes.[281] Once agreements are reached, they are regarded as collective agreements and are binding on all parties to the bargaining council.[282] Application can be made to the Minister to extend the collective agreement to persons who are not party (non-parties) to the bargaining council but who are employed in the sector and area over which the bargaining council has jurisdiction.[283]

An application may be made if one or more of the registered trade unions representing the majority of members and one or more of the employers' organisations whose members employ the majority of employees that are party to the bargaining council support the extension.[284] In addition, ministerial approval is dependent on whether the non-parties fall within the scope of the bargaining council, on whether there exists an independent body to grant exemptions to non-parties and if the terms of the agreement do not discriminate against non-parties.

By extending collective agreements to non-parties, parity and uniformity is maintained in that particular sector in respect of earnings, conditions of service and issues of mutual interest. Non-parties aggrieved by their inclusion are able to argue their cases before an independent person appointed in terms of the collective agreement.

15.5.7.3 The right to engage in collective bargaining and the Constitution

Although the LRA does not impose a legally enforceable obligation on employers to engage in collective bargaining, it is not clear whether this approach is consistent with the right to engage in collective bargaining guaranteed in section 23(5) of the Constitution. In other words, it is not clear whether section 23(5) of the Constitution imposes a legally enforceable obligation on employers to engage in collective bargaining or not.

---

279 Ministerial Legal Task Team (1995) 292.
280 Van Niekerk (2012) 371.
281 S 28 of the LRA.
282 S 31 of the LRA.
283 S 32 of the LRA.
284 S 32 of the LRA.

According to Cheadle, the right to engage in collective bargaining may be divided into three elements:[285]

- First, there is the negative **freedom** to bargain collectively. This freedom may be enforced against the state if it passes legislation that prohibits collective bargaining or has the effect of prohibiting collective bargaining. In addition, it may also be enforced against an employers' organisation or trade union that, by collective agreement or by the exercise of economic power, prevents employers and workers from engaging in collective bargaining.[286]
- Second, there is the right to use economic power. In its judgment in *Certification of the Constitution of The Republic of South Africa, 1996*,[287] the Constitutional Court held that the right to bargain collectively contained within it the right to exercise some economic power against partners in collective bargaining, such as dismissal, the employment of alternative or replacement labour, and the unilateral implementation of new conditions of employment.[288]
- Third, there is the positive **right** to bargain collectively. This right may be enforced against an employer or trade union which refuses to engage in collective bargaining and is usually referred to by its correlative as the duty to bargain. It is the most controversial element because it contains an element of compulsion. In terms of this right, the state may compel employers and trade unions to bargain collectively.[289]

While section 23(5) of the Constitution encompasses the negative freedom to bargain collectively and the right to use economic power, Cheadle argues that it does not include the positive right to bargain collectively for the following three reasons:

- First, a duty to bargain is more than just a right as it involves policy choices such as the form and level of collective bargaining. This results in a complex system that requires a delicate balance to maintain it. To impose a duty to bargain may tip the balance in favour of 'unanticipated and unfortunate effects'.[290]
- Second, international labour standards do not impose a duty to bargain. The ILO Committee of Freedom of Association, for example, has held that collective bargaining will only be effective if it assumes a voluntary quality and does not entail recourse to compulsory measures which will alter the voluntary nature of such bargaining.[291]
- Third, a careful examination of the words of section 23(5) of the Constitution shows that it is restricted to a freedom to bargain collectively and that the forms, processes, institutions and levels are subject matters for the legislature.[292]

In *South African National Defence Union v Minister of Defence and Others*,[293] the SCA adopted the same approach as Cheadle. The Court held that while the Constitution does recognise and protect the central role of collective bargaining in our labour dispensation, it does not impose a legally enforceable duty to bargain on employers and trade unions. Unfortunately, the Constitutional Court did not find it necessary to decide whether the

285 Cheadle (2013) 18.23–18.24.
286 Cheadle (2013) 18.24–18.25.
287 (CCT23/96) [1996] ZACC 26; 1996 (4) SA 744 (CC); 1996 (10) BCLR 1253 (CC) (6 September 1996) paras 64–6.
288 *First Certification* paras 64–6.
289 *First Certification* paras 64–6.
290 Cheadle (2013) 18.23.
291 Cheadle (2013) 18.26.
292 Cheadle (2013) 18.26.
293 2007 (1) SA 402 (SCA).

Constitution imposes a legally enforceable duty to bargain in the same case.[294] It did, however, note that a legally enforceable duty to bargain would draw the courts into controversial and difficult issues:

> **[I]t should be noted that were section 23(5) to establish a justiciable duty to bargain, enforceable by either employers or unions outside of a legislative framework to regulate that duty, Courts may be drawn into a range of controversial industrial relations issues. These issues would include questions relating to the level at which bargaining should take place (ie the level of the workplace, at the level of an enterprise, or at industrial level); the level of union membership required to give rise to that duty; the topics of bargaining and the manner of bargaining. These are difficult issues, which have been regulated in different ways in the recent past in South Africa, as the general principles governing labour relations in South Africa have changed several times since the 1980s when the modern trade union movement emerged.[295]**

PAUSE FOR REFLECTION

Does section 23(5) of the Constitution impose a legally enforceable duty to bargain on employers and trade unions?

As pointed out above, both the SCA and the Constitutional Court considered the question as to whether section 23(5) of the Constitution imposes a legally enforceable duty to bargain on employers and trade unions in their judgments in the case of *South African National Defence Union (II)*.

The facts of this case were as follows. After the Constitutional Court declared section 126B(1) of the Defence Act, which prohibited permanent members of the SANDF from being members of a trade union, unconstitutional and invalid in 1999,[296] the Minister of Defence issued regulations regulating labour relations in the SANDF. These regulations were set out in Chapter 20 of the General Regulations of the South African National Defence Force and the Reserve.

Chapter 20 provided, *inter alia*, that once a union could prove that it had 5 000 SANDF members, it could apply to be registered as a military trade union. Once a military trade union could prove that it had 15 000 SANDF members, it could apply for membership of the Military Bargaining Council (MBC). The purpose of the MBC was to negotiate and bargain collectively to reach agreement on matters of mutual interest between the Department of Defence and members represented by military trade unions.

After the applicant, SANDU, was registered as a military trade union and admitted to the MBC, a number of disputes arose between it and the Department of Defence. Unfortunately, the MBC was unable to resolve most of these disputes. Following the postponement of a number of meetings, SANDU wrote a letter to the Department in which it threatened to engage in labour unrest unless its demands were met.

In response, the Minister of Defence wrote a letter to SANDU indicating that any industrial action by SANDU's members would be unlawful. He also called on SANDU

294 *South African National Defence Union v Minister of Defence (II)* (CCT65/06) [2007] ZACC 10; 2007 (5) SA 400; 2007 (8) BCLR 863 (CC); [2007] 9 BLLR 785 (CC); (2007) 28 ILJ 1909 (CC) (30 May 2007) para 48.

295 *South African National Defence Union (II)* para 55.

296 *South African National Defence Union v Minister of Defence (I)* CCT27/98) [1999] ZACC 7; 1999 (4) SA 469; 1999 (6) BCLR 615 (26 May 1999).

to withdraw its threat and stated that negotiations with SANDU in the MBC would be suspended until it did so. When SANDU received the Minister's letter, it immediately withdrew its threat and asked the Minister to resume negotiations with it. The Minister, however, refused to do so unless certain conditions were met.

Following the Minister's refusal to resume negotiations in the MBC, SANDU brought five different applications against the Minister in the High Court. Two of these were consolidated and heard by Van der Westhuizen J. A further two were also consolidated and heard by Smit J and the remaining application was heard by Bertelsman J. Some of these applications dealt with the disputes that had arisen between SANDU and the Department of Defence and some of them dealt with the Minister's decision to withdraw from negotiations in the MBC.

In so far as the Minister's decision to withdraw from negotiations was concerned, SANDU argued in all three cases that section 23(5) of the Constitution imposes a legally enforceable duty to bargain on employers and that the Minister's decision was therefore unconstitutional and invalid. Smit J and Bertelsman J accepted this argument while Van der Westhuizen J rejected it. All three judgments were then taken on appeal to the SCA.

The SCA rejected SANDU's argument. The Court held that section 23(5) does not impose a legally enforceable duty to bargain on employers and that the Minister's decision was not therefore unconstitutional and invalid.

In its judgment, the SCA began by noting that the phrase 'the right to engage in collective bargaining' was open to at least three possible interpretations:

> **It may mean that the contemplated national legislation to regulate collective bargaining must provide for an employer or a union called upon to bargain to comply with the demand on pain of being ordered to do so. On the other hand it may mean that the envisaged national legislation must provide the framework within which employers, employers' organisations and employees may bargain; or it may mean no more than that no legislative or other governmental act may effectively prohibit collective bargaining.**[297]

When it comes to interpreting the rights guaranteed in the Bill of Rights, the SCA noted further, section 39 of the Constitution provides that a court, tribunal or forum must promote the values that underlie an open and democratic society based on human dignity, equality and freedom, that it must consider international law and that it may consider foreign law.[298]

In so far as international law is concerned, the SCA went on to note, the ILO's Convention on Freedom of Association and Protection of the Right to Organise 1948 as well as its Conventions on the Right to Organise and Collective Bargaining 1949, and on Collective Bargaining 1981, were all particularly helpful because they adopted a voluntarist approach towards collective bargaining.[299]

Taking the approach adopted in these Conventions together with the fact that both the interim Constitution and the LRA adopted a voluntarist approach to collective

297 *South African National Defence Union v Minister of Defence and Others* (*SCA*) para 5.
298 *South African National Defence Union* (*SCA*) para 6.
299 *South African National Defence Union* (*SCA*) paras 7–11.

bargaining,[300] the SCA held that it was quite clear that while the Constitution recognises and protects collective bargaining, it does not impose a legally enforceable duty to bargain on employers or employees.[301]

After losing in the SCA, SANDU appealed to the Constitutional Court. Unfortunately, the Constitutional Court held that it was not necessary for it to consider whether section 23(5) of the Constitution imposes a legally enforceable duty to bargain on employers or employees. This is because Chapter 20 was specifically enacted to give effect to section 23(5) and in those cases in which legislation has been enacted to give effect to a constitutional right, and where the constitutional validity of that legislation has not being challenged, a litigant may not bypass that legislation and rely on the Constitution directly.[302]

This means, the Constitutional Court held further, that:

> a litigant who seeks to assert his or her right to engage in collective bargaining under section 23(5) should in the first place base his or her case on any legislation enacted to regulate the right, not on section 23(5). If the legislation is wanting in its protection of the section 23(5) right in the litigant's view, then that legislation should be challenged constitutionally. To permit the litigant to ignore the legislation and rely directly on the constitutional provision would be to fail to recognise the important task conferred upon the Legislature by the Constitution to respect, protect, promote and fulfil the rights in the Bill of Rights.[303]

In light of these points, the Constitutional Court went on to conclude, it was not necessary for it to decide whether section 23(5) of the Constitution imposes a legally enforceable duty to bargain on the Department of Defence. Instead, it simply had to decide whether Chapter 20 of the Regulations did so.[304] Before turning to consider this question, however, the Court warned that if section 23(5) was interpreted in a manner that did impose a legally enforceable duty to bargain on employers and trade unions outside any legislative framework, the courts would be called on to decide a wide range of controversial and difficult issues, such as the level at which bargaining should take place (i.e. at the level of the workplace, at the level of an enterprise, or at industry level); the level of union membership required to give rise to the duty; the topics of bargaining and the manner of bargaining. This was clearly not desirable.[305]

SUMMARY

Some rights – the right to administrative justice, access to information, access to courts and labour rights among them – enhance the democratic nature of the state as they allow the exercise of many of the other rights in an effective manner. These rights are partly aimed at equalling the playing field by requiring the powerful to adhere to pre-announced rules, to

300 *South African National Defence Union* (*SCA*) paras 14–19.
301 *South African National Defence Union* (*SCA*) para 25.
302 *South African National Defence Union (II)* para 51.
303 *South African National Defence Union (II)* para 52.
304 *South African National Defence Union (II)* para 56.
305 *South African National Defence Union (II)* para 55.

act in a relatively transparent manner and to share information, and to provide individuals with access to courts which will assist them to enforce these and other rights.

To prevent abuse of power in the exercise of discretionary powers, the right to administrative justice guaranteed in section 33 of the Constitution provides that these powers must be exercised in a manner that is lawful, reasonable and procedurally fair. Courts are empowered to review such decisions and to set them aside, not because they are substantively wrong but because they do not conform to the requirements of administrative justice. However, normally when challenging an administrative decision, a litigant will not be able to rely on section 33 of the Constitution, but will rather have to rely on the provisions of the Promotion of Administrative Justice Act (PAJA) which was passed to give effect to section 33. After an applicant has managed to show that the exercise of public power in question falls into the ambit of an administrative action as defined by section 1 of the PAJA, he or she is entitled to claim the administrative rights set out in the PAJA. Among the most important of these administrative rights are the following: the right to lawful administrative action; the right to reasonable administrative action; the right to procedural fairness; and the right to be given reasons for an administrative decision. The content of each of these rights is described in detail in the relevant sections of the PAJA. It is important for lawyers to familiarise themselves with these provisions of the PAJA if they want to have an administrative action reviewed on any of the grounds listed above.

The right of access to information is a pivotal right aimed at enhancing the quality of democracy and protecting our country against the re-establishment of a culture of secrecy that is anathema to open and accountable government. Section 32 of the Constitution thus guarantees for everyone the right of access to any information held by the state and any information that is held by another person and that is required for the exercise or protection of any rights. As is the case with the right to administrative justice guaranteed in section 33, legislation – in this case the Promotion of Access to Information Act (PAIA) – was passed to give effect to the constitutional right. Normally when requesting access to information, litigants will have to rely on the previsions of the PAIA and not on section 32 of the Constitution. The PAIA contains different rules for accessing information held by the state and information held by private parties. As a general rule, a requester must be given access to a record held by a public body if the requester complies with all the procedural requirements set out in the PAIA relating to a request for access to that record and access to that record is not refused in terms of any ground for refusal as set out in the PAIA. As general rule, a requester must be given access to records held by a private body if that record is required for the exercise or protection of any rights, that person complies with the procedural requirements set out in the PAIA relating to a request for access to that record and access to that record is not refused in terms of any ground for refusal set out in the PAIA. However, the PAIA provides for an extensive list of exceptions which allow a private or public body to refuse to provide access to the requested information and it is important to study these exceptions carefully.

The right of access to court is a fundamental component of the rule of a law in a constitutional democracy. Thus, section 34 of the Bill of Rights states that '[e]veryone has the right to have any dispute that can be resolved by the application of law decided in a fair public hearing before a court or, where appropriate, another independent and impartial tribunal or forum.' Some disputes, for example disputes of a purely moral or religious nature, cannot be resolved by the application of law and individuals with such disputes cannot rely on section 34 to gain access to a court for the purposes of the court resolving their dispute. However, when a dispute can be resolved by the application of law, then those involved in the dispute have the right to approach a court although there is no general obligation on the state to fund cases brought to court by individuals.

Section 23 of the Constitution recognises the importance of ensuring fair labour relations and guarantees several rights for employees, employers and trade unions. Section 23 provides not only that everyone has the right to fair labour practices, but also that every worker has the right to join a trade union, that every employer has the right to join an employers' organisation and that every trade union, employers' organisation and employer has the right to engage in collective bargaining. The rights contained in section 23 of the Bill of Rights are largely given effect to in various pieces of legislation, most notably the Labour Relations Act (LRA), the Basic Conditions of Employment Act (BCEA) and the Employment Equity Act (EEA). Litigants with a labour law dispute will normally have to rely on these Acts and not directly on the Constitution when they approach a court. A litigant who wishes to approach a court with a labour related issue will have to make a detailed study of the relevant provisions of the applicable Act.

Chapter 16

Socio-economic rights

16.1 Introduction

As the Constitutional Court has pointed out, South Africa is a society in which there are great disparities in wealth:

> **Millions of people are living in deplorable conditions and in great poverty. There is a high level of unemployment, inadequate social security, and many do not have access to clean water or to adequate health services. These conditions already existed when the Constitution was adopted and a commitment to address them, and to transform our society into one in which there will be human dignity, freedom and equality, lies at the heart of our new constitutional order. For as long as these conditions continue to exist that aspiration will have a hollow ring.**[1]

The constitutional commitment to address these conditions is partly reflected in various provisions of the Bill of Rights, including several provisions that guarantee the social and economic rights of all. The inclusion of so-called 'socio-economic rights' in the Bill of Rights is one of the great innovations found in South Africa's 1996 Constitution. **Socio-economic**

1 *Soobramoney v Minister of Health (Kwazulu-Natal)* (CCT32/97) [1997] ZACC 17; 1998 (1) SA 765 (CC); 1997 (12) BCLR 1696 (27 November 1997) para 8.

rights are rights to the conditions and resources necessary for the material well-being of people. In other words, socio-economic rights are rights to things such as food, water, housing, health care, social assistance, education and a safe, clean and healthy environment. As we pointed out in chapter 1, the inclusion of socio-economic rights in the Constitution provides evidence of the fact that it is a transformative Constitution that engages with the social and economic realities in South Africa.

In this chapter, we survey the legal nature and practical implications of the socio-economic rights in South Africa's Constitution. We describe the rights in the abstract and then investigate the different ways in which they operate as legal entitlements imposing concomitant legal duties on the state and others.

PAUSE FOR REFLECTION

South Africa's Constitution unique with regard to socio-economic rights

It is not simply the fact that socio-economic rights have been included in the South African Constitution that is significant. Many constitutions across the world include at least some of these rights although South Africa's Constitution boasts a longer list of socio-economic rights than most others. Rather, it is the manner in which socio-economic rights are protected in South Africa's Constitution that sets it apart from other comparable documents.

This is true in two ways. First, the socio-economic rights in the South African Constitution are formulated so that they do not only require the state to leave people alone in their access to basic resources such as food, water, housing, education and health care (in other words, the Constitution does not only impose a negative obligation to respect these rights). They also require the state to act - to expend resources and to make and implement plans - to ensure that people indeed have access to those resources (in other words, the Constitution imposes positive obligations on the state to realise these rights). In most other constitutions that include socio-economic rights this is not the case. Generally, these rights are formulated in such a way that they only protect access to resources such as education or housing against unjustified state interference.

Second, the socio-economic rights in South Africa's Constitution are justiciable. In other words, claims may be brought to courts on their basis. Courts have the power authoritatively to interpret these rights, to determine the nature and extent of the duties they impose and to decide whether or not these duties have been complied with. Courts may also impose remedies to ensure that these rights are vindicated. Again, in most other constitutions that include socio-economic rights, this is not the case. Often, for example, socio-economic rights are included in constitutions as so-called directive principles only. This means they are included as goals for the state to pursue without having any legally binding nature.

16.2 Socio-economic rights in the Constitution and related constitutional provisions

Socio-economic rights are found in a variety of provisions of the Constitution:

- Section 24 guarantees everyone's right to a safe and healthy environment and requires the state to protect the environment.
- Section 25(5) requires the state to enable citizens to gain equitable access to land.

- Section 26 provides that everyone has the right to have access to adequate housing and prohibits arbitrary evictions.
- Section 27 guarantees everyone's right to have access to health care services, sufficient food and water, and social security and assistance, and prohibits the refusal of emergency medical treatment.
- Section 28(1)(*c*) entrenches children's rights to shelter and to basic nutrition, social services and health care services.
- Section 29 provides for everyone's right to basic education and to further education.
- Finally, section 35(2)(*e*) guarantees the right of detained persons to be provided with adequate nutrition, accommodation, medical care and reading material.

We can distinguish between three different groups of socio-economic rights.

First, some rights follow a standard formulation, stating that everyone has the right of 'access to' these rights, but circumscribing the positive duties they impose on the state. These rights are circumscribed, first, in that they only provide the right of having 'access' to a particular social good. Second, the positive duties they impose on the state are described as duties to take reasonable steps, within available resources, to achieve their progressive realisation. Standard examples are the section 26(1) right to 'have access to adequate housing' and the section 27(1) right to 'have access to' health care services, including reproductive health care, sufficient food and water, and social security and assistance. The positive duties imposed by these rights are explicitly described in sections 26(2) and 27(2) respectively, but in a manner that limits them, so that the state is required to take only 'reasonable legislative and other measures, within its available resources, to achieve ... [their] progressive realisation ...'

Other qualified socio-economic rights are those in section 24(*b*) which provides that '[e]veryone has the right to have the environment protected ... through **reasonable legislative and other measures**'; section 25(5) which provides that '[t]he state must take **reasonable legislative and other measures, within its available resources**, to foster conditions which enable citizens to **gain access** to land on an equitable basis'; and section 29(1)(*b*) which provides that '[e]veryone has the right to further education, which the state, **through reasonable measures**, must make **progressively** available and **accessible**' (our emphasis).

A second group of rights are neither formulated as access rights nor subjected to the qualifications of 'reasonableness', 'available resources' or 'progressive realisation'. These are the section 29(1)(*a*) right of everyone to 'basic education, including adult basic education'; the section 28(1)(*c*) rights of children to 'basic nutrition, shelter, basic health care services and social services'; and the section 35(2)(*e*) rights of detained persons to 'the provision, at state expense, of adequate accommodation, nutrition, reading material and medical treatment'.

Third, sections 26(3) and 27(3) describe particular elements of the section 26(1) right to have access to adequate housing and the section 27(1)(*a*) right to have access to health care services respectively. These provisions can be viewed as specific, explicitly guaranteed manifestations of the negative obligations imposed by one of the rights contained in that section. In other words, these rights are formulated as prohibitions of certain forms of conduct rather than as rights to particular goods and services. Section 26(3) prohibits arbitrary evictions and section 27(3) prohibits the refusal of emergency medical treatment. These two rights are also not subjected to any of the special qualifications that are typically attached to the qualified socio-economic rights.

16.3 Socio-economic rights and other areas of the law

In addition to the socio-economic rights themselves, it is important to take note of those rights that are not explicitly formulated as rights to material conditions for human welfare, but that can be interpreted to create entitlements to such goods and services. Obvious examples are the section 11 right to life, the section 9 right to equality and the section 33 right to administrative justice. The right to life, for example, can be interpreted as not only requiring the state to refrain from killing, but also requiring it positively to protect and sustain life and to foster and maintain a certain quality of life.[2] Somewhat similarly, the right to equality can be used to ground claims that a particular socio-economic benefit provided to a specific class of needy people should be extended to others.[3] In addition, the section 9(3) and 9(4) prohibition on unfair discrimination is relevant to poverty-related legal claims in the sense that socio-economic status could be recognised as a ground for distinction analogous to the grounds explicitly listed in section 9(3). This would render distinctions made on the basis of socio-economic status actionable as unfair discrimination.[4]

PAUSE FOR REFLECTION

A claim to the right to medical treatment must be based on section 27 of the Constitution

In *Soobramoney v Minister of Health (Kwazulu-Natal)*,[5] the applicant was suffering from chronic renal failure. Although renal dialysis would have prolonged his life, Addington State Hospital refused to place him on its renal dialysis programme. This was because the Hospital's guidelines provided that a person who was suffering from chronic renal failure would only be placed on the dialysis programme if he or she was eligible for a kidney transplant. Its transplant policy provided, in turn, however, that a person would only be eligible for a transplant if he or she was 'free from any significant vascular or cardiac disease'.[6] Unfortunately, Mr Soobramoney suffered from ischaemic heart disease and was not eligible for a transplant. This meant that he was also not eligible for dialysis.

Mr Soobramoney then applied for an order setting aside the Hospital's decision. He based his application, *inter alia*, on the grounds that the Hospital's decision infringed his right to life guaranteed in section 11 of the Constitution. The Constitutional Court, however, rejected this argument on the grounds that, unlike in other countries where the right of access to health care services is not expressly guaranteed in the constitution, the right to medical treatment does not have to be inferred from the right to life. This is because the right to medical treatment is expressly guaranteed in

---

2 See *Soobramoney*.

3 See *Khosa and Others v Minister of Social Development and Others, Mahlaule and Another v Minister of Social Development* (CCT 13/03, CCT 12/03) [2004] ZACC 11; 2004 (6) SA 505 (CC); 2004 (6) BCLR 569 (CC) (4 March 2004).

4 S 34(1)(*a*) of the Promotion of Equality and Prevention of Unfair Discrimination Act 4 of 2000 (PEPUDA) lists socio-economic status as one of a number of grounds that must be considered by the Equality Review Committee established in terms of s 32 of the Act for future inclusion in the list of prohibited grounds. The special consideration accorded socio-economic status in s 34 indicates that, at the very least, socio-economic status will be regarded, for purposes of the PEPUDA, as a ground analogous to the listed grounds. This seems to indicate that the legislature regards it for constitutional purposes also to be a ground analogous to those listed in s 9(3) of the Constitution. See, in general, De Vos, P (2004) The Promotion of Equality and Prevention of Unfair Discrimination Act and socio-economic rights *ESR Review: Economic and Social Rights in South Africa* 5(2):7–11.

5 (CCT32/97) [1997] ZACC 17; 1998 (1) SA 765 (CC); 1997 (12) BCLR 1696 (27 November 1997).

6 *Soobramoney* para 4.

section 27 of the Constitution. A person who wishes to claim the right to medical treatment, therefore, must base his or her case on section 27 of the Constitution and not on section 11.[7]

The administrative justice rights in section 33 of the Constitution are also relevant. Most state decisions affecting access to health care, housing, education, social services, food and water qualify as administrative action and must comply with the standards of procedural fairness, lawfulness and reasonableness. Administrative law grounds of review are potent tools for the protection of socio-economic rights. Courts are comfortable with applying these grounds of review and, particularly in the field of social assistance, a large body of socio-economic rights case law based on administrative law principles has developed.[8]

PAUSE FOR REFLECTION

Using non-rights related constitutional provisions to protect and advance socio-economic rights

Socio-economic rights are not only indirectly protected through other constitutional rights. Litigants can use any number of non-rights related constitutional provisions, which seemingly have nothing whatsoever to do with socio-economic rights, to protect and advance socio-economic rights.

In *Joseph and Others v City of Johannesburg and Others*,[9] for example, the Constitutional Court held that sections 152 and 153 of the Constitution, which set out the objectives of local government, read together with sections 4(2)(*f*) and 73 of the Local Government: Municipal Systems Act[10] impose an obligation on every municipality to provide basic municipal services to their inhabitants irrespective of whether they have a contractual relationship with the municipality or not.[11]

Although, in contrast to water, electricity is not expressly referred to in the Constitution, the Court held further, there is no doubt that electricity is one of the most common and important basic municipal services, especially in urban areas. Municipalities are, therefore, required to provide electricity to their inhabitants as a part of their constitutional duty to provide basic municipal services.[12]

7 *Soobramoney* para 19. For a discussion of the space this leaves for advancing claims for material conditions for welfare through the right to life, see Pieterse, M (1999) A different shade of red: Socio-economic dimensions of the right to life in South Africa *South African Journal on Human Rights* 15(3):372–85 at 384. Mr Soobramoney died a few days after this judgment was handed down.

8 See De Villiers, N (2002) Social grants and the Promotion of Administrative Justice Act *South African Journal on Human Rights* 18(3):320–49 at 320; Van der Walt AJ (2002b) Sosiale geregtigheid, prosedurele billikheid, en eiendom: Alternatiewe perspektiewe op grondwetlike waarborge (Deel Een) *Stellenbosch Law Review* 13(5):59–82 at 59; Van der Walt, AJ 'A South African reading of Frank Michelman's theory of social justice' in Botha, H, Van der Walt, AJ and Van der Walt, JC (2003) *Rights and Democracy in a Transformative Constitution* 172–4, 187–9.

9 (CCT 43/09) [2009] ZACC 30; 2010 (3) BCLR 212 (CC); 2010 (4) SA 55 (CC) (9 October 2009).

10 Act 32 of 2000.

11 *Joseph* para 38.

12 *Joseph* para 39.

16.4 The interpretation of socio-economic rights

16.4.1 Introduction

The interpretation of socio-economic rights is conditioned by two generally applicable provisions of the Constitution: section 7(2) and section 39(1). It is important to understand how these provisions influence the interpretation of the social and economic rights.

16.4.2 Duties: section 7(2)

16.4.2.1 The duty to respect, protect, promote and fulfil

16.4.2.1.1 Introduction

Section 7(2) of the Constitution determines that '[t]he state must respect, protect, promote and fulfil the rights in the Bill of Rights'. Section 7(2) is central to the transformative ethos of the Constitution. It explicitly conveys the idea that the state is not simply required to refrain from interfering with the enjoyment of rights, but must also act so as to protect, enhance and realise the enjoyment of rights.[13] For practical purposes, this provision is important as it indicates the scope and nature of the duties and entitlements that socio-economic rights can create and so shows when and how they can be used to advance legal claims. However, it is important to note that section 7(2) does not only apply to the duties imposed by social and economic rights; it also applies to all rights contained in the Bill of Rights. Although we discuss section 7(2) in this part of the book because it applies so directly and extensively to the duties imposed by social and economic rights, we must never lose sight of its application to every other right contained in the Bill of Rights.

16.4.2.1.2 The duty to respect

The duty to respect requires the state to refrain from interfering with the enjoyment of rights. First, the state must not limit or take away people's existing access to housing, for instance, without good reason and without following proper legal procedure. Second, where the limitation or deprivation of existing access to housing is unavoidable, the state must take steps to mitigate that interference. In the context of state eviction, for example, the state must take steps to find alternative accommodation for the evictees. Third, the state must not place undue obstacles in the way of people gaining access to housing.[14]

---

13 The realisation that rights impose such different kinds of duties is usually attributed to Henry Shue (Shue, H (1980) *Basic Rights: Subsistence, Affluence and US Foreign Policy*). His typology is widely adopted in international law circles. See Van Hoof, GJH (1984) 'The legal nature of economic, social and cultural rights: A rebuttal of some traditional views' in Alston, P and Tomasevski, K (eds) *The Right to Food* (1984) 97, 99; Group of Experts on Limburg Principles (1998) The Maastricht Guidelines on Violations of Economic, Social and Cultural Rights *Human Rights Quarterly* 20(3):691–704 para 6; Committee on ESCR General Comment No 12 *The right to adequate food (art 11 of the Covenant)* UN Doc E/2000/22 para 15; General Comment No 14 *The right to the highest attainable standard of health (art 12 of the Covenant)* UN Doc E/C 12/2000/4 paras 33–7; General Comment No 15 *The right to water (arts 11 and 12 of the Covenant)* UN Doc E/C 12/2002/11 paras 20–9.

14 See *Certification of the Constitution of the Republic of South Africa, 1996* (CCT 23/96) [1996] ZACC 26; 1996 (4) SA 744 (CC); 1996 (10) BCLR 1253 (CC) (6 September 1996) para 78 where the Constitutional Court stated: 'At the very minimum, socio-economic rights can be negatively protected from improper invasion.' See generally De Vos, P (1997) Pious wishes or directly enforceable human rights: Social and economic rights in South Africa's 1996 Constitution *South African Journal on Human Rights* 13(1):67–101 at 79–83; Liebenberg, S (2010) *Socio-Economic Rights: Adjudication Under a Transformative Constitution* 82–7.

16.4.2.1.3 The duty to protect

The duty to protect requires the state to protect against third party interference the existing enjoyment of rights as well as the capacity of people to enhance their enjoyment of rights or to gain access to the enjoyment of rights. The state must, for instance, regulate private health care provision to protect against exploitation by private institutions and must, through such regulation, provide effective legal remedies where such exploitation or other forms of interference occur. An aspect of this duty that is often overlooked is the duty that it places on the courts, through their powers of developing the common law and interpreting legislation, to strengthen existing remedies or develop new remedies for protection against private interference in the enjoyment of rights.[15]

16.4.2.1.4 The duty to promote

The duty to promote is difficult to distinguish from the broader duty to fulfil rights.[16] Liebenberg describes the duty to promote as a duty to raise awareness of rights, that is, through educational programmes, to bring rights and the methods of accessing and enforcing them to the attention of rights holders and to promote the most effective use of existing access to rights.[17] Budlender describes the duty to promote as a duty placed on administrative bodies to use the promotion of socio-economic rights as a primary consideration in their discretionary decision making, much like the constitutional injunction contained in section 28(2) which requires that the best interest of the child be the primary consideration in any decision affecting a child.[18] The duty to promote can also be understood as placing a duty on the state to assist in creating the conditions in which individuals can realise their rights. In other words, it places a duty on the state to use its power to assist individuals in realising their rights.[19]

16.4.2.1.5 The duty to fulfil

The duty to fulfil requires the state to act and to 'adopt appropriate legislative, administrative, budgetary, judicial, promotional and other measures'[20] so that those people who do not currently enjoy access to rights can gain access and so that the existing enjoyment of rights is enhanced. What is required is for the state to take direct steps to fulfil the enjoyment of rights for individuals. For example, the duty to fulfil may require the state to build houses to help meet the needs of individuals without access to housing.

16.4.2.2 Negative and positive duties

On the basis of section 7(2), a distinction is often made between **positive duties** (duties to do something, to act) and **negative duties** (duties to refrain from doing something, not to act). The duty to respect is then classified as a negative duty, whereas the duties to protect,

---

15 De Vos (1997) 83–6.

16 For example, De Vos conflates these two duties in his discussion of s 7(2). See De Vos (1997) 86–91.

17 Liebenberg, S 'The interpretation of socio-economic rights' in Woolman, S and Bishop, M (eds) (2013) *Constitutional Law of South Africa* 2nd ed rev service 5 33.1–33.66.

18 Budlender, G 'Justiciability of socio-economic rights: Some South African experiences' in Ghai, Y and Cottrell, J (eds) (2004) *Economic, Social and Cultural Rights Cultural Rights in Practice: The Role of Judges in Implementing Economic, Social and Cultural Rights* Commonwealth Secretariat 37.

19 See De Vos (1997) 86. See also *Government of the Republic of South Africa and Others v Grootboom and Others* (CCT11/00) [2000] ZACC 19; 2001 (1) SA 46; 2000 (11) BCLR 1169 (4 October 2000) paras 35–6.

20 Committee on ESCR General Comment No 14 *The right to the highest attainable standard of health (art 12 of the Covenant)* UN Doc E/C 12/2000/4 para 33.

promote and fulfil are described as positive duties.[21] This distinction is presented in hierarchical fashion. The negative duty to respect is often seen as more amenable to enforcement through adjudication than the positive duties to protect, promote and fulfil.[22] The argument is that enforcement of a negative duty does not require courts to interfere in allocational choices of the executive or legislature as the enforcement of positive duties inevitably seems to do. By the same token, it is argued that the enforcement of a negative duty does not immerse courts in the field of policy formulation and evaluation to the extent that the enforcement of positive duties supposedly does. However, in reality, the distinction between positive and negative duties contains little more than a simple semantic distinction between acting and not acting.

First, the same conduct of the state can often be described both as an infringement of the positive duty to fulfil a right and as an infringement of the negative duty to respect the right. As Liebenberg points out, in *Minister of Health and Others v Treatment Action Campaign and Others (No 2)*,[23] it was not clear whether the refusal to extend the provision of Nevirapine for purposes of preventing mother-to-child transmission of HIV to all public health facilities, apart from a few select pilot sites, constituted a negative interference of the right to have access to health care services or a failure of the state positively to provide an essential health service. In effect, it could be characterised as both.[24] Similarly, an element of the supposedly negative duty to respect rights - the duty to mitigate interference in the exercise of a right where such interference is unavoidable - clearly requires the state to act rather than to refrain from acting.

Second, the distinction in consequence also does not hold up. Enforcement of a negative duty against the state is as likely to have consequences for expenditure of resources as enforcement of a positive duty. Enforcement of a negative duty also potentially requires a court to interfere as deeply in the policy-making powers of the executive or legislature as does enforcement of a negative duty. Suppose the state seeks to evict a group of illegal occupants from state land with the purpose of developing that land for low-cost housing. The housing will be occupied by a different group of people who are next in line on the housing waiting list. For a court to prevent the state from doing so (to enforce the negative duty to respect the right to have access to adequate housing) will have important resource consequences. The state will have to find other suitable land and buy it, or use other state land, which itself in turn might have been allocated for a different use. Equally, in enforcing the negative duty in this respect, a court would interfere very directly in a complex, multifaceted policy choice about how to decide who gets access to housing first, about where to situate low-cost housing development and so on.[25]

---

21 See *Jaftha v Schoeman and Others, Van Rooyen v Stoltz and Others* (CCT74/03) [2004] ZACC 25; 2005 (2) SA 140 (CC); 2005 (1) BCLR 78 (CC) (8 October 2004) paras 31–4 where the Constitutional Court discusses the distinction between the negative duty to respect the right to have access to adequate housing and the positive duty to fulfil it. See also *Grootboom* para 34.

22 See, for example, the following remarks of the Constitutional Court in the *First Certification* judgment para 78:

> **The objectors argued further that socio-economic rights are not justiciable, in particular because of the budgetary issues their enforcement may raise. The fact that socio-economic rights will almost inevitably give rise to such implications does not seem to us to be a bar to their justiciability. At the very minimum, socio-economic rights can be negatively protected from improper invasion.**

23 (CCT8/02) [2002] ZACC 15; 2002 (5) SA 721; 2002 (10) BCLR 1033 (5 July 2002).

24 Liebenberg (2013) 33.19. By the same token, the provisions of the Social Assistance Act 59 of 1992 that were challenged in *Khosa* could be described as either negative or positive infringements of the right to have access to social assistance.

25 With respect to the blurring of the distinction between positive and negative constitutional duties, see in general Bandes, S (1990) The negative constitution: A critique *Michigan Law Review* 88(8):2271–347.

Nevertheless, despite its porosity, the distinction between positive and negative duties remains important for strategic reasons. As will become clear below, courts are likely to subject negative interferences with socio-economic rights to more robust scrutiny than failures to meet positive duties. This is because the structure of the Constitution seems to demand it and because courts regard themselves as bound by separation of powers concerns to a lesser extent when dealing with negative interferences.

CRITICAL THINKING

Section 7(2) applies equally to all rights

Recall that section 7(2) applies equally to **all** rights, not only social and economic rights. This means that potentially all rights – including all so-called civil and political rights – place both a negative as well as a positive obligation on the state.

The Constitutional Court has recognised in several judgments that section 7(2) places both a negative and a positive obligation on a range of civil and political rights. For example, in *August and Another v Electoral Commission and Others*, the Court recognised the positive duties imposed by the right to vote contained in section 19 of the Constitution, stating that:

> The right to vote by its very nature imposes positive obligations upon the legislature and the executive. A date for elections has to be promulgated, the secrecy of the ballot secured and the machinery established for managing the process. For this purpose the Constitution provides for the establishment of the Commission to manage elections and ensure that they are free and fair ... [T]he Electoral Commission Act ... therefore provides that it is one of the functions of the Commission to '... compile and maintain voters' rolls by means of a system of registering of eligible voters by utilising data available from government sources and information furnished by voters.' This clearly imposes an affirmative obligation on the Commission to take reasonable steps to ensure that eligible voters are registered.[26]

We could similarly think of other civil and political rights which clearly impose positive obligations on the state to ensure their realisation. For example, the right to assemble, demonstrate and picket guaranteed in section 17 of the Constitution may require the police to accompany a protest march to protect marchers from attack, to ensure the keeping of the peace and to regulate traffic flow. These examples show that it would be wrong to associate negative duties with the realisation of civil and political rights and positive duties with the realisation of social and economic rights.

16.4.3 The role of international and foreign law: section 39(1)

Section 39(1) of the Constitution provides that:

> **[w]hen interpreting the Bill of Rights, a court, tribunal or forum:**
> **(*a*) must promote the values that underlie an open and democratic society based on human dignity, equality and freedom;**
> **(*b*) must consider international law; and**
> **(*c*) may consider foreign law.**

26 (CCT8/99) [1999] ZACC 3; 1999 (3) SA 1; 1999 (4) BCLR 363 (1 April 1999) para 16. See also *Minister of Home Affairs v National Institute for Crime Prevention and the Re-Integration of Offenders (NICRO) and Others* (CCT 03/04) [2004] ZACC 10; 2005 (3) SA 280 (CC); 2004 (5) BCLR 445 (CC) (3 March 2004) para 28.

Socio-economic rights are protected as justiciable rights in a large number of national constitutions across the world.[27] However, apart from a few isolated exceptions,[28] they have seldom directly formed the basis of constitutional litigation in these jurisdictions and there remains an absence of domestic case law in this respect. The largest bodies of case law have developed in jurisdictions where socio-economic rights are indirectly recognised through the extended interpretation of other rights or the application of broader constitutional norms. For example, in India, courts have used the so-called 'directive principles of state policy' to read basic socio-economic entitlements into civil and political rights such as the right to life.[29] The German Constitutional Court has used the constitutional 'social state' principle to insulate state conduct intended to protect access to basic socio-economic resources against challenges on the basis of, for instance, freedom of competition.[30] In other jurisdictions, the right to equality and constitutional due process guarantees have been used to protect or establish entitlements to basic socio-economic resources.[31]

In the absence of foreign jurisprudence on socio-economic rights, the focus in South Africa has been on international human rights law. The work of a variety of human rights treaty monitoring or enforcement bodies, in particular, has been influential in shaping both the socio-economic rights provisions of the Constitution[32] and the jurisprudence that has developed around them since their enactment.[33] The primary United Nations (UN) human rights instrument in this respect is the International Covenant on Economic, Social and Cultural Rights of 1996 (ICESCR), which South Africa has signed and at the time of writing was poised to ratify. In various respects, the socio-economic rights provisions of the Constitution are modelled on the ICESCR and it is consequently particularly important as an interpretative source.

---

27 Viljoen, F (2005) The justiciability of socio-economic and cultural rights: Experience and problems (Unpublished paper on file with author) 6 notes that, on the African continent, 'only a handful of states, notably Botswana, Nigeria and Tunisia, ... do not explicitly guarantee any socio-economic ... rights' and that socio-economic rights are included in a large number of Latin-American constitutions.

28 For example, in a recent Colombian decision, the Court held, on the basis of the right to health care, that an AIDS sufferer was entitled to the provision, at state expense, of those health services essential to keep him alive and to restore his health. See Rights of sick persons/AIDS patients, Constitutional Court of Columbia, Judgment No T-505/92, 22 August 1992. A Latvian court held that legislation conditioning access to social security benefits on the payment by employers of contributions on behalf of their employees was invalid on the basis of the right to social security (s 109 of the Latvian Constitution). See Constitutional Court of the Republic of Latvia, Case No 2000-08-0109. Also see Viljoen (2005) 10–11, 15.

29 See, for example, *Paschim Banga Khet Mazdoor Samity and Others v State of West Bengal and Another* (1996) AIR SC 2426 (right to emergency medical treatment read into the right to life) and the references of the Constitutional Court to this case in *Soobramoney* para 18); *Francis Coralie Mullin v The Administrator, Union Territory of Delhi* (1981) 2 SCR 516 529 (right to food read into the right to life).

30 In *Milk and Butterfat* BVerfGE 18, 315, the Court upheld price control regulations against a freedom of competition-based constitutional challenge because it held that the state, in terms of the social state principle, is obliged to combat high food prices so as to protect access to basic foodstuffs.

31 See, for example, with respect to equality, the Canadian case of *Eldridge v British Columbia (Attorney General)* 1997 151 DLR (4th) 577 SCC where the Court held that the state is required to provide sign language interpretation for deaf patients as part of the publicly funded health care system. See with respect to due process, the US cases of *Goldberg v Kelly* 397 US 254 (1970) and *Sniadach v Family Finance Corp* 395 US 337 (1969) where the Courts held that a hearing is required before access to welfare benefits is revoked. For a view that the latter two cases could, when they were decided, have been read to give expression to welfare rights in the US Constitution, see Michelman, FI 'Formal and associational aims in procedural due process' in Pennock, JR and Chapman, JW (eds) (1977) *Due Process (Nomos XVII)* 126.

32 Liebenberg, S (1995) 'The International Covenant on Economic, Social and Cultural Rights and its implications for South Africa *South African Journal on Human Rights* 11(2):359–78 at 359.

33 *Grootboom* para 26. See also, for example, the references in *Grootboom* paras 28 and 45 to the ICESCR and the Committee on ESCR.

The international body that supervises compliance with the ICESCR is the Committee on Economic, Social and Cultural Rights (Committee on ESCR). This Committee receives regular reports from state parties on the realisation of socio-economic rights in the respective countries. In practice, non-governmental organisations (NGOs) also submit 'shadow' reports which the Committee on ESCR considers alongside those of the states when the performance of the state in question is evaluated. The Committee on ESCR also issues General Comments on the ICESCR which are highly influential in the interpretation of socio-economic rights in general.[34]

Other international instruments with strong socio-economic rights dimensions are the Universal Declaration of Human Rights (1948) (Universal Declaration),[35] the Convention on the Elimination of All Forms of Discrimination against Women (1979)[36] and the Convention on the Rights of the Child (1989).[37] South Africa is a state party to the latter two Conventions.

The applicable regional instrument for South Africa is the African Charter on Human and Peoples' Rights (African Charter), to which South Africa is a state party. The African Charter contains civil, political and socio-economic rights which are enforced by the African Court on Human Rights. The African Commission on Human and People's Rights, the predecessor of the African Court on Human Rights, decided few cases in which socio-economic rights played a role.[38]

Other regional instruments that deal with economic and social rights are the European Social Charter (1961) and the Additional Protocol to the American Convention on Human Rights in the area of Economic, Social and Cultural Rights (Protocol of San Salvador) (1988).

On a less formal level, bodies of experts have formulated guidelines that inform the interpretation of socio-economic rights, such as the Limburg Principles on the Implementation of the International Covenant on Economic, Social and Cultural Rights of 1986,[39] the Maastricht Guidelines on Violations of Economic, Social and Cultural Rights of 1997[40] and the Bangalore Declaration and Plan of Action of 1995.[41]

---

34 The Committee has to date published 21 General Comments dealing with a wide range of topics related to the interpretation of the various aspects of the ICESCR. ICESCR (UN Commission on Economic, Social and Cultural Rights) (1990) General Comment No 3 *The nature of States parties obligations (Art. 2, par.1 of the Covenant)*, available at http://www.refworld.org/docid/4538838e10.html, is of particular importance as the Constitutional Court relied partly on it when it developed the South African jurisprudence on social and economic rights enforcement.

35 Arts 22–6.

36 Arts 3 and 10–14.

37 Arts 4, 6(2), 19, 20, 24, 26–9 and 31.

38 An exception is *Social and Economic Rights Action Centre (SERAC) and the Centre for Economic and Social Rights (CESR) v Nigeria* Communication 155/96 (October 2001), a complaint brought against Nigeria for the destruction and wilful neglect, in collusion with an international oil mining consortium, of natural resources, agricultural land and livestock on which the Ogoni people depended for their livelihood. The African Commission found that Nigeria had a duty to protect the socio-economic rights of its citizens against invasion from private sources, that it had facilitated the invasion of these rights by allowing and participating in the actions of oil companies and that it was consequently in violation of arts 2, 4, 14, 16, 18(1), 21 and 24 of the African Charter. See Mbazira, C (2004) Reading the right to food into the African Charter on Human and Peoples' Rights *ESR Review* 5(1):5–7 at 5.

39 See (1987) Limburg Principles on the Implementation of the Covenant on Economic, Social and Cultural Rights *Human Rights Quarterly* 9(2):122–35 at 124.

40 See (1998) The Maastricht Guidelines on Violations of Economic, Social and Cultural Rights *Human Rights Quarterly* 20(3):691–704 at 691.

41 See (1995, December) Bangalore Declaration and Plan of Action reprinted in International Commission of Jurists 55:219–27.

As is the case with section 7(2), remember that section 39(1) applies to all the rights guaranteed in the Bill of Rights. South African courts must therefore take into account international law and may take into account foreign case law when they are called on to interpret the wide range of civil, political, social and economic rights. We discuss section 39(1) here because the scarcity of precedent-setting case law in the field of social and economic rights across the world renders the application of international law of particular importance in the interpretation of social and economic rights.

PAUSE FOR REFLECTION

Socio-economic rights jurisprudence impoverished by the scarcity of case law from other domestic jurisdictions

Despite the valuable guidance that international law provides for the interpretation of the socio-economic rights in the Constitution, the continued absence of directly relevant case law from other domestic jurisdictions arguably impoverishes the development of social and economic rights jurisprudence in South Africa. However, the contribution of international human rights law to the process of gaining recognition for these rights and initiating the development of a viable jurisprudence around them has nevertheless been significant.

The most important of the international socio-economic rights documents, the ICESCR, only recently acquired an individual complaints mechanism through which citizens can lay individual complaints against states for violation of the provisions of the ICESCR.[42] No matters have as yet been dealt with through this mechanism. As a result, the available interpretations that the Committee on ESCR has given to the provisions of ICESCR in its General Comments have not been developed in the context of concrete disputes or complaints, and often take the form of general guidelines.[43]

In addition, up to now there has been no effective method for the actual **enforcement** of the norms developed by the Committee on ESCR in its General Comments. This has meant that little attention has been devoted in international law to the difficult issues of separation of powers and institutional capacity that arise at domestic level in the enforcement of court orders with respect to socio-economic rights.[44]

Both these difficulties dilute the usefulness of international norms as interpretative sources for socio-economic rights at domestic level, particularly as the South African socio-economic rights jurisprudence develops and becomes more concrete and specific.

42 The Optional Protocol to the International Covenant on Economic, Social and Cultural Rights, which establishes an individual complaints mechanism, was adopted in 2008. It achieved the required 10 ratifications to enter into force only in 2013 and entered into force on 5 May 2013.

43 See Brand, D 'The minimum core content of the right to food in context: A response to Rolf Künneman' in Brand, D and Russell, S (eds) (2002b) *Exploring the Core Content of Socio-economic Rights: South African and International Perspectives* 100–2 for a more extensive discussion of this point. See also Craven, M 'Introduction to the International Covenant on Economic, Social and Cultural Rights' in Blyberg, A and Ravindran, DJ (eds) (2000) *A Circle of Rights: Economic, Social and Cultural Rights: A Training Resource* 49, 55. The approach that the Constitutional Court has adopted to the adjudication of socio-economic rights claims – its reasonableness review approach – in many respects amounts to the same kind of generalised policy review method as that applied in the reporting system of the Committee on ESCR. As such, this approach to some extent obviates this particular difficulty with the use of international law norms.

44 Viljoen (2005) 3.

16.5 Socio-economic rights and the legislature and executive

16.5.1 Introduction

As is the case with all constitutional rights, the translation of constitutional socio-economic rights from 'background moral claims'[45] into enforceable legal rights occurs through a variety of 'law-making processes and institutions'.[46] Not only the courts, but at least also the legislature, the executive and the administration, play important roles in this respect to ensure the realisation of these rights.[47] Underlying this discussion is the assumption that social and economic rights – like all other rights – engender specific obligations that the various branches of the state must fulfil. Bilchitz has criticised the Constitutional Court for failing to engage adequately with the need to establish the content of the various social and economic rights and to clarify what the specific obligations are that the various branches of the state need to fulfil. According to Bilchitz, there is a need for the Court to determine what the exact services are to which an individual is entitled when relying on social and economic rights. It is only when these obligations are spelt out that it becomes possible to say with certainty what the obligations are that these rights place on the state.[48] The role that each of these institutions plays in this process is set out below.

PAUSE FOR REFLECTION

The role of the South African Human Rights Commission in the translation of socio-economic rights into enforceable legal rights

Apart from the legislature, the executive and the administration, the South African Human Rights Commission (SAHRC), discussed in chapter 7, also has an important role to play in translating socio-economic rights from background moral claims into enforceable legal rights. In terms of section 184(3) of the Constitution, the SAHRC has a special mandate to monitor the realisation of socio-economic rights. The SAHRC has developed this mandate into a reporting process in terms of which organs of state report to it annually about the steps they have taken to realise socio-economic rights. The SAHRC then drafts a report evaluating the socio-economic rights performance of the state which is tabled in Parliament. This could be referred to as a mechanism for the 'soft protection' of socio-economic rights, emphasising the programmatic involvement of all sectors in government in the implementation of socio-economic rights. The SAHRC is also empowered to receive and deal with complaints of the infringement of socio-economic rights in an extrajudicial fashion.[49]

45 Michelman, FL (2003) The constitution, social rights, and liberal political justification *International Journal of Constitutional Law* 1(1):13–34 at 14.

46 Klare, KE (1998) Legal culture and transformative constitutionalism *South African Journal on Human Rights* 14(1):146–88 at 147.

47 Klare refers in addition to adjudication, legislation and executive and administrative action to police procedure, extra-legal dispute resolution and budgetary processes as 'sites of law-making' at 147.

48 Bilchitz, D (2003) Towards a reasonable approach to the minimum core: Laying the foundations for future socio-economic rights jurisprudence *South African Journal on Human Rights* 19(1):1–26 at 7–9.

49 For a more detailed description of the SAHRC's work in this respect, see Kollapen, J (1999) Monitoring socio-economic rights: What has the SA Human Rights Commission done? *ESR Review* 1(4):18–20; McClain, CV (2002) The SA Human Rights Commission and socio-economic rights: Facing the challenges *ESR Review* 3(1):8–9. For a critique of the SAHRC's work in this respect, see Brand, D (1999) The South African Human Rights Commission: First economic and social rights report *ESR Review* 2(1):18–20; Brand, D and Liebenberg, S (2000) The South African Human Rights Commission: The second economic and social rights report *ESR Review* 2(3):12–6.

16.5.2 Translation through legislation

Socio-economic rights in South Africa are not only entrenched in the Constitution. They are also extensively protected as statutory entitlements in national legislation. The Constitution is replete with commands directed at the legislature to enact legislation to give effect to specific constitutional rights. Examples are found in section 9 in relation to the prohibition on unfair discrimination; in section 32 in relation to the right of access to information; and in section 33 in relation to the right to administrative justice. Along similar lines, several of the socio-economic rights explicitly require statutory measures to be enacted to give effect to them. So, for instance, sections 26(2) and 27(2) require that the state take 'reasonable **legislative** ... measures', among other things, to realise the right to have access to adequate housing and the rights to have access to health care services, food, water and social security and assistance, respectively.[50] The legislature has reacted to these constitutional commands by enacting a wide range of statutes aimed at facilitating, providing and protecting access to basic resources.[51]

The statutory measures envisaged here include legislation that creates and empowers structures and institutions and sets in place processes for the implementation of socio-economic rights.[52] However, an important aspect of such legislation is the creation of statutory socio-economic rights. These statutory socio-economic rights can take the traditional form of subjective legal entitlements of particular persons to particular things or services. Examples are statutory entitlements to receive defined social assistance benefits if an individual meets certain eligibility conditions that can be enforced against the state[53] and entitlements to tenure on land exercised through legal protection against eviction that can be enforced against other private persons.[54]

Importantly, these statutory socio-economic rights also include rights or entitlements of a less traditional nature. Given particularly the liberalised law of standing that applies in Bill of Rights-related litigation in South Africa pursuant to section 38 of the Constitution, it is possible for individuals either on their own behalf, on behalf of a group or class of persons, or in the public interest[55] to enforce broadly phrased statutory duties or statutory commands against the state. A person doing so would not so much be claiming something specific for him or herself (perhaps also that), but the performance of a public statutory duty or commitment on behalf of a larger collective.

---

50 See also sections 24(*b*) and 25(5) of the Constitution.

51 Examples of such legislation with respect to specific socio-economic rights are discussed in detail in other chapters and will not be listed here.

52 See, for example, Chs 3 and 4 of the Social Assistance Act 13 of 2004 and the South African Social Security Agency Act 9 of 2004.

53 See Ch 2 of the Social Assistance Act that creates entitlements for eligible persons to a Child Support Grant, a Care Dependency Grant, a Foster Child Grant, a Disability Grant, a War Veteran's Grant, an Older Person's Grant, a Grant-in-Aid and a Social Relief in Distress Grant.

54 See, for example, ss 8(1) and 11(1), (2) and (3) of the Extension of Security of Tenure Act 62 of 1997 (ESTA).

55 S 38 states:

> **Anyone listed in this section has the right to approach a competent court, alleging that a right in the Bill of Rights has been infringed or threatened, and the court may grant appropriate relief, including a declaration of rights. The persons who may approach a court are –**
> **(*a*) anyone acting in their own interest;**
> **(*b*) anyone acting on behalf of another person who cannot act in their own name;**
> **(*c*) anyone acting as a member of, or in the interest of, a group or class of persons;**
> **(*d*) anyone acting in the public interest; and**
> **(*e*) an association acting in the interest of its members.**

PAUSE FOR REFLECTION

Enforcing statutory duties against the state on behalf of individual complainants and the larger collective

In *Kutumela v Member of the Executive Committee for Social Services, Culture, Arts and Sport in the North West Province*,[56] the plaintiffs had applied for the Social Relief of Distress Grant, but despite clearly being eligible, did not receive it. Their complaint in response was not framed only as an application for each individual complainant to receive the social assistance grant for which they were eligible and to which they each had a subjective statutory right. Instead, the complaint alleged that the state had statutorily committed itself to provide to eligible persons a Social Relief in Distress Grant in terms of the Social Assistance Act and its regulations and had placed a duty on provincial governments to make good that commitment. However, the province in question had not dedicated the necessary human, institutional and financial resources to do so and the grant was therefore available only on paper.

The case was settled and resulted in a particularly wide-ranging order requiring certain relief specific to the parties, but also various forms of general relief. Apart from requiring the provincial government in question to acknowledge its legal responsibility to provide Social Relief of Distress Grants effectively to those eligible for them, the order required it to devise a programme to ensure the effective implementation of Social Relief of Distress Grants and to put in place the necessary infrastructure for the administration and payment of the grant. In essence, the state was ordered to make good on a statutory commitment to give effect to an aspect of the right to have access to social assistance. The result was that the grant would in future be available to all eligible persons in addition to it being paid out to the individual complainants.

The enforcement of socio-economic rights through these kinds of statutory entitlements holds great promise. Statutory entitlements are first likely to be much more detailed and concrete in nature than the vague and generally phrased constitutional rights to which they purport to give effect. They therefore provide a more direct mechanism through which individuals can leverage access to resources. In addition, courts are likely to enforce these statutory entitlements more robustly than they would constitutional rights because they are enforcing a right, duty or commitment defined by the legislature itself rather than a broadly phrased constitutional right to which they have to give content. As such, when courts enforce statutory entitlements, they are not confronted to the same extent with the concerns of separation of powers, institutional legitimacy and technical competence that have so directly shaped and limited their constitutional socio-economic rights jurisprudence. The constitutional validity of such legislative provisions can, of course, also be tested against the relevant social and economic rights provision in cases where litigants believe the legislation is under-inclusive and fails to provide sufficient or equitable access to the guaranteed right.

56 Case 671/2003 23 October 2003 (B). Our thanks to Nick de Villiers, of the Legal Resources Centre in Pretoria, for providing us with a copy of the order.

PAUSE FOR REFLECTION

Statutory entitlements more detailed and concrete in nature

The fact that statutory entitlements are likely to be much more detailed and concrete in nature than the vague and generally phrased constitutional rights forming their background is clearly illustrated by the Regulations Relating to Compulsory National Standards and Measures to Conserve Water.[57]

These regulations have been issued in terms of section 9 of the Water Services Act.[58] They give effect to the constitutional right of access to sufficient water guaranteed in section 27(1)(*b*) of the Constitution by providing that:

> [t]he minimum standard for basic water supply services is a minimum quantity of potable water of 25 litres per person per day or six kilolitres per household per month –
>
> (i) at a minimum flow rate of not less than 10 litres per minute;
>
> (ii) within 200 metres of a household; and
>
> (iii) with an effectiveness such that no consumer is without supply for more than seven full days in any year.

In *Mazibuko and Others v City of Johannesburg and Others*,[59] the Constitutional Court upheld the constitutional validity of this regulation. In arriving at its decision, the Constitutional Court pointed out that the Constitution imposes a positive obligation on the state to adopt legislative and other measures that give content to the socio-economic rights guaranteed in the Constitution.[60] In addition, the Court also pointed out that the enforcement of socio-economic rights through statutory entitlements is consistent with the founding values of the Constitution. This is because the standards adopted by the state inform citizens of what government is seeking to achieve and thus enable citizens to monitor government's performance and to hold it accountable politically if the standard is not achieved or legally if the standard is not reasonable.[61]

In many jurisdictions other than South Africa where socio-economic rights do not enjoy constitutional status, they are protected as statutory entitlements in the ordinary positive law. Possibly the best examples can be found in a number of the Scandinavian countries, in particular Finland, where rights such as the right to social assistance, the right to housing, the right to daycare for small children and rights of specified assistance for the severely handicapped are protected as subjective rights in national legislation.[62] However, in the absence of constitutional socio-economic guarantees, the existence of statutory socio-economic entitlements may be precarious. In the United States, for example, the right to social welfare is not guaranteed in the federal Constitution. The federal government has

57 *Government Gazette* No 22355, Notice R 509 of 2001 (8 June 2001).
58 Act 108 of 1997.
59 (CCT 39/09) [2009] ZACC 28; 2010 (3) BCLR 239 (CC); 2010 (4) SA 1 (CC) (8 October 2009).
60 *Mazibuko* para 66.
61 *Mazibuko* para 70.
62 For a discussion, see Viljoen (2005) 12–3; Scheinin, M 'Economic and social rights as legal rights' in Eide, A, Krause, C and Rosas, A (1995) *Economic, Social and Cultural Rights: A Textbook* 61.

consequently been free gradually to reduce social welfare entitlements as public perceptions have changed about the sustainability of comprehensive welfare provisions.[63]

In South Africa, statutory socio-economic rights are not subject to legislative *fiat* to the same extent as in other jurisdictions where constitutional socio-economic rights are absent. These rights in South Africa are enacted by the legislature to give effect to constitutional socio-economic rights.[64] Legislative interference with a statutory socio-economic right – such as a restrictive legislative redefinition of a social assistance benefit – therefore constitutes an infringement of the constitutional socio-economic right to which the statutory entitlement gives effect. Such legislative interference will only be constitutionally permissible if it is justifiable in terms of the appropriate standard of scrutiny. By the same token, as we pointed out above, the statutory scheme that is intended to give effect to a socio-economic right can be evaluated against that right to see whether or not it gives full effect to that right.[65]

Apart from the corrective or protective background role played by constitutional socio-economic rights in relation to statutory socio-economic rights, constitutional socio-economic rights inform the interpretation of statutory socio-economic rights. Also, the fact that a statutory right or scheme is intended to give effect to a constitutional socio-economic right can in specific cases in a rhetorical sense reinforce the enforcement of that statutory right or scheme. In *Residents of Bon Vista Mansions v Southern Metropolitan Council*,[66] the South Gauteng High Court gave an interim order that the plaintiff's water supply be reconnected on the basis of sections 4(1) and 4(3) of the Water Services Act. Although the decision was based on statutory entitlements, the Court invoked the section 27(1)(*b*) constitutional right to have access to sufficient water to reinforce its finding. In other words, it interpreted the provisions of the Water Services Act expansively and justified this by invoking the constitutional right that guarantees everyone the right of access to water.

The Court proceeded from the assumption that a disconnection of a household water supply was a *prima facie* infringement of the section 27(1)(*b*) constitutional right which had to be justified in order to be constitutionally sound.[67] The Court then held that the provisions of the Water Services Act constituted 'a statutory framework within which such breaches may be justified'.[68] Further, throughout the judgment the Court made reference to the fact that the Act was intended to give effect to the constitutional right and that non-compliance with its provisions constituted an infringement of the constitutional right.[69]

Finally, constitutional socio-economic rights protect statutory socio-economic rights from legal challenge on the basis of other constitutional rights. The case of *City of Cape Town*

63 See Williams, LA 'Welfare and legal entitlements: The social roots of poverty' in Kairys, D (ed) (1998) *The Politics of Law: A Progressive Critique* 570–1; Simon, WH (1986) Rights and redistribution in the welfare system *Stanford Law Review* 38(6):1431–1516 at 1467–77.

64 Much of the social legislation that has so far been enacted is explicit as to this purpose. See, for example, the Preamble of the Social Assistance Act which states that one purpose of the Act is to give effect to section 27(1)(*c*) of the Constitution. Courts, in their interpretation of such legislation, have also emphasised the link between social legislation and the constitutional rights to which it gives effect. See, for example, with respect to the relationship between the Prevention of Illegal Eviction from and Unlawful Occupation of Land Act 19 of 1998 (PIE) and ss 26(3) and 25 of the Constitution, *Port Elizabeth Municipality v Various Occupiers* (CCT 53/03) [2004] ZACC 7; 2005 (1) SA 217 (CC); 2004 (12) BCLR 1268 (CC) (1 October 2004) para 17 and *Cape Killarney Property Investments (Pty) Ltd v Mahamba and Others* 2001 (4) SA 1222 (SCA) para 21.

65 So, for example, in *Grootboom* para 52, with regard to the Housing Act 107 of 1997, the Constitutional Court found the statutory framework for the state's measures to give effect to the right to have access to adequate housing to be lacking in that it made no provision for temporary relief for people in a housing crisis.

66 2002 (6) BCLR 625 (W).

67 *Residents of Bon Vista Mansions* para 20.

68 *Residents of Bon Vista Mansions* para 21.

69 *Residents of Bon Vista Mansions* paras 28–30.

v Rudolph and Others[70] dealt with a constitutional challenge to provisions of the Prevention of Illegal Eviction from and Unlawful Occupation of Land Act (PIE)[71] brought on the basis of section 25 property rights. It was argued that the PIE Act infringed the property rights of individuals because it encouraged 'land grabbing', thus limiting the property rights of the owners of property whose land is occupied. The Court rejected this argument and pointed out that the impugned provisions of the PIE Act were intended to give effect to section 26(3) of the Constitution. The High Court relied on this fact to reject the challenge.[72]

PAUSE FOR REFLECTION

Applying the principle of subsidiarity to socio-economic rights

In recent cases a potential complication in the relationship between constitutional socio-economic rights and legislation enacted to give effect to them has arisen. Drawing on case law dealing with the relationship between, for example, the constitutional right to administrative justice and the Promotion of Administrative Justice Act (PAJA),[73] enacted to give effect to the constitutional right, our courts have intimated that where legislation has been enacted to give effect to a constitutional socio-economic right, litigants may no longer rely directly on the constitutional right in question to review conduct or law that breaches that right.[74] Instead, litigants must use the remedies provided by the legislation in question. The only remaining role for the constitutional right using this approach is as an aid for the interpretation of the legislation in question and as the basis for a possible constitutional challenge to the legislation giving effect to that right. In short, our courts have started to apply the principle of subsidiarity to socio-economic rights.[75]

16.5.3 Translation through executive and administrative action

Apart from the legislature, the executive and state administration can also interpret socio-economic rights and so self-define the duties that those rights impose on them through the adoption of policies or through simple executive or administrative decisions. Courts can then enforce these self-defined duties against the executive or administration as the case may be. The policy formulation or administrative decisions in some sense translate constitutional rights into enforceable legal duties or entitlements.

In *B and Others v Minister of Correctional Services and Others*,[76] for example, four HIV-positive prisoners approached the High Court with an application for an order that the state was constitutionally obliged to provide them with antiretroviral treatment at its own expense. The case turned on the interpretation of the term 'adequate medical treatment' in section 35(2)(*e*) of the Constitution. The Court held that it did not have the requisite medical expertise to determine what adequate medical treatment for the various applicants entailed and whether or not it included antiretroviral medication.

70 2003 (11) BCLR 1236 (C).

71 Act 19 of 1998.

72 *City of Cape Town v Rudolph and Others* 2003 (11) BCLR 1236 (C) 74H–75J.

73 Act 3 of 2000.

74 *Nokotyana and Others v Ekurhuleni Metropolitan Municipality and Others* (CCT 31/09) [2009] ZACC 33; 2010 (4) BCLR 312 (CC) (19 November 2009).

75 See Pieterse-Spies, A (2011) Reasonableness, subsidiarity and service delivery: A case discussion *SA Public Law* 26(1):329–40.

76 1997 (6) BCLR 789 (C).

On this basis it held against two of the applicants.[77] However, the Court did find in favour of a number of the applicants to whom state medical personnel had already prescribed anti-retroviral medication. The Court's reasoning with respect to these prisoners was that, in their case, the state had itself through the prescription determined what 'adequate medical treatment' was for them. In doing so, the state had translated the constitutional right to be provided with adequate medical treatment into a concrete legal entitlement that the Court was willing to enforce.[78]

The relationship between socio-economic rights defined through executive or administrative action in this way, on the one hand, and constitutional socio-economic rights, on the other, is similar to the relationship between constitutional and statutory socio-economic rights described above. In the first place, executive or administrative action that defines duties and entitlements in terms of constitutional socio-economic rights gives effect to those rights. As such, those rights can be protected against challenge on other constitutional grounds.[79] Second, such executive or administrative definition of constitutional socio-economic rights has to comply with the requirements of the right to which it is intended to give effect.[80]

16.6 Socio-economic rights and the courts

16.6.1 Introduction

The socio-economic rights in the Constitution are **justiciable** - that is, when they are infringed, they can be enforced through the courts.[81] In fact, it can be said that courts exercise the primary role in enforcing the statutory socio-economic rights described above. In such cases they 'mechanically' enforce socio-economic rights as predefined by the legislature, often also through particular remedies determined by the legislature. The law-making role of the courts here, although certainly present, is much restricted.

However, courts also directly translate constitutional socio-economic rights into enforceable legal claims through their interpretation and application of these rights. In the process of adjudicating disputes on the basis of constitutional socio-economic rights rather than on the basis of statutory socio-economic rights, courts interpret these rights and give concrete and authoritative expression to the duties they impose and to the entitlements they create in much the same way that the legislature does when giving effect to them through legislation. Courts also, through their orders, enforce the duties and entitlements that they define.

---

77 *B* para 37.

78 *B* paras 35–6 and 60.

79 See *Minister of Public Works and Others v Kyalami Ridge Environmental Association and Others (Mukhwevho Intervening)* (CCT 55/00) [2001] ZACC 19; 2001 (3) SA 1151 (CC); 2001 (7) BCLR 652 (CC) (29 May 2001) where the Court upheld a decision by the appellant to house a group of flood victims on land belonging to it against a challenge on the basis of administrative justice rights partly because the appellant took the decision to give effect to the right to have access to adequate housing.

80 The complaint in *Treatment Action Campaign* was, in essence, that the state's executive definition of its duties in terms of the right to have access to health care services in the context of the prevention of mother-to-child transmission of HIV at birth fell short of the requirements of the right.

81 S 172(1)(*a*) of the Constitution requires and so empowers courts to declare any law or conduct inconsistent with the Constitution invalid to the extent of its inconsistency. Socio-economic rights are included in the scope of this power.

16.6.2 Modes of adjudication: sections 8 and 39(2)

The power of courts to translate socio-economic rights into concrete legal claims in this way is mediated through two provisions of the Constitution. Sections 8 and 39(2) (the application sections) regulate the question of how and under what circumstances fundamental rights, including socio-economic rights, interact with existing law and with conduct. As such, these sections indicate which kinds of legal claims can be launched through the courts on the basis of constitutional socio-economic rights, against whom and how the courts may deal with such claims.

Section 8(1) declares that the Bill of Rights 'applies to all law'[82] and 'binds the legislature, the executive, the judiciary and all organs of state'. Section 8(2) extends the reach of the Bill of Rights to the private sphere, declaring that if the 'nature of [a] right and the nature of any duty imposed by [that] right' allows, the right 'binds a natural or a juristic person'. Section 8(3) provides that when a court has found in terms of section 8(2) that a right in the Bill of Rights is applicable in litigation between private parties and that the right has been limited by one of the parties to the litigation, it must give effect to that right by applying an existing statutory or common law remedy. In the absence of such an existing remedy, the court must develop the common law to create a remedy that will give effect to the right.[83] Finally, section 39(2) determines that when a court interprets legislation or develops the common law, it 'must promote the spirit, purport and objects of the Bill of Rights'. This places a general interpretative injunction on courts to infuse existing law with constitutional values.

Litigants can challenge the constitutionality of any **law** - that is, any statutory rule, common law rule or customary law rule - whether it is the state or a private party that relies on it.[84] The consequence of a successful constitutional challenge to a statutory rule is that the rule is overturned and the situation reverts to the common law position that existed before the particular rule was enacted. This should lead to the legislature enacting new legislation to regulate the same issues, but the court can also itself remedy the constitutional defect by reading words into the impugned provision. If a rule of common law is successfully challenged, a court will employ its inherent power to develop the common law to change that rule or to develop new rules so as to make the common law position consistent with the constitutional right in question.[85]

A statutory provision was challenged in this way as inconsistent with a constitutional socio-economic right in the case of *Khosa and Others v Minister of Social Development and Others, Mahlaule and Another v Minister of Social Development*.[86] This case dealt with

82 See *Du Plessis and Others v De Klerk and Another* (CCT8/95) [1996] ZACC 10; 1996 (3) SA 850; 1996 (5) BCLR 658 (15 May 1996) for a unanimous holding that the same term in section 7(2) of the interim Constitution referred to statute, common law and customary law.

83 A court can also develop a common law rule to limit the right, provided that such a rule would then have to be justifiable in terms of section 36(1) of the Constitution.

84 The textual basis for a Bill of Rights challenge to a statutory or common law rule relied on by the state as against a private entity is s 8(1) of the Constitution. Similarly, the textual basis for a Bill of Rights challenge to a statutory rule relied on by one private entity against another is clearly s 8(1) of the Constitution. However, there is some controversy about whether the textual basis for a challenge to a common law rule relied on by one private entity against another is s 8(1) rather than s 8(2) read with s 8(3). The Constitutional Court in *Khumalo and Others v Holomisa* (CCT53/01) [2002] ZACC 12; 2002 (5) SA 401; 2002 (8) BCLR 771 (14 June 2002) rejected reliance on s 8(1) in a challenge directed at the existing common law rules of defamation relied on by a private party. The Court opted instead to bring the Bill of Rights to bear through s 8(2) and (3).

85 It seems that this would be the case, irrespective of whether the Bill of Rights is brought to bear on a dispute through s 8(1) or s 8(2) and (3).

86 (CCT 13/03, CCT 12/03) [2004] ZACC 11; 2004 (6) SA 505 (CC); 2004 (6) BCLR 569 (CC) (4 March 2004).

provisions of the Social Assistance Act and the Welfare Laws Amendment Act[87] that restricted access to social assistance to South African citizens to the detriment of permanent residents and their children. These provisions were successfully challenged as inconsistent with the section 27(1) right of everyone to have access to social security and assistance and the section 9(3) prohibition on unfair discrimination.[88]

An example of where a common law rule was challenged as inconsistent with a constitutional socio-economic right occurred in *Brisley v Drotsky*.[89] In this case, the existing common law rules regulating private evictions were unsuccessfully challenged as inconsistent with the section 26(3) prohibition on arbitrary evictions. Had the challenge been successful, the Court would have had to develop the common law so as to take adequate account of the section 26(3) injunction that courts take account of 'all relevant factors' before issuing an eviction order. The result would then have been that courts would have a discretion, exercised on the basis of their consideration of relevant circumstances, whether or not to grant the order.[90]

Litigants can challenge state or private **conduct** as inconsistent with a constitutional right. If state conduct is successfully challenged, it would simply be invalid and the court would craft a constitutional remedy to vindicate the right in question. If private conduct is successfully challenged, a court would attempt to find a remedy in the existing statutory or common law that can be adapted to vindicate the right in question. In the absence of such existing remedy, the court would develop the common law so as to provide such a remedy.

An example of a successful constitutional challenge to state conduct as inconsistent with a constitutional socio-economic right is *Treatment Action Campaign (2)* where a policy position of the National Department of Health was successfully challenged as being inconsistent with the section 27(1) right to have access to health care services. The result was that the policy was invalidated and the Court ordered the government to adopt and implement a policy that would be constitutionally sound. There has as yet been no example of a challenge to private conduct as inconsistent with a constitutional socio-economic right.

Finally, litigants can argue that a rule of law on which the other party to the litigation relies is inconsistent, not with a particular right, but with the general tenor of the Bill of Rights, the 'objective value system' that underlies its particular provisions. A court that accepts such a proposition would then interpret the statutory provision in question or develop the common law rule so as to give effect to the 'spirit, purport and objects' of the Bill of Rights.

An example of this kind of interaction between the Bill of Rights and the existing law occurring in the context of socio-economic rights protection is *Afrox Healthcare Bpk v Strydom*.[91] The Supreme Court of Appeal (SCA) was unsuccessfully asked to develop the common law of contract through the rule that contractual terms that conflict with the public interest are unenforceable. This would have rendered unenforceable disclaimers in contracts

---

87 Ss 3(*c*), 4(*b*)(ii) and 4B(*b*)(ii) of the Social Assistance Act 59 of 1992 and s 3 of the Welfare Laws Amendment Act 106 of 1997.

88 The various sections were found to be inconsistent with the Constitution, but were not invalidated to the extent of their inconsistency. Instead, the Court read words into the sections to remedy the constitutional defect. See *Khosa* para 98. See also *Jaftha* where the Court found that provisions of the Magistrates' Courts Act 32 of 1944 allowing for the sale in execution of debtors' homes to satisfy judgment debt were inconsistent with s 26(1) of the Constitution. The Court read words into the Act to remedy the defect.

89 2002 (4) SA 1 (SCA).

90 For a variety of reasons, the use of constitutional socio-economic rights in this indirect, interpretative way to influence the existing law is potentially extremely important.

91 (172/2001) [2002] ZASCA 73; 2002 (6) SA 21 (SCA); [2002] 4 All SA 125 (SCA) (31 May 2002).

between hospitals and their patients that indemnify the hospitals from liability for damage negligently caused to patients.

16.6.3 Constraint in the adjudication of socio-economic rights claims

16.6.3.1 Separation of powers concerns

Courts operate under the control of a set of unwritten constraints related to their institutional legitimacy, their constitutional place and their technical capacity, in particular when they adjudicate claims on the basis of constitutional socio-economic rights in any of the three possible ways described above. Courts are constrained in their law-making role with respect to socio-economic rights by what can loosely be described as separation of powers concerns. Both in the international arena and to a lesser extent in South Africa, the status of socio-economic rights as legal rights has long been questioned, mostly on the basis that these rights are not justiciable.[92]

The arguments along this line all proceed from the same assumption. Socio-economic rights supposedly uniquely create entitlements to affirmative state action and consequently require the expenditure of resources if they are to be realised. Courts, so it is argued, do not have the institutional and technical capacity to deal with the polycentric questions of social and economic policy that claims based on these affirmative rights will inevitably raise. Nor do courts have the democratic legitimacy to question the socio-economic policy choices of the elected political branches of government that will be implicated. Courts are further hampered by the fact that socio-economic rights supposedly do not pose justiciable legal standards according to which these assessments can be made.

If courts engage in the adjudication of socio-economic rights claims, the arguments proceed, this could both erode the legitimacy of the judiciary and the idea of human rights as a whole. Because of economic realities, the state may not be able to deliver the basic services that the courts require the state to provide whatever courts have to say.[93] This places courts in a potentially damaging confrontation with the political branches of government.[94]

The most convincing response to these arguments does not deny that socio-economic rights present problems to the process of adjudication, but does deny that these problems mark them as **essentially different** from other rights. According to this line of argument, already touched on above, all rights impose both affirmative and negative duties on the state,

92 Eide points out that the focus on justiciability, as if that alone determines the relative status of rights, diverts attention from the broader question of the 'effective protection' of socio-economic rights, something that occurs through a variety of mechanisms, including adjudication. See Eide, A 'Future protection of economic and social rights in Europe' in Bloed, A et al (eds) (1993) *Monitoring Human Rights in Europe: Comparing International Procedures and Mechanisms* 214. However, see An-Na'im, AA 'To affirm the full human rights standing of economic, social and cultural rights' in Ghai and Cottrell (2004) 13, who recognises the limitations of the justiciability debate, but points out that 'the claim that judicial enforcement of [socio-economic rights] is not possible or desirable, **undermines the human rights standing of these rights**' (our emphasis) and, accordingly, remains an important focus.

93 The idea that socio-economic rights are justiciable is also criticised from a more promising, radically democratic perspective. The argument is that the judicialisation of issues of socio-economic politics through the entrenchment of justiciable socio-economic rights could stifle social action, impoverish political life and ultimately damage struggles for social justice. As Davis has put it, justiciable socio-economic rights might 'erode the possibility for meaningful public participation in the shaping of the societal good'. See Davis, DM (1992) The case against the inclusion of socio-economic demands in a bill of rights except as directive principles *South African Journal on Human Rights* 8(4):475–90 at 488–90. See also Bakan, J 'What's wrong with social rights' in Bakan, J and Schneiderman, D (eds) (1992) *Social Justice and the Constitution: Perspectives on a Social Union for Canada* 85; Ghai, Y and Cottrell, J 'The role of the courts in the protection of economic, social and cultural rights' in Ghai and Cottrell (2004) 88.

94 Roux, T (2003) Legitimating transformation: Political resource allocation in the South African Constitutional Court *Democratisation* 10:92–111 at 92–3.

depending on the circumstances under which they are enforced. The difficulties attending the judicial enforcement of the affirmative aspects of socio-economic rights also occur in the judicial enforcement of these aspects of other rights. The conclusion is that a rigid categorisation of rights into those that are justiciable and those that are not is simply false. All rights instead fall somewhere along a 'justiciability spectrum' where some are more easily justiciable than others. The 'possibility and role of judicial enforcement ... [should be] assessed and developed in relation to each human right'[95] instead of being denied a whole class or category of rights.

The simple fact that socio-economic rights were eventually included in the Constitution in South Africa as justiciable rights shows that this latter, more nuanced argument regarding their justiciability won the day in South Africa. Nevertheless, an echo of the objection to their inclusion remains in the way some of these rights included in the Bill of Rights, especially sections 26 and 27, have been formulated. The careful limitation of the scope and nature of the positive duties imposed by the qualified socio-economic rights described above seems to be aimed at mediating some of the difficulties with the judicial enforcement of socio-economic rights that those opposed to their entrenchment have raised. In their interpretation of socio-economic rights, our courts have been attuned to this echo.

16.6.3.2 The Constitutional Court's approach to separation of powers concerns

Although the Constitutional Court has from the start emphasised that socio-economic rights are indeed justiciable,[96] it has since been at great pains to show that it regards itself importantly bound by the unwritten separation of powers constraints outlined above.[97] The Court has variously justified what many have described as its restrained, respectful or deferential approach to deciding socio-economic rights cases[98] with reference to its lack of technical expertise in deciding the issues raised in socio-economic rights cases; its lack of democratic accountability in contrast to the executive and legislative branches in this respect;[99] and its institutionally determined inability to access and process the essential information needed to decide the policy, evaluative and allocation questions that arise in such cases.[100] In addition, commentators have pointed out that, in a more strategic sense, the Court's concern for the maintenance of its own institutional integrity in relation to the executive and legislature has had a constraining effect.[101]

95 An-Na'im (2004) 7.

96 See *First Certification* paras 76–8.

97 See *Grootboom* para 41.

98 See Sunstein, CR (2001) Social and economic rights? Lessons from South Africa *Constitutional Forum* 11(4):123–32 at 123.

99 The following quote from Chaskalson P for the Court in *Soobramoney* para 29 shows the Court's concern with both these issues:

> The provincial administration which is responsible for health services in KwaZulu-Natal has to make decisions about the funding that should be made available for health care and how such funds should be spent. **These choices involve difficult decisions to be taken at the political level in fixing the health budget, and at the functional level in deciding upon the priorities to be met. A court will be slow to interfere with rational decisions taken in good faith by the political organs and medical authorities whose responsibility it is to deal with such matters** (our emphasis).

See also Sachs J's concurring judgment in the same case at para 58:

> Courts are not the proper place to resolve the agonising personal and medical problems that underlie these choices. Important though our review functions are, there are areas where **institutional incapacity and appropriate constitutional modesty require us to be especially cautious** (our emphasis).

100 *Grootboom* para 32.

101 Roux (2003).

PAUSE FOR REFLECTION

Separation of powers constraints on the Constitutional Court when interpreting and applying socio-economic rights

The fact that the Constitutional Court regards itself as bound by separation of powers constraints when it interprets and applies socio-economic rights is clearly illustrated in its judgment in the case of *Grootboom* where Yacoob J stated that:

> [t]he precise contours and content of the measures to be adopted are primarily a matter for the Legislature and the Executive. They must, however, ensure that the measures they adopt are reasonable. In any challenge based on s 26 in which it is argued that the State has failed to meet the positive obligations imposed upon it by s 26(2), the question will be whether the legislative and other measures taken by the State are reasonable. A court considering reasonableness will not enquire whether other more desirable or favourable measures could have been adopted, or whether public money could have been better spent. The question would be whether the measures that have been adopted are reasonable. It is necessary to recognise that a wide range of possible measures could be adopted by the State to meet its obligations. Many of these would meet the requirement of reasonableness. Once it is shown that the measures do so, this requirement is met.[102]

In passages like these, we find echoes of the view, discussed in particular in chapters 2 and 6 of this book, that the Constitutional Court views its relationship with the other branches of government within the framework of the separation of powers doctrine as one in which a structured dialogue takes place. This dialogue is one in which each of the parties is designated a particular role to play and in which the dialogue proceeds in a predestined manner – almost like actors speaking the words written by a playwright. In this view, the courts cannot overstep their powers by treading on the terrain of the other branches of government, much like an actor in a play should not tread on the toes of other actors by speaking their lines.

The constraint exercised because of separation of powers concerns shows at two different points in the process of adjudicating socio-economic rights claims. First, it influences the willingness of the Constitutional Court to entertain certain questions at all when it is asked to decide a case.[103] It also determines the extent to which and the manner in which the Court is willing to interrogate those questions that it does feel comfortable dealing with or cannot avoid.[104] Second, it significantly constrains the Court in fashioning orders to enforce its findings where it has held against the state in a socio-economic rights case.[105] Clearly, the extent to which the Court feels itself bound by constraints in specific cases significantly determines the possible outcome of those cases.

102 *Grootboom* para 41.

103 See *Treatment Action Campaign (2)* para 128 where the Court declined to consider the question whether the state is under a duty to provide breastfeeding substitutes to HIV-positive mothers to prevent the transmission of HIV to babies through breastfeeding after birth. The reason the Court gave for this was because this question 'raises complex issues' that are best left to government and health professionals to deal with and because sufficient information was not at the disposal of the Court to make a finding in this respect.

104 See the Court's remarks in *Grootboom* para 41 with respect to the extent to which it is willing to interrogate the relative effectiveness of different policy options in the application of its reasonableness test.

105 See *Treatment Action Campaign (2)* paras 124–33, in particular para 129.

16.6.3.3 Factors influencing separation of powers concerns

16.6.3.3.1 Introduction

A number of factors related to the nature of specific cases and the manner in which they are argued influences the extent to which courts feel themselves bound by separation of powers constraints. It is important to take cognisance of these factors when we want to predict to what extent a court will exercise its powers to enforce social and economic rights in a particular case. It is impossible to provide an encyclopaedic list of such factors or to discuss all the factors in detail in this chapter. However, we identify and discuss the important factors as an illustration of how separation of powers concerns influence social and economic rights adjudication by the judiciary.[106]

16.6.3.3.2 Where the legislature, executive or state administration has defined the legal duties, courts are more likely to intervene

In certain social and economic rights cases, courts are not required to interpret and enforce the rights contained in the Constitution itself. Sometimes courts are merely required to enforce socio-economic rights duties **which the legislature, the executive or the state administration has itself defined**. In such cases, courts feel less constrained as the elected branches of government have chosen to define the duties imposed by social and economic rights themselves and, as it were, invited the courts to police whether these duties are being fulfilled. Arguing a case on the basis of such self-defined duties, rather than directly on the basis of a constitutional socio-economic right, is therefore generally to be preferred.

The most obvious examples of the enforcement of such self-defined duties are cases where courts enforce statutory socio-economic rights in either of the two senses described above.[107] In most such cases, constraint is diluted not only by the fact that courts are not faced with having to define duties to impose on the state themselves, but also because courts are able to use remedies from the existing law to enforce statutorily defined duties. The many instances where courts have enforced statutory entitlements to social assistance through administrative law remedies illustrate this point.[108]

Perhaps the most dramatic example of courts' preference for the enforcement of statutory entitlements is the line of cases culminating in *Ndlovu v Ngcobo; Bekker and Another v Jika.*[109] In terms of the common law, a court **must** grant an eviction order if the applicant can show that he or she is the owner and that the evictee is occupying the land.[110] Section 26(3) of the Constitution, by contrast, determines that a court may only grant an eviction order **after considering all relevant circumstances**. Tenure security laws - most importantly the Prevention of Illegal Eviction from and Unlawful Occupation of Land Act (PIE Act)[111] - require courts in certain instances to consider all relevant circumstances before granting an eviction order and as such to give effect to section 26(3).[112]

106 We refer to only two, in some sense, arbitrary practical factors that influence the extent to which courts feel themselves constrained in adjudicating socio-economic rights claims here. There are, of course, many other, more nuanced factors that also influence constraint such as the extent to which the adjudication of a particular case would involve a court in considering questions of policy, the position of the claimants in society and the extent and degree of deprivation motivating a claim. See in this respect De Vos (1997) 367; Bollyky, TJ (2002) R if C>P+B: A paradigm for judicial remedies of socio-economic rights violations *South African Journal on Human Rights* 18(2):161-200 at 165.

107 Either statutory subjective rights or statutory commands/commitments.

108 See De Villiers (2002) for an overview.

109 2003 (1) SA 113 (SCA). See also *Port Elizabeth Municipality.*

110 *Graham v Ridley* 1931 TPD 476.

111 Act 19 of 1998.

112 See also the ESTA and the Land Reform (Labour Tenants) Act 3 of 1996 (Labour Tenants Act).

However, conflicting decisions in the High Courts raised uncertainty over whether these laws, and particularly the PIE Act, apply also to evictions in cases of holding over. These are cases where initially lawful occupation subsequently became unlawful.[113] In such cases, courts have consequently been faced with the question whether, in lieu of the PIE Act, section 26(3) changed the common law rules of eviction so as to confer discretion on courts.

After a series of conflicting decisions in the High Courts in this respect,[114] the question reached the SCA in *Brisley*. The Court went to somewhat tortuous lengths to avoid developing the common law in line with section 26(3). It held that the section 26(3) 'relevant circumstances' could only be **legally** relevant circumstances. For the Court, the only circumstances legally relevant to the question whether an eviction should be allowed were the common law requirements of whether the evictor was the owner of the land in question and whether the evictee was occupying the land. As a result, the SCA held that section 26(3) did not change the rules of the common law.[115] The only influence that section 26(3) exerted on the existing law was the influence exerted through the tenure security laws. The common law was left intact with respect to those kinds of evictions to which the tenure security laws did not apply.

Five months after *Brisley*, the SCA decided *Ndlovu; Bekker*. In this case, the SCA was faced with the question whether or not the statutory entitlements to security of tenure created by the legislature in the PIE Act applied also to evictions in cases of holding over. The Court extended the PIE Act's application to such evictions.[116] The result in practice was exactly the same as the result would have been had the Court decided *Brisley* differently. Courts would now also have a discretion in cases of holding over, exercised on the basis of a consideration of all relevant circumstances, whether or not to grant an eviction order.[117] What the Court was unwilling to do itself in *Brisley* on the basis of a constitutional right, it was happy to do in *Ndlovu; Bekker* on the basis of the PIE Act's statutory entitlements.

By the same token, courts are more comfortable with enforcing socio-economic rights where they have been defined through executive or administrative action as described above. In *B v Minister of Correctional Services*, the Court was willing to order the state to provide at its own cost antiretroviral medication to the two applicants to whom the state had prescribed it. By contrast, the Court refused to make the same order with respect to the two applicants for whom the medication had not yet been prescribed. This decision turned on the fact that the prescription of the medication to the first two applicants amounted to an administrative self-definition of the state's duty. The Court was willing to enforce that duty because, in doing so, it was not required itself to determine what

---

113 The question was specifically whether the PIE Act applied to such evictions. See, for example, *Ellis v Viljoen* 2001 (4) SA 795 (C) where the Court held that the PIE Act does not apply and *Bekker v Jika* [2001] 4 All SA 573 (SE) where the Court held that the PIE Act does apply.

114 In *Ross v South Peninsula Municipality* 2000 (1) SA 589 (C), the High Court held that section 26(3) changed the common law so that an applicant for an eviction order had to raise circumstance that would persuade the court that it is just and equitable to grant the order in addition to the common law showing. In *Betta Eiendomme (Pty) Ltd v Ekple-Epoh* 2000 (4) SA 468 (W) 473A–D, the High Court held that section 26(3) only applied to evictions by the state and not to evictions by natural or juristic persons.

115 *Brisley* para 42.

116 *Ndlovu; Bekker* para 23.

117 In fact, the result was not exactly the same. Had the SCA developed the common law in line with section 26(3) in *Brisley*, landowners seeking to evict unlawful occupiers in cases of holding over would certainly have had to persuade courts to exercise their discretion in their favour as they have to do in terms of the PIE Act. However, landowners would then not have been subject to the stringent procedural requirements imposed by the PIE Act. The SCA's decision in *Ndlovu; Bekker* has therefore, counter-intuitively, in some respects made it more difficult for landowners to evict unlawful occupiers holding over than it would have been for them had *Brisley* been decided differently.

adequate medical treatment entailed, a task that it felt it did not have the requisite expertise to undertake.[118]

The *Treatment Action Campaign (2)* judgment of the Constitutional Court provides a similar example. This case concerned, however, policy formulated by the Cabinet rather than a decision by the general state administration. In the *TAC* case, the Court was asked to consider the right of access to health care for HIV-positive pregnant mothers. The case involved specifically the question whether they are entitled to a single dose of antiretroviral drugs at the birth of their babies to reduce the transmission of HIV from mother to child. The Court engaged in a relatively robust manner with issues of HIV/AIDS policy and was more willing to impose a precise and intrusive directory order on the state compared with other cases. This can in significant part be explained by the fact that the Court was simply requiring the state to extend to its logical conclusion a policy decision that it had itself already taken. This policy decision was that Nevirapine was suitable and safe to provide to mothers giving birth at select public health facilities and their new-born children to prevent the transmission of HIV. The Court required the state to extend the provision to all public health facilities for the same purpose.[119] Again, an element of self-definition of duties, this time through an executive policy decision, influenced the Court's perception of constraint.

CRITICAL THINKING

Social mobilisation of citizens in addition to litigation

It is sometimes argued that the reasons why the *Treatment Action Campaign (2)* case was successfully litigated go beyond the fact that the Court was required to extend a policy decision already taken by the executive. Mark Heywood, a member of the TAC at the time the case was heard, argues that the TAC was so successful because it used both social mobilisation and litigation - based on the right of access to health care - to pursue clearly defined goals. Heywood argues that in each case in which the TAC invoked constitutional rights and threatened or pursued litigation against private institutions (like drug companies) or the state:

> the litigation was not left to lawyers, but used to strengthen and empower a social movement and backed up by marches, media, legal education, and social mobilization. Without an accompanying social mobilization, the use of the courts may deliver little more than pieces of paper, with a latent untapped potential. For example, one of South Africa's most ground-breaking socio-economic rights judgments (*Government of the RSA and Others v Grootboom and Others*, 2001) concerns the right to housing. It was delivered by the Constitutional Court in 2001. But in 2008, when Irene Grootboom, the first applicant, died she was still without a house ... Some writers ... suggested that this combination of human rights advocacy and litigation will reveal its limitations when it comes up against defences based on arguments about resource constraints and 'available resources'. However, TAC argues that in a system of governance in which rights are supposed to be pivotal to policy making, decisions on resource allocations must be subject to what Pius Langa, the South African Chief Justice, calls the 'culture of justification' ... This means that decisions on spending on crucial

118 *Treatment Action Campaign (2)* para 37. See also paras 35–6 and 60.

119 Brand, D 'The proceduralisation of South African socio-economic rights jurisprudence, or "What are socio-economic rights for?"' in Botha, H, Van der Walt, AJ and Van der Walt, JC (2003) *Rights and Democracy in a Transformative Constitution* 53.

socio-economic rights should not be determined only by what state treasuries (in their own wisdom) decide is affordable.[120]

Heywood is in effect arguing that the broader social mobilisation of citizens around social and economic rights claims is important in pursuing social justice claims and that an over-reliance on the courts to effect social change may backfire or may not produce beneficial results for those citizens most in need.

16.6.3.3.3 Negative rather than positive duties

As a general point of strategy and to avoid separation of powers constraints, it is preferable to characterise infringements of any socio-economic right as a negative rather than a positive infringement of the specific right. As a rule, courts will scrutinise alleged infringements of negative duties imposed by socio-economic rights more strictly than they would failures in meeting positive duties. There is some evidence from the case law that this is a matter of judicial attitude in the first place. Courts simply feel themselves less constrained when adjudicating negative infringements as they perceive the enforcement of negative duties as requiring less interference in the sphere of power of the political branches than the enforcement of positive duties.[121] However, particularly with respect to the qualified socio-economic rights, the difference in degree of judicial constraint at play in cases of enforcement of positive as opposed to negative duties seems simply to be required by the way in which these rights are formulated and by the general structure of constitutional litigation.

As we pointed out in chapter 10, constitutional litigation in South Africa proceeds in two stages. First, the complainant bears the onus of persuading the court that a right in the Bill of Rights has been infringed. Should a court find that the right has in fact been infringed, the state (or where a constitutional duty has been infringed by a private party, the private party in question) bears the onus of justifying and so rendering constitutionally sound its limitation of that right. In principle, the standard of scrutiny in terms of which courts decide whether or not any infringement of any constitutional right, including any socio-economic right, is justified is prescribed by section 36(1), the general limitation section, which applies to all rights.

However, despite the fact that section 36(1) in principle applies to all infringements of all constitutional rights, courts in practice do not apply section 36(1) when they must decide whether or not failures by the state to give effect to the **positive duties** to protect, promote

120 Heywood, M (2009) South Africa's Treatment Action Campaign: Combining law and social mobilization to realize the right to health *Journal of Human Rights Practice* 1(1):14–36 at 22–3.

121 See the Constitutional Court's indication in *Grootboom* that retrogressive steps in the process of giving progressive realisation to socio-economic rights (essentially negative infringements of such rights) 'require the most careful consideration and would need to be fully justified by reference to the totality of the rights provided for in the Covenant and in the context of the full use of the maximum available resources' – that is, that the Court would subject such negative interferences in the exercise of socio-economic rights to especially robust scrutiny. See Committee on ESCR General Comment 3 para 9 as quoted in *Grootboom* para 45. See also *Jaftha* paras 61–4 where the Constitutional Court found that provisions of the Magistrates' Courts Act violated the negative duty to respect the right to have access to adequate housing. These provisions allowed for the sale in execution of a person's home without adequate judicial oversight. The Court proceeded to order the relatively intrusive remedy of reading words into the Magistrates' Courts Act in spite of submissions by the Minister of Justice that the order of invalidity be suspended to allow the legislature to remedy the constitutional defect in the Act. See, further, the discussion below of *Port Elizabeth Municipality* and *Modderfontein Squatters, Greater Benoni City Council v Modderklip Boerdery (Pty) Ltd (Agri SA and Legal Resources Centre, amici curiae); President of the Republic of South Africa and Others v Modderklip Boerdery (Pty) Ltd (Agri SA and Legal Resources Centre, amici curiae)* 2004 (6) SA 40 (SCA).

and fulfil the **qualified socio-economic rights** can be justified.[122] Recall that the positive duties imposed by qualified socio-economic rights in sections 26 and 27 of the Constitution are explicitly described as duties to take reasonable legislative and other measures, within available resources, to achieve the progressive realisation of the rights in question.[123] The Constitutional Court has interpreted these qualifying phrases as an internal limitation clause: in essence, a special standard of reasonableness scrutiny, used instead of section 36(1), according to which the Court decides specifically whether or not failures in meeting the positive duties imposed by qualified socio-economic rights can be justified.

Whether or not the possible justification of an infringement of a socio-economic right is considered in terms of section 36(1) or in terms of the special limitation clause that applies to positive infringements of qualified socio-economic rights significantly determines the degree of constraint under which a court operates. This is so because the standard of scrutiny that is applied under the two tests is different. Section 36(1) first poses a threshold requirement that an infringement of a right must meet in order for it to be capable of justification – the infringement must have occurred in terms of law of general application to be at all justifiable.[124] Second, section 36(1) poses a standard of justification that the infringement must satisfy once it has passed the threshold. The standard of justification or scrutiny required by section 36(1) is relatively intrusive. It has been described by our courts as a proportionality test. A court weighs the purpose and benefits of the infringement against its nature, effect and severity. The court then considers the relative efficacy of the infringing measure in achieving its purpose in deciding whether or not it is justified. As such, it allows courts a fair amount of leeway to interrogate state conduct and to prescribe specific alternative options where state conduct is found to be unjustifiable. By contrast, the reasonableness test that applies in cases of infringements of the positive duties imposed by the qualified socio-economic rights is applied as a shifting standard of scrutiny.

Usually, when the court enquires into whether the state has acted reasonably to protect, promote and fulfil its duties in terms of sections 26 and 27, it will ask whether the means used by the state were effective in achieving the purpose the state set out to achieve. This enquiry gives the state considerable leeway as we pointed out above.[125] Only in exceptional cases does the court apply the reasonableness test in a more searching manner and ask whether there was some proportionality between the actions of the state and the aims it claims to want to achieve.[126]

---

122 Pieterse, M (2003) Towards a useful role for section 36 of the Constitution in social rights cases? *Residents of Bon Vista Mansions v Southern Metropolitan Local Council South African Law Journal* 120(1):41–8 at 41. See also *Khosa* paras 83–4.

123 Remember, however, that some social and economic rights, such as the right to basic education guaranteed in s 29, are not similarly qualified. As there has been no Constitutional Court case directly invoking s 29 to hold the state to its obligation to provide basic education for all, it is impossible to say whether the same separation of powers concerns will arise for the Court when it does so.

124 In general terms, this means that the infringement must have occurred in terms of a rule (as opposed to a once-off decision) that is clear, precise and public (accessible) and that applies in equal measure to all those that it reaches. See the dissenting judgment of Kriegler J in *President of the Republic of South Africa and Another v Hugo* (CCT11/96) [1997] ZACC 4; 1997 (6) BCLR 708; 1997 (4) SA 1 (18 April 1997) para 36. An infringement occasioned by mere conduct, unrelated to law of general application, is incapable of justification – if the mere fact of such an infringement is shown, the conduct in question is unconstitutional.

125 *Grootboom* paras 39–45 and *Treatment Action Campaign (2)* paras 38 and 123. In *Soobramoney* paras 27 and 29, the Court applied an even more lenient basic rationality standard of scrutiny.

126 In *Khosa*, the Constitutional Court confirmed a High Court ruling that the exclusion of permanent residents from social assistance benefits violated the right of access to social assistance (s 27(1)(*c*) of the Constitution). The measures were found unreasonable because the purpose of the exclusion (to prevent people who immigrated to South Africa from becoming a burden on the state) could be achieved through means less restrictive of permanent residents' rights (stricter control of access into the country) (para 65). Also, 'the importance of providing access to social assistance to all who live permanently in South Africa and the impact upon life and dignity that a denial of such access has far outweighs the financial and immigration considerations on which the state relies' (para 82).

This means that the court would not explicitly consider the relative efficacy of challenged state measures compared to other possible measures because, once again, of separation of powers concerns.[127] As a result, infringements of the positive duties imposed by qualified socio-economic rights are usually evaluated against a more lenient standard of scrutiny than the standard that applies to other infringements of rights in terms of section 36(1). In other words, courts are more constrained in their assessment of such infringements than they are with respect to other infringements.

As pointed out above, it is often possible to characterise the same infringement of a socio-economic right as an infringement of either the negative or the positive duties imposed by the right. The special limitation clause that applies to the positive duties of the qualified socio-economic rights in lieu of section 36(1) of course does not also apply to the negative duty to respect those same qualified socio-economic rights[128] or to any of the negative or positive duties imposed by the basic socio-economic rights.[129] Infringements of these rights can still only be justified in terms of section 36(1). As a strategic matter, therefore, it is better to characterise a case brought on the basis of a qualified socio-economic right as a negative infringement of that right where possible. This will involve the application of section 36(1) during the justification phase of the litigation and, as such, will significantly dilute the constraint under which the court operates. By the same token, it is preferable, again where possible, to base a case on one of the unqualified basic socio-economic rights, whether a negative or a positive infringement is at play.

The question whether or not section 36(1) or the special reasonableness limitations clause applies is in a strategic sense important for two further practical reasons unrelated to judicial constraint. First, it has important consequences for the onus of persuasion facing litigants in socio-economic rights cases. As a rule, in Bill of Rights litigation, a party who alleges that a right in the Bill has been infringed must persuade a court that this is indeed so. A complainant has to make a *prima facie* case that the conduct of the respondent has infringed a right in the Bill of Rights. Once such a *prima facie* case has been made, the respondent bears the onus of persuading the court that the infringement is justifiable.[130] The potential benefit of this structure is that it requires very little of a complainant in the way of establishing questions of fact. The complainant usually simply has to propose a certain interpretation of the right he or she alleges is being infringed. The complainant then has to show that the respondent's conduct infringes the right so described, an exercise that mostly involves arguing questions of law on an abstract level.

---

127 *Grootboom* para 41: 'A court considering reasonableness will not enquire whether other more desirable or favourable measures could have been adopted, or whether public money could have been better spent. The question would be whether the measures that have been adopted are reasonable. It is necessary to recognise that a wide range of possible measures could be adopted by the state to meet its obligations. Many of these would meet the requirement of reasonableness. Once it is shown that the measures do so, this requirement is met.'

128 In *Jaftha* para 34, the Court held that a measure negatively breaching the right to have access to adequate housing 'may ... be justified under section 36 of the Constitution'.

129 Clearly, as the basic socio-economic rights are not qualified by the same 'reasonable measures' phrase that applies to the qualified rights, the reasonableness analysis does not apply to them and breaches of these rights fall to be justified in terms of s 36(1). See Liebenberg (2013) 33.55. However, although this seems clear from the text, the Constitutional Court has been ambiguous in its application of these basic rights, in particular the rights of children, in this respect. In both *Grootboom* and *Treatment Action Campaign (2)*, the Court, despite being invited to do so, chose not to decide the dispute on the basis of children's socio-economic rights. Instead, the Court relied on the fact that the state conduct in question also breached these rights to bolster its eventual finding that the conduct was unreasonable in terms of ss 26(2) and 27(2) respectively. See Brand (2004) 48.

130 *S v Zuma and Others* (CCT5/94) [1995] ZACC 1; 1995 (2) SA 642; 1995 (4) BCLR 401 (SA); 1995 (1) SACR 568; [1996] 2 CHRLD 244 (5 April 1995) para 21.

However, in the kinds of socio-economic rights cases referred to above, where the allegation is that the state has failed to take reasonable steps within available resources to achieve the progressive realisation of a qualified socio-economic right, this structure is bedevilled. In such cases, for the complainant to show that the right has in fact been infringed involves making a *prima facie* case that the state's existing measures are unreasonable. The state then has the opportunity to rebut this *prima facie* showing by arguing that its measures are in fact reasonable.[131] The difficulty is that for a complainant to make a *prima facie* showing that the state's measures are unreasonable requires the complainant to establish a wide range of factual questions. These questions mostly relate to information that is more or less uniquely in the knowledge of the complainant's opponent, the state.[132] Often, of course, the typical socio-economic rights complainant would not have the required access to information and resources to do this. This may be another reason why litigation spearheaded by social movements like the Treatment Action Campaign has been successful. TAC's resources allowed it to present an overwhelming amount of persuasive evidence to the court.

Second, the special limitation clause that applies in cases of positive infringements of qualified socio-economic rights potentially allows for the justification of **all** positive infringements of qualified socio-economic rights. This is because it does not also impose a threshold requirement of law of general application as section 36(1) does. Certain infringements that would simply not be capable of justification in terms of section 36(1) – infringements that occur in terms of simple state conduct, for example, unrelated to any law of general application[133] – can be justified in terms of the reasonableness test that applies to the qualified rights.

Both these factors, although not related to constraint as such, additionally indicate a preference for arguing a case as a negative infringement rather than a positive one, or on the basis of a basic rather than a qualified socio-economic right.

PAUSE FOR REFLECTION

Separation of powers concerns overstated

As we have argued throughout this book, separation of powers concerns loom large whenever unelected judges are empowered by the Constitution to declare invalid the actions of members of the executive or of Parliament. These members usually have more democratic legitimacy because of the direct link between voter preferences and the staffing of these institutions. It is sometimes argued that this problem becomes more acute when the courts are empowered – as they are under the Constitution – to enforce social and economic rights. However, we contend that these concerns are often overstated. As the Constitutional Court pointed out in *Treatment Action Campaign (2)*:

> The primary duty of courts is to the Constitution and the law, "which they must apply impartially and without fear, favour or prejudice". The Constitution requires the state to "respect, protect, promote, and fulfil the rights in the Bill of Rights".

131 Liebenberg (2013) 33.53.

132 Liebenberg (2013) 33.53–4; Brand (2004) 52–3.

133 Per Langa J in *City Council of Pretoria v Walker* (CCT8/97) [1998] ZACC 1; 1998 (2) SA 363; 1998 (3) BCLR 257 (17 February 1998) para 82:

> **The rights guaranteed in Chapter 3 of the interim Constitution may be limited in terms of section 33(1) of the interim Constitution. A requirement of section 33(1) is that a right may only be limited by a law of general application. Since the respondent's challenge is directed at the conduct of the council, which was clearly not authorised, either expressly or by necessary implication by a law of general application, section 33(1) is not applicable to the present case.**

> Where state policy is challenged as inconsistent with the Constitution, courts have to consider whether in formulating and implementing such policy the state has given effect to its constitutional obligations. If it should hold in any given case that the state has failed to do so, it is obliged by the Constitution to say so. In so far as that constitutes an intrusion into the domain of the executive, that is an intrusion mandated by the Constitution itself. There is also no merit in the argument ... that a distinction should be drawn between declaratory and mandatory orders against government. Even simple declaratory orders against government or organs of state can affect their policy and may well have budgetary implications. Government is constitutionally bound to give effect to such orders whether or not they affect its policy and has to find the resources to do so.[134]

Moreover, section 1(*d*) of the Constitution explicitly links the democratic nature of the system of government to open, accountable and responsive government.[135] Where courts enforce social and economic rights, they ensure a more accountable and responsive government, thus enhancing and not diminishing the democratic nature of the state. A democratic state is responsive to the needs of those who live in that state and a court that enforces social and economic rights helps the state to be as responsive as financial and other resources available to the state allow that state to be. Thus, it can be argued that the enforcement of social and economic rights by the courts assists the state to be **more** democratic not **less** so.

16.7 Different forms of judicial enforcement of socio-economic rights

The preceding discussion creates the context within which a more detailed description and analysis of the mechanics of the enforcement of socio-economic rights by the courts can take place. We thus proceed to consider each of the different ways in which courts may enforce socio-economic rights in turn, using the constitutional command that these rights must be respected, protected, promoted and fulfilled as a template. While doing so, keep in mind that this taxonomy can be somewhat artificial and that the duties imposed by a specific social or economic right can overlap and can implicate more than one of the commands to 'respect, protect, promote and fufil' the right.

16.7.1 The duty to respect

16.7.1.1 Introduction

The duty to respect socio-economic rights requires the state and others to:

- refrain from interfering with people's existing enjoyment of socio-economic rights
- mitigate interferences with people's existing enjoyment of socio-economic rights when such interferences are unavoidable
- refrain from impairing people's access to socio-economic rights.

134 *Treatment Action Campaign (2)* para 99.

135 S 1 states that South Africa is 'one, sovereign, democratic state' and lists the country's founding values as, *inter alia*, '[u]niversal adult suffrage, a national common voters roll, regular elections and a multi-party system of democratic government, to ensure accountability, responsiveness and openness'.

As pointed out above, the courts are likely to enforce the different elements of this negative duty more robustly than the positive duties to protect, promote and fulfil. The duty to respect, consequently, is a potentially potent tool with which to ensure people's adequate access to basic resources.

16.7.1.2 The duty to refrain from interfering with people's existing enjoyment of socio-economic rights

South Africa's apartheid history provides particularly stark examples of the violation of this element of the duty to respect socio-economic rights. The most obvious of these relate to the right to have access to land and to housing. In terms of the spatial segregationist policies of grand apartheid, large numbers of people were dispossessed of and forcibly removed from their land and their homes. People were also arbitrarily evicted from informal settlements as a result of so-called 'influx control' policies.[136] The statutory measures in terms of which these dispossessions and removals occurred have now been repealed and new legal measures have been put in place preventing a recurrence of such practices. Apart from the fact that the dispossession of land by the state is now regulated by section 25 of the Constitution,[137] the eviction of people from land is heavily regulated by a raft of new laws. Two examples are the Extension of Security of Tenure Act (ESTA)[138] and the PIE Act.[139] Both laws make eviction from land in certain instances more difficult than it would ordinarily be by, *inter alia*, requiring that a court consider whether an eviction would be just and equitable in the light of all relevant circumstances before granting an eviction order.[140] Both the repeal of the old laws and the new legal measures are examples of legislative translations of the duty to respect the rights to have equitable access to land and to housing, and particularly of the prohibition on arbitrary evictions, into concrete legal entitlements.

PAUSE FOR REFLECTION

The notorious removals from District 6

One of the most notorious forced removals occurred in District 6, a suburb close to the city centre of Cape Town. The South African History Archive describes the facts around this removal and the destruction of District 6 by the apartheid state:

> On February 11, 1966, the apartheid government declared Cape Town's District Six a whites-only area under the Group Areas Act of 1950. From 1968, over 60 000 of its inhabitants were forcibly removed to the Cape Flats, over twenty five kilometres away. Except for the local houses of worship, the buildings were systematically bulldozed throughout the 1970s, and by 1982 almost all evidence of the district had been destroyed. Originally named the Sixth Municipal District

136 For an overview of the different ways in which people's access to land and housing was interfered with during this time, see Van der Merwe, D (1989) Land tenure in South Africa: A brief history and some reform proposals *Journal of South African Law* 4:663–92.

137 S 25(2) and (3) of the Constitution. This means that dispossession of land by the state can only occur through regular expropriation, for a public purpose, following the payment of just and equitable compensation, the amount, time and manner of payment of which must be determined after all relevant circumstances have been considered.

138 Act 62 of 1997. The ESTA applies to rural land occupied with the tacit or explicit consent of the owner or person in charge. See s 2(1) of the ESTA and the definitions of 'occupier' and 'consent' in s 1.

139 The PIE Act applies to all land, including state-owned land (see ss 6 and 7). See also the Labour Tenants Act which applies to rural land occupied and used in terms of a labour tenancy agreement (s 1). In practice, this Act does not apply to state land as the labour tenancy agreements that it is intended to regulate are usually with private landowners. The ESTA, the PIE Act and the Labour Tenants Act also regulate private evictions.

140 Ss 8(1) and 11(1), (2) and (3) of the ESTA; ss 4(6) and (7), 5(1)(*b*) and 6(1) and (3) of the PIE Act.

of Cape Town in 1867, the neighbourhood was home to almost ten per cent of the city's population. Its unique culture was a composite of the dynamic and diverse population of Malay, Eastern European, Indian and African immigrants, ex-slaves, artists, musicians and activists. District Six was famed for its proximity to the City Centre, as well as its view of the picturesque Table Mountain and harbour. District Six had experienced a long history of removals, with black residents forcibly removed as early as 1901. This was intensified in the early 1960s, when residents were perfunctorily given notice and informed of their new homes. By the mid 1960s the apartheid government regarded the district as both physically and morally tainted by miscegenation, wholly unfit for rehabilitation. Over the next two decades, they systematically razed it to the ground.[141]

The same pattern was repeated in many other parts of South Africa. The inclusion of a specific provision in the Constitution to prevent the arbitrary eviction of people from their homes is therefore not surprising.

Courts have been involved in the translation of this element of the duty to respect socio-economic rights in different ways. In the first place, courts have enforced legislative translations in this respect. A large body of case law has already developed around the eviction provisions of statutes such as the ESTA and the PIE Act. Second, courts have also directly enforced this element of the duty to respect socio-economic rights by invalidating laws that allowed the state to interfere in the existing enjoyment of socio-economic rights or by preventing the state from interfering in the enjoyment of such rights.

In *Jaftha v Schoeman and Others, Van Rooyen v Stoltz and Others*, for example, the Constitutional Court found that section 66(1)(*a*) of the Magistrates' Courts Act[142] unjustifiably breached the negative duty to respect the right of everyone to have access to adequate housing.[143] These provisions allowed the sale in execution of a person's home to make good a judgment debt without adequate judicial oversight. The Court proceeded to read words into the statute to make provision for appropriate judicial oversight.[144] More recently, the Court reconsidered the execution process in the High Court along similar lines in *Gundwana v Steko Development CC and Others*.[145]

Section 27(3), the right not to be refused emergency medical treatment, can perhaps also be interpreted to give expression to the state's duty to respect socio-economic rights by refraining from interfering in the existing enjoyment of these rights. In *Soobramoney*, the Constitutional Court held this right only required the state not to refuse arbitrarily emergency medical treatment where it exists. This is an inordinately restrictive reading which, as Alston and Scott point out, renders the right virtually redundant.[146] A matter which at this stage remains unclear is the question whether or not section 27(3) of the Constitution could also

141 See District Six: Recalling the forced removals *South African History Archive* available at http://www.saha.org.za/news/2010/February/district_six_recalling_the_forced_removals.htm.

142 Act 32 of 1944.

143 (CCT74/03) [2004] ZACC 25; 2005 (2) SA 140 (CC); 2005 (1) BCLR 78 (CC) (8 October 2004) para 34. The possible justification of this breach was considered by the Court in terms of the s 36(1) proportionality test.

144 *Jaftha* paras 61–4.

145 (CCT 44/10) [2011] ZACC 14; 2011 (3) SA 608 (CC); 2011 (8) BCLR 792 (CC) (11 April 2011).

146 Alston, P and Scott, C (2000) Adjudicating constitutional priorities in a transnational context: A comment on *Soobramoney's* legacy and *Grootboom's* promise *South African Journal on Human Rights* 16(2):206–68 at 245–8.

be used to prohibit the state from disestablishing an emergency medical service at a public health institution to save costs.[147]

16.7.1.3 The duty to mitigate interferences with people's existing enjoyment of socio-economic rights when such interferences are unavoidable

The duty to respect socio-economic rights does not entail an absolute prohibition on the state preventing it from interfering in the existing exercise of such rights. There are many instances in which it is simply unavoidable for the state to interfere, often to advance the public interest in some respect or to protect the rights of others. In such cases, the duty to respect requires that an effort be made to mitigate the effect of the interference in the enjoyment of the right in question by providing some form of alternative access to it. This element of the duty to respect socio-economic rights is potentially quite burdensome and often requires the expenditure of significant resources and significant adjustments in policy. Nevertheless, our courts have shown themselves to be willing to enforce this duty in a robust fashion. The security of tenure laws referred to above again provide a good example of how this constitutional duty has been translated into a statutory entitlement of sorts. These laws, in some instances, require courts to consider to what extent suitable alternative land is available for evictees before granting an eviction order and an eviction order can be denied if such an alternative is absent.[148]

In *Port Elizabeth Municipality v Various Occupiers*,[149] for example, the state had applied for an order to evict illegal occupants from privately owned land in terms of section 6 of the PIE Act. Section 6 allows a court to grant such an order, but only if it is just and equitable to do so taking into account various factors including 'the availability to the unlawful occupier of suitable alternative accommodation or land'.[150] The Constitutional Court confirmed the SCA's decision denying the eviction order.[151] The Court held that section 26(3) of the Constitution, mediated through section 6 of the PIE Act, required that when the state seeks to evict, it must provide suitable alternative accommodation to the evictees. This duty would not be operative in all cases of state-sponsored eviction.[152] A court would have to decide whether or not to enforce this duty on the basis of a consideration of each case's 'own dynamics, its own intractable elements that have to be lived with (at least for the time being), and its own creative possibilities that have to be explored as far as reasonably possible'.[153]

To decide whether or not the duty applied, the Constitutional Court looked in general terms at the position and the conduct of the occupiers, at the conduct of the municipality in its management of the matter and at the conduct of the landowners in question. The Court took the following factors into consideration:

- the fact that the occupiers in this case had lived on the land in question for a long period of time[154]
- that they would be severely affected by any eviction[155]

147 Liebenberg (2013) 33.21.
148 See ss 9(3)(*a*), 10(2) and (3) and 11(3) of the ESTA and s 6(3)(*b*) of the PIE Act.
149 (CCT 53/03) [2004] ZACC 7; 2005 (1) SA 217 (CC); 2004 (12) BCLR 1268 (CC) (1 October 2004).
150 S 6(3)(*c*) of the PIE Act.
151 The SCA decision is reported as *Baartman and Others v Port Elizabeth Municipality* 2004 (1) SA 560 (SCA).
152 *Port Elizabeth Municipality* para 58: 'The availability of suitable alternative accommodation is a consideration in determining whether it is just and equitable to evict the occupiers, it is not determinative of that question.' See also para 28: 'There is therefore no unqualified constitutional duty on local authorities to ensure that in no circumstances should a home be destroyed unless alternative accommodation or land is made available.'
153 *Port Elizabeth Municipality* para 31.
154 *Port Elizabeth Municipality* paras 27, 28, 49 and 59.
155 *Port Elizabeth Municipality* paras 30 and 59.

- that they had occupied the land, not in order to force the municipality to provide to them, in preference to others, alternative land when they were eventually evicted, but because they had been evicted from elsewhere and had nowhere to go[156]
- that there was 'no evidence that either the municipality or the owners of the land need to evict the occupiers in order to put the land to some other productive use'[157]
- that the municipality had made no serious effort to reach an amicable conclusion to the matter, but had rushed to apply for an eviction order and had acted unilaterally.[158]

These factors drove the Court to the conclusion that an eviction order could not be granted unless suitable alternative land or accommodation was provided. Although the municipality had offered to allow the occupiers to move to two possible alternative sites, the Constitutional Court went so far as to find that neither of those sites was suitable, most importantly because the municipality could not guarantee to the evictees security of tenure if they were moved there.[159] As a result, the occupiers were allowed to remain on the land in question.[160]

The robust manner in which the Constitutional Court dealt with this element of the duty to respect socio-economic rights in *Port Elizabeth Municipality* could in part be explained by the fact that the Court was enforcing a statutory duty in terms of the PIE Act. However, there are also indications in the case law that the courts are willing to enforce this burdensome element of the duty to respect socio-economic rights against the state even where a statutory duty to this effect does not apply.

For example, in *Modderfontein Squatters, Greater Benoni City Council v Modderklip Boerdery (Pty) Ltd (Agri SA and Legal Resources Centre, amici curiae); President of the Republic of South Africa and Others v Modderklip Boerdery (Pty) Ltd (Agri SA and Legal Resources Centre, amici curiae)*,[161] the SCA was confronted with a claim brought by a private landowner. The landowner argued that the state was constitutionally obliged effectively to protect his constitutional right to property by enforcing and carrying out an eviction order that he had obtained in terms of section 4 of the PIE Act against a large group of people unlawfully occupying his land. The Court held that the state was indeed obliged to protect the claimant's right to property against invasion by unlawful occupiers.[162] However, at the same time, the state was obliged to protect the right of the unlawful occupiers to have access to adequate housing.[163] On the facts of the particular case, the Court held that this meant that the state, were it to execute the eviction order against the unlawful occupiers, would have to act 'humanely'. This meant, *inter alia*, that the state could not evict the unlawful occupiers unless it 'provide[d] some [alternative] land'.[164] This conclusion led the Court to order the state to pay damages to Modderklip to make good the breach of its right to property and its failure to protect against that breach.[165] The Court also ordered that the unlawful occupiers be allowed to remain on Modderklip's land until alternative land was made available to them by the state.[166]

---

156 *Port Elizabeth Municipality* paras 49 and 55.
157 *Port Elizabeth Municipality* para 59.
158 *Port Elizabeth Municipality* paras 45, 55–7 and 59.
159 *Port Elizabeth Municipality* para 58.
160 *Port Elizabeth Municipality* para 59.
161 2004 (6) SA 40 (SCA). The Constitutional Court affirmed the decision of the SCA in *President of the Republic of South Africa and Another v Modderklip Boerdery (Pty) Ltd* (CCT20/04) [2005] ZACC 5; 2005 (5) SA 3 (CC); 2005 (8) BCLR 786 (CC) (13 May 2005).
162 *Modderfontein Squatters* para 21.
163 *Modderfontein Squatters* para 22.
164 *Modderfontein Squatters* para 26.
165 *Modderfontein Squatters* paras 43 and 52.
166 *Modderfontein Squatters* paras 43 and 52.

In effect, the order required the state to lease the land so that the unlawful occupiers could remain there without continuing to infringe Modderklip Boerdery's property rights.[167] The Court made this intrusive order without considering in any meaningful way the substantial resource consequences that its decision would have for the state and the extent to which its order prescribes a particular policy option to the state in preference to others. This robust approach, as was the case in *Port Elizabeth Municipality*, was justified by the Court with reference to the conduct of the state, the landowner and the unlawful occupiers during the course of the dispute.

The Court pointed out that the state still had no measures in place to deal with the plight of people such as the Modderfontein occupiers despite the Court holding in *Grootboom* that it must introduce measures to take account of the needs of those in housing crisis.[168] The Court also highlighted the fact that the state had, despite various opportunities to do so, failed to attempt to solve the dispute between the unlawful occupiers, the landowner and itself. The state had failed diligently to pursue a settlement and had reneged on agreements reached.[169] This was despite the fact that the state itself had caused the predicament of the unlawful occupiers and the landowner by previously evicting the unlawful occupiers from state land without providing alternative accommodation.[170] As such, the state had made its own bed and now had to lie in it. The conduct of both the unlawful occupiers and the landowner had, in contrast to the state's, been exemplary. The landowner had at all times acted within the law and had throughout sought to effect an amicable solution that would vindicate both his and the occupiers' rights.[171] The unlawful occupiers had occupied the land without intending to force the hand of the state to provide them with land in preference to others and had also sought to reach an amicable solution both with the landowner and the state.[172]

The duty to provide alternative accommodation on eviction has since been applied in a number of further eviction decisions of the Constitutional Court. Significantly, in *City of Johannesburg Metropolitan Municipality v Blue Moonlight Properties 39 (Pty) Ltd and Another*,[173] the duty to provide alternative accommodation was in a limited fashion extended to apply also to private property owners when they seek to evict and not only the state. The case dealt with a group of impoverished people who occupied a disused factory building in downtown Johannesburg. A property developer bought the building in order to develop it. At the time he bought the building he was aware of the presence of the occupiers. When the owner's application for an eviction order eventually landed before the Constitutional Court on appeal, the Court held that the owner could only evict the occupiers once the City had made available alternative accommodation to them. Given that this would take some time, it meant that the owner had to bear some measure of the burden of providing alternative accommodation in allowing the occupiers to remain until alternative accommodation had been found. The Court summarised the position as follows:

> **To the extent that it is the owner of the property and the occupation is unlawful, Blue Moonlight is entitled to an eviction order. All relevant circumstances must be taken**

---

167 Although expressly indicating that it would not be proper for it to order the state to expropriate the land in question (para 41), the Court did point out that in light of its order, it would be the sensible thing for the state to do to expropriate the land (para 43).

168 *Modderfontein Squatters* para 22.

169 *Modderfontein Squatters* paras 35–8.

170 *Modderfontein Squatters* para 35.

171 *Modderfontein Squatters* paras 33, 37 and 38.

172 *Modderfontein Squatters* para 25.

173 (CC) [2011] ZACC 33; 2012 (2) BCLR 150 (CC); 2012 (2) SA 104 (CC) (1 December 2011).

into account though to determine whether, under which conditions and by which date, eviction would be just and equitable. The availability of alternative housing for the Occupiers is one of the circumstances.[174]

CRITICAL THINKING

Unintended consequences of *Blue Moonlight*

The effect of *Blue Moonlight* outlined above should not be overstated. Moreover, it must be noted that the development of the duty to provide alternative accommodation as it was applied in *Blue Moonlight* could have unintended and, it must be said, potentially perverse, consequences in particular with respect to private property owners. Following *Blue Moonlight*, any private person interested in developing land or buildings occupied unlawfully by impoverished people can buy the land or buildings for development in the secure knowledge that the state would have to foot the bill for the relocation of the occupiers. In effect, the state is required to subsidise private property development under such circumstances.

It is also unclear to what extent this decision may have a transformative impact on the law in general. It does not seem to challenge the institution of private property as protected by common law property regulation. This, it can be argued, is because the judgment does not take sufficient notice of its remarks in *Port Elizabeth Municipality* where the Court argued that the Constitution required us:

> ... to move away from a static, typically private-law conceptualist view of the constitution as a guarantee of the status quo to a dynamic, typically public-law view of the constitution as an instrument for social change and transformation under the auspices [and I would add 'and control'] of entrenched constitutional values.[175]

16.7.1.4 The duty to refrain from impairing people's access to socio-economic rights

The duty to respect socio-economic rights may also be violated if the state places obstacles in the way of people gaining access to basic resources or in the way of people enhancing their existing access to such resources. The most obvious way in which the state can fail in this duty is if it arbitrarily refuses to provide access to a basic resource that it has the capacity to provide. In *Soobramoney*, for example, the Constitutional Court held that section 27(3) of the Constitution imposes a duty on the state not to refuse access arbitrarily to emergency medical treatment where it exists.[176]

Although they were dealt with as cases of infringements of the positive duty to fulfil the right of access to health care services and to social assistance respectively, the judgments in *Treatment Action Campaign (No 2)* and *Khosa* are also examples of the state breaching its duty to respect those rights by refusing to provide access to a resource it had the capacity to give. In *Treatment Action Campaign (No 2)*, the policy decision not to make Nevirapine

174 *Blue Moonlight Properties* para 96.

175 *Port Elizabeth Municipality* para 16.

176 This interpretation leaves very little, if any, work for the s 27(3) right that other rights (such as the prohibition on unfair discrimination) and other ordinary legal remedies (such as the rules of the administrative law) do not in any event do. See Alston and Scott (2000).

available generally at public health facilities to prevent mother-to-child transmission of HIV at birth was, in fact, a refusal by the state to provide essential health care to pregnant, HIV-positive women and not only a failure by the state to extend health care provision to those women. Equally, in *Khosa*, the provisions of the Social Assistance Act that excluded permanent residents and their children from access to social assistance benefits were, in fact, a refusal by the state to provide these benefits to them.[177]

Perhaps a less obvious way in which this element of the duty to respect can be breached by the state is where the state impairs access to a basic resource through its administrative inefficiency. In *Mashava v The President of the Republic of South Africa and Others*,[178] for example, the Constitutional Court confirmed an order of the High Court that a presidential proclamation[179] assigning the administration of the Social Assistance Act to provincial governments was invalid. Although the validity of the proclamation was challenged on the grounds that the President was not competent to make the assignment,[180] the case was motivated by the fact that the assignment resulted in the right of access to social assistance of persons eligible for social assistance grants being impaired.

The plaintiff was an indigent disabled person who had applied for and been awarded a disability grant. However, for a period of more than a year after his successful application, he did not receive the grant from the Limpopo Department of Health and Welfare.[181] It was clear that the failure to pay to the plaintiff was caused by the administrative incapacity of the provincial Department of Health and Welfare. Also, the administration of the social welfare system in the province was woefully under-resourced, due to 'demands for the reallocation of social assistance monies to other [provincial] purposes'.[182] The plaintiff contended that the Social Assistance Act (and the payment of his disability grant) could be administered more efficiently and on a more equitable basis by the national government than by the provinces.

As a result, the assignment of the administration of the Social Assistance Act to the provinces constituted a negative impairment of the right to have access to social assistance. In effect, therefore, the decision of the Constitutional Court invalidating the assignment is a decision that the state must give effect to the duty to respect the right to have access to social assistance by removing an impediment to its effective exercise.

16.7.2 The duty to protect

16.7.2.1 Introduction

The duty to protect socio-economic rights requires the state to protect the existing enjoyment of these rights, and the capacity of people to enhance their enjoyment of these rights or newly to gain access to the enjoyment of these rights, against third-party interference.

16.7.2.2 Legislative and executive measures

The state most obviously carries out the duty to protect socio-economic rights by regulating, through legislation or executive/administrative conduct, those instances in which private entities control access to basic resources such as housing, health care services, food, water

177 Liebenberg (2013) 33.19.

178 (CCT 67/03) [2004] ZACC 6; 2005 (2) SA 476 (CC); 2004 (12) BCLR 1243 (CC) (6 September 2004).

179 Proclamation R7 of 1996, *Government Gazette* 16992 GN R7, 23 February 1996. The assignment was made in terms of s 235 of the interim Constitution.

180 *Mashava* para 1.

181 *Mashava* para 9.

182 *Mashava* para 10.

and education. Such regulation could in the first place be aimed at opening up access to these resources. The Rental Housing Act[183] is an example. The purpose of this law is primarily to create mechanisms to open access to the rental housing market, including creating Rental Housing Tribunals to engage in dispute resolution in the rental housing market.

The state can also protect access to socio-economic rights through standard setting in respect of safety and quality in the provision of services and products. The Foodstuffs, Cosmetics and Disinfectants Act (FCDA)[184] is an example here. The purpose of this Act is to regulate fungicide and pesticide residue and additive and preservative levels in food by setting minimum and maximum standards and by creating mechanisms for the monitoring of these levels in foodstuffs.

Finally, the state can exercise its duty to protect socio-economic rights by regulating those instances in which private parties can interfere in the existing enjoyment of socio-economic rights. The tenure security laws discussed above in the context of the duty to respect socio-economic rights[185] provide an example. These laws also protect informal rights to land and housing against private interference in the same way as they protect these rights against the state. They make eviction more difficult than it would otherwise be through imposing additional procedural and substantive safeguards that have to be met before an eviction order can be granted by a court.

16.7.2.3 Judicial measures

Courts can, in a number of important ways, also act so as to protect socio-economic rights. In the first place, courts can protect socio-economic rights by adjudicating constitutional and other challenges to state measures that are intended to advance those rights.[186] In *Minister of Public Works and Others v Kyalami Ridge Environmental Association and Others (Mukhwevho Intervening)*,[187] for example, a state decision to house destitute flood victims temporarily on the state-owned grounds of a prison outside Johannesburg was challenged by surrounding property owners as a violation of their administrative justice rights. The challenge was in part based on the argument that the decision was unlawful as the Minister of Public Works had no statutory authority to take such a decision. The Court rejected this argument primarily because it held that the Minister had the requisite power to take the decision by virtue of the state's common law rights as property owner.[188] Also, the decision was taken in furtherance of a constitutional duty to provide shelter to those in dire straits.[189] Through its decision, the Court effectively protected the right to have access to adequate housing of the flood victims against private interference.

Courts can also protect socio-economic rights when they interpret legislation and develop the common law. As pointed out above, courts are obliged to interpret legislation and develop the common law in such a way that the 'spirit, purport and objects' of the Bill of Rights are promoted.[190] In other words, courts are required to infuse legislation and the common law with the value system underlying the Constitution – to read the rights in the

---

183 Act 50 of 1999.

184 Act 54 of 1972.

185 See the Labour Tenants Act, the ESTA and the PIE Act.

186 See, in general, Heyns, CH (1997) Extended medical training and the Constitution: Balancing civil and political rights and socio-economic rights *De Jure* 30(1):1–17 at 1.

187 (CCT 55/00) [2001] ZACC 19; 2001 (3) SA 1151 (CC); 2001 (7) BCLR 652 (CC) (29 May 2001).

188 *Kyalami Ridge* para 40.

189 *Kyalami Ridge* paras 37–40.

190 See s 39(2) of the Constitution.

Bill of Rights and the values underlying them into the existing law. The power to engage constitutionally with the existing law, particularly with respect to the common law is an extremely important, but much neglected, way in which socio-economic rights can be advanced. In an economy based on private ownership, the common law background rules governing obligations and property determine access to and distribution of basic resources.[191] The development of constitutional socio-economic rights so as to establish new and unique constitutionally based remedies certainly is an important endeavour on its own. However, to explore the full transformative potential of socio-economic rights, sustained critical engagement with these common law background rules is crucial.

Some of these common law background rules have of, course, been significantly adapted through legislation – the impact of the different security of tenure laws on private property rights is a case in point.[192] However, courts retain an important responsibility to extend the protection afforded socio-economic rights in the ordinary law through their powers of interpretation of legislation and development of the common law.

Courts have readily engaged with legislation in attempts to broaden the protection of socio-economic rights. In *Jaftha*, for example, the Constitutional Court considered provisions of the Magistrates' Courts Act[193] that authorised under certain circumstances, without proper judicial oversight, the sale in execution of the home of a debtor to satisfy a judgment debt. On the basis of the section 26(1) right of everyone to have access to adequate housing, the Court adapted the Act through a combination of interpretation and of reading in so that a judgment debtor's home can only be sold in execution if a court has specifically ordered so after considering all relevant circumstances.[194] *Jaftha* was argued and decided on the basis of the negative duty to respect the right to have access to adequate housing.[195] However, in effect, the Court's order amounts to an instance of interpretative law making through which the Court introduces into the Magistrates' Courts Act a measure of **protection** for the right to housing – the Court gave effect to its duty to protect that right.

Unfortunately, the courts have been far less active in engaging with the common law so as to enhance the protection of socio-economic rights than they have been with respect to legislation.[196] In those few cases where the courts have been asked to develop the common law so as better to give effect to socio-economic rights, they have declined. In *Afrox Healthcare*, for example, the SCA was invited to develop the common law of contract so that disclaimers in hospital admission contracts indemnifying the hospitals against damages claims on the basis of the negligence of their staff would be seen as in conflict with the public interest and consequently unenforceable. The argument was that such disclaimers had the effect that patients were not adequately protected against unprofessional conduct at such hospitals and that they as such constituted an impairment of

191 Simon (1986)1433–6; Williams (1998) 575–7.

192 See Van der Walt, AJ (2002a) Exclusivity of ownership, security of tenure, and eviction orders: A model to evaluate South African land-reform legislation *Journal of South African Law* 2:254–89 at 254.

193 S 66(1)(*a*).

194 *Jaftha* paras 61–4 and 67. The factors that the Court lists at para 60 that should considered are: 'the circumstances in which the debt was incurred; ... attempts made by the debtor to pay off the debt; the financial situation of the parties; the amount of the debt; whether the debtor is employed or has a source of income to pay off the debt **and any other factor relevant to the ... facts of the case** ...' (our emphasis).

195 *Jaftha* paras 17, 31–4 and 52.

196 This is certainly due in the first place to the fact that few such cases have been brought to court except in the area of eviction law. See, for example, *Brisley*. Second, courts have in those few cases where the development of the common law to protect socio-economic rights did come into play, readily deferred to the legislature rather than drive the development themselves.

access to health care services.[197] This argument was rejected and the common law position remained intact.[198]

One example of where courts were willing to develop the common law so as to protect socio-economic rights is the case of *Permanent Secretary Department of Welfare, Eastern Cape Provincial Government and Another v Ngxuza and Others*.[199] *Ngxuza* dealt with a class action claim brought in terms of section 38 of the Constitution by a number of social assistance grantees for the reinstatement of disability grants that had unlawfully been terminated by the Eastern Cape Province. The respondents in the case had been granted leave to proceed with such a class action claim by the court *a quo*. The province appealed against this granting of leave to the SCA. The SCA, in the absence of any legislative form having been given to section 38's provision for class actions, proceeded to develop the common law of standing to make provision for such claims. Although the decision certainly opens the door for class action claims, at least where any constitutional right is at play, it is centrally important for the protection of socio-economic rights in particular. As Cameron JA (as he then was) states at the outset of the judgment, for the Court: 'The law is a scarce resource in South Africa. This case shows that justice is even harder to come by. It concerns the way in which the poorest in our country are to be permitted access to both.'[200]

16.7.3 The duty to promote and fulfil

16.7.3.1 Introduction

The duty to fulfil socio-economic rights requires the state to 'adopt appropriate legislative, administrative, budgetary, judicial, promotional and other measures'[201] so that access to basic resources is extended and enhanced. In sum, the state must act affirmatively to realise the rights. The state breaches the duty to fulfil not when it invades the existing exercise of socio-economic rights, but when it does not do enough or does not do the appropriate things fully to realise those rights. For courts to enforce the duty to fulfil requires them directly to evaluate state policy and practice and to decide whether or not those policies and practices are adequate measures to realise the socio-economic rights in question.

Courts are constrained in this evaluation by concerns about technical capacity and institutional legitimacy as well as by a perceived absence of justiciable standards against which to assess state performance. To deal with these difficulties, the Constitutional Court has used a traditional model of judicial review, but has given it new content. As with any breach of any other right, when it is alleged that the duty to fulfil a socio-economic right has been breached and where *prima facie* such a breach is established, the Court considers whether or not it can be justified. However, the Court has developed a special test or standard against which to evaluate the justifiability of state measures to fulfil socio-economic rights that allows it, in different ways, to mediate its concerns with capacity and legitimacy.

Which standard of scrutiny applies to breaches of the duty to fulfil socio-economic rights depends on which socio-economic rights are at issue. If the duty to fulfil a **basic**

---

197 *Afrox Healthcare* para 21.

198 For critiques of this aspect of the judgment, see Brand, D (2002a) Disclaimers in hospital admission contracts and constitutional health rights: Cases *ESR Review* 3(2)17–8; Carstens, PA and Kok, JA (2003) An assessment of the use of disclaimers against medical negligence by South African hospitals in view of constitutional demands, foreign law and medico-legal considerations *SA Public Law* 18(2):430–55 at 430; Tladi, D (2002) One step forward, two steps back for constitutionalising the common law: *Afrox Health Care v Strydom SA Public Law* 17(2):473–78.

199 (493/2000) [2001] ZASCA 85 (31 August 2001).

200 *Ngxuza* para 1.

201 Committee on ESCR General Comment No 14 *The right to the highest attainable standard of health* para 33.

socio-economic right is breached, for example children's rights, rights of detainees or the right to basic education, the section 36(1) proportionality standard applies. If the duty to fulfil a **qualified socio-economic right** is breached, that breach can be justified only in terms of a special standard of scrutiny - the Court's reasonableness standard - developed on the basis of the internal limitation clause attached to these rights.

In determining whether the constitutional duties have been met, the context is all important. The duties on the state may differ depending on the litigants and the broader context within which they find themselves. As the Constitutional Court pointed out in the *Grootboom* judgment with reference to the right of access to adequate housing, 'housing entails more than bricks and mortar. It requires available land, appropriate services such as the provision of water and the removal of sewage and the financing of all of these, including the building of the house itself'.[202] Moreover, it is not only the state which is responsible for the provision of these rights. Other agents in our society, including individuals themselves, must be enabled by legislative and other measures to provide housing. The state must create the conditions for access to the relevant right for people at all economic levels of our society. State policy dealing with housing must therefore take account of different economic levels in our society. There is a difference between the position of those who can afford to pay for housing, even if it is only basic although adequate housing, and those who cannot. For those who can afford to pay for adequate housing, the state's primary obligation lies in unlocking the system, providing access to housing stock and a legislative framework to facilitate self-built houses through planning laws and access to finance.[203]

PAUSE FOR REFLECTION

Applying the reasonableness standard of review to positive duties

The reasonableness standard of review also seems to apply when a positive duty to fulfil arises in terms of section 27(3) of the Constitution, in other words where it is argued that emergency medical services have to be established at an institution **where they do not exist**. This is because in *Soobramoney*, the Constitutional Court intimated that should a positive duty be read into section 27(3), it would be subject to the section 27(2) internal limitation.[204]

16.7.3.2 Reasonableness review

16.7.3.2.1 Introduction

At the heart of the Constitutional Court's approach to the implementation of the duties imposed by social and economic rights - especially those set out in sections 26 and 27 - is the requirement that the state must act reasonably in order to meet its constitutional obligations. Although reasonableness could arguably also be applied when dealing with the duty to protect discussed above, it finds its most direct application in cases of the duty to promote and fulfil and we will therefore discuss it under this subheading. It is important to understand the factors that the courts take into account to determine whether the state has indeed acted reasonably. Before we discuss these factors, we first set out the judicial

202 *Grootboom* para 35.

203 *Grootboom* para 36.

204 *Soobramoney* para 11.

framework within which such a determination will be made. The Constitutional Court has described its reasonableness standard of scrutiny in five cases.

In *Soobramoney*, the Court refused to grant an order instructing Addington State Hospital to provide dialysis treatment to the applicant. The grounds for this decision were that the guidelines according to which the hospital decided whether to provide the treatment were not unreasonable[205] and were applied rationally and in good faith to the applicant.[206] This meant, the Court held, that the Hospital's decision did not breach the section 27(1) right of everyone to have access to health care services.[207]

In *Grootboom*, the respondent applied for an order declaring the state's housing programme to be unconstitutional on the ground that it infringed section 26(1) which guarantees everyone the right of access to adequate housing. The Constitutional Court granted the order. In arriving at its decision, the Court held that the state's housing policy was unreasonable and thus infringed section 26(1) because it did not include people who were homeless and who found themselves in a crisis situation.[208]

In *Treatment Action Campaign (No 2)*, the respondent applied for an order declaring the state's mother-to-child transmission (MTCT) of HIV at birth prevention programme to be unconstitutional on the ground that it infringed section 27(1) which guarantees everyone the right of access to health services. The Constitutional Court granted the order. In arriving at this decision, the Court held that the state's MTCT of HIV at birth programme was unreasonable and thus infringed section 27(1) because it was not implemented at all public health facilities, but only at a limited number of pilot sites.[209]

In *Khosa*, the applicant applied for an order declaring sections of the Social Assistance Act, which excluded permanent residents from access to social assistance grants, to be unconstitutional on the grounds that they infringed section 27(1)(*c*) which guarantees the right of everyone to have access to social security. The Constitutional Court granted the order. In arriving at this decision, the Court held that the relevant sections were unreasonable and thus infringed section 27(1)(*c*) because, first, section 27(1)(*c*) refers to 'everyone' and not just to 'citizens'; second, permanent residents have made South Africa their home; and, third, extending social security grants to permanent residents would not impose an undue financial burden on the state.

In *Mazibuko*, the applicant applied for an order declaring the City of Johannesburg's free water policy which provided each household with 6 kilolitres of free water per month to be unconstitutional on the ground that it infringed section 27(1)(*b*) which guarantees everyone the right of access to sufficient water. The Constitutional Court refused to grant the order. In arriving at this decision, the Court held that the City's policy was reasonable because, first, the majority of households in Johannesburg consisted of four occupants or less; second, 6 kilolitres of free water per household per month was more than adequate for such

205 *Soobramoney* paras 24–8.

206 *Soobramoney* para 29.

207 *Soobramoney* para 36. The application was argued around the s 27(3) right not to be refused emergency medical treatment and a reading of the right to life in terms of which the state is required to keep the applicant alive. The Court denied the application in these respects, holding that because health care rights were explicitly protected in the Constitution, it was unnecessary to give such an interpretation to the right to life (para 19). Also, s 27(3) did not apply to the applicant's case because his was not an emergency situation (para 21). S 27(3) was a right not to be refused emergency medical treatment arbitrarily **where it was available** instead of a positive right to make available emergency medical treatment where it was not (para 20). Having disposed of these two arguments, the Court on its own initiative proceeded to consider the claim on the basis of s 27(1) (para 22).

208 *Grootboom* para 95.

209 *Treatment Action Campaign (No 2)* para 135.

households; and, third, larger households could apply to the City for an additional 4 kilolitres per month.

Although the Constitutional Court has not been explicit about this, it is clear from these cases that the reasonableness standard is a shifting standard of scrutiny. In *Soobramoney,* the Court applied a basic rationality and good faith test.[210] In *Grootboom* and *Treatment Action Campaign (No 2),* the Court applied a more stringent means-end effectiveness test. In *Khosa,* the Court applied a yet stricter proportionality test. In *Mazibuko,* however, the Court retreated from the proportionality test it had adopted in *Khosa* and followed a much more deferential and process based approach.

Unfortunately, the Constitutional Court has not been explicit about which factors determine the strictness of its scrutiny,[211] but the cases indicate that the following factors play a role:

- the position of the claimants in society[212]
- the degree of deprivation they complain of and the extent to which the breach of the right in question affects their dignity[213]
- the extent to which the breach in question involves undetermined, complex policy questions[214]
- whether or not the breach also amounts to a breach of other rights[215]
- the administrative and practical difficulties the provision of the goods and services in question give rise to[216]
- the extent to which the state has continuously reviewed and refined its policies and programmes to ensure that it meets the needs of the poor[217]
- the seriousness with which the state has approached its obligation and the extent to which it accepts that it is obliged to take reasonable steps to fulfil the right in question.[218]

16.7.3.2.2 A means-end effectiveness test

The Constitutional Court derives its reasonableness standard from the state's duty to take reasonable legislative and other measures, within its available resources, to achieve the progressive realisation of socio-economic rights. In describing this duty, the Court has described the standards against which to evaluate the state's measures. The Court has presented its reasonableness test as a means-end effectiveness test. In *Grootboom,* the Court indicated that the state's measures are evaluated to determine whether they are 'capable of

210 With respect to its evaluation of the guidelines according to which the state made this decision, the Court applied a stricter reasonableness test. See *Soobramoney* paras 23–8.

211 See, for comparison, *Bel Porto School Governing Body and Others v Premier of the Western Cape Province and Another* (CCT58/00) [2002] ZACC 2; 2002 (3) SA 265; 2002 (9) BCLR 891 (21 February 2002) para 127 where the Court lists factors that could play a role in determining the strictness of its scrutiny with respect to administrative law reasonableness review.

212 Whether they are a marginalised or especially vulnerable group. See De Vos (2004) 266.

213 *Khosa* para 80.

214 In *Grootboom,* the issues were much less clearly delineated than in either *Treatment Action Campaign (No 2)* or *Khosa.* Also, in *Treatment Action Campaign (No 2),* many of the complex issues the Court had to consider, in other words, the safety/efficacy of Nevirapine and the availability of the necessary infrastructure to provide it properly, had either been determined by specialised bodies empowered to decide such issues, such as the Medicines Control Council, or the Court had dispositive evidence at its disposal with which to decide. In both the latter cases, a stricter standard of scrutiny was applied than in *Grootboom.*

215 In *Khosa,* the impugned provisions also breached s 9(3). In applying this section, the Court used a standard of scrutiny rising to the level of proportionality. It would make little sense to apply s 27(2) to the same breach using a more lenient standard.

216 *Mazibuko* paras 83, 84, 89 and 101.

217 *Mazibuko* para 162.

218 *Mazibuko* para 168.

facilitating the realisation of the right'.[219] The Court has been at pains in all its judgments so far to emphasise that it does not test relative effectiveness, that it 'will not enquire whether other more desirable or favourable measures could have been adopted, or whether public money could have been better spent', but will leave the 'precise contours and content of the measures to be adopted [to render a programme reasonable] ... [to] the legislature and the executive'.[220]

The Constitutional Court quite obviously adopts this distinction between testing effectiveness and testing relative effectiveness to mediate its concern with its institutional capacity and legitimacy and to manage its relationship with the executive and the legislature. However, the distinction is in many cases a fiction. This fiction is useful as it allows the Court to enforce rights without it having to admit to prescribing directly to the state. As such, it helps the Court avoid direct confrontation with the political branches.[221]

In *Grootboom*, the Court was clearly able to maintain the fiction. The policy issue in question – how best to provide for the needs of the 'absolutely homeless' – allowed for a wide variety of different possible solutions. The Court could thus simply declare that the housing programme was inconsistent with the Constitution to the extent that it made no provision for the 'absolutely homeless' and leave the choice of a specific solution to the state.

By contrast, in *Treatment Action Campaign (No 2)*, and particularly in *Khosa*, the specificity of the policy issue that the Court evaluated was such that it did not allow this scope. The Constitutional Court found in *Treatment Action Campaign (No 2)* that the state's restriction of the provision of Nevirapine to the designated pilot sites breached section 27(1). This finding ineluctably led to the state having to provide Nevirapine elsewhere despite its unwillingness to do so.[222] By the same token, in *Khosa*, the Court's finding of unreasonableness left no option but that permanent residents should be included in the social assistance scheme. Indeed, the Court itself read words to this effect into the Social Assistance Act.[223]

The Court's desire to avoid direct confrontation with the political branches is clearly illustrated in *Mazibuko* where the Court downplayed the effect of its decisions in *Grootboom* and *Treatment Action Campaign (No 2)* and emphasised the fact that it respects the policy-making functions of the other two branches of government.

> **The orders made in these two cases illustrate the Court's institutional respect for the policy-making functions of the two other arms of government. The Court did not seek to draft policy or to determine its content. Instead, having found that the policy adopted by the government did not meet the required constitutional standard of reasonableness, the Court, in *Grootboom*, required government to revise its policy to provide for those most in need and, in *Treatment Action Campaign (No 2)*, to remove anomalous restrictions.**
>
> **The Constitution envisages that legislative and other measures will be the primary instrument for the achievement of social and economic rights. Thus it places a positive obligation upon the State to respond to the basic social and economic needs**

219 *Grootboom* para 41.

220 *Grootboom* para 41.

221 See Roux (2003) 92 with respect to a similar fiction operating in the context of the Court's engagement with resource allocation issues.

222 The Court did manage to soften the prescriptive edge of its finding and order by directing that Nevirapine be provided only where the attending physician and the superintendent of the facility in question opined that it was indicated. See *Treatment Action Campaign (No 2)* para 135, para 3(b) of the order.

223 *Khosa* para 98.

of the people by adopting reasonable legislative and other measures. By adopting such measures, the rights set out in the Constitution acquire content, and that content is subject to the constitutional standard of reasonableness.[224]

16.7.3.3 The elements of reasonableness review

16.7.3.3.1 Introduction

The Constitutional Court's reasonableness standard requires first that the state indeed act to give effect to socio-economic rights, and then requires that what the state does meets a standard of reasonableness. In addition, the state is also required to review continuously its plans and policies.

PAUSE FOR REFLECTION

The elements of the reasonableness standard

The different elements that make up the Constitutional Court's reasonableness standard were summarised by O'Regan J in her judgment in *Mazibuko*. In her judgment, O'Regan J stated that:

> the positive obligations imposed upon government by the social and economic rights in our Constitution will be enforced by courts in at least the following ways. If government takes no steps to realise the rights, the courts will require government to take steps. If government's adopted measures are unreasonable, the courts will similarly require that they be reviewed so as to meet the constitutional standard of reasonableness. From *Grootboom*, it is clear that a measure will be unreasonable if it makes no provision for those most desperately in need. If government adopts a policy with unreasonable limitations or exclusions, as in *Treatment Action Campaign No 2*, the Court may order that those are removed. Finally, the obligation of progressive realisation imposes a duty on government continually to review its policies to ensure that the achievement of the right is progressively realised.[225]

16.7.3.3.2 The state must have a plan

The Court's standard requires first that the state must devise and implement measures to realise socio-economic rights – it cannot do nothing.[226] Although these measures need to realise the rights only **progressively** – the need for full realisation is deferred[227] – the state must have measures in place to realise these rights and must implement them. In addition, the state must show progress in implementing these measures and must be able to explain lack of progress or retrogression. In particular, any deliberate retrogression would be a *prima facie* breach that would require convincing justification.[228]

---

224 *Mazibuko* paras 65–6.

225 *Mazibuko* para 67.

226 Ss 26(2) and 27(2) of the Constitution are clearly mandatory provisions with respect to this basic point: 'the state **must** take ... measures ... to achieve the ... realisation of these rights' (our emphasis).

227 *Grootboom* para 45.

228 *Grootboom* para 45. Deliberate retrogression breaches the negative duty to respect rights. As such, it is subject for its justification to s 36(1) rather than to the reasonableness standard that applies uniquely to the positive duties imposed by qualified rights.

16.7.3.3.3 The plan must be reasonable

Those measures that the state does adopt must be reasonably capable of achieving the realisation of the right in question.[229] To be judged as reasonable in this sense, the state's measures must meet at least the following basic standards:

The measures must be comprehensive and co-ordinated.[230] This means that the state's programme with respect to a right must not only address 'critical issues and measures in regard to *all* aspects' of the realisation of that right,[231] but must also be coherent so that responsibilities are clearly allocated to different spheres and institutions within government.

In *Grootboom*, for example, the Constitutional Court held that even though the state had adopted a programme to provide access to housing, it had done nothing with respect to a critical aspect of the right to housing - it had no measures in place with which to provide shelter to people with no roof over their heads. As such, its housing programme was not comprehensive.[232]

To ensure that state measures are comprehensive and co-ordinated, the Committee on ESCR has suggested that states must adopt national strategies or plans of action,[233] which may or may not be presented in national framework laws, through which to give effect to particular socio-economic rights.[234] The Constitutional Court's references in *Grootboom* to the need for a 'national framework' with respect to housing provision, embodied in 'framework legislation'[235] and to the need for a 'coherent public housing programme'[236] seem to endorse this suggestion by the Committee.[237]

Financial and human resources to implement measures must be made available. In *Grootboom*, the Court stated that for a programme to be reasonable, 'appropriate financial and human resources [must be] available'.[238] The Court has as yet not elaborated on this tantalising phrase. It is clear that the Court is loath to prescribe to the state how and on what it must spend its money and to tell it that it must expend resources so as to do something it did not plan to do and does not want to do.[239] However, this phrase does seem to indicate that the Court will not allow the state to adopt mere token measures. Where the state has itself decided and so undertaken to do something, it is under a legal duty, which the Court would be able to enforce, to allocate the resources reasonably necessary to execute its plans.

In *Kutumela*, for example, the plaintiffs had applied for the Social Relief of Distress Grant, but despite clearly qualifying for it, did not receive it. Their complaint was that although in terms of the Social Assistance Act and its regulations, provincial governments were required

229 *Grootboom* para 41.

230 *Grootboom* para 40.

231 Committee on ESCR General Comment 12 *The right to adequate food* para 25.

232 And, according to the various courts' remarks in *Modderklip Boerdery* para 22 and *City of Cape Town v Rudolph* 77B–84H is still not comprehensive.

233 See, for example, Committee on ESCR General Comment 12 *The right to adequate food* paras 21–30; General Comment 14 *The right to the highest attainable standard of health* para 43; General Comment 15 *The right to water* paras 37 and 46–54.

234 See Committee on ESCR, specifically General Comment 12 *The right to adequate food* para 29 and General Comment 15 *The right to water* para 50.

235 *Grootboom* para 40.

236 *Grootboom* para 41.

237 The South African government also seems to understand its duty to fulfil socio-economic rights in this manner. See, for example, the recent adoption by the Department of Agriculture of the Integrated Food Security Strategy in reaction to criticism from various quarters that no coherent and comprehensive plan through which to fulfil the right to food existed in South Africa. The Integrated Food Security Strategy is a framework document seeking to create institutions through which the fulfilment of the right to food can be co-ordinated. This is coupled with the Department's ongoing efforts to enact framework legislation in this respect.

238 *Grootboom* para 39.

239 See below for a discussion of the court's approach to scrutinising the state's budgetary choices.

to provide the grant to qualifying individuals on successful application, the North West Province had not dedicated the necessary human, institutional and financial resources to do so. The grant was consequently available on paper only and not in practice. The case resulted in a settlement order that in essence required the province to dedicate the necessary human, institutional and financial resources to provide the grant. Specifically, it required the province to acknowledge its legal responsibility to provide Social Relief of Distress Grants effectively to those eligible for it and then to devise a programme to ensure its effective provision. This programme must enable it to process applications for Social Relief of Distress Grants on the same day on which they are received, must enable its officials appropriately to assess and evaluate such applications and must enable the eventual payment of the grant. Importantly, the province was ordered to put in place the necessary infrastructure for the administration and payment of the grant, *inter alia*, by training officials in the province in welfare administration.[240]

The state's measures must be both reasonably conceived and reasonably implemented.[241] This element is closely related to the requirement of reasonable resourcing outlined above and means that it is not sufficient for the state merely to adopt measures on paper. These measures must also in fact be implemented effectively. The *Kutumela* case, described above in the context of adequate resourcing, also illustrates this element of the Court's reasonableness standard. In effect, the Court in *Kutumela* ordered the provincial government to implement a measure that existed in concept but not in practice.

The state's measures must be 'balanced and flexible', capable of responding to intermittent crises and to short-, medium- and long-term needs,[242] may not exclude 'a significant segment of society',[243] may not 'leave out of account the degree and extent of the denial' of the right in question and must respond to the extreme levels of deprivation of people in desperate situations.[244] These related requirements of flexibility and 'reasonable inclusion'[245] formed the basis for the Constitutional Court's decisions in both *Grootboom* and *Treatment Action Campaign (No 2)*. In *Grootboom*, the Court found that the state's housing programme was inconsistent with sections 26(1) and (2) because it 'failed to recognise that the state must provide relief for those in desperate need'.[246] In *Treatment Action Campaign (No 2)*, the Court held that the state's measures to prevent MTCT of HIV were inconsistent with the Constitution because they 'failed to address the needs of mothers and their newborn children who do not have access'[247] to the pilot sites where Nevirapine was provided and because the programme as a whole was 'inflexible'.[248]

240 See in this respect also *People's Union for Civil Liberties v Union of India & Ors* in the Supreme Court of India, Civil Original Jurisdiction, Writ Petition, (Civil) No. 196 of 2001. This Indian case dealt with an application in part directed at obtaining orders that the Indian government's existing measures at national and state level to address food insecurity and famine be effectively implemented. The complaint alleged, among other things, that although adequate food reserves existed in India, and although the state had adopted various measures to address food insecurity and famine, these measures were not implemented. This was in part because state governments routinely diverted funds from national government, intended to implement these measures, to other needs. In response, the Indian Supreme Court issued a number of interim orders requiring, among other things, that funds allocated from national level to state governments for use in the public distribution of food and famine measures in fact be used for those purposes.

241 *Grootboom* para 42.

242 *Grootboom* para 43.

243 *Grootboom* para 43.

244 *Grootboom* para 44.

245 See Roux, T (2002) Understanding *Grootboom*: A response to Cass R Sunstein *Constitutional Forum* 12(2):41–51 at 49.

246 *Grootboom* para 66.

247 *Treatment Action Campaign (No 2)* para 67.

248 *Treatment Action Campaign (No 2)* para 80.

In one sense, these different requirements all relate to the idea that the state's programmes must be **comprehensive**. Any state programme designed to fulfil a socio-economic right will be incomplete and, as such, unreasonable unless it includes measures through which short-term crises in accessing the right can be addressed as well as measures that 'provide relief for those in desperate need'.[249] These requirements relate to flexibility and reasonable inclusion, and particularly the Constitutional Court's phrase in *Grootboom* that a programme must take account of the degree and the extent of deprivation with respect to a right.[250] However, the intriguing question raised by these requirements is whether the Court's reasonableness test in this respect requires state measures to prioritise efforts, both with respect to temporal order and resource allocation, according to different degrees of need. Does the test require the state to engage in 'sensible priority-setting, with particular attention to the plight of those in greatest need'?[251]

Roux has made a strong argument that it does not. He points out that the Court's finding in *Grootboom* requires 'merely *inclusion*' and that 'a government programme that is subject to socio-economic rights will [in terms of this finding] be unreasonable if it fails to *cater* to a significant segment of society'.[252] With respect to the finding in *Grootboom*, Roux's reading is correct. The Court there clearly simply required the state to **take account of** the needs of those most desperate without at the same time suggesting that the needs of such people should in any concrete way take precedence over other needs.[253] However, it has been suggested that the Court's reasonableness test can take account of a prioritisation according to need by varying the standard of scrutiny that it applies to particular alleged breaches of socio-economic rights **according to the degree of deprivation suffered by those affected by the breach.**[254] According to this view, a court would scrutinise state measures more rigorously where those complaining of their impact are desperately deprived.

This idea has recently been given credence in *Khosa*. As pointed out above, the Court in *Khosa*, possibly for a variety of reasons, applied a substantially stricter standard of scrutiny to the state's exclusion of permanent residents than it applied to the state's HIV prevention policy in *Treatment Action Campaign (No 2)* or the state's housing programme in *Grootboom*. The Court in *Khosa* applied a proportionality test, weighing the impact that the exclusion had on the dignity and practical circumstances of indigent permanent residents against the purposes for which the state had introduced the exclusion. The Court did not only find that the basic survival interests of the excluded permanent residents should take precedence over the legitimate purposes for their exclusion.[255] It also by implication held that the basic survival needs of the permanent residents should take precedence over further expansion of the social assistance system as it applies to South African citizens. This was illustrated by the rejection of the state's arguments that to include permanent residents in the social assistance scheme would place an undue financial burden on the state and would potentially require the diversion of resources from other social assistance needs.[256] The most important factor determining the Court's robust scrutiny in this respect was 'the severe impact [that the exclusion of permanent residents from the scheme was likely to have] on the dignity of

249 *Grootboom* para 66.
250 *Grootboom* para 44.
251 Sunstein (2001) 127.
252 Roux (2002) 49.
253 Brand (2004) 50.
254 See Brand (2002b) 108 and Bilchitz, D (2003) 15–17.
255 *Khosa* para 82.
256 *Khosa* paras 60–2.

the persons concerned, who, unable to sustain themselves, have to turn to others to enable them to meet the necessities of life and are thus cast in the role of supplicants'.[257]

The state's measures must be transparent in the sense that they must be made known both during their conception and once conceived to all affected.[258] This final element of the Court's reasonableness test was added in *Treatment Action Campaign (No 2)* where the Court held that for a programme to be reasonable, its 'contents must be made known appropriately'.[259] As *Treatment Action Campaign (No 2)* itself illustrated, litigants in socio-economic rights cases face great difficulties if it is not possible to ascertain with certainty what the state's measures entail. In a basic sense, to be able to challenge the state's position, a litigant has to be able to pinpoint what exactly it is. In this respect, the requirement of transparency is practically very important.[260]

PAUSE FOR REFLECTION

Viewing socio-economic rights jurisprudence through the prism of equality

The Constitutional Court's focus on the relative deprivation of the group suffering from the breach - in other words, its insistence on taking account of whether those excluded are vulnerable and in particular need of state intervention to affirm their human dignity - arguably echoes the Court's approach to section 9 of the Constitution. Recall that the Court has stated that in deciding whether there was unfair discrimination in terms of section 9(3) of the Constitution, the Court will have regard to the position of the complainant in society and will ask whether he or she belongs to a group which was previously discriminated against or is still vulnerable. Similarly, when the Court has to decide whether the state has acted reasonably, it will have regard to the vulnerability of the group which is being excluded or is not gaining access to the social and economic benefit to the same degree as others who are less vulnerable. It has therefore been argued that one way of understanding the social and economic rights jurisprudence of the Constitutional Court is to view it through the prism of equality.[261] If viewed thus, the reasonableness requirement can look much like the requirement for contextual fairness which is at the heart of the equality jurisprudence of the Constitutional Court.

16.7.3.3.4 The state must continually review its plan

In *Mazibuko*, the Constitutional Court held that apart from showing that the plan adopted by the state is reasonable, the concept of progressive realisation also imposes an obligation on the state to review and revise continuously its plan to ensure that social and economic rights are progressively achieved.[262] A plan that is set is stone and never revisited, the Constitutional Court held further, is unlikely to be a plan that will result in the progressive realisation of rights consistently with the obligations imposed by the social and economic rights in the Constitution.

257 *Khosa* para 80.
258 *Treatment Action Campaign (No 2)* para 123.
259 *Treatment Action Campaign (No 2)* para 123.
260 See also Liebenberg (2013) 33.37–33.38.
261 See De Vos, P (2001) Grootboom, the right of access to housing and substantive equality as contextual fairness *South African Journal on Human Rights* 17(2):258–76 at 258.
262 *Mazibuko* paras 40, 67 and 162.

16.7.3.4 Meaningful engagement

When a state entity implements social and economic rights, it is required to treat affected individuals and groups with dignity. An excessively technocratic approach that does not take into account the needs and wishes of those affected might not be reasonable. The Constitutional Court therefore developed the notion of meaningful engagement in *Occupiers of 51 Olivia Road, Berea Township and 197 Main Street Johannesburg v City of Johannesburg and Others*.[263]

Although this case dealt with the potential eviction of a large group of individuals from the inner city of Johannesburg, the principle of reasonable accommodation could also be applied to other situations in which the state acts to upgrade services to give effects to the realisation of social and economic rights. This insight stems from the Constitutional Court's remarks in *Grootboom* on the relationship between reasonable state action and the need to treat human beings with the appropriate respect and care for their dignity. In *Grootboom* the Court remarked:

> **All levels of government must ensure that the housing program is reasonably and appropriately implemented in the light of all the provisions in the Constitution. All implementation mechanisms and all State action in relation to housing falls to be assessed against the requirements of s 26 of the Constitution. Every step at every level of government must be consistent with the constitutional obligation to take reasonable measures to provide adequate housing ... The proposition that rights are interrelated and are all equally important is not merely a theoretical postulate. The concept has immense human and practical significance in a society founded on human dignity, equality and freedom. It is fundamental to an evaluation of the reasonableness of State action that account be taken of the inherent dignity of human beings. The Constitution will be worth infinitely less than its paper if the reasonableness of State action concerned with housing is determined without regard to the fundamental constitutional value of human dignity.**[264]

In the context of evictions in *Occupiers of 51 Olivia Road*, the probability arose that people would become homeless as a direct result of their eviction at the state's instance. In these circumstances, those involved in the management of the municipality ought at the very least to have engaged meaningfully with the occupiers both individually and collectively.[265] The Court explained that such an engagement was 'a two-way process' in which all parties needed to engage meaningfully with one another.[266] There is no closed list of the objectives of engagement. However, the Court listed some of the objectives of engagement in cases of pending eviction:

> **(a) what the consequences of the eviction might be;**
> **(b) whether the city could help in alleviating those dire consequences;**
> **(c) whether it was possible to render the buildings concerned relatively safe and conducive to health for an interim period;**

---

263 (24/07) [2008] ZACC 1; 2008 (3) SA 208 (CC); 2008 (5) BCLR 475 (CC) (19 February 2008).

264 *Grootboom* paras 82–3. See also *Port Elizabeth Municipality* para 39 where the Court stated:

> **... the procedural and substantive aspects of justice and equity cannot always be separated. The managerial role of the courts may need to find expression in innovative ways. Thus, one potentially dignified and effective mode of achieving sustainable reconciliations of the different interests involved is to encourage and require the parties to engage with each other in a proactive and honest endeavour to find mutually acceptable solutions. Wherever possible, respectful face-to-face engagement or mediation through a third party should replace arm's-length combat by intransigent opponents.**

265 *Occupiers of 51 Olivia Road* para 13.

266 *Occupiers of 51 Olivia Road* para 114.

> **(d) whether the city had any obligations to the occupiers in the prevailing circumstances; and**
> **(e) when and how the city could or would fulfil these obligations.** [267]

In the case of a pending eviction the authority who wishes to effect the eviction 'must make reasonable efforts to engage' before it can effect such an eviction.[268] The engagement process should preferably be managed by careful and sensitive people on the side of the municipality.[269] This forms part of the general obligation on the state body to act reasonably. In *Grootboom*, the Court remarked that '[e]very step at every level of government must be consistent with the constitutional obligation to take reasonable measures to provide adequate housing'.[270] As the Court stated in *Occupiers of 51 Olivia Road*:

> **It may in some circumstances be reasonable to make permanent housing available and, in others, to provide no housing at all. The possibilities between these extremes are almost endless. It must not be forgotten that the City cannot be expected to make provision for housing beyond the extent to which available resources allow. As long as the response of the municipality in the engagement process is reasonable, that response complies with section 26(2). The Constitution therefore obliges every municipality to engage meaningfully with people who would become homeless because it evicts them. It also follows that, where a municipality is the applicant in eviction proceedings that could result in homelessness, a circumstance that a court must take into account to comply with section 26(3) of the Constitution is whether there has been meaningful engagement.**[271]

However, the process of engagement will work only if both sides act reasonably and in good faith. Civil society organisations that support the peoples' claims should preferably facilitate the engagement process in every possible way.[272] An important prerequisite for meaningful engagement is openness and transparency on the side of the state institution as secrecy is counterproductive to the process of engagement.[273]

16.7.3.5 Within available resources

The state's duty to fulfil socio-economic rights must be exercised 'within its available resources'.[274] Liebenberg points out that this phrase both provides an excuse and imposes a duty on the state.[275] It allows the state to attribute its failure to realise a socio-economic right to budgetary constraints and it requires the state in fact to make resources available with which to realise a right.[276]

The Constitutional Court has been circumspect in scrutinising budgetary issues. In some cases it has avoided them altogether. In *Soobramoney*, the Court simply accepted the state's contention that resources were limited as a given and allowed that fact to determine its decision. The Court interrogated neither the allocation for health purposes from national

267 *Occupiers of 51 Olivia Road* para 14.
268 *Occupiers of 51 Olivia Road* para 115.
269 *Occupiers of 51 Olivia Road* para 15.
270 *Grootboom* para 82.
271 *Occupiers of 51 Olivia Road* para 18.
272 *Occupiers of 51 Olivia Road* para 20.
273 *Occupiers of 51 Olivia Road* para 21.
274 Ss 26(2) and 27(2) of the Constitution.
275 Liebenberg (2013) 33.44.
276 *Grootboom* para 46.

government nor in any rigorous way the manner in which it was used at provincial level.[277] In *Grootboom*, resource constraints were not a direct issue. Equally, in *Treatment Action Campaign (No 2)* with respect to the question whether the provision of Nevirapine should be extended to public health facilities where the necessary counselling and monitoring infrastructure already existed, the question of the availability of resources was obviated. The manufacturers of Nevirapine had undertaken to provide it for free for five years and no additional infrastructural spending was required to proceed with the extension to such facilities.[278]

In those instances where budgetary issues could not be avoided, the Court has required the state to persuade it of its financial constraints.[279] It has then proceeded to scrutinise the state's assertions in this respect but on its own terms – that is, taking the limits of the existing budget allocations as a given. The Court has not scrutinised initial budgetary decisions at macroeconomic level.

In *Treatment Action Campaign (No 2)* with respect to the extension of the programme to prevent MTCT of HIV to facilities without the necessary counselling and monitoring infrastructure, the state indeed objected that it did not have the requisite resources. The Court engaged with and rejected this argument. First, since the litigation between the Treatment Action Campaign and the state had commenced, some provincial governments had proceeded with the extension of the provision of Nevirapine to facilities other than the pilot sites despite the asserted resource constraints.[280] This demonstrated to the Court that in fact 'the requisite political will', rather than resources, was lacking.[281] In addition, while the case was being heard, the state announced that significant additional resources had been allocated to deal with the HIV pandemic.[282] The Court could therefore find that whatever resource constraints had existed previously, existed no longer.[283]

In *Khosa*, the state also objected that it would not have the resources with which to extend social assistance grants to indigent permanent residents.[284] Again, the Court considered and rejected this argument.[285] It could do so first because the state had not provided 'clear evidence to show what the additional cost of providing social grants to ... permanent residents would be'.[286] As a result, the Court could not assess whether the additional cost would place an untenable burden on the state.[287] In addition, the state provided the Court with evidence of current spending on and projected increases in

277 *Soobramoney* paras 24–8.

278 *Treatment Action Campaign (No 2)* para 19. This prompted the Court to hold that the extension of the programme to these sites 'will not attract any significant additional costs' (para 71).

279 That the onus in this respect is indeed on the state rather than on the claimant is most clearly established in *Khosa*.

280 *Treatment Action Campaign (No 2)* para 118.

281 *Treatment Action Campaign (No 2)* para 119.

282 *Treatment Action Campaign (No 2)* para 120.

283 *Treatment Action Campaign (No 2)* para 120.

284 *Khosa* paras 60–1.

285 The Court's willingness to do so is not insignificant. See by way of contrast Ncgobo J, dissenting in *Khosa* at para 128:

> **Mr Kruger ... estimates that the annual cost of including permanent residents could range between R243 million and R672 million. Policymakers have the expertise ... to present a ... prediction about future social conditions. That is ... the work that policymakers are supposed to do. Unless there is evidence to the contrary, courts should be slow to reject reasonable estimates made by policymakers.**

286 *Khosa* para 62.

287 *Khosa* is significant in that it clearly establishes that it is not for the claimant in a socio-economic rights case to show that the state is not constrained by lack of resources, but for the state to show that it is so constrained (paras 60–2). Precisely because the state was unable to make this showing satisfactorily, the Court rejected its objection, seemingly without requiring the claimants to make a contrary showing (para 62).

spending on social assistance.[288] This enabled the Court to point out that even at the most pessimistic estimate of the additional cost occasioned by an extension of social assistance to permanent residents,[289] the additional burden on the state would in relative terms be very small.[290]

The Court's approach to scrutinising budgetary issues and to the consequences of that scrutiny is perhaps best captured in a remark from *Treatment Action Campaign (No 2)*. The Court indicated that its scrutiny is not in itself 'directed at rearranging budgets', but that its scrutiny 'may in fact have budgetary implications'.[291] This remark seems clearly to indicate that the Court will neither directly interrogate nor prescribe the state's initial allocational decisions at macroeconomic level. At the same time, it will not be discouraged from interrogating the reasonableness of state measures according to the standard described above even if a finding of unreasonableness would have the consequence that the state would itself have to rearrange its budget.[292]

This distinction between the Court itself rearranging budgets and taking decisions that have the consequence that the state must rearrange budgets is of course at least sometimes a fiction – as with the distinction between effectiveness and relative effectiveness discussed above. The effect of the decision in *Khosa*, although the Court does not present itself as 'rearranging budgets', is that the state has to allocate additional resources (however slight an amount in relative terms) to an item that it did not want to finance. However, as Roux argues, this is perhaps a useful fiction as it has the singular virtue of allowing the Court to interfere in allocational choices to the extent required to enforce a right without directly admitting to it. As such, it avoids direct confrontation with the executive.[293]

More recently, in *Blue Moonlight Properties*, the City of Johannesburg objected on appeal to the Constitutional Court against a decision of the SCA that it should find the resources to provide temporary alternative housing for people evicted from their homes by private property owners despite the fact that it had not budgeted for this. The City argued that it could not during the course of any given financial year reallocate resources for emergency use to provide such alternative accommodation if this had not been budgeted for. Such expenditure, they continued, would be unlawful. The Constitutional Court responded simply by holding that the City could not avoid its constitutional responsibilities only by asserting that it had not budgeted for that purpose. If it had not done so, it had to find the money, in effect, somewhere.[294]

16.8 Remedies in socio-economic rights cases

In constitutional matters, including matters dealing with socio-economic rights, courts have wide remedial powers. We have already discussed the various remedies that courts can grant to vindicate rights in chapter 11. However, the specific nature of the duties imposed by social and economic rights raises additional questions about the nature of the remedies granted

288 *Khosa* para 60.

289 The state estimated that the additional cost would be between R243 million and R672 million. The wide range itself indicated to the Court the absence of clear evidence as to the possible resource consequences of a finding of inconsistency (para 62).

290 *Khosa* para 62.

291 *Treatment Action Campaign (No 2)* para 38.

292 In *Khosa*, this is precisely what the Court did. Its finding of unreasonableness forced the state to expend resources on providing access to social assistance benefits, something for which the state itself had not budgeted.

293 Roux (2003) 9.

294 *Blue Moonlight Properties* para 74.

by a court in cases dealing with a breach of these rights. We therefore highlight issues relating to the specific vindication of social and economic rights in this subsection. However, this subsection must be read in conjunction with the discussion in chapter 11. Section 38 of the Constitution determines that courts must in such matters provide 'appropriate relief, including a declaration of rights', while section 172 empowers courts to declare invalid law or conduct inconsistent with the Constitution and, in addition, to provide any order that is 'just and equitable'.[295] The Constitutional Court has been clear that these powers allow it to fashion new remedies where necessary to 'protect and enforce the Constitution'.[296] An important consideration for the Court in this respect is that the remedies it provides, whether new or existing, must be effective.[297]

In most of the kinds of socio-economic rights cases described above, providing 'appropriate relief' is unproblematic. It requires courts to do little else than they are used to doing in cases decided on the basis of other rights or indeed cases decided on the basis of the common law or ordinary legislation. However, when courts are required to provide relief in cases where the state has breached the duty to fulfil socio-economic rights, or where the state has interfered in the existing exercise of a socio-economic right and is under a duty to mitigate the impact of that interference, their position is often more difficult. In these cases, the Court's finding requires the state to act affirmatively in order to remedy its breach of the right, to amend its policy or adopt a new policy, or to provide a service that it is not currently providing or to extend a service to people who do not currently qualify for it. Such cases necessarily involve 'amorphous, sprawling party structures, allegations broadly implicating the operations of large public institutions such as schools systems ... mental health facilities ... and public housing authorities, and remedies requiring long term restructuring and monitoring of these institutions', policies and programmes.[298] Courts are consequently faced with having to decide to what extent to prescribe directly to the state what it must do, and to what extent and in what manner to retain control of the implementation of their orders, to see that indeed they will be effective.

An obvious way for courts to retain control of the implementation of their orders is through so-called structural or supervisory interdicts.[299] These orders would usually require the state to draft a plan for its implementation of the order, which could then be submitted to the court and the other party for approval, and then periodically to report back to the court and the other party with respect to its implementation of that plan. The court could manage the supervision on its own, through the other party to the litigation or through a court-appointed supervisor.[300]

In the two cases where such a supervisory interdict could perhaps have played a role, the Constitutional Court has elected not to use it. In *Grootboom*, the Court issued a simple declaratory order, leaving the remedy of the constitutional defect in its housing programme

---

295 Such 'just and equitable' orders could include but are not limited to orders limiting the retrospective effect of an order of invalidity or suspending the operation of an order of invalidity.

296 *Fose v Minister of Safety and Security* (CCT14/96) [1997] ZACC 6; 1997 (7) BCLR 851; 1997 (3) SA 786 (5 June 1997) para 19.

297 *Fose* para 69.

298 Sabel, CF and Simon, WH (2004) Destabilisation rights: How public law litigation succeeds *Harvard Law Review* 117(4):1016–1101 at 1017.

299 See, in this respect, Trengove, W (1999) Judicial remedies for violations of socio-economic rights *ESR Review* 1(4):8–11 at 9–10, and, in general, Sabel and Simon (2004).

300 The Constitutional Court used such a structural interdict in *August* to ensure that the state took the necessary steps to make it possible for prisoners to vote in general elections. The various High Courts have made quite regular use of such interdicts in socio-economic rights cases. See, for example, *Grootboom v Oostenberg Municipality and Others* 2000 (3) BCLR 277 (C).

entirely to the state.[301] In *Treatment Action Campaign (No 2)*, the Court similarly issued a declarator coupled with a mandatory order requiring the state to remedy the constitutional defect in its programme for prevention of MTCT of HIV.[302] However, despite confirming that it did indeed have the power to do so, the Court again declined to issue a supervisory interdict, holding that there was no indication that the state would not implement its order properly.[303]

Although the Court's failure particularly in *Grootboom* to use a supervisory interdict certainly trenched on the effectiveness of its order,[304] it is understandable that the Court is circumspect in its use of these remedies. Structural interdicts have to be very carefully crafted to be effective.[305] More importantly, structural interdicts have the potential to erode the legitimacy of the Court, both because they directly and on an ongoing basis place the Court in confrontation with the executive, and because they can involve the Court in the day-to-day management of public institutions, something at which it is almost bound to fail.[306] Whether or not a structural interdict will be appropriate in a given case will depend on the nature of the breach in question and particularly on the nature of the remedy of that breach.[307]

SUMMARY

Social and economic or socio-economic rights are often distinguished from civil and political rights on the basis that they engender different types of duties. However, although there may be qualitative differences in the nature of the duties imposed by socio-economic rights, in principle there is little difference between these rights and civil and political rights. Both types of rights impose so-called negative and positive duties on the state. Negative duties require the state to refrain from infringing existing rights while positive duties require the state to take positive steps to ensure the enjoyment of the rights.

Socio-economic rights sometimes raise questions about the role of the court in enforcing human rights in the light of the separation of powers doctrine. For reasons relating to pragmatic concerns, courts are therefore often more willing to enforce socio-economic rights in a robust fashion when these rights are given effect to by ordinary legislation or when the court is merely asked to enforce existing policy decisions taken by the executive. Courts also seem to be more willing to enforce socio-economic rights if the infringement is of a negative nature than when it requires positive action from the state to adhere to the duties imposed by these rights.

At the heart of the positive obligations of the state to realise socio-economic rights is the requirement to act reasonably. To be reasonable, the state's measures must be balanced and flexible, capable of responding to intermittent crises and to short-, medium- and long-term

301 *Grootboom* para 99.

302 *Treatment Action Campaign (No 2)* para 135.

303 *Treatment Action Campaign (No 2)* para 129.

304 In a number of recent cases, courts have pointed out that the state has to all intents and purposes simply ignored the order in *Grootboom* and has put in place no discernible measures to take account of the plight of those in housing crises. See, for example, *Modderklip* para 22 and *Rudolph* paras 77B–84H. See also Pillay, K (2002) Implementation of *Grootboom*: Implications for the enforcement of socio-economic rights *Law, Democracy and Development* 6(2):255–77.

305 Sabel and Simon (2004) 1017.

306 *Fose* paras 18–19.

307 It remains an open question, for example, whether or not a structural interdict would indeed have led to the findings in *Grootboom* being implemented effectively by the state or whether, instead, the policy issue in *Grootboom* was so wide and amorphous and required such wide-ranging and complex adjustment on the side of the state that the Court would simply have become bogged down in debilitating detail had it retained jurisdiction.

needs, may not exclude a significant segment of society, may not leave out of account the degree and extent of the denial of the right in question and must respond to the extreme levels of deprivation of people in desperate situations. The measures also need to be comprehensive and co-ordinated. An important factor taken into account by the courts is the degree of deprivation suffered by those affected by the breach. The process through which the state body chooses to implement its obligations is important as this also needs to be reasonable. To this end, the state may well have to engage meaningfully with affected individuals and groups to deal with any possible negative consequences of its actions and to ensure that it treats individuals with the requisite human dignity.[308]

308 This chapter 16 is a modified and updated version of the author's 'Introduction' in D Brand and CH Heyns *Socio-economic rights in South Africa* (2005). To the extent that material from that chapter is reproduced here, the Pretoria University Law Press (PULP) that published the original chapter has given its permission.

Bibliography

Books

Ackermann, L (2012) *Human Dignity: Lodestar for Equality in South Africa* Cape Town: Juta

Akiba, O (ed) (2004) *Constitutionalism and Society in Africa* Aldershot, Hants, England; Burlington VT: Ashgate

Akiba, O 'Constitutional government and the future of constitutionalism in Africa' in Akiba, O (ed) (2004) *Constitutionalism and Society in Africa* Aldershot, Hants, England; Burlington VT: Ashgate

Alston, P and Tomasevski, K (eds) (1984) *The Right to Food* Dordrecht: Martinus Nijhoff Publishers

An-Na'im, AA 'To affirm the full human rights standing of economic, social and cultural rights' in Ghai, Y and Cottrell, J (2004) *Economic, Social and Cultural Rights in Practice: The Role of Judges in Implementing Economic, Social and Cultural Rights* Commonwealth Secretariat

Andrews, P and Ellmann, S (eds) (2001) *The Post-Apartheid Constitutions: Perspectives on South Africa's Basic Law* Johannesburg: Witwatersrand University Press

Badura, P and Dreier, H (eds) (2001) *Festschrift 50 Jahre Bundesverfassungsgericht* Tubingen: Mohr Siebeck

Bakan, J 'What's wrong with social rights' in Bakan, J and Schneiderman, D (eds) (1992) *Social Justice and the Constitution: Perspectives on a Social Union for Canada* Ottawa: Carleton University

Bakan, J and Schneiderman, D (eds) (1992) *Social Justice and the Constitution: Perspectives on a Social Union for Canada* Ottawa: Carleton University

Barkan, JD (ed) (2009) *Legislative Power in Emerging African Democracies* Boulder, Colo: Lynne Rienner Publishers

Basson, DA and Viljoen, HP (1988) *South African Constitutional Law* 2nd ed Cape Town: Juta

Basson, DA and Viljoen, HP (1988) *Suid-Afrikaanse Staatsreg* 2de uitg Cape Town: Juta

Bauman, Z (2007) *Consuming Life* Cambridge; Malden MA: Polity Press

Baxter, L (1984) *Administrative Law* Cape Town: Juta

Beaudoin, GA and Mendes, E (eds) (1996) *The Canadian Charter of Rights and Freedoms* Scarborough, Ont: Carswell Legal

Bennett, T and Murray, C 'Traditional leaders' in Woolman, S and Bishop, M (2013) *Constitutional Law of South Africa* 2nd ed rev service 5, Lansdowne, Cape Town: Juta

Bennett, TW (2004) *Customary Law in South Africa* Cape Town: Juta

Berger, JM and Kapczynski, A 'The story of the TAC case: The potential and limits of socio-economic rights litigation in South Africa' in Hurwitz, DR and Satterthwaite, ML (eds) (2009) *Human Rights Advocacy Stories* New York: Foundation Press

Bickel, AM (1962) *The Least Dangerous Branch: The Supreme Court at the Bar of Politics* Indianapolis: Bobbs-Merrill

Biko, S (1987) *I Write What I Like* London: Heinemann

Bishop, M and Brickhill, J 'Constitutional law' (2010) *Juta's Annual Survey of South African Law* Cape Town: Juta

Bishop, M and Raboshakga, N 'National legislative authority' in Woolman, S and Bishop, M (2013) *Constitutional Law of South Africa* 2nd ed rev service 5 Cape Town: Juta

Bloed, A et al (eds) (1993) *Monitoring Human Rights in Europe: Comparing International Procedures and Mechanisms* Dordrecht: Martinus Nijhoff

Blyberg, A and Ravindran, DJ (eds) (2000) *A Circle of Rights: Economic, Social and Cultural Rights: A Training Resource* New York: International Human Rights Internship Programme/Asian Forum for Human Rights Development

Bogdanor, V (2009) *The New British Constitution* Oxford; Portland Ore: Hart

Botha, H, Van der Walt, AJ and Van der Walt, JC (2003) *Rights and Democracy in a Transformative Constitution* Stellenbosch: African Sun Media

Brand, D 'The minimum core content of the right to food in context: A response to Rolf Künneman' in Brand, D and Russell, S (eds) (2002) *Exploring the Core Content of Socio-economic Rights: South African and International Perspectives* Pretoria: Protea Book House

Brand, D 'The proceduralisation of South African socio-economic rights jurisprudence, or "What are socio-economic rights for?"' in Botha, H, Van der Walt, AJ and Van der Walt, JC (2003) *Rights and Democracy in a Transformative Constitution* Stellenbosch: African Sun Media

Brand, D and Russell, S (eds) (2002) *Exploring the Core Content of Socio-economic Rights: South African and International Perspectives* Pretoria: Protea Book House

Braun, S (2004) *Democracy Off Balance: Freedom of Expression and Hate Propaganda Law in Canada* Toronto: University of Toronto Press

Bronstein, V 'Conflicts' in Woolman, S and Bishop, M (2013) *Constitutional Law of South Africa* 2nd ed rev service 5 Cape Town: Juta

Bronstein, V and Robinson, K 'Constitutional jurisprudence and the Bill of Rights' (1996) *Juta's Annual Survey of South African Law* Cape Town: Juta

Budlender, G 'Justiciability of socio-economic rights: Some South African experiences' in Ghai, Y and Cottrell, J (eds) (2004) *Economic, Social and Cultural Rights in Practice: The Role of Judges in Implementing Economic, Social and Cultural Rights* Commonwealth Secretariat

Calland, R (2013) *The Zuma Years: South Africa's Changing Face of Power* Cape Town: Zebra Press

Carnelley, M and Hoctor, S (eds) (2011) *Law, Order and Liberty: Essays in Honour of Tony Matthews* Pietermaritzburg: UKZN Press

Carpenter, G (1987) *Introduction to South African Constitutional Law* Durban: Butterworths

Chanock, M (2001) *The Making of South African Legal Culture, 1902-1936: Fear, Favour and Prejudice* Cambridge; New York: Cambridge University Press

Chaskalson, M et al (eds) (1996) *Constitutional Law of South Africa* 1st ed Cape Town: Juta

Cheadle, MH 'Labour relations' in Cheadle, MH, Davis, DM and Haysom, NRL (2013) *South African Constitutional Law: The Bill of Rights* 2nd ed Durban: LexisNexis

Cheadle, MH, Davis, DM and Haysom, NRL (2013) *South African Constitutional Law: The Bill of Rights* 2nd ed Durban: LexisNexis

Chemerinsky, E (2009) *Constitutional Law* 3rd ed New York: Wolters Kluwer Law & Business

Chikane, F (2012) *Eight Days in September: The Removal of Thabo Mbeki* Johannesburg: Picador, Africa

Chirwa, DM and Nijzink, L (eds) (2012) *Accountable Government in Africa: Perspectives from Public Law and Political Studies* New York: United Nations University Press

Chothia, F and Jacobs, S 'Remaking the Presidency: The tension between co-ordination and centralisation' in Jacobs, S and Calland, R (eds) (2002) *Thabo Mbeki's World: The Politics and Ideology of the South African President* Pietermaritzburg: University of Natal Press

Claassens, A and Cousins, B (eds) (2008) *Land, Power and Custom: Controversies Generated by South Africa's Communal Land Rights Act* Cape Town: UCT Press; Legal Resources Centre

Courchene, TJ and Allen, JR (eds) (2011) *The Federal Idea: Essays in Honour of Ronald L Watts* Kingston, Ont: Institute of Intergovernmental Relations, Queens University

Craven, M 'Introduction to the International Covenant on Economic, Social and Cultural Rights' in Blyberg, A and Ravindran, DJ (eds) (2000) *A Circle of Rights: Economic, Social and Cultural Rights: A Training Resource* New York: International Human Rights Internship Programme/Asian Forum for Human Rights Development

Crosby, MB (2008) *The Making of a German Constitution: A Slow Revolution* Oxford; New York: Berg

Currie, I and De Waal, J (2005) *The Bill of Rights Handbook* 5th ed Cape Town: Juta

Currie, I and De Waal, J (2013) *The Bill of Rights Handbook* 6th ed Cape Town: Juta

Currie, I and De Waal, J et al (eds) (2001) *The New Constitutional and Administrative Law: Vol 1, Constitutional Law* Cape Town: Juta Law

Curtis, MK et al (2006) *Constitutional Law in Context* 2nd ed vol 1 Durham, NC: Carolina Academic Press

Davenport, TRH (1987) *South Africa: A Modern History* 3rd ed Basingstoke; MacMillan New York: St Martin's Press

Davis D, Chaskalson, M and De Waal, J 'Democracy and constitutionalism: The role of constitutional interpretation' in Van Wyk, DH et al (eds) (1994) *Rights and Constitutionalism: The New South African Legal Order* Cape Town: Juta

De Montesquieu, C (1748) *De l'Esprit des Loix* (Nugent T (tr), Neumann F (ed) (1949) *The Spirit of the Laws*) New York: Hafner Press

De Smith, SA and Brazier, R (1998) *Constitutional and Administrative Law* 8th ed London; New York: Penguin Books

De Ville, J (2005) *Judicial Review of Administrative Action in South Africa* Durban: LexisNexis

De Ville, J and Steytler, N (1996) *Voting in 1999: Choosing an Electoral System* Durban: Butterworths

De Vos, P 'South Africa's experience with proportional representation' in De Ville, J and Steytler, N (1996) *Voting in 1999: Choosing an Electoral System* Durban: Butterworths

De Vos, P (2010) *On 'Shoot the Boer' Hate Speech and the Banning of Struggle Songs* Pretoria: Pretoria University Law Press (PULP)

De Vos, P 'Balancing independence and accountability: The role of Chapter 9 institutions in South Africa's constitutional democracy' in Chirwa, DM and Nijzink, L (eds) (2012) *Accountable Government in Africa: Perspectives from Public Law and Political Studies* New York: United Nations University Press

Devenish, GE (1998) *A Commentary on the South African Constitution* Durban: Butterworths

Dicey, AV (1885; 1959) *Introduction to the Study of the Law of the Constitution* 10th ed Johannesburg: MacMillan

Dlamini, CRM (1995) *Human Rights in Africa: Which Way South Africa*? Durban: Butterworths

Dugard, J (1978) *Human Rights and the South African Legal Order* Princeton, NJ: Princeton University Press

Du Bois, F (ed) (2007) *Wille's Principles of South African Law* 9th ed Cape Town: Juta

Du Plessis, L and Corder, H (1994) *Understanding South Africa's Transitional Bill of Rights* Kenwyn: Juta

Du Plessis, LM (1999) *An Introduction to Law* 3rd ed Kenwyn: Juta

Du Plessis, M and Penfold, G 'Bill of Rights jurisprudence: Operational provisions of the Bill of Rights' (2008) *Juta's Annual Survey of South African Law* Cape Town: Juta

Du Toit, D et al (2006) *Labour Relations Law: A Comprehensive Guide* 5th ed Durban: LexisNexis

Dworkin, R (1978) *Taking Rights Seriously* London: Duckworth

Dworkin, R (1986) *Law's Empire* London: Fontana Press

Dyzenhaus, D (1991) *Hard Cases in Wicked Legal Systems: South African Law in the Perspective of Legal Philosophy* New York: Oxford University Press

Dyzenhaus, D (2003) *Judging the Judges, Judging Ourselves: Truth, Reconciliation and the Apartheid Legal Order* Oxford, England: Hart

Ebrahim, H (1998) *The Soul of a Nation: Constitution-making in South Africa* Cape Town: Oxford University Press

Eide, A, Krause, C and Rosas, A (1995) *Economic, Social and Cultural Rights: A Textbook* Dordrecht: Martinus Nijhoff

Ellmann, SJ (1992) *In a Time of Trouble: Law and Liberty in South Africa's State of Emergency* New York: Oxford University Press

Ely, JH (1980) *Democracy and Distrust: A Theory of Judicial Review* Cambridge: Harvard University Press

Farlam, P 'Freedom of religion, belief and opinion' in Woolman, S and Bishop, M (2013) *Constitutional Law of South Africa* 2nd ed rev service 5 Cape Town: Juta

Forsyth, CF (1985) *In Danger for Their Talents: A Study of the Appellate Division of the Supreme Court of South Africa From 1950-1980* Cape Town: Juta

Friedman, S 'No easy stroll to dominance: Party dominance, opposition and civil society in South Africa' in Giliomee, HB and Simkins, CEW (eds) (1999) *The Awkward Embrace: One Party Domination and Democracy* Australia: Harwood Academic Publishers

Friedman E and Wong J (eds) (2008) *Political Transitions in Dominant Party Systems: Learning to Lose* Abingdon, Oxon; New York: Routledge

Ghai, Y and Cottrell, J (2004) *Economic, Social and Cultural Rights in Practice: The Role of Judges in Implementing Economic, Social and Cultural Rights* Commonwealth Secretariat

Ghai, Y and Cottrell, J 'The role of the courts in the protection of economic, social and cultural rights' in Ghai, Y and Cottrell, J (2004) *Economic, Social and Cultural Rights in Practice: The Role of Judges in Implementing Economic, Social and Cultural Rights* Commonwealth Secretariat

Giliomee, HB and Simkins, CEW (eds) (1999) *The Awkward Embrace: One Party Domination and Democracy* Australia: Harwood Academic Publishers

Ginsburg, T and Dixon, R (eds) (2011) *Comparative Constitutional Law* Cheltenham, UK; Northampton, MA: Edward Elgar

Gordon, A and Bruce, D (2006) *Transformation and Independence of the Judiciary in South Africa* Cape Town: Centre for Study of Violence and Reconciliation

Govindjee, A 'Freedom of expression' in Govindjee, A and Vrancken, P (eds) (2009) *Introduction to Human Rights Law* Durban: LexisNexis

Govindjee, A and Olivier, M 'Finding the boundary: The role of the courts in giving effect to socio-economic rights in South Africa' in Osode, PC and Glover, G (eds) (2010) *Law and Transformative Justice in Post-Apartheid South Africa* Louis Trichardt: Spekboom Publishers

Govindjee, A and Vrancken, P (eds) (2009) *Introduction to Human Rights Law* Durban: LexisNexis

Griffith, JAG and Ryle, M (1989) *Parliament: Functions, Practice and Procedures* London: Sweet & Maxwell

Grogan, J (2009) *Workplace Law* 10th ed Cape Town: Juta

Gumede, WM (2006) *Thabo Mbeki and the Battle for the Soul of the ANC* Cape Town: Zebra Press

Gutto, S (2001) *Equality and Non-Discrimination in South Africa: The Political Economy of Law and Law Making* Cape Town: NAE

Gwyn, WB (1965) *The Meaning of the Separation of Powers: An Analysis of the Doctrine from its Origin to the Adoption of the United States Constitution* New Orleans: Tulane University

Hahlo, HR and Kahn, E (1960) *The Union of South Africa: The Development of its Laws and Constitution* London: Stevens

Hall, DE, Bailey, SJD and Barron, C (2006) *Constitutional Law* Albany, New York: Delmar Pub

Handley, A, Murray, C and Simeon, R 'Learning to lose, learning to win: Government and opposition in South Africa's transition to democracy' in Friedman E and Wong J (eds) (2008) *Political Transitions in Dominant Party Systems: Learning to Lose* Abingdon, Oxon; New York: Routledge

Hassen, E (1998) *The Soul of a Nation: Constitution-Making in South Africa* Cape Town: Oxford University Press

Hatsell, J (1818) *Precedents of Proceedings in the House of Commons: With Observations vol 1* London: Hansard

Haynie, SL (2003) *Judging in Black and White: Decision Making in the South African Appellate Division 1950-1990* New York: P Lang

Haysom, N 'Federal features of the final Constitution' in Andrews, P and Ellmann, S (eds) (2001) *The Post-Apartheid Constitutions: Perspectives on South Africa's Basic Law* Johannesburg: Witwatersrand University Press

Haysom, N 'Dignity' in Cheadle, H, Davis, D and Haysom, N (eds) (2005) *South African Constitutional Law: The Bill of Rights* Durban: LexisNexis

Haysom, N and Kahanovitz, S 'Courts and the State of Emergency' in Moss, G and Obery, I (eds) (1987) *South African Review 4* Johannesburg: Ravan Press

Herman, ES and Chomsky, N (1988) *Manufacturing Consent: The Political Economy of the Mass Media* New York: Pantheon Books

Heun, W (2010) *The Constitution of Germany: A Contextual Analysis* Oxford: Hart

Hiebert, JL 'Constitutional experimentation: Rethinking how a bill of rights functions' in Ginsburg, T and Dixon, R (eds) (2011) *Comparative Constitutional Law* Cheltenham, UK; Northampton, MA: Edward Elgar

Hobsbawm, E and Ranger, T (eds) (1983) *The Invention of Tradition* Cambridge: Cambridge University Press

Hoexter, C (2007) *Administrative Law in South Africa* Cape Town: Juta

Hoexter, C 'The rule of law and the principle of legality in South African administrative law today' in Carnelley, M and Hoctor, S (eds) (2011) *Law, Order and Liberty: Essays in Honour of Tony Matthews* Pietermaritzburg: UKZN Press

Hogg, PW (2007) *Constitutional Law of Canada* 5th ed Scarborough, Ontario: Thomson Carswell

Holness, D and Vrancken, P 'Non-judicial enforcement of human rights' in Govindjee, A and Vrancken, P (eds) (2009) *Introduction to Human Rights Law* Durban: LexisNexis

Holness, D 'The right of access to information' in Govindjee, A and Vrancken, P (2009) *Introduction to Human Rights Law* Durban: LexisNexis

Houston, G (ed) (2001) *Public Participation in Democratic Governance in South Africa* Pretoria: HSRC

Houston, G, Liebenberg, I and Dichaba, W 'The social dynamics of public participation in legislative processes in South Africa' in Houston, G (ed) (2001) *Public Participation in Democratic Governance in South Africa* Pretoria: HSRC

Huglin, TO and Fenna, A (2006) *Comparative Federalism: A Systematic Inquiry* Peterborough: Ontario

Hurwitz, DR and Satterthwaite, ML (eds) (2009) *Human Rights Advocacy Stories* New York: Foundation Press

Institute for Public Policy Research (1991) *A Written Constitution for the United Kingdom* London: Mansell

Kairys, D (ed) (1998) *The Politics of Law: A Progressive Critique* New York: Basic Books

Jacobs, S and Calland, R (eds) (2002) *Thabo Mbeki's World: The Politics and Ideology of the South African President* Pietermaritzburg: University of Natal Press

King, AS (2007) *The British Constitution* Oxford; New York: Oxford University Press

Klaaren, J and Penflod, G 'Just administrative action' in Woolman, S and Bishop, M (eds) (2013) *Constitutional Law of South Africa* 2nd ed rev service 5 Cape Town: Juta

Klaaren, J 'Federalism' in Chaskalson, M et al (eds) (1996) *Constitutional Law of South Africa* 1st ed Cape Town: Juta

Klug, H (2010) *The Constitution of South Africa: A Contextual Analysis* Oxford; Portland Or: Hart

Kommers, DP (1997) *The Constitutional Jurisprudence of the Federal Republic of Germany* Durham, NC: Duke University Press

Kommers, DP, 'The Basic Law of the Federal Republic of Germany: An Assessment After Forty Years' in Merkl, PH (ed) (1989) *The Federal Republic of Germany at Forty*, New York: New York University Press

Kotze, H (1997) *Take Us to Our Leaders: The South African National Assembly and Its Members* Johannesburg: Konrad-Adenauer-Stiftung

Kriel, R and Monadjem, M 'Public finance' in Woolman S and Bishop M (2013) *Constitutional Law of South Africa* 2nd ed rev service 5 Cape Town: Juta

Kunig, P '*Der Rechtsstaat*' in Badura, P and Dreier, H (eds) (2001) *Festschrift 50 Jahre Bundesverfassungsgericht* Tubingen: Mohr Siebeck

Lacey, M (1981) *Working for Boroko: The Origins of a Coercive Labour System in South Africa* Johannesburg: Ravan Press

Le Roux, R 'Employment' in Du Bois, F (ed) (2007) *Wille's Principles of South African Law* 9th ed Cape Town: Juta

Liebenberg, S (2010) *Socio-Economic Rights Adjudication Under a Transformative Constitution* Cape Town: Juta

Liebenberg, S 'The interpretation of socio-economic rights' in Woolman, S and Bishop, M (eds) (2013) *Constitutional Law of South Africa* 2nd ed rev service 5 Cape Town: Juta

Locke, J (1690; 1986) *Second Treatise of Government* Cambridge: Hackett Publishing Co

Mamdani, M (1996) *Citizen and Subject: Contemporary Africa and the Legacy of Late Colonialism* Kampala: Fountain; Cape Town: David Phillip; London: James Currey

Mann, FA (1990) *Further Studies in International Law* Oxford: Clarendon Press

Matlosa, K (2004) *The Politics of State Resources: Party Funding in South Africa* Johannesburg: Konrad-Adenauer-Stiftung

Mendes, E 'The crucible of the Charter' in Beaudoin, GA and Mendes, E (eds) (1996) *The Canadian Charter of Rights and Freedoms* Scarborough, Ont: Carswell Legal

Merkl, PH (ed) (1989) *The Federal Republic of Germany at Forty*, New York: New York University Press

Michelman, F 'The rule of law, legality and the supremacy of the Constitution' in Woolman, S and Bishop, M (2013) *Constitutional Law of South Africa* 2nd ed rev service 5 Cape Town: Juta

Minow, M (1990) *Making All the Difference: Inclusion, Exclusion and American Law* Ithaca: Cornell University Press

Moss, G and Obery, I (eds) (1987) *South African Review 4* Johannesburg: Ravan Press

Motala, Z (1994) *Constitutional Options for a Democratic South Africa: A Comparative Perspective* Washington DC: Howard University Press 1994

Mqeke, RB (1997) *Basic Approaches to Problem Solving in Customary Law: A Study of Conciliation and Consensus Amongst the Cape Nguni* Grahamstown: Grocott & Sherry

Mtshaulana, PM 'The history and role of the Constitutional Court in South Africa' in Andrews, P and Ellmann, S (2001) *The Post-Apartheid Constitutions: Perspectives on South Africa's Basic Law* Johannesburg: Witwatersrand University Press

Munro, CR (1999) *Studies in Constitutional Law* 2nd ed London: Butterworths

Murray, C and Stacey, R 'The President and the National Executive' in Woolman, S and Bishop, M (2013) *Constitutional Law of South Africa* 2nd ed rev service 5 Cape Town: Juta

Nash, A 'Post-apartheid accountability: The transformation of a political idea' in Chirwa, DM and Nijzink, L (2012) *Accountable Government in Africa: Perspectives from Public Law and Political Studies* Cape Town: University of Cape Town Press

Nijzink, L and Murray, C (2002) *Building Representative Democracy: South Africa's Legislatures and the Constitution* Cape Town: Parliamentary Support Programme

Oomen, B (2005) *Chiefs in South Africa, Law, Power and Culture in the Post-Apartheid Era* Oxford: James Currey

Osode, PC and Glover, G (eds) (2010) *Law and Transformative Justice in Post-Apartheid South Africa* Louis Trichardt: Spekboom Publishers

Penfold, G and Reyburn, P 'Public procurement' in Woolman, S and Bishop, M (2013) *Constitutional Law of South Africa* 2nd ed rev service 5 Cape Town : Juta

Pottinger, B (1988) *The Imperial Presidency: PW Botha, The First Ten Years* Stellenbosch: Southern Book Publishers

Pradham, R (ed) (2002) *Legal Pluralism and Unofficial Law in Social, Economic and Political Development* International Centre for the Study of Nature, Environment and Culture

Rautenbach, IM and Malherbe, EFJ (2009) *Constitutional Law* 5th ed Durban: LexisNexis

Rautenbach, IM and Malherbe, EFJ (2012) *Constitutional Law* 6th ed Durban: LexisNexis

Reynolds, A (1999) *Electoral Systems and Democratisation in Southern Africa* New York: Oxford University Press

Roach, K 'Crafting Remedies for Violations of Economic, Social and Cultural Rights' in Squires, J (ed) (2005) *The Road to a Remedy: Current Issues in the Litigation of Economic, Social and Cultural Rights* Geneva, Switzerland: Centre for Housing Rights and Eviction

Roederer, C 'Founding provisions' in Woolman, S and Bishop, M (2013) *Constitutional Law of South Africa* 2nd ed rev service 5 Cape Town : Juta

Roux, T 'Democracy ' in Woolman, S and Bishop, M (2013) *Constitutional Law of South Africa* 2nd ed rev service 5 Cape Town: Juta

Scheinin, M 'Economic and social rights as legal rights' in Eide, A, Krause, C and Rosas, A (1995) *Economic, Social and Cultural Rights: A Textbook* Dordrecht: Martinus Nijhoff

Seedorf, S and Sibanda, S 'Separation of powers' in Woolman, S and Bishop, M (eds) (2013) *Constitutional Law of South Africa* 2nd ed rev service 5 Cape Town: Juta

Shue, H (1980) *Basic Rights: Subsistence, Affluence and US Foreign Policy* Princeton, NJ: Princeton University Press

Sinclair, J (1996) *The Law of Marriage, Vol 1* Cape Town: Juta

Smuts, D and Westcott, S (eds) (1991) *The Purple Shall Govern: A South African A-Z of Nonviolent Action* Cape Town: Oxford University Press, Centre For Intergroup Studies

Sparks, AH (1994) *Tomorrow is Another Country: The Inside Story of South Africa's Revolution* Johannesburg: Struik

Spitz, R and Chaskalson, M (2000) *The Politics of Transition: A Hidden History of South Africa's Negotiated Settlement* Johannesburg: Witwatersrand University Press

Squires, J (ed) (2005) *The Road to a Remedy: Current Issues in the Litigation of Economic, Social and Cultural Rights* Geneva, Switzerland: Centre for Housing Rights and Eviction

Stern, K (1977) *Das Staatsrecht der Bundesrepublik Deutschland vol 1* Munchen: Beck

Steytler, N 'The legislative framework governing party funding in South Africa' in Matlosa, K (2004) *The Politics of State Resources: Party Funding in South Africa* Johannesburg: Konrad-Adenauer-Stiftung

Steytler, N 'Co-operative and coercive models of intergovernmental relations: A South African case study' in Courchene, TJ and Allen, JR (eds) (2011) *The Federal Idea: Essays in Honour of Ronald L Watts* Kingston, Ont: Institute of Intergovernmental Relations, Queens University

Steytler, N and De Visser, J 'Local government' in Woolman, S and Bishop, M (eds) (2013)

Constitutional Law of South Africa 2nd ed rev service 5 Cape Town: Juta

Stone, GR (ed) (1996) *Constitutional Law* 3rd ed Boston: Little, Brown

Tribe, LH (1988) *American Constitutional Law* 2nd ed Foundation Press

Vail, L (ed) (1989) *The Creation of Tribalism in Southern Africa* London: James Currey

Van der Walt, AJ 'A South African reading of Frank Michelman's theory of social justice' in Botha, H, Van der Walt, AJ and Van der Walt, JC (2003) *Rights and Democracy in a Transformative Constitution* Stellenbosch: African Sun Media

Van Hoof, GJH (1984) 'The legal nature of economic, social and cultural rights: A rebuttal of some traditional views' in Alston, P and Tomasevski, K (eds) (1984) *The Right to Food* Dordrecht: Martinus Nijhoff Publishers

Van Niekerk, A (2012) *Law@Work* 2nd ed Durban: LexisNexis

Van Wyk, DH et al (eds) (1994) *Rights and Constitutionalism: The New South African Legal Order* Cape Town: Juta

Vani, MS 'Customary law and modern governance of natural resources in India: Conflicts, prospects for accord and strategies' in Pradham, R (ed) (2002) *Legal Pluralism and Unofficial Law in Social, Economic and Political Development* International Centre for the Study of Nature, Environment and Culture

Venter, F (2000) *Constitutional Comparison: Japan, Germany, Canada and South Africa as Constitutional States* Cape Town: Juta

Vile, MJC (1967) *Constitutionalism and the Separation of Powers* Oxford: Clarendon

Wade, ECS and Bradley, AW (1993) *Constitutional and Administrative Law* 11th ed London: Longman

Waldron, J (1999) *Law and Disagreement* New York: Oxford University Press

White, J 'Constitutional litigation and interpretation, and fundamental rights' (1994) *Annual Survey of South African Law* Cape Town: Juta

Williams, LA 'Welfare and legal entitlements: The social roots of poverty' in Kairys, D (ed) (1998) *The Politics of Law: A Progressive Critique* New York: Basic Books

Woolman, S 'Community rights: Language, culture and religion' in Woolman, S and Bishop, M (2013) *Constitutional Law of South Africa* 2nd ed rev service 5 Cape Town: Juta

Woolman, S 'Application' in Woolman, S and Bishop, M (eds) (2013) *Constitutional Law of South Africa* 2nd ed rev service 5 Cape Town: Juta

Woolman, S 'Assembly, demonstration, picket and petition' in Currie, I and De Waal, J (2013) *The Bill of Rights Handbook* 6th ed Cape Town: Juta

Woolman, S 'Freedom of association' in Woolman, S and Bishop, M (2013) *Constitutional Law of South Africa* 2nd ed rev service 5 Cape Town: Juta

Woolman, S 'The widening gyre of dignity' in Woolman, S and Bishop, M (2013) *Constitutional Law of South Africa* 2nd ed rev service 5 Cape Town: Juta

Woolman, S and Bishop, M (eds) (2013) *Constitutional Law of South Africa* 2nd ed rev service 5 Cape Town: Juta

Woolman, S and Roux, T 'Co-operative government and intergovernmental relations' in Woolman, S and Bishop, M (eds) (2013) *Constitutional Law of South Africa* 2nd ed rev service 5 Cape Town: Juta

Woolman, S and Swanepoel, J 'Constitutional history' in Woolman, S and Bishop, M (eds) (2013) *Constitutional Law of South Africa* 2nd ed rev service 5 Cape Town: Juta

Encyclopaedias

Britannica Academic Edition available at http://www.britannica.com/EBchecked/topic/231865/gerrymandering

Freedman, DW (2009) 'Constitutional law: Bill of Rights' in Joubert, WA (ed) (2012) *Law of South Africa* 2nd ed Vol 5 Part 4 Durban: Butterworths

Freedman, DW (2009) 'Constitutional law: Structures of government' in Joubert, WA (ed) (2012) *Law of South Africa* 2nd ed Vol 5 Part 4 Durban: Butterworths

Kohn, L and Corder, H (2013) 'Judicial regulation of administrative action' *International Encyclopaedia of Laws* available at http://www.ielaws.com/index.htm

Van der Vyver, JD (2009) 'Religion' in Joubert, WA (ed) *Law of South Africa* 2nd ed Vol 23 Durban: Butterworths

Journal Articles

(1987) Limburg Principles on the Implementation of the Covenant on Economic, Social and Cultural Rights *Human Rights Quarterly* 9(2):122–35

(1995, December) Bangalore Declaration and Plan of Action reprinted in International Commission of Jurists 55:219–27.

(1998) The Maastricht Guidelines on Violations of Economic, Social and Cultural Rights *Human Rights Quarterly* 20(3):691–704

Ackerman, B (2000) The new separation of powers *Harvard Law Review* 113(3):633–729

Ackermann, BA (1984) The Storrs Lectures: Discovering the Constitution *Yale Law Journal* 93:1013–72

Albertyn, C and Goldblatt, B (1998) Facing the challenge of transformation: Difficulties in the development of an indigenous jurisprudence of equality *South African Journal on Human Rights* 14(2):248–76

Alence, R (2004) South Africa after apartheid: The first decade *Journal of Democracy* 15(3):78–92

Alston, P and Scott, C (2000) Adjudicating constitutional priorities in a transnational context: A comment on *Soobramoney's* legacy and *Grootboom's* promise *South African Journal on Human Rights* 16(2):206–68

Bandes, S (1990) The negative constitution: A critique *Michigan Law Review* 88(8):2271–347

Basson, D (1987) Judicial activism in a State of Emergency: An examination of recent decisions of the South African courts *South African Journal on Human Rights* 3(1):28–43

Beall, J, Mkhize, S and Vawda, S (2005) Emergent democracy and 'resurgent' tradition: Institutions, chieftancy and transition in KwaZulu-Natal *Journal of Southern African Studies* 31(4):755–71

Beetham, D (2004) Towards a universal framework for democracy assessment *Democratization* 11(2):1–17

Berger, JM (2001) Litigation strategies to gain access to treatment for HIV/AIDS: The case of South Africa's Treatment Action Campaign *Wisconsin International Law Journal* 20:595–614

Berman, G and Feinblatt, J (2001) Problem-solving courts: A brief primer *Law and Policy* 23(2):125–40

Bilchitz, D (2003) Towards a reasonable approach to the minimum core: Laying the foundations for future socio-economic rights jurisprudence *South African Journal on Human Rights* 19(1):1–26

Bilchitz, D (2011) Should religious organisations be entitled to discriminate? *South African Journal on Human Rights* 27(2):219–48

Blaauw-Wolf, L and Wolf, J (1996) A comparison between German and South African limitation provisions *South African Law Journal* 113:267–96

Bollyky, TJ (2002) R if C>P+B: A paradigm for judicial remedies of socio-economic rights violations *South African Journal on Human Rights* 18(2):161–200

Botha, H (2009) Equality, plurality and structural power *South African Journal on Human Rights* 25(1):1–37

Botha, H (2010) Instituting public freedom or extinguishing constituent power? Reflections on South Africa's Constitution-making experiment *South African Journal on Human Rights* 26(1):66–84

Brand, D (1999) The South African Human Rights Commission: First economic and social rights report *ESR Review* 2(1):18–20

Brand, D (2002) Disclaimers in hospital admission contracts and constitutional health rights: Cases *ESR Review* 3(2)17–8

Brand, D and Liebenberg, S (2000) The South African Human Rights Commission: The second economic and social rights report *ESR Review* 2(3):12-6.

Brown, J (2012) Judges' history: On the use of history in the *Malema* judgment *South African Journal on Human Rights* 28(2):316-27

Calabresi, SG, Berghausen, ME and Albertson, S (2012) The rise and fall of the separation of powers *Northwestern University Law Review* 106(2):527-50

Cameron, E (1982) Legal chauvinism, executive-mindedness and justice: LC Steyn's impact on South African law *South African Law Journal* 99(1):38-75

Cameron, E (1993) Sexual orientation and the Constitution: A test case for human rights *South African Journal on Human Rights* 110(3):450-72

Carstens, PA and Kok, JA (2003) An assessment of the use of disclaimers against medical negligence by South African hospitals in view of constitutional demands, foreign law and medico-legal considerations *SA Public Law* 18(2):430-55

Chaskalson, A (2000) The Third Bram Fischer Lecture: Human dignity as a foundational value of our constitutional order *South African Journal on Human Rights* 16(2):193-205

Chemerinsky, E (1989) Foreword: The vanishing Constitution *Harvard Law Review* 103:43-102

Choudry, S (2009) 'He had a mandate': The South African Constitutional Court and the African National Congress in a dominant party democracy *Constitutional Court Review* 2:1-86

Corder, H (2004) Judicial authority in a changing South Africa *Legal Studies* 24(2):253-74

Cowen, S (2001) Can dignity guide South Africa's equality jurisprudence? *South African Journal on Human Rights* 17(1):34-58

Davis, DM (1992) The case against the inclusion of socio-economic demands in a bill of rights except as directive principles *South African Journal on Human Rights* 8(4):475-90

Davis, DM (1999) Equality: The majesty of legoland jurisprudence *South African Law Journal* 116:398-414

Davis, DM (2010) Judicial appointments in South Africa *Advocate* 40-43

Davis, DM (2012) How many positivist legal philosophers can be made to dance on the head of a pin? A reply to Professor Fagan *South African Law Journal* 129(1):59-72

Davis, DM (2013) The importance of reading: A rebuttal to the jurisprudence of Anton Fagan *South African Law Journal* 130(1):52-9

Davis, DM and Klare, K (2010) Transformative constitutionalism and the common and customary law *South African Journal on Human Rights* 26(3):403-509

Davis, RPB (1914) Women as advocates and attorneys *South African Law Journal* 31(4):383-86

De Lange, R and Mevis, PAM (2007) Constitutional guarantees for the independence of the judiciary *Electronic Journal of Comparative Law* 11(1):1-17

De Villiers, B (1994) Intergovernmental relations: The duty to co-operate - A German perspective *SA Public Law* 9(1-2):430-7

De Villiers, N (2002) Social grants and the Promotion of Administrative Justice Act *South African Journal on Human Rights* 18(3):320-49

De Vos, P (1997) Pious wishes or directly enforceable human rights: Social and economic rights in South Africa's 1996 Constitution *South African Journal on Human Rights* 13(1):67-101

De Vos, P (2000) Equality for all? A critical analysis of the equality jurisprudence of the Constitutional Court *Tydskrif vir Hedendaagse Romeins-Hollandse Reg* 63(1):62-75

De Vos, P (2001) A bridge too far? History as context in the interpretation of the South African Constitution *South African Journal on Human Rights* 17(1):1-33

De Vos, P (2001) *Grootboom*, the right of access to housing and substantive equality as contextual fairness *South African Journal on Human Rights* 17(2):258-76

De Vos, P (2004) The Promotion of Equality and Prevention of Unfair Discrimination Act and socio-economic rights *ESR Review* 5(2):7–11

De Vos, P (2009) Freedom of assembly and its limits *Without Prejudice* 9(8):4–5

De Vos, P (2012) The past is unpredictable: Race, redress and remembrance in the South African Constitution *South African Law Journal* 129(1):73–103

Deflem, M (1999) Warfare, political leadership and state formation: The case of the Zulu Kingdom, 1808-1879 *Ethnology* 38(4):371–91

Du Bois, F (2002) Tenure on the Constitutional Court *South African Law Journal* 119(1):1–17

Du Plessis, M (2002) Between apology and utopia: The Constitutional Court and public opinion *South African Journal on Human Rights* 18(1):1–40

Du Plessis, M and Scott, S (2013) The variable standard of rationality review : Suggestions for improved legality jurisprudence *South African Law Journal* 130(3):597–620

Dubow, S (1992) Afrikaner nationalism, apartheid and the conceptualization of race *Journal of African History* 33(2):209–37

Dugard, J (2007) Judging the judges: Towards an appropriate role for the role of the judiciary in South Africa's transformation *Leiden Journal of International Law* 20(4):965–81

Dupper, O (2004) In defence of affirmative action *South African Law Journal* 12(1):187–215

Dupper, O, MacEwan, M and Louw, A (2006) Employment equity in the tertiary sector in the Western Cape *International Journal of Discrimination and the Law* 8(3):191–212

Dyzenhaus, D (2007) The pasts and future of the rule of law in South Africa *South African Law Journal* 124(4):734–61

Elliot, M (2004) United Kingdom: Parliamentary sovereignty under pressure *International Journal of Constitutional Law* 2(3):545–627

Ellmann, SJ (1995) Law and legitimacy in South Africa *Law and Social Inquiry* 20(2):407–79

Fagan, A (1998) Dignity and unfair discrimination: A value misplaced and a right misunderstood *South African Journal on Human Rights* 14(2):220–47

Fagan, A (2010) The secondary role of the spirit, purport and objects of the Bill of Rights in the common law's development *South African Law Journal* 127(3):611–27

Fagan, A (2012) A straw man, three red herrings and a closet rule-worshipper: A rejoinder to Davis JP *South African Law Journal* 129(3):788–98

Forsyth, C (1991) Interpreting a bill of rights: The future task of a reformed judiciary *South African Journal on Human Rights* 7(1):1–23

Freeman, G (1983) The misguided search for the constitutional definition of religion *Georgetown Law Journal* 71(6):1519–66

Friedman, B (2002) The birth of an academic obsession: The history of the counter-majoritarian difficulty Part Five *Yale Law Journal* 112(2):153–260

Gibson, JL and Caldeira, GA (2003) Defenders of democracy? Legitimacy, popular acceptance and the South African Constitutional Court *Journal of Politics* 65(1):1–30

Giliomee, HB (1998) South Africa's emerging dominant-party regime *Journal of Democracy* 9(4):128–42

Giliomee, HB, Myburgh, J and Schlemmer, L (2001) Dominant party rule, opposition parties and minorities in South Africa *Democratization* 8(1):161–82

Group of Experts on Limburg Principles (1998) The Maastricht Guidelines on Violations of Economic, Social and Cultural Rights *Human Rights Quarterly* 20(3):691–704

Hamill, J (2004) The elephant and the mice: Election 2004 and the future of opposition politics in South Africa *The Round Table: The Commonwealth Journal of International Affairs* 93(377):691–708

Hendricks, F and Ntsebeza, L (1999) Chiefs and rural local government in post-apartheid South Africa *African Journal of Political Science* 4(1):99–126

Heyns, CH (1997) Extended medical training and the Constitution: Balancing civil and political rights and socio-economic rights *De Jure* 30(1):1–17

Heywood, M (2009) South Africa's Treatment Action Campaign: Combining law and social mobilization to realize the right to health *Journal of Human Rights Practice* 1(1):14–36

Higginbotham, FM (1994) Sins from the past and lessons for the future: Eliminating apartheid in South African public accommodation and the challenge to an enlightened judiciary *Boston University International Law Journal* 12(1):1–56

Hoexter, C (2004) The principle of legality in South African administrative law *Macquarie Law Journal* 3(4):165–86

Hutchinson, AC (1990) Mice under a chair: Democracy, courts and the administrative state *University of Toronto Law Journal* 40(3):374–404

Iles, K (2007) A fresh look at limitations: Unpacking section 36 *South African Journal on Human Rights* 23(1):68–92

Issacharoff, S (2002) Gerrymandering and political cartels *Harvard Law Review* 116(2):593–648

Kateb, G (1981) The moral distinctiveness of representative democracy *Ethics* 91(3):357–74

Kentridge, S (2003) The highest court: Selecting the judges *Cambridge Law Journal* 62(1):55–71

Kerr, AJ (1984) Back to the problems of a hundred or more years ago: Public policy concerning contracts relating to marriages that are potentially or actually polygamous *South African Law Journal* 101(3):445–56

Klare, K (1998) Legal culture and transformative constitutionalism *South African Journal on Human Rights* 14(1):146–88

Klare, K (2008) Legal subsidiarity and constitutional rights: A reply to AJ Van der Walt *Constitutional Court Review* 1:129–40

Kollapen, J (1999) Monitoring socio-economic rights: What has the SA Human Rights Commission done? *ESR Review* 1(4):18–20

Kuper, A (1997) Review: *The Mfecane Aftermath: Reconstructive Debates in Southern African History* by Carol Hamilton *Current Anthropology* 38(3): 471–3

Kurki, M (2012) Democracy and conceptual contestability: Reconsidering conceptions of democracy in democracy promotion *International Studies Review* 12(3):362–86

Langa, P (2006) Transformative constitutionalism *Stellenbosch Law Review* 17(3):351–60

Larkins, CM (1996) Judicial independence and democratization: A theoretical and conceptual analysis *American Journal of Comparative Law* 44(4):605–25

Lenta, P (2001) Just gaming? The case for postmodernism in South African legal theory *South African Journal on Human Rights* 17(2):173–209

Lenta, P (2004) Democracy, rights disagreements and judicial review *South African Journal on Human Rights* 20(1):1–31

Lenta, P (2012) The right of religious associations to discriminate *South African Journal on Human Rights* 28(2):231–57

Liebenberg, S (1995) 'The International Covenant on Economic, Social and Cultural Rights and its implications for South Africa *South African Journal on Human Rights* 11(2):359–78

Liebenberg, S (2005) The value of human dignity in interpreting socio-economic rights *South African Journal on Human Rights 21(1):1-31*

Lodge, T (2004) The ANC and the development of party politics in modern South Africa *Journal of Modern African Studies* 42(2):189–219

Lowry, MP (2008) Legitimizing elections through the regulation of campaign financing: A comparative constitutional analysis and hope for South Africa *Boston College International and Comparative Law Review* 31(2):185–212

Lucas M (2006) On gay porn *Yale Journal of Law and Feminism* 18(1):299–302

Madala, T (2001) Rule under apartheid and the fledging democracy in post-apartheid South Africa: The role of the judiciary *North Carolina Journal of International Law and Commercial Regulation* 26(3):743–66

Mafunisa, MJ (2008) The role of codes of conduct in promoting ethical conduct in the

South African public service *South African Journal of Labour Relations* 32(1):81–92

Magen, A (2008) The rule of law and its promotion abroad: Three problems of scope *Stanford Journal of International Law* 45(1):51–116

Mahomed, I (1998) The role of the judiciary in a constitutional state *South African Law Journal* 115(1):111–15

Malherbe, EFJ (1998) The South African National Council of Provinces: Trojan horse or white elephant? *Tydskrif vir die Suid-Afrikaanse Reg* 1:77–96

Malherbe, R (2007) Some thoughts on unity, diversity and human dignity in the new South Africa *Journal of South African Law/ Tydskrif vir die Suid-Afrikaanse Reg* 70(1):127–33

Malleson, K (1999) Assessing the performance of the Judicial Service Commission *South African Law Journal* 116(1):36–49

Maseko, TW (2009) The right of blind and visually impaired citizens to vote in secret: Is there a duty to do more? *SA Public Law* 24(2):623–39

Matlosa, K (2004) Electoral systems, constitutionalism and conflict management in Southern Africa *African Journal on Conflict Resolution* 4(2):11–53

Mbazira, C (2004) Reading the right to food into the African Charter on Human and Peoples' Rights *ESR Review* 5(1):5–7

McClain, CV (2002) The SA Human Rights Commission and socio-economic rights: Facing the challenges *ESR Review* 3(1):8–9

McWhinney, E (1957) The German Federal Constitutional Court and the Communist Party decision *Indiana Law Journal* 32(3):295–312

Michelman, FL (2003) The constitution, social rights, and liberal political justification *International Journal of Constitutional Law* 1(1):13–34

Ministerial Legal Task Team (1995, January) Explanatory Memorandum *Industrial Law Journal* 16(2):278–336

Modiri, J (2013) Race, realism and critique: The politics of race and *Afri-forum v Malema* in the Equality Court *South African Law Journal* 130(2):274–93

Moerane, M (2003) The meaning of transformation of the judiciary in the new South African context *South African Law Journal* 120(4):708–18

Mokgoro, Y (2010) Judicial appointments *Advocate* 43–8

Moseneke, D (2009) Transformative constitutionalism: its implications for the law of contract *Stellenbosch Law Review* 20(1):3–13

Motshabi, KB and Volks, SG (1991) Towards democratic chieftaincy: Principles and procedures *Acta Juridica* 104–15

Mureinik, E (1994) A bridge to where? Introducing South Africa's interim Bill of Rights *South African Journal on Human Rights* 10(1):31–48

Murray, C (2001) A constitutional beginning: Making South Africa's final Constitution *University of Arkansas at Little Rock Law Review* 23:809–38

Murray, C (2006) The Human Rights Commission et al: What is the role of South Africa's Chapter 9 institutions? *Potchefstroom Electronic Law Journal* 9(2):122–47

Murray, C and Simeon, R (1999) From paper to practice: The National Council of Provinces after its first year *SA Public Law* 14(1):96–141

Murray, C and Simeon, R (2000) South Africa's financial constitution: Towards better delivery *SA Public Law/Publiekreg* 15(2):477–504

Murray, C and Simeon, R (2006) Tagging Bills in Parliament: Section 75 or 76? *South African Law Journal* 123(2):232–63

Norris, P (1997) Choosing electoral systems: Proportional majoritarian and mixed systems *International Political Science Review* 18(3):297–312

Ntlama, N (2005) Unlocking the future: Monitoring court orders in respect of socio-economic rights *Tydskrif vir*

Hedendaagse Romeins-Hollandse Reg 68(1):81–9

O'Regan, K (2004) Human rights and democracy – A new global debate: Reflections on the first ten years of South Africa's Constitutional Court *International Journal of Legal Information* 38(2):200–16

O'Regan, K (2005) Checks and balances: Reflections on the development of the doctrine of separation of powers under the South African Constitution *Potchefstroom Electronic Law Journal* 8(1):120–50

Pieterse, M (1999) A different shade of red: Socio-economic dimensions of the right to life in South Africa *South African Journal on Human Rights* 15(3):372–85

Pieterse, M (1999) Traditional leaders win battle in undecided war *South African Journal on Human Rights* 15: 179–87

Pieterse, M (2003) Towards a useful role for section 36 of the Constitution in social rights cases? *Residents of Bon Vista Mansions v Southern Metropolitan Local Council South African Law Journal* 120(1):41–8

Pieterse, M (2004) Coming to terms with judicial enforcement of socio-economic rights *South African Journal on Human Rights* 20:383–417

Pieterse, M (2005) What do we mean when we talk about transformative constitutionalism? *SA Public Law/Publiekreg* 20:155–66

Pieterse-Spies, A (2011) Reasonableness, subsidiarity and service delivery: A case discussion *SA Public Law* 26(1):329–40

Pillay, K (2002) Implementation of *Grootboom*: Implications for the enforcement of socio-economic rights *Law, Democracy and Development* 6(2):255–77

Pillay, N and Prinsloo, C (1995) The changing face of 'traditional courts' *De Jure* 1:383

Plasket, C (2007) Post-1994 administrative law in South Africa: The Constitution, the Promotion of Administrative Justice Act 3 of 2000 and the common law *Speculum Juris* 21(1):25–40

Powell, C and Franco, J (2004) The meaning of institutional independence in *Van Rooyen v S South African Law Journal* 121(3):562–79

Pretorius, JL (2001) Constitutional standards for affirmative action in South Africa: A comparative overview *Heidelberg Journal of International Law* 61(8):403–57

Pretorius, JL (2010) Fairness in transformation: A critique of the Constitutional Court's affirmative action jurisprudence *South African Journal on Human Rights* 26(3):536–70

Price, A (2013) The evolution of the rule of law *South African Law Journal* 130:649

Pruitt, LR (2002) No black names on the letterhead? Efficient discrimination and the South African legal profession *Michigan Journal of International Law* 23(3):545–676

Rosenfeld, M (2001) The rule of law and the legitimacy of constitutional democracy *Southern California Law Review* 74(5):1307–52

Roux, T (2002) Understanding *Grootboom*: A response to Cass R Sunstein *Constitutional Forum* 12(2):41–51

Roux, T (2003) Legitimating transformation: Political resource allocation in the South African Constitutional Court *Democratisation* 10:92–111

Roux T (2009) Principle and pragmatism on the Constitutional Court of South Africa *International Journal of Constitutional Law* 7(1):106–38

Sabel, CF and Simon, WH (2004) Destabilisation rights: How public law litigation succeeds *Harvard Law Review* 117(4):1016–1101

Sarakinsky, I (2007) Political party finance in South Africa: Disclosure versus secrecy *Democratization* 14(1):111–28

Scarrow, SE (2001) Direct democracy and institutional change: A comparative investigation *Comparative Political Studies* 34(6):651–65

Scott, IG (1987) The role of the Attorney-General and the Charter of Rights *Criminal Law Quarterly* 29(2):187–99

Sherman, JG (1995) Love speech: The social utility of pornography *Stanford Law Review* 47(4):661–706

Simeon, R and Murray, C (2001) Multi-sphere governance in South Africa: An interim assessment *Publius: The Journal of Federalism* 31(4):65–92

Simon, WH (1986) Rights and redistribution in the welfare system *Stanford Law Review* 38(6):1431–1516

Southall, R (1994) The South African elections of 1994: The remaking of a dominant-party state *The Journal of Modern African Studies* 32(4):629–55

Southall, R (1998) The centralization and fragmentation of South Africa's dominant party system *African Affairs* 97(389):443–69

Southall, R (2001) Conclusion: Emergent perspectives on opposition in South Africa *Democratization* 8(1):275–84

Southall, R (2001) Opposition in South Africa: Issues and problems *Democratization* 8(1):1–24

Southall, R (2005) The 'dominant party debate' in South Africa *Afrika Spectrum* 40(1):61–82

Sprigman, C and Osborne, M (1999) Du Plessis is *not* dead: South Africa's 1996 Constitution and the application of the Bill of Rights to private disputes *South African Journal on Human rights* 15(1):25–51

Steytler, N and Williams, RF (2012) Squeezing out provinces' legislative competence in *Premier: Limpopo Province v Speaker: Limpopo Provincial Legislative and others I and II South African Law Journal* 129(4):621–37

Summers, CW (1964) Freedom of association and compulsory unionism in Sweden and the United States *University of Pennsylvania Law Review* 112(5):674–96

Sunstein, CR (2001) Social and economic rights? Lessons from South Africa *Constitutional Forum* 11(4):123–32

Suttner, R (2006) Party dominance theory: Of what value? *Politikon: SA Journal of Political Studies* 33(3):277–97

Tladi, D (2002) One step forward, two steps back for constitutionalising the common law: *Afrox Health Care v Strydom SA Public Law* 17(2):473–78

Tomaselli, KJ (2008) Exogenous and endogenous democracy: South African politics and media *International Journal of Press/Politics* 13(2):171–80

Trengove, W (1999) Judicial remedies for violations of socio-economic rights *ESR Review* 1(4):8–11

Tshitereke, C (2002) Securing democracy: Party finance and party donations – The South African challenge *Institute for Security Studies* 63:1–12

Van der Merwe, D (1989) Land tenure in South Africa: A brief history and some reform proposals *Journal of South African Law* 4:663–92

Van der Vyver JD (1993) The separation of powers *SA Public Law/Publiekreg* 8:177–91

Van der Walt, AJ (2002) Exclusivity of ownership, security of tenure, and eviction orders: A model to evaluate South African land-reform legislation *Journal of South African Law* 2:254–89

Van der Walt, AJ (2002) Sosiale geregtigheid, prosedurele billikheid, en eiendom: Alternatiewe perspektiewe op grondwetlike waarborge (Deel Een) *Stellenbosch Law Review* 13(5):59–82

Van der Walt, AJ (2008) Normative pluralism and anarchy: Reflections on the 2007 term *Constitutional Court Review* 1:77

Van der Walt, J and Botha, H (2000) Democracy and rights in South Africa: Beyond a constitutional culture of justification *Constellations* 7(3):341–62

Van Reenen, TP (1997) Equality, discrimination and affirmative action: An analysis of section 9 of the Constitution of the Republic of South Africa *SA Publiekreg/Public Law* 12(1):151–65

Van Zyl, D (2009) The judiciary as a bastion of the legal order in challenging times *Potchefstroom Electronic Law Journal* 12(2):1–13

Venter, F (2010) Liberal democracy: The unintended consequence – South African constitution-writing propelled by the winds of globalisation *South African Journal on Human Rights* 26(1):45–65

Wesson, M and Du Plessis, M (2008) Fifteen years on: Central issues relating to the transformation of the South African judiciary *South African Journal on Human Rights* 24(2):187–213

Westen, P (1982) The empty idea of equality *Harvard Law Review* 95(3):537–96

White, S (1997) Freedom of association and the right to exclude *The Journal of Political Philosophy* 5(4):373–91

Woolman, S (2007) The amazing vanishing Bill of Rights *South African Law Journal* 124(4):762–94

Woolman, S (2012) Seek justice elsewhere: An egalitarian pluralist's reply to David Bilchitz on the distinction between differentiation and domination *South African Journal on Human Rights* 28(2):273–95

Woolman, S and Davis, D (1996) The last laugh: *Du Plessis v De Klerk*, classical liberalism, creole liberalism and the application of fundamental rights under the interim and final Constitutions *South African Journal on Human Rights* 12(2):361–404

Papers

Conradie, J (2011, April) The evolution of accounting standards in the public sector, Unpublished Paper, available at http://www.accountancysa.org.za

Cowen, S (2010) Judicial selection in South Africa, Democratic Governance Rights Unit (DGRU) Paper, available at http://www.dgru.uct.ac.za/usr/dgru/downloads/Judicial%20SelectionOct2010.pdf.

Lewis, C (2008, 14 October) The troubled state of South Africa's judiciary, Paper presented at the South African Institute of Race Relations, available at http://www.politicsweb.co.za/politicsweb/view/politicsweb/en/page71619?oid=106544&sn=Detail

Memeza, M (2006) A critical review of the implementation of the Regulation of Gatherings Act 205 of 1993: A local government and civil society perspective available at http://www.fxi.org.za

Ntlama, N (2009, 16–20 July) The Hlophe saga: the question for the institutional integrity of the judiciary, Paper presented at the Law Teachers Conference in Pietermaritzburg, available at http://wenku.baidu.com/view/6c6473f0fab069dc50220111.html

Roux, T (2007) Tactical adjudication: How the Constitutional Court of South Africa survived its first decade 29, available at http://www.saifac.org.za/docs/2007/Tactical%20Adjudication.pdf

The South African National Assembly after ten years of democracy Working paper No 134, Centre for Social Science Research: Democracy in Africa Research Unit, University of Cape Town at 9–11, available at http://www.cssr.uct.ac.za/sites/cssr.uct.ac.za/files/pubs/wp134.pdf

Yacoob, Z (2012) 'The Dynamic Constitution', Keynote Address, University of Cape Town Constitution Week, 12 March 2012, available at http://constitutionallyspeaking.co.za/justice-zac-yacoob-on-the-dynamic-constitution/

Reports

Annual Report of Parliament 1999 and 2000 available at http://www.pmg.org.za/minutes/20011018-sita-annual-report-19992000-briefing

Hendricks, C (2005) 'Party strategy not popular prejudice: Electoral politics in South Africa' in Piper L (ed) *South Africa's 2004 Election: The Quest for Democratic Consolidation, EISA Research Report no 12,* Johannesburg: EISA

Parliament of the Republic of South Africa (2007) *Report of the Ad Hoc Committee on the Review of Chapter 9 and Associated Institutions* A report to the National Assembly of the Parliament of South Africa, Cape Town, South Africa available at http://www.parliament.gov.za/content/chapter_9_report.pdf

Presidential Review Commission (1998) *Report on the Reform and Transformation of the Public Service in South Africa* available at http://www.info.gov.za/otherdocs/1998/prc98/index.html

Report of the Independent Panel Assessment of Parliament (Govender Report) available at http://www.info.gov.za/ view/ DownloadFileAction?id=94365

South Africa Commission of Inquiry into Labour Legislation Wiehahn, NE (1980) *Report of the Commission of Inquiry into Labour Legislation* Republic of South Africa, Department of Manpower Utilisation

South African Human Rights Commission (2006) *The Exclusionary Policies of Voluntary Associates: Constitutional Considerations* Pretoria: South African Human Rights Commission

South African Human Rights Commission (2010) *Golden Key Awards Report on Access to Information in South Africa* (with the Open Democracy Advice Centre) available at http://www.opendemocracy.org.za/ wp-content/uploads/2010/10/2010-GKA-REPORT.pdf.

South African Law Reform Commission (2003) *Customary Law: Report on Traditional Courts and the Judicial Function of Traditional Leaders* Project 90 Pretoria: South African Law Reform Commission

Truth and Reconciliation Commission of South Africa (1998) *Report: Volume 1 Chapter 8 The Destruction of Records* para 24; *Volume 2 Chapter 2 The State Outside SA Between 1960 and 1990*

Newspaper and magazine articles

Allen, J (2005, 14 June) South Africa: President Mbeki relieves Deputy President Zuma of post *AllAfrica* available at http://allafrica.com/stories/200506140114.html

Chaskalson, A (2009, 25 June) Does Hlophe approve of campaign on his behalf? *Cape Times*

Donnelly, L (2011, 23 June) Secrecy bill extension welcomed - concerns remain *Mail & Guardian* Newspapers available at http://mg.co.za/article/2011-06-23-secrecy-bill-extension-welcomed-concerns-remain.

Friedman, S (2012, 6 August) Secrecy Bill *Business Day Live* available at http://www.bdlive.co.za/articles/2011/11/22/ steven-friedman-secrecy-bill

Friedman, S (2012, 6 August) State secrecy is the real threat to our security *Business Day Live* available at http://www. businessday.co.za/ articles/Content.aspx?id=128285

Hartley, R (2008, 23 September) The five big mistakes that cost Mbeki the Presidency *TimesLive* available at http://blogs.timeslive.co.za/hartley/2008/09/23/ the-five-big-mistakes-that-cost-mbeki-the-presidency

Hoffman, P (2011, 2 December) To judge the judgments *Mail & Guardian* available at http://mg.co.za/ article/2011-12-02-to-judge-the-judgments

Malefane, M (2012, 1 April) Turok going juju route? *Sunday World* available at http://www.sundayworld.co.za/ news/2012/04/01/turok-going-juju-route

Mbete, S and February, J (2011, 5 April) Access to Parliament is a right not a privilege *Business Day Live* available at http://www.bdlive.co.za/ articles/2011/04/05/sthembile-mbete-and-judith-february-access-to-parliament-is-a-right-not-a-privilege;jsessionid=8485BDB17C0C6F9F61B042C08A00C41E.present1.bdfm

Mkhabela, M (2011, 19 August) Judiciary must be de-politicised *The Sowetan* available at http://www.sowetanlive.co.za/columnists/ 2011/08/19/judiciary-must-be-de-politicised

Taljaard, R (2012, 20 March) The day my idealism was extinguished *The Star* available at http://www.iol.co.za/the-star/ the-day-my-idealism-was-extinguished-1.1260059#.UGxEGjkWHzI

Blogs

De Vos, P (2008, 8 December) National security, the last refuge of scoundrels? *Constitutionally Speaking* available at http://constitutionallyspeaking.co.za/ national-security-the-last-refuge-of-scoundrels/

De Vos, P (2011, 31 May) Let me tell you a secret ... *Constitutionally Speaking* available at http://constitutionallyspeaking.co.za/ let-me-tell-you-a-secret/

De Vos, P (2011, 12 September) Malema judgment: A re-think on hate speech needed *Constitutionally Speaking* available at http://constitutionallyspeaking.co.za/malema-judgment-a-re-think-on-hate-speech-needed

De Vos, P (2011, 24 November) Cabinet statement on transformation of judicial system *Constitutionally Speaking* available at http://constitutionallyspeaking.co.za/cabinet-statement-on-transformation-of-judicial-system/

De Vos, P (2012, 14 August) Towards a parliament for the people *Constitutionally Speaking* available at http://constitutionallyspeaking.co.za/towards-a-parliament-for-the-people/

De Vos, P (2012, 25 September) Sharp divisions on the Constitutional Court about the right to strike *Constitutionally Speaking* available at http://constitutionallyspeaking.co.za/sharp-divisions-on-the-constitutional-court-about-the-right-to-strike/

De Vos, P (2012, 10 October) One small step for Parliament, one giant leap for Ambrosini *Constitutionally Speaking* available at http://constitutionallyspeaking.co.za/once-small-step-for-parliament-one-giant-leap-for-ambrosini/

De Vos, P (2013, 21 January) Judicial appointments: The JSC's transformation problem *Constitutionally Speaking* available at http://constitutionallyspeaking.co.za/judicial-appointments-the-jscs-transformation-problem/

De Vos, P (2013, 11 April) The JSC must redefine merit to advance judicial transformation *Constitutionally Speaking* available at http://constitutionallyspeaking.co.za/the-jsc-must-redefine-merit-to-advance-judicial-transformation/

Gauntlett, J and Du Plessis, M (2011, 25 August) Ex Parte: Freedom under Law, In re: The Appointment of the Chief Justice Memorandum 10–11 *Constitutionally Speaking* available at http://constitutionallyspeaking.co.za/ful-proposes-changes-to-appointment-of-chief-justice/

Judicial Service Commission, Summary of the Criteria Used by the Judicial Service Commission when Considering Candidates for Judicial Appointments *Constitutionally Speaking* available at http://constitutionallyspeaking.co.za/criteria-used-by-jsc-when-considering-judicial-appointments/

Webliography

African National Congress 53rd National Conference Resolutions 4. Legislature and Governance 4.2.1 28 available at http://www.anc.org.za/docs/res/2013/resolutions53r.pdf

African National Congress Constitution, as amended and adopted at the 52nd National Conference, Polokwane, 2007, available at http://www.anc.org.za/show.php?id=207

African National Congress Constitution, as amended and adopted at the 53nd National Conference, Mangaung, 2012, available at http:// www.anc.org.za/show.php?id=10177

Centre for Human Rights University of Pretoria *Law of Lagos* available at http://www1chr.up.ac.za/images/files/documents/ ahrdd/theme36/rule_of_law_lagos_1961.pdf

Code of Conduct for Assembly and Permanent Council Members available at http://www.parliament.gov. za/live/content.php?Item_ID=235

Congress for a Democratic South Africa (CODESA): *Declaration of Intent signed on 21 December 1991* available at http://www.anc.org.za/show.php?id=3968&t=Transition

Democratic Alliance (2010) *Regulations for the Nomination of Candidates* available at http://www.da.org.za/about.htm?action=view-page&category=469

District Six: Recalling the forced removals *South African History Archive* available at http://www.saha.org.za/news/2010/February/district_six_recalling_the_forced_removals.htm

Donnelly, L (2011, 23 June) Secrecy bill extension welcomed – concerns remain *Mail & Guardian* Newspapers available at http://mg.co.za/article/2011-06-23-secrecy-bill-extension-welcomed-concerns-remain.

Inside Rustenburg's banned protests (2013, 7 March) available at http://www.ru.ac.za/facultyofhumanities/latestnews/name,79323,en.html

Inter-Parliamentary Union (2013) *Women in national parliaments* available at http://www.ipu. org/wmn-e/classif.htm

Kirshner, J and Phokela, C (2010) *Khutsong and xenophobic violence: Exploring the case of the dog that didn't bark* available at http://www.gcro.ac.za/sites/default/files/News_items/Xeno_reports_July2010/case_studies/5_Khutsong_reprint_lowres.pdf

Law, Race and Gender Institute (Centre for Law and Society) (2012) *Submission on the Traditional Courts Bill (B1-2012)* available at http://www.cls.uct.ac.za/usr/lrg/docs/TCB/2012/lrg_feb2012_ncopsubmission.pdf

Lowe Morna, C, Rama, K and Mtonga, L (2009, 15 July) *Gender in the 2009 South African elections, Gender links for equality and justice*, available at http://www.genderlinks.org.za/article/gender-in-the-2009-south-african-elections-2009-07-15

Mandela, N (1992) Press statement available at http://www.sahistory.org.za/archive/press-statement-nelson-r-mandela-president-anc-ancnp-summit-meeting-world-trade-centre-johan

Memeza, M (2006) *A critical review of the implementation of the Regulation of Gatherings Act 205 of 1993: A local government and civil society perspective* available at http://www.fxi.org.za.

Mthembu, J (2012, 4 February) *ANC statement on the National Disciplinary Committee of appeal today* available at http://www.anc.org.za/show.php?id=9363

Parliament of the Republic of South Africa (2009) *Oversight and Accountability Model: Asserting Parliament's Oversight Role in Enhancing Democracy* available at http://www.parliament.gov.za/content/Microsoft%20 Word%20-%20OVAC%20 Model%20-%20edited%20Word%20 version%20-%20Replaced%20 Diagrams,Chapter%20 Upper%20 case_27-Jan-09~1~1.pdf

Parliament of the Republic of South Africa (2011, June) *Rules of the National Assembly* 7th ed available at http://www. pmg.org.za/files/doc/2012/NA%20Rules%207th%20 edition-1.pdf

Parliament of the Republic of South Africa (2008, March) *Rules of the National Council of Provinces* 9th ed available at http://www.pmg.org. za/parlinfo/ncoprules

Policy Framework on the Traditional Justice System under the Constitution, Department of Justice and Constitutional Development 10, available at http://www.pmg.org.za/policy-documents/2009/03/02/policy-framework-traditional-justice-system-under

Role and Functions of the South African Reserve Bank available at http://www.resbank.co.za/AboutUs/Functions/Pages/default.aspx

Segalwe, O (2011, 16 March) *Chief Justice Ngcobo highlights the importance of the Public Protector* available at http://www.pprotect.org.

South Africa: 2009 National Assembly Election Results, Electoral Institute for Sustainable Democracy in Africa, available at http://www.eisa.org.za/WEP/sou2009results1.htm

South African Government News Agency (2009, August) *Address by Defence and Military Veterans Minister, Lindiwe Sisulu, on the Illegal March by SANDF Members to the Union Buildings* available at http://www.sanews.gov.sa/south-africa/address-defence-and-military-veterans-minister-lindiwe-sisulu-illegal-march-sandu

Table of cases

B

C

D

E

F

G

H

I

T

U

Table of legislation

FOREIGN LEGISLATION

Glossary

analogous ground: A ground of discrimination, such as HIV status, not explicitly mentioned in the Constitution, but sufficiently similar to the grounds mentioned in the Constitution because it also deals with different treatment of people who have suffered past discrimination, prejudice or marginalisation because of their membership of the group.

apartheid: A system of absolute racial segregation and political and economic discrimination applied against non-European groups in the Republic of South Africa by the white minority. Grand apartheid envisaged that white South Africans would govern the vast majority of the South African territory while black South Africans would be provided with independent or semi-independent homelands in which they would be 'allowed' to exercise political rights.

apex court: The highest court of law in a country which usually has the final say on any matter of law. A court can be an apex court for certain subject matters like constitutional issues only (as is the case in South Africa) or it can be the apex court for all legal issues (as is the case in the US).

authoritarian system: A system of government that favours a concentration of power in a leader, a political party or an elite who are not democratically elected by the majority of the people, are not accountable to them and do not rule in their best interest.

autonomy: The ability to make decisions freely about your life as an individual without being forced to do so by your family, your community or other cultural or religious institutions.

bicameralism: The legislative system which has two distinct houses of the legislature whose members are elected or appointed in two distinct ways to serve different interests. The houses are jointly tasked with fulfilling the various tasks of the legislature, including the passing of legislation which usually requires the support of a majority of members from both houses of the legislature to become law.

bifurcated state: A state in which different systems of government apply to different people within the same territory, based on the race, ethnicity, language or other characteristics of the governed.

Bill: A draft law that the legislature is discussing and considering. Once the President duly passes and signs the Bill, it becomes an Act of the legislature.

blue rights: The collective name for a group of human rights often distinguished (somewhat arbitrarily) from other types of rights on the basis that they are first generation rights consisting largely of civil and political rights.

branch of government: The name given in constitutional theory to the three pillars of government usually distinguished from each other when discussing the separation of powers doctrine. These three pillars are the legislature, the executive and the judiciary.

burden of proof or justification: The question of which party has to provide evidence to prove or disprove relevant facts and what standard will be used to decide whether the party has managed to prove or disprove the relevant set of facts.

case law: The binding legal principles developed by courts when handing down judgments on the interpretation and application of statutes, common law or customary law.

certification process: The process which required the Constitutional Court to test the final Constitution to determine whether it complied with the 34 Constitutional Principles contained in the interim Constitution.

checks and balances: The concept closely associated with the doctrine of separation of powers which envisages that each of the three branches of government (the legislature, the executive and the judiciary) will act as a check (or brake) on the exercise of power by the other two branches to prevent the abuse of power and to ensure accountable government.

citizenship: The status acquired by individual persons formally associated with (or linked to) a state and consequently who have certain rights and duties in relation to the state. These rights and duties include the right to live and work in the country and to obtain a passport from the state. A person with citizenship in a state is called a citizen of the state.

civil and political rights: The collective name for a group of human rights often distinguished (somewhat arbitrarily) from other types of rights such as social and economic rights on the basis that they are first generation rights as they emerged early in the development of human rights. This set of rights includes rights such as the right to vote, freedom of speech and assembly, freedom of religion and the right to equality.

coalition government: A government formed jointly by the elected representatives of two or more political parties, usually when none of the parties had obtained a majority of more than 50% of seats in the legislature. The government then governs according to principles set out in a coalition agreement concluded by the parties which enter the coalition.

collective accountability: The principle that each member of the executive is accountable for the decisions and actions of all other members of the executive and should, hence, not publically criticise the statements or actions of fellow members of the executive. This principle is based on the assumption that the members of the executive branch of government act as a team and approve all important decisions of the executive.

colonialism: The establishment, maintenance, acquisition and expansion of colonies in one territory by people from another territory. It is a process whereby an economically and militarily powerful government claims the right to govern the people of another territory, imposing its language, values and government structures on the colony and establishing an unequal, exploitative relationship with that colony.

common law: The set of legal rules and principles not contained in legislation duly passed by the legislature, but rather inherited from the colonial powers and which are continuously being developed and enforced by the judiciary.

conscience: The awareness of a moral or ethical aspect to one's conduct together with the urge to prefer right over wrong, regardless of whether that awareness stems from religious beliefs or from ethical commitments not related to religious beliefs at all.

constitutional damages: Where a court finds that a person or institution has infringed the constitutional rights of an individual and (in the absence of other appropriate remedies) orders the person or institution to pay a sum of money to the aggrieved party to remedy the constitutional infringement.

constitutional democracy: Also known as a liberal democracy, this is a common form of representative democracy in which citizens take part in regular, free and fair elections in a competitive political process but a constitution sets out the limits of the powers to be exercised by those representatives elected to represent the people.

contextual analysis: The opposite of considering a legal question in the abstract as if the surrounding circumstances prevalent in a society are irrelevant. Contextual analysis takes into account the differences in the economic position as well as the social status of individuals and the way in which the society is structured to privilege some and disadvantage others.

counter-majoritarianism: The conceptual difficulty associated with the enforcement of the provisions of a supreme constitution by the judiciary. This difficulty arises because unelected judges without a mandate from voters are empowered to thwart the will of the democratically elected legislature and executive by declaring invalid their actions, thus acting in a counter-majoritarian manner.

customary law: Traditional common rule or practice that has become an intrinsic part of the accepted and expected conduct in a community, is enforced by that community and can also be changed over time by that community. In South Africa, customary law usually refers to the laws developed and applied by indigenous peoples and is contrasted to the common law imposed by colonial rulers.

damages: the sum of money a court orders a person or institution to pay to somebody to compensate for the financial or emotional harm or 'damage' suffered by the aggrieved party because of actions taken by the person or institution ordered to pay the damages.

delegation of legislative authority: Where a legislature (parliament or provincial legislature) entrusts the power it originally had to pass primary or subordinate legislation to another body which is then empowered legally to pass the said legislation despite not originally having been entitled to do so.

developing the common law: A process through which judges, hearing specific cases, continuously revisit the general principles of the common law and adapt these rules to ensure that they are in line with the general norms embodied in the Bill of Rights.

dialogic model of the separation of powers: The idea that the tension between the legislature, executive and judiciary, arising from the separation of powers between them, can be resolved by envisaging the relationship between these three branches as one in which a structured conversation shapes the relationship between the branches.

direct discrimination: Where a rule or policy explicitly distinguishes between groups of people to the detriment of one group, based on either a ground listed in section 9(3) of the Constitution or on a similar analogous ground.

disputes of interest: Such disputes arise in the labour law context but, unlike other labour disputes, they are not based on any existing right. Instead, employees or their unions approach the employer to establish a new right. If the employer does not want to give employees what they want and the matter remains unresolved, then the employees may exercise their right to strike after following the appropriate procedures.

diversity: Diversity refers to the fact that not all individuals have the same cultures, languages or religious beliefs, creating a diverse population whose differences must be accommodated without harming others.

divided model of federalism: A model of federalism in which the Constitution strictly divides the subject matters in respect of which policies and laws may be made by each sphere of government. Each level or sphere of government, therefore, has its own exclusive powers and there are very few, if any, concurrent or shared powers.

doctrine of objective invalidity: Also referred to as the doctrine of objective unconstitutionality, this is the principle that any legislative provision or action which is in conflict with the Constitution is assumed to be invalid from the moment that the conflict first arose. When a court confirms the unconstitutionality and hence invalidity of the legislative provision or action, it will automatically be invalid retrogressively from the moment the conflict arose unless the court orders otherwise.

electoral system: The mechanism through which the number of votes cast by voters for each political party is translated into the number of seats for each of the parties in the legislature. Different electoral systems produce different levels of representation for different parties in the legislature.

equitable: A requirement that different institutions, beliefs or practices must be treated fairly, but excluding the requirement that they must be treated in an identical fashion.

final Constitution: The Constitution finally adopted by the democratically elected Constitutional Assembly in 1996 in terms of which South Africa has been governed since 1997.

first generation rights: See the definition for 'civil and political rights'.

formal equality: The idea that individuals are born free and equal and that the law should treat people the same, regardless of their personal circumstances, their history, their social and economic status, and whether they have been discriminated against in the past or still face discrimination in the present. The concept explicitly denies the need to take into account the social and economic context or the differences in power, status and opportunities between individuals or groups of individuals when judging whether the equality injunction has been breached or not.

general administrative law: The principles of administrative law that are applicable to all administrative entities, as opposed to specific administrative law which applies to specific areas such as education, the environment, the police, the revenue service and so on.

good faith: The presumption that a person (in constitutional law often a public official exercising public power) will act in an honest and fair manner and not out of spite or in an arbitrary, capricious, dishonest or corrupt manner.

green rights: Also sometimes (somewhat loosely) referred to as third generation rights. These are a set of rights that emerged recently (towards the end of the twentieth century) and are aimed at protecting society more broadly. The rights include the right to self-determination, the right to development and the right to a healthy environment.

guardian of the Constitution: Normally refers to the judiciary whose task it is to interpret and enforce the Constitution and hence to guard against breaches of the Constitution.

heterogeneous: Made up of different parts. In the context of constitutional law, it refers to the fact that there are many different people from different races, cultures, languages and social and economic backgrounds living in South Africa.

horizontal application: Traditionally, a constitution only binds the state and prohibits it from infringing on the rights of private individuals and institutions (and is said to apply vertically only). The South African Constitution applies horizontally as, in certain cases, it also binds private individuals and institutions and prohibits them from infringing on the rights of others.

horizontal dispute: A legal dispute between private parties (in other words, a dispute in which state institutions are not involved) regarding the scope and content of the duties imposed on such a private party by any of the rights in the Constitution.

human rights: A set of norms and standards contained in a bill of rights or international human rights treaty aimed at protecting the human dignity and other fundamental interests of individuals, which binds the state (and sometimes other parties) and is usually enforced by independent courts or tribunals.

in limine: Literally, 'at the threshold', this Latin term refers to a motion made before a trial begins which asks the court, for example, to rule on a preliminary legal point or on the exclusion of certain evidence.

incidental power: Usually refers to powers that strictly speaking fall outside the matters over which a particular branch in a specific sphere of government has legislative or executive authority, but which are so closely connected to the effective performance of its functions that they are considered to be a part of the matters over which the body has authority.

indigenous populations: Ethnic groups who lived in a territory before the arrival of a colonising power. They are groups of people whose members share a cultural identity that has been shaped by their geographical region and by their experiences of oppression.

indirect discrimination: Different treatment either on grounds listed in section 9(3) or on analogous grounds where the ground for the different treatment is based on a seemingly 'neutral' factor (such as a person's height or where a person lives), but where the differentiation disproportionately affects a group listed in section 9(3) or a group analogous to section 9(3).

individual accountability: The principle that individual members of the executive (members of the cabinet at national level) are responsible for their own portfolios and are accountable for what occurs in their departments.

integrated model of federalism: Where some subject matters are allocated exclusively to one level or sphere of government, but most powers are concurrent or shared and where the subject matters in respect of which policies and laws may be made are thus not strictly divided between the different levels or spheres of government.

interim Constitution: The South African Constitution agreed to by the undemocratic MPNF in 1993, according to which South Africa was governed between 1994 and 1996 while a final Constitution was being negotiated. It contained the 34 Constitutional Principles with which the final Constitution had to comply and prescribed the process for the adoption of the final Constitution.

judicial authority: The term for the power given to judges that allows them to hear a case and to decide in favour of one party.

judicial independence: The notion that judges should be free from interference by the other branches of government or private parties and which is achieved by providing institutional safeguards.

judicial review: The process through which judges review the constitutionality of actions taken by the legislature, executive or private parties and declare such actions invalid if they are in conflict with the Constitution.

judiciary: One of the three branches of government, staffed by judicial officers and led by the Chief Justice.

jurisdiction: The legal authority of members of the judiciary to hear and determine judicial disputes in a specific geographical area or on specific subject matter.

juristic person: An artificial entity through which the law allows a group of natural persons to act as if they were a single composite individual for certain purposes. This legal fiction does not mean these entities are human beings, but rather that the law recognises them and allows them to act as natural persons for some purposes – most commonly lawsuits, property ownership and contracts.

justiciability: Concerns the limits on legal issues over which a court can exercise its judicial authority and thus refers to factual or legal questions capable of being decided by a court.

justiciable: In constitutional law, a matter is justiciable if courts can apply the Constitution to the factual or legal dispute and can declare invalid action in conflict with the Constitution.

law-making power: The power of an institution such as a legislature, derived from a constitution, to pass valid law.

limitation of rights: When law or conduct infringes on one or more of the rights protected in the Bill of Rights, this is called a limitation of the right. A limitation can be justified in terms of section 36 (and is then constitutionally valid) or it can be unjustified (and is then unconstitutional).

material mistake of fact: Ignorance or forgetfulness of the existence or non-existence of a fact important to the creation of a legal obligation which is so central to the dispute that it negates the establishment of a legal obligation.

material mistake of law: Ignorance or forgetfulness of the existence or non-existence of a legal rule important to the creation of a legal obligation which is so central to the dispute that it negates the establishment of a legal obligation.

meaningful engagement: A duty imposed by courts on parties to a dispute that requires them to talk to each other with a view to solving the dispute.

mere differentiation: The distinctions made by the law between groups of people where these distinctions are not based on harmful stereotypes or other problematic personal attributes or characteristics (like a person's race, sex or sexual orientation), but rather on the basis of historically harmless criteria.

nation state: A political unit consisting of an autonomous state inhabited predominantly by a people sharing a common history.

National Assembly: The lower House of the national Parliament of South Africa comprising 400 members elected in a general election through the system of proportional representation to represent the interests of the whole electorate.

National Council of Provinces: The second House of the national Parliament of South Africa comprising 10 delegates from each province, primarily representing the interests of provinces in the national law-making process.

natural person: A human being as opposed to a legal entity and who is treated as the bearer of rights and duties.

negative duties: The legal duties to refrain from acting in a manner in conflict with provisions in the Constitution, often contrasted with positive duties which require those bound by the Constitution to act in a certain manner to give effect to the provisions of the Constitution.

norms: Values or principles that direct proper, or in constitutional law, legally permissible behaviour in a society.

notional severance: A technique of interpretation that focuses on the words of a legal provision and, rather than eliminating specific words in the provision, interprets the provision, usually by narrowing its scope and by indicating circumstances to which the provision is not applicable to ensure it will be interpreted in conformity with the Constitution.

operational provisions of the Bill of Rights: The set of provisions in the Constitution that indicates whom the rights in the Bill of Rights binds, who is protected by the provisions of the Bill of Rights and how these provisions must be applied.

organ of state: Any department of state or administration in the national, provincial or local sphere of government; or any other functionary or institution that exercises a power or performs a function in terms of the Constitution or a provincial constitution; or that exercises a public power or performs a public function in terms of any legislation. However, it does not include a court or a judicial officer.

***par delictum* rule:** The rule that a party must come to court with 'clean hands' and thus denies the aid of the court to parties whose conduct was wrongful.

pardons: Where a person has been convicted of a crime and the President, exercising a Head of State power, decides to excuse the crime, thus wiping the slate clean and allowing the convicted criminal to live as if the conviction had never occurred.

Parliament: In South African constitutional law it is the collective name for the National Assembly and the National Council of Provinces, the two Houses of the national legislature empowered jointly to pass legislation and to fulfil the other duties of the national legislature.

parliamentary privilege: The rule that Members of Parliament have legal immunity that protects them against civil or criminal liability for actions done or statements made in the course of their legislative duties.

parliamentary supremacy: This is also called parliamentary sovereignty or legislative supremacy and is a concept in the constitutional law of some parliamentary democracies. With parliamentary sovereignty, a legislative body (usually the democratically elected parliament) has absolute sovereignty, meaning it is supreme to all other government institutions, including the executive and the judiciary. This means that the legislative body may change or repeal any previous legislation and is not constrained by the constitution in what legislation it can pass.

participatory democracy: The idea that the public has a right and duty to participate in public affairs, including discussions about the passing of legislation and the formulation of government policies.

patterns of disadvantage: The deeply entrenched, historically created and continuing social and economic exclusion experienced by black people, women, gay men and lesbians and other marginalised groups in society.

plenary law-making power: The complete power, bestowed by the constitution on the relevant body, to pass laws on a particular topic with no limitations.

pluralism: A condition or a state in which numerous distinct ethnic, religious or cultural groups are present and in which the beliefs and practices of individuals who belong to such groups are accommodated.

polygynous marriage: A marriage conducted in terms of customary law rules in which a husband is permitted to be married to more than one wife at the same time.

portfolio committees: The various committees of the National Assembly tasked with processing legislation and overseeing the implementation of legislation relating to the portfolio of each member of the Cabinet.

positive duties: The legal duties which require those bound by the Constitution to act in a certain manner to give effect to the provisions of the Constitution, often contrasted with negative duties to refrain from acting in a manner in conflict with provisions in the Constitution,

primogeniture rule: The rule of inheritance that the first-born male child has the right to inherit to the exclusion of other children.

principle of authority: The ideal that a functionary must act within his or her power, thus that a functionary can only exercise public power if authorised to do so by the law.

principle of legality: The legal ideal that requires all exercises of public power to be rational, non-arbitrary and authorised by law that is clear, ascertainable and non-retrospective.

principle of rationality: The legal ideal that the exercise of public power must be for a legitimate purpose and that there should be a rational link between the purpose for which the power is exercised and the action taken.

principle of subsidiarity: The rule that where legislation gives effect to a constitutional right, a litigant must, where possible, rely on the provisions of the legislation and cannot rely directly on the right concerned.

prior restraints: Judicial suppression of material before it can be published or broadcast on the grounds that it is libellous or harmful.

proportional representation: The principle of electoral law that there should be a direct correlation between the percentage of votes cast for a specific political party and the percentage of seats allocated to that party in the legislature.

proportionality: A legal principle used to decide how the right balance should be struck between conflicting interests to accommodate the various interests optimally, usually in a fair and just manner. In limitation analysis this means, broadly speaking, that the interests of the state and of society must be weighed against the interests of those whose rights are being infringed and must be done in a manner that is acceptable in an open and democratic society.

prosecuting authority: The body that makes decisions about who to prosecute and who not to prosecute for the commission of an alleged offence and is responsible for such prosecutions.

public administration: The collective name for the group of individuals employed by the state to implement government policies and programmes, including employees of all organs of state.

public service: The collective name for those persons who work for the national and provincial government departments.

pure proportional representation electoral system: The electoral system in which voters vote for political parties and not individual candidates and in which each party is allocated seats in the legislature in direct proportion to the percentage of votes cast for that party in the election.

quasi-federal system: A system in which the power to pass and implement legislation is distributed between the national government and provincial governments but in which the power of provincial governments is limited.

rational connection: Identifying the purpose to be achieved by a legal provision on the one hand and the nature of the legal provision seeking to achieve that purpose on the other, and asking whether there is a rational link between the two.

rationality: A legal test that is not aimed at enquiring into the wisdom or reasonableness of the impugned legal provision, but rather asks, first, whether the legal provision aims to achieve a legitimate government purpose and, second, whether there is a rational relationship between the legal provision and the purpose sought to be achieved by it.

reading down: The principle of legal interpretation which requires that ordinary legislation is interpreted in line with the spirit, purport and object of the Bill of Rights if the words are reasonably capable of such an interpretation or are not unduly strained.

reading in conformity: The principle of legal interpretation requiring that the courts must prefer interpretations that fall within the boundaries of the Bill of Rights over those that do not, provided that such an interpretation can be reasonably ascribed to the provision.

reasonable accommodation: The need of both private and public institutions to take reasonable steps – within what is financially affordable and practically possible – to accommodate the practices, beliefs and ways of living of diverse groups of people to ensure their full and equal participation in society.

rechtsstaat: Requires that all laws and state conduct must comply with the Constitution and demands that the law and conduct of state actors must strive to protect freedom, justice and legal certainty.

red rights: Also referred to as second generation rights and usually thought to include social and economic rights.

regular intervention: The power of the executive at national or provincial level to intervene in the affairs of the province or municipality respectively when a province or municipality cannot or does not fulfil an executive obligation in terms of the Constitution or legislation.

reparation: Making amends for past injustice by providing those disadvantaged by past unjust acts or laws with opportunities, benefits and rewards to compensate them for the loss incurred by them because of the unjust actions of others in the past.

representative democracy: The notion that the voters are represented by elected representatives serving in legislatures and the executive.

retrospective invalidation of legislation: Where, because of the doctrine of objective invalidity, legislation is declared invalid and renders the legislation invalid from the moment the clash with the Constitution arose.

rights disputes: Disputes in labour law regarding the the interpretation and application of existing rights which are generally arbitrable through the bargaining councils or through the labour courts.

rule of law: An evolving constitutional principle enforceable by courts and closely related to the principle of legality and the *rechtsstaat* which, at a minimum, requires the legislature and the executive in every sphere only to exercise power and perform functions if authorised to do so by law and then only in a rational manner.

rule of *stare decisis:* The basic rule applicable in common law jurisdictions that a court is bound by the legal precedent established by court judgments of a court at the same or higher level of authority.

second generation rights: Refer to rights which were developed after the Second World War, usually social and economic rights.

separation of powers: The principle that there must be some separation of function and, in some cases, personnel of the three branches of government.

severance: The remedy which allows a court to delete those words or phrases from the provision which renders the provision unconstitutional to fix the unconstitutionality of a legal provision.

social and economic rights (also socio-economic rights): Also generally referred to as second generation rights, the set of rights that ensures that the basic social and economic needs of individuals are met.

specific administrative law: the principles of law that are applicable to discrete areas of administration, for example education, the environment, the police, the revenue service and so on.

spirit, purport, and object of Bill of Rights: The human rights based norms and values that are derived from the specific substantive provisions of the Bill of Rights.

standing: The right of either an individual or an organisation to bring a case to a specific court and to have that case heard in that court.

state: An organised political community occupying a certain territory and whose members live under the authority of a constitution. The state is therefore a far broader concept than the government.

statutes: Legislation passed by the duly authorised legislature on a particular topic.

strict party discipline: The principle that elected representatives of a political party are required to obey and follow the decisions made by that political party on a specific policy or legal issue.

structural interdict: A remedy handed down by a court ordering the government to take certain steps and to report back to the court at regular intervals about the steps taken to comply with the Constitution.

substantive provisions of the Bill of Rights: The provisions relating to the protection of specific rights.

suspension of an order of invalidity: A remedy in which the court, after declaring a legal provision constitutionally invalid, suspends that order, allowing the provision to remain in operation, usually for a set period of time to allow the legislature to fix the invalidity of the provision.

teleological interpretation: An interpretative method that asks what the purpose of a specific provision is - why was it included in the Constitution and formulated in the way that it was - to assist with determining the exact meaning of that provision.

tenure: The right to keep a job for life or for a fixed period of time.

third generation rights: See the definition of 'green rights'.

ubi ius ubi remedium: The notion that when a person's right is violated, the victim will have an equitable remedy under law.

ultra vires: Describes actions taken by government bodies or private institutions that exceed the scope of power given to them by law.

values: Important and lasting beliefs or ideals contained in a constitution and/or shared by the members of a culture about what is good or bad and desirable or undesirable.

vertical dispute: A legal dispute between the state and an individual.

vote of no confidence: When the majority of members of a legislature, having decided to stop supporting the government of the day, decide to unseat that government by supporting a vote to that effect.

Westminster system: Also called a parliamentary system, this system of government is based on the British model in which the members of the executive branch (usually the Prime Minister and his or her Cabinet Ministers) are appointed from among the Members of Parliament and obtain their democratic legitimacy from the Parliament. They are members of, as well as accountable to, that body, meaning that the executive and legislative branches are intertwined.

Index

Page numbers in *italics* point to diagrams and tables

E

Q

R